Contents

Plan Your Trip

Discover

Britain & Ireland 50

Italy

Greece

Contents

Discover Europe

Austria, Switzerland, Czech Republic 588

Greece 688

In Focus

Survival Guide

This is Europe

Famed for its iconic landmarks and landscapes, Europe's intricate tapestry of countries and cultures is woven together by rich history, artistic and culinary treasures, enduring traditions and cutting-edge trends.

History is undoubtedly one of Europe's major draws. From Neolithic sites and Grecian ruins to Gothic cathedrals and crumbling castles, taking a trip across Europe can feel like stumbling into the pages of a history textbook. While in many ways one of the world's most forward-looking regions, Europe's past inevitably informs its present and its future. Understanding this continent's turbulent history is essential if you want to get to grips with what makes it tick. Thankfully, there's no shortage of amazing museums to put it all into context, from Paris' palatial Louvre and London's British Museum to Amsterdam's Rijksmuseum.

Europe also understands the finer things in life. And it's never shy about letting you join in the party. It's a place where you can indulge your taste buds, stretch your muscles, shop till you drop and dance into the small hours – all in the same day, should you so desire. Best of all, the next country is never more than a quick trip away. In a few hours you could swap the glittering Mediterranean for Berlin's bars, Rome's ancient ruins or the Madrid's Golden Mile of Art. Few places on earth can offer such a wealth of experiences and adventures. But don't be in too much of a hurry; the journey is a vital part of what makes exploring Europe so fascinating and fun.

Wherever you end up, you're in for an unforgettable trip. So *bon voyage, sichere Fahrt, buen viaje,* happy travels.

" Europe offers more iconic experiences than practically anywhere else on the planet "

Neuschwanstein Castle (p561), Germany

BRIAN LAWRENCE/GETTY IMAGES ©

Europe

NORWAY
Shetland Islands
Orkney Islands
Outer Hebrides
60°N
5°E
10°E
15°W
0° (Greenwich)
Inverness
SCOTLAND
Aberdeen
Oban
Dundee
Skagerrak
NORTHERN IRELAND
18
Glasgow
23
EDINBURGH
DENMARK
Derry
Newcastle-upon-Tyne
North Sea
Belfast
Galway
DUBLIN
ENGLAND
Irish Sea
6
York
Stralsund
IRELAND
Liverpool
Frisian Islands
Wismar
Rostock
BRITAIN
Hamburg
Cork
WALES
NETHERLANDS
BERLIN
Elbe
Bremen
CARDIFF
Oxford
LONDON
8
7
St George's Channel
Hanover
Bath
11
3
AMSTERDAM
Bruges
BRUSSELS
GERMANY
50°N
Plymouth
Brighton
21
English Channel
BELGIUM
Frankfurt-am-Main
Rhine
Channel Islands
Le Havre
20
ATLANTIC OCEAN
Caen
Plzeň
PARIS
2
13
Reims
Quimper
Stuttgart
CHAMPAGNE
Rennes
Danube
Strasbourg
Seine
Munich
22
Loire
17
Tours
Zürich
Nantes
Dijon
Bavarian Alps
FRANCE
BERN
12
45°N
10°W
Geneva
Trento
Limoges
WALAIS
15
ALPS
Bay of Biscay
Bordeaux
Lyon
5
5°W
Mt Blanc (4807m)
Milan
Santiago De Compostela
Chamonix
19
Venice
Po
Turin
Gijón
San Sebastián
ITALY
Bilbao
Nîmes
Genoa
Bologna
Vigo
Toulouse
León
Pisa
Rhône
Nice
Ligurian Sea
Perugia
Pamplona
Montpellier
Golfe du Lion
PYRENEES
Marseille
25
Douro
Ebro
Elba
Salamanca
Zaragoza
Corsica (France)
40°N
14
Barcelona
ROME
1
PORTUGAL
MADRID
Tagus
Sassari
Palma De Mallorca
SPAIN
Badajoz
Valencia
Sardinia (Italy)
Córdoba
Alicante (Alicant)
Balearic Islands
Cagliari
Seville
Murcia
Mediterranean Sea
10
Granada
Cádiz
Málaga
5°E
10°E
Strait of Gibraltar
35°N
ALGERIA
TUNISIA
MOROCCO

25 Top Highlights

1. Rome
2. Eiffel Tower, Paris
3. Nightlife, London
4. Vienna
5. Venice
6. Dublin
7. Berlin
8. Amsterdam
9. Prague
10. Alhambra, Granada
11. Bath
12. Jungfraujoch
13. Champagne Vineyards
14. La Sagrada Família, Barcelona
15. Matterhorn
16. Athens
17. Salzburg
18. Giant's Causeway
19. Chamonix
20. The Rhine
21. Beer & Chocolate, Brussels
22. Beer Drinking, Munich
23. Edinburgh
24. Santorini
25. Tuscany

25 Europe's Top Highlights

Ancient Rome

From the crumbling Colosseum to the ancient Forum and the Appian Way, few sights are more evocative than the ruins of ancient Rome (p369). Two thousand years ago this city was the centre of the greatest empire of the ancient world, where gladiators battled and emperors lived in unimaginable luxury. Nowadays, it's a haunting spot; as you walk the cobbled paths you can almost sense the ghosts in the air. Below: View of the Colosseum (p375) from the Roman Forum

2

Eiffel Tower, Paris

Initially designed as a temporary exhibit for the 1889 Exposition Universelle (World Fair), the elegant, art nouveau design of Paris' Eiffel Tower (p183) has become the defining fixture of the skyline. Its recent 1st-floor refit adds two glitzy glass pavilions housing interactive exhibits; outside them, peer d-o-w-n through glass floor to the ground below. Visit at dusk for best day and night views of the glittering City of Light and make a toast at the sparkling champagne bar.

London's Nightlife

World-famous theatres, landmark cinemas, iconic venues, underground clubs – London's at its liveliest after dark, when there's no better time to take the cultural pulse of the UK capital (p88). Catching a musical or a play in the West End is on most people's itinerary, but that's just the beginning of London's nightlife: you could join the groundlings at Shakespeare's Globe Theatre, watch a blockbuster on Leicester Sq, or experience high culture at the Royal Opera House. The only trick will be finding enough time to sleep. Below: London's West End theatres

3

ALAN COPSON/GETTY IMAGES ©

The Best... City Views

THE PALATINO (PALATINE HILL), ROME
Gaze across the Italian capital from this iconic hill. (p369)

BASILIQUE DU SACRÉ-CŒUR, PARIS
The whole of Paris unfolds below you from this Montmartre landmark. (p182)

THE SHARD, LONDON
London's soaring, splinter-like skyscraper has a bird's-eye view. (p72)

THE CAMPANILE, VENICE
Climb Venice's tallest building for a panoramic perspective. (p404)

THE BELFORT, BRUGES
This medieval bell tower looks over Bruges' most beautiful square. (p503)

The Best... Royal Residences

VERSAILLES
Louis XIV's jaw-dropping statement of architectural excess. (p202)

BUCKINGHAM PALACE
Look for the Royal Standard above the palace to see if the Queen's at home. (p61)

SCHLOSS SCHÖNBRUNN
The Habsburg's rococo summer retreat in Vienna. (p599)

PALACIO REAL
Wander through the 50-odd rooms on show in Madrid's 2800-room palace. (p287)

PRAGUE CASTLE
The Czech monarchs are long gone, but their castle dominates Prague's old city. (p659)

GONZALO AZUMENDI/GETTY IMAGES ©

4 Imperial Vienna

The monumentally graceful Hofburg whisks you back to the age of empires in Vienna (p598) as you marvel at the treasury's imperial crowns, the equine ballet of the Spanish Riding School and the chandelier-lit apartments fit for Empress Elisabeth. The palace, a legacy of the Habsburg era, is rivalled in grandeur only by the 1441-room Schloss Schönbrunn, a Unesco World Heritage Site, and the baroque Schloss Belvedere, both set in exquisite gardens.

Top left: Dining room of the Hofburg (p603)

JEAN-PIERRE LESCOURRET/GETTY IMAGES ©

5 Venice in Winter

Venice (p401) is unquestionably one of the world's most bewitching cities, but its beauty has one drawback – crowds. Venice can feel swamped in summer, but in winter it's a different story: there are far fewer tourists, the light is sharp and clear, and the city is at its most atmospheric. Wander Dorsoduro's shadowy back lanes, then visit two of Venice's top galleries: the Galleria dell'Accademia and the Peggy Guggenheim Collection.

6 Dublin

Whether you're wandering the leafy Georgian terraces of St Stephen's Green or getting acquainted with the past at Kilmainham Gaol, in Dublin (p134) you're never far from a literary or historic sight. And then there are the city's pubs: there are few better places to down a pint than Dublin, and you can even make a pilgrimage to the original Guinness brewery on the city's outskirts. Either way, you'll make a few Irish friends along the way.

Right: Kilmainham Gaol (p137)

7 Berlin

More than 25 years since the fall of the Berlin Wall, it's hard to believe that this most cosmopolitan of cities (p528) once marked the frontier of the Cold War. But reminders of Berlin's divided past still remain: whether you're passing the Brandenburg Gate, gazing at graffiti at the East Side Gallery or soaking up the history at Checkpoint Charlie, it's an essential part of understanding what makes Germany's capital tick. Above: East Side Gallery (p533)

Amsterdam's Canals

To say Amsterdammers love the water is an understatement. Sure, the city (p466) made its first fortune in maritime trade, but that's ancient history. You can stroll next to the canals and check out some of the 2500 houseboats. Or, better yet, go for a ride. From boat level you'll get to see a whole new set of architectural details, like the ornamentation bedecking the bridges. And when you pass the canalside cafe terraces, you can look up and wave.

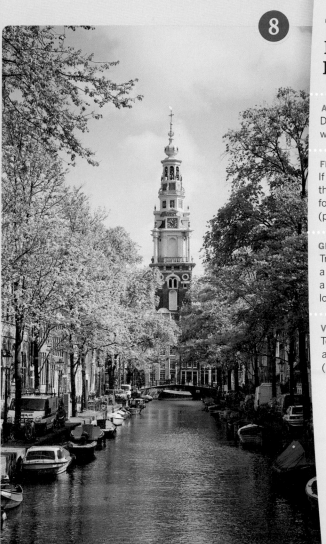

8

FRASER HALL/GETTY IMAGES ©

The Best...

Places for a Drink

A PINT IN A IRISH PUB
Dublin wouldn't be Dublin without its pubs. (p141)

FRENCH VINEYARDS
If you want to learn about the fruits of the vine, head for a Bordeaux vineyard. (p241)

GERMAN BEER GARDENS
Trying the local brews at a Munich beer garden is a great way to meet the locals. (p557)

VIENNA'S KAFFEEHÄUSER
Top spots for coffee, cake and people-watching. (p610)

Historic Prague

Emerging from behind the Iron Curtain, where it slumbered for decades, the capital of the Czech Republic is now one of Europe's most alluring and dynamic places. In some parts Prague (p654) has hardly changed since medieval times – cobbled cul-de-sacs snake through the Old Town, framed by teetering townhouses, baroque buildings and graceful bridges. And if castles are your thing, Prague Castle is an absolute beauty: a 1000-year-old fortress covering around 7 hectares – the world's largest castle complex.

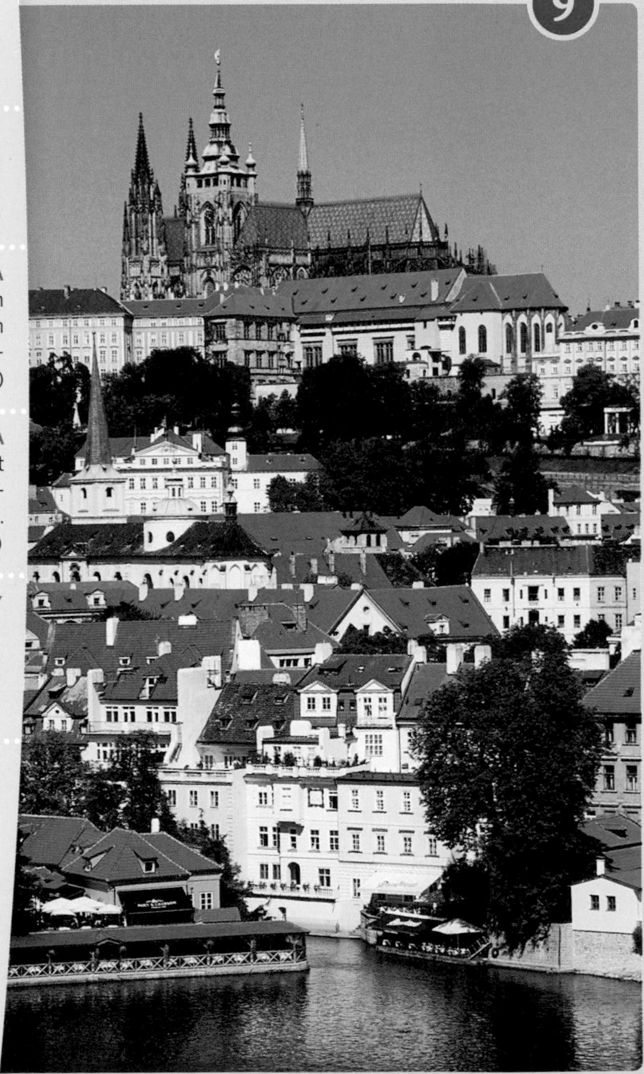

The Best... Sacred Spaces

NOTRE DAME CATHEDRAL
See light filter through the rose windows in Paris' Gothic wonder. (p179)

THE MEZQUITA
Muslim and Christian architecture collide in Córdoba's mosque-cum-cathedral. (p342)

ST PETER'S BASILICA
The Vatican's largest church is among the holiest sites in Christendom. (p374)

WESTMINSTER ABBEY
British monarchs have been crowned at London's Westminster Abbey since 1066. (p60)

ANCIENT DELPHI
Where the oracle sat at the centre of the ancient Greek world. (p711)

9

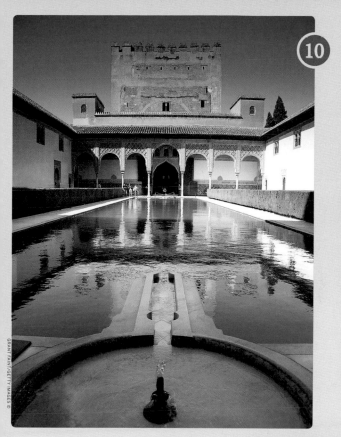

10 Alhambra, Granada

The palace complex of the Alhambra (p346) is perhaps the most refined example of Islamic art anywhere in the world. It's also an enduring symbol of 800 years of Moorish rule in a region that was then known as Al-Andalus. From afar, the Alhambra's red fortress towers dominate the Granada skyline, set against a backdrop of the Sierra Nevada's snow-capped peaks. Up close, the Alhambra's perfectly proportioned Generalife gardens complement the exquisite detail of the Palacio Nazaríes. Put simply, this is Spain's most beautiful monument.

11 Bath's Architecture

Britain boasts many great cities, but Bath (p95) is the belle of the ball. The Romans built a health resort here to take advantage of the hot water bubbling to the surface; the springs were rediscovered in the 18th century and Bath became *the* place to see and be seen by British high society. Today, the stunning Georgian architecture of grand townhouses, sweeping crescents and Palladian mansions (not to mention Roman ruins, a beautiful cathedral and a 21st-century spa) mean that Bath will demand your undivided attention.

Right: Roman baths (p95)

PETER RICHARDSON/GETTY IMAGES ©

12

Jungfraujoch

Travelling through Switzerland often feels like one nonstop scenic adventure, as every bend in the road opens up a new panorama of mind-boggling views. But if it's the ultimate alpine view you're after, then Jungfraujoch (p647) is guaranteed to fit the bill. A gravity-defying train chugs up to Europe's highest railway terminus (at 3471m), opening up an unforgettable vista of icy pinnacles, knife-edge peaks and gleaming glaciers. Dress warmly, don some shades and don't forget the camera.

SLOW IMAGES/GETTY IMAGES ©

13

Champagne Vineyards

For a celebratory tipple, there's only one drink that'll do – and that's a bottle of bubbly. The rolling vineyards around Reims and Épernay in Champagne (p219) are littered with prestigious names, including Mumm, Mercier, De Castellane, Moët & Chandon, most of which offer guided tours and *dégustation* (tasting) in their musty old cellars. There are also over 5000 small-scale *vignerons* (wine makers), all producing their own distinctive champagnes.

La Sagrada Família, Barcelona

Barcelona is famous for its Modernista architecture, much of which is the work of visionary architect Antoni Gaudí. His masterwork is this mighty cathedral (p312), which remains a work in progress close to a century after its creator's death. It's a bizarre combination of crazy and classic: Gothic touches intersect with eccentric experiments and improbable angles. Many decades into its construction, no one is entirely sure when it will be finished; but even half-completed, it's a modern-day wonder.

14

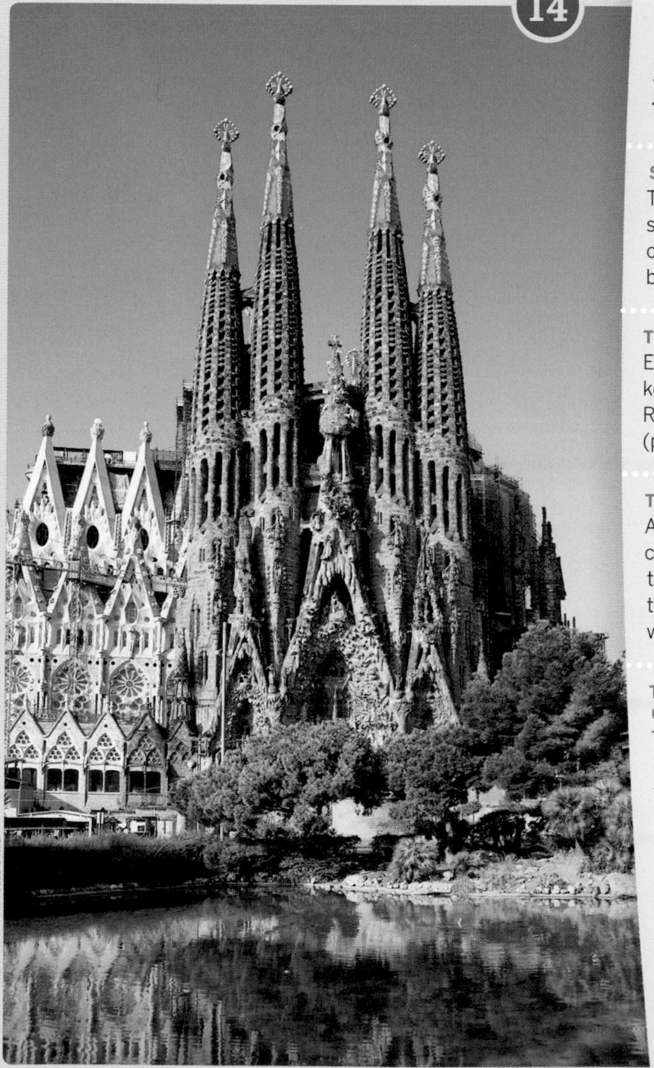

The Best... Ancient Monuments

STONEHENGE
The world's most iconic stone circle is also one of its oldest. Some sections date back to 4500 BC. (p98)

THE ROMAN FORUM
Exploring the streets, markets and temples of ancient Rome is unforgettable. (p369)

THE ACROPOLIS
Athens' ancient temple complex remains an architectural inspiration, more than 2000 years after it was built. (p700)

THE ALIGNEMENTS DE CARNAC
These Neolithic stones stretch for miles across the Breton countryside in France. (p216)

The Best...
Mountain Landscapes

THE FRENCH ALPS Gaze up to Mont Blanc, Europe's highest mountain. (p234)

THE SWISS ALPS Switzerland's mightiest mountain, the Matterhorn, looms over the chalet-filled village of Zermatt. (p638)

THE ISLE OF SKYE, SCOTLAND The misty Cuillin Hills are Britain's most spectacular mountain range. (p133)

HOHE TAUERN NATIONAL PARK, AUSTRIA The largest national park in the Alps, with many 3000m peaks. (p631)

LEFT: MARTIN MOOS/GETTY IMAGES © RIGHT: BRUCE YUANYUE BI/GETTY IMAGES ©

Matterhorn

It graces chocolate-bar wrappers and evokes stereotypical *Heidi* scenes, but nothing prepares you for the allure of the Matterhorn (p639). This mesmerising loner looms above the timber-chalet-filled Swiss village of Zermatt. Gaze at it from a tranquil sidewalk cafe, hike in its shadow along the tangle of alpine paths above town, with cowbells clinking in the distance, or pause on a ski slope and admire its craggy, chiselled peak. Left: The Matterhorn behind the village of Zermatt (p638); Above: Cable car from Zermatt

16 Athens' Ancient Monuments

History looms around every corner in Athens (p698). This 2500-year-old city is awash with architectural reminders of the majesty of the Greek Empire. The grandest of all is the Acropolis, thought by many scholars to be the most perfectly proportioned building ever constructed. Elsewhere you can visit the Ancient Agora (marketplace), make a pilgrimage to the Temple of Olympian Zeus, and browse ancient artefacts at the Acropolis Museum.

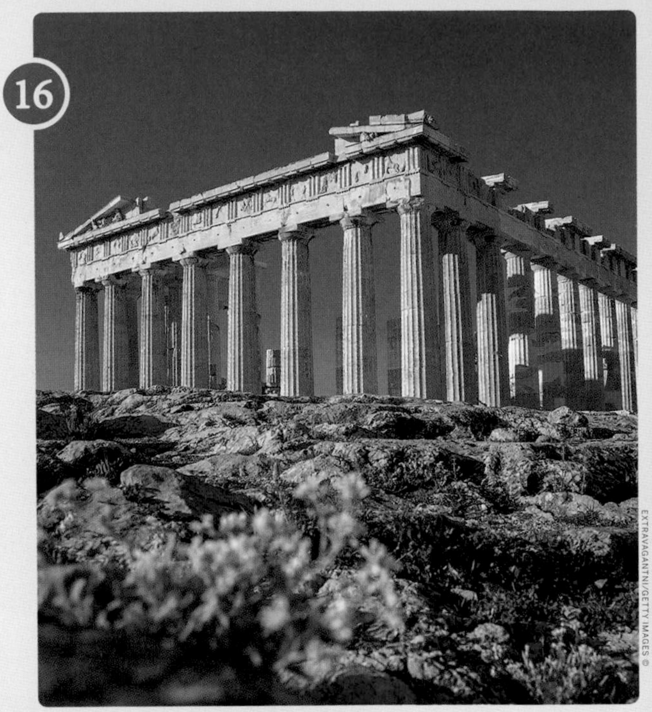

Right: Acropolis (p700)

17 Baroque Salzburg

A castle on a hill, 17th-century cobbled streets, Mozart, the ultimate sing-along – if Salzburg (p616) didn't exist, someone would have to invent it just to keep happy all the acolytes who visit Austria each year. It's hard to say what's most popular, but this is definitely *Sound of Music* country; faster than you can say 'do-re-mi' you will be whisked into gorgeous, steep hills that are alive with tour groups.

Giant's Causeway

This bizarre geological formation (p155) in Northern Ireland consists of more than 40,000 basalt pillars that emerge from the sea on County Antrim's northeastern coast. They're awash with legends (locals claim they're the work of an ancient giant), but were actually caused by a huge volcanic eruption that occurred between 50 and 60 million years ago. Nearby, you can test your nerves on the famous Carrick-a-Rede rope bridge, which dangles 30m above the foaming waves of the Irish Sea.

18

NEALE CLARKE/GETTY IMAGES ©

The Best...
Artistic Icons

MONTMARTRE, PARIS
This Parisian village inspired Toulouse-Lautrec, Dégas, Utrillo and many other artists. (p195)

FLORENCE
The home of the Italian Renaissance. (p418)

MONET'S GARDEN AT GIVERNY
Here in rural Normandy, Claude Monet created his *nymphéas* (water lily) paintings. (p256)

MADRID'S GOLDEN MILE OF ART
From Guernica to Goya, Madrid's big three galleries have few peers. (p286)

MUSEUM HET REMBRANDTHUIS
Visit Rembrandt's original Amsterdam studio. (p472)

SISTINE CHAPEL
Michelangelo's masterpiece decorates the ceiling of this Vatican chapel. (p377)

Chamonix

19

Skiing, mountaineering, trekking, canyoning, rafting, you name it, Chamonix (p234) has it. Not an adrenaline junkie? Hitch a ride to the top of Aiguille du Midi and marvel at the Alpine scenery unfolding.

CHRISTIAN ASLUND/GETTY IMAGES ©

The Best... Natural Wonders

DUNE DU PILAT
Europe's largest sand dune, on France's Atlantic coast near Arcachon. (p242)

DACHSTEIN EISHÖHLE
These ice caves extend 80km into the mountains near Obertraun, Austria. (p622)

SAMARIA GORGE
The walls of this 13km canyon on the Greek island of Crete reach an amazing 1100m. (p728)

GIANT'S CAUSEWAY
Follow in the footsteps of mythical giant Finn McCool on the Northern Irish coast. (p155)

MATTES RENE/GETTY IMAGES ©

20 Slow-Boating the Rhine

A boat ride through the romantic Rhine Valley (p569) between Koblenz and Mainz is one of Germany's most memorable experiences. As you sit back on deck, glorious scenery drifts slowly past like a magic lantern: vineyard-clad hills, idyllic riverside towns and, every now and then, a mighty medieval castle. Stop off for a hearty meal, sample a few of the local wines and spend an hour or two wandering around a half-timbered village - the Rhine is a guaranteed highlight. Left: Pfalzgrafenstein Castle on the Rhine

Belgian Beer & Chocolate

21

Belgium (p490) has a brew for all seasons. From tangy lambics to full-flavoured Trappists, the range of beers is exceptional, and there's no shortage of places to try them, from the breweries of Brussels to the riverside cafes of Bruges and Ghent. Sweet tooths will find plenty of shops selling the delicious chocolates for which Belgium is famous, including melt-in-the-mouth pralines to boozy choc laced with liqueurs.

PASCALE BEROUJON/GETTY IMAGES ©

DAN HERRICK/GETTY IMAGES ©

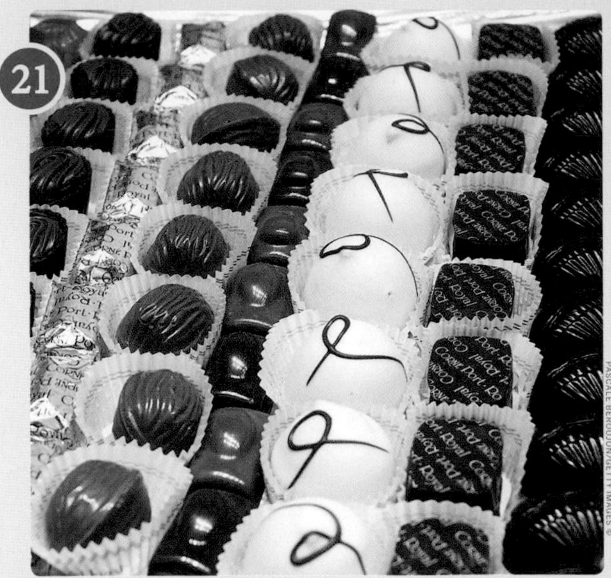

22

Beer Drinking in Munich

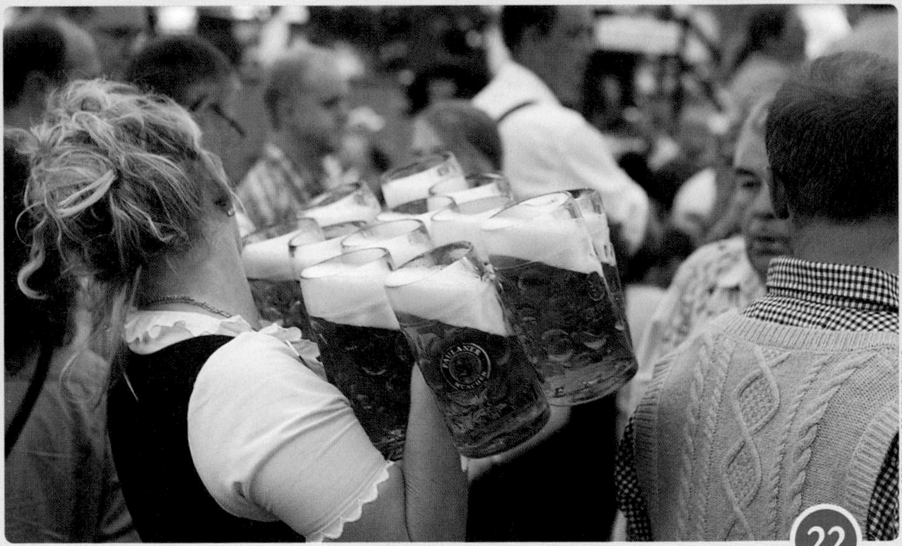

It's not so much that you can drink beer in Munich (p551) – everybody knows you can. It's the variety of places where you can drink that makes this city heaven for beer afficionados. There's Oktoberfest, of course, and then there are the famous beer halls, from the infamous Hofbräuhaus to the wonderful Augustiner Bräustuben, as well as sprawling, high-spirited beer gardens like Chinesischer Turm, where you can enjoy a frothy, refreshing stein.

23

Edinburgh

Edinburgh (p121) is a city of many moods, famous for its amazing festivals and especially lively in the summer. The Scottish capital is also well worth visiting out of season for the sights. View the castle silhouetted against the blue spring sky or, for the atmosphere, fog snagging the spires of the Old Town, rain on the cobblestones and a warm glow beckoning from the window of a pub on a chilly December morning.

Below: View of Edinburgh Castle (p121) from the Ross Fountain, Princes St Gardens

The Best... Shopping Experiences

PARIS' FLEA MARKETS
Paris' *marchés aux puces* are packed with vintage fashion and antiques. (p201)

NUREMBERG'S CHRISTMAS MARKETS
Festive *Christkindlmärkte* are held all across Germany, but Nuremberg has the best. (p568)

PORTOBELLO ROAD MARKET, LONDON
Forget Oxford St – this west London street market has the good stuff. (p91)

MERCAT DE LA BOQUERIA, BARCELONA
Shop for Spanish goodies at the gorgeous Boqueria food market. (p307)

GALERIES ST-HUBERT, BRUSSELS
Shop for dainty lace and handmade chocolates. (p490

Santorini

The idyllic Greek island of Santorini (p719) will grab your attention and won't let go. The submerged caldera, surrounded by lava-layered cliffs topped by villages that resemble a sprinkling of icing sugar, is one of nature's great wonders. It's best experienced by a walk along the clifftops, from the main town of Fira to the northern village of Oia. The precariousness and impermanence of the place is breathtaking. Recover from your efforts with an ice-cold Mythos beer in Oia, as you await its famous sunset.

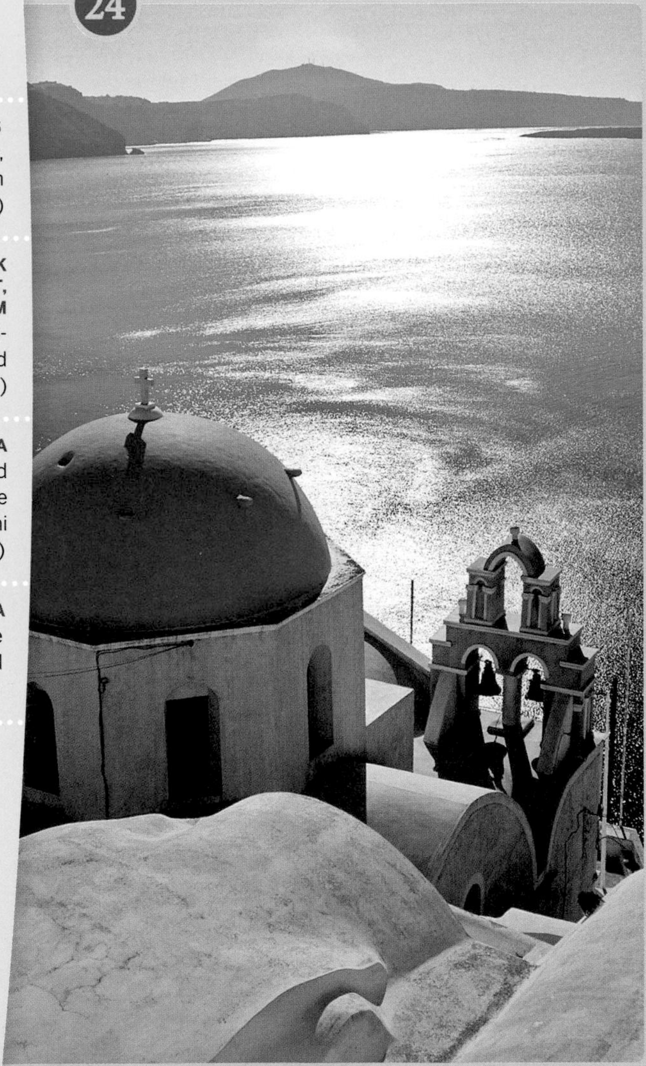

The Best... Weird Buildings

CENTRE POMPIDOU, PARIS
An 'inside-out' building, with pipes and girders on the outside. (p182)

OVERBLAAK DEVELOPMENT, ROTTERDAM
Surreal 'forest' of 45-degree-tilted, cube-shaped apartments. (p485)

LA PEDRERA, BARCELONA
Rooftop sculpture and organic lines from the imagination of Antoni Gaudí. (p311)

LEANING TOWER OF PISA
Tilting in Tuscany since 1173, it still hasn't toppled over. (p433)

ATOMIUM, BRUSSELS
The 102m-tall Atomium has escalators in its connection tubes. (p494)

24

25

Tuscany

The gently rolling hills of Tuscany (p418), bathed in golden light and dotted with vineyards, sum up Italy's attractions in a nutshell. Battalions of books, postcards and lifestyle TV shows try to do this region justice, but nothing beats a visit. Here, picture-perfect hilltop towns vie with magnificent scenery and some of Italy's best food and wine – so it's hardly surprising that this is a tourist hotspot. Visit in spring or autumn to see it at its calmest.

Europe's Top Itineraries

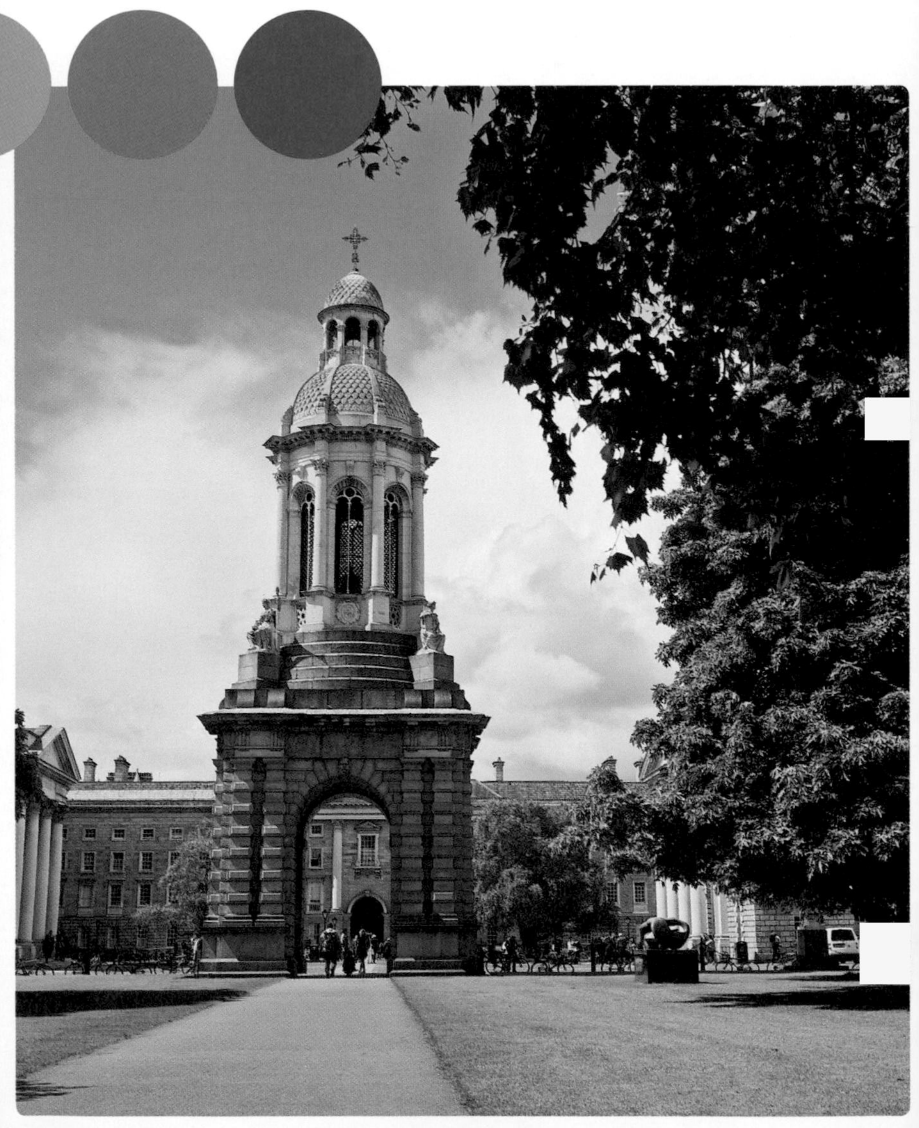

London to Galway England to the Emerald Isle

5 DAYS

This tour begins in Britain's nonstop capital, London, before hopping across the Irish Sea to visit two gems of the Emerald Isle, Dublin and Galway.

1 London (p60)

Samuel Johnson famously quipped that when you're tired of London, you're tired of life, and this is certainly a city that's brimming with unmissable sights. Begin with the British Museum and its treasure trove of artefacts, then mosey around Covent Garden en route to St Paul's Cathedral. Nip across the river to Tate Modern before seeing a play at the Globe Theatre, the rebuilt theatre where Shakespeare premiered many of his plays. On day two, head for Trafalgar Sq, browse the priceless artworks of the National Gallery, snap yourself outside the Houses of Parliament and Westminster Abbey, then picnic in Hyde Park. Finish with dinner and a show in the West End.

LONDON ➔ DUBLIN

✈ **1½ hours**

2 Dublin (p134)

Ireland's capital city makes a fascinating contrast after London. It's an altogether more laid-back city, known for its literary sights and riverside scenery. Among the must-sees are the city's historic seat of learning, Trinity College, the art-filled National Gallery and the impressive main boulevard of O'Connell St. Ale aficionados will definitely want to make time for a visit to the Guinness Brewery before investigating the countless lovely pubs dotted around the Liffey River on a a literary- or musical-themed walking tour. It's worth spending a couple of days in Dublin to soak up the vibe.

DUBLIN ➔ GALWAY

🚗 **2¼ hours** It's 215km along the M6.

3 Galway (p149)

On the opposite side of Ireland, Galway City is known for its rich musical tradition and lively gig scene. If you want to hear some traditional Irish music, this is definitely the place to do it: most of the city's pubs host live music several nights a week. Elsewhere around Galway are the fascinating archaeological remains of the Hall of the Red Earl and a host of excellent restaurants where you can try some cutting-edge Irish grub.

Trinity College (p136), Dublin, Ireland

Paris to Bruges
Northern Highlights

This adventure heads from France into Belgium, via princely Paris, stately Brussels and beautiful Bruges. Taking the train is the most relaxing way to travel, with good rail links between all the stops.

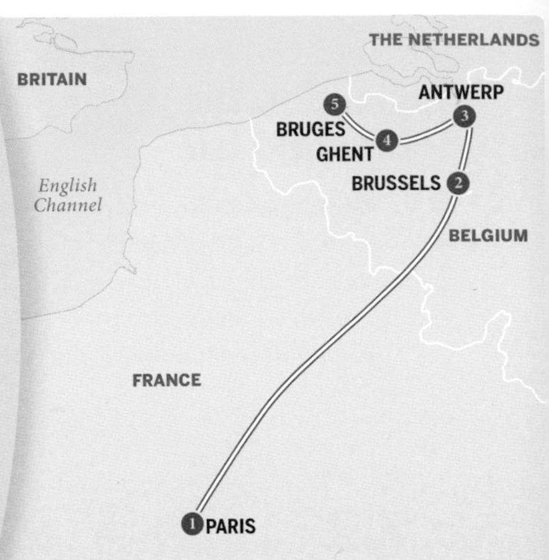

❶ Paris (p174)

The City of Light is a wonderful beginning to this whistle-stop tour. Devote the first morning to the Louvre, wander around the Jardin des Tuileries, then travel down the Seine to Paris' Gothic masterpiece, Cathédrale de Notre Dame – don't miss the panorama from the gargoyle-topped towers. The lively Marais is a great area to explore after dark. On day two, spend the morning on the Left Bank, factoring in a trip up the Eiffel Tower, a walk around the Jardin du Luxembourg and some window-shopping along stylish Blvd St-Germain. Follow up with Impressionist art at the Musée d'Orsay or catch the metro to bohemian Montmartre.

PARIS ➜ BRUSSELS

One hour 20 minutes Via high-speed Eurostar trains **3¼ hours** It's around 320km between Paris and Brussels via the motorways.

❷ Brussels (p490)

Belgium's capital is best known these days as the centre of the European Union, as the European Parliament is based here. But the city has plenty of other attractions. At its heart is the magnificent Grand Place, not only Belgium's finest public square, but one of Europe's grandest. Leave some time for shopping around the elegant arcade of Galeries St-Hubert, where you can pick up delicious pastries, delicate lace and delicious Belgian chocolates.

BRUSSELS ➜ ANTWERP

30 to 45 minutes **45 minutes** It's 45km on the A12 motorway.

❸ Antwerp (p498)

Belgium's second city is often overlooked, but has plenty to recommend it. The Grote Markt is lined with attractive brasseries and cafes, but for most people Antwerp's essential sight is the Rubenshuis, the 17th-century studio of Pieter Paul Rubens, which has been carefully restored and houses 10 of the painter's canvases.

ANTWERP ➜ GHENT

45 minutes **50 minutes** On the main A11.

❹ Ghent (p501)

Nearby Ghent is a medieval canal- and river-woven town which you'll find hard not to fall for, and makes an idyllic stop en route to Bruges.

GHENT ➜ BRUGES

36 minutes **45 minutes** On the E40.

❺ Bruges (p506)

Belgium might not have any big mountains or superstar beaches, but it does have charming towns aplenty – chief among them being Bruges, an impossibly pretty package of cafe-lined squares, cobblestone streets and romantic canals. The essential activity here is a trip to the top of the Belfort (bell tower), one of Belgium's most recognisable landmarks. After dark head for one of the city's cosy pubs, where you can try some of the beers for which Belgium is famous.

Jardin du Luxembourg (p175), Paris, France
EURASIA/GETTY IMAGES ©

Barcelona to Florence Riviera Cruising

This trip tracks the glittering Mediterranean, and takes in some of its key cities including sexy Barcelona, stylish Nice and stately Monaco, before heading over the Italian border to Pisa and Florence.

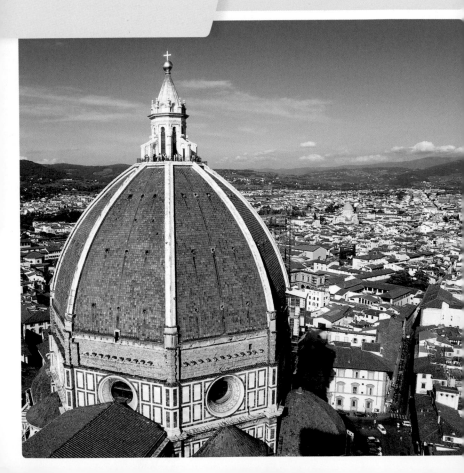

1 Barcelona (p307)

Start the tour in Spain's most bewitching city, Barcelona. The classic areas to wander are the shady lanes of the Barri Gòtic and El Raval, the city's lively waterfront and the gardens of Park Güell. Don't miss Barcelona's celebrated modernista buildings, including the playful Casa Batlló and the outlandish (and unfinished) cathedral, La Sagrada Família.

BARCELONA ➔ MARSEILLE

Seven hours With a change at Narbonne

1¼ hours

2 Marseille (p249)

This old port makes a great place to soak up the sights and sounds of the French Riviera. The heart of the action is around the Vieux Port (Old Harbour), where the city's chaotic fish market takes place, and Le Panier, lined with tempting shops and food stalls. Have lunch at one of the harbourside restaurants, then take a boat trip to the island fort of Château d'If.

MARSEILLE ➔ NICE

2½ hours **2¼ hours** Via the A50 and A8.

3 Nice (p258)

The original Riviera resort, Nice is perennially popular (even if its beaches are pebbly). The street market on cours Saleya is one of France's liveliest, while Vieux Nice is a photogenic tangle of shady alleyways and colourful houses. There are top views from the Parc du Château, at the eastern end of Promenade des Anglais.

NICE ➔ MONACO

20 minutes **30 minutes** It's 20km via A8, 25km to 30km via the roads.

4 Monaco (p266)

A breakneck spin along the corniches (coastal roads) takes you into the millionaire's playground of Monaco, where Europe's high-rollers gamble away fortunes at Monte Carlo casino. If it all gets too much, Monaco's aquarium and hilltop exotic gardens are a peaceful refuge.

MONACO ➔ PISA

Five hours Change in Ventimiglia or Genoa

4½ hours About 350km via A10 and A12.

5 Pisa (p432)

Monaco sits on the Italy border, and nearby Ventimiglia has train links across Italy. Pisa is an essential stop, with its beautiful piazza and, of course, the famously wonky leaning tower. It's worth booking your ticket online to make sure you dodge the inevitable queues.

PISA ➔ FLORENCE

1¼ hours **1¼ hours** It's 88km via the SGC Firenze.

6 Florence (p418)

Florence is where the Italian Renaissance began, and architectural landmarks abound, including the Gothic Duomo and the 14th-century Ponte Vecchio. The city is also renowned for its fabulous artworks, most of which are housed in two renowned galleries, the Galleria degli Uffizi and the Galleria dell'Accademia.

Duomo (p419), Florence, Italy

Bruges to Salzburg
Old Europe

This multicountry trip takes in the best of Belgium, the Netherlands, Germany and Austria. It's doable in 10 days, but will be more fun if you can factor in a bit more time for side trips.

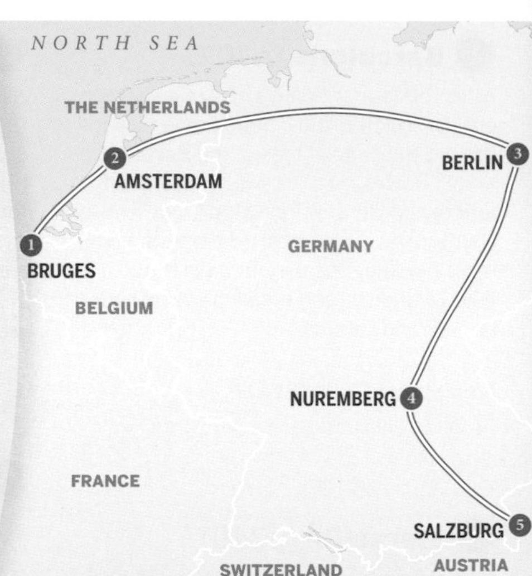

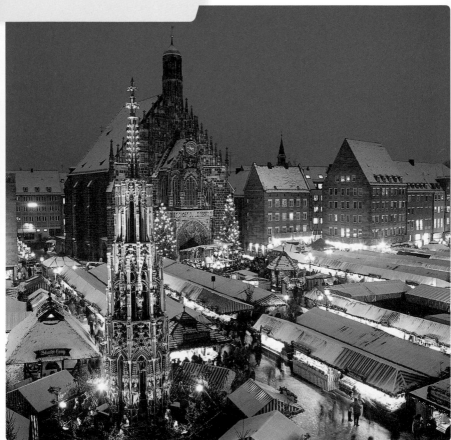

❶ Bruges (p506)

Start off with a leisurely day in Belgium's quintessential canal town, Bruges. It's a compact and relaxed place that's made for aimless ambling: mosey around the medieval centre, climb the Belfort, wander along the waterways, then round the day off with a bowl of *moules-frites* washed down by boutique-brewed Belgian beer.

BRUGES ➔ AMSTERDAM

🚆 **3½ hours** Via Brussels.

❷ Amsterdam (p466)

Regular trains run from Bruges to Brussels – another stately city that's worth a stop – but for this trip we're heading straight to Amsterdam, a city so laid back it's practically horizontal. Amsterdam's compact size means you can cover the centre in a day, squeezing in the Van Gogh Museum, Anne Frank Huis and Rembrandthuis, followed by a canal cruise and a visit to the Red Light District. Two days would allow a day trip to Leiden or Delft.

AMSTERDAM ➔ BERLIN

🚆 **6½ hours** Direct ✈ **1 hour**

❸ Berlin (p528)

Germany's capital ranks alongside London, Paris and Rome in the must-see stakes. Budget at least two days to check off such iconic sights as the Reichstag, the Brandenburg Gate and Checkpoint Charlie, to trace the course of the former Berlin Wall and to throw yourself headlong into some of Europe's most hot-stepping nightlife. With another day, build a visit to Sanssouci Park & Palace in nearby Potsdam into your itinerary.

BERLIN ➔ NUREMBERG

🚆 **Four hours** Direct 🚗 **4¼ hours** About 435km via A10, A9 and A3.

❹ Nuremberg (p565)

Since the dark days of WWII, Nuremberg's Altstadt has been impeccably restored and now hosts one of Europe's most beautiful Christmas markets. The city also has a fine castle, the Kaiserburg, and some excellent museums that confront its troubled past. Best of all, the rest of Bavaria is right on your doorstep with glorious Munich less than two and Neuschwanstein Castle a mere three hours away.

NUREMBERG ➔ SALZBURG

🚆 **Three hours** Change at Munich

🚗 **3½ hours** 300km via E45, E52 and E60.

❺ Salzburg (p616)

Across the Austrian border lies Salzburg, a baroque blockbuster chiefly known for its musical connections: Wolfgang Amadeus Mozart (born here) and *The Sound of Music* (filmed here). The town is at its busiest during the annual Salzburg Festival and Christmas markets, but the Altstadt is always animated – and the Alps are only a quick skip away. All together now – *the hills are alive...*

Christmas market, Nuremberg (p568), Germany

London to Athens The Grand Tour

This is the big one – end to end, top to bottom and back again. You're covering a vast swath of Europe, so travelling times are long, but apart from a few flights, you can mostly watch the scenery unfold from the train.

❶ London (p60)

Two days isn't much time in London, but you should still be able to do the highlights: the Tower of London, Tate Modern, Big Ben and Buckingham Palace, with an extra day for discovering some of the shops, restaurants and theatres of the West End, and perhaps a trip downriver to Greenwich.

LONDON ➔ PARIS

Two hours On the Eurostar **One hour** From Heathrow or Gatwick to Roissy Charles de Gaulle.

❷ Paris (p174)

A high-speed Eurostar train whisks you via the Channel Tunnel to Paris. It's a city you've seen a million times in movies, but somehow nothing prepares you for your first sight of the Eiffel Tower appearing above the rooftops – and that's before you even get started on the Arc de Triomphe, the Louvre and Montmartre.

PARIS ➔ MADRID

Eight hours Via the high-speed TGV line
Two hours

❸ Madrid (p286)

There's nowhere better to experience Spain than Madrid – whether that means dining out on tapas in one of the city's squares, heading for a meal at a top-class *taberna* (tavern), watching authentic flamenco at a traditional tablao, or surveying the national art collection at the Museo del Prado.

MADRID ➔ ROME

Two hours

❹ Rome (p368)

The Eternal City; it is said a lifetime isn't enough to know it. During two days' sightseeing in Rome, choose from among the attractions of the Colosseum, Vatican City, Pantheon, Spanish Steps and the Trevi Fountain. For the perfect pizza, you'll want to head for the *centro storico* (historic centre) or Trastevere.

ROME ➔ VIENNA

13 hours Via direct night train; other trains require change at Bologna, Venice or Florence
Two hours

Temple of Olympian Zeus (p699), Athens, Greece

5 Vienna (p598)

Catch the overnight sleeper train direct to the imperial city of Vienna, where you'll spend a couple of days visiting the monumentally graceful Hofburg, watching the Lipizzaner stallions and whiling away hours over coffee and cake in one of Vienna's many grand cafes.

VIENNA ➔ PRAGUE

4½ hours Direct; longer with connections

Four hours It's 335km via E50.

6 Prague (p654)

Even though it spent decades behind the Iron Curtain, Prague has retained its rich cultural and architectural heritage. This isn't just the Czech Republic's loveliest city, it's also one of the loveliest in Europe, with iconic buildings such as Charles Bridge and Prague Castle contributing to a truly dreamy skyline.

PRAGUE ➔ BERLIN

4½ hours Direct **3½ hours** It's 350km via A13.

7 Berlin (p528)

Another train trip transports you to the German capital where you should spend a day investigating vestiges of the Berlin Wall, the Nazi years and royal Prussia before dedicating another to the dynamic Berlin of today, including its famous nightlife. Kreuzberg is the alternative hub while Mitte is smarter.

BERLIN ➔ ATHENS

Two hours

8 Athens (p698)

Finish with Greece's capital, Athens. The city is a treasure trove of ancient ruins: the Temple of Olympian Zeus, the Ancient Agora and the Theatre of Dionysos are all haunting in their own way, but it's the Parthenon that is guaranteed to stay with you long after you leave for home.

Europe Month by Month

Top Events

Christmas Markets, Germany & Austria, December

Oktoberfest, Germany, September

Venice Carnevale, Italy, February

Edinburgh International Festival, Scotland, August

Notting Hill Carnival, England, August

February

Carnival in all its mania sweeps the Catholic regions of the Continent. Cold temperatures – even in Venice – are forgotten amid masquerades, street festivals and general bacchanalia.

Venice Carnevale

In the period before Ash Wednesday, Venice, Italy, goes mad for masks. Costume balls enliven the social calendar in this storied old city like no other event. Even those without a coveted invite are swept up in the pageantry.

March

Let's hear it for the crocus: the tiny bulb's purple flower breaks through the ice-crusted soil to let Europe know there's a thaw in the air and spring will soon come.

St Patrick's Day

Celebrations are held on 17 March in Irish towns big and small to honour the beloved Saint Patrick. While elsewhere the day is a commercialised romp of green beer, here it's time for watching a parade with friends and family.

April

Spring arrives with a burst of colour, from the glorious bulb fields of the Netherlands to the blooming orchards of Spain.

Semana Santa

Parades of penitents and holy icons take to the streets of Spain, notably Seville, during Easter. Thousands of members of religious brotherhoods parade in traditional garb. Look for the pointed *capirotes* (hoods).

February Venice Carnevale, Italy

Settimana Santa

Italy celebrates Holy Week with processions and passion plays. By Holy Thursday Rome is thronged with the faithful and even non-believers are swept up in the emotion and piety of the hundreds of thousands thronging the Vatican and St Peter's Basilica.

Feria de Abril

Hoods off! This is a week-long party held in Seville in late April to counterbalance the religious peak of Easter. The many old squares in this gorgeous city come alive during Spain's long, warm nights.

Koningsdag (Kings's Day)

On 27 April (26 April if the 27th is a Sunday) the Netherlands celebrates the birthday of King Willem-Alexander nationwide but especially in Amsterdam, where – uproarious partying, music and outrageous orange get-ups aside – there's a giant flea market.

May

Expect nice weather anywhere but especially in the south where the Mediterranean summer is already full steam ahead. Yachts prowl the harbours, while beautiful people ply the sands.

Cannes Film Festival

The famous, not-so-famous and the merely topless converge for a year's worth of movies in little more than a week in Cannes, France. Those winning awards will be sure to tell you about it in film trailers for years to come.

Brussels Jazz Marathon

Around-the-clock jazz performances hit Brussels, Belgium, during the second-last weekend in May (www.brusselsjazzmarathon.be), when the saxophone becomes the instrument of choice for this international-flavoured city's most joyous celebration.

June

The huge summer travel season hasn't burst out yet but the sun has burst through the clouds and the weather is gorgeous, from the hot shores in the south to the cool climes of the north.

Glastonbury Festival

Glastonbury's youthful summer vibe peaks for this long weekend of music, theatre and New Age shenanigans (www.glastonburyfestivals.co.uk). It's one of England's favourite outdoor events and more than 100,000 turn up to writhe around in the grassy fields (or deep mud) at Pilton Farm.

July

Visitors have arrived from around the world and outdoor cafes, beer gardens and beach clubs are hopping. Expect beautiful – even steamy – weather anywhere you go.

Il Palio

Siena's great annual event is the Palio on 2 July and 16 August, a pageant culminating in a bareback horse race round Il Campo. The Italian city is divided into 17 *contrade* (districts), of which 10 compete for the *palio* (silk banner), and emotions explode.

Sanfermines (Running of the Bulls)

Huge male bovines and people who want to be close to them invade Pamplona, Spain, from 6 to 14 July, when the town is overrun with thrill seekers, curious onlookers and, oh yeah, bulls. The *encierro* (running of the bulls) begins at 8am daily. Anything can happen, but it rarely ends well for the bull.

Bastille Day

There's fireworks, balls, processions and more for France's national day, 14 July. It's celebrated in every French town and city: go to the heart of town and get caught up in this patriotic festival.

Notting Hill Carnival

Held over two days in August, this is Europe's largest and London's most vibrant outdoor carnival, where London's Caribbean community shows the city how to party. Food, frolicking and fun are just a part of a vast multicultural celebration.

Edinburgh International Festival

Edinburgh, Scotland, hosts three weeks of drama, comedy, dance and music from around the globe (www.eif.co.uk). For two weeks the International Festival overlaps with the Fringe Festival (www.edfringe.com), which also draws innovative international acts. Expect cutting-edge comedy, drama and productions that defy description.

De Gentse Feesten

Belgium's Ghent is transformed into a 10-day party of music and theatre, a highlight of which is the vast techno celebration called 10 Days Off (www.gentsefeesten.be). This gem of the low country is high on fine bars serving countless kinds of beer.

August

Everybody's going somewhere as half of Europe shuts down to go enjoy the traditional month of holiday with the other half. If it's near the beach, from Germany's Baltic to Spain's Balearic, it's mobbed.

Salzburg Festival

Austria's renowned classical music festival, the Salzburg Festival (www.salzburgfestival.at) attracts international stars from late July to the end of August. That urbane person sitting by you having a glass of wine who looks like a famous cellist probably is.

September

It's cooling off in every sense, from the northern countries to the romance started on a dance floor in Ibiza. This may be the best time to visit: the weather's still good and the crowds have thinned.

Venice International Film Festival

The Mostra del Cinema di Venezia is Italy's top film festival and one of the world's top indie film fests (www.labiennale.org). The judging here is seen as an early indication of what to look for at the next year's Oscars.

Oktoberfest

Germany's legendary beer-swilling party, originates from the marriage celebrations of Crown Prince Ludwig in 1810. Munich's Oktoberfest (www.oktoberfest.de) runs for the 15 days before the first Sunday in October. Millions come for whopping 1L steins of beer and carousing that has no equal.

Festes de la Mercè

Barcelona knows how to party until dawn and it outdoes itself during the four-day Festes de la Mercè (around 24 September). Head for concerts, join the dancing and marvel at *castellers* (human-castle builders), fireworks and *correfocs* – a parade of firework-spitting dragons and devils.

November

Leaves have fallen and snow is about to in much of Europe. Even in the temperate zones around the Med, it can get chilly, rainy and blustery.

Guy Fawkes Night

Bonfires and fireworks flare up across Britain on 5 November recalling the failed antigovernment 'gunpowder plot'from 1605 to blow up the parliament (Fawkes was in charge of the explosives). Go to high ground in London to see glowing explosions erupt everywhere.

December

Christmas is a good excuse for warm cheer despite the weather in virtually every city and town. Decorations transform even the drabbest shopping streets and every region has its own traditions.

Christmas Markets

Christmas markets are held across many European counties, particularly Germany and Austria, whose most famous are Nuremberg's Christkindlmarkt and Vienna's Weihnachtsmarkt. Warm your hands through your mittens holding a hot mug of mulled wine and find that special present.

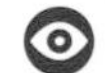

Natale

Italian churches set up intricate cribs or *presepi* (nativity scenes) in the lead-up to Christmas. Some are quite famous, most are works of art and many date back hundreds of years and are venerated for their spiritual ties.

Far left: August Performer at Edinburgh Festival Fringe, Scotland
Left: December Christmas market, Salzburg, Germany

(FAR LEFT) GARETH MCCORMACK/ GETTY IMAGES ©; (LEFT) RICHARD NEBESKY/ GETTY IMAGES ©

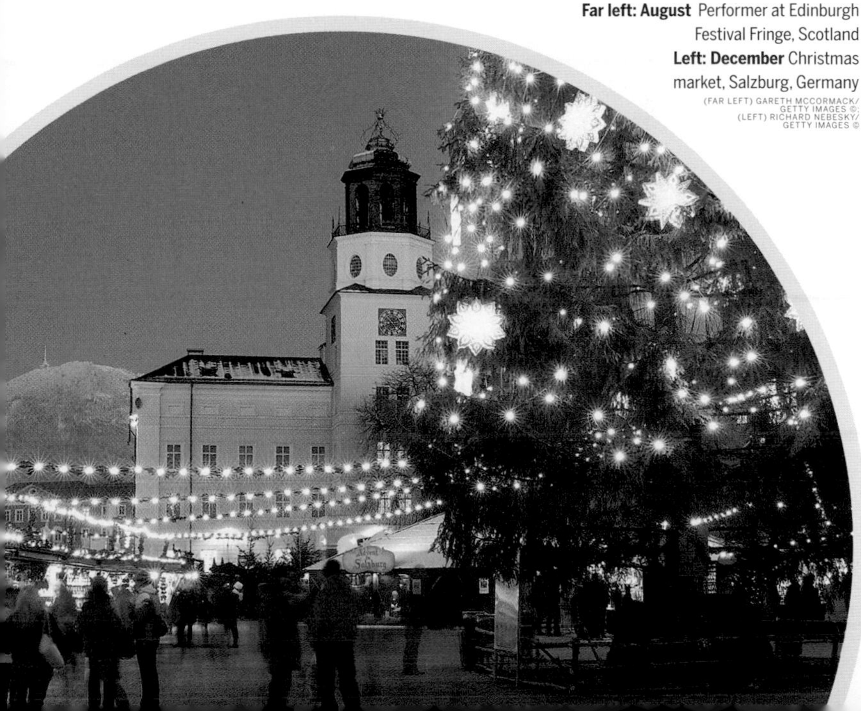

What's New

For this new edition of Discover Europe, our authors hunted down the fresh, the transformed, the hot and the happening. Here are a few of our favourites. For up-to-the-minute recommendations, see lonelyplanet.com/europe.

1 LONDON–AMSTERDAM HIGH-SPEED TRAINS

From late 2016, direct Eurostar services will link London with Amsterdam, stopping at Brussels, Antwerp, Rotterdam and Schiphol airport en route, with a London–Amsterdam journey time of around four hours. (p777)

2 MERCATO CENTRALE

The 1st floor of Florence's covered market has been transformed to house a cooking school, thematic bookshop and stalls selling everything from pizza and pasta to cheese, ice cream and pastries. (p429)

3 DOMQUARTIER

A single ticket provides access to all five sights of the newly opened DomQuartier in Salzburg's historic centre, including the Residenz, Dommuseum and Erzabtei St Peter. (p617)

4 CRUMLIN ROAD GAOL

Belfast's most notorious prison is now a brilliant museum where visitors experience first hand the conditions in which its inmates were kept. (www.crumlinroadgaol.com)

5 ROTTERDAM'S RENAISSANCE

Urban regeneration projects, including a barrelling 1.5m-high surfing wave in an inner-city canal and eye-popping new Markthal (market hall), make Rotterdam one of Europe's most exhilarating cities right now. (p484)

6 THE MAKING OF HARRY POTTER

Prospective Hogwarts pupils can practise their spells during this spectacular new tour at Warner Bros Studios, just outside London. (p94)

7 MUSÉE DES CIVILISATIONS DE L'EUROPE ET DE LA MÉDITERRANÉE

A vertigo-inducing footbridge links the two dramatically contrasting sites of Marseille's stunning new Museum of European & Mediterranean Civilisations: the 13th-century Fort St-Jean and ultracontemporary J4. (p252)

8 BANNOCKBURN VISITOR CENTRE

To mark the 700th anniversary of the Battle of Bannockburn, the National Trust for Scotland unveiled a revamped, high-tech heritage centre on the battlefield. (www.battleofbannockburn.com)

9 STONEHENGE

A £27-million revamp of Britain's most famous prehistoric site has seen the area around the stones returned to grassland, and an impressive new visitor centre. (p98)

10 MUSÉE PICASSO

Finally, after five years of renovations, one of Paris' most beloved art collections – containing 5000 of Picasso's works – has reopened in this beautiful mid-17th-century Marais mansion. (p182)

11 ALBERTINUM

Also fresh from renovations is Dresden's Albertinum museum, displaying masterworks from the 18th to the 20th centuries in its Galerie Neue Meister (New Masters Gallery). (p546)

12 RINGSTRASSE

Vienna's Ringstrasse boulevard encircling the historic centre's trophy sights – from the Gothic-revival Rathaus to the neo-Renaissance Staatsoper – is sparkling from its 150th anniversary celebrations. (p608)

Get Inspired

Books

- **Neither Here nor There: Travels in Europe** Hilarious travelogue by best-selling author Bill Bryson, retracing his European backpacking trip of 20 years before.
- **Europe: A History** Professor Norman Davies' sweeping overview of European history.
- **In Europe: Travels through the Twentieth Century** Fascinating account of journalist Geert Mak's travels.
- **Philip's Multiscale Europe** Plan your European road trip with this continent-wide travel atlas.

Films

- **The Third Man** (1949) Classic tale of wartime espionage in old Vienna, starring Orson Welles and that zither theme.
- **Amélie** (2001) Endearing tale following the quirky adventures of Parisian do-gooder Amélie Poulain.
- **Shaun of the Dead** (2004) Typically quirky British zombie comedy, set in London's streets.
- **Vicky Cristina Barcelona** (2008) Woody Allen rom-com makes use of a beautiful Barcelona backdrop.

Music

- **The Original Three Tenors: 20th Anniversary Edition** Operatic classics courtesy of Pavarotti, Carreras and Domingo.
- **The Best of Edith Piaf** The sound of France, including a selection of the Little Sparrow's greatest hits.
- **Chambao** Feel-good flamenco fused with electronica from Andalucía's deep south.
- **Arctic Monkeys: Whatever People Say I Am, That's What I'm Not** Spiky tunes from northern British songsmiths.

Websites

- **Visit Europe** (www.visiteurope.com) Extensive resource of the European Travel Commission.
- **The Man in Seat Sixty-One** (www.seat61.com) Hands-on advice for European train travel.
- **Eurocheapo** (www.eurocheapo.com) Budget-friendly ideas for hotels, eating, flights and sights.
- **Auto Europe** (www.auto-europe.com) Cheap car hire for all Europe.

Short on time?

This list will give you an instant insight into Europe.

Read *The Europe Book* is a sumptuous Lonely Planet photo-book packed with images of Europe's greatest sights.

Watch *Cinema Paradiso* (1988) tells the heart-warming tale of one boy's cinematic love affair in rural Italy.

Listen Soundtrack your own *Magical Mystery Tour* courtesy of The Beatles.

Log on Visit www.raileurope.com (US) or http://uk.voyages-sncf.com (UK) for the info to plan your pan-European train trip.

Gondolas, Venice (p401), Italy

Need to Know

Currency

Pound sterling (£), euro (€), Swiss franc (Sfr), Czech crown (Kč). For current exchange rates see www.xe.com

Languages

Czech, Dutch, English, French, German, Greek, Italian, Spanish

Visas

Citizens of most Western countries generally don't need visas for tourist visits to Ireland, the UK or any Schengen country for stays of up to 90 days.

Money

ATMs are widespread. Credit-card usage varies by county; Visa and MasterCard are the most widely accepted.

Mobile Phones

Beware high roaming charges. Local SIM cards work in most unlocked mobile phones.

Wi-Fi

Common in most hotels and cafes; usually free.

For more information see Survival Guide (p765)

When to Go

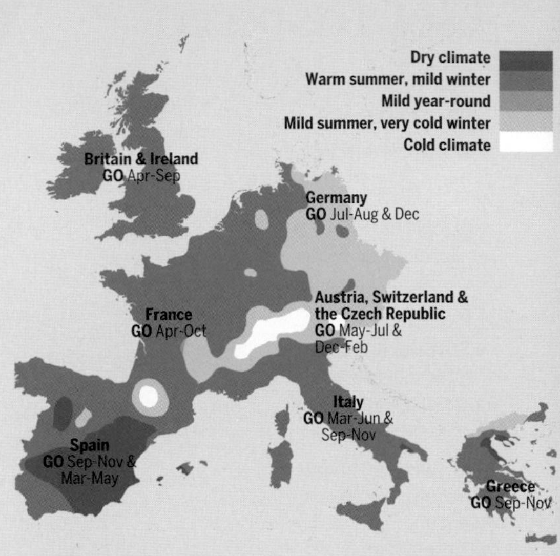

High Season (Jun–Aug)

- Hotel prices take a hefty hike in summer.
- Ski season in the Alps is December to early March.
- Businesses in major cities may have closures around August.

Shoulder Season (Apr–May & Sep–Oct)

- Weather is warm and settled across much of Europe.
- Crowds are lighter, but some attractions keep shorter hours.

Low Season (Nov–Mar)

- Look out for cheap deals on flights and accommodation.
- Some hotels, sights and activities close completely for the winter.

Advance Planning

- **One month before** Book train tickets. Most train companies offer substantial discounts for advance bookings.
- **Two weeks before** Reserve tickets online for popular sights, such as the Alhambra in Granada, the Louvre in Paris and the Colosseum in Rome.
- **When you arrive** Look into buying a travel pass for public transport in major cities; some passes also offer free or discounted admissions.

Daily Costs

Budget Less than €100

- Dorm bed: €20–€50
- Double room in a budget property: €60–€100
- Excellent markets; restaurant mains under around €12
- Local bus/train tickets: €5–€10

Midrange €100–€250

- Double room in a midrange hotel: €80–€160
- Restaurant mains around €12–€25
- Museum admission: free–€15
- Short taxi trip: €10–€20

Top End More than €250

- Iconic hotels
- Destination restaurants
- Duty-free refunds from stylish shopping

What to Bring

- **Passport or EU ID** Remember to bring your driver's licence if you're hiring a car.
- **Travel adaptors** EU countries use two-pin sockets; Ireland and the UK use three-pin sockets.
- **Sturdy shoes** You'll be doing a lot of walking, so good soles are important.
- **Rain gear** In case the weather turns bad.
- **Travel insurance** Check the policy wording on winter sports and flight delays.
- **A corkscrew** Essential for picnics.
- **Phrasebook** Choose one with a good food section for the country you're travelling to.

Tipping

Adding another 5% to 10% to a bill at a restaurant or cafe for good service is common across Europe, although tipping is never expected.

Arriving in Europe

- **London** Trains run from Heathrow Airport to London Paddington (20min), and from Gatwick Airport to London Victoria (20min). Piccadilly tube line runs to Heathrow terminals.
- **Paris** Regular buses (1hr) and trains (30min) run from Charles de Gaulle Airport to Paris.
- **Berlin** Frankfurt Trains (15min) from Frankfurt airport to the centre.
- **Madrid** Line 8 of the Metro (15min) and the Exprés Aeropuerto (40min) run to the city centre.
- **Amsterdam** Regular trains (20min) from Schiphol to Centraal Station.
- **Rome** Buses (1hr) and trains (30min) run from Leonardo da Vinci Airport to the city centre.

Getting Around

- **Car** Huge network of motorways and major roads throughout Europe. Motorways in many countries incur a toll, and petrol is expensive. Rental cars are mostly manual shift.
- **Train** High-speed trains connect major cities throughout Europe; slower trains serve regional towns. Can be faster and cheaper than flying.
- **Air** Internal flights with budget carriers are numerous, but often don't land at major airports.
- **Bus** Useful for smaller towns and rural areas.

Sleeping

- **Hotels** There's a huge choice available, ranging from basic city digs to full-blown luxury.
- **B&Bs** Generally have fewer facilities than hotels, but more local character.
- **Hostels** Nearly every major city has at least one hostel, with a choice of communal dorms or private rooms.
- **Camping** Sleeping under canvas is very popular in Europe, and you'll find plenty of sites to choose from.

Be Forewarned

- **Holiday seasons** Prices skyrocket and accommodation can be hard to find in July and August. Easter is also busy.
- **Pickpocketing** A problem in many cities, especially on public transport and around major attractions.

Britain & Ireland

Few countries are as plagued by cliché as Britain and Ireland. On one side of the Irish Sea, it's all shamrocks and shillelaghs, Guinness and 40 shades of green; over in Britain, it's double-decker buses and red telephone boxes, buttoned-up emotions and stiff upper lips. Yet, while some of the stereotypes are still true, these ancient next-door nations seem to have sloughed off most of the old clichés and turned their gazes firmly towards the future.

Whether it's ancient history or contemporary culture that draws you to Britain's shores, you'll really be spoiled for choice. Travelling around these pocket-sized islands is an absolute breeze, and you'll never be more than a train ride away from the next national park, tumbledown castle, world-class gallery or stately home. There are museums aplenty, galleries galore and mile upon mile of some of the most stunning coast and countryside you'll find anywhere in Europe. So, buckle up – you're in for an awfully big adventure.

Castle Howard (p113), England

KARL BLACKWELL/GETTY IMAGES ©

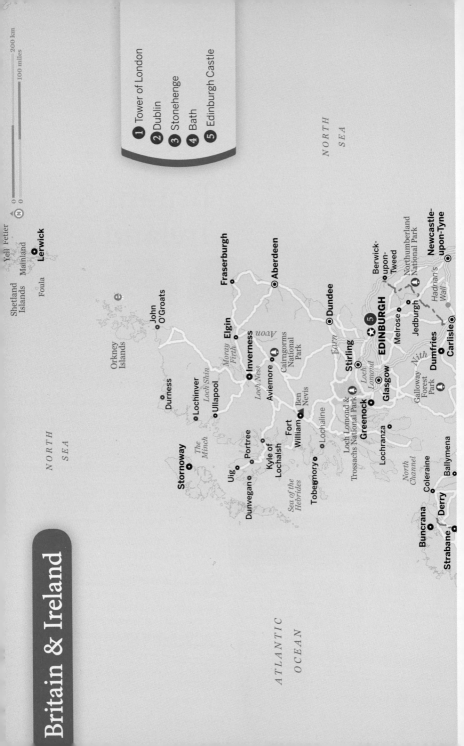

Britain & Ireland

1. Tower of London
2. Dublin
3. Stonehenge
4. Bath
5. Edinburgh Castle

NORTH SEA
Shetland Islands
Yell
Fetlar
Mainland
Foula
Lerwick
0 200 km
0 100 miles
Orkney Islands
John O'Groats
Durness
Stornoway
The Minch
Lochinver
Loch Shin
Ullapool
Moray Firth
Elgin
Fraserburgh
Uig
Dunvegan
Portree
Inverness
Loch Ness
Avon
Kyle of Lochalsh
Aviemore
Aberdeen
Cairngorms National Park
ATLANTIC OCEAN
Sea of the Hebrides
Fort William
Ben Nevis
Tobermory
Lochaline
Dundee
Earn
NORTH SEA
Loch Lomond & Trossachs National Park
Stirling
Greenock
Loch Lomond
EDINBURGH
Berwick-upon-Tweed
Lochranza
Glasgow
Melrose
North Channel
Jedburgh
Northumberland National Park
Galloway Forest Park
Nith
Buncrana
Coleraine
Dumfries
Hadrian's Wall
Newcastle-upon-Tyne
Strabane
Derry
Ballymena
Carlisle

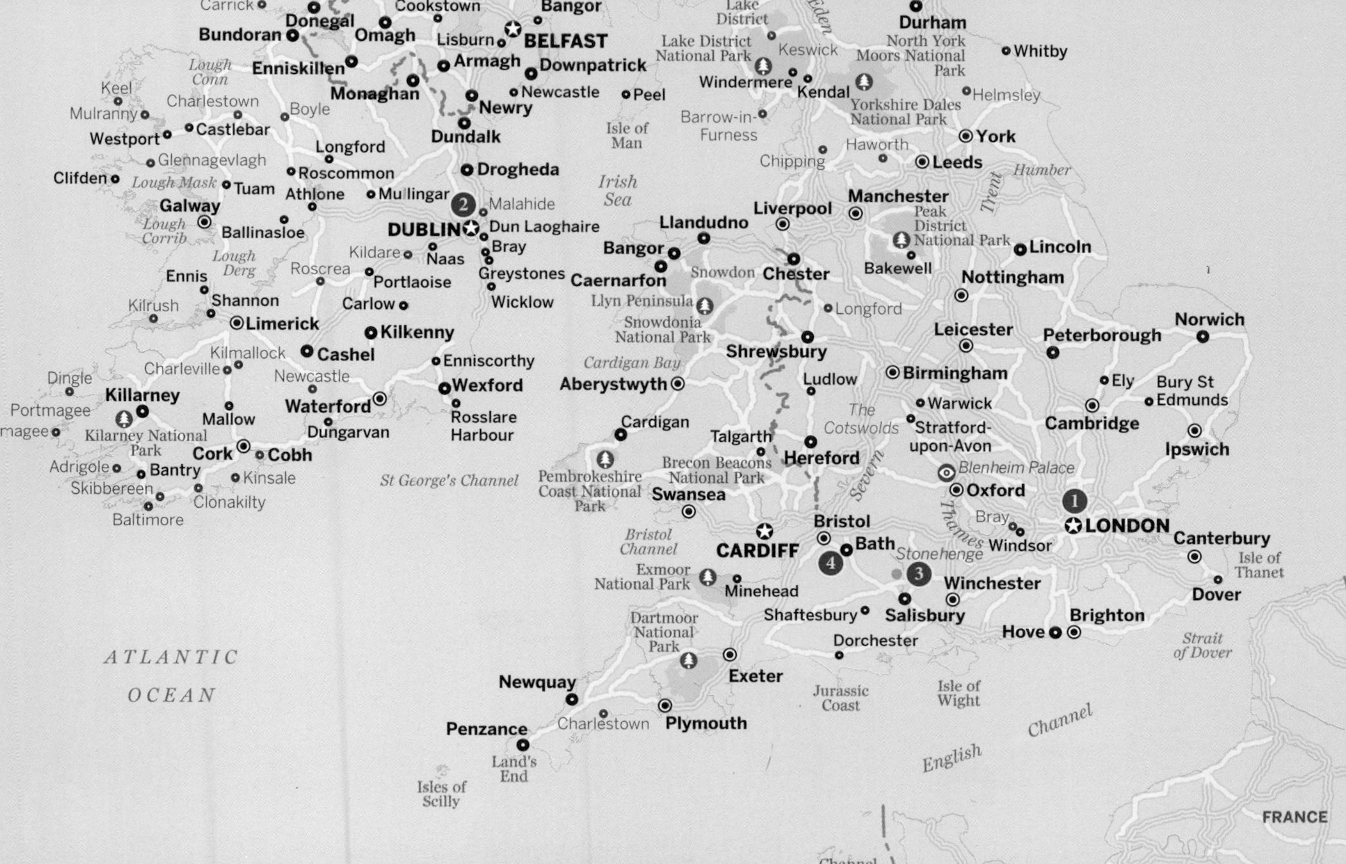

Carrick
Donegal
Bundoran
Omagh
Cookstown
Bangor
Lisburn
BELFAST
Lough Conn
Enniskillen
Armagh
Downpatrick
Monaghan
Newcastle
Newry
Peel
Keel
Mulranny
Charlestown
Boyle
Castlebar
Westport
Dundalk
Isle of Man
Longford
Glennagevlagh
Clifden
Lough Mask
Tuam
Roscommon
Drogheda
Athlone
Mullingar
Malahide
Irish Sea
Galway
Lough Corrib
Ballinasloe
DUBLIN
Dun Laoghaire
Kildare
Naas
Bray
Lough Derg
Ennis
Roscrea
Portlaoise
Greystones
Wicklow
Kilrush
Shannon
Limerick
Carlow
Kilkenny
Kilmallock
Cashel
Enniscorthy
Charleville
Dingle
Newcastle
Wexford
Killarney
Portmagee
Mallow
Waterford
Rosslare Harbour
Portmagee
Kilarney National Park
Dungarvan
Cork
Cobh
Adrigole
Bantry
Kinsale
Skibbereen
Clonakilty
Baltimore
St George's Channel
ATLANTIC OCEAN
Lake District
Eden
Lake District National Park
Keswick
Windermere
Kendal
Barrow-in-Furness
Durham
North York Moors National Park
Whitby
Yorkshire Dales National Park
Helmsley
York
Haworth
Chipping
Leeds
Humber
Trent
Manchester
Liverpool
Peak District National Park
Llandudno
Bangor
Chester
Caernarfon
Snowdon
Bakewell
Lincoln
Nottingham
Llyn Peninsula
Snowdonia National Park
Longford
Shrewsbury
Leicester
Peterborough
Norwich
Cardigan Bay
Aberystwyth
Ludlow
Birmingham
Ely
Bury St Edmunds
Warwick
The Cotswolds
Stratford-upon-Avon
Cambridge
Ipswich
Cardigan
Talgarth
Hereford
Severn
Brecon Beacons National Park
Pembrokeshire Coast National Park
Blenheim Palace
Oxford
Swansea
Bristol
Thames
Bray
Windsor
LONDON
Canterbury
Isle of Thanet
Bristol Channel
CARDIFF
Bath
Stonehenge
Exmoor National Park
Minehead
Winchester
Dover
Shaftesbury
Salisbury
Brighton
Hove
Dartmoor National Park
Dorchester
Strait of Dover
Exeter
Newquay
Jurassic Coast
Isle of Wight
Charlestown
Plymouth
Penzance
Land's End
English Channel
Isles of Scilly
FRANCE
Channel Islands
1
2
3
4

Britain & Ireland Highlights

Tower of London

One of London's world-famous landmarks, the Tower (p66) wraps up almost 1000 years of history within its Thameside turrets and battlements. Famously, it's home to the Crown Jewels, that glittering collection of jewels, sceptres, orbs and crowns used during the coronation of British monarchs. Look out for the Tower's famous flock of ravens and its red-coated Yeoman Warders (or Beefeaters, as they're generally known).

1

MICHAEL ENGLAND/GETTY IMAGES ©

2 Dublin

Ireland's capital (p134) and largest city by some stretch has enough distractions to keep visitors mesmerised for at least a few days. Dublin offers world-class museums and entertainment, superb dining and top-grade hotels. But the real clinchers are Dubliners themselves, who are friendlier, more easy-going and welcoming than the burghers of virtually any other European capital. And it's the home of Guinness.

GEORGE MUNDAY/GETTY IMAGES ©

DAVID NUNUK/GETTY IMAGES ©

3 Stonehenge

You've seen it a million times in photographs, magazines and TV documentaries, but nothing quite prepares you for your first sight of the real Stonehenge (p98). Built by ancient Britons in several stages between 3000 BC and 1600 BC, it's an unforgettable structure. To see the circle at its best, book an after-hours guided tour, which will enable you to dodge the crowds.

KARL BLACKWELL/GETTY IMAGES ©

4 Bath

Say what you like about the Romans, but one thing's for sure – they certainly knew how to build a hot tub. The natural geothermal springs of Bath (p95) have been attracting visitors for more than two thousand years, but this city has so much more to offer than a soothing soak: great restaurants, top-notch shopping and some of the finest Georgian architecture in all of England. Above: Royal Crescent (p95)

5 Edinburgh Castle

Dominating the skyline of Edinburgh from practically every angle, the city's magnificent clifftop fortress (p121) is a sight to behold. It's played a key role in Scotland's history since the 11th century, and with its crenellated battlements, massive walls and brooding watchtowers, it's every inch the image of a classic Scottish castle. Don't miss the view from the Argyle Battery, and try and be around to hear the One O'Clock Gun.

Britain & Ireland's Best...

Beauty Spots

- **Lake District** (p112) Admire the landscape that inspired Wordsworth, Coleridge and Co.
- **Snowdonia** (p119) Climb the highest mountain in Wales.
- **Giant's Causeway** (p155) Explore Northern Ireland's great geological oddity.
- **Scottish Highlands** (p132) Great glens, glassy lochs and snowy mountains.
- **Ring of Kerry** (p148) Home to some of Ireland's most stunning views.

Houses & Palaces

- **Hampton Court Palace** (p75) This glorious Tudor structure is just a quick trip from the British capital.
- **Castle Howard** (p113) Quite possibly the finest stately home in northern England.
- **Buckingham Palace** (p61) Pomp and ceremony galore at the Queen's London residence.
- **Palace of Westminster** (p61) The home of British politics, otherwise known as the Houses of Parliament.
- **Holyroodhouse** (p124) The Queen's official Scottish crash-pad.

Castles

- **Windsor Castle** (p108) Castles don't come much more regal than this royal weekend getaway.
- **Leeds Castle** (p108) Despite the name, this classic castle is an easy trip from London.
- **Warwick Castle** (p108) Is this England's finest fortress? You decide.
- **Edinburgh Castle** (p121) Gaze out from the battlements across Scotland's capital city.
- **Conwy Castle** (p119) A majestic medieval castle overlooking the Welsh coastline.

Literary Locations

- **Stratford-upon-Avon** (p105) The home town of William Shakespeare, Britain's most famous poet and playwright.
- **James Joyce Museum** (p137) Lots of literary memorabilia relating to Ireland's greatest novelist.
- **Bath** (p95) Must-visit location for Jane Austen fans.
- **Hill Top** (p112) Join the crowds at Beatrix Potter's Lake District cottage.
- **Oxford Bar, Edinburgh** (p131) Drink in the pub favoured by Inspector Rebus.

Left: Snowdonia National Park (p119), Wales; **Above:** Houses of Parliament (p61), London

Need to Know

ADVANCE PLANNING

- **As early as possible** Arrange train tickets and car hire. Buying at least a month in advance secures the cheapest deals.
- **One month before** Book hotels and make restaurant reservations, especially in popular cities such as London, Manchester and Bath.
- **One week before** Book guided tours and confirm prices and opening hours.

RESOURCES

- **Visit Britain** (www.visitbritain.com) The UK's main tourism site covers everything from accommodation to outdoor activities.
- **National Rail Enquiries** (www.nationalrail.co.uk) Check out timetables and book train tickets.
- **Traveline** (www.traveline.org.uk) Journey planning for public transport throughout the British Isles.
- **Discover Ireland** (www.ireland.com) Comprehensive info on the Emerald Isle, from places to stay to things to do.

GETTING AROUND

- **Air** Budget flights connect most major British and Irish cities, including London, Edinburgh, Belfast and Dublin.
- **Car** The best option for exploring rural areas, although remember to factor in petrol and parking costs. Road distances in Britain are in miles; Ireland uses kilometres.
- **Train** The best option for intercity travel. There are frequent connections between major towns.
- **Bus** Long-distance coaches and local buses are cheap but slow. Coverage can be patchy outside major towns.

BE FOREWARNED

- **Crowds** Top sights get extremely crowded, especially in summer and on holiday weekends.
- **Bank holidays** Most sights are closed and traffic on main roads can be a nightmare.
- **Nightlife** City centres can be extremely rowdy after dark on weekends.
- **Weather** Notoriously unpredictable, so be prepared. Umbrellas and raincoats essential.

Britain & Ireland Itineraries

It might be great by name, but Britain is surprisingly small by nature. The country's compact geography makes it easy to get around the sights; travelling by train allows you to drink in the scenery and dodge the traffic.

3 DAYS

THE BIG SMOKE & BEYOND

London to Blenheim Palace

World-class museums, historic castles, cutting-edge restaurants: ❶ **London** (p60) is a sightseeing overload, and you could devote your whole holiday to exploring the capital. In one day, you might just about fit in visits to Trafalgar Sq, Westminster, St Paul's Cathedral and the Tower of London, before a lightning-fast detour to the Turbine Hall in Tate Modern, and finishing with an unforgettable performance at Shakespeare's Globe Theatre.

Day two is more leisurely. Hop on a scenic boat along the River Thames to spend a morning at Britain's foremost botanical gardens, ❷ **Kew Gardens** (p75). In the afternoon, catch the boat downriver to visit Henry VIII's ostentatious abode at ❸ **Hampton Court** (p75).

On day three, take an early train to ❹ **Oxford** (p100). Spend the morning wandering the quads and admiring the dreaming spires before catching a bus to ❺ **Blenheim Palace** (p101), not just one of England's finest stately homes, but also the birthplace of Winston Churchill.

Top Left: Shakespeare's Globe (p65), London, England; **Top Right:** Oxford (p100), England

5 DAYS

NORTHERN EXPOSURE

Oxford to Dublin

From ❶ **Oxford** (p100), it's an easy train trip west to the gorgeous Georgian city of ❷ **Bath** (p95), founded as a spa town by the Romans 2000 years ago and still one of England's most desirable addresses. Devote the day to exploring the Roman Baths, soaking in the Thermae Bath Spa and walking along the city's grandest streets, Royal Crescent and the Circus.

From Bath, it's on to Shakespeare's birthplace at ❸ **Stratford-upon-Avon** (p105). The town is packed with sights linked with the Bard, but don't miss the chance to catch his plays in action courtesy of the Royal Shakespeare Company.

On day three, travel northwest to the Viking city of ❹ **York** (p109), with its medieval streets and landmark Minster. Next comes a day in Scotland's capital, ❺ **Edinburgh** (p121), a city renowned for its arts, architecture and history, as well as a brace of stately castles.

Finish your trip with a flight across the Irish Sea to ❻ **Dublin** (p134), a lively river city that's awash with literary heritage, not to mention a cracking pub culture. If you've always wanted to taste an authentic pint of Guinness, this is definitely the place to do it.

Discover Britain & Ireland

At a Glance

- **London** (p60) The big smoke has big thrills to match.
- **Wales** (p117) Celtic nation with its own language and culture.
- **Scotland** (p121) Lochs, mountains, castles and glens galore.
- **Ireland** (p134) From coast to countryside, the Emerald Isle enchants.

Trafalgar Square, London

LONDON

POP 8.3 MILLION

Everyone comes to London with preconceptions shaped by a multitude of books, movies, TV shows and songs. Whatever yours is, prepare to have it exploded by this endlessly fascinating, amorphous city. You could spend a lifetime exploring it and find that the slippery thing's gone and changed on you. One thing is constant: that great serpent of a river enfolding the city in its sinuous loops, linking London both to the green heart of England and to the world.

Sights

WESTMINSTER & ST JAMES

Westminster has been the centre of political power for a millennium, and the area's many landmarks combine to form an awesome display of strength, gravitas and historical import.

Westminster Abbey Church

(Map p70; ☎020-7222 5152; www.westminster-abbey.org; 20 Dean's Yard, SW1; adult/child £20/9, verger tours £5; 🕐9.30am-4.30pm Mon, Tue, Thu & Fri, to 7pm Wed, to 2.30pm Sat; ⊖Westminster)

Westminster Abbey is a mixture of architectural styles, but considered the finest example of Early English Gothic (1190–1300). It's not merely a beautiful place of worship, though. The Abbey serves up the country's history cold on slabs of stone. For centuries the country's greatest have been interred here, including 17 monarchs, from Henry III (died 1272) to George II (1760). Westminster Abbey has never been a cathedral (the seat of a bishop). It's what is called a 'royal peculiar', administered directly by the Crown.

Big Ben

The Houses of Parliament's most famous feature is the clock tower widely known as Big Ben. Strictly speaking, however, Big Ben is the tower's 13-ton bell, named after Benjamin Hall, commissioner of works when the tower was completed in 1858.

Houses of Parliament Historic Building
(Map p70; www.parliament.uk; Parliament Sq, SW1; ⊖Westminster) FREE Officially called the Palace of Westminster, the Houses of Parliament's oldest part is 11th-century Westminster Hall, which is one of only a few sections that survived a catastrophic fire in 1834. Its roof, added between 1394 and 1401, is the earliest known example of a hammerbeam roof. Most of the rest of the building is a neo-Gothic confection built by Charles Barry and Augustus Pugin's in the mid-19th century.

Buckingham Palace Palace
(Map p70; ☎020-7766 7300; www.royalcollection.org.uk; Buckingham Palace Rd, SW1; adult/child £20.50/11.80; ⏱9.30am-7.30pm late Jul–Aug, to 6.30pm Sep; ⊖St James's Park, Victoria, Green Park) Built in 1703 for the Duke of Buckingham, Buckingham Palace replaced St James's Palace as the monarch's official London residence in 1837. When she's not delivering her trademark wave to far-flung parts of the Commonwealth, Queen Elizabeth II divides her time between here, Windsor and, in summer, Balmoral. To check if she's at home, see whether the yellow, red and blue standard is flying.

Tate Britain Gallery
(Map p70; www.tate.org.uk; Millbank, SW1; ⏱10am-6pm, to 10pm 1st Fri of month; ⊖Pimlico) FREE Splendidly refurbished with a stunning new art-deco inspired staircase and a rehung collection, the more elderly and venerable of the two Tate siblings celebrates paintings from 1500 to the present, with works from Blake, Hogarth, Gainsborough, Barbara Hepworth, Whistler, Constable and Turner, as well as vibrant modern and contemporary pieces from Lucian Freud, Francis Bacon, Henry Moore and Tracey Emin. Join free 45-minute **thematic tours** (⏱11am, noon, 2pm & 3pm) and 15-minute **Art in Focus talks** (⏱1.15pm Tue, Thu & Sat)

WEST END

If anywhere is the beating heart of London, it's the West End – a strident mix of culture and consumerism.

Trafalgar Square Square
(Map p70; ⊖Charing Cross) In many ways Trafalgar Sq is where rallies and marches take place, tens of thousands of revellers usher in the New Year and locals congregate for anything from communal open-air cinema and Christmas celebrations to political protests. It is dominated by the 52m-high Nelson's Column and ringed by many splendid buildings, including the National Gallery and St Martin-in-the-Fields.

National Gallery Gallery
(Map p70; www.nationalgallery.org.uk; Trafalgar Sq, WC2; ⏱10am-6pm Sat-Thu, to 9pm Fri; ⊖Charing Cross) FREE With some 2300 European paintings on display, this is one of the world's richest art collections, with seminal paintings from every important epoch in the history of art from the mid-13th to the early 20th century, including works by Leonardo da Vinci, Michelangelo, Titian, Van Gogh and Renoir.

National Portrait Gallery Gallery
(Map p70; www.npg.org.uk; St Martin's Pl, WC2; ⏱10am-6pm Sat-Wed, to 9pm Thu & Fri; ⊖Charing Cross, Leicester Sq) FREE What makes the National Portrait Gallery so compelling is its familiarity; in many cases you'll have heard of the subject (royals, scientists, politicians, celebrities) or the artist (Andy Warhol, Annie Leibovitz, Sam Taylor-Wood). Highlights include the famous 'Chandos portrait' of William Shakespeare, believed to be the only likeness made during the playwright's lifetime, and a touching sketch of novelist Jane Austen by her sister.

Greater London

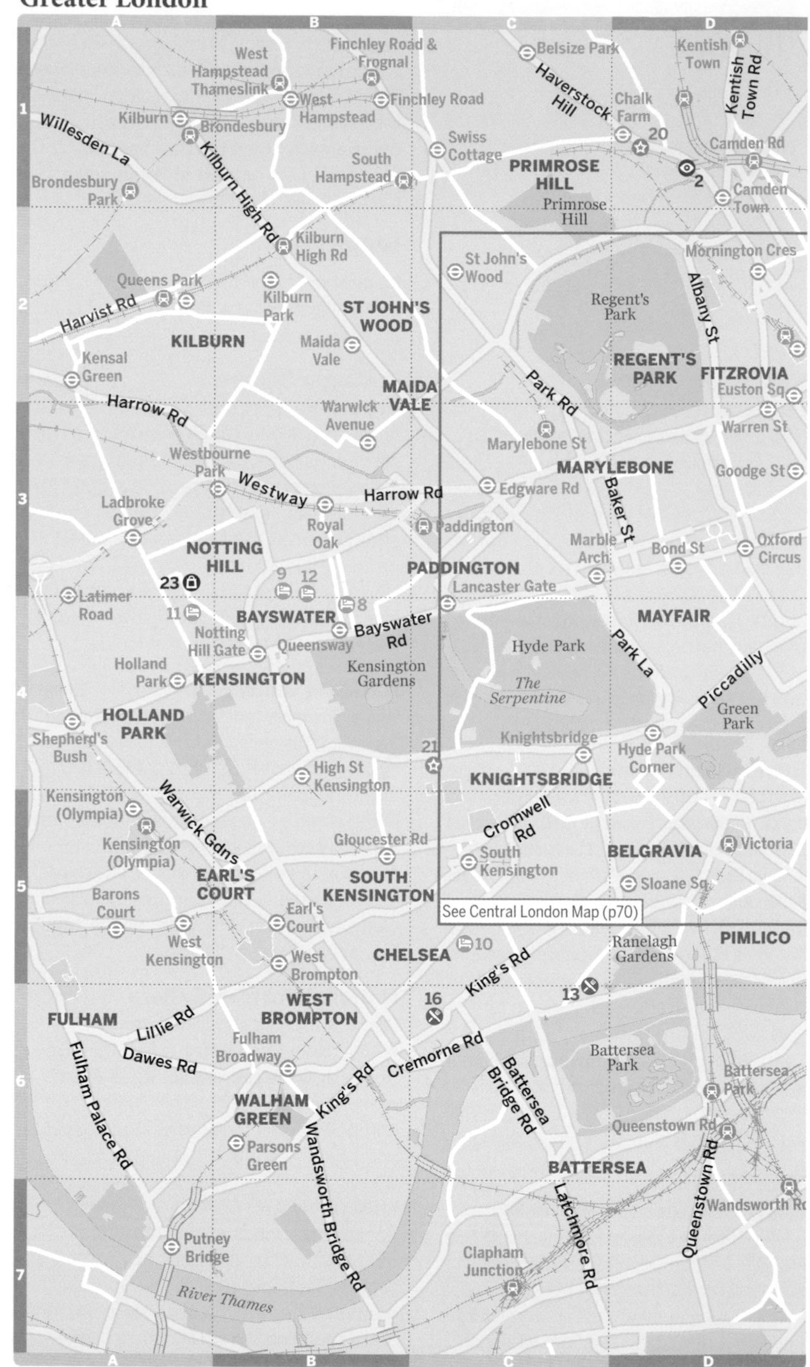

BRITAIN & IRELAND LONDON

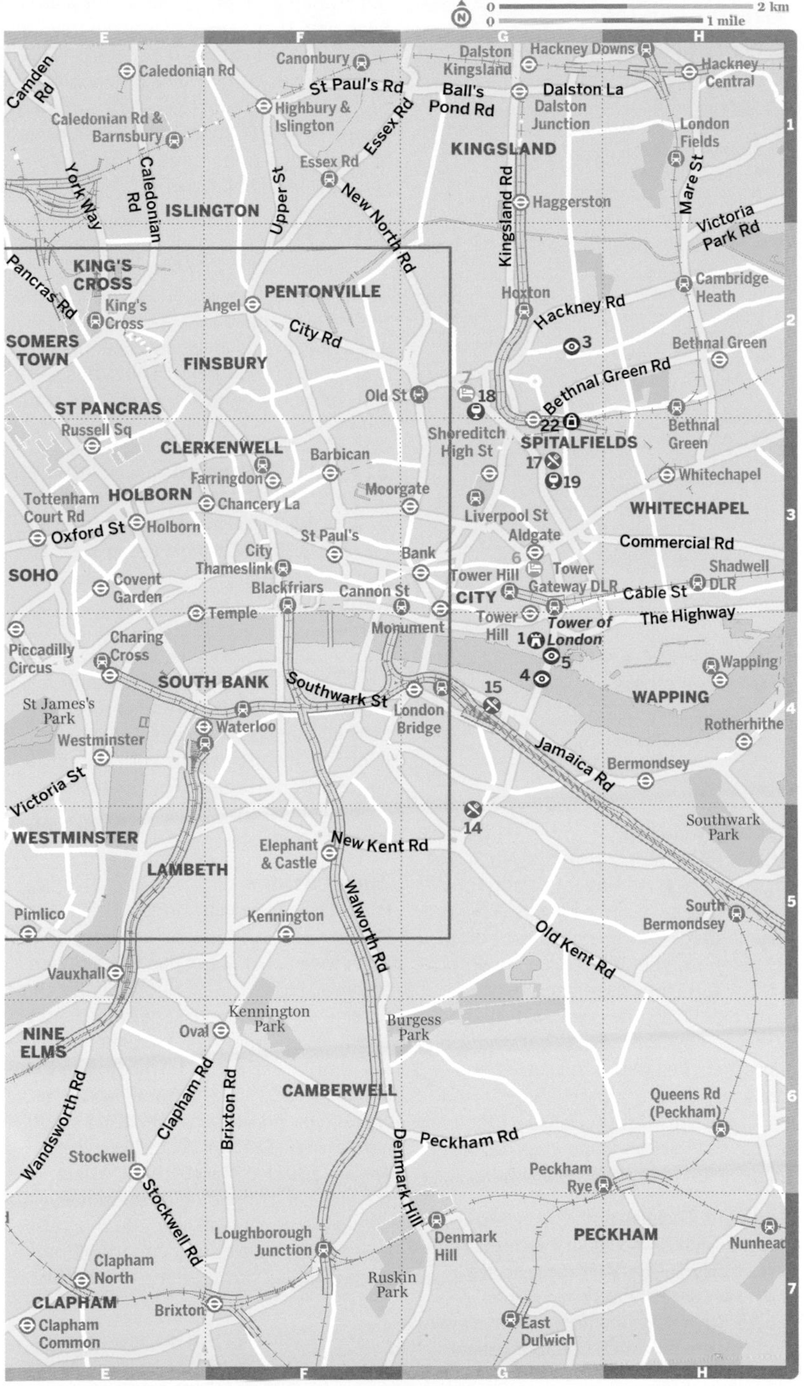

BRITAIN & IRELAND LONDON

Greater London

Don't Miss Sights
1 Tower of London G4

Sights
2 Camden Market D1
3 Columbia Road Flower Market G2
4 Tower Bridge G4
5 Tower Bridge Exhibition G4

Sleeping
6 Hotel Indigo Tower Hill G3
7 Hoxton Hotel G2
8 La Suite West B4
9 New Linden Hotel B3
10 No 90 .... C5
11 Portobello Hotel A4
12 Vancouver Studios B3

Eating
13 Gordon Ramsay C6
14 M Manze G5
15 Magdalen G4
16 Medlar C6
17 Poppies G3

Drinking & Nightlife
18 Book Club G2
19 Ten Bells G3

Entertainment
20 Roundhouse D1
21 Royal Albert Hall C4

Shopping
22 Brick Lane Market G3
23 Portobello Road Market A3

Piccadilly Circus Square

(Map p70; Piccadilly Circus) John Nash had originally designed Regent St and Piccadilly in the 1820s to be the two most elegant streets in town but, curbed by city planners, couldn't realise his dream to the full. He may have been disappointed but he'd have been astonished by Piccadilly Circus today: a traffic maelstrom, deluged with visitors and flanked by flashing advertisement panels. A seething hubbub, 'it's like Piccadilly Circus', as the expression goes, but it's certainly fun.

Madame Tussauds Museum

(Map p70; 0870 400 3000; www.madametussauds.com/london; Marylebone Rd, NW1; adult/child £30/26; 9.30am-5.30pm; Baker St) It may be kitschy and pricey (book online for much cheaper rates), but Madame Tussauds makes for a fun-filled day. There are photo ops with your dream celebrity at the A-List Party (Daniel Craig, Lady Gaga, George Clooney, the Beckhams), the Bollywood gathering (studs Hrithik Roshan and Salman Khan) and the Royal Appointment (the Queen, Harry, William and Kate).

THE CITY

For centuries, the City (note it is spelled with a capital C) *was* London. Its boundaries have changed little from the Roman walls built in this area two millennia ago, and today it's London's central business district (and also known as the 'square mile').

St Paul's Cathedral Church

(Map p70; 020-7246 8350; www.stpauls.co.uk; St Paul's Churchyard, EC4; adult/child £18/8; 8.30am-4.30pm Mon-Sat; St Paul's) Dominating the City of London with the world's second-largest church dome (weighing in at 65,000 tons), St Paul's Cathedral was designed by Sir Christopher Wren after the Great Fire and built between 1675 and 1710; it opened the following year. The site is ancient hallowed ground with four other cathedrals preceding Wren's English Baroque masterpiece here, the first dating from 604.

Tower Bridge Bridge

(Map p62; Tower Hill) London was a thriving port in 1894 when elegant Tower Bridge was built. Designed to be raised to allow ships to pass, electricity has now taken over from the original steam and hydraulic engines. A lift leads up from the northern tower to the **Tower Bridge Exhibition** (**020-7403 3761; www.towerbridge.org.uk; Tower Bridge, SE1; adult/child £9/3.90, incl Monument £10.50/4.70; 10am-6pm Apr-Sep, 9.30am-5.30pm Oct-Mar**), where the story of its building is recounted within the upper walkway. You then walk down to the fascinating Victorian Engine Rooms, which powered the bridge lifts.

SOUTH BANK

Londoners once crossed the river to the area controlled by the licentious Bishops of Southwark for all manner of bawdy frolicking frowned upon in the City. It's a much more seemly area now, but the frisson of theatre and entertainment remains.

Tate Modern Museum

(Map p70; www.tate.org.uk; Queen's Walk, SE1; 10am-6pm Sun-Thu, to 10pm Fri & Sat; ; Blackfriars, Southwark, London Bridge) FREE One of London's most popular attractions, this outstanding modern and contemporary art gallery is housed in the creatively revamped **Bankside Power Station** south of the Millennium Bridge. A spellbinding synthesis of modern art and capacious industrial brick design, Tate Modern has been extraordinarily successful in bringing challenging works to the masses. A stunning extension is aiming for a December 2016 completion date. Free guided highlights tours depart at 11am, noon, 2pm and 3pm daily.

Shakespeare's Globe Theatre

(Map p70; www.shakespearesglobe.com; 21 New Globe Walk, SE1; adult/child £13.50/8; 9am-5.30pm; ; Blackfriars, Southwark or London Bridge) Unlike other venues for Shakespearean plays, the new Globe was designed to resemble the original as closely as possible, which means having the arena open to the fickle London skies, leaving the 700 'groundlings' to stand in London's notorious downpours. Visits to the Globe include tours of the theatre (half-hourly, generally in the morning) as well as access to the exhibition space, which has fascinating exhibits about Shakespeare and theatre in the 17th century.

London Eye Viewpoint

(Map p70; 0871 781 3000; www.londoneye.com; adult/child £21.50/15.50; 10am-8pm; Waterloo) Standing 135m high in a fairly flat city, the London Eye affords views 25 miles in every direction, weather permitting. Interactive tablets provide great information (in six languages) about landmarks as they come up in the skyline. Each rotation takes a gracefully slow 30 minutes. At peak times (July, August and school holidays) it may seem like you'll spend more time in the queue than in the capsule, however. Save time and money by buying tickets online.

London Eye

Don't Miss
Tower of London

The unmissable Tower of London (actually a castle of 20-odd towers) offers a window on to a gruesome and compelling history. This was where two kings and three queens met their death and countless others were imprisoned. Come here to see the colourful Yeoman Warders (or Beefeaters), the spectacular Crown Jewels, the soothsaying ravens and armour fit for a king.

Map p62

0844 482 7777

www.hrp.org.uk/toweroflondon

Tower Hill, EC3

adult/child £22/10, audioguide £4/3

9am-5.30pm Tue-Sat, 10am-5.30pm Sun & Mon Mar-Oct, 9am-4.30pm Tue-Sat, 10am-4.30pm Sun & Mon Nov-Feb

Tower Hill

Crown Jewels

To the east of the Chapel Royal and north of the White Tower is Waterloo Barracks, the home of the Crown Jewels, said to be worth up to £20 billion but, in a very real sense, priceless. Here, you file past film clips of the jewels and their role throughout history, and of Queen Elizabeth II's coronation in 1953, before you reach the vault itself. Once inside you'll be greeted by lavishly bejewelled sceptres, plates, orbs and, naturally, crowns. A travelator carries you past the dozen or so crowns and other coronation regalia.

Tower Green

On the small green in front of the Chapel Royal stood Henry VIII's scaffold, where unlucky nobles were once beheaded. Victims included Anne Boleyn and her cousin Catherine Howard (Henry's second and fifth wives), 16-year-old Lady Jane Grey (who fell foul of Henry's daughter Mary I by attempting to have herself crowned queen), and Robert Devereux, Earl of Essex, once a favourite of Elizabeth I.

Bloody Tower

Opposite Traitors' Gate (the gateway through which prisoners being brought by river entered the tower) is the huge portcullis of the Bloody Tower, taking its nickname from the 'princes in the tower' – Edward V and his younger brother, Richard – who were held here 'for their own safety' and later murdered to annul their claims to the throne. The blame is usually laid (and substantiated by Shakespeare) at the door of their uncle, Richard III, whose remains were unearthed beneath a car park in Leicester in late 2012. An exhibition inside looks at the life and times of Elizabethan adventurer Sir Walter Raleigh, who was imprisoned here three times by the capricious Elizabeth I and her successor James I.

Local Knowledge

Tower of London

RECOMMENDATIONS FROM ALAN KINGSHOTT, CHIEF YEOMAN WARDER AT THE TOWER OF LONDON

1 A TOWER TOUR

To understand the Tower and its history, a guided tour with one of the Yeoman Warders is essential. Very few people realise that the Tower is actually our home as well; all the Warders live inside the outer walls. The Tower is rather like a miniature village – visitors are often surprised to see our washing hanging out beside the castle walls!

2 CROWN JEWELS

Visitors often think the Crown Jewels are the Queen's personal jewellery collection. They're not, of course; the Crown Jewels are actually the ceremonial regalia used during the Coronation. The highlights are the Sceptre and the Imperial State Crown, which contains the celebrated diamond known as the Star of Africa. The Crown Jewels aren't insured (as they could never be replaced).

3 WHITE TOWER

The White Tower is the original royal palace of the Tower of London, but it hasn't been used as a royal residence since 1603. It's the most iconic building here. Inside you can see exhibits from the Royal Armouries, including a suit of armour belonging to Henry VIII.

4 RAVENS

A Tower legend states that if its resident ravens ever left, the monarchy would topple – a royal decree states that we must keep a minimum of six ravens at any time. We currently have nine ravens, looked after by the Ravenmaster and his two assistants.

5 CEREMONY OF THE KEYS

We hold three daily ceremonies: the 9am Official Opening, the Ceremony of the Word (when the day's password is issued) and the 10pm Ceremony of the Keys, when the gates are locked after the castle has closed. Visitors are welcome to attend the last, but must apply directly to the Tower in writing.

Tower of London

TACKLING THE TOWER

Although it's usually less busy in the late afternoon, don't leave your assault on the Tower until too late in the day. You could easily spend hours here and not see it all. Start by getting your bearings on one of the Yeoman Warder (Beefeater) tours; they are included in the cost of admission, entertaining and the easiest way to access the **Chapel Royal of St Peter ad Vincula** ❶, which is where they finish up.

When you leave the chapel, the **Tower Green Scaffold Site** ❷ is directly in front. The building immediately to your left is Waterloo Barracks, where the **Crown Jewels** ❸ are housed. These are the absolute highlight of a Tower visit, so keep an eye on the entrance and pick a time to visit when it looks relatively quiet. Once inside, take things at your own pace. Slow-moving travelators shunt you past the dozen or so crowns that are the treasury's centrepiece, but feel free to double-back for a second or even third pass – particularly if you ended up on the rear travelator the first time around. Allow plenty of time for the **White Tower** ❹, the core of the whole complex, starting with the exhibition of royal armour. As you continue onto the 1st floor, keep an eye out for **St John's Chapel** ❺. The famous **ravens** ❻ can be seen in the courtyard south of the White Tower. Head next through the towers that formed the **Medieval Palace** ❼, then take the **East Wall Walk** ❽ to get a feel for the castle's mighty battlements. Spend the rest of your time poking around the many other fascinating nooks and crannies of the Tower complex.

BEAT THE QUEUES

» **Buy** your fast-track ticket in advance online or at the City of London Information Centre in St Paul's Churchyard.

» **Become a member** An annual Historic Royal Palaces membership allows you to jump the queues and visit the Tower (and four other London palaces) as often as you like.

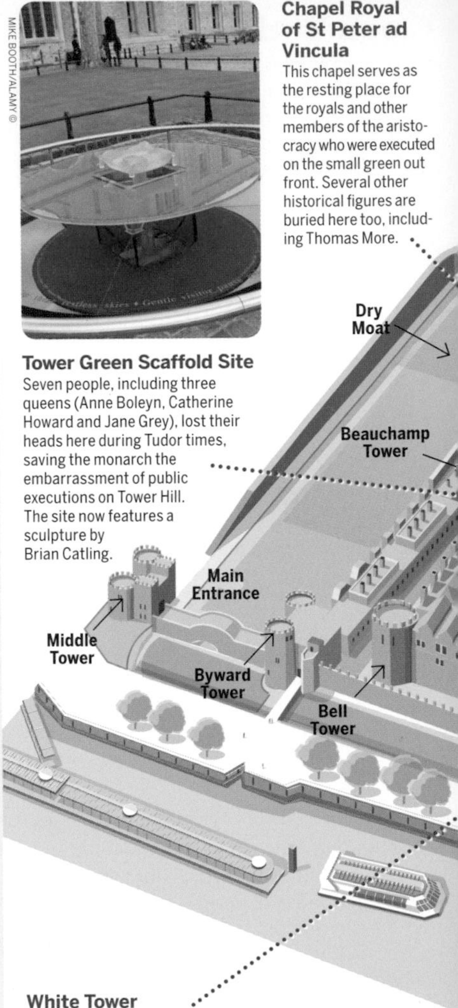

MIKE BOOTH/ALAMY ©

Chapel Royal of St Peter ad Vincula

This chapel serves as the resting place for the royals and other members of the aristocracy who were executed on the small green out front. Several other historical figures are buried here too, including Thomas More.

Tower Green Scaffold Site

Seven people, including three queens (Anne Boleyn, Catherine Howard and Jane Grey), lost their heads here during Tudor times, saving the monarch the embarrassment of public executions on Tower Hill. The site now features a sculpture by Brian Catling.

White Tower

Much of the White Tower is taken up with an exhibition on 500 years of royal armour. Look for the virtually cuboid suit made to match Henry VIII's bloated body, complete with an oversized armoured codpiece to protect, ahem, the crown jewels.

RYAN MCGINNIS/GETTY IMAGES ©

St John's Chapel
Kept as plain and unadorned as it would have been in Norman times, the White Tower's 1st-floor chapel is the oldest surviving church in London, dating from 1080.

Crown Jewels
When they're not being worn for ceremonies of state, Her Majesty's bling is kept here. Among the 23,578 gems, look out for the 530-carat Cullinan I diamond at the top of the Sovereign's Sceptre with cross, the largest part of what was then the largest diamond ever found.

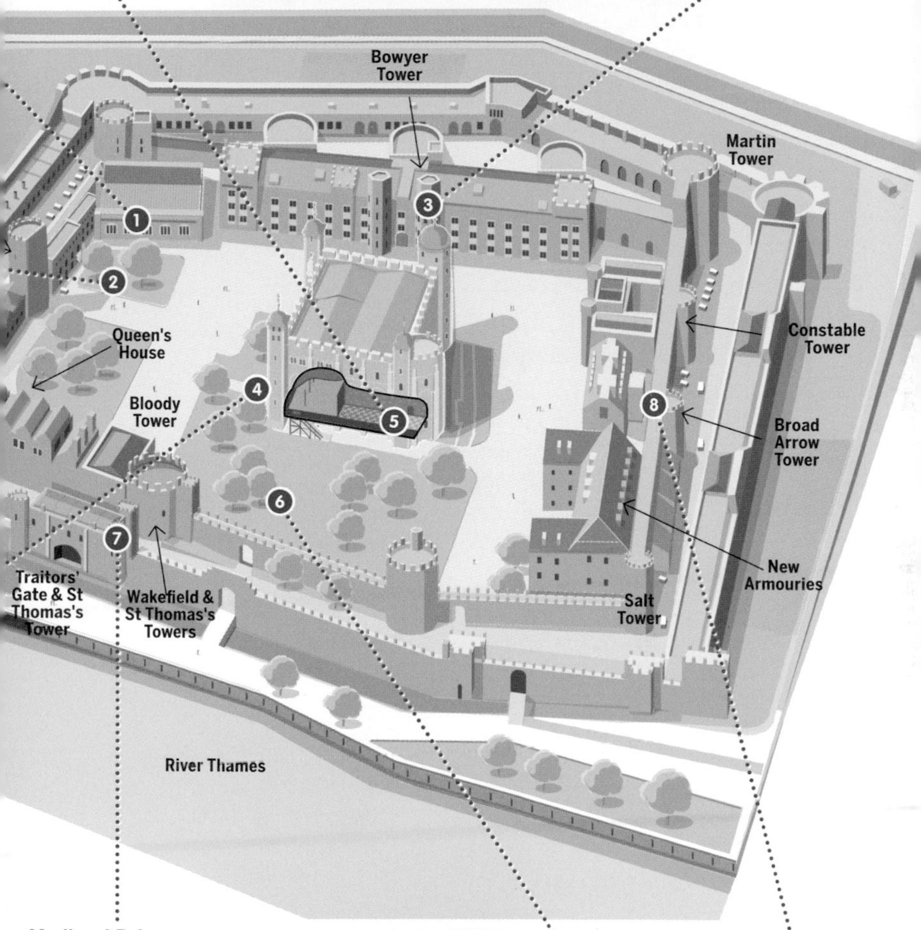

Bowyer Tower
Martin Tower
1
2
3
Queen's House
Constable Tower
Bloody Tower
4
5
8
Broad Arrow Tower
6
7
New Armouries
Traitors' Gate & St Thomas's Tower
Wakefield & St Thomas's Towers
Salt Tower
River Thames

Medieval Palace
This part of the Tower complex was begun around 1220 and was home to England's medieval monarchs. Look for the recreations of the bedchamber of Edward I (1272–1307) in St Thomas's Tower and the throne room of his father, Henry III (1216–72) in the Wakefield Tower.

Ravens
This stretch of green is where the Tower's half-dozen ravens are kept, fed on raw meat and blood-soaked bird biscuits. According to legend, if the birds were to leave the Tower, the kingdom would fall.

East Wall Walk
Follow the inner ramparts, starting from the 13th-century Salt Tower, passing through the Broad Arrow and Constable Towers, and ending at the Martin Tower, where the Crown Jewels were stored till the mid-19th century.

Central London

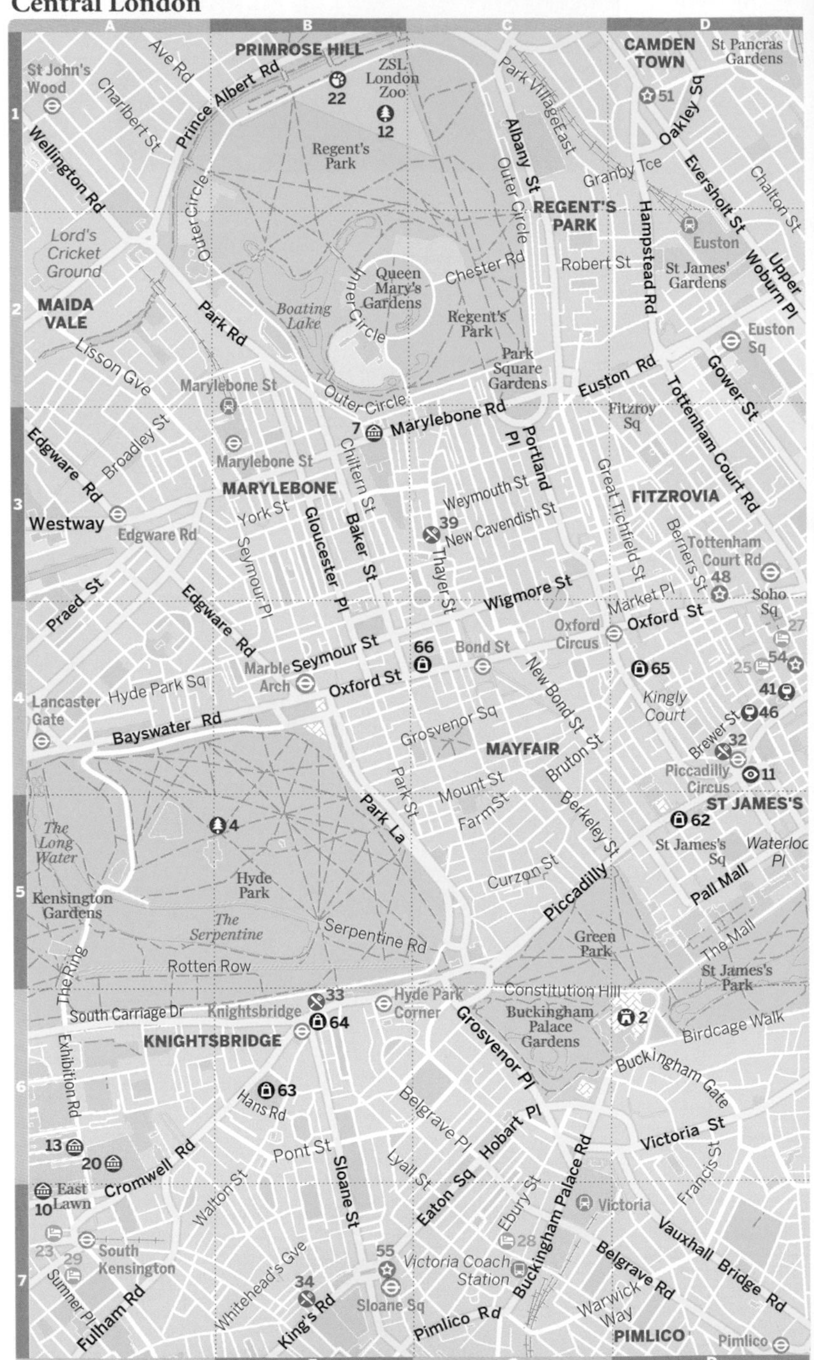

0 1 km
0 0.5 miles
KING'S CROSS
PENTONVILLE
ST PANCRAS
FINSBURY
BLOOMSBURY
CLERKENWELL
HOXTON
CITY
SOUTH BANK
SOUTHWARK
BOROUGH
LAMBETH
WESTMINSTER
King's Cross St Pancras
Russell Sq
Farringdon
Barbican
Moorgate
Old St
Bank
Mansion House
Monument
Cannon St
Blackfriars
Temple
Covent Garden
Waterloo
Waterloo East
London Bridge
Westminster
Elephant & Castle
Kennington
River Thames
British Museum
City of London Information Centre
Smithfield Market
Victoria Embankment Gardens
Trafalgar Square
Horse Guards Parade
Parliament Sq
Archbishop's Park
West Square Gardens
St Andrew's Gardens
Spa Fields
Gray's Inn Gardens
Lincoln's Inn Fields
Bloomsbury Sq
Finsbury Sq
Finsbury Circus
Bunhill Fields
Shoreditch Park
Regent's Canal
City Road Basin
Wenlock Basin
Waterloo Bridge
Blackfriars Bridge
Millennium Bridge
Southwark Bridge
London Bridge
Golden Jubilee Bridge
Westminster Bridge
Lambeth Bridge
Tate Boat
Euston Rd
Pentonville Rd
City Rd
Clerkenwell Rd
Theobald's Rd
High Holborn
Holborn Viaduct
New Oxford St
London Wall
Cheapside
Poultry
White Lion Hill
Southwark St
Union St
Borough Rd
Lambeth Rd
New Kent Rd
Kennington La
Kennington Rd
Newington Butts
London Rd
Blackfriars Rd
Stamford St
Upper Ground
The Strand
Aldwych
Kingsway
Fleet St
Whitehall
Millbank
Horseferry Rd
Goswell Rd
Aldersgate
Moorgate
Long La
Great Dover St
Borough
Old St
Upper St
Rosebery Ave
Farringdon Rd
St John St
Caledonian Rd
York Way
Charing Cross Rd
St Martin's La
Waterloo Rd
York Rd
Belvedere Rd
Carlisle La
Baylis Rd
Morley St
Black Prince Rd
Brook Dr
Harper Rd
Falmouth Rd
Balfour St
Browning St
Webber St
Ufford St
Newcomen St
Park St
Sumner St
Carey St
Tudor St
Greville St
Beech St
Lever St
Bath St
Nile St
East Rd
Provost St
Eagle Wharf Rd
Rheidol Tce
Bunhill Row
City Rd
Muriel St
Coller St
Acton St
Argyle St
Guildford St
Queen Sq
Bloomsbury Sq
Woburn Pl
Marchmont St
Midland Rd
Pancras Rd
Newton St
Drury La
Endell St
Tavistock St
Downing St
John Islip St

Central London

Don't Miss Sights
1 British Museum ... E3

Sights
2 Buckingham Palace ... D6
3 Houses of Parliament ... E6
4 Hyde Park ... B5
5 Imperial War Museum ... F6
6 London Eye ... E5
7 Madame Tussauds ... B3
8 National Gallery ... E5
9 National Portrait Gallery ... E4
National Theatre ... (see 52)
10 Natural History Museum ... A7
11 Piccadilly Circus ... D4
12 Regent's Park ... B1
13 Science Museum ... A6
14 Shakespeare's Globe ... G5
15 Shard ... H5
16 St Paul's Cathedral ... G4
17 Tate Britain ... E7
18 Tate Modern ... G5
19 Trafalgar Square ... E5
20 Victoria & Albert Museum ... A6
21 Westminster Abbey ... E6
22 ZSL London Zoo ... B1

Sleeping
23 Ampersand Hotel ... A7
24 Citizen M ... G5
25 Dean Street Townhouse ... D4
26 Grange St Paul's ... G4
27 Hazlitt's ... D4
28 Lime Tree Hotel ... C7
29 Number Sixteen ... A7
Shangri-La Hotel at the Shard ... (see 15)
30 Zetter Hotel ... G2
31 Zetter Townhouse ... G2

Eating
Arbutus ... (see 27)
32 Brasserie Zédel ... D4
33 Dinner by Heston Blumenthal ... B6
34 Five Fields ... B7
35 Great Queen Street ... E4
36 Hawksmoor Seven Dials ... E4
37 Modern Pantry ... G2
38 National Dining Rooms ... E5
39 Providores & Tapa Room ... C3
Skylon ... (see 56)

Drinking & Nightlife
40 Anchor Bankside ... H5
41 French House ... D4
42 George Inn ... H5
43 Gordon's Wine Bar ... E5
44 Jerusalem Tavern ... G3
45 Lamb & Flag ... E4
Skylon ... (see 56)
46 Spuntino ... D4
47 Ye Olde Cheshire Cheese ... G4

Entertainment
48 100 Club ... D3
49 Barbican ... H3
50 Donmar Warehouse ... E4
51 KOKO ... D1
52 National Theatre ... F5
53 Old Vic ... F5
54 Ronnie Scott's ... D4
55 Royal Court Theatre ... B7
56 Royal Festival Hall ... F5
57 Royal Opera House ... E4
58 Southbank Centre ... F5
59 TKTS ... E4
60 Young Vic ... G5

Shopping
61 Borough Market ... H5
62 Fortnum & Mason ... D5
63 Harrods ... B6
64 Harvey Nichols ... B6
65 Liberty ... D4
66 Selfridges ... C4

Imperial War Museum — Museum

(Map p70; www.iwm.org.uk; Lambeth Rd, SE1; 10am-6pm; Lambeth North) FREE Fronted by a pair of intimidating 15in naval guns, this riveting museum is housed in what was the Bethlehem Royal Hospital, also known as Bedlam. Although the museum's focus is on military action involving British or Commonwealth troops largely during the 20th century, it rolls out the carpet to war in the wider sense. The highlight of the collection are state-of-the-art **First World War Galleries** opened to mark the centenary of the war's outbreak.

Shard — Notable Building

(Map p70; www.theviewfromtheshard.com; 32 London Bridge St, SE1; adult/child £29.95/23.95; 10am-10pm; London Bridge) Puncturing the skies above London, the dramatic splinter-like form of the Shard has rapidly become an icon of the town. The viewing platforms on floors 68, 69 and 72 are open to the public and the views are, as you'd expect from a 244m vantage point, sweeping, but they come at a hefty price – book online at least a day in advance to save £5.

KENSINGTON & HYDE PARK

It's called the Royal Borough of Kensington and Chelsea, and residents are certainly paid royally, earning the highest incomes in the UK (shops and restaurants will presume you do too).

Victoria & Albert Museum — Museum

(V&A; Map p70; www.vam.ac.uk; Cromwell Rd, SW7; 10am-5.45pm Sat-Thu, to 10pm Fri; South Kensington) FREE The Museum of Manufactures, as the V&A was known when it opened in 1852, was part of Prince Albert's legacy to the nation in the aftermath of the successful Great Exhibition of 1851. It houses the world's largest collection of decorative arts, from Asian ceramics to Middle Eastern rugs, Chinese paintings, Western furniture, fashion from all ages and modern-day domestic appliances.

Natural History Museum — Museum

(Map p70; www.nhm.ac.uk; Cromwell Rd, SW7; 10am-5.50pm; South Kensington) FREE This colossal building is infused with the irrepressible Victorian spirit of collecting, cataloguing and interpreting the natural world. The main museum building is as much a reason to visit as the world-famous collection within.

Science Museum — Museum

(Map p70; www.sciencemuseum.org.uk; Exhibition Rd, SW7; 10am-6pm; South Kensington) FREE With seven floors of interactive and educational exhibits, this scientifically spellbinding museum will mesmerise adults and children alike, covering everything from early technology to space travel.

Hyde Park — Park

(Map p70; www.royalparks.org.uk/parks/hyde-park; 5am-midnight; Marble Arch, Hyde Park Corner, Queensway) At 145 hectares, Hyde Park is central London's largest open space. Henry VIII expropriated it from the Church in 1536, when it became a hunting ground and later a venue for duels, executions and horse racing. The 1851 Great Exhibition was held here, and during WWII the park became an enormous potato field. These days, it's an occasional concert venue (Bruce Springsteen, The Rolling Stones, Madonna) and a full-time green space for fun and frolics, including boating on the **Serpentine**.

HAMPSTEAD & NORTH LONDON

London Zoo — Zoo

(Map p70; www.londonzoo.co.uk; Outer Circle, Regent's Park, NW1; adult/child £26/18; 10am-5.30pm Mar-Oct, to 4pm Nov-Feb; 274) These famous zoological gardens have come a long way since being established in 1828, with massive investment making conservation, education and breeding the name of the game. Highlights include **Penguin Beach**, **Gorilla Kingdom**, **Animal Adventure** (the childrens' zoo) and **Butterfly Paradise**. Feeding sessions or talks take place during the day. Arachnophobes can ask about the zoo's Friendly Spider Programme, designed to cure fears of all things eight-legged and hairy.

Regent's Park — Park

(Map p70; www.royalparks.org.uk; 5am-9.30pm; Regent's Park) The most elaborate and ordered of London's many parks, this one was created around 1820 by John Nash, who planned to use it as an estate to build palaces for the aristocracy. Although the plan never quite came off, you can get some idea of what Nash might have achieved from the buildings along the Outer Circle.

GREENWICH

An extraordinary cluster of buildings have earned 'Maritime Greenwich' its place on Unesco's World Heritage list. It's also famous for straddling the hemispheres; this is degree zero, the home of Greenwich Mean Time.

Greenwich is easily reached on the DLR train. Or go by boat: **Thames River Services** **(www.thamesriverservices.co.uk; adult/child single £12.25/6.13, return £16/8)** depart half-hourly from Westminster Pier (one hour, every 40 minutes). **Thames**

FEARGUS COONEY/GETTY IMAGES ©

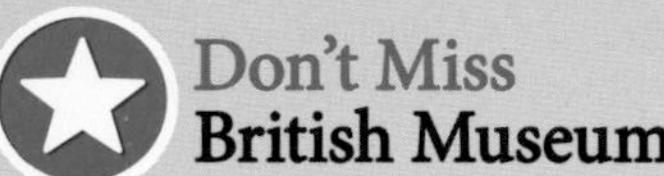

Don't Miss British Museum

The country's largest museum and one of the oldest and finest in the world, this famous museum boasts vast Egyptian, Etruscan, Greek, Roman, European and Middle Eastern galleries, among many others. It is frequently London's most visited attraction, drawing over six million visitors each year.

NEED TO KNOW

Map p70; ☎020-7323 8000; www.britishmuseum.org; Great Russell St, WC1; ⏰10am-5.30pm Sat-Thu, to 8.30pm Fri; ⊖Russell Sq, Tottenham Court Rd

Clippers (www.thamesclippers.com; adult/child £6.50/3.25) are cheaper.

Royal Observatory — Historic Building

(www.rmg.co.uk; Greenwich Park, Blackheath Ave, SE10; adult/child £9.50/5, with Cutty Sark £16.80/7.70; ⏰10am-5pm Oct-Jun, to 6pm Jul-Sep; DLR Cutty Sark, DLR Greenwich, Greenwich) Rising south of Queen's House, idyllic **Greenwich Park** climbs up the hill, affording stunning views of London from the Royal Observatory, which Charles II had built in 1675 to help solve the riddle of longitude. To the north is lovely **Flamsteed House** and the **Meridian Courtyard**, where you can stand with your feet straddling the western and eastern hemispheres; admission is by ticket. The southern half contains the highly informative and free **Astronomy Centre** and the **Peter Harrison Planetarium** (adult/child £6.50/4.50).

Old Royal Naval College — Historic Building

(www.ornc.org; 2 Cutty Sark Gardens, SE10; ⏰grounds 8am-6pm; DLR Cutty Sark) FREE Designed by Christopher Wren, the Old Royal Naval College is a magnificent example of monumental classical architecture. Parts are now used by the

University of Greenwich and Trinity College of Music, but you can still visit the **chapel** and the extraordinary **Painted Hall**, which took artist Sir James Thornhill 19 years to complete. Yeomen-led tours (£6, 1hr) of the complex leave at noon daily, taking in areas not otherwise open to the public.

National Maritime Museum Museum

(www.rmg.co.uk/national-maritime-museum; Romney Rd, SE10; 10am-5pm; DLR Cutty Sark) FREE Narrating the long and eventful history of seafaring Britain, the museum's exhibits are arranged thematically and highlights include *Miss Britain III* (the first boat to top 100mph on open water) from 1933, the 19m-long golden state barge built in 1732 for Frederick, Prince of Wales and the huge ship's propeller and the colourful figureheads installed on the ground floor. Families will love these, as well as the ship simulator and the children's gallery on the 2nd floor.

Cutty Sark Museum

(020-8312 6608; www.rmg.co.uk/cuttysark; King William Walk, SE10; adult/child £12.15/6.30, with Royal Observatory £16.80/7.70; 10am-5pm; DLR Cutty Sark) This Greenwich landmark, the last of the great clipper ships to sail between China and England in the 19th century, is fully operation now after six years and £25 million of extensive renovations largely precipitated by a disastrous fire in 2007. The exhibition in the ship's hold tells her story as a tea clipper at the end of the 19th century (and then wool and mixed cargo).

Emirates Air Line Cable Car

(www.emiratesairline.co.uk; 27 Western Gateway, E16; one way adult/child £4.50/2.30, with Oyster or Travelcard £3.40/1.70; 7am-9pm Mon-Fri, 9am-9pm Sat & Sun, closes 8pm Oct-Mar; DLR Royal Victoria, North Greenwich) Capable of ferrying 2400 people per hour across the Thames in either direction, this cable car makes quick work of the journey from the Greenwich Peninsula to the Royal Docks. Although it's well patronised by tourists for the views over the river, it's also listed on the London Underground map as part of the transport network. Oyster card and Travelcard holders nab discounts for journeys, which are bike-friendly, too.

OUTSIDE CENTRAL LONDON

Kew Gardens Gardens

(www.kew.org; Kew Rd; adult/child £15/3.50; 10am-6.30pm Apr-Aug, earlier closing Sep-Mar; Kew Pier, Kew Bridge, Kew Gardens) In 1759 botanists began rummaging around the world for specimens to plant in the 3-hectare Royal Botanic Gardens at Kew. They never stopped collecting, and the gardens, which have bloomed to 120 hectares, provide the most comprehensive botanical collection on earth (including the world's largest collection of orchids). A Unesco World Heritage Site, the gardens can easily devour a day's exploration; for those pressed for time, the Kew Explorer (adult/child £4.50/1.50) hop-on hop-off road train takes in the main sights.

Hampton Court Palace Palace

(www.hrp.org.uk/HamptonCourtPalace; adult/child/family £17.50/8.75/43.80; 10am-6pm Apr-Oct, to 4.30pm Nov-Mar; Hampton Court Palace, Hampton Court) Built by Cardinal Thomas Wolsey in 1514 but coaxed from him by Henry VIII just before Wolsey (as chancellor) fell from favour, Hampton Court Palace is England's largest and grandest Tudor structure. It was already one of the most sophisticated palaces in Europe when, in the 17th century, Christopher Wren designed an extension. The result is a beautiful blend of Tudor and 'restrained baroque' architecture. You could easily spend a day exploring the palace and its 24 hectares of riverside gardens.

Original Tour Bus Tour

(www.theoriginaltour.com; adult/child £30/15; 8.30am-8.30pm) Another hop-on hop-off option with a river cruise thrown in as well as three themed walks: Changing of the Guard, Rock 'n' Roll and Jack the Ripper.

The River Thames

A FLOATING TOUR

London's history has always been determined by the Thames. The city was founded as a Roman port nearly 2000 years ago and over the centuries since then many of the capital's landmarks have lined the river's banks. A boat trip is a great way to experience the attractions.

There are piers dotted along both banks at regular intervals where you can hop on and hop off the regular services to visit places of interest. The best place to board is Westminster Pier, from where boats head downstream, taking you from the City of Westminster, the seat of government, to the original City of London, now the financial district and dominated by a growing band of skyscrapers. Across the river, the once shabby and neglected South Bank now bristles with as many top attractions as its northern counterpart, including the slender Shard.

In our illustration we've concentrated on the top highlights you'll enjoy from a waterborne vessel.

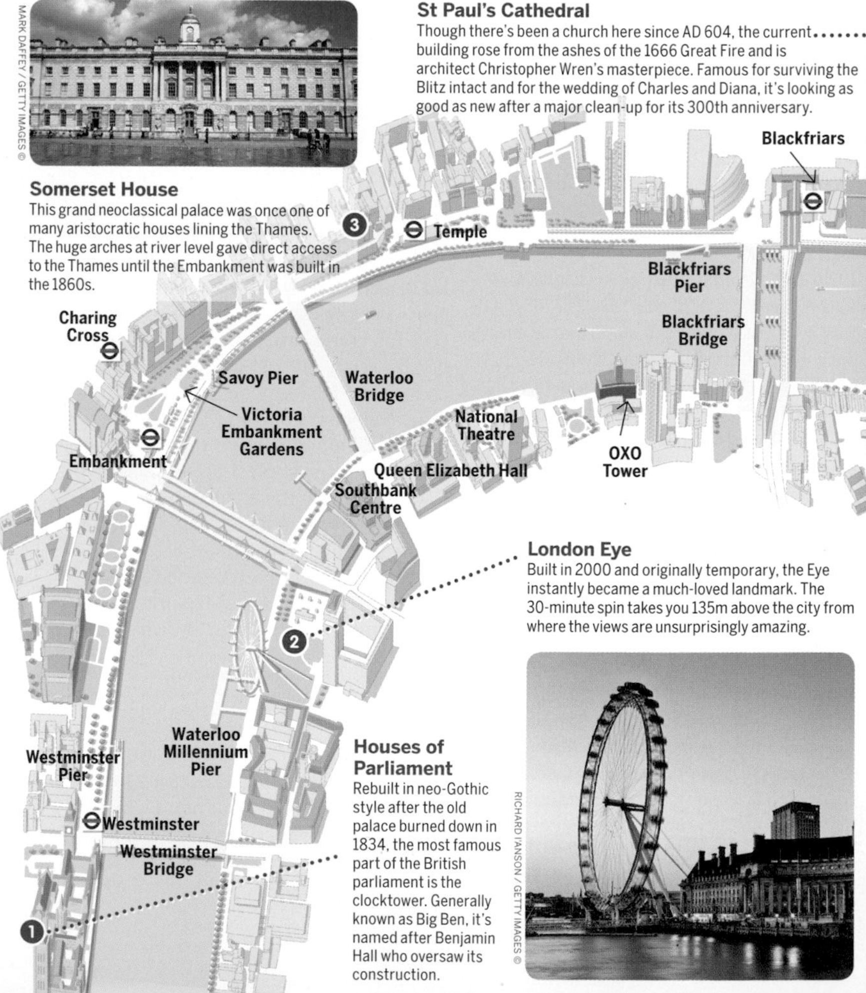

MARK DAFFEY / GETTY IMAGES ©
St Paul's Cathedral
Though there's been a church here since AD 604, the current building rose from the ashes of the 1666 Great Fire and is architect Christopher Wren's masterpiece. Famous for surviving the Blitz intact and for the wedding of Charles and Diana, it's looking as good as new after a major clean-up for its 300th anniversary.
Somerset House
This grand neoclassical palace was once one of many aristocratic houses lining the Thames. The huge arches at river level gave direct access to the Thames until the Embankment was built in the 1860s.
3
Temple
Blackfriars
Blackfriars Pier
Blackfriars Bridge
Charing Cross
Savoy Pier
Waterloo Bridge
Victoria Embankment Gardens
National Theatre
OXO Tower
Embankment
Queen Elizabeth Hall
Southbank Centre
London Eye
Built in 2000 and originally temporary, the Eye instantly became a much-loved landmark. The 30-minute spin takes you 135m above the city from where the views are unsurprisingly amazing.
2
Waterloo Millennium Pier
Westminster Pier
Westminster
Westminster Bridge
Houses of Parliament
Rebuilt in neo-Gothic style after the old palace burned down in 1834, the most famous part of the British parliament is the clocktower. Generally known as Big Ben, it's named after Benjamin Hall who oversaw its construction.
1
RICHARD I'ANSON / GETTY IMAGES ©

These are, from west to east, the **Houses of Parliament** ❶, the **London Eye** ❷, **Somerset House** ❸, **St Paul's Cathedral** ❹, **Tate Modern** ❺, **Shakespeare's Globe** ❻, the **Tower of London** ❼ and **Tower Bridge** ❽.

Apart from covering this central section of the river, boats can also be taken upstream as far as Kew Gardens and Hampton Court Palace, and downstream to Greenwich and the Thames Barrier.

BOAT HOPPING

Thames Clippers hop-on/hop-off services are aimed at commuters but are equally useful for visitors, operating every 15 minutes on a loop from piers at Embankment, Waterloo, Blackfriars, Bankside, London Bridge and the Tower. Other services also go from Westminster. Oyster cardholders get a discount off the boat ticket price.

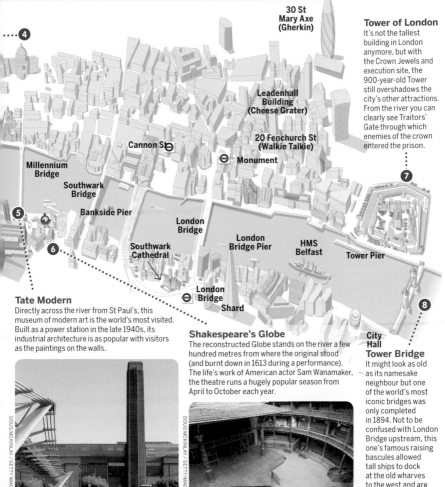

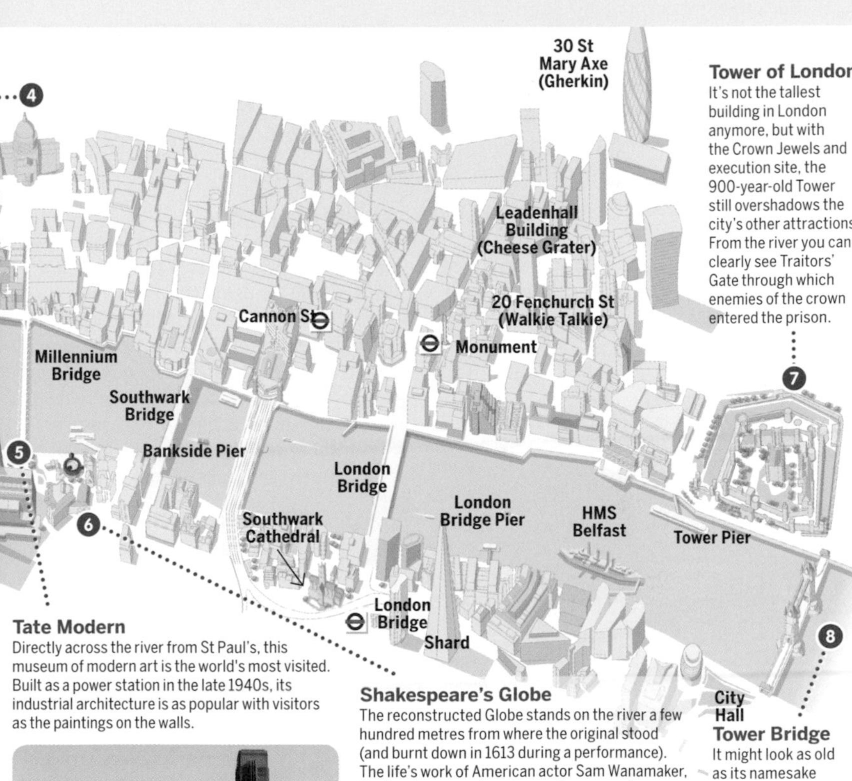

Tower of London
It's not the tallest building in London anymore, but with the Crown Jewels and execution site, the 900-year-old Tower still overshadows the city's other attractions. From the river you can clearly see Traitors' Gate through which enemies of the crown entered the prison.

Tate Modern
Directly across the river from St Paul's, this museum of modern art is the world's most visited. Built as a power station in the late 1940s, its industrial architecture is as popular with visitors as the paintings on the walls.

Shakespeare's Globe
The reconstructed Globe stands on the river a few hundred metres from where the original stood (and burnt down in 1613 during a performance). The life's work of American actor Sam Wanamaker, the theatre runs a hugely popular season from April to October each year.

Tower Bridge
It might look as old as its namesake neighbour but one of the world's most iconic bridges was only completed in 1894. Not to be confused with London Bridge upstream, this one's famous raising bascules allowed tall ships to dock at the old wharves to the west and are still lifted up to 1000 times a year.

DOUG MCKINLAY / GETTY IMAGES ©

DOUG MCKINLAY / GETTY IMAGES ©

Big Bus Tours Bus Tour
(www.bigbustours.com; adult/child £32/13; every 20min 8.30am-6pm Apr-Sep, to 5pm Oct & Mar, to 4.30pm Nov-Feb) Informative commentaries in eight languages. The ticket includes a free river cruise with City Cruises and three thematic walking tours (Royal London, Harry Potter film locations and Ghosts by Gaslight). Online booking discounts available.

London Walks Walking Tour
(020-7624 3978; www.walks.com; adult/child £10/free) A huge choice of walks, including Jack the Ripper tours at 7.30pm daily and 3pm Saturday, Beatles tours at 11.20am Tuesday and Saturday, a Sherlock Holmes tour at 2pm Friday and a tour of Harry Potter film locations at 2pm Saturday and Sunday.

London Mystery Walks Walking Tour
(07957 388280; www.tourguides.org.uk; adult/child/family £10/9/25) Tour Jack the Ripper's old haunts at 7pm on Monday, Wednesday and Friday. You must book in advance.

Capital Taxi Tours Taxi Tour
(020-8590 3621; www.capitaltaxitours.co.uk; 2hr daytime tour per taxi £165, 2½hr evening tour per taxi £235) Takes up to five people on a variety of tours with Blue Badge, City of London and City of Westminster registered guides/drivers – cheeky Cockney Cabbie and foreign language options are available.

Sleeping

When it comes to accommodation, London is one of the most expensive places in the world. Public transport is good, so you don't need to be sleeping at Buckingham Palace to be at the heart of things.

WEST END

Lime Tree Hotel B&B **££**
(Map p70; 020-7730 8191; www.limetreehotel.co.uk; 135-137 Ebury St, SW1; s/tr £115/220, d £175-205; Victoria) Family run for over 40 years, this beautiful Georgian town-house hotel is all comfort, British designs and understated elegance. There is a lovely back garden to catch the late afternoon rays (picnics encouraged on summer evenings). Rates include a hearty full-English breakfast. No lift.

Dean Street Townhouse Boutique Hotel **£££**
(Map p70; 020-7434 1775; www.deanstreettownhouse.com; 69-71 Dean St, W1; r £260-450; Tottenham Court Rd) This 39-room gem in the heart of Soho has a wonderful boudoir atmosphere with its Georgian furniture, retro black-and-white tiled bathroom floors, beautiful lighting, Egyptian cotton sheets and girly touches (Cowshed bathroom products, hair-

Hampton Court Palace (p75)

dryer *and* straighteners in every room!). 'Medium' and 'bigger' rooms have four-poster beds and antique-style bathtubs right in the room.

Hazlitt's Historic Hotel **£££**
(Map p70; ☎020-7434 1771; www.hazlittshotel.com; 6 Frith St, W1; s £216, d/ste from £288/660; ❄ 📶; ⊖Tottenham Court Rd) Built in 1718 and comprising four original Georgian houses, this Soho gem was the one-time home of essayist William Hazlitt (1778–1830). The 30 guest rooms have been furnished with original antiques from the appropriate era and boast a profusion of seductive details, including paneled walls, mahogany four-poster beds, antique desks, Victorian claw-foot tubs, sumptuous fabrics and modern creature comforts.

THE CITY

Grange St Paul's Hotel **££**
(Map p70; ☎020-7074 1000; www.grangehotels.com/hotels-london/grange-st-pauls; 10 Godliman St, EC4; r from £118; ❄ 📶 🏊; ⊖St Paul's) The sheer size of the lobby atrium will have you gasping on entering this contemporary hostelry just south of St Paul's. The 433 well-proportioned rooms are fully loaded with high-tech gadgetry, and there's a 'female friendly' wing designed specifically with women in mind. Add to that a fully equipped health and fitness club and spa with a 20m swimming pool.

Hotel Indigo Tower Hill Boutique Hotel **££**
(Map p62; ☎020-7265 1014; www.hotelindigo.com/lontowerhill; 142 Minories, EC3; r weekend/weekday from £100/260; ❄ 📶; ⊖Aldgate) A welcome addition to the City's accommodation scene is this new branch of the US InterContinental group's boutique-hotel chain. The 46 uniquely styled rooms all feature four-poster beds, iPod docking stations and a 'unique scent' system that allows you to choose your own fragrance. Larger-than-life drawings and photos of the neighbourhood won't let you forget where you are.

Tate-a-tate

To get between London's Tate galleries in style, the **Tate Boat (Map p70; www.tate.org.uk/visit/tate-boat; one-way adult/child £6.50/3.25)** will whisk you from one to the other, stopping en route at the **London Eye** (p65). Services run from 10.10am to 5.28pm daily at 40-minute intervals. A River Roamer hop-on hop-off ticket (purchased on board) costs £12, single tickets £5.

SOUTH BANK

Citizen M Boutique Hotel **££**
(Map p70; ☎020-3519 1680; www.citizenm.com/london-bankside; 20 Lavington St, SE1; r £109-199; ❄ @ 📶; ⊖Southwark) If Citizen M had a motto, it would be 'less fuss, more comfort'. The hotel has done away with things it considers superfluous (room service, reception, bags of space) and instead gone all out on mattress and bedding (heavenly super king-size beds), state-of-the-art technology (everything in the room from mood-lighting to TV is controlled through a tablet computer) and superb decor.

Downstairs, the canteen-restaurant works on a self-service basis so that you can grab a meal whenever you feel like it (breakfast at 1pm and midnight chef encouraged) and the bar-lounge is an uncanny blend of designer and homely.

Shangri-La Hotel at the Shard Hotel **£££**
(Map p70; ☎020-7234 8000; www.shangri-la.com/london/shangrila; 31 St Thomas St, SE1; d/ste £575/3000; ❄ @ 📶 🏊; 🚉London Bridge, ⊖London Bridge) The Shangri-La's first UK opening gives London its first five-star hotel south of the Thames and breathtaking views from the highest hotel (above ground level) in Western Europe, occupying levels 34 to 52 of the Shard. From the 35th floor sky lobby to the rooms, the Shangri-La concocts a stylish blend of

Olympic Park

From 2008, a huge, once-contaminated and largely neglected swathe of industrial East London was ambitiously regenerated and transformed into London's **Olympic Park** (www.queenelizabetholympicpark.co.uk; E20; ⊖Stratford) for the 2012 Games. Complementing its iconic sporting architecture, the Olympic Park was thoughtfully designed with a diverse mix of wetland, woodland, meadow and other wildlife habitats as an environmentally fertile legacy for the future. The twisted, abstract tangle of metal overlooking everything is the ArcelorMittal Orbit, aka the 'Hubble Bubble Pipe', a 115m-high observation tower which opened during the games. Panoramic views of the Olympic Park can also be had from the View Tube on the Greenway, next to the park.

Chinese aesthetics, Asian hospitality and sharp modernity.

The Shard's tapering shape puts the suites on lower floors, while each guest room is slightly different in design. For drop-dead views, zip up to Gŏng on the 52nd floor, but book way ahead.

KENSINGTON & HYDE PARK

These classy zones offer easy access to the museums and big-name fashion stores. It's all a bit sweetie-darling, along with the prices.

No 90 B&B ££

(Map p62; ☎07831-689-1670; www.chelsea-bedbreakfast.com; 90 Old Church St, SW3; s/d £110/130, 📶; ⊖South Kensington) No 90 is a rare thing: a gorgeous yet affordable B&B in the heart of leafy Chelsea. Rooms are a lovely blend of design and homey, with antique furniture and beautiful furnishings. Owner Nina St Charles has lived in the area for nearly 30 years and is a mine of information.
Unusually, breakfast is not included and a two-night minimum stay applies.

Number Sixteen Hotel £££

(Map p70; ☎020-7589 5232; www.firmdalehotels.com/hotels/london/number-sixteen; 16 Sumner Pl, SW7; s from £192, d £240-396; ❄@📶; ⊖South Kensington) With uplifting splashes of colour, choice art and a sophisticated-but-fun design ethos, Number Sixteen is ravishing. There are 41 individually designed rooms, a cosy drawing room and a fully stocked library. And wait till you see the idyllic, long back garden set around a fountain, or have breakfast in the light-filled conservatory. Great amenities for families.

Ampersand Hotel Boutique Hotel £££

(Map p70; ☎020-7589 5895; www.ampersandhotel.com; 10 Harrington Road, SW7; s £170, d £216-360; ❄@📶; ⊖South Kensington) A light, fresh and bubbly feel fills the Ampersand. Smiling staff wear denims and waist coats rather than impersonal dark suits, the common rooms are colourful and airy, and the stylish rooms are decorated with wallpaper designs celebrating the nearby arts and sciences of South Kensington's museums, a short stroll away.

CLERKENWELL, SHOREDITCH & SPITALFIELDS

Hoxton Hotel Hotel £

(Map p62; ☎020-7550 1000; www.hoxtonhotels.com; 81 Great Eastern St, EC2; r from £49; ❄@📶; ⊖Old St) This is hands down the best hotel deal in London. In the heart of Shoreditch, this sleek 208-room hotel aims to make its money by being full each night. You get an hour of free phone calls, free computer terminal access in the lobby, free printing and breakfast from Prêt à Manger. Rooms are small but stylish.

Zetter Hotel Boutique Hotel £££
(Map p70; ☎020-7324 4444; www.thezetter.com; 86-88 Clerkenwell Rd, EC1; d from £222, studio £300-438; ❄📶; ⊖Farringdon) The Zetter comprises two quite different properties, both exemplary in their execution. The original Zetter is a temple of cool with an overlay of kitsch on Clerkenwell's titular street. Built using sustainable materials on the site of a derelict office, its 59 rooms are small but perfectly formed. The **Zetter Townhouse** (Map p70; 49-50 St John's Sq; r £222-294, ste £438-480), on a pretty square behind the Zetter, has just 13 rooms in a characterful Georgian pile.

NOTTING HILL & WEST LONDON

New Linden Hotel Boutique Hotel ££
(Map p62; ☎020-7221 4321; www.newlinden.co.uk; 59 Leinster Sq, W2; s/d from £90/128; 📶; ⊖Bayswater) Light, airy and beautifully designed, the New Linden is a very classy option located between Westbourne Grove and Notting Hill. Some of the rooms are on the small side due to the Georgian buildings' quirky layout, but they feel cosy rather than cramped.

Vancouver Studios Apartment ££
(Map p62; ☎020-7243 1270; www.vancouverstudios.co.uk; 30 Prince's Sq, W2; apt £97-350; @📶; ⊖Bayswater) Everyone will feel at home in this appealing terrace of stylish and affordable apartments, with a restful and charming walled garden. Very well maintained rooms all contain kitchenettes but otherwise differ wildly – ranging from a tiny but well-equipped single to a spacious three-bedroom that sleeps up to six.

La Suite West Boutique Hotel £££
(Map p62; ☎020-7313 8484; www.lasuitewest.com; 41-51 Inverness Tce, W2; r £129-279; ❄@📶; ⊖Bayswater) The black-and-white foyer of the Anouska Hempel–designed La Suite West – bare walls, a minimalist slit of a fireplace, an iPad for guests' use on an otherwise void white marble reception desk – presages the OCD neatness of rooms hidden away down dark corridors. The straight lines, spotless surfaces and sharp angles are accentuated by impeccable bathrooms and softened by comfortable beds and warm service.

Downstairs suites have gardens and individual gated entrances.

Trooping the Colour to celebrate the Queen's birthday in June, London

Right: Shakespeare's Globe (p65), London; **Below:** Covent Garden, London
(LEFT) DAVID WALL PHOTO/GETTY IMAGES ©; (RIGHT) PETER PHIPP/GETTY IMAGES ©

Portobello Hotel Boutique Hotel **£££**
(Map p62; ☎020-7727 2777; www.portobellohotel.co.uk; 22 Stanley Gardens, W11; s/d/feature r from £140/195/240; @📶; ⊖Notting Hill Gate) This splendidly located, 21-room property has been a firm favourite with rock and rollers and movie stars down the decades. Feature rooms are presented with stylish colonial decor, four-poster beds and inviting roll-top baths; room 16 has an ample round bed, a Victorian bathing machine and a roll-call of past celebrity lodgers.

Things are simpler and rooms much smaller lower down the tariff registry, while the overall decor could do with some attention. Rooms at the back have views of the neighbouring properties' beautiful gardens, but the hotel itself has no garden.

Eating

Dining out in London has become so fashionable and the range and quality of eating options has increased massively over the last few decades.

WEST END

Brasserie Zédel French **££**
(Map p70; ☎020-7734 4888; www.brasseriezedel.com; 20 Sherwood St, W1; mains £8.75-30; ⏰11.30am-midnight Mon-Sat, to 11pm Sun; 📶; ⊖Piccadilly Circus) This brasserie in the renovated art deco ballroom of a former Piccadilly hotel is the French-est eatery west of Calais. Choose from among the usual favourites, including *choucroute alsacienne* (sauerkraut with sausages and charcuterie, £14) and duck leg confit with Puy lentils. The set menus (£8.95/11.75 for two/three courses) and plats du jour (£12.95) offer excellent value in a terrific setting.

National Dining Rooms British ££
(Map p70; ☎020-7747 2525; www.peytonandbyrne.co.uk; 1st fl, Sainsbury Wing, National Gallery, Trafalgar Sq, WC2; mains £12.50-17.50; ⏰10am-5.30pm Sat-Thu, to 8.30pm Fri; ⊖Charing Cross) Chef Oliver Peyton's restaurant at the National Gallery styles itself as 'proudly and resolutely British', and what a great idea. The menu features an extensive and wonderful selection of British cheeses for a light lunch. Served from noon, afternoon tea (£17.50) is another fine and particularly tasty indulgence and the all-day bakery churns out fresh cakes and pastries.

Great Queen Street British ££
(Map p70; ☎020-7242 0622; 32 Great Queen St, WC2; mains £14-20; ⏰noon-2.30pm & 6-10.30pm Mon-Sat, 1-4pm Sun; ⊖Holborn) The menu at what is one of Covent Garden's best places to eat is seasonal (and changes daily), with an emphasis on quality, hearty dishes and good ingredients – there are always delicious stews, roasts and simple fish dishes. The atmosphere is lively, with a small cellar bar (open 5pm to midnight Tuesday to Saturday) for cocktails and drinks. The staff are knowledgeable about the food and wine they serve. Booking is essential.

Arbutus Modern European £££
(Map p70; ☎020-7734 4545; www.arbutusrestaurant.co.uk; 63-64 Frith St, W1; mains from £19; ⏰noon-2.30pm & 5-11pm Mon-Sat, noon-3pm & 5.30-10.30pm Sun; 📶; ⊖Tottenham Court Rd) This Michelin-starred brainchild of Anthony Demetre does great British food, focusing on seasonal produce. Try such inventive dishes as pigeon, sweet onion and beetroot tart, squid and mackerel 'burger' or *pieds et paquets* (lamb tripe parcels with pig trotters). Don't miss the bargain set 'working lunch' menu at £17.95 for two courses and £19.95 for three. Booking essential.

Hawksmoor Seven Dials Steakhouse **£££**
(Map p70; 020-7420 9390; www.thehawksmoor.com; 11 Langley St, WC2; steak £18-34, 2-/3-course express menu £24/27; noon-3pm & 5-10.30pm Mon-Sat, noon-9.30pm Sun; ; Covent Garden) Legendary among London carnivores for its mouth-watering and flavour-rich steaks from British cattle breeds, Hawksmoor's sumptuous Sunday roasts, burgers and well-executed cocktails are other show-stoppers. Book ahead.

Providores & Tapa Room Fusion **£££**
(Map p70; 020-7935 6175; www.theprovidores.co.uk; 109 Marylebone High St, W1; 2-/3-/4-/5-course dinner £33/47/57/63; 9am-10.30pm Mon-Fri, 10am-10pm Sat & Sun; ; Baker St) This place is split over two levels: tempting tapas (£2.50 to £17) on the ground floor (no bookings); and outstanding fusion cuisine in the elegant and understated dining room above. The food at Providores is truly original and tastes divine: the Sri Lankan spiced short ribs, Cajun pork belly with Puy lentils, beef fillet with Szechuan-pickled shiitake mushrooms are all recommended..

SOUTH BANK

M Manze British **£**
(Map p62; www.manze.co.uk; 87 Tower Bridge Rd, SE1; mains £2.95-6.65; 11am-2pm Mon-Thu, 10am-2.30pm Fri & Sat; Borough) Dating to 1902, M Manze started off as an ice-cream seller before moving on to selling its legendary staples: pies (minced beef). It's a classic operation, from the ageing tile work to the traditional working-man's menu: pie and mash (£3.70), pie and liquor (£2.95) and you can take your eels jellied or stewed (£4.65).

Skylon Modern European **££**
(Map p70; 020-7654 7800; www.skylon-restaurant.co.uk; 3rd fl, Royal Festival Hall, Southbank Centre, Belvedere Rd, SE1; grill 2-/3-course menu £18/21, restaurant 2-/3-course menu £42/48; grill noon-11pm Mon-Sat & noon-10.30pm Sun, restaurant noon-2.30pm & 5.30-10.30pm Mon-Sat & noon-4pm Sun; ; Waterloo) This excellent restaurant inside the Royal Festival Hall is divided into grill and fine-dining sections by a large **bar** (Map p70; www.skylon-restaurant.co.uk; Royal Festival Hall, Southbank Centre, Belvedere Rd, SE1; noon-1am Mon-Sat, to 10.30pm Sun; Waterloo) (open until 1am). The decor is cutting-edge 1950s: muted colours and period chairs (trendy then, trendier now) while floor-to-ceiling windows bathe you in magnificent views of the Thames and the City. Booking is advised.

Magdalen Modern British **££**
(Map p62; 020-7403 1342; www.magdalenrestaurant.co.uk; 152 Tooley St, SE1; mains £14.50-21, 2-/3-course lunch £15.50/18.50; noon-2.30pm Mon-Fri & 6.30-10pm

Lamb & Flag pub (p86), London
MARK TURNER/GETTY IMAGES ©

Mon-Sat; [wifi]; [tube] London Bridge) You can't go wrong with this formal dining room. The Modern British fare adds its own appetising spin to familiar dishes (grilled calves' kidneys, creamed onion and sage, smoked haddock *choucroute*); the desserts and English cheese selection are another delight. The welcome is warm and the service excellent.

KENSINGTON & HYDE PARK

Dinner by Heston Blumenthal Modern British **£££**
(Map p70; ☎020-7201 3833; www.dinnerbyheston.com; Mandarin Oriental Hyde Park, 66 Knightsbridge, SW1; 3-course set lunch £38, mains £28-42; ⏰noon-2.30pm & 6.30-10.30pm; [wifi]; [tube] Knightsbridge) Sumptuously presented Dinner is a gastronomic tour de force, taking diners on a journey through British culinary history (with inventive modern inflections). Dishes carry historical dates to convey context, while the restaurant interior is a design triumph, from the glass-walled kitchen and its overhead clock mechanism to the large windows onto the park. Book ahead.

Five Fields Modern British **£££**
(Map p70; ☎020-7838 1082; www.fivefieldsrestaurant.com; 8-9 Blacklands Terrace, SW3; 3-course set meal £50; ⏰6.30-10pm Tue-Sat; [wifi]; [tube] Sloane Square) The inventive British cuisine, consummate service and enticingly light and inviting decor of Five Fields are hard to resist, at this triumphant Chelsea restaurant, but you'll need to plan early and book way ahead. It's only open five nights a week.

Medlar Modern European **£££**
(Map p62; ☎020-7349 1900; www.medlarrestaurant.co.uk; 438 King's Rd, SW10; 3-course lunch £28-30, dinner £35-45; ⏰noon-3pm & 6.30-10.30pm; [tube] Fulham Broadway, Sloane Sq) With its uncontrived yet crisply modern green-on-grey design, Medlar has quickly become a King's Rd sensation. With no à la carte menu and scant pretentiousness, the prix fixe modern European cuisine is delightfully assured, with kitchen magic devised by chef Joe Mercer Nairne; prices are equally appetising and service is exemplary.

Gordon Ramsay French **£££**
(Map p62; ☎020-7352 4441; www.gordonramsay.com; 68 Royal Hospital Rd, SW3; 3-course lunch/dinner £55/95; ⏰noon-2.30pm & 6.30-11pm Mon-Fri; [tube] Sloane Sq) One of Britain's finest restaurants and London's longest-running with three Michelin stars, this is hallowed turf for those who worship at the altar of the stove. It's true that it's a treat right from the taster to the truffles, but you won't get much time to savour it all. The blowout tasting Menu Prestige (£135) is seven courses of absolute perfection.

Bookings are made in specific sittings and you dare not linger; book as late as you can to avoid that rushed feeling.

CLERKENWELL, SHOREDITCH & SPITALFIELDS

Poppies Fish & Chips **££**
(Map p62; www.poppiesfishandchips.co.uk; 6-8 Hanbury St, E1; mains £5.90-16; ⏰11am-11pm Mon-Thu, to 11.30pm Fri & Sat, to 10.30pm Sun; [wifi]; [tube] Shoreditch High St) This glorious re-creation of a 1950s East End chippy comes complete with waitresses in pinnies and hairnets, and Blitz memorabilia. As well as the usual fishy suspects, it does those old-time London staples – jellied eels and mushy peas.

Modern Pantry Fusion **££**
(Map p70; ☎020-7553 9210; www.themodernpantry.co.uk; 47-48 St John's Sq, EC1V; mains £17-20, breakfast £5.50-9.80, 2/3-course lunch £23/26; ⏰8am-10.30pm Mon-Fri, 10am-4pm & 6-10.30pm Sat & Sun; [wifi]; [tube] Farringdon) This three-floor Georgian town house in the heart of Clerkenwell has a cracking all-day menu, which gives almost as much pleasure to read as to eat from. Ingredients are combined sublimely into unusual dishes such as miso-marinated onglet steak or panko-crusted turkey escalope. The breakfasts are great, too, though portions can be on the small side.

Right: Chefs at work in a London restaurant;
Below: Ye Olde Cheshire Cheese pub, London
(RIGHT) LONELY PLANET/GETTY IMAGES ©; (BELOW) TIM E WHITE/ALAMY ©

Drinking & Nightlife

WEST END

Gordon's Wine Bar Bar
(Map p70; www.gordonswinebar.com; 47 Villiers St, WC2; ⌚11am-11pm Mon-Sat, noon-10pm Sun; ⊖Embankment) Gordon's is a victim of its own success; it is relentlessly busy and unless you arrive before the office crowd does (generally around 6pm), you can forget about getting a table. It's cavernous and dark, and the French and New World wines are heady and reasonably priced. You can nibble on bread, cheese and olives. Outside garden seating in summer.

French House Bar
(Map p70; www.frenchhousesoho.com; 49 Dean St, W1; ⌚noon-11pm Mon-Sat, to 10.30pm Sun; ⊖Leicester Sq) French House is Soho's legendary boho boozer with a history to match: this was the meeting place of the Free French Forces during WWII, and De Gaulle is said to have drunk here often, while Dylan Thomas, Peter O'Toole and Francis Bacon all ended up on the wooden floor at least once.

Spuntino Bar
(Map p70; www.spuntino.co.uk; 61 Rupert St, W1; mains £6-10; ⌚noon-midnight Mon-Wed, to 1am Thu-Sat, to 11pm Sun; ⊖Piccadilly Circus) Speakeasy decor meets creative fusion American–Italian food at Rupert St cool customer Spuntino. Grab a seat at the bar or one of the counters at the back, but put aside time to queue (no reservations and no phone).

Lamb & Flag Pub
(Map p70; www.lambandflagcoventgarden.co.uk; 33 Rose St, WC2; ⌚11am-11pm Mon-Thu, to 11.30pm Fri & Sat, noon-10.30pm Sun; ⊖Covent Garden) The Lamb & Flag is pocket-sized but brimful of charm and history, squeezed into an alley (where poet John Dryden was mugged in December 1679)

on the site of a pub that dates to at least 1772. Rain or shine, you'll have to elbow your way to the bar through the merry crowd drinking outside. Inside, it's all brass fittings and creaky wooden floors.

THE CITY

Ye Olde Cheshire Cheese Pub

(Map p70; ☎020-7353 6170; Wine Office Court, 145 Fleet St, EC4; ⏰11.30am-11pm Mon-Fri, noon-11pm Sat; ⊖Chancery Lane) The entrance to this historic pub is via a narrow alley off Fleet St. Over its long history locals have included Dr Johnson, Thackeray and Dickens. Despite (or possibly because of) this, the Cheshire feels today like a bit of a museum. Nevertheless it's one of London's most famous pubs and well worth popping in for a pint.

SOUTH BANK

George Inn Pub

(Map p70; ☎020-7407 2056; www.nationaltrust.org.uk/george-inn; 77 Borough High St, SE1; ⏰11am-11pm; ⊖London Bridge) This magnificent old boozer is London's last surviving galleried coaching inn, dating from 1677 (after a fire destroyed it the year before) and mentioned in Dickens' *Little Dorrit*. It is on the site of the Tabard Inn, where the pilgrims in Chaucer's *Canterbury Tales* gathered before setting out (well lubricated, we suspect) on the road to Canterbury, Kent.

Anchor Bankside Pub

(Map p70; 34 Park St, SE1; ⏰11am-11pm Sun-Wed, to midnight Thu-Sat; ⊖London Bridge) Firmly anchored in many guidebooks (including this one) – but with good reason – this riverside boozer dates to the early 17th century (subsequently rebuilt after the Great Fire and again in the 19th century). Trips to the terrace are rewarded with superb views across the Thames, but brace for a constant deluge of drinkers.

CLERKENWELL, SHOREDITCH & SPITALFIELDS

Jerusalem Tavern Pub

(Map p70; www.stpetersbrewery.co.uk; 55 Britton St, EC1M; 11am-11pm Mon-Fri; ; Farringdon) Pick a wood-panelled cubicle to park yourself in at this tiny and highly atmospheric 1720 pub, and select from the fantastic beverages brewed by St Peter's Brewery in North Suffolk. Be warned, it's hugely popular and often very crowded.

Book Club Bar

(Map p62; 020-7684 8618; www.wearetbc.com; 100 Leonard St, EC2A; 8am-midnight Mon-Wed, to 2am Thu & Fri, 10am-2am Sat, to midnight Sun; ; Old St) A creative vibe animates this fantastic one-time Victorian warehouse which hosts DJs and oddball events (life drawing, workshops, twerking lessons, the Crap Film Club) to complement the drinking and enthusiastic ping pong- and pool-playing. Food is served throughout the day and there's a scruffy basement bar below.

Ten Bells Pub

(Map p62; www.tenbells.com; 84 Commercial St, E1; noon-midnight; Shoreditch High St) With its large windows and beautiful tiles, this landmark Victorian pub is perfect positioned for a pint after a wander around Spitalfields Market. The most famous Jack the Ripper pub, it was patronised by his last victim before her grisly end – and possibly by the serial killer himself.

Entertainment

THEATRE

London is a world capital for theatre and there's a lot more than mammoth musicals to tempt you into the West End. On performance days, you can buy half-price tickets for West End productions (cash only) from the official agency **tkts (Map p70; www.tkts.co.uk; Leicester Sq, WC2; 10am-7pm Mon-Sat, noon-4pm Sun; Leicester Sq)**. For more, see www.officiallondontheatre.co.uk or www.theatremonkey.com.

National Theatre Theatre

(Map p70; 020-7452 3000; www.nationaltheatre.org.uk; South Bank, SE1; Waterloo) England's flagship theatre showcases a mix of classic and contemporary plays performed by excellent casts in three theatres (Olivier, Lyttelton and Dorfman).

National Theatre, London

RICHARD I'ANSON/GETTY IMAGES ©

Outstanding artistic director Nicholas Hytner oversaw a golden decade at the theatre, with landmark productions such as *War Horse*. His replacement, Rufus Norris, started in April 2015.

Royal Court Theatre Theatre

(Map p70; 020-7565 5000; www.royalcourttheatre.com; Sloane Sq, SW1; tickets £12-35; Sloane Sq) Equally renowned for staging innovative new plays and old classics, the Royal Court is among London's most progressive theatres and has continued to foster major writing talent across the UK. There are two auditoriums, the main Jerwood Theatre Downstairs, and the much smaller studio Jerwood Theatre Upstairs.

Old Vic Theatre

(Map p70; 0844 871 7628; www.oldvictheatre.com; The Cut, SE1; Waterloo) American actor Kevin Spacey took the theatrical helm of this stalwart of the London theatre scene in 2003 and gave it a new lease of life. He stood down in April 2015 and was succeeded by Matthew Warchus (who directed *Matilda* the musical and the film *Pride*). His aim is to bring an eclectic – and busier – programme to the theatre.

Young Vic Theatre

(Map p70; 020-7922 2922; www.youngvic.org; 66 The Cut, SE1; Southwark, Waterloo) This ground-breaking theatre is as much about showcasing and discovering new talent as it is about people discovering theatre. The Young Vic features actors, directors and plays from across the world, many of whom tackle contemporary political or cultural issues such as the death penalty, racism or corruption, often blending dance and music with acting.

Donmar Warehouse Theatre

(Map p70; 0844 871 7624; www.donmarwarehouse.com; 41 Earlham St, WC2; Covent Garden) The cosy Donmar Warehouse is London's 'thinking person's theatre'. Current artistic director Josie Rourke has staged some intriguing and successful productions, including the well-received comedy *My Night with Reg*.

LIVE MUSIC

KOKO Live Music

(Map p70; www.koko.uk.com; 1a Camden High St, NW1; Mornington Cres) Once the legendary Camden Palace, where Charlie Chaplin, the Goons and the Sex Pistols have all performed, KOKO is keeping its reputation as one of London's better gig venues. The theatre has a dance floor and decadent balconies, and attracts an indie crowd with Club NME on Friday. There are live bands almost every night of the week.

Ronnie Scott's Jazz

(Map p70; 020-7439 0747; www.ronniescotts.co.uk; 47 Frith St, W1; 7pm-3am Mon-Sat, to midnight Sun; Leicester Sq, Tottenham Court Rd) Ronnie Scott originally opened his jazz club on Gerrard St in 1959 under a Chinese gambling den. The club moved to its current location six years later and became widely known as Britain's best jazz club. Gigs are at 8.15pm (8pm Sunday) with a second act at 11.15pm Friday and Saturday, then a late, late show until 2am. Expect to pay between £20 and £50.

100 Club Live Music

(Map p70; 020-7636 0933; www.the100club.co.uk; 100 Oxford St, W1; admission £8-20; check website for gig times; Oxford Circus, Tottenham Court Rd) This legendary London venue has always concentrated on jazz, but also features swing and rock. It's showcased Chris Barber, BB King and the Stones, and was at the centre of the punk revolution and the '90s indie scene. It hosts dancing swing gigs and local jazz musicians, the occasional big name and where-are-they-now bands.

Roundhouse Concert Venue

(Map p62; www.roundhouse.org.uk; Chalk Farm Rd, NW1; Chalk Farm) The Roundhouse was once home to 1960s avant-garde theatre, then was a rock venue, then it fell into oblivion for a while before reopening a few years back. It holds great gigs and brilliant performances, from circus to stand-up comedy, poetry slam and improvisation sessions. The round shape of the building is unique and generally well used in the staging.

GAY & LESBIAN

The West End, particularly Soho, is the visible centre of gay and lesbian London, with numerous venues clustered around Old Compton St; and many other areas have their own mini-scenes.

The easiest way to find out what's going on is to pick up the free press from a venue (*Boyz* or *QX* magazines). The gay section of *Time Out* is useful, as are www.gaydarnation.com (for men) and www.gingerbeer.co.uk (for women).

CLASSICAL MUSIC, OPERA & DANCE

Royal Albert Hall Concert Venue

(Map p62; ☎0845 401 5034; www.royalalberthall.com; Kensington Gore, SW7; ⊖South Kensington) This splendid Victorian concert hall hosts classical-music, rock and other performances, but is most famously the venue for the BBC-sponsored Proms. Booking is possible, but from mid-July to mid-September Proms punters also queue for £5 standing (or 'promenading') tickets that go on sale one hour before curtain-up. Otherwise the box office and prepaid ticket collection counter are both through door 12 (south side of the hall).

Barbican Performing Arts

(Map p70; ☎020-7638 8891;, box office 10am-8pm Mon-Sat, from 11am Sun www.barbican.org.uk; Silk St, EC2; ⊖Barbican) Home to the wonderful London Symphony Orchestra and its associate orchestra, the lesser-known BBC Symphony Orchestra, the arts centre hosts scores of other leading musicians each year as well, focusing in particular on jazz, folk, world and soul artists. Dance is another strong point here.

Southbank Centre Concert Venue

(Map p70; ☎0844 875 0073; www.southbankcentre.co.uk; Belvedere Rd, SE1; ⊖Waterloo) The Southbank Centre's **Royal Festival Hall** seats 3000 in its amphitheatre and is one of the best places for catching world and classical music artists. The sound is fantastic, the programming impeccable and there are frequent free gigs in the wonderfully expansive foyer.

Royal Opera House Opera

(Map p70; ☎020-7304 4000; www.roh.org.uk; Bow St, WC2; tickets £7-250; ⊖Covent Garden) The £210 million redevelopment for the

Royal Albert Hall, London

Roll Out the Barrow

London has more than 350 markets selling everything from antiques and curios to flowers and fish.

Columbia Road Flower Market (Map p62; www.columbiaroad.info; Columbia Rd, E2; 8am-3pm Sun; Hoxton) The best place for East End barrow boy banter ('We got flowers cheap enough for ya muvver-in-law's grave'). Unmissable.

Borough Market (Map p70; www.boroughmarket.org.uk; 8 Southwark St, SE1; 11am-5pm Thu, noon-6pm Fri, 8am-5pm Sat; London Bridge) This farmers' market, sometimes called London's Larder, has become firmly established as a sight in its own right.

Camden Market (Map p62; www.camdenmarket.com; Camden High St, NW1; 10am-6pm; Camden Town) Actually a series of markets spread along Camden High St; the Lock and Stables markets are the place for punk fashion, cheap food, bongs and hippy-dippy stuff.

Portobello Road Market (Map p62; www.portobellomarket.org; Portobello Rd, W10; 8am-6.30pm Mon-Wed, Fri & Sat, to 1pm Thu; Notting Hill Gate, Ladbroke Grove) One of London's most famous (and crowded) street markets; new and vintage clothes, antiques and food.

Brick Lane Market (Map p62; www.visitbricklane.org; Brick Lane, E1; 9am-5pm Sun; Shoreditch High St) A sprawling East End bazaar featuring everything from fruit to paintings and bric-a-brac.

millennium gave classic opera a fantastic setting in London, and coming here for a night is a sumptuous – if pricey – affair. Although the program has been fluffed up by modern influences, the main attractions are still the opera and classical ballet – all are wonderful productions and feature world-class performers.

Shopping

Selfridges Department Store
(Map p70; www.selfridges.com; 400 Oxford St, W1; 9.30am-9pm Mon-Sat, 11.30am-6pm Sun; Bond St) Selfridges loves innovation – it's famed for its inventive window displays by international artists, gala shows and, above all, its amazing range of products. It's the trendiest of London's one-stop shops, with labels such as Boudicca, Luella Bartley, Emma Cook, Chloé and Missoni; an unparalleled food hall; and Europe's largest cosmetics department.

Fortnum & Mason Department Store
(Map p70; www.fortnumandmason.com; 181 Piccadilly, W1; 10am-9pm Mon-Sat, noon-6pm Sun; Piccadilly Circus) With its classic eau-de-nil colour scheme, London's oldest grocery store (into its fourth century), refuses to yield to modern times. Its staff are still clad in old-fashioned tailcoats, its glamorous food hall supplied with hampers, cut marmalade, speciality teas and so forth.

Liberty Department Store
(Map p70; www.liberty.co.uk; Great Marlborough St, W1; 10am-8pm Mon-Sat, noon-6pm Sun; Oxford Circus) An irresistible blend of contemporary styles in an old-fashioned mock-Tudor atmosphere, Liberty has a huge cosmetics department and an accessories floor, along with a breathtaking lingerie section, all at very inflated prices. A classic London souvenir is a Liberty fabric print especially in the form of a scarf.

Oyster Card

To get the most out of London, you need to be able to jump on and off public transport like a local, not scramble to buy a ticket at hefty rates each time. The best and cheapest way to do this is with an Oyster card, a reusable smartcard on which you can load prepaid credit or Travelcards, valid for periods from a day to a year. The card itself is £5, which is fully refundable when you leave.

London is divided into concentric transport zones, although most visitor destinations are in Zones 1 and 2. Travelcard tickets will give you unlimited transport on the tube, buses and rail services within these zones. All you need to do is touch your card to the yellow sensors on the station turnstiles or at the front of the bus.

For pay as you go, the fare will be deducted from the credit on your card at a much lower rate than if you were buying a one-off paper ticket. An Oyster bus trip costs £1.45 as opposed to £2.40 for an individual fare, while a Zone 1 tube journey is £2.20 as opposed to £4.70. Even better, in any single day your fares will be capped at the equivalent of the Oyster day-pass rate for the zones you've travelled in (Zones 1-2 peak/off-peak £8.40/7).

Harrods Department Store
(Map p70; www.harrods.com; 87-135 Brompton Rd, SW1; 10am-9pm Mon-Sat, 11.30am-6pm Sun; Knightsbridge) Garish and stylish in equal measures, perennially crowded Harrods is an obligatory stop for visitors, from the cash strapped to the big, big spenders. The stock is astonishing, as are many of the price tags. High on kitsch, the 'Egyptian Elevator' resembles something out of an Indiana Jones epic, while the memorial fountain to Dodi and Di (lower ground floor) merely adds surrealism.

Harvey Nichols Department Store
(Map p70; www.harveynichols.com; 109-125 Knightsbridge, SW1; 10am-8pm Mon-Sat, 11.30am-6pm Sun; Knightsbridge) At London's temple of high fashion, you'll find Chloé and Balenciaga bags, the city's best denim range, a massive make-up hall with exclusive lines and great jewellery. The food hall and in-house restaurant, **Fifth Floor**, are, you guessed it, on the fifth floor.

Information

City of London Information Centre **(Map p70; www.visitthecity.co.uk; St Paul's Churchyard, EC4; 9.30am-5.30pm Mon-Sat, 10am-4pm Sun; ; St Paul's)** Tourist information, fast-track tickets to City attractions and guided walks (adult/child £6/4).

Getting There & Away

Bus & Coach

The London terminus for long-distance buses (called 'coaches' in Britain) is Victoria Coach Station **(Map p70; 164 Buckingham Palace Rd, SW1; Victoria)**.

Train

Most of London's main-line rail terminals are linked by the Circle line on the tube.

Charing Cross Canterbury

Euston Manchester, Liverpool, Carlisle, Glasgow

King's Cross Cambridge, Hull, York, Newcastle, Scotland

Liverpool Street Stansted airport (Express), Cambridge

London Bridge Gatwick airport, Brighton

Marylebone Birmingham

Paddington Heathrow airport (Express), Oxford, Bath, Bristol, Exeter, Plymouth, Cardiff

St Pancras Gatwick and Luton airports, Brighton, Nottingham, Sheffield, Leicester, Leeds, Paris Eurostar

Victoria Gatwick airport (Express), Brighton, Canterbury

Waterloo Windsor, Winchester, Exeter, Plymouth

Getting Around

To/From the Airports

Gatwick

Gatwick Express (www.gatwickexpress.com; one way/return £19.90/34.90) trains run to/from Victoria 5am to 11.45pm (30 minutes, first/last train 3.30am/12.32am).

Heathrow

The cheapest option from Heathrow is to take the underground (tube). The Piccadilly line is accessible from every terminal (£5.70, one hour to central London, departing from Heathrow every five minutes from around 5am to 11.30pm).

Faster, and much more expensive, is the Heathrow Express (www.heathrowexpress.com; one way/return £21.50/35) train to Paddington station (15 minutes, every 15 minutes from around 5am to 11.30pm).

A taxi to the centre of London will cost between £45 and £85.

Stansted

The Stansted Express (☎0845 850 0150; www.stanstedexpress.com; single/return £19/32) connects with Liverpool Street station (one way/return £23.40/33.20, 46 minutes, every 15 to 30 minutes 6am to 12.30am).

A taxi to/from central London costs about £100–110.

Bicycle

Operating 24 hours a day, **Barclays Cycle Hire Scheme** (www.tfl.gov.uk) allows you to hire a bike from one of 400 docking stations around London. The access fee is £2 for 24 hours or £10 per week; after that, the first 30 minutes is free (making the bikes perfect for short hops), or £1/4/6/15 for one hour/90 minutes/two hours/three hours.

Car

Don't. London was recently rated Western Europe's second most congested city (congratulations Brussels). In addition, you'll pay £8 per day simply to drive into central London from 7am to 6pm on a weekday. If you're hiring a car to continue your trip around Britain, take

Royal Opera House, Covent Garden (p90), London

VISITBRITAIN/JASMINE TEER/GETTY IMAGES ©

the tube or train to a major airport and pick it up from there.

Public Transport

TFL (www.tfl.gov.uk), the city's public transport provider, is the glue that binds the network together.

Boat

Passengers with daily, weekly or monthly travelcards (including an Oyster) get a third off all fares.

Thames Clippers (www.thamesclippers.com) runs regular commuter services between Embankment, Waterloo, Blackfriars, Bankside, London Bridge, Tower, Canary Wharf, Greenwich, North Greenwich and Woolwich piers (adult/child £6.80/3.40) from 6am to between 10pm and midnight (from 9.30am weekends).

Leisure services include the Tate Boat (p79) and Westminster–Greenwich services. There are also boats to Kew Gardens and Hampton Court Palace.

Bus

Single-journey bus tickets (valid for two hours) cost £2.40 (£1.40 on Oyster, capped at £4.40 per day); a weekly pass is £20.20. At stops with yellow signs you must buy your ticket from the automatic machine (or use an Oyster) before boarding.

Buses stop on request, so clearly signal the driver with an outstretched arm.

Underground & DLR

'The tube', as it's universally known, extends its subterranean tentacles throughout London and into the surrounding counties, with services running every few minutes from roughly 5.30am to 12.30am (from 7am to 11.30pm Sunday). The DLR links the City to Docklands, Greenwich and London City Airport.

Taxi

London's famous black cabs are available for hire when the yellow light above the windscreen is lit. Fares are metered, with flag fall of £2.40 and the additional rate dependent on time of day, distance travelled and taxi speed. A 1-mile trip will cost between £5.60 and £8.80.

REST OF ENGLAND

By far the biggest of the three nations that comprise Great Britain, England offers a tempting spread of classic travel experiences, from the grand cathedrals of Canterbury and York to the cloistered colleges of Oxford and Cambridge and the gorgeous landscapes of the Lake District.

Detour: The Making of Harry Potter

Warner Bros Studio Tour: the Making of Harry Potter (**www.wbstudiotour.co.uk; Studio Tour Dr, Leavesden, WD25; adult/child £33/26; 9am-10pm; Watford Junction, then shuttle bus**) Whether you're a fairweather fan or a full-on Pothead, this studio tour (it's near Watford, northwest of London – shuttle buses run from Watford Junction station) is well worth the admittedly hefty admission price. You'll need to prebook your visit for an allocated timeslot and then allow two- to three-hours to do the complex justice. It starts with a short film before you're ushered through giant doors into the actual set of Hogwarts' Great Hall – the first of many 'wow' moments.

Canterbury

POP 151,200

With its jaw-dropping cathedral surrounded by medieval cobbled streets, this World Heritage city has been a Christian pilgrimage site for several centuries, and a tourist attraction for almost as long.

Sights

Canterbury Cathedral Cathedral

(**www.canterbury-cathedral.org; adult/concession £10.50/9.50, tour adult/concession £5/4, audio tour adult/concession £4/3; 9am-5pm Mon-Sat, 12.30pm-2.30pm Sun**) A rich repository of more than 1400 years of Christian history, the Church of England's mother ship is a truly extraordinary place with an absorbing history. This Gothic cathedral, the highlight of the city's World Heritage Sites, is the southeast England's top tourist attraction as well as a place of worship. It's also the site of English history's most famous murder: Archbishop Thomas Becket was done in here in 1170. Allow at least two hours to do the cathedral justice.

Sleeping

House of Agnes Hotel **££**
(☎01227-472185; www.houseofagnes.co.uk; 71 St Dunstan's St; r from £85-130; @ 📶) This rather wonky 13th-century beamed inn, mentioned in Dickens' *David Copperfield*, has eight themed rooms bearing names such as 'Marrakesh' (Moorish), 'Venice' (carnival masks), 'Boston' (light and airy) and 'Canterbury' (antiques and heavy fabrics). If you prefer your room to have straight lines and right angles, there are eight less exciting, but no less comfortable, rooms in an annex in the walled garden.

ABode Canterbury Hotel **£££**
(☎01227-766266; www.abodecanterbury.co.uk; 30-33 High St; r from £143; 📶) The 72 rooms at this supercentral hotel, the only boutique hotel in town, are graded from 'comfortable' to 'fabulous', and for the most part live up to their names. They come with features such as handmade beds, cashmere throws, velour bathrobes, beautiful modern bathrooms and little tuck boxes of locally produced snacks. There's a splendid champagne bar, restaurant and tavern, too.

Getting There & Away

There are two train stations: Canterbury East for London Victoria and Dover; and Canterbury West for London's Charing Cross and St Pancras stations. Connections include Dover Priory (£8, 25 minutes, every 30 minutes), London St Pancras (£34, one hour, hourly) and London Victoria/Charing Cross (£28.40, 1¾ hours, two to three hourly).

Bath

POP 90,144

Britain is littered with beautiful cities, but precious few can hold a candle to Bath. Home to some of the nation's grandest Georgian architecture and stateliest streets – not to mention one of the world's best-preserved Roman bathhouses – this slinky, sophisticated, snooty city has been a tourist draw for nigh-on 2000 years.

Sights

Roman Baths Museum
(www.romanbaths.co.uk; Abbey Churchyard; adult/child £14/9; ⏲9am-9pm Jul & Aug, to 5pm Mar-Jun, Sep & Oct, 9.30am-5pm Nov & Dec, to 4.30pm Jan & Feb) In typically ostentatious style, the Romans constructed a complex of bathhouses above Bath's three natural hot springs, which emerge at a steady 46°C (115°F). Situated alongside a temple dedicated to the healing goddess Sulis Minerva, the baths now form one of the best-preserved ancient Roman spas in the world, encircled by 18th and 19th century buildings. As Bath's premier attraction, the Roman Baths can get very, very busy. Avoid the worst crowds by buying tickets online, visiting early on a midweek morning, and avoiding July and August.

Royal Crescent Architecture
Bath is justifiably celebrated for its glorious Georgian architecture, and it doesn't get any grander than on Royal Crescent, a semicircular terrace of majestic townhouses overlooking the green sweep of Royal Victoria Park. Designed by John Wood the Younger (1728–82) and built between 1767 and 1775, the houses appear perfectly symmetrical from the outside, but the owners were allowed to tweak the interiors to their own specifications; consequently no two houses on the Crescent are quite the same.

Bath Abbey Church
(www.bathabbey.org; requested donation adult/student £2.50/1.50; ⏲9.30am-5.30pm Mon, 9am-5.30pm Tue-Fri, to 6pm Sat, 1-2.30pm & 4.30-5.30pm Sun) Looming above the city

Bath

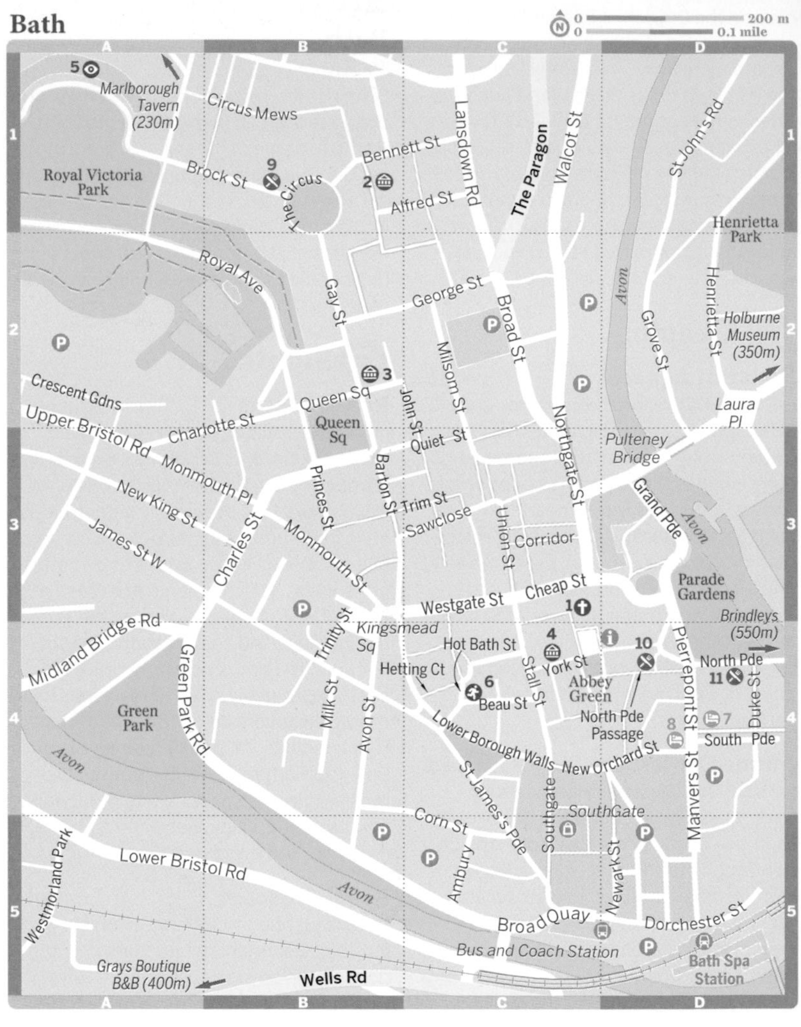

Bath

Sights

1 Bath Abbey C3
2 Bath Assembly Rooms B1
3 Jane Austen Centre B2
4 Roman Baths C4
5 Royal Crescent A1

Activities, Courses & Tours

6 Thermae Bath Spa C4

Sleeping

7 Halcyon D4
8 Henry D4

Eating

9 Circus B1
10 Sally Lunn's D4
11 Sotto Sotto D4

centre, Bath's huge abbey church was built between 1499 and 1616, making it the last great medieval church raised in England. Its most striking feature is the west facade, where angels climb up and down stone ladders, commemorating a dream of the founder, Bishop Oliver King.

Tower tours **(adult/child £6/3; 10am-5pm Apr-Aug, to 4pm Sep & Oct, 11am-4pm Jan & Feb, to 3pm Nov & Dec)** leave on the hour from Monday to Friday, or every half-hour on Saturdays, but don't run on Sundays.

Holburne Museum Gallery

(01225-388569; www.holburne.org; Great Pulteney St; 10am-5pm) FREE Sir William Holburne, the 18th-century aristocrat and art fanatic, amassed a huge art collection that now forms the core of the Holburne Museum, in a lavish mansion at the end of Great Pulteney St. Fresh from a three-year refit, the museum houses a roll-call of works by artists including Turner, Stubbs, William Hoare and Thomas Gainsborough, as well as 18th-century majollica and porcelain.

Bath Assembly Rooms Historic Building

(NT; www.nationaltrust.org.uk/bath-assembly-rooms; 19 Bennett St; 10.30am-5.30pm) FREE Opened in 1771, the city's glorious Assembly Rooms were where fashionable Bath socialites once gathered to waltz, play cards and listen to the latest chamber music. Rooms open to the public include the card room, tearoom and ballroom, all lit by original 18th-century chandeliers. It's free to enter with a ticket to the Fashion Museum.

Jane Austen Centre Museum

(01225-443000; www.janeausten.co.uk; 40 Gay St; adult/child £8/4.50; 9.45am-5.30pm) Bath is known to many as a location in Jane Austen's novels, including *Persuasion* and *Northanger Abbey*. Though Austen only lived in Bath for five years from 1801 to 1806, she remained a regular visitor, and a keen student of the city's social scene. This museum houses memorabilia of the writer's life in Bath, and there's a Regency tearoom that serves crumpets and cream teas in suitably frilly surroundings.

Thermae Bath Spa

Taking a dip in the Roman Baths might be off-limits, but you can still sample the city's curative waters at this fantastic modern **spa complex** **(0844 888 0844; www.thermaebathspa.com; Hot Bath St; Mon-Fri £32, Sat & Sun £35; 9am-9.30pm, last entry 7pm)**, housed in a shell of local stone and plate glass. Tickets includes steam rooms, waterfall showers and a choice of two swimming pools. The showpiece attraction is the open-air rooftop pool, where you can bathe with a backdrop of Bath's cityscape – a mustn't-miss experience, best appreciated at dusk

Sleeping

Henry B&B ££

(01225-424052; www.thehenry.com; 6 Henry St; d £95-125, f £155-165;) This tall townhouse has one of the best positions in Bath, literally steps from the centre. Seven rooms and a self-catering apartment are finished in crisp whites and smooth beiges, and offer decent value considering the location, but there's no parking, and the house's architecture means some rooms feel cramped. Two-night minimum stay at weekends.

Grays Boutique B&B B&B £££

(01225-403020; www.graysbath.co.uk; Upper Oldfield Park; d £120-195;) An elegant B&B straight out of an interiors magazine. All the rooms are individual: some with feminine flowers or polkadot prints, others maritime stripes, but all simple and stylish (we particularly liked Room Two, with its French bed and bay window). Breakfast is served in the conservatory, with eggs, milk and bacon from local farms. The owners run a smaller but equally smart B&B on the east side of town, **Brindleys** **(01225-310444; www.brindleysbath.co.uk; 14 Pulteney Gardens; d £110-185)**.

Don't Miss
Stonehenge

This compelling ring of monolithic stones has been attracting a steady stream of pilgrims, poets and philosophers for the last 5000 years and is easily Britain's most iconic archaeological site.

0870 333 1181

www.english-heritage.org.uk

adult/child incl visitor centre £14/8.30

9am-8pm Jun-Aug, 9.30am-7pm Apr, May & Sep, to 5pm Oct-Mar

The History

Stonehenge was constructed in several phases, starting around 3000 BC. The inner circle of bluestones were somehow hauled here from the Preseli Mountains in south Wales around 2000 BC, followed 500 years later by more stones which were erected in a circle and crowned by lintels to make the trilithons (two vertical stones topped by a horizontal one). Like many stone circles, the inner horseshoes are aligned to coincide with sunrise at the midsummer solstice, which supports the theory that the site was some kind of astronomical calendar.

The Visitor Centre

Stonehenge's swish new visitor centre sees you standing in the middle of an atmospheric 360 degree projection of the stone circle through the ages and seasons – complete with mid-summer sunrise and swirling starscape. Engaging audio-visual displays detail the transportation of the stones and the building stages, while 300 finds from the wider site include flint chippings, bone pins and arrowheads, there's also a striking re-creation of the face of a Neolithic man whose body was found nearby.

Stone Circle Access

A marked pathway leads around the henge, and although you can't walk freely in the circle itself, it's possible to see the stones fairly close up. An audioguide (in 10 languages) is included in the admission price.

Stone Circle Access Visits (**www.english-heritage.org.uk; adult/child £30/18**) enable you to wander round the core of the site, getting up-close views of the iconic bluestones and trilithons. Each visit only takes 26 people; to secure a place book at least two months in advance.

Local Knowledge

Stonehenge

RECOMMENDATIONS FROM PAT SHELLEY, SALISBURY & STONEHENGE GUIDED TOURS

1 THE MAIN CIRCLE

Stonehenge covers a large area but the focal point is, of course, the main circle of stones, including the distinctive trilithons. I've been running tours here for a few years and, for me, nowhere sums up the magic and mystery of ancient Britain better than Stonehenge.

2 INSIDE THE CIRCLE

The main stones are fenced off, and you can't get very close – the only way to actually see inside the circle is on a special access tour, which you need to reserve in advance. It's also worth taking the informative audio tour.

3 THE SLAUGHTER STONE

Look out for the Slaughter Stone, once thought to be a Neolithic altar for human sacrifice. In reality it's a toppled monolith; over the centuries iron ore has mixed with rain in holes in the stone to give the appearance of blood.

4 THE CURSUS AND THE AVENUE

I recommend this short walk to see the route to Stonehenge that Neolithic people would have used. Walk northeast along the bridleway from the car park to reach the Cursus, a long ditchlike earthwork that runs in an east–west line. Turn right to meet the Avenue, an ancient path leading back towards Stonehenge.

5 WOODHENGE AND THE BARROWS

About 2 miles northeast of the stone circle, Woodhenge is an even older site where archaeologists are still discovering new evidence. It was featured on a TV show in the US called *Secrets of Stonehenge*, so many people want to visit. In the area surrounding Woodhenge and Stonehenge, the many hillocks or 'barrows' are ancient burial mounds.

Halcyon Hotel **£££**
(**01225-444100; www.thehalcyon.com; 2/3 South Pde; d £125-145;**) Just what Bath needed: a smart city-centre hotel that doesn't break the bank. Situated on a terrace of townhouses off Manvers St, the Halcyon offers style on a budget: uncluttered rooms, contemporary bed linen and Philippe Starck bath fittings.

Eating

Sally Lunn's Tearoom **£**
(**4 North Pde Passage; mains £5-15; 10am-9pm**) Eating a bun at Sally Lunn's is just one of those things you have to do in Bath. It's all about proper English tea here, brewed in bone-china teapots, with finger sandwiches and dainty cakes served by waitresses in frilly aprons.

Circus Modern British **££**
(**01225-466020; www.thecircuscafeandrestaurant.co.uk; 34 Brock St; mains lunch £10-14, dinner £16.50-18.50; 10am-midnight Mon-Sat**) Chef Ali Golden has turned this bistro into one of Bath's destination addresses. Her taste is for British dishes with a continental twist, à la Elizabeth David: rabbit, guinea-fowl, roast chicken, spring lamb, infused with herby flavours and rich sauces. It occupies the ground floor and basement of a town house near the Circus. Reservations required.

Marlborough Tavern Gastropub **££**
(**01225-423731; www.marlborough-tavern.com; 35 Marlborough Bldgs; lunch £9-13, dinner mains £13.50-21.50; noon-11pm**) The queen of Bath's gastropubs, with food that's closer to a fine-dining restaurant – think duo of venison and pork tenderloin rather than bog-standard meat-and-two-veg. Chunky wooden tables and racks of wine behind the bar give it an exclusive, classy feel.

Sotto Sotto Italian **££**
(**01225-330236; www.sottosotto.co.uk; 10 North Pde; pasta £8.50-10.75, mains £13.50-18.50; noon-2pm & 5-10pm**) Bath's best Italian, hidden away in a vaulted cellar. Ingredients are shipped in from Italy and everything's just like mamma made, from the classic house lasagne to more unusual options such as veal, grilled swordfish and sea bass in parma ham.

Information

Bath Visitor Centre (**0906 711 2000, accommodation bookings 0844 847 5256; www.visitbath.co.uk; Abbey Chambers, Abbey Churchyard; 9.30am-5.30pm Mon-Sat, 10am-4pm Sun**) Sells the Bath Visitor Card (**http://visitbath.co.uk/special-offers/bath-visitor-card; £3**). The general enquiries line is charged at the premium rate of 50p per minute.

Getting There & Away

Bus

Bath's **bus and coach station** (**Dorchester St; 9am-5pm Mon-Sat**) is near the train station.

Train

Bath Spa station is at the end of Manvers St. Many services connect through Bristol (£7.10, 15 minutes, two or three per hour), especially to the north of England. Direct services include London Paddington/London Waterloo (£42, 1½ hours, half-hourly) and Salisbury (£16.90, one hour, hourly).

Oxford

POP 171,000

Oxford is a privileged place, one of the world's most famous university towns. The city is a wonderful place to ramble: the oldest of its 39 separate colleges dates back almost 750 years and little has changed inside the hallowed walls since then (with the notable exception of female admissions, which only began in 1878). With its dreaming spires and dazzling architecture, it opens a fascinating window on the nation's history, but it also provides an ideal gateway for exploring further afield.

Sights

Much of the centre of Oxford is taken up by graceful university buildings, each one individual in its appearance and academic

RELIGIOUS IMAGES/UIG/GETTY IMAGES ©

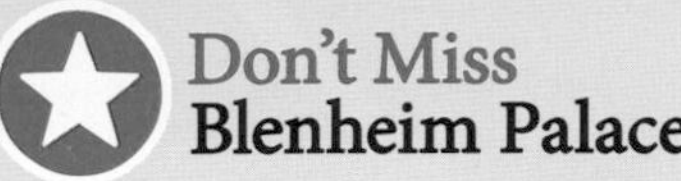

Don't Miss Blenheim Palace

One of the country's greatest stately homes, **Blenheim Palace** is a monumental baroque fantasy and is home to the 11th Duke of Marlborough. Highlights include the Great Hall, a vast space topped by 20m-high ceilings adorned with images of the 1st duke in battle; the opulent Saloon; the three state rooms with their plush decor and priceless china cabinets; and the magnificent 55m Long Library. You can also visit the Churchill Exhibition, dedicated to the life, work and writings of Sir Winston, who was born at Blenheim in 1874. Blenheim Palace is near the town of Woodstock, a few miles northwest of Oxford. To get there, Stagecoach bus S3 (£3.50, 35 minutes, every half-hour, hourly on Sunday) runs from George St in Oxford.

NEED TO KNOW

www.blenheimpalace.com; adult/child £22/12, park & gardens only £13/6.50; 10.30am-5.30pm daily, closed Mon & Tue Nov–mid-Feb

specialities. Not all are open to the public. Check www.ox.ac.uk/colleges for full details.

Ashmolean Museum Museum

(www.ashmolean.org; Beaumont St; 10am-5pm Tue-Sun;) FREE Britain's oldest public museum, second in repute only to London's British Museum, was established in 1683 when Elias Ashmole presented the university with the collection of curiosities amassed by the well-travelled John Tradescant, gardener to Charles I. A 2009 makeover has left the museum with new interactive features, a giant atrium, glass walls revealing galleries on different levels and a beautiful rooftop restaurant.

Christ Church Historic Building

(01865-276150; www.chch.ox.ac.uk; St Aldate's; adult/child £8/6.50; 10am-4.15pm Mon-Sat, 2-4.15pm Sun) The largest of all of

Right: Punting on the River Cherwell (p104), Oxford
Below: Merton College, Oxford

Oxford's colleges and the one with the grandest quad, Christ Church is also its most popular. Its magnificent buildings, illustrious history and latter-day fame as a location for the Harry Potter films have tourists coming in droves. The college was founded in 1524 by Cardinal Thomas Wolsey, who suppressed the monastery existing on the site to acquire the funds for his lavish building project.

Magdalen College College
(☎01865-276000; www.magd.ox.ac.uk; High St; adult/child £5/4; ⏲1-6pm Oct-Jun, noon-7pm Jul-Sep) Set amid 40 hectares of lawns, woodlands, river walks and deer park, Magdalen (*mawd*-lin), founded in 1458, is one of the wealthiest and most beautiful of Oxford's colleges. It has a reputation as an artistic college, and some of its famous students have included writers Julian Barnes, Alan Hollinghurst, CS Lewis, John Betjeman, Seamus Heaney and Oscar Wilde, not to mention Edward VIII, TE Lawrence 'of Arabia' and Dudley Moore.

Merton College College
(www.merton.ox.ac.uk; Merton St; admission £3; ⏲2-5pm Mon-Fri, 10am-5pm Sat & Sun) Founded in 1264, Merton is the oldest of the three original colleges and the first to adopt collegiate planning, bringing scholars and tutors together into a formal community and providing a planned residence for them. Its distinguishing architectural features include large gargoyles whose expressions suggest that they're about to throw up, and the charming 14th-century **Mob Quad** – the first of the college quads.

Bodleian Library Library
(☎01865-287400; www.bodleian.ox.ac.uk/bodley; Catte St; tours £5-13; ⏲9am-5pm Mon-Sat, 11am-5pm Sun) Oxford's Bodleian Library is one of the oldest public libraries in the world and quite possibly the most impressive one you'll ever see. Casual visitors are welcome to wander around

the central quad and visit the exhibition space in the foyer. For £1 you can also access the Divinity School, but the rest of the complex can only be visited on guided tours (check online or at the information desk for times; it pays to book ahead).

Radcliffe Camera Library
(www.admin.ox.ac.uk/sheldonian; Radcliffe Sq) The Radcliffe Camera is the quintessential Oxford landmark and one of the city's most photographed buildings. The spectacular circular library/reading room, filled with natural light, was built between 1737 and 1749 in grand Palladian style, and has Britain's third-largest dome. The only way to see the interior is to join one of the extended tours (£13; 90 minutes) of the Bodleian Library (p102).

 Sleeping

Bath Place Hotel Boutique Hotel **££**
(01865-791812; www.bathplace.co.uk; 4-5 Bath Pl, Holywell St; s/d from £95/120) Comprising several 17th-century weavers' cottages surrounding a tiny, plant-filled courtyard right in the shadow of New College, this is one of Oxford's more unusual hotels. Inside it's all creaky floors, exposed beams, canopied beds and soothing cream walls. The cheapest doubles are on the small side, but the great service and good buffet breakfast make up for it.

Oxford Coach & Horses B&B **££**
(01865-200017; www.oxfordcoachandhorses.co.uk; 62 St Clements St; s/d from £115/130; P) Once a coaching inn, this 18th-century building has been painted powder blue and given a fresh, modern makeover. Rooms are spacious and light-filled, and the ground floor has been converted into a large, attractive breakfast room.

Burlington House B&B **££**
(01865-513513; www.burlington-house.co.uk; 374 Banbury Rd, Summertown; s/d from £70/97; P) Twelve big, bright and elegant rooms with patterned wallpaper and splashes of colour are available at this Victorian merchant's house. The

Punting

Punting is the quintessential Oxford experience. A punt is a flat-bottomed boat, propelled (if that's the word) with a pole instead of oars. Punts are available to rent, and hold five people including the punter. The most central location is **Magdalen Bridge Boathouse** (**☎01865-202643; www.oxfordpunting.co.uk; High St; chauffered 4-person punt per 30min £25, 5-person self-punt per hr £20; ⌚9.30am-dusk Feb-Nov**).

fittings are luxurious and the bathrooms immaculate; the service is attentive; and breakfast comes complete with organic eggs and granola. It has good public transport links to town.

Eating

Edamame Japanese **£**
(**www.edamame.co.uk; 15 Holywell St; mains £6-8; ⌚11.30am-2.30pm Wed-Sat, noon-3.30pm Sun, 5-8.30pm Thu-Sat**) The queue out the door speaks volumes about the quality of food here. This tiny joint, all light wood and friendly bustle, is the best place in town for authentic Japanese cuisine. Arrive early and be prepared to wait.

Rickety Press Modern British **££**
(**☎01865-424581; www.thericketypress.com; 67 Cranham St; mains £13-17; ⌚noon-2.30pm & 6-9.30pm**) Hidden in the back streets of Jericho, this old corner pub serves up beautifully presented, tasty food in casual surrounds. Call in for lunch or before 7pm for a great-value express menu (two/three courses £13/15).

Door 74 Modern British **££**
(**☎01865-203374; www.door74.co.uk; 74 Cowley Rd; mains £10-14; ⌚noon-3pm & 5-11pm Tue-Fri, 10am-11pm Sat, 11am-4pm Sun**) This cosy little place woos its fans with a rich mix of British and Mediterranean flavours and friendly service. The menu is limited and the tables tightly packed, but the food is consistently good and weekend brunches (full English breakfast, pancakes etc) supremely filling. Book ahead.

Drinking & Nightlife

Turf Tavern Pub
(**www.theturftavern.co.uk; 4 Bath Pl; ⌚11am-11pm**) Hidden down a narrow alleyway, this tiny medieval pub (dating from at least 1381) is one of the town's best loved; it's where US president Bill Clinton famously 'did not inhale'. Home to 11 real ales, it's always packed with a mix of students, professionals and lucky tourists who manage to find it. Plenty of outdoor seating.

Bear Inn Pub
(**www.bearoxford.co.uk; 6 Alfred St; ⌚11am-11pm; 📶**) Arguably Oxford's oldest pub (there's been a pub on this site since 1242), this atmospherically creaky place requires all but the most vertically challenged to duck their heads when passing through doorways. There's a curious tie collection on the walls and ceiling (though you can no longer exchange yours for a pint), and there are usually a couple of worthy guest ales.

Information

Tourist Office (**☎01865-686430; www.visitoxfordandoxfordshire.com; 15-16 Broad St; ⌚9.30am-5pm Mon-Sat, 10am-3.30pm Sun**)

Getting There & Away

Bus

Oxford's main bus/coach station is at Gloucester Green, with frequent services to London (£14, 1¾ hours, every 15 minutes). There are also regular buses to/from Heathrow and Gatwick airports.

Train

Oxford's train station has half-hourly services to London Paddington (£25, 1¼ hours). Hourly services also run to Bath (£18, 1½ hours) and Bristol (£28, one to two hours), but require a change at Didcot Parkway.

Stratford-upon-Avon

POP 27,830

William Shakespeare was born in Stratford in 1564 and died here in 1616. The various buildings linked to his life form the centrepiece of a tourist attraction that verges on a cult of personality. Experiences range from the tacky (Bard-themed tearooms) to the humbling (Shakespeare's modest grave in Holy Trinity Church) and the sublime (a play by the world-famous Royal Shakespeare Company).

Sights

Shakespeare's Birthplace Historic Building

(☎01789-204016; www.shakespeare.org.uk; Henley St; incl Nash's House & New Place & Halls Croft £15.90/9.50; ⏱9am-5.30pm Jul-Sep, to 5pm Oct-Jun) Start your Shakespeare quest at the house where the world's most popular playwright supposedly spent his childhood days. In fact, the jury is still out on whether this really was Shakespeare's birthplace, but devotees of the Bard have been dropping in since at least the 19th century, leaving their signatures scratched onto the windows. Set behind a modern facade, the house has restored Tudor rooms, live presentations from famous Shakespearean characters, and an engaging exhibition on Stratford's favourite son.

Anne Hathaway's Cottage Historic Building

(☎01789-204016; www.shakespeare.org.uk; Cottage Lane, Shottery; adult/child £9.50/5.50; ⏱9am-5pm mid-Mar–Oct) Before tying the knot with Shakespeare, Anne Hathaway lived in Shottery, a mile west of the centre of Stratford, in this delightful thatched farmhouse. As well as period furniture, it has gorgeous gardens and an orchard and arboretum, with examples of all the trees mentioned in Shakespeare's plays. A footpath (no bikes allowed) leads to Shottery from Evesham Pl.

Detour: The Cotswolds

Gorgeous villages built of honey-coloured stone, thatched cottages and atmospheric churches draw crowds of visitors to the Cotswolds. If you've ever coveted exposed beams or lusted after a cream tea in the afternoon, there's no finer place to fulfill your fantasies. This is prime tourist territory, however, and the most popular villages can be besieged by traffic in summer.

Travel by public transport requires careful planning and patience; for the most flexibility, and the option of getting off the beaten track, your own car is unbeatable.

Holy Trinity Church Church

(☎01789-266316; www.stratford-upon-avon.org; Old Town; Shakespeare's grave adult/child £2/1; ⏱8.30am-6pm Mon-Sat, 12.30-5pm Sun Apr-Sep, reduced hours Oct-Mar) The final resting place of the Bard is said to be the most visited parish church in all of England. Inside are handsome 16th- and 17th-century tombs (particularly in the Clopton Chapel), some fabulous carvings on the choir stalls and, of course, the grave of William Shakespeare, with its ominous epitaph: 'cvrst be he yt moves my bones'.

Sleeping

White Sails Guesthouse ££

(☎01789-550469; www.white-sails.co.uk; 85 Evesham Rd; d from £100; ❄) Plush fabrics, framed prints, brass bedsteads and shabby-chic tables and lamps set the scene at this gorgeous and intimate guesthouse on the edge of the countryside. The four individually furnished rooms come with flat-screen TVs, climate control and glamorous bathrooms.

Church Street Townhouse Boutique Hotel £££
(☎01789-262222; www.churchstreet-townhouse.com; 16 Church St; d £110-200; 📶) Some of the dozen rooms at this exquisite hotel have free-standing claw-foot bathtubs, and all have iPod docks, flat-screen TVs and luxurious furnishings. Light sleepers should avoid room 1, nearest the bar. The building itself is a centrally located 400-year-old gem with a first-rate restaurant and bar. Minimum two-night stay on weekends.

Eating & Drinking

Lambs Modern European ££
(☎01789-292554; www.lambsrestaurant.co.uk; 12 Sheep St; mains £11.75-18.75; ⌚5-9.30pm Mon & Tue, noon-2pm & 5-9.30pm Wed-Sat, noon-2.30pm & 6-9pm Sun) Lambs swaps Shakespeare chintz in favour of Venetian blinds and modern elegance but throws in authentic 16th-century ceiling beams for good measure. The menu embraces Gressingham duck, deep-fried goats cheese and slow-roasted lamb shank, backed up by a strong wine list.

Edward Moon's Modern British ££
(☎01789-267069; www.edwardmoon.com; 9 Chapel St; mains £10-18; ⌚12.30-3pm & 5-10pm Mon-Fri, noon-10pm Sat & Sun) Named after a famous travelling chef who cooked up the flavours of home for the British colonial service, this snug eatery serves delicious, hearty English dishes, many livened up with herbs and spices from the East.

Dirty Duck Pub
(Black Swan; Waterside; ⌚11am-11pm Mon-Sat, to 10.30pm Sun) Also called the 'Black Swan', this enchanting riverside alehouse is the only pub in England to be licensed under two names. It's a favourite thespian watering hole, with a roll-call of former regulars (Olivier, Attenborough et al) that reads like a who's who of actors.

Entertainment

Royal Shakespeare Company Theatre
(RSC; ☎0844 800 1110; www.rsc.org.uk; Waterside; tickets £10-62.50) Coming to Stratford without seeing a Shakespeare production would be like visiting Beijing and bypassing the Great Wall. The three theatre spaces run by the world-renowned Royal Shakespeare Company have witnessed performances by such legends as Lawrence Olivier, Richard Burton, Judi Dench, Helen Mirren, Ian McKellan and Patrick Stewart.

Information

Tourist Office (☎01789-264293; www.shakespeare-country.co.uk; Bridge Foot; ⌚9am-5.30pm Mon-Sat, 10am-4pm Sun) Just west of Clopton Bridge on the corner with Bridgeway.

Getting There & Away

From Stratford train station, services run to Birmingham (£7.30, 50 minutes, half-hourly) and London Marylebone (£9, 2 hours, up to two per hour).

Cambridge

POP 123,900

Abounding with exquisite architecture, oozing history and tradition, and renowned for its quirky rituals, Cambridge is a university town extraordinaire. The tightly packed core of ancient colleges, the picturesque 'Backs' (college gardens) leading on to the river and the leafy green meadows that surround the city give it a far more tranquil appeal than its historic rival Oxford.

Sights

Cambridge University has 31 colleges, though not all are open to the public.

King's College Chapel Notable Building
(☎01223-331212; www.kings.cam.ac.uk/chapel; King's Pde; adult/child £8/5.50; ⌚9.30am-3.30pm Mon-Fri, to 3.15pm Sat, 1.15-2.30pm

Sun term time, 9.45am-4.30pm Mon, 9.30am-4.30pm Tue-Sun university holidays) In a city crammed with show-stopping buildings, this is the scene-stealer. Grandiose, 16th-century King's College Chapel is one of England's most extraordinary examples of Gothic architecture. Its inspirational, intricate 80m-long, fan-vaulted ceiling is the world's largest and soars upwards before exploding into a series of stone fireworks. This hugely atmospheric space is a fitting stage for the chapel's world-famous choir; hear it in full voice during the magnificent, free, evensong (in term time only – 5.30pm Monday to Saturday, 10.30am and 3.30pm Sunday).

Trinity College College
(www.trin.cam.ac.uk; Trinity St; adult/child £2/1; 10am-4.30pm, closed early Apr–mid-Jun) The largest of Cambridge's colleges, Trinity offers an extraordinary Tudor gateway, an air of supreme elegance and a sweeping Great Court – the largest of its kind in the world. It also boasts the renowned and suitably musty **Wren Library** (noon-2pm Mon-Fri, 10.30am-12.30pm Sat, term time only), containing 55,000 books dated before 1820 and more than 2500 manuscripts. Works include those by Shakespeare, St Jerome, Newton and Swift – and AA Milne's original *Winnie the Pooh;* both Milne and his son, Christopher Robin, were graduates

The Backs Park
Behind the Cambridge colleges' grandiose facades and stately courts, a series of gardens and parks line up beside the river. Collectively known as the Backs, the tranquil green spaces and shimmering waters offer unparalleled views of the colleges and are often the most enduring image of Cambridge for visitors. The picture-postcard snapshots of college life and graceful bridges can be seen from the riverside pathways and pedestrian bridges – or the comfort of a chauffeur-driven punt.

Fitzwilliam Museum Museum
(www.fitzmuseum.cam.ac.uk; Trumpington St; donation requested; 10am-5pm Tue-Sat, noon-5pm Sun) FREE Fondly dubbed 'the Fitz' by locals, this colossal neoclassical pile was one of the first public art museums in Britain, built to house the fabulous treasures that the seventh Viscount Fitzwilliam bequeathed to his old university. Expect Roman and Egyptian grave goods, artworks by many of the great masters and some more quirky collections: banknotes, literary autographs, watches and armour.

Sleeping

Benson House B&B ££
(01223-311594; www.bensonhouse.co.uk; 24 Huntingdon Rd; s £70, d £90-115; P) Lots of little things lift Benson a cut above, meaning you can sleep amongst feather pillows and cotton linen, before breakfasting off Royal Doulton bone china, tucking into kippers, croissants and fresh fruit.

Varsity Boutique Hotel £££
(01223-306030; www.thevarsityhotel.co.uk; Thompson's Lane; d £180-345;) In the 48 individually styled rooms of riverside Varsity, wondrous furnishings and witty features (union-jack footstools, giant postage stamps) sit beside floor-to-ceiling glass windows, monsoon showers and iPod docks. The views from the roof terrace are frankly gorgeous.

Eating & Drinking

Oak Bistro Bistro ££
(01223-323361; www.theoakbistro.co.uk; 6 Lensfield Rd; mains £12-20, set lunch 2/3 courses £13/16; noon-2.30pm & 6-9.30pm Mon-Sat) Truffles (white and black), olive pesto and rosemary jus are the kind of flavour intensifiers you'll find at this friendly but classy neighbourhood eatery where locally sourced duck, fish and beef come cooked just so. The set lunch is a bargain.

Chop House British ££
(www.cambscuisine.com/cambridge-chop-house; 1 Kings Pde; mains £14-20; noon-10.30pm Mon-Sat, to 9.30pm Sun) The window seats here deliver some of the best views in town – onto King's College's hallowed walls. The food is pure English establishment too: hearty steaks and chops and chips, plus a scattering of fish dishes

If You Like... Castles

Two thousand years of history has left England with a wealth of fascinating castles. Some are just crumbling ruins, while others are still impressively intact.

1 **WINDSOR CASTLE** (www.royalcollection.org.uk; Castle Hill; adult/child £19.20/11.30; 9.45am-5.15pm Mar-Oct, to 4.15pm Nov-Feb; 701 or 702 from Victoria coach station, London Waterloo to Windsor Riverside, London Paddington to Windsor Central via Slough) The world's largest and oldest continuously occupied fortress, Windsor Castle is a majestic vision of battlements and towers. It's used for state occasions and is one of the Queen's principal residences; if she's at home, you'll see the Royal Standard flying from the Round Tower.

2 **DOVER CASTLE** (EH; www.english-heritage.org.uk; adult/child £17/10.20; 10am-6pm Apr-Jul & Sep, 9.30am-6pm Aug, to 5pm Oct, 10am-4pm Sat & Sun Nov-Mar; P) Occupying top spot, literally and figuratively, in Dover's townscape, this most impressive of castles was built to bolster the country's weakest point at the shortest sea crossing to mainland Europe. The highlights here are the unmissable **secret wartime tunnels** and the **Great Tower**.

3 **LEEDS CASTLE** (www.leeds-castle.com; adult/child £21/13.50; 10am-6pm Apr-Sep, to 5pm Oct-Mar) This immense moated pile just east of Maidstone is for many the world's most romantic castle, and it's certainly one of the most visited in Britain. It has been home to a who's who of medieval queens, most famously Henry VIII's first wife, Catherine of Aragon.

4 **WARWICK CASTLE** (0871 265 2000; www.warwick-castle.com; castle adult/child £22.80/16.80, castle & dungeon £28.80/24, Kingdom Ticket incl castle, dungeon & exhibition £30.60/27; 10am-6pm Apr-Sep, to 5pm Oct-Mar; P) Founded in 1068 by William the Conqueror, stunningly preserved Warwick Castle is the biggest show in town. As well as waxworks populating the private apartments there are jousting tournaments, daily trebuchet-firings, themed evenings and a dungeon.

and suet puds. Sister restaurant **St John's Chop House** (21-24 Northampton St) sits near the rear entrance to St John's College.

Midsummer House International **£££**
(01223-369299; www.midsummerhouse.co.uk; Midsummer Common; 5/7/10 courses £47.50/82.50/105; noon-1.30pm Wed-Sat, 7-9.30pm Tue-Thu, 6.30-9.30pm Fri & Sat;) At the region's top tables Chef Daniel Clifford's double Michelin-starred creations are distinguished by depth of flavour and immense technical skill. Sample braised oxtail, coal-baked celeriac and scallops with truffle before dollops of dark chocolate, blood orange and marmalade ice cream. Wine flights start at £55.

Eagle Pub
(www.gkpubs.co.uk; Benet St; 9am-11pm Mon-Sat, to 10.30pm Sun) Cambridge's most famous pub has loosened the tongues and pickled the grey cells of many an illustrious academic; among them Nobel Prize–winning scientists Crick and Watson, who discussed their research into DNA here (note the blue plaque by the door). Fifteenth-century, wood-panelled and rambling, its cosy rooms include one with WWII airmen's signatures on the ceiling. The food, served all day, is good too.

Information

Tourist Office (0871 226 8006; www.visitcambridge.org; Peas Hill, Market Sq; 10am-5pm Mon-Sat, 11am-3pm Sun Apr-Oct, 10am-5pm Mon-Sat Nov-Mar)

Getting There & Away

Bus

From Parkside there are regular National Express buses to London Gatwick airport (£20, 4½ hours, hourly), Heathrow airport (£17, four hours, hourly) and Oxford (£15, 3½ hours, every 30 minutes)

Train

The train station is off Station Rd, which is off Hills Rd. Destinations include London Kings Cross (£18, one hour, two to four per hour) and Stansted airport (£15, 30 minutes to 1¼ hours, two per hour).

York

POP 198,000

Nowhere in northern England says 'medieval' quite like York, a city of extraordinary historical wealth that has lost little of its preindustrial lustre. Its spider's web of narrow streets is enclosed by a magnificent circuit of 13th-century walls and the city's rich heritage is woven into virtually every brick and beam.

Sights

If you plan on visiting a lot of sights, you can save yourself some money by using a **York Pass** (**www.yorkpass.com; 1/2/3 days adult £36/48/58, child £20/24/28**). It grants you free access to more than 70 pay-to-visit sights in Yorkshire, including all the major attractions in York.

York Minster Church

(**www.yorkminster.org; Deangate; adult/child £10/free, combined ticket incl tower £15/5; 9am-5.30pm Mon-Sat, 12.45-5.30pm Sun, last admission 5pm**) The remarkable York Minster is the largest medieval cathedral in all of Northern Europe, and one of the world's most beautiful Gothic buildings. Seat of the archbishop of York, primate of England, it is second in importance only to Canterbury, seat of the primate of *all* England – the separate titles were created to settle a debate over the true centre of the English church. If this is the only cathedral you visit in England, you'll still walk away satisfied.

Jorvik Viking Centre Museum

(**www.jorvik-viking-centre.co.uk; Coppergate; adult/child £9.95/6.95; 10am-5pm Apr-Oct, to 4pm Nov-Mar**) Interactive multimedia exhibits aimed at bringing history to life often achieve exactly the opposite, but the much-hyped Jorvik manages to pull it off with aplomb. It's a smells-and-all reconstruction of the Viking settlement unearthed here during excavations in the late 1970s, brought to you courtesy

Shakespeare's birthplace (p105), Stratford-upon-Avon

LAURIE NOBLE/GETTY IMAGES ©

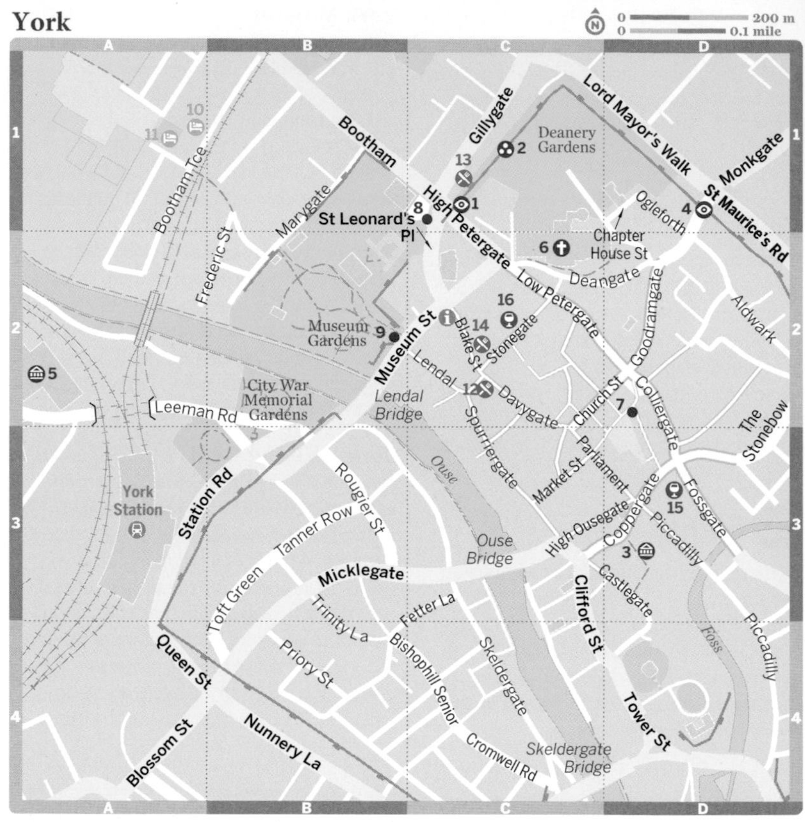

York

Sights

1 Bootham Bar ... C1
2 City Walls ... C1
3 Jorvik Viking Centre ... D3
4 Monk Bar ... D1
5 National Railway Museum ... A2
6 York Minster ... C2

Activities, Courses & Tours

7 Ghost Hunt of York ... D2
8 York Citysightseeing ... C1
9 Yorkwalk ... B2

Sleeping

10 Abbeyfields ... A1
11 Elliotts B&B ... A1

Eating

12 Bettys ... C2
13 Cafe No 8 ... C1
14 Mannion's ... C2

Drinking & Nightlife

15 Blue Bell ... D3
16 Ye Olde Starre ... C2

of a 'time-car' monorail that transports you through 9th-century Jorvik. You can reduce time waiting in the queue by booking your tickets online and choosing the time you want to visit (£1 extra).

City Walls Archaeological Site

(8am-dusk) FREE If the weather's good, don't miss the chance to walk the City Walls, which follow the line of the original Roman walls and give a whole new perspective on the city. Allow 1½ to two hours for the full circuit of 4.5 miles or, if you're pushed for time, the short stretch from **Bootham Bar** to **Monk Bar** is worth doing for the views of the minster.

National Railway Museum Museum

(www.nrm.org.uk; Leeman Rd; ⏲10am-6pm; P 👪) FREE While many railway museums are the sole preserve of lone men in anoraks comparing dog-eared notebooks and getting high on the smell of machine oil, coal smoke and nostalgia, this place is different. York's National Railway Museum – the biggest in the world, with more than 100 locomotives – is so well presented and crammed with fascinating stuff that it's interesting even to folk whose eyes don't mist over at the thought of a 4-6-2 A1 Pacific class thundering into a tunnel.

Tours

Ghost Hunt of York Walking Tour

(www.ghosthunt.co.uk; adult/child £5/3; ⏲tours 7.30pm) The kids will just love this award-winning and highly entertaining 75-minute tour laced with authentic ghost stories. It begins at the Shambles, whatever the weather (it's never cancelled) and there's no need to book, just turn up and wait till you hear the handbell ringing...

Yorkwalk Walking Tour

(www.yorkwalk.co.uk; adult/child £6/5; ⏲tours 10.30am & 2.15pm Feb-Nov) Offers a series of two-hour walks on a range of themes, from the classics – Roman York, the snickelways (narrow alleys) and City Walls – to walks focused on chocolates and sweets, women in York, and the inevitable graveyard, coffin and plague tour. Walks depart from Museum Gardens Gate on Museum St; there's no need to book.

York Citysightseeing Bus Tour

(www.city-sightseeing.com; day ticket adult/child £12/5; ⏲9am-5pm mid-Feb–Nov) Hop-on hop-off route with 16 stops, calling at all the main sights. Buses leave every 20 to 30 minutes from Exhibition Sq near York Minster.

Sleeping

Beds are tough to find midsummer, even with the inflated prices of the high season. The tourist office's accommodation booking service charges £4.

Abbeyfields B&B **££**

(☎01904-636471; www.abbeyfields.co.uk; 19 Bootham Tce; s/d from £55/84; 📶) Expect a warm welcome and thoughtfully arranged bedrooms here, with chairs and bedside lamps for comfortable reading. Breakfasts are among the best in town, with sausage and bacon from the local butcher, freshly laid eggs from a nearby farm and the aroma of newly baked bread.

Elliotts B&B B&B **££**

(☎01904-623333; www.elliottshotel.co.uk; 2 Sycamore Pl; s/d from £55/75; P @ 📶) A beautifully converted 'gentleman's residence', Elliotts leans towards the boutique end of the guesthouse market, with stylish and elegant rooms and some designer touches such as contemporary art and colourful textiles. An excellent location, both quiet and central.

Middlethorpe Hall Hotel **£££**

(☎01904-641241; www.middlethorpe.com; Bishopthorpe Rd; s/d from £139/199; P 📶) This breathtaking 17th-century country house is set in eight hectares of parkland, once the home of diarist Lady Mary Wortley Montagu. The rooms are divided between the main house, restored courtyard buildings and three cottage suites. All the rooms are beautifully decorated with original antiques and oil paintings that have been carefully selected to reflect the period.

Eating

Mannion's Cafe, Bistro **£**

(☎01904-631030; www.mannionandco.co.uk; 1 Blake St; mains £5-9; ⏲9am-5.30pm Mon-Sat, 10am-5pm Sun) Expect to queue for a table at this busy bistro (no reservations), with its maze of cosy, wood-panelled rooms and selection of daily specials. Regulars on the menu include eggs Benedict for

Lake District National Park

A dramatic landscape of ridges, lakes and peaks, including England's highest mountain, Scafell Pike (978m), the Lake District is one of Britain's most scenic corners. The awe-inspiring geography here shaped the literary personae of some of Britain's best-known poets, including William Wordsworth.

Often called simply the Lakes, the national park and surrounding area attract around 15 million visitors annually. But if you avoid summer weekends, and especially if you do a bit of hiking, it's easy enough to miss the crush.

Among the area's many attractions are Beatrix Potter's cottage at **Hill Top** (NT; 015394-36269; www.nationaltrust.org.uk/hill-top; adult/child £9/4.50; 10.30am-4.30pm Sat-Thu mid-Feb–Oct, longer hrs Jul & Aug) near Hawkshead, where she wrote some of her most famous tales, and William Wordsworth's former home at **Dove Cottage** (015394-35544; www.wordsworth.org.uk; adult/child £7.50/4.50; 9.30am-5.30pm), near Grasmere.

To get to the Lake District by train, you need to change at Oxenholme (on the London Euston to Glasgow line) for Kendal and Windermere, which have connections from London Euston (£99, 3½ hours) and Glasgow (£52, 2¾ hours).

breakfast, a chunky Yorkshire rarebit made with home-baked bread, and lunch platters of cheese and charcuterie from the attached deli. Oh, and pavlova for pudding.

Cafe No 8 Cafe, Bistro **££**
(01904-653074; www.cafeno8.co.uk; 8 Gillygate; 2-/3-course meal £18/22, Fri & Sat £22/27; 10am-10pm;) A cool little place with modern artwork mimicking the Edwardian stained glass at the front, No 8 offers a day-long menu of classic bistro dishes using fresh local produce, including duck breast with blood orange and juniper, and Yorkshire pork belly with star anise, fennel and garlic. It also does breakfast daily (mains £5) and Sunday lunch (three courses £25). Booking recommended.

Bettys Tearoom **££**
(www.bettys.co.uk; St Helen's Sq; mains £6-14, afternoon tea £18.50; 9am-9pm;) Old-school afternoon tea, with white-aproned waiters, linen tablecloths and a teapot collection ranged along the walls. The house speciality is the Yorkshire Fat Rascal, a huge fruit scone smothered in melted butter, but the smoked haddock with poached egg and hollandaise sauce (seasonal) is our favourite lunch dish. No bookings – queue for a table at busy times.

Drinking & Nightlife

Blue Bell Pub
(53 Fossgate; 11am-11pm Mon-Sat, noon-10.30pm Sun) This is what a real English pub looks like – a tiny, 200-year-old wood-panelled room with a smouldering fireplace, decor untouched since 1903, a pile of ancient board games in the corner, friendly and efficient bar staff, and Timothy Taylor and Black Sheep ales on tap. Bliss, with froth on top – if you can get in (it's often full).

Ye Olde Starre Pub
(www.taylor-walker.co.uk; 40 Stonegate; 11am-11pm Sun-Wed, to midnight Thu-Sat) Licenced since 1644, this is York's oldest pub – a warren of small rooms and a small beer garden, with a half-dozen real ales on tap. It was used as a morgue by the Roundheads (supporters of parliament) during the Civil War, but the

atmosphere has improved a lot since then.

Information

York Tourist Office (**☎01904-550099; www.visityork.org; 1 Museum St; ⏰9am-6pm Mon-Sat, 10am-5pm Sun Apr-Sep, shorter hours Oct-Mar**) Visitor and transport info for all of Yorkshire, plus accommodation bookings, ticket sales and internet access.

Getting There & Away

York is a major railway hub with frequent direct services to Birmingham (£45, 2¼ hours), Newcastle (£16, one hour), Leeds (£13.50, 25 minutes), London's King's Cross (£80, two hours), Manchester (£17, 1½ hours) and Scarborough (£8, 50 minutes). There are also trains to Cambridge (£65, three hours), changing at Peterborough.

Castle Howard

Stately homes may be two a penny in England, but you'll have to try hard to find one as breathtakingly stately as **Castle Howard** (**www.castlehoward.co.uk; adult/child house & grounds £14/7.50, grounds only £9.50/6; ⏰house 11am-4.30pm Apr-Oct, grounds 10am-5pm Mar-Oct & Dec, to 4pm Nov, Jan & Feb; P**), a work of theatrical grandeur and audacity, and one of the world's most beautiful buildings. It's instantly recognisable from its starring role in the 1980s TV series *Brideshead Revisited* and more recently in the 2008 film of the same name.

Inside, the great house is full of treasures – the breathtaking **Great Hall** with its soaring Corinthian pilasters, Pre-Raphaelite **stained glass** in the chapel, and corridors lined with classical antiquities. Outside, as you wander the grounds (populated by peacocks, naturally), views reveal Vanbrugh's playful **Temple of the Four Winds** and Hawksmoor's stately **mausoleum**, or wider vistas over the surrounding hills.

Castle Howard is 15 miles northeast of York; **Stephenson's of Easingwold** (**www.stephensonsofeasingwold.co.uk**) operates a bus service (£7.50 return, 40 minutes, three times daily Monday to Saturday) from York.

Detour: Hadrian's Wall

Built in AD 122 to mark the edge of the Roman Empire, this 73-mile coast-to-coast barrier across England remains a major feature on the landscape nearly 2000 years later. Named in honour of the emperor who ordered it built, Hadrian's Wall is one of the Roman Empire's greatest engineering projects, a spectacular testament to ambition and the practical Roman mind. It was built to to protect Roman occupied Britain from the unruly Pictish tribes to the north, in the area we know now as Scotland. When completed, the mammoth structure ran from the Solway Firth (west of Carlisle) to the mouth of the Tyne (east of Newcastle).

Several of the original forts that once guarded the wall are still in fairly good repair, including the ones at **Chesters** (**EH; ☎01434-681379; www.english-heritage.org.uk; adult/child £5.60/3.40; ⏰10am-6pm Apr-Sep, to 5pm Oct, 10am-4pm Sat & Sun Nov-Mar**) near Chollerford, Vindolanda near Bardon Mill and Housesteads, between Bardon Mill and Haltwhistle.

Most local tourist offices have reams of information on the wall and the **Hadrian's Wall Path** (www.nationaltrail. co.uk/hadrianswall) which runs along almost the entire length of the wall. For general information, see the informative website at www.hadrians-wall.org.

Hadrian's Wall

ROME'S FINAL FRONTIER

Of all Britain's Roman ruins, Emperor Hadrian's 2nd-century wall, cutting across northern England from the Irish Sea to the North Sea, is by far the most spectacular; Unesco awarded it world cultural heritage status in 1987.

We've picked out the highlights, one of which is the prime remaining Roman fort on the wall, Housesteads, which we've reconstructed here.

Housesteads' granaries
Nothing like the clever underground ventilation system, which kept vital supplies of grain dry in Northumberland's damp and drizzly climate, would be seen again in these parts for 1500 years.

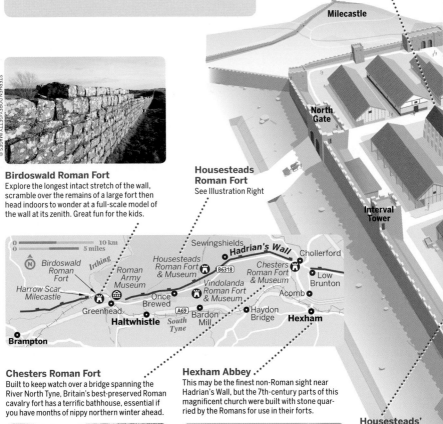

Birdoswald Roman Fort
Explore the longest intact stretch of the wall, scramble over the remains of a large fort then head indoors to wonder at a full-scale model of the wall at its zenith. Great fun for the kids.

Housesteads Roman Fort
See Illustration Right

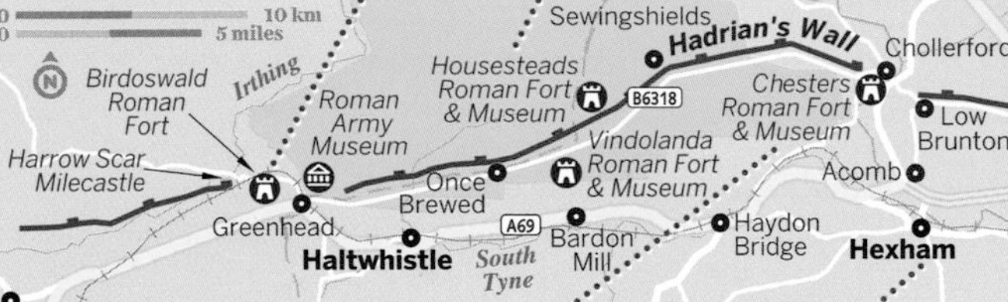

Chesters Roman Fort
Built to keep watch over a bridge spanning the River North Tyne, Britain's best-preserved Roman cavalry fort has a terrific bathhouse, essential if you have months of nippy northern winter ahead.

Hexham Abbey
This may be the finest non-Roman sight near Hadrian's Wall, but the 7th-century parts of this magnificent church were built with stone quarried by the Romans for use in their forts.

Housesteads' hospital
Operations performed at the hospital would have been surprisingly effective, even without anaesthetics; religious rituals and prayers to Aesculapius, the Roman god of healing, were possibly less helpful for a hernia or appendicitis.

Housesteads' latrines
Communal toilets were the norm in Roman times and Housesteads' are remarkably well preserved – fortunately no traces remain of the vinegar-soaked sponges that were used instead of toilet paper.

QUICK WALL FACTS & FIGURES

» **Latin name** Vallum Aelium

» **Length** 73.5 miles (80 Roman miles)

» **Construction date** AD 122–128

» **Manpower for construction** Three legions (around 16,000 men)

» **Features** At least 16 forts, 80 milecastles, 160 turrets

» **Did you know** Hadrian's wasn't the only wall in Britain – the Antonine Wall was built across what is now central Scotland in the AD 140s, but it was abandoned soon after

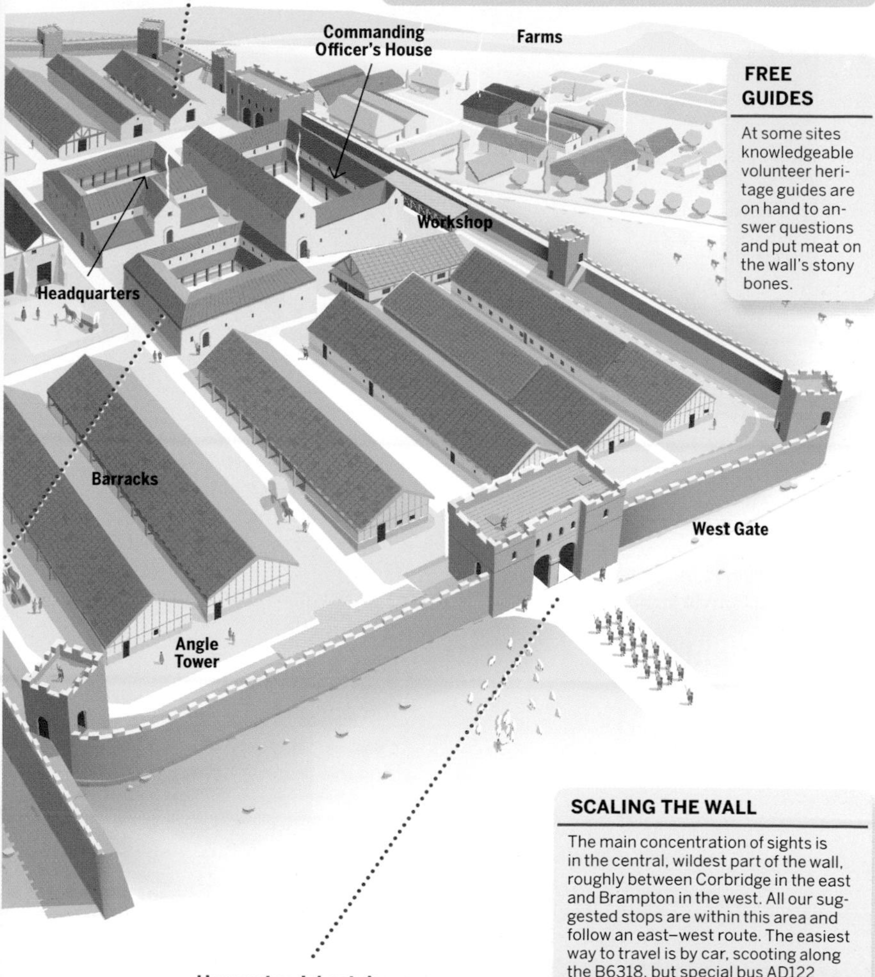

Commanding Officer's House

Farms

Workshop

Headquarters

Barracks

West Gate

Angle Tower

FREE GUIDES

At some sites knowledgeable volunteer heritage guides are on hand to answer questions and put meat on the wall's stony bones.

SCALING THE WALL

The main concentration of sights is in the central, wildest part of the wall, roughly between Corbridge in the east and Brampton in the west. All our suggested stops are within this area and follow an east–west route. The easiest way to travel is by car, scooting along the B6318, but special bus AD122 will also get you there. Hiking along the designated Hadrian's Wall Path (84 miles) allows you to appreciate the achievement up close.

Housesteads' gatehouses
Unusually at Housesteads neither of the gates faces the enemy, as was the norm at a Roman fort – builders aligned them east-west. Ruts worn by cart wheels are still visible in the stone.

Chester

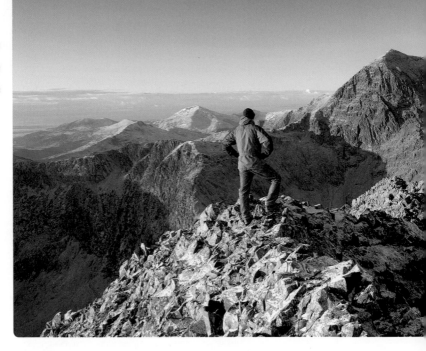

Marvellous Chester is one of English history's greatest legacies. Its red-sandstone wall, which today gift-wraps a tidy collection of Tudor and Victorian buildings, was built during Roman times. The town was then called Castra Devana, and was the largest Roman fortress in Britain.

Sights

City Walls Landmark

A good way to get a sense of Chester's unique character is to walk the 2-mile circuit along the walls that surround the historic centre. Originally built by the Romans around AD 70, the walls were altered substantially over the following centuries but have retained their current position since around 1200. The tourist office's *Walk Around Chester Walls* leaflet is an excellent guide.

Rows Architecture

Besides the City Walls, Chester's other great draw is the Rows, a series of two-level galleried arcades along the four streets that fan out in each direction from the **Central Cross**. The architecture is a handsome mix of Victorian and Tudor (original and mock) buildings that house a fantastic collection of individually owned shops.

Dewa Roman Experience Museum

(☎01244-343407; www.dewaromanexperience.co.uk; Pierpoint Lane; adult/child £5.50/3.75; ⏰9am-5pm Mon-Sat, 10am-5pm Sun) Walk through a reconstructed Roman street to reveal what Roman life was like.

Information

Tourist Office (☎01244-402111; www.visitchester.com; Town Hall, Northgate St; ⏰9am-5.30pm Mon-Sat, 10am-4pm Sun May-Oct, 10am-5pm Mon-Sat Nov-Apr)

Left: Snowdonia National Park (p119), Wales; **Below:** Cardiff Castle, Wales
(LEFT) JAMES OSMOND/GETTY IMAGES ©; (BELOW) BILLY STOCK/GETTY IMAGES ©

Getting There & Away

The train station is about a mile from the city centre. City-Rail Link buses are free for people with rail tickets. Destinations include London Euston (£65, 2½ hours, hourly) and Manchester (£12.60, one hour, hourly).

WALES

Lying to the west of England, Wales is a nation with Celtic roots, its own language and a rich historic legacy. While some areas in the south are undeniably scarred by coal mining and heavy industry, overall Wales boasts a landscape of wild mountains, rolling hills, rich farmland and the bustling capital city of Cardiff.

Cardiff

POP 447,000

The capital of Wales since only 1955, Cardiff has embraced its new role with vigour, emerging as one of Britain's leading urban centres in the 21st century.

Sights

Cardiff Castle Castle

(www.cardiffcastle.com; Castle St; adult/child £12/9, incl guided tour £15/11; 9am-5pm) Cardiff Castle is, quite rightly, the city's leading attraction. There's a medieval keep at its heart, but it's the later additions that capture the imagination of many visitors: during the Victorian era extravagant mock-Gothic features were grafted onto this relic, including a clock tower and a lavish banqueting hall.

Wales Millennium Centre Arts Centre

(029-2063 6464; www.wmc.org.uk; Bute Pl; tours £6; tours 11am & 2.30pm) FREE The centrepiece and symbol of Cardiff Bay's regeneration is the superb Wales Millennium Centre, an architectural masterpiece of stacked Welsh slate in shades of purple, green and grey topped with an overarching bronzed steel shell. Designed by Welsh architect Jonathan Adams, it opened in 2004 as Wales' premier arts complex, housing major cultural organisations such as the Welsh National Opera, National Dance Company, National Orchestra, Literature Wales, HiJinx Theatre and Ty Cerdd (Music Centre of Wales).

Doctor Who Experience Exhibition

(**0844 801 2279; www.doctorwhoexperience.com; Porth Teigr; adult/child £15/11; 10am-5pm (last admission 3.30pm) Wed-Mon, daily school holidays**) The huge success of the reinvented classic TV series *Doctor Who*, produced by BBC Wales, has brought Cardiff to the attention of sci-fi fans worldwide. City locations have featured in many episodes; and the first two series of the spin-off *Torchwood* were also set in Cardiff Bay. Capitalising on Timelord tourism, this interactive exhibition is located right next to the BBC studios where the series is filmed – look out for the Tardis hovering outside.

Sleeping

Jolyons Boutique Hotel Hotel **££**

(**029-2048 8775; www.jolyons.co.uk; 5 Bute Cres; s/d from £76/82;**) A touch of Georgian elegance in the heart of Cardiff Bay, Jolyons has six individually designed rooms combining antique furniture with contemporary colours and crisp cotton sheets. The front rooms face out over Roald Dahl Plass to the Millennium Centre, while one of the rear rooms has its own terrace.

St David's Hotel & Spa Hotel **££**

(**029-2045 4045; www.thestdavidshotel.com; Havannah St; r from £119;**) A glittering, glassy tower topped with a sail-like flourish, St David's epitomises Cardiff Bay's transformation from wasteland to desirable address. Almost every room has a small private balcony with a bay view. The exterior is already showing signs of wear and tear, but the rooms have been recently renovated.

Eating

Goat Major Pub **£**

(**www.sabrain.com/goatmajor; 33 High St; pies £7.50; kitchen noon-6pm Mon-Sat, to 4pm Sun;**) A solidly traditional wood-lined pub with armchairs, a fireplace and Brains Dark real ale on tap, the Goat Major's gastronomic contribution comes in the form of its selection of homemade savoury pot pies served with chips. Try the Wye Valley pie, a mixture of buttered chicken, leek, asparagus and Tintern Abbey cheese.

Conway Gastropub **££**

(**029-2022 4373; www.knifeandforkfood.co.uk; 58 Conway Rd; mains £10-15; noon-11pm;**) With a sun-trap front terrace and a pleasantly laidback vibe, this wonderful corner pub chalks up its delicious 'seasonal, fresh and local' offerings daily. Kids get their own menu, while the grownups can ponder the large selection of wines served by the glass.

Park House Modern British **£££**

(**029-2022 4343; www.parkhouserestaurant.co.uk; 20 Park Pl; mains £26, 2-/3-course lunch £16/21; 11am-10pm Wed-Sat, to 6pm Sun**) The ambience is rather stuffy, but the menu at this private members' club is anything but conservative, adding subtle Indian and Southeast Asian influences to classic European dishes. Dress up and push the buzzer for admittance.

Information

Cardiff Tourist Office (**029-2087 3573; www.visitcardiff.com; Old Library, The Hayes; 9.30am-5.30pm Mon-Sat, 10am-4pm Sun**) Cardiff's main tourist office stocks Ordnance Survey maps and Welsh books, and offers an accommodation booking service and internet access.

Getting There & Away

Arriva Trains Wales (**www.arrivatrainswales.co.uk**) operates all train services in Wales. Direct services from Cardiff include London Paddington (£39, 2¼ hours) and Bristol (£13, 35 minutes).

Snowdonia National Park

Snowdonia National Park (www.eryri-npa.gov.uk) was founded in 1951 (making it Wales' first national park). Around 350,000 people travel to the national park to climb, walk or take the train to the summit of Mt Snowdon, Wales' highest mountain. No Snowdonia experience is complete without coming face-to-face with Snowdon (1085m). On a clear day the views stretch to Ireland and the Isle of Man. Even on a gloomy day you could find yourself above the clouds. At the top is the striking **Hafod Eryri** (**10am to 20min before last train departure;**) visitor centre, opened in 2009 by Prince Charles. Six paths of varying length and difficulty lead to the summit, all taking around six hours return, or you can cheat and catch the **Snowdon Mountain Railway** (**0844 493 8120; www.snowdonrailway.co.uk; return diesel adult/child £27/18, steam £35/25; 9am-5pm mid-Mar–Oct**), opened in 1896 and still the UK's only public rack-and-pinion railway. However you get to the summit, take warm, waterproof clothing, wear sturdy footwear and check the weather forecast before setting out.

Getting There & Away

The Welsh Highland Railway and Snowdon Sherpa (0870 608 2608) buses link various places in Snowdonia with the town of Bangor, which can be reached by train from London Euston (£86, 3¼ hours, hourly).

Conwy

On the north coast of Wales, the historic town of Conwy is dominated by the Unesco-designated cultural treasure of **Conwy Castle** (**Cadw; 01492-592358; www.cadw.wales.gov.uk; Castle Sq; adult/child £5.75/4.35; 9.30am-5pm; P**), the most stunning of all Edward I's Welsh fortresses. Built between 1277 and 1307 on a rocky outcrop, it has commanding views across the estuary and Snowdonia National Park.

If You Like... Cathedrals

Alongside York Minster (p109) and Canterbury (p94), Britain is awash with many stunning houses of worship.

1 **SALISBURY CATHEDRAL** (**01722-555120; www.salisburycathedral.org.uk; Cathedral Close; requested donation adult/child £6.50/3; 9am-5pm Mon-Sat, noon-4pm Sun**) Of the many stunning churches few can hold a candle to the grandeur and sheer spectacle of 13th-century Salisbury Cathedral. This early English Gothic–style structure has an elaborate exterior decorated with pointed arches and flying buttresses, and a sombre, austere interior. Don't miss the daily tower tours and the cathedral's original, 13th-century copy of the Magna Carta.

2 **ELY CATHEDRAL** (**www.elycathedral.org; adult/child £8/free, entry & tower tour £14.50/free; 7am-6.30pm**) Ely Cathedral's stunning silhouette dominates the whole area – it's dubbed the 'Ship of the Fens' because it's so visible across the vast, flat sweeps of land. The early-12th-century nave dazzles with clean, uncluttered lines and a lofty sense of space. Look out too for the entrancing ceiling, the masterly 14th-century Octagon, and the shimmering towers.

3 **DURHAM CATHEDRAL** (**www.durhamcathedral.co.uk; by donation, tower £5, guided tours adult/child £5/free; 7.30am-6pm Mon-Sat, to 5.30pm Sun**) This monumental cathedral is the definitive structure of the Anglo-Norman Romanesque style. Look for the famous Sanctuary Knocker, which medieval felons would strike to gain 37 days asylum in the cathedral before standing trial or leaving the country

4 **WELLS CATHEDRAL** (**Cathedral Church of St Andrew; www.wellscathedral.org.uk; requested donation adult/child £6/3; 7am-7pm**) Wells' gargantuan Gothic cathedral sits plum in the centre of the city. Among its notable features are the West Front, decorated with more than 300 carved figures, and the famous scissor arches – an ingenious solution to the subsidence of the central tower.

Central Edinburgh

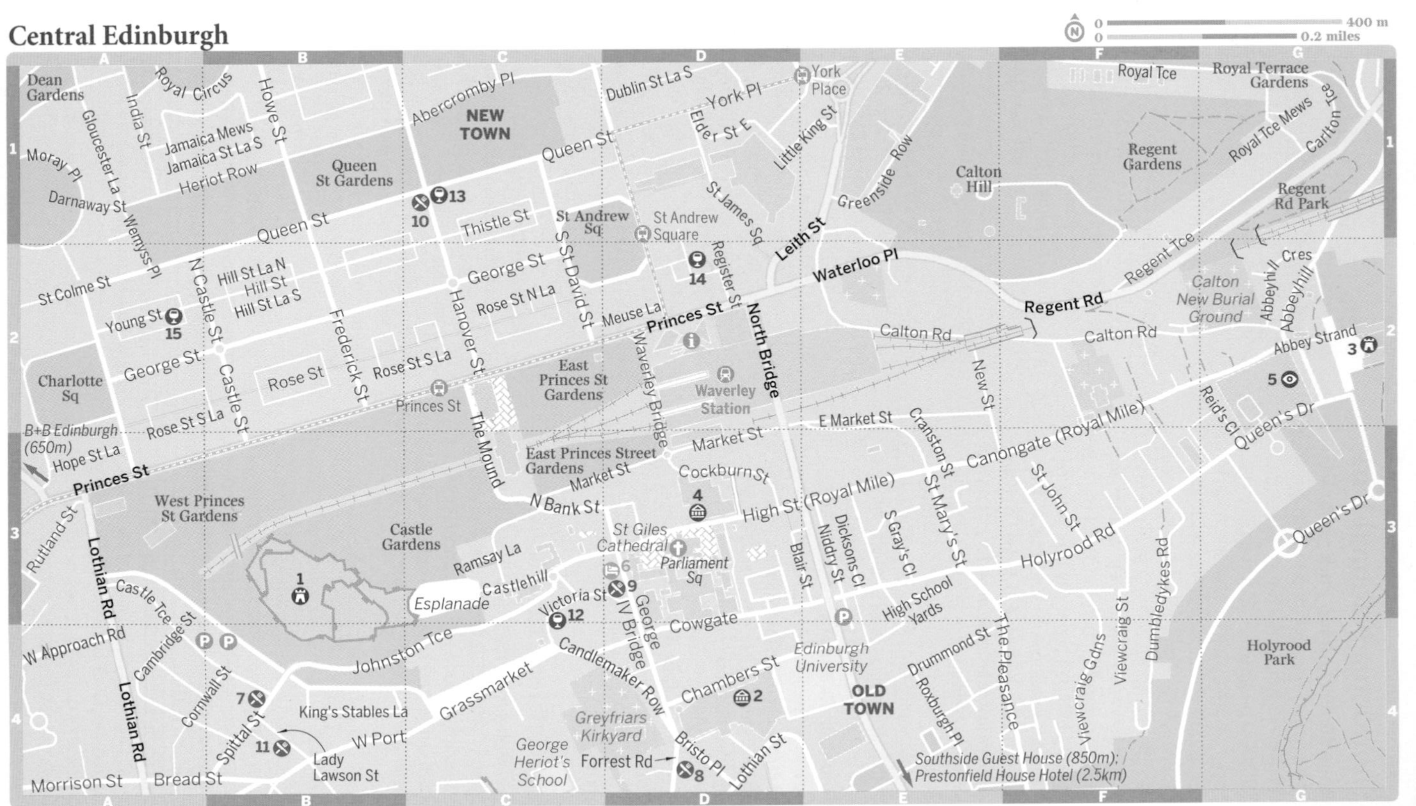

Central Edinburgh

Sights

1 Edinburgh Castle B3
2 National Museum of Scotland D4
3 Palace of Holyroodhouse G2
4 Real Mary King's Close D3
5 Scottish Parliament Building G2

Sleeping

6 Hotel Missoni D3

Eating

7 Castle Terrace B4
8 Mums D4
9 Ondine D3
10 The Dogs C1
11 Timberyard B4

Drinking & Nightlife

12 Bow Bar C3
13 Bramble C1
14 Café Royal Circle Bar D2
15 Oxford Bar A2

SCOTLAND

Despite its small size, Scotland has many treasures crammed into its compact territory – big skies, lonely landscapes, spectacular wildlife, superb seafood and hospitable, down-to-earth people. From the cultural attractions of Edinburgh to the heather-clad hills of the Highlands, there's something for everyone.

Edinburgh

POP 460,400

Edinburgh is a city that just begs to be explored. From the castle to the Palace of Holyroodhouse to the Royal Yacht Britannia, every corner turned reveals sudden views and unexpected vistas – green sunlit hills, a glimpse of rust-red crags, a blue flash of distant sea. But there's more to Edinburgh than sightseeing – there are top shops, world-class restaurants and a bacchanalia of bars to enjoy.

Edinburgh Castle Castle

(www.edinburghcastle.gov.uk; adult/child incl audioguide £16/9.60; 9.30am-6pm Apr-Sep, to 5pm Oct-Mar, last admission 45min before closing; 23, 27, 41, 42) Edinburgh Castle has played a pivotal role in Scottish history, both as a royal residence – King Malcolm Canmore (r 1058–93) and Queen Margaret first made their home here in the 11th century – and as a military stronghold. The castle last saw military action in 1745; from then until the 1920s it served as the British army's main base in Scotland. Today it is one of Scotland's most atmospheric and popular tourist attractions.

Real Mary King's Close Historic Building

(0845 070 6244; www.realmarykingsclose.com; 2 Warriston's Close, High St; adult/child £12.95/7.45; 10am-9pm daily Apr-Oct, to 11pm Aug, 10am-5pm Sun-Thu & 10am-9pm Fri & Sat Nov-Mar; 23, 27, 41, 42) Edinburgh's 18th-century City Chambers were built over the sealed-off remains of Mary King's Close, and the lower levels of this medieval Old Town alley have survived almost unchanged amid the foundations for 250 years. Now open to the public, this spooky, subterranean labyrinth gives a fascinating insight into the everyday life of 17th-century Edinburgh. Costumed characters lead tours through a 16th-century town house and the plague-stricken home of a 17th-century gravedigger. Advance bookings are recommended.

National Museum of Scotland Museum

(www.nms.ac.uk; Chambers St; fee for special exhibitions; 10am-5pm; 2, 23, 27, 35, 41, 42, 45) FREE Broad, elegant Chambers St is dominated by the long facade of the National Museum of Scotland. Its extensive collections are spread between two buildings, one modern, one Victorian – the golden stone and striking modern architecture of the new building, opened in 1998, is one of the city's most distinctive landmarks. The five floors of the museum trace the history of Scotland from geological beginnings to the 1990s, with many imaginative and stimulating exhibits – audioguides are available in several languages.

Royal Mile

A GRAND DAY OUT

Planning your own procession along the Royal Mile involves some tough decisions – it would be impossible to see everything in a single day, so it's wise to decide in advance what you don't want to miss and shape your visit around that. Remember to leave time for lunch, for exploring some of the Mile's countless side alleys and, during festival time, for enjoying the street theatre that is bound to be happening in High St.

The most pleasant way to reach the Castle Esplanade at the start of the Royal Mile is to hike up the zigzag path from the footbridge behind the Ross Bandstand in Princes Street Gardens (in springtime you'll be knee-deep in daffodils). Starting at **Edinburgh Castle** ❶ means that the rest of your walk is downhill. For a superb view up and down the length of the Mile, climb the **Camera Obscura's Outlook Tower** ❷ before visiting **Gladstone's**

Edinburgh Castle

If you're pushed for time, visit the Great Hall, the Honours of Scotland and the Prisons of War exhibit. Head for the Half Moon Battery for a photo looking down the length of the Royal Mile.

ROYAL VISITS TO THE ROYAL MILE

1561: Mary, Queen of Scots arrives from France and holds an audience with John Knox.
1745: Bonnie Prince Charlie fails to capture Edinburgh Castle, and instead sets up court in Holyroodhouse.
2004: Queen Elizabeth II officially opens the Scottish Parliament building.

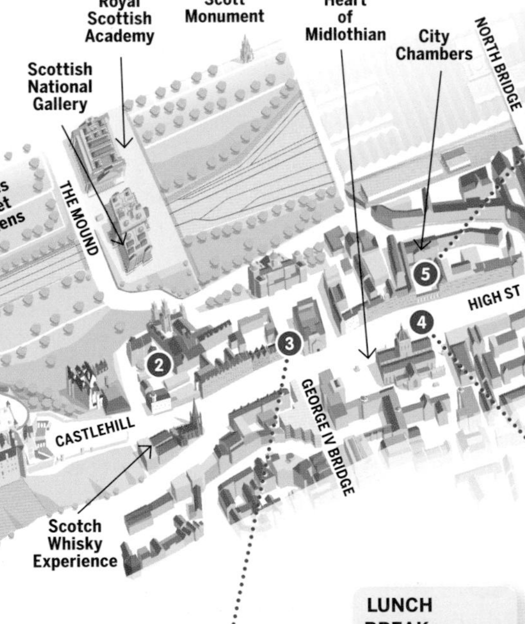

Gladstone's Land

The 1st floor houses a faithful recreation of how a wealthy Edinburgh merchant lived in the 17th century. Check out the beautiful Painted Bedchamber, with its ornately decorated walls and wooden ceilings.

LUNCH BREAK

Burger and a beer at **Holyrood 9A**; steak and chips at **Maxie's Bistro**; slap-up seafood at **Ondine**.

Land ③ and **St Giles Cathedral** ④. If history's your thing, you'll want to add **Real Mary King's Close** ⑤, **John Knox House** ⑥ and the **Museum of Edinburgh** ⑦ to your must-see list.

At the foot of the mile, choose between modern and ancient seats of power – the **Scottish Parliament** ⑧ or the **Palace of Holyroodhouse** ⑨. Round off the day with an evening ascent of Arthur's Seat or, slightly less strenuously, Calton Hill. Both make great sunset viewpoints.

TAKING YOUR TIME

Minimum time needed for each attraction:

» **Edinburgh Castle**: two hours

» **Gladstone's Land**: 45 minutes

» **St Giles Cathedral**: 30 minutes

» **Real Mary King's Close**: one hour (tour)

» **Scottish Parliament**: one hour (tour)

» **Palace of Holyroodhouse**: one hour

Real Mary King's Close
The guided tour is heavy on ghost stories, but a highlight is standing in an original 17th-century room with tufts of horsehair poking from the crumbling plaster, and breathing in the ancient scent of stone, dust and history.

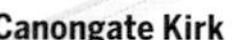

Palace of Holyroodhouse
Find the secret staircase joining Mary, Queen of Scots' bedchamber with that of her husband, Lord Darnley, who restrained the queen while his henchmen stabbed to death her secretary (and possible lover), David Rizzio.

RIEGER BERTRAND/GETTY IMAGES ©

Scottish Parliament
Don't have time for the guided tour? Pick up a 'Discover the Scottish Parliament Building' leaflet from reception and take a self-guided tour of the exterior, then hike up to Salisbury Crags for a great view of the complex.

RICK LEW/GETTY IMAGES © ARCHITECT: ENRIC MIRALLES

St Giles Cathedral
Look out for the Burne-Jones stained-glass window (1873) at the west end, showing the crossing of the River Jordan, and the bronze memorial to Robert Louis Stevenson in the Moray Aisle.

DANITA DELIMONT/GETTY IMAGES ©

Festival City

Edinburgh boasts a frenzy of festivals, especially in August. See www.edinburghfestivals.co.uk for more.

Edinburgh Festival Fringe (☎0131-226 0026; www.edfringe.com) The biggest festival of the performing arts anywhere in the world, held over 3½ weeks in August, the last two weeks overlapping with the first two weeks of the Edinburgh International Festival.

Edinburgh International Festival (☎0131-473 2099; www.eif.co.uk) Three weeks of inspirational music, opera, theatre and dance in August.

Edinburgh Military Tattoo (☎0131-225 1188; www.edintattoo.co.uk) A spectacular display of military marching bands, massed pipes and drums, acrobats, cheerleaders and motorcycle display teams, all played out in front of the magnificent backdrop of the floodlit castle during the first three weeks of August.

Royal Yacht Britannia Ship

(www.royalyachtbritannia.co.uk; Ocean Terminal; adult/child £12.75/7.75; ⏲9.30am-6pm Jul-Sep, to 5.30pm Apr-Jun & Oct, 10am-5pm Nov-Mar, last admission 90min before closing; 🚌11, 22, 34, 35, 36) Built on Clydeside, the former Royal Yacht Britannia was the British royal family's floating holiday home during their foreign travels from the time of her launch in 1953 until her decommissioning in 1997, and is now moored permanently in front of Ocean Terminal. The tour, which you take at your own pace with an audioguide (included in admission fee and available in 20 languages), lifts the curtain on the everyday lives of the royals, and gives an intriguing insight into the Queen's private tastes.

Scottish Parliament Building Notable Building

(☎0131-348 5200; www.scottish.parliament.uk; Horse Wynd; ⏲9am-6.30pm Tue-Thu, 10am-5.30pm Mon, Fri & Sat in session, 10am-6pm Mon-Sat in recess; 🚌35, 36) FREE The Scottish parliament building, built on the site of a former brewery, was officially opened by HM the Queen in October 2005. Designed by Catalan architect Enric Miralles (1955–2000), the ground plan of the parliament complex represents a 'flower of democracy rooted in Scottish soil' (best seen looking down from Salisbury Crags). Free, one-hour guided tours (advance booking recommended) include a visit to the Debating Chamber, a committee room, the Garden Lobby and an MSP's (Member of the Scottish Parliament) office.

Palace of Holyroodhouse Palace

(www.royalcollection.org.uk; Horse Wynd; adult/child £11.30/6.80; ⏲9.30am-6pm Apr-Oct, to 4.30pm Nov-Mar; 🚌35, 36) This palace is the royal family's official residence in Scotland, but is more famous as the 16th-century home of the ill-fated Mary, Queen of Scots. The unfortunate queen spent six turbulent years here, from 1561 to 1567, during which time she debated with John Knox and married both her first and second husbands. The highlight of the tour is **Mary's Bed Chamber**. It was here that her jealous first husband, Lord Darnley, restrained the pregnant queen while his henchmen murdered her secretary – and favourite – Rizzio. A plaque in the neighbouring room marks the spot where he bled to death.

Tours

Majestic Tour Bus Tour

(www.edinburghtour.com; adult/child £13/6; daily year-round except 25 Dec) Hop-on hop-off tour departing every 15 to 20 minutes from Waverley Bridge to the Royal Yacht Britannia at Ocean Terminal via the New Town, Royal Botanic Garden and Newhaven, returning via Leith Walk, Holyrood and the Royal Mile.

City of the Dead Tours Walking Tour

(www.cityofthedeadtours.com; adult/concession £10/8) This tour of Greyfriars Kirkyard is probably the scariest of Edinburgh's 'ghost' tours. Many have reported encounters with the 'Mackenzie Poltergeist', the ghost of a 17th-century judge who persecuted the Covenanters, and now haunts their former prison in a corner of the kirkyard. Not for young children.

Edinburgh Literary Pub Tour Walking Tour

(www.edinburghliterarypubtour.co.uk; adult/student £14/10) An enlightening two-hour trawl through Edinburgh's literary history – and its associated howffs (pubs) – in the entertaining company of Messrs Clart and McBrain. One of the city's best walking tours.

Sleeping

Southside Guest House B&B **££**

(0131-668 4422; www.southsideguesthouse.co.uk; 8 Newington Rd; s/d £75/95;) Though set in a typical Victorian terrace, the Southside transcends the traditional guesthouse category and feels more like a modern boutique hotel. Its eight stylish rooms ooze interior design, standing out from other Newington B&Bs through the clever use of bold colours and modern furniture. Breakfast is an event, with Bucks fizz (champagne mixed with orange juice) on offer to smooth the rough edges off your hangover!

B+B Edinburgh Hotel **££**

(0131-225 5084; www.bb-edinburgh.com; 3 Rothesay Tce; d/ste from £110/170;) Built in 1883 as a grand home for the proprietor of the *Scotsman* newspaper, this Victorian extravaganza of carved oak, parquet floors, stained glass and elaborate fireplaces was given a designer makeover in 2011 to create a striking contemporary hotel. Rooms on the 2nd floor are the most spacious, but the smaller top-floor rooms enjoy the finest views.

Hotel Missoni Boutique Hotel **£££**

(0131-220 6666; www.hotelmissoni.com; 1 George IV Bridge; r £125-290;) The Italian fashion house has established a style icon in the heart of the medieval Old Town with this bold statement of a hotel – modernistic architecture,

Palace of Holyroodhouse, Edinburgh

Detour: Rosslyn Chapel

The success of Dan Brown's novel *The Da Vinci Code* and the subsequent Hollywood film has seen a flood of visitors descend on Scotland's most beautiful and enigmatic church: **Rosslyn Chapel** (Collegiate Church of St Matthew; www.rosslynchapel.org.uk; Chapel Loan, Roslin; adult/child £9/free; 9.30am-5pm Mon-Sat, noon-4.45pm Sun). As well as flowers, vines, angels and biblical figures, the carved stones include many examples of the pagan 'Green Man'; other figures are associated with Freemasonry and the Knights Templar. The symbolism of these images has led some researchers to conclude that Rosslyn might be a secret Templar repository, concealing anything from the Holy Grail or the head of John the Baptist to the body of Christ himself.

The chapel is in Roslin, 7 miles south of Edinburgh's centre.

black-and-white decor with well-judged splashes of colour, impeccably mannered staff and, most importantly, very comfortable bedrooms and bathrooms with lots of nice little touches, from fresh milk in the minibar to plush bathrobes.

Prestonfield House Hotel Boutique Hotel **£££**
(0131-668 3346; www.prestonfield.com; Priestfield Rd; r/ste from £295/375; P) If the blonde wood and brushed steel of modern boutique hotels leave you cold, then this is the place for you. A 17th-century mansion set in 8 hectares of parkland (complete with peacocks and Highland cattle), Prestonfield House is draped in damask and packed with antiques – look out for original tapestries, 17th-century embossed-leather panelling, and £500-a-roll hand-painted wallpaper.

Eating

Mums Cafe **£**
(www.monstermashcafe.co.uk; 4a Forrest Rd; mains £6-9; 9am-10pm Mon-Sat, 10am-10pm Sun; 23, 27, 41, 42) This nostalgia-fuelled cafe serves up classic British comfort food that wouldn't look out of place on a 1950s menu – bacon and eggs, bangers and mash, shepherd's pie, fish and chips. But there's a twist – the food is all top-quality nosh freshly prepared from local produce, including Crombie's gourmet sausages. There's even a wine list, though we prefer the real ales and Scottish-brewed cider.

The Dogs British **££**
(0131-220 1208; www.thedogsonline.co.uk; 110 Hanover St; mains £10-15; noon-4pm & 5-10pm; 23, 27) One of the coolest tables in town, this bistro-style place uses cheaper cuts of meat and lesser-known, more-sustainable species of fish to create hearty, no-nonsense dishes such as lamb sweetbreads on toast, baked coley with *skirlie* (fried oatmeal and onion), and devilled liver with bacon and onions.

Timberyard Scottish **££**
(0131-221 1222; www.timberyard.co; 10 Lady Lawson St; mains £16-21; noon-9.30pm Tue-Sat; ; 2, 35) Ancient worn floorboards, cast-iron pillars, exposed joists and tables made from slabs of old mahogany create a rustic, retro atmosphere in this slow-food restaurant where the accent is on locally sourced produce from artisan growers and foragers. Typical dishes include seared scallop with apple, jerusalem artichoke and sorrel; and juniper-smoked pigeon with wild garlic flowers and beetroot.

DE AGOSTINI / S. VANNINI /GETTY IMAGES ©

Don't Miss
Stirling Castle

Hold Stirling and you control Scotland. This maxim has ensured that a fortress of some kind has existed here since prehistoric times. You cannot help drawing parallels with Edinburgh Castle, but many find Stirling's fortress more atmospheric – the location, architecture, historical significance and commanding views combine to make it a grand and memorable sight. It's best to visit in the afternoon; many tourists come on day trips, so you may have the castle almost to yourself by about 4pm.

The current castle dates from the late 14th to the 16th century, when it was a residence of the Stuart monarchs. The undisputed highlight of a visit is the fabulous, recently restored **Royal Palace**. The idea was that it should look brand new, just as when it was constructed by French masons under the orders of James V in the mid-16th century with the aim of impressing his new (also French) bride and other crowned heads of Europe. The suite of six rooms – three for the king, three for the queen – is a sumptuous riot of colour. Particularly notable are the fine fireplaces, the **Stirling Heads** – modern reproductions of painted oak discs in the ceiling of the king's audience chamber – and the fabulous series of **tapestries** that have been painstakingly woven over many years. Based on originals in New York's Metropolitan Museum, they depict the hunting of a unicorn – an event ripe with Christian metaphor – and are breathtakingly beautiful. Don't miss the palace exterior, studded with beautiful sculptures, or the **Stirling Heads Gallery** above the royal chambers. This displays the original carved oak roundels that decorated the king's audience chamber – a real rogue's gallery of royals, courtiers and classical personalities. In the vaults beneath the palace is a kid-friendly **exhibition** on various aspects of castle life.

NEED TO KNOW

www.stirlingcastle.gov.uk; adult/child £14/7.50; 9.30am-6pm Apr-Sep, to 5pm Oct-Mar

Stirling Castle

PLANNING YOUR ATTACK

Stirling's a sizeable fortress, but not so huge that you'll have to decide what to leave out – there's time to see it all. Unless you've got a working knowledge of Scottish monarchs, head to the **Castle Exhibition** ❶ first: it'll help you sort one James from another. That done, take on the sights at leisure. First, stop and look around you from the **ramparts** ❷; the views high over this flat valley, a key strategic point in Scotland's history, are magnificent.

Track back towards the citadel's heart, stopping for a quick tour through the **Great Kitchens** ❸; looking at all that fake food might make you seriously hungry, though. Then enter the main courtyard. Around you are the principal castle buildings. During summer there are events (such as Renaissance dancing) in the **Great Hall** ❹ – get details at the entrance. The **Museum of the Argyll & Sutherland Highlanders** ❺ is a treasure trove if you're interested in regimental history, but missable if you're not. Leave the best for last – crowds thin in the afternoon – and enter the sumptuous **Royal Palace** ❻.

Take time to admire the beautiful **Stirling Tapestries** ❼, skillfully woven by hand on-site between 2001-2014.

THE WAY UP & DOWN

If you have time, take the atmospheric Back Walk, a peaceful, shady stroll around the Old Town's fortifications and up to the castle's imposing crag-top position. Afterwards, wander down through the Old Town to admire its facades.

TOP TIPS

» **Admission** Entrance is free for Historic Scotland members. If you'll be visiting several Historic Scotland sites a membership will save you plenty.

» **Vital Statistics** First constructed: before 1110; number of sieges: at least nine; last besieger: Bonnie Prince Charlie (unsuccessful); money spent refurbishing the Royal Palace: £12 million.

Museum of the Argyll & Sutherland Highlanders
The history of one of Scotland's legendary regiments – now subsumed into the Royal Regiment of Scotland – is on display here, featuring memorabilia, weapons and uniforms.

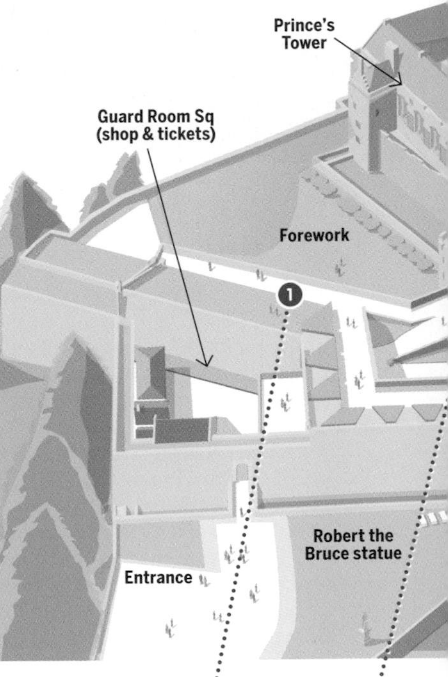

Castle Exhibition
A great overview of the Stewart dynasty here will get your facts straight, and also offers the latest archaeological titbits from the ongoing excavations under the citadel. Analysis of skeletons has revealed surprising amounts of biographical data.

Royal Palace
The impressive new highlight of a visit to the castle is this recreation of the royal lodgings originally built by James V. The finely worked ceiling, ornate furniture and sumptuous unicorn tapestries dazzle.

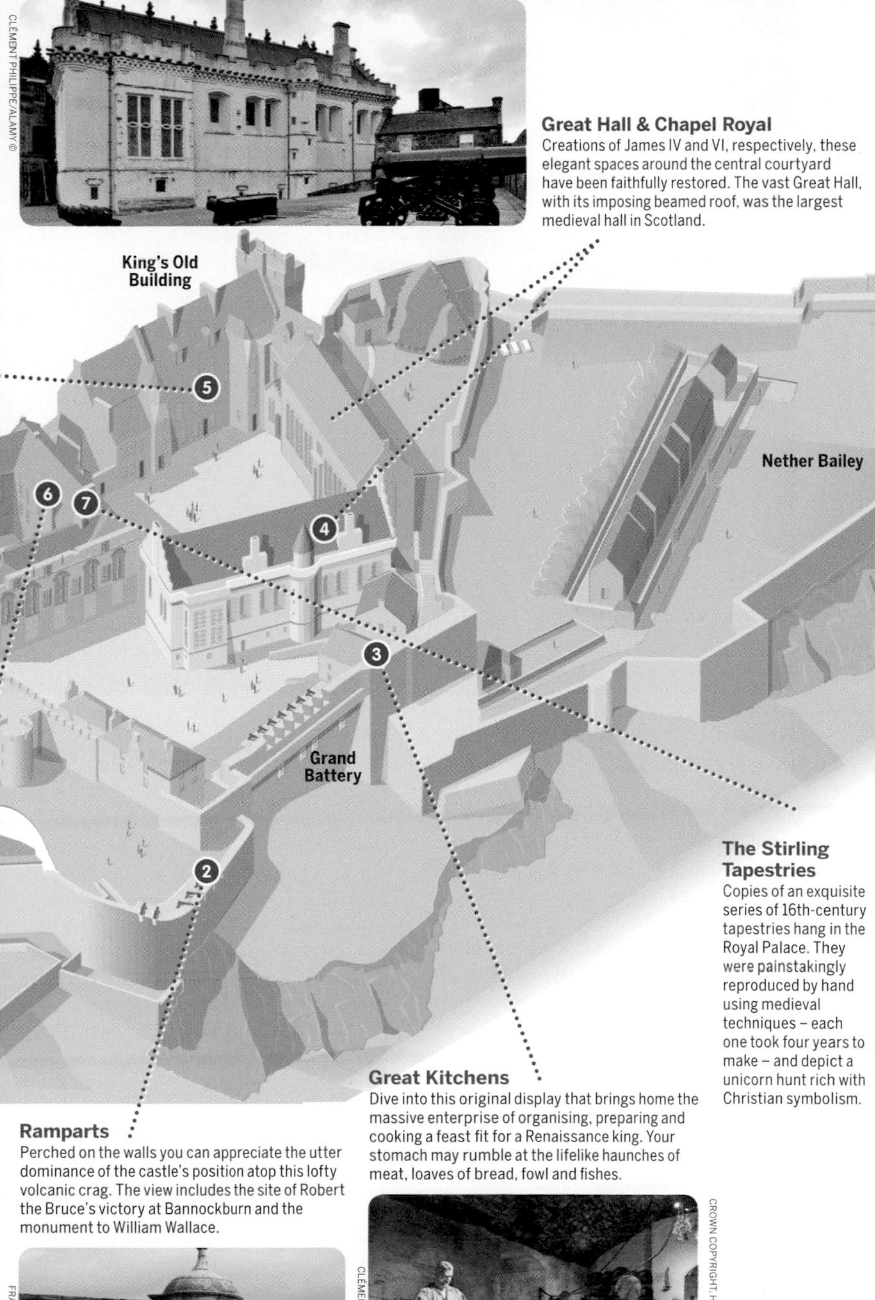

Great Hall & Chapel Royal

Creations of James IV and VI, respectively, these elegant spaces around the central courtyard have been faithfully restored. The vast Great Hall, with its imposing beamed roof, was the largest medieval hall in Scotland.

The Stirling Tapestries

Copies of an exquisite series of 16th-century tapestries hang in the Royal Palace. They were painstakingly reproduced by hand using medieval techniques – each one took four years to make – and depict a unicorn hunt rich with Christian symbolism.

Great Kitchens

Dive into this original display that brings home the massive enterprise of organising, preparing and cooking a feast fit for a Renaissance king. Your stomach may rumble at the lifelike haunches of meat, loaves of bread, fowl and fishes.

Ramparts

Perched on the walls you can appreciate the utter dominance of the castle's position atop this lofty volcanic crag. The view includes the site of Robert the Bruce's victory at Bannockburn and the monument to William Wallace.

Ondine Seafood **£££**

(☎0131-226 1888; www.ondinerestaurant.co.uk; 2 George IV Bridge; mains £14-39, 2-/3-course lunch £22/25; ⏰noon-3pm & 5.30-10pm Mon-Sat; 🚌23, 27, 41, 42) Ondine is one of Edinburgh's finest seafood restaurants, with a menu based on sustainably sourced fish. Take a seat at the curved Oyster Bar and tuck into oysters Kilpatrick, lobster thermidor, a roast shellfish platter or just good old haddock and chips (with minted pea purée, just to keep things posh).

Castle Terrace Scottish **£££**

(☎0131-229 1222; www.castleterracerestaurant.com; 33-35 Castle Tce; mains £25-42, 3-course lunch £28.50; ⏰noon-2pm & 6.30-10pm Tue-Sat; 🚌2) It was little more than a year after opening in 2010 that Castle Terrace was awarded a Michelin star under chef-patron Dominic Jack. The menu is seasonal and applies sharply whetted Parisian skills to the finest of local produce, be it Ayrshire pork, Aberdeenshire lamb or Newhaven crab – even the cheese in the sauces is Scottish.

Drinking & Nightlife

Café Royal Circle Bar Pub

(www.caferoyaledinburgh.co.uk; 17 West Register St; 🚌all Princes St buses) Perhaps *the* classic Edinburgh pub, the Cafe Royal's main claims to fame are its magnificent oval bar and its Doulton tile portraits of famous Victorian inventors. Sit at the bar or claim one of the cosy leather booths beneath the stained-glass windows, and choose from the seven real ales on tap.

Bow Bar Pub

(80 West Bow; 🚌23, 27, 41, 42) One of the city's best traditional-style pubs (it's not as old as it looks), serving a range of excellent real ales and a vast selection of malt whiskies, the Bow Bar often has standing-room only on Friday and Saturday evenings.

Bramble Cocktail Bar

(www.bramblebar.co.uk; 16a Queen St; 🚌23, 27) One of those places that easily earns the sobriquet 'best-kept secret', Bramble

Left & Below: Bow Bar, Edinburgh
(LEFT) KARL BLACKWELL/GETTY IMAGES ©; (BELOW) KARL BLACKWELL/GETTY IMAGES ©

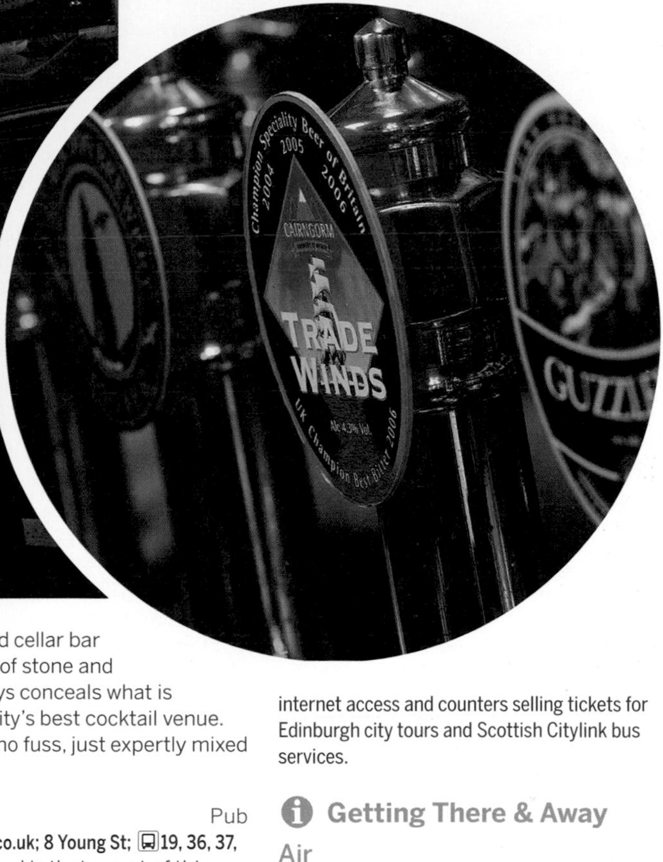

is an unmarked cellar bar where a maze of stone and brick hideaways conceals what is arguably the city's best cocktail venue. No beer taps, no fuss, just expertly mixed drinks.

Oxford Bar Pub
(www.oxfordbar.co.uk; 8 Young St; 🚌19, 36, 37, 41, 47) The Oxford is that rarest of things: a real pub for real people, with no 'theme', no music, no frills and no pretensions. 'The Ox' has been immortalised by Ian Rankin, author of the Inspector Rebus novels, whose fictional detective is a regular here.

Information

Edinburgh Information Centre (**☎0131-473 3868; www.edinburgh.org; Princes Mall, 3 Princes St; ⏲9am-9pm Mon-Sat, 10am-8pm Sun Jul & Aug, 9am-7pm Mon-Sat, 10am-7pm Sun May-Jun & Sep, 9am-5pm Mon-Wed, to 6pm Thu-Sun Oct-Apr**) Includes an accommodation booking service, currency exchange, gift and bookshop, internet access and counters selling tickets for Edinburgh city tours and Scottish Citylink bus services.

Getting There & Away

Air

Edinburgh Airport (**☎0844 448 8833; www.edinburghairport.com**), 8 miles west of the city, has numerous flights to other parts of Scotland and the UK, Ireland and mainland Europe.

Train

The main terminus in Edinburgh is Waverley train station, located in the heart of the city.

First ScotRail (**☎08457 55 00 33; www.scotrail.co.uk**) operates a regular shuttle service between Edinburgh and Glasgow (£13.20, 50 minutes, every 15 minutes), and frequent daily services to all Scottish cities, including Stirling (£8.30, one hour, twice hourly Monday to Saturday, hourly Sunday) and Inverness (£72, 3. hours). There are also regular trains to London Kings Cross (£85, 4. hours, hourly) via York.

Loch Lomond & the Trossachs

The 'bonnie banks' and 'bonnie braes' of Loch Lomond have long been Glasgow's rural retreat, and today the loch's popularity shows no sign of decreasing. The region's importance was recognised when it became the heart of **Loch Lomond & the Trossachs National Park** (www.lochlomond-trossachs.org) – Scotland's first national park, created in 2002.

The main centre for boat trips is Balloch, where **Sweeney's Cruises** (01389-752376; www.sweeneyscruises.com; Balloch Rd) offers a range of trips including a one-hour cruise to Inchmurrin and back (adult/child £8.50/5, departs hourly).

Loch Ness & the Highlands

Deep, dark and narrow, Loch Ness stretches for 23 miles between Inverness and Fort Augustus, in the heart of the Scottish Highlands. Its bitterly cold waters have been extensively explored in search of the elusive **Loch Ness monster**, but most visitors see her only in cardboard cut-out form at the monster exhibitions in the village of Drumnadrochit.

The journey to Loch Ness takes you through majestic Highland scenery, with the option of continuing west to the Isle of Skye.

Sights & Activities

Loch Ness Centre & Exhibition Interpretation Centre

(01456-450573; www.lochness.com; adult/child £7.45/4.95; 9.30am-6pm Jul & Aug, to 5pm Easter-Jun, Sep & Oct, 10am-3.30pm Nov-Easter; P) This Nessie-themed attraction adopts a scientific approach that allows you to weigh the evidence for yourself. Exhibits include the original equipment – sonar survey vessels, miniature submarines, cameras and sediment coring tools – used in various monster hunts, as well as original photographs and film footage of sightings. You'll find out about hoaxes and optical illusions, as well as learning a lot about the ecology of Loch Ness – is there enough food in the loch to support even one 'monster', let alone a breeding population?

Urquhart Castle Castle

(HS; 01456-450551; adult/child £7.90/4.80; 9.30am-6pm Apr-Sep, to 5pm Oct, to 4.30pm Nov-Mar; P) Commanding a brilliant location 1.5 miles east of Drumnadrochit, with outstanding views (on a clear day), Urquhart Castle is a popular Nessie-watching hotspot. A huge visitor centre (most of which is beneath ground level) includes a video theatre (with a dramatic 'unveiling' of the castle at the end of the film) and displays of medieval items discovered in the castle.

Nessie Hunter Boat Tour

(01456-450395; www.lochness-cruises.com; adult/child £15/10; Easter-Oct) One-hour monster-hunting cruises, complete with sonar and underwater cameras. Cruises depart from Drumnadrochit hourly (except 1pm) from 9am to 6pm daily.

Sleeping & Eating

Loch Ness Inn Inn ££

(01456-450991; www.staylochness.co.uk; Lewiston; d/f £90/120; P) The Loch Ness Inn ticks all the weary traveller's boxes, with comfortable bedrooms (the family suite sleeps two adults and two children), a cosy bar pouring real ales from the Cairngorm and Isle of Skye breweries, and a rustic restaurant (mains £9 to £19) serving hearty, wholesome fare such as whisky-flambéed haggis, and roast rump of Scottish lamb. It's conveniently located in the quiet hamlet of Lewiston, between Drumnadrochit and Urquhart Castle.

Rocpool Reserve Boutique Hotel £££

(01463-240089; www.rocpool.com; Culduthel Rd; s/d from £185/220; P) Boutique chic meets the Highlands in this slick and sophisticated little hotel, where an elegant Georgian exterior conceals an oasis of contemporary cool. A gleaming white entrance hall lined with red carpet and contemporary art leads to designer rooms in shades of chocolate, cream and gold; a restaurant by Albert Roux completes the luxury package.

Dores Inn Inn ££

(☎01463-751203; www.thedoresinn.co.uk; Dores; mains £10-14; ⏰pub 10am-11pm, food served noon-2pm & 6-9pm; P 📶) The Dores Inn is a beautifully restored country pub furnished with old church seating, local landscape paintings and fresh flowers. The menu specialises in quality Scottish produce, from haggis, neeps and tatties, and haddock and chips, to steaks, scallops and seafood platters.

The pub garden enjoys a stunning view along Loch Ness, and even has a dedicated monster-spotting vantage point.

Getting There & Away

Scottish Citylink (www.citylink.co.uk) and Stagecoach (www.stagecoachbus.com) buses from Inverness to Fort William run along the shores of Loch Ness (six to eight daily, five on Sunday); those headed for Skye turn off at Invermoriston. There are bus stops at Drumnadrochit (£3.20, 30 minutes) and Urquhart Castle car park (£3.50, 35 minutes).

Isle of Skye

POP 10,000

The Isle of Skye is the second biggest of Scotland's islands (now linked to the mainland by a bridge at Kyle of Lochalsh), a 50-mile-long smorgasbord of velvet moors, jagged mountains, sparkling lochs and towering sea cliffs. It takes its name from the old Norse *sky-a*, meaning 'cloud island', a Viking reference to the often mist-enshrouded **Cuillin Hills**, Britain's most spectacular mountain range. The stunning scenery is the main attraction, including the cliffs and pinnacles of the **Old Man of Storr**, Kilt Rock and the Quiraing, but there are plenty of cosy pubs to retire to when the rainclouds close in. Portree is the main town, with Broadford a close second; both have banks, ATMs, supermarkets and petrol stations.

Sights & Activities

Dunvegan Castle Castle

(☎01470-521206; www.dunvegancastle.com; adult/child £10/7; ⏰10am-5.30pm Apr–mid-Oct; P) Skye's most famous historic building, and one of its most popular tourist attractions, Dunvegan Castle is the seat of the chief of Clan MacLeod. It has played host to Samuel Johnson, Sir Walter Scott and, most famously, Flora MacDonald. The oldest parts are the 14th-century keep and dungeon but most of it dates from the 17th to 19th centuries.

Aonach Dubh, Glen Coe, Scottish Highlands

MARTIN MCCARTHY/GETTY IMAGES ©

Skye Tours Bus Tour
(☎01471-822716; www.skye-tours.co.uk; adult/child £35/30; ⊙Mon-Sat) Five-hour sightseeing tours of Skye in a minibus, departing from the tourist office car park in Kyle of Lochalsh (close to Kyle of Lochalsh train station).

Sleeping & Eating

Ben Tianavaig B&B B&B ££
(☎01478-612152; www.ben-tianavaig.co.uk; 5 Bosville Tce; r £75-88; P 📶) A warm welcome awaits from the Irish-Welsh couple who run this appealing B&B bang in the centre of town. All four bedrooms have a view across the harbour to the hill that gives the house its name and breakfasts include free-range eggs and vegetables grown in the garden. Two-night minimum stay April to October; no credit cards.

Cuillin Hills Hotel Hotel £££
(☎01478-612003; www.cuillinhills-hotel-skye.co.uk; Scorrybreac Rd; r £210-310; P 📶) Located on the eastern fringes of Portree, this luxury hotel enjoys a superb outlook across the harbour towards the Cuillin mountains. The more expensive rooms cosset guests with four-poster beds and panoramic views, but everyone can enjoy the scenery from the glass-fronted restaurant and well-stocked whisky bar.

Harbour View Seafood Restaurant Seafood ££
(☎01478-612069; 7 Bosville Tce; mains £14-19; ⊙noon-3pm & 5.30-11pm Tue-Sun) The Harbour View is Portree's most congenial place to eat. It has a homely dining room with a log fire in winter, books on the mantelpiece and bric-a-brac on the shelves. And on the table, superb Scottish seafood such as fresh Skye oysters, seafood chowder, king scallops, langoustines and lobster.

Getting There & Away

The Isle of Skye became permanently tethered to the Scottish mainland when the Skye Bridge opened in 1995, but a number of ferries still serve the island.

CalMac (www.calmac.co.uk; per person/car £4.65/23.90) operates the Mallaig to Armadale ferry. It's very popular in July and August, so book ahead if you're travelling by car.

Skye Ferry (www.skyeferry.co.uk; car with up to four passengers £15; ⊙Easter–mid-Oct) runs a tiny vessel (six cars only) on the short Glenelg to Kylerhea crossing.

IRELAND

From shamrocks and shillelaghs to leprechauns and lovable rogues, there's a plethora of platitudes to wade through before you reach the real Ireland. But it's well worth looking beyond the tourist tat, for the Emerald Isle is one of Europe's gems, a scenic extravaganza of lakes, mountains, sea and sky.

Dublin

POP 1.27 MILLION

Sultry rather than sexy, Dublin exudes personality as only those who've managed to turn careworn into carefree can.

Dublin

Sights

1 National Museum of Ireland – Archaeology ... D6
2 St Stephen's Green ... C7
3 Trinity College ... C5

Activities, Courses & Tours

4 City Sightseeing ... B2
5 Dublin Literary Pub Crawl ... C6
6 Dublin Musical Pub Crawl ... B4
7 Trinity College Walking Tour ... C5

Sleeping

8 Anchor House ... D2
9 Brooks Hotel ... B6
10 Gresham Hotel ... B2

Eating

11 Chapter One ... A1
12 Fade Street Social ... B6
13 L'Gueuleton ... B6
14 Winding Stair ... B4

Drinking & Nightlife

15 Grogan's Castle Lounge ... B6
16 Stag's Head ... B5
17 Twisted Pepper ... B3

Entertainment

18 Abbey Theatre ... C3

Dublin

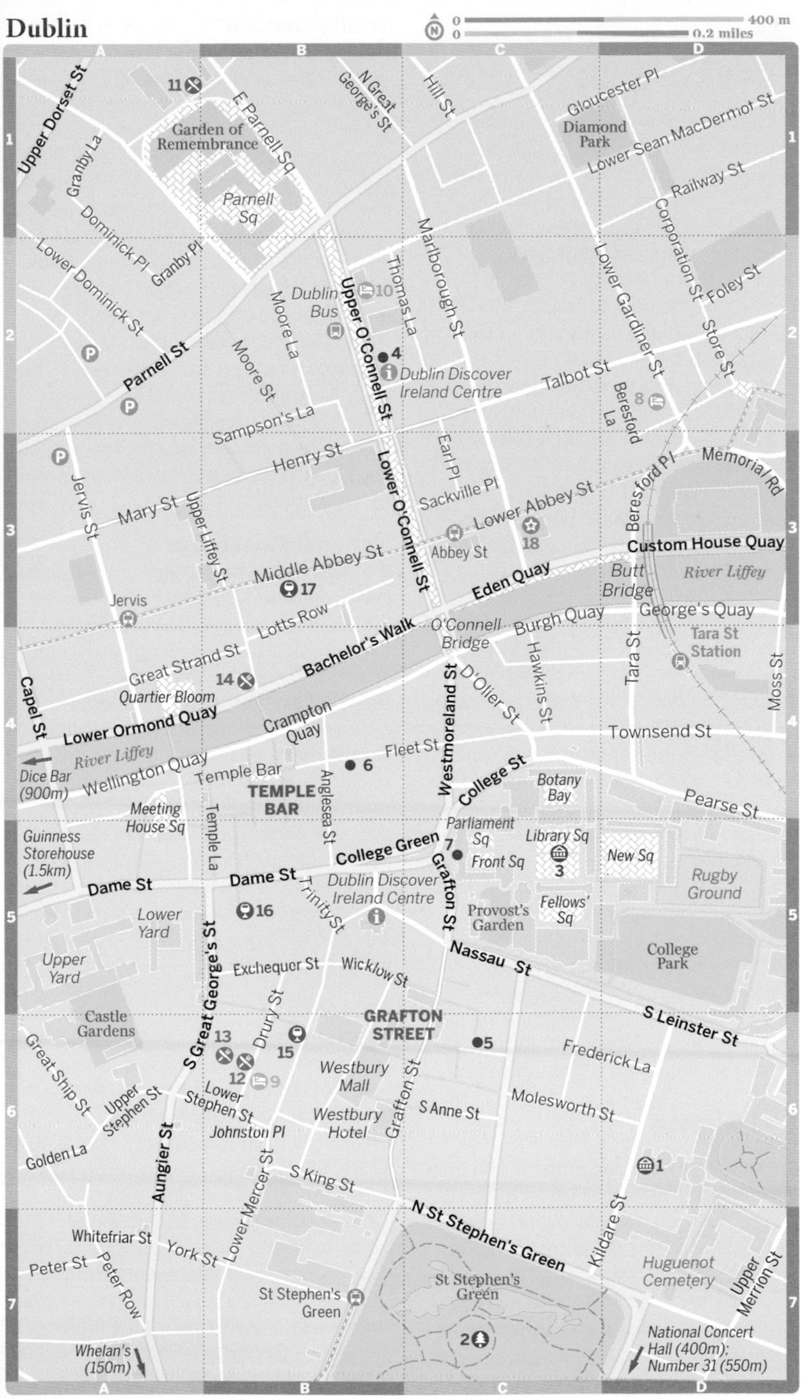
400 m
0.2 miles
Upper Dorset St
Garden of Remembrance
E Parnell Sq
N Great George's St
Hill St
Gloucester Pl
Diamond Park
Lower Sean MacDermot St
Granby La
Parnell Sq
Railway St
Corporation St
Dominick Pl
Granby Pl
Lower Dominick St
Dublin Bus
Upper O'Connell St
Thomas La
Marlborough St
Lower Gardiner St
Foley St
Moore La
Store St
Moore St
Parnell St
Dublin Discover Ireland Centre
Talbot St
Beresford La
Sampson's La
Earl Pl
Henry St
Lower O'Connell St
Beresford Pl
Memorial Rd
Jervis St
Mary St
Sackville Pl
Upper Liffey St
Lower Abbey St
Abbey St
Custom House Quay
Middle Abbey St
Eden Quay
Butt Bridge
River Liffey
Jervis
Lotts Row
O'Connell Bridge
Burgh Quay
George's Quay
Tara St Station
Bachelor's Walk
Hawkins St
Tara St
Moss St
Great Strand St
Capel St
Quartier Bloom
D'Olier St
Westmoreland St
Lower Ormond Quay
Crampton Quay
Townsend St
River Liffey
Fleet St
Dice Bar (900m)
Wellington Quay
Temple Bar
Anglesea St
College St
Botany Bay
TEMPLE BAR
Pearse St
Meeting House Sq
Temple La
Parliament Sq
Library Sq
Guinness Storehouse (1.5km)
College Green
Front Sq
New Sq
Dame St
Grafton St
Rugby Ground
Trinity St
Dublin Discover Ireland Centre
Lower Yard
Provost's Garden
Fellows' Sq
S Great George's St
Nassau St
College Park
Upper Yard
Exchequer St
Wicklow St
Castle Gardens
GRAFTON STREET
S Leinster St
Drury St
Frederick La
Great Ship St
Westbury Mall
Lower Stephen St
Upper Stephen St
Molesworth St
Westbury Hotel
S Anne St
Johnston Pl
Golden La
Aungier St
S King St
Lower Mercer St
Kildare St
N St Stephen's Green
Whitefriar St
York St
Huguenot Cemetery
Upper Merrion St
Peter St
Peter Row
St Stephen's Green
St Stephen's Green
Whelan's (150m)
National Concert Hall (400m); Number 31 (550m)

Book of Kells

The world-famous *Book of Kells*, dating from around AD 800 and thus one of the oldest books in the world, was probably produced by monks at St Colmcille's Monastery on the remote island of Iona. On display in Trinity College, it contains the four gospels of the New Testament, written in Latin, as well as prefaces, summaries and other text. If it were merely words, the *Book of Kells* would simply be a very old book – it's the extensive and amazingly complex illustrations (the illuminations) that make it so wonderful. The superbly decorated opening initials are only part of the story, for the book has smaller illustrations between the lines.

The halcyon days of the Celtic Tiger, when cash cascaded like a free-flowing waterfall, have long since disappeared, and the city has once again been forced to grind out a living. But Dubliners still know how to enjoy life. They do so through their music, their art and their literature – things which Dubs often take for granted but, once reminded, generate immense pride.

There are world-class museums, superb restaurants and the best range of entertainment available anywhere in Ireland – and that's not including the pub, the ubiquitous centre of the city's social life and an absolute must for any visitor.

Sights

Dublin is neatly divided by the River Liffey into the more affluent 'south side' and the less prosperous 'north side'. Immediately south of the river is the pub-packed **Temple Bar** district, Trinity College and, just below it, the lovely **St Stephen's Green** (dawn-dusk; all city centre, St Stephen's Green) FREE.

Trinity College Historic Building
(01-896 1000; www.tcd.ie; College Green; 8am-10pm; all city centre) FREE This calm retreat from the bustle of contemporary Dublin is Ireland's most prestigious university, founded by Elizabeth I in 1592. Not only is it the city's most attractive historic real estate, but it's also home to one of the world's most famous – and most beautiful – books, the gloriously illuminated **Book of Kells**. There's no charge to wander around the grounds on your own, but the student-led **walking tours** (Authenticity Tours; www.tcd.ie/Library/bookofkells/trinity-tours; per person €5, incl Book of Kells €12; 10.15am-3.40pm Mon-Sat, to 3.15pm Sun May-Sep, fewer midweek tours Oct-Apr), departing from the College Green entrance, are recommended.

National Museum of Ireland – Archaeology Museum
(www.museum.ie; Kildare St; 10am-5pm Tue-Sat, 2-5pm Sun; all city centre) FREE Among the highlights of the National Museum's archaeology branch are its superb collection of **prehistoric gold objects**; the exquisite 8th-century **Ardagh Chalice** and **Tara Brooch**, the world's finest examples of Celtic art; and ancient objects recovered from Ireland's bogs, including remarkably well-preserved human bodies. Other exhibits focus on early Christian art, the Viking period and medieval Ireland. There's a lot to see, so ask if there's a guided tour available, or buy a guidebook to help you navigate the exhibits.

Guinness Storehouse Brewery, Museum
(www.guinness-storehouse.com; St James's Gate, South Market St; adult/student/child €16.20/14.50/6.50, connoisseur experience €46.20; 9.30am-5pm Sep-Jun, to 7pm Jul-Aug; 21A, 51B, 78, 78A or 123 from Fleet St, St James's) The most popular visit in town is the beer-lover's Disneyland, a multimedia bells-and-whistles homage to the country's most famous export and the city's most enduring symbol. The old grain storehouse, the only part of the massive, 26-hectare St James's Gate Brewery open to the public, is a suitable cathedral in

which to worship the black gold; it rises seven impressive storeys high around a stunning central atrium. At the top is the **Gravity Bar**, with panoramic views.

Kilmainham Gaol Museum

(www.heritageireland.com; Inchicore Rd; adult/child €7/3; 9.30am-6pm Apr-Sep, 9.30am-5.30pm Mon-Sat, 10am-6pm Sun Oct-Mar; 23, 25, 25A, 26, 68 or 69 from city centre) If you have *any* desire to understand Irish history – especially the juicy bits about resistance to English rule – then a visit to this former prison is a must. This threatening grey building, built between 1792 and 1795, has played a role in virtually every act of Ireland's painful path to independence. An excellent audiovisual introduction to the building is followed by a thought-provoking guided tour of the eerie prison, the largest unoccupied building of its kind in Europe.

James Joyce Tower & Museum Museum

(01-280 9265; www.joycetower.ie; Joyce Tower, Sandycove; 10am-6pm Apr-Sep, 10am-4pm Oct-Mar) FREE Strikingly located in a Martello tower overlooking Dublin Bay in the salubrious seaside suburb of Sandycove, the James Joyce Museum's contents combine memorabilia from the celebrated writer's life with a dramatic setting that has a story all its own. The opening scene of *Ulysses* is set on the tower's roof.

Tours

City Sightseeing Bus Tour

(www.citysightseeingdublin.ie; 14 Upper O'Connell St; adult/student €19/17; every 8-15min 9am-6pm) A typical tour should last around 1½ hours and lead you up and down O'Connell St, past Trinity College and St Stephen's Green, before heading up to the Guinness Storehouse and back around the north quays and Phoenix Park.

Dublin Literary Pub Crawl Walking Tour

(01-670 5602; www.dublinpubcrawl.com; 9 Duke St; adult/student €12/10; 7.30pm daily Apr-Oct, 7.30pm Thu-Sun Nov-Mar) A tour of pubs associated with famous Dublin writers is a sure-fire winner, and this 2½-hour tour by two actors – which includes them acting out the funny bits – is a riotous laugh. There's plenty of drink taken, which makes it all the more popular. It leaves from the Duke on Duke St; get there by 7pm to reserve a spot for the evening tour.

Thomas Burgh Library, Trinity College, Dublin

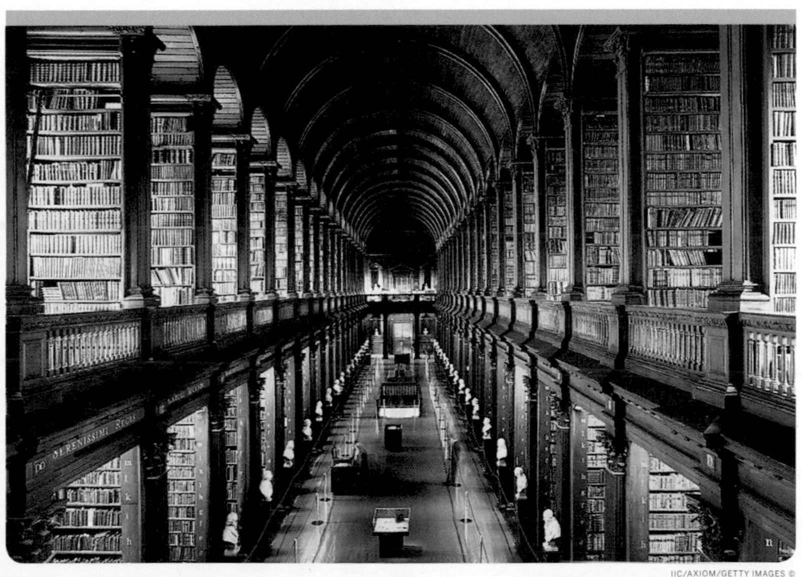

IIC/AXIOM/GETTY IMAGES ©

Trinity College, Dublin

STEP INTO THE PAST

Ireland's most prestigious university, founded on the order of Queen Elizabeth I in 1592, is an architectural masterpiece, a cordial retreat from the bustle of modern life in the middle of the city. Step through its main entrance and you step back in time, the cobbled stones transporting you to another era, when the elite discussed philosophy and argued passionately in favour of empire.

Standing in Front Square, the 30m-high **Campanile** ❶ is directly in front of you with the **Dining Hall** ❷ to your left. On the far side of the square is the Old Library building, the centrepiece of which is the magnificent **Long Room** ❸, which was the inspiration for the computer- generated imagery of the Jedi Archive in Star Wars Episode II: Attack of the Clones. Here you'll find the university's greatest treasure, the **Book of Kells** ❹. You'll probably have to queue to see this masterpiece, and then only for a brief visit, but it's very much worth it.

Just beyond the Old Library is the very modern **Berkeley Library** ❺, which nevertheless fits perfectly into the campus' overall aesthetic: directly in front of it is the distinctive **Sphere Within a Sphere** ❻, the most elegant of the university's sculptures.

DON'T MISS

» Douglas Hyde Gallery, the campus' designated modern art museum.

» Cricket match on pitch, the most elegant of pastimes.

» Pint in the Pavilion Bar, preferably while watching the cricket.

» Visit to the Science Gallery, where science is made completely relevant.

Campanile
Trinity College's most iconic bit of masonry was designed in the mid-19th century by Sir Charles Lanyon; the attached sculptures were created by Thomas Kirk.

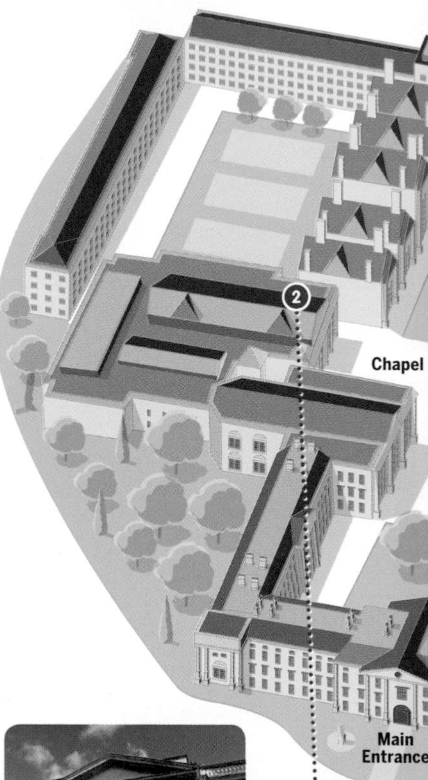

Dining Hall
Richard Cassels' original building was designed to mirror the Examination Hall directly opposite on Front Square: the hall collapsed twice and was rebuilt from scratch in 1761.

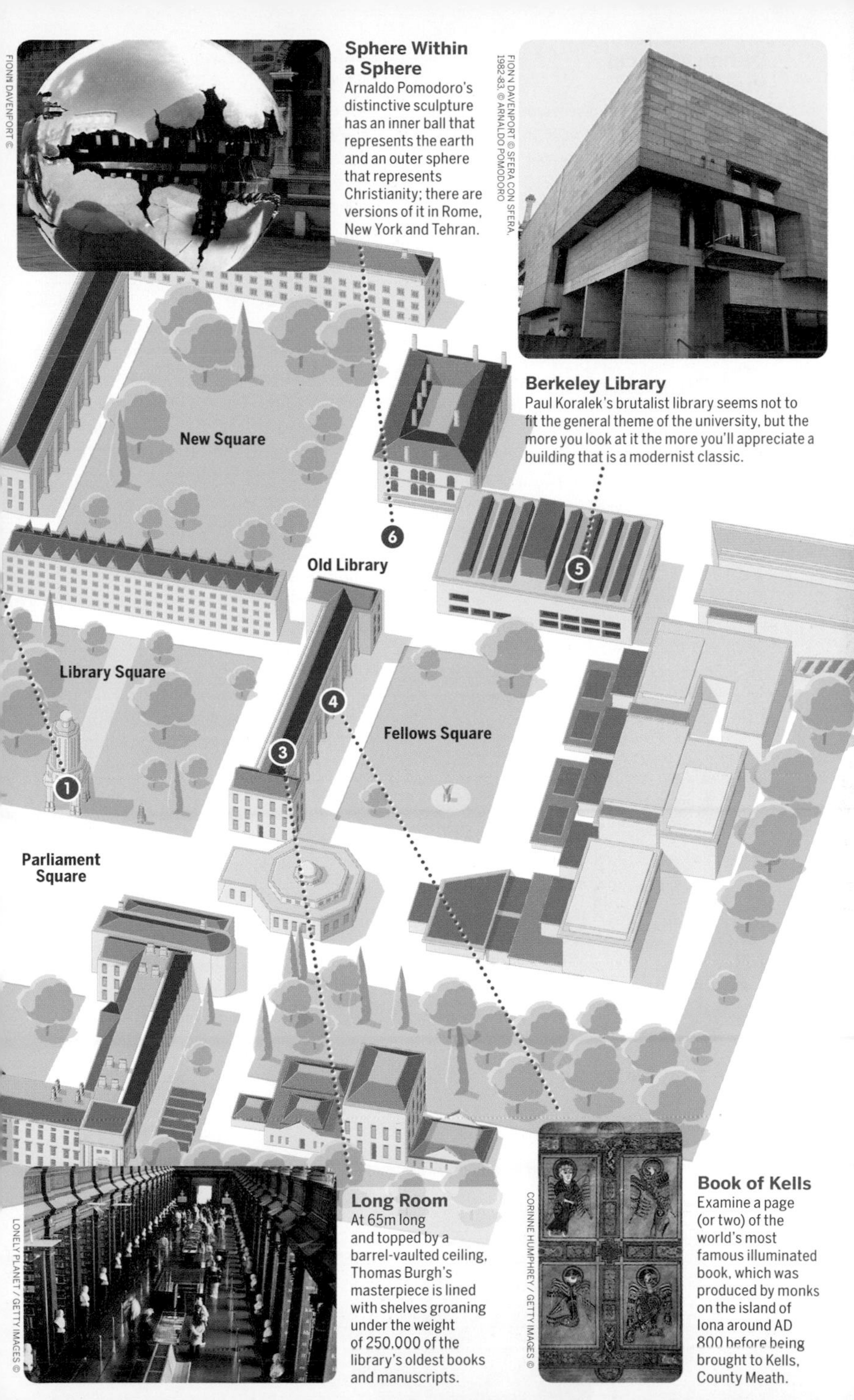

Sphere Within a Sphere

Arnaldo Pomodoro's distinctive sculpture has an inner ball that represents the earth and an outer sphere that represents Christianity; there are versions of it in Rome, New York and Tehran.

FIONN DAVENPORT ©

Berkeley Library

Paul Koralek's brutalist library seems not to fit the general theme of the university, but the more you look at it the more you'll appreciate a building that is a modernist classic.

FIONN DAVENPORT © SFERA CON SFERA, 1982-83, © ARNALDO POMODORO

Long Room

At 65m long and topped by a barrel-vaulted ceiling, Thomas Burgh's masterpiece is lined with shelves groaning under the weight of 250,000 of the library's oldest books and manuscripts.

LONELY PLANET / GETTY IMAGES ©

Book of Kells

Examine a page (or two) of the world's most famous illuminated book, which was produced by monks on the island of Iona around AD 800 before being brought to Kells, County Meath.

CORINNE HUMPHREY / GETTY IMAGES ©

Dublin Musical Pub Crawl Walking Tour
(01-478 0193; www.discoverdublin.ie; Oliver St John Gogarty's, 58-59 fleet St; adult/student €12/10; 7.30pm daily Apr-Oct, 7.30pm Thu-Sat Nov-Mar) The story of Irish traditional music and its influence on contemporary styles is explained and demonstrated by two expert musicians in a number of Temple Bar pubs over 2½ hours. Tours meet upstairs in the Oliver St John Gogarty pub and are highly recommended.

Sleeping

Dublin is *always* bustling, so call ahead or book online, especially on weekends. Don't forget that Dublin Tourism Centres can find and book accommodation for €5, plus a 10% deposit for the first night's stay.

Brooks Hotel Hotel ££
(01-670 4000; www.sinnotthotels.com; 59-62 Drury St; r from €140; P; all cross-city, St Stephen's Green) About 120m west of Grafton St, this small, plush place has an emphasis on familial, friendly service. The decor is nouveau classic with veneer-panelled walls, decorative bookcases and old-fashioned sofas, while bedrooms are extremely comfortable and come fitted out in subtly coloured furnishings. The clincher though, is the king- and superking-size beds in all rooms, complete with...a pillow menu.

Anchor House B&B ££
(01-878 6913; www.anchorhousedublin.com; 49 Lower Gardiner St; s/d from €100/115; P; all city centre, Connolly) Most B&Bs in these parts offer pretty much the same stuff: TV, half-decent shower, clean linen and tea- and coffee-making facilities. The Anchor does all that, but it also has an elegance you won't find in many other B&Bs along this stretch. This lovely Georgian guesthouse, with its delicious wholesome breakfasts, comes highly recommended by readers. They're dead right.

Number 31 Guesthouse £££
(01-676 5011; www.number31.ie; 31 Leeson Close; s/d/tr incl breakfast €200/240/340; P; all city centre) The city's most distinctive property is the former home of modernist architect Sam Stephenson, who successfully fused '60s style with 18th-century grace. Its 21 bedrooms are split between the retro coach house, with its fancy rooms, and the more elegant Georgian house, where rooms are individually furnished with tasteful French antiques and big comfortable beds.

Gresham Hotel Hotel £££
(01-874 6881; www.gresham-hotels.com; Upper O'Connell St; r from €185; P @; all cross-city) This landmark hotel shed its traditional

Irish music pub crawl, Temple Bar, Dublin
HOLGER LEUE/GETTY IMAGES ©

granny's parlour look with a major overhaul some years ago. Despite its brighter, smarter, modern appearance and a fabulous open-plan foyer, its loyal clientele – elderly groups on shopping breaks and well-heeled Americans – continues to find it charming. Rooms are spacious and well serviced, and the location is unbeatable.

Eating

Fade Street Social Modern Irish **££**
(**01-604 0066; www.fadestreetsocial.com; Fade St; mains €19-32, tapas €5-12; 12.30-2.30pm Mon-Fri, 5-10.30pm daily; ; all city centre**) Two eateries in one, courtesy of renowned chef Dylan McGrath: at the front, the buzzy Gastro Bar, which serves up gourmet tapas from a beautiful open kitchen. At the back, the more muted Restaurant does Irish cuts of meat – from veal to rabbit – served with homegrown, organic vegetables. Three-course lunch and early evening menu €25. Reservations suggested.

L'Gueuleton French **££**
(**www.lgueuleton.com; 1 Fade St; mains €22-26; 12.30-3.30pm & 5.30-10pm Mon-Sat, noon-3.30pm & 5.30-9pm Sun; all city centre**) Dubliners have a devil of a time pronouncing the name (which means 'a gluttonous feast' in French) and have had their patience tested with the no-reservations-get-in-line-and-wait policy, but they just can't get enough of this restaurant's robust (read: meaty and filling) take on French rustic cuisine that makes twisted tongues and sore feet a small price to pay.

Chapter One Modern Irish **£££**
(**01-873 2266; www.chapteronerestaurant.com; 18 North Parnell Sq; 2-course lunch €50, 4-course dinner €85; 12.30-2pm Tue-Fri, 7.30-10.30pm Tue-Sat; 3, 10, 11, 13, 16, 19 or 22 from city centre**) Michelin-starred Chapter One is our choice for city's best eatery. It successfully combines flawless haute cuisine with a relaxed, welcoming atmosphere that is at the heart of Irish hospitality. The food is French-inspired contemporary Irish, the menus change regularly and the service is top-notch. The three-course pre-theatre menu (€36.50) is a favourite with those heading to the Gate around the corner.

Winding Stair Modern Irish **£££**
(**01-873 7320; www.winding-stair.com; 40 Lower Ormond Quay; 2-course lunch €19.95, mains €21-28; noon-5pm & 5.30-10.30pm; all city centre**) Housed within a beautiful Georgian building that was once home to the city's most beloved bookshop (the ground floor still is one), the Winding Stair's conversion to elegant restaurant has been faultless. The wonderful Irish menu – creamy fish pie, bacon and organic cabbage, steamed mussels, and Irish farmyard cheeses – coupled with an excellent wine list makes for a memorable meal.

Drinking & Nightlife

Temple Bar, Dublin's 'party district', is almost always packed with raucous stag (bachelor) and hen (bachelorette) parties, scantily clad girls, and loud guys from Ohio wearing Guinness T-shirts. If that's not your style, there's plenty to enjoy beyond Temple Bar.

Stag's Head Pub
(**www.louisfitzgerald.com/stagshead; 1 Dame Ct; 10.30am-1am Mon-Sat, to midnight Sun; all city centre**) The Stag's Head was built in 1770, remodelled in 1895 and thankfully not changed a bit since then. It's a superb pub: so picturesque that it often appears in films and also featured in a postage-stamp series on Irish bars. A bloody great pub, no doubt.

Grogan's Castle Lounge Pub
(**www.groganspub.ie; 15 South William St; 10.30am-11.30pm Mon-Thu, 10.30am-12.30am Fri & Sat, 12.30-11pm Sun**) This place is known simply as Grogan's (after the original owner), and it is a city-centre institution. It has long been a favourite haunt of Dublin's writers and painters, as well as others from the alternative bohemian set, most of whom seem to be waiting for the 'inevitable' moment when they are finally recognised as geniuses.

Right: National Concert Hall, Dublin; **Below:** Blarney Castle (p147)
(RIGHT) DESIGN PICS/GEORGE MUNDAY/GETTY IMAGES ©; (BELOW) LAURA CIAPPONI/GETTY IMAGES ©

Dice Bar Bar

(☎01-674 6710; www.thatsitdublin.com; 79 Queen St; 🕒3pm-midnight Mon-Thu, to 1am Fri & Sat, to 11.30pm Sun; 🚌25, 25A, 66, 67 from city centre, 🚊Museum) Co-owned by Huey from the Fun Lovin' Criminals, the Dice Bar looks like something you might find on New York's Lower East Side. Its dodgy locale, black-and-red painted interior, dripping candles and distressed seating, combined with rocking DJs most nights, make it a magnet for Dublin hipsters. It has Guinness and local craft beers.

Twisted Pepper Club

(☎01-873 4800; www.bodytonicmusic.com/thetwistedpepper; 54 Middle Abbey St; club €8-10; 🕒bar 4pm-late, cafe 8.30am-6pm; 🚌all city centre, 🚊Abbey) Dublin's hippest venue comes in four parts: DJs spin great tunes in the basement; the stage is for live acts; the mezzanine is a secluded bar area above the stage; and the cafe is where you can get an Irish breakfast all day. All run by the Bodytonic crew, one of the most exciting music and production crowds in town.

Entertainment

For events, reviews and club listings, pick up a copy of the fortnightly music review **Hot Press** (www.hotpress.com), or for free cultural events, check out the weekly e-zine *Dublin Event Guide*.

Whelan's Live Music

(☎01-478 0766; www.whelanslive.com; 25 Wexford St; 🚌bus 16, 122 from city centre) A Dublin institution, providing a showcase for Irish singer-songwriters and other lo-fi performers since the 1990s, Whelan's combines a traditional pub upstairs and a popular live-music venue on the ground floor. The old-fashioned ambience belies a progressive music booking policy, with a program that features many breaking new acts from rock and indie to folk and trad.

Abbey Theatre Theatre
(☎01-878 7222; www.abbeytheatre.ie; Lower Abbey St; 🚌all city centre, 🚊Abbey) Ireland's renowned national theatre, founded by WB Yeats in 1904, has been reinvigorated in recent years by director Fiach Mac-Conghaill, who has introduced lots of new blood to what was in danger of becoming a moribund corpse. The current program has a mix of Irish classics (Synge, O'Casey etc), established international names (Shepard, Mamet) and new talent (O'Rowe, Carr et al).

National Concert Hall Live Music
(☎01-417 0000; www.nch.ie; Earlsfort Tce; 🚌all city centre) Ireland's premier orchestral hall hosts a variety of concerts year-round, including a series of lunchtime concerts from 1.05pm to 2pm on Tuesdays, June to August.

ℹ Information

Dublin Discover Ireland Centre (www.visitdublin.com; St Andrew's Church, 2 Suffolk St; 🕒9am-5.30pm Mon-Sat, 10.30am-3pm Sun) The main tourist information centre; there's a second branch at 14 O'Connell St (🕒9am-5pm Mon-Sat).

Getting There & Away

Air

Dublin airport (☎01-814 1111; www.dublinairport.com), about 13km north of the city centre, is Ireland's major international gateway, with direct flights from Europe, North America and Asia.

Boat

There are direct ferries from Holyhead in Wales to Dublin Port, 3km northeast of the city centre, and to Dun Laoghaire, 13km southeast. Boats also sail direct to Dublin Port from Liverpool and from Douglas, on the Isle of Man.

Train

Connolly station is north of the Liffey, with trains to Belfast, Sligo and Rosslare. Heuston station is south of the Liffey and west of the city centre, with trains for Cork, Galway, Killarney, Limerick, and most other points to the south and west. Visit www.irishrail.ie for timetables and fares.

Belfast €38, 2¼ hours, eight daily

Cork €64, 2¾ hours, hourly

Galway €36, 2¾ hours, nine daily

Killarney €67, 3. hours, seven daily

Getting Around

To & From the Airport

- **Aircoach (www.aircoach.ie; one-way/return €7/12)** Buses every 10 to 15 minutes between 6am and midnight, hourly from midnight until 6am.
- **Airlink Express (01-873 4222; www.dublinbus.ie; one way/return €6/3)** Bus 747 runs every 10 to 20 minutes from 5.45am to 11.30pm between the airport, central bus station (Busáras) and Dublin Bus office on Upper O'Connell St.
- **Taxi** There is a taxi rank directly outside the arrivals concourse. It should take about 45 minutes to get into the city centre by taxi and cost about €25, including a supplementary charge of €3 (not applied going to the airport).

Car

Traffic in Dublin is a nightmare and parking is an expensive headache. Better to leave your vehicle at the Red Cow Park & Ride just off Exit 9 on the M50 ring road, and take the **Luas tram** into the city centre (€4.80 return, 30 minutes).

Public Transport

Bus

Dublin Bus (01-873 4222; www.dublinbus.ie; 59 Upper O'Connell St; 9am-5.30pm Mon-Fri, 9am-2pm Sat) Local buses cost from €0.70 to €3.05 for a single journey. You must pay the exact fare when boarding; drivers don't give change. The Freedom Pass (€30) allows three days' unlimited travel on all Dublin buses including Airlink and Dublin Bus hop-on hop-off tour buses.

Train

Dublin Area Rapid Transport (DART; 01-836 6222; www.irishrail.ie) provides quick rail access as far north as Howth and south to Bray; Pearse station is handy for central Dublin.

Tram

Luas runs on two (unconnected) lines; the green line runs from the eastern side of St Stephen's Green southeast to Sandyford, and the red line runs from Tallaght to Connolly station, with stops at Heuston station, the National Museum and Busáras. Single fares range from €1.70 to €3 depending on how many zones you travel through.

Taxi

Taxis in Dublin are expensive; flag fall costs €4.10, plus €1.03 per kilometre. For taxi service, call **National Radio Cabs (01-677 2222; www.radiocabs.ie)**.

Cork

POP 120,000

There's a reason the locals call Cork (Corcaigh) 'Ireland's Real Capital' or 'The People's Republic of Cork'; something special is going on here. The city has long been dismissive of Dublin, and with a burgeoning arts, music and restaurant scene, it has a cultural reputation to rival the capital's.

Sights

The English Market — Market

(www.englishmarket.ie; Princes St; 9am-5.30pm Mon-Sat) It could just as easily be called the Victorian Market for its ornate vaulted ceilings and columns, but the English Market is a true gem, no matter what you name it. Scores of vendors sell some of the very best local produce, meats, cheeses and takeaway food in the region. On decent days, take your lunch to nearby Bishop Lucey Park, a popular al fresco eating spot.

Cork City Gaol — Museum

(021-430 5022; www.corkcitygaol.com; Convent Ave, Sun's Well; adult/child €8/4.50; 9.30am-5pm Apr-Oct, 10am-4pm Nov-Mar) This imposing former prison is well worth a visit, if only to get a sense of how crap life was for prisoners a century ago. An audio tour guides you around the restored cells, which feature models of suffering prisoners and sadistic-looking guards. It's very moving, bringing home the harshness of the 19th-century penal system. The most common crime was that of poverty; many of the inmates were sentenced to hard labour for stealing loaves of bread.

Sleeping

Garnish House B&B ££
(021-427 5111; www.garnish.ie; Western Rd; s/d from €89/98; P) Attention is lavished upon guests at this award-winning B&B. The legendary breakfast menu (30 choices) includes fresh fish and French toast. Typical of the touches here is the freshly cooked porridge, which comes with creamed honey and your choice of whiskey or Baileys. Enjoy it out on the garden terrace. The 14 rooms are very comfortable; reception is open 24 hours.

Crawford House B&B ££
(021-427 9000; www.crawfordhouse.ie; Western Rd; d €60-90; P @) Power showers and large spa baths feature in the 12 rooms of this B&B, along with king-size beds and restrained wooden furnishings. The standard is that of a contemporary hotel (24-hour reception); the atmosphere, that of a family home. Public areas (and four rooms) have wi-fi.

River Lee Hotel Hotel £££
(021-425 2700; www.doylecollection.com; Western Rd; r from €155; P) This modern riverside hotel brings a touch of luxury to the city centre. It has gorgeous public areas with huge sofas, a designer fireplace, a stunning five-storey glass-walled atrium and superb service. There are well-equipped bedrooms (nice and quiet at the back, but request a corner room for extra space) and possibly the best breakfast buffet in Ireland.

Eating

Market Lane Irish, International ££
(021-427 4710; www.marketlane.ie; 5 Oliver Plunkett St; mains €12-26; noon-10.30pm Mon-Sat, 1-9pm Sun;) It's always hopping at this bright corner bistro with an open kitchen and long wooden bar. The broad menu changes often to reflect what's fresh – look out for braised pork marinated in Cork dry gin, and steaks with awesome aioli. The €10 lunch menu is a steal. No reservations; sip a drink at the bar while you wait for a table.

Farmgate Cafe Cafe, Bistro ££
(www.farmgate.ie; Princes St, English Market; mains €6-15; 8.30am-4.30pm Mon-Fri, to 5pm Sat) An unmissable experience at the heart of the English Market, the Farmgate is perched on a balcony overlooking the market below, the source of all that fresh local produce on your plate, everything

Cliffs of Moher (p151), Ireland

Detour: Rock of Cashel

The **Rock of Cashel** (www.heritageireland.com; adult/child €6/2; ⏲9am-5.30pm mid-Mar–mid-Oct, to 7pm mid-Jun–Aug, to 4.30pm mid-Oct–mid-Mar) is one of Ireland's most spectacular archaeological sites. A prominent green hill, banded with limestone outcrops, it rises from a grassy plain on the outskirts of Cashel town and bristles with ancient fortifications. For more than 1000 years it was a symbol of power, and the seat of kings and churchmen who ruled over the region. Sturdy walls circle an enclosure that contains a complete round tower, a roofless abbey and the finest 12th-century Romanesque chapel in Ireland.

Bus Éireann (www.buseireann.ie) runs eight buses daily between Cashel and Cork (€15, 1¾ hours).

from rock oysters to the lamb for an Irish stew. Up the stairs and turn left for table service, right for counter service.

Cafe Paradiso Vegetarian **££**

(☎021-427 7939; www.cafeparadiso.ie; 16 Lancaster Quay; lunch mains €13-14, 2-/3-course dinner €33/40; ⏲noon-2.30pm Fri & Sat, 5.30-10pm Tue-Sat year-round, plus 5.50pm-10pm Mon Jun–late Aug;) A contender for best restaurant in town in any genre, Paradiso serves contemporary vegetarian dishes, including vegan fare: how about sweet chilli–glazed panfried tofu with Asian greens in coconut and lemongrass broth, or spring cabbage dolma of roast squash, caramelised onion and hazelnut, with cardamom yoghurt and saffron-crushed potatoes? Reservations are essential. Dinner, bed and breakfast rates staying in the funky upstairs rooms start from €100 per person.

Drinking & Nightlife

Cork's pub scene is cracking, easily rivalling Dublin's. Locally brewed Murphy's is the stout of choice here, not Guinness. Check www.corkgigs.com for pubs with live music.

Franciscan Well Brewery Pub

(www.franciscanwellbrewery.com; 14 North Mall; ⏲3-11.30pm Mon-Thu, to 12.30am Fri & Sat, to 11pm Sun;) The copper vats gleaming behind the bar give the game away: the Franciscan Well brews its own beer. The best place to enjoy it is in the enormous beer garden at the back. The pub holds regular beer festivals with other small (and often underappreciated) Irish breweries.

Mutton Lane Inn Pub

(www.corkheritagepubs.com; Mutton Lane; ⏲10.30am-11.30pm Mon-Thu, 10.30am-12.30am Fri & Sat, 2-11pm Sun) Tucked down the tiniest of laneways off St Patrick's St, this inviting pub, lit by candles and fairy lights, is one of Cork's most intimate drinking holes. It's minuscule so try to get in early to bag the snug, or perch on beer kegs outside.

Sin É Pub

(www.corkheritagepubs.com; 8 Coburg St; ⏲12.30-11.30pm Sun-Thu, to 12.30am Fri & Sat) You could easily while away an entire day at this great old place, which is everything a craic-filled pub should be – long on atmosphere and short on pretension. There's music most nights (regular sessions Tuesday at 9.30pm, Friday and Sunday at 6.30pm), much of it traditional, but with the odd surprise.

Information

Cork City Tourist Office (☎021-425 5100; www.corkcity.ie; Grand Pde; ⏲9am-6pm Mon-Sat year-round, plus 10am-5pm Sun Jul & Aug) Souvenir shop and information desk. Sells Ordnance Survey maps; **Stena Line** ferries has a desk here.

Getting There & Away

Air

Cork airport (021-431 3131; www.cork-airport.com) is 8km south of the city on the N27. Direct flights to Edinburgh, London, Amsterdam, Barcelona, Munich, Paris, Prague and Rome.

Boat

Brittany Ferries (021-427 7801; www.brittanyferries.ie; 42 Grand Pde) has regular sailings from Cork to Roscoff (France). The ferry terminal is at Ringaskiddy, about 15 minutes by car southeast of the city centre along the N28.

Train

Cork's **Kent train station** (021-450 4777) is across the river from the city centre. Destinations include Dublin (€64, 2¼ hours, eight daily), Galway (€57, four to six hours, seven daily, two or three changes needed) and Killarney (€28, 1½ to two hours, nine daily).

Blarney Castle

Lying just northwest of Cork, the village of Blarney (An Bhlarna) receives a *gazillion* visitors a year, for one sole reason: **Blarney Castle** (021-438 5252; www.blarneycastle.ie; adult/child €12/5; 9am-5.30pm daily year-round, to 6pm Mon-Sat May & Sep, to 7pm Mon-Sat Jun-Aug; P). They come to kiss the castle's legendary **Blarney Stone** and get the 'gift of the gab' (Queen Elizabeth I, exasperated with Lord Blarney's ability to talk endlessly without agreeing to her demands, invented the term 'to talk Blarney' back in the 16th century). The stone is up on the battlements, and bending over backwards to kiss it requires a head for heights, although there's someone there to hold you in position. It also helps if you're not germophobic – there's a greasy mark where millions of lips have been before. (The Blarney stain? Sorry.)

Bus 215 runs from Cork bus station to Blarney (€6.50 return, 30 minutes, every 30 minutes).

Killarney

POP POP 12,750

Killarney is a well-oiled tourism machine set in a sublime landscape of lakes, forests and 1000m peaks. Its manufactured tweeness is renowned, the streets filled with tour-bus visitors shopping for soft-toy shamrocks, and countless placards pointing to trad-music sessions. However,

Blarney Castle, Ireland

CHRIS HILL/GETTY IMAGES ©

it has many charms beyond its proximity to waterfalls, woodlands, mountains and moors. In a town that's been practising the tourism game for more than 250 years, competition keeps standards high, and visitors on all budgets can expect to find superb restaurants, great pubs and good accommodation.

Sights & Activities

Most of Killarney's attractions are just outside the town. The mountain backdrop is part of **Killarney National Park** (www.killarneynationalpark.ie), which takes in beautiful Lough Leane, Muckross Lake and Upper Lake. Besides **Ross Castle** (064-663 5851; www.heritageireland.ie; Ross Rd; adult/child €4/2; 9am-5.45pm Mar-Oct) and **Muckross House** (064-667 0144; www.muckross-house.ie; adult/child €7.50/4, combined ticket with farms €12.50/7; 9am-7pm Jul & Aug, to 5.30pm Sep-Jun), the park also has much to explore by foot, bike or boat, or by hiring a traditional horse-drawn **jaunting car** (064-663 3358; www.killarneyjauntingcars.ie).

In summer the **Gap of Dunloe**, a gloriously scenic mountain pass squeezed between Purple Mountain and Carrauntouhill (at 1040m, Ireland's highest peak), is a tourist bottleneck. Rather than join the crowds taking pony-and-trap rides, **O'Connors Tours** (064-663 0200; www.gapofdunloetours.com; 7 High St, Killarney; Mar-Oct) can arrange a bike and boat circuit (€15; highly recommended) or bus and boat tour (€30) taking in the Gap.

Sleeping & Eating

Crystal Springs B&B ££
(064-663 3272; www.crystalspringsbb.com; Ballycasheen Cross; s/d from €45/70; P) The timber deck of this wonderfully relaxing B&B overhangs the River Flesk, where trout anglers can fish for free. Rooms are richly furnished with patterned wallpapers and walnut timber; private bathrooms (most with spa baths) are huge. The glass-enclosed breakfast room also overlooks the rushing river. It's about a 15-minute stroll into town.

Kingfisher Lodge B&B ££
(064-663 7131; www.kingfisherlodgekillarney.com; Lewis Rd; s/d/f €70/90/120; mid-Feb–Nov; P @) Lovely back gardens are a highlight at this immaculate B&B, whose 11 rooms are done up in vivid yellows, reds and pinks. Owner Donal Carroll is a certified walking guide with a wealth of knowledge on hiking in the area.

Smoke House Steak, Seafood ££
(087 233 9611; High St; lunch mains €11-16, dinner mains €15-29; noon-10pm Mon-Fri, 9am-10pm Sat & Sun) One of Killarney's busiest restaurants, this tiled bistro was the first establishment in Ireland to cook with a Josper (Spanish charcoal oven). Stylish salads include Norwegian king crab, and its Kerry surf 'n turf burger – with prawns and house-made barbecue sauce – has a local following. Early-bird three-course dinner is €25.

Information

Tourist Office (064-663 1633; www.killarney.ie; Beech Rd; 9am-5pm Mon-Sat;) Can handle almost any query, especially dealing with transport intricacies.

Getting There & Away

Operating from the train station, Bus Éireann has regular services to Cork (€27, two hours, hourly), Galway via Limerick (€26, 3¾ hours, four daily) and Rosslare Harbour (€29, seven hours, three daily).

Travelling by train from Cork (€28, 1½ to two hours, nine daily) or Dublin (€67, 3¼ hours, seven daily) sometimes involves changing at Mallow.

The Ring of Kerry

The Ring of Kerry, a 179km circuit around the dramatic coastal scenery of the Iveragh Peninsula, is one of Ireland's premier tourist attractions. Most travellers tackle the ring by bus on guided day trips from Killarney, but you could spend days wandering here.

The Ring is dotted with picturesque villages (**Sneem** and **Portmagee** are worth a stop), **prehistoric sites** (ask for a guide at Killarney tourist office) and spectacular viewpoints, notably at **Beenarourke** just west of Caherdaniel, and **Ladies' View** (between Kenmare and Killarney). The **Ring of Skellig**, at the end of the peninsula, has fine views of the Skellig Rocks and is less busy than the main route.

Getting Around

Bus Éireann runs a once-daily Ring of Kerry bus service (No 280) from late June to late August. Buses leave Killarney at 11.30am and stop at Killorglin, Glenbeigh, Caherciveen (€16.40, 1½ hours), Waterville, Caherdaniel and Molls Gap (€21.50), arriving back at Killarney at 4.45pm.

Travel agencies and hostels in Killarney offer daily coach tours of the Ring for about €20 to €25, year-round, lasting from 10.30am to 5pm.

Galway

POP 75,600

Arty and bohemian, Galway (Gaillimh) is legendary around the world for its entertainment scene. Cafes spill out onto cobblestone streets filled with a frenzy of fiddles, banjos, guitars and bodhráns, and jugglers, painters, puppeteers and magicians in outlandish masks enchant passers-by.

Sights

Galway City Museum Museum

(www.galwaycitymuseum.ie; Spanish Pde; 10am-5pm Tue-Sat year-round, noon-5pm Sun Easter-Sep) FREE This modern museum has exhibits on the city's history from 1800 to 1950, including an iconic Galway Hooker fishing boat, a collection of *currachs* (boats made from animal hides) and a controversial statue of Galway-born writer and hellraiser Pádraic Ó Conaire (1883–1928), which was previously in Eyre Sq.

Spanish Arch Historic Site

The Spanish Arch is thought to be an extension of Galway's medieval city walls, designed to protect ships moored at the nearby quay while they unloaded goods such as wine and brandy from Spain. Today it reverberates to the beat of bongo drums, and the lawns and riverside form

Ross Castle, Ireland

a gathering place for locals and visitors on a sunny day. Many watch kayakers manoeuvre over the tidal rapids of the River Corrib.

Hall of the Red Earl Archaeological Site
(www.galwaycivictrust.ie; Druid Lane; ⏲9.30am-4.45pm Mon-Fri, 10am-1pm Sat) FREE Back in the 13th century when the de Burgo family ran the show in Galway, Richard – the Red Earl – had a large hall built as a seat of power. Here locals would come looking for favours or to do a little grovelling as a sign of future fealty. After the 14 tribes took over, the hall fell into ruin and was lost. Lost that is until 1997 when expansion of the city's Custom House uncovered its foundations. The Custom House was built on stilts overhead, leaving the old foundations open. Artefacts and a plethora of fascinating displays give a sense of Galway life some 900 years ago.

Sleeping

Heron's Rest B&B **££**
(☎091-539 574; www.theheronsrest.com; 16a Longwalk; s/d from €75/160; 📶) Ideally located on the banks of the Corrib, the endlessly thoughtful hosts here will give you deck chairs so you can sit outside and enjoy the scene. Other touches include holiday-friendly breakfast times (8am to 11am), decanters of port and more. Rooms, all with water views, are small and cute.

St Martins B&B B&B **££**
(☎091-568 286; 2 Nun's Island; s/d from €40/70; 📶) This beautifully kept, renovated older house right on the canal has a flower-filled garden overlooking the William O'Brien Bridge and the River Corrib. The four rooms have all the comforts and the breakfast is a few cuts above the norm (fresh-squeezed OJ). Owner Mary Sexton wins rave reviews.

House Hotel Hotel **£££**
(☎091-538 900; www.thehousehotel.ie; Spanish Pde; r €100-220; P 📶) It's a design odyssey at this boutique hotel. Public spaces contrast modern art with trad details and bold accents. Cat motifs abound. The 40 rooms are plush, with beds having conveniently padded headboards and a range of colour schemes. Bathrooms are commodious and ooze comfort.

Eating

Griffin's Cafe **£**
(www.griffinsbakery.com; Shop St; mains €4-8; ⏲8am-6pm Mon-Sat) A local institution which, although it's been run by the Griffin family since 1876, remains as fresh as a bun hot out of the oven. The small bakery counter is laden with treats, including great

Waterville, Ring of Kerry (p148), Ireland

scones. But the real pleasure lies upstairs in the cafe where you can choose from sandwiches, hot specials, luscious desserts and more.

Quay Street Kitchen Irish **££**
(☎091-865 680; The Halls, Quay St; mains €8-18; ⏰11.45am-10.30pm; 📶🌱) Fast and friendly service makes a great first impression at this always-busy bistro. The menu doesn't disappoint either, with a selection of steak, lamb and seafood, good vegetarian and vegan dishes, and hearty daily specials such as pork, leek and stout sausages with mashed potato.

Ard Bia at Nimmo's Modern Irish **££**
(www.ardbia.com; Spanish Arch; mains €7-10 lunch, €19-26 dinner ; ⏰cafe 10am-3.30pm, restaurant 6-10pm, wine bar 6-11pm; closed Sun) In Irish, Ard Bia means 'High Food', and that's somewhat apt, given its location in the 18th-century Custom House near the Spanish Arch. Local seafood and organic produce feature on the seasonal menu in a setting that defines funky chic. The cafe is a perfect place for a coffee and tart.

Drinking & Entertainment

Most of Galway's pubs see musicians performing a few nights a week, either informally or as headline acts, and many have live music every night of the week.

Séhán Ua Neáchtain Pub
(www.tighneachtain.com; 17 Upper Cross St; ⏰noon-11.30pm Mon-Thu, noon-midnight Fri & Sat, noon-11pm Sun) Painted a bright cornflower blue, this 19th-century pub, known simply as Neáchtain's (*nock*-tans) or Naughtons, has a wraparound string of tables outside, many shaded by a large tree. It's a place where a polyglot mix of locals plop down and let the world pass them by – stop and join them for a pint.

Tig Cóilí Pub
(Mainguard St) Two live *céilidh* a day draw the crowds to this authentic fire-engine-red pub, just off High St. It's where musicians go to get drunk or drunks go to become musicians...or something like that. A gem.

Detour: Cliffs of Moher

Star of a million tourist brochures, the Cliffs of Moher in County Clare are one of the most popular sights in Ireland. But like many an ageing star, you have to look beyond the famous facade to appreciate its inherent attributes. In summer the site is overrun with day trippers, but there are good rewards if you're willing to walk along the clifftops for 10 minutes to escape the crowds.

The landscaped **Cliffs of Moher Visitor Centre** (www.cliffsofmoher.ie; adult/child €6/free; ⏰9am-9pm Jul-Aug, to 7pm May-Jun & Sep & Oct, (to 6pm Mar-Apr & Oct, to 5pm Nov-Feb) has exhibitions about the cliffs and their natural history. A number of bus tours leave Galway every morning for the Cliffs of Moher, including **Burren Wild Tours** (☎087 877 9565; www.burrenwalks.com; departs Galway Coach Station; €10-25; ⏰10am-5pm).

Information

Tourist Office (www.discoverireland.ie; Forster St; ⏰9am-5.45pm Mon-Sat, 9am-1.15pm Sun) Large, efficient regional information centre that can help arrange local accommodation and tours.

Getting There & Around

Bus Éireann buses depart from outside the train station. Citylink and GoBus use the coach station a block northeast. Citylink has buses to Dublin (€13, 2½ hours, hourly), while Bus Éireann runs buses to Killarney via Limerick (€26, 3¾ hours, four daily).

Trains run to and from Dublin (€36, three hours, five daily).

NORTHERN IRELAND

When you cross from the Republic into Northern Ireland you notice a couple of changes: the accent is different, the road signs are in miles, and the prices are in pounds sterling. But there's no border checkpoint, no guards, not even a sign to mark the crossing point – the two countries are in a customs union, so there's no passport control, no customs declarations.

Belfast

POP 280,900

Once lumped with Beirut, Baghdad and Bosnia as one of the four 'B's for travellers to avoid, Belfast has pulled off a remarkable transformation from bombs-and-bullets pariah to hip-hotels-and-hedonism party town. Despite the economic downturn, the city's skyline is in a constant state of flux as redevelopment continues. The old shipyards are giving way to the luxury waterfront apartments of the Titanic Quarter; and Victoria Sq, Europe's biggest urban regeneration project, has added a massive city-centre shopping mall to a list of tourist attractions that includes Victorian architecture, a glittering waterfront lined with modern art, foot-stomping music in packed-out pubs and the UK's second-biggest arts festival.

Sights

Titanic Belfast Exhibition

(www.titanicbelfast.com; Queen's Rd; adult/child £15.50/7.25, combination ticket with Thompson Pumphouse & Graving Dock £19/9.25; 9am-7pm Apr & Jun-Aug, 9am-6pm May & Sep, 10am-5pm Oct-Mar) The head of the slipway where the Titanic was built is now occupied by the gleaming, angular edifice of Titanic Belfast, an umissable multimedia extravaganza that charts the history of Belfast and the creation of the world's most famous ocean liner. Cleverly designed exhibits enlivened by historic images, animated projections and soundtracks chart Belfast's rise to turn-of-the-20th-century industrial superpower, followed by a high-tech ride through a noisy, smells-and-all re-creation of the city's shipyards.

Ulster Museum Museum

(www.nmni.com; Stranmillis Rd; by donation; 10am-5pm Tue-Sun) You could spend several hours browsing this revamped museum's beautifully designed displays, but if you're pressed for time don't miss the **Armada Room**, with artefacts retrieved from the wreck of the Spanish galleon *Girona*; the **Egyptian Room's** Princess Takabuti, a 2500-year-old Egyptian mummy unwrapped in Belfast in 1835; and the **Early Peoples Gallery's** bronze Bann Disc, a superb example of Celtic design dating from the Iron Age.

Free tours (10 people maximum; first-come, first served) run at 2.30pm Tuesday to Friday and 1.30pm Sunday.

West Belfast Historic Site

Though scarred by three decades of civil unrest, the former battleground of West Belfast is one of the most compelling places to visit in Northern Ireland. Falls Rd and Shankill Rd are adorned with famous **murals** expressing local political and religious passions, and divided by the infamous **Peace Line** barrier separating Catholic and Protestant districts. Take a taxi tour of the district, or pick up a map from the tourist office and explore on foot.

Tours

Paddy Campbell's Famous Black Cab Tours Taxi Tour

(07990 955227; www.belfastblackcabtours.co.uk; tour per 1-3 people £30) Popular 1½-hour black cab tour.

Titanic Tours Guided Tour

(07852 716655; www.titanictours-belfast.co.uk; adult/child £30/15; on demand) A three-hour luxury tour led by the great-granddaughter of one of the *Titanic*'s crew, visiting various *Titanic*-related sites. For groups of two to five people; includes pick-up and drop-off at your accommodation.

Sleeping

Tara Lodge B&B ££

(☎028-9059 0900; www.taralodge.com; 36 Cromwell Rd; s/d from £79/89; P @) In a great location on a quiet side street just a few paces from the buzz of Botanic Ave, this B&B feels more like a boutique hotel with its clean-cut, minimalist decor, friendly and efficient staff and 24 bright and cheerful rooms. Delicious breakfasts include porridge with Bushmills whiskey.

Old Rectory B&B ££

(☎028-9066 7882; www.anoldrectory.co.uk; 148 Malone Rd; s/d/f from £46/86/120; P @) A lovely Victorian villa with lots of original stained glass, this former rectory has five spacious bedrooms, a comfortable drawing room with leather sofa and fancy breakfasts (home-baked bread, homemade Irish whiskey marmalade, scrambled eggs with smoked salmon, veggie fry-ups, freshly squeezed OJ). A credit card is required to secure your booking but payment is in cash only.

The inconspicuous driveway is on the left, just past Deramore Park South.

Malmaison Hotel Hotel ££

(☎0844 693 0650; www.malmaison-belfast.com; 34-38 Victoria St; d/ste from £95/270; @) Housed in a pair of beautifully restored Italianate warehouses (originally built for rival firms in the 1850s), the Malmaison is a luxurious haven of king-size beds, deep leather sofas and roll-top baths big enough for two, all done up in a decadent decor of black, red, dark chocolate and cream. One rock-star suite even has a purple baize billiard table.

Eating & Drinking

Barking Dog Bistro ££

(☎028-9066 1885; www.barkingdogbelfast.com; 33-35 Malone Rd; mains £14-24, tapas 1/5 dishes £3/12; ⊙noon-3pm & 5.30-10pm Mon-Thu, noon-3pm & 5.30-11pm Fri & Sat, noon-9pm Sun;) Chunky hardwood, bare brick, candlelight and quirky design create the atmosphere of a stylishly restored farmhouse. The menu completes the feeling of cosiness and comfort with simple but sensational dishes such as their signature burger of meltingly tender beef shin with caramelised onion and horseradish cream, and sweet potato ravioli with

Titanic Belfast by Todd Architects + Planners, Ireland

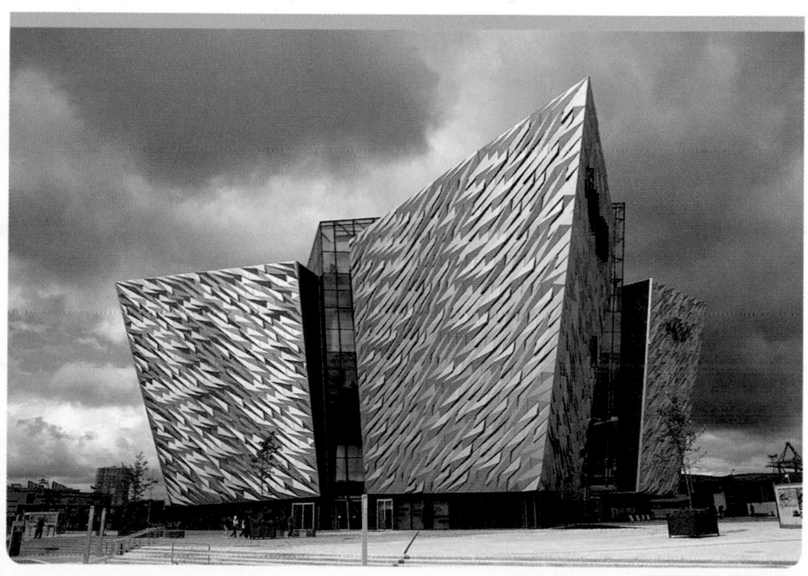

ANDREW MICHAEL/GETTY IMAGES ©

carrot and parmesan crisps. Superb service, too.

OX Irish **££**

(☎028-9031 4121; http://oxbelfast.com; 1 Oxford St; mains lunch £10, dinner £19-25; ⏰noon-2.30pm & 6-9.30pm Tue-Fri, 1-2.30pm & 6-9.30pm Sat) A high-ceilinged space walled with cream-painted brick and furnished with warm golden wood creates a theatre-like ambience for the open kitchen at the back, where Michelin-trained chefs turn out some of Belfast's finest and best-value cuisine. The restaurant works with local suppliers and focuses on fine Irish beef, sustainable seafood, and seasonal vegetables and fruit.

Shu French, Irish **££**

(☎028-9038 1655; www.shu-restaurant.com; 253 Lisburn Rd; mains £12-23, 2-course lunch/dinner menus £13.25/22.50; ⏰noon-2.30pm & 6-10pm Mon-Sat) Lording it over fashionable Lisburn Rd since 2000, Shu is the granddaddy of Belfast chic, and still winning plaudits for its French-influenced food: roast halibut and black rice; wood pigeon with kale and celeriac purée; and wild garlic gnocchi with truffle butter.

Crown Liquor Saloon Pub

(www.nicholsonspubs.co.uk; 46 Great Victoria St; ⏰11.30am-11pm Mon-Wed, 11.30am-midnight Thu-Sat, 12.30-10pm Sun) Despite being a tourist attraction Belfast's most famous bar still fills up with crowds of locals at lunchtime and in the early evening.

Information

Visit Belfast Welcome Centre (☎028-9024 6609; http://visit-belfast.com; 9 Donegall Sq N; ⏰9am-7pm Mon-Sat, 11am-4pm Sun Jun-Sep, 9am-5.30pm Mon-Sat, 11am-4pm Sun Oct-May; wi-fi) Provides information about the whole of Northern Ireland, and books accommodation anywhere in Ireland and Britain. Services include left luggage (not overnight), currency exchange and free wi-fi.

Getting There & Away

Air

Belfast International Airport (BFS; ☎028-9448 4848; www.belfastairport.com), 30km northwest of the city, has flights from the UK, Europe and New York.

Giant's Causeway, Ireland

SLOW IMAGES/GETTY IMAGES ©

Giant's Causeway

This spectacular rock formation – Northern Ireland's only Unesco World Heritage Site – is one of Ireland's most impressive and atmospheric landscape features. When you first see it you'll understand why the ancients thought it wasn't a natural feature – the vast expanse of regular, closely packed, hexagonal stone columns looks for all the world like the handiwork of giants.

The more prosaic explanation is that the columns are simply contraction cracks caused by a cooling lava flow some 60 million years ago. The phenomenon is explained in the **Giant's Causeway Visitor Experience** (☎028-2073 1855; www.nationaltrust.org; adult/child with parking £9/4.50, without parking £7/3.25; ⏲9am-7pm Apr-Sep, to 6pm Feb, Mar & Oct, to 5pm Nov-Jan), a spectacular eco-friendly building half-hidden in a hillside above the sea.

From the centre it's an easy 10- to 15-minute walk downhill to the Causeway itself, but a more interesting approach is to follow the clifftop path northeast for 2km to the **Chimney Tops** headland, then descend the **Shepherd's Steps** to the Causeway.

Eight miles to the east of the causeway, the 20m-long **Carrick-a-Rede rope bridge** (☎028-2076 9839; www.nationaltrust.org.uk/carrick-a-rede; adult/child £5.60/3.10; ⏲10am-7pm Jun-Aug, to 6pm Mar-May, Sep & Oct, 10.30am-3.30pm Nov & Dec) that connects Carrick-a-Rede Island to the mainland, swaying some 30m above the pounding waves, is a classic test of nerve. Note that the bridge is closed in high winds.

The Giant's Causeway is 100km north of Belfast. From April to September the Ulsterbus Antrim Coaster (bus 252) links Belfast with the Giant's Causeway and Bushmills via Larne.

George Best Belfast City Airport (BHD; ☎028-9093 9093; www.belfastcityairport.com; Airport Rd), 6km northeast of the city centre, has flights from the UK, Amsterdam and Barcelona.

Boat

Stena Line ferries to Belfast from Cairnryan (Scotland) and Liverpool (England) dock at Victoria Terminal, 5km north of the city centre; exit the M2 motorway at junction 1. Ferries from the Isle of Man arrive at Albert Quay, 2km north of the centre. Other car ferries to and from Scotland dock at Larne, 30km north of Belfast.

Train

Belfast has two main train stations: Great Victoria St, next to the Europa Bus Centre, and Belfast Central, east of the city centre. If you arrive by train at Central Station, your rail ticket entitles you to a free bus ride into the city centre. A local train also connects with Great Victoria St.

Dublin £30, two hours, eight daily Monday to Saturday, five on Sunday.

Larne Harbour £6.90, one hour, hourly.

SURVIVAL GUIDE

Directory A–Z

Accommodation

Accommodation in the big cities tends to be more expensive, with London in a class all of its own.

- Rates tend to drop in low season (October to April), and rocket during high season (July to September).
- Breakfast is usually included at most B&Bs and hotels, but may be an extra at many hostels and top-end hotels.
- Rates are often quoted per person, rather than per room, and include a private bathroom unless otherwise stated.
- Smoking is banned in all hotels, B&Bs and other accommodation.
- Accommodation can be difficult to find during holidays (especially around Easter and New Year) and major events (such as the Edinburgh Festival Fringe).

Right: View of Dublin (p134), Ireland **Below:** Mural depicting the Titanic, Belfast (p152), Ireland

Price Ranges

Prices are listed at high-season rates (low-season rates can be 15% to 20% less), based on two people sharing a double, and include a private bathroom unless otherwise stated.

Our review rates refer to double rooms with a private bathroom, except in hostels or where otherwise specified.

Britain

£ less than £60 (less than £100 in London)

££ £60 to £130 (£100 to £180 in London)

£££ more than £130 (more than £180 in London)

Ireland

In the Republic of Ireland:

€ less than €60

€€ €60 to €150

€€€ more than €150

In Northern Ireland:

£ less than £50

££ £50 to £120

£££ more than £120

Food

Price Ranges

The prices we quote are for a main course at dinner unless otherwise indicated. The symbols used indicate the following price ranges:

Britain

£ less than £9

££ £9 to £18

£££ more than £18

Ireland

In the Republic of Ireland:

€ less than €12

€€ €12 to €25

€€€ more than €25

In Northern Ireland

£ less than £12

££ £12 to £20

£££ more than £20

Gay & Lesbian Travellers

Most major cities – especially London, Edinburgh and Dublin – have gay and lesbian scenes. Useful resources:

Diva (www.divamag.co.uk)

Gay Community News (www.gcn.ie)

Gay Times (www.gaytimes.co.uk)

ScotsGay (www.scotsgay.co.uk)

Language

Britain

The dominant language of Britain is English. In Wales about 562,000 people (19% of the population) speak Welsh as a first language, while in Scotland, Gaelic – another Celtic language – is spoken by about 57,400 people (1.1% of the population), mainly in the Highlands and Islands.

Ireland

English is the everyday language both in the Republic and in Northern Ireland. While Irish Gaelic is the official language of the Republic of Ireland, it is used daily by only 5% to 10% of the population, mostly in rural areas (known as the Gaeltacht) in counties Cork, Donegal, Galway and Kerry.

Money

ATMs ATMs (often called 'cash machines') are easy to find in cities and even small towns.

Changing Money Most banks and some post offices offer currency exchange services. Check rates at bureaux de change; they may claim 'no commission' but often rates are poor.

Credit & Debit Cards Smaller businesses, such as pubs or B&Bs, prefer debit cards (or charge a fee for credit cards), and some take cash or cheque only. Nearly all credit and debit cards use a 'Chip and PIN' system (instead of signing).

Tipping 10% is fine for restaurants, cafes, taxi drivers and pub meals; if you order drinks and food at the bar, there's no need to tip.

Britain

Currency The currency of Britain is the pound sterling (£). Paper money ('notes') comes in £5, £10, £20 and £50 denominations, although some shops don't accept £50 notes because fakes circulate.

Three Scottish banks issue their own sterling banknotes (including a £1 note), interchangeable with the Bank of England notes used in the rest of the UK.

Ireland

Currency The Irish Republic uses the euro (€), while Northern Ireland uses the British pound sterling (£).

As in Scotland, banks in Northern Ireland issue their own notes which are equivalent to sterling but not readily accepted in mainland Britain.

Opening Hours

Britain

Banks 9.30am to 4pm or 5pm Monday to Friday, 9.30am to 1pm Saturday.

Post offices 9am to 5pm Monday to Friday, 9am to 12.30pm Saturday (main branches to 5pm).

Pubs 11am to 11pm Sunday to Thursday, sometimes to midnight or 1am Friday and Saturday.

Restaurants Lunch noon to 3pm, dinner 6pm to 10pm; hours vary widely.

Shops 9am to 5pm Monday to Saturday (to 5.30pm or 6pm in cities), 10am to 4pm Sunday.

Ireland

Banks 10am to 4pm Monday to Friday, to 5pm Thursday.

Post offices 9am to 5.30pm Monday to Friday and 9am to 12.30pm Saturday in Northern Ireland; 9am to 6pm Monday to Friday and 9am to 1pm Saturday in the Republic.

Pubs Northern Ireland 11.30am to 11pm Monday to Saturday, 12.30pm to 10pm Sunday. Pubs with late licences open until 1am Monday to Saturday and midnight Sunday; Republic 10.30am to 11.30pm Monday to Thursday, 10.30am to 12.30am Friday and Saturday, noon to 11pm Sunday. All pubs close Christmas Day and Good Friday.

Restaurants noon-10.30pm, many close one day of the week.

Shops 9am to 5.30pm or 6pm Monday to Saturday (until 8pm on Thursday and

Buildings along the River Liffey, Dublin (p134), Ireland

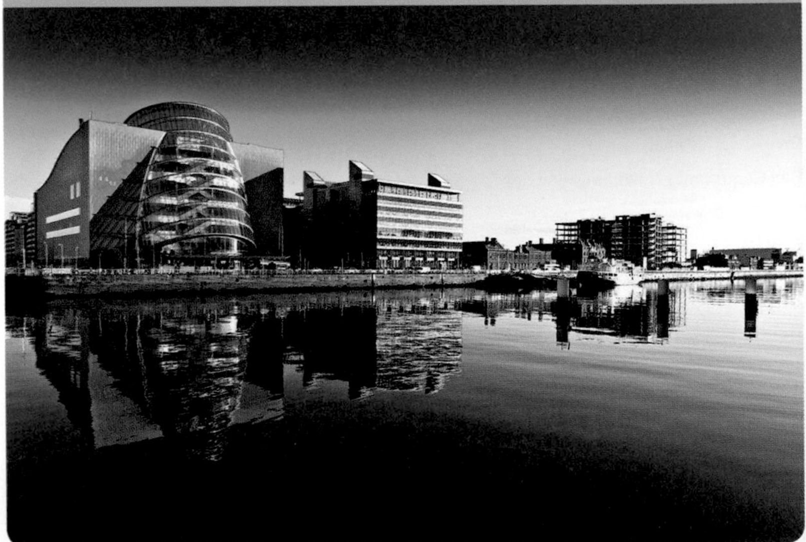

DAVE G KELLY/GETTY IMAGES ©

sometimes Friday), noon to 6pm Sunday (in bigger towns only). Shops in rural towns may close at lunch and one day per week.

Public Holidays

Britain

New Year's Day 1 January (plus 2 January in Scotland)

Easter March/April (Good Friday to Easter Monday inclusive)

May Day First Monday in May

Spring Bank Holiday Last Monday in May

Summer Bank Holiday Last Monday in August

Christmas Day 25 December

Boxing Day 26 December

Ireland

New Year's Day 1 January

St Patrick's Day 17 March

Easter (Good Friday to Easter Monday inclusive) March/April

May Holiday First Monday in May

Christmas Day 25 December

St Stephen's Day (Boxing Day) 26 December

Only Northern Ireland:

Spring Bank Holiday Last Monday in May

Orangemen's Day 12 July (following Monday if 12th is at weekend)

August Bank Holiday Last Monday in August

Only the Republic of Ireland:

June Holiday First Monday in June

August Holiday First Monday in August

October Holiday Last Monday in October

> **Holiday Seasons**
>
> Roads get busy and accommodation prices go up during school holidays.
>
> **Easter Holiday** Week before and week after Easter.
>
> **Summer Holiday** Third week of July to first week of September.
>
> **Christmas Holiday** Mid-December to first week of January.
>
> There are also three week-long 'half-term' school holidays – usually late February (or early March), late May and late October. These vary between Scotland, England and Wales.

Telephone

Britain

Britain uses the GSM 900/1800 network, which covers the rest of Europe, Australia and New Zealand, but isn't compatible with the North American GSM 1900. Most modern mobiles can function on both networks – but check before you leave home just in case.

Area codes in the UK do not have a standard format or length (eg Edinburgh ☎0131, London ☎020). In our reviews, area codes and phone numbers have been listed together, separated by a hyphen. Other codes include ☎0500 or ☎0800 for free calls, ☎0845 for local rates, ☎087 for national rates and ☎089 or ☎09 for premium rates. Mobile phones start with ☎07 and calling them is more expensive than calling a landline.

- Dial ☎100 for an operator and ☎155 for an international operator as well as reverse-charge (collect) calls.
- To call outside the UK, dial ☎00, then the country code (☎1 for USA, ☎61 for Australia etc), the area code (you usually drop the initial zero) and the number.
- For directory enquiries, a host of agencies compete for your business and charge from 10p to 40p; numbers include ☎118 192, ☎118 118, ☎118 500 and ☎118 811.

Ireland

The mobile (cell) phone network in Ireland runs on the GSM 900/1800 system compatible with the rest of Europe and Australia, but not the USA.

Mobile numbers in the Republic begin with ☎085, ☎086 or ☎087 (☎07 in Northern Ireland). A local pay-as-you-go SIM for your mobile will cost from around €10, but may work out free after the standard phone-credit refund (make sure your phone is compatible with the local provider).

To call Northern Ireland from the Republic, do not use ☎0044 as for the rest of the UK. Instead, dial ☎048 and then the local number. To dial the Republic from Northern Ireland, however, use the full international code ☎00 353, then the local number.

Traveline

Traveline (☎ 0871 200 2233; www.traveline.info) is a very useful information service covering bus, coach, taxi and train services all over Britain.

Tourist Information

Most cities and towns, and some villages, have a tourist information centre (TIC) with helpful staff, books and maps, free leaflets and loads of advice although smaller ones may close in winter. They can also assist with booking accommodation.

- **Visit Britain** (www.visitbritain.com)
- **Tourism Ireland** (www.tourismireland.com)

Visas

European Economic Area (EEA) nationals don't need a visa to visit (or work in) Britain and Ireland. Citizens of Australia, Canada, New Zealand, South Africa and the USA can visit the UK for up to six months (three months for the Republic of Ireland), but are prohibited from working.

Getting There & Away

Air

Britain

You can easily fly to Britain from just about anywhere in the world. London is the main hub, but in recent years regional airports around Britain have massively increased their choice – especially on budget ('no-frills') airlines to/from mainland Europe.

Ireland

There are nonstop flights from Britain, Continental Europe and North America to Dublin, Shannon and Belfast International, and nonstop connections from Britain and Europe to Cork.

Land

High-speed **Eurostar** (www.eurostar.com) passenger services shuttle at least 10 times daily between London and Paris (2¼ hours) or Brussels (two hours) via the Channel Tunnel. The normal one-way fare between London and Paris/Brussels costs £140 to £180; advance booking and off-peak travel gets cheaper fares as low as £39 one-way.

Vehicles use the **Eurotunnel** (www.eurotunnel.com) at Folkestone in England or Calais in France. The trains run four times an hour from 6am to 10pm, then hourly. The journey takes 35 minutes. The one-way cost for a car and passengers is between £75 and £165 depending on time of day; promotional fares often bring it down to £55.

Travelling between Ireland and Britain, the main train–ferry–train route is Dublin to London, via Dun Laoghaire and Holyhead. Ferries also run between Rosslare and Fishguard or Pembroke (Wales), with train connections on either side.

Sea

Broker sites covering all routes and options include www.ferrybooker.com and www.directferries.co.uk.

Britain

The main ferry routes between Britain and mainland Europe include Dover to Calais or Boulogne (France), Harwich to Hook of Holland (Netherlands), Hull to Zeebrugge (Belgium) or Rotterdam (Netherlands), and Portsmouth to Santander or Bilbao (Spain). Routes to/from Ireland include Holyhead to Dun Laoghaire.

Ireland

Competition from budget airlines has forced ferry operators to discount heavily and offer flexible fares, meaning great bargains at quiet times of the day or year. For example, the popular route across the Irish Sea between Dublin and Holyhead can be had for as little as €15/£12 for a foot passenger and €90/£75 for a car plus up to four passengers.

Getting Around

When travelling long-distance by train or bus/coach in Britain and Ireland, it's important to realise that there's no such thing as a standard fare. Book long in advance and travel on Tuesday mid-morning, for example, and it's cheap. Buy your ticket on the spot late Friday afternoon, and it'll be a lot more expensive.

Air

Britain's domestic airlines include British Airways (www.britishairways.com), **FlyBe/Loganair** (☎ 0871 700 2000; www.loganair.co.uk), EasyJet (www.easyjet.com) and Ryanair (www.ryanair.com), with regular flights from London to Edinburgh and Inverness, among other destinations Along with Ireland's national carrier **Aer Lingus** (www.aerlingus.com), they also offer flights between Brtiain and Ireland.

Bus

Britain

National Express (www.nationalexpress.com) is the main coach operator in England and Wales. North of the border, Scottish Citylink (☎0871 266 3333; www.citylink.co.uk) is the leading coach company.

Ireland

The Republic of Ireland's national bus line, Bus Éireann (☎01-836 6111; www.buseireann.ie), operates services all over the Republic and into Northern Ireland. Most intercity buses in Northern Ireland are operated by Ulsterbus (☎9066 6600; www.ulsterbus.co.uk).

Car & Motorcycle

EU driving licences are valid in Britain and Ireland; non-EU licences are valid for up to 12 months from the date of entry.

Rental

Car rental is relatively expensive in Britain and Ireland; you'll pay from around £200/€250 per week (including insurance and unlimited mileage). All the major players including Avis, Hertz and Budget operate here.

A minimum age of 21 years may apply; for most hire companies you must be at least 23 and have had a valid driving licence for more than one year. Some companies will not hire to those aged over 70 or 75.

Using a rental-broker site such as UK Car Hire (www.ukcarhire.net), Kayak (www.kayak.com) or Nova (www.novacarhire.com) can help find bargains.

It's illegal to drive a car or motorbike in Britain or Ireland without (at least) third-party insurance. This will be included with all rental cars.

Road Rules

The main ones to remember:

- Always drive on the left
- Give way to your right at junctions and roundabouts
- Always use the left-hand lane on motorways and dual-carriageways, unless overtaking (passing)
- Wear seat belts in cars and crash helmets on motorcycles
- Don't drink and drive; the maximum blood-alcohol level allowed is 80mg/100mL (50mg/10mL in Scotland)
- Yellow lines (single or double) along the edge of the road indicate parking restrictions, red lines mean no stopping whatsoever
- Speed limits are 30mph/50km/h in built-up areas, 60mph/100km/h on main roads, and 70mph/120km/h on motorways and most dual carriageways

Bar tender at the Bow Bar, Edinburgh (p130), Scotland

Right: Grand Canal Square designed by Martha Schwartz Partners, Dublin (p134), Ireland; **Below:** Titanic Dock depth gauge, Titanic Belfast (p152), Ireland (RIGHT) DAVID SOANES PHOTOGRAPHY/GETTY IMAGES ©; (BELOW) NORRIE3699/GETTY IMAGES ©

Train

Britain

About 20 different companies operate train services in Britain. This system can be confusing at first, but information and ticket-buying services are mostly centralised. If you have to change trains, or use two or more train operators, you still buy one ticket – valid for the whole journey. The main railcards and passes are also accepted by all train operators.

National Rail Enquiries (☎08457 48 49 50; www.nationalrail.co.uk) provides booking and timetable information for Britain's entire rail network.

Rail travel has two classes: 1st and standard. Travelling 1st class costs around 50% more than standard. At weekends some train operators offer 'upgrades' for an extra £5 to £25 on top of your standard-class fare.

Costs & Reservations

The earlier you book, the cheaper it gets. You can also save if you travel 'off-peak' (ie the days and times that aren't busy). If you buy online, you can have the ticket posted (UK addresses only), or collect it from station machines on the day of travel.

There are three main fare types:

Anytime Buy any time, travel any time – usually the most expensive option.

Off-peak Buy any time, travel off-peak.

Advance Buy in advance, travel only on specific trains (usually the cheapest option).

Train Passes

For country-wide travel, **BritRail** (www.britrail.com) passes are available for visitors from overseas. They must be bought in your country of origin (not in Britain) from a specialist travel agency. They're available in three different versions (England only; all Britain; UK and Ireland) and for periods from four to 30 days.

Eurail cards are not accepted in Britain, and **InterRail** cards are only valid if bought in another mainland European country.

Ireland

The Republic of Ireland's railway system, **Iarnród Éireann** (Iarnród Éireann; ☎1850 366 222;

www.irishrail.ie), has routes radiating out from Dublin, but there is no direct north–south route along the west coast.

Northern Ireland Railways (NIR; 028-9089 9411; www.nirailways.co.uk; Belfast Central Station) has four lines from Belfast, one of which links up with the Republic's rail system.

Train Passes

Travel passes for trains in Ireland include:

Eurail Pass Valid for train travel in the Republic of Ireland and in Northern Ireland, 30% discount on Irish Ferries and Stena Line crossings to France.

InterRail Pass Valid for train travel in the Republic of Ireland and in Northern Ireland, 30% discount on Irish Ferries and Stena Line crossings to France.

Irish Explorer Rail For train-only travel (five days' travel out of 15) for €160 within the Republic only.

France

Nowhere provokes passion quite like La Belle France. Love it or loathe it, everyone has their own opinion about this Gallic Goliath. Snooty, sexy, superior, chic, infuriating, arrogant, officious and inspired in equal measures, the French have long lived according to their own idiosyncratic rules, and if the rest of the world doesn't always see eye to eye with them, well, *tant pis* (too bad) – that's the price you pay for being a culinary trendsetter, artistic pioneer and cultural icon.

France is a deeply traditional place: castles, chateaux and ancient churches litter the landscape while centuries-old principles of rich food, fine wine and *joie de vivre* underpin everyday life. Yet it is also a country that has one of Western Europe's most multicultural make-ups, not to mention a well-deserved reputation for artistic experimentation and architectural invention. Enjoy.

Carcassonne (p245)

France

ENGLAND
NORTH SEA
Southampton
Portsmouth
Brighton
Folkestone
Dover
Calais
Strait of Dover
BRUSSELS
BELGIUM
Lille
Arras
GERMANY
English Channel (La Manche)
Dieppe
Amiens
Somme
Authie
Sambre
Oise
St- Quentin
LUXEMBOURG CITY
Cherbourg
Baie des Veys
Channel Islands
Le Havre
Rade de Caen
Rouen
Pays de Bray
Côte des Deux Amants
Bayeux
Caen
Chantilly
Aisne
Reims
Verdun
Saarbrücken
Metz
Vernon
Giverny
Evreux
Suisse Normande
Côte des Légendes
Marne
PARIS
Versailles
Sezanne
Nancy
Strasbourg
Brest
Morlaix
St-Malo
Dinan
Mont St-Michel
Fougères
Alençon
Chartres
Troyes
Vittel
Moselle
Quimper
Concarneau
Rennes
Laval
Le Mans
Sens
Seine
Langres
Mulhouse
Îles de Glénan
Vannes
Carnac
Vilaine
Orléans
Auxerre
Blois
Chambord
Presqu'île de Guérande
Angers
Loire
Tours
Yonne
Avallon
Dijon
Besançon
Doubs
Basel
St-Nazaire
Nantes
Cher
Bourges
Château Chinon
Nevers
Autun
Beaune
BERN
SWITZERLAND
Châtellerault
Châteauroux
Parthenay
Poitiers
Allier
Lake Geneva (Lac Léman)
ATLANTIC OCEAN
Montluçon
Mâcon
La Rochelle
Creuse
Vienne
Vichy
Roanne
Saône
Geneva
Aiguille du Midi
A28
A1
A13
A4
A84
A5
A28
A11
A10
A6
A31
N137
A11
A86
A83
A20
A6
A71
A10
1
2
3

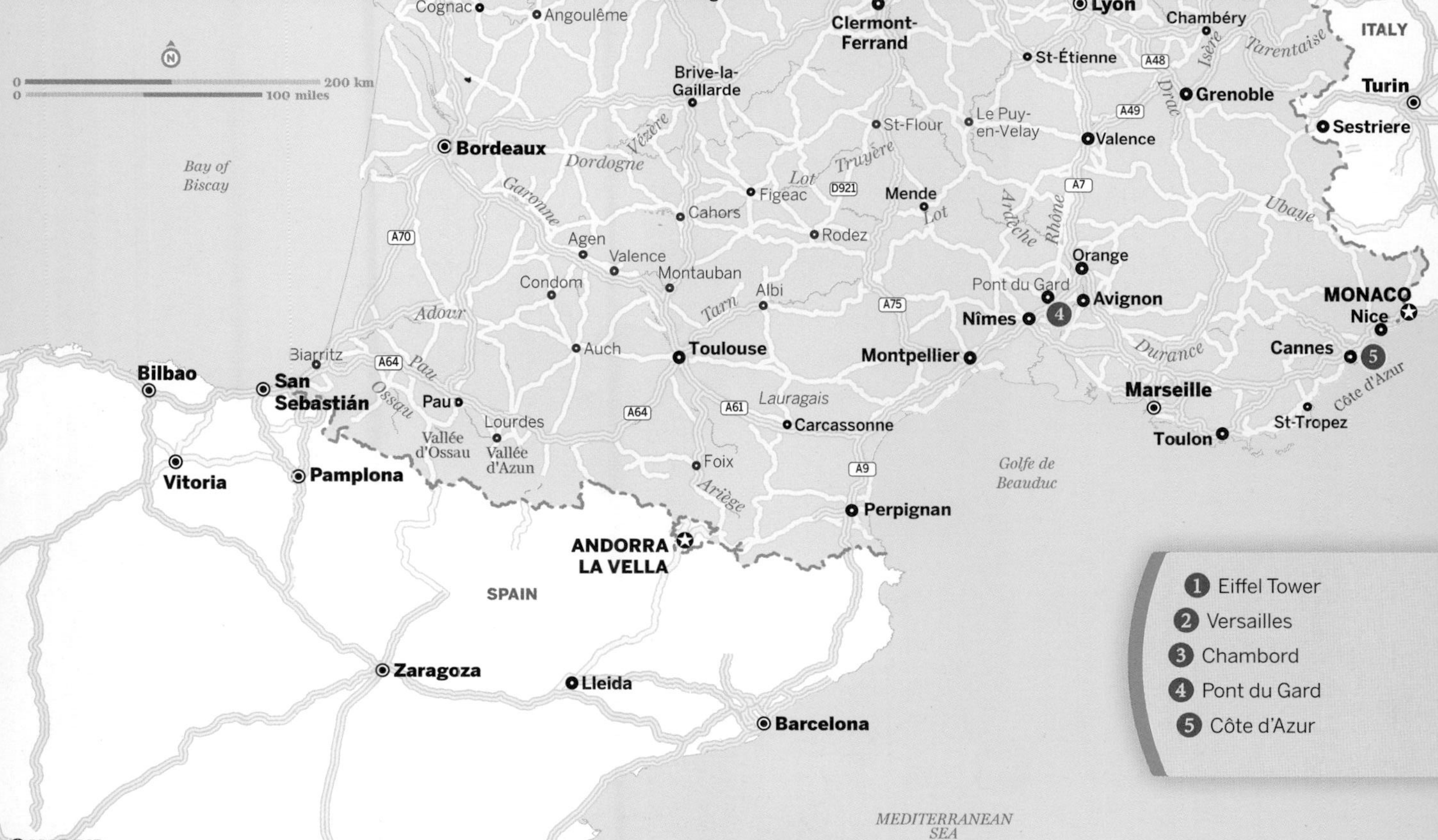

0 200 km
0 100 miles
Bay of Biscay
Cognac
Angoulême
Limoges
Clermont-Ferrand
Lyon
Annecy
Chambéry
ITALY
Turin
Sestriere
St-Étienne
Brive-la-Gaillarde
St-Flour
Le Puy-en-Velay
Grenoble
Valence
Bordeaux
Dordogne
Vézère
Garonne
Lot
Truyère
Figeac
Mende
Cahors
Rodez
Agen
Valence
Montauban
Condom
Albi
Tarn
Adour
Auch
Toulouse
Montpellier
Nîmes
Pont du Gard
Orange
Avignon
Ardèche
Rhône
Durance
Isère
Tarentaise
Drac
Ubaye
MONACO
Nice
Cannes
Côte d'Azur
Marseille
Toulon
St-Tropez
Biarritz
Bilbao
San Sebastián
Pau
Ossau
Lourdes
Vallée d'Ossau
Vallée d'Azun
Lauragais
Carcassonne
Foix
Ariège
Perpignan
Golfe de Beauduc
Vitoria
Pamplona
ANDORRA LA VELLA
SPAIN
Zaragoza
Lleida
Barcelona
MEDITERRANEAN SEA
MADRID
A72
A48
A49
A7
D921
A70
A75
A64
A61
A9
1 Eiffel Tower
2 Versailles
3 Chambord
4 Pont du Gard
5 Côte d'Azur

France Highlights

Eiffel Tower

Spiking into the skyline above the City of Lights, the Eiffel Tower (p183) is quite simply one of the world's most unmistakable sights. Built from cast-iron beams and millions of rivets in the late 19th century, it has managed to transcend its industrial components to become nothing short of a work of art. Climb to the top or catch the lifts, and watch the French capital unfold beneath you. It's the Parisian experience par excellence.

1

2

Versailles

The French monarchs may have lost their heads during the Revolution, but you can still get a glimpse of their pomp and power at the amazing Château de Versailles (p202). It began life as a hunting lodge for Louis XIV, but was expanded by his successors into a showpiece of extravagant art and architecture, from the famous Hall of Mirrors to the fountain-filled grounds. You'll feel royal for a day.

SAMI SARKIS/GETTY IMAGES ©

PAUL THOMPSON/GETTY IMAGES ©

3 Château de Chambord

Versailles isn't the only chateau to explore in France. The Loire Valley is lined with scores more lavish castles, mostly built between the 16th and 18th centuries as country estates for the French aristocracy. Chambord (p224) is perhaps the finest of all. This vast Renaissance retreat built for François I is distinguished by a maze of cupolas, turrets, hallways and state rooms, as well as a famous staircase rumoured to have been designed by Leonardo da Vinci.

DOUG PEARSON/GETTY IMAGES ©

4 Pont du Gard

Two thousand years ago, France (then known as Gaul) was one of the most important provinces of the Roman Empire, and the country is littered with Roman remains. None, however, are as impressive as the Pont du Gard (p246) – an amazing three-tiered aqueduct near Avignon, which was designed to carry 20,000 cubic metres of water per day along the 50km of canals that stretched between Uzès and Nîmes.

5 Côte d'Azur

If there's one place that lives up to its name, it's the Côte d'Azur (French Riviera; p258). Sprinkled with glittering bays, super-exclusive beaches and sunbaked Mediterranean towns, it's been one of Europe's favourite retreats for as long as anyone cares to remember. Nice is essential, but for glitzy Mediterranean glamour you can't beat the pint-sized principality of Monaco, where millionaires step off their yachts straight into Monte Carlo's casino. Above: Monaco (p266)

France's Best...

Food & Drink

- **Lyon** (p229) Famed for its piggy cuisine and delightful restaurant scene.
- **Champagne** (p219) Visit the famous Champagne houses in Épernay for a bubbly tasting.
- **Sweet treats** (p193) Macarons, ice-creams, fancy desserts, Paris will delight the sweet-toothed.
- **Bordeaux wine trail** (p241) Tour the vineyards of the France's most illustrious wine region.
- **Mediterranean cuisine** (p258) Revel in the Riviera's sun-kissed flavours in Nice.

Artistic Sights

- **Musée d'Orsay** (p175) See France's national collection of Impressionist and post-Impressionist art.
- **Centre Pompidou** (p182) Europe's largest modern art collection and radical architecture.
- **Giverny** (p256) Wander among the lily ponds in Monet's beloved gardens.
- **Museé des Beaux Arts** (p231) Admire France's largest collection of sculptures and paintings outside Paris.
- **Vézère Valley** (p239) Home to the world's most important prehistoric paintings.

Historic Locations

- **D-Day Beaches** (p210) Europe's liberation began on Normandy's beaches.
- **Place de la Bastille** (p187) The place where the Revolution originated is now Paris' busiest roundabout.
- **Alignements de Carnac** (p216) Over 3000 *menhirs* make up the world's largest prehistoric monument.
- **Bayeux** (p209) William the Conqueror's invasion of England is recounted in the massive Bayeux Tapestry.
- **Nîmes** (p247) Wander beneath the arches of the largest Roman amphitheatre in France.

Places to Shop

- **Marché aux Puces de St-Ouen** (p201) Paris' fascinating flea market is a paradise for bargain hunters.
- **Sarlat-la-Canéda** (p238) Sarlat's covered and outdoor markets groan with goodies gathered from across the Dordogne.
- **Marché de Noël** (p223) Get into the festive spirit with mulled wine and ginger bread at Strasbourg's month-long Christmas market.
- **Le Panier, Marseille** (p252) Shoppers have been coming to this lively quarter of Marseille since the days of ancient Greece.

Left: Macarons; **Above:** Maison et Jardins de Claude Monet, Giverny (p256)

Need to Know

ADVANCE PLANNING

- **Two months ahead** Book hotels for Paris, Provence, the Côte d'Azur and Corsica.
- **Two weeks ahead** Plan your train travel on the SNCF website.
- **When you arrive** Pick up a Paris Museum Pass or a Paris Visite Pass for discounts on sights and transport.

RESOURCES

- **France Guide** (www.franceguide.com) Detailed advice from the government tourist office.
- **SNCF** (www.sncf-voyages.com) Plan all train travel and buy tickets online.
- **Météo France** (www.meteofrance.com) Get the latest weather forecasts.
- **Paris Convention & Visitors Bureau** (www.parisinfo.com) Paris' tourist site is loaded with useful tips.

GETTING AROUND

- **Air** France's main international airports are Paris' Roissy Charles de Gaulle and Orly; regional airports serve other French cities.
- **Bus** Handy for rural areas; otherwise you're better off with trains.
- **Car** The country's roads are excellent, but tolls operate on most autoroutes.
- **Sea** Cross-channel ferries service Roscoff, St-Malo, Cherbourg and Calais. Nice and Marseille have ferry services to Corsica and Italy.
- **Train** Fast TGVs serve most French cities, while rural areas are served by slower TERs. The Eurostar links Paris' Gare du Nord and London's St Pancras.

BE FOREWARNED

- **Dog poo** Watch where you step, especially in Paris.
- **Closing times** Shops, sights and museums generally shut on Sunday and Monday, and most places close for lunch between noon and 2pm.
- **Manners** It's polite to say *bonjour* (hello) and *au revoir* (goodbye) when entering and leaving shops.
- **Public transport** Remember to stamp your ticket in a *composteur* (validating machine) to avoid being fined.

France Itineraries

France is fascinating enough to fill a lifetime of visits; with these itineraries we've captured the best of both north and south.

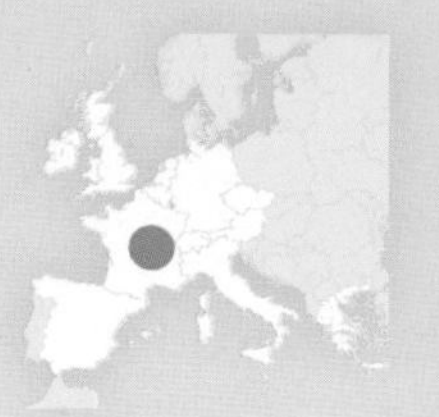

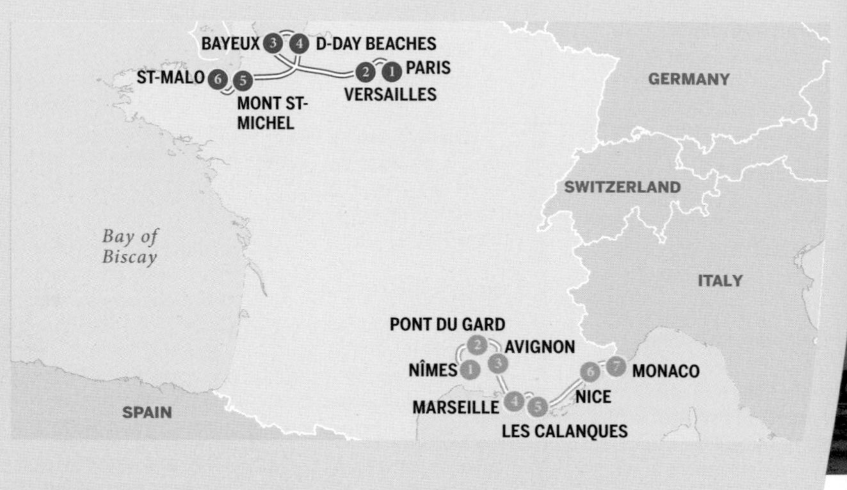

3 DAYS

NORTHERN SIGHTS
Paris to Bayeux

Every French adventure has to begin in ❶ **Paris** (p174). You could fill a month here and still not see every sight, so with just a day you'll have to focus on the essentials: a morning at the Louvre, an afternoon at Notre-Dame Cathedral, and a twilight trip up the Eiffel Tower.

On day two take a day trip by either train or car to ❷ **Versailles** (p202), Louis XIV's monumental pleasure palace. Prebook your tickets online to avoid the queues, and take a guided tour to see the secret parts of the palace. Back in Paris, take an evening cruise along the Seine.

On day three, travel northwest to ❸ **Bayeux** (p209), where you can spend the morning admiring the enormous Bayeux Tapestry before travelling to the ❹ **D-Day Beaches** (p210). Don't miss the moving American Cemetery above Omaha Beach, which you'll recognise from the opening of *Saving Private Ryan*. Unsurprisingly, the beach is still known to veterans as Bloody Omaha.

With a bit of extra time, you could extend the trip with visits to the abbey of ❺ **Mont St-Michel** (p211) and the walled city of ❻ **St-Malo** (p214).

THE SULTRY SOUTH
Nîmes to Monaco

France's sun-drenched south is the perfect place for a road trip. This week-long itinerary begins in 1 **Nîmes** (p247), once one of the great centres of Roman Gaul, where you can still see the remains of the amphitheatre and Roman walls. On day two, stop at the most breathtaking of all Roman sights, the aqueduct of 2 **Pont du Gard** (p246) before making your way to 3 **Avignon** (p255), once the papal seat of power.

After a couple of days in and around Avignon,, head for the coast. Multicultural 4 **Marseille** (p249) comes as something of a shock: it's noisy and chaotic, but if you want to taste authentic *bouillabaisse*, this is the place to do it. If the din gets too much, take a day trip to 5 **Les Calanques** (p249), France's newest national park, to discover one of the Mediterranean's most pristine landscapes.

Finish up in the quintessential city of the Côte d'Azur, 6 **Nice** (p258), where you can while away a few days bronzing yourself on the beach, exploring the Old Town's alleyways or tackling the hairpin curves of the *corniches* (coastal roads) en route to the millionaires' playground, 7 **Monaco** (p266).

Musée du Louvre (p182), Paris

Discover France

At a Glance

- **Paris** (p174) The unforgettable, unmissable city of lights.
- **The Loire Valley** (p224) Home to France's grandest chateaux.
- **The Atlantic Coast** (p240) World-class wines and white sandy beaches.
- **Provence** (p249) France at its most photogenic: hilltop towns, bustling markets, Roman ruins.
- **Côte d'Azur** (p258) The dazzling coastline that has inspired artists for centuries.

PARIS

POP 2.2 MILLION

What can be said about the sexy, sophisticated City of Lights that hasn't already been said a thousand times before? Quite simply, this is one of the world's great metropolises – a trendsetter, market leader and cultural capital for over a thousand years and still going strong. This is the place that gave the world the can-can and the cinematograph, a city that reinvented itself during the Renaissance, bopped to the beat of the jazz age and positively glittered during the belle époque (literally, 'beautiful era').

As you might expect, Paris is strewn with historic architecture, glorious galleries and cultural treasures galore. But the modern-day city is much more than just a museum piece: it's a heady hodgepodge of cultures and ideas – a place to stroll the boulevards, shop till you drop, flop riverside, or simply do as the Parisians do and watch the world buzz by from a streetside cafe. Savour every moment.

Sights

LEFT BANK

Musée du Quai Branly Museum

(Map p176; www.quaibranly.fr; 37 quai Branly, 7e; adult/child €8.50/free; 11am-7pm Tue, Wed & Sun, 11am to 9pm Thu-Sat; M Alma Marceau or RER Pont de l'Alma) No other museum in Paris so inspires travellers, armchair anthropologists and those who simply appreciate the beauty of traditional craftsmanship. A tribute to the diversity of human culture, Musée du Quai Branly presents an overview of indigenous and folk art. Its four main

Musée Rodin, Paris

sections focus on Oceania, Asia, Africa and the Americas.

An impressive array of masks, carvings, weapons, jewellery and more make up the body of the rich collection, displayed in a refreshingly unique interior without rooms or high walls.

Musée d'Orsay Museum

(Map p176; www.musee-orsay.fr; 62 rue de Lille, 7e; adult/child €11/free; ⌚9.30am-6pm Tue, Wed & Fri-Sun, to 9.45pm Thu; Ⓜ Assemblée Nationale or RER Musée d'Orsay) Recently renovated to incorporate richly coloured walls and increased exhibition space, the home of France's national collection from the Impressionist, post-Impressionist and art nouveau movements spanning the 1840s and 1914 is the glorious former Gare d'Orsay railway station – itself an art nouveau showpiece – where a roll-call of masters and their world-famous works are on display.

Top of every visitor's must-see list is the world's largest collection of Impressionist and post-Impressionist art.

Jardin du Luxembourg Park

(Map p188; numerous entrances; ⌚hours vary; Ⓜ St-Sulpice, Rennes or Notre Dame des Champs, or RER Luxembourg) This inner-city oasis of formal terraces, chestnut groves and lush lawns has a special place in Parisians' hearts. Napoléon dedicated the 23 gracefully laid-out hectares of the Luxembourg Gardens to the children of Paris, and many residents spent their childhood prodding 1920s wooden **sailboats (per 30min €3; ⌚Apr-Oct)** with long sticks on the octagonal **Grand Bassin** pond, watching puppets perform Punch & Judy–type shows at the **Théâtre du Luxembourg (Map p188; www.marionnettesduluxembourg.fr; tickets €4.80; ⌚usually 3.30pm Wed, 11am & 3.30pm Sat & Sun, daily during school holidays; Ⓜ Notre Dame des Champs)**, and riding the *carrousel* (merry-go-round) or Shetland ponies.

Musée Rodin Garden, Museum

(Map p176; www.musee-rodin.fr; 79 rue de Varenne, 7e; adult/child museum incl garden €6/free, garden only €2/free; ⌚10am-5.45pm Tue & Thu-Sun, to 8.45pm Wed; Ⓜ Varenne) Sculptor, painter, sketcher, engraver and collector Auguste Rodin donated his entire collection to the French state in 1908 on the proviso that they dedicate his former workshop and showroom, the beautiful 1730 Hôtel Biron, to displaying his works. They're now installed not only in the mansion itself, but in its rose-clambered garden – one of the most peaceful places in central Paris and a wonderful spot to contemplate his famous work *The Thinker*.

Purchase tickets online to avoid queuing.

Museum Tips

- If you're visiting more than two or three museums and monuments, buy a **Paris Museum Pass (http://en.parismuseumpass.com; 2/4/6 days €42/56/69)**, valid for entry to some 60-odd venues including the Louvre, Centre Pompidou, Musée d'Orsay, Musée Rodin and Château de Versailles. Best of all, pass-holders bypass *looong* ticket queues at major attractions. Buy it online, at participating museums, tourist desks at airports, Fnac outlets and major metro stations.
- Most Paris museums are closed on Mondays, but some, including the Louvre and Centre Pompidou, are closed on Tuesdays instead.
- The following are free the first Sunday of the month from November to March: Arc de Triomphe, Conciergerie, Panthéon, Musée du Louvre and the Tours de Notre Dame.

Les Catacombes Cemetery

(Map p176; www.catacombes.paris.fr; 1 av Colonel Henri Roi-Tanguy, 14e; adult/child €8/free; ⌚10am-8pm Tue-Sun (last admission 7pm); Ⓜ Denfert Rochereau) Paris' most macabre sight is its underground tunnels lined with

Greater Paris

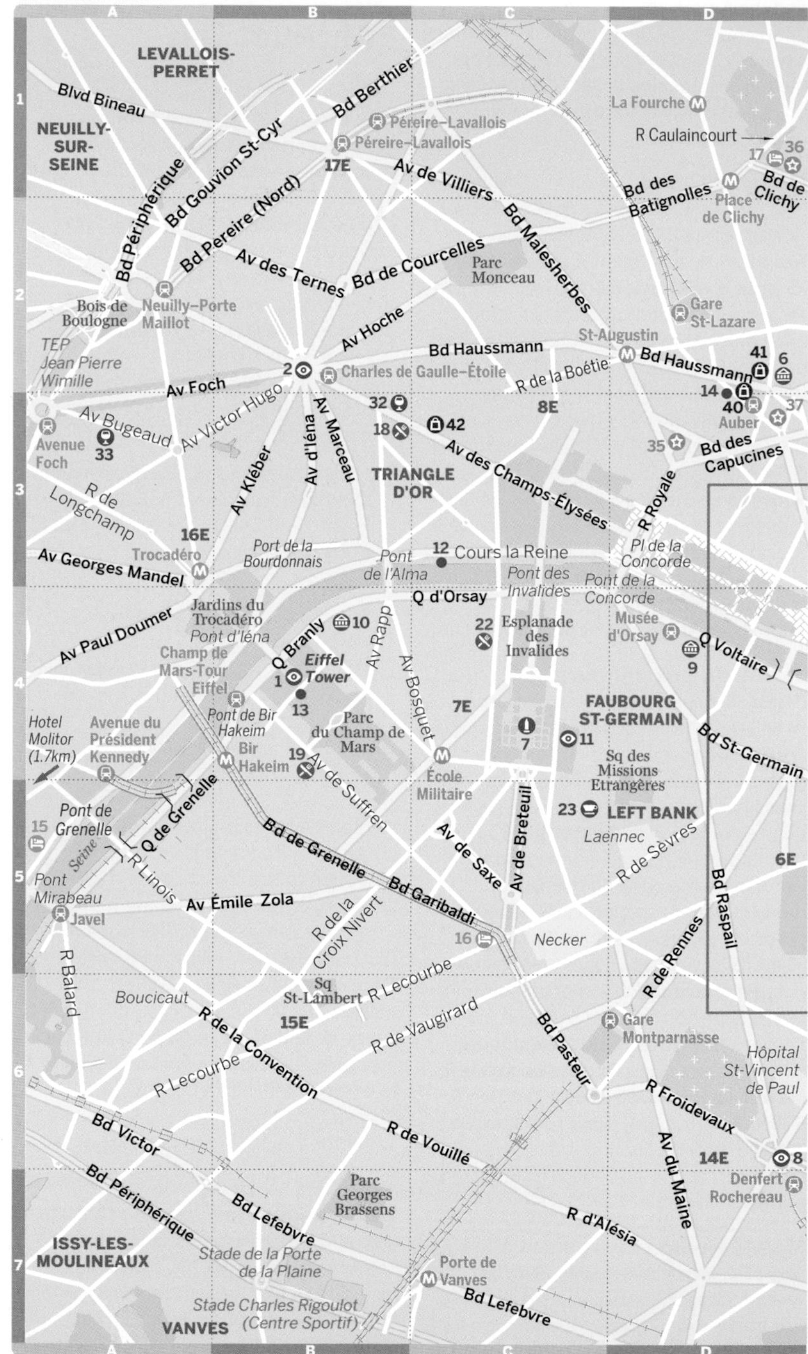
LEVALLOIS-PERRET
NEUILLY-SUR-SEINE
Blvd Bineau
Bd Berthier
Bd Gouvion St-Cyr
Bd Périphérique
Bd Pereire (Nord)
Péreire–Lavallois
17E
Av de Villiers
Bd Malesherbes
La Fourche
R Caulaincourt
Bd des Batignolles
Place de Clichy
Bd de Clichy
Av des Ternes
Bd de Courcelles
Parc Monceau
Bois de Boulogne
Neuilly–Porte Maillot
Av Hoche
Gare St-Lazare
St-Augustin
Bd Haussmann
TEP Jean Pierre Wimille
Av Foch
Charles de Gaulle–Étoile
R de la Boétie
8E
Av Bugeaud
Av Victor Hugo
Avenue Foch
Av d'Iéna
Av Marceau
Auber
Bd des Capucines
Av des Champs-Élysées
Av Kléber
TRIANGLE D'OR
R de Longchamp
R Royale
16E
Trocadéro
Port de la Bourdonnais
Pont de l'Alma
Cours la Reine
Pl de la Concorde
Av Georges Mandel
Pont des Invalides
Pont de la Concorde
Q d'Orsay
Av Paul Doumer
Jardins du Trocadéro
Pont d'Iéna
Q Branly
Av Rapp
Esplanade des Invalides
Musée d'Orsay
Q Voltaire
Champ de Mars-Tour Eiffel
Eiffel Tower
Av Bosquet
7E
FAUBOURG ST-GERMAIN
Hotel Molitor (1.7km)
Avenue du Président Kennedy
Pont de Bir Hakeim
Bir Hakeim
Parc du Champ de Mars
Bd St-Germain
Av de Suffren
École Militaire
Sq des Missions Etrangères
Pont de Grenelle
Q de Grenelle
LEFT BANK
Laennec
Seine
R Linois
Bd de Grenelle
Av de Saxe
Av de Breteuil
R de Sèvres
6E
Pont Mirabeau
Javel
Av Émile Zola
Bd Garibaldi
R de la Croix Nivert
Bd Raspail
Necker
R de Rennes
R Balard
Boucicaut
Sq St-Lambert
R Lecourbe
15E
R de la Convention
R de Vaugirard
Gare Montparnasse
Bd Pasteur
Hôpital St-Vincent de Paul
R Froidevaux
Bd Victor
R de Vouillé
Av du Maine
14E
Denfert Rochereau
Bd Périphérique
Bd Lefebvre
Parc Georges Brassens
R d'Alésia
ISSY-LES-MOULINEAUX
Stade de la Porte de la Plaine
Porte de Vanves
Stade Charles Rigoulot (Centre Sportif)
VANVES

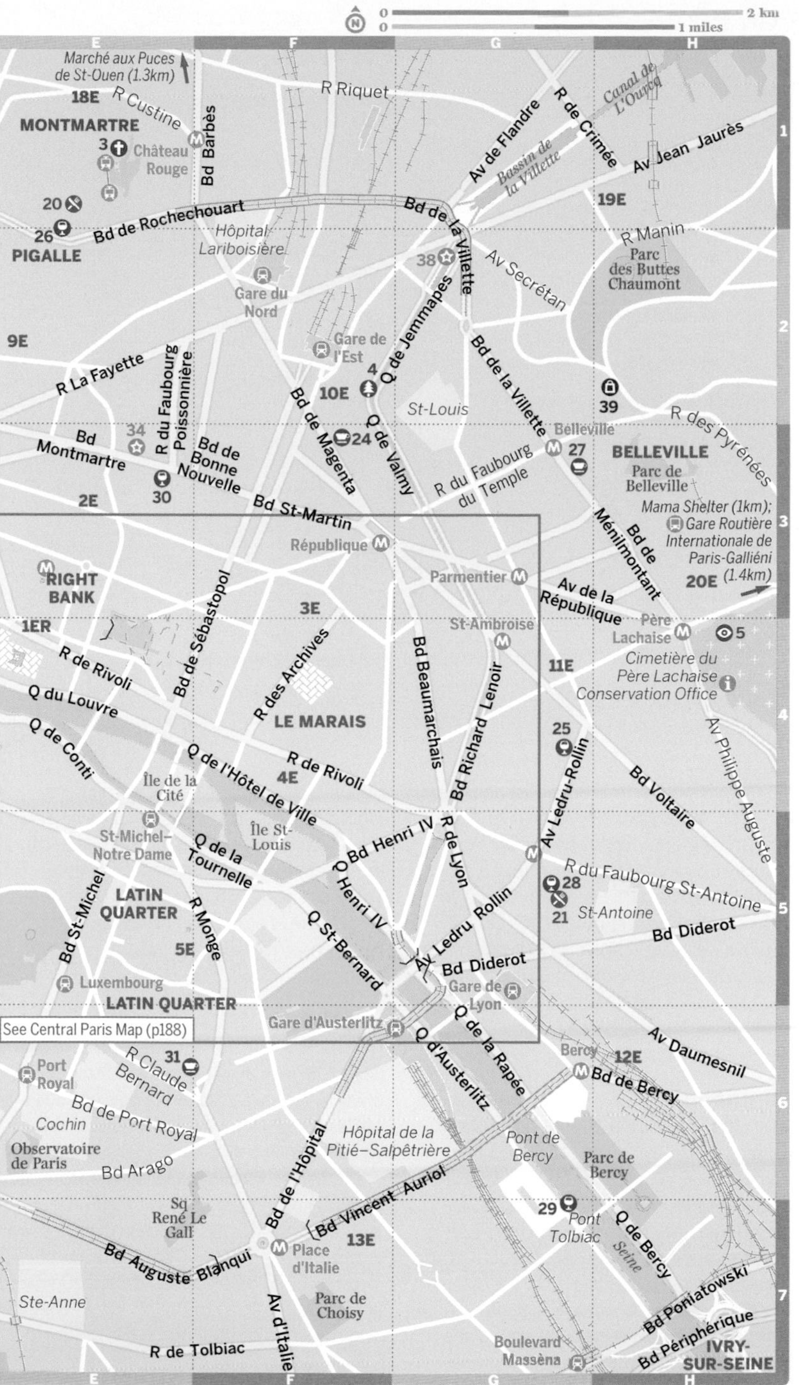

Marché aux Puces de St-Ouen (1.3km)
18E
MONTMARTRE
Château Rouge
PIGALLE
9E
2E
RIGHT BANK
1ER
R Custine
Bd Barbès
R Riquet
Bd de Rochechouart
Hôpital Lariboisière
Gare du Nord
Gare de l'Est
10E
R La Fayette
R du Faubourg Poissonnière
Bd Montmartre
Bd de Bonne Nouvelle
Bd St-Martin
Bd de Magenta
Q de Jemmapes
Q de Valmy
St-Louis
Av de Flandre
R de Crimée
Canal de L'Ourcq
Bassin de la Villette
Av Jean Jaurès
19E
Bd de la Villette
R Manin
Parc des Buttes Chaumont
Av Secrétan
R des Pyrénées
Belleville
BELLEVILLE
Parc de Belleville
R du Faubourg du Temple
Mama Shelter (1km); Gare Routière Internationale de Paris-Galliéni (1.4km)
20E
Bd de Ménilmontant
République
Parmentier
Av de la République
Père Lachaise
Cimetière du Père Lachaise
Conservation Office
3E
St-Ambroise
11E
R de Rivoli
Q du Louvre
Q de Conti
Bd de Sébastopol
R des Archives
LE MARAIS
Bd Beaumarchais
Bd Richard Lenoir
Av Philippe Auguste
4E
Île de la Cité
Q de l'Hôtel de Ville
Île St-Louis
Av Ledru-Rollin
Bd Voltaire
St-Michel–Notre Dame
Q de la Tournelle
Bd Henri IV
R de Lyon
R du Faubourg St-Antoine
LATIN QUARTER
Bd St-Michel
R Monge
Q Henri IV
Q St-Bernard
Av Ledru Rollin
St-Antoine
Bd Diderot
5E
Luxembourg
LATIN QUARTER
Gare de Lyon
See Central Paris Map (p188)
Gare d'Austerlitz
Q de la Rapée
Q d'Austerlitz
Av Daumesnil
Bercy
12E
Bd de Bercy
Port Royal
R Claude Bernard
Bd de Port Royal
Cochin
Observatoire de Paris
Bd Arago
Hôpital de la Pitié–Salpêtrière
Pont de Bercy
Parc de Bercy
Bd de l'Hôpital
Bd Vincent Auriol
Sq René Le Gall
Pont Tolbiac
Q de Bercy
Seine
Bd Auguste Blanqui
Place d'Italie
13E
Ste-Anne
Parc de Choisy
Av d'Italie
R de Tolbiac
Boulevard Massèna
Bd Poniatowski
Bd Périphérique
IVRY-SUR-SEINE
FRANCE

Greater Paris

Don't Miss Sights
1 Eiffel Tower B4

Sights
2 Arc de Triomphe B2
3 Basilique du Sacré-Cœur E1
4 Canal St-Martin F2
5 Cimetière du Père Lachaise H4
6 Galerie des Galeries D2
7 Hôtel des Invalides C4
8 Les Catacombes D6
9 Musée d'Orsay D4
10 Musée du Quai Branly B4
11 Musée Rodin C4
Palais Garnier .... (see 37)

Activities, Courses & Tours
12 Bateaux-Mouches C3
13 Fat Tire Bike Tours B4
14 L'Open Tour D2

Sleeping
15 Hôtel Félicien A5
16 Hôtel Vic Eiffel C5
17 Loft D1
Sublim Eiffel .... (see 16)

Eating
18 Ladurée B3
19 Le Casse Noix B4
20 Le Miroir E1
21 Marché d'Aligre G5
22 Restaurant David Toutain C4

Drinking & Nightlife
23 Coutume C5
24 Holybelly F3
25 La Fée Verte G4
26 La Fourmi E1
27 Le Barbouquin G3
28 Le Baron Rouge G5
29 Le Batofar G7
30 Le Rex Club E3
31 Le Verre à Pied E6
32 Queen B3
33 St James Paris A3

Entertainment
34 Au Limonaire E3
35 Kiosque Théâtre Madeleine D3
36 Moulin Rouge D1
37 Palais Garnier D3
Palais Garnier Box Office .... (see 37)
38 Point Éphémère G2

Shopping
39 Belleville Brûlerie H2
Galeries Lafayette .... (see 6)
40 Galeries Lafayette - Home Design D2
41 Galeries Lafayette - Men's Store D2
42 Guerlain C3

skulls and bones. In 1785 it was decided to rectify the hygiene problems of Paris' overflowing cemeteries by exhuming the bones and storing them in disused quarry tunnels; the Catacombes were created in 1810. After descending 20m (via 130 narrow, dizzying spiral steps) below street level, you follow the dark, subterranean passages to reach the ossuary itself (2km in all). Exit back up 83 steps onto rue Remy Dumoncel, 14e.

Panthéon — Mausoleum

(Map p188; www.monum.fr; place du Panthéon, 5e; adult/child €7.50/free; 10am-6.30pm Apr-Sep, to 6pm Oct-Mar; M Maubert-Mutualité, Cardinal Lemoine or RER Luxembourg) Overlooking the city from its Left Bank perch, the Panthéon's stately neoclassical dome stands out as one of the most recognisable icons in the Parisian skyline. Originally a church and now a mausoleum, it has served since 1791 as the resting place of some of France's greatest thinkers, including Voltaire, Rousseau, Braille and Hugo. An architectural masterpiece, the interior is impressively vast (if slightly soulless) and certainly worth a wander. The dome is closed for renovations through 2015 (other structural work will continue through 2022).

Hôtel des Invalides — Monument, Museum

(Map p176; www.musee-armee.fr; 129 rue de Grenelle, 7e; adult/child €9.50/free; 7.30am-7pm daily, to 9pm Tue Apr-Sep, hours can vary; M Invalides) Fronted by the 500m-long Esplanade des Invalides lawns, the Hôtel des Invalides was built in the 1670s by Louis XIV to house 4000 *invalides* (disabled war veterans). On 14 July 1789, a mob broke into the building and seized 32,000 rifles before heading on to the prison at Bastille and the start of the French Revolution.

NEALE CLARK/GETTY IMAGES ©

Don't Miss
Cathédrale Notre Dame de Paris

Notre Dame, Paris' most visited unticketed site with upwards of 14 million visitors crossing its threshold a year, is a masterpiece of French Gothic architecture. It was the focus of Catholic Paris for seven centuries, its vast interior accommodating 6000-plus worshippers. Highlights include its three spectacular **rose windows**, **treasury**, and bell **towers** which can be climbed. From the North Tower, 400-odd steps spiral to the top of the western facade, where you'll find yourself face-to-face with frightening gargoyles and a spectacular view of Paris.

NEED TO KNOW

Map p188; ☎01 53 10 07 00; www.cathedraledeparis.com; 6 place du Parvis Notre Dame, 4e; cathedral free, towers adult/child €8.50/free, treasury €2/1; ⏱cathedral 7.45am-6.45pm Mon-Sat, to 7.15pm Sun, towers 10am-6.30pm, to 11pm Fri & Sat Jul & Aug; Ⓜ Cité

Admission includes entry to all Hôtel des Invalides sights. Hours for individual sites often vary – check the website for updates.

Église St-Sulpice — Church

(Map p188; http://pss75.fr/saint-sulpice-paris; place St-Sulpice, 6e; ⏱7.30am-7.30pm; Ⓜ St-Sulpice) In 1646 work started on the twin-towered Church of St Sulpicius, lined inside with 21 side chapels, and it took six architects 150 years to finish. What draws most visitors isn't its striking Italianate facade with two rows of superimposed columns, its Counter-Reformation-influenced neoclassical decor or even its frescoes by Eugène Delecroix but its setting for a murderous scene in Dan Brown's *The Da Vinci Code*. You can hear the monumental, 1781-built organ during 10.30am Mass on Sunday or the occasional Sunday-afternoon concert.

Notre Dame

TIMELINE

1160 Maurice de Sully becomes bishop of Paris. Mission: to grace growing Paris with a lofty new cathedral.

1182–90 The **choir with double ambulatory** ❶ is finished and work starts on the nave and side chapels.

1200–50 The **west façade** ❷, with rose window, three portals and two soaring towers, goes up. Everyone is stunned.

1345 Some 180 years after the foundation stone was laid, the Cathédrale de Notre Dame is complete. It is dedicated to notre dame (our lady), the Virgin Mary.

1789 Revolutionaries smash the original **Gallery of Kings** ❸, pillage the cathedral and melt all its bells except the great bell Emmanuel. The cathedral becomes a Temple of Reason then a warehouse.

1831 Victor Hugo's novel *The Hunchback of Notre Dame* inspires new interest in the half-ruined Gothic cathedral.

1845–50 Architect Viollet-le-Duc undertakes its restoration. Twenty-eight new kings are sculpted for the west façade. The heavily decorated **portals** ❹ and **spire** ❺ are reconstructed. The neo-Gothic **treasury** ❻ is built.

1860 The area in front of Notre Dame is cleared to create the parvis, an alfresco classroom where Parisians can learn a catechism illustrated on sculpted stone portals.

1935 A rooster bearing part of the relics of the Crown of Thorns, St Denis and St Geneviève is put on top of the cathedral spire to protect those who pray inside.

1991 The architectural masterpiece of Notre Dame and its Seine-side riverbanks become a Unesco World Heritage Site.

2013 Notre Dame celebrates 850 years since construction began with a bevy of new bells and restoration works.

Virgin & Child
Spot all 37 artworks representing the Virgin Mary. Pilgrims have revered the pearly-cream sculpture of her in the sanctuary since the 14th century. Light a devotional candle and write some words to the *Livre de Vie* (Book of Life).

North Rose Window
See prophets, judges, kings and priests venerate Mary in vivid blue and violet glass, one of three beautiful rose blooms (1225–70), each almost 10m in diameter.

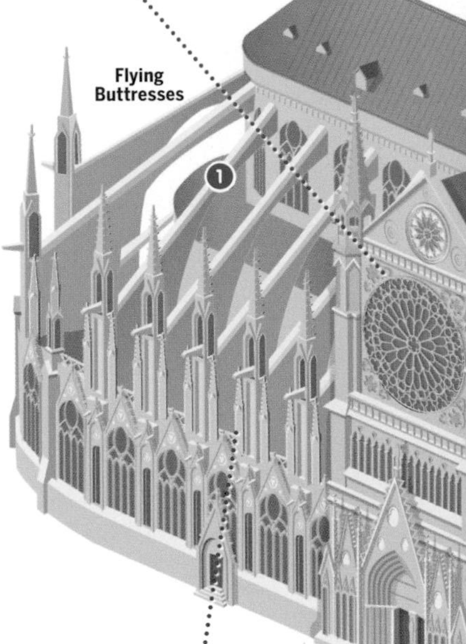

Choir Screen
No part of the cathedral weaves biblical tales more evocatively than these ornate wooden panels, carved in the 14th century after the Black Death killed half the country's population. The faintly gaudy colours were restored in the 1960s.

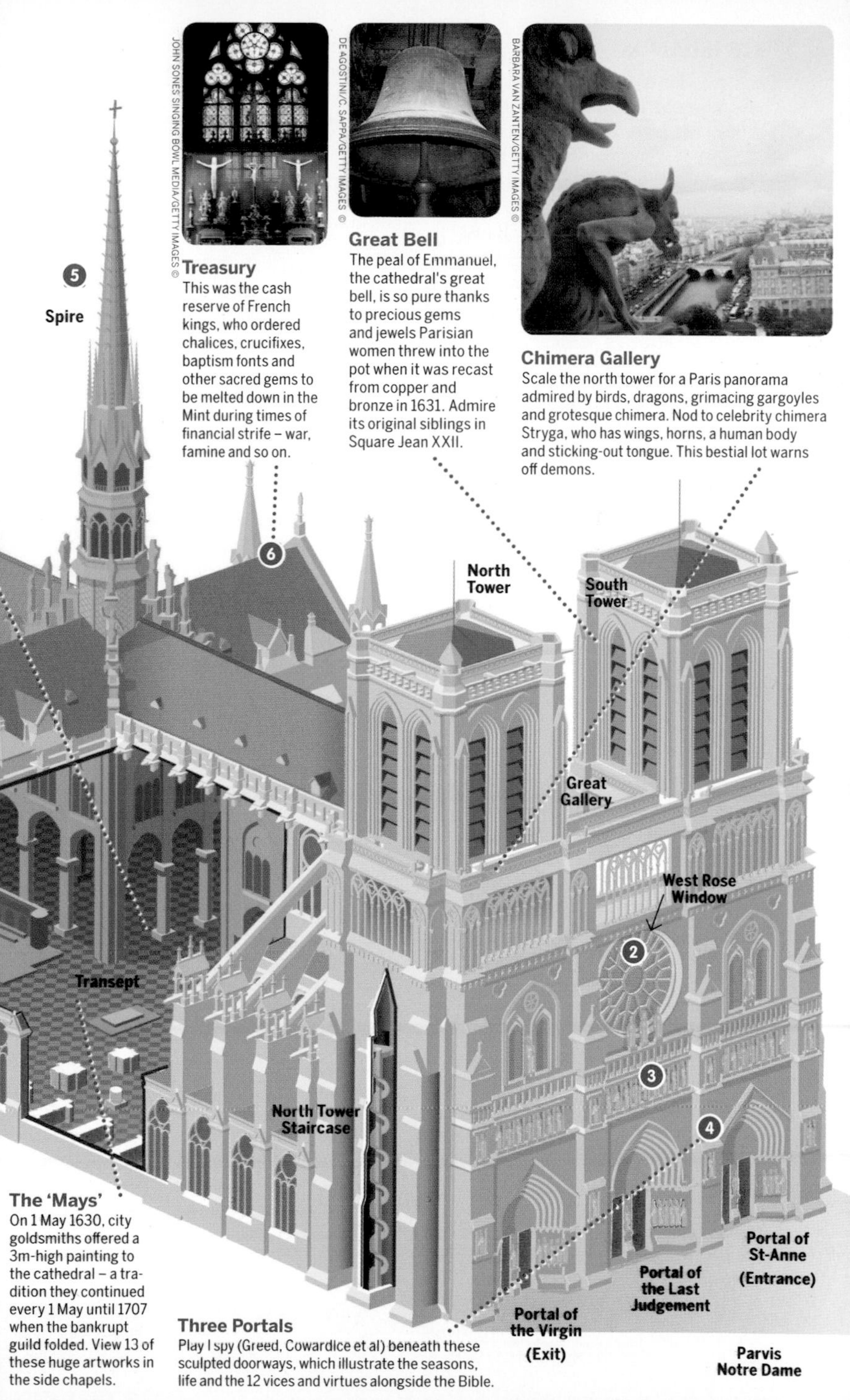
JOHN SONES SINGING BOWL MEDIA/GETTY IMAGES ©
DE AGOSTINI/C. SAPPA/GETTY IMAGES ©
BARBARA VAN ZANTEN/GETTY IMAGES ©
Treasury
This was the cash reserve of French kings, who ordered chalices, crucifixes, baptism fonts and other sacred gems to be melted down in the Mint during times of financial strife – war, famine and so on.
Great Bell
The peal of Emmanuel, the cathedral's great bell, is so pure thanks to precious gems and jewels Parisian women threw into the pot when it was recast from copper and bronze in 1631. Admire its original siblings in Square Jean XXII.
Chimera Gallery
Scale the north tower for a Paris panorama admired by birds, dragons, grimacing gargoyles and grotesque chimera. Nod to celebrity chimera Stryga, who has wings, horns, a human body and sticking-out tongue. This bestial lot warns off demons.
5
Spire
6
North Tower
South Tower
Great Gallery
West Rose Window
2
3
4
Transept
North Tower Staircase
The 'Mays'
On 1 May 1630, city goldsmiths offered a 3m-high painting to the cathedral – a tradition they continued every 1 May until 1707 when the bankrupt guild folded. View 13 of these huge artworks in the side chapels.
Three Portals
Play I spy (Greed, Cowardice et al) beneath these sculpted doorways, which illustrate the seasons, life and the 12 vices and virtues alongside the Bible.
Portal of the Virgin (Exit)
Portal of the Last Judgement
Portal of St-Anne (Entrance)
Parvis Notre Dame

THE ISLANDS

Paris' twin set of islands could not be more different. **Île de la Cité** is bigger, full of sights and very touristy (few people live here). The seven decorated arches of Paris' oldest bridge, **Pont Neuf**, have linked Île de la Cité with both banks of the River Seine since 1607. Smaller **Île St-Louis** is residential and quieter, with just enough boutiques and restaurants – and a legendary ice-cream maker – to attract visitors.

Conciergerie — Monument

(Map p188; www.monuments-nationaux.fr; 2 bd du Palais, 1er; adult/child €8.50/free, joint ticket with Sainte-Chapelle €12.50; ⌚9.30am-6pm; M Cité) A royal palace in the 14th century, the Conciergerie later became a prison. During the Reign of Terror (1793–94) alleged enemies of the Revolution were incarcerated here before being brought before the Revolutionary Tribunal next door in the **Palais de Justice**. Top-billing exhibitions take place in the beautiful, Rayonnant Gothic **Salle des Gens d'Armes**, Europe's largest surviving medieval hall.

RIGHT BANK

Musée du Louvre — Museum

(Map p188; ☎01 40 20 53 17; www.louvre.fr; rue de Rivoli & quai des Tuileries, 1er; admission/child €12/free; ⌚9am-6pm Mon, Thu, Sat & Sun, to 9.45pm Wed & Fri; M Palais Royal–Musée du Louvre) Few art galleries are as prized or daunting as the Musée du Louvre, Paris' pièce de résistance no first-time visitor to the city can resist. This is, after all, one of the world's largest and most diverse museums. Showcase to 35,000 works of art – from Mesopotamian, Egyptian and Greek antiquities to masterpieces by artists such as da Vinci, Michelangelo and Rembrandt – it would take nine months to glance at every piece, rendering advance planning essential.

Arc de Triomphe — Landmark

(Map p176; www.monuments-nationaux.fr; place Charles de Gaulle, 8e; adult/child €9.50/free; ⌚10am-11pm Apr-Sep, to 10.30pm Oct-Mar; M Charles de Gaulle–Étoile) If anything rivals the Eiffel Tower as the symbol of Paris, it's this magnificent 1836 monument to Napoleon's 1805 victory at Austerlitz, which he commissioned the following year. The intricately sculpted triumphal arch stands sentinel in the centre of the Étoile ('star') roundabout. From the viewing platform on top of the arch (50m up via 284 steps and well worth the climb) you can see the dozen avenues.

Centre Pompidou — Museum

(Map p188; ☎01 44 78 12 33; www.centrepompidou.fr; place Georges Pompidou, 4e; museum, exhibitions & panorama adult/child €13/free; ⌚11am-9pm Wed-Mon; M Rambuteau) The Pompidou Centre has amazed and delighted visitors ever since it opened in 1977, not just for its outstanding collection of modern art – the largest in Europe – but also for its radical architectural statement. The dynamic and vibrant arts centre delights with its irresistible cocktail of galleries and cutting-edge exhibitions, hands-on workshops, dance performances, cinemas and other entertainment venues. The exterior, with its street performers and fanciful fountains (place Igor Stravinsky), is a fun place to linger.

Basilique du Sacré-Cœur — Basilica

(Map p176; www.sacre-coeur-montmartre.com; place du Parvis du Sacré-Cœur; dome adult/child €6/4, cash only; ⌚6am-10.30pm, dome 9am-7pm Apr-Sep, to 5.30pm Oct-Mar; M Anvers) Although some may poke fun at Sacré-Cœur's unsubtle design, the view from its parvis is one of those perfect Paris postcards. More than just a basilica, Sacré-Cœur is a veritable experience, from the musicians performing on the steps and the groups of friends picnicking on the hillside park. Touristy, yes. But beneath it all, Sacré-Cœur's heart still shines gold.

Musée Picasso — Art Museum

(Map p188; ☎01 42 71 25 21; www.museepicassoparis.fr; 5 rue de Thorigny, 3e; admission €11; ⌚11.30am-6pm Tue-Fri, 9.30am-6pm Sat & Sun ; M St-Paul or Chemin Vert) One of Paris' most beloved art collections reopened its doors after a massive renovation and much controversy in late 2014. Housed in the stunning, mid-17th-century Hôtel Salé, the Musée Picasso woos art lovers with 5000

NEALE CLARK/GETTY IMAGES ©

Don't Miss
Eiffel Tower

No one could imagine Paris today without it, but Gustave Eiffel only constructed this elegant, 320m-tall signature spire as a temporary exhibit for the 1889 World Fair. Luckily, the art nouveau tower's popularity assured its survival. Prebook tickets online to avoid long ticket queues.

Lifts ascend to the tower's three levels; change lifts on the 2nd level for the final ascent to the top. Energetic visitors can walk as far as the 2nd level using the south pillar's 704-step stairs.

NEED TO KNOW

Map p176; ☎08 92 70 12 39; www.tour-eiffel.fr; Champ de Mars, 5 av Anatole France, 7e; lift to top adult/child €15/10.50, lift to 2nd fl €9/4.50, stairs to 2nd fl €5/3, lift 2nd fl to top €6; ⏰lifts & stairs 9am-midnight mid-Jun–Aug, lifts 9.30am-11pm, stairs 9.30am-6.30pm Sep–mid-Jun; Ⓜ Bir Hakeim or RER Champ de Mars-Tour Eiffel

drawings, engravings, paintings, ceramic works and sculptures by the *grand maître* (great master) Pablo Picasso (1881–1973). The extraordinary collection was donated to the French government by the artist's heirs in lieu of paying inheritance tax.

Place des Vosges Square

(Map p188; place des Vosges, 4e; Ⓜ St-Paul or Bastille) Inaugurated in 1612 as place Royale and thus Paris' oldest square, place des Vosges is a strikingly elegant ensemble of 36 symmetrical houses with ground-floor arcades, steep slate roofs and large dormer windows arranged around a leafy square with four symmetrical fountains and an 1829 copy of a mounted statue of Louis XIII. The square received its present name in 1800 to honour the Vosges *département* (administrative division) for being the first in France to pay its taxes.

The Louvre

A HALF-DAY TOUR

Successfully visiting the Louvre is a fine art. Its complex labyrinth of galleries and staircases spiralling three wings and four floors renders discovery a snakes-and-ladders experience. Initiate yourself with this three-hour itinerary – a playful mix of Mona Lisa obvious and up-to-the-minute unexpected.

Arriving by the stunning main entrance, pick up colour-coded floor plans at the lower-ground-floor **information desk** ❶ beneath IM Pei's glass pyramid, ride the escalator up to the Sully Wing and swap passport for multimedia guide (there are limited descriptions in the galleries) at the wing entrance.

The Louvre is as much about spectacular architecture as masterly art. To appreciate this zip up and down Sully's Escalier Henri II to admire **Venus de Milo** ❷, then up parallel Escalier Henri IV to the palatial displays in **Cour Khorsabad** ❸. Cross room 1 to find the escalator up to the 1st floor and staircase-as-art **L'Esprit d'Escalier** ❹. Next traverse 25 consecutive galleries (thank you, floor plan!) to flip conventional contemplation on its head with Cy Twombly's **The Ceiling** ❺, and the hypnotic **Winged Victory of Samothrace sculpture** ❻ – just two rooms away – which brazenly insists on being admired from all angles. End with the impossibly famous **The Raft of Medusa** ❼, **Mona Lisa** ❽ and **Virgin & Child** ❾.

TOP TIPS

➡ **Floor Plans** Don't even consider entering the Louvre's maze of galleries without a Plan/Information Louvre brochure, free from the information desk in the Hall Napoléon

➡ **Crowd dodgers** The Denon Wing is always packed; visit on late nights Wednesday or Friday or trade Denon in for the notably quieter Richelieu Wing

➡ **2nd floor** Not for first-timers: save its more specialist works for subsequent visits

MISSION MONA LISA

If you just want to venerate the Louvre's most famous lady, use the Porte des Lions entrance (closed Tuesday and Friday), from where it's a five-minute walk. Go up one flight of stairs and through rooms 26, 14 and 13 to the Grande Galerie and adjoining room 6.

L'Esprit d'Escalier
Escalier Lefuel, Richelieu
Discover the 'Spirit of the Staircase' through François Morellet's contemporary stained glass, which casts new light on old stone. **DETOUR»** Napoleon III's gorgeous gilt apartments.

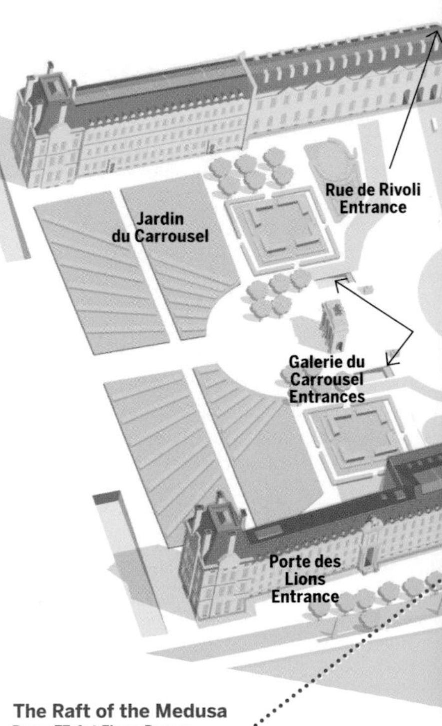

The Raft of the Medusa
Room 77, 1st Floor, Denon
Decipher the politics behind French romanticism in Théodore Géricault's *Raft of the Medusa*.

DEA/G.DAGLI ORTI/GETTY IMAGES ©

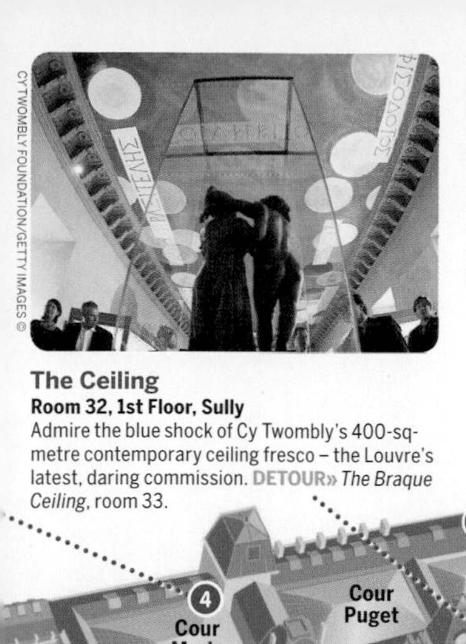

CY TWOMBLY FOUNDATION/GETTY IMAGES ©

The Ceiling

Room 32, 1st Floor, Sully

Admire the blue shock of Cy Twombly's 400-sq-metre contemporary ceiling fresco – the Louvre's latest, daring commission. **DETOUR»** *The Braque Ceiling*, room 33.

Cour Khorsabad

Ground Floor, Richelieu

Time travel with a pair of winged human-headed bulls to view some of the world's oldest Mesopotamian art. **DETOUR»** Night-lit statues in Cour Puget.

JOHN SONES SINGING BOWL MEDIA/ GETTY IMAGES ©

Venus de Milo

Room 16, Ground Floor, Sully

No one knows who sculpted this seductively realistic goddess from Greek antiquity. Naked to the hips, she is a Hellenistic masterpiece.

Mona Lisa

Room 6, 1st Floor, Denon

No smile is as enigmatic or bewitching as hers. Da Vinci's diminutive *La Joconde* hangs opposite the largest painting in the Louvre – sumptuous, fellow Italian Renaissance artwork *The Wedding at Cana*.

Virgin & Child

Room 5, Grande Galerie, 1st Floor, Denon

In the spirit of artistic devotion save the Louvre's most famous gallery for last: a feast of Virgin-and-child paintings by Raphael, Domenico Ghirlandaio, Giovanni Bellini and Francesco Botticini.

MITCH DIAMOND/GETTY IMAGES ©

Winged Victory of Samothrace

Escalier Daru, 1st Floor, Sully

Draw breath at the aggressive dynamism of this headless, handless Hellenistic goddess. **DETOUR»** The razzle-dazzle of the Apollo Gallery's crown jewels.

Canal St-Martin Park

(Map p176; M République, Jaurès or Jacques Bonsergent) The tranquil, 4.5km-long Canal St-Martin was inaugurated in 1825 to provide a shipping link between the Seine and the northeastern Parisian suburbs. Emerging from below ground near place République, its shaded towpaths take you past locks, metal bridges and ordinary Parisian neighbourhoods. It's a great place for a romantic stroll or cycle.

Note that some of the neighbourhood bistros here are closed or have limited hours on Sunday and Monday.

Cimetière du Père Lachaise Cemetery

(Map p176; ☎01 43 70 70 33; www.pere-lachaise.com; 16 rue du Repos & bd de Ménilmontant, 20e; ⏰8am-6pm Mon-Fri, 8.30am-6pm Sat, 9am-6pm Sun; M Père Lachaise or Gambetta) FREE The world's most visited cemetery, Père Lachaise, opened in 1804, and today its 70,000 ornate, even ostentatious, tombs of the rich and/or famous form a verdant, 44-hectare sculpture garden.

The most visited are those of 1960s rock star Jim Morrison (division 6) and Oscar Wilde (division 89). Pick up cemetery maps at the **conservation office** **(Map p176; 16 rue du Repos, 20e; ⏰8.30am-12.30pm & 2-5pm Mon-Fri; M Père Lachaise)**; near the main bd de Ménilmontant entrance.

Musée Carnavalet Museum

(Map p188; www.carnavalet.paris.fr; 23 rue de Sévigné, 3e; ⏰10am-6pm Tue-Sun; M St-Paul, Chemin Vert or Rambuteau) FREE This engaging history museum, spanning Gallo-Roman times to modern day, is in two *hôtels particuliers:* mid-16th-century Renaissance-style Hôtel Carnavalet and late-17th-century Hôtel Le Peletier de St-Fargeau. Some of the nation's most important documents, paintings and other objects from the French Revolution are here.

Don't miss Georges Fouquet's stunning art nouveau jewellery shop

Left: Cathédrale Notre Dame de Paris (p179); **Below:** Cruise boat on the River Seine, Paris

(LEFT) AUSTROPHOTO AUSTROPHOTO/GETTY IMAGES ©; (BELOW) RICHARD I'ANSON/GETTY IMAGES ©

from rue Royale, and Marcel Proust's cork-lined bedroom from his bd Haussmann apartment where he wrote his 7350-page literary cycle *À la Recherche du Temps Perdu* (Remembrance of Things Past).

Palais Garnier Opera House

(Map p176; ☎08 25 05 44 05; www.operade-paris.fr; cnr rues Scribe & Auber, 9e; unguided tour adult/child €10/6, guided tour adult/child €14/12.50; ⌚unguided tour 10am-5pm, to 1pm on matinee performance days, guided tour by reservation; M Opéra) The fabled 'phantom of the opera' lurked in this opulent opera house designed in 1860 by Charles Garnier (then an unknown 35-year-old architect). You can reserve a spot on an English-language guided tour or take an unguided tour of the attached museum, with posters, costumes, backdrops, original scores and other memorabilia, which includes a behind-the scenes peek (except during matinees and rehearsals).

Highlights include the Grand Staircase and horseshoe-shaped, gilded auditorium with red velvet seats, a massive chandelier and Chagall's gorgeous ceiling mural.

Place de la Bastille Square

(Map p188; M Bastille) The Bastille, a 14th-century fortress built to protect the city gates, is the most famous monument in Paris that no longer exists. Nothing remains of the prison it became under Cardinal Richelieu, which was mobbed on 14 July 1789, igniting the French Revolution, but you can't miss the 52m-high green-bronze column topped by a gilded, winged Liberty. Revolutionaries from the uprising of 1830 are buried beneath. Now a frantically busy roundabout, it's still Paris' most symbolic destination for political protests.

Central Paris

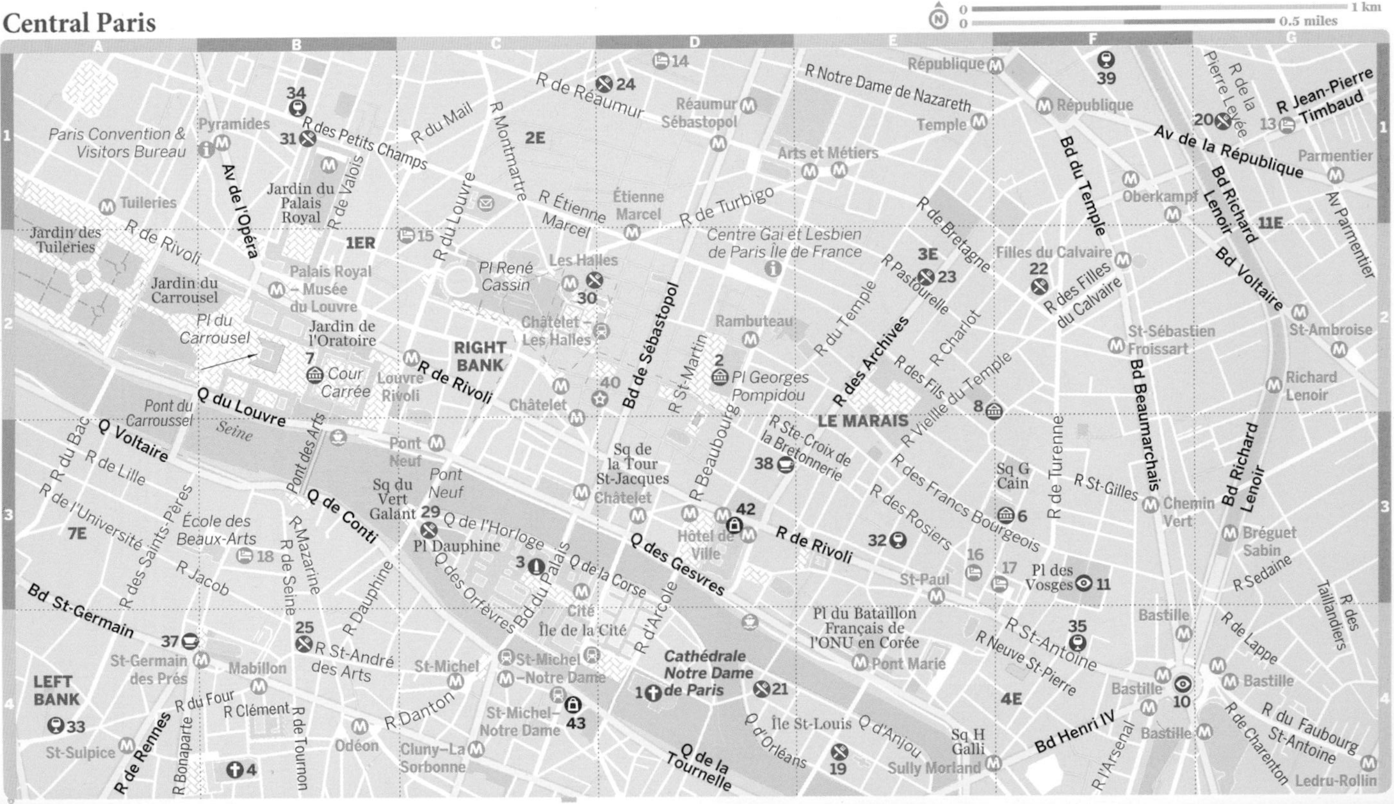

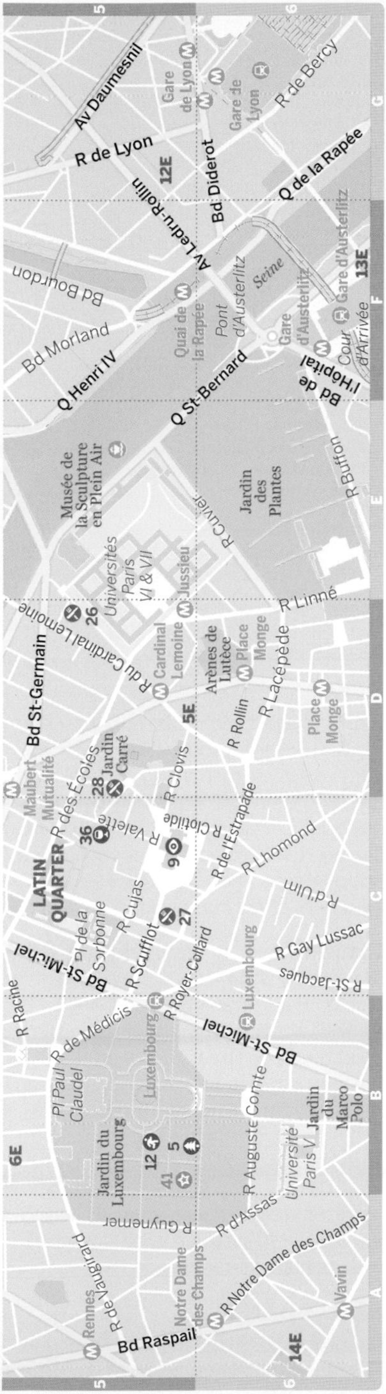

 Tours

Bateaux-Mouches Boat Tour
(Map p176; ☎01 42 25 96 10; www.bateaux-mouches.com; Port de la Conférence, 8e; adult/child €13.50/5.50; ⏲Apr-Dec; Ⓜ Alma Marceau) The largest river cruise company in Paris and a favourite with tour groups. Cruises (70 minutes) run regularly from 10.15am to 11pm April to September and 13 times a day between 11am and 9pm the rest of the year. Commentary is in French and English. It's located on the Right Bank, just east of the Pont de l'Alma.

L'Open Tour Bus Tour
(Map p176; www.parisopentour.com; one-day pass adult/child €31/16) Hop-on hop-off bus tours aboard open-deck buses with four different circuits and 50 stops to jump on/off at – tops for a whirlwind city tour.

Paris Walks Walking Tour
(☎01 48 09 21 40; www.paris-walks.com; adult/child €12/8) Long established and highly rated by our readers, Paris Walks offers two-hour thematic walking tours (art, fashion, chocolate, the French Revolution etc).

Fat Tire Bike Tours Cycling Tour
(Map p176; ☎01 56 58 10 54; www.fattirebike-tours.com) Day and night bike tours of the city, both in central Pais and further afield to Versailles and Monet's garden in Giverny.

 Sleeping

The Paris Convention & Visitors Bureau (p206) can find you a place to stay (no booking fee, but you need a credit card), though queues can be long in high season; it also has information on bed-and-breakfast accommodation.

If you plan to stay a few nights, a great option is to rent a furnished apartment. **Paris Attitude (www.parisattitude.com)** has excellent listings.

LEFT BANK

The 15e offers particularly good value accommodation – being relatively close

Central Paris

to Mme Eiffel, yet affordable. The Latin Quarter is good for mid-range whilst St-Germain-des-Prés comes up trumps for top end charmers.

Hôtel Vic Eiffel Boutique Hotel **€**
(Map p176; www.hotelviceiffel.com; 92 bd Garibaldi, 15e; s/d from €99/109; ; M Sèvres-Lecourbe) Outstanding value for money, this pristine hotel with chic orange and oyster-grey rooms (two are wheelchair accessible) is a short walk from the Eiffel Tower, with the metro on the doorstep. Budget-priced Classic rooms are small but perfectly functional; midrange Superior and Privilege rooms offer increased space. Friendly staff go out of their way to help.

Sublim Eiffel Design Hotel **€€**
(Map p176; 01 40 65 95 95; www.sublimeiffel.com; 94 bd Garibaldi, 15e; d from €140; ; M Sèvres-Lecourbe) There's no forgetting what city you're in with the Eiffel Tower motifs in reception and rooms (along with Parisian street-map carpets and metro-tunnel-shaped bedheads) plus glittering tower views from upper-floor windows. Edgy design elements also include cobblestone staircase carpeting (there's also a lift/elevator) and, fittingly in *la ville lumière*, technicoloured in-room fibre optic lighting. The small wellness centre/hammam offers massages.

L'Hôtel Boutique Hotel **€€€**
(Map p188; 01 44 41 99 00; www.l-hotel.com; 13 rue des Beaux Arts, 6e; d €275-495; ; M St-Germain des Prés) In a quiet quayside street, this award-winning hostelry is the stuff of romance, Parisian myths and urban legends. Rock- and film-star patrons fight to sleep in room 16, where Oscar Wilde died in 1900 and which is now decorated with a peacock motif, or in the art deco room 36 (which entertainer Mistinguett once stayed in), with its huge mirrored bed.

RIGHT BANK

Popular areas on the Right Bank incude Le Marais and Bastille for their buzzing nightlife. Also high on many people's list is Montmartre for its bohemian village feel.

Mama Shelter Design Hotel €

(☎01 43 48 48 48; www.mamashelter.com; 109 rue de Bagnolet, 20e; s/d from €79/89; ❄@📶; 🚌76, Ⓜ Alexandre Dumas or Gambetta) Coaxed into its zany new incarnation by uberdesigner Philippe Starck, this former car park offers what is surely the best-value accommodation in the city. Its 170 super-comfortable rooms feature iMacs, trademark Starck details like a chocolate-and-fuchsia colour scheme, concrete walls and even microwave ovens, while a rooftop terrace and cool pizzeria add to the hotel's street cred.

Cosmos Hôtel Hotel €

(Map p188; ☎01 43 57 25 88; www.cosmos-hotel-paris.com; 35 rue Jean-Pierre Timbaud, 11e; s €62-75, d €68-75, tr/q €85/94; 📶; Ⓜ République) Cheap, brilliant value and just footsteps from the nightlife of rue JPT, Cosmos is a shiny star with retro style on the budget-hotel scene. It has been around for 30-odd years but, unlike most other hotels in the same price bracket, Cosmos has been treated to a thoroughly modern makeover this century. Breakfast €8.

Hôtel Félicien Boutique Hotel €€

(Map p176; ☎01 83 76 02 45; www.hotelfelicien-paris.com; 21 rue Félicien David, 16e; d €120-280; ❄@📶🏊; Ⓜ Mirabeau) The price–quality ratio at this chic boutique hotel, squirrelled away in a 1930s building, is outstanding. Exquisitely designed rooms feel more five-star than four, with 'White' and 'Silver' suites on the hotel's top 'Sky floor' more than satisfying their promise of indulgent cocooning. Romantics, eat your heart out.

Loft Apartment €€

(Map p176; ☎06 14 48 47 48; www.loft-paris.fr; 7 cité Véron,18e; apt €100-270; 📶; Ⓜ Blanche) Book months in advance to secure one of the stylish apartments in this gem, which offers an intimacy that simply cannot be replicated in a hotel. Just around the corner from the Moulin Rouge, this apartment block offers choices ranging from a two-person studio to a loft that can fit a large family or group. The owner, a culture journalist, is a great resource.

Hôtel Jeanne d'Arc Hotel €€

(Map p188; ☎01 48 87 62 11; www.hoteljeannedarc.com; 3 rue de Jarente, 4e; s €72, d €98-120,

Palais Garnier (p187), Paris

JULIAN ELLIOTT PHOTOGRAPHY/GETTY IMAGES ©

q €250; ; M St-Paul) About the only thing wrong with this gorgeous address is everyone knows about it; book well in advance. Games to play, a painted rocking chair for tots in the bijou lounge, knick knacks everywhere and the most extraordinary mirror in the breakfast room create a real 'family home' air in this 35-room house.

Hôtel Emile Design Hotel **€€**
(Map p188; ☎01 42 72 76 17; www.hotelemile.com; 2 rue Malher, 4e; s €170, d €180-230, ste €350; ; M St-Paul) Prepare to be dazzled – literally. Retro B&W, geometrically patterned carpets, curtains, wallpapers and drapes dress this chic hotel, wedged between boutiques and restaurants in the Marais. Pricier 'top floor' doubles are just that, complete with breathtaking outlook over Parisian roofs and chimney pots. Breakfast, included in the price, is on bar stools in the lobby; open the cupboard to find the 'kitchen'.

Edgar Boutique Hotel **€€**
(Map p188; ☎01 40 41 05 19; www.edgarparis.com; 31 rue d'Alexandrie, 2e; d €235-295; ; M Strasbourg St-Denis) Twelve playful rooms, each decorated by a different team of artists or designers, await the lucky few who secure a reservation at this former convent/seamstress workshop. Milagros conjures up all the magic of the Far West, while Dream echoes the rich imagination of childhood with surrealist installations. Breakfast is served in the popular downstairs restaurant, and the hidden tree-shaded square is a fabulous location.

Hôtel Molitor Boutique Hotel **€€€**
(☎01 56 07 08 50; www.mltr.fr; 2 av de la porte Molitor, 16e; d from €270; ; M Michel Ange Molitor) Famed as Paris' swishest swimming pool in the 1930s (where the bikini made its first appearance, no less) and hot spot for graffiti art in the 1990s, the Molitor is one seriously mythical address. The art deco complex, built in 1929 and abandoned from 1989, has been restored to stunning effect.

Hôtel Crayon Boutique Hotel **€€€**
(Map p188; ☎01 42 36 54 19; www.hotelcrayon.com; 25 rue du Bouloi, 1er; s/d €311/347; ; M Les Halles or Sentier) Line drawings by French artist Julie Gauthron bedeck walls and doors at this creative boutique hotel. The pencil *(le crayon)* is the theme, with 26 rooms sporting a different shade of each floor's chosen colour – we love the coloured-glass shower doors and the books on the bedside table guests can swap and take home. Online deals often slash rates by over 50%.

Buskers in the Latin Quarter, Paris

Eating

LEFT BANK

Rue Mouffetard in the Latin Quarter is famed for its food market and food shops; while its side streets, especially pedestrianised rue du Pot au Fer, cook up fine budget dining.

JSFP Traiteur Delicatessen €
(Map p188; http://jsfp-traiteur.com; 8 rue de Buci, 6e; dishes €3.40-5.70; 9.30am-8.30pm; ; M Mabillon) Brimming with big bowls of salad, terrines, pâté and other prepared delicacies, this deli is a brilliant bet for quality Parisian 'fast food' such as quiches in a variety of flavour combinations (courgette and chive, mozzarella and basil, salmon and spinach...) to take to a nearby park, square or stretch of riverfront.

Le Comptoir du Panthéon Cafe, Brasserie €
(Map p188; 01 43 54 75 56; 5 rue Soufflot, 5e; salads €11-13, mains €12.40-15.40; 7am-1.45am; ; M Cardinal Lemoine or RER Luxembourg) Enormous, creative meal-size salads are the reason to pick this as a dining spot. Magnificently placed across from the domed Panthéon on the shady side of the street, its pavement terrace is big, busy and oh so Parisian – turn your head away from Voltaire's burial place and the Eiffel Tower pops into view.

Le Casse Noix Modern French €€
(Map p176; 01 45 66 09 01; www.le-cassenoix.fr; 56 rue de la Fédération, 15e; 2-/3-course lunch menus €21/26, 3-course dinner menu €33; noon-2.30pm & 7-10.30pm Mon-Fri; M Bir Hakeim) Proving that a location footsteps from the Eiffel Tower doesn't mean compromising on quality, quantity or authenticity, 'the nutcracker' is a neighbourhood gem with a cosy retro interior, affordable prices and exceptional cuisine that changes by season and by the inspiration of owner/chef Pierre Olivier Lenormand, who has honed his skills in some of Paris' most fêted kitchens. Book ahead.

Top Three for Sweet Treats

The French have something of a sweet tooth – from breakfast viennoiseries, to fabulous desserts, crêpes and ice creams – sweets are part and parcel of the gastronomy. Here are our top Parisian picks for a treat:

Ladurée (Map p176; www.laduree.com; 75 av des Champs-Élysées, 8e; pastries from €1.50; 7.30am-11.30pm Mon-Fri, 8.30am-12.30am Sat, 8.30am-11.30pm Sun; M George V) Paris' most historic and decadent baker; inventor of the *macaron*.

Berthillon (Map p188; 31 rue St-Louis en l'Île, 4e; 2-/3-/4-ball cone or tub €2.50/5.50/7; 10am-8pm Wed-Sun; M Pont Marie) Berthillon is to ice cream what Château Lafite Rothschild is to wine: the Holy Grail. Seventy-odd flavours to choose from, including seasonal ones.

Dessance (Map p188; 01 42 77 23 62; www.dessance.fr; 74 rue des Archives, 3e; desserts à la carte €19, 4-course dessert menu €36-44; 3-11pm Wed-Fri, noon-midnight Sat & Sun; ; M Arts et Métiers) Incredible as it sounds, this restaurant only serves desserts – although some of the 'dishes' may surprise you.

Les Pipos Wine Bar €€
(Map p188; 01 43 54 11 40; www.les-pipos.com; 2 rue de l'École Polytechnique, 5e; mains €13.90-26.90; 8am-2am Mon-Sat; M Maubert-Mutualité) A feast for the eyes and the senses, this *bar à vins* is above all worth a visit for its food. The bistro standards (bœuf bourguignon) and *charcuteries de terroir* (regional cold meats and sausages) are mouth-watering, as is the cheese board, which includes all the gourmet names (bleu d'Auvergne, St-Félicien and St-Marcellin). No credit cards.

Right: Berthillon ice cream shop (p193), Paris;
Below: Breakfast outside the Café Saint Régis, Paris

L'AOC Traditional French **€€**
(Map p188; ☎01 43 54 22 52; www.restoaoc.com; 14 rue des Fossés St-Bernard, 5e; 2-/3-course lunch menus €21/29, mains €19-36; ⊙noon-2.30pm & 7.30-10.30pm Tue-Sat; Ⓜ Cardinal Lemoine) *'Bistrot carnivore'* is the strapline of this ingenious restaurant concocted around France's most respected culinary products. The concept is Appellation d'Origine Contrôlée (AOC), meaning everything has been reared or produced according to strict guidelines. The result? Only the best! Choose between meaty favourites (steak tartare) or the rotisserie menu, ranging from roast chicken to suckling pig.

Restaurant David Toutain Gastronomic **€€€**
(Map p176; ☎01 45 51 11 10; http://davidtoutain.com; 29 rue Surcouf, 7e; lunch menus €42, lunch & dinner menus €68-98; ⊙noon-2.30pm & 8-10pm Mon-Fri; Ⓜ Invalides) Prepare to be wowed: David Toutain pushes the envelope at his eponymous new restaurant with some of the most creative high-end cooking in Paris today. Mystery degustation courses include unlikely combinations such as smoked eel in green-apple and black-sesame mousse, or candied celery and truffled rice pudding with artichoke praline (stunning wine pairings available).

THE ISLANDS

Café Saint Régis Cafe **€**
(Map p188; http://cafesaintregisparis.com; 6 rue Jean du Bellay, 4e; salads & mains €14.50-28; ⊙7am-2am; 📶; Ⓜ Pont Marie) Hip and historical with an effortless dose of retro vintage thrown in, Le Saint Régis – as those in the know call it – is a deliciously Parisian hang-out any time of day. From pastries for breakfast to a mid-morning pancake, brasserie lunch or early-evening oyster platter, Café St-Regis gets it just right. Come midnight it morphs into a late-night hot spot.

Les Voyelles Modern French **€€**
(Map p188; ☎01 46 33 69 75; www.les-voyelles.com; 74 quai des Orfèvres, 4e; plat du jour €12, 2-/3-course menus €17/22.50; ⏰8am-midnight Tue-Sat; Ⓜ Pont Neuf) This new kid on the block is worth the short walk from Notre Dame. The Vowels – spot the letters casually scattered between books and beautiful objects on the shelves lining the intimate 'library' dining room – is thoroughly contemporary, with a menu ranging from finger food to full-blown dinner to match. Its pavement terrace is Paris gold.

RIGHT BANK

The Marais is one of Paris' premier dining neighbourhoods; book ahead for weekend dining. Montmartre is another hot spot, with plenty of funky neobistros and world cuisine – mind the tourist traps however.

Candelaria Mexican **€**
(Map p188; www.candelariaparis.com; 52 rue Saintonge; tacos €3.20-3.75, quesadillas & tostadas €3.50, lunch menu €11.50; ⏰noon-midnight Thu-Sat, to 11pm Sun-Wed; ❄; Ⓜ Filles du Calvaire) You need to know about this terribly cool *taqueria* to find it. Made of pure, unadulterated hipness in that brazenly nonchalant manner Paris does so well, clandestine Candelaria serves delicious homemade tacos, quesadillas and tostadas in a laidback setting – squat at the bar in the front or lounge out back around a shared table with bar stools or at low coffee tables.

Le Miroir Bistro **€€**
(Map p176; ☎01 46 06 50 73; http://restaurantmiroir.com; 94 rue des Martyrs, 18e; lunch menu €19.50, dinner menus €27-34; ⏰noon-2.30pm & 7.30-11pm Tue-Sat; Ⓜ Abbesses) This unassuming modern bistro is smack in the middle of the Montmartre tourist trail, yet it remains a local favourite. There are lots of delightful pâtés and rillettes to start off with – guinea hen with dates, duck with mushrooms, haddock and lemon – followed by well-prepared standards like stuffed veal shoulder.

Pirouette Neobistro €€

(Map p188; ☎01 40 26 47 81; 5 rue Mondétour, 1er; lunch menu €18, 3-/6-course dinner menu €40/60; ⏰noon-2.30pm & 7.30-10.30pm Mon-Sat; M Les Halles) In one of the best restaurants in the vicinity of the old 'belly of Paris', chef Tomy Gousset's kitchen crew is working wonders at this cool loft-like space, serving up tantalising creations that range from seared duck, asparagus and Buddha's hand fruit to rum baba with chantilly and lime. Some unique ingredients and a new spin for French cuisine.

Blue Valentine Modern French €€

(Map p188; ☎01 43 38 34 72; http://bluevalentine-restaurant.com; 13 rue de la Pierre Levée, 11e; 2-/3-course menu €29/36, 8-course tasting menu €54; ⏰noon-2.30pm & 7.30-11pm Wed-Sun, bar 7pm-2am; M République) This thoroughly modern bistro with retro decor in the increasingly gourmet 11e was a hit the moment it opened in late 2013. A hip crowd flocks here for well-crafted cocktails and Japanese chef Terumitsu Saito's exquisite dishes flavoured with edible flowers and a profusion of herbs. The menu is small – just three dishes to choose from per course – but memorable.

Frenchie Bistro €€€

(Map p188; ☎01 40 39 96 19; www.frenchie-restaurant.com; 5-6 rue du Nil, 2e; prix fixe menu €48; ⏰7-11pm Mon-Fri; M Sentier) Tucked down an alley you wouldn't venture down otherwise, this bijou bistro with wooden tables and old stone walls is iconic. Frenchie is always packed and for good reason: excellent-value dishes are modern, market-driven (the menu changes daily with a choice of two dishes) and prepared with just the right dose of unpretentious creative flair by French chef Gregory Marchand.

Verjus Modern American €€€

(Map p188; ☎01 42 97 54 40; www.verjusparis.com; 52 rue de Richelieu, 1er; prixe-fixe menu €60; ⏰7-10pm Mon-Fri; M Bourse or Palais Royal–Musée du Louvre) Opened by American duo Braden Perkins and Laura Adrian, Verjus was born out of a wildly successful clandestine supper club known as the Hidden Kitchen. The restaurant builds on that tradition, offering a chance to sample some excellent, creative cuisine (gnocchi with shiitake relish and parmesan, wild-boar confit with cherry compote) in a casual space. The tasting menu is a series

Cheese for sale at Rue Mouffetard market (p193), Paris

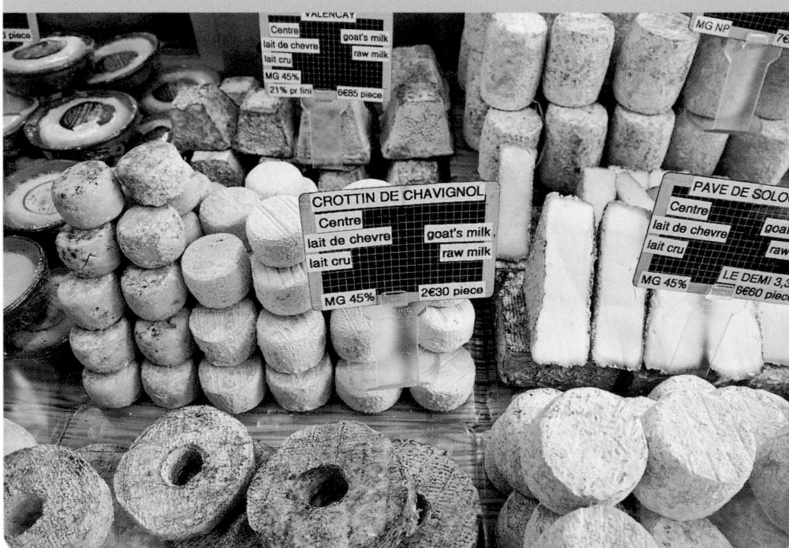

of small plates, using ingredients sourced straight from producers.

 Drinking & Nightlife

The line between bars, cafes and bistros is blurred at best. Sitting at a table costs more than standing at the counter, more on a fancy square than a backstreet, more in the 8e than in the 18e. After 10pm many cafes charge a pricier *tarif de nuit* (night rate).

LEFT BANK

Au Sauvignon Wine Bar

(Map p188; 80 rue des St-Pères, 7e; 8.30am-10pm Mon-Sat, to 9pm Sun; M Sèvres-Babylone) Grab a table in the evening sun at this wonderfully authentic *bar à vin* or head to the quintessential bistro interior, with an original zinc bar, tightly packed tables and hand-painted ceiling celebrating French viticultural tradition. A plate of *casse-croûtes au pain Poilâne* – toast with ham, pâté, terrine, smoked salmon and foie gras is the perfect accompaniment.

Le Batofar Club

(Map p176; www.batofar.org; opp 11 quai François Mauriac, 13e; bar 12.30pm-midnight Tue, to 6am Wed-Fri, 6pm-6am Sat; M Quai de la Gare or Bibliothèque) This much-loved, red-metal tugboat has a rooftop bar that's terrific in summer, and a respected restaurant, while the club underneath provides memorable underwater acoustics between its metal walls and portholes. Le Batofar is known for its edgy, experimental music policy and live performances, mostly electro-oriented but also incorporating hip-hop, new wave, rock, punk or jazz.

Le Verre à Pied Cafe

(Map p176; http://leverreapied.fr; 118bis rue Mouffetard, 5e; 9am-9pm Tue-Sat, 9.30am-4pm Sun; M Censier Daubenton) This *café-tabac* is a pearl of a place where little has changed since 1870. Its nicotine-hued mirrored wall, moulded cornices and original bar make it part of a dying breed, but the place oozes the charm, glamour and romance of an old Paris everyone loves, including stall holders from the rue Mouffetard market who yo-yo in and out.

Coffee Revolution

Bitter Parisian coffee is becoming a thing of the past: the city is in the throes of a coffee revolution, with local roasteries priming cafes citywide for outstanding brews made by professional baristas, often using cutting-edge extraction techniques. Caffeine fiends are now spoilt for choice and while there's still plenty of substandard coffee in Paris, you don't have to go far to avoid it. Leading the charge:

Belleville Brûlerie **(Map p176; 09 83 75 60 80; http://cafesbelleville.com; 10 rue Pradier, 19e; 300g packet €13-16; 11.30am-6.30pm Sat; M Belleville)** Groundbreaking roastery with Saturday morning tastings and cuppings.

Holybelly **(Map p176; http://holybel.ly; 19 Rue Lucien Sampaix, 10e; 9am-6pm Thu-Mon, from 10am Sat & Sun; M Jacques Bonsergent)** The flagbearer for Canal St-Martin's new crop of coffee specialists; distressed decor, a serious kitchen and a pinball machine.

Coutume **(Map p176; http://coutumecafe.com; 47 rue Babylone, 7e; 8am-7pm Mon-Fri, from 10am Sat & Sun; ; M St-François Xavier or Vaneau)** Artisan roasters of premium beans, with a fab flagship cafe.

Les Deux Magots Cafe

(Map p188; www.lesdeuxmagots.fr; 170 bd St-Germain, 6e; 7.30am-1am; M St-Germain des Prés) If ever there were a cafe that summed up St-Germain des Prés' early-20th-century literary scene, it's this former hangout of anyone who was anyone. You will spend *beaucoup* to sip a coffee in a wicker chair on the terrace shaded by dark-green awnings and geraniums spilling from window boxes, but it's an undeniable piece of Parisian history.

Le Pub St-Hilaire Pub

(Map p188; 2 rue Valette, 5e; ⏲3pm-2am Mon-Thu, 3pm-4am Fri, 4pm-4am Sat, 4pm-midnight Sun; Ⓜ Maubert-Mutualité) 'Buzzing' fails to do justice to the pulsating vibe inside this student-loved pub. Generous happy hours last several hours and the place is kept packed with a trio of pool tables, board games, music on two floors, hearty bar food and various gimmicks to rev up the party crowd (a metre of cocktails, 'be your own barman' etc).

RIGHT BANK

St James Paris Bar

(Map p176; ☎01 44 05 81 81; www.saint-james-paris.com; 43 rue Bugeaud, 16e; drinks €15-25, Sun brunch €65; ⏲7-11pm; 📶; Ⓜ Porte Dauphine) It might be a hotel bar, but a drink at St James might well be one of your most memorable in Paris. Tucked behind a stone wall, this historic mansion opens its bar each evening to non-guests – and the setting redefines extraordinary. Winter drinks are in the library, in summer they're in the impossibly romantic garden.

Le Barbouquin Cafe

(Map p176; www.lebarbouquin.fr; 3 rue Ramponeau, 20e; ⏲10.30am-6pm Tue-Sat; Ⓜ Belleville) There is no lovelier spot to relax in a vintage armchair over a cup of organic tea or freshly juiced carrot and apple cocktail after a hectic morning at Belleville market. Second-hand books – to be borrowed, exchanged or bought – line one wall and the twinset of pavement-terrace tables outside sit on magnificently graffitied rue Dénoyez. Breakfast and weekend brunch.

Le Baron Rouge Wine Bar

(Map p176; 1 rue Théophile Roussel, 12e; ⏲10am-2pm & 5-10pm Tue-Fri, 10am-10pm Sat, 10am-4pm Sun; Ⓜ Ledru-Rollin) Just about the ultimate Parisian wine-bar experience, this place has barrels stacked against the bottle-lined walls. As unpretentious as you'll find, it's a local meeting place where everyone is welcome and it's especially busy on Sunday after the **Marché d'Aligre (Map p176; http://marchedaligre.free.fr; rue d'Aligre, 12e; ⏲8am-1pm & 4-7.30pm Tue-Sat, 8am-1.30pm Sun; Ⓜ Ledru-Rollin)** wraps up. All the usual suspects – cheese, charcuterie and oysters – will keep your belly full.

Le Cap Horn Bar

(Map p188; 8 rue de Birague, 4e; ⏲10am-1am; Ⓜ St-Paul or Chemin Vert) On summer evenings the ambience at this laid-back, Chilean bar is electric. The crowd spills onto the pavement, parked cars doubling as table tops for well-shaken pina coladas, punch cocos and cocktails made with pisco, a fiery Chilean grape eau-de-vie. Find it steps from place des Vosges.

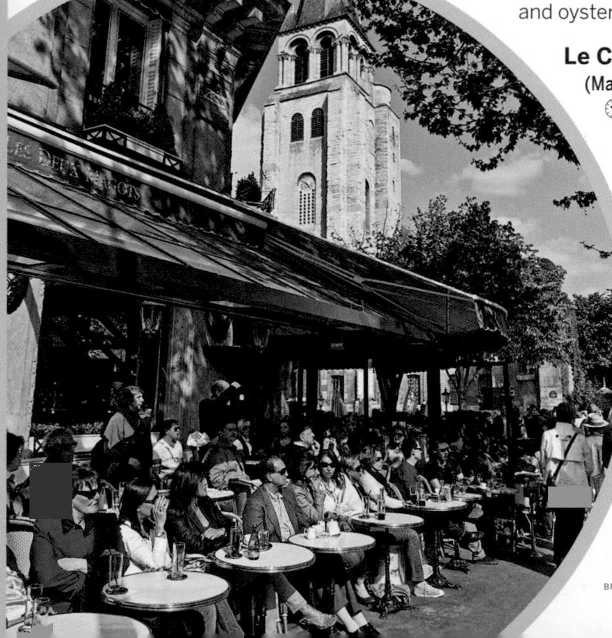

Les Deux Magots cafe (p197), Paris

La Fourmi Bar

(Map p176; 74 rue des Martyrs, 18e; ⏰8am-1am Mon-Thu, to 3am Fri & Sat, 10am-1am Sun; M Pigalle) A Pigalle institution, La Fourmi hits the mark with its high ceilings, long zinc bar and unpretentious vibe. Get up to speed on live music and club nights or sit down for a reasonably priced meal and drinks.

Le Rex Club Club

(Map p176; www.rexclub.com; 5 bd Poissonnière, 2e; ⏰midnight-7am Thu-Sat; M Bonne Nouvelle) Attached to the art-deco Grand Rex cinema, this is Paris' premier house and techno venue where some of the world's hottest DJs strut their stuff on a 70-speaker, multidiffusion sound system.

La Fée Verte Bar

(Map p176; 108 rue de la Roquette, 11e; ⏰8am-2am Mon-Sat, 9am-2am Sun; 📶; M Voltaire) You guessed it, the 'Green Fairy' specialises in absinthe (served traditionally with spoons and sugar cubes), but this fabulously old-fashioned neighbourhood cafe and bar also serves terrific food.

Entertainment

To find out what's on, buy *Pariscope* (€0.50) or *Officiel des Spectacles* (€0.50, www.offi.fr, in French) at Parisian news kiosks. The most comvenient place to buy concert, performance or event tickets is megastore **Fnac (www.fnacspectacles.com)**, which has numerous branches in town.

If you go on the day of a performance, you can snag a half-price ticket (plus €3 commission) for ballet, theatre, opera and other performances at the discount-ticket outlet **Kiosque Théâtre Madeleine (Map p176; opp 15 place de la Madeleine, 8e; ⏰12.30-8pm Tue-Sat, to 4pm Sun; M Madeleine)**.

Moulin Rouge Cabaret

(Map p176; ☎01 53 09 82 82; www.moulinrouge.fr; 82 bd de Clichy, 18e; M Blanche) Immortalised in the posters of Toulouse-Lautrec and later on screen by Baz Luhrmann, the Moulin Rouge twinkles beneath a 1925 replica of its original red windmill. Yes, it's rife with bus-tour crowds. But from the opening bars of music to the last high kick it's a whirl of fantastical costumes, sets, choreography and Champagne. Booking advised.

Gay & Lesbian Paris

The Marais (4e), especially the areas around the intersection of rue Ste-Croix de la Bretonnerie and rue des Archives, and eastwards to rue Vieille du Temple, has been Paris' main centre of gay nightlife for some three decades.

The single best source of info on gay and lesbian Paris is the **Centre Gai et Lesbien de Paris (CGL; Map p188; ☎01 43 57 21 47; www.centrelgbtparis.org; 63 rue Beaubourg, 3e; ⏰centre & bar 3.30-8pm Mon-Fri, 1-7pm Sat, library 6-8pm Mon-Wed, 3.30-6pm Fri, 5-7pm Sat; M Rambuteau or Arts et Métiers)**, with a large library and happening bar.

Our top choices include:

Open Café (Map p188; www.opencafe.fr; 17 rue des Archives, 4e; ⏰11am-2am; M Hôtel de Ville) The wide pavement terrace in the Marais is prime for people-watching.

Scream Club (Map p188; www.scream-paris.com; 18 rue du Faubourg du Temple, 11e; admission €15; ⏰midnight-7am Sat; M Belleville or Goncourt) Saturday night's the night at 'Paris' biggest gay party'.

3W Kafé (Map p188; 8 rue des Écouffes, 4e; ⏰8pm-3am Wed & Thu, to 5.30am Fri & Sat; M St-Paul) For women.

Queen (Map p176; ☎01 53 89 08 90; www.queen.fr; 102 av des Champs-Élysées, 8e; ⏰11.30pm-6.30am; M George V) Don't miss disco nights.

La Champmeslé (Map p188; www.lachampmesle.com; 4 rue Chabanais, 2e; ⏰4pm-dawn Mon-Sat; M Pyramides) Cabaret nights, fortune-telling and art exhibitions attract an older lesbian crowd.

Right: View of Paris from the Eiffel Tower;
Below: Croissants for sale
(RIGHT) BREMECR/GETTY IMAGES ©; (BELOW) DAMIEN POLEGATO/GETTY IMAGES ©

Au Limonaire Live Music

(Map p176; ☎01 45 23 33 33; http://limonaire.free.fr; 18 cité Bergère, 9e; ⌚6pm-2am Tue-Sat, from 7pm Sun & Mon; Ⓜ Grands Boulevards) This perfect little wine bar is one of the best places to listen to traditional French *chansons* and local singer-songwriters. Performances begin at 10pm Tuesday to Saturday and 7pm on Sunday. Entry is free; reservations are recommended if you plan on dining.

Palais Garnier Opera

(Map p176; ☎08 92 89 90 90; www.operadeparis.fr; place de l'Opéra, 9e; Ⓜ Opéra) The city's original opera house is smaller than its Bastille counterpart, but has perfect acoustics. Due to its odd shape, some seats have limited or no visibility – book carefully. Ticket prices and conditions (including last-minute discounts) are available from the **box office (Map p176; cnr rues Scribe & Auber; ⌚11am-6.30pm Mon-Sat)**.

Point Éphémère Live Music

(Map p176; www.pointephemere.org; 200 quai de Valmy, 10e; ⌚12.30pm-2am Mon-Sat, 12.30-11pm Sun; 📶; Ⓜ Louis Blanc) This arts and music venue by the Canal St-Martin attracts an underground crowd for drinks, meals, concerts, dance nights and even art exhibitions. At the time of writing there were three different food trucks setting up shop here three days a week after 7pm.

Le Baiser Salé Live Music

(Map p188; www.lebaisersale.com; 58 rue des Lombards, 1er; ⌚daily; Ⓜ Châtelet) Known for its Afro and Latin jazz, and jazz fusion concerts, the Salty Kiss combines big names and unknown artists. The place has a relaxed vibe, with sets usually starting at 7.30pm or 9.30pm.

Shopping

Key areas to mooch with no particular purchase in mind are the maze of back-street lanes in the Marais (3e and 4e), around St-Germain des Prés (6e), and parts of Montmartre and Pigalle (9e and 18e). There are also some particularly noteworthy flea markets.

Guerlain Perfume

(Map p176; ☎spa 01 45 62 11 21; www.guerlain.com; 68 av des Champs-Élysées, 8e; ⏰10.30am-8pm Mon-Sat, noon-7pm Sun; Ⓜ Franklin D Roosevelt) Guerlain is Paris' most famous parfumerie, and its shop (dating from 1912) is one of the most beautiful in the city. With its shimmering mirror and marble art-deco interior, it's a reminder of the former glory of the Champs-Élysées. For total indulgence, make an appointment at its decadent spa.

Paris Rendez-Vous Concept Store

(Map p188; 29 rue de Rivoli, 4e; ⏰10am-7pm Mon-Sat; Ⓜ Hôtel de Ville) Only the city of Paris could be so chic as to have its own designer line of souvenirs, sold in its own uber-cool concept store inside the Hôtel de Ville. Shop here for everything from clothing and homewares to Paris-themed books, toy sailing boats and signature Jardin du Luxembourg's Fermob chairs. *Quel style!*

Marché aux Puces de St-Ouen Market

(www.marcheauxpuces-saintouen.com; rue des Rosiers, av Michelet, rue Voltaire, rue Paul Bert & rue Jean-Henri Fabre; ⏰9am-6pm Sat, 10am-6pm Sun, 11am-5pm Mon; Ⓜ Porte de Clignancourt) This vast flea market, founded in the late 19th century and said to be Europe's largest, has more than 2500 stalls grouped into a dozen *marchés* (market areas), each with its own speciality (eg Paul Bert for 17th-century furniture, Malik for clothing, Biron for Asian art). There are miles upon miles of 'freelance' stalls; come prepared to spend some time.

Don't Miss
Versailles

Louis XIV transformed his father's hunting lodge into the monumental Château de Versailles in the mid-17th century, and it remains France's most famous, grandest palace. Versailles, 28km southwest of Paris, was the seat for the royal court from 1682 to 1789 when revolutionaries massacred the palace guard and dragged Louis XVI and Marie Antoinette back to Paris to be guillotined.

☎ 01 30 83 78 00

www.chateauversailles.fr

passport ticket incl estate-wide access adult/child €18/free, with musical events €25/free, palace €15/free

⏲ 9am-6.30pm Tue-Sat, to 6pm Sun Apr-Oct, to 5.30pm Tue-Sun Nov-Mar

M RER Versailles-Château–Rive Gauche

Highlights

Created by architect Louis Le Vau, painter and interior designer Charles Le Brun, and landscape artist André Le Nôtre, the chateau was designed as the last word in luxury. Among the most dazzling features are the **Galerie des Glaces** (Hall of Mirrors), a 75m-long ballroom lined with 17 huge mirrors, and the 17th-century **Bassin de Neptune** (Neptune's Fountain).

Versailles Tours

You can access off-limits areas of the chateau with a **guided tour** (**☎01 30 83 77 88; www.chateauversailles.fr; tours €7 plus palace admission; ⏰English-language tours Tue-Sun, tour times vary**) of the Private Apartments of Louis XV and Louis XVI and the Opera House or Royal Chapel. They can be prebooked online. If you're short on time, consider renting an **electric car, a boat or bicycle** (**☎01 39 66 97 66; per hr €32/15/ 6.50**) to get around the vast estate.

Dodging the Crowds

Pre-purchase your tickets on the chateau's website, or arrive as early as you can to avoid the midday queues. Steer clear of Tuesday and Sunday (which are the busiest days), and Monday (when the chateau is closed).

Local Knowledge

Versailles

RECOMMENDATIONS FROM SYLVAIN POSTOLLE, OFFICIAL GUIDE

1 KING'S PRIVATE APARTMENT

This is the most fascinating part of the palace as it shows the king as a man and very much reflects his daily life in the 18th century. Of the 10 or so rooms, the most famous is his bedroom where he not only slept but also held ceremonies. Up to 150 courtiers and people would watch him have supper here each evening!

2 KING LOUIS XIV'S LIBRARY

This is a lovely room – full of books, a place where you can really imagine the king coming to read for hours and hours. Louis XVI loved geography and his copy of *The Travels of James Cook* – in English – is still here.

3 HERCULES SALON

I love one particular perspective inside the palace: from the Hercules Salon you can see all the rooms comprising the King's State Apartment, and to the right, through the gallery leading to the opera house. The salon served as a passageway for the king to go from his state apartment to the chapel to celebrate daily Mass.

4 ROYAL CHAPEL

This is an exquisite example of the work of a very important architect of the time, Jules Hardouin-Mansart (1646–1708). The paintings are also stunning: they evoke the idea that the French king was chosen by God and was his lieutenant on earth. The chapel is where the future king Louis XVI wed Marie Antoinette in 1770.

5 ENCELADE GROVE

Versailles' gardens are extraordinary but my favourite spot has to be this grove, typical of the gardens created for Louis XIV by André Le Nôtre. A gallery of trellises surround a pool with a statue of Enceladus, chief of the Titans who was punished for his pride by the gods from Mount Olympus. The fountains are impressive.

PHOTO: LAURENT LOMBARDI

Versailles

A DAY IN COURT

Visiting Versailles – even just the State Apartments – may seem overwhelming at first, but think of it as a house where people ate, drank, worked, slept and conspired and you'll be on the right path.

Some two decades into his long reign, Louis XIV began turning his father's hunting lodge into a palace large enough to house his entire court (to keep closer tabs on the 6000-strong army of courtiers). Sparing no expense, the Sun King employed the greatest artists and craftspeople of the day and by 1682 he'd created the most extravagant dormitory in history.

The royal schedule was as accurate and predictable as a Swiss watch. By following this itinerary of rooms you can recreate the king's day, starting with the **King's Bedchamber** ❶ and the **Queen's Bedchamber** ❷, where the royal couple was roused at about the same time. The royal procession then leads through the **Hall of Mirrors** ❸ to the **Royal Chapel** ❹ for morning Mass and returns to the **Council Chamber** ❺ for late-morning meetings with ministers. After lunch the king might ride or hunt or visit the **King's Library** ❻. Later he could join courtesans for an 'apartment evening' starting from the **Hercules Drawing Room** ❼ or play billiards in the **Diana Drawing Room** ❽ before supping at 10pm.

VERSAILLES BY NUMBERS

- **Rooms** 700 (11 hectares of roof)
- **Windows** 2153
- **Staircases** 67
- **Gardens and parks** 800 hectares
- **Trees** 200,000
- **Fountains** 50 (with 620 nozzles)
- **Paintings** 6300 (measuring 11km laid end to end)
- **Statues and sculptures** 2100
- **Objets d'art and furnishings** 5000
- **Visitors** 5.3 million per year

Queen's Bedchamber
Chambre de la Reine
The queen's life was on constant public display and even the births of her children were watched by crowds of spectators in her own bedchamber. **DETOUR »** The Guardroom, with a dozen armed men at the ready.

LUNCH BREAK

Diner-style food at Sister's Café, crêpes at Le Phare St-Louis or picnic in the park.

Guardroom

South Wing

King's Library
Bibliothèque du Roi
The last resident, bibliophile Louis XVI, loved geography and his copy of *The Travels of James Cook* (in English, which he read fluently) is still on the shelf here.

SAVVY SIGHTSEEING

Avoid Versailles on Monday (closed), Tuesday (Paris' museums close, so visitors flock here) and Sunday, the busiest day. Also, book tickets online so you don't have to queue.

Hall of Mirrors

Galerie des Glaces

The solid-silver candelabra and furnishings in this extravagant hall, devoted to Louis XIV's successes in war, were melted down in 1689 to pay for yet another conflict. **DETOUR»** The antithetical Peace Drawing Room, adjacent.

King's Bedchamber

Chambre du Roi

The king's daily life was anything but private and even his *lever* (rising) at 8am and *coucher* (retiring) at 11.30pm would be witnessed by up to 150 sycophantic courtiers.

Council Chamber

Cabinet du Conseil

This chamber, with carved medallions evoking the king's work, is where the monarch met his various ministers (state, finance, religion etc) depending on the days of the week.

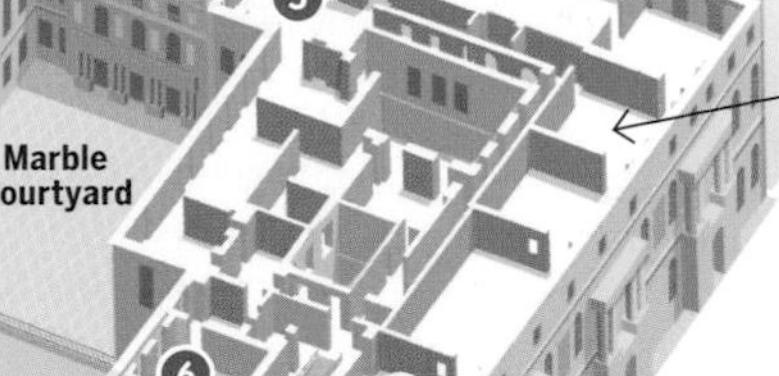

Diana Drawing Room

Salon de Diane

With walls and ceiling covered in frescos devoted to the mythical huntress, this room contained a large billiard table reserved for Louis XIV, a keen player.

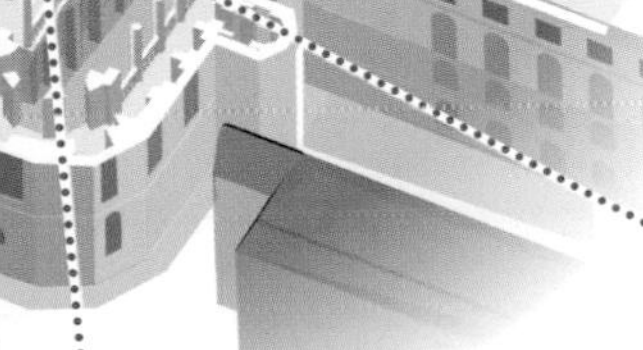

Royal Chapel

Chapelle Royale

This two-storey chapel (with gallery for the royals and important courtiers, and the ground floor for the B-list) was dedicated to St Louis, patron of French monarchs. **DETOUR»** The sumptuous Royal Opera.

CHRISTOPHE LEHENAFF/GETTY IMAGES ©

Hercules Drawing Room

Salon d'Hercule

This salon, with its stunning ceiling fresco of the strong man, gave way to the State Apartments, which were open to courtiers three nights a week. **DETOUR»** Apollo Drawing Room, used for formal audiences and as a throne room.

Shakespeare & Company Books
(Map p188; www.shakespeareandcompany.com; 37 rue de la Bûcherie, 5e; ⌚10am-11pm Mon-Fri, from 11am Sat & Sun; M St-Michel) This bookshop is the stuff of legends. A kind of spell descends as you enter, weaving between nooks and crannies overflowing with new and secondhand English-language books. The original shop (12 rue l'Odéon, 6e; closed by the Nazis in 1941) was run by Sylvia Beach and became the meeting point for Hemingway's 'Lost Generation'. Readings by emerging and illustrious authors take place at 7pm most Mondays; it also hosts workshops and festivals.

Galeries Lafayette Department Store
(Map p176; http://haussmann.galerieslafayette.com; 40 bd Haussmann, 9e; ⌚9.30am-8pm Mon-Sat, to 9pm Thu; M Auber or Chaussée d'Antin) *Grande dame* department store Galeries Lafayette is spread across the main store (whose magnificent stained-glass dome is over a century old), **men's store (Map p176)** and **homewares (Map p176)** store, and includes a gourmet emporium.

Catch modern art in the **gallery (Map p176; www.galeriedesgaleries.com; 1st fl; ⌚11am-7pm Tue-Sat)** FREE, or take in a **fashion show (☎bookings 01 42 82 30 25; ⌚3pm Fri Mar-Jul & Sep-Dec by reservation)**; a free, windswept rooftop panorama; or a break at one of its 19 restaurants and cafes.

Information

Dangers & Annoyances

Metro stations best avoided late at night include: Châtelet-Les Halles and its corridors; Château Rouge in Montmartre; Gare du Nord; Strasbourg St-Denis; Réaumur Sébastopol; and Montparnasse Bienvenüe. Pickpocketing and thefts from handbags and packs is a problem wherever there are crowds (especially of tourists).

Tourist Information

Paris Convention & Visitors Bureau (Office du Tourisme et des Congrès de Paris; Map p188; www.parisinfo.com; 27 rue des Pyramides, 1er; ⌚9am-7pm May-Oct, 10am-7pm Nov-Apr; M Pyramides) Main branch of the Paris Convention & Visitors Bureau, about 500m northwest of the Louvre.

Getting There & Away

Air

There are three main airports in Paris:

Aéroport Charles de Gaulle (p272) Most international airlines fly to CDG, 28km northeast of the centre of Paris. In French, the airport is commonly called 'Roissy'.

Aéroport d'Orly (ORY; ☎01 70 36 39 50; www.aeroportsdeparis.fr) Located 19km south of Paris but not as frequently used by international airlines.

Aéroport de Beauvais (BVA; ☎08 92 68 20 66; www.aeroportbeauvais.com) Not really Paris at all (it's 75km north of Paris) but used by some low-cost carriers.

Bus

Gare Routière Internationale de Paris-Galliéni (☎08 92 89 90 91; 28 av du Général de Gaulle; M Galliéni) The city's international bus terminal is in the eastern suburb of Bagnolet; it's about a 15-minute metro ride to the more central République station.

Train

Paris has six major train stations.

Gare du Nord (rue de Dunkerque, 10e; M Gare du Nord) Trains to/from the UK, Belgium, Germany and northern France.

Gare de l'Est (bd de Strasbourg, 10e; M Gare de l'Est) Trains to/from Germany, Switzerland and eastern areas of France.

Gare de Lyon (bd Diderot, 12e; M Gare de Lyon) The terminus for trains to Provence, the Riviera, the Alps and Italy. Also serves Geneva.

Gare d'Austerlitz (bd de l'Hôpital, 13e; M Gare d'Austerlitz) Trains to/from Spain and Portugal, and non-TGV trains to southwestern France.

Gare Montparnasse (av du Maine & bd de Vaugirard, 15e; M Montparnasse Bienvenüe) Trains to/from western France (Brittany, Atlantic Coast) and southwest.

Gare St-Lazare (rue St-Lazare & rue d'Amsterdam, 8e; M St-Lazare) Trains to Normandy.

Getting Around

To/From the Airports

Getting into town is straightforward and inexpensive thanks to a host of public-transport

options. Bus drivers sell tickets. Children aged four to 11 years pay half-price on most services.

Aéroport Roissy Charles de Gaulle

RER B line (€9.50, approximately 50 minutes, every 10 to 15 minutes) Stops at Gare du Nord, Châtelet–Les Halles and St-Michel-Notre Dame stations in the city centre. Trains run from 5am to 11pm; there are fewer trains on weekends.

Roissybus (€10.50, 45 to 60 minutes, every 15 minutes, 5.30am to 11pm) Links the airport with Opéra.

Taxi Costs €50, more at nights and weekends. Allow 40 minutes to the centre, more at rush hour.

Aéroport d'Orly

RER B & Orlyval (€10.90, 35 minutes, every 4 to 12 minutes, 6am to 11pm) The nearest RER station to the airport is Antony, where you connect on the dedicated Orlyval.

Air France bus 1 (€12.50, one hour, every 20 minutes, 5am to 11pm) Links the airport with Gare Montparnasse, Invalides and Arc de Triomphe.

Taxi Costs around €40, more at nights and weekends. Allow 30 minutes to the centre, more at rush hour.

Aéroport Paris-Beauvais

The **Beauvais shuttle** (€17, 1¼ hours) links the airport with metro station Porte Maillot.

Bicycle

The **Vélib (http://en.velib.paris.fr; day/week subscription €1.70/8, bike hire up to 30min/60min/90min/2hr free/€1/2/4)** bike share scheme puts 20,000-odd bikes at the disposal of Parisians and visitors to get around the city. There are around 1800 docking stations; bikes are available around the clock.

Boat

Batobus (www.batobus.com; Port de Solférino, 7e; 1-/2-day pass €16/18; ⏲10am-9.30pm Apr-Aug, to 7pm rest of year) Batobus runs glassed-in trimarans that dock every 20 to 25 minutes at eight small piers along the Seine; Eiffel Tower, Musée d'Orsay, St-Germain des Prés, Notre Dame, Jardin des Plantes, Hôtel de Ville, Musée du Louvre and Champs-Élysées. Buy tickets online, at ferry stops or tourist offices. You can also buy a 2-/3-day ticket covering L'Open Tour buses too for €45/49.

Public Transport

Paris' public transit system is operated by the **RATP** (www.ratp.fr).

- The same RATP tickets are valid on the metro, RER, buses, trams and Montmartre funicular. A single ticket/*carnet* of 10 costs €1.70/13.70.
- One ticket covers travel between any two metro stations (no return journeys) for 1½ hours; you can transfer between buses and between buses and trams, but not from metro to bus or vice versa.
- Keep your ticket until you exit the station or risk a fine.

Moulin Rouge cabaret (p199), Paris

Bus

Buses run from 5.30am to 8.30pm Monday to Saturday, with certain evening lines continuing until midnight or 12.30am, when hourly Noctilien (www.noctilien.fr) night buses kick in.

Metro & RER

Paris' underground network consists of the 14-line metro and the five-line RER, a network of suburban train lines. The last metro train on each line begins sometime between 12.35am and 1.15am (2.15am Friday and Saturday), before starting up again around 5.30am.

Tourist Passes

The **Mobilis Card** allows unlimited travel for one day in two to five zones (€6.80 to €16.10) on the metro, the RER, buses, trams and suburban trains; while the **Paris Visite** 'Paris+Suburbs+Airports' pass allows unlimited travel (including to/from airports) plus discounted entry to museums and activities and costs €22.85/34.70/59.50 for 1/2/5 days.

Passes are sold at larger metro and RER stations, SNCF stations and the airports.

Taxi

- The flag fall is €2.50, plus €1 per kilometre within the city limits from 10am and 5pm Monday to Saturday (Tarif A; white light on meter)
- It's €1.24 per kilometre from 5pm to 10am, all day Sunday, and public holidays (Tarif B; orange light on meter).
- The first piece of luggage is free; additional bags cost €1.
- Taxis will often refuse to take more than three passengers.
- You can flag taxis on the street, wait at official stands or phone/book online with Taxis G7 (3607; www.taxisg7.fr) or Taxis Bleus (01 49 36 10 10; www.taxis-bleus.com).

AROUND PARIS

Bordered by five rivers – the Epte, Aisne, Eure, Yonne and Marne – the area around Paris looks rather like a giant island, and indeed is known as Île de France. Centuries ago this was where French kings retreated to extravagant chateaux in Versailles and Fontainebleau. These days such royal castles have been joined by a kingdom of an altogether different kind.

Disneyland Resort Paris

In 1992, Mickey Mouse, Snow White and chums set up shop on reclaimed sugar-beet fields 32km east of Paris at a cost of €4.6 billion. Though not quite as over-the-top as its American cousin, France's Disneyland packs in the crowds nonetheless.

The main **Disneyland Park** (10am-11pm May-Aug, to 10pm Sep, to 6pm Oct-Apr, hours can vary) comprises five *pays* (lands), including: the 1900s idealised **Main St USA**, a re-creation of the American Wild West in **Frontierland** with the legendary Big Thunder Mountain ride, futuristic **Discoveryland**; and the exotic-themed **Adventureland**, where you'll find the Pirates of the Caribbean and the spiralling 360-degrees roller coaster, Indiana Jones and the Temple of Peril. Pinocchio, Snow White and other fairy-tale characters come to life in the candy-coated heart of the park, **Fantasyland**.

Adjacent **Walt Disney Studios Park** (10am-7pm May-Sep, to 6pm Oct-Apr, hours can vary) has a sound stage, backlot and animation studios illustrating how films, TV programs and cartoons are produced.

Standard admission fees at **Disneyland Resort Paris** (hotel bookings 01 60 30 60 30, restaurant reservations 01 60 30 40 50; www.disneylandparis.com; one day adult/child €64/58; hours vary; M RER Marne-la-Vallée/Chessy) include admission to either Disneyland Park or Walt Disney, but there's always a multitude of different passes, special offers and accommodation/transport packages on offer.

Marne-la-Vallée/Chessy, Disneyland's RER station, is served by line A4; trains run every 15 minutes or so from central Paris (€7.50, 35 to 40 minutes).

NORMANDY

Famous for cows, cider and Camembert, this largely rural region (www.normandie-tourisme.fr) is one of France's most traditional – and most visited thanks to world-renowned sights such as the Bayeux Tapestry, historic D-Day beaches, and spectacular Mont St-Michel.

Bayeux

POP 13,350

Bayeux has become famous throughout the English-speaking world thanks to a 68m-long piece of painstakingly embroidered cloth: the 11th-century Bayeux Tapestry, whose 58 scenes vividly tell the story of the Norman invasion of England in 1066. The town is also one of the few in Normandy to have survived WWII practically unscathed, with a centre crammed with 13th- to 18th-century buildings, wooden-framed Norman-style houses, and a spectacular Norman Gothic cathedral.

Sights

Bayeux Tapestry Tapestry

(02 31 51 25 50; www.tapestry-bayeux.com; rue de Nesmond; adult/child incl audioguide €9/4; 9am-6.30pm mid-Mar–mid-Nov, to 7pm May-Aug, 9.30am-12.30pm & 2-6pm mid-Nov–mid-Mar) The world's most celebrated embroidery depicts the conquest of England by William the Conqueror in 1066 from an unashamedly Norman perspective. Commissioned by Bishop Odo of Bayeux, William's half-brother, for the opening of Bayeux' cathedral in 1077, the 68.3m-long cartoon strip tells the dramatic, bloody tale with verve and vividness.

Musée d'Art et d'Histoire Baron Gérard Museum

(MAHB; 02 31 92 14 21; www.bayeuxmuseum.com; 37 rue du Bienvenu; adult/child €7/4; 9.30am-6.30pm May-Sep, 10am-12.30pm & 2-6pm Oct-Apr) Opened in 2013, this is one of France's most gorgeously presented provincial museums. The exquisite exhibits cover everything from Gallo-Roman archaeology to medieval art to paintings from the Renaissance to the 20th century, including a fine work by Gustave Caillebotte. Other highlights include impossibly delicate local lace and Bayeux-made porcelain. Housed in the former bishop's palace.

Engraving showing a detail of the Bayeux Tapestry

 Sleeping

Les Logis du Rempart B&B €
(02 31 92 50 40; www.lecornu.fr; 4 rue Bourbesneur; d €60-100, tr €110-130;) The three rooms of this delightful *maison de famille* ooze old-fashioned cosiness. Our favourite, the Bajocasse, has parquet floor and Toile de Jouy wallpaper. The shop downstairs is the perfect place to stock up on top-quality, homemade cider and *calvados* (apple brandy).

Hôtel d'Argouges Hotel €€
(02 31 92 88 86; www.hotel-dargouges.com; 21 rue St-Patrice; d/tr/f €140/193/245; closed Dec & Jan; P) Occupying a stately 18th-century residence with a lush little garden, this graceful hotel has 28 comfortable rooms with exposed beams, thick walls and Louis XVI–style furniture. The breakfast room, hardly changed since 1734, still has its original wood panels and parquet floors.

La Reine Mathilde Patisserie €
(47 rue St-Martin; cakes from €2.20; 9am-7.30pm Tue-Sun) This sumptuously decorated patisserie and *salon de thé* (tearoom), ideal for a sweet breakfast or a relaxing cup of afternoon tea, hasn't changed much since it was built in 1898.

Le Pommier Norman €€
(02 31 21 52 10; www.restaurantlepommier.com; 38-40 rue des Cuisiniers; lunch menus €15-18, other menus €21-39.50; noon-2pm & 7-9pm, closed Sun Nov-Feb;) At this romantic restaurant, delicious Norman classics include steamed pollock and Caen-style tripe. A vegetarian menu – a rarity in Normandy – is also available, with offerings such as soybean steak in Norman cream.

Information

Tourist Office (02 31 51 28 28; www.bayeux-bessin-tourisme.com; pont St-Jean; 9.30am-12.30pm & 2-6pm Mon-Sat) Covers both Bayeux and the surrounding Bessin region, including the D-Day beaches. Has a walking-tour map of town and bus and train schedules, and sells books on the D-Day landings in English. Charges €2 to book hotels and B&Bs.

Getting There & Away

Trains link Bayeux with Caen (€6.60, 20 minutes, hourly), from where there are connections to Paris' Gare St-Lazare.

D-Day Beaches

The D-Day landings, code-named 'Operation Overlord', rank among the largest military operations in history. Early on 6 June 1944, Allied troops came ashore along 80km of beaches north of

WWII memorial near Omaha Beach (p214)

BERTHOLD TRENKEL/GETTY IMAGES ©

Don't Miss
Mont St-Michel

On a rocky island opposite the coastal town of Pontorson, connected to the mainland by a narrow causeway, the sky-scraping turrets of the **Abbaye du Mont St-Michel** (☎02 33 89 80 00; www.monuments-nationaux.fr; adult/child incl guided tour €9/free; ⏰9am-7pm, last entry 1hr before closing) provide one of France's iconic sights.

The surrounding bay is notorious for its fast-rising tides: at low tide the Mont is surrounded by bare sand for miles around; at high tide, just six hours later, the bay, causeway and nearby car parks can be submerged. From the **tourist office** (☎02 33 60 14 30; www.ot-montsaintmichel.com; ⏰9am-12.30pm & 2-6pm Sep-Jun, 9am-7pm Jul & Aug), at the base of the mount, a cobbled street winds up to the **Église Abbatiale** (Abbey Church), incorporating elements of both Norman and Gothic architecture.

Other notable sights include the arched **cloître** (cloister), the barrel-roofed **réfectoire** (dining hall), and the Gothic **Salle des Hôtes** (Guest Hall), dating from 1213. English-language tours run hourly in summer, twice daily (11am and 3pm) in winter. In July and August, Monday to Saturday, there are illuminated *nocturnes* (night-time visits) with music from 7pm to 10pm.

Check the *horaire des marées* (tide table) at the tourist office. When the tide is out, you can walk all the way around Mont St-Michel, a distance of about 1km. Stray too far from the Mont and you risk getting stuck in wet sand.

There are two to three daily trains to Pontorson from Bayeux (€23.90, 1¾ hr).

Bayeux, code-named (from west to east) Utah, Omaha, Gold, Juno and Sword. The landings on D-Day – called 'Jour J' in French – were followed by the Battle of Normandy, which ultimately led to the liberation of Europe from Nazi occupation. Memorial museums in Caen and Bayeux

(Continued on page 214)

Mont St-Michel

TIMELINE

708 Inspired by a vision of **St Michael** ❶, Bishop Aubert is inspired to 'build here and build high'.

966 Richard I, Duke of Normandy, gives the Mont to the Benedictines. The three levels of the **abbey** ❷ reflect their monastic hierarchy.

1017 Development of the abbey begins. Pilgrims arrive to honour the cult of St Michael. They walk barefoot across the mudflats and up the **Grande Rue** ❸ to be received in the almonry (now the bookshop).

1203 The monastery is burnt by the troops of Philip Augustus, who later donates money for its restoration and the Gothic 'miracle', **La Merveille** ❹, is constructed.

1434 The Mont's **ramparts** ❺ and fortifications ensure it withstands the English assault during the Hundred Years War. It is the only place in northern France not to fall.

1789 After the Revolution, Monasticism is abolished and the Mont is turned into a prison. During this period the **treadmill** ❻ is built to lift up supplies.

1878 The Mont is linked to the mainland by a **causeway** ❼.

1979 The Mont is declared a Unesco World Heritage Site.

2014 The causeway is replaced by a bridge.

TOP TIPS

➡ Pick up a picnic lunch at the supermarket in La Caserne to avoid the Mont's overpriced fast food.

➡ Allow 45 minutes to an hour to get from the new parking lot in La Caserne to the Mont.

➡ If you step off the island pay close attention to the tides - they can be dangerous.

➡ Don't forget to pick up the Abbey's excellent audioguide – it tells some great stories.

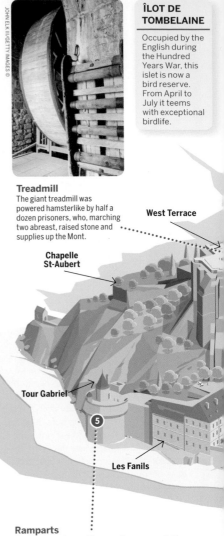

JOHN ELK III/GETTY IMAGES ©

ÎLOT DE TOMBELAINE

Occupied by the English during the Hundred Years War, this islet is now a bird reserve. From April to July it teems with exceptional birdlife.

Treadmill
The giant treadmill was powered hamsterlike by half a dozen prisoners, who, marching two abreast, raised stone and supplies up the Mont.

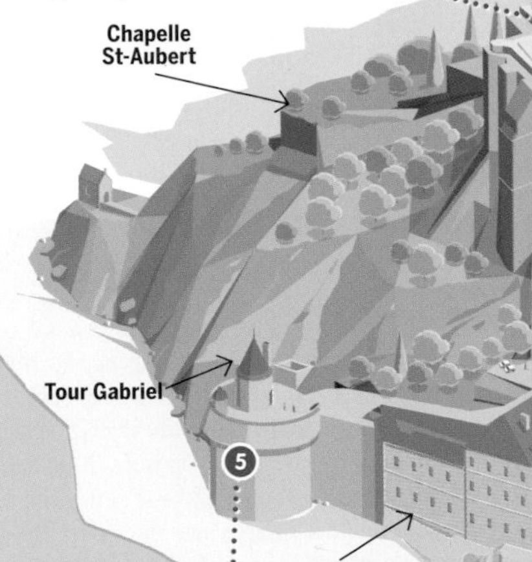

Ramparts
The Mont was also a military garrison surrounded by machicolated and turreted walls, dating from the 13th to 15th centuries. The single entrance, Porte de l'Avancée, ensured its security in the Hundred Years War. Tip: Tour du Nord (North Tower) has the best views.

ROCCO FASANO/GETTY IMAGES ©

Abbey

The abbey's three levels reflect the monastic order: monks lived isolated in church and cloister, the abbot entertained noble guests at the middle level, and lowly pilgrims were received in the basement. Tip: night visits run from mid-July to August.

HUGHES HERVÉ/GETTY IMAGES ©

St Michael Statue & Bell Tower

A golden statue of the winged St Michael looks ready to leap heavenward from the bell tower. He is the patron of the Mont, having inspired St Aubert's original devotional chapel.

IZZET KERIBAR/GETTY IMAGES ©

La Merveille

The highlights of La Merveille are the vast refectory hall lit through embrasured windows, the Knights Hall with its elegant ribbed vaulting, and the cloister (above), which is one of the purest examples of 13th-century architecture to survive here.

Grande Rue

The main thoroughfare of the small village below the abbey, Grande Rue has its charm despite its rampant commercialism. Don't miss the famous Mère Poulard shop here, for souvenir cookies.

DAVID TOMLINSON/GETTY IMAGES ©

New Bridge

In 2014, the Mont's 136-year-old causeway was replaced by a bridge designed to allow seawater to circulate and thus save the island from turning into a peninsula.

ART WIDAK/DEMOTIX/CORBIS ©

BEST VIEWS

The view from the Jardin des Plantes in nearby Avranches is unique, as are the panoramas from Pointe du Grouin du Sud near the village of St-Léonard.

(Continued from page 211)

provide a comprehensive overview, and there are many small D-Day museums dotted along the coast. For context, see www.normandiememoire.com and www.6juin1944.com.

The most brutal fighting on D-Day took place 15km northwest of Bayeux along the stretch of coastline now known as **Omaha Beach**, today a glorious stretch of fine golden sand partly lined with sand dunes and summer homes. **Circuit de la Plage d'Omaha**, trail-marked with a yellow stripe, is a self-guided tour along the beach, surveyed from a bluff above by the huge **Normandy American Cemetery & Memorial** (www.abmc.gov; Colleville-sur-Mer; 9am-6pm mid-Apr–mid-Sep, to 5pm rest of the year). Featured in the opening scenes of Steven Spielberg's *Saving Private Ryan*, this is the largest American cemetery in Europe.

Caen's hi-tech, hugely impressive **Mémorial – Un Musée pour la Paix** (Memorial – A Museum for Peace; 02 31 06 06 44; www.memorial-caen.fr; esplanade Général Eisenhower; adult/child €19/11.50; 9am-7pm daily mid-Feb–mid-Nov, 9.30am-6.30pm Tue-Sun mid-Nov–mid-Feb, closed 3 weeks in Jan) uses sound, lighting, film, animation and lots of exhibits to graphically explore and evoke the events of WWII, D-Day landings and the ensuing Cold War.

Tours

An organised minibus tour is an excellent way to get a sense of the D-Day beaches and their place in history. Bayeux tourist office (p210) handles reservations.

Normandy Tours Guided Tour
(02 31 92 10 70; www.normandy-landing-tours.com; 26 place de la Gare, Bayeux; adult/student €62/55) Offers well-regarded four- to five-hour tours of the main sites starting at 8.15am and 1.15pm on most days, as well as personally tailored trips. Based at Bayeux' Hôtel de la Gare, facing the train station.

Tours by Mémorial – Un Musée pour la Paix Minibus Tour
(02 31 06 06 45; www.memorial-caen.fr; adult/child morning €64/64, afternoon €81/64; 9am & 2pm Apr-Sep, 1pm Oct-Mar, closed 3 weeks in Jan) Excellent year-round minibus tours (four to five hours), with cheaper tours in full-size buses (€39) from June to August. Rates include entry to Le Mémorial – Un Musée pour la Paix. Book online.

Getting There & Away

Bus Verts (www.busverts.fr) bus 70 (two or three daily Monday to Saturday, more in summer) goes northwest from Bayeux to Colleville-sur-Mer and Omaha Beach (€2.40, 35 minutes).

BRITTANY

Brittany is for explorers. Its wild, dramatic coastline, medieval towns, thick forests and the eeriest stone circles this side of Stonehenge make a trip here well worth the detour from the beaten track.

St-Malo

POP 48,800

The mast-filled port of fortified St-Malo is inextricably tied up with the deep briny blue: the town became a key harbour during the 17th and 18th centuries, functioning as a base for merchant ships and government-sanctioned privateers, and these days it's a busy cross-Channel ferry port and summertime getaway.

Sights

Walking on top of the city's sturdy 17th-century ramparts (1.8km) affords fine views of the old walled city known as **Intra-Muros** ('within the walls') or Ville Close – access the ramparts from any of the city gates.

Cathédrale St-Vincent Cathedral
(place Jean de Châtillon; 9.30am-6pm) The city's centrepiece was constructed between the 12th and 18th centuries. During the ferocious fighting of August 1944 the cathedral was badly hit; much of its original structure (including its spire) was reduced to rubble. The cathedral was subsequently rebuilt and reconsecrated in 1971. A mosaic plaque on the floor of

the nave marks the spot where Jacques Cartier received the blessing of the bishop of St-Malo before his 'voyage of discovery' to Canada in 1535.

Fort National Ruin

(www.fortnational.com; adult/child €5/3; ⌚Easter, school holidays & Jun-Sep) The St-Malo ramparts' northern stretch looks across to the remains of this former prison, built by Vauban in 1689. Standing atop a rocky outcrop, the fort can only be accessed at low tide. Ask at the tourist office for times of tours.

Musée d'Histoire de St-Malo Museum

(☎02 99 40 71 57; www.ville-saint-malo.fr/culture/les-musees; Château; adult/child €6/3; ⌚10am-12.30pm & 2-6pm Apr-Sep, Tue-Sun Oct-Mar) Within **Château de St-Malo**, built by the dukes of Brittany in the 15th and 16th centuries, this museum looks at the life and history of the city through nautical exhibits, model boats and marine artefacts, as well as an exhibition covering the city's cod-fishing heritage. There's also background info on the city's sons, including Cartier, Surcouf, Duguay-Trouin and the writer Chateaubriand.

Sleeping

Hôtel San Pedro Hotel €

(☎02 99 40 88 57; www.sanpedro-hotel.com; 1 rue Ste-Anne; s €65-69, d €75-83; P 📶) Tucked at the back of the old city, the San Pedro has a cool, crisp, neutral-toned decor with subtle splashes of yellow paint, friendly service, great breakfast, private parking (€10) and a few bikes available for free. It features 12 rooms on four floors served by a miniature lift (forget those big suitcases!); two rooms come with sea views.

Accroche Cœur B&B €€

(☎02 99 40 43 63, 06 07 10 80 22; www.accrochecoeursaintmalo.fr; 9 rue Thévenard; d incl breakfast €120-145; 📶) Is this St-Malo's best-kept secret? There are five upper-crust *chambres d'hôte* in this solid townhouse tucked into a side street in the historic centre. Top of the heap is the vast Brieg suite, which is suitable for a family, but the Mac Low, which boasts polished wood beams, elegant furniture and sparkling bathroom, isn't a bad backup.

Beach at St-Malo

Detour: The Morbihan Megaliths

Pre-dating Stonehenge by about a hundred years, **Carnac** comprises the world's greatest concentration of megalithic sites. There are more than 3000 of these upright stones scattered across the countryside between **Carnac-Ville** and **Locmariaquer** village, most of which were erected between 5000 BC and 3500 BC. No one's quite sure what purpose these sites served, although theories abound. A sacred site? Phallic fertility cult? Or maybe a celestial calendar? Even more mysterious is the question of their construction – no one really has the foggiest idea how the builders hacked and hauled these vast granite blocks several millennia before the wheel arrived in Brittany, let alone mechanical diggers.

Because of severe erosion, the sites are usually fenced off to allow vegetation to regrow. **Guided tours** (€6) run in French year-round and in English from early July to late August. Sign up at the **Maison des Mégalithes** (☎02 97 52 29 81; www.carnac.monuments-nationaux.fr; rte des Alignements; tour adult/child €6/free; ⏲9.30am-7.30pm Jul & Aug, to 5pm Sep-Apr, to 6pm May & Jun).

Eating & Drinking

Le Corps de Garde Crêperie €

(☎02 99 40 91 46; www.le-corps-de-garde.com; 3 montée Notre-Dame; mains €4-10; ⏲noon-10pm) The main draw of this unfussy crêperie is its location right beside the ramparts – be sure to ask for an outside table if you're a sucker for sunset views. Crêpes and *galettes* (savoury buckwheat crêpes) form the menu's backbone.

L'Absinthe Modern French €€

(☎02 99 40 26 15; www.restaurant-absinthe-cafe.fr; 1 rue de l'Orme; mains €18-24, menus €28-45; ⏲noon-2pm & 7-10pm) Hidden away in a quiet street near the covered market, this fab (and very French) eatery is housed in an imposing 17th-century building. Ingredients fresh from the nearby market are whipped into shape by the talented chef, Stéphane Brebel, and served in cosy surrounds. The wine list is another hit, with an all-French cast from white to red and rosé.

La Cafe du Coin d'en Bas de la Rue du Bout de la Ville d'en Face du Port... La Java Cafe

(☎02 99 56 41 90; www.lajavacafe.com; 3 rue Ste-Barbe; ⏲8.51am-8.44pm Mon-Fri, 9.31am-11.32pm Sat, 9.31am-8.44pm Sun, 8.51am-11.32pm daily mid-Jul–mid-Aug) The word 'eccentric' must have been coined to describe the extraordinary and insanely named cafe. Think part-museum, part–toy shop and a work of art from an ever-so-slightly-twisted mind. Traditional French accordion music plays in the background and the beady eyes of hundreds of dolls and puppets keep watch from shelves and alcoves in the walls. Customers sit on swings, not chairs.

Information

Tourist Office (☎08 25 13 52 00; www.saint-malo-tourisme.com; esplanade St-Vincent; ⏲9am-7.30pm Mon-Sat, 10am-6pm Sun) Just outside the walls.

Getting There & Away

TGV trains go to **Paris' Gare Montparnasse** (€52 to €64, three hours, up to 10 daily).

Cancale

No day trip from St-Malo is tastier than one to Cancale, an idyllic Breton fishing port 14km east, that's famed for its offshore *parcs à huîtres* (oyster beds).

Learn all about oyster farming at the **Ferme Marine** (☎02 99 89 69 99; www.ferme-marine.com; corniche de l'Aurore; adult/child €7/3.70; ⏰guided tours in French 11am, 3pm & 5pm Jul–mid-Sep, in English 2pm) and shop for oysters fresh from their beds at the **Marché aux Huîtres** (Pointe des Crolles; 12 oysters from €4; ⏰9am-6pm), the local oyster market atmospherically clustered around the Pointe des Crolles lighthouse.

Le Coquillage (☎02 99 89 64 76; www.maisons-de-bricourt.com; D155, rte du Mont St-Michel, Le Buot; lunch menu €31, other menus €75-139; ⏰noon-2pm & 7-9pm), the sumptuous, Michelin-starred kitchen of superchef Olivier Roellinger, is housed in the gobsmackingly impressive Château Richeux, 4km south of Cancale. Crown the culinary experience with lunch or dinner here.

CHAMPAGNE

Known in Roman times as Campania, meaning 'plain', the agricultural region of Champagne is synonymous these days with its world-famous bubbly. This multimillion-dollar industry is strictly protected under French law, ensuring that only grapes grown in designated Champagne vineyards can truly lay claim to the hallowed title. The town of Épernay, 30km south of the regional capital of Reims, is the best place to head for *dégustation* (tasting), and a self-drive **Champagne Route** wends its way through the region's most celebrated vineyards.

Reims

POP 184,652

Over the course of a millennium (816 to 1825), some 34 sovereigns – among them two dozen kings – began their reigns in Reims' famed cathedral. Meticulously reconstructed after WWI and again following WWII, the city – whose name is pronounced something like 'rance' and is often anglicised as Rheims – is endowed with handsome pedestrian zones, well-tended parks, lively nightlife and a state-of-the-art tramway.

Tram, Reims

DAVID FREUND/GETTY IMAGES ©

Sights

Cathédrale Notre Dame Cathedral
(www.cathedrale-reims.culture.fr; place du Cardinal Luçon; tower adult/child €7.50/free, incl Palais du Tau €11/free; 7.30am-7.30pm, tower tours hourly 11am-4pm Tue-Sun May-Sep) Imagine the egos and extravagance of a French royal coronation. The focal point of such bejewelled pomposity was Reims' resplendent Gothic cathedral, begun in 1211 on a site occupied by churches since the 5th century. The interior is a rainbow of stained glass windows; the finest are the western facade's 12-petalled **great rose window**, the north transept's **rose window** and the vivid **Chagall** creations (1974) in the central axial chapel. The tourist office rents audioguides (€6) for self-paced cathedral tours.

Basilique St-Rémi Basilica
(place du Chanoine Ladame; 8am-7pm) FREE This 121m-long former Benedictine abbey church, a Unesco World Heritage Site, mixes Romanesque elements from the mid-11th century (the worn but stunning nave and transept) with early Gothic features from the latter half of the 12th century (the choir, with a large triforium gallery and, way up top, tiny clerestory windows). Next door, **Musée St-Rémi** (53 rue Simon; adult/child €4/free; 2-6.30pm Mon-Fri, to 7pm Sat & Sun), in a 17th- and 18th-century abbey, features local Gallo-Roman archaeology, tapestries and 16th- to 19th-century military history.

Tours

The great-value **Pass Reims** (€9), available at the tourist office, gives you entry to a museum of your choice, an audio-guide tour of the city, plus discounts on Champagne house tours.

Mumm Champagne House
(03 26 49 59 70; www.mumm.com; 34 rue du Champ de Mars; one-hour tours incl tasting €14-25; tours 9am-5pm daily, shorter hrs & closed Sun winter) Mumm (pronounced 'moom'), the only *maison* in central Reims, was founded in 1827 and is now the world's third-largest producer (almost eight million bottles a year). Engaging and edifying one-hour tours take you through cellars filled with 25 million bottles of fine bubbly. Wheelchair accessible. Phone ahead if possible.

Taittinger Champagne House
(03 26 85 45 35; www.taittinger.com; 9 place St-Niçaise; tours €16.50-45; 9.30am-5.30pm, shorter hrs & closed Sun in winter) The headquarters of Taittinger are an excellent place to come for a clear, straightforward presentation on how Champagne is actually made – there's no claptrap about 'the Champagne mystique' here. Parts of the cellars occupy 4th-century Roman stone quarries; other bits were excavated by 13th-century

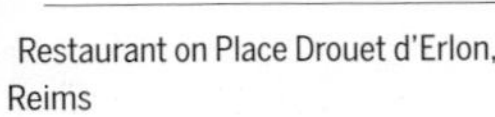

Restaurant on Place Drouet d'Erlon, Reims
GUIZIOU FRANCK/GETTY IMAGES ©

Benedictine monks. No need to reserve. Situated 1.5km southeast of Reims centre; take the Citadine 1 or 2 bus to the St-Niçaise or Salines stops.

Sleeping

Les Telliers B&B **€€**
(☎09 53 79 80 74; http://telliers.fr; 18 rue des Telliers; s €67-83, d €79-114, tr €115-134, q €131-155; P 📶) Enticingly positioned down a quiet alley near the cathedral, this bijou B&B extends one of Reims' warmest *bienvenues*. The high-ceilinged rooms are big on art-deco character, handsomely decorated with ornamental fireplaces, polished oak floors and the odd antique. Breakfast costs an extra €9 and is a generous spread of pastries, fruit, fresh-pressed juice and coffee.

Château Les Crayères Luxury Hotel **€€€**
(☎03 26 24 90 00; www.lescrayeres.com; 64 bd Henry-Vasnier; d €400-850; P ❄ @ 📶) Such class! If you've ever wanted to stay in a palace, this romantic château on the fringes of Reims is the real McCoy. Manicured lawns sweep to the graceful turn-of-the-century estate, where you can play golf or tennis, dine in two-Michelin-starred finery, and stay in the lap of luxury in exuberantly furnished, chandelier-lit interiors – all at a price, naturally.

Eating

L'Éveil des Sens Bistro **€€**
(☎03 26 35 16 95; www.eveildessens-reims.com; 8 rue Colbert; menus €30-38; ⌚12.15-2pm & 7.15-10pm, closed Sun & Wed) The 'awakening of the senses' is a fitting name for this terrific bistro. Monochrome hues and white linen create a chic yet understated setting for market-fresh cuisine delivered with finesse. Nicolas Lefèvre's specialities appear deceptively simple on paper, but the flavours are profound – be it scallops with tangy Granny Smith apple or braised beef ravioli on white bean velouté.

Le Millénaire Gastronomic **€€€**
(☎03 26 08 26 62; www.lemillenaire.com; 4-6 rue Bertin; menus €35-94; ⌚noon-1.45pm & 7.30-9.30pm Mon-Fri, 7.30-9.30pm Sat) Sand and claret hues and contemporary art-works create an air of intimate sophistication at this Michelin-starred haunt. Chef Laurent Laplaige keeps flavours crisp and seasonal with specialities such as wild sea bass with celery, truffle risotto and Champagne sauce.

Tourist Office (☎03 26 77 45 00; www.reims-tourisme.com; 2 rue Guillaume de Machault; ⌚9am-7pm Mon-Sat, 10am-6pm Sun)

Getting There & Away

Direct trains link Reims with **Épernay** (€6.80, 30 minutes, 19 daily) and **Paris' Gare de l'Est** (€36 to €44, one hour, 12 to 17 daily).

Épernay

POP 24,600

Prosperous Épernay, 25km south of Reims, is the self-proclaimed *capitale du Champagne* and home to many of the world's most celebrated Champagne houses.

Sights & Activities

Avenue de Champagne Street
Épernay's handsome avenue de Champagne fizzes with *maisons de Champagne* (Champagne houses). The boulevard is lined with mansions and neoclassical villas, rebuilt after WWI. Peek through wrought-iron gates at Moët's private **Hôtel Chandon**, an early 19th-century pavilion-style residence set in landscaped gardens, which counts Wagner among its famous past guests. The haunted-looking **Château Perrier**, a redbrick mansion built in 1854 in neo-Louis XIII style, is aptly placed at number 13! The roundabout presents photo-ops with its giant cork and bottle-top.

Moët & Chandon Champagne House
(☎03 26 51 20 20; www.moet.com; 20 av de Champagne; adult incl 1/2 glasses €21/28, 10-18yr €10; ⌚tours 9.30am-11.30am & 2-4.30pm, closed Sat & Sun late Jan–mid-Mar) Flying the

Right: Vineyard, Alsace; **Below:** Glasses of champagne
(RIGHT) GÃ©RARD LABRIET/GETTY IMAGES ©; (BELOW) DASHA PETRENKO/SHUTTERSTOCK ©

Moët, French, European and Russian flags, this prestigious *maison* offers frequent one-hour tours that are among the region's most impressive, offering a peek at part of their 28km labyrinth of *caves* (cellars). At the shop you can pick up a 15L bottle of Brut Impérial for just €1500; a standard bottle will set you back €31.

Champagne Domi Moreau Vineyard Tour
(**06 30 35 51 07, after 7pm 03 26 59 45 85; www.champagne-domimoreau.com; tours €25-30; tours 9.30am & 2.30pm except Wed & 2nd half of Aug)** This company runs scenic and insightful three-hour minibus tours, in French and English, of nearby vineyards. Pick-up is across the street from the tourist office. It also organises two-hour vineyard tours by bicycle (€25). Call ahead for reservations.

Sleeping

Parva Domus B&B **€€**
(**06 73 25 66 60; www.parvadomusrimaire.com; 27 av de Champagne; d €100, ste €110;**) Brilliantly situated on the avenue de Champagne, this vine-swathed B&B is kept spick and span by the amiable Rimaire family. Rooms have a countrified feel, with wood floors, floral fabrics and pastel colours. Sip a glass of house Champagne on the terrace or in the elegant living room.

La Villa Eugène Boutique Hotel **€€€**
(**03 26 32 44 76; www.villa-eugene.com; 84 av de Champagne; d €154-333, ste €375-390;** P) Sitting handsomely astride the avenue de Champagne in its own grounds with an outdoor pool, La Villa Eugène is a class act. It's lodged in a beautiful 19th-century town mansion that once belonged to the Mercier family. The roomy doubles exude understated elegance, with soft, muted hues and

the odd antique. Splash out more for a private terrace or four-poster.

Eating & Drinking

La Grillade Gourmande Regional Cuisine **€€**

(**☎03 26 55 44 22; www.lagrilladegourmande.com; 16 rue de Reims; menus €19-57; ⏲noon-2pm & 7.30-10pm Tue-Sat)** This chic, red-walled bistro is an inviting spot to try char-grilled meats and dishes rich in texture and flavour, such as crayfish pan-fried in Champagne and lamb cooked until meltingly tender in rosemary and honey. Diners spill out onto the covered terrace in the warm months.

C. Comme Champagne Bar

(**www.c-comme.fr; 8 rue Gambetta; light meals €7.50-14.50, 6-glass Champagne tasting €33-39; ⏲10am-8.30pm Sun-Wed, 10am-11pm Thu, 10am-midnight Fri & Sat)** The downstairs cellar has a stash of 300 different varieties of Champagne; sample them (from €5.50 a glass) in the softly lit bar-bistro upstairs. Accompany with a tasting plate of regional cheese, charcuterie and *rillettes* (pork pâté). We love the funky bottle-top tables and relaxed ambience.

Information

Tourist Office (**☎03 26 53 33 00; www.ot-epernay.fr; 7 av de Champagne; ⏲9.30am-12.30pm & 1.30-7pm Mon-Sat, 10.30am-1pm & 2-4.30pm Sun;** wi-fi) The super-friendly team here hand out English brochures and maps with walking, cycling and driving tour options. They can make cellar visit reservations. Free wi-fi.

Getting There & Away

Direct trains link **Reims** (€6.80, 30 minutes, 19 daily) and **Paris' Gare de l'Est** (€23.60, 1¼ hours, 16 daily).

ALSACE

Alsace is a one-off cultural hybrid. With its Germanic dialect and French sense of fashion, love of foie gras and *choucroute* (sauerkraut), fine wine *and* beer, this distinctive region often leaves you wondering quite where you are.

No matter whether you're planning to get behind the wheel for a morning or pedal leisurely through the vineyards for a week, the picture-book **Route des Vins d'Alsace** (Alsace Wine Route) is a must. Swinging 170km from Marlenheim to Thann, the road is like a 'greatest hits' of Alsace, with its pastoral views, welcoming *caves* (cellars) and half-timbered villages. Go to www.alsace-route-des-vins.com to start planning.

Strasbourg

POP 271,708

Strasbourg is the perfect overture to all that is idiosyncratic about Alsace – walking a fine tightrope between France and Germany and between a medieval past and a progressive future, it pulls off its act in inimitable Alsatian style.

Tear your gaze away from that mesmerising Gothic cathedral for just a minute and you'll be roaming the old town's twisting alleys lined with crooked half-timbered houses à la Grimm; feasting in cosy *winstubs* (Alsatian taverns) by the canalside in Petite France; and marvelling at how a city that does Christmas markets and gingerbread so well can also be home to the glittering EU Quarter and France's second-largest student population.

Sights

The **Strasbourg Pass** (adult/child €15/7.50), a coupon book valid for three consecutive days, includes a visit to one museum, access to the cathedral platform, half a day's bicycle rental and a boat tour, plus hefty discounts on other tours.

Admission to all of Strasbourg's museums (www.musees-strasbourg.org), and to the cathedral's platform, is free on the first Sunday of the month.

Cathédrale Notre-Dame Cathedral
(place de la Cathédrale; astronomical clock adult/child €2/1.50, platform adult/child €5/2.50; 7am-7pm, astronomical clock tickets sold 9.30am-11am, platform 9am-7.15pm; Grand'Rue) Nothing prepares you for your first glimpse of Strasbourg's Cathédrale Notre-Dame, completed in all its Gothic grandeur in 1439. The lace-fine façade lifts the gaze little by little to flying buttresses, leering gargoyles and a 142m spire. The interior is exquisitely lit by 12th- to 14th-century **stained-glass windows**, including the western portal's jewel-like rose window. The Gothic-meets-Renaissance **astronomical clock** strikes solar noon at 12.30pm with a parade of figures portraying the different stages of life and Jesus with his apostles.

Old Town, Strasbourg
WERNER DIETERICH/GETTY IMAGES ©

Grande Île Historic Quarter
(Grand'Rue) History seeps through the twisting lanes and cafe-rimmed plazas of Grande Île, Strasbourg's Unesco World Heritage-listed island bordered by the River Ill. These streets – with their photogenic line-up of wonky, timber-framed houses in sherbet colours – are made for aimless ambling. They cower beneath the soaring magnificence of the cathedral and its sidekick, the gingerbready 15th-century **Maison Kammerzell** (rue des Hallebardes), with its ornate carvings and leaded windows. The alleys are at their most atmospheric when lantern-lit at night.

Sleeping

Villa Novarina Design Hotel **€€**
(03 90 41 18 28; www.villanovarina.com; 11 rue Westercamp; s €87-157, d €117-257, ste €237-537; P; Droits de l'Homme) New-wave design is pitched just right at this light-flooded 1950s villa near Parc de l'Orangerie. Slick without being soulless, rooms and suites are liberally sprinkled with art and overlook gardens. Breakfast places the accent on organic, regional produce. There's a heated pool, whirlpool and spa for quiet moments. It's a 10-minute walk south of Droits de l'Homme tram stop.

Cour du Corbeau Boutique Hotel **€€€**
(03 90 00 26 26; www.cour-corbeau.com; 6-8 rue des Couples; r €140-175, ste €220-260; Porte de l'Hôpital) A 16th-century inn lovingly converted into a boutique hotel, Cour du Corbeau wins you over with its half-timbered charm and location, just steps from the river. Gathered around a courtyard, rooms blend original touches like oak parquet and Louis XV furnishings with mod cons like flat-screen TVs.

Eating

Bistrot et Chocolat Cafe **€**
(www.bistrotetchocolat.net; 8 rue de la Râpe; snacks €7.50-11, brunch €12.50-26.50; 11am-7pm Mon-Thu, 10am-9pm Fri-Sun; ; Grand'Rue) Chilled bistro hailed for its solid and liquid organic chocolate (ginger is superb), day specials and weekend brunches.

La Cuiller à Pot Alsatian **€€**
(03 88 35 56 30; www.lacuillerapot.com; 18b rue Finkwiller; €17.50-26.50; noon-2.30pm & 7-10.30pm Tue-Fri, 7-10.30pm Sat; Musée d'Art Moderne) Run by a talented husband-wife team, this little Alsatian dream of a restaurant rustles up fresh regional cuisine. Its well-edited menu goes with the seasons, but might include such dishes as filet of beef with wild mushrooms and homemade gnocchi and escargots in parsley jus. Quality is second to none.

Strasbourg's Christmas Market

Mulled wine, spicy *bredele* (biscuits) and a Santa-loaded children's village are all part and parcel of Strasbourg's sparkly **Marché de Noël** (Christmas Market; www.noel.strasbourg.eu), running from the last Saturday in November until 31 December.

Information

Main Tourist Office (03 88 52 28 28; www.otstrasbourg.fr; 17 place de la Cathédrale; 9am-7pm daily; Grand'Rue) A city-centre walking map with English text costs €1; bus/tram and cycling maps are free. *Strolling in Strasbourg* (€4.50) details six architectural walking tours.

Getting There & Away

Air

Strasbourg's international **airport** (03 88 64 67 67; www.strasbourg.aeroport.fr) is 17km southwest of the city centre (towards Molsheim).

Train

Direct services go to both European and French cities. Destinations include:

Brussels-Nord €80-180, 5¼ hours, three daily

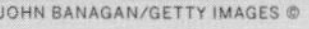

Don't Miss
Château de Chambord

For full-blown château splendour, you can't top Chambord, one of the crowning examples of French Renaissance architecture, and by far the largest, grandest and most visited château in the Loire Valley. Begun in 1519 as a weekend hunting lodge by François I, it quickly snowballed into one of the most ambitious (and expensive) architectural projects ever attempted by any French monarch. This cityscape of turrets, chimneys and lanterns crowns some 440 rooms, 365 fireplaces and 84 staircases, including a famous **double-helix staircase**, reputedly designed by the king's chum, Leonardo da Vinci.

NEED TO KNOW

information 02 54 50 40 00, tour & spectacle reservations 02 54 50 50 40; www.chambord.org; adult/child €11/9, parking €4; 9am-6pm Apr-Sep, 10am-5pm Oct-Mar

Lyon €75-145, 4½ hours, 14 daily

Marseille €161, 6¾ hours, 16 daily

Paris Gare de l'Est €75-134, 2¼ hours, 19 daily

THE LOIRE VALLEY

One step removed from the French capital, the Loire was historically the place where princes, dukes and notable nobles established their country getaways, and the countryside is littered with some of the most extravagant architecture outside Versailles.

Many private companies offer a choice of well-organised itineraries, taking in various combinations of chateaux (plus wine-tasting tours). Half-day trips cost between €23 and €36; full-day trips range from €50 to €54. Entry to the chateaux isn't included, although you'll likely get a discount on tickets. Reserve via the tourist offices in Tours or Amboise, from where most tours depart.

Blois

POP 48,393

Blois' historic chateau was the feudal seat of the powerful counts of Blois, and its grand halls, spiral staircases and sweeping courtyards provide a whistlestop tour through the key periods of French architecture.

Sights

Château Royal de Blois Château (☎02 54 90 33 33; www.chateaudeblois.fr; place du Château; adult/child €9.80/5, audioguide €4, English tours Jul & Aug free; ⏰9am-6.30pm Apr-Sep, to 7pm Jul & Aug, shorter hours rest of year) Intended more as an architectural showpiece (look at that ornately carved facade!) than a military stronghold, Blois' chateau bears the creative mark of several successive French kings. It makes an excellent introduction to the châteaux of the Loire Valley, with elements of Gothic (13th century), Flamboyant Gothic (1498–1503), early Renaissance (1515–24) and classical (1630s) architecture in its four grand wings.

The most famous feature of the Renaissance wing, the royal apartments of François I and Queen Claude, is the **loggia staircase**, decorated with salamanders and curly Fs (heraldic symbols of François I).

Getting There & Away

The train station is 600m uphill from the chateau, on av Jean Laigret.

Amboise €7, 20 minutes, 10 daily

Paris Gares d'Austerlitz and **Montparnasse** from €28.60, 1½ to two hours, 26 daily

Around Blois

CHÂTEAU DE CHEVERNY

Thought by many to be the most perfectly proportioned château of all, **Cheverny** (☎02 54 79 96 29; www.chateau-cheverny.fr; adult/child €9.50/6.50; ⏰9am-7pm Apr-Sep, 10am-5pm Oct-Mar) represents the zenith of French classical architecture: the perfect blend of symmetry, geometry and aesthetic order. Since its construction between 1625 and 1634 by Jacques Hurault, an intendant to Louis XII, the castle has hardly been altered, and its interior decoration includes some of the most sumptuous furnishings, tapestries and objets d'art anywhere in the Loire Valley.

Tintin fans might find the château's facade oddly familiar: Hergé used it as a model (minus the two end towers) for Moulinsart (Marlinspike) Hall, the ancestral home of Tintin's irascible sidekick, Captain Haddock. A dynamic exhibition, Les Secrets de Moulinsart, explores the Tintin connections with re-created scenes, thunder and other special effects.

Cheverny is 16km southeast of Blois.

Amboise

POP 13,375

The childhood home of Charles VIII and final resting place of Leonardo da Vinci, elegant Amboise, 23km northeast of Tours, is pleasantly perched along the southern bank of the Loire and overlooked by its fortified chateau.

Sights

Château Royal d'Amboise Château (☎02 47 57 52 23; www.chateau-amboise.com; place Michel Debré; adult/child €10.70/7.20, with audioguide €14.70/10.20; ⏰9am-7pm Jul & Aug, to 6pm Apr-Oct, shorter hours Nov-Mar) Elegantly tiered on a rocky escarpment above town, this easily defendable castle presented a formidable prospect to would-be attackers – but saw little military action. It was more often a weekend getaway from the official royal seat at Blois. Charles VIII (r 1483–98), born and bred here, was responsible for the château's Italianate remodelling in 1492. Today just a few of the original 15th- and 16th-century structures survive, notably the Flamboyant Gothic wing and Chapelle

St-Hubert, the final resting place of Leonardo da Vinci. They have thrilling views to the river, town and gardens.

Le Clos Lucé Historic Building

(**02 47 57 00 73; www.vinci-closluce.com; 2 rue du Clos Lucé; adult/child €14/9, joint family tickets reduced; 9am-8pm Jul & Aug, 9am-7pm Feb-Jun & Sep-Oct, 9am-6pm Nov & Dec, 10am-6pm Jan;**) Leonardo da Vinci took up residence at this grand manor house in 1516 on the invitation of François I. An admirer of the Italian Renaissance, François named da Vinci 'first painter, engineer and king's architect'. Already 64 by the time he arrived, da Vinci spent his time sketching, tinkering and dreaming up new contraptions, scale models of which are now displayed throughout the home and its expansive **gardens**. Visitors tour rooms where da Vinci worked and the bedroom where he drew his last breath on 2 May 1519.

Sleeping

Au Charme Rabelaisien B&B **€€**

(**02 47 57 53 84; www.au-charme-rabelaisien.com; 25 rue Rabelais; d incl breakfast €92-179;**) At this calm haven in the centre, Sylvie offers the perfect small B&B experience. Mixing modern fixtures with antique charm, three comfy rooms share a flower-filled garden, pool and free enclosed parking. The spacious Chambre Nature is delightfully secluded and only a few steps from the pool. Breakfasts are fab.

Le Clos d'Amboise Historic Hotel **€€€**

(**02 47 30 10 20; www.leclosamboise.com; 27 rue Rabelais; r €140-210, ste €210-295;**) Backed by a vast grassy lawn, complete with 200-year-old trees, a heated pool and parking, this posh pad offers a taste of country living in the heart of town. Stylish features abound, from luxurious fabrics to wood-panelling and antique beds. The best rooms have separate sitting areas, original fireplaces or garden-front windows.

Eating

Chez Bruno Bistro **€**

(**02 47 57 73 49; www.bistrotchezbruno.com; 38-40 place Michel Debré; mains €8-12; lunch**

Hôtel-Dieu des Hospices de Beaune

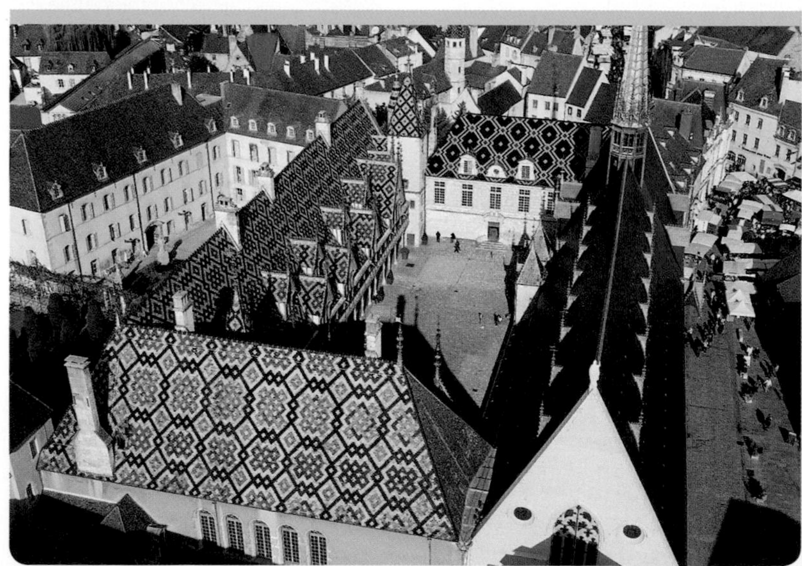

& dinner Tue-Sat) Uncork a host of local vintages in a lively contemporary setting just beneath the towering château. Tables of chatting visitors and locals alike dig into delicious, inexpensive regional cooking. If you're after Loire Valley wine tips, this is the place.

La Fourchette Traditional **€€**
(☎06 11 78 16 98; 9 rue Malebranche; lunch/dinner menus €15/24; ⏲noon-1.30pm Tue-Sat, 7-9.30pm Fri & Sat) Tucked into a back alley behind the tourist office, this is Amboise's favourite address for straightforward home cooking. Chef Christine makes you feel like you've been invited to her house for lunch... It's small so reserve ahead.

Information

Tourist Office (☎02 47 57 09 28; www.amboise-valdeloire.com; quai du Général de Gaulle; ⏲9.30am-6pm Mon-Sat, 10am-1pm & 2-5pm Sun, closed Sun Nov-Mar) Sells walking and cycling maps, plus discount ticket combinations for the château, Clos Lucé and the Pagode de Chanteloup, and offers walking tours. Amboise Tour is their free app. Located riverside.

Getting There & Around

From the **train station (bd Gambetta)**, 1.5km north of the chateau on the opposite side of the Loire, there are services to **Blois** (€7, 20 minutes, 13 daily) and **Paris Gare d'Austerlitz** (€15, 1¾ hours, four daily).

BURGUNDY & THE RHÔNE VALLEY

If there's one place in France where you're really going to find out what makes the nation tick, it's Burgundy. Two of the country's enduring passions – food and wine – come together in this gorgeously rural region, and if you're a sucker for hearty food and the fruits of the vine, you'll be in seventh heaven.

If You Like... French Chateaux

For architecture aficionados, touring the Loire is a never-ending pleasure. Start with Chambord and Cheverny, then seek out these other sumptuous chateaux.

1 **CHATEAU DU CHENONCEAU**
(☎02 47 23 90 07; www.chenonceau.com; adult/child €12.50/9.50, with audioguide €17/13.50; ⏲9am-7pm Apr-Sep, shorter hours rest of year) With its supremely graceful arches spanning the languid Cher River, Chenonceau is one of the most elegant and unusual chateaux in the Loire Valley. Don't miss the 60m-long Grande Gallerie. It's 20km south of Amboise.

2 **CHATEAU D'AZAY-LE-RIDEAU**
(☎02 47 45 42 04; www.azay-le-rideau.monuments-nationaux.fr/en; adult/child €8.50/free; ⏲9.30am-6pm Apr-Sep, to 7pm Jul & Aug, 10am-5.15pm Oct-Mar) Built in the 1500s, this romantic chateau is surrounded by a glassy moat that throws back reflections of its turreted facade. It's particularly well-known for its loggia staircase and night-time summer spectacles. It's 26km southwest of Tours.

Beaune

POP 22,620

Beaune (pronounced 'bone'), 44km south of Dijon, is the unofficial capital of the Côte d'Or. This thriving town's raison d'être and the source of its joie de vivre is wine: making it, tasting it, selling it, but most of all, drinking it. Consequently, Beaune is one of the best places in all of France for wine tasting.

Sights & Activities

Hôtel-Dieu des Hospices de Beaune Historic Building
(www.hospices-de-beaune.com; rue de l'Hôtel-Dieu; adult/child €7/3; ⏲9am-6.30pm) Built in 1443, this magnificent Gothic hospital (until 1971) is famously topped by stunning turrets and pitched rooftops covered

Burgundy Vineyards

Burgundy's most renowned vintages come from the **Côte d'Or** (Golden Hillside), a range of hills made of limestone, flint and clay that runs south from Dijon for about 60km. The northern section, the **Côte de Nuits**, stretches from Marsannay-la-Côte south to Corgoloin and produces reds known for their robust, full-bodied character. The southern section, the **Côte de Beaune**, lies between Ladoix-Serrigny and Santenay and produces great reds and whites.

Tourist offices provide brochures: *The Burgundy Wine Road* is an excellent free booklet published by the Burgundy Tourist Board (www.bourgogne-tourisme.com) and *Roadmap to the Wines of Burgundy* is a useful map. There's also the **Route des Grands Crus** (www.road-of-the-fine-burgundy-wines.com), a signposted road route of some of the most celebrated Côte de Nuits vineyards. Mandatory tasting stops for oenophiles after nirvana include 16th-century **Château du Clos de Vougeot** (03 80 62 86 09; www.closdevougeot.fr; Vougeot; adult/child €5/2.50; 9am-6.30pm Apr-Sep, 9-11.30am & 2-5.30pm Oct-Mar, closes 5pm Sat year-round) (excellent guided tours) and **L'Imaginarium** (03 80 62 61 40; www.imaginarium-bourgogne.com; av du Jura, Nuits-St-Georges; adult incl basic/grand cru tasting €8/15, child €5; 2-7pm Mon, 10am-7pm Tue-Sun) (entertaining wine museum) in Nuits-St-Georges.

Wine & Voyages (03 80 61 15 15; www.wineandvoyages.com; tours from €53) and **Alter & Go** (06 23 37 92 04; www.alterandgo.fr; tours from €70), with an emphasis on history and winemaking methods, run minibus tours in English; reserve online or at the Dijon tourist office.

in multicoloured tiles. Interior highlights include the barrel-vaulted **Grande Salle** (look for the dragons and peasant heads up on the roof beams); the mural-covered **St-Hughes Room**; an 18th-century **pharmacy** lined with flasks once filled with elixirs and powders; and the multipanelled masterpiece **Polyptych of the Last Judgement** by 15th-century Flemish painter Rogier van der Weyden, depicting Judgment Day in glorious technicolour.

Moutarderie Fallot Mustard Factory

(Mustard Mill; 03 80 22 10 10; www.fallot.com; 31 rue du Faubourg Bretonnière; adult/child €10/8; tasting room 9.30am-6pm Mon-Sat; tours 10am & 11.30am Mon-Sat mid-Mar–mid-Nov, plus 3.30pm & 5pm Jun-Sep, by arrangement rest of year) Burgundy's last family-run stone-ground mustard company offers guided tours through its mustard museum, focusing on mustard's history, folklore and traditional production techniques, with kid-friendly opportunities for hand-milling mustard seeds. An alternate tour focuses on Fallot's modern mustard production facility. Reserve tours ahead at Beaune's tourist office. Drop-ins can sample and purchase over a dozen varieties in the brand-new *dégustation* room.

Marché aux Vins Wine Tasting

(www.marcheauxvins.com; 2 rue Nicolas Rolin; 10am-7pm Apr-Oct, 10am-noon & 2-7pm Nov-Mar) Sample seven wines for €11, or 10 for €15, in the candle-lit former Église des Cordeliers and its cellars. Wandering among the vintages takes about an hour. The finest wines are at the end; look for the *premier crus* and the *grand cru* (wine of exceptional quality).

Sleeping

Les Jardins de Loïs B&B **€€**

(03 80 22 41 97; www.jardinsdelois.com; 8 bd Bretonnière; incl breakfast r €149, ste €180-190, apt €280-350;) An unexpected oasis

in the middle of the city, this luxurious B&B encompasses several ample rooms, including two suites and a 135-sq-metre top floor apartment with drop-dead gorgeous views of Beaune's rooftops. The vast garden, complete with rose bushes and fruit trees, makes a dreamy place to sit and enjoy wine grown on the hotel's private *domaine*. Free parking.

Chez Marie B&B **€€**
(**☎06 64 63 48 20; www.chezmarieabeaune.com; 14 rue Poissonnerie; incl breakfast d €85-115, tr/q €135/155;**) At this peaceful haven on a residential street only a five-minute stroll from central Beaune, Marie and Yves make visitors feel right at home, sharing conversation and travel-planning advice (especially for cyclists) over breakfast in the sweet central garden. The four rooms, including two family-friendly apartments with kitchenettes, are impeccably simple and airy. Bikes (regular and electric) are available for rent.

Eating

Le Bacchus Modern Burgundian **€€**
(**☎03 80 24 07 78; 6 Faubourg Madeleine; lunch menus €14-16.50, dinner menus €26.50-33; noon-1.30pm & 7-10pm**) The welcome is warm and the food exceptional at this small restaurant just outside Beaune's centre. Multilingual co-owner Anna works the tables while her partner Olivier whips up market-fresh menus that blend classic flavours (steak with Fallot mustard) with tasty surprises (gazpacho with tomato-basil ice cream). Save room for splendid desserts such as Bourbon vanilla crème brûlée, flambéed at your table.

Loiseau des Vignes Gastronomic **€€€**
(**☎03 80 24 12 06; www.bernard-loiseau.com; 31 rue Maufoux; lunch menus €20-28, dinner menus €59-95; noon-2pm & 7-10pm Tue-Sat**) For that special meal with your significant other, this culinary shrine is the place to go. Expect stunning concoctions ranging from caramelised pigeon to *quenelles de sandre* (dumplings made from pike fish), all exquisitely presented. And even the most budget-conscious can indulge – lunch menus are a bargain. In summer, the verdant garden is a plus.

Information

Tourist Office (**☎03 80 26 21 30; www.beaune-tourisme.fr; 6 bd Perpreuil; 9am-6.30pm Mon-Sat, 9am-6pm Sun**) Sells Pass Beaune and has lots of brochures about the town and nearby vineyards. An annexe (**1 rue de l'Hôtel-Dieu; 10am-1pm & 2-6pm**) opposite the Hôtel-Dieu keeps shorter hours.

Getting There & Away

Train

Lyon-Part Dieu €26.50, 1¾ hours, 16 daily

Nuits-St-Georges from €3.60, 10 minutes, eight daily

Paris Gare de Lyon TGV €75, 2¼ hours, two daily; non-TGV €49, 3½ hours, seven daily

Lyon

POP 499,800

Gourmets, eat your heart out: Lyon is *the* gastronomic capital of France, with a lavish table of piggy-driven dishes and delicacies to savour. The city has been a commercial, industrial and banking powerhouse for the past 500 years, and is still France's third-largest city, with outstanding art museums, a dynamic nightlife, green parks and a Unesco-listed Old Town.

Sights

The **Lyon City Card** (**www.en.lyon-france.com/Lyon-City-Card; 1/2/3 days adult €22/32/42, child €13.50/18.50/23.50**) covers admission to every Lyon museum and a number of attractions. The card also includes unlimited travel on buses, trams, the funicular and metro. Buy it online or from the tourist office.

VIEUX LYON

Cathédrale St-Jean Cathedral
(**place St-Jean, 5e; 8.15am-7.45pm Mon-Fri, to 7pm Sat & Sun; M Vieux Lyon**) Lyon's partly Romanesque cathedral was built between

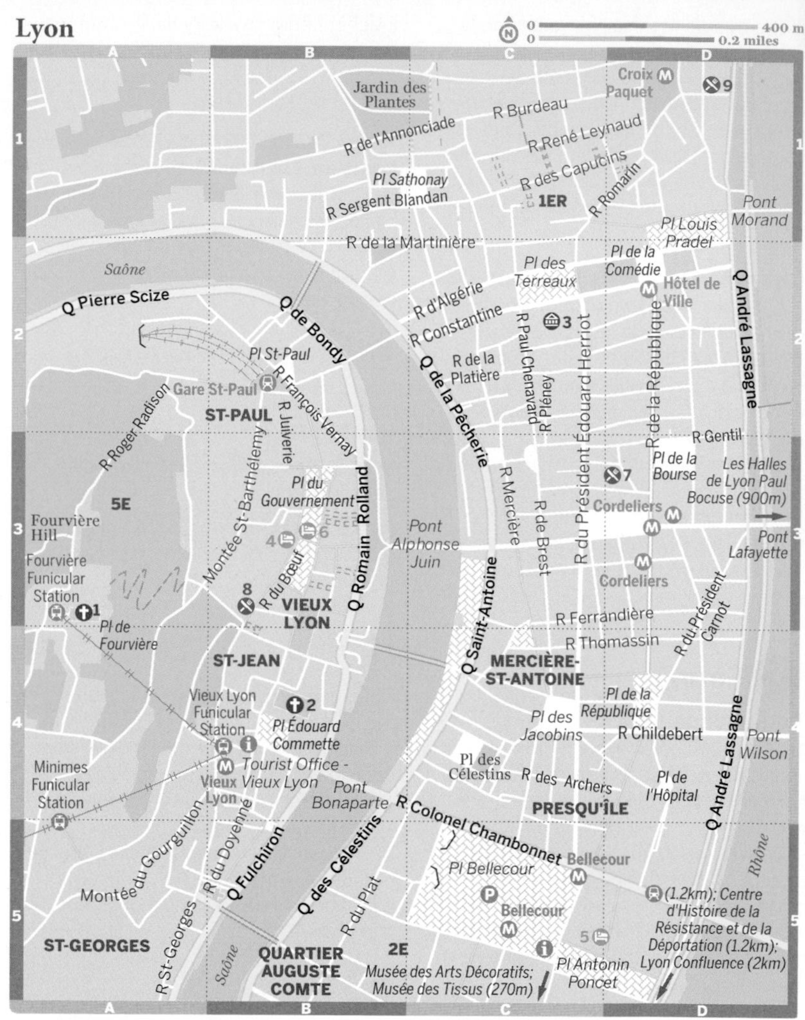

Lyon

Sights

1 Basilique Notre Dame de Fourvière A3
2 Cathédrale St-Jean B4
3 Musée des Beaux-Arts C2

Sleeping

4 Cour des Loges B3
5 Jardin d'Hiver C5
6 Lyon Renaissance B3

Eating

7 Le Musée D3
8 Les Adrets B3
9 L'Ourson qui Boit D1

the late 11th and early 16th centuries. The portals of its Flamboyant Gothic façade, completed in 1480, are decorated with 280 square stone medallions. Inside, the highlight is the **astronomical clock** in the north transept. It was recently off-limits due to restoration work, but is expected to resume its regular daily chiming (at noon, 2pm, 3pm and 4pm) by the time you read this.

Medieval & Renaissance Architecture Architecture
(Ⓜ Vieux Lyon) Lovely old buildings line rue du Bœuf, rue St-Jean and rue des Trois Maries. Crane your neck upwards to see gargoyles and other cheeky stone characters carved on window ledges along rue Juiverie, home to Lyon's Jewish community in the Middle Ages.

FOURVIÈRE

Over two millennia ago, the Romans built the city of Lugdunum on the slopes of Fourvière. Today, Lyon's 'hill of prayer' – topped by a basilica and the **Tour Métallique**, an Eiffel Tower–like structure built in 1893 and used as a TV transmitter – affords spectacular views of the city and its two rivers. Footpaths wind uphill, but the **funicular** (place Édouard Commette, 5e; one-way €1.70) is the least taxing way up.

Crowning Fourvière hill is the **Basilique Notre Dame de Fourvière** (www.fourviere.org; place de Fourvière, 5e; rooftop tour adult/child €6/3; 🕗8am-7pm; funicular Fourvière), an iconic, 27m-high basilica, a superb example of exaggerated 19th-century ecclesiastical architecture.

PRESQU'ÎLE & CONFLUENCE

The centrepiece of **place des Terreaux** is a 19th-century fountain sculpted by Frédéric-Auguste Bartholdi, creator of the Statue of Liberty. The **Musée des Beaux-Arts** (www.mba-lyon.fr; 20 place des Terreaux, 1er; adult/child incl audioguide €7/free; 🕗10am-6pm Wed, Thu & Sat-Mon, 10.30am-6pm Fri; Ⓜ Hôtel de Ville) showcases France's finest collection of sculptures and paintings outside Paris.

Lyonnais silks are showcased at the **Musée des Tissus** (www.musee-des-tissus.com; 34 rue de la Charité, 2e; adult/child €10/7.50, after 4pm €8/5.50; 🕗10am-5.30pm Tue-Sun; Ⓜ Ampère). Next door, the **Musée des Arts Décoratifs** (34 rue de la Charité, 2e; free with Musée des Tissus ticket; 🕗10am-noon & 2-5.30pm Tue-Sun) displays 18th-century furniture, tapestries, wallpaper, ceramics and silver.

Laid out in the 17th century, **place Bellecour** – one of Europe's largest public squares – is pierced by an equestrian **statue of Louis XIV**. South of here, past **Gare de Perrache**, lies the once-downtrodden industrial area of **Lyon Confluence** (www.lyon-confluence.fr), where the Rhône and Saône meet. Trendy

Basilique Notre Dame de Fourvière, Lyon

restaurants now line its quays, and the ambitious **Musée des Confluences** (**www.museedesconfluences.fr; 28 Boulevard des Belges, 6e**), a science-and-humanities museum inside a futuristic steel-and-glass transparent crystal, will open here in 2014.

RIVE GAUCHE

Musée Lumière — Museum

(**www.institut-lumiere.org; 25 rue du Premier Film, 8e; adult/child €6.50/5.50; ⏲10am-6.30pm Tue-Sun; M Monplaisir-Lumière**) Cinema's glorious beginnings are showcased at the art-nouveau home of Antoine Lumière, who moved to Lyon with sons Auguste and Louis in 1870. The brothers shot the first reels of the world's first motion picture, *La Sortie des Usines Lumières* (*Exit of the Lumières Factories*) here on 19 March 1895.

Centre d'Histoire de la Résistance et de la Déportation — Museum

(**www.chrd.lyon.fr; 14 av Berthelot, 7e; adult/child €6/free; ⏲10am-6pm Wed-Sun; M Perrache or Jean Macé**) The WWII headquarters of Gestapo commander Klaus Barbie evokes Lyon's role as the 'Capital of the Resistance' through moving multimedia exhibits. Extensively remodelled in 2012, the museum includes sound recordings of deportees and Resistance fighters, plus a varied collection of everyday objects associated with the Resistance (including the parachute Jean Moulin used to re-enter France in 1942).

Sleeping

Lyon Renaissance — Apartment €€

(**☎04 27 89 30 58; www.lyon-renaissance.com; 3 rue des Tourelles, 5e; apt €95-115; 📶; M Vieux Lyon**) Friendly owners Françoise and Patrick rent these two superbly situated Vieux Lyon apartments with beamed ceilings and kitchen facilities. The smaller third-floor walk-up sleeps two, with windows overlooking a pretty tree-shaded square. A second unit, opposite Vieux Lyon's most famous medieval tower, has a spacious living room with ornamental fireplace and fold-out couch, plus a mezzanine with double bed.

Cathédrale St-Jean (p229) and Basilique Notre Dame de Fourvière (p231), Lyon

Jardin d'Hiver B&B **€€**
(☎04 78 28 69 34; www.guesthouse-lyon.com; 10 rue des Marronniers, 2e; s/d incl breakfast €120/140, 1-/2-bedroom apt per week from €520/550; ❄ 📶; M Bellecour) Chic and centrally located, this 3rd-floor B&B (no lift) has two beautifully maintained en-suite rooms replete with modern conveniences – one in understated purple and pistachio, the other in vivid purple and orange. Friendly owner Annick Bournonville serves 100% organic breakfasts in the foliage-filled breakfast room. Next door, her son rents out apartments with kitchen and laundry facilities.

Cour des Loges Hotel **€€€**
(☎04 72 77 44 44; www.courdesloges.com; 2-8 rue du Bœuf, 5e; d €190-485, junior ste €340-655; ❄ @ 📶 ≋; M Vieux Lyon) Four 14th- to 17th-century houses wrapped around a *traboule* (secret passage) with preserved features such as Italianate loggias make this an exquisite place to stay. Individually decorated rooms woo with designer bathroom fittings and bountiful antiques, while decadent facilities include a spa, an elegant restaurant (*menus* €85 to €105), swish cafe (lunch *menu* €17.50, mains €22 to €30) and cross-vaulted bar.

Eating

Les Halles de Lyon Paul Bocuse Market **€**
(www.hallespaulbocuse.lyon.fr; 102 cours Lafayette, 3e; ⏲7am-10.30pm Tue-Sat, to 4.30pm Sun; M Part-Dieu) Lyon's famed indoor food market has nearly five dozen stalls selling countless gourmet delights. Pick up a round of runny St Marcellin from legendary cheesemonger Mère Richard, and a knobbly Jésus de Lyon from Charcuterie Sibilia. Or enjoy a sit-down lunch of local produce, especially enjoyable on Sundays when local families congregate for shellfish and white-wine brunches.

Le Musée Bouchon **€€**
(☎04 78 37 71 54; 2 rue des Forces; lunch/dinner menus €23/28; ⏲noon-2pm & 7.30-9.30pm Tue-Sat; M Cordeliers) Housed in the stables of Lyon's former Hôtel de Ville, this delightful *bouchon* serves a splendid array of meat-heavy Lyonnais classics alongside veggie-centric treats such as roasted peppers with fresh goat cheese. The daily changing *menu* features 10 appetisers and 10 main dishes, plus five scrumptious desserts, all served on cute china plates at long family-style tables.

L'Ourson qui Boit Fusion **€€**
(☎04 78 27 23 37; 23 rue Royale, 1er; lunch/dinner menus €18/28; ⏲noon-1.30pm & 7.30-9.30pm Mon, Tue & Thu-Sat; M Croix Paquet) On the fringes of Croix Rousse, Japanese chef Akira Nishigaki puts his own splendid spin on French cuisine, with plenty of locally sourced fresh vegetables and light, clean flavours. The ever-changing *menu* of two daily appetisers and two main dishes is complemented by good wines, attentive service and scrumptious desserts. Well worth reserving ahead.

Les Adrets Lyonnais **€€**
(☎04 78 38 24 30; 30 rue du Bœuf, 5e; lunch menu €17.50, dinner menus €27-45; ⏲noon-1.30pm & 7.45-9pm Mon-Fri; M Vieux Lyon) This atmospheric spot serves an exceptionally good-value lunch *menu* (€17.50 including wine and coffee). The mix is half classic *bouchon* fare, half alternative choices such as Parma ham and truffle risotto, or duck breast with roasted pears.

Drinking & Entertainment

Cafe terraces on place des Terreaux buzz with all-hours drinkers, as do the British, Irish and other-styled pubs on nearby rue Ste-Catherine, 1er, and rue Lainerie and rue St-Jean, 5e, in Vieux Lyon.

Floating bars with DJs and live bands rock until around 3am aboard the string of *péniches* (river barges) moored along the Rhône's left bank. Scout out the section of quai Victor Augagneur between Pont Lafayette (metro Cordeliers or Guichard) and Pont de la Guillotière (metro Guillotière).

Le Sucre Live Music
(www.le-sucre.eu; 50 quai Rambaud, 2e; ⏲6pm-midnight Wed & Thu, 7pm-6am Fri & Sat) Down in the Confluence neighbourhood, Lyon's

newest and most innovative club hosts DJs, live shows and eclectic arts events on its super-cool roof terrace atop a 1930s sugar factory, La Sucrière.

 Information

Tourist Office (☎04 72 77 69 69; www.lyon-france.com; place Bellecour, 2e; ⏰9am-6pm; Ⓜ Bellecour) In the centre of Presqu'île, Lyon's exceptionally helpful, multilingual and well-staffed main tourist office offers a variety of city walking tours and sells the Lyon City Card. There's a smaller branch (Av du Doyenné, 5e; ⏰10am-5.30pm; Ⓜ Vieux Lyon) just outside the Vieux Lyon metro station.

 Getting There & Away

Air

Lyon-St-Exupéry Airport (www.lyonaeroports.com), 25km east of the city, serves 120 direct destinations across Europe and beyond, including many budget carriers.

Train

Lyon has two main-line train stations: Gare de la Part-Dieu (Ⓜ Part-Dieu), 1.5km east of the Rhône, and Gare de Perrache (Ⓜ Perrache).

Destinations by direct TGV include:

Marseille from €52, 1¾ hours, every 30 to 60 minutes

Paris Gare de Lyon from €73, two hours, every 30 to 60 minutes

Paris Charles de Gaulle Airport from €95, two hours, at least 11 daily

 Getting Around

Tramway Rhônexpress (www.rhonexpress.fr; adult/youth/child €15.70/13/free) links the airport with Part-Dieu train station in under 30 minutes.

Buses, trams, a four-line metro and two funiculars linking Vieux Lyon to Fourvière are run by TCL (www.tcl.fr). Public transport runs from around 5am to midnight. Tickets cost €1.70. Time-stamp tickets on all forms of public transport or risk a fine.

Bikes are available from 200-odd bike stations thanks to Vélo'v (www.velov.grandlyon.com; first 30min free, next 30min €1, each subsequent 30min period €2).

THE FRENCH ALPS & JURA

Hiking, skiing, majestic panoramas – the French Alps have it all when it comes to the great outdoors. But you'll also find great gastronomy, good nightlife and plenty of history.

Chamonix

POP 9050 / ELEV 1037M

With the pearly white peaks of the Mont Blanc massif as sensational backdrop, being an icon comes naturally to Chamonix. First 'discovered' by Brits William Windham and Richard Pococke in 1741, this is the mecca of mountaineering. Its knife-edge peaks, plunging slopes and massive glaciers have enthralled generations of adventurers and thrill-seekers ever since. Its après-ski scene is equally pumping.

Sights

Le Brévent Viewpoint

The highest peak on the western side of the Chamonix Valley, Le Brévent (2525m) has tremendous views of the Mont Blanc massif, myriad hiking trails, ledges to paraglide from and the summit restaurant **Le Panoramic**. Reach it on the **Télécabine de Planpraz** (www.compagniedumontblanc.co.uk; adult/child one-way €13.20/11.20, return €16/13.60), 400m west of the tourist office, and then the **Téléphérique du Brévent** (www.compagniedumontblanc.co.uk; 29 rte Henriette d'Angeville; adult/child one-way €22/18.70, return €29.50/25; ⏰mid-Dec–mid-Apr & mid-Jun–mid-Sep). Plenty of family-friendly trails begin at **Planpraz** (2000m).

Mer de Glace Glacier

France's largest glacier, the glistening 200m-deep Mer de Glace (Sea of Ice) snakes 7km down the northern side of Mont Blanc, moving up to 1cm an hour (about 90m a year). The **Train du Montenvers** (www.compagniedumontblanc.co.uk; adult/child one-way €24/20.40, return €29.50/25; ⏰closed late Sep–mid-Oct), a picturesque, 5km-long cog railway opened in 1909, links Chamonix' Gare du Monten-

JOHN ELK/GETTY IMAGES ©

Don't Miss Aiguille du Midi

A jagged finger of rock soaring above glaciers, snowfields and rocky crags, 8km from the hump of Mont Blanc, the Aiguille du Midi (3842m) is one of Chamonix' most distinctive geographical features. If you can handle the altitude, the 360-degree views of the French, Swiss and Italian Alps from the summit are (quite literally) breathtaking. Year-round, you can float in a cable car from Chamonix to the Aiguille du Midi on the vertiginous **Téléphérique de l'Aiguille du Midi** (www.compagniedumontblanc.co.uk; place de l'Aiguille du Midi; adult/child return to Aiguille du Midi €55/47, to Plan de l'Aiguille summer €29.50/25, winter €16/14; 1st ascent btwn 7.10am & 8.30am, last ascent btwn 3.30pm & 5pm).

vers with Montenvers (1913m), from where a cable car takes you down to the glacier and the **Grotte de la Mer de Glace** (closed last half of May & late Sep–mid-Oct), an ice cave whose frozen tunnels and ice sculptures change colour like mood rings.

Musée des Cristaux Museum

(Esplanade St-Michel, Espace Tiarraz; adult/child €5/free; 2-6pm daily, closed mid-Nov–early Dec) Has a truly dazzling collection of crystals, rocks and minerals, many from around Mont Blanc. **L'Espace Alpinisme** focuses on the art and science of mountaineering with creative interactive displays and spectacular photos and videos of seemingly impossible ascents. Situated behind the church.

Activities

The ski season runs from mid-December to mid-April. Summer activities – hiking, canyoning, mountaineering etc – generally start in June and end in September. The **Compagnie des Guides de Chamonix** (04 50 53 00 88; www.chamonix-guides.com; 190 place de l'Église, Maison de la Montagne; 8.30am-noon & 2.30-7.30pm, closed Sun & Mon late Apr–mid-Jun & mid-Sep–mid-Dec) is

Right: French and Swiss Alps, near Chamonix;
Below: Mer de Glace train (p234), Chamonix

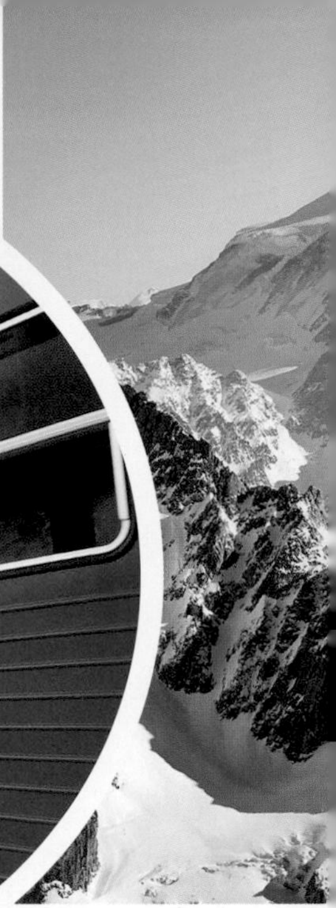

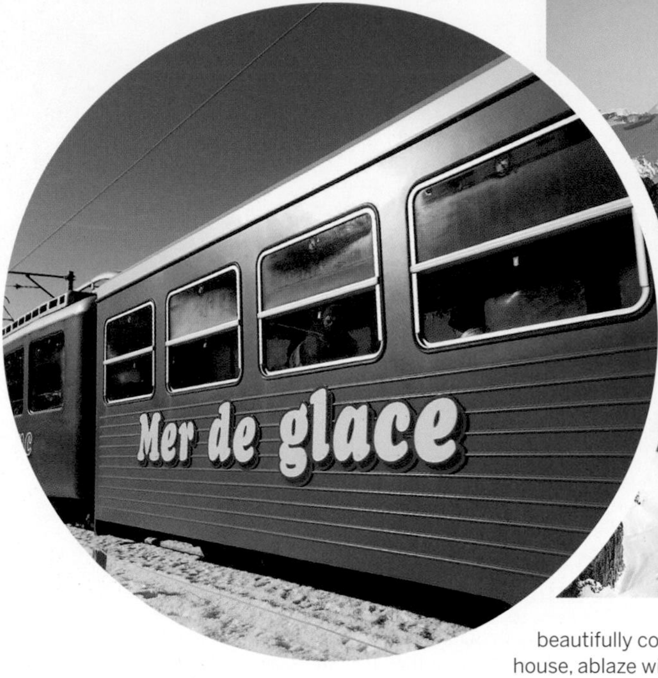

the most famous of all the guide companies and has guides for virtually every activity, whatever the season.

Sleeping

Hôtel Richemond Hotel **€€**
(☎04 50 53 08 85; www.richemond.fr; 228 rue du Docteur Paccard; s/d/tr €75/120/153; ⏲closed mid-Apr–mid-Jun & mid-Sep–mid-Dec; 📶) In a grand old building constructed in 1914 (and run by the same family ever since), this hotel – as friendly as it is central – has 52 spacious rooms with views of either Mont Blanc or Le Brévent; some are pleasantly old-fashioned, others recently renovated in white, black and beige, and three still have cast-iron bathtubs. Outstanding value.

Auberge du Manoir Hotel **€€**
(☎04 50 53 10 77; www.aubergedumanoir.com; 8 rte du Bouchet; s/d/tr €130/150/220; ⏲closed 2 wks in late Apr & 2 wks in autumn; 📶) This beautifully converted farmhouse, ablaze with geraniums in summer, offers 18 pine-panelled rooms that are quaint but never cloying, pristine mountain views, an outdoor hot tub, a sauna and a bar whose open fire keeps things cosy. Family-owned.

Hotel L'Oustalet Hotel **€€**
(☎04 50 55 54 99; www.hotel-oustalet.com; 330 rue du Lyret; d/q €148/190; ⏲closed mid-May–mid-Jun & mid-Oct–mid-Dec; 📶🏊) A block from the Aiguille du Midi cable car, this lift-equipped hotel has 15 decent rooms, snugly built of thick pine, that open onto balconies with Mont Blanc views. To unwind, you can curl up by the fire with a *chocolat chaud* or loll about in the jacuzzi, hamam or sauna – or, in summer, take a dip in the garden pool.

Eating

Papillon Cafe **€**
(416 rue Joseph Vallot; mains €5-8; ⏲11am-8pm Mon-Sat, 4-8pm Sun mid-Dec–early May &

mid-Jun–early Oct;) A British-owned hole-in-the-wall take-out place that does great home-made curries, chilli con carne, Italian-style meatballs, noodle soup and deli-style sandwiches. Has plenty of vegie, vegan and gluten-free options.

Le Cap Horn French **€€**
(04 50 21 80 80; www.caphorn-chamonix.com; 78 rue des Moulins; lunch menu €20, other menus €29-39; noon-2pm & 7-10pm daily year-round) Housed in a gorgeous, two-storey chalet decorated with model sailboats – joint homage to the Alps and Cape Horn – this highly praised restaurant, opened in 2012, serves French and Asian-inflected dishes such as pan-seared duck breast with honey and soy sauce, fisherman's stew and, for dessert, *souffle au Grand Marnier*. Reserve for dinner Friday and Saturday.

Munchie Fusion **€€**
(04 50 53 45 41; www.munchie.eu; 87 rue des Moulins; mains €19-24; 7pm-2am daily, closed 2 weeks May & mid-Oct–Nov) Franco-Asian fusion has been the lip-smacking mainstay of this casual, Swedish-skippered restaurant since 1997. Specialities such as steak with spicy Béarnaise sauce are presented with panache. Reservations recommended during the ski season.

Drinking & Nightlife

MBC Microbrewery
(Micro Brasserie de Chamonix; www.mbchx.com; 350 rte du Bouchet; 4pm-2am Mon-Thu, 10am-2am Fri-Sun) Run by four Canadians, this trendy microbrewery is fab. Be it with their phenomenal burgers (€10 to €15), cheesecake of the week, live music (Sunday from 9.30pm) or amazing beers, MBC delivers. Busiest from 5pm to 11pm.

Chambre Neuf Bar
(272 av Michel Croz; 7am-1pm daily year-round;) Chamonix' most spirited après-ski party (4pm to 8pm), fuelled by a Swedish band and dancing on the tables, spills out the front door of Chambre Neuf. Wildly popular with seasonal workers.

Information

Tourist Office (☎04 50 53 00 24; www.chamonix.com; 85 place du Triangle de l'Amitié; ⏲9am-12.30pm & 2-6pm, longer hrs winter & summer) Information on accommodation, activities, the weather and cultural events.

Getting There & Away

Bus

From **Chamonix bus station** (☎04 50 53 01 15; place de la Gare; ⏲8-11.30am & 1.15-6.15pm in winter, shorter hrs rest of yr), next to the train station, **SAT-Mont-Blanc** (☎04 50 78 05 33; www.sat-montblanc.com) operates five daily buses run to/from Geneva airport (one way/return €30/50, 1½ to two hours). Advanced booking only.

Train

The Mont Blanc Express narrow-gauge train trundles from St-Gervais-Le Fayet station, 23km west of Chamonix, to Martigny in Switzerland, stopping en route in Chamonix. There are nine to 12 return trips daily between Chamonix and St-Gervais (€10, 45 minutes).

From St-Gervais-Le Fayet there are trains to most major French cities.

THE DORDOGNE

If it's French heart and soul you're after, look no further. Tucked in the country's southwestern corner, the Dordogne fuses history, culture and culinary sophistication in one unforgettably scenic package. The region is best known for its sturdy *bastides* (fortified towns), clifftop chateaux and spectacular prehistoric cave paintings, neighboured to the southwest by the Mediterranean-tinged region of **the Lot,** with its endless vintage vineyards.

Sarlat-La-Canéda

POP 10,105

A gorgeous tangle of honey-coloured buildings, alleyways and secret squares make up this unmissable Dordogne village – a natural if touristy launchpad into the Vézère Valley.

Sights

Part of the fun of Sarlat is getting lost in its twisting alleyways and backstreets. **Rue Jean-Jacques Rousseau** or **rue Landry** are good starting points, but for the grandest buildings and *hôtels particuliers*, explore **rue des Consuls**.

Sarlat Markets Market

(place de la Liberté & rue de la République; ⏲8.30am-1pm Wed & 8.30am-6pm Sat) For an introductory French market experience visit Sarlat's heavily touristed Saturday market, which takes over the streets around Cathédrale St-Sacerdos. Depending on the season, delicacies include local mushrooms and duck- and goose-based products such as foie gras. Get *truffe noir* (black truffle) at the winter **Marché aux Truffes** (⏲Sat morning Dec-Feb). An atmospheric largely organic **night market** (⏲6-10pm) operates on Thursday. Seasoned market-goers may prefer others throughout the region.

Cathédrale St-Sacerdos Cathedral

(place du Peyrou) Once part of Sarlat's Cluniac abbey, the original abbey church was built in the 1100s, redeveloped in the early 1500s and remodelled again in the 1700s, so it's a real mix of styles. The belfry and western façade are the oldest parts of the building, while the nave, organ and interior chapels are later additions.

Place du Marché aux Oies Square

A life-size statue of three bronze geese stands in the centre of beautiful place du Marché aux Oies (Goose Market Sq), where live geese are still sold during the Fest'Oie. The square's architecture is exceptional.

Sleeping

Villa des Consuls B&B **€€**

(☎05 53 31 90 05; www.villaconsuls.fr; 3 rue Jean-Jacques Rousseau; d €95-110, apt €150-190; @📶) Despite its Renaissance exterior, the enormous rooms here are modern through and through, with shiny wood floors and sleek furnishings. Several delightful self-contained apartments dot the town, all offering the same mix of period plushness – some also have terraces overlooking the town's rooftops.

La Maison des Peyrat Hotel **€€**
(**05 53 59 00 32; www.maisondespeyrat.com; Le Lac de la Plane; r €80-109**) This beautifully renovated 17th-century house, formerly a nuns' hospital and later an aristocratic hunting lodge, is set on a hill about 1.5km from Sarlat centre. Eleven generously sized rooms are decorated in modern farmhouse style; the best have views over gardens and the countryside beyond. Good restaurant too.

Eating

Le Quatre Saisons Regional Cuisine **€€**
(**05 53 29 48 59; www.4saisons-sarlat-perigord.com; 2 côte de Toulouse; menus from €19; 12.30-2pm & 7.30-9.30pm Thu-Mon;**) A reliable local favourite, hidden in a beautiful stone house on a narrow alley leading uphill from rue de la République. The food is honest and unfussy, taking its cue from market ingredients and regional flavours. The most romantic tables have cross-town views.

Le Grand Bleu Gastronomic **€€€**
(**05 53 31 08 48; www.legrandbleu.eu; 43 av de la Gare; menus €54-125; 12.30-2pm Thu-Sun, 7.30-9.30pm Tue-Sat**) This eminent Michelin-starred restaurant run by chef Maxime Lebrun is renowned for its creative cuisine with elaborate *menus* making maximum use of luxury produce: truffles, lobster, turbot and scallops, with a wine list to match. Cooking courses (€40) are also available. Located 1.5km south of the centre.

Information

Tourist Office (**05 53 31 45 45; www.sarlat-tourisme.com; 3 rue Tourny; 9am-7pm Mon-Sat, 10am-1pm & 2-6pm Sun May-Aug, shorter hours Sep-Apr;**) Sarlat's tourist office is packed with info, but often gets overwhelmed by visitors; the website has it all.

Getting There & Away

The **train station** (**av de la Gare**), 1.3km south of the old city, serves Périgueux (€15.90, 1¾ hours, four daily) and Les Eyzies (€9.80, 50 minutes to 2½ hours, four daily), both via Le Buisson.

Les Eyzies-de-Tayac-Sireuil

POP 842

A hot base for touring the extraordinary cave collection of the **Vézère Valley**, this village is essentially a clutch of touristy shops strung along a central street. Its **Musée National de Préhistoire** (**05 53 06 45 45; www.musee-prehistoire-eyzies.fr; 1 rue du Musée; adult/child €6/4.50, 1st Sun of month free; 9.30am-6.30pm daily Jul &**

Old houses and cave dwellings, Les Eyzies

Prehistoric Paintings

Fantastic prehistoric **caves** with some of the world's finest **cave art** is what makes the Vézère Valley so very special. Most of the caves are closed in winter, and get very busy in summer. Visitor numbers are strictly limited, so you'll need to reserve well ahead.

Of the valley's 175 known sites, the most famous include **Grotte de Font de Gaume** (☎05 53 06 86 00; http://eyzies.monuments-nationaux.fr; adult/child €7.50/free; guided tours 9.30am-5.30pm Sun-Fri mid-May–mid-Sep, 9.30am-12.30pm & 2-5.30pm Sun-Fri mid-Sep–mid-May), 1km northeast of Les Eyzies. About 14,000 years ago, prehistoric artists created the gallery of over 230 figures, including bison, reindeer, horses, mammoths, bears and wolves, of which 25 are on permanent display.

About 7km east of Les Eyzies, **Abri du Cap Blanc** (☎05 53 06 86 00; adult/child €7.50/free; guided tours 9.30am-5.30pm Sun-Fri mid-May–mid-Sep, 9.30am-12.30pm & 2-5.30pm Sun-Fri mid-Sep–mid-May) showcases an unusual sculpture gallery of horses, bison and deer.

Then there is **Grotte de Rouffignac** (☎05 53 05 41 71; www.grottederouffignac.fr; Rouffignac-St-Cernin-de-Reilhac; adult/child €7/4.60; 9-11.30am & 2-6pm Jul & Aug, 10-11.30am & 2-5pm mid-Apr–Jun & Sep-Oct, closed Nov–mid-Apr), sometimes known as the 'Cave of 100 Mammoths' because of its painted mammoths. Access to the caves, hidden in woodland 15km north of Les Eyzies, is aboard a trundling electric train.

Star of the show goes hands down to **Grotte de Lascaux** (Lascaux II; ☎05 53 51 95 03; www.semitour.com; adult/child €8.80/6; 9.30am-6pm), 2km southeast of Montignac, featuring an astonishing menagerie including oxen, deer, horses, reindeer and mammoth, as well as an amazing 5.5m bull, the largest cave drawing ever found. The original cave was closed to the public in 1963 to prevent damage to the paintings, but the most famous sections have been meticulously recreated in a second cave nearby – a massive undertaking that required some 20 artists and took 11 years.

Aug, 9.30am-6pm Wed-Mon Jun & Sep, 9.30am-12.30pm & 2-5.30pm Wed-Mon Oct-May), rife with amazing prehistoric finds, makes a great introduction to the area.

About 250m north of the museum is the Cro-Magnon shelter of **Abri Pataud** (☎05 53 06 92 46; www.mnhn.fr; 20 rue du Moyen Âge; adult/child €5/free; 10am-noon & 2-6pm Sun-Thu, daily Jul & Aug, Mon-Fri Apr–mid-Oct, closed mid-Oct–Mar), with an ibex carving dating from about 19,000 BC. Admission includes a guided tour (some in English).

Train services link Les Eyzies with Sarlat-la-Canéda.

THE ATLANTIC COAST

With quiet country roads winding through vine-striped hills and wild stretches of coastal sands interspersed with misty islands, the Atlantic coast is where France gets back to nature.

If you're a surf nut or a beach bum, then the sandy bays around Biarritz will be right up your alley, while oenophiles can sample the fruits of the vine in the high temple of French winemaking, Bordeaux. Towards the Pyrenees you'll find the Basque Country, which in many ways is closer to the culture of northern Spain than to the rest of France.

Bordeaux

POP 236,000

The new millennium was a turning point for the city long nicknamed La Belle au Bois Dormant (Sleeping Beauty), when the mayor, ex-Prime Minister Alain Juppé, roused Bordeaux, pedestrianising its boulevards, restoring its neoclassical architecture, and implementing a hi-tech public-transport system. Today the city is a Unesco World Heritage Site and, with its merry student population and 2.5 million-odd annual tourists, scarcely sleeps at all.

Sights

Cathédrale St-André Cathedral

(Place Jean Moulin) Lording over the city, and a Unesco World Heritage Site prior to the city's classification, the cathedral's oldest section dates from 1096; most of what you see today was built in the 13th and 14th centuries. Exceptional masonry carvings can be seen in the north portal.

Even more imposing than the cathedral itself is the gargoyled, 50m-high Gothic belfry, **Tour Pey-Berland** **(Place Jean Moulin; adult/child €5.50/free; 10am-1.15pm & 2-6pm Jun-Sep, 10am-12.30pm & 2-5.30pm Oct-May)**, erected between 1440 and 1466. Its spire was added in the 19th century, and in 1863 it was topped off with the statue of Notre Dame de l'Aquitaine (Our Lady of Aquitaine). Scaling the tower's 231 narrow steps rewards you with a spectacular panorama of the city.

Musée d'Aquitaine Museum

(www.musee-aquitaine-bordeaux.fr; 20 cours Pasteur; 11am-6pm Tue-Sun) FREE Gallo-Roman statues and relics dating back 25,000 years are among the highlights at the impressive Musée d'Aquitaine. Ask to borrow an English language catalogue.

CAPC Musée d'Art Contemporain Gallery

(rue Ferrére, Entrepôt 7; temporary exhibitions adult/child €5/2.50; 11am-6pm Tue & Thu-Sun, to 8pm Wed) FREE Built in 1824 as a warehouse for French colonial produce like coffee, cocoa, peanuts and vanilla, the cavernous Entrepôts Lainé creates a dramatic backdrop for cutting-edge modern art at the CAPC Musée d'Art Contemporain. Entry to the permanent collection is free but there is a cover charge for any temporary exhibitions.

On the Wine Trail

Thirsty? The 1000-sq-km wine-growing area around the city of Bordeaux is, along with Burgundy, France's most important producer of top-quality wines. Whet your palate with Bordeaux tourist office's introduction wine-and-cheese courses (€25).

Serious students of the grape can enrol in a two-hour (€39) or two- to three-day course (€390 to €690) at the **École du Vin** (Wine School; 05 56 00 22 66; www.bordeaux.com) inside the **Maison du Vin de Bordeaux** (3 cours du 30 Juillet).

Bordeaux has over 5000 estates where grapes are grown, picked and turned into wine. Smaller chateaux often accept walk-in visitors, but at many places, especially better-known ones, you have to reserve in advance. If you have your own wheels, one of the easiest to visit is **Château Lanessan** (05 56 58 94 80; www.lanessan.com; Cussac-Fort-Medoc; 9am-noon & 2-6pm).

Favourite vine-framed villages brimming with charm and tasting/buying opportunities include medieval **St-Émilion**, port town **Pauillac** and **Listrac-Médoc**. In **Arsac-en-Médoc**, Philippe Raoux's vast glass-and-steel wine centre, **La Winery** (05 56 39 04 90; www.winery.fr; Rond-point des Vendangeurs, D1; 10am-7pm), stuns with concerts and contemporary art exhibitions alongside tastings to determine your *signe œnologique* ('wine sign'; booking required).

Many chateaux close during October's *vendange* (grape harvest).

Detour: Dune du Pilat

This colossal sand dune (sometimes referred to as the Dune de Pyla because of its location in the resort town of Pyla-sur-Mer), 65km west of Bordeaux, stretches from the mouth of the Bassin d'Arcachon southwards for almost 3km. Already the largest in Europe, it's spreading eastwards at 4.5m a year – it has swallowed trees, a road junction and even a hotel.

The view from the top – approximately 114m above sea level – is magnificent. To the west you can see the sandy shoals at the mouth of the Bassin d'Arcachon, including the **Banc d'Arguin bird reserve** and Cap Ferret. Dense dark-green pine forests stretch from the base of the dune eastwards almost as far as the eye can see.

Take care swimming in this area: powerful currents swirl out to sea from the deceptively tranquil *baïnes* (little bays).

Although an easy day trip from Bordeaux, the area around the dune is an enjoyable place to kick back for a while. Most people choose to camp in one of the swag of seasonal campgrounds. Lists and information on all of these (and more bricks-and-mortar-based accommodation) can be found at www.bassin-arcachon.com.

Sleeping

Ecolodge des Chartrons — B&B €€

(☎05 56 81 49 13; www.ecolodgedeschartrons.com; 23 rue Raze; s €107-205, d €119-228; wifi) Hidden away in a little side street off the quays in Bordeaux's Chartrons wine-merchant district. The owner-hosts of this *chambre d'hôte*, Veronique and Yann, have stripped back and limewashed the stone walls of an old house, scrubbed the wide floorboards and brought in recycled antique furniture to create a highly memorable place to stay.

Les Chambres au Coeur de Bordeaux — B&B €€

(☎05 56 52 43 58; www.aucoeurdebordeaux.fr; 28 rue Boulan; r €105-155; wifi) This renovated townhouse is now a swish B&B run like a small boutique hotel. Its five charming rooms are a very Bordeaux-appropriate mix of the old and the new, and most evenings your hosts offer an *apero* and tapas tasting session (€20-25) at 7pm.

L'Hôtel Particulier — Boutique Hotel €€€

(☎05 57 88 28 80; www.lhotel-particulier.com; 44 rue Vital-Carles; apt from €89, d from €203; wifi) When you step into this fabulous boutique hotel, with its secret courtyard garden, and find a thousand eyes staring at you from the reception walls and lampshades made only of feathers, you realise you've stumbled upon somewhere special. The rooms don't disappoint – they are highly extravagant affairs with huge fireplaces, carved ceilings, free-standing bathtubs and quality furnishings.

Eating

Le Cheverus Café — Bistro €

(☎05 56 48 29 73; 81-83 rue du Loup; menus from €12.50; ⏰noon-3pm & 7-9pm Mon-Sat) In a city full of neighbourhood bistros, this one, smack in the city centre, is one of the most impressive. It's friendly, cosy and chaotically busy (be prepared to wait for a table at lunchtime). The food tastes fresh and home-cooked and it dares to veer slightly away from the bistro standards of steak and chips.

La Boîte à Huîtres — Oysters €€

(☎05 56 81 64 97; 36 cours du Chapeau Rouge; lunch menu €20, 6 oysters from €8; ⏰noon-2pm & 7-11pm) This rickety, wood-panelled little place feels like an Arcachon fisherman's hut. It's a sensation that's quite appropriate because this is by far the best place in Bordeaux to munch on fresh Arcachon oysters. Traditionally they're served with sausage but you can have them in a number of different forms, including with that other southwest delicacy, foie gras.

La Tupina Regional Cuisine **€€€**
(**05 56 91 56 37; www.latupina.com; 6 rue Porte de la Monnaie; menus €18-74, mains €27-45)** Filled with the aroma of soup simmering inside an old *tupina* ('kettle' in Basque) over an open fire, this white-tableclothed place is feted far and wide for its seasonal southwestern French specialities such as a minicasserole of foie gras and eggs, milk-fed lamb or goose wings with potatoes and parsley.

Information

Main Tourist Office (**05 56 00 66 00; www.bordeaux-tourisme.com; 12 cours du 30 Juillet; 9am-7pm Mon-Sat, 9.30am-6pm Sun)** Runs an excellent range of city and regional tours. There's a small-but-helpful branch (**05 56 91 64 70; 9am-noon & 1-6pm Mon-Sat, 10am-noon & 1-3pm Sun)** at the train station.

Getting There & Away

Air

Bordeaux airport (**www.bordeaux.aeroport.fr**) is in Mérignac, 10km west of the city centre, with domestic and some international services.

Train

From Gare St-Jean, 3km from the centre, at least 16 trains a day serve **Paris Gare Montparnasse** (€73, three hours).

Biarritz

POP 26,067

Edge your way south along the coast towards Spain and you arrive in stylish Biarritz, just as ritzy as its name suggests. The resort took off in the mid-19th century (Napoléon III had a rather soft spot for the place) and it still shimmers with architectural treasures from the belle époque and art deco eras.

Sights & Activities

Biarritz' raison d'être is its fashionable beaches, particularly central **Grande Plage** and **Plage Miramar**, lined end to end with sunbathing bodies on hot

Biarritz

summer days. North of Pointe St-Martin, the adrenaline-pumping surfing beaches of **Anglet** (the final 't' is pronounced) continue northwards for more than 4km. Take bus 10 or 13 from the bottom of av Verdun (just near av Édouard VII).

Musée de la Mer Museum
(**☎05 59 22 75 40; www.museedelamer.com; esplanade du Rocher de la Vierge; adult/child €14/10; ⏰9.30am-midnight Jul-Aug, 9.30am-8pm Apr-Jun & Sep-Oct, shorter hrs rest of yr)** Housed in a wonderful art-deco building, Biarritz's Musée de la Mer is seething with underwater life from the Bay of Biscay and beyond, including huge aquariums of sharks and dainty tropical reef fish, as well as exhibits on fishing recalling Biarritz's whaling past. It's the seals, though, that steal the show (feeding time, always a favourite with children, is at 10.30am and 5pm). In high season it's possible to have the place almost to yourself by visiting late at night.

Cité de l'Océan Museum
(**☎05 59 22 75 40; www.citedelocean.com; 1 av de la Plage; adult/child €11/7.30; ⏰10am-10pm Jul-Aug, 10am-7pm Easter, Apr-Jun & Sep-Oct, shorter hours rest of year)** We don't really know whether it's fair to call the Cité de l'Océan a mere 'museum'. At heart it's simply a museum of the ocean, but this is entertainment, cutting-edge technology, theme park and science museum all rolled into one. During a visit you will learn all you ever wanted to know about the ocean and (sort-of) ride in a submarine to watch giant squid and sperm whales do battle.

Sleeping

Hôtel Mirano Boutique Hotel **€€**
(**☎05 59 23 11 63; www.hotelmirano.fr; 11 av Pasteur; d €72-132; P ᯤ)** Squiggly purple, orange and black wallpaper and oversize orange perspex light fittings are some of the rad '70s touches at this boutique retro hotel. Oh, and there's a flirty Betty Boop in the bar. The staff go above and beyond the call of duty in order to please. All up, it's one of the best deals in town.

Hôtel Villa Koegui Boutique Hotel **€€€**
(**☎05 59 50 07 77; www.hotel-villakoegui-biarritz.fr; 7 rue de Gascogne; r from €200; ❄ ᯤ)** This fab little place has swanky,

Château Comtal (p247) and the medieval ramparts of Carcassonne

bright rooms filled with locally made furnishings and decorations and is set around a leafy courtyard garden. What really makes it stand out though is that it's run with the kind of warmth and care normally only found in small, family-run B&Bs.

Eating

Restaurant le Pim'pi French **€€**
(☎05 59 24 12 62; 14 av Verdun; menus €14-28, mains €17; ⏲noon-2pm Tue, noon-2pm & 7-9.30pm Wed-Sat) A small and resolutely old-fashioned place unfazed by all the razzmatazz around it. The daily specials are chalked up on a blackboard – most are of the classic French bistro style but are produced with such unusual skill and passion that many consider this one of the town's better places to eat.

Bistrot des Halles Basque **€€**
(☎05 59 24 21 22; 1 rue du Centre; mains €17-19; ⏲noon-2pm & 7.30-10.30pm Tue-Sat) One of a cluster of restaurants along rue du Centre that get their produce directly from the nearby covered market, this bustling place stands out from the pack for serving excellent fish and other fresh modern French market fare from the blackboard menu, in an interior adorned with old metallic advertising posters. Open daily during Easter and the summer holidays.

Drinking & Nightlife

Miremont Cafe
(☎05 59 24 01 38; www.miremont-biarritz.com; 1bis place Georges-Clemenceau; hot chocolate from €5; ⏲9am-8pm) Operating since 1880, this grande dame harks back to the time when belle-époque Biarritz was the beach resort of choice for the rich and glamorous. Today it still attracts perfectly coiffed hairdos (and that's just on the poodles) but the less chic are also welcome to come and partake of a fine selection of tea and cakes.

Ventilo Caffé Bar
(rue du Port Vieux; ⏲closed Tue Oct-Easter) Dressed up like a boudoir, this funky place continues its domination of the Biarritz young and fun bar scene.

Tourist information

Tourist Office (☎05 59 22 37 10; www.biarritz.fr; square d'Ixelles; ⏲9am-7pm Jul-Aug, shorter hrs rest of yr) In July and August there are tourist-office annexes at the airport, train station and at the roundabout just off the Biarritz *sortie* (exit) 4 from the A63.

Getting There & Away

Air

Biarritz-Anglet-Bayonne Airport (www.biarritz.aeroport.fr), 3km southeast of Biarritz, is served by several low-cost carriers.

Train

Biarritz-La Négresse train station, 3km south of town, is linked to the centre by bus A1.

LANGUEDOC-ROUSSILLON

Languedoc-Roussillon comes in three distinct flavours: Bas-Languedoc (Lower Languedoc), land of bullfighting, rugby and robust red wines, where the region's major sights are found; sunbaked Nîmes with its fine Roman amphitheatre; and fairy-tale Carcassonne, crowned with a ring of witch-hat turrets.

Inland, Haut Languedoc (Upper Languedoc) is a mountainous, sparsely populated terrain made for lovers of the great outdoors; while to the south sits Roussillon, snug against the rugged Pyrenees and frontier to Spanish Catalonia.

Carcassonne

Perched on a rocky hilltop and bristling with zig-zag battlements, stout walls and spiky turrets, the fortified city of Carcassonne looks like something out of a children's storybook from afar. It's most people's perfect idea of a medieval castle, and it's undoubtedly an impressive spectacle – not to mention one of the Languedoc's biggest tourist draws.

Unfortunately, the medieval magic's more than a tad tarnished by an annual

PHILIP GAME/GETTY IMAGES ©

Don't Miss Pont du Gard

Southern France has some fine Roman sites, but nothing can top the Unesco World Heritage Site–listed Pont du Gard, 21km northeast of Nîmes. This fabulous three-tiered aqueduct was once part of a 50km-long system of water channels, built around 19 BC to transport water from Uzès to Nîmes. The scale is huge: 48.8m high, 275m long and graced with 35 precision-built arches; the bridge was sturdy enough to carry up to 20,000 cubic metres of water per day.

Each block was carved by hand and transported from nearby quarries – no mean feat, considering the largest blocks weighed over 5 tonnes. Amazingly, the height of the bridge descends by just 2.5cm across its length, providing just enough gradient to keep the water flowing – an amazing demonstration of the precision of Roman engineering. The **Musée de la Romanité** provides background on the bridge's construction, and the **Ludo** play area helps kids to learn in a fun, hands-on way.

You can walk across the tiers for panoramic views over the River Gard, but the best perspective on the bridge is from downstream, along the 1.4km **Mémoires de Garrigue** walking trail. Early evening is a good time to visit, as admission is cheaper and the bridge is stunningly illuminated after dark.

There are large car parks on both banks of the river, 400m walk from the bridge. Several buses stop nearby, including Edgard bus B21 (hourly Monday to Saturday, two or three on Sunday) from Nîmes to Alès.

NEED TO KNOW

☎ 04 66 37 50 99; www.pontdugard.fr; car & up to 5 passengers €18, after 8pm €10; ⏰ visitor centre & museum 9am-8pm Jul & Aug, shorter hours rest of year

influx of over four million visitors and it can be a tourist hell in high summer.

The old city, **La Cité**, is dramatically illuminated at night and enclosed by two rampart walls punctuated by 52 stone towers, Europe's largest city fortifications. Successive generations of Gauls, Romans, Visigoths, Moors, Franks and Cathars reinforced the walls, but only the lower sections are original; the rest, including the turrets, were stuck on by the 19th-century architect Viollet-le-Duc.

A drawbridge leads to the old gate of **Porte Narbonnaise** and rue Cros Mayrevieille en route to place Château and the 12th-century **Château Comtal** (adult/child €8.50/free; 10am-6.30pm Apr-Sep). South is **Basilique St-Nazaire** (9-11.45am & 1.45-5pm), illuminated by delicate medieval rose windows.

Carcassonne is on the main rail line to/from Toulouse (€14, 50 minutes).

Nîmes

POP 146,500

This buzzy city boasts some of France's best-preserved classical buildings, including a famous Roman amphitheatre, although the city is most famous for its sartorial export, *serge de Nîmes* – better known to cowboys, clubbers and couturiers as denim – and for its bullfighting festivals, the *ferias* (held in May and September).

Sights

A **Pass Nîmes Romaine** (adult/child €11.50/9), valid for three days, covers all three sights; buy one at the first place you visit.

Les Arènes Roman Sites

(www.arenes-nimes.com; place des Arènes; adult/child €9.50/free; 9am-8pm Jul & Aug, shorter hours rest of year) Nîmes' twin-tiered amphitheatre is the best preserved in France. Built around 100 BC, the arena would have seated 24,000 spectators and staged gladiatorial contests and public executions, and it still provides an impressive venue for gigs, events and summer bullfights. An audioguide provides context as you explore the arena, seating areas, stairwells and corridors (rather marvellously known to Romans as *vomitories*), and afterwards you can view replicas of

Château Comtal, Carcassonne

DALLAS STRIBLEY/GETTY IMAGES ©

gladiatorial armour and original bullfighters' costumes in the museum.

Maison Carrée Roman Sites
(place de la Maison Carrée; adult/child €5.80/free; 10am-8pm Jul & Aug, shorter hours rest of year) Constructed in gleaming limestone around AD 5, this temple was built to honour Emperor Augustus' two adopted sons. Despite the name, the Maison Carrée (Square House) is actually rectangular – to the Romans, 'square' simply meant a building with right angles. The building is beautifully preserved, complete with stately columns and triumphal steps. There's no need to go inside unless you are interested in the relatively cheesy 22-minute 3D film.

Jardins de la Fontaine Roman Sites
(Tour Magne adult/child €3.40/free; Tour Magne 9.30am-6.30pm) The elegant Jardins de la Fontaine conceal several Roman remains, most notably the 30m-high **Tour Magne**, raised around 15 BC. Built as a display of imperial power, it's the largest of a chain of towers that once punctuated the city's 7km-long Roman ramparts. At the top of its 140 steps, there's an orientation table to help you interpret the panoramic views over Nîmes.

Sleeping & Eating

Look out for *cassoulet* (pork, sausage and white bean stew, sometimes served with duck), aïoli and *rouille* (a spicy chilli mayonnaise).

Hôtel de l'Amphithéâtre Hotel **€€**
(04 66 67 28 51; www.hoteldelamphitheatre.com; 4 rue des Arènes; s/d/f €72/92/130) Down a narrow backstreet leading away from Les Arènes, this tall townhouse ticks all the boxes: smart rooms with shabby-chic furniture and balconies overlooking place du Marché; a sleek palette of greys, whites and taupes; and a great buffet breakfast. It's run by an expat Cornishman and his French wife.

Le Cerf à Moustache Bistro **€€**
(09 81 83 44 33; 38 bd Victor Hugo; mains €14-35; 11.45am-2pm & 7-11pm Tue-Sat) Despite its weird name, the Deer with the Moustache has quickly established itself as one of Nîmes' top bistros, with quirky decor (including reclaimed furniture and a wall full of old-book doodles), matched

Lavender field, Provence

by chef Julien Salem's creative take on the classics. Go basic with burgers and risotto, or upmarket with crusted lamb and chunky steaks.

Information

Tourist Office (☎04 66 58 38 00; www.ot-nimes.fr; 6 rue Auguste; ⊙8.30am-8pm Mon-Fri, 9am-7pm Sat, 10am-6pm Sun Jul & Aug, shorter hours rest of year; 📶) There's also a seasonal annexe (⊙10am-6pm Mon-Sat Apr-Sep, to 5pm Mon-Fri Oct-Mar) on esplanade Charles de Gaulle.

Getting There & Away

More than 12 TGVs daily run to/from **Paris Gare de Lyon** (€62.50 to €111, three hours). Local destinations include **Arles** (€9, 30 minutes) and **Avignon** (€8.50, 30 minutes).

PROVENCE

Provence conjures up images of rolling lavender fields, blue skies, gorgeous villages, wonderful food and superb wine. It certainly delivers on all those fronts, but it's not just worth visiting for its good looks – dig a little deeper and you'll also discover the multicultural metropolis of Marseille, Avignon's rich history and the landscapes that inspired Impressionists.

Marseille

POP 858,902

There was a time when Marseille was the butt of French jokes. No more. The *cité phocéenne* has made an unprecedented comeback, undergoing a vast makeover. Marseillais will tell you that the city's rough-and-tumble edginess is part of its charm and that, for all its flaws, it is a very endearing place. They're right: Marseille grows on you with its unique history, souklike markets, millennia-old port and spectacular *corniches* (coastal roads) – all good reasons indeed why Marseille was chosen European Capital of Culture in 2013.

Les Calanques

Marseille abuts the wild and spectacular Les Calanques, a protected 20km stretch of high, rocky promontories rising from the bright turquoise sea. Sheer cliffs are occasionally interrupted by idyllic beach-fringed coves, many only possible to reach with kayak. They've been protected since 1975 and became a national park in 2012.

Marseille's tourist office leads guided hikes in Les Calanques and has information on walking trails (shut July and August due to forest-fire risk). For great views from out at sea hop aboard a boat trip from the wine-producing port of **Cassis**, 30km east along the coast.

Sights

Buy a cent-saving **City Pass** (one-/two-day €24/31) at the tourist office. It covers admission to museums, a city tour, unlimited public-transport travel, boat trips and so on.

Vieux Port Historic Quarter

(Ⓜ Vieux Port) Ships have docked for more than 26 centuries at the city's birthplace, the colourful Old Port. The main commercial docks were transferred to the Joliette area north of here in the 1840s, but the old port remains a thriving harbour for fishing boats, pleasure yachts and tourists. Guarding the harbour are **Fort St-Nicolas** (⊙8am-7.45pm May-Aug, shorter hours rest of year; Ⓜ Vieux Port) FREE on the south side and, across the water, **Fort St-Jean** (Ⓜ Vieux Port) FREE, founded in the 13th century by the Knights Hospitaller of St John of Jerusalem, and home to MuCEM (p252), the state-of-the-art museum.

Vieux Port

AN ITINERARY

Start with an early morning coffee on the balcony at La Caravelle, with views of the boats bobbing in the harbor and Basilique Notre Dame de la Garde across the way. Mosey down the quay to the sparkling **MuCEM** ❶ and its cantilevered neighbour **Villa Méditerranée** ❷ for a morning of art and culture. You'll enter through Fort St-Jean, and wind through roof-top gardens to reach the state-of-the-art museums. Alternatively, take in green-and-white striped **Cathédrale de la Major** ❸ then explore the apricot-coloured alleys of **Le Panier** ❹, browsing the exhibits at the **Centre de la Vieille Charité** ❺, and shopping in the neighbourhood's tiny boutiques.

In the afternoon, hop on the free cross-port ferry to the harbour's south side and take a **boat trip** ❻ to Château d'If, made famous by the Dumas novel The Count of Monte Cristo. Or, stroll under Norman Foster's mirrored pavilion, then wander into the **Abbaye St-Victor** ❼, to see the bones of martyrs enshrined in gold. As evening nears, you can catch the sunset from the stone benches in the **Jardin du Pharo** ❽. Then as the warm southern night sets in, join the throngs on cours Honoré d'Estienne d'Orves, where you can drink pastis and people-watch beneath a giant statue of a lion devouring a man – the **Milo de Croton** ❾.

Cathédrale de Marseille Notre Dame de Major
The striped facade of Marseille's cathedral is made from local Cassis stone and green Florentine marble. Its grand north staircase leads from Le Panier to La Joliette quarter

Musée des Civilisations de l'Europe et de la Méditerranée (MuCEM)
Explore the icon of modern Marseille, this stunning museum designed by Rudi Ricciotti and linked by vertigo-inducing foot-bridge to 13th-century Fort St-Jean. You'll get stupendous views of the Vieux Port and the Mediterranean.

Centre de la Vieille Charité

Before the 18th century, beggar hunters rounded up the poor for imprisonment. The Vieille Charité almshouse, which opened in 1749, improved their lot by acting as a workhouse. It's now an exhibition space and only the barred windows recall its original use.

Le Panier

The site of the Greek town of Massilia, Le Panier woos walkers with its sloping streets. Grand Rue follows the ancient road and opens out into place de Lenche, the location of the Greek market. It is still the place to shop for artisanal products.

GARDEL BERTRAND/GETTY IMAGES ©

Frioul If Express

Catch the Frioul If Express to Château d'If, France's equivalent to Alcatraz. Prisoners were housed according to class: the poorest at the bottom in windowless dungeons, the wealthiest in paid-for private cells, with windows and a fireplace.

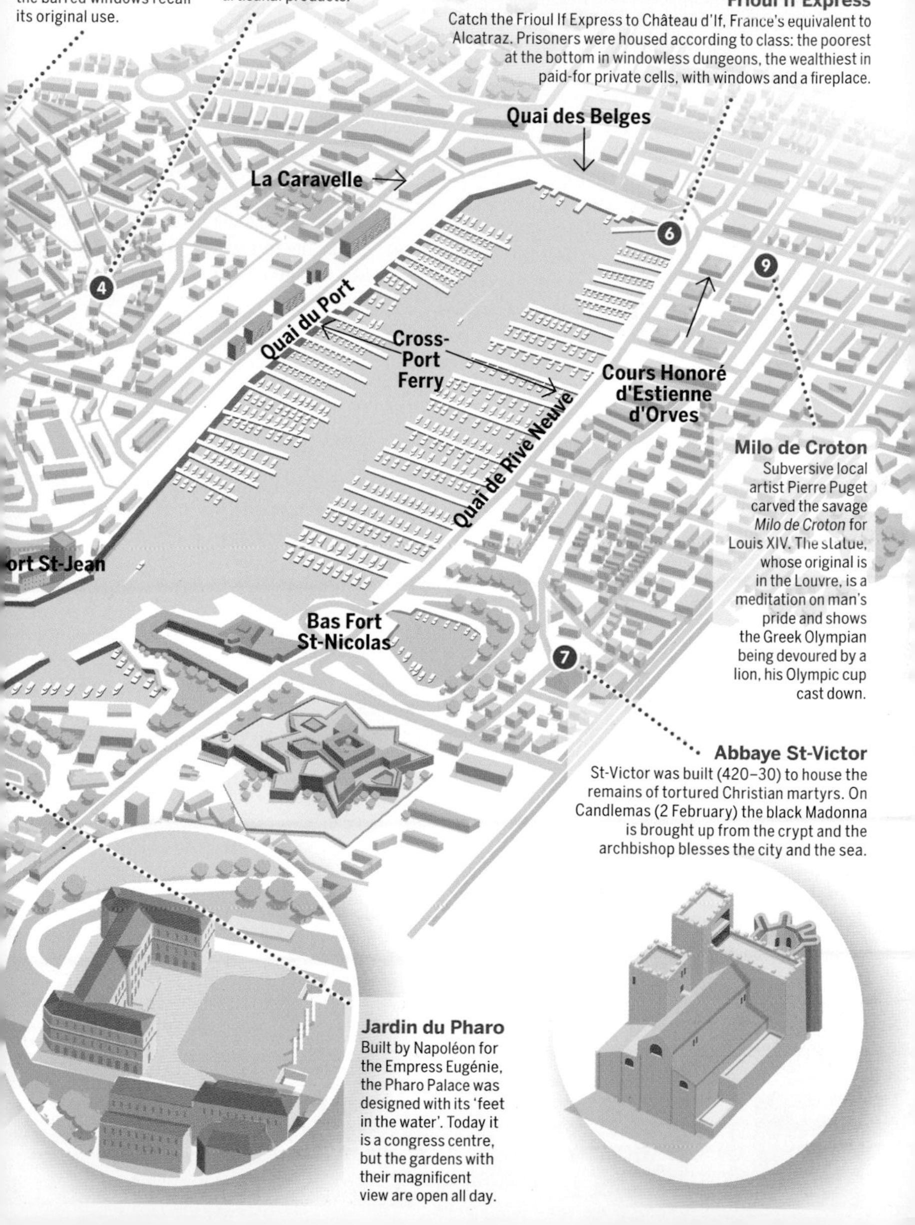

Quai des Belges

La Caravelle

6

9

4

Quai du Port

Cross-Port Ferry

Cours Honoré d'Estienne d'Orves

Quai de Rive Neuve

Fort St-Jean

Bas Fort St-Nicolas

7

Milo de Croton

Subversive local artist Pierre Puget carved the savage *Milo de Croton* for Louis XIV. The statue, whose original is in the Louvre, is a meditation on man's pride and shows the Greek Olympian being devoured by a lion, his Olympic cup cast down.

Abbaye St-Victor

St-Victor was built (420–30) to house the remains of tortured Christian martyrs. On Candlemas (2 February) the black Madonna is brought up from the crypt and the archbishop blesses the city and the sea.

Jardin du Pharo

Built by Napoléon for the Empress Eugénie, the Pharo Palace was designed with its 'feet in the water'. Today it is a congress centre, but the gardens with their magnificent view are open all day.

Musée des Civilisations de l'Europe et de la Méditerranée Museum

(MuCEM, Museum of European & Mediterranean Civilisations; ☎04 84 35 13 13; www.mucem.org; 7 Promenade Robert Laffont; J4 adult/child €5/free, plus temporary exhibitions €8/free, 1st Sun of month free; ⏰10am-8pm Wed-Mon Jul & Aug, 11am-7pm Wed-Mon Sep, Oct, May & Jun, 11am-6pm Wed-Mon Nov-Apr; 👪; Ⓜ Vieux Port or Joliette) The icon of modern Marseille, this stunning museum explores the history, culture and civilisation of the Mediterranean region through anthropological exhibits, rotating art exhibitions and film. The collection sits in a bold, contemporary building, **J4**, designed by Algerian-born, Marseille-educated architect Rudi Ricciotti. It is linked by a vertigo-inducing **foot bridge** to the 13th-century **Fort St-Jean**, from which there are stupendous views of the Vieux Port and the Mediterranean. The fort grounds and their gardens are free to explore.

Le Panier Historic Quarter

(Ⓜ Vieux Port) From the Vieux Port, hike north up to this fantastic history-woven quarter, which is fabulous for a wander with its artsy ambience, cool hidden squares and sun-baked cafes. In Greek Massilia it was the site of the *agora* (marketplace), hence its name, which means 'the basket'. During WWII the quarter was dynamited and afterwards rebuilt. Today it's a mishmash of lanes hiding artisan shops, *ateliers* (workshops) and terraced houses strung with drying washing.

Basilique Notre Dame de la Garde Church

(Montée de la Bonne Mère; www.notredamedelagarde.com; rue Fort du Sanctuaire; ⏰7am-8pm Apr-Sep, to 7pm Oct-Mar; 🚌60) FREE This opulent 19th-century Romano-Byzantine basilica occupies Marseille's highest point, **La Garde** (162m). Built between 1853 and 1864, it is ornamented with coloured marble, murals depicting the safe passage of sailing vessels and superb mosaics. The hilltop gives 360-degree panoramas of the city. The church's bell tower is crowned by a 9.7m-tall gilded **statue of the Virgin Mary** on a 12m-high pedestal. It's a 1km walk from the Vieux Port, or take bus 60 or the tourist train.

Château d'If Island, Castle

(www.if.monuments-nationaux.fr; adult/child €5.50/free; ⏰9.30am-6.10pm mid-May–mid-Sep, shorter hours rest of year) Immortalised in Alexandre Dumas' classic 1844 novel *Le Comte de Monte Cristo (The Count of Monte Cristo)*, the 16th-century fortress-turned-prison Château d'If sits on the tiny island, Île d'If, 3.5km west of the Vieux Port. Political prisoners were incarcerated here, along with hundreds of Protestants, the Revolutionary

Les Arènes (p247), Nîmes
GLENN BEANLAND/GETTY IMAGES ©

hero Mirabeau, and the Communards of 1871.

Frioul If Express (www.frioul-if-express.com; 1 quai des Belges) boats leave for Château d'If (€10.50 return, 20 minutes, around 9 daily) from the Vieux Port.

Sleeping

Hôtel Hermès — Design Hotel €

(☎04 96 11 63 63; www.hotelmarseille.com; 2 rue Bonneterie; s €64, d €85-102; ❄ 📶; M Vieux Port) Nothing to do with the Paris design house, this excellent-value hotel has a rooftop terrace with panoramic Vieux Port views. Grab breakfast (€9) on a tray in the bright ground-floor breakfast room and ride the lift to the 5th floor for breakfast à la rooftop. Contemporary rooms have white walls and a splash of lime-green or red to complement their Scandinavian-like design.

Hôtel Edmond Rostand — Design Hotel €€

(☎04 91 37 74 95; www.hoteledmondrostand.com; 31 rue Dragon; d €90-115, tr €127-141; ❄ @ 📶; M Estrangin-Préfecture) Turn a blind eye to the grubby outside shutters of this excellent-value Logis de France hotel in the Quartier des Antiquaires. Inside, decor is a hip mix of contemporary design and vintage, with a great sofa area for lounging and 16 rooms dressed in crisp white and soothing natural hues. Some rooms overlook a tiny private garden, others the Basilique Notre Dame de la Garde.

Au Vieux Panier — B&B €€

(☎04 91 91 23 72; www.auvieuxpanier.com; 13 rue du Panier; d €100-140; M Vieux Port) The height of Le Panier shabby chic, this super-stylish *maison d'hôte* woos art lovers with original works of art. Each year artists are invited to redecorate, meaning its six rooms change annually. Staircases and corridors are like an art gallery and a drop-dead gorgeous rooftop terrace peeks across terracotta tiles to the sea on the horizon.

Eating

The Vieux Port overflows with restaurants, but choose carefully. Head to Cours Julien and its surrounding streets for world cuisine.

Café Populaire — Bistro €€

(☎04 91 02 53 96; http://cafepopulaire.com; 110 rue Paradis; tapas €6-16, mains €17-22; ⏲noon-2.30pm & 8-11pm Tue-Sat; M Estrangin-Préfecture) Vintage furniture, old books on the shelves and a fine collection of glass soda bottles lend a retro air to this trendy, 1950s-styled *jazz comptoir* (counter) – a restaurant despite its name. The crowd is chic and smiling chefs in the open kitchen mesmerise with daily specials like king prawns *à la plancha* or beetroot and coriander salad.

Le Café des Épices — Modern French €€

(☎04 91 91 22 69; www.cafedesepices.com; 4 rue du Lacydon; lunch/dinner menus from €25/45; ⏲noon-3pm & 6-11pm Tue-Fri, noon-3pm Sat; 👪; M Vieux Port) One of Marseille's best chefs, Arnaud de Grammont, infuses his cooking with a panoply of flavours: squid-ink spaghetti with sesame and perfectly cooked scallops, or coriander- and citrus-spiced potatoes topped by the catch of the day. Presentation is impeccable, the decor playful, and the colourful outdoor terrace between giant potted olive-trees nothing short of superb.

Le Rhul — Seafood €€€

(☎04 91 52 01 77; www.lerhul.fr; 269 corniche Président John F Kennedy; bouillabaisse €53; ⏲noon-2pm & 5-9pm; 🚌83) This long-standing classic has atmosphere (however kitschy): a 1940s seaside hotel with Mediterranean views. This is one of the most reliably consistent spots for authentic *bouillabaisse* but go the classic one better and get the *bourride* (minimum two persons), a hard-to-find variation brimming with garlic in white sauce.

Right: Marseille harbour with view of Basilique Notre Dame de la Garde (p252); **Below:** Rue Saint Saens, Vieux Port, Marseille

Drinking & Entertainment

La Caravelle Bar
(34 quai du Port; ⌚7am-2am; Ⓜ Vieux Port) Look up or miss this standout upstairs hideaway, styled with rich wood and leather, a zinc bar and yellowing murals. If it's sunny, snag a coveted spot on the port-side terrace. On Fridays, there's live jazz from 9pm to midnight.

Espace Julien Live Music
(☎ 04 91 24 34 10; www.espace-julien.com; 39 cours Julien; Ⓜ Notre Dame du Mont-Cours Julien) Rock, *opérock*, alternative theatre, reggae, hip hop, Afro groove and other cutting-edge entertainment all appear on the bill; the website lists gigs.

Information

Dangers & Annoyances

Petty crimes and muggings are common. Avoid the Belsunce area (southwest of the train station, bounded by La Canebière, cours Belsunce and rue d'Aix, rue Bernard du Bois and blvd d'Athènes) at night. Walking La Canebière is annoying, but generally not dangerous; expect to encounter kids peddling hash.

Tourist information

Tourist Office (☎ 04 91 13 89 00; www.marseille-tourisme.com; 11 La Canebière; ⌚9am-7pm Mon-Sat, 10am-5pm Sun; Ⓜ Vieux Port) Marseille's useful tourist office has plenty of information on everything, including guided tours on foot or by bus, electric tourist train or boat.

Getting There & Away

Air

Aéroport Marseille-Provence (p272), 25km northwest in Marignane, has numerous budget flights to various European destinations. **Shuttle**

buses link it with Marseille train station (€8.20; 25 minutes, every 20 minutes).

Train

From Marseille's Gare St-Charles, trains including TGVs go all over France and Europe.

Avignon €29.50, 35 minutes

Lyon €65, 1¾ hours

Nice €37, 2½ hours

Paris Gare de Lyon €113, three hours

Getting Around

Marseille has two metro lines, two tram lines and an extensive bus network, all run by **RTM** (**04 91 91 92 10; www.rtm.fr; 6 rue des Fabres; 8.30am-6pm Mon-Fri, 8.30am-noon & 1-4.30pm Sat; M Vieux Port**), where you can obtain information and transport tickets (€1.50).

Avignon

POP 92,078

Hooped by 4.3km of superbly preserved stone ramparts, this graceful city is the belle of Provence's ball. Famed for its annual performing arts festival (held in July) and fabled bridge, Avignon is an ideal spot from which to step out into the surrounding region. Wrapping around the city, Avignon's defensive ramparts were built between 1359 and 1370, and are punctuated by a series of sturdy *portes* (gates).

Sights

Discount card, *Avignon Passion*, yields discounts of 10% to 50% on city museums, tours and monuments (pay full price at the first site, then discounts at each susbsequent site). The pass covers five people and is valid for 15 days. Available from the tourist office and tourist sites.

Palais des Papes Palace
(Papal Palace; www.palais-des-papes.com; place du Palais; adult/child €11/9, with Pont St-Bénezet €13.50/10.50; 9am-8pm Jul, to 8.30pm Aug, shorter hours Sep-Jun) Palais des Papes, a

If You Like… Artistic Landmarks

From marvellous art museums to inspirational Impressionists, France is littered with fascinating artistic sights.

1 VAN GOGH IN ARLES

If Arles seems familiar, it's hardly surprising: Vincent Van Gogh lived here for much of his life and the town regularly featured in his paintings. Follow in his footsteps along the evocative **Van Gogh Walking Circuit**. The **tourist office** (04 90 18 41 20; www.arlestourisme.com; esplanade Charles de Gaulle, Blvd des Lices; 9am-6.45pm Apr-Sep, to 4.45pm Mon-Fri & 12.45pm Sun Oct-Mar;) has maps (€1). There are frequent trains to Arles from Nîmes, Marseille and Avignon.

2 CÉZANNE SIGHTS

The town of Aix-en-Provence is famous for its connections with local-born Impressionist Paul Cézanne. His **studio** (04 42 21 06 53; www.atelier-cezanne.com; 9 av Paul Cézanne; adult/child €5.50/free; 10am-6pm Jul & Aug, reduced hours rest of year) is a poignant insight into his work. Numerous buses and trains between Aix and Marseille.

3 MAISON ET JARDINS DE CLAUDE MONET

Monet's **home** (02 32 51 28 21; www.fondation-monet.com; 84 rue Claude Monet; adult/child €9.50/5, incl Musée des Impressionnismes Giverny €16.50/8; 9.30am-6pm Apr-Oct) for the last 43 years of his life is now a delightful house-museum. Monet bought the **Jardin d'Eau** (water garden) in 1895 and set about creating the famous lily pond and Japanese bridge. The nearest station is Vernon, from where there are regular trains to Paris.

4 CENTRE POMPIDOU-METZ

With a curved roof resembling a space-age Chinese hat, the satellite branch of Paris' **Centre Pompidou in Metz** (www.centrepompidou-metz.fr; 1 parvis des Droits de l'Homme; adult/child €7/free; 11am-6pm Mon & Wed-Fri, 10am-8pm Sat, 10am-6pm Sun) draws on Europe's largest collection of modern art to stage ambitious temporary exhibitions. Metz can be reached by direct train from Paris or Strasbourg.

Unesco World Heritage Site, is the world's largest Gothic palace. Built when Pope Clement V abandoned Rome in 1309, it was the papal seat for 70-odd years. The immense scale testifies to the papacy's wealth; the 3m-thick walls, portcullises and watchtowers show their insecurity.

It takes imagination to picture the former luxury of these bare, cavernous stone halls, but multimedia audioguides (€2) assist. Highlights include 14th-century chapel frescoes by Matteo Giovannetti, and the Chambre du Cerf with medieval hunting scenes.

Pont St-Bénezet Bridge

(bd du Rhône; adult/child 24hr ticket €5/4, with Palais des Papes €13.50/10.50; 9am-8pm Jul, to 8.30pm Aug, shorter hours Sep-Jun) Legend says Pastor Bénezet had three saintly visions urging him to build a bridge across the Rhône. Completed in 1185, the 900m-long bridge with 20 arches linked Avignon with Villeneuve-lès-Avignon. It was rebuilt several times before all but four of its spans were washed away in the 1600s. If you don't want to pay to visit the bridge, admire it free from Rocher des Doms park, Pont Édouard Daladier or on Île de la Barthelasse's chemin des Berges.

Musée Angladon Museum

(www.angladon.com; 5 rue Laboureur; adult/child €6.50/4.50; 1-6pm Tue-Sun mid-Mar–Nov, closed Mon & Tue mid-Nov–mid-Mar) Tiny Musée Angladon harbours Impressionist treasures, including *Railway Wagons*, the only Van Gogh in Provence (look closely and notice the 'earth' isn't paint, but bare canvas). Also displayed are a handful of early Picasso sketches and artworks by Cézanne, Sisley, Manet and Degas; upstairs are antiques and 17th-century paintings.

Sleeping

Hôtel Mignon Hotel **€**

(04 90 82 17 30; www.hotel-mignon.com; 12 rue Joseph Vernet; s €40-60, d €65-77, tr €80-99, q €105;) Bathrooms might be tiny and the stairs up, steep and narrow, but Hôtel Mignon (literally 'Cute Hotel') remains excellent value. Its 16 rooms are clean and comfortable, and the hotel sits on Avignon's smartest shopping street. Breakfast €7.

Le Limas B&B **€€**

(📞04 90 14 67 19; www.le-limas-avignon.com; 51 rue du Limas; s/d/tr from €130/150/250; ❄@🛜) This chic B&B in an 18th-century townhouse, like something out of *Vogue Living*, is everything designers strive for when mixing old and new: state-of-the-art kitchen and minimalist white decor complementing antique fireplaces and 18th-century spiral stairs. Breakfast on the sun-drenched terrace is divine, darling.

Ginette et Marcel Cafe **€**

(📞04 90 85 58 70; 27 place des Corps Saints; tartines €4-7; ⏲11am-11pm Wed-Mon; 👪) With tables and chairs on one of Avignon's most happening plane-tree-shaded squares, this vintage cafe styled like a 1950s grocery is a charming spot to hang out and people-watch over a *tartine* (open-faced sandwich), tart, salad or other light dish – equally tasty for lunch or an early evening *apéro*. Kids adore Ginette's cherry- and violet-flavoured cordials, and Marcel's glass jars of old-fashioned sweets.

83.Vernet French **€€**

(📞04 90 85 99 04; www.83vernet.com; 83 rue Joseph Vernet; menus lunch €19.50, dinner €24-30; ⏲noon-3pm & 7pm-1am Mon-Sat) Forget flowery French descriptions. The menu is straightforward and to the point at this strikingly contemporary address, magnificently at home in the 18th-century cloistered courtyard of a medieval college. Expect pan-seared scallops, squid *à la plancha* and beef steak in pepper sauce on the menu, and watch for weekend events that transform the lounge-style restaurant into the hippest dance floor in town.

Information

Tourist Office (📞04 32 74 32 74; www.avignon-tourisme.com; 41 cours Jean Jaurès; ⏲9am-6pm Mon-Fri, to 6pm Sat, 10am-noon Sun Apr-Oct, shorter hours rest of year) Offers guided walking tours and information on other tours and activities, including boat trips on the River Rhône and wine-tasting trips to nearby vineyards. Smartphone apps too.

Getting There & Away

Avignon has two stations. **Gare Avignon TGV**, 4km southwest in Courtine; and **Gare Avignon Centre**, with multiple daily services to/from: Arles (€7.50, 20 minutes) and Nîmes (€9.70, 30 minutes). Some TGVs to/from **Paris** (€123, 3½ hours) stop at Gare Avignon Centre, but TGVs to/from **Marseille** (€25, 30 minutes) and **Nice** (€60, 3¼ hours) only use Gare TGV.

Palais des Papes (p255), Avignon
JEAN-PIERRE LESCOURRET/GETTY IMAGES ©

THE FRENCH RIVIERA & MONACO

With its glistening seas, idyllic beaches and fabulous weather, the French Riviera (Côte d'Azur in French) screams exclusivity, extravagance and excess. It has been a favourite getaway for wealthy Europeans since Victorian times and there is nowhere more chichi or glam in France than St-Tropez, Cannes and super-rich, sovereign Monaco.

Nice

POP 348,195

Riviera queen Nice is what good living is all about – shimmering shores, the very best of Mediterranean food, a unique historical heritage, free museums, a charming Old Town, exceptional art and Alpine wilderness within an hour's drive. To get stuck-in straight away, make a beeline upon arrival for **Promenade des Anglais,** Nice's curvaceous palm-lined seafront that follows its busy pebble beach for 6km from the city centre to the airport.

Sights & Activities

Vieux Nice Historic Quarter

Nice's old town, an atmospheric mellow-hued rabbit warren, has scarcely changed since the 1700s and getting lost in it is a highlight. Cue **cours Saleya**: this joyous, thriving market square hosts a well-known **flower market** (6am-5.30pm Tue-Sat, to 1.30pm Sun) and a thriving **food market** (6am-1.30pm Tue-Sun), a staple of local life. A **flea market** (8am-5pm Mon) takes over on Monday, and the spill over from bars and restaurants seems to be a permanent fixture.

Promenade des Anglais Architecture

Palm-lined promenade des Anglais, paid for by Nice's English colony in 1822, is a fine stage for a stroll and a flop on one of its iconic sea-blue chairs, immortalised by Niçoise sculptor Sabine Géraudie with her strikingly giant seafront sculpture **La Chaise de SAB** (2014). Historic highlights from the early 20th century include the magnificent **Hôtel Negresco** (04 93 16 64 00; www.hotel-negresco-nice.com; 37 promenade des Anglais) and art deco

Beach near the Promenade des Anglais, Nice

Palais de la Méditerranée (☎04 92 14 77 30; www.lepalaisdelamediterranee.com; 13-15 promenade des Anglais; d €345; ❄@📶🏊). The promenade follows the complete 4km sweep of the **Baie des Anges** with a cycle and skating lane.

Musée Matisse Art Museum
(☎04 93 81 08 08; www.musee-matisse-nice.org; 164 av des Arènes de Cimiez; ⏰10am-6pm Wed-Mon) FREE This museum, 2km north in the leafy Cimiez quarter, houses a fascinating assortment of works by Matisse, including oil paintings, drawings, sculptures, tapestries and Matisse's signature famous paper cut-outs. The permanent collection is displayed in a red-ochre 17th-century Genoese villa in an olive grove. Temporary exhibitions are in the futuristic basement building. Matisse is buried in the **Monastère de Cimiez cemetery**, across the park from the museum.

Trans Côte d'Azur Boat Tour
(www.trans-cote-azur.com; quai Lunel; ⏰Apr-Oct) Trans Côte d'Azur runs one-hour boat cruises along the Baie des Anges and Rade de Villefranche (adult/child €17.50/12) April to October. Mid-June to mid-September it sails to Île Ste-Marguerite (€39/29, one hour), St-Tropez (€64/49, 2½ hours), Monaco (€37/28.50, 45 minutes) and Cannes (€39/29, one hour).

Sleeping

Nice Pebbles Self-Contained €€
(☎04 97 20 27 30; www.nicepebbles.com; 1-/2-/3-bedroom apt from €110/190/330; ❄📶) Nice Pebbles' concept is simple: offering the quality of a four-star boutique hotel in holiday flats. Apartments and villas (one to five bedrooms) are gorgeous and equipped to high standards. Guests can expect wi-fi, flat-screen TV, DVD players, fully equipped kitchens and linen bedding in most flats, and in some cases, swimming pool, balcony or terrace.

Nice Garden Hôtel Boutique Hotel €€
(☎04 93 87 35 62; www.nicegardenhotel.com; 11 rue du Congrès; s/d/tr from €75/90/138; ⏰reception 8am-9pm; ❄📶) Behind heavy iron gates hides this gem: nine beautifully appointed rooms – the work of the exquisite Marion – are a subtle blend of old and new and overlook a delightful garden with a glorious orange tree. Amazingly, all this charm and peacefulness is just two blocks from the promenade. Breakfast is €9.

Hôtel La Pérouse Boutique Hotel €€€
(☎04 93 62 34 63; www.hotel-la-perouse.com; 11 quai Rauba Capeu; d from €330; ❄@📶🏊) Built into the rock cliff next to Tour Bellanda, La Pérouse evokes the spirit of a genteel villa. Lower-floor rooms face a lemon-tree-shaded courtyard and pool; upper-floor rooms have magnificent sea vistas. Smart accent colours add flair to the traditional decor. Best rates are online. Breakfast €18.

Eating

Niçois nibbles include *socca* (a thin layer of chickpea flour and olive oil batter), *salade niçoise* and *farcis* (stuffed vegetables). Restaurants in Vieux Nice are a mixed bag, so choose carefully.

La Rossettisserie French €
(☎04 93 76 18 80; www.larossettisserie.com; 8 rue Mascoïnat; mains €14.50-€15.50; ⏰noon-2pm & 7.30-10pm Mon-Sat) The Rossettisserie (a lovely play of words on rotisserie – roast house – and Rossetti, the name of the nearby square) is a retro grocery-style space known for its succulent roast meat. Pair your choice of beef, chicken, veal or lamb with heavenly homemade mash or sautéed potatoes and ratatouille or salad. The vaulted dining room in the basement is stunning.

Chez Palmyre French €
(☎04 93 85 72 32; 5 rue Droite; menu €17; ⏰noon-1.30pm & 7-9.30pm Mon-Fri) A new chef has breathed new life into this fabulously atmospheric little restaurant,

Nice

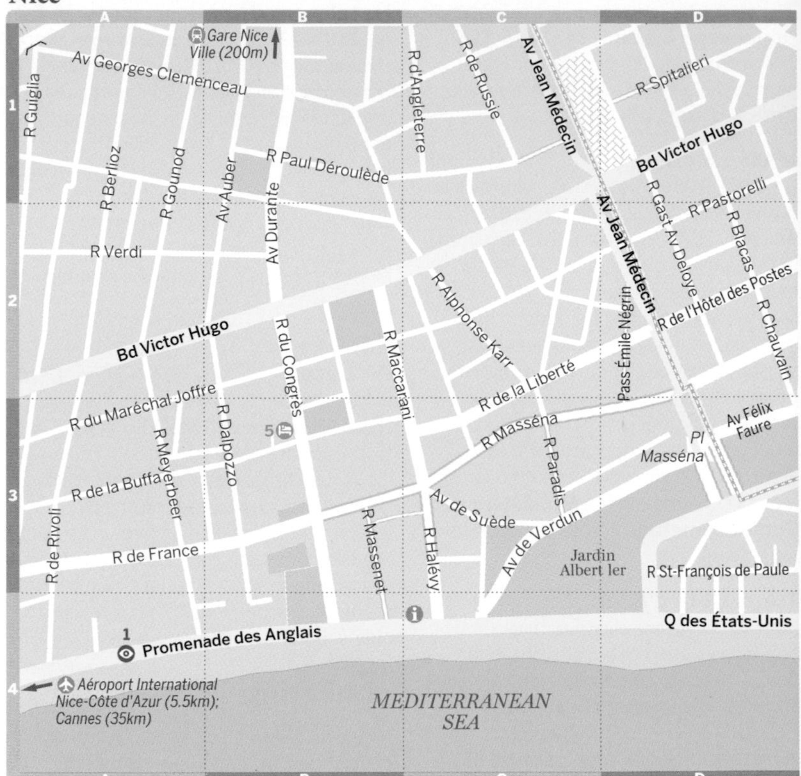

seemingly unchanged for its long life. The kitchen churns out Niçois standards with a light hand, service is sweet and the price fantastic; book ahead, even for lunch.

Fenocchio Ice Cream €

(www.fenocchio.fr; 2 place Rossetti; 1/2/3 scoops €2/3.50/5; ⏲9am-midnight Feb-Oct) Bags of spots sell it but the best in Nice without a doubt is by this *maître glacier* (master ice-cream maker), in the biz since 1966. Eschew predictable favourites and indulge in a new taste sensation: black olive, thyme, lavender, ginger chocolate, violet or typical Niçois *tourte de blette* (a sweet Swiss chard tart made with raisins, pine kernels and parmesan cheese).

L'Escalinada Niçois €€

(☎04 93 62 11 71; 22 rue Pairolière; mains €20-25; ⏲noon-2.30pm & 7-11pm) L'Escalinada has been brilliant for grassroots Niçois cuisine for the last half-century: *petits farcis* (stuffed vegetables), homemade gnocchi with tasty *daube* (Provençal beef stew) and Marsala veal stew see tables packed jaw to jowl on a tiny pavement terrace in Vieux Nice. The complimentary aperitif is a welcome touch. No credit cards.

Jan Modern French €€€

(☎04 97 19 32 23; www.restaurantjan.com; 12 rue Lascaris; 2-/3-course lunch menu €25/32, dinner menus €52 & €72, mains €26-32; ⏲6.30-10pm Tue-Thu & Sat, noon-2pm & 6.30-10pm Fri) An advance reservation (which must then be confirmed by phone the day you dine) is essential at this elegant dining room,

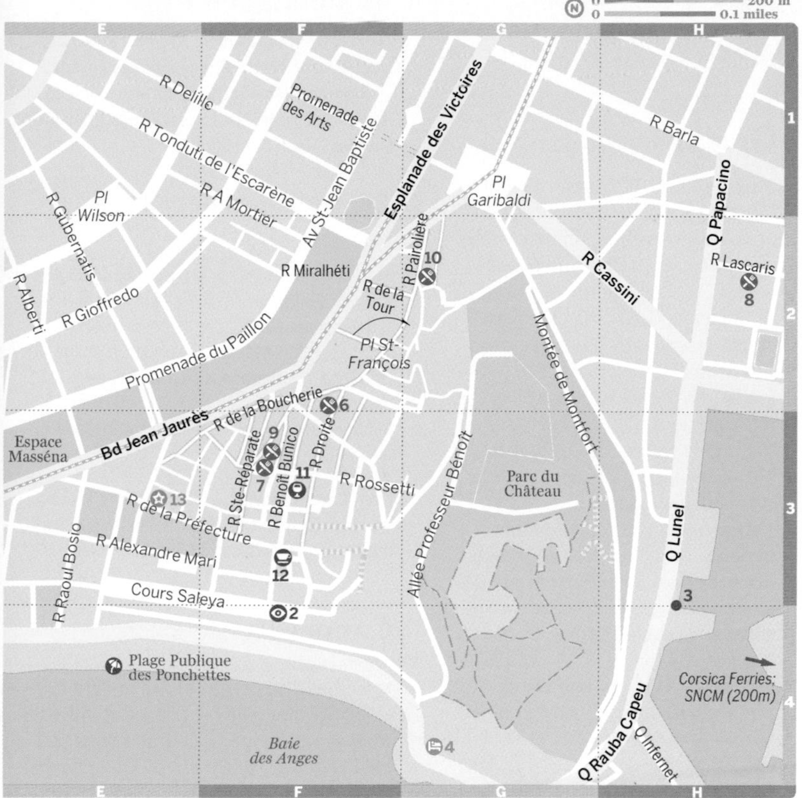

gourmet kingdom of South African wonder chef Jan Hendrik van der Westhuizen. Antipodean influences are light in the menu but more pronounced in the wine list. There is no à la carte menu – just a divine choice of market-sourced tasting menus.

Drinking & Entertainment

Les Distilleries Idéales Cafe

(www.lesdistilleriesideales.fr; 24 rue de la Préfecture; 9am-12.30am) Whether you're after *un café* or *apéro* with cheese or charcuterie platter, Les Distilleries is one atmospheric bar. Watch the world go by on the narrow street terrace or hang out inside with the 'happy hour' crowd and a good-value cocktail from 6pm to 8pm.

Nice

Sights

1 Promenade des Anglais A4
2 Vieux Nice F4

Activities, Courses & Tours

3 Trans Côte d'Azur H3

Sleeping

4 Hôtel La Pérouse G4
5 Nice Garden Hôtel B3

Eating

6 Chez Palmyre F2
7 Fenocchio F3
8 Jan H2
9 La Rossettisserie F3
10 L'Escalinada G2

Drinking & Nightlife

11 L'Abat-Jour F3
12 Les Distilleries Idéales F3

Entertainment

13 Chez Wayne's E3

Detour: Grasse

Mosey some 20km northwest of Cannes to inhale the sweet smell of lavender, jasmine, mimosa and orange-blossom fields. In **Grasse**, one of France's leading perfume producers, dozens of perfumeries create essences to sell to factories (for aromatically enhanced foodstuffs and soaps) as well as to prestigious couture houses – the highly trained noses of local perfume-makers can identify 3000 scents in a single whiff.

Learn about three millennia of perfume-making at the **Musée International de la Parfumerie** (MIP; www.museesdegrasse.com; 2 bd du Jeu de Ballon; adult/child €4/free; 10am-7pm Wed-Mon Apr-Sep, 10.30am-5.30pm Wed-Mon Oct-Mar;) and watch the process first-hand during a guided tour at **Fragonard** (04 93 36 44 65; www.fragonard.com; 20 bd Fragonard; 9am-7pm Jul & Aug, 9am-12.30pm & 2-6.30pm Sep-Jun) FREE perfumery, the easiest to reach by foot.

L'Abat-Jour Bar, Club

(25 rue Benoît Bunico; 6.30pm-2.30am Tue-Sat) With its vintage furniture, basement DJ sessions and alternative music, L'Abat-Jour is all the rage with trendies. Check its Facebook page for events.

Chez Wayne's Live Music

(www.waynes.fr; 15 rue de la Préfecture; 10am-2am) Raucous watering hole Chez Wayne's is a typical English pub, with live bands every night. The pub is also sports-mad and shows every rugby, football, Aussie Rules, tennis and cricket game worth watching.

Information

Tourist Office (08 92 70 74 07; www.nicetourisme.com; 5 Promenade des Anglais; 9am-6pm Mon-Sat) There's also a branch in front of the train station (av Thiers; 8am-7pm Mon-Sat, 10am-5pm Sun).

Getting There & Away

Air

Nice-Côte d'Azur airport (08 20 42 33 33; www.nice.aeroport.fr;) is 6km west of Nice, by the sea. A taxi to Nice centre costs around €30.

Buses 98 and 99 link the airport terminal with Nice's centre and Nice train station (€6, 35 minutes, every 20 minutes). Bus 110 (€20, 30 minutes, hourly) links the airport with Monaco.

Train

From **Gare Nice Ville**, 1.2km north of the beach, there are frequent services to Cannes (€5.80, 40 minutes) and Monaco (€3.30, 25 minutes).

Cannes

POP 73,671

Most have heard of Cannes and its celebrity film festival. The latter only lasts for two weeks in May, but the buzz and glitz linger all year thanks to regular visits from celebrities who come here to indulge in designer shopping, beaches and the palace hotels of the Riviera's glammest seafront, blvd de la Croisette.

Sights & Activities

La Croisette Architecture

The multi-starred hotels and couture shops lining the iconic bd de la Croisette (aka La Croisette) may be the preserve of the rich and famous, but anyone can enjoy strolling the palm-shaded promenade – a favourite pastime among Cannois at night when it twinkles with bright lights. Views of the Bay of Cannes and nearby Estérel mountains are beautiful, and seafront hotel palaces dazzle in all their stunning art deco glory.

Îles de Lérins Islands

Although just 20 minutes away by boat, these tranquil islands feel far from the madding crowd. **Île Ste-Marguerite**, where the mysterious Man in the Iron Mask was incarcerated during the late 17th century, is known for its bone-white beaches, eucalyptus groves and small marine museum. Tiny **Île St-Honorat** has been a monastery since the 5th century: you can visit the church and small chapels and stroll through the monks' vineyards.

Boats leave Cannes from quai des Îles on the western side of the harbour. **Riviera Lines** (**04 92 98 71 31; www.riviera-lines.com; quai Laubeuf**) runs ferries to Île Ste-Marguerite and **Compagnie Planaria** (**www.cannes-ilesdelerins.com; quai Laubeuf**) covers Île St-Honorat.

Sleeping

Hôtel Alnea Hotel **€**
(**04 93 68 77 77; www.hotel-alnea.com; 20 rue Jean de Riouffe; s/d/tr €76/88/99;**) A breath of fresh air in a town of stars, Noémi and Cédric have put their heart and soul into their hotel, with bright, colourful two-star rooms, original paintings and numerous little details such as the afternoon coffee break, the honesty bar and the bike or *boules* (to play *pétanque*) loans. Breakfast €8.50.

Hôtel de Provence Hotel **€€**
(**04 93 38 44 35; www.hotel-de-provence.com; 9 rue Molière; s €118-139, d €161-189;**) This traditional Provençal townhouse with buttermilk walls and lavender-blue shutters disguises a minimalist chic interior. Almost every room sports a balcony, climaxing with a 7th-floor suite with stunning rooftop terrace. The Provence also has self-catering studios for three to six people in the neighbourhood. Breakfast €9.80.

Eating

PhilCat Sandwiches **€**
(**Promenade de la Pantiéro; sandwiches & salads €3.50-6; 7am-7pm;**) Phillipe and Catherine's prefab cabin on the waterfront is one of Cannes' finest lunch dates. Join knowing locals on its terrace with seaview for giant salads, panini and the best *pan bagna* (€5) on the Riviera (a gargantuan bread bun filled with tuna, onion, red pepper, lettuce and tomato, and dripping in olive oil. The 'super' version (€5.30) throws anchovies into the mouthwatering Provençal mix.

Mantel Modern European **€€€**
(**04 93 39 13 10; www.restaurantmantel.com; 22 rue St-Antoine; menus €35-60, mains €34-45; noon-2pm Fri-Mon, 7.30-10pm Thu-Tue**) Discover why Noël Mantel is the hotshot of the Cannois gastronomic scene at his refined old-town restaurant. Service is stellar and the seasonal cuisine divine: try the wonderfully tender glazed veal shank in balsamic vinegar or the original poached octopus *bourride*-style.

Sea Sens Fusion **€€€**
(**04 63 36 05 06; www.five-hotel-cannes.com; 1 rue Notre Dame; lunch menus €29 & €39, dinner menus €65-115, mains €23-68; 7.30-11pm Tue-Sat;**) Perched on the 5th floor of the Five Seas Hotel, this single Michelin-starred restaurant blends French gastronomy and Asian elegance with panoramic views of Le Suquet and Cannes' rooftops. Pastry chef Jerôme De Oliveira's champion desserts are the sweet highlight. Lunch here is excellent value.

The Corniches

Some of the Riviera's most spectacular scenery stretches east between Nice and Monaco. A trio of corniches (coastal roads) hugs the cliffs between the two seaside cities, each higher up the hill than the last. The middle corniche ends in Monaco; the upper and lower continue to Menton near the French-Italian border.

The most wonderful stop is **Èze** on the middle corniche: a small, medieval village spectacularly located on a rocky outcrop, it has dazzling views of the Mediterranean and incredibly atmospheric lanes.

Information

Tourist Office (04 92 99 84 22; www.cannes-destination.fr; 1 bd de la Croisette; 9am-8pm Jun-Aug, 10am-7pm Sep-May)

Getting There & Away

From Cannes train station there are at least hourly services to/from:

Grasse €4.30, 30 minutes

Marseille €32, two hours

Monaco €9.40, one hour

Nice €6.80, 40 minutes

St-Tropez

POP 4571

In the soft autumn or winter light, it's hard to believe the pretty terracotta fishing village of St-Tropez is a stop on the Riviera celebrity circuit. It seems far removed from its glitzy siblings further up the coast, but come spring or summer, it's a different world: the population increases tenfold, prices triple and fun-seekers pile in to party till dawn, strut around the luxury-yacht-packed Vieux Port and enjoy the creature comforts of exclusive A-listers' beaches in the Baie de Pampelonne.

Sights & Activities

About 4km southeast of town is the start of **Plage de Tahiti** and its continuation, the famous **Plage de Pampelonne**, studded with St-Tropez's most legendary party spots.

Vieux Port Port

Yachts line the harbour and visitors stroll the quays at the picturesque old port. In front of the sable-coloured townhouses, the **Bailli de Suffren statue**, cast from a 19th-century cannon, peers out to sea. The bailiff (1729–88) was a sailor who fought with a Tropezien crew against Britain and Prussia during the Seven Years War. As much of an institution as the bailiff is portside cafe **Sénéquier** (www.senequier.com; quai Jean Jaurès; 8am-1am year-round).

Place des Lices Square

St-Tropez's legendary and very charming central square is studded with plane trees, cafes and *pétanque* players. Simply sitting on a cafe terrace watching the world go by or jostling with the crowds at its extravaganza of a twice-weekly **market** (place des Lices; 8am-1pm Tue & Sat), jam-packed with everything from fruit and veg to antique mirrors and sandals, is an integral part of the St-Tropez experience.

Musée de l'Annonciade Art Museum

(place Grammont; adult/child €6/free; 10am-1am & 2-6pm Wed-Mon) In a gracefully converted 16th-century chapel, this small but famous art museum showcases an impressive collection of modern art infused with that legendary Côte d'Azur light. Pointillist Paul Signac bought a house in St-Tropez in 1892 and introduced others to the area. The museum's collection includes his *St-Tropez, Le Quai* (1899) and *St-Tropez, Coucher de Soleil au Bois de Pins* (1896).

Sleeping

Hôtel Lou Cagnard Hotel **€€**

(04 94 97 04 24; www.hotel-lou-cagnard.com; 18 av Paul Roussel; d €81-171; Mar-Oct;) Book well ahead for this great-value courtyard charmer, shaded by lemon and fig trees, and owned by schooled hoteliers. The pretty Provençal house with lavender shutters has its very own jasmine-scented garden, strung with fairy lights at night. Bright and beautifully clean rooms are decorated with painted Provençal furniture. Five have ground-floor garden terraces. The cheapest rooms have private washbasin and stand-up bathtub but share a toilet; most rooms have air-con.

Pastis Design Hotel **€€€**

(04 98 12 56 50; www.pastis-st-tropez.com; 61 av du Général Leclerc; d from €375;) This stunning townhouse-turned-hotel is the brainchild of an English couple besotted with Provence and passionate about modern art. You'll die for the

pop-art-inspired interior, and long for a swim in the emerald-green pool. Every room is beautiful although those overlooking av Leclerc are noisy.

Quai Jean Jaurès at the Vieux Port is lined with restaurants and cafés but prices are high and quality average.

La Tarte Tropézienne Cafe, Boulangerie **€**
(www.latartetropezienne.fr; place des Lices; mains €13-15; ⌚6.30am-7.30pm, lunch noon-3pm) This cafe-bakery is the original creator of the eponymous cake, and therefore the best place to buy St-Tropez's delicacy. But to start, choose from delicious daily specials, salads and sandwiches which you can enjoy in the bistro inside or on the little terrace outside. Several of their bakeries dot St-Tropez as well, and you'll see them around the Côte d'Azur – perfect for catering to your sweet tooth.

La Plage des Jumeaux Seafood **€€€**
(☎04 94 58 21 80; www.plagedesjumeaux.com; rte de l'Épi, Plage de Pampelonne; mains €25-40; ⌚noon-3pm; 🍹👪) The top pick of St-Tropez's beach restaurants, Les Jumeaux serves beautiful seafood (including fabulous whole fish, ideal to share) and sun-bursting salads on its dreamy white-and-turquoise striped beach. Families are well catered for, with playground equipment, beach toys and a kids' menu.

Information

Tourist Office (☎08 92 68 48 28; www.sainttropeztourisme.com; quai Jean Jaurès; ⌚9.30am-1.30pm & 3-7.30pm Jul & Aug, 9.30am-12.30pm & 2-7pm Apr-Jun & Sep-Oct, to 6pm Mon-Sat Nov-Mar) Occasional walking tours April to October. Has a kiosk in Parking du Port in July and August.

Getting There & Away

From the **bus station (☎04 94 56 25 74; av du Général de Gaulle)**, buses run by **VarLib (☎04 94 24 60 00; www.varlib.fr)** go to Toulon-Hyères airport (€3, 1½ hours).

St-Tropez

ELENATHEWISE/GETTY IMAGES ©

Monaco

POP 32,020

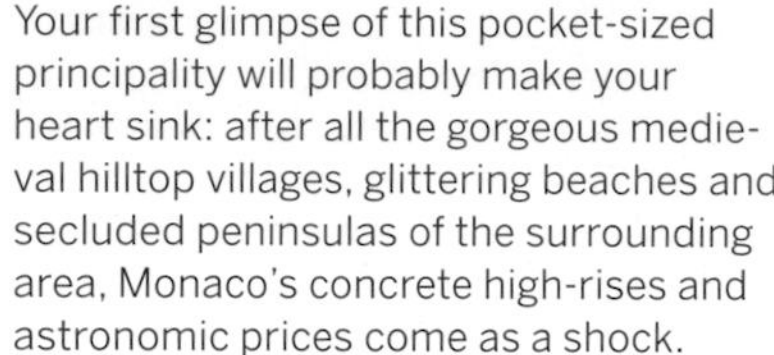

Your first glimpse of this pocket-sized principality will probably make your heart sink: after all the gorgeous medieval hilltop villages, glittering beaches and secluded peninsulas of the surrounding area, Monaco's concrete high-rises and astronomic prices come as a shock.

But Monaco is beguiling. The world's second-smallest state (the Vatican is smaller), it is as famous for its tax-haven status as for its glittering casino, sports scene (Formula One, world-famous circus festival and tennis open) and a royal family on a par with British royals for best gossip fodder.

In terms of practicalities, Monaco is a sovereign state but has no border control. It has its own flag (red and white), national holiday (19 November) and telephone country code (☎377), but the official language is French and the country uses the euro even though it is not part of the European Union.

Most visit Monaco as a day trip from Nice, a 20-minute train ride away.

Sights

Musée Océanographique de Monaco — Aquarium

(www.oceano.mc; av St-Martin; adult/child €14/7; ⌚9.30am-8pm Jul & Aug, 10am-7pm Apr, May, Jun & Sep, to 6pm Oct-Mar) Stuck dramatically to the edge of a cliff since 1910, the world-renowned Musée Océanographique de Monaco, founded by Prince Albert I (1848–1922), is a stunner. Its centrepiece is its **aquarium** with a 6m-deep lagoon where sharks and marine predators are separated from colourful tropical fishes by a coral reef. Upstairs, two huge colonnaded rooms retrace the history of oceanography and marine biology (and Prince Albert's contribution to the field) through photographs, old equipment, numerous specimens and interactive displays.

Le Rocher — Historic Quarter

Monaco Ville, also called Le Rocher, is the only part of Monaco to have retained small, windy medieval lanes. The old town thrusts skywards on a pistol-shaped rock, its strategic location overlooking the sea became the stronghold

Monaco harbour

of the Grimaldi dynasty in 1297. To access Le Rocher, from place aux Armes in the Condamine area, visitors can walk up the 16th-century red-brick Rampe Major, past the statue of the late Prince Rainier looking down on his beloved Monaco by Dutch artist Kees Verkade.

Jardin Exotique Garden

(www.jardin-exotique.mc; 62 bd du Jardin Exotique; adult/child €7.20/3.80; ⌚9am-7pm May-Sep, to 6pm Feb-Apr & Oct, to 5pm Nov-Jan) Home to the world's largest succulent and cactus collection, from small echinocereus to 10m-tall African candelabras, the gardens tumble down the slopes of Moneghetti through a maze of paths, stairs and bridges. Views of the principality are spectacular. Admission includes the **Musée d'Anthropologie** displaying prehistoric remains unearthed in Monaco and a 35-minute guided tour of the **Grotte de l'Observatoire**. The prehistoric, stalactite- and stalagmite-laced cave is bizarre – it's the only cave in Europe where the temperature rises as you descend. Bus 2 links Jardin Exotique with the town centre.

Eating

Casino Supermarket €

(17 bd Albert 1er; pizza slices & sandwiches from €3.20; ⌚8.30am-midnight Mon-Sat, to 9pm Sun; 🖉) It's not so much the supermarket that's worth knowing about as its excellent street-side bakery and pizzeria, which churns out freshly prepared goodies. A saviour for those keen to watch the pennies.

La Montgolfière Fusion €€€

(☎97 98 61 59; www.lamontgolfiere.mc; 16 rue Basse; 3-/4-course menu €45/52; ⌚noon-2pm & 7.30-9.30pm Mon-Tue & Thu-Sat) This pocket-sized restaurant is a local favourte amid the touristy jumble of Monaco's historic quarter. The Hot Air Balloon is the culinary creation of Henri and Fabienne Geraci, a couple whose time in Malaysia was clearly well spent based on Henri's outstanding fusion cuisine. In winter, he boils up *bourride* (a salted cod stew typical of Monaco and Nice) every day.

Café Llorca Modern French €€

(☎99 99 29 29; www.cafellorca.mc; 10 av Princesse Grace, Grimaldi Forum; 2-course menu €22, mains €16-19; ⌚11.30am-3pm Mon-Fri) This chic bistro on the 1st floor of the Grimadi Forum conference centre is Michelin-starred chef Alain Llorca's gift to lunch-goers: fabulous modern French cuisine with a fusion twist at affordable prices. The two-course lunch menu, including a glass of wine, is a steal. In spring/summer, make a beeline (and book) for the tables on the terrace overlooking the sea.

Drinking & Entertainment

Brasserie de Monaco Microbrewery

(www.brasseriedemonaco.com; 36 rte de la Piscine; ⌚4pm-1am Mon-Fri, noon-3am Sat, noon-1am Sun) Tourists and locals rub shoulders at Monaco's only microbrewery, which crafts rich organic ales and lager, and serves tasty lunch and snacking grub too. Watch out for live music and sports-event TV screenings. Happy hour 6pm to 8pm.

Casino de Monte Carlo Casino

(www.montecarlocasinos.com; place du Casino; admission 9am-noon adult/child €10, admission from 2pm Salons Ordinaires/Salons Privées €10/20; ⌚visits 9am-noon, gaming 2pm-2am or 4am or when last game ends) Peeping inside Monte Carlo's legendary marble-and-gold casino is a Monaco essential. The building, open to visitors every morning, is Europe's most lavish example of belle epoque architecture. Prince Charles III came up with the idea of the casino and in 1866, three years' after its inaugeration, the name 'Monte Carlo' – Ligurian for 'Mount Charles' in honour of the prince – was coined. To gamble or watch the poker-faced play visit after 2pm (when a strict over 18s only admission rule kicks in).

Monte Carlo Casino

TIMELINE

1863 Charles III inaugurates the first Casino on Plateau des Spélugues. The **atrium** ❶ is a small room with a wooden podium from which an orchestra entertains while punters purchase entrance tickets.

1864 Hôtel de Paris opens and the area becomes known as the 'Golden Square'.

1865 Construction of **Salle Europe** ❷. Cathedral-like, it is lined with onyx columns and lit by eight Bohemian crystal chandeliers weighing 150kg each.

1868 The steam train arrives in Monaco and **Café de Paris** ❸ is completed.

1878–79 Gambling moves to Hôtel de Paris while Charles Garnier is charged with building a new casino with a miniature replica of the Paris Opera House, **Salle Garnier** ❹.

1890 The advent of electricity casts a glow on architect Jules Touzet's newly added **gaming rooms** ❺ for high rollers.

1903 Inspired by female gamblers, Henri Schmit decorates **Salle Blanche** ❻ with caryatids and the painting *Les Grâces Florentines*.

1904 Smoking is banned in the gaming rooms and **Salon Rose** ❼, a new smoking room, is added.

1910 **Salle Médecin** ❽, immense and grand, hosts the high-spending Private Circle.

1966 Celebrations mark 100 years of uninterrupted gambling despite two world wars.

TOP TIPS

➡ After 2pm when gaming begins, admission is strictly for 18 years and over. Photo ID is obligatory.

➡ Don't wear trainers. A jacket for men is not obligatory, but is recommended, in the gaming rooms.

➡ In the main room, the minimum bet is €5/25 for roulette/blackjack.

➡ In the Salons Privés, the minimum bet is €15, with no maximum.

SLOW IMAGES/GETTY IMAGES ©

Atrium
The casino's 'lobby', so to speak, is paved in marble and lined with 28 Ionic columns, which support a balustraded gallery canopied with an engraved glass ceiling.

Hôtel de Paris

HÔTEL DE PARIS

Notice the horse's shiny leg (and testicles) on the lobby's statue of Louis XIV on horseback? Legend has it that rubbing them brings good luck in the casino.

Salon Rose
Smoking was banned in the gaming rooms following a fraud involving a croupier letting his ash fall on the floor. The Salon Rose (Pink Room; today a restaurant) was therefore opened in 1903 for smokers – the gaze of Gallelli's famous cigarillo-smoking ladies follow you around the room.

Salle Garnier
Taking eight months to build and two years to restore (2004–2006), the opera's original statuary is rehabilitated using original moulds saved by the creator's grandson. Individual air-con and heating vents are installed beneath each of the 525 seats.

DEA/G. DAGLI ORTI/GETTY IMAGES ©

ANNE GALKOVSKAYA/GETTY IMAGES ©

Salle Europe

The oldest part of the casino, where they continue to play *trente-et-quarante* and European roulette, which have been played here since 1865. Tip: the bull's-eye windows around the room originally served as security observation points.

Café de Paris

With the arrival of Diaghilev as director of the Monte Carlo Opera in 1911, Café de Paris becomes the go-to address for artists and gamblers. It retains the same high-glamour ambience today. Tip: snag a seat on the terrace and people-watch.

JEAN-PIERRE LESCOURRET/GETTY IMAGES ©

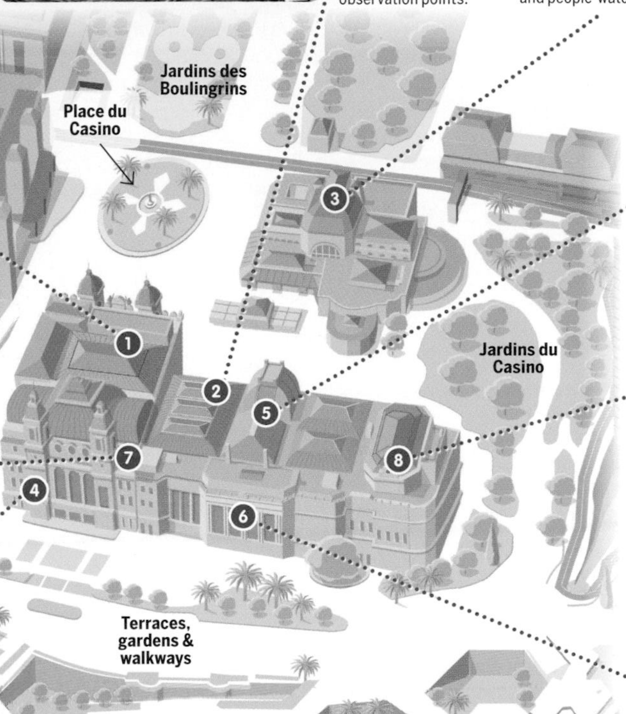

Salles Touzet

This vast partitioned hall, 21m by 24m, is decorated in the most lavish style: oak, Tonkin mahogany and oriental jasper panelling are offset by vast canvases, Marseille bronzes, Italian mosaics, sculptural reliefs and stained-glass windows.

Salle Médecin

Also known as Salle Empire because of its extravagant Empire-style decor, Monégasque architect François Médecin's gaming room was originally intended for the casino's biggest gamblers. Part of it still remains hidden from prying eyes as a Super Privé room.

Salle Blanche

Today a superb bar-lounge, the Salle Blanche (White Room) opens onto an outdoor gaming terrace, a must on balmy evenings. The caryatids on the ceiling were modelled on fashionable courtesans such as La Belle Otéro, who placed her first bet here aged 18.

BEST VIEWS

Wander behind the casino through manicured gardens and gaze across Victor Vasarely's vibrant op-art mosaic, *Hexagrace*, to views of the harbour and the sea.

MARVIN E. NEWMAN/GETTY IMAGES ©

Corsica

The rugged island of Corsica (Corse in French) is officially a part of France, but remains fiercely proud of its own culture, history and language. It's one of the Mediterranean's most dramatic islands, with a bevy of beautiful beaches, glitzy ports and a mountainous, maquis-covered interior to explore, as well as a wild, independent spirit all of its own.

The island has long had a love-hate relationship with the mother mainland – you'll see plenty of anti-French slogans and 'Corsicanised' road signs – but that doesn't seem to deter the millions of French tourists who descend on the island every summer. Prices skyrocket and accommodation is at a premium during the peak season between July and August, so you're much better off saving your visit for spring and autumn.

Regular flights and ferries cross from Marseille and Nice to Corsica's main towns, Ajaccio and Bastia. For ferry schedules, see SNCM (www.sncm.fr). Air France (www.airfrance.com) has the most frequent flights, but other budget carriers including Easyjet also serve the island.

Information

Telephone

Calls between Monaco and France are international calls. Dial 00 followed by Monaco's country code (377) when calling Monaco from France or elsewhere abroad. To phone France from Monaco, dial 00 and France's country code (33).

Tourist information

Tourist Office **(www.visitmonaco.com; 2a bd des Moulins; 9am-7pm Mon-Sat, 11am-1pm Sun)** For tourist information by the port, head to the seasonal kiosk run by the tourist office near the cruise ship terminal on Esplanade des Pêcheurs.

Getting There & Away

Monaco's train station **(av Prince Pierre)** has frequent trains to Nice (€3.80, 20 minutes). Bus 100 goes to Nice (€1.50, 45 minutes) along the Corniche Inférieure.

SURVIVAL GUIDE

Directory A–Z

Accommodation

France has accommodation to suit every taste, pocket and mood.

- Budget covers everything from bare-bones hostels to simple family-run places; midrange means a few extra creature comforts such as satellite TV, air-conditioning and free wi-fi; while top-end places stretch from luxury five-star chains with the mod cons and swimming pools to boutique-chic chalets in the Alps.
- Many tourist offices make room reservations, often for a fee of €5, but many only do so if you stop by in person.
- French hotels almost never include breakfast in their advertised nightly rates.

Price Ranges

Our reviews refer to the cost of a double room with private bathroom, except in hostels or where otherwise specified. Quoted rates are for high season, which is July and August in southern France (Provence and the French Riviera, Languedoc-Roussilon, Corsica) and December to March in the French Alps.

€ less than €90 (€130 in Paris)

€€ €90 to €190 (€130 to €200 in Paris)

€€€ more than €190 (€200 in Paris)

Food

Price ranges refer to a two-course meal:

€ less than €20

€€ €20 to €40

€€€ more than €40

Gay & Lesbian Travellers

Gay mayors, artists and film directors, camper-than-camp fashion designers...the rainbow flag flies high in France, one of Europe's most liberal countries when it comes to homosexuality.

- Major gay and lesbian organisations are based in Paris.
- Bordeaux, Lyon, Nice and many other towns have active communities.
- Attitudes towards homosexuality tend to be more conservative in the countryside.

Money

Credit and debit cards are accepted almost everywhere in France.

- Some places (eg 24hr petrol stations and some *autoroute* toll machines) only take credit cards with chips and PINs.
- In Paris and major cities, *bureaux de change* (exchange bureaux) are fast, easy, open longer hours and offer competitive exchange rates.

Opening Hours

- French business hours are regulated by a maze of government regulations, including the 35-hour working week.
- The midday break is uncommon in Paris but, in general, gets longer the further south you go.
- French law requires most businesses to close Sunday; exceptions include grocery stores, *boulangeries,* florists and businesses catering to the tourist trade.
- In many places shops close on Monday.
- Restaurants generally close one or two days of the week.
- Most (but not all) national museums are closed on Tuesday, while most local museums are closed on Monday, though in summer some open daily. Some museums close for lunch.

Public Holidays

New Year's Day (Jour de l'An) 1 January

Easter Sunday & Monday (Pâques & lundi de Pâques) March or April

May Day (Fête du Travail) 1 May – traditional parades.

Victoire 1945 8 May – commemorates the Allied victory in Europe that ended WWII.

Ascension Thursday May – celebrated on the 40th day after Easter.

Pentecost/Whit Sunday & Whit Monday (Pentecôte & lundi de Pentecôte) Mid-May to mid-June – celebrated on the seventh Sunday after Easter.

Bastille Day/National Day (Fête Nationale) 14 July – *the* national holiday.

Assumption Day (Assomption) 15 August

All Saints' Day (Toussaint) 1 November

Remembrance Day (L'onze novembre) 11 November – marks the WWI armistice.

Christmas (Noël) 25 December

Telephone

Mobile Phones

French mobile phones numbers begin with ☎06 or ☎07.

- France uses GSM 900/1800, compatible with the rest of Europe and Australia but not with the North American GSM 1900 or the totally different system in Japan (though some North Americans have tri-band phones that work here).
- It's usually cheaper to buy your own French SIM card from one of France's mobile phone companies, **Bouygues**, **Orange**, **SFR** or **Free**.
- Recharge cards are sold at *tabacs* (tobacconists) and newsagents.

Phone Codes

Calling France from abroad Dial your country's international access code, ☎33 (France's country code), and the 10-digit local number *without* the initial 0.

Calling internationally from France Dial ☎00 (the international access code), the country code, area code (without the initial zero if there is one) and local number.

Directory inquiries For France Telecom's *service des renseignements* (directory inquiries), dial ☎11 87 12 or use the online service for free www.118712.fr.

International directory inquiries For numbers outside France, dial ☎11 87 00.

Emergency number ☎112, can be dialled from public phones without a phonecard.

Toilets

- Public toilets, signposted WC or *toilettes,* are not always plentiful in France.
- Love them (sci-fi geek) or loathe them

Right: Eiffel Tower (p183), Paris; **Below:** River view, Paris
(RIGHT) LILLISPHOTOGRAPHY/GETTY IMAGES ©; (BELOW) MATHIEURIVRIN/GETTY IMAGES ©

(claustrophobe), France has its fair share of 24hr self-cleaning toilets, €0.50 in Paris and free elsewhere.

- Some older cafes and restaurants still have the hole-in-the-floor squat toilets.
- The French are blasé about unisex toilets; save your blushes when tiptoeing past the urinals to reach the loo.

Visas

- EU nationals and citizens of Iceland, Norway and Switzerland need only a passport or national identity card to enter France and stay in the country, even for stays of over 90 days.
- Citizens of Australia, the USA, Canada, Israel, Hong Kong, Japan, Malaysia, New Zealand, Singapore, South Korea and many Latin American countries do not need visas to visit France as tourists for up to 90 days.
- Other people wishing to come to France as tourists have to apply for a **Schengen Visa**.

Getting There & Away

Entering the Country

Entering France from other parts of the EU should be a breeze – no border checkpoints or customs thanks to Schengen Agreements signed by all of France's neighbours except the UK, the Channel Islands and Andorra.

Major Airports

Aéroport de Charles de Gaulle (CDG; www.aeroportsdeparis.fr)

Paris Orly (www.aeroportsdeparis.fr)

Aéroport Lyon-St Exupéry (www.lyonaeroports.com)

Aéroport Marseille-Provence (MRS; ☎04 42 14 14 14; www.marseille.aeroport.fr) Located 25km northwest of Marseille in Marignane; it is also called Aéroport Marseille-Marignane.

Aéroport Nice Côte d'Azur (http://societe.nice.aeroport.fr)

Land

Car & Motorcycle

A right-hand-drive vehicle brought to France from the UK or Ireland must have deflectors affixed to the headlights to avoid dazzling oncoming traffic.

Departing from the UK, **Eurotunnel Le Shuttle** (**in France 08 10 63 03 04, in UK 08443-35 35 35; www.eurotunnel.com**) trains whisk bicycles, motorcycles, cars and coaches in 35 minutes from Folkestone through the Channel Tunnel to Coquelles, 5km southwest of Calais. The earlier you book, the less you pay. Fares for a car, including up to nine passengers, start at €30.

Train

Rail services – including a dwindling number of overnight services to/from Spain, Italy and Germany – link France with virtually every country in Europe. Book tickets and get train information from **Rail Europe** (**www.raileurope.com**). In France ticketing is handled by **SNCF** (**from abroad +33 8 92 35 35 35, in France 36 35; http://en.voyages-sncf.com**); internet bookings are possible but they won't post tickets outside France.

High-speed train travel between France and the UK, Belgium, the Netherlands, Germany and Austria is covered by **Railteam** (**www.railteam.co.uk**) and TGV-Europe.

Eurostar (**in France 08 92 35 35 39, in UK 08432 186 186; www.eurostar.com**) Runs from London St-Pancras station to Paris Gare du Nord in 2¼ hours, with easy onward connections available to destinations all over France.

Sea

Regular ferries travel to France from Italy, the UK, Channel Islands and Ireland. Several ferry companies ply the waters between Corsica and Italy.

Getting Around

Air

Air France (**www.airfrance.com**) and its subsidiaries **Hop!** (**www.hop.com**) and **Transavia** (**www.transavia.com**) control the lion's share of France's domestic airline industry.

Budget carriers offering flights within France include **EasyJet** (**www.easyjet.com**), **Twin Jet** (**www.twinjet.net**) and **Air Corsica** (**www.aircorsica.com**).

Priority to the Right

Under the *priorité à droite* (priority to the right) rule, any car entering an intersection from a road on your right has the right of way, unless the intersection is marked *'vous n'avez pas la priorité'* (you do not have right of way) or *'cédez le passage'* (give way).

Bus

You're nearly always better off travelling by train in France if possible, as the SNCF domestic railway system is heavily subsidised by the government and is much more reliable than local bus companies. Nevertheless, buses are widely used for short-distance travel within *départements*, especially in rural areas with relatively few train lines (eg Brittany and Normandy).

Bicycle

Most French cities and towns have at least one bike shop that rents out mountain bikes (VTT; around €15 a day), road bikes (VTCs) and cheaper city bikes. You have to leave ID and/or a deposit (often a credit-card slip) that you forfeit if the bike is damaged or stolen. A growing number of cities have automatic bike rental systems.

Car & Motorcycle

Bringing Your Own Vehicle

All foreign motor vehicles entering France must display a sticker or licence plate identifying its country of registration. If you're bringing a right-hand-drive vehicle remember to fix deflectors on your headlights to avoid dazzling oncoming traffic.

Driving Licence & Documents

All drivers must carry a national ID card or passport; a valid driving licence (*permis de conduire;* most foreign licences can be used in France for up to a year); car-ownership papers, known as a *carte grise* (grey card); and proof of third party (liability) insurance.

Fuel & Tolls

Essence (petrol), also known as *carburant* (fuel), costs around €1.40-1.70 per litre for 95 unleaded (Sans Plomb 95 or SP95, usually available from a green pump), and €1.30-1.50 for diesel (*diesel, gazole* or *gasoil*, usually available from a yellow pump).

Many French motorways (*autoroutes*) are fitted with toll *(péage)* stations that charge a fee based on the distance you've travelled; factor in these costs when driving.

Hire

To hire a car you'll usually need to be over 21 and in possession of a valid driving licence and a credit card. Auto transmissions are *very* rare in France; you'll need to order one well in advance.

Insurance

Unlimited third-party liability insurance is mandatory in France. Third-party liability insurance is provided by car-rental companies, but collision-damage waivers (CDW) vary between companies. When comparing rates check the *franchise* (excess). Your credit card may cover CDW if you use it to pay for the car rental.

Road Rules

Cars drive on the right in France. Speed limits on French roads are as follows:

- 50km/h in built-up areas
- 90km/h (80km/h if it's raining) on N and D highways
- 110km/h (100km/h if it's raining) on dual carriageways
- 130km/h (110km/h if it's raining) on *autoroutes*

Child-seat rules are as follows:

- Children under 10 are not permitted to ride in the front seat (unless the back is already occupied by other children under 10).
- A child under 13kg must travel in a backward-facing child seat (permitted in the front seat only for babies under 9kg and if the airbag is deactivated).
- Up to age 10 and/or a minimum height of 140cm, children must use a size-appropriate type of front-facing child seat or booster.

Other key rules of the road:

- Blood-alcohol limit is 0.05% (0.5g per litre of blood) – the equivalent of two glasses of wine for a 75kg adult. Police often conduct random breathalyser tests and penalties can be severe, including imprisonment.
- Mobile phones may be used only if they are equipped with a hands-free kit or speakerphone.
- All passengers must wear seatbelts.
- All vehicles must carry a reflective safety

jacket (stored inside the car, not the trunk/boot), a reflective triangle, and a portable, single-use breathalyser kit. The fine for not carrying any of these items is €90.

- Riders of any type of two-wheeled vehicle with a motor (except motor-assisted bicycles) must wear a helmet.
- North American drivers, remember: turning right on a red light is illegal.

Train

France's superb rail network is operated by the state-owned **SNCF** (**www.sncf.com**); many rural towns not on the SNCF train network are served by SNCF buses.

The flagship trains on French railways are the superfast TGVs, which reach speeds in excess of 200mph and can whisk you from Paris to the Côte d'Azur in as little as three hours.

Many non-high-speed lines are also served by TGV trains; otherwise you'll find yourself aboard a non-TGV train, referred to as a *corail* or TER *(train express régional)*.

- 1st-class travel, where available, costs 20% to 30% extra.
- The further in advance you reserve, the lower the fares.
- Children under four travel for free (€9 to any destination if they need a seat).
- Children aged four to 11 travel for half price.

Discount Tickets

Prem's The SNCF's most heavily discounted, use-or-lose tickets, sold online, by phone and at ticket windows/machines a maximum of 90 days and minimum 14 days before you travel.

Bons Plans A grab-bag of cheap options for different routes/dates, advertised online under the tab '*Dernière Minute*' (Last Minute).

iDTGV Cheap tickets on advance-purchase TGV travel between about 30 cities; only sold at www.idtgv.com.

Tickets

Buying online at the various SNCF websites can reward with you some great reductions on fares, but be warned – these are generally intended for domestic travellers, and if you're buying abroad be aware of the pitfalls. Many tickets can't be posted outside France, and if you buy with a non-French credit card, you might not be able to use it in the automated ticket collection machines at many French stations.

Before boarding any train, you must validate *(composter)* your ticket by time-stamping it in a *composteur,* one of those yellow posts located on the way to the platform. If you forget (or don't have a ticket for some other reason), find a conductor on the train before they find you – or risk an unwelcome fine.

Rail Passes

The **InterRail One Country Pass** (**www.interrailnet.com; 3/4/6/8 days €216/237/302/344, 12–25yr €147/157/199/222**), valid in France, entitles residents of Europe who do not live in France to unlimited travel on SNCF trains for three to eight days over a month.

Spain

Feisty, fiery and full of life – that pretty much sums up Spain in a nutshell. This sunbaked corner of southern Europe knows all about the good things in life, and certainly isn't shy about wearing its emotions on its sleeve.

It's an intoxicating place that seems to march to its own beguiling beat. Whether it's exploring the shady lanes of Barcelona's Barri Gòtic, watching some authentic flamenco in a Seville *tablao* (flamenco venue) or trying delicious tapas on Madrid's backstreets, Spain offers a wealth of enticing experiences that seem to seep into your soul, and will stay with you long after you've left for home. From the sexy cities of Madrid and Barcelona to the Moorish-influenced towns of Granada and Seville and the hilltop *pueblos blancos* (white villages), there are many different aspects to Spain, each providing a new perspective on this fascinating country. Dance till dawn, hike the hills, bask on a beach or savour a siesta – they're all part of the essential Spanish experience. Enjoy every moment.

Palau de la Música Catalana (p311), Barcelona
NEIL SETCHFIELD/GETTY IMAGES ©

Spain
Punta da Estaca de Bares
Cabo Ortegal
Rías Altas
Ferrol
Costa da Morte
La Coruña
Santiago de Compostela
Lugo
Serra dos Ancares
Rías Baixas
Pontevedra
A Ribeira Sacra
Ourense
Cabo de Home
Vigo
Valença do Minho
Aviles
Gijón
Oviedo
Santander
Torrelavega
Museo Guggenheim
Carmona
Bilbao
Parque Nacional de los Picos de Europa
Vitoria
Miranda de Ebro
León
Logroño
Benavente
Palencia
Soria
Valladolid
Río Duero
Zamora
Porto
Rio Duero
Salamanca
Segovia
Guadalajara
Ávila
Coimbra
MADRID
2
4
Talavera de la Reina
Río Tejo
Toledo
Parque Nacional de Monfragüe
Rio Tejo
Cáceres
Trujillo
Montes de Toledo
Alcázar de San Juan
PORTUGAL
Ciudad Real
Badajoz
Mérida
Río Guadiana
Manzanares
LISBON
Almaden
Valdepeñas
Zafra
Barrancos
Rio Sado
Córdoba
Montoro
Jaen
Baza
Seville
Carmona
Huelva
Granada
3
Guadix
Ponta da Piedade
Faro
Parque Natural de Doñana
Río Genil
Parque Natural Sierra Nevada
Golfo di Cádiz
Parque Natural Sierra de Grazalema
Ronda
Málaga
Adra
Almería
Marbella
Cádiz
Gibraltar
Tarifa
Ceuta (Spain)
Tangier
MOROCCO
Málaga-Melilla
Almería-Melilla

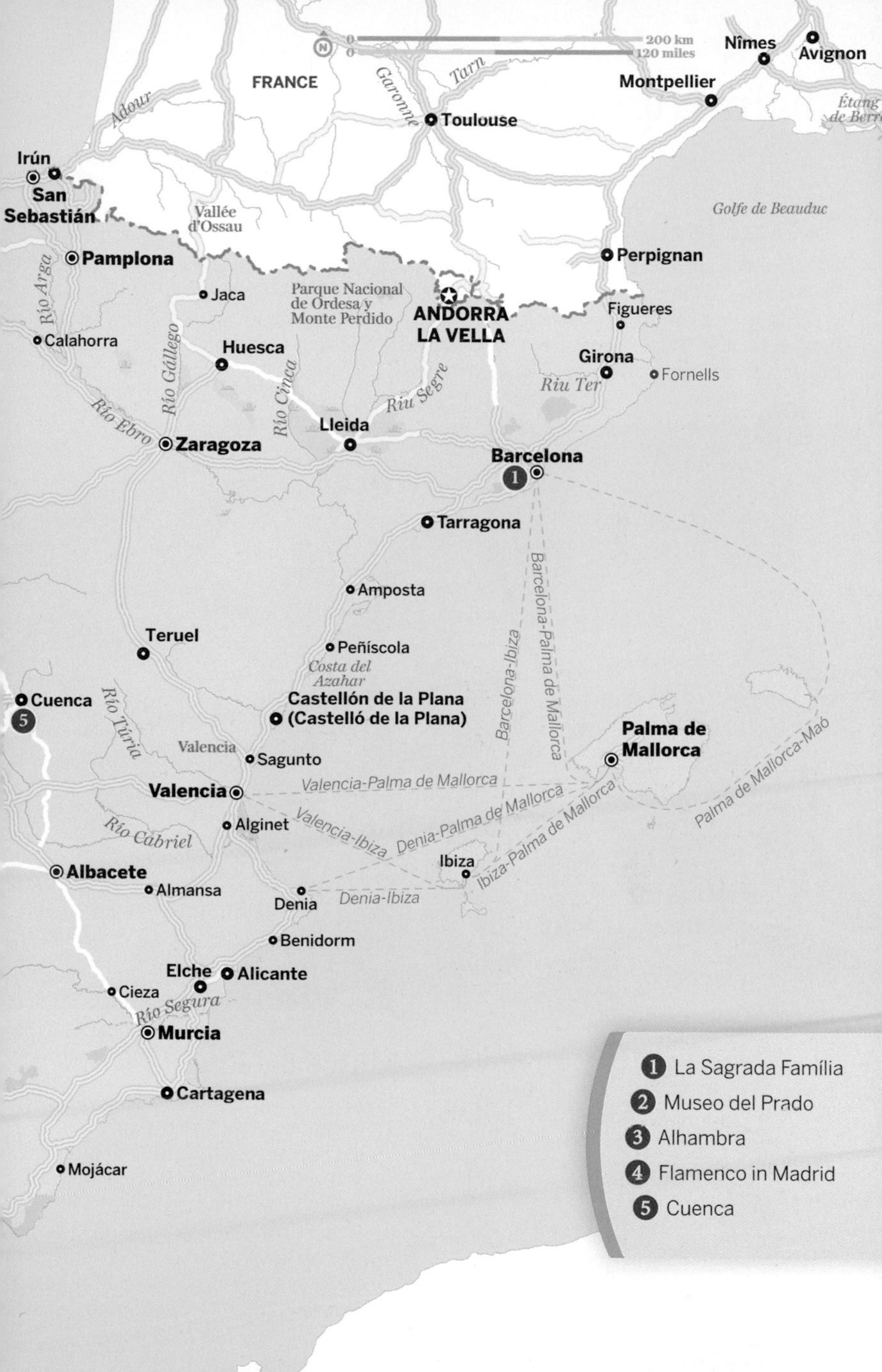

0
200 km
0
120 miles
FRANCE
Garonne
Tarn
Nîmes
Avignon
Montpellier
Étang de Berre
Adour
Toulouse
Irún
San Sebastián
Vallée d'Ossau
Golfe de Beauduc
Pamplona
Perpignan
Río Arga
Jaca
Parque Nacional de Ordesa y Monte Perdido
ANDORRA LA VELLA
Figueres
Calahorra
Río Gállego
Huesca
Girona
Fornells
Riu Ter
Río Cinca
Riu Segre
Río Ebro
Lleida
Zaragoza
Barcelona
Tarragona
Barcelona-Palma de Mallorca
Barcelona-Ibiza
Amposta
Teruel
Peñíscola
Costa del Azahar
Cuenca
Río Túria
Castellón de la Plana (Castelló de la Plana)
Palma de Mallorca
Valencia
Sagunto
Palma de Mallorca-Maó
Valencia-Palma de Mallorca
Valencia
Alginet
Valencia-Ibiza
Denia-Palma de Mallorca
Ibiza-Palma de Mallorca
Río Cabriel
Ibiza
Albacete
Almansa
Denia
Denia-Ibiza
Benidorm
Elche
Alicante
Cieza
Río Segura
Murcia
Cartagena
Mojácar
ALGERIA
1 La Sagrada Família
2 Museo del Prado
3 Alhambra
4 Flamenco in Madrid
5 Cuenca

Spain Highlights

La Sagrada Família

Halfway between an architectural experiment and a monumental artwork, this fantastical cathedral (p312) in the centre of Barcelona has been under construction since 1882, and is still thought to be several decades away from completion. It's the work of the visionary architect Antoni Gaudí, whose playful buildings can be seen along many of Barcelona's boulevards, as well as the lovely Parc Güell.

Museo del Prado

Housed in a glorious 18th-century palace (enhanced by a modern extension) in the heart of old Madrid, the Museo del Prado (p286) is Spain's foremost art museum and houses the nation's top artistic treasures. Around 7000 pieces are on show: Rubens, Rembrandt and Van Dyck are all represented, but it's th Spanish boys, Goya and Velazquez, whc inevitably take the prize.

SYLVAIN SONNET/GETTY IMAGES ©

KARL BLACKWELL/GETTY IMAGES ©

3 Alhambra

This fabulous Moorish palace (p346) in Granada is one of Spain's architectural marvels. It was built for the Muslim rulers of Granada between the 13th and 15th centuries, although parts of the structure date back to the 11th century. Seeing the medieval Palacio Nazaríes (Nasrid Palace) illuminated at twilight is an image that will linger. Right: Palacio Nazaríes

TRAVEL INK/GETTY IMAGES ©

4 Flamenco

Nothing sums up the Spanish spirit better than flamenco. This ancient dance form has been a cornerstone of Spanish culture for centuries, and is still going strong – although you'll have to choose carefully if you want to see the real thing. The best places to see authentic flamenco are Madrid and Seville, where you can watch some of the country's top performers strut their fiery stuff. Above: Flamenco dancer at Casa Patas (p300), Madrid

5 Cuenca

Spain has plenty of clifftop villages, but few of them can hold a candle to the *casas colgadas* (hanging houses) of Cuenca (p307). These balconied houses seem to have been carved straight from the cliff face, and perch precariously above the deep ravine of Río Huécar – a true marvel of medieval engineering. Unsurprisingly, the village has been named a Unesco World Heritage Site.

Spain's Best...

Festivals

- **Semana Santa** (p335) This holy week is a highlight of the pre-Easter calendar.
- **Sanfermines** (p330) See the brave (and the barmy) run with the bulls during Pamplona's hair-raising street race.
- **Carnaval Cádiz** Spain's wildest carnival kicks off on the streets of Cádiz in February.
- **Feria de Abril** (p335) Seville's six-day street party in April is packed with Andalucian passion.

Sacred Sites

- **Montserrat** (p328) Make a pilgrimage to this otherworldly mountain monastery near Barcelona.
- **Santiago de Compostela** Join the pilgrims on the last leg of the Camino de Santiago.
- **The Mezquita** (p342) Córdoba's Moorish mosque-cum-cathedral is almost as impressive as the Alhambra.
- **Toledo Cathedral** (p304) Considered to be the heart of Catholic Spain.
- **Burgos Cathedral** Pay your respects at the tomb of Spain's national hero, El Cid.

Spanish Experiences

- **Markets** (p307) Drink in the sights, sounds and smells of Barcelona's Boqueria market.
- **Flamenco** (p341) Experience traditional flamenco in an Andalucían *tablao*.
- **Zarzuela** (p301) Catch this Spanish blend of dance, music and theatre.
- **Cafe life** Drink till dawn with the locals: there's always tomorrow for a siesta.
- **Football** (p327) Watch the soccer superstars in action at Barcelona's Camp Nou.

Culinary Specialities

- **Tapas** (p296) Join the locals over Spanish snacks in Madrid's lively tapas bars.
- **Pintxos** (p331) Try this Basque version of tapas in San Sebastián.
- **Chocolate and churros** (p298) Savour this sweet pick-me-up at Madrid's Chocolatería de San Ginés.
- **Cochinillo asado** Madrid or San Sebastián are both great places to try roast suckling pig.
- **Basque cooking** (p331) San Sebastián is a great place to experience Basque cuisine.

Left: Women in flamenco dresses at Feria de Abril; **Above:** *Pintxos* in San Sebastián

Need to Know

ADVANCE PLANNING

- **Three months before** Book hotels and transport tickets, especially during festival season.
- **One month before** Arrange theatre, opera and flamenco tickets, and book tables at top restaurants.
- **One week before** Beat the queues at the Alhambra by buying your ticket online for a €1 supplement.

RESOURCES

- **Turespaña** (www.spain.info, www.tourspain.es) The national tourism site.
- **Renfe** (www.renfe.es) Plan your train travel.
- **Fiestas.net** (www.fiestas.net) Handy online guide to fiestas and festivals.
- **Tour Spain** (www.tourspain.org) Useful resource for culture and food, with links to hotels and transport.

GETTING AROUND

- **Bus** Spain's bus network is extensive but chaotic. ALSA (www.alsa.es) is one of the largest companies.
- **Car** Traffic and parking can be a nightmare around the big cities, so it's more convenient to hire cars from airport kiosks. Major motorways are called *autopistas;* tolls are compulsory on many routes.
- **Sea** Frequent ferries connect Spain with the UK, Italy, Morocco and Algeria. Major ports are in Santander, Bilbao and Barcelona.
- **Train** Spain's railways are run by Renfe (www.renfe.es). High-speed AVE trains link Madrid, Barcelona and major towns in between, and travel across the Pyrenees into France.

BE FOREWARNED

- **Public holidays** Most of Spain goes on holiday during August and Semana Santa (the week before Easter Sunday).
- **Smoking** 'Officially' banned in most public places, but many Spanish people don't seem to take much notice.
- **Scams** Watch out for pickpocketing and bag snatching, and be wary of common scams.

Spain Itineraries

Spain is famous for its laid-back approach to life – this is, after all, the land that invented the siesta – so take things slowly if you want to make the most of the sights.

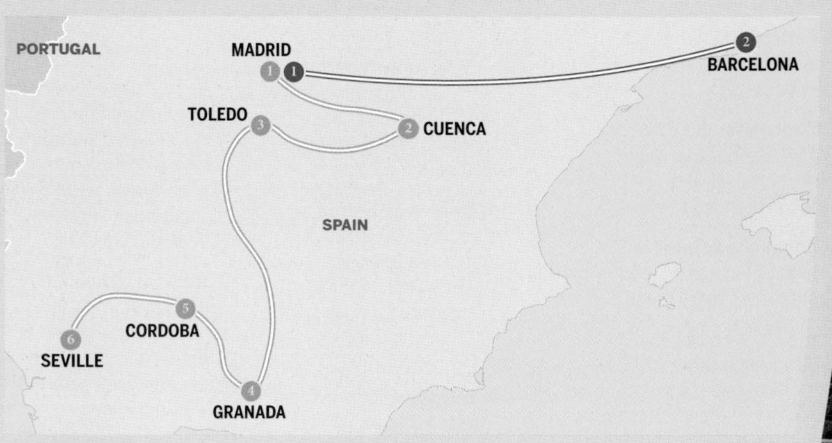

3 DAYS

CITY SIGHTS
Madrid to Barcelona

This trip gives you a taste of both of Spain's must-see cities. Start out in ❶**Madrid** (p286), with incredible art at the Museo del Prado, the Museo Thyssen-Bornemisza and the Caixa Forum, followed by a spot of people-watching on the Plaza Mayor and an after-dark visit to the *tabernas* (taverns) and tapas bars of La Latina, Chueca and Los Austrias. Book yourself a spot at a *tablao* for some late-night flamenco.

On day two, spend the morning at the Palacio Real, the monarch's Madrid residence, then visit one of the city's markets and take a picnic to Parque del Buen Retiro. In the late afternoon, it's on to ❷**Barcelona** (p307); thanks to the high-speed AVE trains, the trip now takes under three hours, leaving you plenty of time to check in before delving into the bars and bistros of the Barri Gòtic.

Day three's for sightseeing. Top of the list is La Sagrada Família, Gaudí's fantasy cathedral. Spend the afternoon at the Museu Picasso, have an early evening mooch around the shops and boutiques of El Raval and La Ribera, before finishing up with sophisticated Spanish food in the restaurants of L'Eixample.

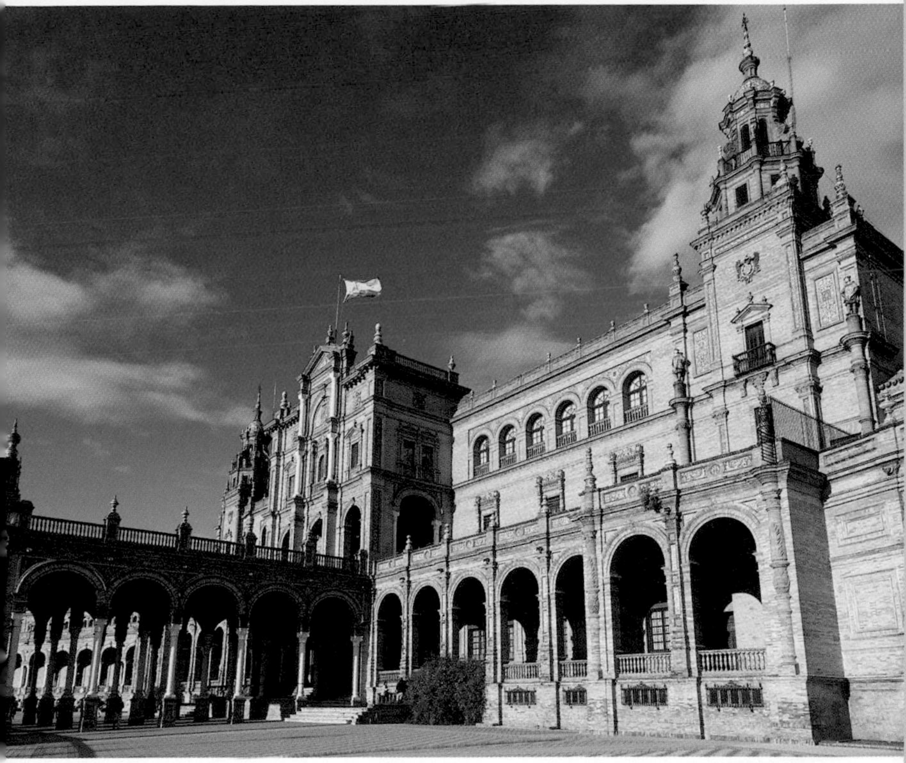

THE SOUTH
5 DAYS Madrid to Seville

This adventure heads into Spain's sultry, sun-drenched south, a region that's full of flamboyant passion. Start in 1 **Madrid** (p286), and make a detour southwest to see the marvellous 'hanging houses' of 2 **Cuenca** (p307), a Unesco site. On day two you can either backtrack to the capital or head west to the elegant city of 3 **Toledo** (p304), renowned for its cathedral.

Next comes 4 **Granada** (p346), where you can visit one of the great monuments of Spain's Moorish past, the mighty Alhambra, built as a palace and fortress for the region's rulers during the 14th century, and impressively preserved.

There's another Moorish structure in nearby 5 **Córdoba** (p342): the stunning Mezquita, a unique combination of Muslim and Christian cultures.

Finish off your trip in sexy 6 **Seville** (p335), the archetypal Andalucian city. This is the spiritual home of flamenco, and its lively bars and *tablaos* are probably the best places in Spain to experience this ancient art form. In summer, bars spring up along both sides of the river, and the action doesn't really get going till midnight – so it's best just to forget your watch and join the party.

Seville (p335)
WALTER BIBIKOW/GETTY IMAGES ©

Discover Spain

At a Glance

- **Madrid** (p286) Spain's sophisticated capital never seems to sleep.
- **Catalonia** (p307) Historic region that's home to Spain's most exciting city, Barcelona.
- **Basque Country** (p329) A country within a country, governed by its own language and culture.
- **Andalucía** (p335) The spiritual home of flamenco, full of fiery passion.

Statue of Felipe III, Plaza Mayor, Madrid

MADRID

POP 3.26 MILLION

No city on earth is more alive than Madrid, a beguiling place whose sheer energy carries a simple message: *madrileños* know how to live. Explore the old streets of the centre, relax in the plazas, soak up the culture in Madrid's excellent art museums and spend at least one night exploring the city's legendary nightlife scene.

Sights

Get under the city's skin by walking its streets, sipping coffee and beer in its plazas and relaxing in its parks. Madrid de los Austrias, the maze of mostly 15th- and 16th-century streets that surround Plaza Mayor, is the city's oldest district. Tapas-crazy La Latina, alternative Chueca, bar-riddled Huertas and Malasaña, and chic Salamanca are other districts that reward pedestrian exploration.

Museo del Prado Museum

(Map p294; www.museodelprado.es; Paseo del Prado; adult/child €14/free, free 6-8pm Mon-Sat & 5-7pm Sun, audioguides €3.50, admission plus official guidebook €23; 10am-8pm Mon-Sat, 10am-7pm Sun; ; M Banco de España)

Welcome to one of the world's premier art galleries. The more than 7000 paintings held in the Museo del Prado's collection (although only around 1500 are currently on display) are like a window into the historical vagaries of the Spanish soul, at once grand and imperious in the royal paintings of Velázquez, darkly tumultuous in *Las pinturas negras* (The Black Paintings) of Goya, and outward-looking with sophisticated works of art from all across Europe.

Museo Thyssen-Bornemisza Museum

(Map p294; ☎902 760511; www.museothyssen.org; Paseo del Prado 8; adult/concession/child €10/7/free, free for all Mon; ⏰10am-7pm Tue-Sun, noon-4pm Mon; M Banco de España) The Thyssen is one of the most extraordinary private collections of predominantly European art in the world. Where the Prado or Reina Sofía enable you to study the body of work of a particular artist in depth, the Thyssen is the place to immerse yourself in a breathtaking breadth of artistic styles. Most of the big names are here, sometimes with just a single painting, but the Thyssen's gift to Madrid and the art-loving public is to have them all under one roof.

Centro de Arte Reina Sofía Museum

(Map p290; ☎91 774 10 00; www.museoreinasofia.es; Calle de Santa Isabel 52; adult/concession €8/free, free 1.30-7pm Sun, 7-9pm Mon & Wed-Sat; ⏰10am-9pm Mon & Wed-Sat, 10am-7pm Sun, closed Tue; M Atocha) Home to Picasso's *Guernica,* arguably Spain's single most famous artwork, the Centro de Arte Reina Sofía is Madrid's premier collection of contemporary art. In addition to plenty of paintings by Picasso, other major drawcards are works by Salvador Dalí (1904–1989) and Joan Miró (1893–1983). The collection principally spans the 20th century up to the 1980s. The occasional non-Spaniard artist makes an appearance (including Francis Bacon's *Lying Figure;* 1966), but most of the collection is strictly peninsular.

Caixa Forum Museum, Architecture

(Map p294; ☎91 330 73 00; obrasocial.lacaixa.es/nuestroscentros/caixaforummadrid_es.html; Paseo del Prado 36; admission free, exhibitions from €4; ⏰10am-8pm; M Atocha) This extraordinary structure is one of Madrid's most eye-catching landmarks. Seeming to hover above the ground, this brick edifice is topped by an intriguing summit of rusted iron. On an adjacent wall is the *jardín colgante* (hanging garden), a lush vertical wall of greenery almost four storeys high. Inside there are four floors of exhibition and performance space awash in stainless steel and with soaring ceilings. The exhibitions here are always worth checking out and include photography, contemporary painting and multimedia shows.

Palacio Real Palace

(Map p294; ☎91 454 88 00; www.patrimonionacional.es; Calle de Bailén; adult/concession €11/6, guide/audioguide €4/4, EU citizens free last two hours Mon-Thu; ⏰10am-8pm Apr-Sep, 10am-6pm Oct-Mar; M Ópera) Spain's lavish Palacio Real is a jewel box of a palace, although it's used only occasionally for royal ceremonies; the royal family moved to the modest Palacio de la Zarzuela years ago. When the Alcázar burned down on Christmas Day 1734, Felipe V, the first of the Bourbon kings, decided to build a palace that would dwarf all its European counterparts. Felipe died before the palace was finished, which is perhaps why the Italianate baroque colossus has a mere 2800 rooms, just one-quarter of the original plan.

Plaza Mayor Square

(Map p294; Plaza Mayor; M Sol) Madrid's grand central square, a rare but expansive opening in the tightly packed streets of central Madrid, is one of the prettiest open spaces in Spain, a winning combination of imposing architecture, picaresque historical tales and vibrant street life coursing across its cobblestones. At once beautiful in its own right and a reference point for so many Madrid days, it also hosts the city's main tourist office (p302), a Christmas market in December and arches leading to so many laneways that lead out into the labyrinth.

Tours

Visitas Guiadas Oficiales Guided Tour

(Official Guided Tours; Map p294; ☎902 221 424902 221 424; www.esmadrid.com/programa-visitas-guiadas-oficiales; Plaza Mayor 27; per person €17-21; M Sol) Over 40 highly recommended walking, cycling and roller-blade tours conducted in Spanish and English. Organised by the Centro de Turismo de Madrid (p302). Stop by the office and pick up its *M – Visitas Guiadas/Guided Tours* catalogue.

Museo del Prado

PLAN OF ATTACK

Begin on the 1st floor with **Las meninas** ❶ by Velázquez. Although it alone is worth the entry price, it's a fine introduction to the 17th-century golden age of Spanish art; nearby are more of Velázquez' royal paintings and works by Zurbarán and Murillo. While on the 1st floor, seek out Goya's **La maja vestida and La maja desnuda** ❷ with more of Goya's early works in neighbouring rooms. Downstairs at the southern end of the Prado, Goya's anger is evident in the searing **El dos de mayo and El tres de mayo** ❸, and the torment of Goya's later years finds expression in the adjacent rooms with his **Las pinturas negras** ❹, or Black Paintings. Also on the lower floor, Hieronymus Bosch's weird and wonderful **The Garden of Earthly Delights** ❺ is one of the Prado's signature masterpieces. Returning to the 1st floor, El Greco's **Adoration of the Shepherds** ❻ is an extraordinary work, as is Peter Paul Rubens' **Las tres gracias** ❼ which forms the centrepiece of the Prado's gathering of Flemish masters. (Note: this painting may be moved to the 2nd floor.) A detour to the 2nd floor takes in some lesser-known Goyas, but finish in the **Edificio Jerónimos** ❽ with a visit to the cloisters and the outstanding bookshop.

ALSO VISIT:

Nearby are Museo Thyssen-Bornemisza and Centro de Arte Reina Sofía. They form an extraordinary trio of galleries.

TOP TIPS

» **Book online** Purchase your ticket online (www.museodelprado.es) and avoid the queues.

» **Best time to visit** As soon after opening time as possible.

» **Free tours** The website (www.museodelprado.es/coleccion/que-ver/) has self-guided tours for one- to three-hour visits.

Las meninas (Velázquez)
This masterpiece depicts Velázquez and the Infanta Margarita, with the king and queen whose images appear, according to some experts, in mirrors behind Velázquez.

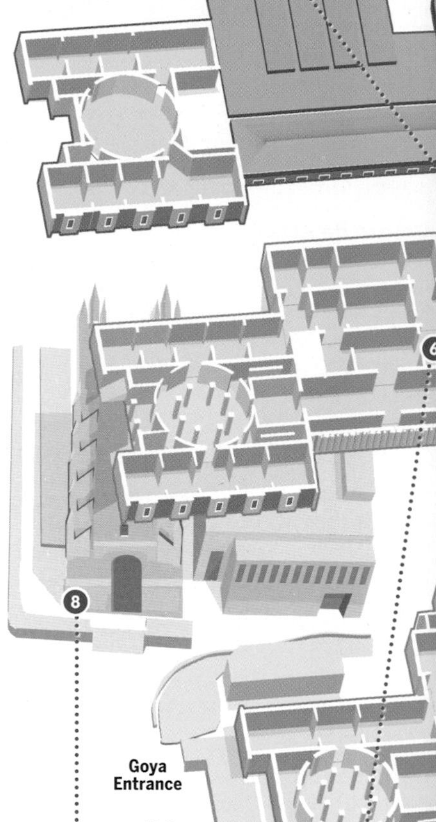

Edificio Jerónimos
Opened in 2007, this state-of-the-art extension has rotating exhibitions of Prado masterpieces held in storage for decades for lack of wall space, and stunning 2nd-floor granite cloisters that date back to 1672.

Adoration of the Shepherds (El Greco)
There's an ecstatic quality to this intense painting. El Greco's distorted rendering of bodily forms came to characterise much of his later work.

Las tres gracias (Rubens)

A late Rubens masterpiece, *The Three Graces* is a classical and masterly expression of Rubens' preoccupation with sensuality, here portraying Aglaia, Euphrosyne and Thalia, the daughters of Zeus.

La maja vestida & La maja desnuda (Goya)

These enigmatic works scandalised early 19th-century Madrid society, fuelling the rumour mill as to the woman's identity and drawing the ire of the Spanish Inquisition.

Edificio Villanueva

1

7

2

El dos de mayo & El tres de mayo (Goya)

Few paintings evoke a city's sense of self quite like Goya's portrayal of Madrid's valiant but ultimately unsuccessful uprising against French rule in 1808.

Las pinturas negras (Goya)

Las pinturas negras are Goya's darkest works. *Saturno devorando a su hijo* evokes a writhing mass of tortured humanity, while *La romería de San Isidro* and *El aquelarre* are profoundly unsettling.

Jerónimos Entrance (Main Entrance)

Information Counter & Audioguides

Gift Shop

Cafeteria

Murillo Entrance

5

3

4

Velázquez Entrance

The Garden of Earthly Delights (Bosch)

A fantastical painting in triptych form, this overwhelming work depicts the Garden of Eden and what the Prado describes as 'the lugubrious precincts of Hell' in exquisitely bizarre detail.

Greater Madrid

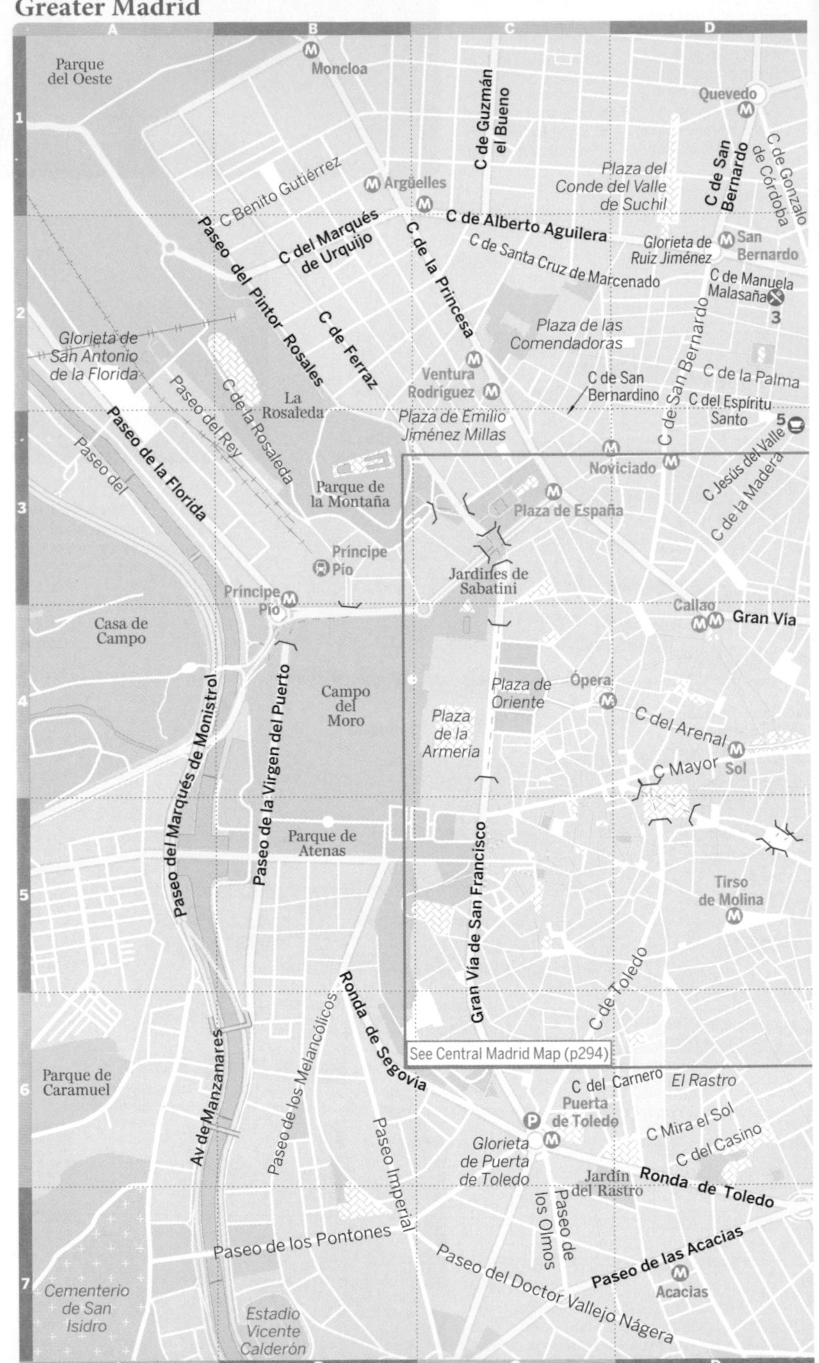

Parque del Oeste
Moncloa
C de Guzmán el Bueno
Quevedo
C de San Bernardo
C de Gonzalo de Córdoba
Plaza del Conde del Valle de Suchil
Argüelles
C Benito Gutiérrez
C de Alberto Aguilera
C del Marqués de Urquijo
Paseo del Pintor Rosales
C de la Princesa
C de Santa Cruz de Marcenado
Glorieta de Ruiz Jiménez
San Bernardo
C de Manuela Malasaña
3
C de Ferraz
Plaza de las Comendadoras
Glorieta de San Antonio de la Florida
Paseo del Rey
C de la Rosaleda
La Rosaleda
Ventura Rodríguez
C de San Bernardino
C de San Bernardo
C de la Palma
C del Espíritu Santo
5
Plaza de Emilio Jiménez Millas
Paseo de la Florida
Paseo del
Noviciado
C Jesús del Valle
C de la Madera
Parque de la Montaña
Plaza de España
Príncipe Pío
Jardines de Sabatini
Casa de Campo
Callao
Gran Vía
Campo del Moro
Plaza de Oriente
Ópera
Paseo del Marqués de Monistrol
Paseo de la Virgen del Puerto
Plaza de la Armería
C del Arenal
Sol
C Mayor
Parque de Atenas
Gran Vía de San Francisco
Tirso de Molina
C de Toledo
Ronda de Segovia
Paseo de los Melancólicos
Av de Manzanares
See Central Madrid Map (p294)
Parque de Caramuel
C del Carnero
El Rastro
Puerta de Toledo
C Mira el Sol
C del Casino
Paseo Imperial
Glorieta de Puerta de Toledo
Jardín del Rastro
Ronda de Toledo
Paseo de los Olmos
Paseo de los Pontones
Paseo de las Acacias
Acacias
Paseo del Doctor Vallejo Nágera
Cementerio de San Isidro
Estadio Vicente Calderón

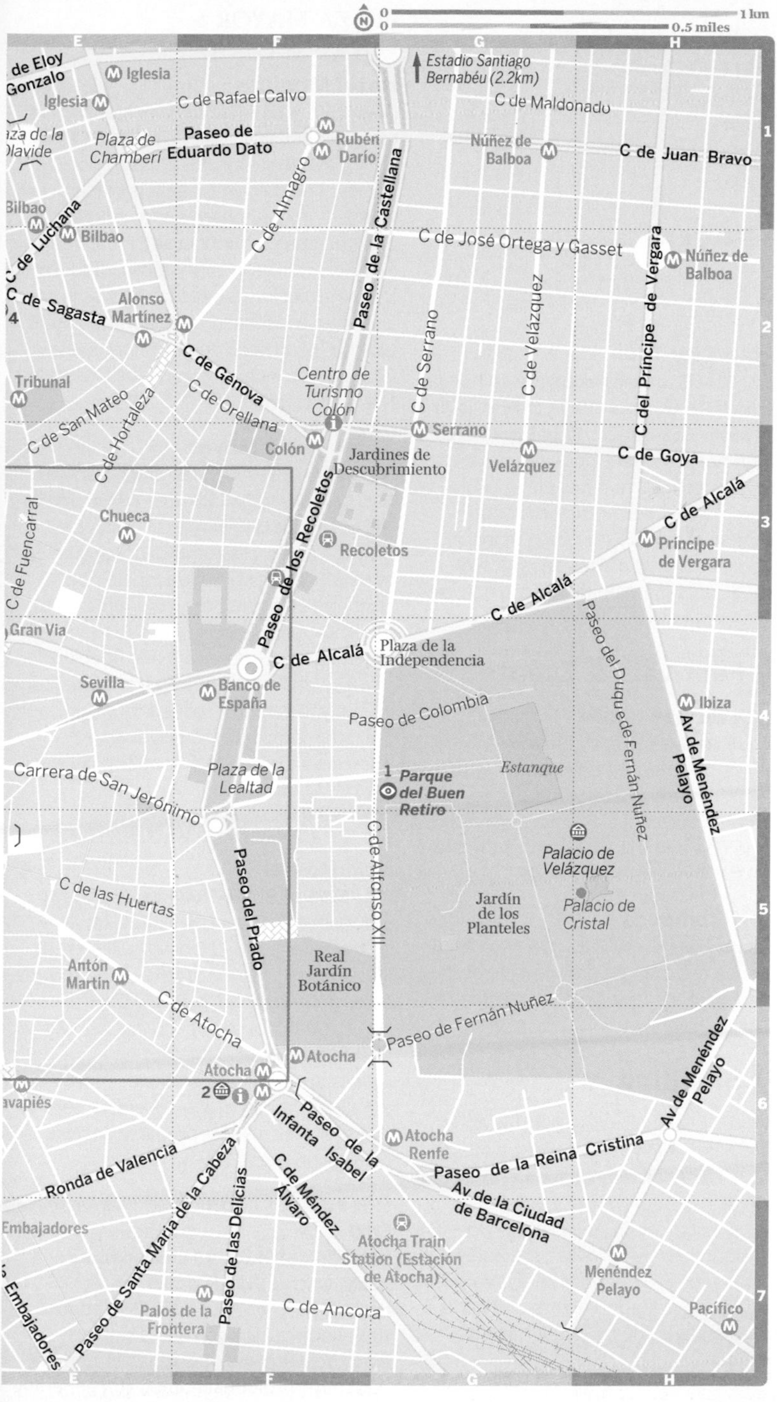

Estadio Santiago Bernabéu (2.2km)
C de Rafael Calvo
C de Maldonado
Iglesia
Paseo de Eduardo Dato
Plaza de Chamberí
Rubén Darío
Núñez de Balboa
C de Juan Bravo
C de Almagro
Paseo de la Castellana
Bilbao
C de Luchana
C de José Ortega y Gasset
Núñez de Balboa
C de Sagasta
Alonso Martínez
C de Serrano
C de Velázquez
C del Príncipe de Vergara
C de Génova
C de Orellana
Tribunal
Centro de Turismo Colón
C de San Mateo
C de Hortaleza
Serrano
Colón
Jardines de Descubrimiento
Velázquez
C de Goya
C de Alcalá
C de Fuencarral
Chueca
Paseo de los Recoletos
Recoletos
Príncipe de Vergara
Gran Via
C de Alcalá
Plaza de la Independencia
Paseo del Duque de Fernán Nuñez
Sevilla
Banco de España
Paseo de Colombia
Ibiza
Av de Menéndez Pelayo
Carrera de San Jerónimo
Plaza de la Lealtad
1 Parque del Buen Retiro
Estanque
C de Alfonso XII
Palacio de Velázquez
Paseo del Prado
C de las Huertas
Jardín de los Planteles
Palacio de Cristal
Real Jardín Botánico
Antón Martín
C de Atocha
Paseo de Fernán Nuñez
Atocha
2
Paseo de la Infanta Isabel
Atocha Renfe
Av de Menéndez Pelayo
Ronda de Valencia
Paseo de Santa María de la Cabeza
Paseo de las Delicias
C de Méndez Álvaro
Paseo de la Reina Cristina
Av de la Ciudad de Barcelona
Embajadores
Atocha Train Station (Estación de Atocha)
Menéndez Pelayo
Palos de la Frontera
C de Ancora
Pacífico
1 km
0.5 miles

Greater Madrid

Madrid City Tour Bus Tour
(902 024758; www.madridcitytour.es; 1-/2-day ticket adult €21/25, child €10/13, children under 7 free; 9am-10pm Mar-Oct, 10am-6pm Nov-Feb) Hop-on hop-off open-topped buses that run every 10 to 20 minutes along two routes: Historical Madrid and Modern Madrid. Information, including maps, is available at tourist offices, most travel agencies and some hotels, or you can get tickets on the bus.

Festivals & Events

Fiesta de San Isidro Cultural
(www.esmadrid.com) Around 15 May Madrid's patron saint is honoured with a week of nonstop processions, parties and bullfights. Free concerts are held throughout the city, and this week marks the start of the city's bullfighting season.

Suma Flamenca Flamenco
(www.madrid.org/sumaflamenca) A soul-filled flamenco festival that draws some of the biggest names in the genre to the Teatros del Canal in June.

Sleeping

Where you decide to stay will play an important role in your experience of Madrid. Los Austrias, Sol and Centro put you in the heart of the busy downtown area, while La Latina (the best *barrio* – neighbourhood – for tapas), Lavapiés and Huertas (good for nightlife) are ideal for those who love Madrid nights and don't want to stagger too far to get back to their hotel.

PLAZA MAYOR & ROYAL MADRID

Hotel Meninas Boutique Hotel **€€**
(Map p294; 91 541 28 05; www.hotelmeninas.com; Calle de Campomanes 7; s/d from €75/95; M Ópera) This is a classy, cool choice. The colour scheme is blacks, whites and greys, with dark-wood floors and splashes of fuchsia and lime green. Flat-screen TVs in every room, modern bathroom fittings, internet-access points, and even a laptop in some rooms, round out the clean lines and latest innovations. Past guests include Viggo Mortensen and Natalie Portman.

Hotel Plaza Mayor Hotel **€€**
(Map p294; 91 360 06 06; www.h-plazamayor.com; Calle de Atocha 2; s/d from €37/47; M Sol, Tirso de Molina) We love this place. Sitting just across from the Plaza Mayor, here you'll find stylish decor, helpful staff and charming original elements of this 150-year-old building. The rooms are attractive, some with a light colour scheme and wrought-iron furniture. The pricier attic rooms boast dark wood and designer lamps, and have lovely little terraces with wonderful rooftop views of central Madrid.

LA LATINA & LAVAPIÉS

Mad Hostel Hostel **€**
(Map p294; 91 506 48 40; www.madhostel.com; Calle de la Cabeza 24; dm €20-24; @; M Antón Martín) Mad Hostel is filled with life. The 1st-floor courtyard – with retractable roof – re-creates an old Madrid *corrala* (traditional patio) and is a wonderful place to chill, while the four- to eight-bed rooms are smallish but clean. There's a small, rooftop gym..Guests get access to Cat's Hostel, a sister property nearby, for those who like to party.

Posada del León de Oro Boutique Hotel **€€**
(Map p294; 91 119 14 94; www.posadadelleondeoro.com; Calle de la Cava Baja 12; r from €105; M La Latina) Next door to Posada del Dragón and a similarly spectacular place, this rehabilitated inn has muted colour schemes and generally

KRZYSZTOF DYDYNSKI/GETTY IMAGES ©

Don't Miss
Parque del Buen Retiro

The glorious gardens of El Retiro are as beautiful as any you'll find in a European city. Littered with marble monuments, landscaped lawns, the occasional elegant building (the Palacio de Cristal is especially worth seeking out) and abundant greenery, it's quiet and contemplative during the week but comes to life on weekends. Put simply, this is one of our favourite places in Madrid.

NEED TO KNOW

Map p290; 6am-midnight May-Sep, to 11pm Oct-Apr; M Retiro, Príncipe de Vergara, Ibiza, Atocha

large rooms. There's a *corrala* its core, and thoroughly modern rooms along one of Madrid's best-loved streets. The downstairs bar is terrific.

SOL, SANTA ANA & HUERTAS

Praktik Metropol Boutique Hotel **€€**
(Map p294; 91 521 29 35; www.hotelpraktikmetropol.com; Calle de la Montera 47; s/d from €89/99; ; M Gran Vía) You'd be hard-pressed to find better value anywhere in Europe than here in this recently overhauled hotel. The rooms have a fresh, contemporary look with white wood furnishings, and some (especially the corner rooms) have brilliant views down to Gran Vía and out over the city. It's spread over six floors and there's a roof terrace if you don't have a room with a view.

Hotel Alicia Boutique Hotel **€€**
(Map p294; 91 389 60 95; www.room-matehoteles.com; Calle del Prado 2; d €100-175, ste from €200; ; M Sol, Sevilla, Antón Martín) One of the landmark properties of the designer Room Mate chain of hotels, Hotel Alicia overlooks Plaza de Santa Ana with beautiful, spacious rooms. The style (the work of designer Pascua Ortega) is

Central Madrid

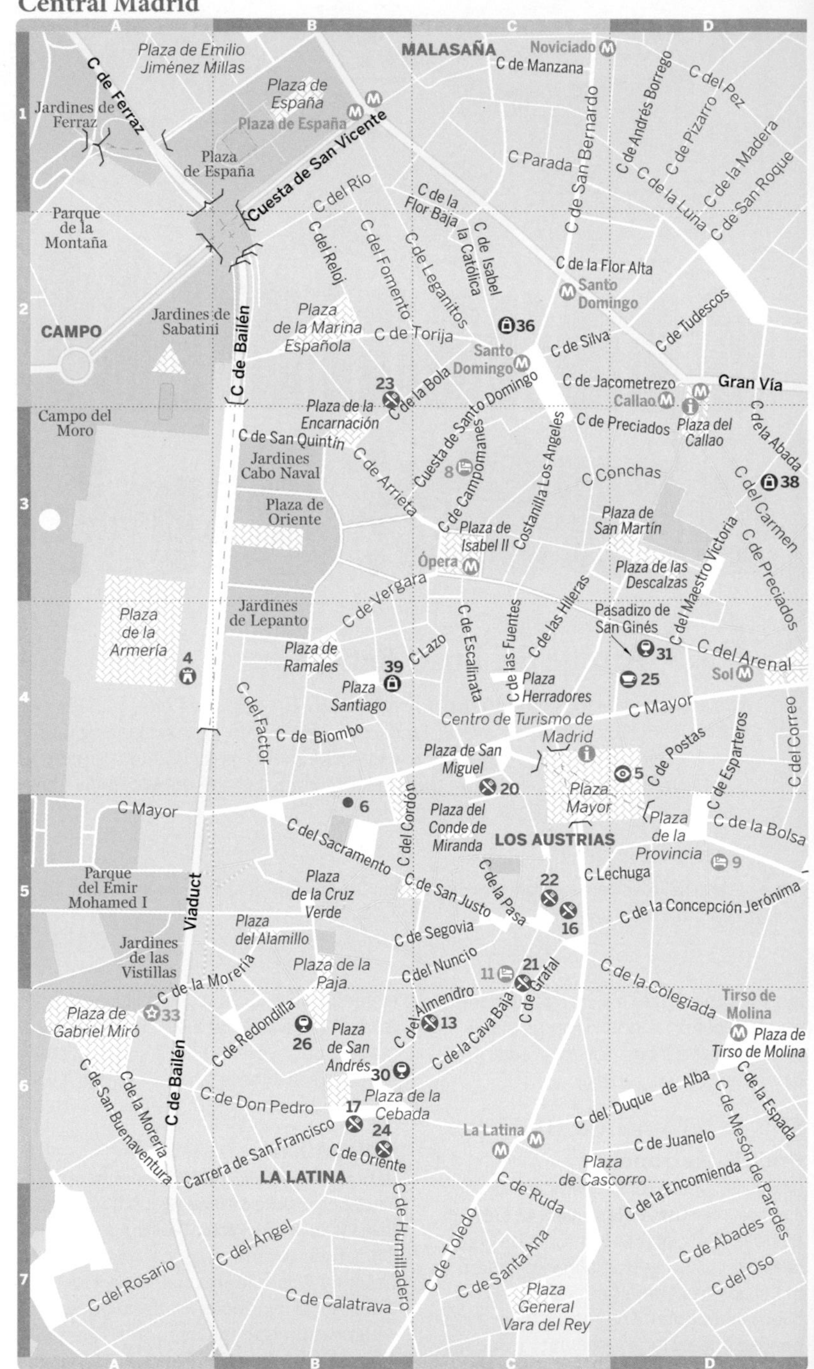
MALASAÑA
Noviciado
Plaza de Emilio Jiménez Millas
C de Ferraz
Jardines de Ferraz
Plaza de España
Plaza de España
Cuesta de San Vicente
C de Manzana
C de San Bernardo
C Parada
C de Andrés Borrego
C del Pez
C de Pizarro
C de la Madera
C de la Luna
C de San Roque
Parque de la Montaña
C del Río
C de la Flor Baja
C del Reloj
C del Fomento
C de Leganitos
C de la Católica
C de Isabel
C de la Flor Alta
Santo Domingo
CAMPO
Jardines de Sabatini
C de Bailén
Plaza de la Marina Española
C de Torija
36
C de Silva
C de Tudescos
Santo Domingo
C de la Bola
23
C de Jacometrezo
Gran Vía
Callao
Plaza de la Encarnación
Cuesta de Santo Domingo
C de Preciados
Plaza del Callao
C de la Abada
Campo del Moro
C de San Quintín
Jardines Cabo Naval
C de Arrieta
C de Campomanes
8
Costanilla Los Angeles
C Conchas
38
C del Carmen
Plaza de Oriente
Plaza de Isabel II
Plaza de San Martín
C del Maestro Victoria
C de Preciados
Ópera
Plaza de las Descalzas
C de Vergara
Plaza de la Armería
Jardines de Lepanto
C de Escalinata
C de las Fuentes
C de las Hileras
Pasadizo de San Ginés
31
C del Arenal
4
Plaza de Ramales
39
C Lazo
Plaza Santiago
Plaza Herradores
25
Sol
C del Factor
C de Biombo
Centro de Turismo de Madrid
C Mayor
C de Postas
C de Esparteros
C del Correo
Plaza de San Miguel
5
20
C Mayor
6
C del Cordón
Plaza Mayor
Plaza del Conde de Miranda
LOS AUSTRIAS
Plaza de la Provincia
C de la Bolsa
C del Sacramento
9
Parque del Emir Mohamed I
Viaduct
Plaza de la Cruz Verde
C de San Justo
C de la Pasa
22
C Lechuga
16
C de la Concepción Jerónima
Plaza del Alamillo
C de Segovia
Jardines de las Vistillas
C de la Morería
Plaza de la Paja
C del Nuncio
11
21
C de Grafal
C de la Colegiada
Tirso de Molina
Plaza de Gabriel Miró
33
C de Redondilla
26
C del Almendro
13
C de la Cava Baja
Plaza de Tirso de Molina
Plaza de San Andrés
30
C de la Morería
C de San Buenaventura
C de Don Pedro
Plaza de la Cebada
17
24
C del Duque de Alba
C de la Espada
C de Mesón de Paredes
Carrera de San Francisco
C de Oriente
La Latina
C de Juanelo
LA LATINA
Plaza de Cascorro
C de Ruda
C de la Encomienda
C de Humilladero
C del Ángel
C de Toledo
C de Abades
C de Santa Ana
C del Oso
C del Rosario
C de Calatrava
Plaza General Vara del Rey
A
B
C
D
1
2
3
4
5
6
7

C de Colón
C San Lucas
C de Piamonte
C del Almirante
CHUECA
Plaza de Chueca
Chueca
C de Gravina
C de Pelayo
C de Augusto Figueroa
C de Prim
C de San Marcos
C de Hortaleza
C de Fuencarral
C del Valverde
C del Barco
C de la Reina
C de las Infantas
Plaza del Rey
C de la Libertad
C de Barquillo
Paseo de los Recoletos
Paseo del Prado
Gran Via
Gran Vía
Plaza de la Red de San Luis
C del Caballero de Gracia
Banco de España
Plaza de la Cibeles
C de Alcalá
CENTRO
C de los Jardines
Plaza del Carmen
C de la Aduana
Sevilla
C de la Montera
C de Tetuán
C de la Salud
C de los Madrazo
C de los Cedaceros
C de Marqués de Cubas
Sol
Plaza de la Puerta del Sol
C de Arlabán
Plaza de Canalejas
C de Zorrilla
Plaza de la Lealtad
C del Pozo
Carrera de San Jerónimo
SOL
Plaza de las Cortes
Plaza de Neptuno (Plaza de Cánovas del Castillo)
C Felipe IV
C de Carretas
C de Espoz y Mina
C de la Cruz
C del Príncipe
C de Echegaray
C del Prado
HUERTAS
Museo del Prado
Plaza del Ángel
C del Infante
C de Cervantes
Plaza de Jesús
C de Lope de Vega
JERÓNIMOS
Plaza de Matute
C de León
C de Atocha
C de Santa María
C de las Huertas
C de Moratín
C de los Relatores
C de Luiz Vélez de Guevera
C del Amor de Dios
Antón Martín
Plaza de Antón Martín
C de la Magdalena
Plaza de Bravo Murillo
C de Cabeza
C de Verónica
C del Gobernador
C de la Alameda
Real Jardín Botánico
C del Calvario
C del Olmo
C del Olivar
C del Ave María
C del Duque de Fernán Núñez
C Almadén
C de Jesús y María
C Tres Peces
C San Ildefonso
ATOCHA
C de Cenicero
C de San Carlos
C de Buena Vista
LAVAPIÉS
C de Santa Isabel
C de Zurita
C de Salitre
Plaza de Lavapiés
Atocha
400 m
0.2 miles
SPAIN MADRID

Central Madrid

Sights

1 Caixa Forum H6
2 Museo del Prado H5
3 Museo Thyssen-Bornemisza G4
4 Palacio Real A4
5 Plaza Mayor D4

Activities, Courses & Tours

6 Visitas Guiadas Oficiales B5

Sleeping

7 Hotel Alicia F5
8 Hotel Meninas C3
9 Hotel Plaza Mayor D5
10 Mad Hostel E6
11 Posada del León de Oro C5
12 Praktik Metropol E3

Eating

13 Almendro 13 .... C6
14 Bazaar G2
15 Casa Alberto F5
16 Casa Revuelta C5
17 Juana La Loca B6
18 La Finca de Susana F4
19 Lhardy E4
20 Mercado de San Miguel C4
21 Posada de la Villa C5
22 Restaurante Sobrino de Botín C5
23 Taberna La Bola B2
24 Txirimiri B6

Drinking & Nightlife

25 Chocolatería de San Ginés D4
26 Delic B6
27 Kapital H7
28 La Venencia F4
29 Museo Chicote F3
30 Taberna Tempranillo B6
31 Teatro Joy Eslava D4

Entertainment

32 Casa Patas E6
33 Corral de la Morería A6
34 Teatro de la Zarzuela G4
35 Villa Rosa E5

Shopping

36 Antigua Casa Talavera C2
37 Casa de Diego E4
38 Casa de Diego D3
39 El Flamenco Vive B4

a touch more muted than in other Room Mate hotels, but the supermodern look remains intact, the downstairs bar is oh-so-cool, and the service is young and switched on.

Eating

It's possible to find just about any kind of cuisine and eatery in Madrid, from traditional to trendy fusion. From the chaotic tapas bars of La Latina to countless neighbourhood favourites, you'll have no trouble tracking down specialities like *cochinillo asado* (roast suckling pig) or *cocido madrileño* (a hearty stew made of chickpeas and various meats).

PLAZA MAYOR & ROYAL MADRID

Mercado de San Miguel Tapas **€€**
(Map p294; www.mercadodesanmiguel.es; Plaza de San Miguel; tapas from €1; 10am-midnight Sun-Wed, 10am-2am Thu-Sat; M Sol) One of Madrid's oldest and most beautiful markets, the Mercado de San Miguel has undergone a stunning major renovation. Within the early-20th-century glass walls, the market has become an inviting space strewn with tables. You can order tapas and sometimes more substantial plates at most of the counter-bars, and everything here (from caviar to chocolate) is as tempting as the market is alive.

Taberna La Bola Madrileño **€€**
(Map p294; 91 547 69 30; www.labola.es; Calle de la Bola 5; mains €16-24; 1.30-4.30pm & 8.30-11pm Mon-Sat, 1.30-4.30pm Sun, closed Aug; M Santo Domingo) Taberna La Bola (going strong since 1870 and run by the sixth generation of the Verdasco family) is a much-loved bastion of traditional Madrid cuisine. If you're going to try *cocido madrileño* (€20) while in Madrid, this is a good place to do so. It's busy and noisy and very Madrid.

Restaurante Sobrino de Botín Castilian **€€€**
(Map p294; 91 366 42 17; www.botin.es; Calle de los Cuchilleros 17; mains €19-27; 1-4pm & 8pm-midnight; M La Latina, Sol) It's not every day that you can eat in the oldest restaurant in the world (the *Guinness Book of*

A Tapas Tour of Madrid

Almendro 13 (Map p294; ☎91 365 42 52; Calle del Almendro 13; mains €7-15; ⏰1-4pm & 7.30pm-midnight Sun-Thu, 1-5pm & 8pm-1am Fri & Sat; Ⓜ La Latina) Almendro 13 is a charming, wildly popular *taberna* (tavern) where you come for traditional Spanish tapas with an emphasis on quality rather than frilly elaborations. A full *racion* of the famously good *huevos rotos* (literally, 'broken eggs') served with *jamón* (ham) and thin potato slices is a meal in itself. The only problem is that the wait for a table (low, with wooden stools) requires the patience of a saint, so order a fine wine or *manzanilla* (dry sherry) and soak up the buzz.

Juana La Loca (Map p294; ☎91 364 05 25; Plaza de la Puerta de Moros 4; tapas from €5, mains €8-19; ⏰noon-1am Tue-Sun, 8pm-1am Mon; Ⓜ La Latina) Juana La Loca does a range of creative tapas with tempting options lined up along the bar, and more on the menu that they prepare to order. But we love it above all for its *tortilla de patatas* (potato and onion omelette), which is distinguished from others of its kind by the caramelised onions – simply wonderful.

Txirimiri (Map p294; ☎91 364 11 96; www.txirimiri.es; Calle del Humilladero 6; tapas from €4; ⏰noon-4.30pm & 8.30pm-midnight Mon-Sat, closed Aug; Ⓜ La Latina) This *pintxo* (Basque tapas) bar is a great little discovery just down from the main La Latina tapas circuit. Wonderful wines, gorgeous *pinchos* (tapas; the *tortilla de patatas* is superb) and fine risottos add up to a pretty special combination.

Casa Revuelta (Map p294; ☎91 366 33 32; Calle de Latoneros 3; tapas from €2.80; ⏰10.30am-4pm & 7-11pm Tue-Sat, 10.30am-4pm Sun, closed Aug; Ⓜ Sol, La Latina) Casa Revuelta puts out some of Madrid's finest tapas of *bacalao* (cod) bar none - the fact that the octogenarian owner, Señor Revuelta, painstakingly extracts every fish bone in the morning and serves as a waiter in the afternoon wins the argument for us. Early on a Sunday afternoon, as the Rastro crowd gathers here, it's filled to the rafters.

Records has recognised it as the oldest – established in 1725). And it has also appeared in many novels about Madrid, from Ernest Hemingway to Frederick Forsyth. Roasted meats are the speciality.

LA LATINA & LAVAPIÉS

Posada de la Villa Madrileño €€€
(Map p294; ☎91 366 18 80; www.posadadelavilla.com; Calle de la Cava Baja 9; mains €19-28; ⏰1-4pm & 8pm-midnight Mon-Sat, 1-4pm Sun, closed Aug; Ⓜ La Latina) This wonderfully restored 17th-century *posada* (inn) is something of a local landmark. The atmosphere is formal, the decoration sombre and traditional (heavy timber and brickwork), and the cuisine decidedly local – roast meats, *cocido*, *callos* (tripe) and *sopa de ajo* (garlic soup).

SOL, SANTA ANA & HUERTAS

Casa Alberto Spanish, Tapas €€
(Map p294; ☎91 429 93 56; www.casaalberto.es; Calle de las Huertas 18; tapas €4-10, raciones €6.50-16, mains €14-21; ⏰restaurant 1.30-4pm & 8pm-midnight Tue-Sat, 1.30-4pm Sun, bar 12.30pm-1.30am Tue-Sat & 12.30-4pm Sun, closed Sun Jul & Aug; Ⓜ Antón Martín) One of the most atmospheric old *tabernas* of Madrid, Casa Alberto has been around since 1827. The secret to its staying power is vermouth on tap, excellent tapas at the bar and fine sit-down meals; Casa Alberto's *rabo de toro* (bull's tail) is famous among aficionados.

Hot Chocolate & Churros

Chocolatería de San Ginés
(Map p294; ☎91 365 65 46; www.chocolateriasangines.com; Pasadizo de San Ginés 5; ⏲24hr; Ⓜ Sol) One of the grand icons of the Madrid night, this *chocolate con churros* (Spanish doughnuts with chocolate) cafe sees a sprinkling of tourists throughout the day, but locals pack it out in their search for sustenance on their way home from a nightclub sometime close to dawn. Only in Madrid...

La Finca de Susana Spanish **€**
(Map p294; ☎91 369 35 57; www.grupandilana.com/es/restaurantes/la-finca-de-susana; Calle de Arlabán 4; mains €7-12; ⏲1-3.45pm & 8.30-11.30pm Sun-Wed, 1-3.45pm & 8.15pm-midnight Thu-Sat; Ⓜ Sevilla) It's difficult to find a better combination of price, quality cooking and classy atmosphere anywhere in Huertas. The softly lit dining area is bathed in greenery and the sometimes innovative, sometimes traditional food draws a hip young crowd. The duck confit with plums, turnips and couscous is a fine choice. No reservations, so you may have to wait..

Lhardy Spanish **€€€**
(Map p294; ☎91 521 33 85; www.lhardy.com; Carrera de San Jerónimo 8; mains €19-38; ⏲1-3.30pm & 8.30-11pm Mon-Sat, 1-3.30pm Sun, closed Aug; Ⓜ Sol, Sevilla) This Madrid landmark (since 1839) is an elegant treasure trove of takeaway gourmet tapas downstairs, while the six upstairs dining areas are the upmarket preserve of traditional Madrid dishes with an occasional hint of French influence. House specialities include *cocido a la madrileña* (€35.50), pheasant and wild duck in an orange perfume. The quality and service are unimpeachable.

A favourite haunt of royalty in the 19th century, Lhardy has drawn the great and good of Madrid ever since.

MALASAÑA & CHUECA

Bazaar Spanish **€**
(Map p294; ☎91 523 39 05; www.restaurantbazaar.com; Calle de la Libertad 21; mains €6.50-10; ⏲1.15-4pm & 8.30-11.30pm Sun-Wed, 1.15-4pm & 8.15pm-midnight Thu-Sat; Ⓜ Chueca) Bazaar's popularity among the well heeled and famous shows no sign of abating. Its pristine white interior design, with theatre-style lighting and wall-length windows, may draw a crowd that looks like it stepped out of the pages of *Hola!* magazine, but the food is extremely well priced and innovative and the atmosphere is casual.

Albur Tapas, Spanish **€€**
(Map p290; ☎91 594 27 33; www.restaurantealbur.com; Calle de Manuela Malasaña 15; mains €11-16; ⏲1-5pm & 8pm-12.30am Mon-Fri, 1pm-1am Sat & Sun; Ⓜ Bilbao) One of Malasaña's best deals, this place has a wildly popular tapas bar and a classy but casual restaurant out the back. Albur is known for terrific rice dishes and tapas, and has a well-chosen wine list. The restaurant waiters never seem to lose their cool, and the extremely well-priced rice dishes are the stars of the show, although in truth you could order anything here and leave well satisfied.

Drinking & Nightlife

The essence of Madrid lives in its streets and plazas, and bar-hopping is a pastime enjoyed by young and old alike. If you're after the more traditional, with tiled walls and flamenco tunes, head to Huertas. For gay-friendly drinking holes, Chueca is the place. Malasaña caters to a grungy, funky crowd, while La Latina has friendly bars that guarantee atmosphere most nights of the week.

The bulk of Madrid bars open to 2am Sunday to Thursday, and to 3am or 3.30am Friday and Saturday.

Don't expect dance clubs or *discotecas* (nightclubs) to get going until after 1am at the earliest. Standard entry fee is €12, which usually includes the first drink, although megaclubs and swankier places charge a few euros more.

PLAZA MAYOR & ROYAL MADRID

Museo Chicote Cocktail Bar

(Map p294; ☎91 532 67 37; grupomercadodelareina.com/en/museo-chicote-en/; Gran Vía 12; 🕑5pm-3am Mon-Thu, to 3.30am Fri & Sat; M Gran Vía) The founder of this Madrid landmark (complete with 1930s-era interior) is said to have invented more than 100 cocktails, which the likes of Hemingway, Ava Gardner, Grace Kelly, Sophia Loren and Frank Sinatra have all enjoyed at one time or another. It's at its best after midnight, when a lounge atmosphere takes over, couples cuddle on the curved benches and some of the city's best DJs do their stuff.

Teatro Joy Eslava Club

(Joy Madrid; Map p294; ☎91 366 37 33; www.joy-eslava.com; Calle del Arenal 11; admission €12-15; 🕑11.30pm-6am; M Sol) The only things guaranteed at this grand old Madrid dance club (housed in a 19th-century theatre) are a crowd and the fact that it'll be open (it claims to have operated every single day for the past 29 years). The music and the crowd are a mixed bag, but queues are long and invariably include locals and tourists, and even the occasional *famoso* (celebrity).

LA LATINA & LAVAPIÉS

Delic Bar

(Map p294; ☎91 364 54 50; www.delic.es; Costanilla de San Andrés 14; 🕑11am-2am Sun & Tue-Thu, 11am-2.30am Fri & Sat; M La Latina) We could go on for hours about this long-standing cafe-bar, but we'll reduce it to its most basic elements: nursing an exceptionally good mojito (€8) or three on a warm summer's evening at Delic's outdoor tables on one of Madrid's prettiest plazas is one of life's great pleasures. Bliss.

Taberna Tempranillo Wine Bar

(Map p294; Calle de la Cava Baja 38; 🕑1-3.30pm & 8pm-midnight Tue-Sun, 8pm-midnight Mon; M La Latina) You could come here for the tapas, but we recommend Taberna

Mercado de San Miguel (p296), Madrid

MATTES RENÉ/GETTY IMAGES ©

Tempranillo primarily for its wines; it has a selection that puts many Spanish bars to shame and many are sold by the glass. It's not a late-night place, but it's always packed in the early evening and on Sundays after El Rastro.

SOL, SANTA ANA & HUERTAS

La Venencia Bar

(Map p294; ☎91 429 73 13; Calle de Echegaray 7; ⏲12.30-3.30pm & 7.30pm-1.30am; Ⓜ Sol, Sevilla) La Venencia is a *barrio* classic, with fine sherry from Sanlúcar and manzanilla from Jeréz poured straight from the dusty wooden barrels, accompanied by a small selection of tapas with an Andalucían bent. Otherwise, there's no music, no flashy decorations; it's all about you, your *fino* (sherry) and your friends. As one reviewer put it, it's 'a classic among classics'.

Kapital Club

(Map p294; ☎91 420 29 06; www.grupo-kapital.com; Calle de Atocha 125; admission from €15; ⏲5.30-10.30pm & midnight-6am Fri & Sat, midnight-6am Thu & Sun; Ⓜ Atocha) One of the most famous megaclubs in Madrid, this seven-storey club has something for everyone: from cocktail bars and dance music to karaoke, salsa, hip hop and more chilled spaces for R&B and soul, as well as an area devoted to 'Made in Spain' music. It's such a big place that a cross-section of Madrid society (VIPs and the Real Madrid set love this place) hangs out here without ever getting in each other's way.

MALASAÑA & CHUECA

Café Comercial Cafe

(Map p290; ☎91 521 56 55; www.cafecomercial.es; Glorieta de Bilbao 7; ⏲7.30am-1am; 📶; Ⓜ Bilbao) This glorious old Madrid cafe proudly fights a rearguard action against progress with heavy leather seats, abundant marble and old-style waiters. It dates back to 1887 and has changed little since those days, although the clientele has broadened to include just about anyone, from writers and their laptops to old men playing chess.

Lolina Vintage Café Cafe

(Map p290; ☎91 523 58 59; www.lolinacafe.com; Calle del Espíritu Santo 9; ⏲10am-12.30am Sun-Thu, 10am-2am Fri & Sat; Ⓜ Tribunal) Lolina Vintage Café seems to have captured the essence of the *barrio* in one small space. With a studied retro look (comfy old-style chairs and sofas, gilded mirrors and 1970s-era wallpaper), it confirms that the new Malasaña is not unlike the old but is a whole lot more sophisticated. It's low-key, full from the first breakfast to closing time and caters to every taste with salads and cocktails.

Entertainment

Corral de la Morería Flamenco

(Map p294; ☎91 365 84 46; www.corraldelamoreria.com; Calle de la Morería 17; admission incl drink from €38.90, set menus from €39.90; ⏲7pm-12.15am, shows 9pm & 10.55pm; Ⓜ Ópera) This is one of the most prestigious flamenco stages in Madrid, with 50 years' experience as a leading flamenco venue and top performers most nights. The stage area has a rustic feel, and tables are pushed up close. The performances have a far better price-quality ratio than the meals.

Casa Patas Flamenco

(Map p294; ☎91 369 04 96; www.casapatas.com; Calle de Cañizares 10; admission incl drink €36; ⏲shows 10.30pm Mon-Thu, 9pm & midnight Fri & Sat; Ⓜ Antón Martín, Tirso de Molina) One of the top flamenco stages in Madrid, this *tablao* (flamenco venue) always offers flawless quality that serves as a good introduction to the art. It's not the friendliest place in town, especially if you're only here for the show, and you're likely to be crammed in a little, but no one complains about the standard of the performances.

Villa Rosa Flamenco

(Map p294; ☎91 521 36 89; www.tablaoflamencovillarosa.com; Plaza de Santa Ana 15; adult/child from €32/17; ⏲11pm-6am Mon-Sat, shows 8.30pm & 10.45pm Sun-Thu, 8.30pm, 10.45pm & 12.15am Fri & Sat; Ⓜ Sol) The extraordinary tiled facade (the 1928 work of Alfonso Romero, who was responsible for the

ALEX LIVESEY/STAFF/GETTY IMAGES ©

Don't Miss
Real Madrid Tickets

El Estadio Santiago Bernabéu (☎ **91 398 43 00, 902 291709; www.realmadrid.com; Avenida de Concha Espina 1; tour adult/child €19/13;** ⏲ **10am-7pm Mon-Sat, 10.30am-6.30pm Sun, except match days;** Ⓜ **Santiago Bernabéu)** is one of the world's great football arenas; watching a game here is akin to a pilgrimage for sports fans and doing so alongside 80,000 passionate Madridistas (Real Madrid supporters) in attendance will send chills down your spine. Those who can't come to a game can at least stop by for a tour, a peek at the trophies or to buy Real Madrid memorabilia in the club shop.

The Spanish football season runs from September (or the last weekend in August) until May, with a two-week break just before Christmas until early in the New Year. Unless you book your Real Madrid ticket through a ticket agency, turn up at the Estadio Santiago Bernabéu ticket office at Gate 42 on Calle de Conche de Espina early in the week before a scheduled game (eg a Monday morning for a Sunday game). Tickets can also be bought on the website; click on 'Entradas'.

tilework in Madrid's Plaza de Toros) of this longstanding nightclub is a tourist attraction in itself; the club even appeared in the Pedro Almodóvar film *Tacones Lejanos* (High Heels; 1991). It's been going strong since 1914 and has seen many manifestations – it made its name as a flamenco venue and has recently returned to its roots with well-priced shows and meals that won't break the bank.

Teatro de la Zarzuela Theatre

(Map p294; ☎ **91 524 54 00; teatrodelazarzuela.mcu.es; Calle de Jovellanos 4; tickets €5-50;** ⏲ **box office noon-6pm Mon-Fri, 3-6pm Sat & Sun;** Ⓜ **Banco de España, Sevilla)** This theatre, built in 1856, is the premier place to see *zarzuela*. It also hosts a smattering of classical music and opera, as well as the cutting edge Compañía Nacional de Danza.

Shopping

The key to shopping Madrid-style is knowing where to look. Salamanca is the home of upmarket fashions, with chic boutiques lining up to showcase the best that Spanish and international designers have to offer. Some of it spills over into Chueca, but Malasaña is Salamanca's true alter ego, home to fashion that's as funky as it is offbeat and ideal for that studied underground look that will fit right in with Madrid's hedonistic after-dark crowd. Central Madrid – Sol, Huertas or La Latina – offers plenty of individual surprises.

Antigua Casa Talavera Ceramics
(Map p294; 91 547 34 17; www.antiguacasatalavera.com; Calle de Isabel la Católica 2; 10am-1.30pm & 5-8pm Mon-Fri, 10am-1.30pm Sat; M Santo Domingo) The extraordinary tiled facade of this wonderful old shop conceals an Aladdin's cave of ceramics from all over Spain. This is not the mass-produced stuff aimed at a tourist market, but comes from the small family potters of Andalucía and Toledo, ranging from the decorative (tiles) to the useful (plates, jugs and other kitchen items). The old couple who run the place are delightful.

El Flamenco Vive Flamenco
(Map p294; 91 547 39 17; www.elflamencovive.es; Calle Conde de Lemos 7; 10am-1.45pm & 5-9pm Mon-Sat & 1st Sun of month; M Ópera) This temple to flamenco has it all, from guitars and songbooks to well-priced CDs, polka-dotted dancing costumes, shoes, colourful plastic jewellery and literature about flamenco. It's the sort of place that will appeal as much to curious first-timers as to serious students of the art. It also organises classes in flamenco guitar.

Casa de Diego Accessories
(Map p294; www.casadediego.com; Plaza de la Puerta del Sol 12; 9.30am-8pm Mon-Sat; M Sol) This classic shop has been around since 1858, making, selling and repairing Spanish fans, shawls, umbrellas and canes. Service is old-style and occasionally grumpy, but the fans are works of antique art. There's another **branch** (Map p294; 91 531 02 23; www.casadediego.com; Calle del los Mesoneros Romanos 4; 9.30am-1.30pm & 4.45-8pm Mon-Sat; M Callao, Sol) nearby.

Information

Tourist Information

Centro de Turismo de Madrid (Map p294; 91 531 00 74, 91 454 44 10, 91 588 16 36; www.esmadrid.com; Plaza Mayor 27; 9.30am-8.30pm; M Sol) Excellent city tourist office with a smaller office underneath Plaza de Colón (Map p290; www.esmadrid.com; Plaza de Colón 1; 9.30am-8.30pm; M Colón) and the Palacio de Cibeles (Map p294; 91 480 00 08; www.centrocentro.org; Plaza de

El Rastro flea market, Madrid

Cibeles 1; 10am-8pm Tue-Sun; M Plaza de España), as well as information points at Plaza de la Cibeles (Map p294; www.esmadrid.com; Plaza de la Cibeles; 9.30am-8.30pm; M Banco de España), Plaza del Callao (closed for renovations at the time of writing), outside the Centro de Arte Reina Sofía (Map p290; www.esmadrid.com; cnr Calle de Santa Isabel & Plaza del Emperador Carlos V; 9.30am-8.30pm; M Atocha) and at the T2 and T4 terminals at Barajas airport.

Safe Travel

Madrid is a generally safe city although, as in most European cities, you should be wary of pickpockets in the city centre, on the metro and around major tourist sights.

Getting There & Away

Air

Madrid's international Barajas airport (MAD), 15km northeast of the city, is Europe's fifth-busiest airport (depending on the year), with flights coming in from all over Europe and beyond.

Car & Motorcycle

The city is surrounded by two main ring roads, the outermost M-40 and the inner M-30; there are also two additional partial ring roads, the M-45 and the more-distant M-50.

Train

Renfe (902 240202; www.renfe.es) operates high-speed Tren de Alta Velocidad Española (AVE) services connecting Madrid with Seville (via Córdoba), Valladolid (via Segovia), Toledo, Valencia, Málaga and Barcelona (via Zaragoza and Tarragona).

Puerta de Atocha (www.renfe.es; M Atocha Renfe) This is one of the main train stations at the southern end of the city centre. The bulk of trains for Spanish destinations depart from Atocha, especially those going south. For bookings, contact Renfe.

Estación de Chamartín (902 432343; M Chamartín) North of the city centre, Estación de Chamartín has numerous long-distance rail services, especially those to/from northern Spain. This is also where long-haul international trains arrive from Paris and Lisbon.

Getting Around

To/From the Airport

Bus

AeroCITY (902 151654, 91 747 75 70; www.aerocity.com; per person from €17.85, express service from €34 per minibus) This excellent, private minibus service takes you door-to-door between central Madrid and the airport (T1 in front of Arrivals Gate 2, T2 between gates 5 and 6, and T4 arrivals hall). It operates 24 hours and you can book by phone or online. You can reserve a seat or the entire minibus; the latter operates like a taxi.

Exprés Aeropuerto (Airport Express; www.emtmadrid.es; per person €5; 24hr;) The Exprés Aeropuerto runs between Puerta de Atocha train station and the airport. Buses run every 13 to 23 minutes from 6am to 11.30pm, and every 35 minutes throughout the rest of the night. The trip takes 40 minutes. From 11.55pm until 5.35am, departures are from the Plaza de la Cibeles, not the train station.

Metro

Line 8 of the metro (entrances in T2 and T4) runs to the Nuevos Ministerios transport interchange, which connects with lines 10 and 6. It operates from 6.05am to 2am. A one-way ticket to/from the airport costs €4.50. The journey from the airport to Nuevos Ministerios takes around 15 minutes, around 25 minutes from T4.

Taxi

There is now a fixed rate for taxis from the airport to the city centre (€30). If you're going to an airport hotel, you'll pay €20.

Public Transport

Madrid's metro (www.metromadrid.es) is extensive and well maintained. A single ride costs €1.50 and a 10-ride ticket is €12.20. The metro is quick, clean, relatively safe and runs from 6.05am until 2am.

Taxi

You can pick up a taxi at ranks throughout town or simply flag one down. Flag fall is €2.15 from 6am to 10pm daily, €2.20 from 10pm to 6am Sunday to Friday and €3.10 from 10pm Saturday to 6am Sunday. Several supplementary charges, usually posted inside the taxi, apply.

If You Like… Spanish Architecture

From Córdoba's Mezquita to the hanging houses of Cuenca, the Spanish certainly have a taste for eye-catching architecture.

1 **MUSEO GUGGENHEIM**
(www.guggenheim-bilbao.es; Avenida Abandoibarra 2; adult/student/child €13/7.50/free; 10am-8pm, closed Mon Sep-Jun) Opened in September 1997, Bilbao's shimmering titanium Museo Guggenheim is one of the iconic buildings of modern architecture and it almost single-handedly lifted Bilbao out of its postindustrial depression and into the 21st century.

2 **MURALLAS**
(adult/child under 12yr €5/free; 10am-8pm Tue-Sun;) Ávila's splendid 12th-century walls stretch for 2.5km atop the remains of earlier Roman and Muslim battlements and rank among the world's best-preserved medieval defensive perimeters. Two sections of the walls can be climbed: a 300m stretch that can be accessed from just inside the **Puerta del Alcázar**, and a longer 1300m stretch that runs the length of the old city's northern perimeter.

3 **ALCÁZAR**
(921 46 07 59; www.alcazardesegovia.com; Plaza de la Reina Victoria Eugenia; adult/concession/child under 6yr €5/3/free, tower €2, EU citizens free 3rd Tue of month; 10am-6pm Oct-Mar, 10am-7pm Apr-Sep;) Rapunzel towers, turrets topped with slate witches' hats and a *deep* moat at its base make the Alcázar at Segovia a prototype fairy-tale castle. Fortified since Roman days, the site takes its name from the Arabic *al-qasr* (fortress). It was rebuilt in the 13th and 14th centuries, but the whole lot burned down in 1862. What you see today is an evocative, over-the-top reconstruction of the original.

4 **RONDA**
Ronda is the most dramatically sited of Andalucía's *pueblos blancos* (white villages). Look out for the amazing 18th-century Puente Nuevo (New Bridge) to the old town, and the Plaza de Toros, considered the national home of bullfighting.

Radio-Teléfono Taxi (91 547 82 00; www.radiotelefono-taxi.com)

Tele-Taxi (91 371 21 31; www.tele-taxi.es)

CASTILLA-LA MANCHA

Known as the stomping ground of Don Quijote and Sancho Panza, Castilla-La Mancha conjures up images of lonely windmills, medieval castles and bleak, treeless plains. The characters of Miguel de Cevantes provide the literary context, but the richly historic cities of Toledo and Cuenca are the most compelling reasons to visit.

Toledo

POP 85,593

Toledo is Spain's equivalent of a downsized Rome. Commanding a hill rising above the Tajo River, it's crammed with monuments that attest to the waves of conquerors and communities – Roman, Visigoth, Jewish, Muslim and Christian – who have called the city home during its turbulent history. It's one of the country's major tourist attractions.

Sights

Catedral Cathedral
(www.catedralprimada.es; Plaza del Ayuntamiento; adult/child €11/free; 10.30am-6.30pm Mon-Sat, 2-6.30pm Sun) Toledo's cathedral reflects the city's historical significance as the heart of Catholic Spain and it's one of the most extravagant cathedrals in the country. The heavy interior, with sturdy columns dividing the space into five naves, is on a monumental scale. Every one of the numerous side chapels has artistic treasures, with the other main highlights being the *coro,* Capilla Mayor, Transparente, *sacristia* and bell tower (for €3 extra).

Alcázar

Fortress, Museum

(Museo del Ejército; Calle Alféreces Provisionales; adult/child €5/free, free for all Sun; 11am-5pm Thu-Tue) At the highest point in the city looms the foreboding Alcázar. Rebuilt under Franco, it has been reopened as a vast military museum. The usual displays of uniforms and medals are here, but the best part is the exhaustive historical section, with an in-depth overview of the nation's history in Spanish and English.

Sinagoga del Tránsito

Synagogue

(925 22 36 65; museosefardi.mcu.es; Calle Samuel Leví; adult/child €3/1.50, Sat after 2pm & all day Sun free; 9.30am-7.30pm Tue-Sat Mar-Oct, 9.30am-6pm Tue-Sat Nov-Feb, 10am-3pm Sun year-round) This magnificent synagogue was built in 1355 by special permission of Pedro I. The synagogue now houses the **Museo Sefardí**. The vast main prayer hall has been expertly restored and the Mudéjar decoration and intricately carved pine ceiling are striking. Exhibits provide an insight into the history of Jewish culture in Spain, and include archaeological finds, a memorial garden, costumes and ceremonial artefacts.

Monasterio San Juan de los Reyes

Monastery

(www.sanjuandelosreyes.org; Calle San Juan de los Reyes 2; admission €2.50; 10am-6.30pm Jun-Sep, 10am-5.30pm Oct-May) This imposing 15th-century Franciscan monastery and church was provocatively founded in the heart of the Jewish quarter by the Catholic monarchs Isabel and Fernando to demonstrate the supremacy of their faith. The rulers had planned to be buried here but eventually ended up in their prize conquest, Granada. The highlight is the amazing two-level cloister, a harmonious fusion of late ('flamboyant') Gothic downstairs and Mudéjar architecture upstairs, with superb statuary, arches, vaulting, elaborate pinnacles and gargoyles surrounding a lush garden with orange trees and roses.

Mezquita del Cristo de la Luz

Mosque

(Calle Cristo de la Luz; admission €2.50; 10am-2pm & 3.30-5.45pm Mon-Fri, 10am-5.45pm Sat & Sun) On the northern slopes of town you'll find a modest, yet beautiful, mosque (the only one remaining of Toledo's 10) where architectural traces of Toledo's medieval

Catedral, Toledo

DANIEL VIÑÉ GARCIA/GETTY IMAGES ©

Muslim conquerors are still in evidence. Built around AD 1000, it suffered the usual fate of being converted into a church (hence the religious frescoes), but the original vaulting and arches survived.

Sleeping

Accommodation is often full, especially from Easter to September. Many visitors choose to come on a day trip from Madrid.

Casa de Cisneros Boutique Hotel **€€**
(**925 22 88 28; www.hostal-casa-de-cisneros.com; Calle del Cardenal Cisneros; s/d €40/66;**) Right by the cathedral, this lovely 16th-century house was once the home of the cardinal and Grand Inquisitor Cisneros (often known as Ximénes). It's a top choice, with cosy, seductive rooms with original wooden beams and walls and voguish bathrooms. Archaeological works have revealed the remains of Roman baths and part of an 11th-century Moorish palace in the basement.

La Posada de Manolo Boutique Hotel **€€**
(**925 28 22 50; www.laposadademanolo.com; Calle de Sixto Ramón Parro 8; s/d €33/61;**) This memorable hotel has themed each floor with furnishings and decor reflecting one of the three cultures of Toledo: Christian, Islamic and Jewish. There are stunning views of the old town and cathedral from the terrace.

Eating

Kumera Modern Spanish **€**
(**925 25 75 53; www.restaurantekumera.com; Calle Alfonso X El Sabio 2; meals €9-10, set menus €20-35; 8am-2.30am Mon-Fri, 11am-2.30am Sat & Sun**) With arguably the best price-quality ratio in town, this place serves up innovative takes on local traditional dishes such as *cochinito* (suckling pig), *rabo de toro* (bull's tail) or *croquetas* (croquettes, filled with *jamón*, squid, cod or wild mushrooms), alongside gigantic toasts and other creatively conceived dishes. The dishes with foie gras as the centrepiece are especially memorable.

Café Comercial (p300), Madrid

La Abadía Castilian, Tapas **€€**
(www.abadiatoledo.com; Plaza de San Nicolás 3; raciones €4-15) In a former 16th-century palace, this atmospheric bar and restaurant has arches, niches and subtle lighting are spread over a warren of brick-and-stone-clad rooms. The menu includes lightweight dishes and tapas, but the 'Menú de Montes de Toledo' (€19) is a fabulous collection of tastes from the nearby mountains.

Information

Main Tourist Office (925 25 40 30; www.toledo-turismo.com; Plaza del Ayuntamiento; 10am-6pm) Within sight of the cathedral. There's another branch **(Estación de Renfe; 10am-3pm)** at the train station.

Getting There & Away

The high-speed AVE service runs every hour or so to Madrid (€12.70, 30 minutes).

CATALONIA

Home to stylish Barcelona, ancient Tarragona, romantic Girona, and countless alluring destinations along the coast, in the Pyrenees and in the rural interior, Catalonia (Catalunya in Catalan, Cataluña in Castilian) is a treasure box waiting to be opened.

Barcelona

POP 1.62 MILLION

Barcelona is one of Europe's coolest cities. Despite two millennia of history, it's a forward-thinking place, always on the cutting edge of art, design and cuisine. Whether you explore its medieval palaces and plazas, admire the Modernista masterpieces, shop for designer fashions along its bustling boulevards, sample its exciting nightlife or just soak up the sun on the beaches, you'll find it hard not to fall in love with this vibrant city.

Detour: Cuenca

A World Heritage Site, Cuenca is one of Spain's most memorable small cities, its old centre a stage set of evocative medieval buildings. Most emblematic are the 14th-century *casas colgadas*, the hanging houses that jut out precariously over the steep defile of Río Huécar. Inside one of the houses is the **Museo de Arte Abstracto Español (Museum of Abstract Art; www.march.es/arte/cuenca; Calle Canónigos; adult/concession/child €3/1.50/free; 11am-2pm & 4-6pm Tue-Fri, 11am-2pm & 4-8pm Sat, 11am-2.30pm Sun)**. Cuenca is also famous for its Semana Santa (Holy Week) processions; stop by the **Museo de la Semana Santa (www.msscuenca.org; Calle Andrés de Cabrera 13; adult/child €3/free; 11am-2pm & 4.30-7.30pm Thu-Sat, 11am-2pm Sun;)** to see why.

There's a **tourist office (969 24 10 51; turismo.cuenca.es; Calle Alfonso VIII 2; 9am-9pm Mon-Sat, to 2.30pm Sun)**, and Cuenca is most easily reached along the Madrid–Valencia rail line.

Sights

LA RAMBLA

Mercat de la Boqueria Market
(Map p318; 93 318 25 84; www.boqueria.info; La Rambla 91; 8am-8.30pm Mon-Sat, closed Sun; M Liceu) Mercat de la Boqueria is possibly La Rambla's most interesting building, not so much for its Modernista-influenced design (it was actually built over a long period, from 1840 to 1914, on the site of the former St Joseph monastery), but for the action of the food market within.

Greater Barcelona

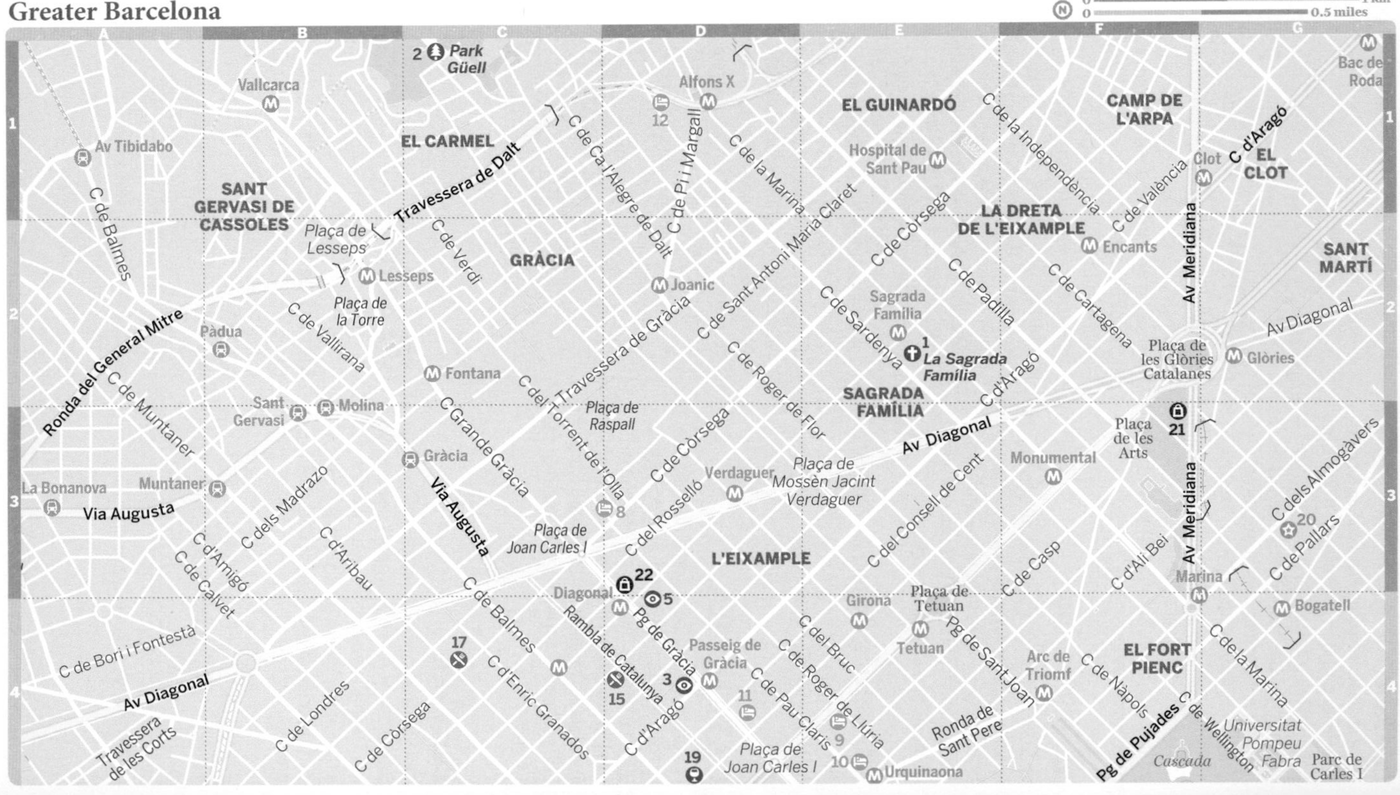

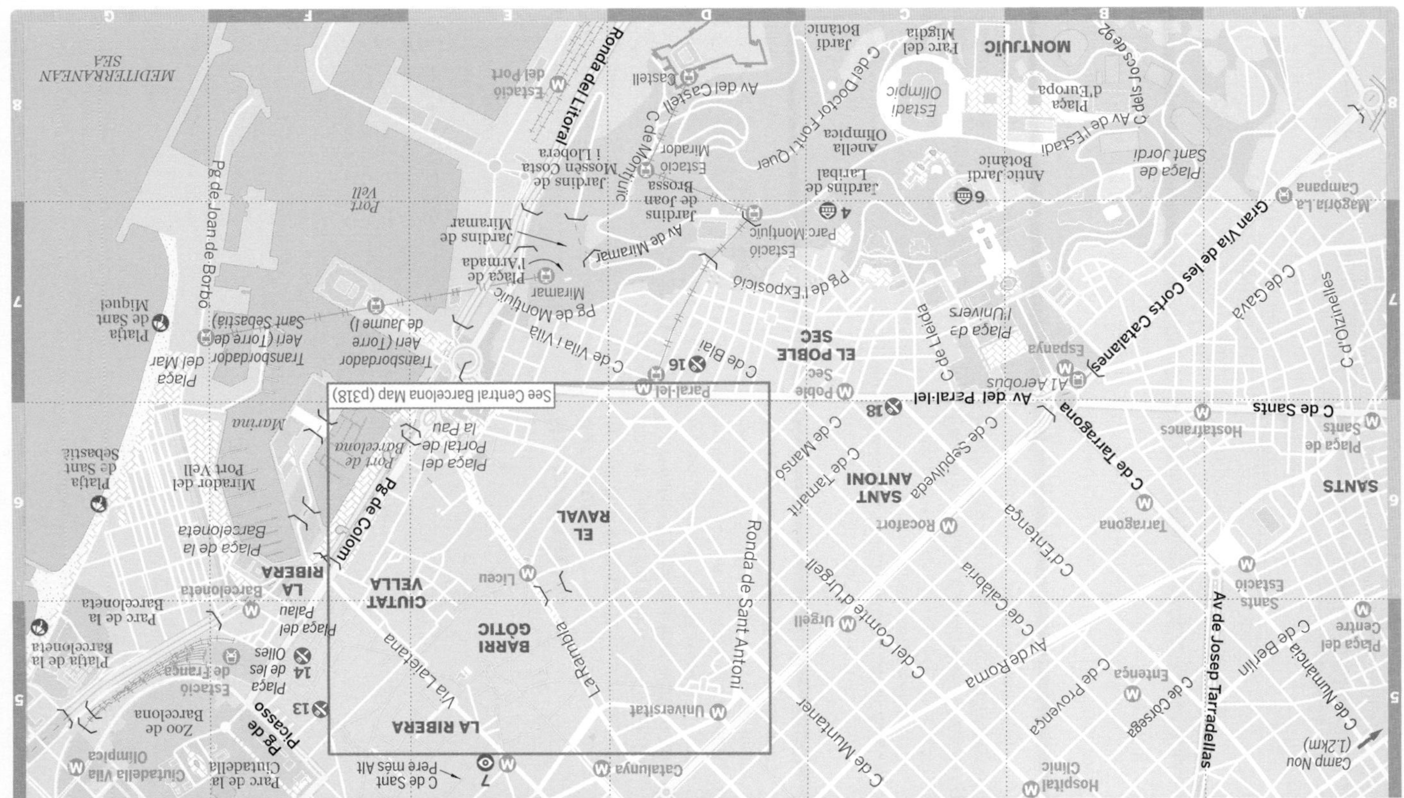

MEDITERRANEAN SEA
Pg de Joan de Borbó
Port Vell
Marina
Port de Barcelona
Ronda del Litoral
Estació del Port
Platja de Sant Miquel
Plaça del Mar
Transbordador Aeri (Torre de Sant Sebastià)
Transbordador Aeri (Torre de Jaume I)
Platja de Sant Sebastià
Mirador del Port Vell
Plaça de la Barceloneta
Barceloneta
LA RIBERA
Parc de la Barceloneta
Platja de la Barceloneta
Plaça del Palau
Plaça de les Olles
14
13
Estació de França
Zoo de Barcelona
Pg de Picasso
Parc de la Ciutadella
Ciutadella Vila Olímpica
C de Sant Pere més Alt
7
LA RIBERA
Via Laietana
BARRI GÒTIC
CIUTAT VELLA
Pg de Colom
Liceu
La Rambla
EL RAVAL
Plaça del Portal de la Pau
See Central Barcelona Map (p318)
Catalunya
Universitat
Ronda de Sant Antoni
Paral·lel
16
C de Blai
C de Vila i Vilà
Pg de Montjuïc
Miramar
Plaça de l'Armada
Jardins de Miramar
Av de Miramar
Jardins de Mossèn Costa i Llobera
C de Montjuïc
Estació Mirador
Jardins de Joan Brossa
Av del Castell
Castell
C del Doctor Font i Quer
Estació Parc Montjuïc
Pg de l'Exposició
EL POBLE SEC
Poble Sec
4
Jardins de Laribal
Anella Olímpica
Jardí Botànic
Estadi Olímpic
Parc del Migdia
MONTJUÏC
6
Antic Jardí Botànic
Plaça d'Europa
Av de l'Estadi
C dels Jocs de 92
Plaça de Sant Jordi
Magòria La Campana
Gran Via de les Corts Catalanes
C de Gavà
C d'Olzinelles
Plaça de l'Univers
C de Lleida
Espanya
A1 Aerobús
Av del Paral·lel
18
C de Mansó
C de Tamarit
SANT ANTONI
C de Sepúlveda
Rocafort
C de Tarragona
Tarragona
Hostafrancs
C de Sants
Plaça de Sants
SANTS
Urgell
C del Comte d'Urgell
C de Muntaner
C d'Entença
C de Calàbria
Av de Roma
C de Provença
C de Còrsega
Entença
Hospital Clínic
Sants Estació
Av de Josep Tarradellas
C de Berlín
C de Numància
Plaça del Centre
Camp Nou (1.2km)

Greater Barcelona

Don't Miss Sights
1 La Sagrada Família ... E2
2 Park Güell ... C1

Sights
3 Casa Batlló ... D4
4 Fundació Joan Miró ... C7
5 La Pedrera ... D4
6 Museu Nacional d'Art de Catalunya (MNAC) ... C8
7 Palau de la Música Catalana ... E5

Sleeping
8 Aparteasy ... D3
9 Barcelona On Line ... E4
10 Five Rooms ... E4
11 Hostal Oliva ... D4
12 Rent a Flat in Barcelona ... D1

Eating
13 Bormuth ... F5
14 Cal Pep ... F5
15 Cerveseria Catalana ... D4
16 Quimet i Quimet ... D7
17 Speakeasy ... C4
18 Tickets ... C6

Drinking & Nightlife
Dry Martini ... (see 17)
19 Monvínic ... D4

Entertainment
Palau de la Música Catalana ... (see 7)
20 Razzmatazz ... G3

Shopping
21 Els Encants Vells ... F3
22 Vinçon ... D3

Plaça Reial Square

(Map p318; M Liceu) One of the most photogenic squares in Barcelona, the Plaça Reial is a delightful retreat from the traffic and pedestrian mobs on the nearby Rambla. Numerous eateries, bars and nightspots lie beneath the arcades of 19th-century neoclassical buildings, with a buzz of activity at all hours.

BARRI GÒTIC

La Catedral Church

(Map p318; ☎ 93 342 82 62; www.catedralbcn.org; Plaça de la Seu; admission free, special visit €6, choir admission €2.80; ⏰ 8am-12.45pm & 5.15-7.30pm Mon-Sat, special visit 1-5pm Mon-Sat, 2-5pm Sun & holidays; M Jaume I) Barcelona's central place of worship presents a magnificent image. The richly decorated main facade, laced with gargoyles and the stone intricacies you would expect of northern European Gothic, sets it quite apart from other churches in Barcelona. The facade was actually added in 1870, although the rest of the building was built between 1298 and 1460. The other facades are sparse in decoration, and the octagonal, flat-roofed towers are a clear reminder that, even here, Catalan Gothic architectural principles prevailed.

Museu d'Història de Barcelona Museum

(Map p318; ☎ 93 256 21 00; www.museuhistoria.bcn.cat; Plaça del Rei; adult/child €7/free, 1st Sun of month & 3-8pm Sun free; ⏰ 10am-7pm Tue-Sat, 10am-8pm Sun; M Jaume I) One of Barcelona's most fascinating museums takes you back through the centuries to the very foundations of Roman Barcino. You'll stroll over ruins of the old streets, sewers, laundries and wine- and fish factories that flourished here following the town's founding by Emperor Augustus around 10 BC. Equally impressive is the building itself, which was once part of the Palau Reial Major (Grand Royal Palace) on Plaça del Rei, among the key locations of medieval princely power in Barcelona.

LA RIBERA

In medieval days, La Ribera was a stone's throw from the Mediterranean and the heart of Barcelona's foreign trade, with homes belonging to numerous wealthy merchants. Now it's a trendy district full of boutiques, restaurants and bars.

Basílica de Santa Maria del Mar Church

(Map p318; ☎ 93 310 23 90; Plaça de Santa Maria del Mar; ⏰ 9am-1.30pm & 4.30-8.30pm, opens at 10.30am Sun; M Jaume I) FREE At the southwest end of Passeig del Born stands the apse of Barcelona's finest Catalan Gothic church, Santa Maria del Mar (Our Lady of the Sea). Built in the 14th century with record-breaking alacrity for the time (it took just 54 years), the church is remarkable for its architectural harmony and simplicity.

Palau de la Música Catalana — Architecture

(Map p308; ☎93 295 72 00; www.palaumusica.org; Carrer de Sant Francesc de Paula 2; adult/child €17/free; ⏰guided tours 10am-3.30pm daily; Ⓜ Urquinaona) This concert hall is a high point of Barcelona's Modernista architecture, a symphony in tile, brick, sculpted stone and stained glass. Built by Domènech i Montaner between 1905 and 1908 for the Orfeo Català musical society, it was conceived as a temple for the Catalan Renaixença (Renaissance).

L'EIXAMPLE

Modernisme, the Catalan version of art nouveau, transformed Barcelona's cityscape in the early 20th century. Most Modernista works were built in L'Eixample, the grid-plan district that was developed from the 1870s on.

La Pedrera — Architecture

(Casa Milà; Map p308; ☎902 202 138; www.lapedrera.com; Carrer de Provença 261-265; adult/student/child €20.50/16.50/10.25 ; ⏰9am-8pm Mar-Oct, to 6.30pm Nov-Feb; Ⓜ Diagonal) This undulating beast is a madcap Gaudí masterpiece, built from 1905 to 1910 as a combined apartment and office block. Formally called Casa Milà, after the businessman who commissioned it, it is better known as La Pedrera (the Quarry) because of its uneven grey stone facade, which ripples around the corner of Carrer de Provença.

Casa Batlló — Architecture

(Map p308; ☎93 216 03 06; www.casabatllo.es; Passeig de Gràcia 43; adult/concession/child under 7yr €21.50/€18.50/free; ⏰9am-9pm daily; Ⓜ Passeig de Gràcia) One of the strangest residential buildings in Europe, this is Gaudí at his hallucinogenic best. The facade, sprinkled with bits of blue, mauve and green tiles and studded with wave-shaped window frames and balconies, rises to an uneven blue-tiled roof with a solitary tower.

MONTJUÏC

Museu Nacional d'Art de Catalunya (MNAC) — Museum

(Map p308; ☎93 622 03 76; www.museunacional.cat; Mirador del Palau Nacional; adult/student/ senior & child under 16yr €12/€8.40/free, 1st Sun of month free; ⏰10am-8pm Tue-Sat, to 3pm Sun, library 10am-6pm Mon-Fri; Ⓜ Espanya) From across the city, the bombastic neobaroque silhouette of the **Palau Nacional** can be seen on the slopes of Montjuïc. Built for the 1929 World Exhibition and restored in 2005, it houses a vast collection of mostly Catalan art spanning the early Middle Ages to the early 20th century. The high point is the collection of extraordinary Romanesque frescoes.

Fundació Joan Miró — Museum

(Map p308; ☎93 443 94 70; www.fundaciomirobcn.org; Parc de Montjuïc; adult/child €11/free; ⏰10am-8pm Tue-Sat, to 9.30pm Thu, to 2.30pm Sun & holidays; 🚌55, 150, funicular Paral·lel) Joan Miró, the city's best-known 20th-century artistic progeny, bequeathed this art foundation to his home town in 1971. Its light-filled buildings, designed by close friend and architect Josep Lluís Sert (who also built Miró's Mallorca studios), are crammed with seminal works, from Miró's earliest timid sketches to paintings from his last years.

 Festivals & Events

Festes de la Mercè — City Festival

(www.bcn.cat/merce) The city's biggest party involves four days of concerts, dancing, *castellers* (human-castle builders), a fireworks display synchronised with the Montjuïc fountains, dances of giants on the Saturday, and *correfocs* – a parade of fireworks-spitting monsters and demons who run with the crowd – on the Sunday. Held around 24 September.

Don't Miss
La Sagrada Família

If you have time for only one sight-seeing outing in Barcelona, this should be it. La Sagrada Família inspires awe by its sheer verticality and, in the manner of the medieval cathedrals it emulates, it's still under construction after more than 100 years. When completed, the highest tower will be more than half as high again as those that stand today.

Map p308

93 207 30 31

www.sagradafamilia.cat

Carrer de Mallorca 401

adult/senior & student/child under 11yr €14.80 /12.80/ free

9am-8pm Apr-Sep, to 6pm Oct-Mar

M Sagrada Família

Design

Gaudí devised a temple 95m long and 60m wide, able to seat 13,000 people, with a central tower 170m high above the transept (representing Christ) and another 17 towers of 100m or more. It's a slender structure devoted to geometric perfection and sacred symbolism. It's also a work in progress, spanning the generations but never losing Gaudí's breathtaking originality and architectural synthesis of natural forms. Some of the many highlights include the apse, Nativity Facade, Passion Facade, Glory Facade and the Museu Gaudí.

The Present Day

Unfinished though it may be, La Sagrada Família still attracts around 2.8 million visitors a year and is the most visited monument in Spain. The most important recent tourist was Pope Benedict XVI, who consecrated the church in a huge ceremony in November 2010.

Local Knowledge

La Sagrada Família

RECOMMENDATIONS FROM JORDI FAULÍ, DEPUTY ARCHITECTURAL DIRECTOR FOR LA SAGRADA FAMÍLIA

1 **PASSION FACADE**

Among the Fachada de la Pasión's stand-out features are the angled columns, dramatic scenes from Jesus' last hours, an extraordinary rendering of the Last Supper and a bronze door that reads like a sculpted book. But the most surprising view is from inside the door on the extreme right.

2 **MAIN NAVE**

The majestic Nave Principal showcases Gaudí's use of tree motifs for columns to support the domes: he described this space as a forest. But it's the skylights that give the nave its luminous quality as light floods onto the apse and main altar from the skylight 75m above the floor.

3 **SIDE NAVE & NATIVITY TRANSEPT**

Although beautiful in its own right with windows that project light into the interior, this is the perfect place to view the sculpted treelike columns and get an overall perspective of the main nave. Turn around and you're confronted with the inside of the Nativity Facade, an alternative view that most visitors miss; the stained-glass windows are superb.

4 **NATIVITY FACADE**

The Fachada del Nacimiento is Gaudí's grand hymn to Creation. Begin by viewing it front-on from a distance, then draw close enough (but to one side) to make out the details of its sculpted figures. The complement to the finely wrought detail is the majesty of the four parabolic towers that reach for the sky and are topped by Venetian stained glass.

5 **THE MODEL OF COLÒNIA GÜELL**

Of the many original models used by Gaudí on display in the Museu Gaudí, the most interesting is the church at Colònia Güell. From the side you can, thanks to the model's ingenious use of rope and cloth, visualise the harmony and beauty of the interior.

La Sagrada Família

A TIMELINE

1882 Francesc del Villar is commissioned to construct a neo-Gothic church.

1883 Antoni Gaudí takes over as chief architect, and plans a far more ambitious church to hold 13,000 faithful.

1926 Death of Gaudí; work continues under Domènec Sugrañes. Much of the **apse** ❶ and **Nativity Facade** ❷ is complete.

1930 **Bell towers** ❸ of the Nativity Facade completed.

1936 Construction is interrupted by Spanish Civil War; anarchists destroy Gaudí's plans.

1939-40 Architect Francesc de Paula Quintana i Vidal restores the crypt and meticulously reassembles many of Gaudí's lost models, some of which can be seen in the **museum** ❹.

1976 Completion of **Passion Facade** ❺.

1986-2006 Sculptor Josep Subirachs adds sculptural details to the Passion Facade including the panels telling the story of Christ's last days, amid much criticism for employing a style far removed from what was thought typical of Gaudí.

2000 **Central nave vault** ❻ completed.

2010 Church completely roofed over; Pope Benedict XVI consecrates the church; work begins on a high-speed rail tunnel that will pass beneath the church's **Glory Facade** ❼.

2026–28 Projected completion date.

TOP TIPS

» **Light** The best light through the stained-glass windows of the Passion Facade bursts through into the heart of the church in the late afternoon.

» **Time** Visit at opening time on week-days to avoid the worst of the crowds.

» **Views** Head up the Nativity Facade bell towers for the views, as long queues generally await at the Passion Facade towers.

Spiral staircase

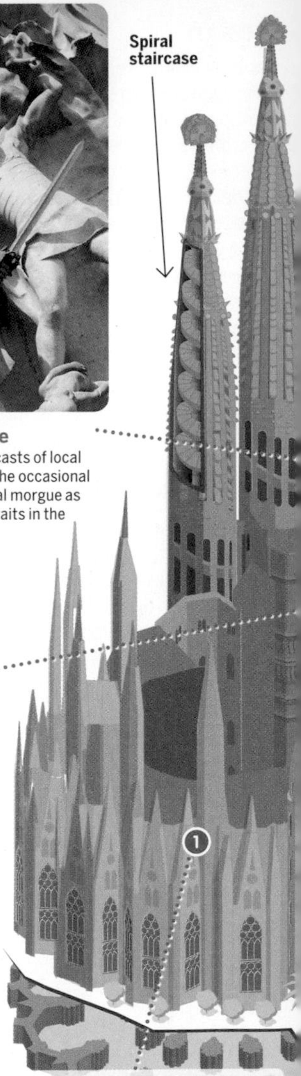

Nativity Facade
Gaudí used plaster casts of local people and even of the occasional corpse from the local morgue as models for the portraits in the Nativity scene.

Central nave vault

❶

Apse
Built just after the crypt in mostly neo-Gothic style, it is capped by pinnacles that show a hint of the genius that Gaudí would later deploy in the rest of the church.

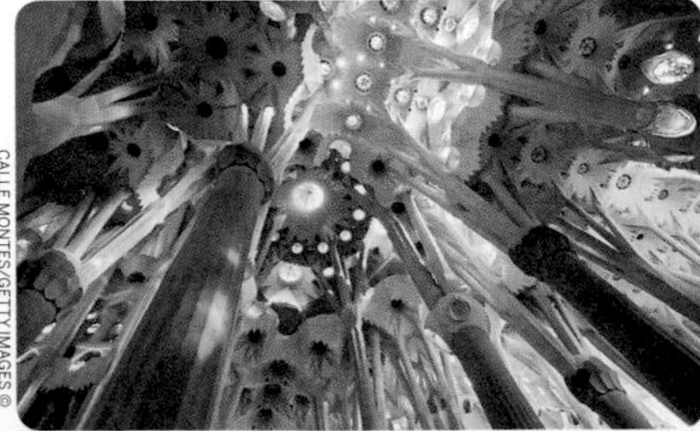

Bell towers
The towers (eight completed) of the three facades represent the 12 Apostles. Lifts whisk visitors up one tower of the Nativity and Passion Facades (the latter gets longer queues) for fine views.
NIKADA/GETTY IMAGES ©
Completed church
Along with the Glory Facade and its four towers, six other towers remain to be completed. They will represent the four Evangelists, the Virgin Mary and, soaring above them all over the transept, a 170m colossus symbolising Christ.
Glory Facade
This will be the most fanciful facade of all, with a narthex boasting 16 hyperboloid lanterns topped by cones that will look something like an organ made of melting ice cream.
Museu Gaudí
Jammed with old photos, drawings and restored plaster models that bring Gaudí's ambitions to life, the museum also houses an extraordinarily complex plumb-line device he used to calculate his constructions.
Escoles de Gaudí
Crypt
The first completed part of the church, the crypt is in largely neo-Gothic style and lies under the transept. Gaudí's burial place here can be seen from the Museu Gaudí.
JEKATERINA NIKITINA/GETTY IMAGES ©
Passion Facade
See the story of Christ's last days from Last Supper to burial in an S-shaped sequence from bottom to top of the facade. Check out the cryptogram in which the numbers always add up to 33, Christ's age at his death.
STEPHEN SAKS/GETTY IMAGES ©

Dia de Sant Joan Midsummer

This is a colourful midsummer celebration on 24 June with bonfires, even in the squares of L'Eixample, and fireworks marking the evening that precedes this holiday

Tours

Barcelona Walking Tours Walking Tour

(Map p318; ☎93 285 38 34; www.barcelonaturisme.com; Plaça de Catalunya 17-S; M Catalunya) The Oficina d'Informació de Turisme de Barcelona organises guided walking tours. One explores the **Barri Gòtic** (adult/child €15.50/free; ⏰in English 9.30am daily); another follows in the footsteps of **Picasso** (adult/child €21.50/7; ⏰in English 3pm Tue, Thu & Sat) and winds up at the Museu Picasso, entry to which is included in the price, and a third takes in the main jewels of **Modernisme** (adult/child €15.50/free; ⏰in English 4pm Fri). Also offered is a **gourmet tour** (adult/child €21.50/7; ⏰in English 10am Fri & Sat) of traditional purveyors of fine foodstuffs across the old city; it includes chances to taste some of the products.

Bus Turístic Bus Tour

(☎93 285 38 32; www.barcelonabusturistic.cat/en; day ticket adult/child €27/16; ⏰9am-8pm) This hop-on hop-off service covers three circuits (44 stops) linking virtually all the major tourist sights. Tourist offices, TMB transport authority offices and many hotels have leaflets explaining the system. Each of the two main circuits takes approximately two hours. The third circuit, from Port Olímpic to El Fòrum, runs from April to September and is less interesting. Possession of a Bus Turístic ticket entitles you to discounts to some museums.

Sleeping

There's no shortage of hotels in Barcelona. Those looking for cheaper accommodation close to the action should check out the Barri Gòtic and El Raval. Some good lower-end *pensiones* are scattered about L'Eixample, as well as a broad range of midrange and top-end places, most in easy striking distance of the old town.

Numerous private apartment-rental companies operate in Barcelona. These can often be a better deal than staying in a hotel. Start your search at **Aparteasy** (Map p308; ☎93 451 67 66; www.aparteasy.com; Carrer de Santa Tecla 3; M Diagonal), **Barcelona On Line** (Map p308; ☎902 887017, 93 343 79 93; www.barcelona-on-line.es; Gran Vía de les Corts Catalanes, 662, 1º 1A) and **Rent a Flat in Barcelona** (Map p308; ☎93 342 73 00; www.rentaflatinbarcelona.com; Ronda del Guinardó 2).

LA RAMBLA & BARRI GÒTIC

Vrabac Guesthouse **€€**

(Map p318; ☎663 494029; vrabacguesthouse.wordpress.com; Carrer de Portaferrissa 14; d €95-145, s/d without bathroom from €55/65; ❄📶; M Liceu or Catalunya) In a central location just off La Rambla, Vrabac is set in a beautifully restored heritage building complete with original decorative ceilings, exposed sandstone walls and large oil paintings. Rooms vary in size and equipment – the best have elegant ceramic tile floors and sizeable balconies with private bathrooms. The cheapest are small and basic and lack a bathroom, and aren't recommended. Cash only.

EL RAVAL

Barceló Raval Design Hotel **€€**

(Map p318; ☎93 320 14 90; www.barceloraval.com; Rambla del Raval 17-21; r from €128; ❄@; M Liceu) Part of the city's plans to pull the El Raval district up by the bootstraps, this oval-shaped designer hotel tower makes a 21st-century splash. The rooftop terrace offers fabulous views and the B-Lounge bar-restaurant is the toast of the town for meals and cocktails. Rooms have slick aesthetics (white with lime green or ruby red splashes of colour), Nespresso machines and iPod docks.

Chic & Basic Ramblas Design Hotel **€€**

(Map p318; ☎93 302 71 11; www.chicandbasicramblashotel.com; Passatge Gutenberg 7; s & d €106-116; ❄📶; M Drassanes) The latest

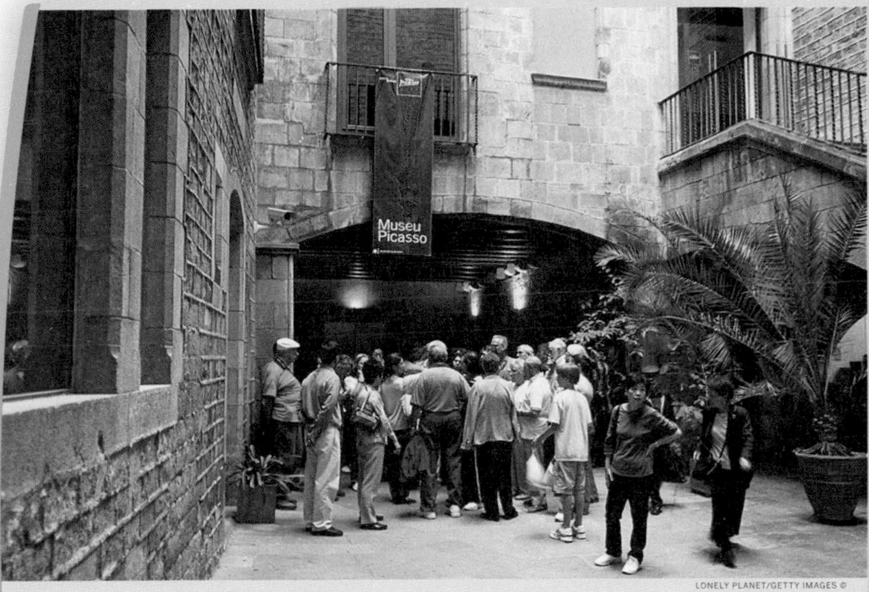

LONELY PLANET/GETTY IMAGES ©

Don't Miss
Museu Picasso

The setting alone, in five contiguous medieval stone mansions, makes the Museu Picasso unique (and worth the probable queues). The pretty courtyards, galleries and staircases preserved in the first three of these buildings are as delightful as the collection inside.

NEED TO KNOW

Map p318; ☎93 256 30 00; www.museupicasso.bcn.cat; Carrer de Montcada 15-23; adult/child €14/free, temporary exhibitions adult/child €6.50/free, 3-8pm Sun & 1st Sun of month free; ⏰9am-7pm, to 9.30pm Thu; 📶; M Jaume I

in the Chic & Basic chain is the most riotous to date, with quirky and colourful interiors that hit you from the second you walk in and see a vintage Seat 600 in the foyer. The rooms themselves are solid blocks of colour, and each loosely pays homage to an aspect of Barcelona life in the 1960s. All have balconies and small kitchens. Note that the name is misleading – the hotel is a couple of blocks into the Raval.

LA RIBERA & LA BARCELONETA

Hotel Banys Orientals Boutique Hotel **€€**

(Map p318; ☎93 268 84 60; www.hotelbanysorientals.com; Carrer de l'Argenteria 37; s €96, d €115.50-143; ❄📶; M Jaume I) Book well ahead to get into this magnetically popular designer haunt. Cool blues and aquamarines combine with dark-hued floors to lend this clean-lined, boutique hotel a quiet charm. All rooms, on the small side, look onto the street or back lanes. There are more spacious suites in two other nearby buildings.

Central Barcelona

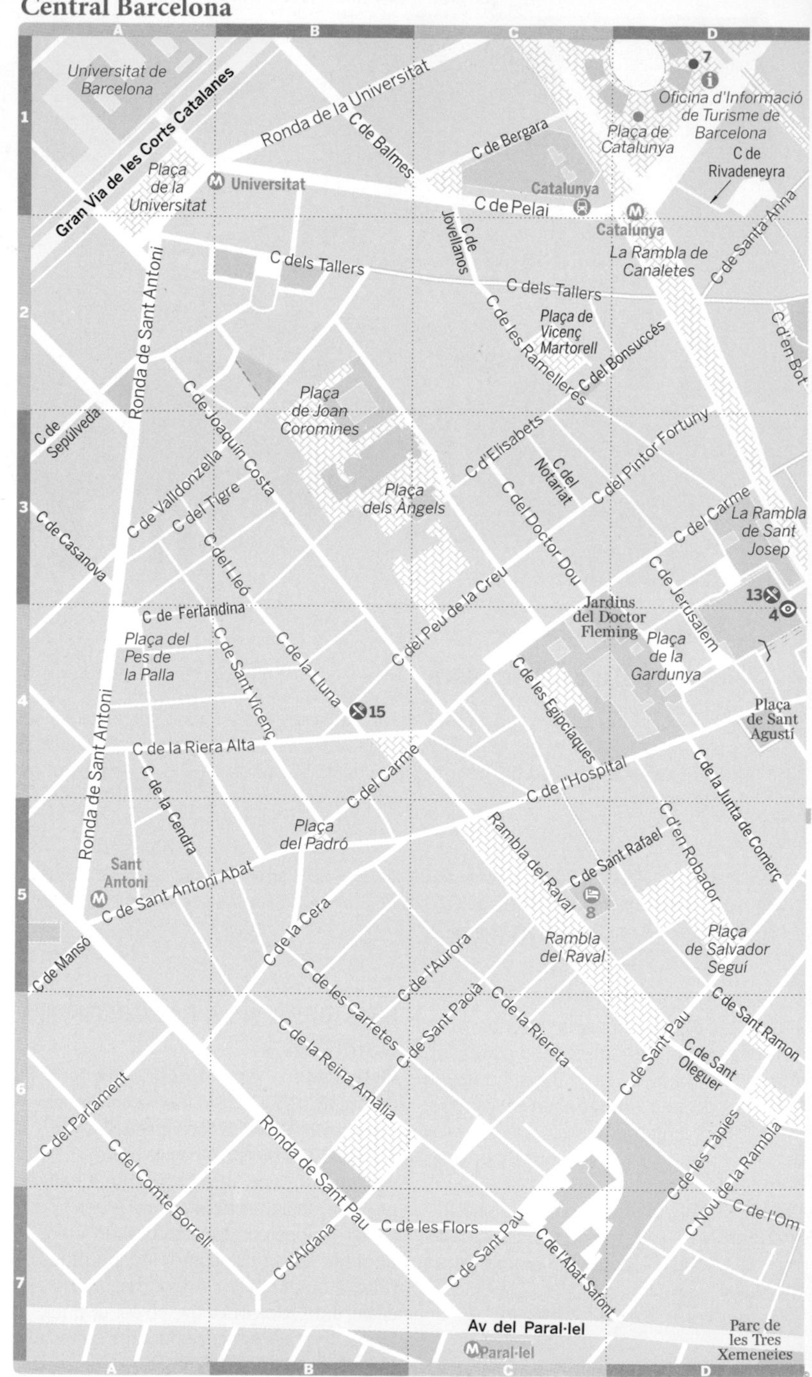

Universitat de Barcelona
Gran Via de les Corts Catalanes
Ronda de la Universitat
C de Balmes
C de Bergara
Plaça de Catalunya
Oficina d'Informació de Turisme de Barcelona
C de Rivadeneyra
Plaça de la Universitat
Universitat
Catalunya
C de Pelai
C de Jovellanos
C dels Tallers
La Rambla de Canaletes
C de Santa Anna
C d'en Bot
Ronda de Sant Antoni
Plaça de Vicenç Martorell
C de les Ramelleres
C del Bonsuccés
Plaça de Joan Coromines
C de Joaquín Costa
C de Sepúlveda
C d'Elisabets
C del Notariat
C del Pintor Fortuny
C de Valldonzella
C del Tigre
Plaça dels Àngels
C del Doctor Dou
C del Carme
La Rambla de Sant Josep
C de Casanova
C del Lleó
C del Peu de la Creu
C de Jerusalem
C de Ferlandina
Jardins del Doctor Fleming
Plaça de la Gardunya
Plaça del Pes de la Palla
C de Sant Vicenç
C de la Lluna
C de les Egipcíaques
15
13
4
Plaça de Sant Agustí
C de la Riera Alta
C del Carme
C de l'Hospital
C de la Junta de Comerç
C de la Cendra
Rambla del Raval
C d'en Robador
Plaça del Padró
C de Sant Rafael
Sant Antoni
C de Sant Antoni Abat
8
C de la Cera
Rambla del Raval
Plaça de Salvador Seguí
C de Mansó
C de l'Aurora
C de les Carretes
C de Sant Pacià
C de la Riereta
C de Sant Pau
C de Sant Ramon
C de Sant Oleguer
C de la Reina Amàlia
C del Parlament
C de les Tàpies
C Nou de la Rambla
C del Comte Borrell
Ronda de Sant Pau
C de l'Om
C d'Aldana
C de les Flors
C de Sant Pau
C de l'Abat Safont
Av del Paral·lel
Paral·lel
Parc de les Tres Xemeneies

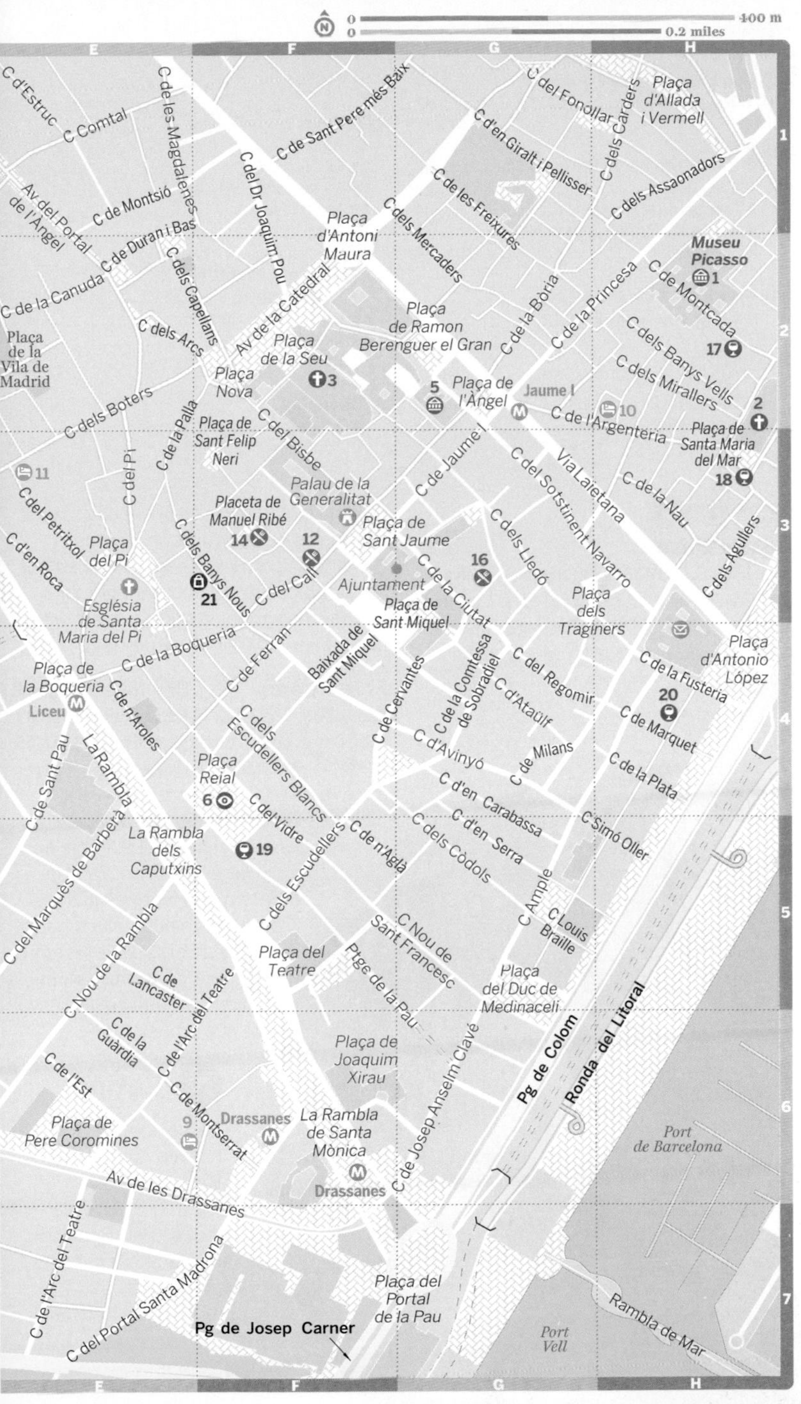
0 400 m
0 0.2 miles
C d'Estruc
C Comtal
C de les Magdalenes
C de Sant Pere més Baix
C del Fonollar
C dels Carders
Plaça d'Allada i Vermell
C d'en Giralt i Pellisser
C dels Assaonadors
C de les Freixures
C del Dr Joaquim Pou
Av del Portal de l'Àngel
C de Montsió
C de Duran i Bas
Plaça d'Antoni Maura
C dels Mercaders
Museu Picasso
C de la Canuda
C dels Capellans
Av de la Catedral
Plaça de Ramon Berenguer el Gran
C de la Bòria
C de la Princesa
C de Montcada
Plaça de la Vila de Madrid
C dels Arcs
Plaça de la Seu
C dels Banys Vells
C dels Miralles
Plaça Nova
Plaça de l'Àngel
Jaume I
C de l'Argenteria
C dels Boters
C de la Palla
Plaça de Sant Felip Neri
C del Bisbe
C de Jaume I
Via Laietana
Plaça de Santa Maria del Mar
C del Pi
C del Sotstinent Navarro
C de la Nau
Palau de la Generalitat
C del Petritxol
Placeta de Manuel Ribé
Plaça de Sant Jaume
C dels Lledó
C dels Agullers
C d'en Roca
Plaça del Pi
C dels Banys Nous
C del Call
C de la Ciutat
Ajuntament
Església de Santa Maria del Pi
Plaça de Sant Miquel
Plaça dels Traginers
C de la Boqueria
C de Ferran
Baixada de Sant Miquel
C de la Comtessa de Sobradiel
C del Regomir
Plaça d'Antonio López
Plaça de la Boqueria
C de Cervantes
C d'Ataülf
C de la Fusteria
Liceu
C de n'Aroles
C dels Escudellers Blancs
C d'Avinyó
C de Milans
C de Marquet
C de Sant Pau
La Rambla
Plaça Reial
C de la Plata
C d'en Carabassa
C del Vidre
C de n'Aglà
C d'en Serra
C Simó Oller
La Rambla dels Caputxins
C del Marquès de Barberà
C dels Escudellers
C dels Còdols
C Ample
C Louis Braille
C Nou de la Rambla
C Nou de Sant Francesc
Plaça del Teatre
Ptge de la Pau
Plaça del Duc de Medinaceli
C de Lancaster
C de l'Arc del Teatre
C de la Guàrdia
Plaça de Joaquim Xirau
C de Josep Anselm Clavé
Pg de Colom
Ronda del Litoral
C de l'Est
C de Montserrat
Plaça de Pere Coromines
Drassanes
La Rambla de Santa Mònica
Port de Barcelona
Av de les Drassanes
C de l'Arc del Teatre
C del Portal Santa Madrona
Plaça del Portal de la Pau
Rambla de Mar
Port Vell
Pg de Josep Carner

Central Barcelona

L'EIXAMPLE

Hostal Oliva Hostal €

(Map p308; ☎93 488 01 62; www.hostaloliva.com; Passeig de Gràcia 32; d €51-91, s/d without bathroom €41-71; ❄ 📶; M Passeig de Gràcia) A picturesque antique lift wheezes its way up to this 4th-floor *hostal*, a terrific, reliable cheapie in one of the city's most expensive neighbourhoods. Some of the single rooms can barely fit a bed but the doubles are big enough, light and airy (some with tiled floors, others with parquet and dark old wardrobes).

Five Rooms Boutique Hotel €€

(Map p308; ☎93 342 78 80; www.thefiverooms.com; Carrer de Pau Claris 72; s/d from €155/165; ❄ @ 📶; M Urquinaona) Like it says, there are five rooms (standard rooms and suites) in this 1st-floor flat virtually on the border between L'Eixample and the old centre of town. Each is different and features include broad, firm beds, stretches of exposed brick wall, restored mosaic tiles and minimalist decor. There are also two apartments.

Eating

Barcelona is foodie heaven. Although Barcelona has a reputation as a hot spot of 'new Spanish cuisine', you'll still find local eateries serving up time-honoured local

Seafood platter, Barcelona
OLIVER STREWE/GETTY IMAGES ©

grub, from squid-ink *fideuà* (a satisfying paella-like noodle dish) to pigs' trotters, rabbit with snails, and *butifarra* (a tasty local sausage).

LA RAMBLA & BARRI GÒTIC

Skip the overpriced traps along La Rambla and get into the winding lanes of the Barri Gòtic.

Allium Catalan, Fusion **€€**
(Map p318; ☎93 302 30 03; Carrer del Call 17; mains €8-16; ⊙noon-4pm Mon-Tue, to 10.30pm Wed-Sat; Ⓜ Liceu) This inviting newcomer to Barri Gòtic serves beautifully prepared tapas dishes and changing specials (including seafood paella for one). The menu, which changes every two or three weeks, focuses on seasonal, organic cuisine. Its bright, modern interior sets it apart from other neighbourhood options; it's also open continuously, making it a good bet for those who don't want to wait until 9pm for a meal.

La Vinateria del Call Spanish **€€**
(Map p318; ☎93 302 60 92; www.lavinateriadelcall.com; Carrer de Sant Domènec del Call 9; small plates €7-12; ⊙7.30pm-1am; Ⓜ Jaume I) In a magical setting in the former Jewish quarter, this tiny jewel box of a restaurant serves up tasty Iberian dishes including Galician octopus, cider-cooked chorizo and the Catalan *escalivada* (roasted peppers, aubergine and onions) with anchovies. Portions are small and made for sharing, and there's a good and affordable selection of wines.

Pla Fusion **€€€**
(Map p318; ☎93 412 65 52; www.elpla.cat; Carrer de la Bellafila 5; mains €18-25; ⊙7.30pm-midnight; 🚭; Ⓜ Jaume I) One of Gòtic's longstanding favourites, Pla is a stylish, romantically lit medieval dining room where the cooks churn out such temptations as oxtail braised in red wine, seared tuna with oven-roasted peppers, and polenta with seasonal mushrooms. It has a tasting menu for €38 Sunday to Thursday.

EL RAVAL

Mam i Teca Catalan **€€**
(Map p318; ☎93 441 33 35; Carrer de la Lluna 4; mains €9-12; ⊙1-4pm & 8pm-midnight Mon, Wed-Fri & Sun, closed Sat lunch; Ⓜ Sant Antoni) A tiny place with half a dozen tables, Mam i Teca is as much a lifestyle choice as a restaurant. Locals drop in and hang about at the bar, and diners are treated to Catalan dishes made with locally sourced products and adhering to Slow Food principles. Try, for example, cod fried in olive oil with garlic and red pepper, or pork ribs with chickpeas.

Bar Pinotxo Tapas **€€**
(Map p318; www.pinotxobar.com; Mercat de la Boqueria; mains €8-15; ⊙6am-4pm Mon-Sat; Ⓜ Liceu) Bar Pinotxo is arguably La Boqueria's, and even Barcelona's, best tapas bar. It sits among the half-dozen or so informal eateries within the market, and the popular owner, Juanito, might serve up chickpeas with a sweet sauce of pine nuts and raisins, a fantastically soft mix of potato and spinach sprinkled with coarse salt, soft baby squid with cannellini beans, or a quivering cube of caramel-sweet pork belly.

LA RIBERA & WATERFRONT

Bormuth Tapas **€**
(Map p308; ☎93 310 21 86; Carrer del Rec 31; tapas from €3.50; ⊙5pm-midnight Mon & Tue, noon-1am Wed, Thu & Sun, noon-2.30am Fri & Sat; Ⓜ Jaume I) Opened on the pedestrian Carrer del Rec in 2013, Bormuth has tapped into the vogue for old-school tapas with modern-times service and decor, and serves all the old favourites – *patatas bravas, ensaladilla* (Russian salad), tortilla – along with some less predictable and superbly prepared numbers (try the chargrilled red pepper with black pudding). The split-level dining room is never less than animated, but there's a more peaceful space with a single long table if you can assemble a group.

Cal Pep Tapas €€

(Map p308; ☎93 310 79 61; www.calpep.com; Plaça de les Olles 8; mains €12-20; ⏰7.30-11.30pm Mon, 1-3.45pm & 7.30-11.30pm Tue-Fri, 1-3.45pm Sat, closed last 3 weeks Aug; Ⓜ Barceloneta) It's getting a foot in the door here that's the problem – there can be queues out into the square with people trying to get in. And if you want one of the five tables out the back, you'll need to call ahead. Most people are happy elbowing their way to the bar for some of the tastiest gourmet seafood tapas in town.

L'EIXAMPLE & GRÀCIA

Cerveseria Catalana Tapas €

(Map p308; ☎93 216 03 68; Carrer de Mallorca 236; tapas €4-11; ⏰9.30am-1.30am; Ⓜ Passeig de Gràcia) The 'Catalan Brewery' is good for breakfast, lunch and dinner. Come for your morning coffee and croissant, or wait until lunch to enjoy choosing from the abundance of tapas and *montaditos* (tapas served on a slice of bread). You can sit at the bar, on the pavement terrace or in the restaurant at the back. The variety of hot tapas, salads and other snacks draws a well-dressed crowd of locals and outsiders.

MONTJUÏC

Quimet i Quimet Tapas €€

(Map p308; ☎93 442 31 42; Carrer del Poeta Cabanyes 25; tapas €4-11; ⏰noon-4pm & 7-10.30pm Mon-Fri, noon-4pm Sat & Sun; Ⓜ Paral·lel) Quimet i Quimet is a family-run business that has been passed down from generation to generation. There's barely space to swing a calamar in this bottle-lined, standing-room-only place, but it is a treat for the palate, with *montaditos* made to order. Let the folk behind the bar advise you, and order a drop of fine wine to accompany the food.

Tickets Modern Spanish €€€

(Map p308; www.ticketsbar.es; Avinguda del Paral·lel 164; tapas €6-15; ⏰7-11.30pm Tue-Fri, 1.30-3.30pm & 7-11.30pm Sat, closed Aug; Ⓜ Paral·lel) This is, literally, one of the sizzling tickets in the restaurant world, a tapas bar opened by Ferran Adrià, of the legendary El Bulli, and his brother Albert. And unlike El Bulli, it's an affordable venture – if you can book a table, that is (you can only book online, and two months in advance).

It's a fairly flamboyant and modern affair in terms of decor, playing with circus images and theatre lights, while the food has kept some of the El Bulli greats such as the 'air baguette' (a crust larded with Iberico ham), or the slightly bonkers 'cotton candy tree', with fruit-studded candyfloss clouds served on a small bush. The seafood bar serves a slightly more serious option of oysters, tuna belly, and delicate fish skin in a paper cone.

Drinking & Nightlife

Barcelona abounds with daytime cafes, laid-back lounges and lively night-time bars. Closing time is generally 2am from Sunday to Thursday, and 3am Friday and Saturday.

Barcelona clubs are spread a little more thinly than bars across the city. They tend to open from around midnight until 6am. Entry can cost from nothing to €20 (one drink usually included).

BARRI GÒTIC

Ocaña Bar

(Map p318; ☎93 676 48 14; www.ocana.cat; Plaça Reial 13; ⏰5pm-2.30am Mon-Fri, from 11am Sat & Sun; Ⓜ Liceu) Named after a flamboyant artist who once lived on Plaça Reial, Ocaña is a beautifully designed space with fluted columns, stone walls, candlelit chandeliers and plush furnishings. Have a seat on the terrace and watch the passing people parade, or head downstairs to the Moorish-inspired Apotheke bar or the chic lounge a few steps away, where DJs spin for a mix of beauties and bohemians on weekend nights.

Sor Rita Bar

(Map p318; Carrer de la Mercè 27; ⏰7pm-2.30am; Ⓜ Jaume I) A lover of all things kitsch, Sor Rita is pure eye candy, from its leopard-print wallpaper to its high-heel festooned ceiling, and deliciously irreverent decorations inspired by the films of Almodóvar. It's a fun and festive scene,

HIROSHI HIGUCHI/GETTY IMAGES ©

Don't Miss Park Güell

North of Gràcia and about 4km from Plaça de Catalunya, Park Güell is where Gaudí turned his hand to landscape gardening. It's a strange, enchanting place where his passion for natural forms really took flight – to the point where the artificial almost seems more natural than the natural.

NEED TO KNOW

Map p308; ☎93 409 18 31; www.parkguell.cat; Carrer d'Olot 7; adult/child €7/€4.50 admission to central area; ⏰8am-9.30pm daily; 🚌24 or 32, Ⓜ Lesseps or Vallcarca

with special-event nights throughout the week, including tarot readings on Mondays, €5 all-you-can-eat snack buffets on Tuesdays, karaoke Wednesdays and gin specials on Thursdays.

LA RIBERA

La Vinya del Senyor — Wine Bar

(Map p318; ☎93 310 33 79; www.lavinyadelsenyor.com; Plaça de Santa Maria del Mar 5; ⏰noon-1am Mon-Thu, noon-2am Fri & Sat, noon-midnight Sun; Ⓜ Jaume I) Relax on the terrace, which lies in the shadow of Basílica de Santa Maria del Mar, or crowd inside at the tiny bar. The wine list is as long as *War and Peace* and there's a table upstairs for those who opt to sample by the bottle rather than the glass.

El Xampanyet — Wine Bar

(Map p318; ☎93 319 70 03; Carrer de Montcada 22; ⏰noon-3.30pm & 7-11pm Tue-Sat, noon-4pm Sun; Ⓜ Jaume I) Nothing has changed for decades in this, one of the city's best-known cava bars. Plant yourself at the bar or seek out a table against the decoratively tiled walls for a glass or three of the cheap house cava and an assortment of tapas, such as the tangy *boquerons en vinagre* (fresh anchovies in vinegar).

Montjuïc

A ONE-DAY ITINERARY

Montjuïc, perhaps once the site of pre-Roman settlements, is today a hilltop green lung looking over city and sea. Interspersed across varied gardens are major art collections, a fortress, an Olympic stadium and more. A solid one-day itinerary can take in the key spots.

Alight at Espanya metro stop and make for **CaixaForum** ❶, always host to three or four free top-class exhibitions. The nearby **Pavelló Mies van der Rohe** ❷ is an intriguing study in 1920s futurist housing by one of the 20th century's greatest architects. Uphill, the Romanesque art collection in the **Museu Nacional d'Art de Catalunya** ❸ is a must, and its restaurant is a pleasant lunch stop. Escalators lead further up the hill towards the **Estadi Olímpic** ❹, scene of the 1992 Olympic Games. The road leads east to the **Fundació Joan Miró** ❺, a shrine to the master surrealist's creativity. Contemplate ancient relics in the **Museu d'Arqueologia de Catalunya** ❻, then have a break in the peaceful **Jardins de Mossèn Cinto Verdaguer** ❼, the prettiest on the hill, before taking the cable car to the **Castell de Montjuïc** ❽. If you pick the right day, you can round off with the gorgeously kitsch **La Font Màgica** ❾ sound and light show, followed by drinks and dancing in an open-air nightspot in **Poble Espanyol** ❿.

TOP TIPS

» **Moving views** Ride the Transbordador Aeri from Barceloneta for a bird's eye approach to Montjuïc. Or take the Teleféric de Montjuïc cable car to the Castell for more aerial views.

» **Summer fun** The Castell de Montjuïc features outdoor summer cinema and concerts (see http://sala montjuic.org).

» **Beautiful bloomers** Bursting with colour and serenity, the Jardins de Mossèn Cinto Verdaguer are exquisitely laid out with bulbs, especially tulips, and aquatic flowers.

JEAN-PIERRE LESCOURRET/GETTY IMAGES ©

CaixaForum
This former factory and barracks designed by Josep Puig i Cadafalch is an outstanding work of Modernista architecture; like a Lego fantasy in brick.

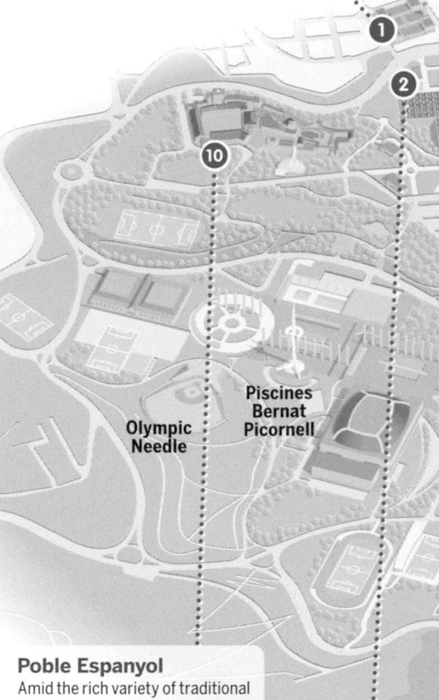

Poble Espanyol
Amid the rich variety of traditional Spanish architecture created in replica for the 1929 Barcelona World Exhibition, browse the art on show in the Fundació Fran Daurel.

TRAVEL INK/GETTY IMAGES ©

Pavelló Mies van der Rohe
Admire the inventiveness of the great German architect Ludwig Mies van der Rohe in this recreation of his avant garde German pavillion for the 1929 World Exhibition.

La Font Màgica
Take a summer evening to behold the Magic Fountain come to life in a unique 15-minute sound and light performance, when the water glows like a cauldron of colour.

Museu Nacional d'Art de Catalunya
Make a beeline for the Romanesque art selection and the 12th-century polychrome image of Christ in majesty, which was recovered from the apse of a country chapel in northwest Catalonia.

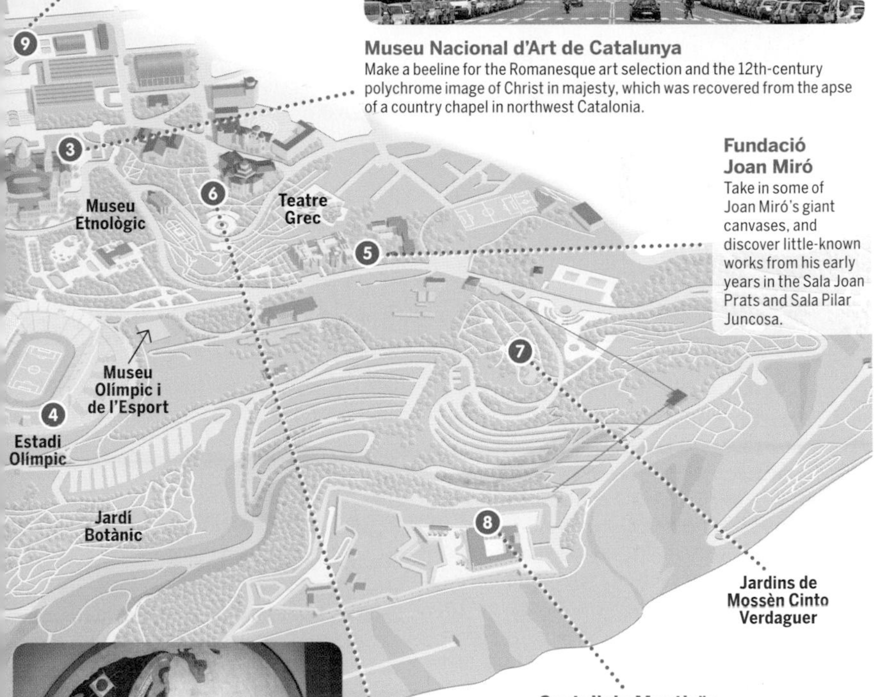

9

3

6

Museu Etnològic

Teatre Grec

5

Museu Olímpic i de l'Esport

4

Estadi Olímpic

7

Jardí Botànic

8

Fundació Joan Miró
Take in some of Joan Miró's giant canvases, and discover little-known works from his early years in the Sala Joan Prats and Sala Pilar Juncosa.

Jardins de Mossèn Cinto Verdaguer

Castell de Montjuïc
Enjoy the sweeping views of the sea and city from atop this 17th-century fortress, once a political prison and long a symbol of oppression.

Museu d'Arqueologia de Catalunya
Seek out the Roman mosaic depicting the Three Graces, one of the most beautiful items in this museum, which was dedicated to the ancient past of Catalonia and neighbouring parts of Spain.

L'EIXAMPLE & GRÀCIA

Dry Martini Bar

(Map p308; ☎93 217 50 72; www.javierdelasmuelas.com; Carrer d'Aribau 162-166; ⏰1pm-2.30am Mon-Thu, 6pm-3am Fri & Sat; Ⓜ Diagonal) Waiters with a discreetly knowing smile will attend to your cocktail needs here. The house drink, taken at the bar or in one of the plush green leather lounges, is a safe bet. The gin and tonic comes in an enormous mug-sized glass – a couple of these and you're well on the way. Out the back is a restaurant, **Speakeasy** (Map p308; ☎93 217 50 80; www.javierdelasmuelas.com; Carrer d'Aribau 162-166; mains €19-28; ⏰1-4pm & 8pm-midnight Mon-Fri, 8pm-midnight Sat, closed Aug; Ⓜ Diagonal).

Monvínic Wine Bar

(Map p308; ☎93 272 61 87; www.monvinic.com; Carrer de la Diputació 249; ⏰wine bar 1.30-11pm Mon-Sat; Ⓜ Passeig de Gracia) Proclaimed as 'possibly the best wine bar in the world' by the *Wall Street Journal,* and apparently considered unmissable by El Bulli's sommelier, Monvínic is an ode, a rhapsody even, to wine loving. The interactive wine list sits on the bar for you to browse on a digital tablet similar to an iPad and boasts more than 3000 varieties.

☆ Entertainment

Razzmatazz Live Music

(Map p308; ☎93 320 82 00; www.salarazzmatazz.com; Carrer de Pamplona 88; admission €12-32; ⏰midnight-3.30am Thu, to 5.30am Fri & Sat; Ⓜ Marina, Bogatell) Bands from far and wide occasionally create scenes of near hysteria in this, one of the city's classic live-music and clubbing venues. Bands can appear throughout the week (check the website), with different start times. On weekends the live music then gives way to club sounds.

Palau de la Música Catalana Classical Music

(Map p308; ☎93 295 72 00; www.palaumusica.org; Carrer de Sant Francesc de Paula 2; ⏰box office 9.30am-9pm Mon-Sat; Ⓜ Urquinaona) A feast for the eyes, this Modernista confec-

Left: Flamenco dancers, Madrid; **Below:** Casa Batlló (p311), Barcelona
(LEFT) INGOLF POMPE 85/ALAMY©; (BELOW) SERGIO PITAMITZ/GETTY IMAGES ©

tion is also the city's most traditional venue for classical and choral music, although it has a wide-ranging program, including flamenco, pop and – particularly – jazz. Just being here for a performance is an experience. Sip a preconcert tipple in the foyer, its tiled pillars all a-glitter. Head up the grand stairway to the main auditorium, a whirlpool of Modernista whimsy.

Camp Nou Spectator Sport
(**☎902 189900; www.fcbarcelona.com; Carrer d'Aristides Maillol; tickets €20-265; ⌚box ofice 10am-7.45pm Mon-Sat, to 2.15pm Sun, 11am to kick-off on match days; M Palau Reial or Collblanc)** Seeing an FC Barcelona football match inside massive Camp Nou stadium is an experience not to be missed. You can purchase tickets at the stadium box office, at tourist offices and online.

Shopping

Most mainstream fashion stores are along a shopping 'axis' that runs from Plaça de Catalunya along Passeig de Gràcia, then left (west) along Avinguda Diagonal.

The El Born area in La Ribera is awash with tiny boutiques, especially those purveying young, fun fashion. There are plenty of shops scattered throughout the Barri Gòtic (stroll Carrer d'Avinyò and Carrer de Portaferrissa). For secondhand stuff, head for El Raval, especially Carrer de la Riera Baixa.

Empremtes de Catalunya Handicrafts
(**Map p318; ☎93 467 46 60; Carrer dels Banys Nous 11; ⌚10am-8pm Mon-Sat, to 2pm Sun; M Liceu)** A celebration of Catalan products, this nicely designed store is a great place to browse for unique gifts. You'll find jewellery with designs inspired by Roman iconography (as well as works that reference Gaudí and Barcelona's Gothic era), plus pottery, wooden toys, silk scarves, notebooks, housewares and more.

Detour: Monestir de Montserrat

The monks who built the Monestir de Montserrat (Monastery of the Serrated Mountain), 50km northwest of Barcelona, chose a spectacular spot. The Benedictine **monastery** (www.abadiamontserrat.net) sits on the side of a 1236m-high mountain of weird, bulbous peaks. The monastery was founded in 1025 and pilgrims still come from all over Christendom to kiss the Black Virgin (La Moreneta), the 12th-century wooden sculpture of the Virgin Mary.

If you're around the basilica at the right time, you'll catch a brief performance by the **Montserrat Boys' Choir** (www.escolania.cat; performances 1pm Mon-Fri, noon Sun, 6.45pm Sun-Thu).

You can explore the mountain above the monastery on a web of paths leading to some of the peaks and to 13 empty and rather dilapidated hermitages. Running every 20 minutes, the **Funicular de Sant Joan** (one way/return €5.85/9; every 20min 10am-6.50pm, closed mid-Jan–Feb) will carry you up the first 250m from the monastery.

Montserrat is an easy day trip from Barcelona. The R5 line trains operated by FGC run from Plaça d'Espanya station in Barcelona to Monistrol de Montserrat up to 18 times daily starting at 5.16am. They connect with the **cremallera** (902 312020; www.cremallerademontserrat.com; one way/return €5.40/8.60), a rack-and-pinion train which takes 17 minutes to make the upwards journey.

Els Encants Vells Market

(Fira de Bellcaire; Map p308; 93 246 30 30; www.encantsbcn.com; Plaça de les Glòries Catalanes; 8am-8pm Mon, Wed, Fri & Sat; M Glòries) In a gleaming open-sided complex near Plaça de les Glòries Catalanes, the 'Old Charms' flea market is the biggest of its kind in Barcelona. Over 500 vendors ply their wares beneath massive mirrorlike panels. It's all here, from antique furniture through to secondhand clothes. A lot of it is junk, but occasionally you'll stumble across a *ganga* (bargain).

Vinçon Homewares

(Map p308; 93 215 60 50; www.vincon.com; Passeig de Gràcia 96; 10am-8.30pm Mon-Fri, 10.30am-9pm Sat; M Diagonal) An icon of the Barcelona design scene, Vinçon has the slickest furniture and household goods (particularly lighting), both local and imported. Not surprising, really, since the building, raised in 1899, belonged to the Modernista artist Ramon Casas. Head upstairs to the furniture area – from the windows and terrace you get close side views of La Pedrera.

Information

Tourist Information

Oficina d'Informació de Turisme de Barcelona (Map p318; 93 285 38 34; www.barcelonaturisme.com; underground at Plaça de Catalunya 17-S; 9.30am-9.30pm; M Catalunya) The main Barcelona tourist information office sells walking tours, bus tours, discount cards, transport passes and tickets to shows, and can help book accommodation. The branch in the airport's EU arrivals hall has information on all of Catalonia; a smaller office at the international arrivals hall opens the same hours. The train-station branch has limited city information. There's also a branch in the *ajuntament* (town hall).

Safe Travel

Purse snatching and pickpocketing are major problems, especially around Plaça de Catalunya, La Rambla and Plaça Reial.

Getting There & Away

Air

Barcelona's airport, El Prat de Llobregat (☎902 404704; www.aena.es), is 12km southwest of the city centre.

Train

Virtually all trains travelling to and from destinations within Spain stop at Estació Sants (Plaça dels Països Catalans; Ⓜ Estació Sants). High-speed trains to Madrid via Lleida and Zaragoza take as little as two hours and 40 minutes; prices vary wildly. Other trains run to Valencia (€35 to €45, three to 4½ hours, 15 daily).

There are also international connections with French cities from the same station.

Getting Around

To/From the Airport

The A1 Aerobús (Map p308; ☎902 100104; www.aerobusbcn.com; one way/return €5.90/10.20) runs from Terminal 1 to Plaça de Catalunya from 6.05am to 1.05am, taking 30 to 40 minutes. A2 Aerobús does the same run from Terminal 2, from 6am to 12.30am. Buy tickets on the bus.

Renfe's R2 Nord train line runs between the airport and Passeig de Gràcia (via Estació Sants) in central Barcelona (about 35 minutes). Tickets cost €3.60, unless you have a T-10 multitrip public-transport ticket.

A taxi to/from the centre, about a half-hour ride depending on traffic, costs around €25 to €30.

Public Transport

Barcelona's metro system spreads its tentacles around the city in such a way that most places of interest are within a 10-minute walk of a station. Buses and suburban trains are needed only for a few destinations. A single metro, bus or suburban train ride costs €2.15, but a T-1 ticket, valid for 10 rides, costs €10.30.

Taxi

Barcelona's black-and-yellow taxis are plentiful and reasonably priced. The flag fall is €2.10. If you can't find a street taxi, call ☎93 303 30 33.

BASQUE COUNTRY

Known to Basques as Euskadi or Euskal Herria ('the land of Basque Speakers') it combines wild coastal scenery with lofty mountain peaks.

San Sebastián

POP 183,300

Stylish San Sebastián (Donostia in Basque) has the air of an upscale resort, complete with an idyllic location on the shell-shaped Bahía de la Concha. The natural setting – crystalline waters, a flawless beach, green hills on all sides – is captivating. But this is one of Spain's true culinary capitals, with more Michelin stars (14) per capita here than anywhere else on earth.

Playa de la Concha (p330), San Sebastián

Detour: Pamplona's Running of the Bulls

Immortalised by Ernest Hemingway in *The Sun Also Rises*, the pre-Pyrenean city of Pamplona (Iruña in Basque) is home of the wild Sanfermines (aka Encierro or Running of the Bulls) festival, but is also an extremely walkable city that's managed to mix the charm of old plazas and buildings with modern shops and a lively nightlife.

The Sanfermines festival is held from 6 to 14 July, when Pamplona is overrun with thrill-seekers, curious onlookers and, yes, bulls. The Encierro (Running of the Bulls) begins at 8am daily, when bulls are let loose from the Coralillos Santo Domingo. The 825m race lasts just three minutes, and rarely ends well for the bull. The safest place to watch the Encierro is on TV. If that's too tame for you, try to sweet-talk your way onto a balcony or book a room in a hotel with views. The anti-bullfighting event, the Running of the Nudes, takes place two days earlier.

The extremely well-organised **tourist office** (www.turismo.navarra.es; Calle de Esclava 1; 9am-8pm Mon-Sat, to 2pm Sun) has plenty of information about the city and Navarra.

Sights

Playa de la Concha Beach

Fulfilling almost every idea of how a perfect city beach should be formed, Playa de la Concha and its westerly extension, **Playa de Ondarreta**, are easily among the best city beaches in Europe. Throughout the long summer months a fiesta atmosphere prevails, with thousands of tanned and toned bodies spread across the sands. The swimming is almost always safe.

Monte Igueldo Viewpoint

(www.monteigueldo.es; 10am-10pm Jun-Sep, shorter hours rest of year) The views from the summit of Monte Igueldo, just west of town, will make you feel like a circling hawk staring over the vast panorama of the Bahía de la Concha and the surrounding coastline and mountains. The best way to get there is via the old-world **funicular railway** (www.monteigueldo.es; Plaza del Funicular; return adult/child €3.15/2.35; 10am-9pm Mon-Fri, 10am-10pm Sat-Sun Jul, 10am-10pm Aug, 10am-9pm Sep, shorter hours rest of year) to the **Parque de Atracciones** (admission €2.20; 11.15am-2pm & 4-8pm Mon-Fri, until 8.30pm Sat & Sun Jul-Sep, shorter hours rest of year), a slightly tacky mini theme park at the top of the hill. Individual rides (which include roller coasters, boat rides, carousels and pony rides) cost between €1 and €2.50 extra. Trains on the funicular railway depart every 15 minutes.

Sleeping

Pensión Aida Boutique Hotel **€€**

(943 32 78 00; www.pensionesconencanto.com; Calle de Iztueta 9; s €62, d €84-90, studios €132-152;) The owners of this excellent *pensión* read the rule book on what makes a good hotel and have complied exactly. The rooms are bright and bold, full of exposed stone, and everything smells fresh and clean. The communal area, stuffed with soft sofas and mountains of information, is a big plus.

Pensión Amaiur Boutique Hotel **€€**

(943 42 96 54; www.pensionamaiur.com; Calle de 31 de Agosto 44; s €45, d €90-100;) The young and friendly owners of this top-notch guesthouse, which has a prime old-town location, have really created something different here. The look of the place is 'old-granny cottage' with bright floral wallpapers and bathrooms tiled in Andalucían blue and white.

Eating

San Sebastián is paradise for food lovers. Considered the birthplace of *nueva cocina española* (Spanish nouvelle cuisine), this area is home to some of the country's top chefs. Yet not all the good food is pricey. Head to the Parte Vieja for San Sebastián's *pintxos,* Basque-style tapas.

Pintxo etiquette is simple. Ask for a plate and point out what *pintxos* you want. Keep the toothpicks and go back for as many as you'd like. Accompany with *txakoli,* a cloudy white wine poured like cider to create a little fizz. When you're ready to pay, hand over the plate with all the toothpicks and tell bar staff how many drinks you've had.

Restaurante Alberto Seafood **€**
(☎943 42 88 84; Calle de 31 de Agosto 19; mains €12-15, menus €15; ⏰noon-4pm and 7pm-midnight Thu-Tue) A charming old seafood restaurant with a fishmonger-style window display of the day's catch. It's small and friendly and the pocket-sized dining room feels like it was once someone's living room. The food is earthy (well, OK, salty) and good, and the service swift.

La Fábrica Modern Basque **€€**
(☎943 98 05 81; www.restaurantelafabrica.es; Calle del Puerto 17; mains €15-20, menus from €25; ⏰12.30-4pm & 7.30-11.30pm Mon-Fri, 1-4pm & 8-11pm Sat-Sun) The red-brick interior walls and white tablecloths lend an air of class to a resturant whose modern takes on Basque classics have been making waves with San Sebastián locals over the last couple of years. At just €24, the multidish tasting menu is about the best-value deal in the city. Advance reservations are almost essential.

Arzak Contemporary Basque **€€€**
(☎+34 943 27 84 65; www.arzak.info; Avenida Alcalde Jose Elosegui 273; meals around €195; ⏰closed Sun-Mon, and Nov & late Jun) With three shining Michelin stars, acclaimed chef Juan Mari Arzak takes some beating when it comes to *nueva cocina vasca* and his restaurant is, not surprisingly, considered one of the best places to eat in Spain. Arzak is now assisted by his daughter Elena and they never cease to innovate. Reservations, well in advance, are obligatory.

Sanfermines festival, Pamplona

MATTHEW MICAH WRIGHT/GETTY IMAGES ©

If You Like... Spanish Art

After exploring the Prado (p286) in Madrid and the Guggenheim in Bilbao, you might feel inspired to seek out some of Spain's other artistic landmarks.

1 **TEATRE-MUSEU DALÍ**
(www.salvador-dali.org; Plaça de Gala i Salvador Dalí 5; admission incl Dalí Joies & Museu de l'Empordà adult/child under 9 yr €12/free; 9am-8pm Jul-Sep, 9.30am-6pm Tue-Sun Mar-Jun & Oct, 10.30am-6pm Tue-Sun Nov-Feb) The first name that comes into your head when you lay your eyes on this red castle-like building, topped with giant eggs and stylised Oscar-like statues and studded with plaster-covered croissants, is Dalí. An entirely appropriate final resting place for the master of surrealism, its entrance watched over by medieval suits of armour balancing baguettes on their heads, it has assured his immortality. 'Theatre-museum' is an apt label for this trip through the incredibly fertile imagination of one of the great showmen of the 20th century.

2 **MUSEO PICASSO MÁLAGA**
(902 443377; www.museopicassomalaga.org; Calle San Agustín 8; admission €7, incl temporary exhibition €10; 10am-8pm Tue-Thu & Sun, to 9pm Fri & Sat;) The Museo Picasso has an enviable collection of 204 works, 155 donated and 49 loaned to the museum by Christine Ruiz-Picasso (wife of Paul, Picasso's eldest son) and Bernard Ruiz-Picasso (his grandson), and includes some wonderful paintings of the family, including the heartfelt *Paulo con gorro blanco* (Paulo with a white cap), a portrait of Picasso's eldest son painted in the 1920s.

3 **MUSEO DE BELLAS ARTES**
(San Pío V; www.museobellasartesvalencia.gva.es; Calle de San Pío V 9; 10am-7pm Tue-Sun, 11am-5pm Mon) Bright and spacious, the Museo de Bellas Artes in Valencia ranks among Spain's best. Highlights include the grandiose Roman *Mosaic of the Nine Muses*, a collection of magnificent late-medieval altarpieces, and works by El Greco, Goya, Velázquez, Murillo and Ribalta, plus artists such as Sorolla and Pinazo of the Valencian Impressionist school.

Information

Oficina de Turismo **(943 48 11 66; www.sansebastianturismo.com; Alameda del Boulevard 8; 9am-8pm Mon-Sat, 10am-7pm Sun)** This friendly office offers comprehensive information on the city and the Basque Country in general.

Getting There & Away

Renfe Train Station **(Paseo de Francia)** The main station is just across Río Urumea, on a line linking Paris to Madrid. There are several services daily to Madrid (five hours) and two to Barcelona (six hours).

VALENCIA

A warm climate, an abundance of seaside resorts and interesting cities make this area of Spain a popular destination.

Valencia

POP 792,300

Valencia, where paella first simmered over a wood fire, is a vibrant, friendly, slightly chaotic place. It has two outstanding fine-arts museums, an accessible old quarter, Europe's newest cultural and scientific complex, and one of Spain's most exciting nightlife scenes.

Sights

Ciudad de las Artes y las Ciencias Notable Buildings
(City of Arts & Sciences; www.cac.es; combined ticket for Oceanogràfic, Hemisfèric & Museo de las Ciencias Príncipe Felipe adult/child €36.25/27.55) The aesthetically stunning City of Arts & Sciences occupies a massive 350,000-sq-metre swath of the old Turia riverbed. It's mostly the work of world-famous, locally born architect Santiago Calatrava. He's a controversial figure for many Valencians, who complain about the expense, and various design flaws that have necessitated major re-

pairs. Nevertheless, if your taxes weren't involved, it's awe-inspiring stuff, and pleasingly family-oriented.

Barrio del Carmen Historic Site

You'll see Valencia's best face by simply wandering around the Barrio del Carmen. Valencia's Romanesque-Gothic-baroque-Renaissance **catedral** (Plaza de la Virgen; adult/child incl audioguide €5/3.50; 10am-5.30pm or 6.30pm Mon-Sat, 2-5.30pm Sun, closed Sun Nov-Feb) is a compendium of centuries of architectural history and home to the **Capilla del Santo Cáliz**, a chapel said to contain the Holy Grail (the chalice Christ supposedly used in the Last Supper). Climb the 207 stairs of the **Micalet bell tower** (adult/child €2/1; 10am-7pm or 7.30pm) for sweeping city views.

Plaza del Mercado Historic Site

Over on Plaza del Mercado, two emblematic buildings, each a masterpiece of its era, face each other. Valencia's Modernista covered market, the **Mercado Central** (www.mercadocentralvalencia.es; Plaza del Mercado; 8am-2.30pm Mon-Sat) recently scrubbed and glowing as new, was constructed in 1928. With over 900 stalls, it's a swirl of smells, movement and colour. **La Lonja** (Calle de la Lonja; adult/child €2/1; 10am-6pm or 7pm Tue-Sat, to 3pm Sun) is a splendid late-15th-century building, a Unesco World Heritage Site and was originally Valencia's silk and commodity exchange.

Sleeping

Ad Hoc Monumental Hotel **€€**

(963 91 91 40; www.adhochoteles.com; Calle Boix 4; s/d €72/84;) Friendly Ad Hoc offers comfort and charm deep within the old quarter and also runs a splendid small restaurant (open for dinner Monday to Saturday). The late-19th-century building has been restored to its former splendour with great sensitivity, revealing original ceilings, mellow brickwork and solid wooden beams.

Caro Hotel Hotel **€€€**

(963 05 90 00; www.carohotel.com; Calle Almirante 14; r €143-214; P) Housed in a sumptuous 19th-century mansion, this hotel sits atop some 2000 years of Valencian history, with restoration revealing a hefty hunk of the Arab wall, Roman column bases and Gothic arches. Each room is furnished in soothing dark shades, has a great king-sized bed and varnished cement floors. Bathrooms are tops. For that very special occasion, reserve the 1st-floor grand suite, once the ballroom. Savour, too, its excellent restaurant Alma del Temple.

Street in Barrio de Santa Cruz (p335), Seville

DIANA MAYFIELD/GETTY IMAGES ©

Eating

Carosel Valencian €

(☎961 13 28 73; www.carosel.es; Calle Taula de Canvis 6; mains €7-16, menu €15; ⏰1-4pm & 9-11pm Tue-Sat, 1-4pm Sun) Jordi and his partner, Carol, run this delightful small restaurant with outdoor seating on a square. The freshest of produce from the nearby market is blended with Alicante and Valencia traditions to create salads, cocas, rices and other delicious titbits. Top value and warmly recommended.

Lonja del Pescado Fish €€

(www.restaurantelalonjapescadovalencia.com; Calle de Eugenia Viñes 243; dishes €8-15; ⏰1-3.30pm Sat & Sun, 8-11.30pm Tue-Sun Mar-Oct, 1-3.30pm Fri-Sun, 8-11.30pm Fri & Sat Nov-Feb) One block back from the beach at Malvarrosa, this busy, informal place has plenty of atmosphere and offers unbeatable value for fresh fish. Grab an order form as you enter and fill it in at your table. The tram stops outside.

Information

Turismo Valencia Tourist Office (VLC; ☎963 15 39 31; www.turisvalencia.es; Plaza de la Reina 19; ⏰9am-7pm Mon-Sat, 10am-2pm Sun) Has several other branches around town, including Plaza del Ayuntamiento (Plaza del Ayuntamiento; ⏰9am-7pm Mon-Sat, 10am-2pm Sun), the AVE station and airport arrivals area.

Getting There & Away

Air

Aeropuerto de Manises (VLC; ☎902 404704) Valencia's airport is 10km west of the city centre along the A3, direction Madrid.

Train

From Valencia's **Estación del Norte** (Calle Xàtiva; 📶), major destinations include the following:

TO	PRICE (€)	DURATION (HR)	FREQUENCY (PER DAY)
Alicante	17-30	1½-2	11-13
Barcelona	40-44	3-4¼	14-18
Madrid	27-73	1¾-6½	13-20

Participants in parade for Semana Santa, Seville

IAN CUMMING/GETTY IMAGES ©

ANDALUCÍA

Images of Andalucía are so potent, so quintessentially Spanish that it's sometimes difficult not to feel a sense of déjà vu. It's almost as if you've already been there in your dreams: a solemn Easter parade, an ebullient spring festival, exotic nights in the Alhambra.

Seville

POP 703,000

A sexy, gutsy and gorgeous city, Seville is home to two of Spain's most colourful festivals, fascinating and distinctive *barrios* (neighbourhoods) and a local population that lives life to the fullest. A fiery place (as you'll soon see in its packed and noisy tapas bars), it is also hot climatewise – avoid July and August!

Sights

Catedral & Giralda Church

(www.catedraldesevilla.es; adult/child €9/free; 11am-3.30pm Mon, 11am-5pm Tue-Sat, 2.30-6pm Sun) Seville's immense cathedral, one of the largest Christian churches in the world, is awe-inspiring in its scale and sheer majesty. It stands on the site of the great 12th-century Almohad mosque, with the mosque's minaret (the Giralda) still towering beside it.

Alcázar Castle

(www.alcazarsevilla.org; adult/child €9.50/free; 9.30am-7pm Apr-Sep, 9:30am-5pm Oct-Mar) If heaven really *does* exist, then let's hope it looks a little bit like the inside of Seville's Alcázar. Built primarily in the 1300s during the so-called 'dark ages' in Europe, the architecture is anything but dark. Unesco agreed, making it a World Heritage Site.

Archivo de Indias Museum

(Calle Santo Tomás; 9.30am-4.45pm Mon-Sat, 10am-2pm Sun) FREE Housed in the former Casa de la Contratación (Merchants Exchange) on the western side of Plaza del Triunfo, the Archivo de Indias has, since 1785, been the main archive on Spain's American empire, with 80 million pages of documents dating from 1492 through to the end of the empire in the 19th century – a most effective statement of Spain's power and influence during its Golden Age.

Barrio de Santa Cruz Historic Site

Seville's medieval *judería* (Jewish quarter), east of the cathedral and Alcázar, is today a tangle of atmospheric, winding streets and lovely plant-decked plazas perfumed with orange blossom. Among its most characteristic plazas is **Plaza de Santa Cruz**, which gives the barrio its name. Plaza de Doña Elvira is perhaps the most romantic small square in Andalucía, especially in the evening.

Museo del Baile Flamenco Museum

(www.museoflamenco.com; Calle Manuel Rojas Marcos 3; adult/concession €10/8; 10am-7pm) The brainchild of *sevillana* flamenco dancer Cristina Hoyos, this museum spread over three floors of an 18th-century palace makes a noble effort to showcase the mysterious art with sketches, paintings, photos of erstwhile (and contemporary) flamenco greats, plus a collection of dresses and shawls. Better than all of that though are the fantastic nightly concerts (7pm; €20) in the onsite courtyard.

Festivals & Events

Semana Santa Religious

(www.semana-santa.org) Every day from Palm Sunday to Easter Sunday, large, life-sized *pasos* (sculptural representations of events from Christ's Passion) are carried from Seville's churches through the streets to the cathedral, accompanied by processions that may take more than an hour to pass. The processions are organised by over 50 different *hermandades* or *cofradías* (brotherhoods, some of which include women).

Feria de Abril Spring Fair

The April fair, held in the second half of the month (sometimes edging into May), is the jolly counterpart to the sombre Semana Santa. The biggest and most colourful of all Andalucía's ferias is less invasive (and also less inclusive) than the Easter celebration. It takes place on El Real

Seville

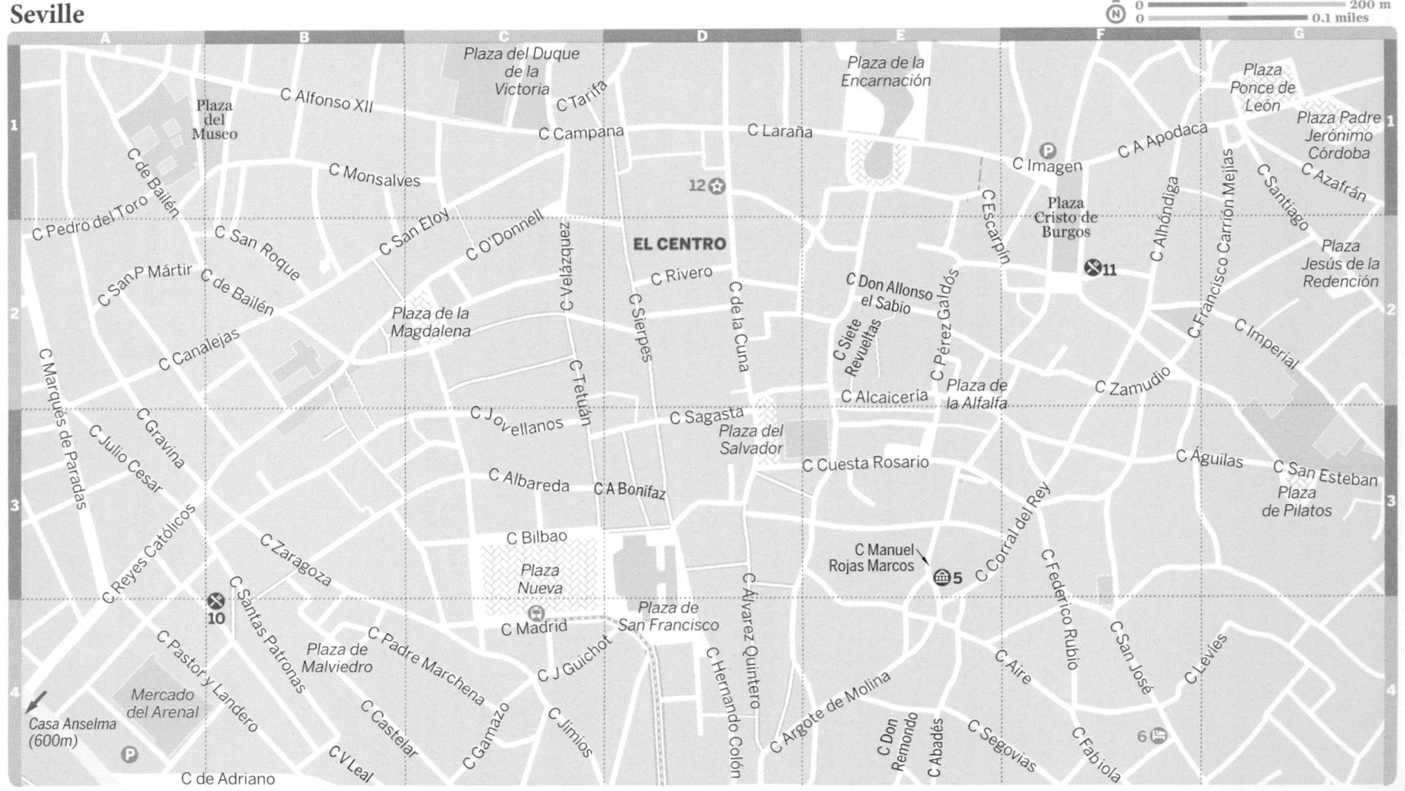
0 200 m
0 0.1 miles
A
B
C
D
E
F
G
1
2
3
4
Plaza del Duque de la Victoria
Plaza de la Encarnación
Plaza Ponce de León
Plaza Padre Jerónimo Córdoba
Plaza del Museo
C Alfonso XII
C Tarifa
C Campana
C Laraña
C A Apodaca
C Imagen
C Monsalves
12
C de Bailén
C Pedro del Toro
C San Roque
C San Eloy
C O'Donnell
C Velázquez
EL CENTRO
C Rivero
C Escarpín
Plaza Cristo de Burgos
C Alhóndiga
C Francisco Carrión Mejías
C Santiago
C Azafrán
Plaza Jesús de la Redención
11
C San P Mártir
C de Bailén
Plaza de la Magdalena
C Sierpes
C de la Cuna
C Don Allonso el Sabio
C Pérez Galdós
C Siete Revueltas
C Imperial
C Canalejas
C Marqués de Paradas
C Tetuán
C Alcaicería
Plaza de la Alfalfa
C Zamudio
C Jovellanos
C Sagasta
Plaza del Salvador
C Gravina
C Julio Cesar
C Cuesta Rosario
C Águilas
C San Esteban
Plaza de Pilatos
C Albareda
C A Bonifaz
C Corral del Rey
C Reyes Católicos
C Zaragoza
C Bilbao
C Manuel Rojas Marcos
5
Plaza Nueva
C Álvarez Quintero
C Federico Rubio
10
C Santas Patronas
C Madrid
Plaza de San Francisco
C Pastor y Landero
Plaza de Malviedro
C Padre Marchena
C J Guichot
C Hernando Colón
C Aire
C San José
C Levíes
Mercado del Arenal
Casa Anselma (600m)
C Castelar
C Gamazo
C Jimios
C Argote de Molina
C Don Remondo
C Abadés
C Segovias
C Fabiola
6
C V Leal
C de Adriano

Seville

Sights

1	Alcázar	E6
2	Archivo de Indias	D6
3	Barrio de Santa Cruz	F5
4	Catedral & Giralda	D5
5	Museo del Baile Flamenco	E3

Sleeping

6	Hotel Amadeus	F4
7	Hotel Casa 1800	E5
8	Un Patio en Santa Cruz	G5

Eating

9	Bodega Santa Cruz	E5
10	La Brunilda	B4
11	Los Coloniales	F2

Entertainment

12	Casa de la Memoria	D1
13	La Casa del Flamenco	F5

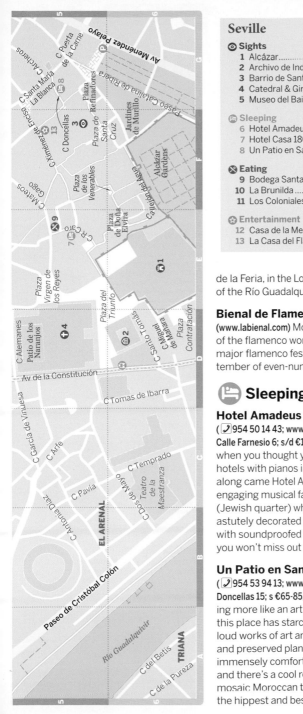

de la Feria, in the Los Remedios area west of the Río Guadalquivir.

Bienal de Flamenco Flamenco
(www.labienal.com) Most of the big names of the flamenco world participate in this major flamenco festival. Held in the September of even-numbered years.

Sleeping

Hotel Amadeus Hotel **€€**
(☎954 50 14 43; www.hotelamadeussevilla.com; Calle Farnesio 6; s/d €100/114; P ❄ ᯤ) Just when you thought you could never find hotels with pianos in the rooms anymore, along came Hotel Amadeus. It's run by an engaging musical family in the old *judería* (Jewish quarter) where several of the astutely decorated rooms come complete with soundproofed walls and pianos, so you won't miss out on your daily practice.

Un Patio en Santa Cruz Hotel **€€**
(☎954 53 94 13; www.patiosantacruz.com; Calle Doncellas 15; s €65-85, d €65-120; ❄ ᯤ) Feeling more like an art gallery than a hotel, this place has starched white walls with loud works of art and strange sculptures and preserved plants. The rooms are immensely comfortable, staff are friendly and there's a cool rooftop terrace with mosaic Moroccan tables. It's easily one of the hippest and best-value hotels in town.

Seville Cathedral

'We're going to construct a church so large future generations will think we were mad,' declared the inspired architects of Seville in 1402 at the beginning of one of the most grandiose building projects in medieval history. Just over a century later their madness was triumphantly confirmed.

WHAT TO LOOK FOR

To avoid getting lost, orient yourself by the main highlights. Directly inside the southern (main) entrance is the grand **tomb of Columbus** ❶. Turn right here and head into the south-eastern corner to uncover some major art treasures: a Goya in the Sacristía de los Cálices, a Zurbarán in the **Sacristía Mayor** ❷, and Murillo's shining Immaculada in the Sala Capitular. Skirt the cathedral's eastern wall taking a look inside the **Capilla Real** ❸ with its important royal tombs. By now it's impossible to avoid the lure of **Capilla Mayor** ❹ with its fantastical altarpiece. Hidden over in the northwest corner is the **Capilla de San Antonio** ❺ with a legendary Murillo. That huge doorway almost in front of you is the rarely opened **Puerta de la Asunción** ❻. Make for the **Giralda** ❼ next, stealing admiring looks at the high, vaulted ceiling on the way. After looking down on the cathedral's immense footprint, descend and depart via the **Patio de los Naranjos** ❽.

TOP TIPS

» **Pace yourself** Don't visit the Alcazar and Cathedral on the same day. There is far too much to take in.

» **Viewpoints** Take time to admire the cathedral from the outside. It's particularly stunning at night from the Plaza Virgen de los Reyes, and from across the river in Triana.

Capilla Mayor

Behold! The cathedral's main focal point contains its greatest treasure, a magnificent gold-plated altarpiece depicting various scenes in the life of Christ. It constitutes the life's work of one man, Flemish artist Pieter Dancart.

Patio de los Naranjos

Inhale the perfume of 60 Sevillan orange trees in a cool patio bordered by fortress-like walls – a surviving remnant of the original 12th-century mosque. Exit is gained via the horseshoe-shaped Puerta del Perdón.

Puerta del Perdón

8

5

Iglesia del Sagrario

6

Puerta del Bautismo

Puerta de la Asunción

Located on the western side of the cathedral and also known as the Puerta Mayor, these huge, rarely opened doors are pushed back during Semana Santa to allow solemn processions of Catholic *hermanadades* (brotherhoods) to pass through.

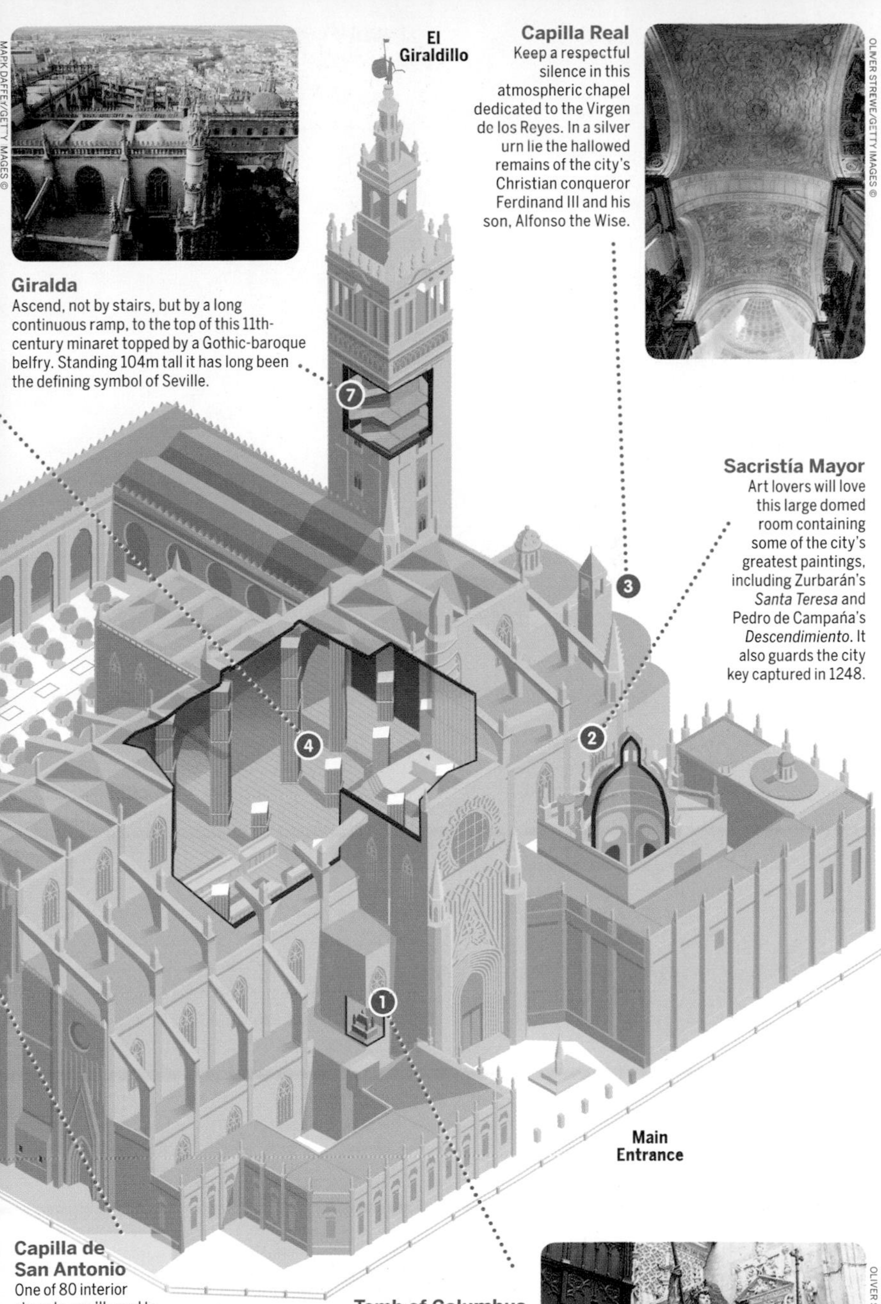

MARK DAFFEY/GETTY IMAGES ©
El Giraldillo
Capilla Real
Keep a respectful silence in this atmospheric chapel dedicated to the Virgen de los Reyes. In a silver urn lie the hallowed remains of the city's Christian conqueror Ferdinand III and his son, Alfonso the Wise.
OLIVER STREWE/GETTY IMAGES ©
Giralda
Ascend, not by stairs, but by a long continuous ramp, to the top of this 11th-century minaret topped by a Gothic-baroque belfry. Standing 104m tall it has long been the defining symbol of Seville.
7
Sacristía Mayor
Art lovers will love this large domed room containing some of the city's greatest paintings, including Zurbarán's *Santa Teresa* and Pedro de Campaña's *Descendimiento*. It also guards the city key captured in 1248.
3
2
4
1
Main Entrance
Capilla de San Antonio
One of 80 interior chapels, you'll need to hunt down this little gem notable for housing Murillo's 1666 painting, *The Vision of St Anthony*. The work was pillaged by thieves in 1874 but later restored.
Tomb of Columbus
Buried in Valladolid in 1506, the remains of Christopher Columbus were moved four times before they arrived in Seville in 1898 encased in an elaborately carved catafalque. Or were they? A longstanding debate rages about whether these are actually Columbus' remains or if, in a postdeath mix-up, he still resides in the Dominican Republic.
OLIVER STREWE/ GETTY IMAGES ©

Hotel Casa 1800 Luxury Hotel **€€€**
(954 56 18 00; www.hotelcasa1800sevilla.com; Calle Rodrigo Caro 6; r from €195;) Reigning as number one in Seville's 'favourite hotel' charts is this postively regal Santa Cruz pile where the word 'casa' (house) is taken seriously. This really is your home away from home (albeit a posh one!), with charming staff catering for your every need. Historic highlights include a complimentary afternoon-tea buffet, plus a quartet of penthouse garden suites with Giralda views.

Eating

Bodega Santa Cruz Tapas **€**
(Calle Mateos Gago; tapas €2; 11.30am-midnight) This forever-crowded bodega is where eating tapas becomes a physical contact sport. Watch out for flying elbows, hold tight to your drink and admire those dexterous waiters who bob and weave like prizefighters amid the chaos. The fiercely traditional tapas are best enjoyed alfresco with a cold beer as you watch marching armies of Santa Cruz tourists go squeezing past.

La Brunilda Tapas, Fusion **€€**
(954 22 04 81; Calle Galera 5; tapas €3.50-6.50; 1-4pm & 8.30-11.30pm Tue-Sat, 1-4pm Sun) Seville's crown as Andalucia's tapas capital is regularly attacked by well-armed rivals from the provinces, meaning it constantly has to reinvent itself and offer up fresh competition. Enter Brunilda, a newish font of fusion tapas sandwiched into a inconspicuous backstreet in the Arenal quarter where everything – including the food staff and clientele – is pretty.

Los Coloniales Andalucían **€€**
(www.tabernacoloniales.es; cnr Calle Dormitorio & Plaza Cristo de Burgos; mains €10-12; 12.30pm-12.15am) The quiet ones are always the best. It might not look like

Left: Mezquita (p342), Córdoba;
Below: Women dancing at Seville's Feria de Abril (p335)
(LEFT) MICHELE FALZONE/GETTY IMAGES ©; (BELOW) ALEX SEGRE/ALAMY ©

much from the outside, but take it on trust that Los Coloniales is something very special. The quality plates line up like models on a catwalk: *chorizo a la Asturiana,* a divine spicy sausage in an onion sauce served on a bed of lightly fried potato; eggplants in honey; and pork tenderloin *al whiskey* (a whiskey-flavoured sauce).

Entertainment

Seville is arguably Spain's flamenco capital and you're most likely to catch a spontaneous atmosphere (of unpredictable quality) in one of the bars staging regular nights of flamenco with no admission fee.

La Casa del Flamenco Flamenco
(**955 02 99 99; www.lacasadelflamenco sevilla.com; Calle Ximénenz de Enciso, 28; tickets adult/child €18/10; 8.30pm)** When Seville's **Casa de la Memoria (954 56 06 70; www.casadelamemoria.es; Calle Cuna 6; €18; shows 7.30pm & 9pm)** moved its flamenco centre to El Centro in 2012, its former location – a beautiful patio in an old Sephardic Jewish mansion in Santa Cruz – was filled by La Casa del Flamenco. Fortunately, not much else has changed and the performances on a stage hemmed in by seating on three sides are mesmerizing.

Casa Anselma Flamenco
(Calle Pagés del Corro 49; midnight-late Mon-Sat) True, the music is often more folkloric than flamenco, but Casa Anselma is the antithesis of a touristy flamenco *tablaos,* with cheek-to-jowl crowds, zero amplification and spontaneous outbreaks of dexterous dancing. Beware: there's no sign, just a doorway embellished with *azulejos* tiles.

Information

Seville Tourism (www.turismo.sevilla.org) The city's official tourism site; its 'Accessible Guide' is especially useful for travellers with a disability.

Getting There & Away

Twenty or more superfast AVE trains, reaching speeds of 280km/h, whiz daily to/from Madrid (€76, 2½ hours). Other services include Cádiz (€16, 1¾ hours, 13 daily), Córdoba (€30, 40 minutes to 1½ hours, 21 or more daily), Granada (€30, three hours, four daily) and Málaga (€43, two hours, 11 daily).

Estación Santa Justa (☎902 432343; Avenida Kansas City) Seville's Estación Santa Justa is 1.5km northeast of the centre.

Córdoba

POP 328,659

Córdoba was once one of the most enlightened Islamic cities on earth, and enough remains to place it in the contemporary top three Andalucian draws. The centrepiece is the gigantic and exquisitely rendered Mezquita. Surrounding it is an intricate web of winding streets, geranium-sprouting flower boxes and cool intimate patios that are at their most beguiling in late spring.

Sights & Activities

Mezquita Mosque, Cathedral

(Mosque; ☎957 47 05 12; www.catedraldecordoba.es; Calle Cardenal Herrero; adult/child €8/4, 8.30-9.30am Mon-Sat free; ⌚8.30-9.30am & 10am-7pm Mon-Sat, 8.30-11.30am & 3-7pm Sun, closes 6pm Nov-Feb) It's impossible to overemphasise the beauty of Córdoba's great mosque, with its remarkably serene (despite tourist crowds) and spacious interior. One of the world's greatest works of Islamic architecture, the Mezquita hints, with all its lustrous decoration, at a refined age when Muslims, Jews and Christians lived side by side and enriched their city with a heady interaction of diverse vibrant cultures.

Centro Flamenco Fosforito Museum

(☎957 47 68 29; www.centroflamencofosforito.cordoba.es; Plaza del Potro; admission €2; ⌚8.30am-7.30pm Tue-Fri, 8.30am-2.30pm

Córdoba

SYOLACAN/GETTY IMAGES ©

Sat, 9.30am-2.30pm Sun) Possibly the best flamenco museum in Andalucía, this recently opened centre has exhibits, film and information panels in English and Spanish telling you the history of the guitar and all the flamenco greats, and touch-screen videos showing all the important techniques of flamenco song, guitar, dance and percussion – and you can try your hand at beating out the *compás* (rhythm) of different *palos* (song forms). Regular live flamenco performances are held here too.

Judería Historic Neighbourhood

Jews were among the most dynamic and prominent citizens of Islamic Córdoba. The medieval *judería*, extending northwest from the Mezquita almost to Avenida del Gran Capitán, is today a maze of narrow streets and whitewashed buildings with flowery window boxes.

Medina Azahara Ruin

(Madinat al-Zahra; admission €1.50, EU citizens free; ⌚10am-6.30pm Tue-Sat, to 8.30pm May–mid-Sep, to 2pm Sun) Even in the cicada-shrill heat and stillness of a summer afternoon, the Medina Azahara whispers of the power and vision of its founder, Abd ar-Rahman III. The self-proclaimed caliph began the construction of a magnificent new capital 8km west of Córdoba around 936, and took up full residence around 945. Medina Azahara was a resounding declaration of his status, a magnificent trapping of power. It was destroyed in the 11th century and just 10% of the site has been excavated.

Hammam Baños Árabes Bathhouse

(☎957 48 47 46; cordoba.hammamalandalus.com; Calle del Corregidor Luis de la Cerda 51; bath/bath & massage €24/36; ⌚2hr sessions 10am, noon, 2pm, 4pm, 6pm, 8pm & 10pm) Follow the lead of the medieval Cordobans and dip your toe in these beautifully renovated Arab baths, where you can enjoy an aromatherapy massage, with tea, hookah and Arabic sweets in the cafe afterwards.

Sleeping

Bed and Be Hostel **€**

(☎661 420733; www.bedandbe.com; Calle Cruz Conde 22; dm €17-20, d without bathroom €50-80; ❄📶) An exceptionally good hostel option a bit north of Plaza de las Tendillas. Staff are clued up about what's on and what's new in Córdoba, and they offer a social event every evening – anything from a bike tour to a tapas tour to a sushi dinner. The assortment of double and dorm rooms are all super-clean and as gleaming white as a *pueblo blanco*.

Hotel Mezquita Hotel **€€**

(☎957 47 55 85; www.hotelmezquita.com; Plaza Santa Catalina 1; s €50-65, d €65-140; ❄📶) This former mansion stands right opposite its namesake monument and sports a broad miscellany of art and antiques in its common areas. There are some large, elegant rooms with marble floors and balconies overlooking the great mosque, and some smaller (though still comfortable) abodes in a recently added interior section.

Eating

Casa Mazal Jewish, Andalucian **€€**

(☎957 94 18 88; www.casamazal.com; Calle Tomás Conde 3; mains €9-20; ⌚12.30-4pm & 7.30-11pm; 🖉) A meal here makes a fine complement to the nearby Casa de Sefarad museum, as it brings the Sephardic tradition to the table, along with some *andalusí* dishes (originating in Moorish Spain). A sort of culinary diaspora, Sephardic cuisine has diverse roots in Al-Andalus, Turkey, Italy and North Africa, with such varied items as Syrian lentil-and-rice salad, an array of couscous options, and *seniyeh* lamb pie on the menu.

Getting There & Away

From Córdoba's train station, destinations include Seville (€10.60 to €32.10, 90 minutes, 23 or more daily), Madrid (€52 to €66.30, 1¾ to 6¼ hours, 23 or more daily), Málaga (€21 to €39.60, one to 2½ hours, nine daily) and Barcelona (€59.40 to €133, 4½ hours, four daily).

Mezquita

TIMELINE

600 Foundation of the Christian Visigothic church of St Vincent on the site of the present Mezquita.

785 Salvaging Visigoth and Roman ruins, Emir Abd ar-Rahman I converts the Mezquita into a mosque.

822–5 Mosque enlarged in reign of Abd ar-Rahman II.

912–961 A new minaret is ordered by Abd ar-Rahman III.

961–6 Mosque enlarged by Al-Hakam II who also enriches the **mihrab** ❶.

987 Mosque enlarged for the last time by Al-Mansur Ibn Abi Aamir. With the addition of the **Patio de los Naranjos** ❷, the building reaches its current dimensions.

1236 Mosque reconverted into a Christian church after Córdoba is recaptured by Ferdinand III of Castile.

1271 Instead of destroying the mosque, the overawed Christians elect to modify it. Alfonso X orders the construction of the **Capilla de Villaviciosa** ❸ and **Capilla Real** ❹.

1300s Original minaret is replaced by the baroque **Torre del Alminar** ❺.

1520s A Renaissance-style cathedral nave is added by Charles V. 'I have destroyed something unique to the world,' he laments on seeing the finished work.

2004 Spanish Muslims petition to be able to worship in the Mezquita again. The Vatican doesn't consent.

TOP TIPS

» **Among the oranges** The Patio de los Naranjos can be enjoyed free of charge at any time.

» **Early birds** Entry to the rest of the Mezquita is offered free every morning except Sunday between 8.30am and 9.30am.

» **Quiet time** Group visits are prohibited before 10am, meaning the building is quieter and more atmospheric in the early morning.

The mihrab
Everything leads to the mosque's greatest treasure – a scallop-shell-shaped prayer niche facing Mecca that was added in the 10th century. Cast your eyes over the gold mosaic cubes crafted by imported Byzantium sculptors.

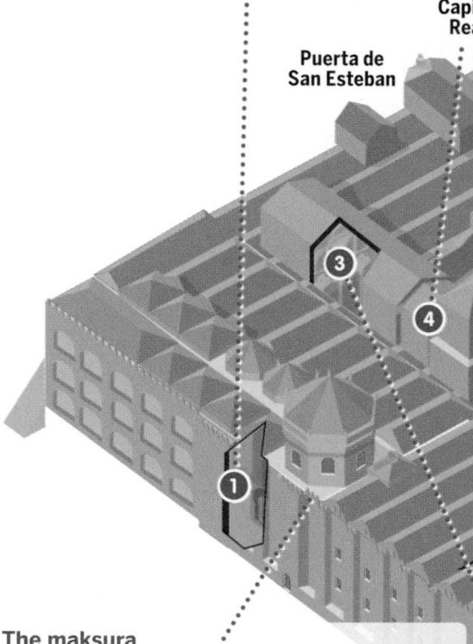

The maksura
Guiding you towards the mihrab, the maksura is a former royal enclosure where the caliphs and their retinues prayed. Its lavish, elaborate arches were designed to draw the eye of worshippers towards the mihrab and Mecca.

OLIVER STREWE/GETTY IMAGES ©

The cathedral choir

Few ignore the impressive *coro* (choir): a late-Christian addition dating from the 1750s. Once you've admired the skilfully carved mahogany choir stalls depicting scenes from the Bible, look up at the impressive baroque ceiling.

RUTH TOMLINSON / GETTY IMAGES ©

5

Torre del Alminar

This is the Mezquita's cheapest sight because you don't have to pay to see it. Rising 93m and viewable from much of the city, the baroque-style bell tower was built over the mosque's original minaret.

KARL BLACKWELL /GETTY IMAGES ©

The Mezquita arches

No, you're not hallucinating. The Mezquita's most defining characteristic is its unique terracotta-and-white striped arches that support 856 pillars salvaged from Roman and Visigoth ruins. Glimpsed through the dull light they're at once spooky and striking.

Puerta del Perdón

2

Patio de los Naranjos

Abandon architectural preconceptions all ye who enter here. The ablutions area of the former mosque is a shady courtyard embellished with orange trees that acts as the Mezquita's main entry point.

Capilla Mayor

A Christian monument inside an Islamic mosque sounds beautifully ironic, yet here it is: a Gothic church commissioned by Charles V in the 16th century and planted in the middle of the world's third largest mosque.

KRZYSZTOF DYDYNSKI/GETTY IMAGES ©

Capilla de Villaviciosa

Sift through the building's numerous chapels till you find this gem, an early Christian modification added in 1277 which fused existing Moorish features with Gothic arches and pillars. It served as the Capilla Mayor until the 1520s.

IZZET KERIBAR/GETTY IMAGES ©

Granada

Granada's eight centuries as a Muslim capital are symbolised in its keynote emblem, the remarkable Alhambra, one of the most graceful architectural achievements in the Muslim world. Islam was never completely expunged here, and today it seems more present than ever in the shops, restaurants, tearooms and the mosque of a growing North African community in and around the maze of the Albayzín.

Sights

The Alhambra may be the star of the show, but the **Albayzín** (Granada's old Muslim quarter), on the hill facing the Alhambra across the Darro valley, is an open-air museum in which you can lose yourself for a whole morning. The cobblestone streets are lined with gorgeous *cármenes* (large mansions with walled gardens, from the Arabic *karm* for garden). It survived as the Muslim quarter for several decades after the Christian conquest in 1492.

Alhambra Palace

(☎902 441221; www.alhambra-tickets.es; adult/under 12yr €14/free, Generalife only €7; ⏰8.30am-8pm 15 Mar-14 Oct, to 6pm 15 Oct-14 Mar, night visits 10-11.30pm Tue-Sat Mar-Oct, 8-9.30pm Fri & Sat Oct-Mar) Andalucian poet, Federico Lorca, once declared that the Alhambra is where the water from the Sierra Nevada's bubbling streams 'lies down to die' and where Granada's air is 'so beautiful, it is almost thought'. Part palace, part fort, part World Heritage Site, part lesson in medieval architecture; the Alhambra has long enchanted a never-ending line of expectant visitors. As a historic monument, it is unlikely it will ever be surpassed – at least not in the lifetime of anyone reading this book. As a tourist sight, it is an essential pilgrimage and, as a result, predictably crowded. Try to book in advance for the very earliest or latest time slot.

Left: Granada; **Below:** Courtyard of the Palacio de Carlos V, Alhambra, Granada

(LEFT) INGRAM PUBLISHING/GETTY IMAGES ©; (BELOW) MARQUES/SHUTTERSTOCK ©

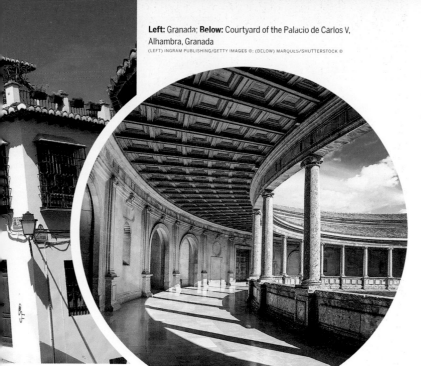

Capilla Real
Historic Building

(www.capillarealgranada.com; Calle Oficios; admission €4; ⌚10.15am-1.30pm & 3.30-6.30pm Mon-Sat, 11am-1.30pm & 2.30-5.30pm Sun) Here they lie, Spain's notorious Catholic Monarchs, entombed in a chapel adjoining Granada's cathedral, far more peaceful in death than their tumultuous lives would have suggested. Isabella and Ferdinand commissioned the elaborate Isabelline-Gothic-style mausoleum that was to house them, but it was not completed until 1521, hence their temporary interment in the Alhambra's Convento de San Francisco.

Sleeping

Hotel Posada del Toro
Hotel €

(☎958 22 73 33; www.posadadeltoro.com; Calle de Elvira 25; d from €50; ❄📶) A lovely small hotel with rooms set around a tranquil central patio. Walls are coloured like Italian gelato in a combination of pale pistachio, peach and cream. The rooms are similarly tasteful with parquet floors, Alhambra-style stucco, rustic-style furniture and small but perfectly equipped bathrooms with double sinks and hydro-massage showers. The restaurant dishes up Spanish dishes like Galician octopus, as well as pastas and pizza.

Carmen de la Alcubilla del Caracol
Historic Hotel €€

(☎958 21 55 51; www.alcubilladelcaracol.com; Calle del Aire Alta 12; s/d €100/120; ❄@📶) This much sought after small hotel inhabits a tradtional *carmen* on the slopes of the Alhambra. It feels more like a B&B than a hotel thanks to the attentiveness of its Granada-loving host, Manuel. The seven rooms are washed in pale pastel colours and furnished luxuriously, but not ostentatiously.

Alhambra

TIMELINE

900 The first reference to al-qala'at al-hamra (red castle) atop Granada's Sabika Hill.

1237 Founder of the Nasrid dynasty, Muhammad I, moves his court to Granada. Threatened by belligerent Christian armies he builds a new defensive fort, the **Alcazaba** ❶.

1302–09 Designed as a summer palace-cum-country estate for Granada's foppish rulers, the bucolic **Generalife** ❷ is begun by Muhammad III.

1333–54 Yusuf I initiates the construction of the **Palacio Nazaríes** ❸, still considered the highpoint of Islamic culture in Europe.

1350–60 Up goes the **Palacio de Comares** ❹, taking Nasrid lavishness to a whole new level.

1362–91 The second coming of Muhammad V ushers in even greater architectural brilliance exemplified by the construction of the **Patio de los Leones** ❺.

1527 The Christians add the **Palacio de Carlos V** ❻. Inspired Renaissance palace or incongruous crime against Moorish art? You decide.

1829 The languishing, half-forgotten Alhambra is 'rediscovered' by American writer Washington Irving during a protracted sleep-over.

1954 The Generalife gardens are extended southwards to accommodate an outdoor theatre.

TOP TIPS

» **Queue-dodger** Reserve tickets in advance online at www.alhambra-tickets.es

» **Money-saver** You can visit the general areas of the palace free of charge any time by entering through the Puerta de Justica.

» **Stay over** Two fine hotels are encased in the grounds: Parador de Granada (expensive) and Hotel América (more economical).

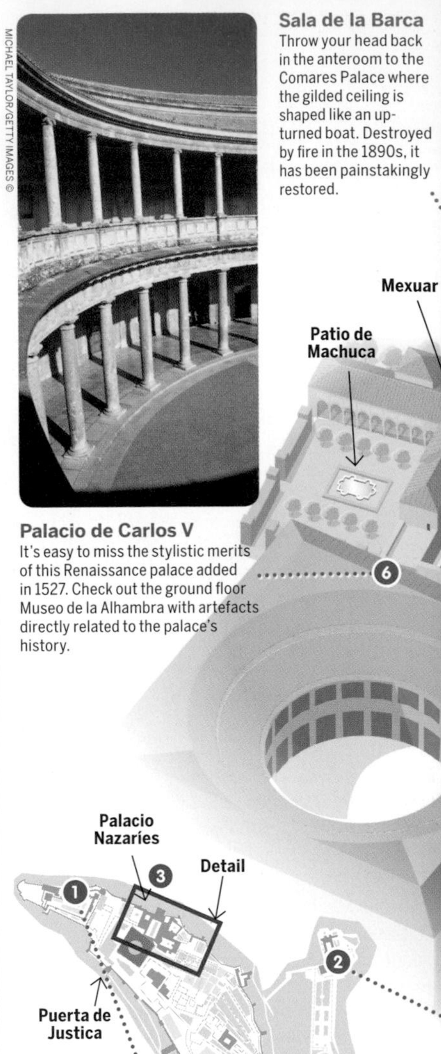

Sala de la Barca
Throw your head back in the anteroom to the Comares Palace where the gilded ceiling is shaped like an upturned boat. Destroyed by fire in the 1890s, it has been painstakingly restored.

Palacio de Carlos V
It's easy to miss the stylistic merits of this Renaissance palace added in 1527. Check out the ground floor Museo de la Alhambra with artefacts directly related to the palace's history.

Alcazaba
Find time to explore the towers of the original citadel, the most important of which – the Torre de la Vela – takes you, via a winding staircase, to the Alhambra's best viewpoint.

JOHN ELK III/GETTY IMAGES ©

Patio de Arrayanes

If only you could linger longer beside the rows of *arrayanes* (myrtle bushes) that border this calming rectangular pool. Shaded porticos with seven harmonious arches invite further contemplation.

DAVID C TOMLINSON/GETTY IMAGES ©

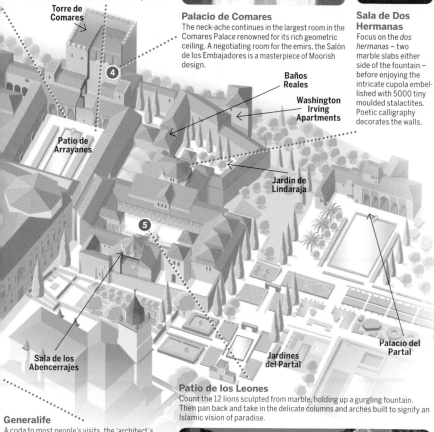

Palacio de Comares

The neck-ache continues in the largest room in the Comares Palace renowned for its rich geometric ceiling. A negotiating room for the emirs, the Salón de los Embajadores is a masterpiece of Moorish design.

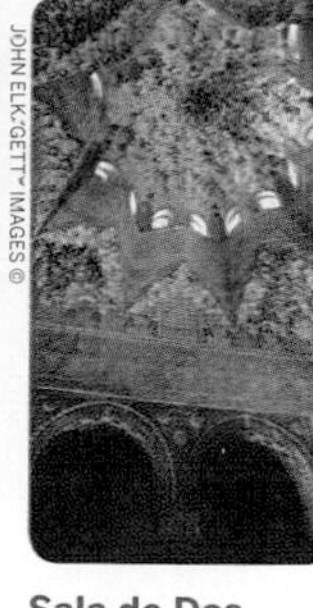

JOHN ELK/GETTY IMAGES ©

Sala de Dos Hermanas

Focus on the *dos hermanas* – two marble slabs either side of the fountain – before enjoying the intricate cupola embellished with 5000 tiny moulded stalactites. Poetic calligraphy decorates the walls.

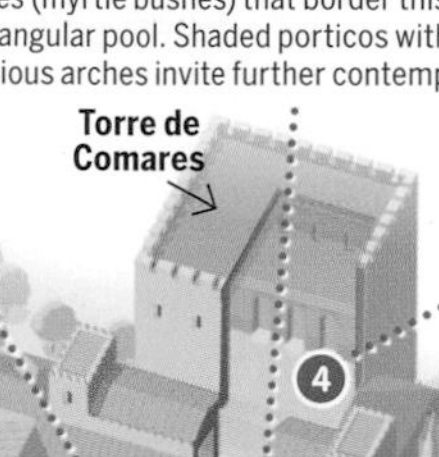

Patio de los Leones

Count the 12 lions sculpted from marble, holding up a gurgling fountain. Then pan back and take in the delicate columns and arches built to signify an Islamic vision of paradise.

JOHN ELK/GETTY IMAGES ©

Generalife

A coda to most people's visits, the 'architect's garden' is no afterthought. While Nasrid in origin, the horticulture is relatively new: the pools and arcades were added in the early 20th century.

Alhambra Access

Tickets are timed for either morning (from 8.30am) or afternoon (after 2pm) entry to the grounds, and, more important, for admission to the Palacios Nazaríes within a 30-minute period (you can stay as long as you like). Allow three hours or more to see the whole complex, and at least 10 minutes to walk from the Generalife to the Palacios Nazaríes.

Same-day tickets sell out early, so it's more convenient to buy tickets up to three months ahead. Pick up phone or internet orders at the yellow machines to the right of the ticket office, using the credit card with which you made the purchase. When full-access tickets are sold out, you can still buy a ticket to the Generalife and gardens (€7). The Palacios Nazaríes are open for **night visits** (€8; 10-11.30pm Tue-Sat Mar-Oct, 8-9.30pm Fri & Sat Nov-Feb), good for atmosphere rather than detail.

Walk up one of three ways: Cuesta de Gomérez, through woods to the **Puerta de la Justicia** (enter here if you already have your ticket) or, further along, to the ticket office; Cuesta de los Chinos, to the east end of the complex; and up Cuesta de Realejo via the Alhambra Palace Hotel.

Buses 30, 32 and (less directly) 34 run from near Plaza Nueva from 7am to 11pm, stopping at the ticket office and in front of the Alhambra Palace. By car, follow 'Alhambra' signs from the highway to the car park, just uphill from the ticket office.

Hotel Hospes Palacio de Los Patos Luxury Hotel **€€€**
(958 53 57 90; www.hospes.com; Solarillo de Gracia 1; r/ste €200/400; P ❄ @ ☰ ≋) Put simply, the best hotel in Granada, offering lucky guests sharp modernity and never-miss-a-beat service in a palatial Unesco-protected building. You could write a novella about its many memorable features: the grand staircase, the post-modern chandeliers, the Arabian garden, the Roman Emperor spa, the carnations left on your bed in the afternoon....

Eating

Granada is one of the last bastions of that fantastic practice of free tapas with every drink, and some have an international flavour.

Arrayanes Moroccan **€€**
(958 22 84 01; www.rest-arrayanes.com; Cuesta Marañas 4; mains €15; 1.30-4.30pm & 7.30-11.30pm Sun-Fri 1.30-4.30pm Sat;) The best Moroccan food in a city that is well known for its Moorish throwbacks? Recline on lavish patterned seating, try the rich, fruity tagine casseroles and make your decision. Note that Arrayanes does not serve alcohol.

La Botillería Tapas, Fusion **€€**
(958 22 49 28; Calle Varela 10; mains €13-20; 1pm-1am Wed-Sun, 1-8pm Mon) Establishing a good reputation for nouveau tapas, La Botillería is just around the corner from the legeandary La Tana bar, to which it has family connections. It's a more streamlined modern place than its cousin, where you can *tapear* (eat tapas) at the bar or sit down for the full monty Andalucían-style. The *solomillo* (pork tenderloin) comes in a rich, wine sauce.

Information

Provincial Tourist Office (www.turismodegranada.org; Plaza de Mariana Pineda 10; 9am-8pm Mon-Fri, 10am-7pm Sat, 10am-3pm Sun) Information on whole of Granada province.

Getting There & Away

The **train station** (☎958 24 02 02; Avenida de Andaluces) is 1.5km west of the centre. Trains run to/from Seville (€30, three hours, four daily), Ronda (€20, three hours, three daily), Algeciras (€30, 4½ hours, three daily), Madrid (€68, four to five hours, one or two daily), Valencia (€32, 7½ to eight hours, one daily) and Barcelona (€70, 12 hours, one daily).

SURVIVAL GUIDE

Directory A–Z

Accommodation

Budget options include everything from dorm-style youth hostels to family-style *pensiones* and slightly better-heeled *hostales*. At the upper end of this category you'll find rooms with air-conditioning and private bathrooms. Midrange *hostales* and hotels are more comfortable and most offer standard hotel services. Business hotels, trendy boutique hotels and luxury hotels are usually in the top-end category.

Price Ranges

Our reviews refer to double rooms with a private bathroom, except in hostels or where otherwise specified. Quoted rates are for high season, generally May to September (though this varies greatly from region to region).

€ less than €65 (less than €75 for Madrid/Barcelona)

€€ €65 to €140 (€75 to €200 for Madrid/Barcelona)

€€€ more than €140 (more than €200 for Madrid/Barcelona)

Business Hours

Banks 8.30am to 2pm Monday to Friday; some also open 4pm to 7pm Thursday and 9am to 1pm Saturday

Central post offices 8.30am to 9.30pm Monday to Friday, 8.30am to 2pm Saturday

Nightclubs Midnight or 1am to 5am or 6am

Restaurants Lunch 1pm to 4pm, dinner 8.30pm to midnight or later

Shops 10am to 2pm and 4.30pm to 7.30pm or 5pm to 8pm; big supermarkets and department stores generally open from 10am to 10pm Monday to Saturday

Food

Each eating review is accompanied by one of the following (the price relates to a main course):

€ less than €10

€€ €10 to €20

€€€ more than €20

Spices for sale, Granada (p346)

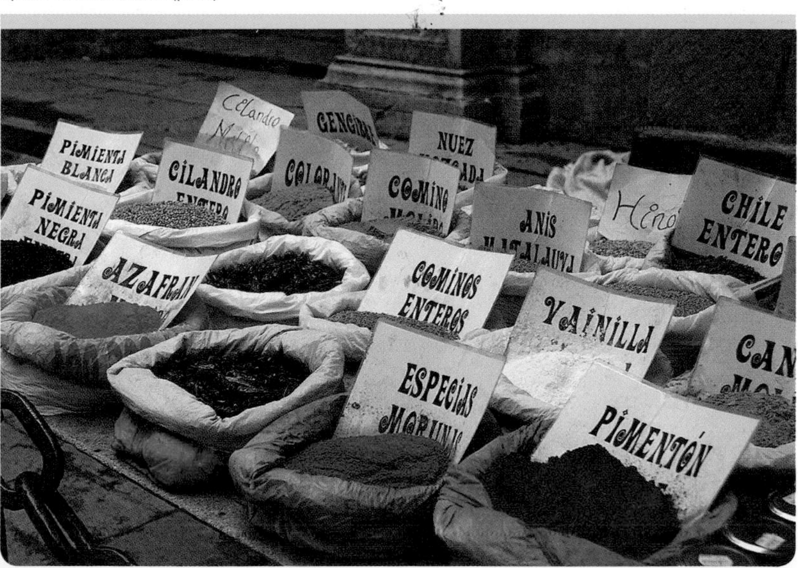

PHILIP LANGE/SHUTTERSTOCK ©

Right: Cafes in the old quarter, Valencia (p332); **Below:** Market stall selling fresh vegetables, Barcelona (p307)

Gay & Lesbian Travellers

Homosexuality is legal in Spain. In 2005 the Socialists gave the country's conservative Catholic foundations a shake with the legalisation of same-sex marriages in Spain.

Lesbians and gay men generally keep a fairly low profile, but are quite open in the cities. Madrid, Barcelona, Sitges, Torremolinos and Ibiza have particularly lively scenes.

Legal Matters

Drugs Cannabis is legal but only for personal use and in very small quantities. Public consumption of any drug is illegal.

Smoking Not permitted in any enclosed public space, including bars, restaurants and nightclubs.

Money

ATMs Many credit and debit cards can be used for withdrawing money from *cajeros automáticos* (automatic teller machines) that display the relevant symbols such as Visa, MasterCard, Cirrus.

Cash Most banks will exchange major foreign currencies and offer the best rates. Ask about commissions and take your passport.

Credit & debit cards Can be used to pay for most purchases. You'll often be asked to show your passport or some other form of identification, or to type in your pin. The most widely accepted cards are Visa and MasterCard.

Money changers Exchange offices, indicated by the word *cambio* (exchange), offer longer opening hours than banks, but worse exchange rates and higher commissions.

Taxes & refunds In Spain, value-added tax (VAT) is known as IVA (*ee*-ba; *impuesto sobre el valor añadido*). Visitors are entitled to a refund of the 18% IVA on purchases costing more than €90.16 from any shop if they are taking them out of the EU within three months.

Tipping Menu prices include a service charge. Most people leave some small change. Taxi drivers don't have to be tipped but a little rounding up won't go amiss.

Public Holidays

The two main periods when Spaniards go on holiday are Semana Santa (the week leading up to Easter Sunday) and July or August.

There are at least 14 official holidays a year, some observed nationwide, some locally. National holidays:

Año Nuevo (New Year's Day) 1 January

Viernes Santo (Good Friday) March/April

Fiesta del Trabajo (Labour Day) 1 May

La Asunción (Feast of the Assumption) 15 August

Fiesta Nacional de España (National Day) 12 October

La Inmaculada Concepción (Feast of the Immaculate Conception) 8 December

Navidad (Christmas) 25 December

Regional governments set five holidays and local councils two more. Common dates include the following:

Epifanía (Epiphany) or **Día de los Reyes Magos** (Three Kings' Day) 6 January

Día de San José (St Joseph's Day) 19 March

Jueves Santo (Good Thursday) March/April; not observed in Catalonia and Valencia

Corpus Christi June; the Thursday after the eighth Sunday after Easter Sunday

Día de San Juan Bautista (Feast of St John the Baptist) 24 June

Día de Santiago Apóstol (Feast of St James the Apostle) 25 July

Día de Todos los Santos (All Saints Day) 1 November

Día de la Constitución (Constitution Day) 6 December

Safe Travel

Most visitors to Spain never feel remotely threatened, but a sufficient number have unpleasant experiences to warrant an alert. The main thing to be wary of is petty theft (which may of course not seem so petty if your passport, cash, travellers cheques, credit card and camera go missing). What follows is intended as a strong warning rather than alarmism. In other words, be careful but don't be paranoid.

Common scams include the following:

- Kids crowding around you asking for directions or help.
- A person pointing out bird droppings on your shoulder (some substance their friend has sprinkled on you) – as they help clean it off they are probably emptying your pockets.
- The guys who tell you that you have a flat tyre. While your new friend and you check the tyre, his pal is emptying the car.
- The classic snatch-and-run. Never leave your purse, bag, wallet, mobile phone etc unattended or alone on a table.
- An old classic: the ladies offering flowers for good luck. We don't know how they do it, but your pockets always wind up empty.

Telephone

Blue public payphones are common and fairly easy to use. They accept coins, phonecards and, in some cases, credit cards. Phonecards come in €6 and €12 denominations and, like postage stamps, are sold at post offices and tobacconists.

International reverse-charge (collect) calls are simple to make: dial ☎900 99 followed by the appropriate code. For example: ☎900 99 00 61 for Australia, 900 99 00 44 for the UK, ☎900 99 00 11 (AT&T) for the USA etc.

To speak to an English-speaking Spanish international operator, dial 1008 (for calls within Europe) or 1005 (rest of the world).

Mobile Phones

All Spanish mobile-phone companies (Telefónica's MoviStar, Orange and Vodafone) offer *prepagado* (prepaid) accounts for mobiles. The SIM card costs from €50, which includes some prepaid phone time.

Mobile-phone numbers in Spain start with the number 6.

Phone Codes

Telephone codes in Spain are an integral part of the phone number. All numbers are nine digits and you just dial that nine-digit number.

Numbers starting with 900 are national toll-free numbers, while those starting 901 to 905 come with varying costs; most can only be dialled from within Spain. In a similar category are numbers starting with 800, 803, 806 and 807.

Tourist Information

All cities and many smaller towns have an *oficina de turismo* (tourist office).

Turespaña (www.spain.info) **Turespaña** is the country's national tourism body, and it operates branches around the world. Check the website for office locations.

High-speed train, Spain

QUINTANILLA/GETTY IMAGES ©

Transport from France

CAR & MOTORCYCLE

The main road crossing into Spain from France is the highway that links up with Spain's AP7 tollway, which runs down to Barcelona and follows the Spanish coast south (with a branch, the AP2, going to Madrid via Zaragoza). A series of links cut across the Pyrenees from France and Andorra into Spain, as does a coastal route that runs from Biarritz in France into the Spanish Basque Country.

TRAIN

The main rail lines into Spain cross the Franco–Spanish frontier along the Mediterranean coast and via the Basque Country. Another minor route runs inland across the Pyrenees from Latour-de-Carol to Barcelona.

TGV (high-speed) trains connect Paris Montparnasse with Irún, where you change to a normal train for the Basque Country and on towards Madrid. Up to three TGVs also put you on track to Barcelona (leaving from Paris Gare de Lyon), with a change at Montpellier or Narbonne.

The new high-speed rail link from Paris to Madrid has brought travel times down to an impressive eight hours.

Visas

Spain is one of 26 member countries of the Schengen Convention and Schengen visa rules apply.

Getting There & Away

Air

Flights from all over Europe, including numerous budget airlines, serve main Spanish airports. All of Spain's airports share the user-friendly website and flight information telephone number of Aena (**902 404704; www.aena.es**), the national airports authority.

Madrid's Aeropuerto de Barajas is Spain's busiest (and Europe's fifth-busiest) airport.

Land

Spain shares land borders with France, Portugal and Andorra.

In addition to the rail services connecting Spain with France and Portugal, there are direct trains between Zurich and Barcelona (via Bern, Geneva, Perpignan and Girona), and between Milan and Barcelona (via Turin, Perpignan and Girona). For these and other services, visit the website of Renfe (**for international trips 902 24 34 02; www.renfe.com**), the Spanish national railway company.

Sea

Ferries run to mainland Spain regularly from the Canary Islands, Italy, North Africa (Algeria, Morocco and the Spanish enclaves of Ceuta and Melilla) and the UK. Most services are run by the Spanish national ferry company, **Acciona Trasmediterránea** (**902 454645; www.trasmediterranea.es**).

Getting Around

Air

Air Europa (**www.aireuropa.com**) Madrid to Ibiza, Palma de Mallorca, Vigo, Bilbao and Barcelona as well as other routes between Spanish cities.

Iberia (**www.iberia.com**) Spain's national airline and its subsidiary, Iberia Regional-Air Nostrum, have an extensive domestic network.

Vueling (**www.vueling.com**) Spanish low-cost company with loads of domestic flights within Spain, especially from Barcelona.

Boat

Regular ferries connect the Spanish mainland with the Balearic Islands.

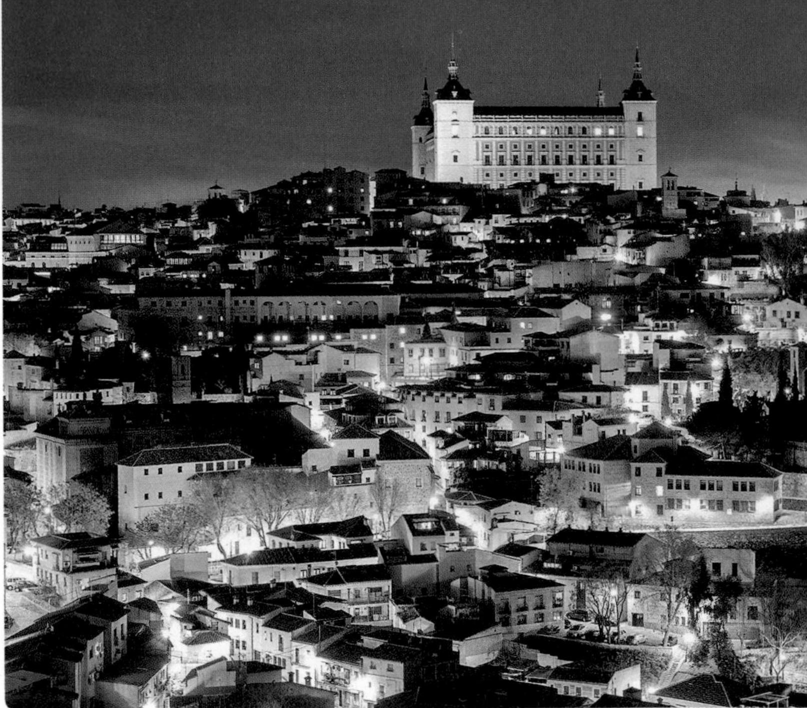

Bus

Spain's bus network is operated by countless independent companies, and reaches into the most remote towns and villages. Many towns and cities have one main station for arrivals and departures, which usually has an information desk. Tourist offices can also help with information on bus services.

ALSA (**902 422242; www.alsa.es**) The biggest player, this company has routes all over the country in association with various other companies.

Car & Motorcycle

Spain's roads vary but are generally good. Fastest are the *autopistas;* on some, you have to pay hefty tolls.

Every vehicle should display a nationality plate of its country of registration and you must always carry proof of ownership of a private vehicle. Third-party motor insurance is required throughout Europe. A warning triangle and a reflective jacket (to be used in case of breakdown) are compulsory.

Driving Licences

All EU member states' driving licences are recognised. Other foreign licences should be accompanied by an International Driving Permit (although in practice local licences are usually accepted). These are available from automobile clubs in your country and valid for 12 months.

Hire

To rent a car in Spain you have to have a licence, be aged 21 or over and have a credit or debit card. Rates vary widely: the best deals tend to be in major tourist areas, including airports. Prices are especially competitive in the Balearic Islands. Expect a compact car to cost from €30 and up per day.

Road Rules

Blood-alcohol limit 0.05%.

Legal driving age for cars Eighteen.

Legal driving age for motorcycles & scooters Sixteen (80cc and over) or fourteen (50cc and under). A licence is required.

Motorcyclists Must use headlights at all times and wear a helmet if riding a bike of 125cc or more.

Left: View of Toledo (p304); **Below:** Street scene, Seville (p335)
(LEFT) DANIEL VIÑÉ GARCIA/GETTY IMAGES ©; (BELOW) ZU SANCHEZ PHOTOGRAPHY/GETTY IMAGES ©

Side of the road Drive on the right.

Speed limits In built-up areas 50km/h (and in some cases, such as inner-city Barcelona, 30km/h), which increases to 100km/h on major roads and up to 120km/h on *autovías* and *autopistas* (toll-free and tolled dual-lane highways, respectively). Cars towing caravans are restricted to a maximum speed of 80km/h.

Train

Renfe (☎902 240202; www.renfe.es) is the national railway company. Trains are mostly modern and comfortable, and late arrivals are the exception rather than the rule. The high-speed network is in constant expansion.

Passes are valid for all long-distance Renfe trains; Inter-Rail users pay supplements on Talgo, InterCity and AVE trains.

All long-distance trains have 2nd and 1st classes, known as *turista* and *preferente*, respectively. The latter is 20% to 40% more expensive.

CLEMENS XII PONT MAX
AQVAM VIRGINEM
COPIA ET SALVBRITATE COMMENDATA
CVLTV MAGNIFICO ORNAVIT
ANNO DOMINI MDCCXXXV PONTIF VI

Italy

Italy, the land that has turned its lifestyle into a designer accessory, is one of Europe's great seducers. Ever since the days of the 18th-century Grand Tour, travellers have been falling under its spell, and still today it stirs strong emotions. The rush of seeing the Colosseum for the first time or cruising down Venice's surreal canals are experiences you'll remember for life.

Of course, Italy is not all about ancient ruins, Michelangelo masterpieces and frescoed churches. There's also the food, imitated the world over, and a landscape that boasts beautiful Alpine peaks, stunning coastlines and remote, silent valleys. So if the noise, heat and chaos of the cities start getting to you – as they do many locals – change gear and head out to the country and rural villages for a taste of the sun-kissed slow life.

Trevi Fountain (p379), Rome

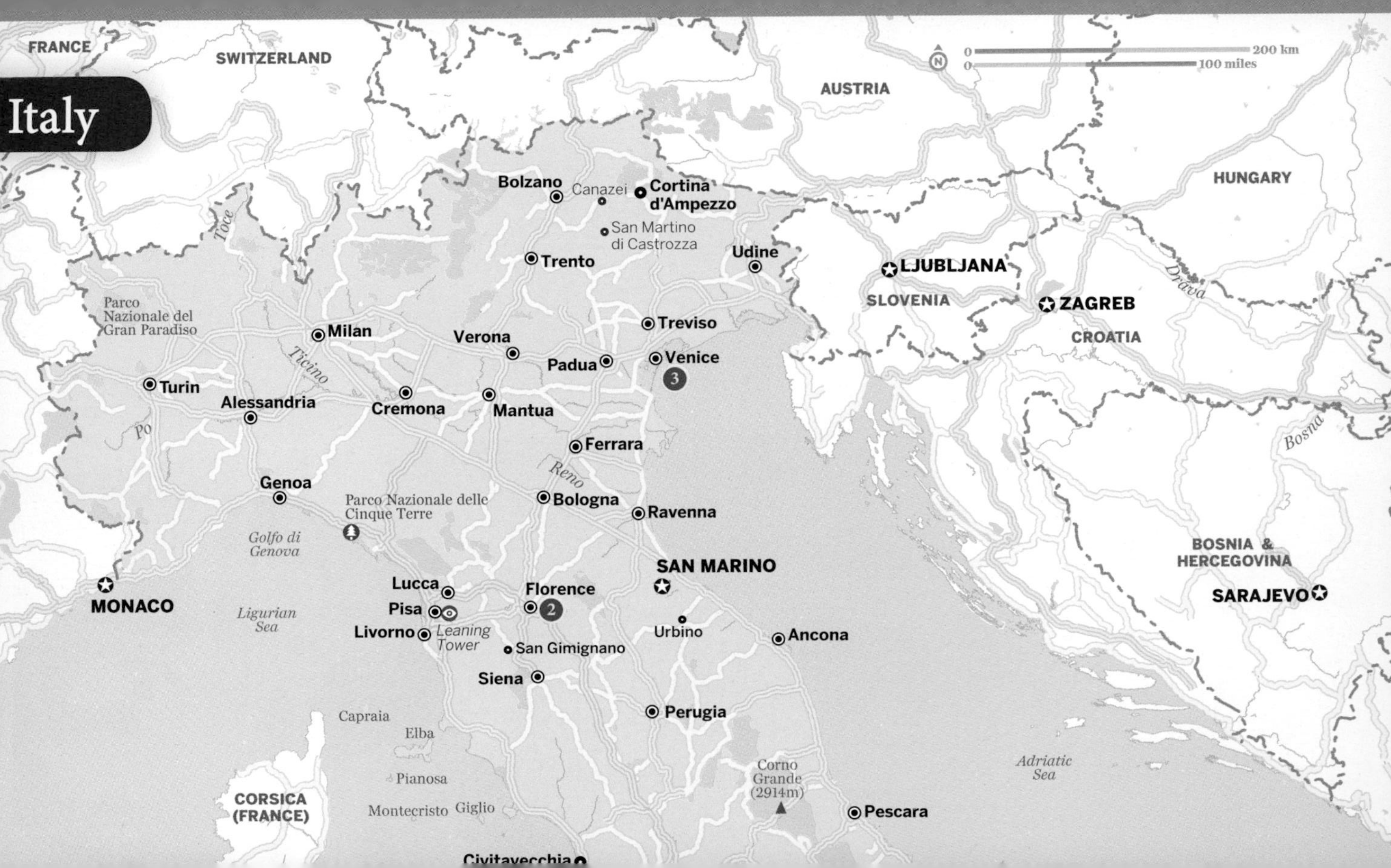
Italy
FRANCE
SWITZERLAND
AUSTRIA
HUNGARY
0 200 km
0 100 miles
Bolzano
Canazei
Cortina d'Ampezzo
San Martino di Castrozza
Trento
Udine
LJUBLJANA
SLOVENIA
ZAGREB
CROATIA
Drava
Toce
Parco Nazionale del Gran Paradiso
Milan
Verona
Treviso
Padua
Venice
3
Ticino
Turin
Alessandria
Cremona
Mantua
Po
Ferrara
Reno
Bosna
Genoa
Parco Nazionale delle Cinque Terre
Bologna
Ravenna
Golfo di Genova
BOSNIA & HERCEGOVINA
SAN MARINO
MONACO
Lucca
Florence
2
SARAJEVO
Pisa
Ligurian Sea
Livorno
Leaning Tower
San Gimignano
Urbino
Ancona
Siena
Perugia
Capraia
Elba
Adriatic Sea
Corno Grande (2914m)
Pianosa
CORSICA (FRANCE)
Montecristo
Giglio
Pescara
Civitavecchia

ROME
1
Fiumicino
Ostia Antica
Monte Cassino (1669m)
Parco Nazionale del Gargano
Îles Lavezzi
Golfo Aranci
Olbia
Porto Torres
Alghero
Bosa
Dorgali
Arbatax
SARDINIA
Cagliari
Palmarola
Ventotene
Tyrrhenian Sea
Naples
Pompeii
Herculaneum
Procida
Sorrento
Capri
Amalfi
4
5
Avellino
Bari
Matera
Brindisi
Taranto
Agri
Gallipoli
Golfo di Taranto
Parco Nazionale del Cilento e Vallo di Diano (Cilento National Park & the Valley of Diana)
Parco Nazionale del Pollino
Cosenza
Crotone
Catanzaro
AEOLIAN ISLANDS
Stromboli
Filicudi
Alicudi
Panarea
Lipari
Vulcano
Ustica
MEDITERRANEAN SEA
Messina
Reggio di Calabria
Ionian Sea
Palermo
Trapani
Taormina
Mt Etna (3340m)
SICILY
Catania
Agrigento
Syracuse
Golfo di Gela
Pantelleria
1 Colosseum
2 Florence
3 Venice's Canals
4 Pompeii
5 Amalfi Coast

Italy Highlights

Colosseum

Even before setting foot in this ancient stadium, most visitors are gobsmacked to find the Colosseum (p375) looming before them in all its glory as soon as they leave the metro station. Not only is this Roman arena impressive for its size and endurance, but its well-preserved condition makes for an unparalleled insight into the life of ancient Rome.

1

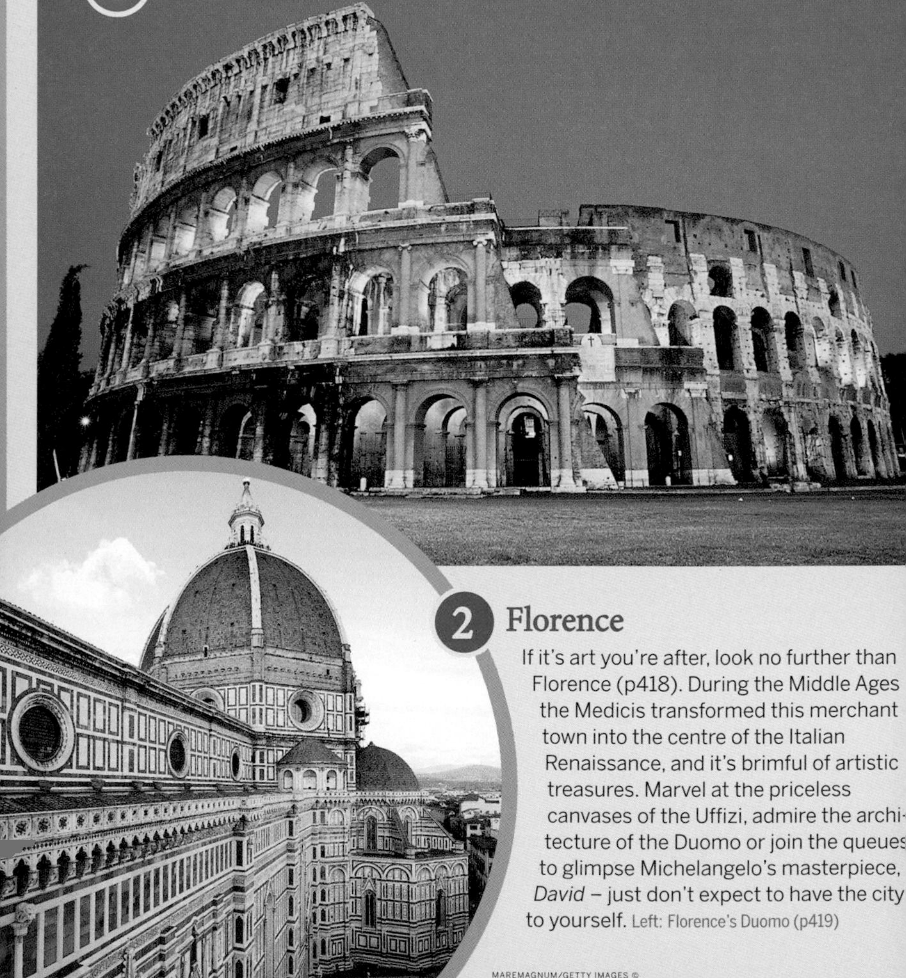

2 Florence

If it's art you're after, look no further than Florence (p418). During the Middle Ages the Medicis transformed this merchant town into the centre of the Italian Renaissance, and it's brimful of artistic treasures. Marvel at the priceless canvases of the Uffizi, admire the architecture of the Duomo or join the queues to glimpse Michelangelo's masterpiece, *David* – just don't expect to have the city to yourself. Left: Florence's Duomo (p419)

GLENN BEANLAND/GETTY IMAGES ©

3 Venice's Canals

What else is there to say about Venice (p401)? Quite simply, this is one of the world's unmissable cities, renowned for its glorious architecture, romantic canals, historic churches and stunning museums. Whether you're riding the gondolas, wandering the alleyways or joining the throngs in Piazza San Marco, you'll find it impossible not to fall head over heels for this Italian beauty.

GLENN BEANLAND/GETTY IMAGES ©

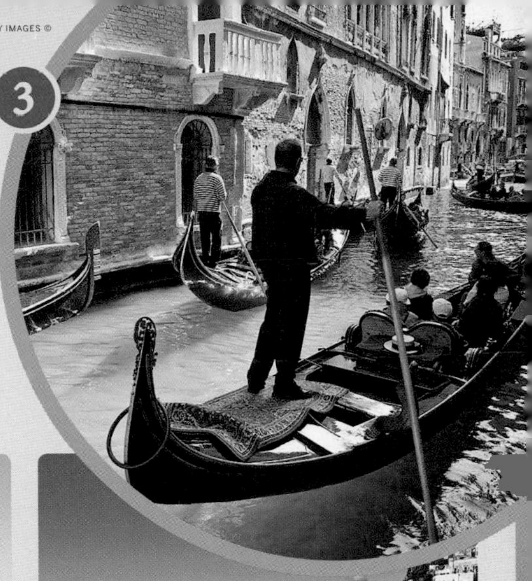

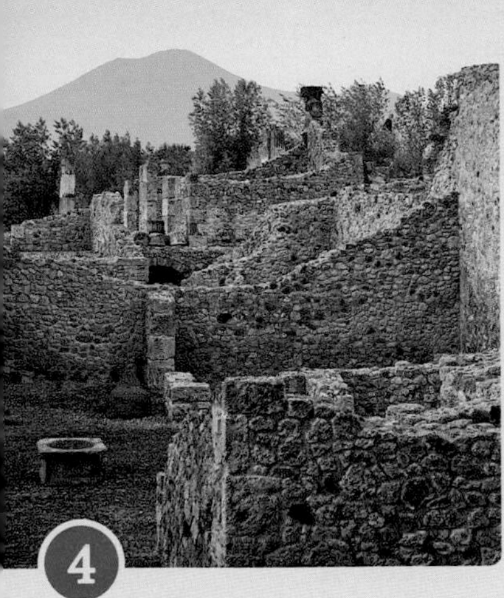

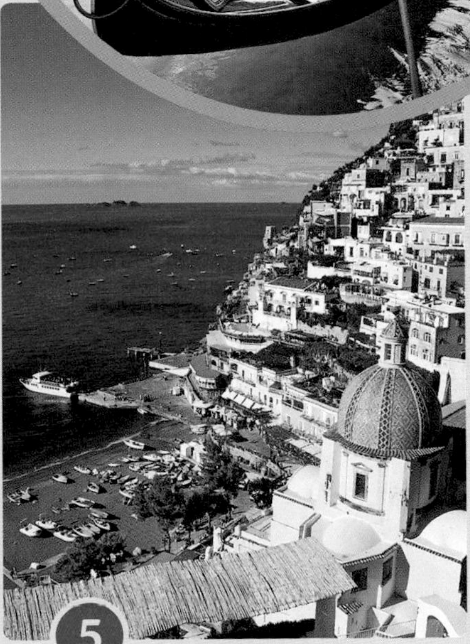

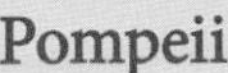

4 Pompeii

You know the story: 2000 years ago, the bustling town of Pompeii (p441) was devastated by a catastrophic eruption from Mt Vesuvius. But nothing can prepare you for the eerie experience of standing in Pompeii itself; the deserted streets and squares and spooky body casts bring a whole new meaning to the term 'ghost town'. It's an unmissable experience, and probably gives you a better insight into the reality of ancient Rome than anywhere else on earth.

5 Amalfi Coast

For a classic Italian road trip, nothing can hold a candle to the Amalfi Coast (p448). Stretching for 50km along the southern Sorrento Peninsula, this glittering coastline is one of the most beautiful spots in the Mediterranean – studded with sparkling beaches, secluded bays and cliffside towns. It's tailor-made for cruising with the top down… just watch out for those hairpin bends. Above: Positano (p448)

Italy's Best...

Artistic Treasures

- **David** (p426) Michelangelo's masterpiece in the Galleria dell'Accademia in Florence is a celebration of the human form.
- **Sistine Chapel** (p377) This incredible ceiling fresco needs no introduction.
- **St Peter's Basilica** (p374) Rome's most impressive architectural landmark.
- **Ravenna Mosaics** (p417) Amazing mosaics mentioned in Danté's *Divine Comedy*.
- **Galleria degli Uffizi** (p419) Famous Florence gallery crammed with Botticellis, da Vincis and Raphaels.

Roman Remains

- **Colosseum** (p375) See where the gladiators slugged it out.
- **Roman Forum** (p369) Stand in the heart of the Roman Republic.
- **Pompeii** (p441) Shiver at ancient horrors as you wander Italy's legendary ruined city.
- **Villa Adriana** (p383) Take a day trip from Rome to Hadrian's incredible weekend retreat.
- **Ostia Antica** (p383) Explore the quays of ancient Rome's port.

Festivals

- **Carnevale** (p409) Don your costume for Venice's crazy carnival.
- **Scoppio del Carro** (p426) Fireworks explode above Florence on Easter Sunday.
- **Il Palio** (p436) Siena's annual horse races are a lively spectacle.
- **Venice International Film Festival** (p409) Italy's most prestigious film festival brings big-name stars to the city.
- **Natale di Roma** (p384) Rome celebrates its birthday in style.

City Views

Leaning Tower of Pisa (p433) Where else?

Campanile, Florence (p424) Climb the Duomo's campanile for the quintessential Florence photo op.

Basilica di San Marco (p405) See Venice's Piazza San Marco from atop the basilica's bell tower.

Il Vittoriano (p374) Magnificent 360-degree views over Rome.

Torre degli Asinelli (p416) Gaze over Bologna's medieval rooftops.

Left: Copy of Michelangelo's *David*, Piazza della ...gnoria (p424), Florence; **Above:** Duomo (p432) and the Leaning Tower of Pisa (p433), Pisa

Need to Know

ADVANCE PLANNING

- **As early as possible** Book accommodation in Rome, Venice and Florence.
- **Two weeks before** Beat the queues by booking online for the Colosseum, the Vatican Museums, the Leaning Tower of Pisa and the Galleria degli Uffizi.
- **When you arrive** Pick up discount cards for Rome, Venice and Florence's museums.

RESOURCES

- **Italia** (www.italia.it) Inspiration, ideas and planning tips.
- **Trenitalia** (www.trenitalia.com) Plan your train trips.
- **Agriturismo** (www.agriturismo.com) Find the perfect Italian farm stay.
- **Turismo Roma** (www.turismoroma.it) Rome Tourist Board's website.
- **Coop Culture** (www.coopculture.it) Online booking for many museums and monuments.

GETTING AROUND

- **Air** Italy's largest airport is Leonardo da Vinci (aka Fiumicino) in Rome. International flights also serve Milan, Pisa, Venice, Florence and other main cities.
- **Train** Italy's main rail hubs are Rome, Milan Bologna and Venice. High-speed services operate on the main line from Milan to Rome/Naples via Bologna and Florence. Other routes operate local *regionale* or faster InterCity (IC) services.
- **Sea** Dozens of options to France, Spain and other Mediterranean destinations; main ports are in Genoa, Civitavecchia, Ancona, Naples and Bari.
- **Bus** Extensive, and often the only option to many rural areas.
- **Car** Autostradas (motorways) are quick but often charge a toll; regional roads are better for sightseeing.

BE FOREWARNED

- **Scams** Watch out for pickpockets and moped thieves in Rome, Florence and Venice, and count your change carefully.
- **Driving** Expect the unexpected – Italians have a notoriously relaxed attitude to road rules.
- **Prices** Prices for everything skyrocket during peak season and major holidays.

Italy Itineraries

Maybe it's the art, maybe it's the architecture or maybe it's just the atmosphere – but there's something about Italy that seems to get under your skin. Don't be surprised if you're smitten.

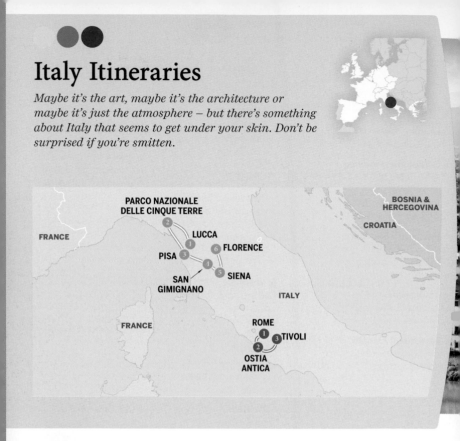

3 DAYS

ROME TO TIVOLI

Exploring Ancient Rome

Its empire may have long since sailed into the sunset, but there's still nowhere better to experience Italy at its passionate, pompous, pizza-spinning best than ❶**Rome** (p368). There are too many sights to squeeze into a couple of days, so you'll need to plan carefully. On day one, you could cover the Colosseum and the Roman Forum, followed by an early evening visit to the Pantheon, dinner at Casa Coppelle and a late-night wander around vibrant Trastevere. Devote day two to the Vatican, allowing time for St Peter's Basilica, the Vatican Museums and, of course, the jaw-dropping Sistine Chapel.

On day three, take a trip outside the city to see some of the other landmarks of ancient Rome. Spend the morning at the great port of ❷**Ostia Antica** (p383), where you can still see the ruins of restaurants, shops, houses and even the place where the Romans used to do their laundry. Then head up to Emperor Hadrian's lavish country retreat near ❸**Tivoli** (p383), the Villa Adriana, one of the best-preserved villas in Italy, and a fine example of the extravagant tastes of Rome's all-powerful emperors.

LUCCA TO FLORENCE
A Taste of Tuscany

If anywhere encapsulates the Italian character, it's Tuscany. This sunbaked corner of Italy is one of the country's most rewarding regions for culture vultures. ❶ **Lucca** (p438) makes a fine place to start thanks to its handsome centre, but even it can't hold a candle to the scenic splendour of ❷ **Parco Nazionale delle Cinque Terre** (p394), in the neighbouring region of Liguria. Spend a day exploring the national park before braving the crowds at ❸ **Pisa**'s (p433) punch-drunk tower.

On day four, swing south via one of Tuscany's heart-meltingly beautiful hilltop towns, ❹ **San Gimignano** (p437). From here it's a short drive to ❺ **Siena** (p434), renowned for its medieval buildings and fabulous restaurants. The annual horse race, Il Palio, takes over the town for two hectic days in July and August, but you'll need to book way ahead if you plan to join the party.

Complete your Tuscan trip in ❻ **Florence** (p418), a city that's brimming with artistic and architectural treasures. From landmark buildings such as the Duomo to the priceless artworks housed at the Uffizi and the Galleria dell'Accademia, Florence is a place where it's impossible not to feel inspired.

Florence (p418)
RICHARD I'ANSON/GETTY IMAGES ©

Discover Italy

At a Glance

- **Rome** (p368) Few cities have more history and chutzpah than the Italian capital.
- **Northern Italy** (p394) Italy's affluent north: from stately cities to cliff-top towns.
- **Tuscany** (p418) Home to Italy's artistic and cultural highlights.
- **Southern Italy** (p440) Hot, fiery, chaotic and quintessentially Italian.

Piazza Navona (p375), Rome
P. EOCHE/GETTY IMAGES ©

ROME

POP 2.86 MILLION

Even in this country of exquisite cities, Rome is special. Pulsating, seductive and utterly disarming, the Italian capital is an epic, monumental metropolis that will steal your heart and haunt your soul. They say a lifetime's not enough *(Roma, non basta una vita),* but even on a short visit you'll be swept off your feet by its artistic and architectural masterpieces, its operatic piazzas, romantic corners and cobbled lanes.

History

According to legend, Rome was founded by Romulus and Remus in 753 BC. Historians debate this, but archaeological evidence has confirmed the existence of a settlement on the Palatine Hill in that period.

The city was originally ruled by a king, but in 509 BC the Roman Republic was founded. Over the next five centuries the Republic flourished, growing to become the dominant force in the Western world. The end came in the 1st century BC when internal rivalries led to the murder of Julius Caesar in 44 BC and the outbreak of civil war between Octavian and Mark Antony. Octavian emerged victorious and was made Rome's first emperor with the title Augustus.

The Roman Empire thrived and by about AD 100 Rome was the undisputed *caput mundi* (capital of the world). But within 375 years, the Empire had fallen and Rome was routed by the invading Vandals.

Christianity had been spreading since the 1st century AD, and under Constantine it received official recognition. Pope Gregory I (590–604) did much to strengthen the

Church's grip over the city, laying the foundations for its later role as capital of the Catholic Church.

Under the Renaissance popes of the 15th and 16th centuries, Rome was given an extensive facelift.

By the 17th century Rome needed rebuilding, and turned to baroque masters Bernini and Borromini. With their exuberant churches, fountains and *palazzi* (palaces), these two bitter rivals changed the face of the city.

Sights

Most of Rome's sights are concentrated in the area between Stazione Termini and the Vatican. Halfway between the two, the Pantheon and Piazza Navona lie at the heart of the *centro storico* (historic cente), while to the southeast, the Colosseum lords it over the city's ancient core.

A sightseeing and transport card, the **Roma Pass** comes in two forms: the **Classic Pass** (€36; valid for three days) provides free admission to two museums or sites, as well as reduced entry to extra sites, unlimited city transport, and discounted entry to other exhibitions and events; the **48-hour Pass** (€28; valid for 48 hours) gives free admission to one museum or site and then as per the classic pass. Both are available online, from tourist information points or participating museums.

ANCIENT ROME

Palatino Archaeological Site

(Palatine Hill; Map p378; ☎06 3996 7700; www.coopculture.it; Via di San Gregorio 30 & Via Sacra; adult/reduced incl Colosseum & Roman Forum €12/7.50; ⏱8.30am-1hr before sunset; Ⓜ Colosseo) Sandwiched between the Roman Forum and the Circo Massimo, the Palatino (Palatine Hill) is an atmospheric area of towering pine trees, majestic ruins and memorable views. It was here that Romulus supposedly founded the city in 753 BC, and Rome's emperors lived in unabashed luxury. Look out for the stadio (stadium), the ruins of the Domus Flavia (the imperial palace), and the grandstand views over the Roman Forum from the **Orti Farnesiani**.

Roman Forum Archaeological Site

(Foro Romano; Map p378; ☎06 3996 7700; www.coopculture.it; Largo della Salara Vecchia & Via Sacra; adult/reduced incl Colosseum & Palatino €12/7.50; ⏱8.30am-1hr before sunset; 🚌Via dei Fori Imperiali) Nowadays an impressive – if rather confusing – sprawl of ruins, the Roman Forum was ancient Rome's showpiece centre, a grandiose district of temples, basilicas and vibrant public spaces. The site, which was originally an Etruscan burial ground, was first developed in the 7th century BC, growing over time to become the social, political and commercial hub of the Roman Empire. Landmark sights include the **Arco di Settimio Severo** (Arch of Septimius Severus) the **Curia**, and the **Casa delle Vestali** (House of the Vestal Virgins).

Piazza del Campidoglio Piazza

(Map p378; 🚌Piazza Venezia) Designed by Michelangelo in 1538, this is one of Rome's most beautiful piazzas. You can reach it from the Roman Forum, but the most dramatic approach is via the **Cordonata (Map p378)**, the graceful staircase that leads up from Piazza d'Ara Coeli.

The piazza is flanked by **Palazzo Nuovo** and **Palazzo dei Conservatori,** together home to the Capitoline Museums, and **Palazzo Senatorio**, seat of Rome's city council. In the centre is a copy of an equestrian **statue** of Marcus Aurelius.

Capitoline Museums Museum

(Musei Capitolini; Map p378; ☎06 06 08; www.museicapitolini.org; Piazza del Campidoglio 1; adult/reduced €11.50/9.50; ⏱9.30am-7.30pm, last admission 6.30pm; 🚌Piazza Venezia) Dating to 1471, the Capitoline Museums are the world's oldest national museums. Their collection of classical sculpture is one of Italy's finest, including crowd-pleasers such as the iconic *Lupa capitolina* (Capitoline Wolf), a sculpture of Romulus and Remus under a wolf, and the *Galata morente* (Dying Gaul). There's also a formidable picture gallery with masterpieces by the likes of Titian, Tintoretto, Van Dyck, Rubens and Caravaggio.

Roman Forum

In ancient times, a forum was a market place, civic centre and religious complex all rolled into one, and the greatest of all was the Roman Forum (Foro Romano). Situated between the Palatino (Palatine Hill), ancient Rome's most exclusive neighbourhood, and the Campidoglio (Capitoline Hill), it was the city's busy, bustling centre. On any given day it teemed with activity. Senators debated affairs of state in the **Curia** ❶ shoppers thronged the squares and traffic-free streets, crowds gathered under the **Colonna di Foca** ❷, to listen to politicians holding forth from the **Rostrum** ❸. Elsewhere, lawyers worked the courts in basilicas including the **Basilica di Massenzio** ❸, while the Vestal Virgins quietly went about their business in the **Casa delle Vestali** ❹.

Special occasions were also celebrated in the Forum: religious holidays were marked with ceremonies at temples such as the **Tempio di Saturno** ❺ and the Tempio di **Castore e Polluce** ❻, and military victories were honoured with dramatic processions up Via Sacra and the building of monumental arches like the Arco di **Settimio Severo** ❼ and the **Arco di Tito** ❽.

The ruins you see today are impressive but they can be confusing without a clear picture of what the Forum once looked like. This spread shows the Forum in its heyday, complete with temples, civic buildings and towering monuments to heroes of the Roman Empire.

TOP TIPS

» Get grandstand views of the Forum from the Palatino and Campidoglio.

» Visit first thing in the morning or late afternoon; crowds are worst between 11am and 2pm.

» In summer it gets hot in the Forum and there's little shade, so take a hat and plenty of water.

Campidoglio (Capitoline Hill)

Colonna di Foca & Rostrum

The free-standing, 13.5m-high Column of Phocus is the Forum's youngest monument, dating to AD 608. Behind it, the Rostrum provided a suitably grandiose platform for pontificating public speakers.

5

ADMISSION

Although valid for two days, admission tickets only allow for one entry into the Forum, Colosseum and Palatino.

Tempio di Saturno

Ancient Rome's Fort Knox, the Temple of Saturn was the city treasury. In Caesar's day it housed 13 tonnes of gold, 114 tonnes of silver and 30 million sestertii worth of silver coins.

Tempio di Castore e Polluce

Only three columns of the Temple of Castor and Pollux remain. The temple was dedicated to the Heavenly Twins after they supposedly led the Romans to victory over the Etruscans.

LONELY PLANET/GETTY IMAGES ©

Arco di Settimio Severo
One of the Forum's signature monuments, this imposing triumphal arch commemorates the military victories of Septimius Severus. Relief panels depict his campaigns against the Parthians.

Curia
This big barnlike building was the official seat of the Roman Senate. Most of what you see is a reconstruction, but the interior marble floor dates to the 3rd-century reign of Diocletian.

DUNCAN GARWOOD ©

Basilica di Massenzio
Marvel at the scale of this vast 4th-century basilica. In its original form the central hall was divided into enormous naves; now only part of the northern nave survives.

JULIUS CASEAR
Julius Caesar was cremated on the site where the Tempio di Giulio Cesare now stands.

1 7 2 3 6 4 8

Via Sacra

Tempio di Giulio Cesare

Casa delle Vestali
White statues line the grassy atrium of what was once the luxurious 50-room home of the Vestal Virgins. The virgins played an important role in Roman religion, serving the goddess Vesta.

LONELY PLANET/GETTY IMAGES ©

Arco di Tito
Said to be the inspiration for the Arc de Triomphe in Paris, the well-preserved Arch of Titus was built by the emperor Domitian to honour his elder brother Titus.

DUNCAN GARWOOD ©

Greater Rome

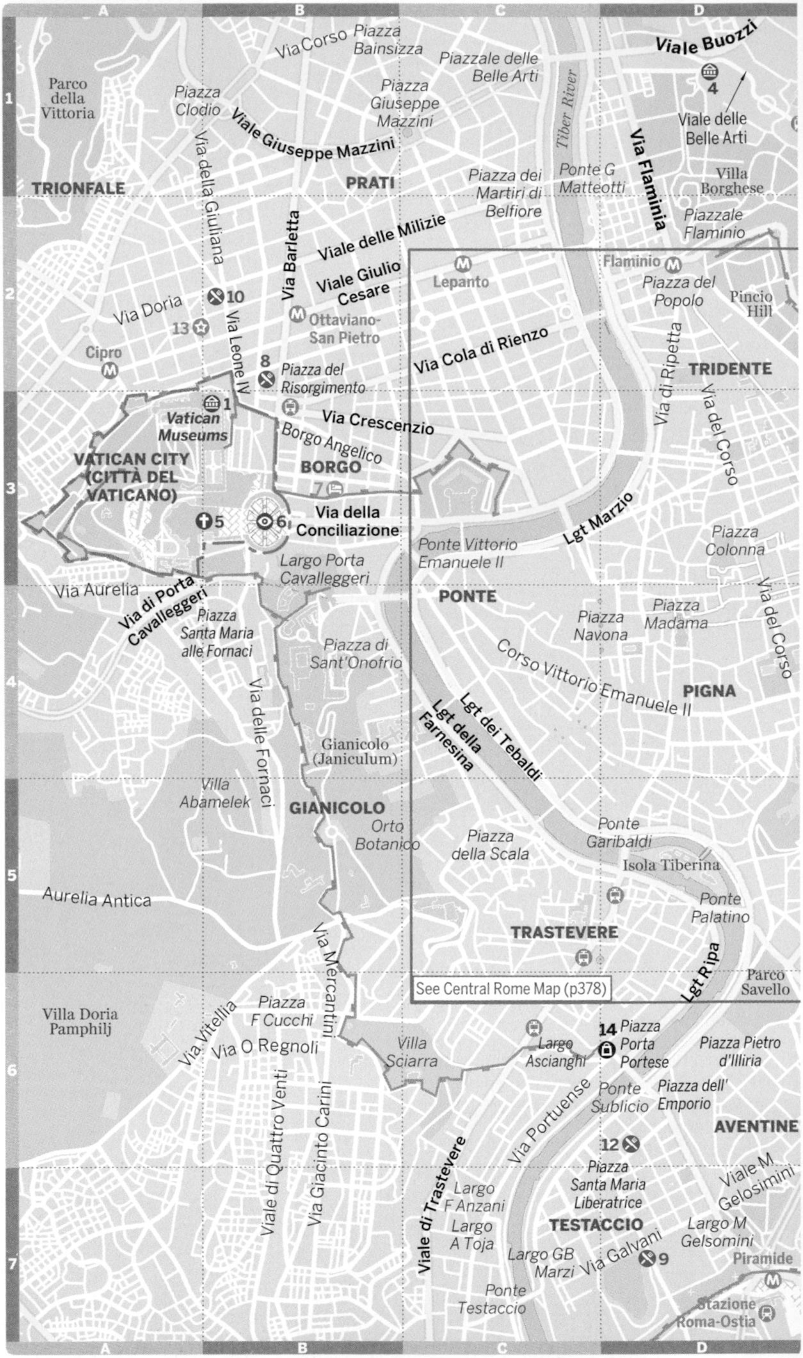

A B C D

1 2 3 4 5 6 7

Via Corso
Piazza Bainsizza
Piazzale delle Belle Arti
Viale Buozzi
4
Parco della Vittoria
Piazza Clodio
Viale Giuseppe Mazzini
Piazza Giuseppe Mazzini
Tiber River
Viale delle Belle Arti
Via della Giuliana
Via Flaminia
Villa Borghese
TRIONFALE
PRATI
Piazza dei Martiri di Belfiore
Ponte G Matteotti
Piazzale Flaminio
Via Barletta
Viale delle Milizie
Viale Giulio Cesare
Lepanto
Flaminio
Piazza del Popolo
Pincio Hill
Via Doria
10
13
Via Leone IV
Ottaviano-San Pietro
Cipro
8
Piazza del Risorgimento
Via Cola di Rienzo
Via di Ripetta
TRIDENTE
1
Vatican Museums
Via Crescenzio
Via del Corso
Borgo Angelico
VATICAN CITY (CITTÀ DEL VATICANO)
BORGO
7
5
6
Via della Conciliazione
Lgt Marzio
Piazza Colonna
Ponte Vittorio Emanuele II
Largo Porta Cavalleggeri
Via Aurelia
Via di Porta Cavalleggeri
PONTE
Piazza Santa Maria alle Fornaci
Piazza Navona
Piazza Madama
Via del Corso
Piazza di Sant'Onofrio
Corso Vittorio Emanuele II
Via delle Fornaci
PIGNA
Lgt della Farnesina
Lgt dei Tebaldi
Gianicolo (Janiculum)
Villa Abamelek
GIANICOLO
Orto Botanico
Piazza della Scala
Ponte Garibaldi
Isola Tiberina
Aurelia Antica
Ponte Palatino
TRASTEVERE
Via Mercantini
Lgt Ripa
Parco Savello
See Central Rome Map (p378)
Villa Doria Pamphilj
Piazza F Cucchi
Via Vitellia
Via O Regnoli
Villa Sciarra
Largo Ascianghi
14 Piazza Porta Portese
Piazza Pietro d'Illiria
Via Portuense
Ponte Sublicio
Piazza dell' Emporio
Viale di Quattro Venti
Via Giacinto Carini
AVENTINE
12
Viale di Trastevere
Piazza Santa Maria Liberatrice
Viale M Gelosimini
Largo F Anzani
Largo A Toja
TESTACCIO
Largo M Gelsomini
Largo GB Marzi
Via Galvani
9
Piramide
Ponte Testaccio
Stazione Roma-Ostia

0 1 km
0 0.5 miles
Via Ulisse Aldrovandi
Piazzale Scipione Borghese
Viale dell'Uccelliera
Piazzale del Museo Borghese
Largo Aqua Felix
Piazza di Siena
3
VILLA BORGHESE
Viale del Museo Borghese
Galoppatoio
Via Savoia
SALARIO
Viale Regina Margherita
Corso Trieste
Via Nomentana
Piazza Salerno
Piazza Galeno
Piazza Porta Pia
Villa Medici
SALLUSTIANO
Porta Pia
Viale del Policlinico
Policlinico
Castro Pretorio
Viale del Policlinico
Viale Regina Elena
Spagna
Via Sistina
Via XX Settembre
TREVI
Barberini
Via del Tritone
Repubblica
Viale dell' Università
Autostazione Tiburtina (300m); Stazione Tiburtina (400m)
Viale P Gobetti
Giardino del Quirinale
Quirinale
Via Torino
Termini
Piazza dei Cinquecento
Stazione Termini
Via della Pilotta
Via Nazionale
Via Tiburtina
Piazza Santa Maria Maggiore
Via Giovanni Giolitti
Piazza dei Siculi
Via dei Volsci
Via Panisperna
Vittorio Emanuele
Via Giovanni Lanza
Cavour
SAN LORENZO
Via dei Fori Imperiali
Via Merulana
Via di Porta Maggiore
Roman Forum
Colosseo
Parco del Colle Oppio
Piazza del Colosseo
Manzoni
Via di San Giovanni in Laterano
Via Statilia
Piazza di Porta Maggiore
Palatino
Parco del Celio
Via dei Cerchi
Viale Carlo Felice
Piazza di SS Giovanni E Paolo
SAN GIOVANNI
2
Via La Spezia
TUSCOLANO
Via dell'Amba Aradam
Villa Celimontana
San Giovanni
Via Appia Nuova
Via Magna Grecia
Aventine Hill
Circo Massimo
CELIAN HILL
Via Aosta
Viale Aventino
11
Via Druso
Re di Roma
Viale Metronio
Via Appia Nuova
Piazza Gian Lorenzo Bernini
Viale Guido
Viale delle Terme di Caracalla
Piazza Epiro
Via Britannia
Ponte Lungo
Parco San Sebastiano
Piazzale Ostiense
Via Appia Antica (1km)
ITALY ROME

Greater Rome

Don't Miss Sights
1 Vatican Museums B3

Sights
2 Basilica di San Giovanni in Laterano G6
3 Museo e Galleria Borghese F1
4 Museo Nazionale Etrusco di Villa Giulia D1
5 St Peter's Basilica B3
6 St Peter's Square B3

Sleeping
7 Hotel Bramante B3

Eating
8 Fa-Bìo B2
9 Flavio al Velavevodetto D7
10 Hostaria Dino e Tony B2
11 Il Gelato E6
12 Pizzeria Da Remo D6

Entertainment
13 Alexanderplatz A2

Shopping
14 Porta Portese Market D6

Il Vittoriano Monument
(Map p378; Piazza Venezia; 9.30am-5.30pm summer, to 4.30pm winter; Piazza Venezia) FREE Love it or loathe it, as most locals do, you can't ignore Il Vittoriano (aka the Altare della Patria; Altar of the Fatherland), the mountain of white marble overlooking Piazza Venezia. Begun in 1885 to honour Italy's first king, Victor Emmanuel II, it incorporates the **Museo Centrale del Risorgimento** (www.risorgimento.it; adult/reduced €5/2.50; 9.30am-6.30pm, closed 1st Mon of month), a museum documenting Italian unification, and the **Tomb of the Unknown Soldier**.

For Rome's best 360-degree views, take the **Roma dal Cielo** (adult/reduced €7/3.50; 9.30am-6.30pm Mon-Thu, to 7.30pm Fri-Sun) lift to the top.

Bocca della Verità Monument
(Mouth of Truth; Map p378; Piazza Bocca della Verità 18; donation €0.50; 9.30am-5.50pm summer, to 4.50pm winter; Piazza Bocca della Verità) A round piece of marble that was once part of a fountain, or possibly an ancient manhole cover, the Bocca della Verità (Mouth of Truth) is one of Rome's most popular curiosities. Legend has it that if you put your hand in the carved mouth and tell a lie, it will bite your hand off. The mouth lives in the portico of the **Chiesa di Santa Maria in Cosmedin**, a beautiful medieval church.

THE VATICAN

The world's smallest sovereign state (it covers just 0.44 sq km), the Vatican is the modern vestige of the Papal States, the papal empire that encompassed Rome and much of central Italy until Italian unification in 1861. It was formally established under the terms of the 1929 Lateran Treaty, signed by Mussolini and Pope Pius XI.

St Peter's Basilica Basilica
(Basilica di San Pietro; Map p372; www.vatican.va; St Peter's Sq; 7am-7pm summer, to 6.30pm winter; M Ottaviano-San Pietro) FREE In this city of outstanding churches, none can hold a candle to the Basilica di San Pietro, Italy's most spectacular cathedral. Built atop an earlier 4th-century church, it was completed in 1626 after 150 years of construction. It contains many spectacular works of art, including three of Italy's most celebrated masterpieces: Michelangelo's *Pietà*, his soaring dome, and Bernini's 29m-high baldachin (canopy)over the papal altar.
Note that the basilica attracts up to 20,000 people on a busy day, so expect queues in peak periods.

St Peter's Square Piazza
(Piazza San Pietro; Map p372; M Ottaviano-San Pietro) Overlooked by St Peter's Basilica, the Vatican's central square was laid out between 1656 and 1667 to a design by baroque artist Gian Lorenzo Bernini. Seen from above, it resembles a giant keyhole with two semicircular colonnades, each consisting of four rows of Doric columns, encircling a giant ellipse that straightens out to funnel believers into the basilica. The effect was deliberate – Bernini described the colonnades as representing 'the motherly arms of the church'.

MATTEO COLOMBO/GETTY IMAGES ©

Don't Miss Colosseum

Rome's great gladiatorial arena is the most thrilling of the city's ancient sights. Inaugurated in AD 80, the 50,000-seat Colosseum, originally known as the Flavian Amphitheatre, was clad in travertine and covered by a huge canvas awning held aloft by 240 masts. Inside, tiered seating encircled the arena, itself built over an underground complex (the hypogeum) where animals were caged and stage sets prepared. Games involved gladiators fighting wild animals or each other.

NEED TO KNOW

Colosseo; Map p378; ☎06 3996 7700; www.coopculture.it; Piazza del Colosseo; adult/reduced incl Roman Forum & Palatino €12/7.50; ⏰8.30am-1hr before sunset; Ⓜ Colosseo

HISTORIC CENTRE

Pantheon — Church

(Map p378; Piazza della Rotonda; ⏰8.30am-7.30pm Mon-Sat, 9am-6pm Sun; 🚌Largo di Torre Argentina) FREE A striking 2000-year-old temple, now church, the Pantheon is the best preserved of Rome's ancient monuments, and one of the most influential buildings in the Western world. Built by Hadrian over Marcus Agrippa's earlier 27 BC temple, it has stood since AD 120, and although its greying, pockmarked exterior is looking its age, it's still an exhilarating experience to pass through its vast bronze doors and gaze up at the largest unreinforced concrete dome ever built.

Piazza Navona — Piazza

(Map p378; 🚌Corso del Rinascimento) With its ornate fountains, baroque *palazzi* (mansions) and colourful cast of street artists, hawkers and tourists, Piazza Navona is central Rome's showcase square. Built over the 1st-century Stadio di Domiziano (Domitian's Stadium), it was paved over in the 15th century and for almost 300 years hosted the city's main market. Its

(Continued on page 379)

Don't Miss
Vatican Museums

With some 7km of exhibitions and more masterpieces than many small countries, this vast museum complex, housed in the 5.5-hectare Palazzo Apostolico Vaticano, contains one of the world's greatest art collections.

Musei Vaticani

Map p372

06 6988 4676

http://mv.vatican.va

Viale Vaticano

adult/reduced €16/8, last Sun of month free

9am-4pm Mon-Sat, 9am-12.30pm last Sun of month

M Ottaviano-San Pietro

Pinacoteca

The papal picture gallery boasts some 460 paintings with works by Giotto, Fra Angelico, Filippo Lippi, Guido Reni, Guercino, Nicholas Poussin, Van Dyck and Pietro da Cortona. Look out for Raphael's *Madonna di Foligno* (Madonna of Folignano) and his last painting, *La Trasfigurazione* (Transfiguration), which was completed by his students after his death.

Museo Pio-Clementino

This spectacular museum contains some of the Vatican Museums' finest classical statuary. Many pieces are to be found in in the **Cortile Ottagono** (Octagonal Courtyard), including the *Apollo Belvedere*, one of the great masterpieces of classical sculpture, and the 1st-century *Laocoön* (pictured left). Another must-see is the *Torso Belvedere* in the **Sala delle Muse**.

Stanze di Raffaello

Even in the shadow of the Sistine Chapel, the Raphael Rooms stand out. These four chambers were part of Pope Julius II's private apartment and in 1508 he commissioned the relatively unknown 25-year-old Raphael to decorate them. Of the resulting frescoes, the most celebrated is *La Scuola di Atene* (The School of Athens) in the **Stanza della Segnatura**.

Sistine Chapel

The chapel where the papal conclave meets to elect a new pope, the Cappella Sistina is home to two of the world's most famous works of art: Michelangelo's ceiling frescoes and his *Giudizio Universale* (*Last Judgment*). The 800-sq-metre ceiling design, painted between 1508 and 1512, is centred on nine central panels depicting the Creation, Adam and Eve, the Fall, and the plight of Noah. On the west wall, the *Giudizio Universale* shows Christ passing sentence over the souls of the dead as they are torn from their graves.

Local Knowledge

Vatican Museums

BY SILVIA PROSPERI, TOUR GUIDE

1 CORTILE OTTAGONO (OCTAGONAL COURTYARD)

This used to be an orange-tree garden for the guests of Pope Julius II. It is decorated with masterpieces of Greek-Roman classical art, such as the *Laocoön*, *Apollo*, *Venus* and *Hermes*. These spectacular statues inspired Renaissance artists such as Michelangelo and Raffaello.

2 PAINTING GALLERY

This shows the evolution of Italian art from Giotto to Caravaggio and beyond. The fragments of the fresco *Christ in Glory Between Angels and Apostles* by Melozzo da Forlì represent an incredible rescue – they were saved when the apse of the Church SS Apostoli was demolished, and are a true example of angelic beauty.

3 STANZE DI RAFFAELLO

In the Raphael Rooms, look carefully at the *Liberation of St Peter* in the Heliodorus Room. This was proof of the great talent of the young Raphael, who had just arrived in Rome, as night scenes with different sources of light are particularly hard to realise in fresco.

4 SISTINE CHAPEL

The entire chapel is overwhelming and captivating, and it is impossible to pick the best of thousands of characters, all defined in intricate detail. However, the Lybian Sybil is amazing evidence of Michelangelo's development over five years working on the chapel: the transparent veil over the sybil's legs, the brilliance of her orange dress, and the feminine twist of her body all show the touch of a genius.

5 MUSEO GREGORIANO PROFANO

The mosaic of the 'unswept floor' (which includes a little mouse nibbling leftovers!) is a good example of the level of perfection reached by the Greek-Roman artists in this art form.

Central Rome

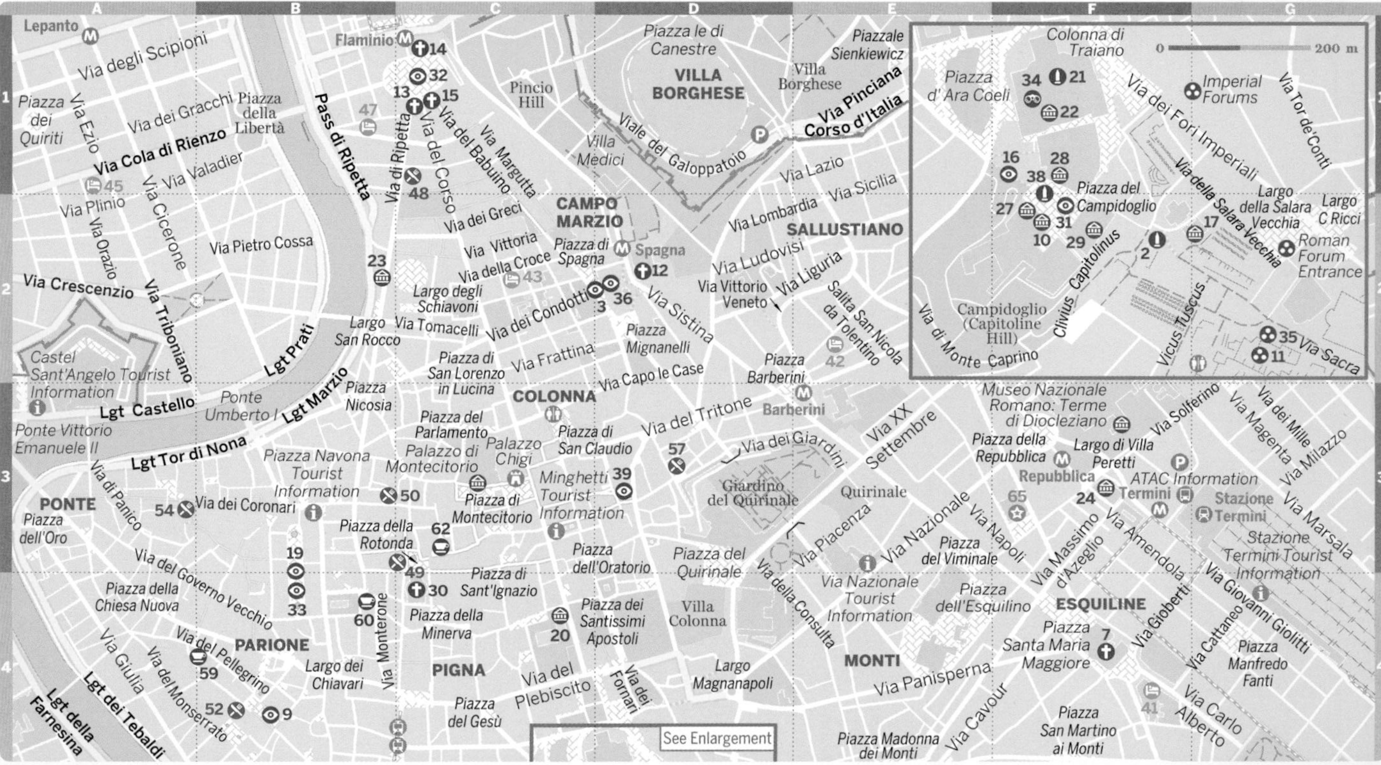

(Continued from page 375)

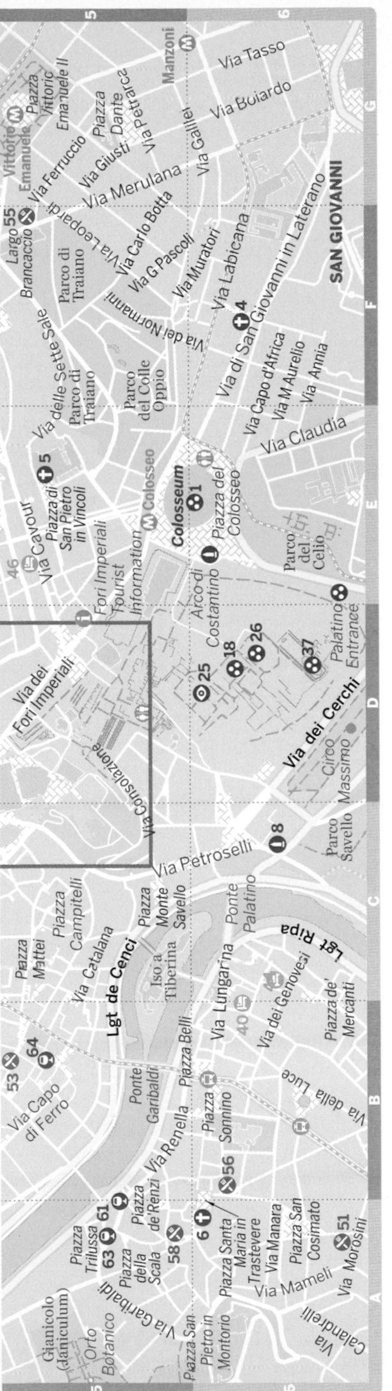

grand centrepiece, Bernini's **Fontana dei Quattro Fiumi** (Fountain of the Four Rivers), is an ornate, showy work depicting personifications of the rivers Nile, Ganges, Danube and Plate.

Campo de' Fiori — Piazza

(Map p378; Corso Vittorio Emanuele II) Noisy, colourful 'Il Campo' is a major focus of Roman life: by day it hosts a much-loved market, while at night it morphs into a raucous open-air pub. For centuries it was the site of public executions, and it was here that philosopher monk Giordano Bruno was burned at the stake for heresy in 1600. The spot is today marked by a sinister statue of the hooded monk, created by Ettore Ferrari and unveiled in 1889.

Galleria Doria Pamphilj — Gallery

(Map p378; 06 679 73 23; www.dopart.it; Via del Corso 305; adult/reduced €11/7.50; 9am-7pm, last admission 6pm; Via del Corso) Hidden behind the grimy grey exterior of Palazzo Doria Pamphilj, this wonderful gallery boasts one of Rome's richest private art collections, with works by Raphael, Tintoretto, Brueghel, Titian, Caravaggio, Bernini and Velázquez. Masterpieces abound, but the undisputed star is Velázquez' portrait of an implacable Pope Innocent X, who grumbled that the depiction was 'too real'. Compare it with Gian Lorenzo Bernini's sculptural interpretation of the same subject.

Trevi Fountain — Fountain

(Fontana di Trevi; Map p378; Piazza di Trevi; M Barberini) The Fontana di Trevi, scene of Anita Ekberg's dip in *La Dolce Vita*, is Rome's largest and most famous fountain. A flamboyant baroque ensemble of mythical figures, wild horses and cascading rock falls, it takes up the entire side of the 17th-century Palazzo Poli.

The famous tradition is to toss a coin into the water, thus ensuring that one day you'll return to the Eternal City. On average about €3000 is thrown in every day.

Central Rome

Don't Miss Sights
1 Colosseum ... E6

Sights
2 Arco di Settimio Severo ... F2
3 Barcaccia ... D2
4 Basilica di San Clemente ... F6
5 Basilica di San Pietro in Vincoli ... E5
6 Basilica di Santa Maria in Trastevere ... A6
7 Basilica di Santa Maria Maggiore ... F4
8 Bocca della Verità ... C6
9 Campo de' Fiori ... B4
10 Capitoline Museums ... F2
11 Casa delle Vestali ... G2
12 Chiesa della Trinità dei Monti ... D2
13 Chiesa di Santa Maria dei Miracoli ... C1
14 Chiesa di Santa Maria del Popolo ... C1
15 Chiesa di Santa Maria in Montesanto ... C1
16 Cordonata ... F1
17 Curia ... G2
18 Domus Flavia ... D6
19 Fontana dei Quattro Fiumi ... B3
20 Galleria Doria Pamphilj ... C4
21 Il Vittoriano ... F1
22 Museo Centrale del Risorgimento ... F1
23 Museo dell'Ara Pacis ... B2
24 Museo Nazionale Romano: Palazzo Massimo alle Terme ... F3
Obelisk ... (see 32)
25 Orti Farnesiani ... D6
26 Palatino ... D6
27 Palazzo dei Conservatori ... F2
28 Palazzo Nuovo ... F1
29 Palazzo Senatorio ... F2
30 Pantheon ... C4
31 Piazza del Campidoglio ... F2
32 Piazza del Popolo ... C1
33 Piazza Navona ... B4
34 Roma dal Cielo ... F1
35 Roman Forum ... G2
36 Spanish Steps ... D2
37 Stadio ... D6
38 Statue of Marcus Aurelius ... F1
39 Trevi Fountain ... D3

Sleeping
40 Arco del Lauro ... B6
41 Blue Hostel ... F4
42 Daphne Inn ... E2
43 Hotel Panda ... C2
44 La Casa di Kaia ... C6
45 Le Stanze di Orazio ... A1
Maria-Rosa Guesthouse ... (see 44)
46 Nicolas Inn ... E5
47 Okapi Rooms ... B1

Eating
48 Al Gran Sasso ... C1
49 Armando al Pantheon ... C3
50 Casa Coppelle ... B3
51 Fatamorgana - Trastevere ... A6
52 Forno di Campo de' Fiori ... B4
53 Forno Roscioli ... B5
54 Gelateria del Teatro ... A3
55 Panella l'Arte del Pane ... F5
56 Paris ... B6
57 San Crispino ... D3
58 Trattoria degli Amici ... A5

Drinking & Nightlife
59 Barnum Cafe ... B4
60 Caffè Sant'Eustachio ... B4
61 Freni e Frizioni ... A5
62 La Casa del Caffè Tazza d'Oro ... C3
63 Ma Che Siete Venuti a Fà ... A5
64 Open Baladin ... B5

Entertainment
65 Teatro dell'Opera di Roma ... F3

Spanish Steps — Staircase

(Scalinata della Trinità dei Monti; Map p378; Piazza di Spagna; M Spagna) Rising from Piazza di Spagna, the Spanish Steps have been attracting visitors since the 18th century. The piazza was named after the nearby Spanish Embassy, but the staircase, designed by Italian Francesco De Sanctis and built in 1725 with French money, leads to the French **Chiesa della Trinità dei Monti** **(Map p378; Piazza Trinità dei Monti; 6.30am-8pm Tue-Sun; M Spagna)**. At the the foot of the stairs, the boat-shaped **Barcaccia** (1627) fountain is believed to be by Pietro Bernini (father of Gian Lorenzo Bernini).

Piazza del Popolo — Piazza

(Map p378; M Flaminio) This dazzling piazza was laid out in 1538 to provide a grandiose entrance to what was then Rome's main northern gateway. It has since been remodelled several times, most recently by Giuseppe Valadier in 1823.

Guarding its southern approach are Carlo Rainaldi's twin 17th-century churches, **Chiesa di Santa Maria dei Miracoli** **(Map p378; M Flaminio)** and **Chiesa**

di Santa Maria in Montesanto (Map p378; Ⓜ Flaminio). In the centre, the 36m-high **obelisk** (Map p378; Ⓜ Flaminio) was brought by Augustus from ancient Egypt and originally stood in Circo Massimo.

Chiesa di Santa Maria del Popolo — Church

(Map p378; Piazza del Popolo; ⏲7am-noon & 4-7pm Mon-Sat, 7.30am-1.30pm & 4.30-7.30pm Sun; Ⓜ Flaminio) A magnificent repository of art, this is one of Rome's earliest and richest Renaissance churches. Of the numerous works of art on display, it is the two Caravaggio masterpieces – the *Conversione di San Paolo* (Conversion of St Paul) and the *Crocifissione di San Pietro* (Crucifixion of St Peter) – that draw the most onlookers but it contains numerous other fine works.

Museo dell'Ara Pacis — Museum

(Map p378; ☎06 06 08; http://en.arapacis.it; Lungotevere in Auga; adult/reduced €10.50/8.50, audioguide €4; ⏲9am-7pm, last admission 6pm; Ⓜ Flaminio) The first modern construction in Rome's historic centre since WWII, Richard Meier's controversial and widely detested glass-and-marble pavilion houses the *Ara Pacis Augustae* (Altar of Peace), Augustus' great monument to peace. One of the most important works of ancient Roman sculpture, the vast marble altar – measuring 11.6m by 10.6m by 3.6m – was completed in 13 BC.

VILLA BORGHESE

Just north of the historic centre, Villa Borghese is Rome's best-known park. The grounds, which were created in the 17th century by Cardinal Scipione Borghese, are accessible from Piazzale Flaminio, Pincio Hill and the top of Via Vittorio Veneto. Bike hire is available at various points, typically costing €5 per hour.

Museo e Galleria Borghese — Museum

(Map p372; ☎06 3 28 10; www.galleriaborghese.it; Piazzale del Museo Borghese 5; adult/reduced €11/6.50; ⏲9am-7pm Tue-Sun; 🚌 Via Pinciana) If you only have the time (or inclination) for one art gallery in Rome, make it this one. Housing what's generally considered the 'queen of all private art collections', it boasts paintings by Caravaggio, Botticelli and Raphael, as well as some spectacular sculptures by Bernini. There are highlights at every turn, but look out for Bernini's

Piazza del Popolo, Rome

Ratto di Proserpina (Rape of Persephone) and Canova's *Venere vincitrice* (Conquering Venus).

To limit numbers, visitors are admitted at two-hourly intervals, so you'll need to book your ticket and get an entry time.

Museo Nazionale Etrusco di Villa Giulia — Museum

(Map p372; www.villagiulia.beniculturali.it; Piazzale di Villa Giulia; adult/reduced €8/4; 8.30am-7.30pm Tue-Sun; Via delle Belle Arti) Italy's finest collection of Etruscan treasures is considerately displayed in Villa Giulia, Pope Julius III's 16th-century pleasure palace, and the nearby Villa Poniatowski. Exhibits, many of which came from burial tombs in the surrounding Lazio region, range from bronze figurines and black *bucchero* tableware to temple decorations, terracotta vases and a dazzling display of sophisticated jewellery.

Must-sees include a polychrome terracotta statue of Apollo, the 6th-century-BC *Sarcofago degli Sposi* (Sarcophagus of the Betrothed) and the *Euphronios Krater,* a celebrated Greek vase.

TRASTEVERE

Trastevere is one of central Rome's most vivacious neighbourhoods, a tightly packed warren of ochre *palazzi,* ivy-clad facades and photogenic lanes. Taking its name from the Latin *trans Tiberium,* meaning 'over the Tiber', it was originally a working-class district, but has since been gentrified and is today a trendy hang-out full of bars, trattorias and restaurants.

Basilica di Santa Maria in Trastevere — Basilica

(Map p378; Piazza Santa Maria in Trastevere; 7.30am-9pm; Viale di Trastevere, Viale di Trastevere) Nestled in a quiet corner of Trastevere's focal square, this is said to be the oldest church dedicated to the Virgin Mary in Rome. In its original form it dates to the early 3rd century, but a major 12th-century makeover saw the addition of a Romanesque bell tower and glittering facade. The portico came later, added by Carlo Fontana in 1702.

Inside, the 12th-century mosaics are the headline feature.

Piazza di Santa Maria, Trastevere, Rome

TERMINI & ESQUILINE

The largest of Rome's seven hills, the Esquiline (Esquilino) extends from the Colosseum up to Stazione Termini, Rome's main transport hub.

Museo Nazionale Romano: Palazzo Massimo alle Terme — Museum

(Map p378; ☎06 3996 7700; www.coopculture.it; Largo di Villa Peretti 1; adult/reduced €7/3.50; ⏲9am-7.45pm Tue-Sun; Ⓜ Termini) One of Rome's great unheralded museums, this is a fabulous treasure trove of classical art. The ground and 1st floors are devoted to sculpture with some breathtaking pieces: check out the *Pugile* (Boxer), a 2nd-century-BC Greek bronze; the graceful 2nd-century-BC *Ermafrodite dormiente* (Sleeping Hermaphrodite); and the idealised *Il discobolo* (Discus Thrower). It's the magnificent and vibrantly coloured frescoes on the 2nd floor, however, that are the real highlight.

Basilica di San Pietro in Vincoli — Basilica

(Map p378; Piazza di San Pietro in Vincoli 4a; ⏲8am-12.20pm & 3-7pm summer, to 6pm winter; Ⓜ Cavour) Pilgrims and art lovers flock to this 5th-century basilica for two reasons: to marvel at Michelangelo's colossal *Moses* (1505) sculpture and to see the chains that supposedly bound St Peter when he was imprisoned in the Carcere Mamertino (near the Roman Forum).

Access to the church is via a flight of steps through a low arch that leads up from Via Cavour.

Basilica di Santa Maria Maggiore — Basilica

(Map p378; Piazza Santa Maria Maggiore; basilica/museum/loggia/archaeological site free/€3/5/5; ⏲7am-7pm, museum & loggia 9am-5.30pm; 🚌 Piazza Santa Maria Maggiore) One of Rome's four patriarchal basilicas, this monumental 5th-century church stands on the summit of the Esquiline Hill, on the spot where snow is said to have

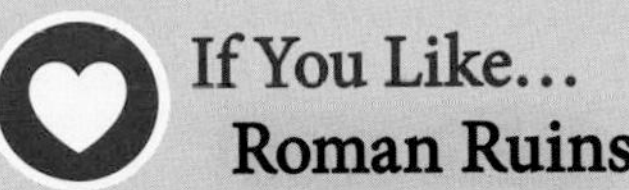

If You Like… Roman Ruins

Beyond the crumbling Colosseum and the remains of Pompeii, Italy is littered with countless other ruins created during the heyday of the Roman Empire.

1 SCAVI ARCHEOLOGICI DI OSTIA ANTICA

(☎06 5635 0215; www.ostiaantica.beniculturali.it; Viale dei Romagnoli 717; adult/reduced €10/6; ⏲8.30am-6.15pm Tue-Sun summer, earlier closing winter) An easy train ride from Rome, Ostia Antica is one of Italy's most under-appreciated archaeological sites. The ruins of ancient Rome's main seaport are spread out and you'll need a few hours to do them justice. Highlights include the Terme di Nettuno (Baths of Neptune) and steeply stacked amphitheatre.

2 VIA APPIA ANTICA

(Appian Way; ☎06 513 53 16; www.parcoappiaantica.it; bike hire hour/day €3/15; ⏲Info Point 9.30am-1pm & 2-5.30pm Mon-Fri, 9.30am-6.30pm Sat & Sun, to 5pm winter; 🚌 Via Appia Antica) Named after consul Appius Claudius Caecus, who laid the first 90km section in 312 BC, ancient Rome's *regina viarum* (queen of roads) was extended in 190 BC to reach Brindisi on Italy's southern Adriatic coast. Nowadays, Via Appia Antica (the Appian Way) is one of Rome's most exclusive addresses, a beautiful cobbled thoroughfare flanked by grassy fields, ancient ruins and towering pine trees.

3 VILLA ADRIANA

(☎0774 38 27 33; www.villaadriana.beniculturali.it; adult/reduced €8/4, incl temporary exhibition €11/7; ⏲9am-1hr before sunset) Some 5km outside Tivoli proper, Emperor Hadrian's sumptuous summer residence set new standards of luxury when it was built between AD 118 and 134. Spread over 120 hectares (of which about 40 are open to the public) the site is more like a small town than a villa and you'll need several hours to explore it. Consider hiring an audioguide (€5), which gives a helpful overview.

miraculously fallen in the summer of AD 358. Much altered over the centuries, it's something of an architectural hybrid with a 14th-century Romanesque belfry, an 18th-century baroque facade, a largely baroque interior, and a series of glorious 5th-century mosaics.

SAN GIOVANNI & CAELIAN HILL

Basilica di San Giovanni in Laterano — Basilica

(Map p372; Piazza di San Giovanni in Laterano 4; basilica/cloister free/€5; 7am-6.30pm, cloister 9am-6pm; M San Giovanni) For a thousand years this monumental cathedral was the most important church in Christendom. Commissioned by the Emperor Constantine and consecrated in AD 324, it was the first Christian basilica built in the city and, until the late 14th century, was the pope's main place of worship. It's still Rome's official cathedral and the pope's seat as the bishop of Rome.

The basilica has been revamped several times, most notably by Borromini in the 17th century, and by Alessandro Galilei who added the vast 18th-century facade.

Basilica di San Clemente — Basilica

(Map p378; www.basilicasanclemente.com; Via di San Giovanni in Laterano; excavations adult/reduced €10/5; 9am-12.30pm & 3-6pm Mon-Sat, 12.15-6pm Sun; Via Labicana) Nowehere better illustrates the various stages of Rome's turbulent past than this fascinating multilayered church. The ground-level 12th-century basilica sits atop a 4th-century church, which, in turn, stands over a 2nd-century pagan temple and 1st-century Roman house. Beneath everything are foundations dating from the Roman Republic.

Festivals & Events

Easter — Religious

On Good Friday, the pope leads a candlelit procession around the Colosseum. At noon on Easter Sunday he blesses the crowds in St Peter's Square.

Natale di Roma — Cultural

Rome celebrates its birthday on 21 April with music, historical re-creations, fireworks and free entry to many museums.

Festa de'Noantri — Cultural

Trastevere's annual party, held in the third week of July, involves plenty of food, wine, prayer and dancing.

Festa del Cinema di Roma — Film

(www.romacinemafest.it) Held at the Auditorium Parco della Musica in late October, Rome's film festival rolls out the red carpet for big-screen big shots.

St Peter's Basilica (p374), Rome

Sleeping

Rome has plenty of accommodation, but rates are universally high. The best, most atmospheric places to stay are the historic centre, the Prati area near the Vatican and Trastevere. Always try to book ahead, even if it's just for the first night.

ANCIENT ROME

Nicolas Inn B&B €€

(Map p378; ☎06 9761 8483; www.nicolasinn.com; 1st fl, Via Cavour 295, ; s €95-160, d €100-180; ❄ 📶; M Cavour) This sunny B&B offers a warm welcome and convenient location, a stone's throw from the Roman Forum. Run by a friendly couple, it has four big rooms, each with homely furnishings, colourful pictures and large en suite bathrooms. No children under five.

THE VATICAN

Le Stanze di Orazio B&B €€

(Map p378; ☎06 3265 2474; www.lestanzediorazio.com; Via Orazio 3; r €85-135; ❄ @ 📶; M Lepanto) This small boutique B&B is excellent value for money. Its five bright rooms feature soothing tones and playful decor – think shimmering rainbow wallpaper, lilac accents and grey designer bathrooms. There's a small breakfast area and rooms come with kettles and tea-making kit.

Hotel Bramante Historic Hotel €€

(Map p372; ☎06 6880 6426; www.hotelbramante.com; Vicolo delle Palline 24-25; s €100-160, d €140-240, tr €175-260, q €190-300; ❄ 📶; 🚌 Borgo Sant'Angelo) Nestled under the Vatican walls, the Bramante exudes country-house charm with its cosy internal courtyard, eggshell blue walls, wood-beamed ceilings and antique furniture. It's housed in the 16th-century building where architect Domenico Fontana once lived.

HISTORIC CENTRE

Okapi Rooms Hotel €

(Map p378; ☎06 3260 9815; www.okapirooms.it; Via della Penna 57; s €65-80, d €85-120, tr €110-140, q €120-180; ❄ 📶; M Flaminio) The Okapi is a smart, value-for-money choice near Piazza del Popolo. Rooms, spread over six floors of a narrow townhouse, are simple and airy with cream walls, terracotta floors and the occasional stone frieze. Some are smaller than others and several have small terraces. No breakfast.

Hotel Panda Pension €

(Map p378; ☎06 678 01 79; www.hotelpanda.it; Via della Croce 35; s €65-90, d €85-130, tr €120-150, q €160-190; ❄ 📶; M Spagna) Near the Spanish Steps, in an area where a bargain is a Bulgari watch bought at the sales, the Panda flies the flag for budget accommodation. It's a friendly place with high-ceilinged rooms and simple, tasteful decor. Air-con is free in summer, but €6 in other periods.

Daphne Inn Boutique Hotel €€

(Map p378; ☎06 8745 0086; www.daphne-rome.com; Via di San Basilio 55; s €115-180, d €130-240, ste €190-290, without bathroom s €70-130, d €90-160; ❄ 📶; M Barberini) Run by an American-Italian couple, the Daphne has helpful English-speaking staff and chic, comfortable rooms. They come in various shapes and sizes, but the overall look is smart contemporary. There's a second branch, Daphne Trevi, offering more of the same at Via degli Avignonesi 20.

TRASTEVERE

Maria-Rosa Guesthouse B&B €

(Map p378; ☎338 7700067; www.maria-rosa.it; Via dei Vascellari 55; s €45-65, d €65-80, tr €80-120; @ 📶; 🚌 Viale di Trastevere, 🚋 Viale di Trastevere) This is a delightful B&B on the 3rd floor of a Trastevere townhouse. It's a simple affair with two guest rooms sharing a single bathroom and a small living room, but the homey decor, pot plants and books create a lovely, warm atmosphere. The owner, Sylvie, also has a further three rooms on the floor above at **La Casa di Kaia** (Map p378; ☎338 7700067; www.kaia-trastevere.it; Via dei Vascellari 55; without bathroom s €45-55, d €65-75; 📶; 🚌 Viale di Trastevere, 🚋 Viale di Trastevere). No lift.

Arco del Lauro B&B €€

(Map p378; ☎346 2443212, 9am-2pm 06 9784 0350; www.arcodellauro.it; Via Arco de' Tolomei 27; s €72-132, d €132-145; ❄ 📶;

Viale di Trastevere, Viale di Trastevere) A real find, this fab six-room B&B occupies a centuries-old *palazzo* on a narrow cobbled street. Its gleaming white rooms combine rustic charm with a modern low-key look and comfortable beds. The owners extend a warm welcome and are always ready to help.

TERMINI & ESQUILINE

Blue Hostel Hostel €

(Map p378; 340 9258503; www.bluehostel.it; Via Carlo Alberto 13, 3rd fl; d €60-150, apt €100-180; ; M Vittorio Emanuele) A hostel in name only, this pearl offers small, hotel-standard rooms, each with its own en-suite bathroom, and decorated in tasteful low-key style – beamed ceilings, wooden floors, French windows, black-and-white framed photos. There's also an apartment, with kitchen, that sleeps up to four. No lift and no breakfast.

Eating

Eating out is one of the great joys of visiting Rome and everywhere you go you'll find trattorias, pizzerias, gelaterie (ice-cream shops) and restaurants. Traditional Roman cooking holds sway but *cucina creativa* (creative cooking) has taken off in recent years and there are plenty of exciting, contemporary restaurants to try.

The best areas are the historic centre and Trastevere, but there are also excellent choices in San Lorenzo east of Termini and Testaccio. Watch out for overpriced tourist traps around Termini and the Vatican.

Roman specialities include *cacio e pepe* (pasta with pecorino cheese, black pepper and olive oil), *pasta all'amatriciana* (with tomato, pancetta and chilli), *fiori di zucca* (fried courgette flowers) and *carciofi alla romana* (artichokes with garlic, mint and parsley).

THE VATICAN

Fa-Bìo Sandwiches €

(Map p372; 06 6452 5810; www.fa-bio.com; Via Germanico 43; sandwiches €5; 10am-5.30pm Mon-Fri, to 4pm Sat) Sandwiches, salads and smoothies are all prepared with speed, skill and organic ingredients at this tiny takeaway. Locals in the know come here to grab a quick lunchtime bite, and if you can squeeze in the door you'd do well to follow suit.

Display of gelato and desserts

Gelato Galore

To get the best out of Rome's gelaterie (ice cream shops) look for the words *'produzione proprio'*, meaning 'own production'. As a rough guide, expect to pay from €2 for a *cono* (cone) or *coppa* (tub).

Fatamorgana (Map p378; Via Roma Libera 11, Piazza San Cosimato; cones/tubs from €2; noon-midnight summer, to 10.30pm winter; Viale di Trastevere, Viale di Trastevere) Creative flavours at one of Rome's new breed of gourmet gelaterie.

Il Gelato (Map p372; Viale Aventino 59; gelati €2-4.50; 10am-midnight summer, 11am-9pm winter; Viale Aventino) Creative, preservative-free combos from Rome's gelato king Claudio Torcè.

Gelateria del Teatro (Map p378; Via dei Coronari 65; gelati from €2.50; 11.30am-midnight; Corso del Rinascimento) Seasonal fruit and spicy chocolate flavours in the heart of the *centro storico*.

San Crispino (Map p378; 06 679 39 24; Via della Panetteria 42; tubs from €2.70; 11am-12.30am Sun-Thu, to 1.30am Fri & Sat; M Barberini) Near the Trevi Fountain, it serves natural, seasonal flavours – think *fichi secci* (dried figs) and *miele* (honey) – in tubs only.

Hostaria Dino e Tony Trattoria €€
(Map p372; 06 3973 3284; Via Leone IV 60; meals €25-30; 12.30-3pm & 7-11pm, closed Sun & Aug; M Ottaviano-San Pietro) An authentic old-school trattoria, Dino e Tony offers simple, no-frills Roman cooking. Kick off with the monumental antipasto, a minor meal in its own right, before plunging into its signature *rigatoni all'amatriciana* (pasta tubes with pancetta, chilli and tomato sauce). No credit cards.

HISTORIC CENTRE

Forno Roscioli Pizza, Bakery €
(Map p378; Via dei Chiavari 34; pizza slices from €2, snacks from €1.50; 7am-7.30pm Mon-Sat; Via Arenula) This is one of Rome's top bakeries, much loved by lunching locals who crowd here for sliced pizza, prize pastries and hunger-sating *supplì* (fried rice balls). There's also a counter serving hot pastas and vegetable side dishes.

Forno di Campo de'Fiori Pizza, Bakery €
(Map p378; Campo de' Fiori 22; pizza slices about €3; 7.30am-2.30pm & 4.45-8pm Mon-Sat; Corso Vittorio Emanuele II) This buzzing bakery on Campo de' Fiori does a roaring trade in *panini* and delicious fresh-from-the-oven *pizza al taglio* (by the slice). Aficionados swear by the *pizza bianca* ('white' pizza with olive oil, rosemary and salt), but the *panini* and *pizza rossa* ('red' pizza, with olive oil, tomato and oregano) taste plenty good, too.

Casa Coppelle Ristorante €€
(Map p378; 06 6889 1707; www.casacoppelle.it; Piazza delle Coppelle 49; meals €35-40; 12-3.30pm & 6.30-11.30pm; Corso del Rinascimento) Intimate and romantic, Casa Coppelle serves modern Italian and French-inspired food on a small piazza near the Pantheon. There's a full range of starters and pastas, but the real tour de force are the deliciously tender steaks and meat dishes. Service is quick and attentive. Book ahead.

Armando al Pantheon Trattoria €€
(Map p378; 06 6880 3034; www.armandoalpantheon.it; Salita dei Crescenzi 31; meals €40; 12.30-3pm & 7-11pm Mon-Fri, 12.30-3pm Sat; Largo di Torre Argentina) A Roman institution, wood-panelled Armando is a rare find – a genuine family-run trattoria in the touristy Pantheon area. It's been on the

go for more than 50 years and has served its fair share of celebs, but the focus remains fixed on traditional, earthy Roman food. Reservations recommended.

Al Gran Sasso Trattoria **€€**
(Map p378; ☎06 321 48 83; www.algransasso.com; Via di Ripetta 32; meals €35; ⏲12.30-2.30pm & 7.30-11.30pm Sun-Fri; Ⓜ Flaminio) A top lunchtime spot, this is a classic, dyed-in-the-wool trattoria specialising in old-school country cooking. It's a relaxed place with a welcoming vibe, garish murals on the walls (strangely often a good sign) and tasty, value-for-money food. The fried dishes are excellent; daily specials are chalked on the board ooutside.

TRASTEVERE

Trattoria degli Amici Trattoria **€€**
(Map p378; ☎06 580 60 33; www.trattoriadegliamici.org; Piazza Sant'Egidio 6; meals €35; ⏲12.30-3pm & 7.30-11.30pm; 🚌 Viale di Trastevere, 🚋 Viale di Trastevere) Boasting a prime location on a pretty piazza, this cheerful trattoria is staffed by volunteers and people with disabilities who welcome guests with a warmth not always apparent in this touristy neck of the woods. Grab a squareside table and dig into fried starters and fresh, well-prepared classics.

Paris Ristorante **€€€**
(Map p378; ☎06 581 53 78; www.ristoranteparis.it; Piazza San Calisto 7a; meals €45-55; ⏲7.30-11pm Mon, 12.30-3pm & 7.30-11pm Tue-Sun; 🚌 Viale di Trastevere, 🚋 Viale di Trastevere) An old-school restaurant set in a 17th-century building with tables on a small piazza, Paris – named for its founder, not the French capital – is the best place outside the Ghetto to sample Roman-Jewish cuisine. Signature dishes include *gran fritto vegetale con baccalà* (deep-fried vegetables with salt cod) and *carciofi alla giudia* (fried artichoke).

TESTACCIO

Pizzeria Da Remo Pizza **€**
(Map p372; ☎06 574 62 70; Piazza Santa Maria Liberatrice 44; pizzas from €5.50; ⏲7pm-1am Mon-Sat; 🚌 Via Marmorata) For an authentic Roman experience, join the noisy crowds at this popular pizzeria. It's a spartan place, but the thin-crust Roman pizzas are the business, and there's a cheerful, boisterous vibe. To order, tick your choices on the sheet of paper slapped

Pantheon (p375), Rome

JEAN-PIERRE LESCOURRET/GETTY IMAGES ©

down by an overstretched waiter. Expect to queue after 8.30pm.

Flavio al Velavevodetto Trattoria €€
(Map p372; ☎06 574 41 94; www.ristorantevelavevodetto.it; Via di Monte Testaccio 97-99; meals €30-35; ⏰12.30-3pm & 7.45-11pm; 🚌Via Galvani) This welcoming eatery is the sort of place that gives Roman trattorias a good name. Housed in a rustic Pompeian-red villa, complete with covered courtyard and open-air terrace, it specialises in earthy, no-nonsense Roman food. Expect antipasti of cheeses and cured meats, huge helpings of homemade pastas, and uncomplicated meat dishes.

TERMINI & ESQUILINE

Panella l'Arte del Pane Bakery, Cafe €
(Map p378; ☎06 487 24 35; Via Merulana 54; snacks about €3.50; ⏰8am-11pm Mon-Thu, to midnight Fri & Sat, 8.30am-4pm Sun; Ⓜ Vittorio Emanuele) With a magnificent array of *pizza al taglio, arancini* (Sicilian rice balls), focaccia, fried croquettes and pastries, this smart bakery-cum-cafe is good any time of the day. The outside tables are ideal for a leisurely breakfast or chilled evening drink, or you can perch on a high stool and lunch on something from the sumptuous counter display.

Drinking & Nightlife

Rome has plenty of drinking venues, ranging from neighbourhood hang-outs to elegant streetside cafes, dressy lounge bars and Irish-theme pubs.

Barnum Cafe Cafe
(Map p378; www.barnumcafe.com; Via del Pellegrino 87; ⏰9am-10pm Mon, 8.30am-2am Tue-Sat; 📶; 🚌Corso Vittorio Emanuele II) A relaxed, friendly spot to check your email over a freshly squeezed orange juice or spend a pleasant hour reading a newspaper on one of the tatty old armchairs in the white bare-brick interior. Come evenings and the scene is cocktails, smooth tunes and dressed-down locals.

Caffè Sant'Eustachio Cafe
(Map p378; www.santeustachioilcaffe.it; Piazza Sant'Eustachio 82; ⏰8.30am-1am Sun-Thu, to 1.30am Fri, to 2am Sat; 🚌Corso del Rinascimento) This small, unassuming cafe, generally three deep at the bar, is reckoned to serve the best coffee in town. Created by beating the first drops of espresso and several teaspoons of sugar into a frothy paste, then adding the rest of the coffee, it's superbly smooth and guaranteed to put some zing into your sightseeing.

Open Baladin Bar
(Map p378; www.openbaladinroma.it; Via degli Specchi 6; ⏰noon-2am; 📶; 🚋Via Arenula) A hip, shabby-chic lounge bar near Campo de' Fiori, Open Baladin is a leading light in Rome's thriving beer scene with more than 40 beers on tap and up to 100 bottled brews, many from artisanal microbreweries. There's also a decent food menu with *panini,* burgers and daily specials.

La Casa del Caffè Tazza d'Oro Cafe
(Map p378; www.tazzadorocoffeeshop.com; Via degli Orfani 84-86; ⏰7am-8pm Mon-Sat, 10.30am-7.30pm Sun; 🚌Via del Corso) A busy, stand-up cafe with burnished 1940s fittings, this is one of Rome's best coffee houses. Its espresso hits the mark nicely and there's a range of delicious coffee concoctions, including a cooling *granita di caffè,* a crushed-ice coffee drink served with whipped cream.

Ma Che Siete Venuti a Fà Pub
(Map p378; www.football-pub.com; Via Benedetta 25; ⏰11am-2am; 🚌Piazza Trilussa) Named after a football chant, which translates politely as 'What did you come here for?', this pint-sized Trastevere pub is a beer-buff's paradise, packing in a huge number of international craft beers.

Freni e Frizioni Bar
(Map p378; ☎06 4549 7499; www.freniefrizioni.com; Via del Politeama 4-6; ⏰6.30pm-2am; 🚌Piazza Trilussa) This cool Trastevere bar is housed in a former mechanic's workshop – hence its name ('brakes and clutches'). It draws a young *spritz*-loving crowd that

swells onto the small piazza outside to sip well-priced cocktails (from €7) and to enjoy the daily *aperitivo* (7pm to 10pm).

Entertainment

Rome has a thriving cultural scene, with a year-round calendar of concerts, performances and festivals. In summer, the **Estate Romana** (**www.estateromana.comune.roma.it**) festival sponsors hundreds of cultural events, many staged in atmospheric parks, piazzas and churches.

Upcoming events are also listed on www.turismoroma.it, www.060608.it and www.auditorium.com.

Auditorium Parco della Musica Concert Venue

(**06 8024 1281; www.auditorium.com; Viale Pietro de Coubertin 30; Viale Tiziano**) Rome's main concert venue, this modernist complex combines architectural innovation with perfect acoustics. Designed by Renzo Piano, its three concert halls and 3000-seat open-air arena host everything from classical-music concerts to tango exhibitions, book readings and film screenings.

To get to the auditorium, take tram 2 from Piazzale Flaminio.

Alexanderplatz Jazz

(**Map p372; 06 3972 1867; www.alexanderplatzjazzclub.com; Via Ostia 9; 8.30pm-2am, concerts 9.45pm; M Ottaviano-San Pietro**) Small and intimate, Rome's bes- known jazz joint attracts top Italian and international performers and a respectful, cosmopolitan crowd. Book a table if you want to dine to the tunes.

Teatro dell'Opera di Roma Opera

(**Map p378; 06 481 70 03; www.operaroma.it; Piazza Beniamino Gigli; ballet €12-80, opera €17-150; 9am-5pm Tue-Sat, to 1.30pm Sun; M Repubblica**) Rome's premier opera house boasts a plush and gilt interior, a Fascist 1920s exterior and an impressive history: it premiered Puccini's *Tosca* and Maria Callas once sang here. Opera and ballet performances are staged between September and June.

Shopping

Rome boasts the usual cast of flagship chain stores and glitzy designer outlets, but what makes shopping here fun is its legion of small, independent shops: historic, family-owned delis, small-label fashion boutiques, artists' studios, neighbourhood markets. For designer clothes head to Via dei Condotti and the area around Piazza di Spagna, while for something more left-field check out the vintage shops and boutiques on Via del Governo Vecchio, around Campo de' Fiori, and in the Monti neighbourhood.

Rome's markets are great places for bargain hunting. The most

Fontana dei Quattro Fiumi, Piazza Navona (p375), Rome

famous, **Porta Portese** (Map p372; Piazza Porta Portese; 6am-2pm Sun; Viale di Trastevere, Viale di Trastevere), is held every Sunday morning near Trastevere, and sells everything from antiques to clothes, bikes, bags and furniture.

Information

Dangers & Annoyances

Rome is not a dangerous city but petty theft can be a problem. Watch out for pickpockets around the big tourist sites, at Stazione Termini and on crowded public transport – the 64 Vatican bus is notorious.

Medical Services

Pharmacy (06 488 00 19; Piazza dei Cinquecento 51; 7am-11.30pm Mon-Fri, 8am-11.30pm Sat & Sun) There's also a pharmacy in Stazione Termini, next to platform 1, open 7.30am to 10pm daily.

Ospedale Santo Spirito (06 6 83 51; Lungotevere in Sassia 1) Near the Vatican.

Policlinico Umberto I (06 4 99 71; www.policlinicoumberto1.it; Viale del Policlinico 155) Near Stazione Termini.

Money

Most midrange and top-end hotels accept credit cards, as do most restaurants and large shops. Some cheaper *pensioni*, trattorias and pizzerias only accept cash. Don't rely on credit cards at museums or galleries.

There are money-exchange booths at Stazione Termini and Fiumicino and Ciampino airports.

Tourist Information

For phone enquiries, the Comune di Roma runs a multilingual **tourist information line** (06 06 08; 9am-9pm).

There are tourist information points at **Fiumicino** (Terminal 3, International Arrivals; 8am-7.30pm) and **Ciampino** (International Arrivals, baggage claim area; 9am-6.30pm) airports, and at the following locations.

Castel Sant'Angelo Tourist Information (Map p378; Piazza Pia; 9.30am-7.15pm)

Fori Imperiali Tourist Information (Map p378; Via dei Fori Imperiali; 9.30am-7.15pm)

Piazza Navona Tourist Information (Map p378; 9.30am-7.15pm) Near Piazza delle Cinque Lune.

Stazione Termini Tourist Information (Map p378; 8am-7.45pm) In the hall adjacent to platform 24.

Minghetti Tourist Information (Map p378; Via Marco Minghetti; 9.30am-7.15pm) This tourist point is closer to Via del Corso than the fountain.

Via Nazionale Tourist Information (Map p378; Via Nazionale; 9.30am-7.15pm)

Websites

060608 (www.060608.it) Provides information on sites, shows, transport etc.

Coop Culture (www.coopculture.it) Information and ticketing for Rome's monuments, museums and galleries.

Turismo Roma (www.turismoroma.it) Rome's official tourist website.

Vatican (www.vatican.va) The Vatican's official website.

Getting There & Away

Air

Rome's main international airport, Leonardo da Vinci (p453), better known as Fiumicino, is on the coast 30km west of the city. The much smaller Ciampino airport (p453), 15km southeast of the city centre, is the hub for low-cost carrier **Ryanair** (895 895 8989; www.ryanair.com).

Boat

Rome's port is at Civitavecchia, about 80km north of Rome.

Ferries sail here from Spain and Tunisia, as well as Sicily and Sardinia.

Ferry bookings can be made at the Termini-based **Agenzia 365** (06 488 16 78; www.agenzie365.it; 7am-9pm), at travel agents or online at www.traghettionline.net. You can also buy directly at the port.

Half-hourly trains depart from Roma Termini to Civitavecchia (€5 to €10, 40 minutes to 1¼ hours). On arrival, it's about 700m to the port (to your right) as you exit the station.

Car & Motorcycle

Driving into central Rome is a challenge, involving traffic restrictions, one-way systems, a shortage of street parking and aggressive drivers.

Car hire is available at the airport and Stazione Termini.

Train

Almost all trains arrive at and depart from Stazione Termini.

Left luggage (Stazione Termini; 1st 5hr €6, 6-12hr per hour €0.90, 13hr & over per hour €0.40; 6am-11pm) is on the lower ground floor under platform 24.

Rome's other principal train stations are Stazione Tiburtina and Stazione Roma-Ostiense.

Getting Around

To/From the Airport

Fiumicino

The easiest way to get to/from Fiumicino is by train but there are also bus services. The set taxi fare to the city centre is €48 (valid for up to four people with luggage).

Leonardo Express Train (one way €14) Runs to/from Stazione Termini. Departures from the airport every 30 minutes between 6.38am and 11.08pm; from Termini between 5.50am and 10.50pm. Journey time is 30 minutes.

FL1 Train (one way €8) Connects to Trastevere, Ostiense and Tiburtina stations, but not Termini. Departures from the airport every 15 minutes (hourly on Sunday and public holidays) between 5.57am and 10.42pm; from Tiburtina every 15 minutes between 5.46am and 7.31pm, then half-hourly to 10.02pm.

Ciampino

The best option is to take one of the regular bus services into the city centre. The set taxi fare is €30.

SIT Bus (06 591 68 26; www.sitbusshuttle.com; from/to airport €4/6) Regular departures from the airport to Via Marsala outside Stazione Termini between 7.15am and 10.30pm, and from Termini between 4.30am and 9.30pm. Get tickets on the bus. Journey time is 45 minutes.

Terravision Bus (www.terravision.eu; one way €6, online €4) Twice-hourly departures to/from Via Marsala outside Stazione Termini. From the airport services are between 8.15am and 12.15am; from Via Marsala between 4.30am and 9.20pm. Buy tickets at Terracafè in front of the Via Marsala bus stop. Journey time is 40 minutes.

Car & Motorcycle

Most of the historic centre is closed to normal traffic from 6.30am to 6pm Monday to Friday, from 2pm to 6pm Saturday, and from 11pm to 3am Friday to Sunday; see http://muovi.roma.it for details of the capital's limited traffic zones (*zone a traffico limitato;* ZTL).

Spiral staircase, Vatican Museums (p376), Rome

Detour: Villa d'Este

The town of Tivoli is home to two Unesco-listed sites: Emperor Hadrian's lavish villa (p383), and **Villa d'Este** (0774 31 20 70; www.villadestetivoli.info; Piazza Trento; adult/reduced €8/4; 8.30am-1hr before sunset Tue-Sun), a sumptuous Renaissance residence. The villa was originally a Benedictine convent before Lucrezia Borgia's son, Cardinal Ippolito d'Este, transformed it into a pleasure palace in 1550. Later, in the 19th century, the composer Franz Liszt lived and worked here.

More than the villa itself, it's the elaborate gardens and fountains that are the main attraction. Highlights include the **Fountain of the Organ**, an extravagant baroque ensemble that uses water pressure to play music through a concealed organ, and the 130m-long **Avenue of the Hundred Fountains**.

Tivoli is 30km east of Rome and accessible by Cotral bus (€2.30, 50 minutes, every 15 to 20 minutes) from Ponte Mammolo metro station. The fastest route by car is on the Rome–L'Aquila autostrada (A24).

Parking

Blue lines denote pay-and-display parking spaces with tickets available from meters (coins only) and *tabacchi* (tobacconists). Expect to pay about €1.20 per hour between 8am and 8pm (11pm in some places). After 8pm (or 11pm) parking is generally free until 8am the next morning. If your car gets towed away, check with the traffic police (06 676 92 303).

Public Transport

Rome's public transport system includes buses, trams, metro and a suburban train network.

Tickets

Tickets are valid for all forms of transport and come in various forms:

Single (BIT; €1.50) Valid for 100 minutes, during which time you can use as many buses or trams as you like but can only go once on the metro.

Daily (BIG; €6) Unlimited travel until midnight of the day of purchase.

Three-day (BTI; €16.50) Unlimited travel for three days.

Weekly (CIS; €24) Unlimited travel for seven days.

Buy tickets at *tabacchi*, news stands and from vending machines at main bus stops and metro stations. They must be purchased before you start your journey and validated in the machines on buses, at the entrance gates to the metro or at train stations. Ticketless riders risk an on-the-spot €50 fine. Children under 10 travel free.

Bus

Buses and trams are run by ATAC (06 5 70 03; www.atac.roma.it). The main bus station is in front of Stazione Termini on Piazza dei Cinquecento, where there's an information booth (Map p378; 7.30am-8pm).

Metro

Rome's two main metro lines, A (orange) and B (blue), cross at Termini, the only point at which you can change from one line to the other.

Take line A for the Trevi Fountain (Barberini), Spanish Steps (Spagna) and Vatican (Ottaviano-San Pietro); line B for the Colosseum (Colosseo).

Trains run between 5.30am and 11.30pm (to 1.30am on Friday and Saturday).

Taxi

Official licensed taxis are white with an ID number and *Roma capitale* on the sides. Always go with the metered fare, never an arranged price (the set fares to and from the airports are exceptions).

There are major taxi ranks at the airports, Stazione Termini, Largo di Torre Argentina, Piazza della Repubblica and the Colosseum. You can book a taxi by phoning the Comune di Roma's automated taxi line (06 06 09) or calling a taxi company direct:

La Capitale (06 49 94)

Radio 3570 (06 35 70; www.3570.it)

Samarcanda (06 55 51; www.samarcanda.it)

NORTHERN ITALY

Italy's well-heeled north is a fascinating area of historical wealth and natural diversity. Bordered by the northern Alps and boasting some of the country's most spectacular coastline, it also encompasses Italy's largest lowland area, the fertile Po valley plain.

Cinque Terre

Liguria's eastern Riviera boasts some of Italy's most dramatic coastline, the highlight of which is the Unesco-listed **Parco Nazionale delle Cinque Terre** (Cinque Terre National Park) just north of La Spezia. Running for 18km, this awesome stretch of plunging cliffs and vine-covered hills is named after its five tiny villages: Riomaggiore, Manarola, Corniglia, Vernazza and Monterosso.

The area's beauty masks its vulnerability; in autumn 2011 heavy rainfall caused severe flooding and mudslides, leaving four people dead. Further problems arose a year later when four Australian tourists were injured by rockfalls on the coast's most popular trail. The villages are now up and running again but several paths remain closed.

It gets very crowded in summer, so try to come in spring or autumn.

Sights & Activities

The Cinque Terre villages are linked by the 12km **Sentiero Azzurro** (Blue Trail; admission with Cinque Terre Card), a magnificent, mildly challenging five-hour trail. At the time of writing, the Sentiero was closed between Riomaggiore and Corniglia after the floods in 2011 and rockfalls in 2012. Check www.parconazionale5terre.it for the latest situation.

Sleeping

L'Eremo sul Mare B&B **€**
(☎339 268 56 17; www.eremosulmare.com; d €70-100; ❄ 📶) To spend a romantic night in Vernazza, try L'Eremo sul Mare, a charming cliffside villa with just three rooms and a lovely panoramic terrace. It's a 15-minute walk from the village; follow the Sentiero Azzurro towards Corniglia.

Hotel Pasquale Hotel **€€**
(☎0187 81 74 77; www.hotelpasquale.it; Via Fegina 4, Monterosso; s €80-160, d €140-220, tr €170-300; 🕐Mar–mid-Nov; ❄ 📶) Offering soothing views and stylish, modern guest rooms, this friendly seafront hotel is built into Monterosso's medieval sea walls. To find it, exit the train station and go left through the tunnel towards the *centro storico*.

Hotel Ca' d'Andrean Hotel **€€**
(☎0187 92 00 40; www.cadandrean.it; Via Doscovolo 101, Manarola; s €80-90, d

Riomaggiore, Cinque Terre

€90-150; ⏲Mar–mid-Nov; ❄📶) An excellent family-run hotel in the upper part of Manarola. Rooms are big and cool, with white-grey tones and designer bathrooms, and some have private terraces. Breakfast (€7) is optional. No credit cards.

Eating

Ristorante Belvedere Seafood **€€**
(☎0187 81 70 33; www.ristorante-belvedere.it; Piazza Garibaldi 38, Monterosso; meals €30; ⏲noon-3pm & 6.15-10.30pm Wed-Mon) With tables overlooking the beach, this unpretentious seafood restaurant is a good place to try the local bounty. Start with *penne con scampi* (pasta tubes with scampi) before diving into a rich *zuppa di pesce* (fish soup).

Dau Cila Modern Italian **€€**
(☎0187 76 00 32; www.ristorantedaucila.com; Via San Giacomo 65, Riomaggiore; meals €40; ⏲8am-2am Mar-Oct) Perched within pebble-lobbing distance of Riomaggiore's twee harbour, Dau Cila is a smart restaurant-cum-winebar, specialising in classic seafood and local wines.

Information

Information office (www.parconazionale5terre.it; ⏲8am-8pm summer, 9am-5pm winter) the most convenient office is at Riomaggiore train station.

Getting There & Away

Boat

Between June and September, **Golfo Paradiso** (☎0185 77 20 91; www.golfoparadiso.it) operates excursions from Genoa's Porto Antico to Vernazza and Monterosso. These cost €18 one way, €33 return.

From late March to October, **Consorzio Marittimo Turistico 5 Terre** (☎0187 73 29 87; www.navigazionegolfodeipoeti.it) runs daily ferries between La Spezia and four of the villages (not Corniglia). One-way tickets cost €12 to/from Riomaggiore or Manarola, or €16 to/from Vernazza or Monterosso. Return trips are covered by a daily ticket (weekdays/weekends €25/27).

Cinque Terre Card

To walk the Sentiero Azzurro or any other of the Cinque Terre paths, you'll need a Cinque Terre Trekking Card. This comes in two forms:

- **Cinque Terre Trekking Card** (one/two days €7.50/14.50) Available at all park offices.
- **Cinque Terre Treno Card** (one/twodays €12/23) As for the Cinque Terre Card plus unlimited train travel between La Spezia and the five villages.

Train

From Genoa Brignole direct trains run to Riomaggiore (€6.80, 1½ to two hours, 18 daily), stopping at each of the Cinque Terre villages.

Between 4.30am and 11.46pm, one to three trains an hour crawl up the coast from La Spezia to Levanto, stopping at all of the villages en route. If you're using this route and want to stop at all the villages, get the Cinque Terre Treno Card.

Milan

POP 1.32 MILLION

Few Italian cities polarise opinion like Milan, Italy's financial and fashion capital. Some people love the cosmopolitan, can-do atmosphere, the vibrant cultural scene and the sophisticated shopping; others grumble that the city's dirty, ugly and expensive. Certainly, it lacks the picture-postcard beauty of many Italian towns, but in among the urban hustle are some truly great sights: Leonardo da Vinci's *Last Supper*, the immense Duomo and the world-famous La Scala opera house.

Sights

Duomo Cathedral
(www.duomomilano.it; Piazza del Duomo; roof terraces adult/reduced stairs €8/4, lift €13/7, Battistero di San Giovanni €4/2; ⏲Duomo

Central Milan

Central Milan

Sights

1	Castello Sforzesco	A1
2	Duomo	C3
3	Galleria Vittorio Emanuele II	C3
4	Museo del Novecento	C3
5	Museo Teatrale alla Scala	C2
6	Pinacoteca di Brera	C1
7	Teatro alla Scala	C2

Eating

8	Luini	C3

Shopping

9	Cavalli e Nastri	C2
10	Peck	B3

7am-6.40pm, roof terraces 9am-6.30pm, Battistero di San Giovanni 10am-6pm Tue-Sun; M Duomo) A vision in pink Candoglia marble, Milan's extravagant Gothic cathedral aptly reflects the city's creativity and ambition. Commissioned in 1387 and finished nearly 600 years later, it boasts a pearly white facade adorned with 135 spires and 3200 statues, and a vast interior punctuated by the largest stained-glass windows in Christendom. Underground, you can see the remains of the saintly Carlo Borromeo in the crypt and explore ancient ruins in the Battistero di San Giovanni. Up top, the spired roof terraces command stunning views.

Museo del Novecento Gallery

(☎02 8844 4061; www.museodelnovecento.org; Via Marconi 1; adult/reduced €5/3; 2.30-7.30pm Mon, 9.30am-7.30pm Tue, Wed, Fri & Sun, to 10.30pm Thu & Sat; M Duomo) Overlooking Piazza del Duomo, with fabulous views of the cathedral, is Mussolini's **Arengario**, from where he would harangue huge crowds in his heyday. Now it houses Milan's museum of 20th-century art. Built around a futuristic spiral ramp (an ode to the Guggenheim), the lower floors are cramped, but the heady collection, which includes the likes of Umberto Boccioni, Campigli, de Chirico and Marinetti, more than distracts.

Teatro alla Scala — Opera House

(La Scala; www.teatroallascala.org; Via Filodrammatici 2; M Duomo) Giuseppe Piermarini's grand 2800-seat theatre was inaugurated in 1778 with Antonio Salieri's *Europa Riconosciuta,* replacing the previous theatre, which burnt down in a fire after a carnival gala. Costs were covered by the sale of *palchi* (private boxes), of which there are six gilt-and-crimson tiers.

In the theatre's **museum (La Scala Museum; Largo Ghiringhelli 1; admission €7; 9am-12.30pm & 1.30-5.30pm; M Duomo)**, harlequin costumes and a spinet inscribed with the command 'Inexpert hand, touch me not!' hint at centuries of Milanese musical drama.

The Last Supper — Artwork

(Il Cenacolo; 02 9280 0360; www.vivaticket.it; Piazza Santa Maria delle Grazie 2; adult/reduced €8/4.75; 8.15am-7pm Tue-Sun; M Cadorna) Milan's most famous mural, Leonardo Da Vinci's *The Last Supper* is hidden away on a wall of the refectory adjoining the **Basilica di Santa Maria delle Grazie**. Depicting Christ and his disciples at the dramatic moment when Christ reveals he's aware of his betrayal, it's a masterful psychological study and one of the world's most iconic images.

To see it you must book in advance or sign up for a guided city tour.

Pinacoteca di Brera — Gallery

(02 7226 3264; www.brera.beniculturali.it; Via Brera 28; adult/reduced €10/7; 8.30am-7.15pm Tue-Sun; M Lanza, Montenapoleone) Located upstairs from the centuries-old Accademia di Belle Arti (still one of Italy's most prestigious art schools), this gallery houses Milan's most impressive collection of old masters, much of the bounty 'lifted' from Venice by Napoleon. Rembrandt, Goya and Van Dyck all have a place in the collection, but you're here to see the Italians: Titian, Tintoretto, glorious Veronese, groundbreaking Mantegna, the Bellini brothers and a Caravaggio.

Duomo (p395), Milan

Sleeping

Hotel Aurora Hotel €€

(02 204 79 60; www.hotelauroramilano.com; Corso Buenos Aires 18; s €60-135, d €80-140; M Porta Venezia) Clean, quiet rooms in a strategic location await at this modest two-star hotel. The decor is businesslike and fairly unforgettable, but the rates compare well with other places in town and rooms are comfortable enough. No breakfast.

Antica Locanda Leonardo Hotel €€

(02 4801 4197; www.anticalocandaleonardo.com; Corso Magenta 78; s €95-170, d €110-225; @; M Conciliazione) A charmer hidden in a 19th-century residence near Leonardo's *Last Supper*. Rooms exude homey comfort, from the period furniture and parquet floors to the plush drapes, while breakfast is served in the small, scented garden.

Eating & Drinking

Local specialities include *risotto alla milanese* (saffron-infused risotto cooked in bone-marrow stock) and *cotoletta alla milanese* (breaded veal cutlet).

Luini Fast Food €

(www.luini.it; Via Santa Radegonda 16; panzerotti €2.50; 10am-3pm Mon, to 8pm Tue-Sat; M Duomo) This historic joint is the go-to place for *panzerotti*, delicious pizza-dough parcels stuffed with a combination of mozzarella, spinach, tomato, ham or spicy salami, and then fried or baked in a wood-fired oven.

Rinomata Gelateria €

(Ripa di Porta Ticinese; cones/tubs €2.50-4.50; noon-2am; M Porta Genova) If dining in Navigli, skip dessert and grab an ice cream from this hole-in-the-wall gelateria. Its fabulous interior features old-fashioned fridges and glass-fronted cabinets filled with cones – and the gelato is good, too.

Al Bacco Milanese €€

(02 5412 1637; Via Marcona 1; meals €35; 12.30-2.30pm & 7.30-11pm Mon-Fri, 7pm-1am Sat; Corso XXII Marzo) Search out this cosy, Slow Food–recommended restaurant east of the city centre – a block north of Corso XXII Marzo – for lovingly prepared Milanese classics. Try *tortino di riso giallo allo zafferano* (yellow rice tart with saffron) followed by *cotoletta alla milanese* (breaded veal cutlet).

BQ Navigli Bar

(Birra Artigianale di Qualità; Via Alzaia Naviglio Grande 44; 6pm-2am; M Porta Genova) This Navigli canalside bar has a fine selection of craft beers, ranging from light lagers to robust hop-heavy bitters. Soak it all up with *panini* and *piadine* (stuffed pitta breads).

Shopping

For designer clobber head to the so-called Golden Quad, the area around Via della Spiga, Via Sant'Andrea, Via Monte Napoleone and Via Alessandro Manzoni. Hip younger labels can be found in Brera and Corso Magenta, while Corso Porta Ticenese and Navigli are home to Milan's street scene. Chain stores line Corso Vercelli and Corso Buenos Aires. A stroll through the neoclassical Galleria Vittorio Emanuele II is a must.

Peck Food, Wine

(02 802 31 61; www.peck.it; Via Spadari 9; 3.30-7.30pm Mon, 9.30am-7.30pm Tue-Sat; M Duomo) Milan's historic deli is smaller than its reputation suggests, but what it lacks in space it makes up for in variety, with a mind-boggling selection of *parmigiano reggiano* (Parmesan) and myriad other treasures: chocolates, pralines, pastries, freshly made gelato, seafood, caviar, pâtés, fruit and vegetables, truffle products, olive oils and balsamic vinegars.

Cavalli e Nastri Clothing

(02 7200 0449; www.cavallienastri.com; Via Brera 2; 3.30-7.30pm Mon, 10.30am-6.30pm Tue-Sat; M Montenapoleone) This gorgeously colourful Brera shop is known for its vintage clothes and accessories.

It specialises in lovingly curated frocks, bags, jewellery and even shoes, sourced from early- and mid-20th-century Italian fashion houses, and priced accordingly.

Information

There are tourist offices at **Piazza Castello** (**☎02 8845 6555; www.turismo.milano.it; Galleria Vittorio Emanuele II 11-12; 9am-7pm Mon-Fri, 9am-6pm Sat, 10am-6pm Sun; M Duomo**) and Stazione Centrale.

Useful websites include www.visitamilano.it and www.hellomilano.it.

Getting There & Away

Air

Most international flights fly into Malpensa Airport (p453), about 50km northwest of Milan. Domestic and some European flights use **Linate airport** (**LIN; ☎02 23 23 23; www.milanolinate-airport.com**), about 7km east of the city. Low-cost airlines often use **Orio al Serio airport** (**Aeroporto Il Caravaggio; ☎035 32 63 23; www.sacbo.it**), near Bergamo.

Train

Regular daily trains depart Stazione Centrale for Venice (€37.50, 2½ hours), Bologna (€40, one hour), Florence (€50, 1¾ hours), Rome (€86, three hours) and other Italian and European cities. Note that these prices are for the fast Frecce services.

Getting Around

To/From the Airport

Malpensa

Malpensa Shuttle (**www.malpensashuttle.it; one-way/return €10/16**) Coaches run to/from Piazza Luigi di Savoia next to Stazione Centrale. Departures run from the station every 20 minutes between 3.45am and 12.30am; from the airport 5am to 12.30am. Journey time 50 minutes.

Malpensa Express (**☎02 7249 4949; www.malpensaexpress.it; one-way €12**) From 4.28am to 12.26am, trains run every 30 minutes between Terminal 1, Cadorna Stazione Nord (35 minutes) and Stazione Centrale (45 minutes). Passengers for Terminal 2 will need to take the free shuttle bus to/from Terminal 1.

Orio al Serio

Orio al Serio Bus Express (**☎02 7200 1304; www.autostradale.it; one-way €5**) This Autostradale service departs Piazza Luigi di Savoia approximately every half hour between

Galleria Vittorio Emanuele II, Milan

TODD KEITH/GETTY IMAGES ©

ITALY MILAN

2.45am and 11.30pm; from Orio between 4.30am and 1am. The journey takes one hour.

Bus & Metro

Milan's excellent public transport system is run by **ATM (Azienda Trasporti Milano; ☎02 4860 7607; www.atm.it)**. Tickets (€1.50) are valid for one underground ride or up to 90 minutes' travel on city buses and trams. A day ticket costs €4.50.

Verona

POP 260,000

Wander Verona's atmospheric streets and you'll understand why Shakespeare set *Romeo and Juliet* here – this is one of Italy's most beautiful and romantic cities. Known as *piccola Roma* (little Rome) for its importance in imperial days, its heyday came in the 13th and 14th centuries when it was ruled by the Della Scala (aka Scaligeri) family, who built *palazzi* and bridges, sponsored Giotto, Dante and Petrarch, oppressed their subjects and feuded with everyone else.

Sights

The **VeronaCard** (2/5 days €15/20), available from tourist offices, sites and tobacconists, covers city transport and the city's main monuments and churches.

Roman Arena Ruin

(☎045 800 32 04; www.arena.it; Piazza Brà; adult/reduced €10/7.50, incl Museo Maffeiano €11/8, or with VeronaCard, first Sun of month Oct-May €1; ⏰1.30-7.30pm Mon, 8.30am-7.30pm Tue-Sun) Verona's Roman amphitheatre, built of pink-tinged marble in the 1st century AD, survived a 12th-century earthquake to become the city's legendary open-air opera house, with seating for 30,000 people. You can visit the arena year-round, though it's at its best during the summer opera festival.

Casa di Giulietta Museum

(Juliet's House; ☎045 803 43 03; Via Cappello 23; adult/reduced €6/4.50, or with VeronaCard; ⏰1.30-7.30pm Mon, 8.30am-7.30pm Tue-Sun) Never mind that Romeo and Juliet were completely fictional characters, and that there's hardly room for two on the narrow stone balcony: romantics flock to this 14th-century house to add their lovelorn pleas to the graffiti on the courtyard gateway.

Piazza delle Erbe Square

Originally a Roman forum, Piazza delle Erbe is ringed with buzzing cafes and some of Verona's most sumptuous buildings, including the elegantly baroque **Palazzo Maffei**, which now houses several shops at its northern end.

Just off the piazza, the monumental arch known as the **Arco della Costa** is hung with a whale's rib. Legend holds that the rib will fall on the first just person to walk beneath it.

View over Piazza dei Signori, Verona

So far, it remains intact, despite visits by popes and kings.

Piazza dei Signori Square

Verona's beautiful open-air salon is ringed by a series of elegant Renaissance *palazzi*. Chief among these are the **Palazzo degli Scaligeri** (aka Palazzo Podestà), the 14th-century residence of Cangrande I Della Scala; the arched **Loggia del Consiglio**, built in the 15th century as the city council chambers; and the brick and tufa stone **Palazzo della Ragione**.

In the middle of the piazza is a statue of **Dante**, who was given refuge in Verona after he was exiled from Florence in 1302.

Sleeping

Corte delle Pigne B&B **€€**

(**☎333 7584141; www.cortedellepigne.it; Via Pigna 6a; s €60-90, d €90-130, tr & q €110-150; P ❄ 📶**) In the heart of the historic centre, this three-room B&B is set around a quiet internal courtyard. It offers tasteful rooms and plenty of personal touches: a communal sweet jar, luxury toiletries, and even a jacuzzi for one lucky couple.

Hotel Aurora Hotel **€€**

(**☎045 59 47 17; www.hotelaurora.biz; Piazzetta XIV Novembre 2; d €100-250, tr €130-280; ❄ 📶**) This friendly three-star hotel is right in the thick of it, overlooking Piazza delle Erbe. Its light-filled rooms, some of which have piazza views, offer a mix of modern and classic decor. Breakfast can be enjoyed on the the sunny terrace.

Eating

Hostaria La Vecchia Fontanina Trattoria **€**

(**☎045 59 11 59; www.ristorantevecchiafontanina.com; Piazzetta Chiavica 5; meals €25; ⌚noon-2.30pm & 7-10.30pm Mon-Sat**) With tables on a pint-sized piazza, cosy indoor rooms, and excellent food, this historic eatery stands out from the crowd. The menu features typical Veronese dishes alongside a number of more unusual creations such as *bigoli con ortica e ricotta affumicata* (thick spaghetti with nettles and smoked ricotta) and several heavenly desserts.

Al Pompiere Trattoria **€€**

(**☎045 803 05 37; www.alpompiere.com; Vicolo Regina d'Ungheria 5; meals €45; ⌚12.40-2pm & 7.40-10.30pm Mon-Sat**) The fireman's *(pompiere)* hat is still on the wall, but the focal point at this local hot spot is the vast cheese selection and famed house-cured *salumi* platter. Make a meal of the starters with wine by the glass, or graduate to plates of risotto and oven-cooked pork knuckle. Reserve ahead.

Information

Tourist office (**☎045 806 86 80; www.tourism.verona.it; Via degli Alpini 9; ⌚9am-7pm Mon-Sat, 10am-4pm Sun**) Information, opera tickets and hotel reservations are available at this central office, just off Piazza Brà.

Getting There & Around

Direct trains connect with Milan (€12.05 to €17.20, one hour 20 minutes to two hours, up to three hourly), Venice (€8.55 to €18.40, 50 minutes to 2¼ hours, twice hourly) and Bologna (€9.75 to €18.40, 50 minutes to 1½ hours, 20 daily).

Venice

POP 264,500

Venice (Venezia) is a hauntingly beautiful city. At every turn you're assailed by unforgettable images: tiny bridges crossing limpid canals, delivery barges jostling chintzy gondolas, excited tourists posing on Piazza San Marco. Its celebrated sights are legion and its labyrinthine backstreets exude a unique, almost eerie, atmosphere, redolent of dark passions and dangerous secrets. Parts of the Cannaregio, Dorsoduro and Castello *sestieri* (districts) rarely see many tourists, and you can lose yourself for hours in the lanes between the Accademia and train station.

Venice's origins date to the 5th and 6th centuries when barbarian invasions forced the Veneto's inhabitants to seek refuge on the lagoon's islands. Initially the city was ruled by the Byzantines from Ravenna, but in 726 the Venetians went it alone and elected their first doge (duke). Over successive centuries, the

Venice

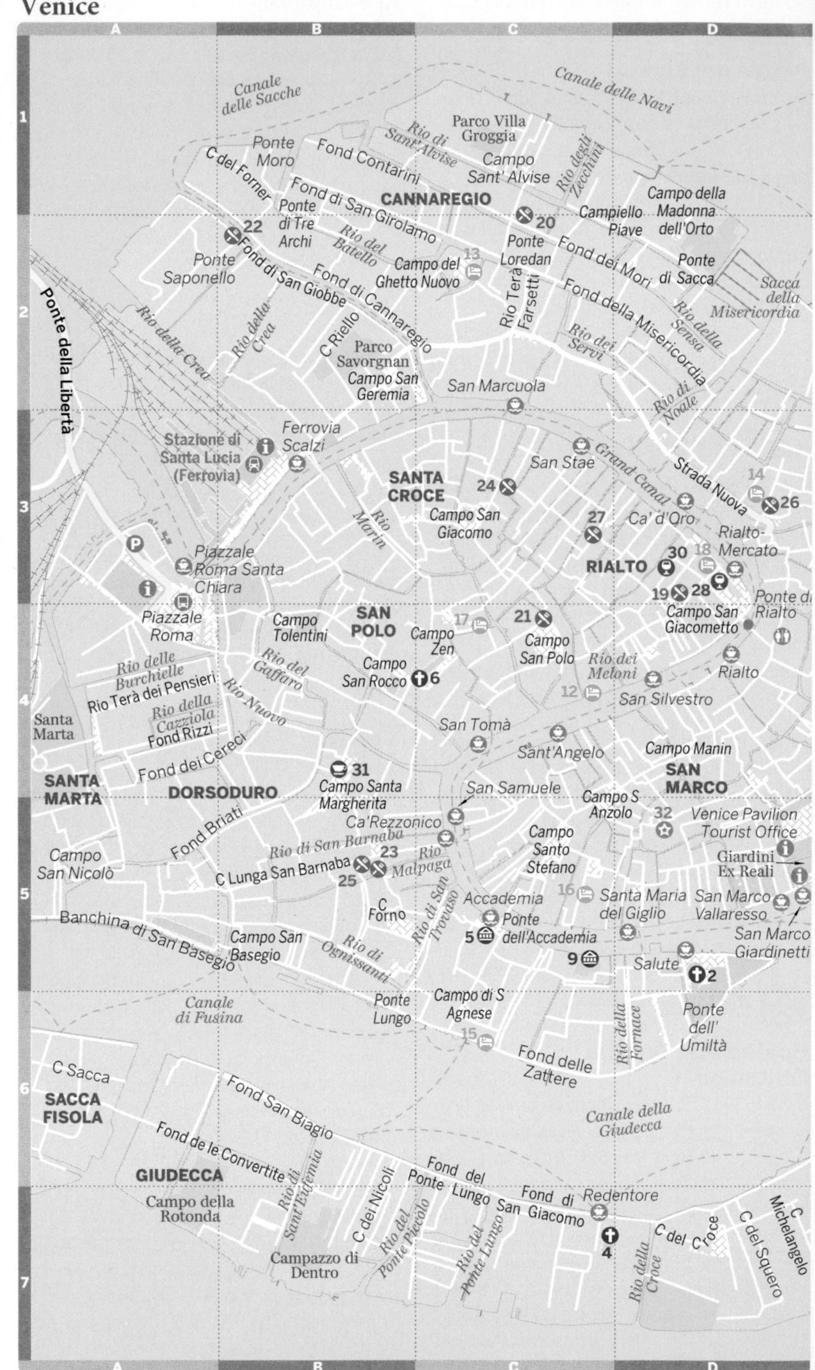

Canale delle Sacche
Canale delle Navi
CANNAREGIO
SANTA CROCE
SAN POLO
DORSODURO
SANTA MARTA
SAN MARCO
RIALTO
SACCA FISOLA
GIUDECCA
Grand Canal
Canale della Giudecca
Canale di Fusina
Ponte della Libertà
Stazione di Santa Lucia (Ferrovia)
Piazzale Roma
Campo San Rocco
Campo Santa Margherita
Ca'Rezzonico
Accademia
Ponte dell'Accademia
Salute
Ponte di Rialto
Venice Pavilion Tourist Office
Giardini Ex Reali
San Marco Vallaresso
San Marco Giardinetti
Fond delle Zattere
Strada Nuova
Fond della Misericordia
Fond di Cannaregio
Fond San Biagio
Campo Sant' Alvise
Campo del Ghetto Nuovo
Campo San Polo
Campo Santo Stefano
Campo Manin
Redentore

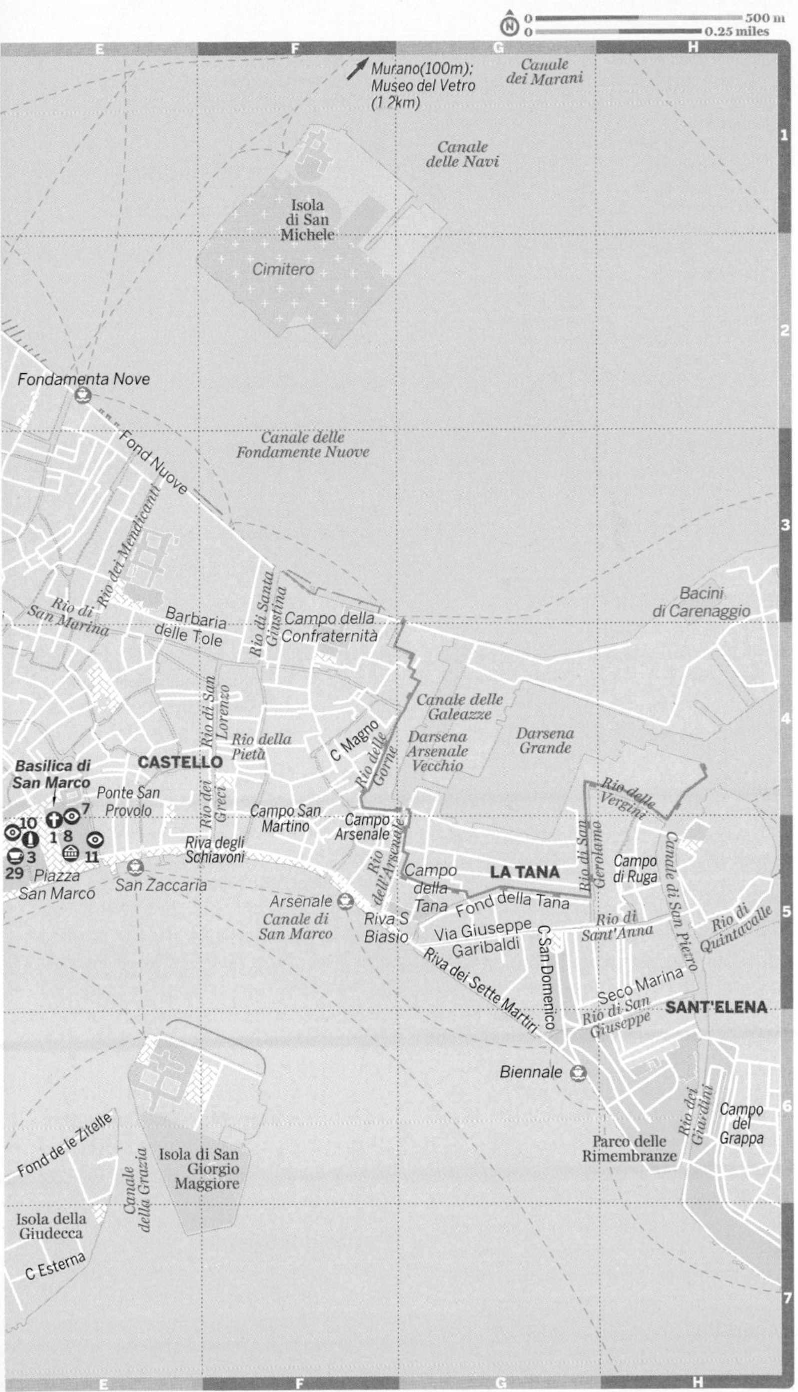

0 500 m
0 0.25 miles
Murano(100m); Museo del Vetro (1.2km)
Canale dei Marani
Canale delle Navi
Isola di San Michele
Cimitero
Fondamenta Nove
Canale delle Fondamente Nuove
Fond Nuove
Rio dei Mendicanti
Rio di San Marina
Barbaria delle Tole
Rio di Santa Giustina
Campo della Confraternità
Bacini di Carenaggio
Rio di San Lorenzo
Canale delle Galeazze
Darsena Arsenale Vecchio
Darsena Grande
Rio della Pietà
C Magno
Rio delle Gorne
Basilica di San Marco
CASTELLO
Ponte San Provolo
Rio dei Greci
Campo San Martino
Campo Arsenale
Rio delle Vergini
Riva degli Schiavoni
Rio dell'Arsenale
Campo della Tana
LA TANA
Rio di San Gerolamo
Campo di Ruga
Canale di San Pietro
Piazza San Marco
San Zaccaria
Arsenale
Canale di San Marco
Fond della Tana
Riva S Biasio
Via Giuseppe Garibaldi
C San Domenico
Rio di Sant'Anna
Rio di Quintavalle
Riva dei Sette Martiri
Seco Marina
Rio di San Giuseppe
SANT'ELENA
Biennale
Rio dei Giardini
Campo del Grappa
Parco delle Rimembranze
Fond de le Zitelle
Isola di San Giorgio Maggiore
Canale della Grazia
Isola della Giudecca
C Esterna

Venice

Don't Miss Sights
1 Basilica di San Marco E5

Sights
2 Basilica di Santa Maria della Salute D5
3 Campanile E5
4 Chiesa del Santissimo Redentore C7
5 Gallerie dell'Accademia C5
6 I Frari C4
7 Pala d'Oro E4
8 Palazzo Ducale E5
9 Peggy Guggenheim Collection C5
10 Piazza San Marco E5
11 Ponte dei Sospiri E5

Sleeping
12 Ca' Angeli C4
13 Giardino dei Melograni C2
14 Hotel Bernardi D3
15 Hotel La Calcina C6
16 Novecento C5
17 Oltre il Giardino C4
18 Pensione Guerrato D3

Eating
19 All'Arco D3
20 Anice Stellato C2
21 Birraria La Corte C4
22 Dalla Marisa B2
23 Grom B5
24 Osteria La Zucca C3
25 Ristorante La Bitta B5
26 Trattoria da Bepi Già "54" D3
27 Vecio Fritolin C3

Drinking & Nightlife
28 Al Mercà D3
29 Caffè Florian E5
30 Cantina Do Spade D3
31 Il Caffè Rosso B4

Entertainment
32 Teatro La Fenice D5

Venetian Republic grew into a great merchant power, dominating half the Mediterranean and the trade routes to the Levant – it was from Venice that Marco Polo set out for China in 1271. Decline began in the 16th century and in 1797 the city authorities opened the gates to Napoleon, who, in turn, handed the city over to the Austrians. In 1866, Venice was incorporated into the Kingdom of Italy.

Sights

Whet your sightseeing appetite by taking *vaporetto* (small passenger ferry) number 1 along the **Grand Canal**, lined with rococo, Gothic, Moorish and Renaissance palaces. Alight at Piazza San Marco, Venice's main square.

SAN MARCO

Piazza San Marco — Piazza

(St Mark's Sq; San Marco) This grand showpiece square beautifully encapsulates the splendour of Venice's past and its tourist-fuelled present. Flanked by the arcaded **Procuratie Vecchie** and **Procuratie Nuove**, it's filled for much of the day with tourists, pigeons and tour guides. To get a bird's eye view, the Basilica di San Marco's free-standing 99m **campanile (Bell Tower; www.basilicasanmarco.it; Piazza San Marco; admission €8; 9am-9pm summer, to 7pm spring & autumn, 9.30am-3.45pm winter; San Marco)** commands stunning 360-degree panoramas.

Palazzo Ducale — Museum

(Ducal Palace; 041 271 59 11; www.palazzoducale.visitmuve.it; Piazzetta San Marco 52; incl Museo Correr adult/reduced €17/10; 8.30am-7pm summer, to 5.30pm winter; San Zaccaria) This grand Gothic palace was the Doge's official residence from the 9th century, and seat of the Venetian Republic's government (and prisons) for nearly seven centuries. The Doge's Apartments are on the 1st floor, but it's the lavishly decorated 2nd-floor chambers that are the real highlight. These culminate in the echoing **Sala del Maggior Consiglio** (Grand Council Hall), home to the Doge's throne and a 22m-by-7m *Paradise* painting by Tintoretto's son Domenico.

Ponte dei Sospiri — Bridge

One of Venice's most photographed sights, the Bridge of Sighs connects Palazzo Ducale to the 16th-century Priggione Nove (New Prisons). It's named after the sighs that condemned

DANITA DELIMONT/GETTY IMAGES ©

Don't Miss Basilica di San Marco

With its tapering spires, Byzantine domes, luminous mosaics and lavish marblework, Venice's signature church is an unforgettable sight. It was originally built to house St Mark's corpse, but the first chapel burnt down in 932 and a new basilica was constructed over it in 1094. For the next 500 years it was a work in progress as successive doges added mosaics and embellishments looted from the east.

Of the many jewels inside, look out for the **Pala d'Oro** (admission €2), a stunning gold altarpiece.

NEED TO KNOW

St Mark's Basilica; ☎041 270 83 11; www.basilicasanmarco.it; Piazza San Marco; 🕘9.45am-5pm Mon-Sat, 2-5pm Sun summer, to 4pm Sun winter; ⛴San Marco

prisoners – including Giacomo Casanova – emitted as they were led down to the cells.

DORSODURO

Gallerie dell'Accademia Gallery

(☎041 520 03 45; www.gallerieaccademia.org; Campo della Carità 1050; adult/reduced €11/8 plus supplement during special exhibitions, first Sun of the month free; 🕘8.15am-2pm Mon, to 7.15pm Tue-Sun; ⛴Accademia) Venice's historic gallery traces the development of Venetian art from the 14th to 18th centuries with works by Bellini, Titian, Tintoretto, Veronese and Canaletto among others. Housing it, the former Santa Maria della Carità convent complex maintained its serene composure for centuries until Napoleon installed his haul of Venetian art trophies here in 1807, since when there's been nonstop visual drama inside its walls.

Grand Canal

The 3.5km route of vaporetto (passenger ferry) No 1, which passes some 50 palazzi (mansions), six churches and scene-stealing backdrops featured in four James Bond films, is public transport at its most glamorous.

The Grand Canal starts with controversy: **Ponte di Calatrava** ❶ a luminous glass-and-steel bridge that cost triple the original €4 million estimate. Ahead are castle-like **Fondaco dei Turchi** ❷, the historic Turkish trading-house; Renaissance **Palazzo Vendramin** ❸, housing the city's casino; and double-arcaded **Ca' Pesaro** ❹. Don't miss **Ca' d'Oro** ❺, a 1430 filigree Gothic marvel.

Points of Venetian pride include the **Pescaria** ❻, built in 1907 on the site where fishmongers have been slinging lagoon crab for 600 years, and neighbouring **Rialto Market** ❼ stalls, overflowing with island-grown produce. Cost overruns for 1592 **Ponte di Rialto** ❽ rival Calatrava's, but its marble splendour stands the test of time.

The next two canal bends could cause architectural whiplash, with Sanmicheli-designed Renaissance **Palazzo Grimani** ❾ and Mauro Codussi's **Palazzo Corner-Spinelli** ❿ followed by Giorgio Masari-designed **Palazzo Grassi** ⓫ and Baldassare Longhena's baroque jewel box, **Ca' Rezzonico** ⓬.

Wooden **Ponte dell'Accademia** ⓭ was built in 1930 as a temporary bridge, but the beloved landmark was recently reinforced. Stone lions flank the **Peggy Guggenheim Collection** ⓮, where the American heiress collected ideas, lovers and art. You can't miss the dramatic dome of Longhena's **Chiesa di Santa Maria della Salute** ⓯ or **Punta della Dogana** ⓰, Venice's triangular customs warehouse reinvented as a contemporary art showcase. The Grand Canal's grand finale is pink Gothic **Palazzo Ducale** ⓱ and its adjoining **Ponte dei Sospiri** ⓲.

LONELY PLANET/GETTY IMAGES ©
Palazzo Grassi
French magnate François Pinault scandalised Paris when he relocated his contemporary art collection here, where there are galleries designed by Gae Aulenti and Tadao Ando.
1
Ca' Rezzonico
See how Venice lived in baroque splendour at this 18th-century art museum with Tiepolo ceilings, silk-swagged boudoirs and even an in-house pharmacy.
12
11
13 Ponte dell'Accademia
14
Peggy Guggenheim Collection
Chiesa di Santa Maria delle Salute
15
16
Punta della Dogana
Minimalist architect Tadao Ando creatively repurposed abandoned warehouses as galleries, which now host contemporary art installations from François Pinault's collection.
ALVARO LEIVA/GETTY IMAGES ©

RUSSELL MOUNTFORD/GETTY IMAGES ©

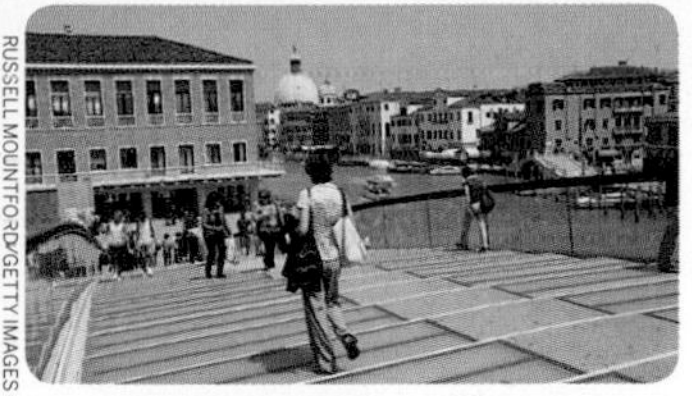

Ponte di Calatrava
With its starkly streamlined fish-fin shape, the 2008 bridge is the first to be built over the Grand Canal in 75 years.

Fondaco dei Turchi
Recognisable by its double colonnade, watchtowers, and dugout canoe parked at the Museo di Storia Naturale's ground-floor loggia.

JEAN-PIERRE LESCOURRET/GETTY IMAGES ©

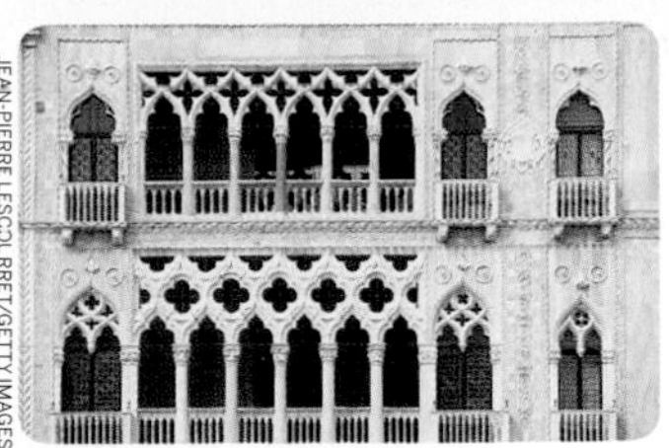

Ca' d'Oro
Behind the triple Gothic arcades are priceless masterpieces: Titians looted by Napoleon, a rare Mantegna and semiprecious stone mosaic floors.

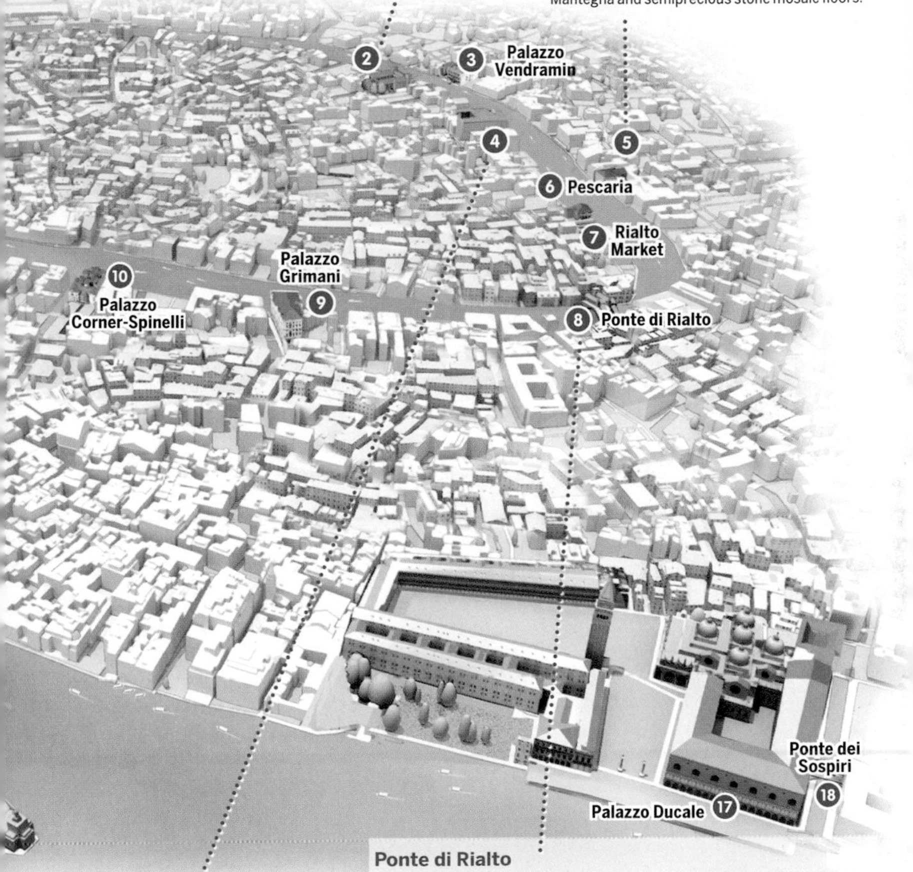

2
3 Palazzo Vendramin
4
5
6 Pescaria
7 Rialto Market
Palazzo Grimani 9
10 Palazzo Corner-Spinelli
8 Ponte di Rialto
Ponte dei Sospiri 18
Palazzo Ducale 17

Ponte di Rialto
Antonio da Ponte beat out Palladio for the commission of this bridge, but construction costs spiralled to 250,000 Venetian ducats – about €19 million today.

KRZYSZTOF DYDYNSKI/GETTY IMAGES ©

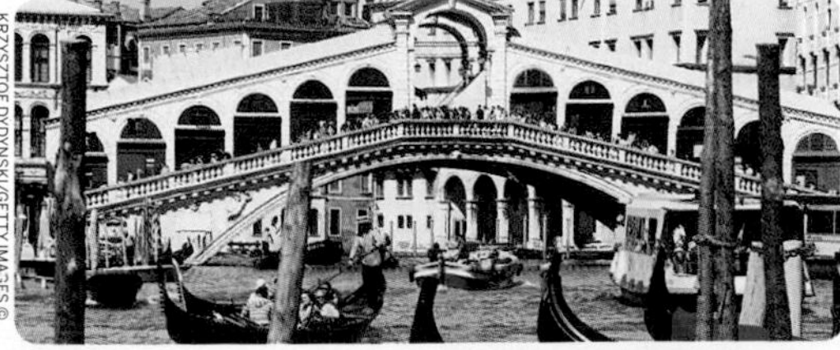

Ca' Pesaro
Originally designed by Baldassare Longhena, this palazzo was bequeathed to the city in 1898 to house the Galleria d'Arte Moderna and Museo d'Arte Orientale.

Peggy Guggenheim Collection Museum

(041 240 54 11; www.guggenheim-venice.it; Palazzo Venier dei Leoni 704; adult/reduced €15/9; 10am-6pm Wed-Mon; Accademia) After losing her father on the *Titanic,* heiress Peggy Guggenheim became one of the great collectors of the 20th century. Her palatial canalside home, Palazzo Venier dei Leoni, showcases her stockpile of surrealist, futurist and abstract expressionist art with works by up to 200 artists, including her ex-husband Max Ernst, Jackson Pollock (among her many rumoured lovers), Picasso and Salvador Dalí.

Basilica di Santa Maria della Salute Basilica

(La Salute; 041 241 10 18; www.seminariovenezia.it; Campo della Salute 1b; admission free, sacristy adult/reduced €3/1.50; 9am-noon & 3-5.30pm; Salute) Guarding the entrance to the Grand Canal, this 17th-century domed church was commissioned by Venice's plague survivors as thanks for salvation. Baldassare Longhena's uplifting design is an engineering feat that defies simple logic, and in fact the church is said to have mystical curative properties. Titian eluded the plague until age 94, leaving a legacy of masterpieces in the Salute's sacristy.

SAN POLO & SANTA CROCE

I Frari Church

(Basilica di Santa Maria Gloriosa dei Frari; Campo dei Frari, San Polo 3072; adult/reduced €3/1.50; 9am-6pm Mon-Sat, 1-6pm Sun; ; San Tomà) This soaring Italian-brick Gothic church features marquetry choir stalls, Canova's pyramid mausoleum, Bellini's achingly sweet *Madonna with Child* triptych in the sacristy and Longhena's creepy Doge Pesaro funereal monument – yet visitors are inevitably drawn to the small altarpiece. This is Titian's 1518 *Assumption,* in which a radiant red-cloaked Madonna reaches heavenward, steps onto a cloud and escapes this mortal coil. Titian himself died in 1576 and is buried here near his celebrated masterpiece.

GIUDECCA

Chiesa del Santissimo Redentore Church

(Church of the Redeemer; Campo del SS Redentore 194; adult/reduced €3/1.50, or with Chorus Pass free; 10am-5pm Mon-Sat; Redentore) Built to celebrate the city's deliverance from the Black Death, Palladio's *Il Redentore* was completed under Antonio da Ponte (of Rialto bridge fame) in 1592. Inside there are works by Tintoretto, Veronese and Vivarini, but the most striking is Paolo Piazza's 1619 *Gratitude of Venice for Liberation from the Plague*.

Grand Canal and the Basilica di Santa Maria della Salute, Venice

Venice Discounts

- **Civic Museum Pass** (www.visitmuve.it, adult/reduced €24/18) is valid for single entry to 11 civic museums, or just the five museums around Piazza San Marco (adult/reduced €16/10). Buy online or at participating museums.
- **Chorus Pass** (www.chorusvenezia.org, adult/reduced €12/8) Covers admission to 11 churches. Buy at particpating sites.
- **Venezia Unica City Pass** (www.veneziaunica.it, adult/reduced €39.90/29.90) Combines the Civic Museum and Chorus Passes as well as providing discounted entry to other sites. Check the website for details and to buy. Also available at HelloVenezia booths.

THE ISLANDS

Murano Island

(**4.1, 4.2**) Murano has been the home of Venetian glass-making since the 13th century. Tour a factory for a behind-the-scenes look at production or visit the **Museo del Vetro** (**Glass Museum; 041 527 47 18; www.museovetro.visitmuve.it; Fondamenta Giustinian 8; adult/reduced €10/7.50; 10am-6pm summer, to 5pm winter; Museo**) near the Museo *vaporetto* stop. Note that at the time of writing the museum was undergoing a major overhaul.

Activities

Be prepared to pay through the nose for that quintessential Venetian experience, a **gondola ride**. Official rates start at €80 or €100 from 7pm to 8am; these prices are per gondola (maximum six people). Additional time is charged in 20-minute increments (day/night €40/50). Haggling is unlikely to get you a reduction but you can save money by taking a gondola tour with the tourist office or a reliable tour operator.

Festivals & Events

Carnevale Carnival

(**www.carnevale.venezia.it**) Masquerade madness stretches over two weeks in February before Lent. Tickets to masked balls start at €140, but there's a free-flowing wine fountain to commence Carnevale, public costume parties in every *campo* (square) and a Grand Canal flotilla marking the end of festivities.

Venice Biennale Art

(**www.labiennale.org**) This major exhibition of international visual arts is held every odd-numbered year from June to November.

Venice International Film Festival Film

(**Mostra del Cinema di Venezia; www.labiennale.org/en/cinema**) The only thing hotter than a Lido beach in August is the Film Festival's star-studded red carpet, usually rolled out from the last weekend in August through the first week of September.

Regata Storica Cultural

(**www.regatastoricavenezia.it**) Sixteenth-century costumes, eight-oared gondolas and ceremonial barques feature in this historical procession (usually held in September), which re-enacts the arrival of the Queen of Cyprus and precedes gondola races.

Sleeping

Venice is Italy's most expensive city. It's always advisable to book ahead, especially at weekends, in May and September, and during Carnevale and other holidays.

Right: Burano, near Venice ; **Below:** Glass vase from Murano (p409)

SAN MARCO

Novecento Boutique Hotel **€€€**
(☎041 241 37 65; www.novecento.biz; Calle del Dose 2683/84; d €160-340; ❄📶; ⛴Santa Maria del Giglio) Sporting a boho-chic look, the Novocento is a real charmer. Its nine individually designed rooms ooze style with Turkish kilim pillows, Fortuny draperies and 19th-century carved bedsteads. Outside, its garden is a lovely spot to linger over breakfast.

DORSODURO

Hotel La Calcina Hotel **€€€**
(☎041 520 64 66; www.lacalcina.com; Fondamenta Zattere ai Gesuati 780, Dorsoduro; s €100-190, d €170-370; ❄📶; ⛴Zattere) A historic waterfront landmark, this classy three-star hotel boasts a panoramic rooftop terrace, an elegant canalside restaurant, and airy, parquet-floored rooms, several facing the Giudecca Canal and Redentore church. Book ahead for rooms with views, especially No 2, where John Ruskin stayed while he wrote his classic 1876 *The Stones of Venice*.

SAN POLO & SANTA CROCE

Ca' Angeli Boutique Hotel **€€**
(☎041 523 24 80; www.caangeli.it; Calle del Traghetto de la Madoneta 1434, San Polo; d €95-225, ste from €200; ❄📶; ⛴San Silvestro) Murano-glass chandeliers, polished parquet floors and grandstand canal views await at this refined retreat. Guest rooms are a picture with beamed ceilings, antique carpets and big bathrooms, while the dining room, where hearty organic breakfasts are served, looks out onto the Grand Canal.

Pensione Guerrato Pension **€€**
(☎041 528 59 27; www.pensioneguerrato.it; Calle Drio la Scimia 240a, San Polo; d/tr/q €145/165/185; ❄📶; ⛴Rialto Mercato) In a 1227 tower that was once a hostel for knights headed to the Third Crusade, smart guest rooms haven't lost their

sense of history – some have frescoes or glimpses of the Grand Canal. A prime Rialto Market location and helpful owners add to the package. Wi-fi in lobby. No lift.

Oltre il Giardino Boutique Hotel **€€€**
(**📞041 275 00 15; www.oltreilgiardino-venezia.com; Fondamenta Contarini, San Polo 2542; d €180-250, ste €200-500; ❄📶; ⛴San Tomà)** Live the dream in this garden villa, the 1920s home of Alma Mahler, the composer's widow. Hidden behind a lush walled garden, its six high-ceilinged guest rooms brim with historic charm and modern comfort, marrying precious antiques with discreet mod cons and pale ivory backdrops.

CANNAREGIO

Hotel Bernardi Hotel **€**
(**📞041 522 72 57; www.hotelbernardi.com; SS Apostoli Calle dell'Oca 4366, Cannaregio; s €48-110, d €57-90, f €75-140, without bathroom s €25-32, d €45-62; ❄📶)** Hospitable owners, a convenient location just off the main thoroughfare, and keen prices mean that the Bernardi is always heavily booked. Some of the best rooms – think timber-beamed ceilings, Murano chandeliers and gilt furniture – are in the annexe round the corner.

Giardino dei Melograni Guesthouse **€€**
(**📞041 822 61 31; www.pardesrimonim.net; Ghetto Nuovo, Cannaregio 2873/c; s €70-100, d €80-180, tr €110-210, q €140-240; ❄📶; ⛴Ferrovia Santa Lucia)** Run by Venice's Jewish community, to which all proceeds go, the 'Garden of Pomegranates' is a sparkling kosher residence. It's located on the charming Campo Ghetto Nuovo just a short walk from the train station, and offers 14 bright, modern rooms.

Eating

Venetian specialities include *risi e bisi* (pea soup thickened with rice) and *sarde in saor* (fried sardines marinated

Navigating Venice

Everybody gets lost in Venice. It's impossible not to in a city of 117 islands, 150-odd canals and 400 bridges (only four of which – the Rialto, Accademia, Scalzi and Costituzione – cross the Grand Canal). To make matters worse, Venetian addresses are all but meaningless without detailed walking directions. Instead of a street and civic number, addresses generally consist of no more than the *sestiere* (Venice is divided into six *sestieri* or districts: Cannaregio, Castello, San Marco, Dorsoduro, San Polo and Santa Croce) followed by a long number.

You'll also need to know that in Venice a street is called a *calle, ruga* or *salizada;* beside a canal it's a *fondamenta.* A canal is a *rio,* a filled canal-turned-street a *rio terrà,* and a square a *campo* (Piazza San Marco is Venice's only piazza).

When walking around, the most helpful points of reference are Santa Lucia train station (signposted as *ferrovia*) and Piazzale Roma in the northwest, and Piazza San Marco (St Mark's Sq) in the south. The signposted path from the station to Piazza San Marco (Venice's main drag) is a good 40- to 50-minute walk.

in vinegar and onions). Also look out for *cicheti*, traditional Venetian bar snacks.

DORSODURO

Grom Gelateria €

(**041 099 17 51; www.grom.it; Campo San Barnaba 2461; gelati €2.50-5.50; 10.30am-11pm Sun-Thu, 10am-12.30am Fri & Sat, shorter hours winter; Ca' Rezzonico)** One of several Grom branches across town. The consistently good gelato, made with prime, seasonal ingredients (lemons from the Amalfi Coast, pistachios from Sicily, hazelnuts from Piedmont), makes for a perfect pick-me-up.

Ristorante La Bitta Ristorante €€

(**041 523 05 31; Calle Lunga San Barnaba 2753a; meals €35-40; 6.45-10.45pm Mon-Sat; Ca' Rezzonico)** A cosy, woody restaurant near lively Campo Santa Margherita. The daily menu arrives on an artist's easel, and the hearty, rustic fare looks like a still life and tastes like a carnivore's dream: steak comes snugly wrapped in bacon, veal is braised with *chiodini* mushrooms. Reservations essential. Cash only.

SAN POLO & SANTA CROCE

All'Arco Venetian €

(**041 520 56 66; Calle dell'Ochialer 436, San Polo; cicheti from €1.50; 8am-8pm Wed-Fri, to 3pm Mon, Tue & Sat ; Rialto-Mercato)** Search out this authentic neighbourhood *osteria* for some of the best *cicheti* (bar snacks) in town. Armed with ingredients from the nearby Rialto market, father-son team Francesco and Matteo serve miniature masterpieces such as poached white asparagus with seasoned pancetta, and *otrega* (butterfish) *crudo* with mint-and-olive-oil marinade.

Osteria La Zucca Modern Italian €€

(**041 524 15 70; www.lazucca.it; Calle del Tentor 1762, Santa Croce; meals €35; 12.30-2.30pm & 7-10.30pm Mon-Sat; San Stae)** With its menu of seasonal vegetarian creations and classic meat dishes, this cosy wood-panelled restaurant consistently hits the mark. Herbs and spices are used to great effect in dishes such as cinnamon-tinged pumpkin flan and lamb with dill and pecorino. The small interior can get toasty, so reserve canalside seats in summer.

Birraria La Corte Pizza **€€**
(☎041 275 05 70; Campo San Polo 2168, San Polo; pizzas €7-14, meals €35; ⏰noon-3pm & 6-10.30pm; 📶; ⛴San Tomà) This one-time bull stable became a brewery in the 19th century to keep Venice's Austrian occupiers occupied, and beer and beef remain reliable bets. There's also pizza and much coveted piazza-side seating.

Vecio Fritolin Venetian, Seafood **€€€**
(☎041 522 28 81; www.veciofritolin.it; Calle della Regina 2262, Santa Croce; meals €45, traditional 3-course set menu €38; ⏰7.30-10.30pm Tue, noon-2.30pm & 7-10.30pm Wed-Sun; ⛴San Stae) Traditionally, a *fritolin* was an eatery where diners sat at a communal table and tucked into fried fish. This is the modern equivalent, albeit smarter and more sophisticated. The menu includes meat and vegetable dishes, but the star act is the top-quality seafood, sourced daily from the nearby Rialto market.

CANNAREGIO

Dalla Marisa Venetian **€€**
(☎041 72 02 11; Fondamenta di San Giobbe 652b, Cannaregio; set menus lunch/dinner €15/35; ⏰noon-3pm daily & 7-11pm Tue & Thu-Sat; ⛴Crea) At this Cannaregio institution, you'll be seated where there's room and have whatever Marisa's cooking, though you will be informed whether the fixed-price menu is meat- or fish-based when you book. Venetian regulars confess Marisa's *fegato alla veneziana* (Venetian calf's liver) is better than their grandmothers'. No credit cards.

Trattoria da Bepi Già 54 Venetian **€€**
(☎041 528 50 31; www.dabepi.it; Campo SS Apostoli 4550; meals €30-40; ⏰noon-2.30pm & 7-10pm Fri-Wed; ⛴Ca' d'Oro) One of the better eateries on the touristy main drag (actually it's just a few metres off it near Santi Apostoli) this is a classic old-school trattoria with a few outside tables and a cheerfully cluttered wood-lined interior. The food is traditional Venetian with an emphasis on seafood.

Anice Stellato Venetian **€€€**
(☎041 72 07 44; www.osterianicestellato.com; Fondamenta della Sensa 3272; bar snacks €13.50, meals €45-50; ⏰10.30am-3.30pm & 6.30pm-midnight Wed-Sun; ⛴Madonna dell'Orto) Tin lamps, unadorned rustic tables and a small wooden bar set the scene for quality seafood at this excellent canalside *bacaro* (traditional Venetian *osteria*). You can munch on barside *cicheti* (bar snacks) or go for the full à la carte menu and swoon over juicy scampi in *saor* (vinegar marinade) and grilled tuna.

Drinking & Nightlife

Cantina Do Spade Bar
(☎041 521 05 83; www.cantinadospade.com; Calle delle Do Spade 860, San Polo; ⏰10am-3pm & 6-10pm; 📶; ⛴Rialto) Since 1488 this

Piazza San Marco (p404), Venice
HANS-PETER MERTEN/GETTY IMAGES ©

cosy, brick-clad bar has kept Venice in good spirits, and the young, laid-back management extends a warm welcome to *spritz*-sipping Venetian regulars and visiting connoisseurs drinking double-malt beer and bargain Venetian cab franc. Come early for market-fresh *fritture* (batter-fried seafood).

Al Mercà Wine Bar

(Campo Cesare Battisti 213, San Polo; 10am-2.30pm & 6-9pm Mon-Thu, to 9.30pm Fri & Sat; Rialto) Discerning drinkers throng to this cupboard-sized counter on a Rialto market square to sip on top-notch *prosecco* and wines by the glass (from €2). Arrive by 6.30pm for mini-*panini* (€1 to €2.50) and easy bar access, or mingle with crowds stretching to the Grand Canal docks.

Il Caffè Rosso Cafe

(041 528 79 98; Campo Santa Margherita 2963; 7am-1am Mon-Sat; ; Ca' Rezzonico) Affectionately known as *'il rosso'*, this red-fronted cafe has been at the centre of the bar scene on Campo Santa Margherita since the late 1800s. It's at its best in the early evening, when locals snap up the sunny piazza seating to sip on inexpensive *spritzes*.

Caffè Florian Cafe

(041 520 56 41; www.caffeflorian.com; Piazza San Marco 56/59; drinks €10-25; 9am-midnight; San Marco) One of Venice's most famous cafes, Florian maintains rituals (if not prices) established c 1720: white-jacketed waiters serve cappuccino on silver trays, lovers canoodle in plush banquettes and the orchestra strikes up a tango as the sunset illuminates San Marco's mosaics.

Entertainment

Upcoming events are listed in the *Shows & Events* guide (€1), available at tourist offices, and at www.veneziadavivere.com. Tickets for most events are sold at **HelloVenezia** (**041 24 24; Piazzale Roma; transport tickets 7am-8pm, events tickets 8.30am-6.30pm; Piazzale Roma**). The ticket booth is in front of the train station.

Teatro La Fenice Opera

(041 78 65 11, theatre tours 041 78 66 75; www.teatrolafenice.it; Campo San Fantin 1965; theatre visits adult/reduced €9/6, concert/

Caffè Florian, Venice

KRZYSZTOF DYDYNSKI/GETTY IMAGES ©

opera tickets from €15/45; ⏲tours 9.30am-6pm; ⛴Santa Maria dei Giglio) La Fenice, one of Italy's top opera houses, hosts a rich program of opera, ballet and classical music. With advance booking you can tour the theatre, but the best way to see it is with the *loggionisti* – opera buffs in the cheap top-tier seats. Get tickets at the theatre, online or through HelloVenezia.

Information

Emergency

Police station (Santa Croce 500; ⛴Santa Chiara)

Medical Services

Ospedale Civile (☎041 529 41 11; Campo SS Giovanni e Paolo 6777; ⛴Ospedale) Venice's main hospital; for emergency care and dental treatment.

Tourist Information

Tourist office (☎041 529 87 11; www.turismovenezia.it). Has branches at:

Airport **(Arrivals Hall, Marco Polo Airport; ⏲8.30am-7.30pm)**

Piazzale Roma **(Ground fl, multistorey car park, Piazzale Roma; ⏲8.30am-2.30pm; ⛴Santa Chiara)**

San Marco **(Piazza San Marco 71F; ⏲8.30am-7pm; ⛴San Marco)**

Santa Lucia Station **(Stazione di Santa Lucia; ⏲8.30am-7pm; ⛴Ferrovia Santa Lucia)**

Venice Pavilion **(Ex Giardini Reali, San Marco 30124; ⏲8.30am-7pm; ⛴San Marco)**

Getting There & Away

Air

Most European and domestic flights land at Marco Polo airport (p453), 12km outside Venice. Ryanair flies to **Treviso airport (TSF; ☎0422 31 51 11; www.trevisoairport.it; Via Noalese 63)**, about 30km away.

Boat

Venezia Lines (☎041 882 11 01; www.venezialines.com) operates high-speed boats to/from several ports in Croatia between mid-April and early October, including Pula (€69 to €74).

Train

Venice's Stazione di Santa Lucia is directly linked by regional trains to Padua (€4.05 to €13, 50 minutes, every 10 minutes) and Verona (€7.40 to €18.40, 1¼ to 2¼ hours, half-hourly), and has fast services to/from Bologna, Milan, Rome and Florence. International trains run to/from points in France, Germany, Austria and Switzerland.

Getting Around

To/From the Airport

To get to/from Marco Polo airport there are several options.

Alilaguna (☎041 240 17 01; www.alilaguna.it) operates three fast-ferry lines (€8/15 to Murano/Venice, approximately half-hourly) – the Arancio (Orange) line goes to Piazza San Marco via Rialto and the Grand Canal; the Blu (Blue) line stops off at Murano, the Lido and San Marco; and the Rosso (Red) line runs to Murano and the Lido.

There is an **ATVO (☎0421 59 46 71; www.atvo.it)** shuttle bus to/from Piazzale Roma (€6/11 one way/return, 20 minutes, half-hourly).

The set taxi fare to/from the train station is €40. A water taxi will cost about €115 for two people with luggage.

For Treviso airport, there's an ATVO shuttle bus (one way/return €7/13, 70 minutes, six times daily) to/from Piazzale Roma.

Boat

The city's main mode of public transport is the *vaporetto.* Useful routes include:

Route 1 From Piazzale Roma to the train station and down the Grand Canal to San Marco and the Lido.

Route 2 From San Zaccaria (near San Marco) to the Lido via Giudecca, Piazzale Roma, the train station and Rialto.

Route 4.1 To/from Murano via Fondamente Nove, the train station, Piazzale Roma, Giudecca and San Zaccaria.

Route 9 From Burano to Torcello and vice versa.

Tickets, available from ACTV booths at the major *vaporetti* stops and the HelloVenezia booth at Piazzale Roma, are expensive:

€7 for a single trip;
€18 for 12 hours;
€20 for 24 hours;
€25 for 36 hours;

€30 for two days;
€35 for three days;
€50 for seven days.

The poor man's gondola, traghetti (€2 per crossing), are used to cross the Grand Canal where there's no nearby bridge.

Bologna

POP 384,200

Boasting a boisterous bonhomie rare in Italy's reserved north, Bologna is one of Italy's great unsung destinations. Its medieval centre, one of Italy's finest, is an eye-catching ensemble of red-brick *palazzi,* Renaissance towers and 40km of arcaded porticoes, and there are enough sights to excite without exhausting. A university town since 1088 (Europe's oldest), it is also one of Italy's foremost foodie destinations, home to the eponymous bolognese sauce *(ragù)* as well as tortellini (pasta pockets stuffed with meat), lasagne and *mortadella* (aka baloney or Bologna sausage).

Sights

The **Bologna Welcome Card** (€20), available in tourist offices, gives free entrance to city-run museums, discounts in shops and restaurants, and a choice of one of the following: a city guided tour, free public transport for 24 hours or a free ticket for the airport shuttle bus.

Basilica di San Petronio Church
(Piazza Maggiore; 7.45am-2pm & 3-6.30pm) Bologna's hulking Gothic basilica is the world's fifth-largest church, measuring 132m by 66m by 47m. Work began on it in 1390, but it was never finished and still today its main facade remains incomplete. Inside, look out for the huge sundial that stretches 67.7m down the eastern aisle. Designed in 1656 by Gian Cassini and Domenico Guglielmi, this was instrumental in discovering the anomalies of the Julian calendar and led to the creation of the leap year.

Torre degli Asinelli Tower
(Piazza di Porta Ravegnana; admission €3; 9am-7pm Apr-Sep, to 5pm Oct-Mar) Bologna's two leaning towers are the city's

Gondola on the Grand Canal (p406), Venice

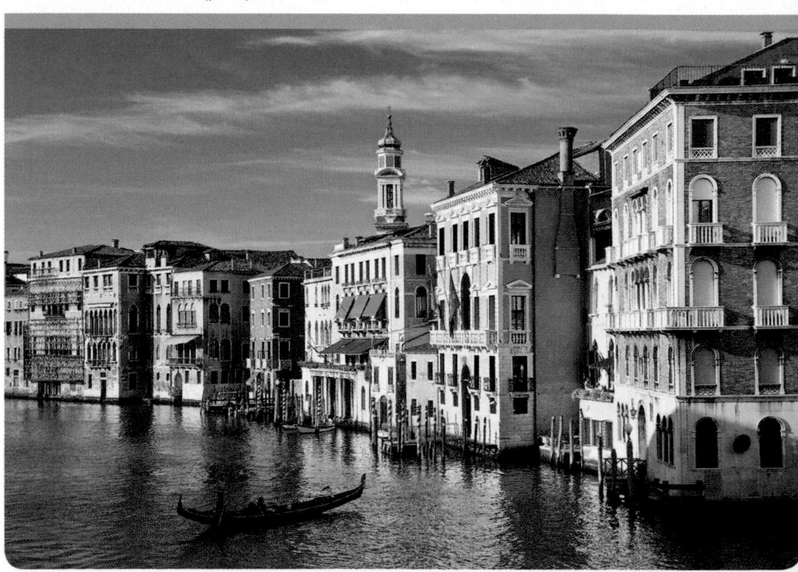

Detour: Ravenna

A rewarding and worthwhile day trip from Bologna, the refined town of Ravenna is famous for its early Christian mosaics. These Unesco-listed treasures have been impressing visitors since the 13th century when Dante described them in his *Divine Comedy* (much of which was written in Ravenna).

The mosaics are spread over five sites in the town centre: the **Basilica di San Vitale** (Via Fiandrini; ⏰9am-7pm Apr-Sep, 9am-5.30pm Mar & Oct, 9.30am-5pm Nov-Feb), the **Mausoleo di Galla Placidia** (Via Fiandrini; ⏰9am-7pm Apr-Sep, 9am-5.30pm Mar & Oct, 9.30am-5pm Nov-Feb), the **Museo Arcivescovile** (Piazza Arcivescovado; ⏰9am-7pm Apr-Sep, 9.30am-5.30pm Mar & Oct, 10am-5pm Nov-Feb), the **Battistero Neoniano** (Piazza del Duomo; ⏰9am-7pm Apr-Sep, 9.30am-5.30pm Mar & Oct, 10am-5pm Nov-Feb), the **Basilica di Sant'Apollinare Nuovo** (Via di Roma; ⏰9am-7pm Apr-Sep, 9.30am-5.30pm Mar & Oct, 10am-5pm Nov-Feb). These are covered by a single ticket (€9.50 or €11.50 between March and June), available at any of the sites.

Outside of town, you'll find further mosaics at the **Basilica di Sant'Apollinare in Classe** (Via Romea Sud; adult/reduced €5/2.50, Sun morning free; ⏰8.30am-7.30pm).

The website www.ravennamosaici.it has more information.

Regional trains run to/from Bologna (€7.10, 1½ hours, hourly) and destinations on the east coast.

main symbol. The taller of the two, the 97.6m-high Torre degli Asinelli is open to the public, though it's not advisable for the weak-kneed (there are 498 steps) or for superstitious students (local lore says if you climb it you'll never graduate). Built by the Asinelli family between 1109 and 1119, it today leans 1.3m off vertical.

Its shorter twin, the 48m-high **Torre Garisenda** is sensibly out of bounds given its drunken 3.2m tilt.

Quadrilatero — Area

To the east of Piazza Maggiore, the grid of streets around Via Clavature (Street of Locksmiths) sits on what was once Roman Bologna. Known as the Quadrilatero, this compact district is a great place for a wander with its market stalls, cafes and lavishly stocked delis.

Sleeping

Albergo delle Drapperie — Hotel €€

(☎051 22 39 55; www.albergodrapperie.com; Via delle Drapperie 5; s €58-70, d €85-115, ste €115-140; ❄📶) In the atmospheric Quadrilatero neighbourhood, the Drapperie is snugly ensconced in the upper floors of a large building. Buzz in at ground level and climb the stairs to discover 19 attractive rooms with wood-beamed ceilings, the occasional brick arch and colourful ceiling frescoes. Breakfast is €5 extra.

Hotel University Bologna — Hotel €€

(☎051 22 97 13; www.hoteluniversitybologna.com; Via Mentana 7; d €70-250; ❄📶) Student digs never felt so good. This low-key hotel offers a hospitable welcome and decent three-star rooms in the heart of the university district.

Eating

Trattoria del Rosso — Trattoria €

(☎051 23 67 30; www.trattoriadelrosso.com; Via A Righi 30; meals €21-25; ⏰noon-3pm & 7-10pm) The Rosso, said to be the city's oldest trattoria, is a great example of what they do so well in Bologna. A bustling, workaday eatery, it serves healthy portions of home-style local fare at honest prices and without a frill in sight.

Osteria de' Poeti Ristorante **€€**
(**051 23 61 66; www.osteriadepoeti.com; Via de' Poeti 1b; meals €30-40; 12.30-2.30pm & 7.30pm-3am Tue-Fri, 7.30pm-3am Sat, 12.30-2.30pm Sun**) In the wine cellar of a 14th-century *palazzo,* this historic eatery is one place to get to grips with Bologna's much-lauded cuisine. Take a table by the stone fireplace and try staples such as *tortelloni al doppio burro e salvia* (homemade ravioli with butter and sage).

Information

Tourist office (**051 23 96 60; www.bolognawelcome.it; Piazza Maggiore 1e; 9am-7pm Mon-Sat, 10am-5pm Sun**) Also has an office at the airport.

Getting There & Around

Air

European and domestic flights serve Guglielmo Marconi airport (**051 647 96 15; www.bologna-airport.it**), 8km northwest of the city. From the airport, an Aerobus shuttle (€6, 30 minutes, every 15 to 30 minutes) connects with the main train station; tickets can be bought on board.

Train

From the central train station on Piazza delle Medaglie d'Oro, regular fast trains run to Milan (€33 to €40, one to two hours), Venice (€30, 1½ hours), Florence (€24, 40 minutes) and Rome (€56, 2½ hours).

TUSCANY

Tuscany is one of those places that well and truly lives up to its hype. The fabled landscape of rolling, vine-covered hills dotted with cypress trees and stone villas has long been considered the embodiment of rural chic, and its historically intact cities are home to a significant portfolio of the world's medieval and Renaissance art.

Florence

POP 371,300

Visitors have rhapsodised about the beauty of Florence (Firenze) for centuries, and once here you'll appreciate why. An essential stop on every Italian itinerary, this Renaissance time capsule is busy year-round, but even the enormous and inevitable crowds of tourists fail to diminish its lustre. A list of the city's famous sons reads like a Renaissance who's who – under 'M' alone you'll find Medici, Machiavelli and Michelangelo – and its treasure trove of galleries, museums and churches showcases a magnificent array of Renaissance artworks. Florence's golden age flourished under the auspices of the Medici family. They ruled the city between the 14th and 17th centuries and their visionary patronage of writers, artists and thinkers culminated in the Renaissance.

Piazza Maggiore, Bologna
RUTH EASTHAM & MAX PAOLI/GETTY IMAGES ©

JUERGEN RICHTER/LOOK-FOTO/GETTY IMAGES ©

Don't Miss
Galleria degli Uffizi

Home to the world's greatest collection of Italian Renaissance art, Florence's premier gallery occupies Palazzo degli Uffizi, a handsome palace built between 1560 and 1580 to house government offices. The collection, which was bequeathed to the city by the Medici family in 1743 on condition that it never leave Florence, contains some of Italy's best-known paintings, including Piero della Francesco's profile portaits of the duke and duchess of Urbino and Sandro Botticelli's *La nascita di Venere* (The Birth of Venus).

NEED TO KNOW

Uffizi Gallery; www.uffizi.firenze.it; Piazzale degli Uffizi 6; adult/reduced €8/4, incl temporary exhibition €12.50/6.25; 8.15am-6.50pm Tue-Sun

Sights

PIAZZA DEL DUOMO

Duomo Cathedral

(Cattedrale di Santa Maria del Fiore; www.operaduomo.firenze.it; Piazza del Duomo; 10am-5pm Mon-Wed & Fri, to 4.30pm Thu, to 4.45pm Sat, 1.30-4.45pm Sun) FREE Florence's Duomo is the city's most iconic landmark. Capped by Filippo Brunelleschi's red-tiled **cupola (Dome; incl cupola, baptistry, campanile, crypt & museum adult/reduced €10/free; 8.30am-6.20pm Mon-Fri, to 5pm Sat)**, it's a staggering construction and its breathtaking pink, white and green marble facade and graceful *campanile* (bell tower) dominate the medieval cityscape. Sienese architect Arnolfo di Cambio began work on it 1296, but construction took almost 150 years and it wasn't consecrated until 1436. In the echoing interior, look out for frescoes by Vasari and Zuccari and up to 44 stained-glass windows.

The Uffizi

JOURNEY INTO THE RENAISSANCE

Navigating the Uffizi's chronologically-ordered art collection is straightforward enough: knowing which of the 1500-odd masterpieces to view before gallery fatigue strikes is not. Swap coat and bag (travel light) for floor plan and audioguide on the ground floor, then meet 16th-century Tuscany head-on with a walk up the *palazzo's* magnificent bust-lined staircase (skip the lift – the Uffizi is as much about masterly architecture as art).

Allow four hours for this journey into the High Renaissance. At the top of the staircase, on the 2nd floor, show your ticket, turn left and pause to admire the full length of the first corridor sweeping south towards the Arno river. Then duck left into room 2 to witness first steps in Tuscan art – shimmering altarpieces by **Giotto** ❶ et al. Journey through medieval art to room 8 and **Piero della Francesca's** ❷ impossibly famous portrait, then break in the corridor with playful **ceiling art** ❸. After Renaissance heavyweights **Botticelli** ❹ and **da Vinci** ❺, meander past the Tribuna (potential detour) and enjoy the daylight streaming in through the vast windows and panorama of the **riverside second corridor** ❻. Lap up soul-stirring views of the Arno, crossed by Ponte Vecchio and its echo of four bridges drifting towards the Apuane Alps on the horizon. Then saunter into the third corridor, pausing between rooms 25 and 34 to ponder the entrance to the enigmatic Vasari Corridor. End on a high with High Renaissance maestro **Michelangelo** ❼.

The Ognissanti Madonna
Room 2
Draw breath at the shy blush and curvaceous breast of Giotto's humanised Virgin (*Maestà*; 1310) – so feminine compared with those of Duccio and Cimabue painted just 25 years before.

Portraits of the Duke & Duchess of Urbino
Room 8
Revel in realism's voyage with these uncompromising, warts-and-all portraits (1472–75) by Piero della Francesca. No larger than A3 size, they originally slotted into a portable, hinged frame that folded like a book.

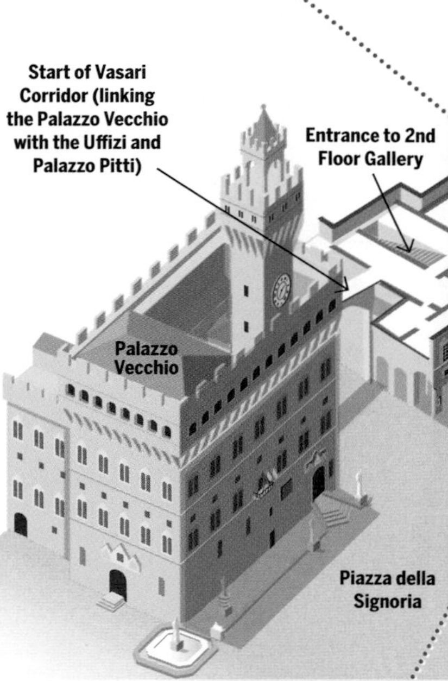

Grotesque Ceiling Frescoes
First Corridor
Take time to study the make-believe monsters and most unexpected of burlesques (spot the arrow-shooting satyr outside room 15) waltzing across this eastern corridor's fabulous frescoed ceiling (1581).

JUERGEN RICHTER/GETTY IMAGES ©

The Genius of Botticelli
Room 10–14

The miniature form of *The Discovery of the Body of Holofernes* (c 1470) makes Botticelli's early Renaissance masterpiece all the more impressive. Don't miss the artist watching you in *Adoration of the Magi* (1475), left of the exit.

BETHUNE CARMICHAEL/GETTY IMAGES ©

View of the Arno

Indulge in intoxicating city views from this short glassed-in corridor – an architectural masterpiece. Near the top of the hill, spot one of 73 outer towers built to defend Florence and its 15 city gates below.

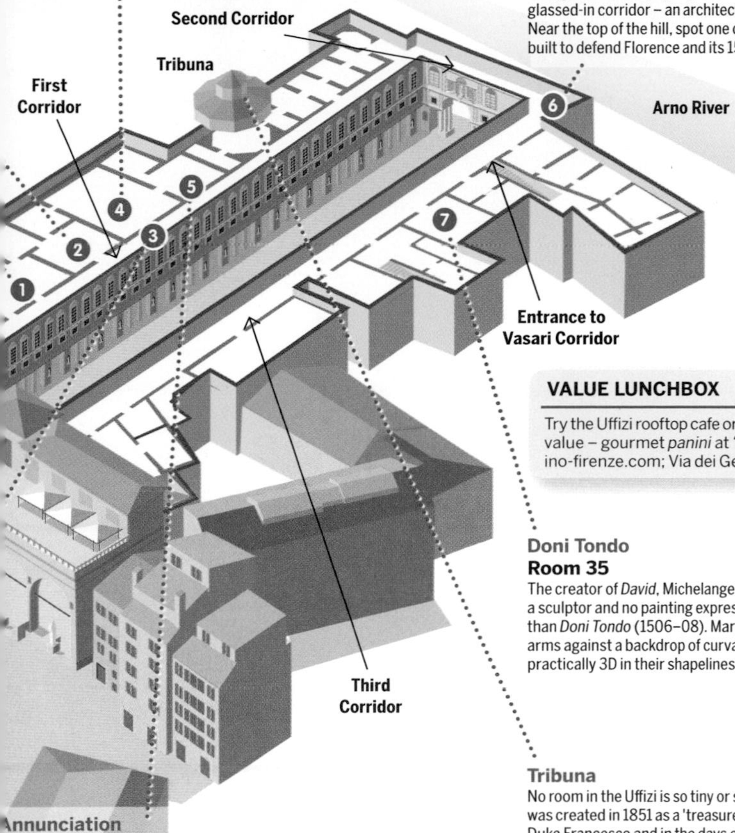

VALUE LUNCHBOX

Try the Uffizi rooftop cafe or – better value – gourmet *panini* at 'Ino (www.ino-firenze.com; Via dei Georgofili 3-7r).

Doni Tondo
Room 35

The creator of *David*, Michelangelo, was essentially a sculptor and no painting expresses this better than *Doni Tondo* (1506–08). Mary's muscular arms against a backdrop of curvaceous nudes are practically 3D in their shapeliness.

Tribuna

No room in the Uffizi is so tiny or so exquisite. It was created in 1851 as a 'treasure chest' for Grand Duke Francesco and in the days of the Grand Tour, the Medici Venus here was a tour highlight.

Annunciation
Room 15

Admire the exquisite portrayal of the Tuscan landscape in this painting (c 1472), one of few by Leonardo da Vinci to remain in Florence.

MATTER OF FACT

The Uffizi collection spans the 13th to 18th centuries, but its 15th- and 16th-century Renaissance works are second to none.

DEA PICTURE LIBRARY/GETTY IMAGES ©

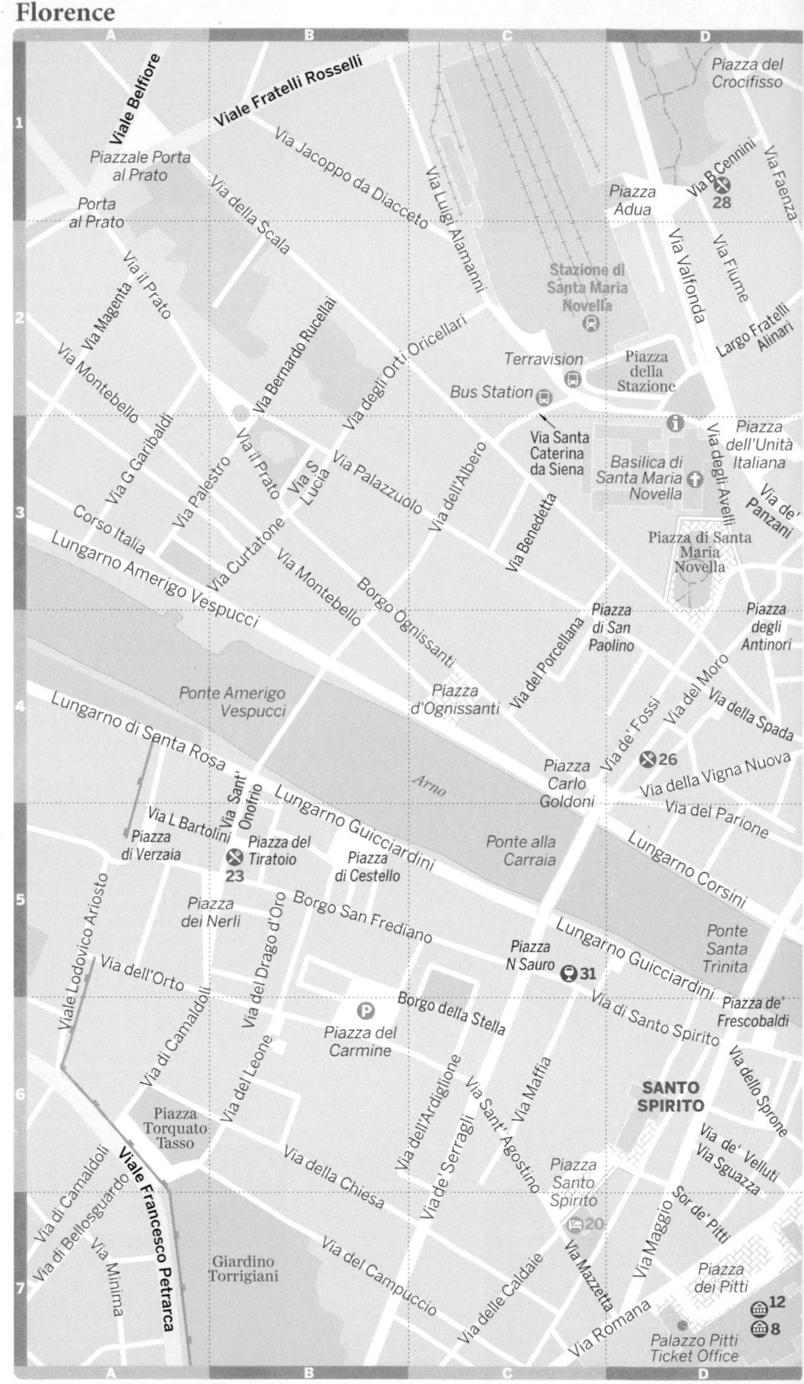
Viale Belfiore
Viale Fratelli Rosselli
Piazza del Crocifisso
Piazzale Porta al Prato
Porta al Prato
Via Jacoppo da Diacceto
Via della Scala
Via Luigi Alamanni
Piazza Adua
Via B Cennini
28
Via Faenza
Via Valfonda
Via Fiume
Stazione di Santa Maria Novella
Via il Prato
Via Magenta
Via Bernardo Rucellai
Via degli Orti Oricellari
Largo Fratelli Alinari
Terravision
Piazza della Stazione
Via Montebello
Bus Station
Via G Garibaldi
Via Santa Caterina da Siena
Piazza dell'Unità Italiana
Via il Prato
Via S Lucia
Via Palazzuolo
Via dell'Albero
Basilica di Santa Maria Novella
Via degli Avelli
Via Palestro
Via de' Panzani
Corso Italia
Via Benedetta
Piazza di Santa Maria Novella
Lungarno Amerigo Vespucci
Via Curtatone
Via Montebello
Borgo Ognissanti
Piazza di San Paolino
Piazza degli Antinori
Via del Porcellana
Via del Moro
Ponte Amerigo Vespucci
Piazza d'Ognissanti
Via della Spada
Lungarno di Santa Rosa
Via de' Fossi
26
Piazza Carlo Goldoni
Via della Vigna Nuova
Arno
Via Sant' Onofrio
Lungarno Guicciardini
Via del Parione
Via L Bartolini
Piazza di Verzaia
Piazza del Tiratoio
23
Piazza di Cestello
Ponte alla Carraia
Lungarno Corsini
Viale Lodovico Ariosto
Piazza dei Nerli
Borgo San Frediano
Via del Drago d'Oro
Lungarno Guicciardini
Ponte Santa Trìnita
Piazza N Sauro
31
Via dell'Orto
Via di Camaldoli
Borgo della Stella
Piazza de' Frescobaldi
Piazza del Carmine
Via di Santo Spirito
Via del Leone
Via dello Sprone
Via dell'Ardiglione
Via Sant' Agostino
Via Maffia
SANTO SPIRITO
Piazza Torquato Tasso
Via de' Serragli
Via de' Velluti
Via Sguazza
Via della Chiesa
Piazza Santo Spirito
Via di Camaldoli
Viale Francesco Petrarca
Via di Bellosguardo
Sdr de' Pitti
20
Via Maggio
Via del Campuccio
Via Mazzetta
Via Minima
Giardino Torrigiani
Via delle Caldaie
Piazza dei Pitti
Via Romana
12
8
Palazzo Pitti Ticket Office
ITALY FLORENCE

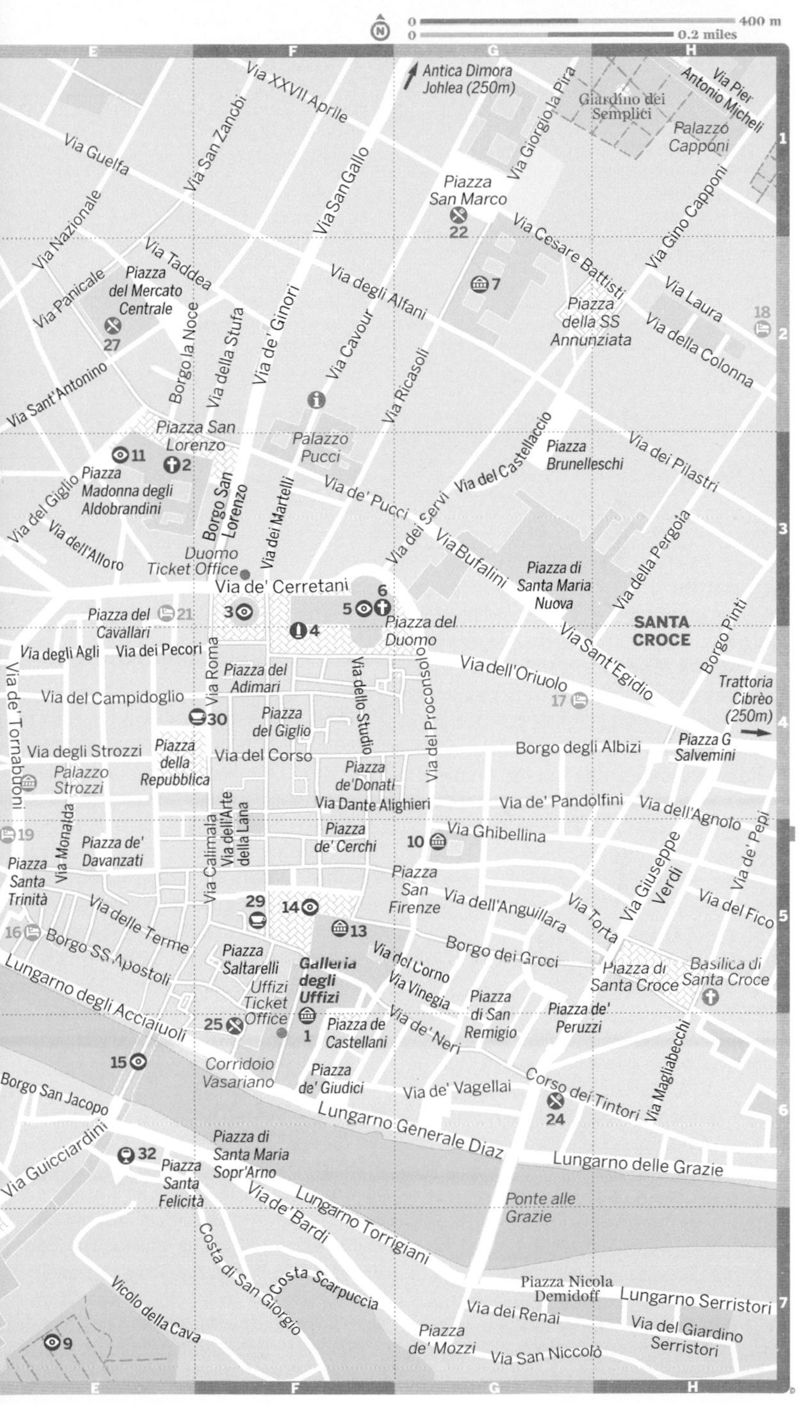
0 400 m
0 0.2 miles
Antica Dimora Johlea (250m)
Via XXVII Aprile
Via Guelfa
Via San Zanobi
Via San Gallo
Via Giorgio la Pira
Giardino dei Semplici
Via Pier Antonio Micheli
Palazzo Capponi
Piazza San Marco
22
Via Nazionale
Via Cesare Battisti
Via Gino Capponi
Via Taddea
Via Panicale
Piazza del Mercato Centrale
27
Via degli Alfani
7
Piazza della SS Annunziata
Via Laura
18
Via della Colonna
Borgo la Noce
Via della Stufa
Via de' Ginori
Via Cavour
Via Ricasoli
Via Sant'Antonino
Palazzo Pucci
Via del Castellaccio
Piazza Brunelleschi
Via dei Pilastri
Piazza San Lorenzo
11
2
Piazza Madonna degli Aldobrandini
Via del Giglio
Borgo San Lorenzo
Via dei Martelli
Via de' Pucci
Via dei Servi
Via Bufalini
Via della Pergola
Via dell'Alloro
Duomo Ticket Office
Via de' Cerretani
6
5
Piazza di Santa Maria Nuova
Piazza del Cavallari
21
3
4
Piazza del Duomo
SANTA CROCE
Borgo Pinti
Via degli Agli
Via dei Pecori
Via Roma
Piazza del Adimari
Via dello Studio
Via del Proconsolo
Via dell'Oriuolo
Via Sant'Egidio
Via de' Tornabuoni
Via del Campidoglio
30
Piazza del Giglio
17
Trattoria Cibrèo (250m)
Via degli Strozzi
Piazza della Repubblica
Via del Corso
Borgo degli Albizi
Piazza G Salvemini
Palazzo Strozzi
Piazza de'Donati
Via Dante Alighieri
Via de' Pandolfini
Via dell'Agnolo
19
Via Monalda
Via Calimala
Via dell'Arte della Lana
Piazza de' Cerchi
10
Via Ghibellina
Via Giuseppe Verdi
Via de' Pepi
Piazza de' Davanzati
Piazza Santa Trinità
Piazza San Firenze
Via dell'Anguillara
Via Torta
Via del Fico
29
14
13
Via delle Terme
16
Borgo SS Apostoli
Borgo dei Greci
Piazza Saltarelli
Galleria degli Uffizi
Via del Corno
Via Vinegia
Piazza di Santa Croce
Basilica di Santa Croce
Lungarno degli Acciaiuoli
Uffizi Ticket Office
Piazza di San Remigio
Piazza de' Peruzzi
25
1
Piazza de Castellani
Via de' Neri
Via Magliabecchi
15
Corridoio Vasariano
Piazza de' Giudici
Via de' Vagellai
Corso dei Tintori
Borgo San Jacopo
24
Lungarno Generale Diaz
Via Guicciardini
32
Piazza di Santa Maria Sopr'Arno
Lungarno delle Grazie
Piazza Santa Felicità
Via de' Bardi
Lungarno Torrigiani
Ponte alle Grazie
Costa di San Giorgio
Costa Scarpuccia
Piazza Nicola Demidoff
Lungarno Serristori
Vicolo della Cava
Via dei Renai
Via del Giardino Serristori
9
Piazza de' Mozzi
Via San Niccolò

Florence

Don't Miss Sights

1 Galleria degli Uffizi F6

Sights

2 Basilica di San Lorenzo E3
3 Battistero di San Giovanni F3
4 Campanile F4
5 Cupola F3
6 Duomo F3
7 Galleria dell'Accademia G2
8 Galleria Palatina D7
9 Giardino di Boboli E7
10 Museo del Bargello G5
11 Museo delle Cappelle Medicee E3
12 Palazzo Pitti D7
13 Palazzo Vecchio F5
14 Piazza della Signoria F5
15 Ponte Vecchio E6

Sleeping

16 Hotel Cestelli E5
17 Hotel Dalí G4
18 Hotel Morandi alla Crocetta H2
19 Hotel Scoti E5
20 Palazzo Guadagni Hotel C7
21 Relais del Duomo E3

Eating

22 Accademia Ristorante G1
23 All'Antico Ristoro di' Cambi B5
24 Del Fagioli G6
25 'Ino F6
26 L'Osteria di Giovanni D4
27 Mercato Centrale E2
28 Trattoria I Due G D1

Drinking & Nightlife

29 Caffè Rivoire F5
30 Gilli F4
31 Il Santino C5
32 Le Volpi e l'Uva E6

Campanile — Bell Tower

(www.operaduomo.firenze.it; Piazza del Duomo; adult/reduced inc cathedral dome & baptistry €10/free; 8.30am-7.30pm) Begun in 1334 by Giotto, the Duomo's soaring bell tower rises nearly as high as the dome. Its elaborate Gothic facade, including 16 life-size statues, was worked on by a who's who of 14th-century artists, including Giotto, Andrea Pisano, Donatello and Luca Della Robbia. Climb its 414 steps for nearly the same superb views as those from Brunelleschi's dome, but without the snaking queues.

Battistero di San Giovanni — Landmark

(Baptistry; Piazza di San Giovanni; adult/reduced incl cupola, campanile & museum €10/free; 8.15-10.15am & 11.15am-7pm Mon-Sat, 8.30am-2pm Sun & 1st Sat of month) Across from the Duomo is the 11th-century Romanesque baptistry, an octagonal striped structure of white and green marble with three sets of doors conceived as panels on which to tell the story of humanity and the Redemption. Most celebrated of all are Lorenzo Ghiberti's gilded bronze doors at the eastern entrance, known as the *Porta del Paradiso* (Gate of Paradise). What you see today, though, are copies – the originals are in the Grande Museo del Duomo.

PIAZZA DELLA SIGNORIA & AROUND

Piazza della Signoria — Piazza

The hub of local life since the 13th century, this animated piazza is where Florentines flock to meet friends and chat over early-evening *aperitivi* at historic cafes. Presiding over eveything is **Palazzo Vecchio**, Florence's city hall, and the 14th-century **Loggia dei Lanzi**, an open-air gallery showcasing Renaissance sculptures, including Giambologna's *Rape of the Sabine Women* (c 1583), Benvenuto Cellini's bronze *Perseus* (1554) and Agnolo Gaddi's *Seven Virtues* (1384–89).

Palazzo Vecchio — Museum

(055 276 82 24; www.musefirenze.it; Piazza della Signoria; archaeology tour €2, museum adult/reduced €10/8, tower €10/8, museum & tower €14/12; museum 9am-midnight Mon-Wed & Fri-Sun, to 2pm Thu summer, 9am-7pm Mon-Wed & Fri-Sun, to 2pm Thu winter, tower 9am-9pm Fri-Wed, to 2pm Thu summer, 10am-5pm Fri-Wed, to 2pm Thu winter) This fortress palace, with its crenellations and 94m-high tower, was designed by Arnolfo di

Cambio between 1298 and 1314 for the *signoria* (city government). From the top of the **Torre d'Arnolfo** (tower), you can revel in unforgettable rooftop views, while inside, Michelangelo's *Genio della Vittoria* (Genius of Victory) sculpture graces the **Salone dei Cinquecento**, a magnificent painted hall created for the city's 15th-century ruling Consiglio dei Cinquecento (Council of 500).

Ponte Vecchio Bridge

Dating to 1345, Ponte Vecchio was the only Florentine bridge to survive destruction at the hands of retreating German forces in 1944. Above the jewellers' shops on the eastern side, the **Corridoio Vasariano** is a 16th-century passageway between the Uffizi and Palazzo Pitti that runs around, rather than through, the medieval **Torre dei Mannelli** at the bridge's southern end.

Museo del Bargello Museum

(www.polomuseale.firenze.it; Via del Proconsolo 4; adult/reduced €4/2; ⌚8.15am-4.50pm summer, to 1.50pm winter, closed 1st, 3rd & 5th Sun & 2nd & 4th Mon of month) It was behind the stark walls of Palazzo del Bargello, Florence's earliest public building, that the *podestà* meted out justice from the late 13th century until 1502. Today the building safeguards Italy's most comprehensive collection of Tuscan Renaissance sculpture, with some of Michelangelo's best early works and a hall full of Donatello's.

SAN LORENZO

Basilica di San Lorenzo Basilica

(Piazza San Lorenzo; admission €4.50, incl Biblioteca Medicea Laurenziana €7; ⌚10am-5.30pm Mon-Sat, plus 1.30-5pm Sun winter) Considered one of the most harmonious examples of Renaissance architecture in Florence, this unfinished basilica was the Medici parish church and mausoleum – many members of the family are buried here. It was designed by Brunelleschi in 1425 for Cosimo the Elder, who lived nearby, and built over an earlier 4th-century church. In the solemn interior look out for Brunelleschi's austerely beautiful **Sagrestia Vecchia** (Old Sacristy) with its sculptural decoration by Donatello.

Fountain of Neptune, Piazza della Signoria, Florence

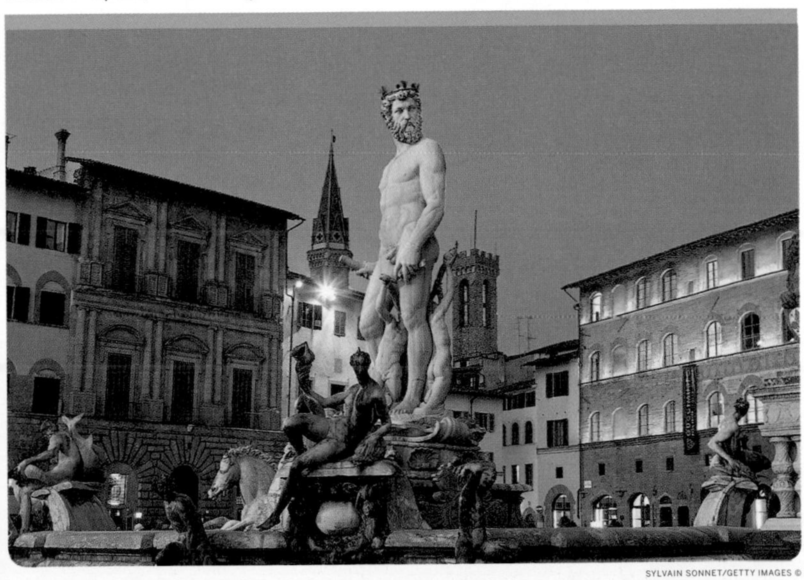

SYLVAIN SONNET/GETTY IMAGES ©

Museo delle Cappelle Medicee Mausoleum
(Medici Chapels; ☎055 294 883; www.polomuseale.firenze.it; Piazza Madonna degli Aldobrandini; adult/reduced €6/3; ⏰8.15am-1.50pm, closed 2nd & 4th Sun & 1st, 3rd & 5th Mon of month) Nowhere is Medici conceit expressed so explicitly as in their mausoleum, the Medici Chapels. Sumptuously adorned with granite, precious marble, semi-precious stones and some of Michelangelo's most beautiful sculptures, it is the burial place of 49 members of the dynasty.

SAN MARCO

Galleria dell'Accademia Gallery
(www.polomuseale.firenze.it; Via Ricasoli 60; adult/reduced €8/4; ⏰8.15am-6.50pm Tue-Sun) A lengthy queue marks the door to this gallery, built to house one of the Renaissance's most iconic masterpieces, Michelangelo's *David.* Fortunately, the world's most famous statue is worth the wait. The subtle detail of the real thing – the veins in his sinewy arms, the leg muscles, the change in expression as you move around the statue – *is* impressive.

OLTRARNO

Palazzo Pitti Museum
(www.polomuseale.firenze.it; Piazza dei Pitti; ⏰8.15am-6.50pm Tue-Sun, reduced hours winter) Commissioned by banker Luca Pitta and designed by Brunelleschi in 1457, this vast Renaissance palace was later bought by the Medici family. Over the centuries, it served as the residence of the city's rulers until the Savoys donated it to the state in 1919. Nowadays it houses several museums including the art-rich **Galleria Palatina** (adult/reduced incl Appartamenti Reali & Galleria d'Arte Moderna €8.50/4.25 ; ⏰8.15am-6.50pm Tue-Sun summer, reduced hours winter). Behind it, you can explore the palace's 17th-century gardens, the **Giardino di Boboli** (Piazza Pitti; adult/reduced incl Museo degli Argenti, Museo delle Porcellane & Galleria del Costume €7/3.50; ⏰8.15am-7.30pm summer, reduced hours winter).

Festivals & Events

Scoppio del Carro Fireworks
A cart of fireworks is exploded in front of the cathedral at 11am on Easter Sunday.

Maggio Musicale Fiorentino Arts
(www.operadifirenze.it) Italy's oldest arts festival features world-class performances of theatre, classical music, jazz and dance; April to June.

Festa di San Giovanni Religious
Florence celebrates its patron saint, John, with a *calcio storico* (historic

Michelangelo's *David*, Galleria dell'Accademia, Florence
ROGER ANTROBUS/GETTY IMAGES ©

Cutting the Queues

Sightseeing in Florence can entail hours spent in queues. Fortunately, there are two ways of saving time – one of which can also save you money.

For €4 extra per museum you can book tickets for the Uffizi and Galleria dell'Accademia (the museums with the longest queues) through **Firenze Musei** (**Florence Museums; ☎055 29 48 83; www.firenzemusei.it**). Book online in advance, or purchase tickets in person before your visit from the ticket desks at Palazzo Pitti or at the rear of the Chiesa di Orsanmichele.

If you are planning to visit most of the major museums, consider purchasing a **Firenze Card** (€72). This is valid for 72 hours and allows the holder to bypass both advance booking and queues. It can be purchased online, at the Via Cavour tourist office, at Palazzo Pitti, Palazzo Vecchio or the Uffizi. Check details at www.firenzecard.it.

football) match on Piazza di Santa Croce and fireworks over Piazzale Michelangelo; 24 June.

Sleeping

PIAZZA DEL DUOMO & AROUND

Hotel Dalí Hotel €

(**☎055 234 07 06; www.hoteldali.com; Via dell'Oriuolo 17; d €90, s/d without bathroom €40/70, apt from €95; P 📶**) A warm welcome from hosts Marco and Samanta awaits at this lovely small hotel. A stone's throw from the Duomo, it has 10 sunny rooms, some overlooking a leafy inner courtyard, decorated in a low-key modern way and equipped with kettles, coffee and tea. No breakfast, but there is free parking available.

Relais del Duomo B&B €

(**☎055 21 01 47; www.relaisdelduomo.it; Piazza dell'Olio 2; s €40-90, d €70-130; ❄ 📶**) Location is the prime selling point of this B&B on a quiet, traffic-free street around the corner from the Duomo. Its four elegant, pastel-coloured rooms come with parquet floors and simple, down-to-earth decor.

PIAZZA DELLA SIGNORIA & AROUND

Hotel Cestelli Hotel €

(**☎055 21 42 13; www.hotelcestelli.com; Borgo SS Apostoli 25; d €70-100, f €80-115, without bathroom s €40-60, d €50-80; ⏲closed 4 weeks Jan-Feb, 2-3 weeks Aug; 📶**) Housed in a 12th-century *palazzo* a stiletto-hop from fashionable Via de' Tornabuoni, this intimate eight-room hotel is a gem. Rooms reveal an understated style, tastefully combining polished antiques with spangly chandeliers, vintage art and silk screens. Owners Alessio and Asumi are a mine of local information and are happy to share their knowledge. No breakfast.

Hotel Scoti Pension €€

(**☎055 29 21 28; www.hotelscoti.com; Via de' Tornabuoni 7; s/d/tr/q €75/130/160/185; 📶**) Wedged between the designer stores on Florence's smartest shopping strip, this hidden *pensione* is a splendid mix of old-fashioned charm and value for money. Its 16 traditionally styled rooms are spread across the 2nd floor of a towering 16th-century *palazzo*, with some offering lovely rooftop views. The star of the show, though, is the frescoed lounge from 1780. Breakfast €5.

Right: Galleria Palatina in Palazzo Pitti (p426), Florence; **Below:** Palazzo Vecchio (p424), Florence
(RIGHT) JEAN-PIERRE LESCOURRET/GETTY IMAGES ©; (BELOW) IZZET KERIBAR/GETTY IMAGES ©

SAN MARCO

Antica Dimora Johlea B&B **€€**
(055 463 32 92; www.johanna.it; Via San Gallo 80; d €90-220;) A way out from the centre, this impeccable residence is a lovely retreat. There's an air of old-world elegance about the six guest rooms with their four-poster beds, creaking parquet floors, high ceilings and period furniture. Help yourself to a drink from the honesty bar and head up to the small terrace to enjoy views over to the Duomo.

Hotel Morandi alla Crocetta Boutique Hotel **€€**
(055 234 47 47; www.hotelmorandi.it; Via Laura 50; s/d/tr/q €105/170/197/227; P) This medieval convent-turned-hotel away from the madding crowd in San Marco is a stunner. Rooms are refined and traditional in look – think antique furnishings, wood beams and oil paintings – with a quiet, old-world ambience. Pick of the bunch is frescoed room No 29, the former chapel.

OLTRARNO

Palazzo Guadagni Hotel Hotel **€€**
(055 265 83 76; www.palazzoguadagni.com; Piazza Santo Spirito 9; d €150, extra bed €45;) This delightful hotel overlooking Florence's liveliest summertime square is legendary – Zefferelli shot scenes from *Tea with Mussolini* here. Housed in an artfully revamped Renaissance palace, it has 15 spacious, tastefully styled rooms and an impossibly romantic loggia terrace with wicker chairs and predictably dreamy views.

Eating

Classic Tuscan dishes include *ribollita*, a heavy vegetable soup, and *bistecca alla fiorentina* (Florentine steak served rare). Chianti is the local tipple.

PIAZZA DEL DUOMO & AROUND

'Ino Sandwiches €

(www.inofirenze.com; Via dei Georgofili 3r-7r; panini €5-8; 11.30am-4.30pm summer, noon-3.30pm Mon-Fri, 11.30am-4.30pm Sat & Sun winter) Artisanal ingredients sourced locally and mixed creatively is the secret behind this gourmet sandwich bar near the Uffizi. Create your own filling or go for a house special such as *finocchiona* (a local Tuscan salami) paired with herbed pecorino and pepper mustard.

SANTA MARIA NOVELLA

L'Osteria di Giovanni Tuscan €€€

(055 28 48 97; www.osteriadigiovanni.it; Via del Moro 22; meals €50; 7-10pm Mon-Fri, noon-3pm & 7-10pm Sat & Sun) It's not the decor that stands out at this smart neighbourhood eatery, it's the cuisine: sumptuous Tuscan. Imagine truffles, tender steaks and pastas such as *pici al sugo di salsiccia e cavolo nero* (thick spaghetti with a sauce of sausage and black cabbage). Throw in a complimentary glass of *prosecco* and you'll want to return time and again.

SAN LORENZO

Mercato Centrale Market, Fast Food €

(055 239 97 98; www.mercatocentrale.it; Piazza del Mercato Centrale 4; dishes €7-15; 10-1am, food stalls noon-3pm & 7pm-midnight;) The food-court concept has arrived in Florence. The 1st floor of the covered Mercato Centrale has been transformed into a vibrant food fair with a dedicated bookshop, a cookery school, wine bars and stalls selling everything from steaks and grilled burgers to smoothies, pizzas, gelato, pastries and fresh pasta. Load up and sit at the nearest free table.

Trattoria I Due G Tuscan €€

(055 21 86 23; www.trattoriai2g.com; Via B Cennini 6r; meals €30; noon-2.30pm & 7.30-10pm Mon-Sat) Near the train station, this is a quintessential family-run trattoria specialising in earthy Tuscan cooking. Start off with a classic *parpadelle al cinghiale* (pasta ribbons with a boar-meat sauce) before getting your teeth into a tasty hunk of tender chargrilled steak.

SAN MARCO

Accademia Ristorante Tuscan **€€**
(**☎055 21 73 43; www.ristoranteaccademia.it; Piazza San Marco 7r; pizzas €7-18, meals €35-40; ⏰noon-3pm & 7-11pm**) Friendly staff, cheerful decor and consistently good food mean that this family-run restaurant is perennially packed. The focus is traditional regional cuisine, so expect antipasti of *crostini*, cured meats and cheeses, homemade pastas, meaty mains and a good selection of wood-fired pizzas.

SANTA CROCE

Trattoria Cibrèo Tuscan **€€**
(**www.edizioniteatrodelsalecibreofirenze.it; Via dei Macci 122r; meals €30; ⏰12.50-2.30pm & 6.50-11pm Tue-Sat, closed Aug**) Dine here and you'll instantly understand why a queue gathers outside before it opens. Once inside, revel in top-notch Tuscan cuisine: perhaps *pappa al pomodoro* (a thick soupy mash of tomato, bread and basil) followed by *polpettine di pollo e ricotta* (chicken and ricotta meatballs). No reservations, no credit cards, no coffee, and arrive early to snag a table.

Del Fagioli Tuscan **€€**
(**☎055 24 42 85; Corso Tintori 47r; meals €25-30; ⏰12.30-2.30pm & 7.30-10.30pm Mon-Fri, closed Aug**) This cosy, woody eatery near the Basilica di Santa Croce is the archetypal Tuscan trattoria. It opened in 1966 and has been serving well-priced soups and boiled meats to throngs of appreciative local workers and residents ever since. No credit cards.

OLTRARNO

All'Antico Ristoro di' Cambi Tuscan **€€**
(**☎055 21 71 34; www.anticoristorodicambi.it; Via Sant'Onofrio 1r; meals €35; ⏰noon-2.30pm & 6-10.30pm Mon-Sat**) Founded as a wine shop in 1950, this Oltrarno institution sticks closely to the traditional, with its long list of fine Tuscan wines, dried meats hanging from brick-vaulted ceilings and a glass case proudly displaying its highly regarded *bistecca alla fiorentina*. Meat aficionados will also enjoy the succulent *tagliata di cinta Senese* (steak of Sienese pork).

Drinking & Nightlife

Il Santino Wine Bar
(**Via Santo Spirito 60r; ⏰12.30-11pm**) This pocket-sized wine bar is packed every evening. Inside, squat modern stools contrast with old brick walls, but the real action is outside, from around 9pm, when the buoyant wine-loving crowd spills onto the street.

Le Volpi e l'Uva Wine Bar
(**www.levolpieluva.com; Piazza dei Rossi 1; ⏰11am-9pm Mon-Sat**) This intimate spot with a marble-topped bar crowning two oak wine barrels chalks up an impressive list of Italian wines, from Tuscan Chiantis to rich Piedmontese reds and chardonnays from the Valle d'Aosta. To attain true bliss, nibble on *crostini* or Tuscan cheeses as you sip.

Caffè Rivoire Cafe
(**Piazza della Signoria 4; ⏰7am-11pm Tue-Sun**) Dating to 1872, this pricey number offers unbeatable people-watching on Piazza della Signoria – an ideal antidote to art overload brought on in the nearby Uffizi. Speciality of the house is its exquisite chocolate.

Gilli Cafe
(**www.gilli.it; Piazza della Repubblica 39r; ⏰7.30am-1.30am**) The city's grandest cafe, Gilli has been serving excellent coffee and delicious cakes since 1733. Claiming a table on the piazza is *molto* expensive – we prefer standing at the spacious Liberty-style bar.

Information

Tourist Information

Central Tourist Office (☎055 29 08 32; www.firenzeturismo.it; Via Cavour 1r; ⏰9am-6pm Mon-Sat)

Infopoint Stazione (☎055 21 22 45; www.firenzeturismo.it; Piazza della Stazione 5; ⏰9am-7pm Mon-Sat, to 2pm Sun)

Getting There & Away

Air

The main airport serving Florence is Pisa International Airport (p453). There's also the small, city **Florence airport** (Aeroport Vespucci; ☎055 306 13 00; www.aeroporto.firenze.it; Via del Termine), 5km northwest of Florence.

Bus

The main **bus station** (Via Santa Caterina da Siena 17r) is near the train station. Buses leave for Siena (€7.80, 1¼ hours, at least hourly) and San Gimignano via Poggibonsi (€6.80, 1¼ to two hours, up to 16 daily).

Car & Motorcycle

Florence is connected by the A1 autostrada to Bologna and Milan in the north and Rome and Naples to the south. The A11 links Florence with Pisa and the coast, and a *superstrada* (expressway) joins the city to Siena.

Train

Florence's **Stazione di Santa Maria Novella** is on the main Rome–Milan line. There are regular services to/from Pisa (€8, 45 minutes to 1½ hours), Rome (€20.65 to €35.90, 1½ to 3½ hours), Venice (€22.45 to €45, two hours) and Milan (€28 to €50, 1¾ to four hours).

Getting Around

To/From the Airport

ATAF runs the Volainbus (one way €6) between the bus station and Florence airport. Departures are roughly every 20 minutes between 5.30am and 12.30am. Journey time is about 25 minutes. **Terravision** (www.terravision.eu; single/return €6/10) runs a bus service between Pisa (Galileo Galilei) airport and the paved bus park in front of Stazione Santa Maria Novella (one way/return €6/10, one hour, 18 daily). In Florence, buy your tickets at the Terravision desk inside Deanna Café, opposite the station.

Taxis charge a fixed rate of €20 plus €1 per bag (€23.30 at night) for the trip between Florence airport and the historic centre.

Car & Motorcycle

Note that there is a strict limited traffic zone (ZTL) in the historic centre from 7.30am to 7.30pm Monday to Friday and 7.30am to 6pm on Saturday. Fines are hefty if you enter the centre during these times without a special permit having been organised by your hotel in advance.

Sweets for sale at Gilli, Florence

LONELY PLANET/GETTY IMAGES ©

If You Like... Historic Towns

From hilltop San Gimignano (p466) to lovely Lucca (p465), every Italian town seems to have its own historical tale to tell.

1 PADUA
Medieval Padua (Padova) sees only a fraction of the visitors who pile into Venice, but it's just as fascinating: Galileo taught astronomy here, Shakespeare set parts of *The Taming of the Shrew* here and Giotto painted one of Italy's greatest works of art in the city's **Cappella degli Scrovegni**. Padua is 40km west of Venice.

2 PERUGIA
With its hilltop medieval centre and international student population, Perugia is Umbria's largest and most cosmopolitan city. Each year, it plays host to two top festivals: **Umbria Jazz** in July and **Eurochocolate** in late October. Perugia is 110km southeast of Siena.

3 ASSISI
Famous as the birthplace of St Francis, this medieval town is a major pilgrimage destination. Its major sight is the **Basilica di San Francesco**, a treasure trove of Renaissance frescoes spread across two churches. Dress modestly: no shorts, miniskirts or low-cut tops. Assisi is 25km east of Perugia.

4 MATERA
Set atop two rocky gorges, Matera is one of Italy's most remarkable towns. Dotting the ravines are a number of prehistoric cave dwellings known as *sassi*, where up to half the town's population lived until the late 1950s. Matera is 65km southwest of Bari.

5 LECCE
Lecce is known as 'the Florence of the South' thanks to its wonderful baroque architecture. Among the town's highlights are the **Basilica di Santa Croce** and its elaborately carved facade, and the grand **Piazza del Duomo**, a baroque masterpiece. Lecce is 40km southeast of Brindisi.

The ZTL means that the best option is to leave your car in a car park, such as Porto al Prato, and use public transport to access the centre. Details of car parks are available at www.firenzeparcheggi.it.

Pisa

POP 88,600

Most people know Pisa as the home of an architectural project gone terribly wrong, but the Leaning Tower is just one of a number of noteworthy sights in this compact and compelling university city.

Sights

The Leaning Tower and Pisa's main sights are on Piazza dei Miracoli, a beautiful walled lawn 1.5km from the bus and train stations. To walk there follow Viale F Crispi north, cross the Ponte Solferino over the Arno, and continue straight up Via Roma.

Duomo — Cathedral

(www.opapisa.it; Piazza dei Miracoli; 10am-8pm summer, 10am-12.45pm & 2-5pm winter) FREE Pisa's magnificent Romanesque Duomo was begun in 1064 and consecrated in 1118. Its striking tiered exterior, with cladding of green and cream marble bands, gives on to a vast columned interior capped by a gold wooden ceiling. The elliptical dome, the first of its kind in Europe at the time, was added in 1380.

Note that while admission is free, you'll need an entrance coupon from the ticket office or a ticket from one of the other Piazza dei Miracoli sights.

Battistero — Religious Site

(Baptistry; www.opapisa.it; Piazza dei Miracoli; adult/reduced €5/3, combination ticket with Camposanto & Museo delle Sinópie 2/3 sights adult/reduced €7/8, €4/5; 8am-8pm summer, 10am-5pm Nov-Feb) Pisa's unusual round baptistry has one dome piled on top of another, each roofed half in lead, half in tiles, and topped by a gilt bronze John the Baptist (1395). Construction

LUIS DAVILLA/GETTY IMAGES ©

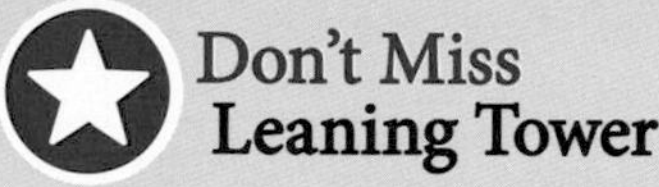

One of Italy's signature sights, the Torre Pendente truly lives up to its name, leaning a startling 3.9 degrees off the vertical. The 56m-high tower, officially the Duomo's *campanile* (bell tower), took almost 200 years to build, but was already listing when it was unveiled in 1372. Over time, the tilt, caused by a layer of weak subsoil, steadily worsened until it was finally halted by a major stabilisation project in the 1990s.

NEED TO KNOW

Torre Pendente; www.opapisa.it; Piazza dei Miracoli; admission €18; ⌚9am-8pm summer, 10am-5pm winter

began in 1152, but it was remodelled and continued by Nicola and Giovanni Pisano more than a century later and finally completed in the 14th century. Inside, the hexagonal marble pulpit (1260) by Nicola Pisano is the highlight.

Sleeping

Hotel Pisa Tower Hotel **€**
(**☎050 520 00 19; www.hotelpisatower.com; Via Pisano 23; d €75-90, tr €90-100, q €110-119;** ❄📶) Superb value for money, a superlative location and spacious, high-ceilinged rooms – this polished newcomer is one of Pisa's best deals. Chandeliers, marble floors and old framed prints adorn the classically attired interiors, while out back, a pristine lawn adds a soothing dash of green.

Eating & Drinking

Osteria La Toscana Osteria **€€**
(**☎050 96 90 52; Via San Frediano 10; meals €25-30; ⌚7-11pm daily & noon-3pm Sat & Sun**) This relaxed spot is one of several excellent eateries on Via San Frediano, a lively street off Piazza dei Cavalieri. Subdued lighting, bare brown walls and

Detour: Orvieto

This spectacularly sited hilltop town has one major drawcard: its extraordinary Gothic **Cattedrale** (0763 34 24 77; www.opsm.it; Piazza Duomo 26; admission €3; 9.30am-6pm Mon-Sat, 1-5.30pm Sun, shorter hours in winter).

Dating to 1290, this soul-stirring structure sports a black and white banded exterior fronted by what is perhaps the most astonishing facade to grace any Italian church, a mesmerising display of rainbow frescoes, jewel-like mosaics, bas-reliefs and delicate braids of flowers and vine. Inside, the highlight is Luca Signorelli's magnificent fresco cycle, the *Giudizio Universale* (Last Judgment), in the Cappella di San Brianzo.

For further town information, there's a **tourist office** (0763 34 17 72; www.orvieto.regioneumbria.eu; Piazza Duomo 24; 8.15am-1.50pm & 4-7pm Mon-Fri, 10am-1pm & 3-6pm Sat & Sun) opposite the cathedral.

Orvieto, 80km southwest of Perugia, is on the main Rome–Florence train line. If you arrive by train, you'll need to take the **funicular** (€1.30; every 10min 7.15am-8.30pm Mon-Sat, every 15mins 8am-8.30pm Sun) up to the historic centre.

background jazz set the stage for ample pastas and delectable grilled meats served with a smile and quiet efficiency.

biOsteria 050 Vegetarian **€€**
(050 54 31 06; www.biosteria050.it; Via San Francesco 36; meals €25-30; 12.30-2.30pm & 7.30-10.30pm Tue-Sat, 7.30-10.30pm Mon & Sun;) Everything that Marco and Raffaele at Zero Cinquanta cook up is strictly seasonal, local and organic, with products from farms within a 50km radius of Pisa. Feast on dishes like risotto with almonds and asparagus or go for one of the excellent-value lunch specials.

Information

For city information, check www.pisaunicaterra.it or pop into the tourist office at the airport or in the city centre.

Getting There & Around

Pisa International Airport (p453) is linked to the city centre by the PisaMover bus (€1.30, eight minutes, every 10 minutes).

A taxi between the airport and the city centre costs about €15 (€20 at night).

Frequent trains run to Lucca (€3.40, 30 minutes), Florence (€8, 45 minutes to 1¼ hours), and La Spezia (€7.20 to €11.60, 45 minutes to 1½ hours) for the Cinque Terre.

Siena

POP 54,120

Siena is one of Italy's most enchanting medieval towns. Its walled centre, a beautifully preserved warren of dark lanes punctuated with Gothic *palazzi,* has at its centre Piazza del Campo, the sloping square that is the venue for the city's famous annual horse race, Il Palio.

According to legend, Siena was founded by the sons of Remus (one of the founders of Rome).

Sights

If you're planning to blitz Siena's sights consider buying the **OPA Si Pass** (€12/8 summer/winter, valid three days) which covers admission to the Duomo, Libraria Piccolomini, Battistero, Museo dell' Opera del Duomo and Panoramic Terrace. It's available at the Duomo ticket office.

Piazza del Campo Piazza
This sloping piazza, popularly known as Il Campo, has been Siena's civic and social centre since being staked out by the *Con-*

siglio dei Nove in the mid-12th century. It was built on the site of a former Roman marketplace, and its pie-piece paving design is divided into nine sectors to represent the number of members of the council. At its lowest point, the graceful Gothic **Palazzo Comunale** houses the town's finest museum, the Museo Civico.

Museo Civico — Museum

(Palazzo Comunale, Piazza del Campo; adult/reduced €9/8; 10am-7pm summer, to 6pm winter) Siena's most famous museum occupies rooms richly frescoed by artists of the Sienese school. These are unusual in that they were commissioned by the governing body of the city, rather than by the Church, and many depict secular subjects instead of the favoured religious themes of the time. The highlight is Simone Martini's celebrated *Maestà* (Virgin Mary in Majesty; 1315) in the **Sala del Mappamondo** (Hall of the World Map).

Duomo — Cathedral

(www.operaduomo.siena.it; Piazza del Duomo; summer/winter €4/free, when floor displayed €7; 10.30am-7pm Mon-Sat, 1.30-6pm Sun summer, 10.30am-5.30pm Mon-Sat, 1.30-5.30pm Sun winter) A triumph of Romanesque-Gothic architecture, Siena's cathedral is one of Italy's most awe-inspiring churches. According to tradition it was consecrated in 1179, but work continued on it for centuries and many of Italy's top artists contributed: Giovanni Pisano designed the intricate white, green and red marble facade; Nicola Pisano carved the elaborate pulpit; Pinturicchio painted frescoes; and Michelangelo, Donatello and Gian Lorenzo Bernini all produced sculptures. Also of note is the extraordinary inlaid floor.

Battistero di San Giovanni — Baptistry

(Piazza San Giovanni; admission €4; 10.30am-7pm summer, to 5.30pm winter) Behind the Duomo, down a steep flight of steps, is the Baptistry, richly decorated with frescoes. At its centre is a hexagonal marble font by Jacopo della Quercia, decorated with bronze panels depicting the life of St John the Baptist by artists including Lorenzo Ghiberti *(Baptism of Christ* and *St John in Prison)* and Donatello *(The Head of John the Baptist Being Presented to Herod)*.

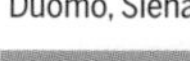

Duomo, Siena

RICHARD I'ANSON/GETTY IMAGES ©

Museo dell'Opera del Duomo Museum

(www.operaduomo.siena.it; Piazza del Duomo 8; admission €7; ⏲10.30am-7pm summer, to 5.30pm winter) The collection here showcases artworks that formerly adorned the cathedral, including 12 statues of prophets and philosophers by Giovanni Pisano that originally stood on the facade. These were designed to be viewed from ground level, which is why they look so distorted as they crane uncomfortably forward. The museum's highlight is Duccio di Buoninsegna's striking *Maestà* (1311), which was painted on both sides as a screen for the Duomo's high altar.

Festivals & Events

Palio Cultural

(**⏲2 Jul & 16 Aug**), Siena's great annual event, a pageant culminating in a bareback horse race round Il Campo. The city is divided into 17 *contrade* (districts), of which 10 are chosen annually to compete for the *palio* (silk banner).

Palio, Siena

SIMEONE HUBER/GETTY IMAGES ©

Sleeping

It's always advisable to book in advance, but for August and the Palio, it's essential.

Hotel Alma Domus Hotel **€**

(**☎0577 4 41 77; www.hotelalmadomus.it; Via Camporegio 37; s €40-52, d €60-€122, q €95-140;** ❄📶) Owned by the church and still home to several Dominican nuns, this convent hotel is a lovely, peaceful oasis. Rooms, on the 3rd and 4th floors, represent excellent value for money with a smart, modern look and pristine bathrooms. Some, for which you'll pay more, have views over to the Duomo.

Antica Residenza Cicogna B&B **€**

(**☎0577 28 56 13; www.anticaresidenzacicogna.it; Via delle Terme 76; s €70-95, d €95-115, ste €120-155;** ❄@📶) Charming host Elisa welcomes guests to her 13th-century family *palazzo*. The seven guest rooms are clean and well maintained, with painted ceilings, brick floors and the occasional patch of original fresco. There's also a tiny lounge where you can relax over complimentary Vin Santo and *cantuccini* (hard, sweet almond biscuits).

Campo Regio Relais Boutique Hotel **€€€**

(**☎0577 22 20 73; www.camporegio.com; Via della Sapienza 25; d €220-400, ste €450;** ❄📶) This fetching hotel has only six rooms, all individually decorated and elegantly appointed. Breakfast is served in the sumptuously decorated lounge or on the terrace, with a sensational view of the Duomo and Torre del Mangia.

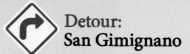

Detour: San Gimignano

This tiny hilltop town deep in the Tuscan countryside is a mecca for day trippers from Florence and Siena. Its nickname is 'The Medieval Manhattan' courtesy of the 11th-century towers that soar above its pristine *centro storico*. Originally 72 were built as monuments to the town's wealth but only 14 remain. The Romanesque cathedral, known as the **Collegiata** (Duomo or Basilica di Santa Maria Assunta; Piazza del Duomo; adult/reduced €4/2; 10am-7pm Mon-Fri, to 5pm Sat, 12.30-7pm Sun summer, to 4.30pm winter), boasts an interior covered with 14th-century frescoes by Bartolo di Fredi, Lippo Memmi and Tadeo di Bartolo. The small **Cappella di Santa Fina** off the south aisle features frescoes by Domenico Ghirlandaio.

Regular buses link San Gimignano with Florence (€6.80, 1¼ to two hours, up to 16 daily) via Poggibonsi. There are also services to/from Siena (€6, 1¼ hours, hourly).

Eating & Drinking

Among many traditional Sienese dishes are *panzanella* (summer salad of soaked bread, basil, onion and tomatoes), *pappardelle con la lepre* (ribbon pasta with hare) and *panforte* (a rich cake of almonds, honey and candied fruit).

Osteria Nonna Gina Trattoria €
(0577 28 72 47; www.osterianonnagina.com; Pian dei Mantellini 2; meals €25; 12.30-2.30pm & 7.30-10.30pm Tue-Sun) This cheery eatery is the picture of an old-school family-run trattoria. An oddment of accumulated clutter provides the decor as family members run between the kitchen and cosy dining room delivering steaming plates of pasta and Tuscan stews.

Morbidi Deli €
(www.morbidi.com; Via Banchi di Sopra 75; lunch buffet €12; 8am-8pm Mon-Thu, to 9pm Fri & Sat) Duck under the ground-floor deli for Morbidi's excellent lunch buffet. For a mere €12, you can pick and choose from antipasti, salads, risottos, pastas and a dessert of the day. Bottled water is supplied, wine and coffee cost extra.

Enoteca I Terzi Modern Tuscan €€
(0577 4 43 29; www.enotecaiterzi.it; Via dei Termini 7; meals €35-40; 11am-1am summer, 11am-4pm & 6.30pm-midnight winter, closed Sun) Close to the Campo, this historic *enoteca* (wine bar) is a favourite with locals, who linger over working lunches, *aperitivi*, and casual dinners featuring top-notch Tuscan *salumi*, delicate handmade pasta and wonderful wines.

Information

Tourist office (0577 28 05 51; www.terresiena.it; Piazza del Duomo 1; 9am-6pm daily summer, 10am-5pm Mon-Sat, to 1pm Sun winter) Opposite the Duomo. Reserves accommodation, organises car and scooter hire, and sells train tickets (commission applies). Also takes bookings for a range of day tours.

Getting There & Away

Siena is not on a main train line, so it's easier to arrive by bus. From the bus station on Piazza Gramsci, **Siena Mobilità** (800 922984; www.sienamobilita.it) buses run to/from Florence (€7.80, 1¼ hours, at least hourly), San Gimignano (€6, 1¼ hours, hourly), either direct or via Poggibonsi, and Pisa International Airport (€14, two hours, one daily).

Sena (www.sena.it) operates services to/from Rome Tiburtina (€24, 3 hours, nine daily), two of which continue to Fiumicino Airport. It also

Right: Piazza Anfiteatro, Lucca; **Below:** Dining in Lucca
(RIGHT) CARLOS SANCHEZ PEREYRA/GETTY IMAGES ©; (BELOW) TIM E WHITE/GETTY IMAGES ©

serves Milan (€36, 4½ hours, four daily), Perugia (€18, 1½ hours, two daily) and Venice (€32, 5½ hours, two daily).

Lucca

POP 89,200

Lucca is a love-at-first-sight type of place. Hidden behind monumental Renaissance walls, its historic centre is chock-full of handsome churches, excellent restaurants and tempting *pasticcerie*. Founded by the Etruscans, it became a city state in the 12th century and stayed that way for 600 years. Most of its streets and monuments date from this period.

Sights

Opera buffs should visit in July and August, when the **Puccini Festival** is held in a purpose-built outdoor theatre in the nearby settlement of Torre del Lago.

City Wall Wall

Lucca's monumental *mura* (wall) was built around the old city in the 16th and 17th centuries and remains in almost perfect condition. Twelve metres high and 4km long, the ramparts are crowned with a tree-lined footpath that looks down on the *centro storico* and out towards the Apuane Alps. This path is a favourite location for the locals' daily *passeggiata* (traditional evening stroll).

Cattedrale di San Martino Cathedral

(www.museocattedralelucca.it; Piazza San Martino; adult/reduced €3/2, with museum & Chiesa e Battistero dei SS Giovanni & Reparata €7/5; ⌚9.30am-5pm Mon-Fri, to 6pm Sat, 11.30am-5pm Sun) Lucca's predominantly Romanesque cathedral dates to the start of the 11th century. Its stunning facade was constructed in the prevailing Lucca-Pisan style and designed to accommodate the pre-existing *campanile* (bell tower). The reliefs over the left doorway of the portico are believed to be by Nicola Pisano, while inside, treasures include the **Volto Santo** (literally, Holy Countenance) crucifix sculpture and a wonderful 15th-century tomb in the **sacristy**.

Sleeping

Piccolo Hotel Puccini Hotel €

(0583 5 54 21; www.hotelpuccini.com; Via di Poggio 9; s/d €75/100;) In an enviable central position, this welcoming three-star hotel hides behind a discreet brick exterior. Its small guest rooms reveal an attractive look with wooden floors, vintage ceiling fans and colourful, contemporary design touches.

Alla Corte degli Angeli Boutique Hotel €€

(0583 46 92 04; www.allacortedegliangeli.com; Via degli Angeli 23; s/d/ste €150/250/400;) This boutique hotel oozes charm. Set in a 15th-century townhouse, its lovely beamed lounge gives onto 21 sunny rooms adorned with frescoed ceilings, patches of exposed brick and landscape murals. Breakfast is €10 extra.

Eating

Da Felice Pizza €

(www.pizzeriadafelice.it; Via Buia 12; focaccias €1-3, pizza slices €1.30; 11am-8.30pm Mon, 10am-8.30pm Tue-Sat) This buzzing spot behind Piazza San Michele is where the locals come for wood-fired pizza, *cecina* (salted chickpea pizza) and *castagnacci* (chestnut cakes).

La Pecora Nera Trattoria €€

(0583 46 97 38; www.lapecoraneralucca.it; Piazza San Francesco 1; pizzas €5.50-9, meals €25-30; 7-11pm Wed-Fri, 11am-3pm & 7-11pm Sat & Sun) A pretty *centro storico* piazza sets the scene for alfresco dining at this laid-back trattoria. Staffed in part by young disabled people, it's a lovely spot for a pizza or dinner of earthy Tuscan fare.

Information

Tourist office (**☎0583 58 31 50; www.luccaitinera.it; Piazzale Verdi; ⌚9am-7pm summer, to 5pm winter**) Holds luggage (€7.50 per day), offers toilet facilities (€0.60), hires bicyles (€2.50 per hour), and supplies free maps and information.

Getting There & Around

Lucca is on the Florence–Pisa–Viareggio train line. Regional trains run to/from Florence (€7.20, 1½ hours, every 30 to 90 minutes) and Pisa (€8, one hour, half-hourly).

There are plenty of car parks around the walls. Most charge €1.50 per hour between 8am and 6.30pm.

SOUTHERN ITALY

A sun-bleached land of spectacular coastlines and rugged landscapes, southern Italy is a robust contrast to the more genteel north. Its stunning scenery, baroque towns and classical ruins exist alongside ugly urban sprawl and scruffy coastal development, sometimes in the space of just a few kilometres.

Yet for all its flaws, *il mezzogiorno* (the midday sun, as southern Italy is known) is an essential part of every Italian itinerary, offering charm, culinary good times and architectural treasures.

Capri

POP 14,100

The most visited of the islands in the Bay of Naples, Capri deserves more than a quick day trip. Beyond the glamorous veneer of chichi cafes and designer boutiques is an island of rugged seascapes, desolate Roman ruins and a surprisingly unspoiled rural interior.

The island is easily reached from Naples and Sorrento. Hydrofoils and ferries dock at Marina Grande, from where it's a short funicular ride up to Capri, the main town. A further bus ride takes you up to the island's second settlement, Anacapri.

For the best views on the island, take the **seggiovia** (**☎081 837 14 38; www.capriseggiovia.it; single/return €7.50/10; ⌚9.30am-5pm summer, to 3.30pm winter**) up from Piazza Vittoria to the summit of **Mt Solaro** (589m), Capri's highest point.

Southern coast of Capri

WOJTEK BUSS/GETTY IMAGES ©

Don't Miss Pompeii & Herculaneum

On 24 August AD 79 Mt Vesuvius erupted, submerging the thriving port of Pompeii in *lapilli* (burning fragments of pumice stone) and Herculaneum in mud. Both places were quite literally buried alive, leaving thousands of people dead. The Unesco-listed ruins of both provide remarkable models of working Roman cities, complete with streets, temples, houses, baths, forums, taverns, shops, even a brothel.

Visitors can choose to visit one site, or can purchase a combination ticket that covers both and is valid for three days.

To visit **Herculaneum** (081 732 43 27; www.pompeiisites.org; Corso Resina 187, Ercolano; adult/reduced €11/5.50, incl Pompeii €20/10; 8.30am-7.30pm summer, to 5pm winter; Circumvesuviana to Ercolano-Scavi), take the Circumvesuviana train from Naples (€2.20, 15 minutes), alight at the Ercolano stop and walk straight down the main street to reach the archaeological site. Highlights include the Casa d'Argo, the Casa di Nettuno e Anfitrite and the Casa dei Cervi.

For **Pompeii** (pictured above; 081 857 53 47; www.pompeiisites.org; entrances at Porta Marina, Piazza Esedra & Piazza Anfiteatro; adult/reduced €11/5.50, incl Herculaneum €20/10; 8.30am-7.30pm summer, to 5pm winter), take the Circumvesuviana to the Pompeii Scavi-Villa dei Misteri stop (€2.90, 35 minutes), located right next to the Porta Marina entrance to the ruins. There's a huge amount to see here, but be sure not to miss the Lupanare (Brothel), the *foro* (forum), the *anfiteatro* (ampitheatre) and the Villa dei Misteri with its extraordinary frescoes.

Tragedy in Pompeii

24 AUGUST AD 79

8am Buildings including the **Terme Suburbane** ❶ and the **foro** ❷ are still undergoing repair after an earthquake in AD 63 caused significant damage to the city. Despite violent earth tremors overnight, residents have little idea of the catastrophe that lies ahead.

Midday Peckish locals pour into the **Thermopolium di Vetutius Placidus** ❸. The lustful slip into the **Lupanare** ❹, and gladiators practise for the evening's planned games at the **anfiteatro** ❺. A massive boom heralds the eruption. Shocked onlookers witness a dark cloud of volcanic matter shoot some 14km above the crater.

3pm–5pm Lapilli (burning pumice stone) rains down on Pompeii. Terrified locals begin to flee; others take shelter. Within two hours, the plume is 25km high and the sky has darkened. Roofs collapse under the weight of the debris, burying those inside.

25 AUGUST AD 79

Midnight Mudflows bury the town of Herculaneum. Lapilli and ash continue to rain down on Pompeii, bursting through buildings and suffocating those taking refuge within.

4am–8am Ash and gas avalanches hit Herculaneum. Subsequent surges smother Pompeii, killing all remaining residents, including those in the **Orto dei Fuggiaschi** ❻. The volcanic 'blanket' will safeguard frescoed treasures like the **Casa del Menandro** ❼ and **Villa dei Misteri** ❽ for almost two millennia.

TOP TIPS

- » Visit in the afternoon
- » Allow three hours
- » Wear comfortable shoes and a hat
- » Bring drinking water
- » Don't use flash photography

Terme Suburbane
The *laconicum* (sauna), *caldarium* (hot bath) and large, heated swimming pool weren't the only sources of heat here; scan the walls of this suburban bathhouse for some of the city's raunchiest frescoes.

Foro
An ancient Times Square of sorts, the forum sits at the intersection of Pompeii's main streets and was closed to traffic in the 1st century AD. The plinths on the southern edge featured statues of the imperial family.

Villa dei Misteri
Home to the world-famous *Dionysiac Frieze* fresco. Other highlights at this villa include *trompe l'oeil* wall decorations in the *cubiculum* (bedroom) and Egyptian-themed artwork in the *tablinum* (reception).

Lupanare
The prostitutes at this brothel were often slaves of Greek or Asian origin. Mattresses once covered the stone beds and the names engraved in the walls are possibly those of the workers and their clients.

Thermopolium di Vetutius Placidus
The counter at this ancient snack bar once held urns filled with hot food. The *lararium* (household shrine) on the back wall depicts Dionysus (the god of wine) and Mercury (the god of profit and commerce).

EYEWITNESS ACCOUNT

Pliny the Younger (AD 61–c 112) gives a gripping, first-hand account of the catastrophe in his letters to Tacitus (AD 56–117).

Casa dei Vettii

Porta del Vesuvio

Porta di Nola

Casa della Venere in Conchiglia

Porta di Sarno

3

7

6

Grande Palestra

5

Tempio di Iside

Orto dei Fuggiaschi
The Garden of the Fugitives showcases the plaster moulds of 13 locals seeking refuge during Vesuvius' eruption – the largest number of victims found in any one area. The huddled bodies make for a moving scene.

Anfiteatro
Magistrates, local senators and the games' sponsors and organisers enjoyed front-row seating at this veteran amphitheatre, home to gladiatorial battles and the odd riot. The parapet circling the stadium featured paintings of combat, victory celebrations and hunting scenes.

Casa del Menandro
This dwelling most likely belonged to the family of Poppaea Sabina, Nero's second wife. A room to the left of the atrium features Trojan War paintings and a polychrome mosaic of pygmies rowing down the Nile.

 Sights

Grotta Azzurra — Cave

(Blue Grotto; admission €13; ⏲9am-1hr before sunset) Capri's single most famous attraction is the Grotto Azzura, a stunning sea cave illuminated by an other-worldly blue light.

The easiest way to visit is to take a tour from Marina Grande. This costs €26.50, comprising the return boat trip, a rowing boat into the cave, and the cave's admission fee. Allow a good hour.

Giardini di Augusto — Gardens

(Gardens of Augustus; admission €1; ⏲9am-1hr before sunset) Escape the crowds by seeking out these colourful gardens near the 14th-century Certosa di San Giacomo. Founded by the Emperor Augustus, they rise in a series of flowered terraces to a viewpoint offering breathtaking views over to the **Isole Faraglioni**, a group of three limestone stacks that rise vertically out of the sea.

Villa Jovis — Ruin

(Jupiter's Villa; Via Amaiuri; admission €2; ⏲11am-3pm, closed Tue 1st-15th of month, closed Sun rest of month) Some 2km east of Capri along Via Tiberio, Villa Jovis was the largest and most sumptuous of the island's 12 Roman villas and Tiberius' main Capri residence. A vast pleasure complex, now reduced to ruins, it famously pandered to the emperor's debauched tastes, and included imperial quarters and extensive bathing areas set in dense gardens and woodland.

 Sleeping

Hotel Villa Eva — Hotel €€

(☎081 837 15 49; www.villaeva.com; Via La Fabbrica 8; d €110-180, tr €160-210, apt per person €55-70; ⏲Easter-Oct; ❄@📶🏊) Nestled amid fruit and olive trees in the countryside near Anacapri, Villa Eva is an idyllic retreat, complete with swimming pool, lush gardens and sunny rooms and apartments. Stained-glass windows and vintage fireplaces add character, while the location ensures peace and quiet.

La Minerva — Boutique Hotel €€€

(☎081 837 70 67; www.laminervacapri.com; Via Occhio Marino 8; d €190-550; ❄📶🏊) This gleaming hotel is a model of Capri style. Rooms, which cascade down the hillside, feature gleaming blue and white ceramic tiles, silk drapes and cool 100% linen sheets, while terraces come with sun loungers, and jacuzzis boast sea views. And then there's the gorgeous pool, surrounded by lush greenery

 Eating

Be warned that restaurants on Capri are overpriced and underwhelming. Many close between November and Easter.

Marina Grande (p440), Capri

Lo Sfizio Trattoria, Pizza **€€**
(**☎081 837 41 28; Via Tiberio 7; pizzas €7-11, meals €30; ⏰noon-3pm & 7pm-midnight Wed-Mon Apr-Dec)** On the path up to Villa Jovis, this trattoria-cum-pizzeria is ideally placed for a post-sightseeing meal. It's a relaxed, down-to-earth place with a few roadside tables and a typical island menu, ranging from pizza and handmade pasta to grilled meats and baked fish.

Pulalli Ristorante **€€**
(**☎081 837 41 08; Piazza Umberto 1; meals €35-40; ⏰noon-3pm & 7-11.30pm daily Aug, closed Tue Sep-Jul)** Climb the clock-tower steps to the right of the tourist office in the town of Capri and your reward is this lofty local hang-out where fabulous wine meets a discerning selection of cheese, charcuterie and more substantial fare such as *risotto al limone* (lemon risotto). Try for a seat on the terrace or, best of all, the coveted table on its own balcony.

Information

Information is available online at www.capritourism.com or from one of the three tourist offices: Marina Grande (**☎081 837 06 34; Banchina del Porto, Marina Grande**), Capri Town (**☎081 837 06 86; Piazza Umberto I, Capri Town; ⏰9am-1pm & 3-6.15pm Mon-Sat, 9am-1pm Sun**) and Anacapri. (**☎081 837 15 24; Via Giuseppe Orlandi 59, Anacapri; ⏰9am-3pm**)

Getting There & Around

There are year-round hydrofoils and ferries to Capri from Naples. Timetables and fare details are available online at www.capritourism.com; look under 'Shipping timetable'. Services are regular and tickets cost from €12 (ferry) to €19.10 (hydrofoil).

There are services to/from Sorrento (hydrofoil €18.30, fast ferry €17.10), and from Easter to November there are also services to Positano (€17).

On the island, buses run from Capri Town to/from Marina Grande, Anacapri and Marina Piccola. There are also buses from Marina Grande to Anacapri. Single tickets cost €1.80 on all routes, as does the funicular that links Marina Grande with Capri Town.

If You Like... Italian Islands

If you've been dazzled by the seaside charms of Capri (p440), you might feel like venturing across the Med to explore some of Italy's other islands.

1 SARDINIA

Just to the south of the French island of Corsica, Sardinia is renowned for its golden beaches and glorious coastline. The island is Italy's favourite summer getaway, and fancy resorts litter the coastline, but inland the island reveals a more rugged side: granite peaks, dizzying valleys and remote villages. It gets very busy in summer, so it's best to visit in spring or autumn. Flights from major Italian cities land in Cagliari and Alghero, while ferries arrive from various Italian ports, including Genoa, Livorno, Piombino, Civitavecchia, Naples and Palermo.

2 SICILY

Dominated by the smoking summit of Mt Etna, the Mediterranean's largest island has always marched to its own tune: geographically, linguistically, politically and gastronomically. From sunbaked plains to sparkling coast, Greek ruins to baroque cities, it's a fascinating island that feels several steps removed from the rest of Italy. Flights from Italy's main cities land at Palermo and Catania, and ferries cross regularly from Calabria.

3 AEOLIAN ISLANDS

Rising out of the cobalt-blue seas off Sicily's northeastern coast, the Aeolian Islands (Isole Eolie) have been seducing visitors since Odysseus' time. The seven islands (Lipari, Salina, Vulcano, Stromboli, Alicudi, Filicudi and Panarea) comprise a ridge of ancient volcanoes, many of which are still active: Stromboli still regularly supplies spectacular fire shows, while on Vulcano you can tackle a dip in hot volcanic mud. Ustica Lines (www.usticalines.it) runs hydrofoils from the islands to/from Messina (€22.70, 1¾ hours) and Milazzo (€23.70, one hour).

Right: Positano (p448); **Below:** Seafood pasta dish
(RIGHT) SLOW IMAGES/GETTY IMAGES ©; (BELOW) VINCENZO VERGELLI/GETTY IMAGES ©

Boat operators based at Marina Grande offer two-hour tours of the island (€17) and one-hour excursions to the Faraglioni (€16).

Sorrento

POP 16,640

A stunning location overlooking the Bay of Naples and Mt Vesuvius makes Sorrento a popular package-holiday destination despite the fact that it has no decent beach. Its profusion of sweet-smelling citrus trees and laid-back local lifestyle are certainly attractive, and its relative proximity to the Amalfi Coast, Pompeii and Capri make it a good base for those who don't wish to deal with the chaos and cacophany of Naples.

Sights & Activities

You'll probably spend most of your time in the *centro storico,* which is full of narrow streets lined with shops, cafes, churches and restaurants.

To the north, the **Villa Comunale Park** (8am-midnight summer, to 10.30pm winter) commands grand views over the sea to Mt Vesuvius.

The two main swimming spots are **Marina Piccola** and **Marina Grande**, although neither is especially appealing. Nicer by far is **Bagni Regina Giovanna**, a rocky beach set among the ruins of a Roman villa, 2km west of town.

Sleeping

Casa Astarita B&B €

(081 877 49 06; www.casastarita.com; Corso Italia 67; d €90-130, tr €110-150;) Housed in a 16th-century *palazzo* on Sorrento's main strip, this charming B&B reveals a colourful, eclectic look with original vaulted ceilings, brightly painted doors and maiolica-tiled floors. Its six simple but well-equipped rooms surround a central parlour, where breakfast is served on a large rustic table.

Eating

Raki Gelateria €

(www.rakisorrento.com; Via San Cesareo 48; cones/tubs from €2; ⏲11am-late) There are numerous gelaterie in Sorrento, but this new kid on the block is making a mark with its homemade, preservative-free ice cream in a number of exciting flavours. Try ricotta, walnut and honey, or vanilla and ginger, which packs a surprisingly spicy punch.

O'Puledrone Seafood €€

(☎081 012 41 34; Via Marina Grande 150; meals €25-30; ⏲noon-3pm & 6.30pm-late Easter-Oct) The small harbour at Marina Grande is the place for seafood. This no-frills trattoria, run by a cooperative of local fishers, is as good a spot as any for fried fish starters, pastas and a mountainous *risotto alla pescatora* (seafood risotto).

Information

The main **tourist office** **(☎081 807 40 33; www.sorrentotourism.com; Via Luigi De Maio 35; ⏲8.30am-8pm Mon-Sat, 9am-1pm Sun Jul-Sep)** is near Piazza San Antonino, but there are also information points at the **Circumvesuviana station** **(⏲10am-1pm & 3-7pm summer, to 5pm winter)** and **Piazza Tasso** **(cnr Corso Italia & Via Correale; ⏲10am-1pm & 4-9pm summer, to 7pm winter)**. Note that their opening hours can be erratic, especially in the low season.

Getting There & Away

Circumvesuviana trains run half-hourly between Sorrento and Naples (€4.10, 65 minutes) via Pompeii (€2.90, 35 minutes) and Ercolano (€2.20, 15 minutes). A daily ticket covering stops at Ercolano, Pompeii and Sorrento costs €6.30 (€3.50 on weekends).

From Marina Piccola, hydrofoils (€18.30) and fast ferries (€17.10) sail to Capri (25 minutes, up to 16 daily). There are also summer sailings to Naples (€12.30, 35 minutes), Positano (return €32) and Amalfi (return €34).

Amalfi Coast

Stretching 50km along the southern side of the Sorrentine Peninsula, the Amalfi Coast (Costiera Amalfitana) is a postcard-perfect vision of shimmering blue water fringed by vertiginous cliffs to which whitewashed villages with terraced lemon groves cling. This Unesco-protected area is one of Italy's top tourist destinations, attracting hundreds of thousands of visitors each year (70% of them between June and September).

Getting There & Away

There are two main entry points to the Amalfi Coast: Sorrento and Salerno. Both can be accessed by train from Naples (Sorrento on the Circumvesuviana and Salerno on Trenitalia).

Buses run from Sorrento to Positano (€2.50, 40 minutes) and Amalfi (€3.80, 90 minutes), and from Salerno to Amalfi (€3.80, 75 minutes).

Boat services generally run between April and October. Alicost (**089 87 14 83; www.alicost.it**) operates daily boats from Salerno (Molo Manfredi) to Amalfi (€8), Positano (€12) and Capri (€21.80). Travelmar (**089 87 29 50; www.travelmar.it**) has up to seven daily sailings from Salerno (Piazza Concordia) to Amalfi (€8) and Positano (€12).

By car, take the SS163 coastal road at Vietri sul Mare.

POSITANO

POP 3950

Approaching Positano by boat, you will be greeted by an unforgettable view of colourful, steeply stacked houses clinging to near-vertical green slopes.

Activities

The **tourist office** (**089 87 50 67; Via del Saracino 4; 9am-7pm Mon-Sat, to 2pm Sun summer, 9am-4pm Mon-Sat winter**) can provide information on walking in the densely wooded Lattari Mountains, including details of the spectacular 12km **Sentiero degli Dei** (Path of the Gods) between Positano and Praiano, and the **Via degli Incanti** (Trail of Charms) between Positano and Amalfi.

Sleeping

Hotel Villa Gabrisa Boutique Hotel €€€

(**089 81 14 98; www.villagabrisa.it; Via Pasitea 219-227; €250-320;**) This lovely four-star hotel occupies an 18th-century *palazzo* near the top of town. Rooms exude Italian style with painted furniture from Tuscany coupled with traditional wrought-iron beds, Murano-glass chandeliers and maiolica tiles. There's also an elegant wine bar and restaurant serving sophisticated regional cuisine.

Eating & Drinking

C'era una volta Trattoria, Pizza €

(**089 81 19 30; Via Marconi 127; pizzas €6, meals €25; noon-3pm & 6.30pm-late**) Up in the high part of town, this authentic trattoria is a good bet for honest, down-to-earth Italian grub. Alongside regional staples like *gnocchi alla sorrentina* (gnocchi served in a tomato and basil sauce), there's a decent selection of pizzas (to eat in or take away) and a full menu of pastas and fail-safe mains.

Next2 Ristorante €€

(**089 812 35 16; www.next2.it; Viale Pasitea 242; meals €45; 6.30-11.30pm**) Understated elegance meets creative cuisine at this contemporary set-up. Local and organic ingredients are put to impressive use in beautifully presented dishes such as ravioli stuffed with aubergine and prawns or seabass with tomatoes and lemon-scented peas. Desserts are wickedly delicious and the alfresco sea-facing terrace is summer perfection.

AMALFI

POP 5170

Amalfi, the main hub on the coast, makes a convenient base for exploring the surrounding coastline. It's a pretty place with a tangle of narrow alleyways, stacked whitewashed houses and sun-drenched piazzas, but can get get very busy in summer as day trippers pour in to peruse its loud souvenir shops and busy eateries.

Sights

Cattedrale di Sant'Andrea Cathedral

(☎089 87 10 59; Piazza del Duomo; ⏰cathedral 7.30am-7.45pm, cloister 9am-7.45pm) A melange of architectural styles, Amalfi's cathedral, one of the few relics of the town's past as an 11th-century maritime superpower, makes a striking impression at the top of its sweeping flight of stairs. Between 10am and 5pm entrance is through the adjacent **Chiostro del Paradiso**, a 13th-century cloister, where you have to pay an admission fee of €3.

Grotta dello Smeraldo Cave

(admission €5; ⏰9.30am-4pm) Four kilometres west of Amalfi, this grotto is named after the eerie emerald colour that emanates from the water. Stalactites hang down from the 24m-high ceiling, while stalagmites grow up to 10m tall. Buses regularly pass the car park above the cave entrance (from where you take a lift or stairs down to the rowing boats). Alternatively, Coop Sant'Andrea runs boats from Amalfi (€10 return, plus cave admission). Allow 1½ hours for the return trip.

Sleeping & Eating

Hotel Lidomare Hotel €€

(☎089 87 13 32; www.lidomare.it; Largo Duchi Piccolomini 9; s/d €65/145; ❄📶) Family-run, this old-fashioned hotel has real character. The large luminous rooms have an air of gentility, with their appealingly haphazard decor, vintage tiles and fine antiques. Some have jacuzzi bathtubs, others have sea views and a balcony, some have both. Breakfast is laid out, rather unusually, on top of a grand piano.

Hotel Centrale Hotel €€

(☎089 87 26 08; www.amalfihotelcentrale.it; Largo Piccolomini 1; r €100-120; ❄@📶) For the money, this is one of the best-value hotels in Amalfi. The entrance is on a tiny little piazza in the *centro storico*, but many of the small but tastefully decorated rooms overlook Piazza del Duomo. The aquamarine ceramic tiling lends it a vibrant fresh look and the views from the rooftop terrace are magnificent.

Marina Grande Seafood €€€

(☎089 87 11 29; www.ristorantemarinagrande.com; Viale Delle Regioni 4; tasting menu lunch/dinner €25/60, meals €45; ⏰noon-3pm & 6.30-11pm Tue-Sun Mar-Oct) 🌿 Run by the third generation of the same family, this beachfront restaurant serves fish so fresh it's almost flapping. It prides itself on its use of locally sourced organic produce, which, in Amalfi, means high-quality seafood. Reservations recommended.

Grotto dello Smeraldo
AGF SRL/ALAMY ©

SURVIVAL GUIDE

Directory A–Z

Accommodation

The bulk of Italy's accommodation is made up of *alberghi* (hotels) and *pensioni* – often housed in converted apartments. Other options are youth hostels, camping grounds, B&Bs, *agriturismi* (farm-stays), mountain *rifugi* (Alpine refuges), monasteries and villa/apartment rentals.

High-season rates apply at Easter, in summer (mid-June to August) and over the Christmas to New Year period.

The north of Italy is generally more expensive than the south.

Many city-centre hotels offer discounts in August to lure clients from the crowded coast. Check hotel websites for last-minute offers.

Most hotels in coastal resorts shut for winter, typically from November to March. The same applies to *agriturismi* and villa rentals in rural areas.

Price Ranges

In this chapter prices quoted are for rooms with a private bathroom, and unless otherwise stated include breakfast.

The following price indicators apply (for a high-season double room):

€ less than €110

€€ €110 to €200

€€€ more than €200

Hotel Tax

Most Italian hotels apply a room-occupancy tax (*tassa di soggiorno*) which is charged on top of your regular hotel bill. The exact amount, which varies from city to city, depends on your type of accommodation, but as a rough guide reckon on €1 to €3 per person per night in a one-star hotel, €3 to €3.50 in a B&B, €3 to €4 in a three-star hotel etc.

Note that prices quoted in this book do not include the tax.

Food

The following price ranges refer to the cost of a two-course meal, glass of house wine and *coperto* (cover charge):

€ under €25

€€ €25 to €45

€€€ over €45

Gay & Lesbian Travellers

Homosexuality is legal in Italy, but same-sex couples have no shared rights to property, social

Venice (p401)

DAVID C TOMLINSON/GETTY IMAGES ©

security and inheritance. There is a push to legalise gay marriage, but this seems unlikely in the near future.

Homosexuality is well tolerated in major cities but overt displays of affection could attract a negative response, particularly in small towns and in the more conservative south.

Italy's main gay and lesbian organisation is Arcigay (☎051 1095 7241; www.arcigay.it; Via Don Minzoni 18, Bologna), based in Bologna.

Internet Access

Most hotels, hostels, B&Bs and *pensioni* offer free wi-fi.

Internet cafes are thin on the ground. Charges are typically around €5 per hour.

To use internet points in Italy you must present photo ID.

Money

Italy's currency is the euro.

ATMs, known in Italy as *bancomat,* are widespread and will accept cards displaying the appropriate sign. Visa and MasterCard are widely recognised, as are Cirrus and Maestro; American Express is less common.

Credit cards are widely accepted, although many small trattorias, pizzerias and *pensioni* only take cash. Don't assume museums, galleries and the like accept credit cards.

If your credit/debit card is lost, stolen or swallowed by an ATM, telephone toll-free to block it: Amex (☎800 928 391); MasterCard (☎800 870866); and Visa (☎800 819014).

Opening Hours

Many museums, galleries and archaeological sites operate summer and winter opening hours. Typically, winter hours will apply between November and late March or early April.

Banks 8.30am-1.30pm & 2.45-4.30pm Mon-Fri

Bars & Cafes 7.30am-8pm; many open earlier and some stay open until the small hours; pubs often open noon-2am

Discos & Clubs 10pm-4am

Pharmacies 9am-1pm & 4-7.30pm Mon-Fri, to 1pm Sat; outside of these hours, pharmacies open on a rotation basis – all are required to post a list of places open in the vicinity

Post offices Major offices 8am-7pm Mon-Fri, to 1.15pm Sat; branch offices 8.30am-2pm Mon-Fri, to 1pm Sat

Restaurants noon-3pm & 7.30-11pm or midnight; most restaurants close one day a week

Shops 9am-1pm & 3.30-7.30pm, or 4-8pm Mon-Sat; in larger cities many chain stores and supermarkets open from 9am to 7.30pm Mon-Sat; some also open Sun morning, typically 9am -1pm; food shops are generally closed Thu afternoon; some other shops are closed Mon morning

Post

Italy's postal system, Poste Italiane (☎80 31 60; www.poste.it), is reasonably reliable.

The standard service is *posta prioritaria*. Registered mail is known as *posta raccomandata,* insured mail as *posta assicurato*.

Francobolli (stamps) are available at post offices and *tabacchi* (tobacconists); look for a big white 'T' against a blue/black background.

Public Holidays

Most Italians take their annual holiday in August. This means that many businesses and shops close down for at least a part of the month, usually around Ferragosto (15 August). Easter is another busy holiday.

New Year's Day (Capodanno) 1 January

Epiphany (Epifania) 6 January

Anniversary of the Unification of Italy (Anniversario dell'Unità d'Italia) 17 March

Easter Monday (Pasquetta) March/April

Liberation Day (Giorno delle Liberazione) 25 April

Labour Day (Festa del Lavoro) 1 May

Republic Day (Festa della Repubblica) 2 June

Feast of the Assumption (Ferragosto) 15 August

All Saints' Day (Ognisanti) 1 November

Day of National Unity and the Armed Forces (Giornata dell'Unità Nazionale e delle Forze Armate) 4 November

Feast of the Immaculate Conception (Immacolata Concezione) 8 December

Christmas Day (Natale) 25 December

Boxing Day (Festa di Santo Stefano) 26 December

Individual towns also have holidays to celebrate their patron saints:

St Mark (Venice) 25 April

St John the Baptist (Florence, Genoa and Turin) 24 June

Sts Peter and Paul (Rome) 29 June

St Rosalia (Palermo) 15 July

St Janarius (Naples) First Sunday in May, 19 September and 16 December

St Ambrose (Milan) 7 December

Safe Travel

Petty theft is prevalent in Italy. Be on your guard against pickpockets and moped thieves in popular tourist centres such as Rome, Florence and Venice, and especially in Naples.

Don't take it for granted that cars will stop at red lights.

Telephone

Area codes are an integral part of all Italian phone numbers and must be dialled even when calling locally.

To call Italy from abroad, dial ☎0039 and then the area code, including the first zero.

To call abroad from Italy, dial ☎00, then the relevant country code followed by the telephone number.

Skype is available on many hostel computers.

Mobile Phones

Italy uses the GSM 900/1800 network, which is compatible with the rest of Europe and Australia, but not with the North American GSM 1900 or the Japanese system (although some GSM 1900/900 phones do work here).

If you can unlock your phone (check with your service provider), the cheapest way to make calls is to buy an Italian SIM card.

These are available from **TIM (Telecom Italia Mobile; www.tim.it)**, **Tre (www.tre.it)**, **Wind (www.wind.it)** and **Vodafone (www.vodafone.it)**.

You'll need ID when you buy one.

Phone Codes

Italy's country code is ☎39.

Mobile-phone numbers begin with a three-digit prefix starting with a ☎3.

Toll-free (free-phone) numbers are known as *numeri verdi* and start with ☎800. These are not always available if calling from a mobile phone.

Tourist Information

For pre-trip information, check out the website of the **Ministro del Turismo (www.italia.it)**.

Travellers with Disabilities

Italy is not an easy country for travellers with disabilities. Cobbled streets, blocked pavements and tiny lifts all make life difficult. Rome-based **Consorzio Cooperative Integrate (CO.IN; www.coinsociale.it)** is the best point of reference for travellers with disabilities.

Main International Ferry Routes

FROM	TO	COMPANY	MIN-MAX FARE (€)	DURATION (HR)
Ancona	Igoumenitsa	Minoan, Superfast, Anek	69-100	16½-22
Ancona	Patra	Minoan, Superfast, Anek	69-100	22-29
Ancona	Split	Jadrolinija, SNAV	48-57.50	10¾
Bari	Igoumenitsa	Superfast	78-93	8-12
Bari	Patra	Superfast	78-93	16
Bari	Dubrovnik	Jadrolinija	48-57.50	10-12
Bari	Bar	Montenegro	50-55	9
Brindisi	Igoumenitsa	Endeavor	52-83	8
Brindisi	Patra	Endeavor	56-94	14
Brindisi	Corfu	Endeavor	52-83	6½-11½
Brindisi	Kefallonia	Endeavor	56-94	12½
Genoa	Barcelona	SNAV	90	19½
Genoa	Tunis	SNAV	111	23½

If you're travelling by train, Trenitalia (p455) runs a telephone info line (☎199 30 30 60) with details of assistance available at stations.

Visas

Schengen visa rules apply for entry to Italy.

Non-EU citizens who want to study in Italy must obtain a study visa from their nearest Italian embassy or consulate.

A *permesso di soggiorno* (permit to stay) is required by all non-EU nationals who stay in Italy longer than three months. You must apply within eight days of arriving in Italy. Check the exact documentary requirements at www.polizia distato.it.

Getting There & Away

Air

Italy's main international airports:

Malpensa Airport (MXP; ☎**02 23 23 23; www. milanomalpensa-airport.com**) About 50km northwest of Milan; northern Italy's main international airport.

Marco Polo Airport (VCE; ☎**flight information 041 260 92 60; www.veniceairport.it**) Some 12km outside Venice, east of Mestre.

Pisa International Airport (**Galileo Galilei Airport;** ☎**050 84 93 00; www.pisa-airport.com**) Tuscany's main international airport, a 10-minute drive south of Pisa; flights to most major European cities.

Rome Ciampino (☎**06 6 59 51; www.adr.it/ciampino**) Hub for European low-cost carrier Ryanair.

Rome Leonardo da Vinci (**Fiumicino;** ☎**06 6 59 51; www.adr.it/fiumicino**) Italy's main international airport; also known as Fiumicino.

Land

Border Crossings

Italy borders France, Switzerland, Austria and Slovenia. The main points of entry:

From France The coast road from Nice; the Mont Blanc tunnel; Fréjus tunnel .

From Switzerland The Grand St Bernard tunnel; the Simplon tunnel; the Lötschberg Base tunnel.

From Austria The Brenner Pass.

Car & Motorcycle

If traversing the Alps, note that border crossings from the Brenner Pass and Grand St Bernard tunnel are open year-round. Other mountain passes are often closed in winter and sometimes even in spring and autumn.

Burano, near Venice

It's obligatory to carry snow chains in your car when driving on mountain roads in winter, typically between November and March.

Train

Direct international trains connect with various cities:

Milan To/from Paris, Marseille, Geneva, Zürich, Vienna.

Rome To/from Munich, Vienna.

Venice To/from Paris, Munich, Innsbruck, Salzburg, Vienna.

There are also international trains from Verona, Padua, Bologna and Florence. Get details at www.trenitalia.com.

Voyages-sncf (**0844 848 5848; http://uk.voyages-sncf.com**) can provide fare information on journeys from the UK to Italy, most of which require a change at Paris. Another excellent resource is www.seat61.com.

Eurail and Inter-Rail passes are both valid in Italy.

Sea

Dozens of ferry companies connect Italy with other Mediterranean countries. Timetables are seasonal, so always check ahead; you'll find details of routes, companies and online booking at www.traghettiweb.it.

Getting Around

Bicycle

- Tourist offices can generally provide details of designated bike trails and bike hire (at least €10 per day).
- Bikes can be taken on regional and international trains carrying the bike logo, but you'll need to pay a supplement (€3.50 on regional trains, €12 on international trains). Bikes can be carried free if dismantled and stored in a bike bag.
- Bikes generally incur a small supplement on ferries, typically €10 to €15.

Boat

Navi (large ferries) service Sicily and Sardinia; *traghetti* (smaller ferries) and *aliscafi* (hydrofoils) cover the smaller islands.

The main embarkation points for Sardinia are Genoa, Piombino, Livorno, Civitavecchia and Naples; for Sicily, it's Naples and Villa San Giovanni in Calabria.

Bus

- Italy boasts an extensive and largely reliable bus network.
- Buses are not necessarily cheaper than trains, but in mountainous areas they are often the only choice.
- In larger cities, companies have ticket offices or operate through agencies but in most villages and small towns tickets are sold in bars or on the bus.
- Reservations are only necessary for high-season long-haul trips.

Car & Motorcycle

- Roads are generally good and there's an excellent system of autostradas (motorways).
- There's a toll to use most autostradas, payable in cash or by credit card at exit barriers.
- Autostradas are indicated

Vernazza, Cinque Terre (p394)

by an A with a number (eg A1) on a green background; *strade statali* (main roads) are shown by an S or SS and number (eg SS7) against a blue background.

- Italy's motoring organisation **Automobile Club d'Italia** (ACI; **☎803 116, from a foreign mobile 800 116 800; www.aci.it**) provides 24-hour roadside assistance.
- Cars use unleaded petrol *(benzina senza piombo)* and diesel *(gasolio);* both are expensive but diesel is slightly cheaper.
- All EU driving licences are recognised in Italy. Holders of non-EU licences must get an International Driving Permit (IDP) to accompany their national licence.

Hire

To hire a car you must:

- have a valid driving licence (plus IDP if required)
- have had your licence for at least a year
- be 21 or over; under-25s will often have to pay a young-driver's supplement on top of the usual rates
- have a credit card.

Make sure you understand what is included in the price (unlimited kilometres, tax, insurance, collision damage waiver etc) and what your liabilities are. For the best rental rates, book your car before leaving home. Note also that most cars have manual gear transmission.

In addition to major rental agencies, local firms often offer competitive deals.

Insurance

If driving your own car, carry your vehicle registration certificate, driving licence, and proof of third party liability insurance cover.

Road Rules

- Drive on the right, overtake on the left and give way to cars coming from the right.
- It's obligatory to wear seatbelts, to drive with your headlights on when outside built-up areas, and to carry a warning triangle and fluorescent waistcoat in case of breakdown.
- Wearing a helmet is compulsory on all two-wheeled vehicles.
- The blood alcohol limit is 0.05%, or zero for drivers who have had their licence for less than three years.

Unless otherwise indicated, speed limits are as follows:

- 130km/h (in rain 110km/h) on autostradas
- 110km/h (in rain 90km/h) on all main, non-urban roads
- 90km/h on secondary, non-urban roads
- 50km/h in built-up areas.

Most major Italian cities operate a limited traffic zone (ZTL; Zona a Traffico Limitato) in their historic centres. You can enter a on a *motorino* (moped/scooter) but not in private or hire cars.

Train

Italy has an extensive rail network. Most services are run by **Trenitalia** (**☎89 20 21; www.trenitalia.com**) but **Italo Treno** (**☎06 07 08; www.italotreno.it**) high-speed trains also connect Salerno, Naples, Rome, Florence, Bologna, Milan, Turin, Padua and Venice.

- InterCity and fast Frecce trains require a supplement, which is incorporated in the ticket price.
- Generally, it's cheaper to buy all local train tickets in Italy.
- If your ticket doesn't include a reservation with an assigned seat, you must validate it before boarding by inserting it into one of the machines dotted around stations.
- Some services offer 'ticketless' travel; book and pay for your seat at www.trenitalia.com and then communicate your booking code to the controller on board.

The Netherlands & Belgium

They might be next-door neighbours, but Belgium and the Netherlands couldn't be more different in attitude and outlook. On the one side, there's Belgium: best known for its bubbly beer, top-quality chocolate and political position at the heart of the EU. But look beyond these well-worn clichés and you'll discover an eccentric little nation packed with centuries of history, art and architecture, not to mention a longstanding identity crisis between its Flemish and Walloon sides.

On the other side is the Netherlands: liberal, laid-back and flat as a pancake, famous for its brown cafes, spinning windmills and colourful tulip fields. But again, the stereotypes tell only half the story. Look beyond Amsterdam's canals and you'll discover a whole different side to the Netherlands, from buzzing urban centres like Rotterdam, gorgeous medieval towns such as Leiden and Delft, and wide-open spaces such as the stunning national park of Hoge Veluwe.

Woman cycling on frozen river, the Netherlands

The Netherlands & Belgium

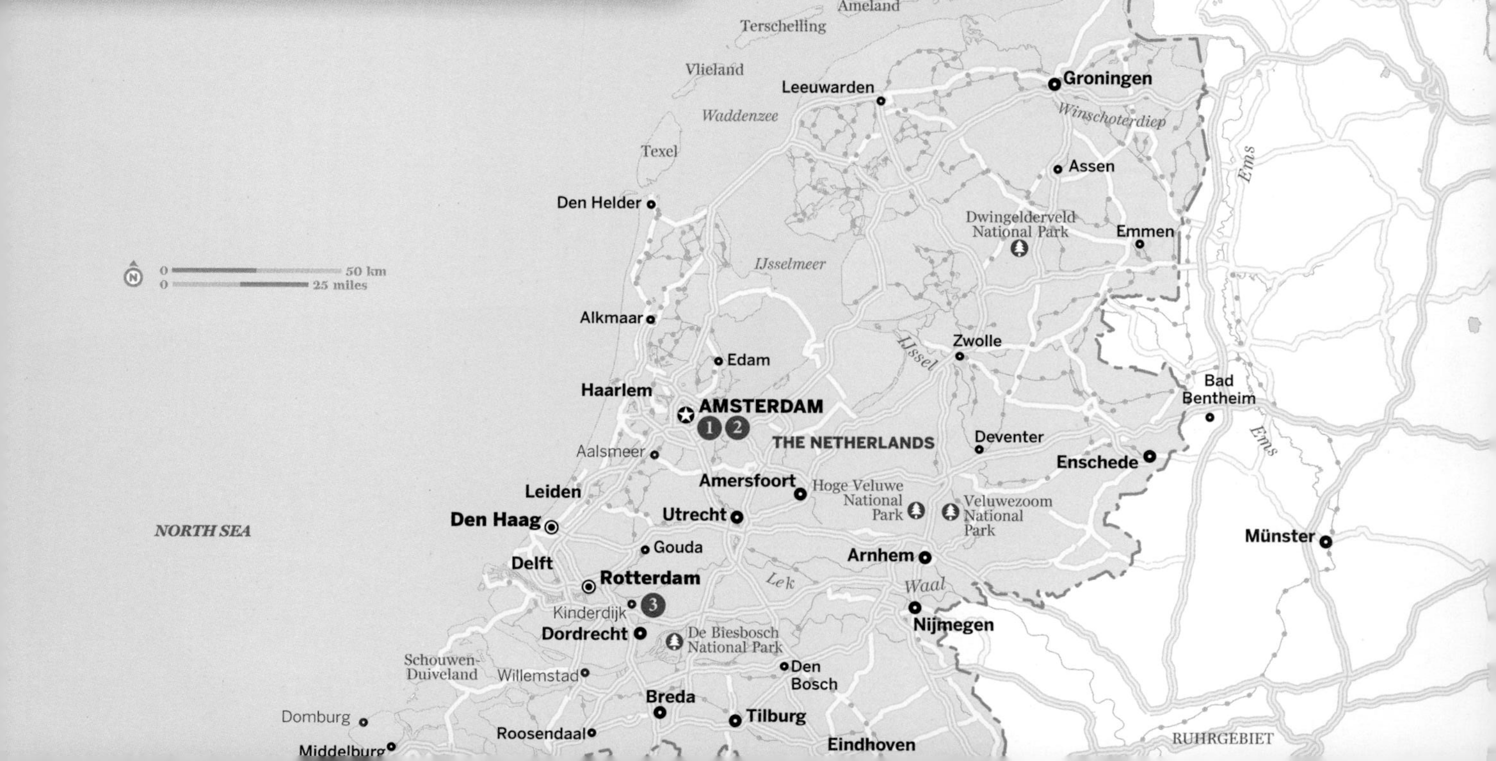

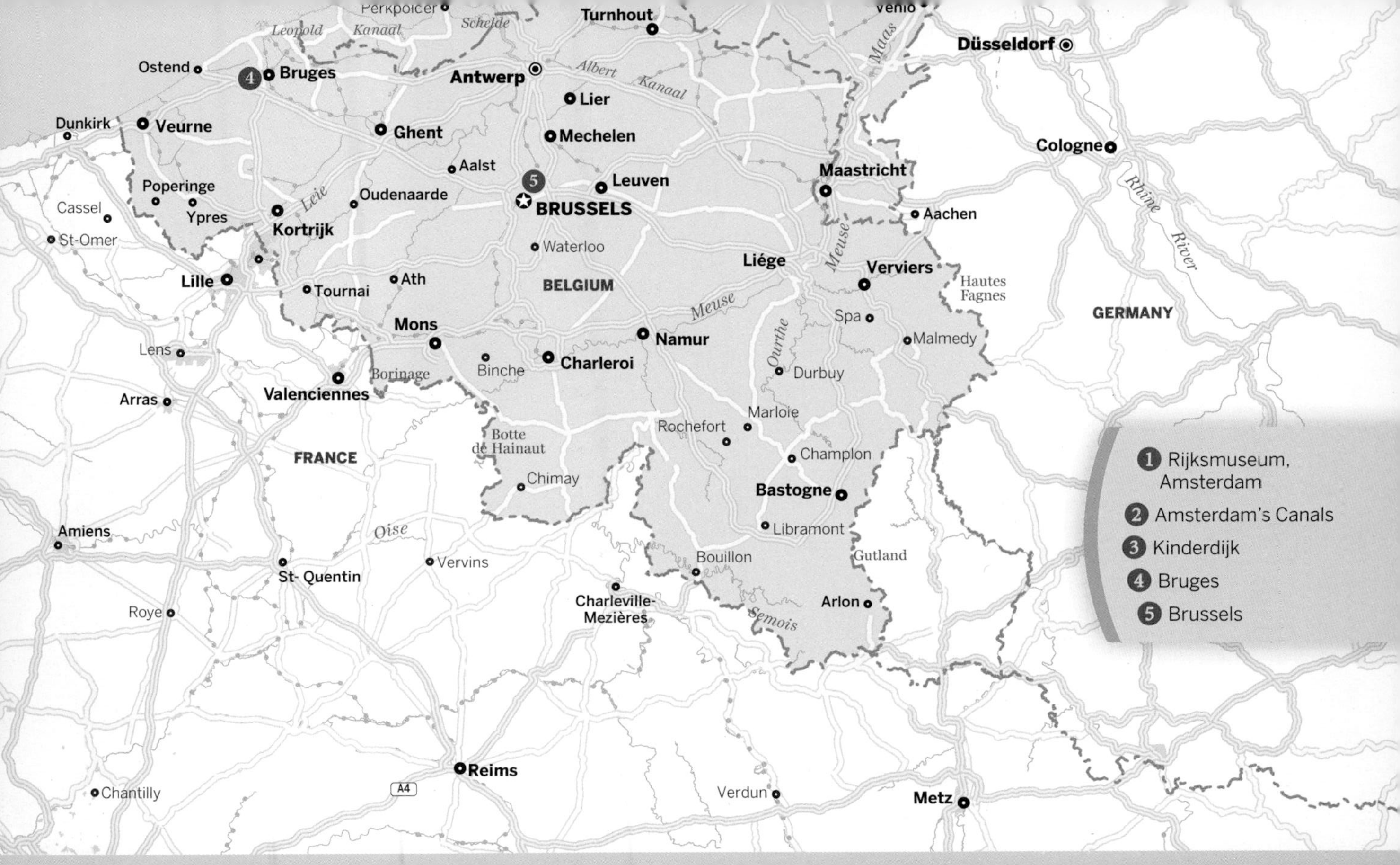

1 Rijksmuseum, Amsterdam
2 Amsterdam's Canals
3 Kinderdijk
4 Bruges
5 Brussels
Turnhout
Düsseldorf
Leopold
Kanaal
Schelde
Ostend
Bruges
Antwerp
Albert
Kanaal
Lier
Maas
Dunkirk
Veurne
Ghent
Mechelen
Cologne
Aalst
Leuven
Maastricht
Poperinge
Leie
Oudenaarde
BRUSSELS
Cassel
Ypres
Kortrijk
Aachen
Rhine
St-Omer
Waterloo
River
Liége
Meuse
Verviers
Lille
Ath
Tournai
BELGIUM
Hautes Fagnes
Meuse
GERMANY
Spa
Mons
Namur
Malmedy
Lens
Ourthe
Charleroi
Binche
Durbuy
Borinage
Valenciennes
Arras
Marloie
Rochefort
Botte de Hainaut
Champlon
FRANCE
Chimay
Bastogne
Amiens
Oise
Libramont
Vervins
Bouillon
Gutland
St- Quentin
Charleville-Mezières
Arlon
Roye
Semois
Reims
Chantilly
A4
Verdun
Metz

The Netherlands & Belgium Highlights

Rijksmuseum

The Netherlands' national museum (p468) is simply unmissable. From priceless Delft pottery to ancient Egyptian artefacts, it's a dazzling affair. But it's the museum's unmatched collection of Dutch art that steals the show, with famous names such as Bosch, Cranach, van Gogh, Vermeer and Rubens all represented, and the biggest draw of all, Rembrandt's masterpiece *Night Watch*.

1

2 Amsterdam's Canals

If any European city was tailor-made for a romantic break, it's Amsterdam (p466). The city is criss-crossed by a web of waterways left over from its days as a maritime hub, and they're still a fundamental part of the city's laid-back character. Take a river cruise, hire a houseboat, cycle along the cobbled quays or just sit back in a canalside cafe and watch the world spin by.

CHRIS MELLOR/GETTY IMAGES ©

3 Kinderdijk

Kinderdijk is perhaps the quintessential Dutch landscape. This Unesco-protected landscape southeast of Rotterdam (p486) boasts some of the Netherlands' oldest dikes and windmills, built during the 18th century to drain agricultural land. Regular boat cruises run from Rotterdam, and bikes are readily available for hire once you arrive.

JOHN ELK III/GETTY IMAGES ©

4 Bruges

With a beautiful medieval centre and charmingly old-world atmosphere, Bruges (p506) is a Belgian treasure. The city's most famous landmark is the huge Belfort (83m; bell tower) overlooking the central marketplace – 366 winding steps lead to the top for one of the best views in Belgium. The only drawback is its popularity – try to visit in the low season if you can.

5 Brussels

With its impressive squares, colonnaded arcades and art nouveau architecture, Brussels (p490) is a city that oozes grace and sophistication. Browse for antiques, taste handmade chocolates and shop till you drop, then sit back and immerse yourself in the city's famous cafe culture on Grand Place.

The Netherlands & Belgium's Best...

Historic Towns

- **Haarlem** (p478) The Netherlands in a nutshell: canals, cobbles, churches and cosy bars.
- **Delft** (p481) This pretty Dutch town is famous for its delicate blue-and-white pottery.
- **Ghent** (p501) Just as beautiful as Bruges, but much less crowded.
- **Utrecht** (p487) Parts of this canal city date back to the 13th century.
- **Ypres** (p510) Home to one of Belgium's grandest public squares, the Grote Markt.

Views

- **The Canal Belt** (p467) Watch narrowboats putter past in Amsterdam's canal quarter.
- **Belfort, Bruges** (p506) Bruges' iconic bell tower offers knockout views across the city.
- **Euromast** (p485) This striking 185m-high tower soars above Rotterdam's historic harbour.
- **Kinderdijk** (p486) The classic Dutch landscape: pancake-flat fields and spinning windmills.
- **Domtoren** (p487) Climb 465 steps to the top of Utrecht's church tower.

Architectural Landmarks

- **The Bourse** (p490) Brussels' 19th-century stock exchange is a neoclassical landmark.
- **Grand Place** (p491) Grand by name and nature: the finest public square in Belgium.
- **Overblaak** (p485) Piet Blom's controversial cube-shaped apartment block dates from the early 1980s.
- **Atomium** (p494) A giant molecule built for the 1958 World Fair.

Art Museums

- **Rijksmuseum** (p468) Still the daddy of Dutch art galleries.
- **Van Gogh Museum** (p467) The world's largest collection of Vincent's works.
- **Museum Boijmans van Beuningen** (p484) Admire Dutch old masters, surrealists and pop artists at this Rotterdam landmark.
- **Rembrandthuis** (p472) Rembrandt's former Amsterdam studio is now a museum.
- **SMAK** (p503) Belgium's top contemporary gallery, near Ghent.

Left: Delftware pottery (p482), the Netherlands; **Above:** Utrecht (p487), the Netherlands

Need to Know

ADVANCE PLANNING

- **Two months before** Book accommodation for popular cities, especially Amsterdam, Bruges and Ghent.
- **At least a month before** Book Eurostar tickets for the cheapest deals.
- **When you arrive** Pick up a Museumkaart, which covers entry to 400 Dutch museums.

RESOURCES

- **Netherlands Tourism Board** (www.holland.com) Hotels, sights, restaurants and more.
- **Dutch Railways** (www.ns.nl) Plan your travel on the Dutch train system.
- **Flanders** (www.visitflanders.com) Specific information for the Flanders region.
- **Brussels** (www.brusselsinternational.be and visitbrussels.be) The latest lowdown on Belgium's capital.
- **USE-IT**(use-it.travel) Quirky maps made by locals, giving you the lowdown on the major Belgian cities.

GETTING AROUND

- **Air** The Netherlands' main airports are at Schiphol (Amsterdam) and Rotterdam. Most Belgian flights land in Brussels, Antwerp, Charleroi or Liège. All airports have shuttle buses and/or trains to relevant cities.
- **Bus** Regular buses serve major Dutch cities plus Brussels, Antwerp, Ghent and Liège.
- **Car** Rental costs and petrol can be pricey.
- **Train** Both countries have good rail networks; high-speed trains (Thalys in Belgium; Hispeed in the Netherlands) connect several major cities.

BE FOREWARNED

- **Public transport** The prepaid *OV-chipkaart* covers all public transport in the Netherlands.
- **Drugs** In the Netherlands, soft drugs are tolerated, but hard drugs are a serious crime. You can smoke pot *without* tobacco in coffee shops (but not cafes!).
- **Languages** Belgium has three official languages: French, German and Dutch (also called Flemish). Many Dutch people speak excellent English.

The Netherlands & Belgium Itineraries

The Netherlands and Belgium both have a lot to offer – great museums, groundbreaking architecture and some of Europe's most interesting cities.

3 DAYS

THE DUTCH ESSENTIALS
Amsterdam to Rotterdam

For an introduction to the Netherlands, you simply can't beat ❶ **Amsterdam** (p466). It won't take you long to fall head over heels for this lovely, laid-back city. On day one head to the Rijksmuseum, Van Gogh Museum and Rembrandtshuis, and spend the evening in an atmospheric brown cafe.

On day two visit Anne Frank's house, where the teenager penned her diary during the Nazi occupation. Spend the afternoon exploring the canals along Prinsengracht and Herengracht and the lovely area around Jordaan. Finish up with the essential Amsterdam experience – a romantic canal cruise.

On your last day, hop on a train to ❷ **Rotterdam** (p484), Holland's cool second city, and home to some of its eclectic architecture. Don't miss the experimental Overblaak Development and the 185m-tall Euromast, but make sure you leave time for the city's arts museum, the Museum Boijmans van Beuningen. Spend the evening dining and drinking in the old harbour area, Delfshaven.

Top Left: Overblaak Development (p485), Rotterdam, the Netherlands; **Top Right:** Grand Place (p491), Brussels, Belgium

5 DAYS

THE ROAD TO BELGIUM

Delft to Ghent

After the cities, it's time to explore further afield. Two historic towns are within easy reach of Rotterdam – 1 **Delft** (p481), famous for its decorative china, and 2 **Leiden** (p480), Rembrandt's home town. Frequent train links make travelling to either town a breeze, so devote a day to each. Then it's on to 3 **Kinderdijk** (p486), a wonderfully Dutch landscape of antique windmills spinning above pancake-flat polders. The best transport there is the Waterbus from central Rotterdam.

On day four, catch the train south into Belgium and hop off at 4 **Antwerp** (p498), a fascinating old city whose main claim to fame is as the birthplace of Rubens; you can even visit the artist's original studio.

On day five, catch the train south to 5 **Brussels** (p490), Belgium's elegant capital and one of the EU's most important cities. All roads lead to Grand Place, the magnificent main square, where you can browse for Belgian goodies in the historic Galeries St-Hubert before sampling locally brewed beers in one of the many *belle époque* cafes.

Finish with a visit to gorgeous 6 **Ghent** (p501): with its haphazard streets, old squares and waterfront cafes, it feels a lot like Bruges but without the crowds.

Discover the Netherlands & Belgium

At a Glance

- **Amsterdam** (p466) Edgy and eccentric, cut through by canals, this is the Netherlands' must-see city.
- **The Randstad** (p478) Picture-postcard Netherlands, from windmills and dikes to revitalised harbours.
- **Brussels** (p490) Sip a coffee on Belgium's grandest Grand Place, then shop for the world's finest chocolate.
- **Flanders** (p498) Half-Belgian, half-Flemish, and crammed with history.

Windmill and canal, the Netherlands
DAVID HENDERSON/GETTY IMAGES ©

THE NETHERLANDS

Amsterdam

☎020 / POP 811,200

If Amsterdam were a staid place it would still be one of Europe's most beautiful and historic cities, right up there with Venice and Paris. But add in the qualities that make it Amsterdam – the cool and mellow bars, brown cafes full of characters, pervasive irreverence, whiffs of pot and an open-air marketplace for sleaze and sex – and you have a literally intoxicating mix.

Wander the 17th-century streets, tour the iconic canals, stop off to enjoy a masterpiece, discover a funky shop and choose from food from around the world. Walk or ride a bike around the concentric rings of the centre then explore the historic lanes of the Jordaan district or the Plantage, and bask in the many worlds-within-worlds, where nothing ever seems the same twice.

Sights

CITY CENTRE

The not-overly-impressive **Royal Palace** (Koninklijk Paleis; ☎620 40 60; www.paleisamsterdam.nl; Dam; adult/child €10/free; ⏲11am-5pm; 🚋4/9/16/24 Dam) and the square that puts the 'Dam' in Amsterdam anchor Amsterdam's oldest quarter. This is the busiest part of town for tourists: many leave the train station and head straight for the coffee shops and the Red Light District.

Begijnhof Historic Building

(☎622 19 18; www.begijnhofamsterdam.nl; off Gedempte Begijnensloot; ⏰9am-5pm; 🚋1/2/5/13/17 Spui) FREE This enclosed former convent dates from the early 14th century. It's a surreal oasis of peace, with tiny houses and postage-stamp gardens around a well-kept courtyard. The Beguines were a Catholic order of unmarried or widowed women who cared for the elderly and lived a religious life without taking monastic vows. The last true Beguine died in 1971.

CANAL BELT

Created in the 17th century as an upscale neighbourhood, the Canal Belt, especially in the west and south, remains Amsterdam's top district. Wandering here amid architectural treasures and their reflections on the narrow waters of the Prinsengracht, Keizersgracht and Herengracht can cause days to vanish quicker than some of Amsterdam's more lurid pursuits. No two buildings are alike, yet they combine in ever-changing, ever-pleasing harmony.

Anne Frank Huis Museum

(☎556 71 00; www.annefrank.org; Prinsengracht 267; adult/child €9/4.50; ⏰9am-9pm, hours vary seasonally; 🚋13/14/17 Westermarkt) The Anne Frank Huis draws almost one million visitors annually (prepurchase tickets online to minimise the queues). With its reconstruction of Anne's melancholy bedroom and her actual diary – sitting alone in its glass case, filled with sunnily optimistic writing tempered by quiet despair – it's a powerful experience.

MUSEUMPLEIN

Van Gogh Museum Museum

(☎570 52 00; www.vangoghmuseum.nl; Paulus Potterstraat 7; adult/child €15/free, audio guide €5; ⏰9am-6pm Sat-Thu, to 10pm Fri; 🚋2/3/5/12 Van Baerlestraat) Framed by a gleaming new glass entrance hall, the world's largest Van Gogh collection offers a superb line-up of masterworks. Trace the artist's life from his tentative start through his giddy-coloured sunflower phase, and on to the black cloud that descended over him and his work. There are also paintings by contemporaries Gauguin, Toulouse-Lautrec, Monet and Bernard.

Queues can be huge; pre-booked e-tickets and discount cards expedite the process with fast-track entry. Opening hours vary seasonally.

Stedelijk Museum Museum

(☎573 29 11; www.stedelijk.nl; Museumplein 10; adult/child €15/free, audio guide €5; ⏰10am-6pm Fri-Wed, to 10pm Thu; 🚋2/3/5/12 Van Baerlestraat) Built in 1895 to a neo-Renaissance design by AM Weissman, the Stedelijk Museum is the permanent home of the National Museum of Modern Art. Amassed by postwar curator Willem Sandberg, the modern classics here are among the world's most admired. The permanent collection includes all the blue chips of 19th- and 20th-century painting – Monet, Picasso and Chagall among them – as well as sculptures by Rodin, abstracts by Mondrian and Kandinsky, and much, much more.

Vondelpark Park

(www.vondelpark.nl; 🚋2/5 Hobbemastraat) The lush urban idyll of the Vondelpark is one of Amsterdam's most magical places – sprawling, English-style gardens, with ponds, lawns, footbridges and winding footpaths. On a sunny day, an open-air party atmosphere ensues when tourists, lovers, cyclists, in-line skaters, pram-pushing parents, cartwheeling children, football-kicking teenagers, spliff-sharing friends and champagne-swilling picnickers all come out to play.

JORDAAN

Originally a stronghold of the working class, the Jordaan is now one of the most desirable areas to live in Amsterdam. It's a pastiche of modest 17th- and 18th-century merchants' houses, humble workers' homes and a few modern carbuncles, squashed in a grid of tiny lanes peppered with bite-sized cafes and shops. Its intimacy is contagious, and now the average Jordaan dweller is more likely to be a gallery owner than a labourer.

Don't Miss Rijksmuseum

Fresh from a 10-year renovation, the Netherlands' foremost museum reopened its doors in 2013, revealing more than 1.5km of refurbished galleries lined with old master paintings, priceless artefacts and historical oddities.

National Museum

☎900 07 45

www.rijksmuseum.nl

Museumstraat 1

adult/child €17.50/free

⏰9am-5pm

🚋2/5 Hobbemastraat

The Building

One of the main attractions of the renovated Rijksmuseum is the building itself. The 19th-century facade has been thoroughly spruced up during its 10-year refit, and and shines once again in crimson-and-cream stone. Of particular note are the wonderful entrance hall, with its mosaic and stained glass, and the new Asian Pavilion, which provides a bold, modern contrast to the museum's classical surroundings. The original architect, Pierre Cuypers, would no doubt be thrilled with the care, attention and expense that's been lavished on his most famous building.

The Old Masters

The Rijksmuseum owns the world's finest collection of paintings from the golden age of Dutch art (7500 in all). Among its priceless canvases are four of 35 Vermeers, as well as an array of works by notable names such as Franz Hals and Jan Steen. But it's Rembrandt's iconic *Night Watch* (1642) which takes pride of place: it's the museum's prize painting and is displayed to suitably dramatic effect in its very own gallery.

Other Highlights

The Rijksmuseum isn't just about paintings, though. It also houses one of the world's great collections of Delftware, the delicate blue-and-white pottery that was all the rage in aristocratic Europe during the 17th and 18th centuries. There are also countless curiosities to seek out, from antique dolls' houses to vintage weaponry and insanely detailed model ships. In fact, you could spend every day of your trip here and still only scratch the surface.

Local Knowledge

The Rijksmuseum

RECOMMENDATIONS FROM PIETER ROELOFS, CURATOR OF 17TH CENTURY PAINTING AT THE RIJKSMUSEUM

1 WOMAN IN BLUE READING A LETTER BY JOHANNES VERMEER

Painted around 1660, this is one of four Vermeer paintings in the museum's collection. It shows a woman standing in the corner of a room reading a letter from her lover. It's a classic Vermeer composition, and is remarkable for its intense blues: blue was by far the most expensive colour to use at the time, as it had to be made from lapis lazuli brought to the Netherlands all the way from Afghanistan.

2 THE BATTLE OF WATERLOO BY JAN WILLEM PIENEMAN

Painted in 1824, this huge painting is the largest in the museum's collection, measuring around 8m by 6m. It's full of drama and movement, and features all the key characters from the Battle of Waterloo, including the Duke of Wellington and the wounded Dutch prince, Willem II, lying on a stretcher.

3 THE BEUNING ROOM

This beautiful room illustrates what life was like in Amsterdam in the mid-18th century. It was originally part of a canal house, but the original building was demolished and the entire mahogany room has been reconstructed inside the museum, complete with original stucco and painted decorations.

4 TERRACOTTA BUST OF THE WEEPING MADONNA

This wonderful medieval bust, with its slightly opened mouth, was made by an Italian sculptor who was working in Flanders around 1500. It's so lifelike and full of emotion, and demonstrates incredible skill.

5 THE F.K. 23 BANTAM BIPLANE

This aeroplane was built in 1917 by the Dutch engineer Frederick Koolhoven as a WWI fighter plane. The wooden fuselage was made by hand, including the propeller, which is a work of art in itself. People don't expect to see a full-sized aeroplane inside the Rijksmuseum, so it comes as quite a surprise!

Central Amsterdam

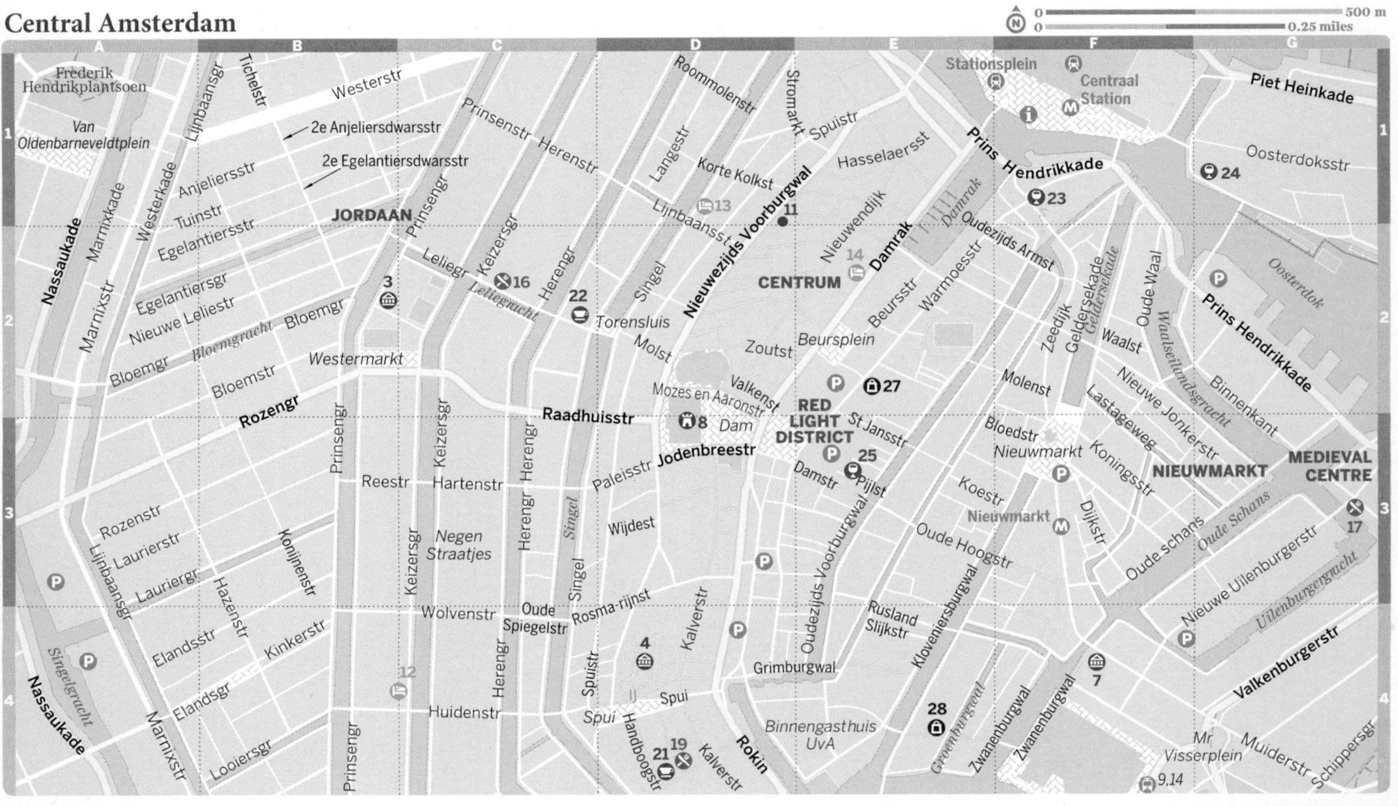

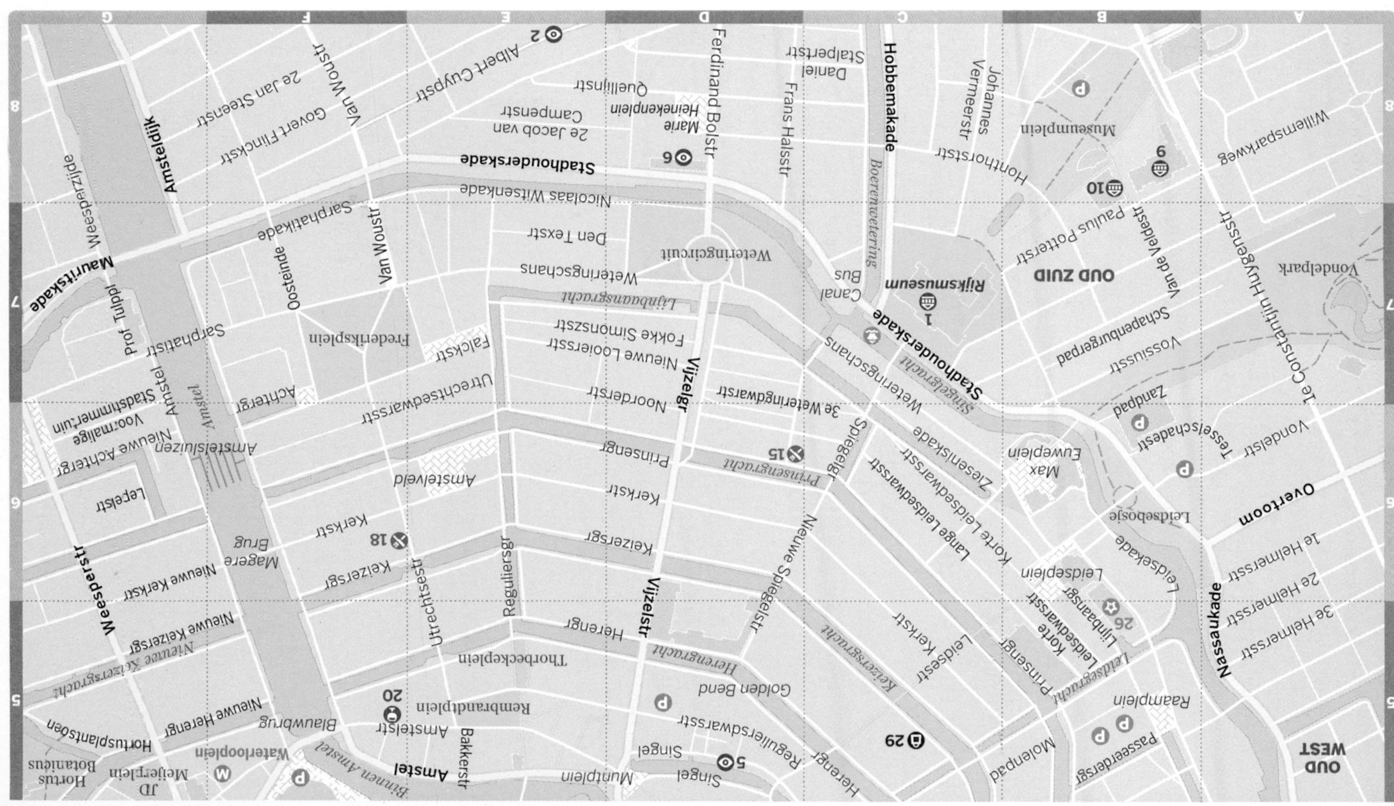
Weesperstr
Weesperzijde
Mauritskade
Amsteldijk
Amstel
Prof Tulppl
Sarphatistr
Sarphatikade
Stadhouderskade
Nicolaas Witsenkade
Weteringschans
Weteringcircuit
Den Texstr
Vijzelstr
Vijzelgr
Ferdinand Bolstr
Frans Halsstr
Daniel Stalpertstr
Hobbemakade
Boerenwetering
Canal Bus
Rijksmuseum
OUD ZUID
Museumplein
Paulus Potterstr
Van de Veldestr
Johannes Vermeerstr
Honthorststr
Willemsparkweg
Vondelpark
1e Constantijn Huygensstr
Vossiusstr
Schapenburgerpad
Zandpad
Tesselschadestr
Vondelstr
Overtoom
Leidsebosje
Leidsekade
Leidseplein
Max Euweplein
Zieseniskade
Korte Leidsedwarsstr
Lange Leidsedwarsstr
Lijnbaansgr
Leidsegracht
Leidsestr
Kerkstr
Keizersgracht
Prinsengr
Prinsengracht
Raamplein
Passeerdersgr
Molenpad
Nassaukade
1e Helmersstr
2e Helmersstr
3e Helmersstr
OUD WEST
Herengr
Herengracht
Singel
Muntplein
Reguliersdwarsstr
Golden Bend
Nieuwe Spiegelstr
Spiegelgr
3e Weteringdwarstr
Singelgracht
Noorderstr
Nieuwe Looiersstr
Fokke Simonszstr
Lijnbaansgracht
Keizersgr
Reguliersgr
Thorbeckeplein
Rembrandtplein
Utrechtsestr
Amstelstr
Bakkerstr
Blauwbrug
Binnen Amstel
Waterlooplein
JD Meijerplein
Hortus Botanicus
Hortusplantsoen
Nieuwe Herengr
Nieuwe Keizersgr
Nieuwe Keizersgracht
Nieuwe Kerkstr
Magere Brug
Amstelveld
Utrechtsedwarsstr
Falckstr
Frederiksplein
Van Woustr
Oosteinde
Achtergr
Amstelsluizen
Nieuwe Achtergr
Voormalige Stadstimmertuin
Lepelstr
Stadhouderskade
2e Jacob van Campenstr
Marie Heinekenplein
Quellijnstr
Albert Cuypstr
Govert Flinckstr
2e Jan Steenstr
1
2
5
6
9
10
15
18
20
26
29
A
B
C
D
E
F
G
5
6
7
8

Central Amsterdam

Don't Miss Sights

1 Rijksmuseum C7

Sights

2 Albert Cuypmarkt E8
3 Anne Frank Huis B2
4 Begijnhof D4
5 Bloemenmarkt D5
6 Heineken Experience D8
7 Museum het Rembrandthuis F4
8 Royal Palace D3
9 Stedelijk Museum B8
10 Van Gogh Museum B8

Activities, Courses & Tours

11 Yellow Bike D1

Sleeping

12 Dylan C4
13 Hotel Brouwer D1
14 Hotel The Exchange E2

Eating

15 Buffet van Odette D6
16 De Luwte C2
17 Greetje G3
18 Tempo Doeloe F6
19 Vleminckx D4

Drinking & Nightlife

20 Air F5
21 Dampkring D4
22 Grey Area C2
23 In 't Aepjen F1
24 SkyLounge G1
25 Wynand Fockink E3

Entertainment

26 Melkweg B5

Shopping

27 Condomerie Het Gulden Vlies E2
28 Droog E4
29 Young Designers United C5

DE PIJP

Heineken Experience Brewery
(523 94 35; www.heinekenexperience.com; Stadhouderskade 78; adult/child €18/12.50; 10.30am-9pm Jul & Aug, 11am-7.30pm Mon-Thu, 10.30am-9pm Fri-Sun Sep-Jun; 16/24 Stadhouderskade) On the site of the company's old brewery, the crowning glory of this self-guided 'Experience' (samples aside) is a multimedia exhibit where you 'become' a beer by getting shaken up, sprayed with water and subjected to heat. True beer connoisseurs will shudder, but it's a lot of fun. Admission includes a 15-minute shuttle boat ride to the Heineken Brand Store near Rembrandtplein. Prebooking tickets online saves you €2 on the entry fee and allows you to skip the ticket queues.

NIEUWMARKT & PLANTAGE

Museum het Rembrandthuis Museum
(Rembrandt House Museum; 520 04 00; www.rembrandthuis.nl; Jodenbreestraat 4; adult/child €12.50/4; 10am-6pm; 9/14 Waterlooplein) You almost expect to find the master himself at the Museum het Rembrandthuis, where Rembrandt van Rijn ran the Netherlands' largest painting studio, only to lose the lot when profligacy set in, enemies swooped and bankruptcy came a-knocking. The museum has scores of etchings and sketches. Ask for the free audio guide at the entrance. You can buy advance tickets online, though it's not as vital here as at some of the other big museums.

Tours

There are bike tours as well as canal boat tours of Amsterdam that let you hop on and hop off.

Sleeping

Book ahead for weekends and in summer. Wi-fi is near universal but elevators are not.

Hotel Brouwer Hotel €€
(624 63 58; www.hotelbrouwer.nl; Singel 83; s €71-79, d €115-128, tr €148-178; @; 1/2/5/13/17 Nieuwezijds Kolk) A bargain-priced (for Amsterdam) favourite, Brouwer has just eight rooms in a house dating back to 1652. Each chamber is named for a Dutch painter and furnished with simplicity, but all have canal views. There's a mix of Delft-blue tiles and early-20th-century decor, plus a tiny lift. Staff

dispense friendly advice. Reserve well in advance. Cash only.

Hotel The Exchange Boutique Hotel €€
(☎523 00 89; www.hoteltheexchange.com; Damrak 50; d 1-/2-/3-/4-/5-star from €93/110/128/162/196; @📶; 🚋1/2/5/13/17 Nieuwezijds Kolk) The Exchange's 61 rooms have been dressed 'like models' in eye-popping style by students from the Amsterdam Fashion Institute. Anything goes, from oversized button-adorned walls to a Marie Antoinette dress tented over the bed. If you like plain decor, this isn't your place. Rooms range from small and viewless to spacious sanctums but all have en-suite bathrooms.

Frederic Rentabike Houseboat €€
(☎624 55 09; www.frederic.nl; Brouwersgracht 78; houseboat from €145; 📶; 🚌18/21/22 Brouwersstraat) Frederic offers nicely outfitted houseboats on the Prinsengracht, Brouwersgracht and Bloemgracht that are bona fide floating holiday homes with all mod cons. On land, the company also has various rooms and apartments in central locations. (And yes, bikes too.)

Dylan Hotel €€€
(☎530 20 10; www.dylanamsterdam.com; Keizersgracht 384; d/ste from €350/500; ❄@📶; 🚋1/2/5 Spui) Exquisite boutique hotel the Dylan occupies an 18th-century Keizersgracht canal house ensconcing a herringbone-paved, topiary-filled inner courtyard. Bespoke furniture such as silver-leaf and mother-of-pearl drinks cabinets adorn its 40 individually decorated rooms and suites (some duplex). Its Michelin-starred Restaurant Vinkeles also hosts private chef's tables aboard its boat, the *Muze*, as it cruises the canals.

Eating

Happy streets for hunting include Utrechtsesraat, Spuistraat and any of the little streets lining and connecting the west canals, such as Berenstraat.

Red Light District

Just southeast of Centraal Station, on and around the parallel neon-lit canals Oudezijds Voorburgwal and Oudezijds Achterburgwal, is the warren of medieval alleyways making up Amsterdam's Red Light District (locally known as De Wallen). It is a carnival of vice, seething with skimpily clad prostitutes in brothel windows, raucous bars, haze-filled 'coffeeshops', strip shows, sex shows, mindboggling museums and shops selling everything from cartoonish condoms to S&M gear and herbal highs. The area is generally safe, but keep your wits about you and don't photograph or film prostitutes in the windows – out of respect, and to avoid having your camera flung in a canal by their enforcers. Seriously.

Foodhallen Food Hall €
(www.foodhallen.nl; Bellamyplein 51; most dishes €5-15; ⏰11am-8pm Sun-Wed, to 9pm Thu-Sat; 🚋17 Ten Katestraat) Inside the converted tram sheds housing the cultural and design complex De Hallen, this glorious international food hall has 20 stands surrounding an airy open-plan eating area. Some are offshoots of popular Amsterdam eateries, such as the Butcher (burgers) and Wild Moa Pies; look out for De Ballenbar *(bitterballen)*. It's adjacent to the lively street market Ten Katemarkt.

Vleminckx Fast Food €
(Voetboogstraat 31; fries €2.10-4.10, sauces €0.60; ⏰noon-7pm Sun & Mon, 11am-7pm Tue, Wed, Fri & Sat, 11am-9pm Thu; 🚋1/2/5 Koningsplein) This hole-in-the-wall takeaway has drawn the hordes for its monumental *frites* (French fries) since 1887. The standard is smothered in mayonnaise, though you can ask for ketchup, peanut sauce or a variety of spicy toppings.

De Luwte International €€
(☎625 85 48; www.restaurantdeluwte.nl; Leliegracht 26; mains €19.50-28.50; ⏰6-11pm; 🚋13/17 Westermarkt) Fabulously designed with a vertical 'living wall' garden and recycled timbers, the star of the show here is the artfully presented Mediterranean-inspired food: slow-cooked rack of pork with risotto croquettes; cod with creamed pumpkin and truffle polenta with mushroom foam; or the house-specialty black Angus tomahawk steak for two. Great cocktails too.

Buffet van Odette Cafe €€
(☎423 60 34; www.buffet-amsterdam.nl; Prinsengracht 598; lunch mains €7.50-15.50, dinner €14.50-20.50; ⏰kitchen 10am-10pm; 🥕; 🚋7/10 Spiegelgracht) Not a buffet but an airy, white-tiled sit-down cafe with a beautiful canal-side terrace, where Odette and Yvette show how good simple cooking can taste when you start with great ingredients and a dash of creativity. Soups, sandwiches, pastas and quiches are mostly organic with smart little extras like pine nuts or truffle cheese.

Greetje Contemporary Dutch €€€
(☎779 74 50; www.restaurantgreetje.nl; Peperstraat 23-25; mains €23-27; ⏰6-10pm Sun-Fri, to 11pm Sat; 🚌22/34/35/48 Prins Hendrikkade) 🍃 Using market-fresh organic produce, Greetje resurrects and re-creates traditional Dutch recipes like beet-crusted North Sea cod, Veluwe deer stew with red cabbage and Elstar apple, or roasted Alblasserwaard pheasant with melted duck liver. A good place to start is the two-person Big Beginning, with a sampling of hot and cold starters.

If you can't decide on dessert (which, with dishes like *stroopwafel* mousse with coffee parfait, or crème brûlée with sweet wood extract and liquorice ice cream, is no easy feat), go for the Grand Finale (for two people) to share all six.

Tempo Doeloe Indonesian €€€
(☎625 67 18; www.tempodoeloerestaurant.nl; Utrechtsestraat 75; mains €23.50-38.50, rijsttafel & set menus €28.50-49; ⏰6-11.30pm Mon-Sat; 🥕; 🚋4 Prinsengracht) Consistently ranked among Amsterdam's finest Indonesian restaurants, Tempo Doeloe's setting and service are elegant without being overdone. The same applies to the *rijsttafel*: a ridiculously overblown affair at many places, here it's a fine sampling of the range of flavours found in the country. Warning: dishes marked 'very hot' are indeed like napalm. The wine list is excellent.

Drinking & Nightlife

A particular Amsterdam joy is discovering your own brown cafe. They are found everywhere, often tucked into the most atmospheric of locations, and many serve food. We've also listed a tasting house and cocktail bar.

In 't Aepjen Brown Cafe
(Zeedijk 1; ⏰noon-1am Mon-Thu, to 3am Fri & Sat; 🚋4/9/16/24 Centraal Station) Candles burn even during the day at this bar based in a mid-16th-century house, which is one of two remaining wooden buildings in the city. The name allegedly comes from the bar's role in the 16th and 17th centuries as a crash pad for sailors from the Far East, who often toted *aapjes* (monkeys) with them.

Wynand Fockink Tasting House
(www.wynand-fockink.nl; Pijlsteeg 31; ⏰3-9pm; 🚋4/9/16/24 Dam) This small tasting house (dating from 1679) serves scores of *jenever* and liqueurs in an arcade behind Grand Hotel Krasnapolsky. Although there are no seats or stools, it's an intimate place to knock back a shot-glass or two. Guides give an English-language tour of the distillery every Saturday at 2pm (€17.50, reservations not required).

SkyLounge Cocktail Bar
(http://doubletree3.hilton.com; Oosterdoksstraat 4; ⏰11am-1am Sun-Thu, to 3am Fri & Sat; 🚋1/2/4/5/9/14/16/24 Centraal Station) An unrivalled 360-degree panorama of Amsterdam extends from the glass-walled SkyLounge on the 11th floor of the DoubleTree Amsterdam Centraal Station hotel – and just gets better when you head out to its vast SkyTerrace, with an outdoor bar and timber decking strewn

with sofas. Deliberate over more than 500 different cocktails; DJs regularly hit the decks.

 Entertainment

Find out what's on in Amsterdam (www.iamsterdam.com/en-GB/experience/what-to-do/whats-on/event-guide).

GAY & LESBIAN AMSTERDAM

Gay Amsterdam (www.gayamsterdam.com) Lists hotels, shops, restaurants and clubs, and provides maps.

COFFEE SHOPS

Cafes have coffee, 'coffee shops' are where you buy marijuana.

In coffee shops, ask at the bar for the menu of cannibis-related goods on offer, usually packaged in small bags. Alcohol and tobacco products are not permitted in coffee shops.

Don't light up anywhere besides a coffee shop without checking that it's OK to do so.

Dampkring Coffee Shop

(www.dampkring-coffeeshop-amsterdam.nl; Handboogstraat 29; ⌚10am-1am; 📶; 🚋1/2/5 Koningsplein) With an interior that resembles a larger-than-life lava lamp, Dampkring is a consistent Cannabis Cup winner, and known for having the most comprehensive menu in town (including details about smell, taste and effect). Its name means the ring of the earth's atmosphere where smaller items combust.

Grey Area Coffee Shop

(www.greyarea.nl; Oude Leliestraat 2; ⌚noon-8pm; 🚋1/2/5/13/14/17 Dam) Owned by a couple of laid-back American guys, this tiny shop introduced the extra-sticky, flavoursome 'Double Bubble Gum' weed to the city's smokers. Organic coffee includes free refills.

NIGHTCLUBS

Air Club

(www.air.nl; Amstelstraat 16-24; ⌚Thu-Sun, hours vary; 🚋4/9/14 Rembrandtplein) One of Amsterdam's 'it' clubs, Air has an environmentally friendly design by Dutch designer Marcel Wanders including a unique tiered dance floor. Bonuses include lockers and refillable cards that preclude fussing with change at the bar. The awesome sound system attracts cutting-edge DJs spinning everything from disco to house and techno to hip-hop. Dress to impress.

LIVE MUSIC

Melkweg Live Music

(www.melkweg.nl; Lijnbaansgracht 234a; ⌚6pm-1am; 🚋1/2/5/7/10 Leidseplein) In a former dairy, the nonprofit 'Milky Way' is a dazzling galaxy of diverse music. One

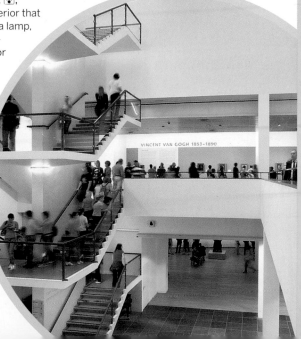

Van Gogh Museum (p467), Amsterdam
JEAN-PIERRE LESCOURRET/GETTY IMAGES ©

Markets

Markets of just about every description are scattered across the city. Amsterdam's largest and busiest market, **Albert Cuypmarkt** (www.albertcuypmarkt.nl; Albert Cuypstraat, btwn Ferdinand Bolstraat & Van Woustraat; 9am-5pm Mon-Sat; 16/24 Albert Cuypstraat) is 100 years old. Food of every description, flowers, souvenirs, clothing, hardware and household goods can be found here.

Bloemenmarkt (Flower Market; Singel, btwn Muntplein & Koningsplein; 9am-5.30pm Mon-Sat, 11am-5.30pm Sun; 1/2/5 Koningsplein) is a touristy 'floating' flower market that's actually on pilings. Still, at the stalls that actually stock flowers (as opposed to plastic clogs), the vibrant colours burst forth.

night it's electronica, the next reggae or punk, and next heavy metal. Roots, rock and mellow singer-songwriters all get stage time too. Check out the website for cutting-edge cinema, theatre and multimedia offerings.

Shopping

Droog Design, Homewares
(www.droog.com; Staalstraat 7; 11am-6pm Tue-Sun; 4/9/14/16/24 Muntplein) Droog means 'dry' in Dutch, and this slick local design house's products are strong on dry wit. You'll find all kinds of smart items you never knew you needed, like super-powerful suction cups. Also here is a gallery space, whimsical blue-and-white cafe, and fairytale-inspired courtyard garden that Alice in Wonderland would love, as well as a top-floor apartment (double €275).

Young Designers United Clothing
(YDU; www.ydu.nl; Keizersgracht 447; 1-6pm Mon, 10am-6pm Tue, Wed, Fri & Sat, 10am-8pm Thu; 1/2/5 Keizersgracht) Racks are rotated regularly at this affordable boutique showcasing young designers working in the Netherlands. You might spot durable basics by Agna K, minimalist knits by Andy ve Eirn, geometric dresses by Fenny Faber and soft, limited-edition knits by Mimoods. Accessorise with YDU's select range of jewellery and bags.

Condomerie Het Gulden Vlies Specialty Shop
(www.condomerie.com; Warmoesstraat 141; 11am-6pm Mon-Sat, 1-5pm Sun; 4/9/14/16/24 Dam) Perfectly positioned for the Red Light District, this boutique sells condoms in every imaginable size, colour, flavour and design (horned devils, marijuana leaves, Delftware tiles...), along with lubricants and saucy gifts.

Information

I Amsterdam Card (www.iamsterdam.com; per 24/48/72hr €47/57/67) Provides admission to more than 30 museums, a canal cruise, and discounts at shops, attractions and restaurants. Also includes a GVB transit pass. Available at VVV offices (tourist offices) and some hotels.

Tourist Office (VVV; 702 60 00; www.iamsterdam.nl; Stationsplein 10; 9am-5pm Mon-Sat, to 4pm Sun; 4/9/16/24/25 Centraal Station) Maps, guides and transit passes.

Getting There & Away

Air

Most major airlines serve Schiphol airport, 18km southwest of the city centre.

Train

Amsterdam's main train station is fabled **Centraal Station** (Stationsplein; 8am-10pm Mon-Sat, 9am-10pm Sun; 4/9/16/24/25 Centraal Station), with services to the rest of the country and major European cities.

Getting Around

To/From the Airport

A **taxi** into Amsterdam from Schiphol airport takes 25 to 45 minutes and costs about €55. **Trains** to Centraal Station leave every few minutes, take 15 to 20 minutes, and cost €4/8 per single/return.

Bicycle

Amsterdam is cycling nirvana: flat, beautiful, with dedicated bike paths. About 150,000 bicycles are stolen each year in Amsterdam, so always lock up. Rental agencies include the following:

Bike City (626 37 21; www.bikecity.nl; Bloemgracht 68-70; bike rental per day from €14; 9am-6pm; 13/14/17 Westermarkt) These black bikes have no advertising on them, so you can free-wheel like a local.

Yellow Bike (620 69 40; www.yellowbike.nl; Nieuwezijds Kolk 29; bike rental per day €12, city/countryside tours €25/31.50; 9.30am-5pm; 1/2/5/13/17 Nieuwezijds Kolk) The original. Choose from city tours or the longer countryside tour through the pretty Waterland district to the north.

Boat

Amsterdam's **canal boats** are a popular way to tour the town but most are actually a bit claustrophobic, with steamed-up glass windows surrounding passengers. Look for a boat with an open seating area.

There are also free **ferries** from behind Centraal Station to destinations around the IJ, notably Amsterdam Noord.

Canal Bus (217 05 00; www.canal.nl; Weteringschans 26; day pass adult/child €22/11; 10am-6pm; ; 1/2/5 Leidseplein) Offers a unique hop-on hop-off service, with docks around the city near big museums and attractions.

Canal Motorboats (422 70 07; www.canalmotorboats.com; Zandhoek 10a; 1st hr €50; 9am-sunset; 48 Barentszplein) This operator has small, electric aluminium boats (maximum six passengers) that are easy to drive (no boat licence required). Staff give you a map and plenty of advice, and will come and rescue you if need be. Credit-card imprint or €150 cash deposit required. Reduced rates after the first hour.

Car & Motorcycle

Amsterdam is horrendous for parking, with charges averaging €5 per hour. Your best bet is to ditch the car at an outlying train station and ride in.

Public Transport

Services – including Amsterdam's iconic **trams** – are run by the local transit authority, GVB. Its highly useful **GVB information office** (www.gvb.nl; Stationsplein 10; 7am-9pm Mon-Fri, 8am-9pm Sat & Sun; 1/2/4/5/9/14/16/24 Centraal

Vondelpark (p467), Amsterdam

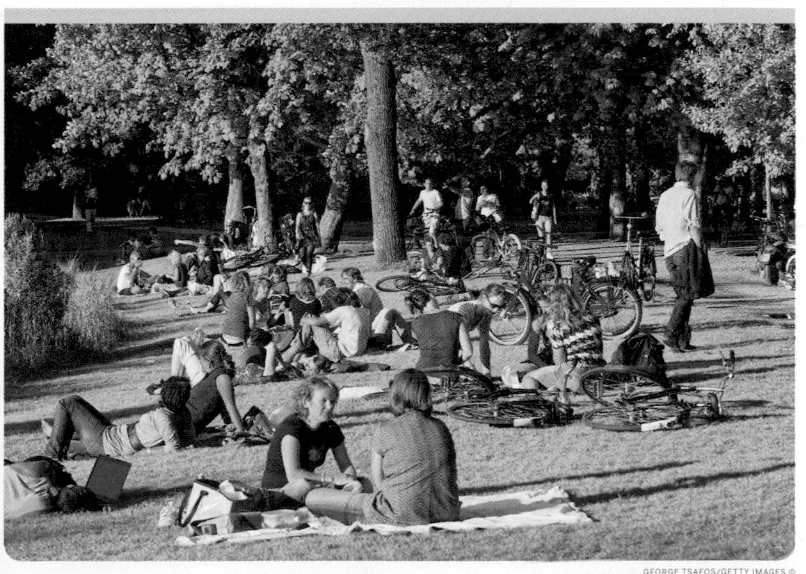

Detour: Zaanse Schans

Zaanse Schans Windmills (www.dezaanseschans.nl; site free, windmills adult/child €3.50/2; windmills 10am-5pm Apr-Nov, hours vary Dec-Mar) The working, inhabited village Zaanse Schans functions as an open-air windmill gallery on the Zaan river. Popular with tourists, its mills are completely authentic and operated with enthusiasm and love. You can explore the windmills at will, seeing the vast moving parts first-hand.

The impressive **Zaans Museum (075-616 28 62; www.zaansmuseum.nl; Schansend 7; adult/child €9/5; 10am-5pm)** shows how wind and water were harnessed.

From Amsterdam Centraal Station (€3, 17 minutes, four times hourly) take the train towards Alkmaar and get off at Koog Zaandijk – it's a well-signposted 1km walk to Zaanse Schans.

Station) is located across the tram tracks from the Centraal Station main entrance. You can avoid the often-long lines by buying day passes at the adjoining VVV office instead.

Public transport in Amsterdam uses the OV-chipkaart. Rides cost €2.90 when bought on the tram or bus. Unlimited-ride passes are available for between one to seven days (€7.50–32), valid on trams, most buses and the metro are good value.

Night buses take over shortly after midnight, which is when the trams and regular buses stop running.

Taxi

Amsterdam taxis are expensive, even over short journeys. Try **Taxicentrale Amsterdam** (TCA; 777 77 77; www.tcataxi.nl).

Around Amsterdam

ALKMAAR

072 / POP 94,000

This picturesque town stages its famous cheese market in the historic main square. The market dates from the 17th century. Dealers in officious white smocks insert a hollow rod to extract cheese samples, sniffing and crumbling for fat and moisture content. Then the porters, wearing colourful hats to signify their cheese guild, heft the cheeses on wooden sledges to a large scale. An average 30 tonnes of cheese is on display at the Alkmaar market at any one time.

Arrive early for more than fleeting glimpses. There are four trains per hour from Amsterdam Centraal Station (€7.40, 30 to 40 minutes).

The Randstad

When people think of the Netherlands outside of Amsterdam, they are often really thinking about the Randstad. One of the most densely populated places on the planet, it stretches from Amsterdam to Rotterdam and features the classically Dutch towns and cities of Den Haag, Utrecht, Haarlem, Leiden, Delft and Gouda. Most people focus their visit to the Netherlands here, enjoying the cycling network that links the towns amid tulip fields.

HAARLEM

023 / POP 150,000

Haarlem is the Netherlands in microcosm, with canals, gabled buildings and cobblestone streets. Its historic buildings, grand churches, museums, cosy bars, good restaurants and antique shops draw scores of day trippers – it's only 15 minutes by train from Amsterdam.

Sights

A couple of hours' stroll – with stops for refreshments – will cover Haarlem's tidy centre, which radiates out from the **Grote Markt**, where there are markets on many days.

Town Hall Historic Building

(Grote Markt 2) At the western end of the Grote Markt stands the florid, 14th-century town hall, which sprouted many extensions including a balcony where judgments from the high court were pronounced. It only opens to the public on Open Monuments Day in the second weekend of September.

Grote Kerk van St Bavo Church

(www.bavo.nl; Oude Groenmarkt 22; adult/child €2.50/1.25; ⌚10am-5pm Mon-Sat) Topped by a towering 50m-high steeple, the Gothic Grote Kerk van St Bavo cathedral contains some fine Renaissance artworks, but the star attraction is its stunning Müller organ – one of the most magnificent in the world, standing 30m high with about 5000 pipes. It was played by Handel and Mozart, the latter when he was just 10. Free hour-long **organ recitals** take place at 8.15pm Tuesday and 4pm Thursday from May to October.

Frans Hals Museum Gallery

(www.franshalsmuseum.nl; Groot Heiligland 62; adult/child €15.50/free; ⌚11am-5pm Tue-Sat, from noon Sun) A short stroll south of Grote Markt, the Frans Hals Museum is a must for anyone interested in the Dutch Masters. Kept in a poorhouse where Hals spent his final years, the collection focuses on the 17th-century Haarlem School; its pride and joy are eight group portraits of the Civic Guard that reveal Hals' exceptional attention to mood and psychological tone. Look out for works by other greats such as Pieter Bruegel the Younger, and Jacob van Ruysdael.

 Eating & Drinking

Lange Veerstraat has a bounty of cafes, while Schagchelstraat is lined with restaurants. The Saturday morning market on Grote Markt is one of the Netherland's best; try the fresh *stroopwafels* (small caramel-filled waffles).

De Haerlemsche Vlaamse Fast Food €

(Spekstraat 3; frites €2-3; ⌚11am-6.30pm Mon-Wed & Fri, to 9pm Thu, to 5pm Sat, noon-5pm Sun) Practically on the doorstep of the Grote Kerk, this minuscule *frites* (French fries) joint is a local institution. Line up for its crispy, golden fries made from

Grote Kerk van St Bavo, Haarlem, the Netherlands

fresh potatoes and one of a dozen sauces including three kinds of mayonnaise.

Jopenkerk Brewery

(www.jopenkerk.nl; Gedempte Voldersgracht 2; ⌚brewery & cafe 10am-1am, restaurant 5.30pm-late Tue-Sat) Haarlem's most atmospheric place to drink and/or dine is this independent brewery inside a stained-glass-windowed, 1910-built church. Enjoy brews like citrusy Hopen, fruity Lente Bier or chocolatey Koyt and classic snacks (*bitterballen*, cheeses) beneath the gleaming vats, or head to the mezzanine for mains (€16.50 to €23.50) made from locally sourced, seasonal ingredients and Jopenkerk's beers, with pairings available.

Information

The tourist office is located in a free-standing glass house in the middle of the main shopping district.

Getting There & Away

Trains serve Haarlem's stunning art deco station, a 10-minute walk from the centre. Destinations include Amsterdam (€4.10, 15 minutes, five to eight services per hour), Den Haag (€8.20, 35 to 40 minutes, four to six per hour) and Rotterdam (€11.90, 50 minutes, four per hour).

LEIDEN

☎071 / POP 122,000

Leiden is a busy, vibrant town that is another popular day trip from Amsterdam. Claims to fame: it's Rembrandt's birthplace, it's home to the Netherlands' oldest university (and 20,000 students) and it's where America's pilgrims raised money to lease the leaky *Mayflower* that took them to the New World in 1620.

Sights

The best way to experience Leiden is by strolling the historic centre, especially along the Rapenburg canal.

Follow the huge steeple of **Pieterskerk** **(Pieterskerkhof; admission €2; ⌚11am-6pm)**, which shines after a grand restoration (a good thing as it's been prone to collapse since it was built in the 14th century). Across the plaza, look for the **Gravensteen** **(Pieterskerkhof 6)**, which dates to the 13th century and once was a prison.

Lakenhal Museum

(www.lakenhal.nl; Oude Singel 32; adult/child €7.50/free; ⌚10am-5pm Tue-Fri, noon-5pm Sat & Sun) Get your Rembrandt fix at the 17th-century Lakenhal, which houses the Municipal Museum, with an assortment of works by old masters, as well as period rooms and temporary exhibits. The 1st floor has been restored to the way it would have looked when Leiden was at the peak of its prosperity.

Decorated bicycle in Amsterdam

Rijksmuseum van Oudheden Museum

(National Museum of Antiquities; www.rmo.nl; Rapenburg 28; adult/child €9.50/3; ⏲10am-5pm Tue-Sun) This museum has a world-class collection of Greek, Roman and Egyptian artefacts, the pride of which is the extraordinary **Temple of Taffeh**, a gift from former Egyptian president Anwar Sadat to the Netherlands for helping to save ancient Egyptian monuments from flood.

Sleeping

Nieuw Minerva Hotel €€

(☎512 63 58; www.nieuwminerva.nl; Boommarkt 23; s/d from €84/88; @ ☎) Located in canal-side houses dating from the 16th century, this central hotel has a mix of 40 regular (ie nothing special) and very fun themed rooms, including a room with a bed in which King Lodewijk Bonaparte (aka Louis Bonaparte) slept, the 'room of angels' – a luminous vision of white, the 'Delft blue room', and the Rembrandt room.

Eating & Drinking

Oudt Leyden Pancakes €

(www.oudtleyden.nl; Steenstraat 49; pancakes €8-15, mains €12.50-24.50; ⏲11.30am-9.30pm;) Get ready to meet giant Dutch-style pancakes with creative fillings that make kids and adults alike go wide-eyed. Whether you're feeling savoury (marinated salmon, sour cream and capers), sweet (apple, raisins, almond paste, sugar and cinnamon) or simply adventurous (ginger and bacon!), this welcoming cafe hits the spot every time.

Proeverij de Dames Wine Bar

(www.proeverijdedames.nl; Nieuwe Rijn 37; lunch mains €7-9.50, dinner €17-20.50; ⏲10am-10pm) Run by two women with excellent taste, this stylish canal-side cafe/wine bar opening out to a terrace has an excellent range of coffees and wines by the glass. There's a long list of small plates for nibbling, sharing or combining into a meal. House-made baked goods include double-chocolate cake and apple pie.

Detour: Keukenhof Gardens

One of the Netherlands' top attractions is near Lisse, between Haarlem and Leiden. **Keukenhof (www.keukenhof.nl; Lisse; adult/child €16/8, parking €6; ⏲8am-7.30pm mid-Mar–mid-May, last entry 6pm)** is the world's largest bulb-flower garden, attracting nearly 800,000 visitors during a season almost as short-lived as the blooms on the millions of multicoloured tulips, daffodils and hyacinths.

Buses 50 and 54 travel from Leiden Centraal Station to Keukenhof (30 minutes, four times per hour). All tickets can be purchased online, which helps avoid huge queues.

Information

The **tourist office** **(☎516 60 00; www.vvvleiden.nl; Stationsweg 41; ⏲7am-7pm Mon-Fri, 10am-4pm Sat, 11am-3pm Sun)**, across from the train station, has good maps and historic info.

Getting There & Away

Buses leave from directly in front of Centraal Station. **Train** destinations, all with six departures per hour, include Amsterdam (€8.80, 34 minutes), Den Haag (€3.40, 10 minutes) and Schiphol airport (€5.70, 15 minutes).

DELFT

☎015 / POP 99,700

Compact, charming and relaxed, Delft may be the perfect Dutch day trip. Founded around 1100, it maintains tangible links to its romantic past despite the pressures of modernisation and tourist hordes. Many of the canalside vistas could be scenes from the *Girl with a Pearl Earring*, the novel about Golden Age painter

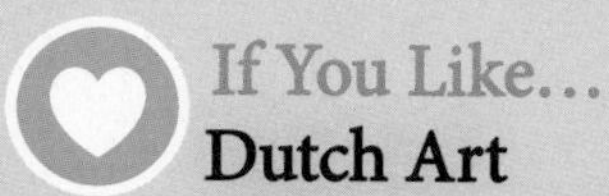

If You Like... Dutch Art

Amsterdam's Rijksmuseum (p468) and the Van Gogh Museum (p467) attract the most attention, but the Netherlands has some other stellar art institutions.

1 **MAURITSHUIS**
(www.mauritshuis.nl; Plein 29; adult/child €14/free, combined ticket with Galerij Prins Willem V €17.50; 1-6pm Mon, 10am-5pm Tue, Wed & Fri-Sun, to 8pm Thu) For a comprehensive introduction to Dutch and Flemish art, visit the Mauritshuis in The Hague, a jewel-box of a museum in an old palace and brand-new wing. Almost every work is a masterpiece, among them Vermeer's *Girl with a Pearl Earring*, and Rembrandt's wistful self-portrait from the year of his death, 1669, as well as *The Anatomy Lesson of Dr Nicolaes Tulp*. A five-minute walk southwest, the newly restored **Galerij Prins Willem V (www.mauritshuis.nl; Buitenhof 35; adult/child €5/2.50, combined ticket with Mauritshuis €17.50; noon-5pm Tue-Sun)** contains 150 old masters (Steen, Rubens, Potter, et al).

2 **GEMEENTEMUSEUM**
(Municipal Museum; www.gemeentemuseum.nl; Stadhouderslaan 41; adult/child €17/free; 10am-5pm Tue-Sun) Admirers of De Stijl, and in particular of Piet Mondrian, mustn't miss the Berlage-designed Gemeentemuseum, The Hague,. It houses a large collection of works by neoplasticist artists and others from the late 19th century, as well as extensive exhibits of applied arts, costumes and musical instruments. Take tram 17 from CS and HS to the Statenwartier stop.

3 **BONNEFANTENMUSEUM**
(www.bonnefanten.nl; Ave Cèramique 250; adult/child €9/4.50; 11am-5pm Tue-Sun) The Bonnefantenmuseum in Maastricht features a 28m tower that's a local landmark. Designed by Aldo Rossi, the museum opened in 1995, and is well laid out with collections divided into departments, each on its own floor: Old Masters and medieval sculpture are on one floor, contemporary art by Limburg artists on the next, linked by a dramatic sweep of stairs. Make time for the world-class Neuteling collection of medieval art.

Johannes Vermeer, which was made into a movie (and partially shot here) in 2003. Delft is also famous for its 'delftware', the distinctive blue-and-white pottery originally duplicated from Chinese porcelain by 17th-century artisans.

Sights

The 14th-century **Nieuwe Kerk (New Church; www.oudeennieuwekerkdelft.nl; Markt; adult/child incl Oude Kerk €3.75/2.25, Nieuwe Kerk tower €3.50/2; 9am-6pm Mon-Sat Apr-Oct, hours vary Nov-Mar)** houses the crypt of the Dutch royal family and the mausoleum of Willem the Silent. The fee includes entrance to the **Oude Kerk (Old Church; http://oudeennieuwekerkdelft.nl; Heilige Geestkerkhof 25; adult/child incl Nieuwe Kerk €3.50/2; 9am-6pm Apr-Oct, 11am-4pm Nov-Mar, closed Sun)**. The latter, 800 years old, is a surreal sight: its tower leans 2m from the vertical.

Vermeer Centrum Delft — Museum

(www.vermeerdelft.nl; Voldersgracht 21; adult/child €8/4; 10am-5pm) As the place where Vermeer was born, lived, and worked, Delft is 'Vermeer Central' to many art-history and old-masters enthusiasts. Along with viewing life-sized images of Vermeer's oeuvre, you can tour a replica of Vermeer's studio, which reveals the way the artist approached the use of light and colour in his craft. A 'Vermeer's World' exhibit offers insight into his environment and upbringing, while temporary exhibits show how his work continues to inspire other artists.

De Candelaer — Studio

(www.candelaer.nl; Kerkstraat 13; 9.30am-6pm Mon-Sat, 11am-6pm Sun) The most central and modest Delftware outfit is de Candelaer, just off the Markt. It has five artists, a few of whom work most days. When it's quiet they'll give you a detailed tour of the manufacturing process.

Sleeping

Hotel de Plataan Boutique Hotel **€€**
(212 60 46; www.hoteldeplataan.nl; Doelenplein 9-11; s/d from €105/115;) On a pretty canal-side square in the old town, this family-run gem has small but elegant standard rooms and wonderfully opulent theme rooms, including the 'Garden of Eden'; the Eastern-style 'Amber', with a Turkish massage shower; or the desert-island 'Tamarinde'. Modesty alert: many en suites are only partially screened from the room. Rates include breakfast and secure parking.

Eating & Drinking

De Visbanken Seafood **€**
(www.visbanken.nl; Camaretten 2; dishes €2-7; 10am-6pm Mon, 9am-6pm Tue-Fri, 9am-5pm Sat, 10am-5pm Sun) Fish has been sold on this spot since 1342. Display cases in the old open-air pavilion entice with fresh and marinated, smoked and fried fishy treats.

Spijshuis de Dis Contemporary Dutch **€€**
(213 17 82; www.spijshuisdedis.com; Beestenmarkt 36; mains €17-24.50; 5-10pm Tue-Sat;) Fresh fish and amazing soups served in bread bowls take centre stage at this romantic foodie haven, but meat eaters and vegetarians are well catered for too. Creative starters include smoked, marinated mackerel on sliced apple with horseradish. Don't skip the Dutch pudding served in a wooden shoe.

Locus Publicus Brown Cafe
(www.locuspublicus.nl; Brabantse Turfmarkt 67; 11am-1am Mon-Thu, to 2am Fri & Sat, noon-1am Sun) Cosy little Locus Publicus is filled with cheery locals quaffing their way through the 175-strong beer list. There's great people-watching from the front terrace.

Information

The **tourist office** (VVV; 215 40 51; www.delft.nl; Kerkstraat 3; hours vary) has free internet; the thematic walking guides are excellent.

Keukenhof Gardens (p481), the Netherlands

ℹ Getting There & Away

The area around the **train station** will be a vast construction site for years to come as the lines are moved underground. Train services include Amsterdam (€12.70, one hour, two per hour), Den Haag (€3, 12 minutes, four per hour) and Rotterdam (€3.50, 12 minutes, four per hour).

ROTTERDAM

☎010 / POP 619,800

Rotterdam bursts with energy. Vibrant nightlife, a diverse, multi-ethnic community, an intensely interesting maritime tradition and a wealth of top-class museums all make it a must-see part of any visit to the Netherlands, especially if you are passing by on the high-speed trains.

The Netherlands' 'second city', central Rotterdam was bombed flat during WWII and spent the following decades rebuilding. You won't find the classic Dutch medieval centre here – it was swept away along with the other rubble and detritus of war. In its place is an architectural aesthetic that's unique in Europe, a progressive, perpetual-motion approach to architecture that's clearly a result of the city's postwar, postmodern, anything-goes philosophy (a fine example of this is the Paul McCarthy statue titled *Santa with Butt Plug* that the city placed in the main shopping district).

Sights

Rotterdam is split by the vast Nieuwe Maas shipping channel, which is crossed by a series of tunnels and bridges, notably the fabulously postmodern Erasmusbrug. The centre is on the north side of the water and is easily strolled. The historic neighbourhood of Delfshaven is 3km west.

Museum Boijmans van Beuningen — Museum

(www.boijmans.nl; Museumpark 18-20; adult/child €15/free; 🕓11am-5pm Tue-Sun) Among Europe's very finest museums, the Museum Boijmans van Beuningen has a permanent collection spanning all eras of Dutch and European art, including superb old masters. Among the highlights are *The Marriage Feast at Cana* by Hieronymus Bosch, the *Three Maries at the Open Sepulchre* by Van Eyck, the minutely detailed *Tower of Babel* by Pieter Brueghel the Elder, and *Portrait of Titus* and *Man in a Red Cap* by Rembrandt.

Statue of Willem Van Oranje (Willem the Silent), Nieuwe Kerk (p482), Delft, the Netherlands

Overblaak Development Notable Building
Designed by Piet Blom and built from 1978 to 1984, this development near Blaak metro station is marked by its pencil-shaped tower and 'forest' of 45-degree-tilted, cube-shaped apartments on hexagonal pylons. One apartment, the **Kijk-Kubus Museum-House** (**www.kubuswoning.nl; Overblaak 70; admission €3; 11am-5pm**), is open to the public; the **Stayokay Rotterdam** youth hostel occupies the super-sized cube at the southern end.

Euromast Viewpoint
(**www.euromast.nl; Parkhaven 20; adult/child from €9.25/5.90; 9.30am-10pm Apr-Sep, from 10am Oct-Mar**) A 1960-built landmark, the 185m Euromast offers unparalleled 360-degree views of Rotterdam from its 100m-high observation deck. Extra diversions here include a brasserie and summertime abseiling (€52.50). The tower's two suites start from €385 including breakfast.

RiF010 Surfing
(**www.rif010.nl; Steigersgracht**) From May 2015, surfers, bodyboarders, stand-up paddleboarders and kayakers can take a wild 14-second ride on a naturally purified, barrelling 1.5m-high wave in an inner-city canal. Its water-level beach-house cafe provides up-close views of the action.

Sleeping

King Kong Hostel Boutique Hostel €
(**818 87 78; www.kingkonghostel.com; Witte de Withstraat 74; dm/d/q from €22.50/75/110;** @) Outdoor benches made from salvaged timbers and garden hoses by Sander Bokkinga sit outside King Kong, a design haven on Rotterdam's coolest street. Artist-designed rooms and dorms are filled with vintage and industrial furniture; fab features include hammocks, lockers equipped with device-charging points, a gourmet self-catering kitchen, roof garden and barbecue area, and Netflix.

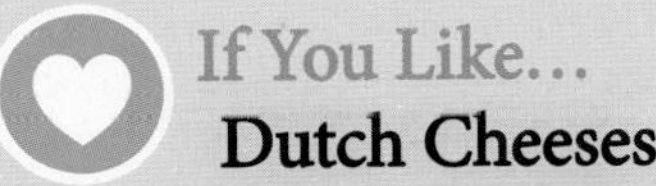

If You Like... Dutch Cheeses

If your taste buds have been tickled by the amazing cheese market in Alkmaar, there are a couple more iconic Dutch cheeses you simply have to try.

1 **EDAM**
This spherical, semi-hard cheese is undoubtedly the best-known Dutch cheese, and is instantly recognisable thanks to its coat of red paraffin wax. You'll see it for sale everywhere.

2 **GOUDA**
The first mention of the Netherlands' second-most famous *fromage* was allegedly in 1184, making it one of the world's oldest cheeses. Gouda is a hugely attractive little town, with many old buildings and quaint canals, as well as a huge cheese market, held on the main square every Thursday in summer.

Hotel New York Historic Hotel €€€
(**439 05 00; www.hotelnewyork.nl; Koninginnenhoofd 1; d €99-270;** @) An art-nouveau showpiece, the Holland-America passenger-ship line's former HQ has sweeping vistas, superb dining options (including an oyster bar), a barber shop, and a water taxi ferrying guests across the Nieuwe Maas to the city centre. Rooms retain original, painstakingly restored fittings and decor; styles range from standard to timber-panelled suites in the old boardrooms with fireplaces.

Eating

De Jong Contemporary Dutch €€
(**465 79 55; www.restaurantdejong.nl; Rampoortstraat 38; 4-course menu €40; 6-11pm Wed-Sun;**) In the hip Station Hofplein complex – the former train station of the disused Hofpleinlijn railway, whose viaduct arches are being transformed into cultural and creative spaces – adventurous chef Jim De Jong wows diners with surprise four-course menus (meat/fish

FRANS LEMMENS/GETTY IMAGES ©

Don't Miss Kinderdijk

In 1740 a series of windmills were built to drain a polder about 12km southeast of Rotterdam. Today 19 of the Dutch icons survive at Kinderdijk, a Unesco monument. You can wander the dikes for over 3km amid the spinning sails and go inside one of the windmills. It's a good bicycle ride; you can rent bikes once here or travel from Rotterdam (16km); get a map from the tourist office.

NEED TO KNOW

www.kinderdijk.nl; adult/child €7.50/5.50; 9am-5.30pm mid-Mar–Oct, 11am-4pm mid-Feb–mid-Mar & Nov-Dec, closed Jan–mid-Feb

or vegetarian; no à la carte) made from seasonal produce including herbs and flowers from the restaurant's garden.

Ter Marsch & Co Burgers, Steak **€€**
(www.termarschco.nl; Witte de Withstraat 70; burgers €7-12.50, mains €21-40; noon-10pm) Butcher shop–turned–bar/restaurant Ter Marsch & Co sizzles up monumental burgers (such as Scottish black Angus, pancetta and truffle mayo) and succulent steaks.

Drinking & Nightlife

De Witte Aap Brown Cafe
(www.dewitteaap.nl; Witte de Withstraat 78; 1pm-4am;) Anchoring this artist-filled 'hood, the fabulous 'White Monkey' has live music on Wednesdays and DJs on Saturdays and is always crowded with locals. The front opens right up and a huge awning keeps inclement weather at bay.

Stadsbrouwerij De Pelgrim Brewery
(www.pelgrimbier.nl; Aelbrechtskolk 12; ⏲noon-midnight Wed-Sat) This brewery is named for the religious folk who passed through on their way to America. You can take your own voyage through the various beers brewed in the vintage surrounds. In addition to seasonal brews, specialities include its Mayflower Triple and Rotterdam's Stoonbier. There's a restaurant too.

Shopping

Markthal Rotterdam Food & Drink
(http://markthalrotterdam.nl; Nieuwstraat; ⏲10am-8pm Mon-Thu & Sat, to 9pm Fri, noon-6pm Sun) The Netherlands' inaugural indoor food market hit headlines around the world when it opened in 2014 due to its extraordinary inverted-U-shaped design, with glass-walled apartments arcing over the foodhall's fantastical fruit- and vegetable-muralled ceiling. There's a tantalising array of produce, prepared food and drinks; shops continue downstairs, while the **Blaak** (⏲8am-5pm Tue & Sat) street market unfurls outside twice weekly.

Information

The Rotterdam Welcome Card (from adult/child €10/7) offers discounts for sights, hotels and restaurants, and free public transport. Buy it from the tourist office.

Tourist Office (☎790 01 85; www.rotterdam.info; Coolsingel 197; ⏲9.30am-6pm) The main tourist office; there's a smaller branch at the main train station (Centraal Station; ⏲9am-5.30pm).

Getting There & Away

DESTINATION	PRICE (€)	TIME (MIN)	FREQUENCY (PER HR)
Amsterdam via Leiden	14.80	65	5
Amsterdam (high speed)	17.10	43	2
Brussels	29-62	70-76	1-2
Schiphol airport	11.90-14.20	25-50	4-5
Utrecht	10.10	40	4

Rotterdam Centraal Station is a new architectural stunner that opened in 2014. There are direct services to Brussels and Paris; from late 2016, Eurostar trains linking Amsterdam with London will stop here.

Getting Around

Rotterdam's trams, buses and metro are provided by RET (www.ret.nl). Most converge in front of CS, where there is an information booth (⏲7am-10pm) that also sells tickets. Day passes are sold for varying durations: 1/2/3 days costs €7/10.50/14. A single-ride ticket purchased from a bus driver or tram conductor costs €3.

UTRECHT

☎030 / POP 330,700

Utrecht is one of the Netherlands' oldest cities and boasts a beautiful, vibrant, old-world city centre, ringed by striking 13th-century canal wharves. The wharves, well below street level, are unique to Utrecht. Canalside streets alongside brim with shops, restaurants and cafes.

Initial impressions may be less auspicious. When you step off the train you'll find yourself lost in the maze that is the Hoog Catharijne shopping centre. The Hoog is huge...and it's attached to the station...and it seemingly goes on forever...and ever. It's really a nightmare but a vast construction project (www.nieuwhc.nl) is transforming the entire area.

Sights

Focus your wanderings on the **Domplein** and south along the tree-lined **Oudegracht**. The tourist office has a good booklet that covers Utrecht's myriad small museums, which feature everything from waste water to old trains.

Domtoren Historic Building
(Cathedral Tower; www.domtoren.nl; Domplein; tower tour adult/child €9/5; ⏲11am-4pm) Finished in the 14th century after almost 300 years' construction, the cathedral and its tower are Utrecht's most striking medieval landmarks. In 1674 the North Sea winds reached hurricane force and

Right: Erasmusbrug bridge, Rotterdam (p484), the Netherlands;
Below: Oudegracht, Utrecht, the Netherlands
(RIGHT) GLENN VAN DER KNIJFF/GETTY IMAGES ©; (BELOW) ALLAN BAXTER/GETTY IMAGES ©

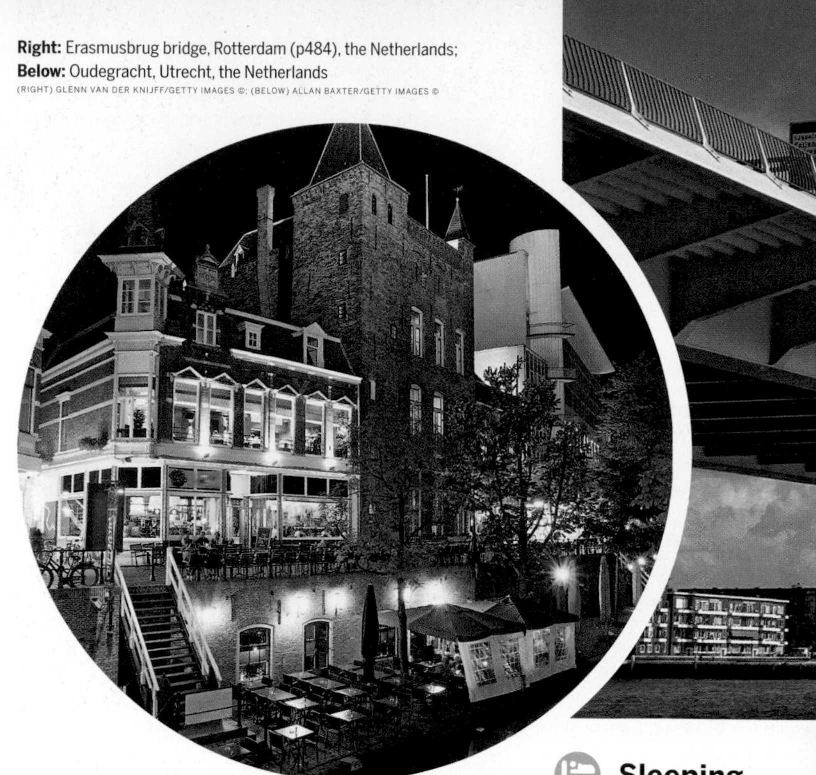

blew down the cathedral's nave, leaving the tower and transept behind.

The Domtoren is 112m high, with 50 bells. It's worth the tough haul up 465 steps to the top for unbeatable city views; on a clear day you can see Amsterdam.

Centraal Museum Museum
(www.centraalmuseum.nl; Nicolaaskerkhof 10; adult/child €9/4; 11am-5pm Tue-Sun) The Centraal Museum has a wide-ranging collection. It displays applied arts dating back to the 17th century, as well as paintings by some of the Utrecht School artists and a bit of De Stijl to boot – including the world's most extensive Gerrit Rietveld collection, a dream for all minimalists. There's even a 12th-century Viking longboat that was dug out of the local mud, plus a sumptuous 17th-century dollhouse.

Sleeping

B&B Utrecht Guesthouse **€**
(06 5043 4884; www.hostelutrecht.nl; Lucas Bolwerk 4; dm/s/d/tr from €19.50/57.50/65/90; @ **)** Straddling the border between hostel and hotel, this spotless inn in an elegant old building has a communal kitchen and free breakfast, lunch and dinner ingredients. Wi-fi, scanners, printers etc are also free, along with a huge range of musical instruments and DVDs.

Mary K Hotel Hotel **€€**
(230 48 88; www.marykhotel.com; Oudegracht 25; d from €120;) A bevy of Utrecht artists decorated the rooms at this ideally situated canal house. Rooms come in three basic sizes ('cosy', medium and large) but no two are alike. All make use of the original 18th-century features and you may find a timber beam running through your bathroom or a stuffed animal snoozing in the rafters.

Eating

GYS Cafe €

(http://gysutrecht.nl; Voorstraat 77; dishes €7-10; ⌚10am-10pm Mon-Sat; 📶) Organic produce at this bright, airy, design-filled cafe is used in burgers (such as tofu with grilled peppers and hummus, or lamb with pumpkin and mint), sandwiches (like tempeh with sweet potato, avocado and watercress, or smoked mackerel with beetroot mousse), soups, salads and hot dishes like eggplant schnitzel with salsa, plus tasting platters.

Karaf International €€

(☎233 11 04; www.restaurantkaraf.nl; Lange Nieuwstraat 71; mains €18-23.50; ⌚5-10pm) Exquisitely presented dishes such as seabass in smoked butter, and Scottish grouse stuffed with Merquez sausage served with mulberry jus are among the reasons Karaf became an instant hit following its recent opening – along with its cool, contemporary Dutch dining room and stunning wine list.

Drinking & Nightlife

't Oude Pothuys Brown Cafe

(www.pothuys.nl; Oudegracht 279; ⌚3pm-2am Mon & Tue, noon-3am Wed-Sun) In a darkened barrel-vaulted medieval cellar, this wonderfully cosy pub has nightly music, from jam sessions and emerging bands to funk and soul, jazz and blues, electro and established acts. Enjoy drinks on the canal-side pier.

Information

The **tourist office** (VVV; ☎0900 128 87 32; www.visit-utrecht.com; Domplein 9; ⌚noon-5pm Sun & Mon, 10am-5pm Tue-Sat) sells maps and tours of the nearby Domtoren.

Getting There & Away

The train station is a major connection point and is the Netherland's busiest. It is on the line linking Amsterdam to Cologne. Sample fares include Amsterdam (€7.40, 30 minutes, four per hour), Maastricht (€23.10, two hours, two per hour) and Rotterdam (€10.10, 40 minutes, four per hour).

BELGIUM

Stereotypes of comic books, chips and sublime chocolates are just the start in eccentric little Belgium; its self-deprecating people have quietly spent centuries producing some of Europe's finest art and architecture. Bilingual Brussels is the dynamic yet personable EU capital, but also sports what's arguably the world's most beautiful city square. Flat, Dutch-speaking Flanders has many other alluring medieval cities, all easily linked by regular train hops. In hilly, French-speaking Wallonia, the attractions are contrastingly rural – castle villages, outdoor activities and extensive cave systems.

Brussels

POP 1.14 MILLION

Like the country it represents, Brussels (Bruxelles, Brussel) is a surreal, multilayered place pulling several disparate identities into one enigmatic core. It subtly seduces with great art, tempting chocolate shops and classic cafes. Meanwhile a confusing architectural smorgasbord pits awesome art-nouveau and 17th-century masterpieces against shabby suburbanism and the disappointingly soulless glass-faced anonymity of the EU area. Note that Brussels is officially bilingual, so all names – from streets to train stations – have both Dutch and French versions, but for simplicity we use only the French versions in this chapter.

Sights

The **BrusselsCard** (www.brusselscard.be; 24/48/72hr €24/36/43) allows free visits to over 30 Brussels-area museums, various other discounts, plus unlimited free use of city public transport. You'll need to be a seriously hyperactive museum fan to save much money, but it's fun trying. Remember that most museums close Mondays. On the first Wednesday afternoon of each month many museums are free.

CENTRAL BRUSSELS

Galeries St-Hubert Covered Arcade
(www.galeries-saint-hubert.com; off Rue du Marché aux Herbes; M Gare Centrale) When opened in 1847 by King Léopold I, the glorious Galeries St-Hubert formed Europe's very first shopping arcade. Many enticing shops lie behind its neoclassical glassed-in arches flanked by marble pilasters. Several eclectic cafes spill tables onto the gallery terrace, safe from rain beneath the glass roof.

Bourse Stock Exchange
(Place de la Bourse; Bourse) The Belgian Stock Exchange occupies a grandiose neoclassical edifice from 1873. The cream facade is festooned with friezes and sculptures of exotic fruits, reclining nudes, lunging horses and a multitude of allegorical figures. One of the statues is by Rodin.

Manneken Pis Monument
(cnr Rue de l'Étuve & Rue du Chêne; M Gare Centrale) From Rue Charles Buls, Brussels' most unashamedly touristy shopping street, chocolate and trinket shops lead the camera-toting hoards three blocks to the Manneken Pis. This fountain-statue of a little boy taking a leak is comically tiny and a perversely perfect national symbol for surreal Belgium. Most of the time the tiny statue's nakedness is largely hidden beneath a costume relevant to an anniversary, national day or local event: his ever-growing wardrobe is partly displayed at the **Maison du Roi** (Musée de la Ville de Bruxelles; Grand Pl; M Gare Centrale).

Musées Royaux des Beaux-Arts Gallery
(Royal Museums of Fine Arts; 02-508 32 11; www.fine-arts-museum.be; Rue de la Régence 3; adult/6–25yrs/BrusselsCard €8/2/free, with Magritte Museum €13; 10am-5pm Tue-Sun; M Gare Centrale, Parc) This prestigious museum incorporates the **Musée d'Art Ancien** (ancient art); the **Musée d'Art Moderne** (modern art), with works by surrealist Paul Delvaux and fauvist Rik Wouters; and the purpose-built **Musée Magritte**. The 15th-century Flemish

ALAN COPSON/GETTY IMAGES ©

Don't Miss
Grand Place

Brussels' incomparable central square tops any itinerary. Its splendidly spired Gothic **Hôtel de Ville** was the only building to escape bombardment by the French in 1695, quite ironic considering that it was their main target. Today the pedestrianised square's splendour is due largely to its intact **guildhalls**, rebuilt by merchant guilds after 1695 and fancifully adorned with gilded statues.

NEED TO KNOW

M Gare Centrale

Primitives are wonderfully represented in the Musée d'Art Ancien: there's Rogier Van der Weyden's *Pietà* with its hallucinatory dawn sky, Hans Memling's refined portraits, and the richly textured *Madonna With Saints* by the Master of the Legend of St Lucy.

IXELLES

Musée Horta Museum

(**02-543 04 90; www.hortamuseum.be; Rue Américaine 25; adult/child €8/4; 2-5.30pm Tue-Sun; M Horta, 91, 92**) The typically austere exterior doesn't give much away, but Victor Horta's former home (designed and built 1898–1901) is an art-nouveau jewel. The stairwell is the structural triumph of the house – follow the playful knots and curlicues of the banister, which become more exuberant as you ascend, ending at a tangle of swirls and glass lamps at the skylight, glazed with citrus-coloured and plain glass.

HEYSEL

A 15-minute metro ride to Brussels' northern edge brings you to an area of trade fairs and the national stadium.

Central Brussels

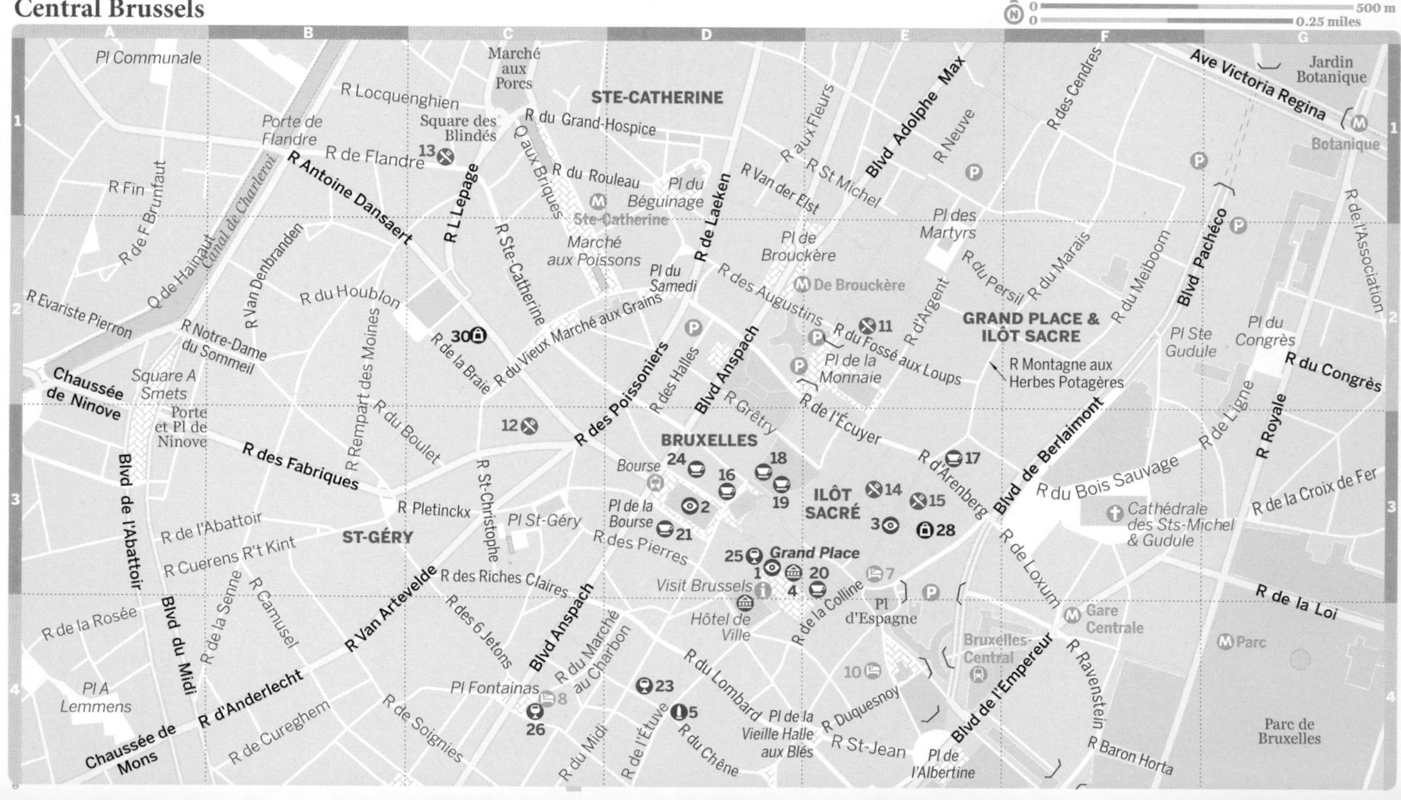

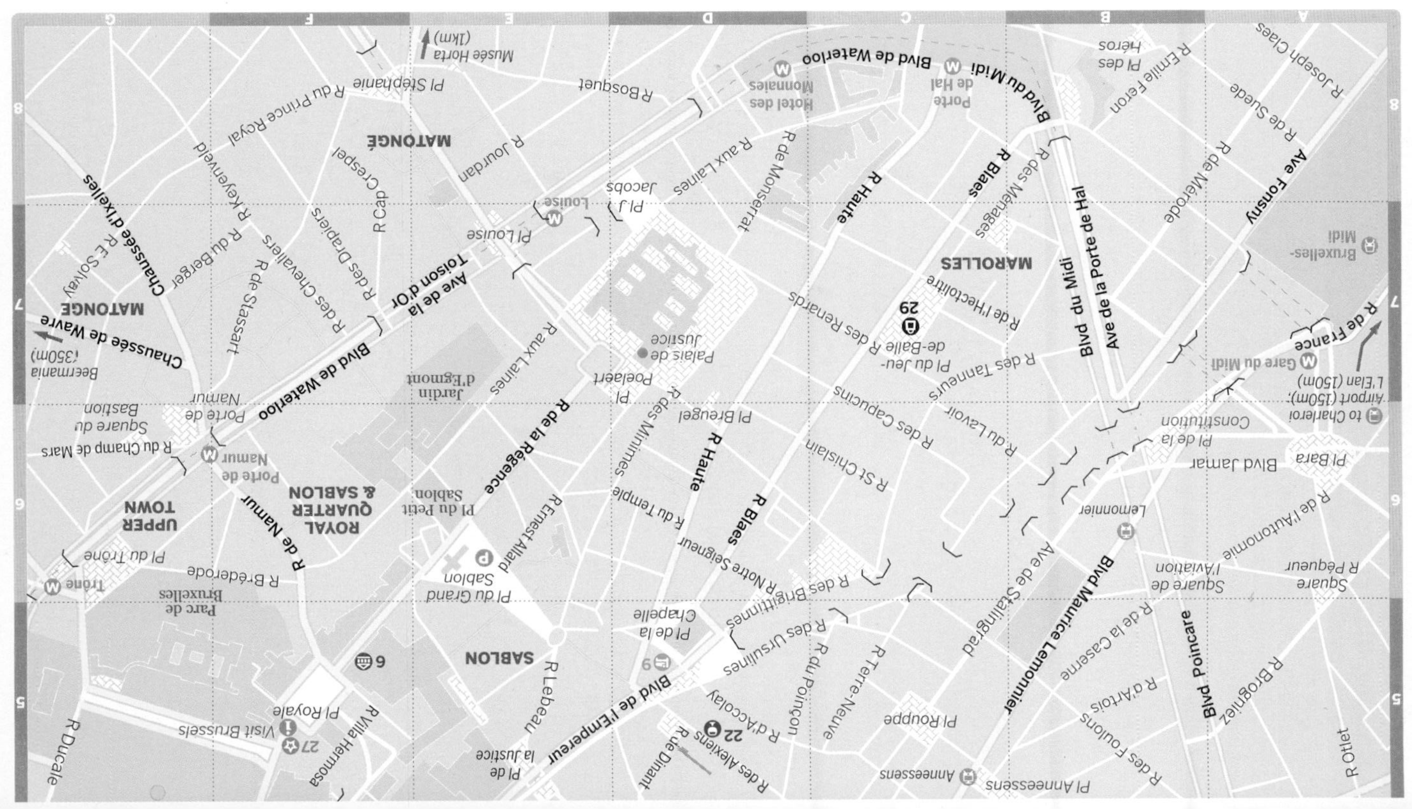
UPPER TOWN
ROYAL QUARTER & SABLON
SABLON
MATONGE
MATONGÉ
MAROLLES
Parc de Bruxelles
Jardin d'Egmont
Palais de Justice
Visit Brussels
Trône
Porte de Namur
Louise
Hotel des Monnaies
Porte de Hal
Gare du Midi
Bruxelles-Midi
Anneessens
Lemonnier
Beermania (350m)
Musée Horta (1km)
to Charleroi Airport (150m); L'Elan (150m)
Blvd de Waterloo
Ave de la Toison d'Or
R de la Régence
R Haute
R Blaes
Blvd de l'Empereur
Blvd du Midi
Ave de la Porte de Hal
Blvd Maurice Lemonnier
Blvd Poincare
Blvd Jamar
Ave Fonsny
Chaussée d'Ixelles
Chaussée de Wavre
R de Namur
Pl Royale
Pl du Grand Sablon
Pl du Petit Sablon
Pl Poelaert
Pl Louise
Pl Stéphanie
Pl de la Chapelle
Pl du Jeu-de-Balle
Pl Rouppe
Pl Anneessens
Pl de la Constitution
Pl Bara
Pl des Héros
Pl de la Justice
Pl J Jacobs
Pl Breugel
Pl du Trône
Square du Bastion
Square de l'Aviation
Square R Pequeur
R Ducale
R Villa Hermosa
R Bréderode
R du Champ de Mars
R de Stassart
R du Berger
R E Solvay
R Keyenveld
R des Chevaliers
R des Drapiers
R Cap Crespel
R du Prince Royal
R Jourdan
R Bosquet
R aux Laines
R de Monserrat
R Ernest Allard
R Lebeau
R des Minimes
R du Temple
R Notre Seigneur
R des Brigittines
R des Ursulines
R d'Accolay
R des Alexiens
Rue Dinant
R du Poinçon
R Terre-Neuve
R St Ghislain
R des Capucins
R des Renards
R du Lavoir
R des Tanneurs
R de l'Hectolitre
R des Ménages
Ave de Stalingrad
R de la Caserne
R d'Artois
R des Foulons
R Brogniez
R Otlet
R de l'Autonomie
R de France
R de Mérode
R Emile Feron
R de Suède
R Joseph Claes
6
9
22
27
29
5
6
7
8
A
B
C
D
E
F
G

Central Brussels

Don't Miss Sights
1 Grand Place ... D3

Sights
2 Bourse ... D3
3 Galeries St-Hubert ... E3
4 Maison du Roi ... D3
5 Manneken Pis ... D4
6 Musées Royaux des Beaux-Arts ... F5

Sleeping
7 Chambres d'Hôtes du Vaudeville ... E3
8 Downtown-BXL ... C4
9 HI Hostel John Bruegel ... D5
10 Hôtel Le Dixseptième ... E4
La Casa-BXL ... (see 8)

Eating
11 Belga Queen Brussels ... E2
12 Fin de Siècle ... C3
13 Henri ... C1
14 L'Ogenblik ... E3
15 Mokafé ... E3

Drinking & Nightlife
16 À la Bécasse ... D3
17 À la Mort Subite ... E3
18 A l'Image de Nostre-Dame ... D3
19 Au Bon Vieux Temps ... D3
20 Chaloupe d'Or ... E3
21 Falstaff ... D3
22 La Fleur en Papier Doré ... D5
23 Le Cercle des Voyageurs ... D4
24 Le Cirio ... D3
25 Le Roy d'Espagne ... D3
26 Moeder Lambic Fontainas ... C4

Entertainment
27 Arsène50 ... F5

Shopping
28 Délices et Caprices ... E3
29 Flea Market ... C7
30 Stijl ... C2

Atomium Monument, Museum
(www.atomium.be; Sq de l'Atomium; adult/students/BrusselsCard €11/6/9; 10am-6pm; M Heysel, 51) The space-age Atomium looms 102m over north Brussels' suburbia, resembling a steel alien from a '60s Hollywood movie. It consists of nine house-sized metallic balls linked by steel tube-columns containing escalators and lifts. The balls are arranged like a school chemistry set to represent iron atoms in their crystal lattice...except these are 165 billion times bigger. It was built as a symbol of postwar progress for the 1958 World's Fair and became an architectural icon, receiving a makeover in 2006.

Sleeping

With much of Brussels' accommodation scene aimed squarely at Eurocrats and business travellers, many business hotels drop their rates dramatically at weekends and in summer.

Beware that several otherwise decent hotels around Rogier and Bruxelles-Nord lie uncomfortably close to a seedy red-light district. Nicer Ste-Catherine area is central but calm, St-Gilles offers a more 'local' experience.

Brussels has a reasonable network of B&Bs, many bookable through Bed & Brussels (www.bnb-brussels.be) and Airbnb (www.airbnb.com).

HI Hostel John Bruegel Hostel €
(02-511 04 36; www.jeugdherbergen.be/brussel.htm; Rue du Saint Esprit 2; dm/tw €27.20/63.30, youth €24.45/57.90; lockout 10am-2pm, curfew 1am-7am; M Louise) Superbly central but somewhat institutional with limited communal space. The attic singles are a cut above the other hostels. Internet €2 per hour, wi-fi free, lockers €1.50. There's a 10% discount for HI members.

Downtown-BXL B&B €€
(0475 29 07 21; www.downtownbxl.com; Rue du Marché au Charbon 118-120; r €99-119; ; Anneessens) Near the capital's gay district, this B&B is superbly located if you're partying the night away. From the communal breakfast table and help-yourself coffee bar, a classic staircase winds up to good-value rooms featuring zebra-striped cushions and Warhol Marilyn prints. One room features a round bed. Adjacent **Casa-BXL (0475 29 07 21; www.lacasabxl.com; Rue du Marché au Charbon 16; €109-119)** offers three rooms in a more Moroccan-Asian style.

Chambres d'Hôtes du Vaudeville B&B €€
(☎0471 47 38 37; www.theatreduvaudeville.be; Galerie de la Reine 11; d from €120; 📶; 🚇Bruxelles Central) This classy B&B has an incredible location right within the gorgeous (if reverberant) Galeries St-Hubert. Delectable decor styles include African, modernist and 'Madame Loulou' (with 1920s nude sketches). Larger front rooms have clawfoot bathtubs and *galerie* views, but can be noisy with clatter that continues all night. Get keys via the art-deco-influenced Café du Vaudeville, where breakfast is included. Vaudeville's unique house beer is provided free in the minibar.

Hôtel Le Dixseptième Boutique Hotel €€€
(☎02-517 17 17; www.ledixseptieme.be; Rue de la Madeleine 25; s/d/ste from €120/140/250, weekend from €120/120/200; ❄📶; 🚇Bruxelles Central) A hushed magnificence greets you in this alluring boutique hotel, partly occupying the former 17th-century residence of the Spanish ambassador. The coffee-cream breakfast room retains original cherub reliefs. Spacious executive suites come with four-poster beds. Across a tiny enclosed courtyard-garden in the cheaper rear section, the Creuz Suite has its bathroom tucked curiously into a 14th-century vaulted basement. Lifts stop between floors so you'll need to deal with some stairs.

Eating

Mokafé Waffles €
(☎02-511 78 70; Galerie du Roi; waffles from €3; ⏰7.30am-11.30pm; Ⓜ De Brouckère) Locals get their waffles in this old-fashioned cafe under the glass arch of the Galeries-St Hubert. It's a little timeworn and dowdy inside, but wicker chairs in the beautiful arcade provide you with a view of passing shoppers.

Fin de Siècle Belgian €
(Rue des Chartreux 9; mains €11.25-20; ⏰bar 4.30pm-1am, kitchen 6pm-12.30am; 🚇Bourse) From *carbonade* (beer-based hot-pot) and *kriek* (cherry beer) chicken to mezzes and tandoori chicken, the food is as eclectic as the decor in this low-lit cult place. Tables are rough, music constant and ceilings purple. To quote the barman,

Galeries St-Hubert (p490), Brussels, Belgium

'there's no phone, no bookings, no sign on the door…we do everything to put people off but they still keep coming'.

Henri Fusion **€€**
(**02-218 00 08; www.restohenri.be; Rue de Flandre 113; mains €15-20; noon-2pm Tue-Fri & 6-10pm Tue-Sat; M Ste-Catherine)** In an airy white space on this street to watch, Henri concocts tangy fusion dishes like tuna with ginger, soy and lime, artichokes with scampi, lime and olive tapenade, or Argentinean fillet steak in parsley. There's an astute wine list, and staff who know their stuff.

Belga Queen Brussels Belgian **€€**
(**02-217 21 87; www.belgaqueen.be; Rue du Fossé aux Loups 32; mains €16-25, weekday lunch €16; noon-2.30pm & 7pm-midnight; M De Broukère)** Belgian cuisine is given a chic, modern twist within a magnificent, if reverberant, 19th-century bank building. Classical stained-glass ceilings and marble columns are hidden behind an indecently hip oyster counter and wide-ranging beer and cocktail bar (open noon till late). In the former bank vaults beneath, there's a cigar lounge that morphs into a nightclub after 10pm Wednesday to Saturday.

L'Ogenblik French **€€€**
(**02-511 61 51; www.ogenblik.be; Galerie des Princes 1; mains €23-29, lunch €12; noon-2.30pm & 7pm-midnight; Bourse)** It may be only a stone's throw from Rue des Bouchers, but this timeless bistro with its lace curtains, resident cat, marble-topped tables and magnificent wrought-iron lamp feels a world away. They've been producing French classics here for more than 30 years, and the expertise shows. Worth the price for a special meal in the heart of town.

Drinking & Nightlife

Cafe culture is one of Brussels' greatest attractions. On the Grand Place itself, 300-year-old gems, like **Le Roy d'Espagne (www.roydespagne.be; Grand Place 1; 10am-1am; M Gare Centrale)** and **Chaloupe d'Or (Grand Place 24; M Gare Centrale)** are magnificent but predictably pricey. Somewhat cheaper classics lie around the Bourse, with livelier pubs ranged around Place St-Géry and further south around fashion-conscious Flagey.

Moeder Lambic Fontainas Beer Hall
(**www.moederlambic.com; Place Fontainas 8; 11am-1am Sun-Thu, to 2am Fri & Sat; Annessens, Bourse)** At the last count they were serving 46 artisinal beers here, in a contemporary rather than old-world setting: walls are bare brick and hung with photos and the booths are backed with concrete. They dish up great quiches and cheese and meat platters. The mood is upbeat and the music loud.

Le Cirio cafe, Brussels, Belgium

Bourse Area Cafes

Many of Brussels' most iconic cafes are within stumbling distance of the Bourse. Don't miss century-old **Falstaff** (www.lefalstaff.be; Rue Henri Maus 17; 10am-1am; Bourse) with its festival of stained glass ceilings, or **Le Cirio** (Rue de la Bourse 18; 10am-midnight; Bourse), a sumptuous yet affordable 1866 marvel full of polished brasswork serving great-value pub meals. Three more classics are hidden up shoulder-wide alleys: the medieval yet unpretentious **A l'Image de Nostre-Dame** (off Rue du Marché aux Herbes 5; noon-midnight Mon-Fri, 3pm-1am Sat, 4-10.30pm Sun; Bourse); the 1695 Rubenseque **Au Bon Vieux Temps** (Impasse Saint Michel; 11am-midnight; Bourse), which sometimes stocks ultra-rare Westvletteren beers (€10!); and lambic specialist **À la Bécasse** (www.alabecasse.com; Rue de Tabora 11; 11am-midnight, to 1am Fri & Sat; M Gare Centrale), with its vaguely Puritanical rows of wooden tables.

À la Mort Subite Cafe
(02-513 13 18; www.alamortsubite.com; Rue Montagne aux Herbes Potagères 7; 11am-1am Mon-Sat, noon-midnight Sun; M Gare Centrale) An absolute classic unchanged since 1928, with lined-up wooden tables, arched mirror panels and entertainingly brusque service.

Le Cercle des Voyageurs Brasserie
(02-514 39 49; www.lecercledesvoyageurs.com; Rue des Grands Carmes 18; mains €15-21; 11am-midnight; ; M Annessens, Bourse) Invite Phileas Fogg for coffee to this delightful bistro featuring globes, an antique-map ceiling and a travel library. If he's late, flick through an old *National Geographic* in your colonial leather chair. The global brasserie food is pretty good, and the free live music fantastic: piano jazz on Tuesdays and experimental on Thursdays. Other gigs in the cave have a small entrance fee.

La Fleur en Papier Doré Brown Cafe
(www.goudblommekeinpapier.be; Rue des Alexiens 53; 11am-midnight Tue-Sat, to 7pm Sun; Bruxelles Central) The nicotine-stained walls of this tiny cafe, adored by artists and locals, are covered with writings, art and scribbles by Magritte and his surrealist pals, some of which were reputedly traded for free drinks. 'Ceci n'est pas un musée', quips a sign on the door reminding visitors to buy a drink and not just look around.

Shopping

Tourist-oriented shops selling chocolate, beer, lace and Atomium baubles stretch between the Grand Place and Manneken Pis. For better **chocolate shops** in calmer, grander settings, peruse the resplendent Galeries St-Hubert (p490) or the upmarket Sablon area. In the Marolles, Rue Haute and Rue Blaes are full of quirky **interior design shops**, while Place du Jeu-de-Balle has a daily **flea market** (6am-2pm). Rue Antoine Dansaert has most of Brussels' **high-fashion boutiques**, with **Stijl** (www.stijl.be; Rue Antoine Dansaert 74; M Ste-Catherine) hosting many cutting-edge collections.

Supermarkets sell a range of **Belgian beers** relatively cheaply. For wider selections and the relevant glasses, try **Beermania** (www.beermania.be; Chaussée de Wavre 174; 11am-9pm Mon-Sat; M Porte de Namur) or the very personal little **Délices et Caprices** (www.the-belgian-beer-tasting-shop.be; Rue des Bouchers 68; 2-8pm Thu-Mon; M Gare Centrale).

Information

Tourist Information

Visit Brussels (02-513 89 40; www.visitbrussels.be; Hôtel de Ville; 9am-6pm; Bourse) Visit Brussels has stacks of city-specific information as well as handy fold-out guides (independently researched) to the best shops, restaurants and pubs in town. The Rue Royale (02-513 89 40; http://visitbrussels.be; rue Royale 2; 9am-6pm Mon-Fri, 10am-6pm Sat-Sun; M Parc) office is much less crowded than the Grand Place one. Here you'll also find the Arsène50 (02-512 57 45; www.arsene50.be; Rue Royale 2; 12.30-5.30pm Tue-Sat; M Parc) desk, which provides great discounts for cultural events.

Getting There & Away

Train

Eurostar, TGV and Thalys high-speed trains stop only at Bruxelles-Midi (Brussel-Zuid). Jump on any local service for the four-minute hop to conveniently central Bruxelles-Central. All domestic trains, plus some Amsterdam services, stop there anyway. Consult www.belgianrail.be for timetable information.

Getting Around

To/From the Airports

Brussels Airport

Taxi

Fares start around €35. Very bad idea in rush hour traffic.

Train

Four per hour (5.30am to 11.50pm), €8.50. Takes 20 minutes to Bruxelles-Central, 24 minutes to Bruxelles-Midi.

Charleroi ('Brussels-South') Airport

Bus

Direct services operated by L'Elan (www.voyages-lelan.be) run to/from a stop behind Bruxelles-Midi station roughly every half hour (single/return €14/23); last services to/from the airport are 8.30pm/11.45pm. Should take around an hour but allow far more at rush hour.

Train

The nearest mainline train station, Charleroi-Sud, is linked to Charleroi Airport by TEC bus A (€5, 18 minutes) twice hourly on weekdays, hourly at weekends. A combined bus-and-rail ticket never costs more than €14 to anywhere in Belgium if pre-purchased. Brussels-Charleroi-Sud trains take around 50 minutes.

Public Transport

Costs

Tickets valid for one hour are sold at metro stations, STIB/MIVB kiosks, newsagents and on buses and trams. Single-/five-/10-journey STIB/MIVB tickets cost €2.10/8/12.50 including transfers. Unlimited one/two/three-day passes cost €7/13/17. Airport buses are excluded. Tickets must be machine-validated before travel or you could face a €60 fine.

Information

Fare/route information: www.stib.be.

Operating hours

From 6am to midnight daily. Limited 'Noctis' buses (rates as per STIB) run from midnight to 3am Friday and Saturday.

Taxi

Taxis (www.autolux.be) cost €2.40 flag fall plus €1.35 per kilometre in Brussels, €2.70 per kilometre beyond city limits, with a €2 surcharge from 10pm to 6am. There are taxis ranks at Bruxelles-Midi and Madeleine (prebook 02-268 00 00, 02-349 49 49). Flagging down cabs London-style doesn't work.

Flanders

ANTWERP

POP 511,700

Cosmopolitan, confident and full of contrasts, Antwerp (Antwerpen in Dutch, Anvers in French) was one of northern Europe's foremost cities in the 17th century when it also was home to Pieter Paul Rubens, diplomat, philosopher and northern Europe's greatest baroque artist. Today it once again revels in fame and fortune attracting art lovers and fashion moguls, club queens and diamond dealers.

City Centre

Website www.antwerpforfree.be lists a daily calendar of free concerts and events. Most major city-run museums are free on the last Wednesday of each month. At other times a 48-hour **Antwerp Card** **(www.visitantwerpen.be; 24/48/72hr €25/32/37)** will save you money if you visit four of the city's splendid museums.

Brabo Fountain — Statue

(Grote Markt) As with every great Flemish city, Antwerp's medieval heart is a classic Grote Markt (Market Sq). Here the triangular, pedestrianised space features the voluptuous, baroque Brabo Fountain depicting Antwerp's hand-throwing legend. Flanked on two sides by very photogenic guildhalls, the square is dominated by an impressive Italo-Flemish Renaissance-style **stadhuis (Town Hall; Grote Markt)**, completed in 1565.

Onze-Lieve-Vrouwekathedraal — Cathedral

(www.dekathedraal.be; Handschoenmarkt; adult/concession €6/4; ⌚10am-5pm Mon-Fri, to 3pm Sat, to 4pm Sun) Belgium's finest Gothic cathedral was 169 years in the making (1352–1521). Wherever you wander in Antwerp, its gracious 123m-high spire has a habit of popping unexpectedly into view and rarely fails to jolt a gasp of awe. The sight is particularly well framed when looking up Pelgrimstraat in afternoon light.

Museum Plantin-Moretus — Historic Building

(www.museumplantinmoretus.be; Vrijdag Markt 22; adult/child €8/1; ⌚10am-5pm Tue-Sun) The idea of giving a museum Unesco World Heritage status might seem odd, until you've seen this fabulous place. Once home to the world's first industrial printing works, it has been a museum since 1876. The medieval building and 1622 **courtyard garden** alone are worth the visit. Highlights include the 1640 **library**, the historic **bookshop** (room 4), and rooms 11 and 21 for their gilt leather 'wallpaper'. Then there's a priceless collection of manuscripts, tapestries and the world's oldest printing press.

Brabo Fountain in the Grote Markt, Antwerp, Belgium

TIBOR BOGNÁR/GETTY IMAGES ©

Rubenshuis Museum

(www.rubenshuis.be; Wapper 9-11; adult/child €8/1, audio guide €2; ⌚10am-5pm Tue-Sun) Restored along original lines, the 1611 building was built as home and studio by celebrated painter Pieter Paul Rubens. Rescued from ruins in 1937, the building is architecturally indulgent with baroque portico, rear facade and formal garden. The furniture dates from Rubens' era but was not part of the original decor. Ten Rubens canvases are displayed, including one where Eve appears to glance lustfully at Adam's fig-leaf.

Station Area

Antwerpen-Centraal train station is an attraction in itself.

Diamond Quarter Neighbourhood

(www.awdc.be) An astounding 80% of all the world's uncut diamonds are traded in Antwerp's architecturally miserable diamond district, immediately southwest of Antwerpen-Centraal station. For the cost of a smile you can see gem polishers at work at Diamondland, which is essentially a zero-pressure lure to get visitors into a diamond salesroom. The well-explained Diamond Museum has changing jewellery 'treasure shows' and similar live gem-polishing demonstrations.

Sleeping

Pulcinella Hostel €

(☎03-234 03 14; www.jeugdherbergen.be; Bogaardeplein 1; dm/tw €26.80/32.40; @ wifi) This giant, tailor-made HI Hostel is hard to beat for its Fashion District location and cool modernist decor. HI members save €3.

Bed, Bad & Brood B&B €€

(☎03-248 15 39; www.bbantwerp.com; Justitiestraat 43; s/d/q €75/85/135; non-smoking @) In a 1910, belle-epoque-style townhouse near the vast Gerechtshof (former courthouse), BB&B has squeaky wooden floors, high ceilings, some old-fashioned furniture and a remarkable spaciousness for a B&B in this price range. Owners are assiduously keen to help. Get off trams 12 or 24 at the Gerechtshof with its verdigris statues of justice. A two-night minimum stay often applies.

Onze-Lieve-Vrouwekathedraal (p499), Antwerp, Belgium

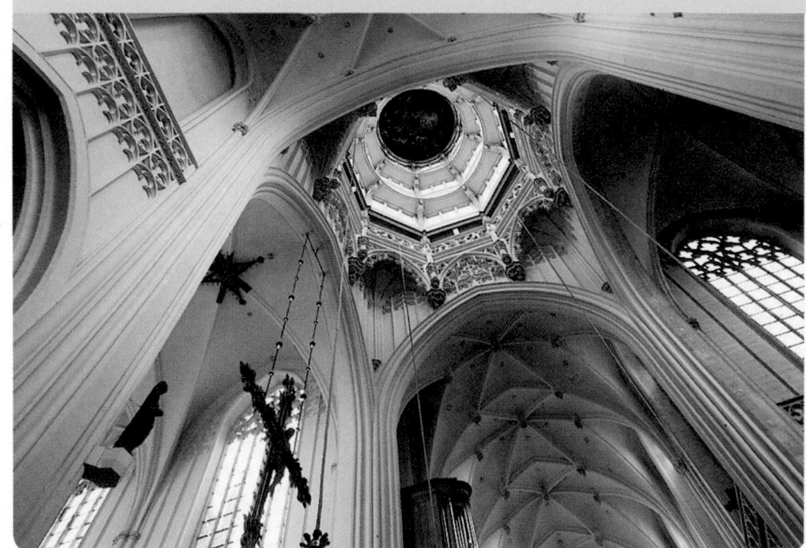

Hotel O Hotel **€€**
(☎03-500 89 50; www.hotelokathedral.com; Handschoenmarkt 3; €89-129) The immediate selling point here is an unbeatable location, opposite the cathedral. Behind an intriguing little foyer of 1950s radios, the all-black decor is relieved by midsized rooms with giant Rubens prints spilling over onto the ceilings. Note that there's a second Hotel O above Nero Brasserie in Het Zuid.

Eating

De Groote Witte Arend Belgian **€€**
(☎03-233 50 33; www.degrootewittearend.be; Reyndersstraat 18; mains €13-24; 10.30am-midnight, kitchen 11.30am-3pm & 5-10pm;) Retaining the Tuscan stone arcade of a 15th- and 17th-century convent building, this relaxed central gem combines the joys of a good beer bar with the satisfaction of well-cooked, sensibly priced Flemish home cuisine, notably *stoemp*, *stoofvlees/carbonnades* and huge portions of rabbit in rich Westmalle sauce.

Kathedraalcafe Belgian **€€**
(Torfbrug 10; mains €14-24.50, sandwiches €8.50; noon-11pm) This ivy-clad medieval masterpiece has an astounding interior decked with angels, saints, pulpits and several deliciously sacrilegious visual jokes. Good, if pricey, sandwiches supplement the mussels, vol-au-vents and other typical local favourites. Outside dining hours, or after 11pm, come for a beer.

Drinking & Nightlife

To sound like a local, stride into a pub and ask for a *bolleke*. Don't worry, that means a 'little bowl' (ie glass) of De Koninck, the city's favourite ale. Cheap places to try it include classic cafes **Oud Arsenaal** (Pijpelincxstraat 4; 10am-10pm Wed-Fri, 7.30am-7.30pm Sat & Sun), **De Kat** (Wolstraat 22) and the livelier **Pelikaan** (www.facebook.com/cafepelikaan; Melkmarkt 14; 8.30am-3am).

Den Bengel Pub
(www.cafedenengel.be; Grote Markt 5; 9am-2am) Sixteenth-century guildhall pub with fabulous cathedral views from the terrace.

Bierhuis Kulminator Pub
(Vleminckveld 32; 4pm-midnight Tue-Sat, from 8pm Mon) Classic beer pub boasting 700 mostly Belgian brews, including notably rare 'vintage' bottles laid down to mature for several years like fine wine.

Information

Tourism Antwerp (☎03-232 01 03; www.visitantwerpen.be; Grote Markt 13; 9am-5.45pm Mon-Sat, to 4.45pm Sun & holidays) is a central tourist office with a branch on level zero of Antwerpen-Centraal train station.

Getting There & Away

Train

Located 1.5km east of the historic centre, Antwerpen-Centraal Station (Diamant) is a veritable cathedral of a building, considered to be among the world's most handsome stations.

DESTINATION	FARE (€)	TIME (MIN)	FREQUENCY (PER HR)
Amsterdam	from 28	135/74	1
Bruges	14.80	75	2
Brussels	7.30	35-49	5
Ghent-Dampoort	9.40	46	3
Leuven	7.30	42-63	4
Lier	2.90	17	5
Mechelen-Nekkerspoel	3.90	15	2
Paris	110	138	9 daily

Getting Around

Franklin Rooseveltplaats and Koningin Astridplein are hubs for the integrated network of De Lijn buses and trams (some running underground metro-style).

GHENT

POP 248,200

Known as Gent in Dutch and Gand in French, Ghent is Flanders' unsung historic city. Like a grittier Bruges without the crush of tourists, it sports photogenic canals, medieval towers, great cafes and some of Belgium's most inspired museums.

Ghent Centre

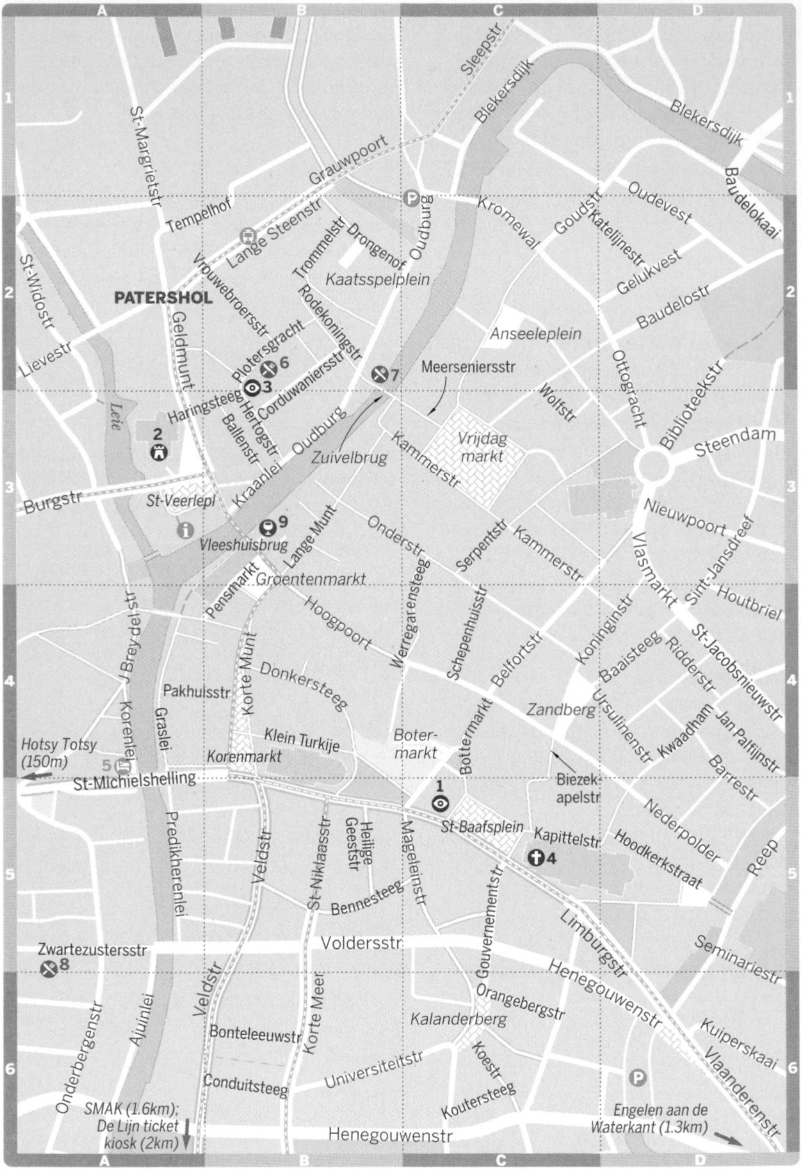

Sights

The main sights are strolling distance from Korenmarkt, the westernmost of three interlinked squares that form the heart of Ghent's historic core.

The good value **CityCard Gent** (www.visitgent.be; 2-/3-day ticket €30/35) provides three days' entrance to a number of sights and attractions (except for boat tours), and travel on all city transport. It's

Ghent Centre

Sights

1 Belfort ... C5
2 Gravensteen ... A3
3 Patershol ... B2
4 St-Baafskathedraal ... C5

Sleeping

5 Uppelink ... A4

Eating

6 Amadeus ... B2
7 Soup Lounge ... B2
8 't Oud Clooster ... A5

Drinking & Nightlife

9 Het Waterhuis aan de Bierkant ... B3

sold at museums, De Lijn booths and the tourist office.

St-Baafskathedraal Church

(www.sintbaafskathedraal.be; St-Baafsplein; 8.30am-6pm Apr-Oct, to 5pm Nov-Mar) St-Baafs cathedral's towering interior has some fine stained glass and an unusual combination of brick vaulting with stone tracery. A €0.20 leaflet guides you round the cathedral's numerous art treasures, including a big original Rubens opposite the stairway that leads down into the partly muralled crypts. However, most visitors come to see just one magnificent work – the Van Eycks' 1432 'Flemish Primitive' masterpiece, *The Adoration of the Mystic Lamb* (adult/child/audio guide €4/1.50/1).

Belfort Belfry

(Botermarkt; adult/concession €6/2; 10am-5.30pm) Ghent's soaring, Unesco-listed, 14th-century belfry is topped by a large dragon. That's a weathervane not a fire breather, and it's become something of a city mascot. You'll meet two previous dragon incarnations on the climb to the top (mostly by lift), but other than some bell-making exhibits the real attraction is the view. Enter through the **Lakenhalle**, Ghent's cloth hall that was left half-built in 1445 and only completed in 1903.

Gravensteen Castle

(www.gravensteengent.be; St-Veerleplein; adult/child €10/6; 10am-6pm Apr-Oct, 9am-5pm Nov-Mar) The counts of Flanders' quintessential 12th-century stone castle comes complete with moat, turrets and arrow slits. It's all the more remarkable considering that during the 19th century the site was converted into a cotton mill. Meticulously restored since, the interior sports the odd suit of armour, a guillotine and torture devices. The relative lack of furnishings is compensated with a hand-held 45-minute movie guide, which sets a tongue-in-cheek historical costumed drama in the rooms, prison pit and battlements.

Patershol Neighbourhood

(www.patershol.be) Dotted with half-hidden restaurants, enchanting Patershol is a web of twisting cobbled lanes whose old-world houses were once home to leather tradesmen and to the Carmelite Fathers (Paters), hence the name. An aimless wander here is one of the city's great pleasures.

SMAK Gallery

(Museum of Contemporary Art; www.smak.be; Citadelpark; adult/youth €12/2, 10am-1pm Sun free; 10am-6pm Tue-Sun; 5) Ghent's highly regarded Museum of Contemporary Art features regularly changing exhibitions of provocative, cutting-edge installations which (as in TRAK 2012) sometimes spill out right across the city.

 Sleeping

Websites www.gent-accommodations.be and www.bedandbreakfast-gent.be help you judge availability in the city's numerous appealing B&Bs.

Engelen aan de Waterkant B&B €€

(09-223 08 83; www.engelenaandewaterkant.be; Ter Platen 30; s/d €120/140) Two 'angel' rooms are an opportunity for the interior-designer owner to experiment and for guests to soak up the special atmosphere in a 1900 townhouse overlooking the tree-lined canal.

Uppelink Hostel €€

(09-279 44 77; www.hosteluppelink.com; Sint-Michielsplein 21; dm €27.50-37.50, s €52, tw €62) Within a classic step-gabled canalside

Right: Museum Plantin-Moretus (p499), Antwerp, Belgium;
Below: Brabo Fountain and Onze-Lieve-Vrouwekathedraal (p499), Antwerp, Belgium
(RIGHT) JOHN ELK/GETTY IMAGES ©; (BELOW) RELIGIOUS IMAGES/UIG/GETTY IMAGES ©

house, the show-stopping attraction at this super-central new hostel is the unbeatable view of Ghent's main towers as seen from the breakfast room and from the biggest, cheapest dorms. Smaller rooms have little view, if any.

Eating

't Oud Clooster Tavern €
(☎09-233 78 02; www.toudclooster.be; Zwartezusterstraat 5; mains €9-18; ⏰noon-2.30pm & 6-10.30pm Mon-Fri, noon-2.30pm & 5-10.30pm Sat, 5-10.30pm Sun) Mostly candlelit at night, this atmospheric double-level 'pratcafe' is built into sections of what was long ago a nunnery, hence the sprinkling of religious statues and cherub lamp-holders. Well-priced cafe food is presented with unexpected style and the kitchen is open until midnight. Try their original curry-cream *Spaghetti Oud Clooster* (€9).

Soup Lounge Soup €
(www.souplounge.be; Zuivelbrug 4; small/large soup €4/5, sandwiches 2.80; ⏰10am-6pm) At this bright, central retro-70s soup kitchen, each bowlful comes with add-your-own cheese and croutons, two rolls and a piece of fruit. Canal views are free.

Amadeus Ribs €
(☎09-225 13 85; www.amadeusspareribrestaurant.be; Plotersgracht 8/10; mains €13.75-18.75; ⏰6.30-11pm) All-you-can-eat spare ribs (€15.95) at four Ghent addresses, all within ancient buildings that are full of atmosphere, bustle and cheerful conversation.

Drinking & Nightlife

Hotsy Totsy Jazz Bar
(www.hotsytotsy.be; Hoogstraat 1; ⏰6pm-1am Mon-Fri, 8pm-2am Sat & Sun) A 1930s vamp pouts above the zinc of this classic artist's cafe with silver-floral wallpaper, black-and-white film photos and free live

jazz at 9pm most Thursdays (October to April). It was founded by the brothers of famous Flemish author Hugo Claus.

Het Waterhuis aan de Bierkant — Pub

(www.waterhuisaandebierkant.be; Groentenmarkt 12; ⌚11am-1am) Sharing an enticing waterfront terrace with the atmospherically austere *jenever* bar 't Dreupelkot (open from 4pm), this photogenic classic beer pub has an interior draped in dried hops and three exclusive house beers amid the wide possible selection.

Information

Ghent Tourist Office (☎09-266 56 60; www.visitgent.be; Oude Vismijn, St-Veerleplein 5; ⌚9.30am-6.30pm mid-Mar–mid-Oct, to 4.30pm mid-Oct–mid-Mar) Very helpful for free maps and accommodation bookings.

Getting There & Away

Train

Gent-Dampoort, 1km west of the old city, is the handiest station with useful trains to Antwerp (€9.40, fast/slow 42/64 minutes, three per hour), Bruges (€6.90, 36 minutes, hourly) and Kortrijk (€6.90, 35 minutes, hourly).

The main station, **Gent-St-Pieters** (2.5km south of centre), has more choice, including Brussels (€8.90, 36 minutes, twice hourly), Bruges (fast/slow 24/42 minutes, five per hour), Kortrijk (€6.60, fast/slow 26/33 minutes) and Ostend (€9.40, fast/slow 38/55 minutes).

Getting Around

Driving a car in Ghent is purgatory. Park it and walk or ride.

Bicycle

Max Mobiel (www.max-mobiel.be; Vokselslaan 27; per day/week/month €9/25/30) Two minutes' walk south of Gent-St-Pieters station. Branch kiosk at Gent-Dampoort station.

Bus & Tram

One-hour/all-day tickets cost €1.30/5 if purchased ahead of time from ticket machines or De Lijn offices beside **Gent-St-Pieters** (7am-1.30pm & 2-7pm Mon-Fri) or in the centre. Handy tram 1 runs from Gent-St-Pieters to and through the centre passing walkably close to most major sites.

BRUGES

POP 117,400

Cobblestone lanes, dreamy canals, soaring spires and whitewashed old almshouses combine to make central Bruges (Brugge in Dutch) one of Europe's most picture-perfect historic cities. The only problem is that everyone knows.

Sights

A **Bruges City Card** (www.bruggecitycard.be; 48/72hr €46/€49) gives entry to all the main city museums, plus private attractions including Choco-Story and De Halve Maan brewery. You'll also score a canal boat ride and discounts on bicycle rental, concerts, films and theatre.

Groeningemuseum Gallery

(www.brugge.be; Dijver 12; adult/concession €8/6; 9.30am-5pm Tue-Sun) Bruges' most celebrated art gallery has an astonishingly rich collection whose strengths are in superb Flemish Primitive and Renaissance works, depicting the conspicuous wealth of the city with glitteringly realistic artistry. In room 2 are meditative works including Jan Van Eyck's 1436 radiant masterpiece *Madonna with Canon George Van der Paele* (1436) and the *Madonna* by the Master of the Embroidered Foliage, where the rich fabric of the Madonna's robe meets the 'real' foliage at her feet with exquisite detail.

Markt Square

The heart of ancient Bruges, the old market square is lined with pavement cafes beneath step-gabled facades. The buildings aren't always quite as medieval as they look, but together they create a fabulous scene and even the neo-Gothic **post office** is architecturally magnificent. The scene is dominated by the **Belfort**, Belgium's most famous belfry whose iconic octagonal tower is arguably better appreciated from afar than by climbing 366 claustrophobic steps to the top.

Burg Square

Bruges' 1420 **Stadhuis** (City Hall; Burg 12) is smothered in statuettes and contains a breathtaking **Gotische Zaal** (Gothic Hall; Burg; adult/concession €4/3; 9.30am-5pm), featuring dazzling polychromatic ceilings, hanging vaults and historicist murals. Tickets include entry to part of the early baroque **Brugse Vrije** (Burg 11a; 9.30am-noon & 1.30-4.30pm) next door. With its gilt highlights and golden statuettes, this palace was once the administrative centre for a large autonomous territory ruled from Bruges between 1121 and 1794.

Historium Museum

(www.historium.be; Markt 1; adult/child €11/5.50; 10am-6pm) An 'immersive' one-hour audio and video tour, the lavish Historium aims to take you back to medieval Bruges: you can survey the old port or watch Van Eyck paint. It's a little light on facts so for many it will be a diversion from the real sights of the city, perhaps best for entertaining kids on a rainy day.

Begijnhof Begijnhof

(Wijngaardstraat; 6.30am-6.30pm) FREE Bruges' delightful *begijnhof* originally dates from the 13th century. Although the last *begijn* has long since passed away, today residents of the pretty, whitewashed garden complex include a convent of Benedictine nuns. Despite the hoards of summer tourists, the *begijnhof* remains a remarkably tranquil haven. In spring a carpet of daffodils adds to the quaintness of the scene. Outside the 1776 gateway bridge lies a tempting, if predictably tourist-priced, array of terraced restaurants, lace shops and waffle peddlers.

Brouwerij De Halve Maan Brewery

(050 33 26 97; www.halvemaan.be; Walplein 26; 10.30am-6pm, closed mid-Jan) Founded in 1856, this is the last family *brouwerij* (brewhouse) in central Bruges. Multi-

lingual **guided visits (tours €7.50; 11am-4pm, to 5pm Sat)**, lasting 45 minutes, depart on each hour. They include a tasting but can sometimes be rather crowded. Alternatively you can simply sip one of their excellent *Brugse Zot* (Bruges Fool, 7%) or *Straffe Hendrik* (Strong Henry, 9%) beers in the appealing brewery *café*.

 Sleeping

Although there are well over 250 hotels and B&Bs, accommodation can still prove oppressively overbooked from Easter to September, over Christmas and, especially, at weekends, when two-night minimum stays are commonly required.

't Keizershof Hotel **€**

(**050 33 87 28; www.hotelkeizershof.be; Oostermeers 126; s €35-47, d €47; P**) Remarkably tasteful and well kept for this price, the seven simple rooms with shared bathrooms are above a former brasserie-cafe decorated with old radios (now used as the breakfast room). Free parking.

Bauhaus Hostel **€**

(**050 34 10 93; www.bauhaus.be; Langestraat 145; hostel dm/tw €16/50, 2-4 person apt per weekend from €240; @**) One of Belgium's most popular hang-outs for young travellers, this virtual backpacker 'village' incorporates a bustling hostel, apartments, a nightclub, internet cafe and a little chill-out room that's well hidden behind the reception and laundrette section at Langestraat 145. Simple and slightly cramped dorms are operated with key cards; hotel-section double rooms have private shower cubicles; bike hire is also available. Take bus 6 or 16 from the train station.

B&B Dieltiens B&B **€€**

(**050 33 42 94; www.bedandbreakfastbruges.be; Waalsestraat 40; s €60-80, d €70-90, tr €90-100**) Old and new art fills this lovingly restored classical mansion, which remains an appealingly real home run by charming musician hosts. Superbly central yet quiet. They also operate a holiday flat nearby in a 17th-century house.

Baert B&B B&B **€€**

(**050 33 05 30; www.bedandbreakfastbrugge.be; Westmeers 28; s/d €80/90**) In a 1613 former stable this is one of very few places in Bruges where you'll get a private canalside terrace (flower-decked, though not on the loveliest canal section). Floral rooms have bathrooms across the landing; bathrobes are provided. A big breakfast spread is served in a glass verandah, and extras include a welcome drink and a pack of chocolates.

 Eating

Touristy terraces crowd the Markt and line pedestrianised St-Amandsstraat

Guild houses in Markt, Bruges, Belgium
LOUISE HEUSINKVELD/GETTY IMAGES ©

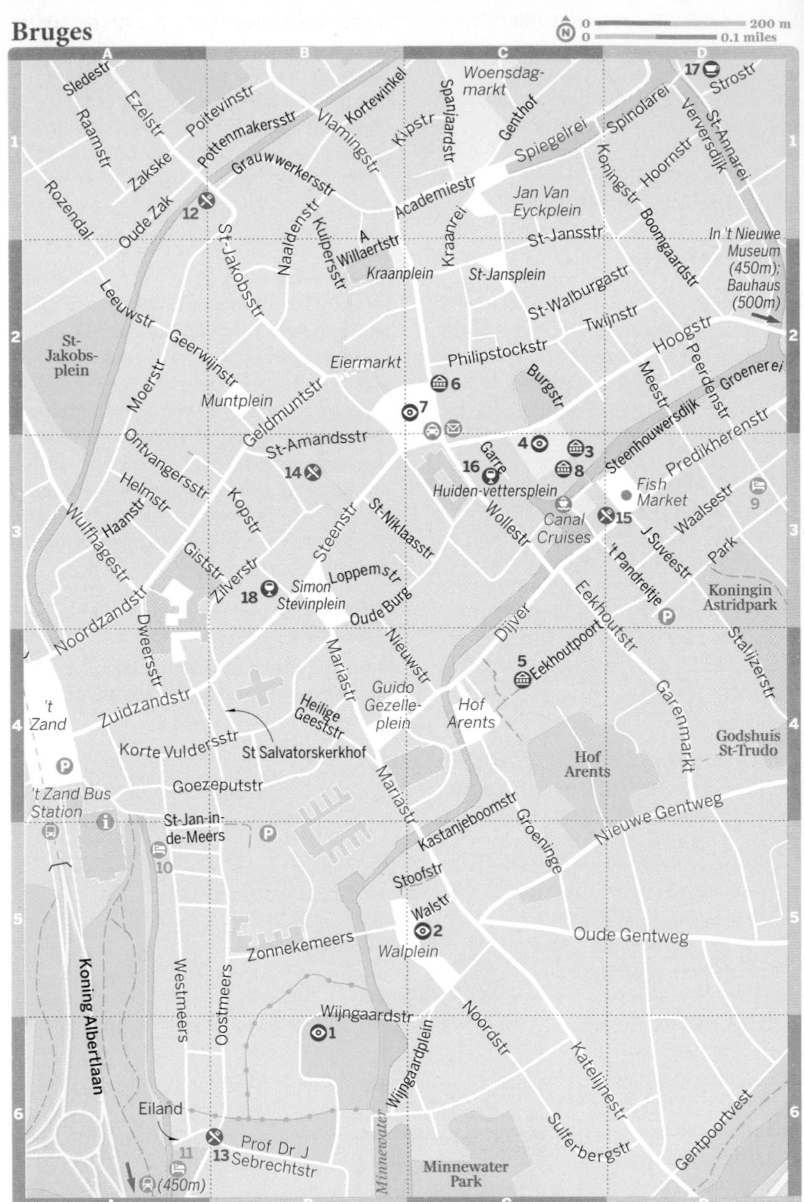

where there are many cheaper eateries. Along eclectic Langestraat (the eastward extension of Hoogstraat), you'll find everything from kebabs to Michelin stars.

Est Wijnbar Tapas **€**

(**050 33 38 39; www.wijnbarest.be; Braambergstraat 7; mains €9.50-12.50, tapas €3.50-9.50; 4pm-midnight Wed-Sun;**) This attractive little wine bar – the building dates back to 1637 – is an especially lively

Bruges

Sights

Sleeping

Eating

Drinking & Nightlife

spot on Sunday nights, when you can catch live jazz, blues and occasionally other musical styles from 8.30pm. It's also a pleasantly informal supper spot, with raclette, pasta, snacks and salads on the menu, and tasty desserts.

De Stove Gastronomic **€€**
(**☎050 33 78 35; www.restaurantdestove.be; Kleine St-Amandsstraat 4; mains €19-33, menu without/with wine €48/65; ⊙noon-1.30pm Sat & Sun, 7-9pm Fri-Tue)** Just 20 seats keep this gem intimate. Fish caught daily is the house speciality, but the monthly changing menu also includes the likes of wild boar fillet on oyster mushrooms. Everything, from the bread to the ice cream, is homemade. Despite perennially rave reviews, this calm, one-room, family restaurant remains friendly, reliable and inventive, without a hint of tourist-tweeness.

In 't Nieuwe Museum Brown Cafe **€€**
(**☎050 33 12 22; www.nieuw-museum.com; Hooistraat 42; mains €16-22; ⊙noon-2pm & 6-10pm Thu-Tue, closed lunch Sat)** So called because of the museumlike collection of brewery plaques, money boxes and other mementos of cafe life adorning the walls, this family-owned local favourite serves five kinds of *dagschotel* (dish of the day) for lunch (€7 to €12.50), and succulent meat cooked on a 17th-century open fire in the evenings.

De Bottelier Mediterranean **€€**
(**☎050 33 18 60; www.debottelier.com; St-Jakobsstraat 63; mains from €16; ⊙lunch & dinner Tue-Fri, dinner Sat)** Decorated with hats and old clocks, this adorable little restaurant sits above a wine shop overlooking a delightful handkerchief of canalside garden. Pasta/veg dishes cost from €9/13.50. Diners are predominantly local. Reservations are wise.

De Stoepa Bistro **€€**
(**☎050 33 04 54; www.stoepa.be; Oostmeers 124; ⊙noon-2pm & 6pm-midnight Tue-Sat, noon-3pm & 6-11pm Sun)** A gem of a place in a peaceful residential setting with a slightly hippy/Buddhist feel. Oriental statues, terracotta-coloured walls, a metal stove and wooden floors and furniture give a homey but stylish feel. Best of all though is the leafy terrace garden. Tuck into their upmarket bistro-style food.

Drinking & Nightlife

't Brugs Beertje Brown Cafe
(**www.brugsbeertje.be; Kemelstraat 5; ⊙4pm-midnight Mon, Thu & Sun, to 1am Fri & Sat)** Legendary throughout Bruges, Belgium and beyond for its hundreds of Belgian brews, this cosy *bruin café* is filled with old advertising posters and locals who are part of the furniture. It's one of those perfect beer-bars with smoke-yellowed walls, enamel signs, hop-sprig ceilings and knowledgeable staff to help you choose from a book full of brews.

Herberg Vlissinghe Cafe
(**☎050 34 37 37; www.cafevlissinghe.be; Blekerstraat 2; ⊙11am-10pm Wed & Thu, to midnight Fri & Sat, to 7pm Sun)** Luminaries have frequented Bruges' oldest pub since 1515; local legend has it that Rubens once painted an imitation coin on the table here and then did a runner. The interior is

gorgeously preserved with wood panelling and a wood-burning stove, but in summer the best seats are in the shady garden where you can play boules.

De Garre Pub
(050 34 10 29; www.degarre.be; Garre 1; noon-midnight Mon-Fri, to 1am Fri & Sat) Nowhere else on the planet serves the fabulous 11% Garre draught beer, which comes with a thick floral head in a glass that's almost a brandy balloon. But that's not all. This hidden two-floor *estaminet* (tavern) also stocks dozens of other fine Belgian brews including remarkable Struise Pannepot (€3.50).

Information

The **tourist office** (050 44 46 46; www.brugge.be; 't Zand 34; 10am-6pm Mon-Sun) is situated at street level of the Concertgebouw with a branch at the train station. Standard city maps cost €0.50, comprehensive guide pamphlets €2. Excellent *Use-It* guide-maps (www.use-it.be) are free.

Getting There & Away

Bruges' train station is about 1.5km south of the Markt, a lovely walk via the Begijnhof. It offers the following services:

Antwerp (€14.80, 75 minutes) Twice hourly

Brussels (€14.10, one hour) Twice hourly

Ghent (€6.50, fast/slow 24/42 minutes) Five hourly; two continue to more central Gent-Dampoort

Ypres (Ieper in Dutch) Take a train to Roeselare (€5, fast/slow 22/33 minutes), then bus 94 or 95: both buses pass key WWI sites en route.

Getting Around

Horse-Drawn Carriage

Up to five people per carriage (€44) on a well-trodden, 35-minute route from the Markt.

YPRES

Especially when viewed from the south-east, the Grote Markt of Ypres (Ieper in Dutch, pronounced 'eepr' in French and English) is one of the most breathtaking market squares in Flanders. It's all the more astonishing once you discover that virtually all of its convincingly 'medieval' buildings are in fact 20th-century copies. The originals were brutally bombarded into oblivion between 1914 and 1918 when the historic city failed to capitulate to German WWI advances. WWI battles in the surrounding poppy fields, known as the Ypres Salient, killed hundreds of thousands of soldiers. A century later, countless lovingly tended cemeteries remain, along with numerous widely spread WWI-based museums and trench remnants. Together they present a thoroughly moving introduction to the horrors and futility of war.

Sights

Central Ypres

Grote Markt Square
The brilliantly rebuilt **Lakenhallen**, a vast Gothic edifice originally serving as the 13th-century cloth market, dominates this very photogenic central square. It sports a 70m-high belfry, reminiscent of London's Big Ben, and hosts the gripping museum **In Flanders Fields** (www.inflandersfields.be; Lakenhalle, Grote Markt 34; adult/youths €9/4-5; 10am-6pm Apr–mid-Nov, to 5pm Tue-Sun mid-Nov–Mar), a multimedia WWI experience honouring ordinary people's experiences of wartime horrors. The ticket allows free entry to three other minor city museums.

Ypres Salient

Many Salient sites are awkward to reach without a car or tour bus. But the following are all within 600m of Ypres–Roeselare bus routes 94 and 95 (once or twice hourly on weekdays, five daily on weekends), so could be visited en route to or from Bruges.

Memorial Museum Passchendaele 1917 Museum
(www.passchendaele.be; Ieperstraat 5; admission €7.50; 10am-6pm Feb-Nov; 94) In central Zonnebeke village, **Kasteel Zonnebeke** (www.zonnebeke.be) is a lake-fronted Normandy chalet-style mansion built in 1922 to replace a castle bombarded into rubble

Detour: Moselle Valley

Welcome to wine country. Smothering the Moselle River's steeply rising banks are the neatly clipped vineyards that produce balanced rieslings, fruity rivaners and excellent crémants (sparkling *méthode traditionelle* wines). The region's various wine towns aren't architecturally memorable but **Ahn** and hillside **Wellenstein** are gently picturesque villages, while bigger **Remich** offers one-hour summer **river cruises** (www.navitours.lu; adult/child/dog €7/4/1). About 1.5km north of Remich's bus terminal (bus 175 from Luxembourg City), **St-Martin** (☎23 69 97 74; www.cavesstmartin.lu; 53 Route de Stadtbredimus; tour with one taster €5.20; ⏰10am, 1.30pm & 3pm Tue-Sun Apr-Oct) has wine caves that really are caves – cool, damp tunnels hewn deep into the rock face. To join its hour-long tours it's worth reserving. In contrast, bookings are unnecessary if you continue to the grand **Caves Bernard-Massard** (☎75 05 45 1; www.bernard-massard.lu; 8 Rue du Pont; tour adult/child from €7/4; ⏰9.30am-6pm Apr-Oct) in central **Grevenmacher** where frequent 20-minute **winery tours** (adult/child from €7/4) are multilingual, spiced with humour and culminate in a genteel sampling cafe. The Enner der Bréck bus stop outside is on bus routes 130 (to Rue Heine in Luxembourg City) and 450 to Remich.

Bicycles from **Rentabike Miselerland** (www.entente-moselle.lu/rentabike-miselerland; per day €10) can be picked up at Remich bus station and returned at Grevenmacker's Butterfly Garden (amongst various other points) allowing visits en route to Ehnen's **wine museum** (☎76 00 26; 115 Route du Vin; adult/child €3.50/1.50; ⏰9.30-11.30am & 2-5pm Tue-Sun Apr-Oct) and winery **Poll-Fabaire** (☎76 82 11; www.pollfabaire.lu; 115 Route du Vin; tours €4; ⏰tours 1pm-5.30pm, tasting room 10.30am-8pm May-Oct, 10.30am-6pm Nov-Apr).

during WWI. It now hosts a tourist office, cafe and particularly polished WWI museum charting local battle progressions with plenty of multilingual commentaries. The big attraction here is descending into its multiroom 'trench experience' with low-lit, wooden-clad subterranean bunk rooms and a soundtrack to add wartime atmosphere. Entirely indoors, explanations are much more helpful here than in 'real' trenches elsewhere.

Tyne Cot Cemetery
(⏰24hr, visitor centre 9am-6pm Feb-Nov; 🚌94)
FREE Probably the most visited Salient site, this is the world's biggest British Commonwealth war cemetery, with 11,956 graves. A huge semicircular wall commemorates another 34,857 lost-in-action soldiers whose names wouldn't fit on Ypres' Menin Gate. The name Tyne Cot was coined by Northumberland Fusiliers who fancied that German bunkers on the hillside here looked like Tyneside cottages. Two such dumpy concrete bunkers sit amid the graves, with a third partly visible through the metal wreath beneath the central white Cross of Sacrifice.

Deutscher Soldatenfriedhof Cemetery
FREE The area's main German WWI cemetery is smaller than Tyne Cot but arguably more memorable, amid oak trees and trios of squat, mossy crosses. Some 44,000 corpses were grouped together here, up to 10 per granite grave slab, and four eerie silhouette statues survey the site. Entering takes you through a black concrete 'tunnel' that clanks and hisses with distant war sounds, while four short video montages commemorate the

Damme

Historic, quaint but often tourist-jammed, the inland port-village of **Damme** (www.toerismedamme.be) makes a popular summer excursion by canal **paddle steamer** (adult/child one way €7.50/5.50, return €10/8; 10am-5pm Easter–mid-Oct), departing every two hours from Bruges' Noorweegse Kaai (bus 4 from Markt). Consider cycling instead: it's only 5km and, by continuing 2km further along the idyllic canal, you'll escape from the worst of the visitor overload. If you're still energetic, consider then heading 10km northwest via Dudzele and **Hof Ter Doest** (www.terdoest.be) to sweet little **Lissewege** (www.lissewege.be), an artists village from which hourly trains return to Bruges.

Quasimodo (050 37 04 70; www.quasimodo.be) visits most of these by minibus on its Triple Treat tours, adding castles at **Loppem** and **Tillegem** and fascinating **WWII coastal defences** near Ostend. The same company's Flanders Fields tours visit Ypres Salient.

tragedy of war. It's beyond the northern edge of Langemark on bus route 95.

Tours

There are dozens more WWI sites to seek out. Two bookshops towards Menin Gate sell a range of useful guidebooks and specialist publications and each offer guided minibus tours of selected war sites (advance booking suggested):

Over the Top Bookshop, Tours
(0472 34 87 47; www.overthetoptours.be; Meensestraat 41; tours €40; 9am-12.30pm, 1.30-5.30pm & 7.30-8.30pm) A WWI specialist bookshop towards the Menin Gate, offering twice-daily, half-day guided minibus tours of the Ypres Salient.

British Grenadier Bookshop, Tours
(057 21 46 57; www.salienttours.be; Meensestraat 5; short/long tour €30/38; 9.30am-1pm, 2-6pm & 7.30-8.30pm) Two Ypres tours – the 2½-hour option takes in Hill 60, the Caterpillar Crater and the German Bayernwald trench complex, while the standard four-hour tour covers every site on the Salient.

Getting There & Around

Train

Services run hourly to Ghent (€11.50, one hour) and Brussels (€17.50, 1¾ hours) via Kortrijk (€5.30, 30 minutes), where you could change for Bruges or Antwerp.

SURVIVAL GUIDE

Directory A–Z

Accommodation

The Netherlands

Always book accommodation ahead, especially during high season; note that many visitors choose to stay in Amsterdam even if travelling elsewhere. Many Dutch hotels have steep, perilous stairs but no lifts, although most top-end and some midrange hotels are exceptions.

Prices quoted here include private bathrooms unless otherwise stated and are high-season rates. Breakfast is not included unless specified.

€ less than €80

€€ €80 to €160

€€€ more than €160

Belgium

Tourist offices are superb sources of accommodation assistance, usually free.

B&Bs Rooms rented in local homes *(gastenkamers/chambres d'hôtes)* can be cheap and cheerful but some offer standards equivalent to a boutique hotel (up to €160 double). Discounts of around €10 per room are common if you stay at least a second night.

Holiday houses *(gîtes)* Are easily rented in Wallonia (www.gitesdewallonie.be), but minimum stays apply and there's a hefty 'cleaning fee' on top of quoted rates.

Short term apartments Bookable through sites including www.airbnb.com and www.wimdu.com.

Hostels Typically charge €22 to €28 for dormitory beds, somewhat less in Bruges. HI hostels (*jeugdherbergen* in Dutch, *auberges de jeunesse* in French) affiliated with Hostelling International (www.hihostels.com), charge €3 less for members, and some take off €2 for under-26-year-olds. Prices usually include sheets and a basic breakfast. Always read the conditions.

Our sleeping reviews refer to double rooms with a private bathroom, except in hostels or where otherwise specified.

€ less than €60; expect shared bathrooms and only basic facilities.

€€ €60 to €140; good B&B or relatively functional hotel.

€€€ more than €140; note that top-end business establishments in Brussels often cut prices radically at weekends and in summer.

Business Hours

The Netherlands

Opening hours given in the text are for high season. Many tourism-based businesses reduce their hours off season.

Banks 9am to 3.30pm Monday to Friday, Saturday mornings too in Luxembourg

Brasseries 11am to midnight

Clubs 11pm to 6am Friday to Sunday

Pubs & cafes till 1am or later

Restaurants 11.30am to 2.30pm & 6.30 to 10.30pm

Shops 10am to 6pm Monday to Saturday, some close for lunch. Limited opening Sunday in Belgium.

Supermarkets 9am-8pm Monday to Saturday, some open Sundays.

Belgium

Banks & government offices 9.30am-4pm Mon-Fri

Bars & cafes 11am-1am

Clubs Mostly 10pm-4am

Museums Most closed Monday

Post offices 9am-6pm Mon-Fri

Restaurants 10am-10pm or 11am-10pm, with a 3-6pm break

Shops Noon-6pm Mon, 9am-6pm Tue-Sat (also Sun in large cities), to 9pm Thu; supermarkets to 8pm

Food

The Netherlands

Price ranges for average main courses are as follows:

€ less than €15

€€ €15 to €25

€€€ more than €25

Belgium

The following price categories are for the cost of a main course.

€ less than €12

€€ €12 to €25

€€€ more than €25

Legal Matters

Drugs are actually illegal in the Netherlands. Possession of soft drugs up to 5g is tolerated but larger amounts can get you jailed. Hard drugs are treated as a serious crime.

Smoking is banned in all public places, including most bars (except for tiny family-run pubs). In a uniquely Dutch solution, you can still smoke pot in coffee shops as long as there's no tobacco mixed in.

Money

The Netherlands

Credit Cards All major international credit cards are recognised in the Netherlands, and you will find most hotels, restaurants and sights will accept them (although not the Dutch railway).

ATMs Can be found outside banks and at train stations.

Tipping Not essential as restaurants, hotels, bars etc all include a service charge.

Belgium

Banks usually offer better exchange rates than **exchange bureaux** (*wisselkantoren* in Dutch, *bureaux de change* in French), though often only for their banking clients, especially in Luxembourg.

ATMs Widespread, but often hidden within bank buildings.

Tipping Not expected in restaurants or cabs: service and VAT are always included.

Public Holidays

The Netherlands

Nieuwjaarsdag New Year's Day

Goede Vrijdag Good Friday

Eerste Paasdag Easter Sunday

Tweede Paasdag Easter Monday

Koningsdag (King's Day) 30 April

Bevrijdingsdag (Liberation Day) 5 May

Hemelvaartsdag Ascension Day

Eerste Pinksterdag Whit Sunday (Pentecost)

Tweede Pinksterdag Whit Monday

Eerste Kerstdag (Christmas Day) 25 December

Tweede Kerstdag (Boxing Day) 26 December

Belgium

School holidays are July and August (slightly later in Luxembourg), one week in early November; two weeks at Christmas; one week around Carnival; two weeks at Easter; one week in May (Ascension).

Public holidays are as follows:

New Year's Day 1 January

Easter Monday March/April

Labour Day 1 May

Ascension Day Fortieth day after Easter

Whit Monday Seventh Monday after Easter

National Day (Luxembourg) 23 June

Flemish Community Festival 11 July (Flanders only)

National Day (Belgium) 21 July

Assumption 15 August

Francophone Community Festival 27 September (Wallonia only)

All Saints' Day 1 November

Armistice Day 11 November

German-Speaking Community Festival 15 November (eastern cantons only)

Christmas Day 25 December

Telephone

The Netherlands

Most public phones will accept credit cards as well as various phonecards.

Country code ☎31

Collect call (gesprek) domestic ☎0800 01 01; international ☎0800 04 10

International access code ☎00

International directory inquiries ☎0900 84 18

National directory inquiries ☎1888

Operator assistance ☎0800 04 10

Belgium

Dial full numbers: there's no optional area code.

International operator Belgium/Luxembourg ☎1324/12410

Directory Enquiries Belgium www.whitepages.be, Luxembourg www.editus.lu/ed/en

Visas

Schengen visa rules apply. Embassies are listed at www.diplomatie.belgium.be/en and www.mae.lu.

Getting There & Away

Air

The Netherlands

Huge **Schiphol Airport** (6am-10pm) is the Netherlands' main international airport. **Rotterdam Airport** (RTM; www.rotterdamthehagueairport.nl) and **Eindhoven Airport** (EIN; www.eindhovenairport.nl) are small.

Belgium

Antwerp airport (www.antwerpairport.be) is tiny with just a few flights to the UK on CityJet (www.cityjet.com).

Brussels airport (BRU; www.brusselsairport.be) is Belgium's main long-haul gateway. Domestic airline Brussels Airlines (www.brusselsairlines.com)

flies from here to numerous European and African destinations. Brussels is also a European hub for Chinese airline Hainan Airlines (www.hainanairlines.com), Gulf-based Etihad (www.etihad.com) and Qatar Airways (www.qatarairways.com), and Indian airline Jet Airways (www.jetairways.com), with useful connections to North America and throughout Asia.

Budget airlines **Ryanair (www.ryanair.com)** and WizzAir use the misleadingly named **Brussels-South Charleroi Airport (CRL; ☎07 125 12 11; www.charleroi-airport.com)**, which is actually 55km south of Brussels, 6km north of the ragged, post-industrial city of Charleroi.

Train

The Netherlands

The Netherlands has good train links to Germany, Belgium and France. All Eurail, Inter-Rail, Europass and Flexipass tickets are valid on the Dutch national train service, **Nederlandse Spoorwegen (Netherlands Railway; NS; www.ns.nl)**. Many international services, including those on the high-speed line to Belgium, are operated under the NS International (www.nsinternational.nl). In addition, **Thalys (www.thalys.com)** fast trains serve Brussels (where you can connect to Eurostar) and Paris.

The high-speed line from Amsterdam (via Schiphol and Rotterdam) speeds travel times to Antwerp (70 minutes), Brussels (two hours) and Paris (3¼ hours).

German ICE high-speed trains run six times a day between Amsterdam and Cologne (2½ hours) via Utrecht. Many continue on to Frankfurt (four hours) via Frankfurt Airport.

Belgium

For comprehensive timetables and international bookings, see www.belgianrail.be or www.cfl.lu.

International high-speed trains have compulsory pre-booking requirements and charge radically different prices according to availability, so advance booking can save a packet.

Thalys (www.thalys.com) operates on the following routes:

Brussels Midi–Liege–Aachen–Cologne 2¾ hours, 5 daily

Brussels Midi–Paris-Nord 82 minutes, 12 daily

Brussels Midi–Antwerp–Rotterdam–Schiphol–Amsterdam 109 minutes

SNCB (www.b-europe.com) runs trains from both Brussels Midi and Brussels Central to Amsterdam (€25 to €54, two hours) 10 times daily via Antwerp, Rotterdam and Schiphol.

Eurostar (www.eurostar.com) runs Brussels Midi–Lille–London St Pancras (two hours) up to 10 times daily.

Bottling machine at Brouwerij De Halve Maan brewery (p506), Bruges, Belgium

Deutsche Bahn (www.deutschebahn.com) runs Brussels Midi–Liège–Aachen–Frankfurt (3¼ hours, three daily) via Cologne (2¼ hours) and Frankfurt airport (three hours).

TGV (www.sncf.com) runs Bruxelles Midi–Paris CDG Airport-Marne-la-Vallée (for Eurodisney, 1¾ hours) continuing to various southern French cities. TGVs from Brussels don't stop in central Paris, but those from Luxembourg reach Paris–Est in 2¼ hours.

Sea

The Netherlands

There are several companies operating car/passenger ferries between the Netherlands and the UK, including the following:

DFDS Seaways (www.dfdsseaways.co.uk) DFDS Seaways has overnight sailings (15 hours) between Newcastle and IJmuiden, 30km northwest of Amsterdam, linked to Amsterdam by bus (one-way €6, 40 minutes).

P&O Ferries (www.poferries.com) P&O Ferries operates an overnight ferry every evening (11¾ hours) between Hull and Europoort, 39km west of central Rotterdam. Book bus tickets (€10, 40 minutes) to/from the city when you reserve your berth.

Stena Line (www.stenaline.co.uk) Stena Line has overnight crossings between Harwich and Hoek van Holland, 31km northwest of Rotterdam, linked to central Rotterdam by train (€5.50, 30 minutes).

Belgium

Most UK-bound motorists drive a couple of hours west to Calais in France. However there is a direct option from Zeebrugge in Belgium to Hull:

P&O (www.poferries.com) Fourteen-hour overnight service costs from UK£121 one-way for pedestrians. A very useful connecting bus to/from Bruges train station can be prebooked through P&O.

Getting Around

Bicycle

The Netherlands

The Netherlands has more than 20,000km of dedicated bike paths (*fietspaden*), which makes it the most bike-friendly place on the planet. You can criss-cross the country on the motorways of cycling: the LF routes. Standing for *landelijke fietsroutes* (long-distance routes), but virtually always simply called LF, there are more than 25 routes comprising close to 7000km.

Grote Markt (p499), Antwerp, Belgium

Independent rental shops are available in abundance. Many day trippers avail themselves of the train-station bicycle shops, called **Rijwiel shops** (www.ov-fiets.nl), which are found in more than 100 stations. Operating long hours (6am to midnight is common), the shops hire out bikes from €3 to €12 per day, with discounts by the week. You'll have to show an ID and leave a deposit (usually €25 to €100).

You may bring your bicycle onto any train as long as there is room; a day pass is required for bicycles (*dagkaart fiets*; €6).

Belgium

Cycling is a great way to get around in flat Flanders, less so in chaotic Brussels or undulating Wallonia. The Belgian countryside is riddled with cycling routes and most tourist offices sell helpful regional cycling maps.

In Belgium it costs €5 one-way (or €8 all day) on top of the rail fare to take bikes on the train. A few busy city-centre train stations don't allow bicycle transportation.

Bike hire is available in or near most major train stations. Short hop hire schemes are available in Brussels, Antwerp and Namur.

Car & Motorcycle

The Netherlands

- You'll need the vehicle's registration papers, third-party insurance and an international driver's permit plus your domestic licence.
- Traffic travels on the right and the minimum driving age is 18 for vehicles and 16 for motorcycles. Seat belts are required and children under 12 must ride in the back if there's room.
- Speed limits are 50km/h in built-up areas, 80km/h in the country, 100km/h on major through-roads, and 120km/h on freeways (sometimes 100km/h, clearly indicated).
- Outside Amsterdam, car-hire companies can be in inconvenient locations if you're arriving by train. You must be at least 23 years of age to hire a car in the Netherlands.

Belgium

- Speed limits are 50km/h in most towns (30km/h near schools), 70km/h to 90km/h on inter-town roads, and 120/130km/h on motorways in Belgium/Luxembourg.
- The maximum legal blood alcohol limit is 0.05%.
- Car hire is available at airports and major train stations, but is usually cheaper from city centre offices.
- A driving licence from your home country will usually suffice for foreign drivers.
- Priorité à droite – give way to the right.

Train

The Netherlands

The train network is run by **NS** (Nederlandse Spoorwegen; www.ns.nl). Several ticket types are available:

Enkele reis One way; you can break your journey along the direct route.

Dagretour Day return; 10% to 15% cheaper than two one-way tickets.

Weekendretour Weekend return; costs the same as a normal return and is valid from 7pm Friday to 4am Monday.

Dagkaart Day pass; allows unlimited train travel throughout the country. Only good value if you're planning to spend the day on the train.

Keep in mind that:

- Only some ticket machines accept cash, and those are coins-only, so you need a pocketful of change.
- Ticket windows do not accept credit or ATM cards, although they will accept paper euros. Lines are often quite long and there is a surcharge for the often-unavoidable need to use a ticket window.
- Discounted tickets for Hispeed and Fyra trains sold on the web require a Dutch credit card. The cheap fares can't be bought at ticket windows.

Belgium

NMBS/SNCB trains are completely non-smoking. Special fare categories include the following:

Children After 9am, kids under 12 travel for free if accompanied by an adult.

Seniors People over 65 pay only €5 for a return 2nd-class trip anywhere in Belgium (some exclusions apply).

B-Excursions Good-value one-day excursion fares including return rail ticket plus selected entry fees.

Go Pass/Rail Pass Ten one-way 2nd-class trips to anywhere in Belgium (except frontier points) cost €50/76 for people under/over 26 years.

Weekend Return Tickets Valid from 7pm Friday to Sunday night, for just 20% more than a single.

Germany

Prepare for a roller coaster of feasts, treats and temptations.

Germany offers soul-stirring scenery, spirit-lifting culture, old and bold architecture, big-city beauties, romantic castles and half-timbered towns. Few countries have had as much impact on the world as Germany, which has given us the printing press, the automobile, aspirin and MP3 technology. This is the birthplace of Martin Luther, Albert Einstein and Karl Marx, of Bach, Beethoven, the Brothers Grimm and other heavyweights who, each in their own way, have left their mark on human history.

If anything, though, Germany's story-book landscapes will likely leave an even bigger imprint on your memories. There's simply something undeniably artistic in the way the scenery unfolds from the windswept maritime north to the off-the-charts splendour of the Alps. As much fun as it may be to rev up the engines on the autobahn, do slow down to fully appreciate this complex and fascinating country.

Reichstag (p529), Berlin
RAIMUND KOCH/GETTY IMAGES ©

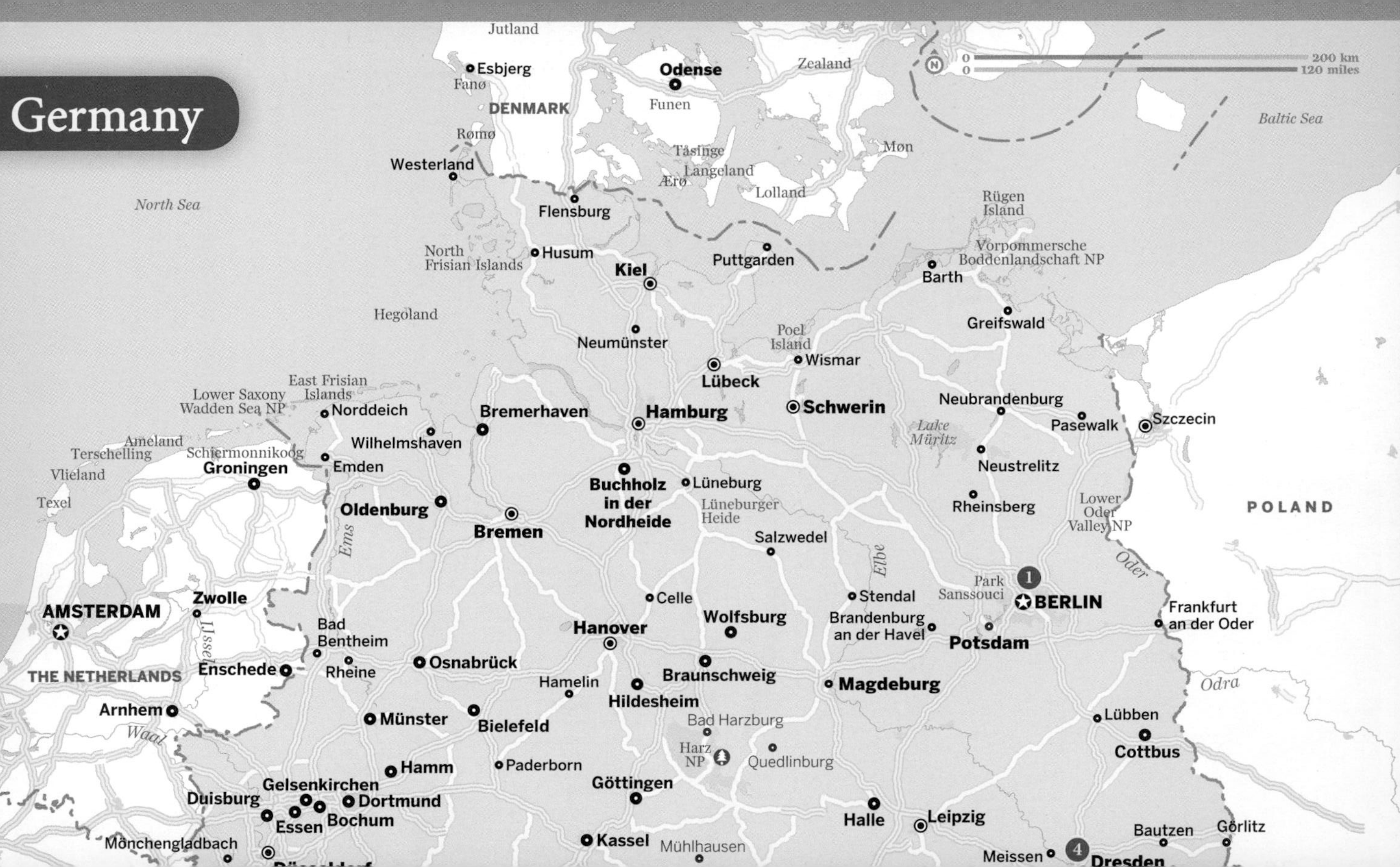

Germany
0 200 km
0 120 miles
Baltic Sea
North Sea
Jutland
Esbjerg
Fanø
DENMARK
Rømø
Westerland
Odense
Funen
Zealand
Tåsinge
Langeland
Ærø
Lolland
Møn
Flensburg
North Frisian Islands
Husum
Kiel
Puttgarden
Rügen Island
Vorpommersche Boddenlandschaft NP
Barth
Greifswald
Hegoland
Neumünster
Poel Island
Wismar
Lübeck
East Frisian Islands
Lower Saxony Wadden Sea NP
Norddeich
Bremerhaven
Hamburg
Schwerin
Neubrandenburg
Pasewalk
Szczecin
Lake Müritz
Neustrelitz
Ameland
Terschelling
Schiermonnikoog
Vlieland
Texel
Groningen
Wilhelmshaven
Emden
Buchholz in der Nordheide
Lüneburg
Lüneburger Heide
Oldenburg
Bremen
Rheinsberg
Lower Oder Valley NP
POLAND
Ems
Salzwedel
Elbe
Oder
Park Sanssouci
BERLIN
Stendal
Frankfurt an der Oder
AMSTERDAM
Zwolle
IJssel
Bad Bentheim
Celle
Wolfsburg
Brandenburg an der Havel
Hanover
Potsdam
THE NETHERLANDS
Enschede
Rheine
Osnabrück
Braunschweig
Magdeburg
Hamelin
Hildesheim
Odra
Arnhem
Münster
Bielefeld
Bad Harzburg
Lübben
Waal
Harz NP
Quedlinburg
Cottbus
Hamm
Paderborn
Gelsenkirchen
Göttingen
Duisburg
Dortmund
Essen
Bochum
Halle
Leipzig
Bautzen
Görlitz
Mönchengladbach
Kassel
Mühlhausen
Meissen
Dresden

1 Cold War Berlin
2 Munich Resicenz
3 Schloss Neuschwanstein
4 Dresden's Grünes Gewölbe
5 Kölner Dom
BELGIUM
Aachen
Bonn
Siegen
Marburg
Gotha
Weimar
Gera
Chemnitz
Zwickau
Saalfeld
Suhl
Giessen
Fulda
Plauen
Hof
Coburg
Meuse
Naturpark
Hohes
Venn-Eifel
Koblenz
Frankfurt-am-Main
Offenbach
Wiesbaden
Mainz
Cochem
Moselle
Bitburg
Bacharach
Aschaffenburg
Schweinfurt
Marktredwitz
PRAGUE
CZECH REPUBLIC
LUXEMBOURG
Gutland
Trier
Darmstadt
Würzburg
Bamberg
Bayreuth
Main
Erlangen
Worms
Ludwigshafen
Mannheim
Heidelberg
Kaiserslautern
Speyer
Rothenburg ob der Tauber
Nuremberg
Schwandorf
Saarbrücken
Heilbronn
Karlsruhe
Pforzheim
Stuttgart
Baden-Baden
Nördlingen
Altmühltal Nature Park
Ingolstadt
Regensburg
Landshut
FRANCE
Nancy
Strasbourg
Offenburg
Tübingen
Danube
Ulm
Augsburg
Dachau
Munich
Freiburg im Breisgau
Memmingen
Lake Starnberg
Rosenheim
Chiemsee
Berchtesgaden
Singen
Meersburg
Kempten
Oberammergau
Inn
Konstanz
Lindau
Füssen
Mittenwald
Kufstein
Berchtesgaden NP
AUSTRIA
Basel
Lake Constance
Oberstdorf
Salzach
Zürich
Besançon
Innsbruck
Graz
VADUZ
Bressanone
Klagenfurt
Wörthersee
SWITZERLAND
ITALY
SLOVENIA

Germany Highlights

Cold War Berlin

Few events in history have the power to move the entire world. The Kennedy assassination; the moon landing; 9/11. And, of course, the fall of the Berlin Wall in 1989. If you were alive back then you will remember the crowds cheering and dancing at the Brandenburger Tor (Brandenburg Gate). Although little is left of the physical barrier, it lives on in the imagination and in such places as Checkpoint Charlie (p529), the Gedenkstätte Berliner Mauer and the East Side Gallery.

1

2 Munich Residenz

Vast, sprawling and impressive, the Munich Residenz (p554), is a suitably gran palace that reflects the splendour and power of the Wittelsbach clan, the Bavarian rulers who lived here from 1385 to 1918. Badly bombed in WWII, it was meticulously restored and is again a sparkling repository of fine art, furnitu and architectural detail.

PIOTR JACZEWSKI/GETTY IMAGES ©

3 Schloss Neuschwanstein

Commissioned by Bavaria's most celebrated (and loopiest) 19th-century monarch, Ludwig II, the chambers and halls of Neuschwanstein Castle (p561) reflect the king's obsession with the mythical Teutonic past and his admiration of the composer Richard Wagner. This sugary folly is said to have inspired Walt's castle at Disney World; now it inspires tourist masses to make the pilgrimage along the Romantic Road, which culminates at its gates.

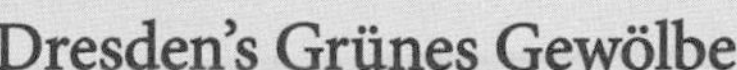

ALLAN BAXTER/GETTY IMAGES ©

4 Dresden's Grünes Gewölbe

WWII bombs reduced Germany's 'Florence on the Elbe' into a smouldering pile of bricks, but Dresden is a survivor. A star among many reconstructed baroque jewels is the royal Residenz, home to the Grünes Gewölbe (p547), one of the world's richest treasure chests, spilling over with fanciful objects crafted from gold, silver, gems, ivory and other precious materials.

5 Kölner Dom

At unexpected moments you see it: Cologne's cathedral (p578), the twin-towered icon of the city towering over an urban vista, dominating the view up a road. And why shouldn't it? This perfectly formed testament to faith and conviction was started in 1248 and consecrated a 'mere' six centuries later. Ponder the passage of time as you sit in its cavernous, stained-glass-lit interior.

Germany's Best...

Cold War & WWII Sites

- **Checkpoint Charlie** (p529) This infamous checkpoint between East and West Berlin was once a symbol of divided Germany.
- **Dokumentationszentrum Reichsparteitagsgelände** (p566) This fascinating exhibit delves into the Nazi regime on the site where the mass rallies were held.
- **Dachau** (p558) Pay your respects at this chilling concentration camp.
- **Eagle's Nest** (p558) Savour the gorgeous scenery of Berchtesgaden from Hitler's mountain-top retreat.

Relaxation Spots

- **Park Sanssouci** (p544) Explore the stately palaces and gardens of this landscaped Potsdam park.
- **Tiergarten** (p533) Kick back with the locals in Berlin's idyllic city park.
- **Baden-Baden** (p570) Lose your inhibitions and bathe like a German – in the nude.
- **Berchtesgaden** (p558) Enjoy the sublime scenery of jagged Alps and a crystalline lake.
- **The Rhine** (p569) Take a soothing cruise along this great river.

Historic Buildings

- **Reichstag** (p529) This landmark Berlin building was built to house the German parliament.
- **Kölner Dom** (p578) Germany's most celebrated church: a masterpiece of Gothic grandeur.
- **Residenz, Munich** (p554) Bavarian rulers lived in this vast palace for over six centuries.
- **Frauenkirche** (p546) Completely rebuilt, this Dresden landmark baroque church still exudes the gravitas of age.

Places for a Drink

- **Beer gardens, Munich** (p557) There's nowhere better to sink a few German brews than Munich's Englischer Garten.
- **Bars of Kreuzberg** (p541) Drink and dance till dawn in Berlin's hippest quarter.
- **Bars in Hamburg** (p583) Fun libation stations and live music clubs abound in the St Pauli district.
- **Moselle Valley** (p571) Take a tipple in one Germany's most celebrated wine regions.

eft: Lion statues in Berlin's Tiergarten (p533)
Above: Beer garden, Munich (p557)

Need to Know

ADVANCE PLANNING

- **As early as possible** In summer book accommodation early, especially in popular spots such as the Black Forest, Moselle and Rhine Valleys and Bavarian Alps.
- **One month before** Arrange hotel accommodation and car hire.
- **Two weeks before** Book city tours in Berlin, Munich and other cities, and plan train journeys using Deutsche Bahn (www.bahn.de).

RESOURCES

- **German National Tourist Office** (www.germany-tourism.de) The official site for the German National Tourist Board.
- **Facts about Germany** (www.tatsachen-ueber-deutschland.de) Full of fascinating facts about the German nation.
- **Online German Course** (www.deutsch-lernen.com) Brush up your Deutsch before you go.

GETTING AROUND

- **Air** Germany is well served by major airlines, but budget carriers often use small regional airports. Frankfurt and Munich are the main hubs.
- **Car** Germany's road system is fast and efficient; autobahns (motorways) are fastest, but regional roads are much more pleasant. Traffic can be a problem on summer weekends and around holidays.
- **Train** Germany's rail system, mostly operated by Deutsche Bahn, is one of the best in Europe. Trains are frequent, fast and very comfortable.
- **Bus** Buses are much less comfortable and efficient than trains, but are often the only option for rural towns and villages.

BE FOREWARNED

- **Autobahns** Unless otherwise indicated, there is no official speed limit on German motorways.
- **Accommodation** Can be hard to come by in peak seasons such as Oktoberfest and the Christmas markets.

Germany Itineraries

From sophisticated cities to snowy mountains, Germany offers a smorgasbord of contrasting experiences. It's a place where old and new worlds collide; the real trick is finding enough time to see it all in one trip.

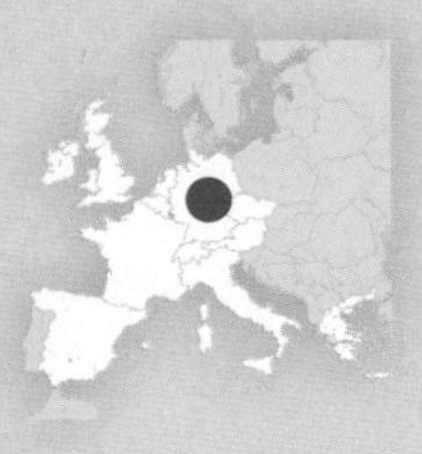

3 DAYS

BERLIN & BEYOND

Berlin to Dresden

Since the Berlin Wall came down a little over a quarter century ago, ❶ **Berlin** (p528) has evolved into one of Europe's most exciting cosmopolitan cauldrons that deep down maintains the unpretentious charm of a global village. Spend one day sampling its blockbuster sights – like the Reichstag, the Brandenburger Tor (Brandenburg Gate), Checkpoint Charlie and the East Side Gallery – then the next day plunge in and discover what makes the city truly tick by wandering the streets of a neighbourhood or two (the Scheunenviertel and Kreuzberg are recommended), popping into cafes, indie boutiques and galleries. After dark, Berlin kicks into high gear with nightlife that is as diverse as it is unbridled. Bring stamina!

On day three, travel south to ❷ **Dresden** (p546), a city effectively wiped off the map during WWII. Thankfully, the city's baroque centre has been rebuilt in elegant style with the crowning glory being the resurrection of the landmark cathedral, the Frauenkirche. For more local flavour, cross the Elbe River to explore the Neustadt's latest bars and restaurants.

Top Left: Frauenkirche (p546), Dresden;
Top Right: Schloss Nymphenburg (p555), Munich

5 DAYS

A BAVARIAN ADVENTURE

Munich to Würzburg

Start this trip in ❶ **Munich** (p551), an ideal launch pad for a foray around Bavaria, Germany's largest, most scenic and sight-packed region. Budget half a day exploring the city's historic centre and refuelling on regional gourmet fare at the Viktualienmarkt before marvelling at the treasures filling the vast Residenz (royal residence) and wrapping up the day in a boisterous beer hall or leafy beer garden.

Point your compass south next to breathe the fresh mountain air of the Bavarian Alps, a dream destination for hikers, skiers and other outdoorsy types. History buffs especially should have ❷ **Berchtesgaden** (p558) on their radar; its idyllic setting was tainted in the 1930s when Hitler established a second seat of Nazi power here.

A key sight for royal groupies is 'Mad' King Ludwig's fantasy palace of ❸ **Neuschwanstein** (p561) in Füssen, a small town that also marks the beginning of the Romantic Road, one of Germany's most popular themed holiday routes. On its gentle 400km meander north it passes through such medieval gems as ❹ **Rothenburg ob der Tauber** (p560) before culminating in ❺ **Würzburg** (p563), famous for its fine wine and dazzling baroque palace. From here, Frankfurt is only an hour's ride away.

Discover Germany

At a Glance

- **Berlin** (p528) Germany's historic and happening capital city.
- **Munich** (p551) So much more than beer halls, oompah bands and lederhosen.
- **Rhine & Moselle** (p569) All-star waterways flanked by steep vineyards, medieval castles and half-timbered villages.
- **Romantic Road** (p560) Idyllic route that culminates in fairy-tale Schloss Neuschwanstein.
- **Dresden** (p546) 'Come-back-city' with stunning baroque treasures and a lively pub quarter.

Brandenburger Tor, Berlin

BERLIN

030 / POP 3.5 MILLION

There's just no escaping history in Berlin. You might be distracted by the trendy, edgy, gentrified streets, by the bars bleeding a laid-back cool factor, by the galleries sprouting talent and pushing the envelope, but make no mistake – reminders of the German capital's past assault you while modernity sits around the corner. Norman Foster's Reichstag dome, Peter Eisenman's Holocaust Memorial and the iconic Brandenburger Tor (Brandenburg Gate) are all contained within a few neighbouring blocks. Potsdamer Platz and its shiny Sony Center hosts Berlin's star-studded film festival each year, on the very site where only 25 years ago you could climb up a viewing platform in the West and peer over the Berlin Wall for a glimpse behind the Iron Curtain.

Renowned for its diversity and its tolerance, its alternative culture and its night-owl stamina, the best thing about Berlin is the way it reinvents itself and isn't shackled by its mind-numbing history.

Sights

Key sights like the Reichstag, Brandenburger Tor, Checkpoint Charlie and Museumsinsel cluster in the historic city centre – Mitte – which is also home to a mazelike hipster quarter around Hackescher Markt. North of here, residential Prenzlauer Berg has a lively cafe and restaurant scene, while to the south loom the contemporary high-rises of Potsdamer Platz. Further south, gritty but cool Kreuzberg is party central, as is student-flavoured Friedrichshain east across the Spree River and home to the East Side

Gallery stretch of the Berlin Wall. Western Berlin's hub is Charlottenburg, with great shopping and a famous royal palace.

REICHSTAG & UNTER DEN LINDEN

Linking the government quarter with Museuminsel, Unter den Linden is eastern Berlin's grand boulevard and is lined by structures built under various Prussian kings. In coming years, though, it will mostly be a giant construction zone thanks to an U-Bahn (subway) extension and the reconstruction of the Berlin City Palace.

Reichstag Historic Building

(Map p536; www.bundestag.de; Platz der Republik 1, Service Center: Scheidemannstrasse; lift ride 8am-midnight, last entry 11pm, Service Center 8am-8pm Apr-Oct, 8am-6pm Nov-Mar; 100, S Bundestag, Hauptbahnhof, Brandenburger Tor) FREE One of Berlin's most iconic buildings, the 1894 Reichstag was burned, bombed, rebuilt, buttressed by the Berlin Wall, wrapped in fabric and eventually turned into the home of Germany's parliament, the Bundestag, by Lord Norman Foster. Its most distinctive feature, the glittering glass dome, is accessible by lift (reservations mandatory, see www.bundestag.de) and affords fabulous 360-degree city views. Those without a reservation can try scoring leftover tickets in the Service Center. Bring ID.

At the top, pick up a free auto-activated audioguide to learn about the building, landmarks and the workings of parliament while following the ramp spiraling up around the dome's mirror-clad central cone.

Brandenburger Tor Landmark

(Map p536; Pariser Platz; 24hr; S Brandenburger Tor, Brandenburger Tor) FREE A symbol of division during the Cold War, the landmark Brandenburg Gate now epitomises German reunification. Modelled after the Acropolis in Athens, the triumphal arch was completed in 1791 as the royal city gate and is crowned by the *Quadriga* sculpture – a winged goddess of victory piloting a horse-drawn chariot.

Holocaust Memorial Memorial

(Memorial to the Murdered European Jews; Map p536; 030-2639 4336; www.stiftung-denkmal.de; Cora-Berliner-Strasse 1; audioguide adult/concession €4/2; field 24hr, information centre 10am-8pm Tue-Sun Apr-Sep, to 7pm Oct-Mar, last entry 45min before closing; S Brandenburger Tor, Brandenburger Tor) FREE Inaugurated in 2005, this football-field-sized memorial by American architect Peter Eisenman consists of 2711 sarcophagi-like concrete columns rising in sombre silence from undulating ground. You're free to access this maze at any point and make your individual journey through it. For context visit the subterranean **Ort der Information**, the exhibits of which will leave no one untouched. Audioguides are available.

Hitler's Bunker Historic Site

(Map p536; cnr In den Ministergärten & Gertrud-Kolmar-Strasse; 24hr; S Brandenburger Tor, Brandenburger Tor) Berlin was burning and Soviet tanks advancing relentlessly when Adolf Hitler committed suicide on 30 April 1945, alongside Eva Braun, his long-time female companion, hours after their marriage. Today, a parking lot covers the site, revealing its dark history only via an information panel with a diagram of the vast bunker network, construction data and the site's post-WWII history.

Checkpoint Charlie Historic Site

(Map p530; cnr Zimmerstrasse & Friedrichstrasse; 24hr; S Kochstrasse, Stadtmitte) Checkpoint Charlie was the principal gateway for foreigners and diplomats between the two Berlins from 1961 to 1990. Unfortunately, this potent symbol of the Cold War has become a tacky tourist trap, although a free open-air exhibit that illustrates milestones in Cold War history is one redeeming aspect.

MUSEUMSINSEL & SCHEUNENVIERTEL

Museumsinsel (Museum Island) is a cluster of five museums showing off 6000 years' worth of art, artefacts, sculpture and architecture from Europe and the Middle East. Opposite, the Berlin City Palace is being constructed, while to the

Berlin

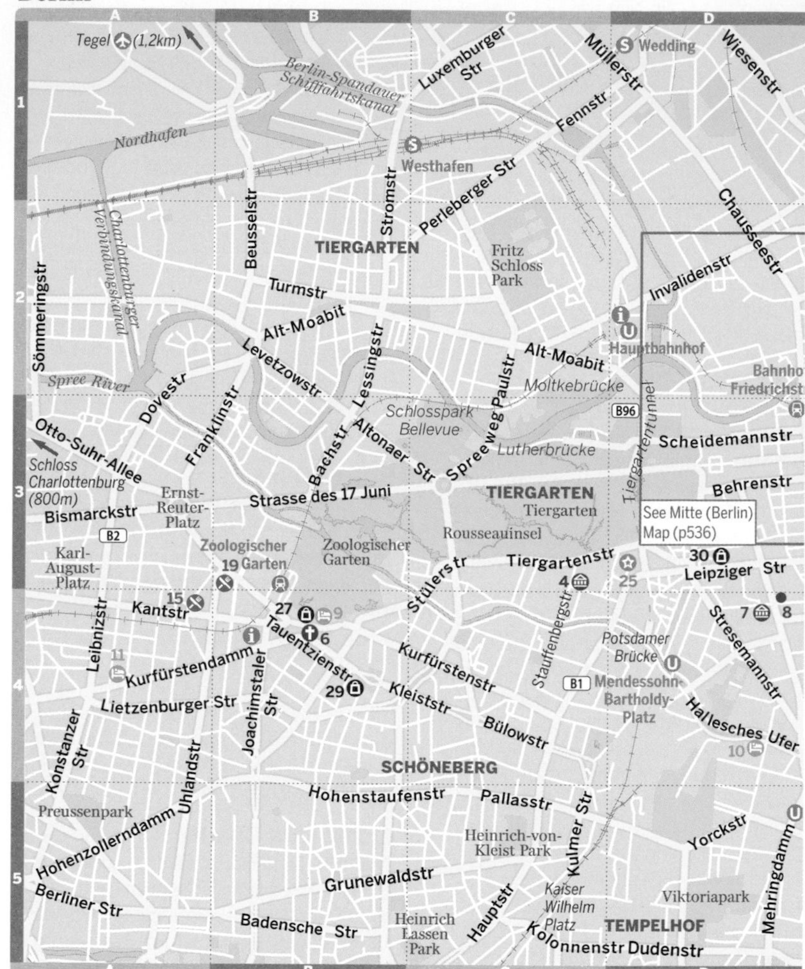

northwest the Scheunenviertel, Berlin's historic Jewish quarter, is filled with idyllic courtyards, cafes, galleries and boutiques.

Neues Museum — Museum

(New Museum; Map p536; ☎030-266 424 242; www.smb.museum; Bodestrasse 1-3; adult/ concession €12/6; ⏲10am-6pm Fri-Wed, 10am-8pm Thu; 🚌100, 200, 🚆Hackescher Markt) David Chipperfield's reconstruction of the bombed-out Neues Museum is now the residence of Queen Nefertiti, the show-stopper of the Egyptian Museum that also features mummies, sculptures and sarcophagi. Pride of place of the Museum of Pre- and Early History in the same building goes to Trojan antiquities, a Neanderthal skull and a 3000-year-old gilded conical ceremonial hat. Museum tickets are only valid for admission during a designated half-hour time slot. Skip the queue by buying advance tickets online.

Berliner Dom — Church

(Berlin Cathedral; Map p536; ☎030-2026 9136; www.berlinerdom.de; Am Lustgarten; adult/

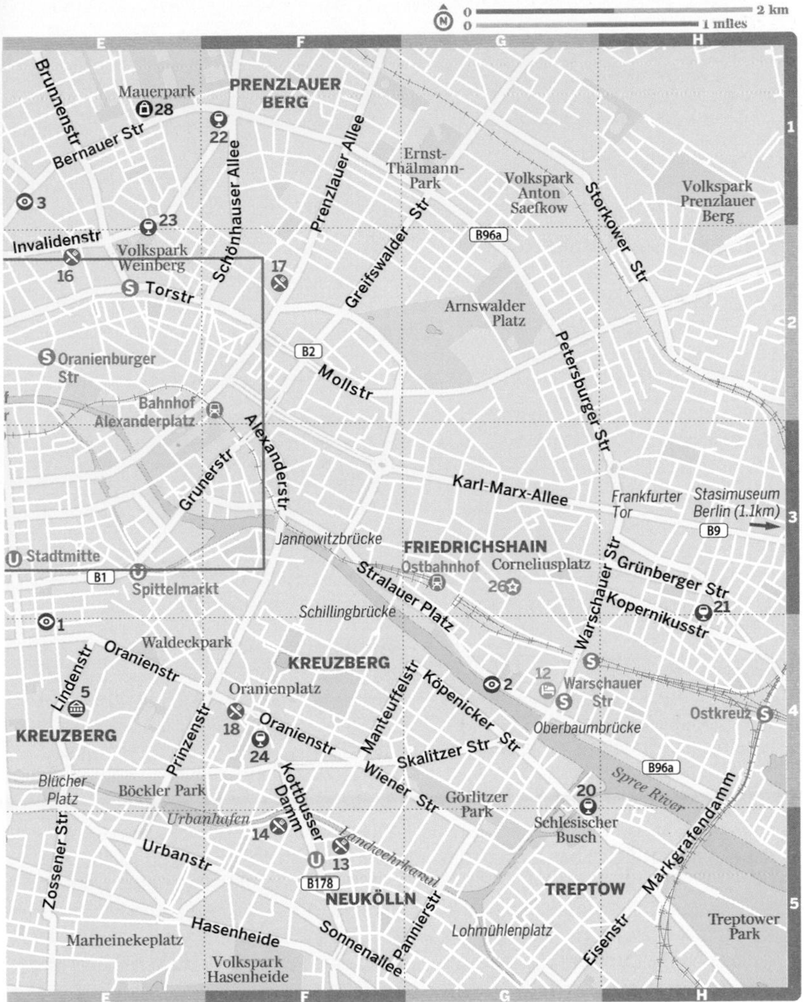

concession/under 18yr €7/5/free; ⌚9am-8pm Apr-Oct, to 7pm Nov-Mar; 🚌100, 200, 🚆Hackescher Markt) Pompous yet majestic, the Italian Renaissance–style former royal court church (1905) does triple duty as house of worship, museum and concert hall. Inside it's gilt to the hilt and outfitted with a lavish marble-and-onyx altar, a 7269-pipe Sauer organ and elaborate royal sarcophagi. Climb up the 267 steps to the gallery for glorious city views.

DDR Museum Museum

(GDR Museum; Map p536; ☎030-847 123 731; www.ddr-museum.de; Karl-Liebknecht-Strasse 1; adult/concession €7/4; ⌚10am-8pm Sun-Fri, 10am-10pm Sat; 👪; 🚌100, 200, 🚆Hackescher Markt) This interactive museum does a delightful job at pulling back the iron curtain on an extinct society. Find out that East German kids were put through collective potty training, engineers earned little more than farmers and everyone, it seems, went on nudist holidays. A highlight is a simulated ride in a Trabi.

Berlin

Sights
1 Checkpoint Charlie ... E4
2 East Side Gallery ... G4
3 Gedenkstätte Berliner Mauer ... E1
4 Gemäldegalerie ... C3
5 Jüdisches Museum ... E4
6 Kaiser-Wilhelm-Gedächtniskirche ... B4
7 Topographie des Terrors ... D4

Activities, Courses & Tours
8 Trabi Safari ... D4

Sleeping
9 25hours Hotel Bikini Berlin ... B4
10 Grand Hostel Berlin ... D4
11 Hotel Askanischer Hof ... A4
12 Michelberger Hotel ... G4

Eating
13 Cafe Jacques ... F5
14 Defne ... F5
15 Dicke Wirtin ... A4
16 Katz Orange ... E2
17 La Soupe Populaire ... F2
18 Max und Moritz ... F4
19 Restaurant am Steinplatz ... B3

Drinking & Nightlife
Berghain/Panorama Bar ... (see 26)
20 Club der Visionäre ... G4
21 Hops & Barley ... H3
22 Prater ... F1
23 Weinerei ... E1
24 Würgeengel ... F4

Entertainment
25 Berliner Philharmonie ... D3
26 Kantine am Berghain ... G3

Shopping
27 Bikini Berlin ... B4
28 Flohmarkt am Mauerpark ... E1
29 KaDeWe ... B4
30 LP12 Mall of Berlin ... D3

The more sinister sides of daily life are also addressed, including the chronic supply shortages and Stasi surveillance.

Humboldt-Box — Museum

(Map p536; ☎01805 030 707; www.humboldt-box.com; Schlossplatz; ⊙10am-7pm Apr-Sep, to 6pm Nov-Mar; 🚌100, 200, S Hausvogteiplatz) FREE This futuristic five-floor structure opens up a window on the Berlin City Palace, to be called 'Humboldt-Forum', the reconstruction of which has been underway since 2013. On display are interactive teasers from each future resident – the Ethnological Museum, the Museum of Asian Art and the Central Library – along with a fantastically detailed model of the historic city centre. Great views from the upstairs cafe terrace.

Fernsehturm — Landmark

(TV Tower; Map p536; ☎030-247 575 875; www.tv-turm.de; Panoramastrasse 1a; adult/child €13/8.50, Fast View ticket €19.50/12; ⊙9am-midnight Mar-Oct, 10am-midnight Nov-Feb; S Alexanderplatz, 🚆Alexanderplatz) Germany's tallest structure, the 368m-high TV Tower is as iconic to Berlin as the Eiffel Tower is to Paris. On clear days, views from the panorama level at 203m are unbeatable. The upstairs Restaurant Sphere (mains €14 to €28) makes one revolution per hour. To skip the line, buy tickets online.

Hackesche Höfe — Historic Site

(Map p536; ☎030-2809 8010; www.hackesche-hoefe.com; enter from Rosenthaler Strasse 40/41 or Sophienstrasse 6; S Weinmeisterstrasse, 🚋M1, 🚆Hackescher Markt) FREE Thanks to its congenial mix of cafes, galleries, boutiques and entertainment venues, this attractively restored complex of eight interlinked courtyards is hugely popular with the tourist brigade. **Court I**, festooned with patterned art nouveau tiles, is the prettiest. **Court VII** leads off to the romantic **Rosenhöfe**, a single courtyard with a sunken rose garden and tendril-like balustrades.

Gedenkstätte Berliner Mauer — Memorial

(Berlin Wall Memorial; Map p530; ☎030-467 986 666; www.berliner-mauer-gedenkstaette.de; Bernauer Strasse btwn Schwedter Strasse & Gartenstrasse; ⊙visitor center 9.30am-7pm Apr-Oct, to 6pm Nov-Mar, open-air exhibit 8am-10pm; 🚆Nordbahnhof, Bernauer Strasse, Eberswalder Strasse) FREE The central memorial site of German division extends for 1.4km along Bernauer Strasse and incorporates a section of original Wall, vestiges of the border installations and escape tunnels, a chapel and a monument. It's the only place where you can see how border fortifications developed over time. Multimedia stations, 'archaeological windows' and markers provide context and details about events that took place along here. For a great overview climb up the viewing platform at the Documentation Centre near Ackerstrasse.

POTSDAMER PLATZ & TIERGARTEN

The Potsdamer Platz quarter was forged in the 1990s from ground once bisected by the Berlin Wall and is a showcase of contemporary architecture. The adjacent Kulturforum harbours art museums, while the sweeping Tiergarten park makes for a perfect sightseeing respite.

Gemäldegalerie Gallery

(Gallery of Old Masters; Map p530; ☎030-266 424 242; www.smb.museum/gg; Matthäikirchplatz 8; adult/concession €10/5; ⏲10am-6pm Tue, Wed & Fri, 10am-8pm Thu, 11am-6pm Sat & Sun; 🚌M29, M41, 200, S Potsdamer Platz, U Potsdamer Platz) The principal Kulturforum museum boasts one of the world's finest and most comprehensive collections of European art from the 13th to the 18th centuries. Wear comfy shoes when exploring the 72 galleries: a walk past masterpieces by Rembrandt, Dürer, Hals, Vermeer, Gainsborough and many more old masters covers almost 2km.

Topographie des Terrors Museum

(Topography of Terror; Map p530; ☎030-2548 0950; www.topographie.de; Niederkirchner Strasse 8; ⏲10am-8pm, grounds until dusk or 8pm latest; 👪; S Potsdamer Platz, U Potsdamer Platz) FREE In the same spot where once stood the most feared institutions of Nazi Germany (including the Gestapo headquarters and the SS central command), this compelling exhibit chronicles the stages of terror and persecution, puts a face on the perpetrators and details the impact these brutal institutions had on all of Europe. A second exhibit outside zeroes in on how life changed for Berlin and its people after the Nazis made it their capital.

Discount Cards

- **Berlin Museum Pass** (adult/concession €24/12) Buys admission to the permanent exhibits of about 50 museums for three consecutive days, including big draws like the Pergamonmuseum. Sold at tourist offices and participating museums.
- **Berlin Welcome Card** (travel in AB zones 48/72 hours €18.50/25.50, 48 hours including Potsdam and up to three children under 15 years €20.50, 72 hours including Museuminsel €40.50) Unlimited public transport and up to 50% discount to 200 sights, attractions and tours for periods of two, three or five days. Sold online, at tourist offices, at U-Bahn and S-Bahn vending machines and on buses.

KREUZBERG & FRIEDRICHSHAIN

Kreuzberg has a split personality: while its western section (around Bergmannstrasse) has an upmarket, genteel air, eastern Kreuzberg (around Kottbusser Tor) is a multicultural mosaic and raucous nightlife hub. You'll find more after-dark action along with some Cold War relics (including Karl-Marx-Allee, East Berlin's showcase socialist boulevard) in student-flavoured Friedrichshain across the Spree.

East Side Gallery Landmark

(Map p530; www.eastsidegallery-berlin.de; Mühlenstrasse btwn Oberbaumbrücke & Ostbahnhof; ⏲24hr; S Warschauer Strasse, U Ostbahnhof, Warschauer Strasse) FREE The year was 1989. After 28 years, the Berlin Wall, that grim and grey divider of humanity, finally met its maker. Most of it was quickly dismantled along the Spree, and a 1.3km stretch became the East Side Gallery, the world's largest open-air mural collection. In more than 100

STEVE RAYMER/GETTY IMAGES ©

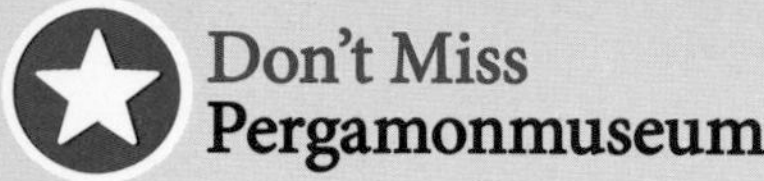

Don't Miss Pergamonmuseum

Even while undergoing renovation, the Pergamonmuseum still opens a fascinating window onto the ancient world. The palatial three-wing complex unites a rich feast of classical sculpture and monumental architecture from Greece, Rome, Babylon and the Middle East, including such famous stunners as the radiant-blue **Ishtar Gate** from Babylon, the Roman **Market Gate of Miletus** and the **Caliph's Palace** of Mshatta. Note that the namesake Pergamon Altar will be off limits until 2019.

NEED TO KNOW

Map p536; ☎030-266 424 242; www.smb.museum; Bodestrasse 1-3; adult/concession €12/6; ⏲10am-6pm Fri-Wed, to 8pm Thu; 🚌100, 🚆Hackescher Markt, Friedrichstrasse

paintings, dozens of international artists translated the era's global euphoria and optimism into a mix of political statements, drug-induced musings and truly artistic visions.

Jüdisches Museum Museum

(Jewish Museum; Map p530; ☎030-2599 3300; www.jmberlin.de; Lindenstrasse 9-14; adult/concession €8/3, audioguide €3; ⏲10am-10pm Mon, to 8pm Tue-Sun, last entry 1hr before closing; S Hallesches Tor, Kochstrasse) In a landmark building by American-Polish architect Daniel Libeskind, Berlin's Jewish Museum offers a chronicle of the trials and triumphs in 2000 years of Jewish history in Germany. The exhibit smoothly navigates through all major periods, from the Middle Ages via the Enlightenment to the community's current renaissance. Find out about Jewish cultural contributions, holiday traditions, the difficult road to emancipation and outstanding individuals such as the philosopher Moses Mendelssohn, jeans inventor Levi Strauss and the painter Felix Nussbaum.

Stasimuseum
Museum

(☎030-553 6854; www.stasimuseum.de; Haus 1, Ruschestrasse 103; adult/concession €6/4.50; ⏰10am-6pm Mon-Fri, noon-6pm Sat & Sun; S Magdalenenstrasse) The former head office of the Ministry of State Security is now a museum, where you can marvel at cunningly low-tech surveillance devices (hidden in watering cans, rocks, even neckties), a prisoner transport van with teensy, lightless cells and the obsessively neat offices of Stasi chief Erich Mielke.

Stasi Prison
Memorial

(Gedenkstätte Hohenschönhausen; ☎030-9860 8230; http://en.stiftung-hsh.de; Genslerstrasse 66; adult/concession €5/2.50; ⏰German tours hourly 10am-4pm Apr-Oct, 11am-3pm Mon-Fri & 10am-4pm Sat & Sun Nov-Mar, English tours 11.30am Apr-Oct, 2.30pm year-round; 🚋M5 to Freienwalder Strasse) Victims of Stasi persecution often ended up in this grim remand prison, now a memorial site officially called Gedenkstätte Hohenschönhausen. Tours reveal the full extent of the terror and cruelty perpetrated upon thousands of suspected regime opponents, many utterly innocent. A new exhibit documents the history of the prison. To get here, take tram M5 from Alexanderplatz to Freienwalder Strasse, then walk 10 minutes along Freienwalder Strasse.

CHARLOTTENBURG

The glittering heart of West Berlin during the Cold War, Charlottenburg has been eclipsed by historic Mitte and other eastern districts since reunification, but is now trying hard to stage a comeback with major construction and redevelopment around Zoo station. Its main artery is the 3.5km-long Kurfürstendamm (Ku'damm for short), Berlin's busiest shopping strip.

Schloss Charlottenburg
Palace

(☎030-320 910; www.spsg.de; Spandauer Damm 10-22; admission varies by building, day pass to all four adult/concession €17/13; ⏰hours vary by building; 🚌M45, 109, 309, S Richard-Wagner-Platz, Sophie-Charlotte-Platz) The grandest of Berlin's surviving royal pads consists of the main palace and three smaller buildings dotted around the lovely palace park. The Schloss has origins as the summer residence of Sophie Charlotte, wife of King Friedrich I, and was later enlarged by Frederick the Great. Highlights include opulently furnished private royal apartments, richly festooned festival halls, collections of precious porcelain and paintings by French 18th-century masters, and lots of silver, vases, tapestries and other items representative of a royal lifestyle.

Kaiser-Wilhelm-Gedächtniskirche
Church

(Kaiser Wilhelm Memorial Church; Map p530; ☎030-218 5023; www.gedaechtniskirche.com; Breitscheidplatz; ⏰church 9am-7pm, memorial hall 10am-6pm Mon-Fri, 10am-5.30pm Sat, noon-5.30pm Sun; 🚌100, S Zoologischer Garten, Kurfürstendamm, 🚆Zoologischer Garten) FREE The bombed-out tower of this landmark church, consecrated in 1895, serves as an antiwar memorial, standing quiet and dignified amid the roaring traffic. The adjacent octagonal hall of worship, added in 1961, has amazing midnight-blue glass walls and a giant 'floating' Jesus.

Tours

Most of these English-language tours don't require reservations; just check the website for the latest meetings points and show up.

Alternative Berlin Tours
Walking Tour

(☎0162-819 8264; www.alternativeberlin.com) Pay-what-you-want twice-daily subculture tours that get beneath the skin of the city, plus a street-art workshop, an alternative pub crawl and the hard-core 'Twilight Tour'.

Berlin Walks
Walking Tour

(☎030-301 9194; www.berlinwalks.de; adult €12-15, concession €10-12) Berlin's longest-running English-language walking-tour company also does tours of Sachsenhausen Concentration Camp and Potsdam.

Mitte (Berlin)

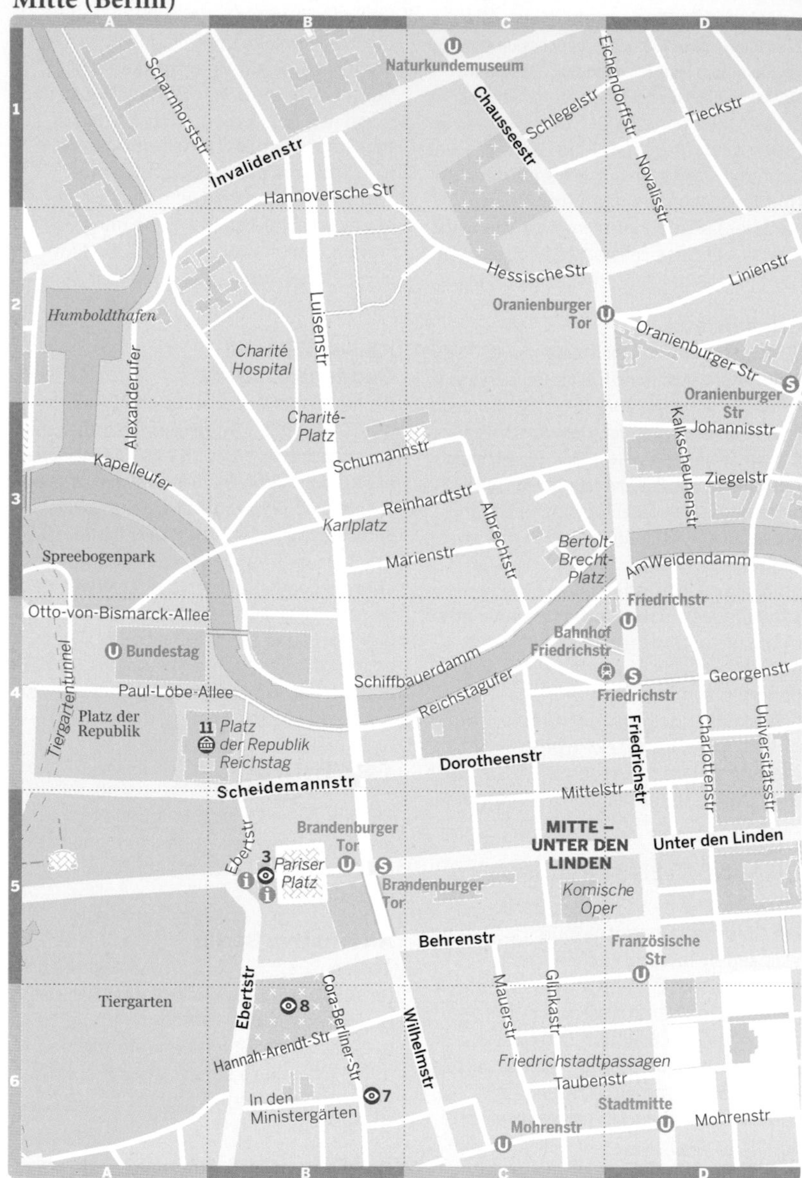

Fat Tire Bike Tours Bicycle Tour

(Map p536; ☎030-2404 7991; www.fattirebiketours.com/berlin; Panoramastrasse 1a; adult/concession €24/22; S Alexanderplatz, Alexanderplatz) Has classic city, Nazi and Berlin Wall tours as well as a fascinating 'Raw: Berlin Exposed' tour that gets under the city's urban, subcultural skin. Tours leave from the TV Tower main entrance. E-bike tours available. Reservations recommended (and for some tours required).

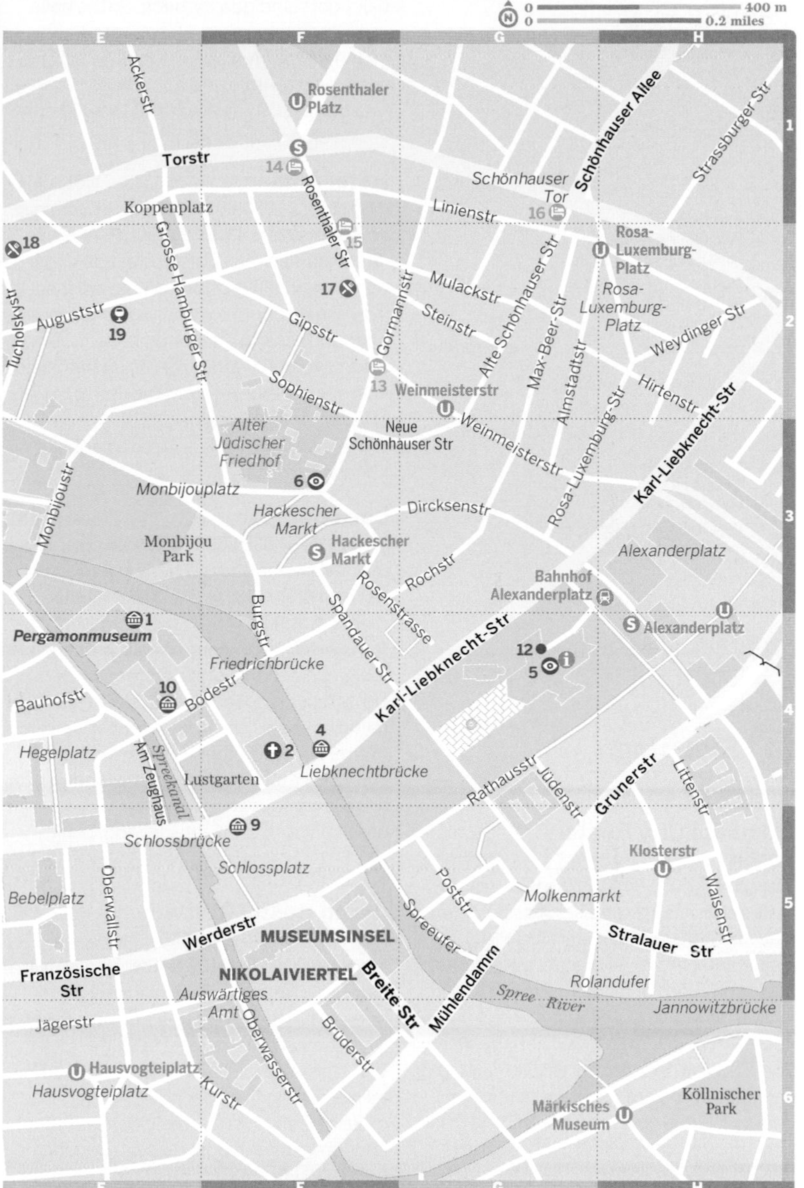

Trabi Safari Car Tour

(Map p530; ☎030-2759 2273; www.trabi-safari.de; Zimmerstrasse 97; per person €34-60, Wall Ride €79-89; Ⓢ Kochstrasse) Catch the *Good Bye, Lenin!* vibe on tours of Berlin's classic sights or the 'Wild East' with you driving or riding as a passenger in a convoy of GDR-made Trabant cars (Trabi) with live commentary (in English by prior arrangement) piped into your vehicle.

Mitte (Berlin)

Don't Miss Sights
1 Pergamonmuseum.............................E4

Sights
2 Berliner Dom.......................................F4
3 Brandenburger Tor & Pariser Platz...B5
4 DDR Museum.......................................F4
5 Fernsehturm..G4
6 Hackesche Höfe...................................F3
7 Hitler's Bunker.....................................B6
8 Holocaust Memorial............................B6
9 Humboldt-Box.......................................F5
10 Neues Museum...................................E4
11 Reichstag..A4

Activities, Courses & Tours
12 Fat Tire Bike Tours..............................G4

Sleeping
13 Casa Camper.......................................F2
14 Circus Hotel...F1
15 Hotel Amano..F2
16 Wombats City Hostel Berlin...............G1

Eating
17 Chèn Chè...F2
18 Schwarzwaldstuben.............................E2

Drinking & Nightlife
19 Clärchens Ballhaus..............................E2

Sleeping

SCHEUNENVIERTEL

Wombats City Hostel Berlin Hostel €
(Map p536; ☎030-8471 0820; www.wombats-hostels.com; Alte Schönhauser Strasse 2; dm/d €26/78; @📶; S Rosa-Luxemburg-Platz) Sociable and central, Wombats gets hostelling right. From backpack-sized in-room lockers to individual reading lamps and a guest kitchen with dishwasher, the attention to detail here is impressive. Spacious en suite rooms are as much part of the deal as freebie linen and a welcome drink, best enjoyed with fellow party pilgrims at the 7th-floor Wombar.

Circus Hotel Hotel €€
(Map p536; ☎030-2000 3939; www.circus-berlin.de; Rosenthaler Strasse 1; d €85-120; @📶; S Rosenthaler Platz) At our favourite budget boutique hotel none of the mod rooms are alike, but all feature upbeat colours, thoughtful design details, sleek oak floors and quality beds. Baths have walk-in rain showers. Unexpected perks include a roof terrace with summertime yoga, bike rentals and a fabulous breakfast buffet (€9) served until 1pm. Simply good value all around.

Hotel Amano Hotel €€
(Map p536; ☎030-809 4150; www.amanogroup.de; Auguststrasse 43; d €90-190; P❄@📶; S Rosenthaler Platz) This budget designer hotel has inviting public areas, dressed in brushed-copper walls and cocoa-hued banquettes, and efficiently styled rooms, where white furniture teams up with oak floors and natural-toned fabrics to create crisp cosiness. Breakfast €15. Space-cravers should book an apartment with kitchenette.

Casa Camper Hotel €€€
(Map p536; ☎030-2000 3410; www.casacamper.com; Weinmeisterstrasse 1; r/ste incl breakfast from €194/338; P📶; S Weinmeisterstrasse) Catalan shoemaker Camper has translated its concept of chic yet sensible footwear into this style-pit for trend-conscious travellers. Rooms are mod if minimalist and come with day-lit bathrooms and beds that invite hitting the snooze button. Minibars are eschewed for a top-floor lounge with stellar views, free breakfast and 24/7 snacks and drinks.

KREUZBERG

Grand Hostel Berlin Hostel €
(Map p530; ☎030-2009 5450; www.grandhostel-berlin.de; Tempelhofer Ufer 14; dm from €14, d €58; @📶; S Möckernbrücke) Afternoon tea in the library bar? Check. Rooms with stucco-ornamented ceilings? Got 'em. Canal views? Yup. OK, the Grand Hostel may be no five-star hotel, but it is one of Berlin's most supremely comfortable and atmospheric hostels. Ensconced in a fully renovated 1870s building are private rooms and dorms with quality single beds (linen costs €3.60) and large lockers.

Michelberger Hotel Hotel €€
(Map p530; ☎030-2977 8590; www.michelbergerhotel.com; Warschauer Strasse 39; d €105-196; 📶; S Warschauer Strasse, 🚆 Warschauer Strasse) The ultimate in creative crash

pads, Michelsberger perfectly encapsulates Berlin's offbeat DIY spirit without being self-consciously cool. Rooms don't hide their factory pedigree, but are comfortable and come in sizes suitable for lovebirds, families or rock bands. Staff are friendly and clued-in, and there's a popular restaurant, and live music in the lobby on some nights. Optional breakfast is €16.

CHARLOTTENBURG

25hours Hotel Bikini Berlin Hotel €€

(Map p530; ☎030-120 2210; www.25hours-hotels.com; Budapester Strasse 40; r from €80; ❄@📶; S Zoologischer Garten, 🚌 Zoologischer Garten) The 'urban jungle' theme of this hip lifestyle outpost is a reflection of its location between the city's zoo and main shopping district. Rooms are stylish, if a tad compact, with the nicer ones facing the animal park.

The hotel is part of the iconic Bikini Berlin redevelopment and popular with locals for its 10th-floor Monkey Bar and Neni restaurant. Optional breakfast is €18.

Hotel Askanischer Hof Hotel €€

(Map p530; ☎030-881 8033; www.askanischer-hof.de; Kurfürstendamm 53; d incl breakfast €80-160; 📶; S Adenauerplatz) If you're after character and vintage flair, you'll find heaps of both at this 17-room jewel with a Roaring Twenties pedigree. An ornate oak door leads to a quiet oasis where no two rooms are alike, but all are filled with antiques, lace curtains, frilly chandeliers and time-worn oriental rugs. The quaint Old Berlin charms make a popular setting for fashion shoots.

Eating

SCHEUNENVIERTEL

Chèn Chè Vietnamese €€

(Map p536; www.chenche-berlin.de; Rosenthaler Strasse 13; dishes €7-11; ⏰noon-midnight; 🌶; S Rosenthaler Platz, 🚋M1) Settle down in the charming Zen garden or beneath the hexagonal chandelier of this exotic Vietnamese tea house and pick from the small menu of steaming *pho* (soups), curries and noodle dishes served in traditional clay pots. Exquisite tea selection and small store.

Dome of the Reichstag (p529), Berlin

Schwarzwaldstuben German €€
(Map p536; ☎030-2809 8084; Tucholskystrasse 48; mains €7-14; ⏰9am-midnight; 🚊M1, 🚆Oranienburger Strasse) In the mood for a Hansel and Gretel moment? Then join the other 'lost kids' for satisfying southern German food amid tongue-in-cheek forest decor. Thumbs up for the *Spätzle* (mac 'n' cheese), *Maultaschen* (ravioli-like pasta) and giant schnitzel, all best washed down with a crisp Rothaus Tannenzäpfle beer, straight from the Black Forest.

La Soupe Populaire German €€
(Map p530; ☎030-4431 9680; www.lasoupepopulaire.de; Prenzlauer Allee 242; mains €14-21; ⏰noon-midnight Thu-Sat; S Rosa-Luxemburg-Strasse, 🚊M2) Local top toque Tim Raue's newest gastro destination embraces the soulful goodness of German home-cooking, with a best seller being his riff on *Königsberger Klopse* (veal meatballs in caper sauce). It's all served in an industrial-chic space within a defunct 19th-century brewery where patrons sit at vintage tables overlooking a gallery space showcasing changing contemporary art.

Katz Orange International €€€
(Map p530; ☎030-983 208 430; www.katzorange.com; Bergstrasse 22; mains €18-26; ⏰6-11pm; S Rosenthaler Platz, 🚊M8) With its gourmet organic farm-to-table menu, feel-good country styling, and swift and smiling servers, the 'Orange Cat' hits a gastro grand slam. It will have you purring for Duroc pork that's been slow-roasted for 12 hours giving extra rich flavour. The setting in a castlelike former brewery is stunning, especially in summer when the patio opens.

KREUZBERG

Cafe Jacques International €€
(Map p530; ☎030-694 1048; Maybachufer 14; mains €12-20; ⏰6pm-late; S Schönleinstrasse) A favourite with off-duty chefs and local foodies, Jacques infallibly charms with flattering candlelight, arty-elegant decor, fantastic wine and uberfriendly staff. It's the perfect date spot but, quite frankly, you only have to be in love with good food to appreciate the French- and North African–inspired blackboard menu. The cold appetiser platter is big enough for sharing, fish and meat are always tops and the pasta is homemade. Reservations essential.

Max und Moritz German €€
(Map p530; ☎030-6951 5911; www.maxundmoritzberlin.de; Oranienstrasse 162; mains €9.50-17; ⏰5pm-midnight; S Moritzplatz) The patina of yesteryear hangs over this ode-to-old-school brewpub named for the cheeky Wilhelm Busch cartoon characters. Since 1902 it has packed hungry diners and drinkers into its rustic tile-and-stucco ornamented rooms for sudsy home brews and granny-style Berlin fare. A menu favourite is the *Kutschergulasch* (goulash cooked with beer).

Defne Turkish €€
(Map p530; ☎030-8179 7111; www.defne-restaurant.de; Planufer 92c; mains €8-20; ⏰4pm-1am Apr-Sep, 5pm-1am Oct-Mar; S Kottbusser Tor, Schönleinstrasse) If you thought Turkish cuisine stopped at the doner kebab, canalside Defne will teach you otherwise. The appetiser platter alone elicits intense cravings (fabulous walnut-chilli paste!), but inventive mains such as *ali nacik* (sliced lamb with puréed eggplant and yoghurt) also warrant repeat visits. Lovely summer terrace.

CHARLOTTENBURG

Dicke Wirtin German €€
(Map p530; ☎030-312 4952; www.dicke-wirtin.de; Carmerstrasse 9; mains €6-16; ⏰11am-late; 🚆Savignyplatz) Old Berlin charm oozes from every nook and cranny of this been-here-forever pub which pours eight draught beers (including the superb Kloster Andechs) and nearly three dozen homemade schnapps varieties. Hearty local fare like roast pork, fried liver or breaded schnitzel keeps brains balanced. Bargain lunches.

Restaurant am Steinplatz German €€€
**(Map p530; ☎030-312 6589; www.marriott.de; Hardenbergstrasse 12; mains €16-26; ⏰breakfast, lunch & dinner; 🚌M45, S Ernst-

Reuter-Platz, Bahnhof Zoologischer Garten, **Bahnhof Zoologischer Garten)** The 1920s gets a 21st-century makeover both in the kitchen and the decor at this stylish outpost. The dining room is anchored by an open kitchen where veteran chef Marcus Zimmer uses mostly regional products to execute classic Berlin recipes. Even rustic beer-hall dishes such as *Eisbein* (boiled pork knuckle) are imaginatively reinterpreted and beautifully plated.

 Drinking & Nightlife

With no curfew, Berlin is a notoriously late city, where bars stay packed from dusk to dawn and beyond and some clubs don't hit their stride until 6am. Kreuzberg and Friedrichshain are currently the edgiest bar-hopping grounds, with swanky Mitte and Charlottenburg being more suited for date nights than late nights.

Hops & Barley — Pub

(Map p530; 030-2936 7534; Wühlischstrasse 40; from 5pm Mon-Fri, from 3pm Sat & Sun; S Warschauer Strasse, Warschauer Strasse) Conversation flows as freely as the unfiltered Pilsner, malty *Dunkel* (dark), fruity *Weizen* (wheat) and potent cider produced right at this congenial microbrewery inside a former butcher's shop. For variety, the brewers produce seasonal blackboard specials such as a malty Bernstein or a robust Indian Pale Ale.

Würgeengel — Bar

(Map p530; www.wuergeengel.de; Dresdener Strasse 122; from 7pm; S Kottbusser Tor) For a swish night out, point the compass to Würgeengel, a stylish art deco–style bar with lots of chandeliers and shiny black surfaces. It's always busy but especially so after the final credits roll at the adjacent Babylon cinema.

Weinerei — Wine Bar

(Map p530; 030-440 6983; www.weinerei.com; Veteranenstrasse 14; 8pm-late; ; S Rosenthaler Platz, M1) This living-room-style wine bar works on the honour principle: you 'rent' a wine glass for €2, then help yourself to as much vino as you like and in the end decide what you want to pay. Please be fair and do not take advantage of this fantastic concept.

Jüdisches Museum (p534), Berlin

PAOLO CORDELLI/GETTY IMAGES ©

GERMANY BERLIN

Gay & Lesbian Berlin

Berlin's legendary liberalism has spawned one of the world's biggest and most diverse LGBTIQ playgrounds. The historic 'gay village' is near Nollendorfplatz in Schöneberg (Motzstrasse and Fuggerstrasse especially; get off U-Bahn station Nollendorfplatz) where the rainbow flag has proudly flown since the 1920s. The crowd skews older and leather. Current hipster central is Kreuzberg, where free-wheeling party pens cluster around Mehringdamm and Oranienstrasse. Check *Siegessäule* (www.siegesaeule.de), the weekly freebie 'bible' to all things gay and lesbian in town, for the latest happenings.

Prater Beer Garden

(Map p530; 030-448 5688; www.pratergarten.de; Kastanienallee 7-9; noon-late Apr-Sep, weather permitting; S Eberswalder Strasse) This place has seen beer-soaked nights since 1837, making it Berlin's oldest beer garden. It's kept much of its traditional charm and is still perfect for guzzling a custom-brewed Prater pilsner beneath the ancient chestnut trees (self-service). Kids can romp around the small play area. In foul weather or winter, the adjacent beer hall is a fine place to sample classic Berlin dishes (mains €8 to €19).

Clärchens Ballhaus Club

(Map p536; 030-282 9295; www.ballhaus.de; Augustrasse 24; 11am-late, dancing from 9pm or 9.30pm; M1, Oranienburger Strasse) Yesteryear is right now at this late, great 19th-century dance hall where groovers and grannies hoof it across the parquet without even a touch of irony. There are different sounds nightly – salsa to swing, tango to disco – and a live band on Saturday.

Club der Visionäre Club

(Map p530; 030-6951 8942; www.clubdervisionaere.com; Am Flutgraben 1; from 2pm Mon-Fri, from noon Sat & Sun; S Schlesisches Tor, Treptower Park) It's cold beer, crispy pizza and fine electro at this summertime chill and party playground in an old canal-side boatshed. Park yourself beneath the weeping willows, stake out some turf on the upstairs deck or hit the teensy dance floor. At weekends party people invade. The toilets suck.

Berghain/Panorama Bar Club

(Map p530; www.berghain.de; Wriezener Bahnhof; midnight Fri-Mon morning; Ostbahnhof) Only world-class DJs heat up this hedonistic bass-junkie hellhole inside a labyrinthine ex–power plant. Hard-edged minimal techno dominates the ex–turbine hall (Berghain) while house dominates at Panorama Bar one floor up. Strict door, no cameras. Check the website for mid-week concerts and record-release parties at the main venue and the adjacent **Kantine am Berghain** (Map p530; 030-2936 0210; www.berghain.de; Am Wriezener Bahnhof; hours vary; Ostbahnhof).

Entertainment

Berliner Philharmonie Classical Music

(Map p530; tickets 030-2548 8301; www.berliner-philharmoniker.de; Herbert-von-Karajan-Strasse 1; 200, S Potsdamer Platz, Potsdamer Platz) This world-famous concert hall has supreme acoustics and, thanks to Hans Scharoun's clever terraced vineyard design, not a bad seat in the house. It's the home turf of the Berliner Philharmoniker, which will be led by Sir Simon Rattle until 2018. Chamber-music concerts take place at the adjacent Kammermusiksaal.

Shopping

Berlin's main shopping boulevard is Kurfürstendamm and its extension Tauentzienstrasse, which are chock-a-bloc with the usual-suspect high-street chains and the famous **KaDeWe** (Map p530; 030-212 10; www.kadewe.de; Tauentzienstrasse 21-24;

⏲10am-8pm Mon-Thu, 10am-9pm Fri, 9.30am-8pm Sat; **S** Wittenbergplatz), continental Europe's largest department store. Also nearby is the new **Bikini Berlin** (Map p530; www.bikiniberlin.de; Budapester Strasse 38-50; ⏲9am-9pm Mon-Sat; **S** Bahnhof Zoologischer Garten, **U** Bahnhof Zoologischer Garten), an edgy 'concept mall' with idiosyncratic local designers. Berlin's newest mall is the chic **Mall of Berlin** (Map p530; www.mallofberlin.de; Leipziger Platz 12; 🚌200, **S** Potsdamer Platz, **U** Potsdamer Platz) near Potsdamer Platz. The most popular flea market is **Flohmarkt am Mauerpark** (Map p530; www.mauerparkmarkt.de; Bernauer Strasse 63-64; ⏲10am-5pm Sun; **S** Eberwalder Strasse) in Prenzlauer Berg.

Information

Visit Berlin (Map p536; www.visitberlin.de), the Berlin tourist board, operates four walk-in offices, info desks at the airports, and a **call centre** (☎030-2500 2333; ⏲9am-7pm Mon-Fri, 10am-6pm Sat, 10am-2pm Sun) with multilingual staff who field general questions and make hotel and ticket bookings.

Brandenburger Tor (Map p536; Brandenburger Tor, Pariser Platz; ⏲9.30am-7pm Apr-Oct, to 6pm Nov-Mar; **S** Brandenburger Tor, **U** Brandenburger Tor)

Hauptbahnhof (Map p530; Hauptbahnhof, Europaplatz entrance, Ground fl; ⏲8am-10pm; **S** Hauptbahnhof, **U** Hauptbahnhof)

Neues Kranzler Eck (Map p530; Kurfürstendamm 22, Neues Kranzler Eck; ⏲9.30am-8pm Mon-Sat; **S** Kurfürstendamm)

TV Tower (Map p536; TV Tower, Ground fl; ⏲10am-6pm Apr-Oct, to 4pm Nov-Mar; 🚌100, 200, **S** Alexanderplatz, **U** Alexanderplatz)

Getting There & Away

Air

Since the opening of the new Berlin Brandenburg Airport has been delayed indefinitely, flights continue to land at the city's **Tegel** (TXL; ☎030-6091 1150; www.berlin-airport.de) and **Schönefeld** (SXF; ☎030-6091 1150; www.berlin-airport.de) Airports.

Bus

Most long-haul buses arrive at the **Zentraler Omnibusbahnhof** (ZOB; ☎030-302 5361; www.iob-berlin.de; Masurenallee 4-6; **S** Kaiserdamm, **U** Messe/ICC Nord) near the trade-fair grounds in far western Berlin. The U2 U -Bahn line links to the city centre. Some bus operators also stop at Alexanderplatz and other points around town.

Train

Berlin is well connected by train to other German cities, as well as to popular European destinations, including Prague, Warsaw and Amsterdam. There are several mainline train stations but all long-distance services converge at the **Hauptbahnhof** (www.berlin-hauptbahnhof.de; Europaplatz, Washingtonplatz; **S** Hauptbahnhof, **U** Hauptbahnhof).

Schloss Charlottenburg (p535), Berlin

HANS BACH/STIFTUNG PREUSSISCHE SCHLÖSSER UND GÄRTEN BERLIN-BRANDENBURG/FOTOTHEK ©

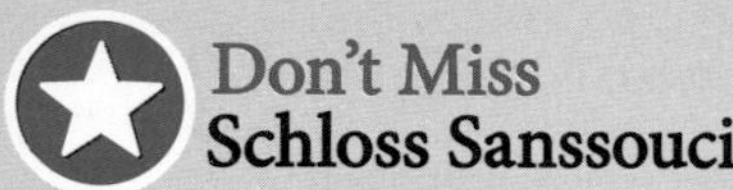

Don't Miss Schloss Sanssouci

Frederick the Great's famous summer palace, Schloss Sanssouci, was designed by Georg Wenzeslaus von Knobelsdorff in 1747; the rococo jewel sits daintily above vine-draped terraces with the king's grave nearby. Admission is limited and by timed ticket only; book online to avoid wait times and/or disappointment. Otherwise, only city tours booked through the tourist office guarantee entry to the Schloss.

Standouts on the audioguided tours include the **Konzertsaal** (Concert Hall), whimsically decorated with vines, grapes and even a cobweb where sculpted spiders frolic. The king himself gave flute recitals here. Also note the intimate **Bibliothek** (Library), lidded by a gilded sunburst ceiling, where the king would seek solace amid 2000 leather-bound tomes ranging from Greek poetry to the latest releases by his friend Voltaire. Another highlight is the **Marmorsaal** (Marble Room), an elegant white Carrara-marble symphony modelled after the Pantheon in Rome.

As you exit the palace, don't be fooled by the **Ruinenberg**, a pile of classical 'ruins' looming in the distance – they're merely a folly conceived by Frederick the Great.

NEED TO KNOW

0331-969 4200; www.spsg.de; Maulbeerallee; adult/concession incl audioguide €12/8; 10am-6pm Tue-Sun Apr-Oct, 10am-5pm Nov-Mar; 650, 695

Getting Around

To/From the Airport

Tegel

Bus TXL bus to Alexanderplatz (€2.60, 40 minutes) via Haupbahnhof every 10 minutes. Bus X9 for Kurfürstendamm and Zoo station, (€2.60, 20 minutes).

U-Bahn Closest U-Bahn station is Jakob-Kaiser-Platz, served by buses 109 and X9. From here, the U7 goes straight to Schöneberg and Kreuzberg (€2.60).

Schönefeld

The airport train station is about 400m from the terminals. Free shuttle buses run every 10 minutes; walking takes five to 10 minutes.

Airport-Express Regular Deutsche Bahn regional trains, identified as RE7 and RB14 in timetables, go to central Berlin twice hourly (€3.20, 30 minutes).

S-Bahn The S9 runs every 20 minutes and is handy for Friedrichshain or Prenzlauer Berg. For the Messe (trade-fair grounds), take the S45 to Südkreuz and change to the S41. Tickets cost €3.20.

Public Transport

One ticket is valid on all forms of public transport, including the U-Bahn, buses, trams and ferries. Most trips within Berlin require an AB ticket (€2.60). which is valid for two hours (interruptions and transfers allowed, but not round trips).

Tickets are available from bus drivers, vending machines at U- and S-Bahn stations (English instructions available), vending machines aboard trams and from station offices. Expect to pay cash (change given) and be sure to validate (stamp) your ticket or risk a €40 fine.

Services operate from 4am until just after midnight on weekdays, with half-hourly Nachtbuses (night buses) in between. At weekends, the U-Bahn and S-Bahn run all night long (except the U4 and U55).

For trip planning, check the website or call the 24-hour **hotline** (**☎030-194 49; www.bvg.de**).

Taxi

You can order a **taxi** (**☎030-20 20 20, 030-44 33 11**) by phone, flag one down or pick one up at a rank. Tip about 10%. A special feature in Berlin is the *Kurzstrecke*: short trips of 2km costing only €4 provided you flag down a cab and request a *Kurzstrecke* before the driver has activated the meter.

Elbe River, Dresden

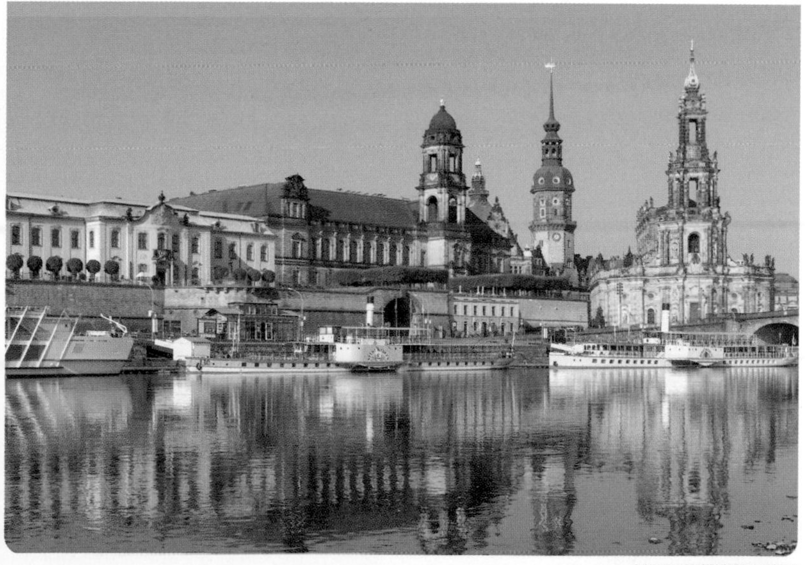

DRESDEN

☎0351 / POP 512,000

Proof that there is life after death, Dresden has become one of Germany's most popular attractions, and for good reason. Restorations have returned the city to its 18th-century heyday when it was famous throughout Europe as 'Florence on the Elbe'. Scores of Italian artists, musicians, actors and master craftsmen flocked to the court of Augustus the Strong, bestowing countless masterpieces upon the city. The devastating bombing raids in 1945 levelled most of these treasures. But Dresden is a survivor and many of the most important landmarks have since been rebuilt, including the elegant Frauenkirche.

Sights

Dresden straddles the Elbe River, with the attraction-studded Altstadt (old town) in the south and the Neustadt (new town) pub and student quarter to the north.

Frauenkirche Church

(www.frauenkirche-dresden.de; Neumarkt; audioguide €2.50; usually 10am-noon & 1-6pm) FREE The domed Frauenkirche – Dresden's most beloved symbol – has literally risen from the city's ashes. The original graced its skyline for two centuries before collapsing after the February 1945 bombing. After reunification a grassroots movement helped raise funds to rebuild the landmark. A spitting image of the original, it may not bear the gravitas of age but that only slightly detracts from its beauty. The altar, reassembled from nearly 2000 fragments, is especially striking.

Zwinger Museum

(☎0351-4914 2000; www.skd.museum; Theaterplatz 1; adult/under 17yr €14/free; 10am-6pm Tue-Sun) The sprawling Zwinger, one of the most ravishing baroque buildings in Germany, today houses several important museums. The most important collection, the **Gemäldegalerie Alte Meister** (Old Masters Gallery), displays a roll call of such art-world darlings as Botticelli, Titian, Rubens, Vermeer and Dürer. A key work is the 500-year-old *Sistine Madonna* by Raphael. Fans of precious porcelain from Meissen and East Asia gravitate to the **Porzellansammlung**, while technotypes will like the historic scientific instruments (clocks, telescopes etc) at the **Mathematisch-Physikalischer Salon**.

Albertinum Museum

(☎0351-4914 2000; www.skd.museum; enter from Brühlsche Terrasse or Georg-Treu-Platz 2; adult/concession/under 17yr €10/7.50/free; 10am-6pm Tue-Sun; P) After massive renovations following severe 2002 flood damage, the Renaissance-era former arsenal is now the stunning home of the **Galerie Neue Meister** (New Masters Gallery), which displays an arc of paintings by prime practitioners from the 18th to the 20th centuries – Caspar David Friedrich to Claude Monet and Gerhard Richter – in gorgeous rooms orbiting a light-filled courtyard.

Tours

NightWalk Dresden Walking Tour

(☎0172 781 5007; www.nightwalk-dresden.de; Albertplatz; tours €13; tour 9pm) Dresden is not all about baroque beauties, as you will discover on this intriguing 'behind the scenes' walking tour of it's most interesting quarter, the Outer Neustadt. See fabulous street art, learn about what life was like in the former East Germany and visit fun pubs and bars. The meeting point is normally at Albertplatz but call ahead and confirm.

Grosse Stadtrundfahrt Bus Tour

(☎0351-899 5650; www.stadtrundfahrt.com; Theaterplatz; day pass adult/concession €20/18; 9.30am-10pm Apr-Oct, 9.30am-8pm Nov-Mar) Narrated hop-on hop-off tour with 22 stops and optional short guided tours tick off all major sights. Buses leave every 15 to 30 minutes.

Sleeping

Hostel Mondpalast Hostel **€**

(☎0351-563 4050; www.mondpalast.de; Louisenstrasse 77; dm €13-19.50, d €56, linen €2; @) Check in at the out-of-this-world

/GETTY IMAGES ©

Don't Miss Grünes Gewölbe

Dresden's fortresslike Renaissance city palace was home to the Saxon rulers from 1485 to 1918 and now shelters a dazzling collection of precious objects amassed by Augustus the Strong in the 18th century. Spilling over with intricate trinkets wrought by hand from gold, ivory, silver, diamonds and jewels, this real-life 'Aladdin's Cave' is so big that displays are spread over two separate museums: the Historisches Grünes Gewölbe (Historic Green Vault) and the modern Neues Grünes Gewölbe (New Green Vault).

If you only have time for one, make it the former, largely because objects are displayed in a series of lavishly decorated baroque-style rooms just as they were during Augustus' time. Admission is by timed ticket only and visitor numbers are limited. It's best to get advance tickets online or show up before the ticket office opens.

Don't be too disappointed, though, if you can't get into the historic chambers, for trinkets displayed in the modern New Green Vault are just as stunning. Combination tickets are also good for the other palace collections (coins, armour, prints and drawings) as well as the Hausmannturm (tower).

NEED TO KNOW

Green Vault; ☎0351-4914 2000; www.skd.museum; Residenzschloss; adult/under 17yr incl audioguide €14/free, combination ticket €23/free; ⏲10am-6pm Wed-Mon

bar-cafe (with cheap drinks) before being 'beamed up' to your room in the Moon Palace, each one designed to reflect a sign of the zodiac. Bonus points for the bike rentals and the well-equipped kitchen. Breakfast is €6.50.

Aparthotel am Zwinger Apartment €€
(☎0351-8990 0100; www.pension-zwinger.de; Maxstrasse 3; apt €60-112; ⏰reception 7am-10pm Mon-Fri, 9.30am-6pm Sat & Sun or by arrangement; P @ 📶) Self-caterers, families and space-cravers will appreciate these bright, functional and stylish rooms and apartments with basic kitchens. Units are spread over several buildings, but all are supercentral and fairly quiet. Breakfast costs €9.50.

Hotel Martha Dresden Hotel €€
(☎0351-817 60; www.hotel-martha-dresden.de; Nieritzstrasse 11; d €113-121; 📶) Fifty rooms with big windows, wooden floors and Biedermeier-inspired furnishings combined with an attractive winter garden and a smiley welcome make for a pleasant place to hang your hat. Breakfast costs €10. The entire hotel is wheelchair accessible. Bike rentals are available.

Eating

The Neustadt has oodles of cafes and restaurants, especially along Königstrasse and the streets north of Albertplatz. The latter is also Dresden's nightlife hub. Altstadt restaurants are mostly tourist-geared.

Villandry Mediterranean €€
(☎0351-899 6724; www.villandry.de; Jordanstrasse 8; mains €9-22; ⏰6.30-11.30pm Mon-Sat) The folks in the kitchen here sure know how to coax maximum flavour out of even the simplest ingredients, and to turn them into supertasty Mediterranean treats for your eyes and palate. Meals are best enjoyed in the lovely courtyard.

Raskolnikoff International €€
(☎0351-804 5706; www.raskolnikoff.de; Böhmische Strasse 34; mains €7-24; ⏰10am-2am Mon-Fri, 9am-2am Sat & Sun) An artist squat before the Wall came down, Raskolnikoff now brims with grown-up artsy-bohemian flair, especially in the sweet little garden at the back. The seasonally calibrated menu showcases the fruits of regional terroir in globally inspired dishes, and the beer is brewed locally. Upstairs are seven handsomely done-up rooms (single/double €45/62) and one studio with kitchenette (€55/72).

Cafe Alte Meister International €€
(☎0351-481 0426; www.altemeister.net; Theaterplatz 1a; mains €9-20; ⏰10am-1am) If you've worked up an appetite from museum-hopping or need a break from culture overload, retreat to this elegant filling station between the Zwinger and the Semperoper for creative and seasonal bistro fare in its artsy interior

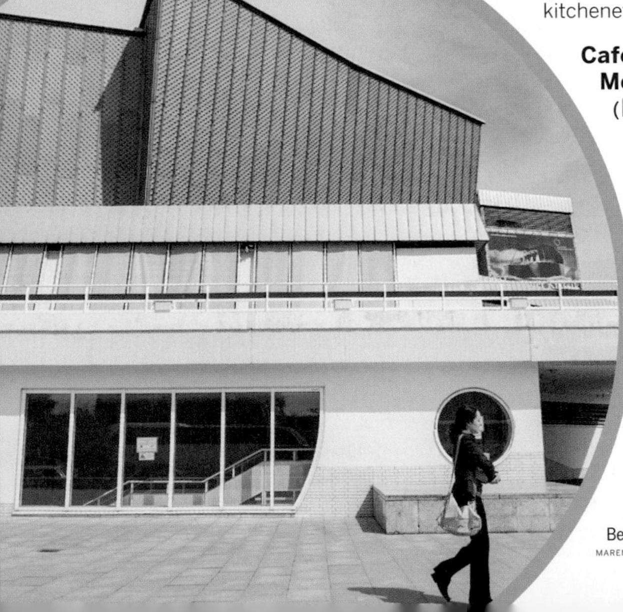

Berliner Philharmonie (p542), Berlin

or on the terrace. At night, the ambience is a bit more formal.

Information

Tourist office Frauenkirche (**0351-501 501; www.dresden.de; Neumarkt 2; 10am-7pm Mon-Fri, to 6pm Sat, to 3pm Sun**) Books rooms and tours, rents out audioguides and sells Dresden Cards for tourist discounts.

Tourist office Hauptbahnhof (**0351-501 501; www.dresden.de; Main train station, Wiener Platz; 8am-8pm**) Small office inside the main train station.

Getting There & Away

Air **Dresden Airport** (**DRS; www.dresden-airport.de**) is about 9km north of the city centre and linked by S2 train to the city centre several times hourly (€2.20, 20 minutes). Taxis are about €23.

Train Direct destinations include Leipzig (from €23.80, 70 to 100 minutes), Berlin (€40, 2¼ hours). Most trains stop at the Hauptbahnhof and at Dresden-Neustadt station across the Elbe River.

WEIMAR

03643 / POP 65,500

Neither a monumental town nor a medieval one, Weimar appeals to those whose tastes run to cultural and intellectual pleasures. Over the centuries, it has been home to an entire pantheon of intellectual and creative giants, including Goethe, Schiller, Cranach, Bach, Herder, Liszt and Nietzsche. In the 20th century, Weimar made a name for itself as the the birthplace of the seminal Bauhaus design movement.

Sights

Goethe-Nationalmuseum — Museum

(**03643-545 400; www.klassik-stiftung.de; Frauenplan 1; adult/concession/under 16yr €12/8.50/free; 9am-6pm Tue-Sun Apr-Oct, to 4pm Nov-Mar**) This museum has the most comprehensive and insightful exhibit about Johann Wolfgang von Goethe, who is to the Germans what Shakespeare is to the British. It incorporates his home of 50 years, left pretty much as it was upon his death in 1832. This is where Goethe worked, studied, researched and penned *Faust* and other immortal works. In a modern annex, documents and objects shed light on the man and his achievements, not only in literature but also in art, science and politics.

Schiller-Museum — Museum

(**03643-545 400; www.klassik-stiftung.de; Schillerstrasse 12; adult/concession/under 16yr €7.50/6/free; 9.30am-6pm Tue-Sun Apr-Oct, to 4pm Nov-Mar**) The dramatist Friedrich von Schiller (and close friend of Goethe's) lived in Weimar from 1799 until his early death in 1805. Study up on the man, his family and life in Thuringia in a recently revamped exhibit before plunging on to the private quarters, including the study with his deathbed and the desk where he wrote *Wilhelm Tell* and other famous works.

Park an der Ilm — Park

The sprawling Park an der Ilm provides a buccolic backdrop to the town and is also home to a trio of historic houses, most notably the **Goethe Gartenhaus** (where Goethe lived from 1776 to 1782), the **Römisches Haus** (the local duke's summer retreat, with period rooms and an exhibit on the park) and the **Liszt-Haus** (where the composer resided in 1848 and again from 1869 to 1886, and wrote the *Faust Symphony*).

Bauhaus Museum — Museum

(**03643-545 400; www.klassik-stiftung.de; Theaterplatz 1; adult/concession/under 16yr €4.50/3/free; 10am-6pm Apr-Oct, 10am-4pm Nov-Mar**) Considering that Weimar is the 1919 birthplace of the influential Bauhaus school of art, design and architecture, this museum is a rather modest affair. A new, representative museum is expected to open in 2018.

Sleeping

Casa dei Colori — B&B €€

(**03643-489 640; www.casa-colori.de; Eisfeld 1a; d incl breakfast €95-125; P**) Possibly

Right: Neues Rathaus and Marienplatz, Munich;
Below: Residenz-Café, Weimar

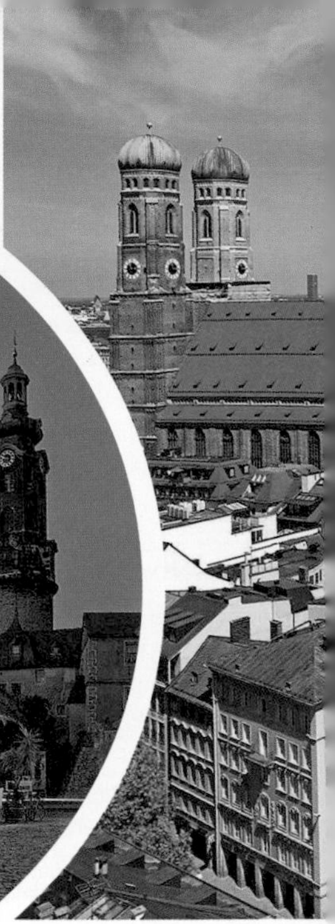

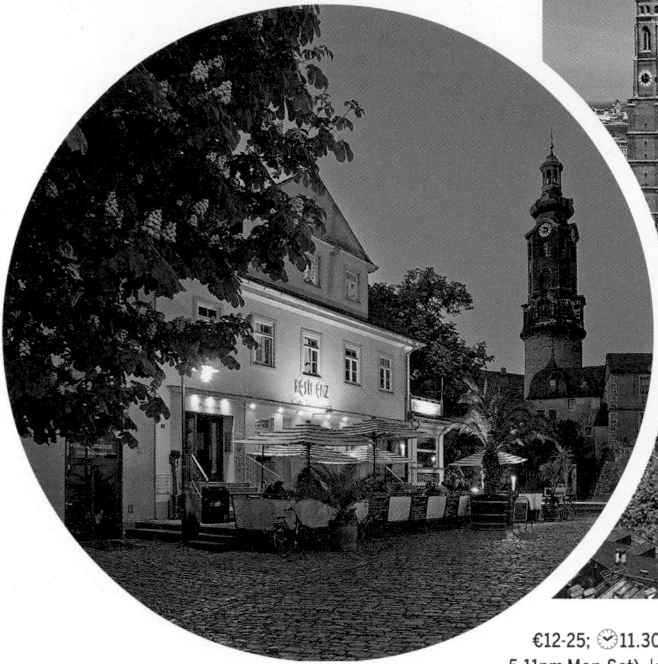

Weimar's most charming boutique *Pension*, the Casa convincingly imports cheerfully exuberant Mediterranean flair to central Europe. The mostly good-sized rooms are dressed in bold colours and come with a small desk, a couple of comfy armchairs and a stylish bathroom.

Amalienhof Hotel **€€**
(**03643-5490; www.amalienhof-weimar.de; Amalienstrasse 2; d incl breakfast & parking €97-125;** P) The charms of this hotel are manifold: classy antique furnishings, richly styled rooms that point to history without burying you in it, and a late breakfast buffet for those who take their holidays seriously. It's a splendid choice.

Eating

JoHanns Hof German **€€**
(**03643-493 617; www.restaurant-weimar.com; Scherfgasse 1; lunch special €6.50, mains €12-25; 11.30am-2.30pm & 5-11pm Mon-Sat)** JoHanns is a breezy and elegant port of call for inspired modern German cuisine and perfectly prepared choice cuts of steak, paired with a carefully curated selection of wines from the nearby Saale-Unstrut region. For a break from sightseeing, tuck into the value-priced weekday lunch specials in the cosy courtyard.

Residenz-Café International **€€**
(**03643-594 08; www.residenz-cafe.de; Grüner Markt 4; breakfast €2.90-6.40, mains €5-12; 8am-1am;**) Locally adored 'Resi' is a Viennese-style coffee house and a jack of all trades – everyone should find something to their taste here no matter where the hands on the clock. The 'Lovers' Breakfast' comes with sparkling wine, the cakes are delicious and the salads crisp, but perhaps the most creativity goes into the weekly specials.

Information

Tourist office (**☎03643-7450; www.weimar.de; Markt 10; ⌚9.30am-7pm Mon-Sat, to 3pm Sun Apr-Oct, 9.30am-6pm Mon-Fri, to 2.30pm Sat & Sun Nov-Mar**) Sells the WeimarCard (per day €14.50) for free or discounted museum admissions and travel on city buses and other benefits.

Getting There & Away

Train Weimar's Hauptbahnhof is a 20-minute walk or ride on bus 1 from the centre. Frequent direct connections include Erfurt (€5.30, 15 minutes), Eisenach (€15.30, one hour), Leipzig (€19.20, 1¾ hours), Dresden (€47, 2½ hours) and Berlin (€58, 2¼ hours).

MUNICH

☎089 / POP 1.38 MILLION

Munich is a flourishing success story that revels in its own contradictions. It's the natural habitat of well-heeled power dressers and lederhosen-clad thigh-slappers, Mediterranean-style street cafes and olde-worlde beer halls, high-brow art and high-tech industry. If you're looking for Alpine clichés, they're all here, but the Bavarian capital also has plenty of unexpected cards down its dirndl.

Sights

ALTSTADT

Marienplatz Square

(**S Marienplatz**) The heart and soul of the Altstadt, Marienplatz is a popular gathering spot and packs a lot of personality into a compact frame. It's anchored by the Mariensäule (Mary's Column), built in 1638 to celebrate the victory over Swedish forces during the Thirty Years' War. At 11am and noon (also 5pm March to October), the square jams up with tourists craning their necks to take in the cute carillon in the Neues Rathaus (New Town Hall)

Central Munich

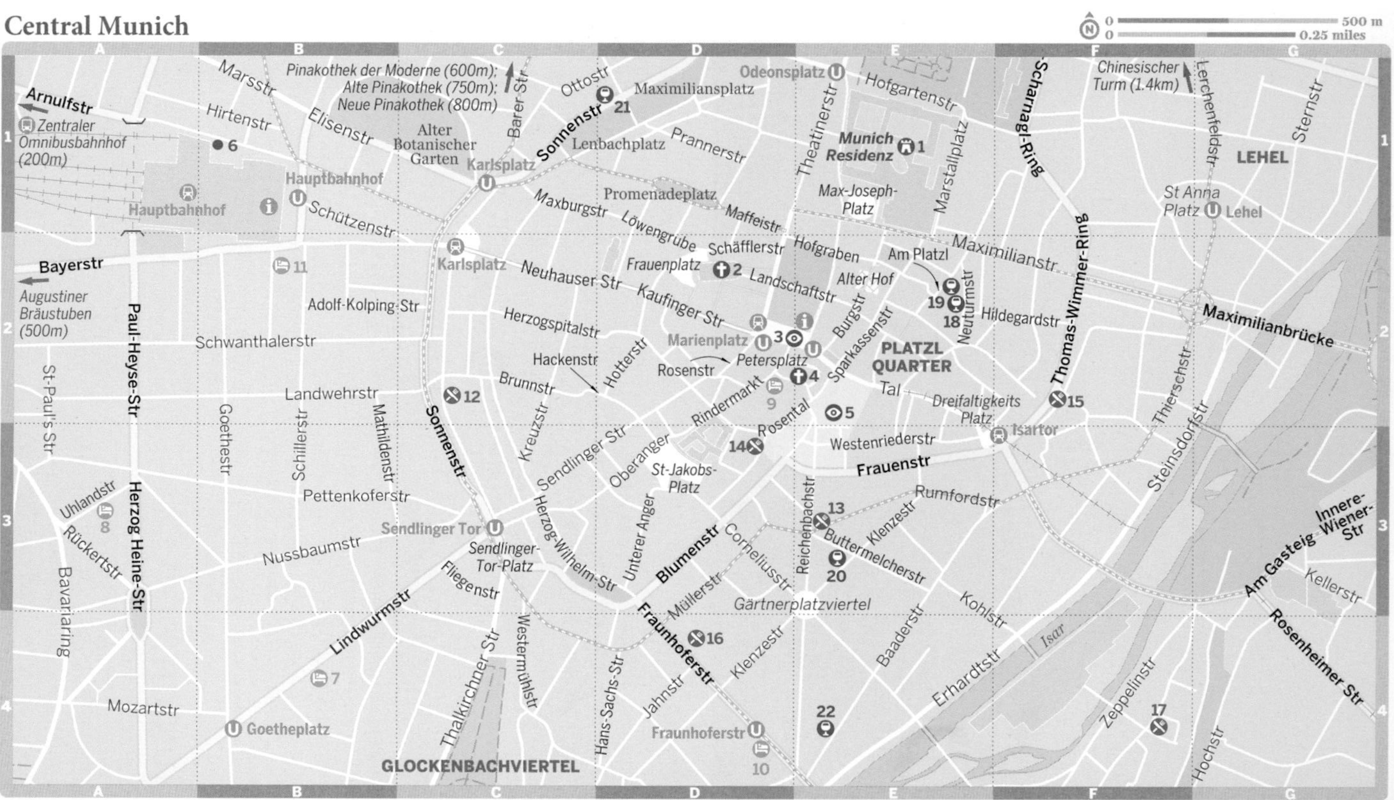

Central Munich

Don't Miss Sights
1 Munich Residenz E1

Sights
2 Frauenkirche D2
3 Marienplatz D2
4 St Peterskirche E2
5 Viktualienmarkt E2

Activities, Courses & Tours
6 Radius Tours & Bike Rental B1

Sleeping
7 Hotel Cocoon B4
8 Hotel Uhland A3
9 Louis Hotel D2
10 The Flushing Meadows D4
11 Wombats City Hostel Munich B2

Eating
12 Café Cord C2
13 Kochspielhaus E3
14 Schmalznudel D3
15 Vegelangelo F2
16 Wirtshaus Fraunhofer D4
17 Wirtshaus in der Au F4

Drinking & Nightlife
18 Atomic Café E2
19 Hofbräuhaus E2
20 Niederlassung E3
21 Rote Sonne D1
22 Zephyr Bar E4

St Peterskirche — Church

(Church of St Peter; Rindermarkt 1; admission church free, tower adult/child €2/1; tower 9am-7pm Mon-Fri, from 10am Sat & Sun May-Oct, closes 1hr earlier Nov-Apr; S Marienplatz, Marienplatz) Some 306 steps divide you from the best view of central Munich from the 92m tower of St Peterskirche, Munich's oldest church (1150). Inside awaits a virtual textbook of art through the centuries. Worth taking a closer peek at are the Gothic St-Martin-Altar, the baroque ceiling fresco by Johann Baptist Zimmermann and rococo sculptures by Ignaz Günther.

Viktualienmarkt — Market

(Mon-Fri & Sat morning; S Marienplatz, Marienplatz) Fresh fruits and vegetables, piles of artisan cheeses, tubs of exotic olives, hams and jams, chanterelles and truffles – Viktualienmarkt is a feast of flavours and one of central Europe's finest gourmet markets.

Frauenkirche — Church

(Church of Our Lady; 089-290 0820; www.muenchner-dom.de; Frauenplatz 1; 7am-7pm Sat-Wed, to 8.30pm Thu, to 6pm Fri; S Marienplatz) The landmark Frauenkirche, built between 1468 and 1488, is Munich's spiritual heart and the Mt Everest among its churches. No other building in the central city may stand taller than its onion-domed twin towers, which reach a skyscraping 99m.

MAXVORSTADT, SCHWABING & ENGLISCHER GARTEN

North of the Altstadt, Maxvorstadt is home to Munich's main university and top-drawer art museums. It segues into equally cafe-filled Schwabing which rubs up against the vast Englischer Garten, one of Europe's biggest city parks and a favourite playground for locals and visitors alike.

Alte Pinakothek — Museum

(089-238 0526; www.pinakothek.de; Barer Strasse 27; adult/child €4/2, Sun €1, audioguide €4.50; 10am-8pm Tue, to 6pm Wed-Sun; Pinakotheken, Pinakotheken) Munich's main repository of old European masters is crammed with all the major players that decorated canvases between the 14th and 18th centuries. This neoclassical temple was masterminded by Leo von Klenze and is a delicacy even if you can't tell your Rembrandt from your Rubens. The collection is world famous for its exceptional quality and depth, especially when it comes to German masters. Note that some sections are closed for renovation.

Neue Pinakothek — Museum

(089-2380 5195; www.pinakothek.de; Barer Strasse 29; adult/child €7/5, Sun €1; 10am-6pm Thu-Mon, to 8pm Wed; Pinakotheken, Pinakotheken) The Neue Pinakothek harbours a well-respected collection of 19th- and early-20th-century paintings and sculpture, from rococo to *Jugendstil* (art nouveau). All the world-famous household names get wall space here, including crowd-pleasing French impressionists such as Monet, Cézanne and Degas as

ALTRENDO TRAVEL/GETTY IMAGES ©

Don't Miss
Munich Residenz

Generations of Bavarian rulers expanded a medieval fortress into this vast and palatial compound that served as their primary residence and seat of government from 1508 to 1918. Today it's an Aladdin's cave of fanciful rooms and collections through the ages that can be seen on an audioguided tour of what is called the Residenzmuseum. Allow at least two hours to see everything at a gallop.

Highlights include the fresco-smothered Antiquarium banqueting hall and the exuberantly rococo Reiche Zimmer (Ornate Rooms). The Schatzkammer (Treasure Chamber) displays a veritable banker's bonus worth of jewel-encrusted bling of yesteryear, from golden toothpicks to finely crafted swords, miniatures in ivory to gold-covered cosmetics trunks.

NEED TO KNOW

089-290 671; www.residenz-muenchen.de; Max-Joseph-Platz 3; Museum & Schatzkammer each adult/concession/under 18yr €7/6/free; 9am-6pm Apr-mid-Oct, 10am-5pm mid-Oct-Mar, last entry 1hr before closing

well as Van Gogh, whose bold pigmented *Sunflowers* (1888) radiates cheer.

Pinakothek der Moderne Museum (**089-2380 5360; www.pinakothek.de; Barer Strasse 40; adult/child €10/7, Sun €1; 10am-6pm Tue, Wed & Fri-Sun, 10am-8pm Thu; Pinakotheken, Pinakotheken)** Germany's largest modern-art museum unites four significant collections under a single roof: 20th-century art, applied design from the 19th century to today, a graphics collection and an architecture museum. It's housed in a spectacular building by Stephan Braunfels, whose four-storey interior centres on a vast eyelike dome, from which soft natural light filters throughout blanched white galleries.

AROUND MUNICH

Schloss Nymphenburg Palace

(www.schloss-nymphenburg.de; adult/concession/under 18yr €6/5/free; 9am-6pm Apr–mid-Oct, 10am-4pm mid-Oct–Mar; Schloss Nymphenburg) The Bavarian royal family's summer residence and its lavish gardens sprawl around 5km northwest of the city centre. A self-guided tour kicks off in the Gallery of Beauties, where 38 portraits of attractive females chosen by an admiring King Ludwig I peer prettily from the walls. Other highlights include the Queen's Bedroom with the sleigh bed on which Ludwig II was born, and the King's Chamber resplendent with trompe l'œil ceiling frescoes.

Tours

Radius Tours & Bike Rental Guided Tour

(089-5502 9374; www.radiustours.com; Arnulfstrasse 3; office 8.30am-6pm Apr-Oct, to 2pm Nov-Mar) Entertaining and informative English-language tours include the donation-based city tour, a Third Reich tour and a beer-themed tour. Also does day trips to Neuschwanstein, Nuremberg and Salzburg. Bikes rent for €17 for 24 hours.

City Bus 100 Bus Tour

Ordinary city bus that runs from the Hauptbahnhof to the Ostbahnhof via 21 sights, including the Residenz and the Pinakothek museums.

Sleeping

Book way ahead during Oktoberfest and the busy summer. Many budget places cluster in the cheerless streets around the train station.

Wombats City Hostel Munich Hostel €

(089-5998 9180; www.wombats-hostels.com; Senefelderstrasse 1; dm €19-29, d €76; P @; S Hauptbahnhof, Hauptbahnhof) Munich's top hostel is a professionally run affair with a whopping 300 dorm beds plus private rooms. Dorms are painted in cheerful pastels and outfitted with wooden floors, en suite facilities, sturdy lockers and comfy pine bunks, all in a central location near the train station. A free welcome drink awaits in the bar. Breakfast costs €3.90.

Hotel Uhland Hotel €€

(089-543 350; www.hotel-uhland.de; Uhlandstrasse 1; s/d incl breakfast from €75/95; P; S Theresienwiese) The Uhland is an enduring favourite with regulars who like their hotel to feel like a home away from home. Free wi-fi and parking, a breakfast buffet with organic products, and minibar drinks that won't dent your budget are just some of the thoughtful features. Rooms have extra large waterbeds.

Flushing Meadows Design Hotel €€

(089-5527 9170; www.flushingmeadowshotel.com; Fraunhoferstrasse 32; studios €115-165; reception 6am-11pm; P; S Fraunhoferstrasse) Urban explorers keen on up-to-the-minute design cherish this new contender on the top two floors of a former postal office in the hip Glockenbachviertel. Each

Oktoberfest

Hordes come to Munich for **Oktoberfest** (www.oktoberfest.de), running the 15 days before the first Sunday in October. Go early in the day so you can grab a seat in one of the hangar-sized beer tents spread across the Theresienwiese grounds, about 1km southwest of the Hauptbahnhof (central train station). While there is no entrance fee, those €11 1L steins of beer (called *Mass*) add up fast.

Although its origins are in the marriage celebrations of Crown Prince Ludwig in 1810, there's nothing regal about this beery bacchanalia now: expect mobs, expect to meet new and drunken friends, expect decorum to vanish as night sets in and you'll have a blast.

of the 11 concrete-ceilinged lofts reflects the vision of a locally known creative type, while three of the five penthouse studios have a private terrace. Breakfast costs €11.

Hotel Cocoon Design Hotel **€€**
(☎089-5999 3907; www.hotel-cocoon.de; Lindwurmstrasse 35; s/d from €69/89; **S** Sendlinger Tor, 🚊 Sendlinger Tor) Fans of retro design will strike gold in this central lifestyle hotel. Things kick off in the reception with its faux. '70s veneer and dangling '60s ball chairs, and continue in the rooms. All are identical, decorated in retro oranges and greens and equipped with LCD TV, iPod dock and a 'laptop cabin'. Breakfast costs €9.

Louis Hotel Hotel **€€€**
(☎089-411 9080; www.louis-hotel.com; Viktualienmarkt 6/Rindermarkt 2; r €159-289; **S** Marienplatz) An air of relaxed sophistication pervades the scene-savvy Louis, where good-sized rooms are furnished in nut and oak, natural stone and elegant tiles and equipped with the gamut of 'electronica', including iPod docks and flat screens with Sky TV. All have small balconies facing either the courtyard or the Viktualienmarkt. Views are also terrific from the rooftop bar and restaurant. Breakfast costs €24.50.

Eating

Schmalznudel Cafe **€**
(Cafe Frischhut; ☎089-2602 3156; Prälat-Zistl-Strasse 8; pastries €1.70; ⏲7am-6pm Mon-Fri, 5am-5pm Sat; **S** Marienplatz, 🚆 Marienplatz) Officially called Cafe Frischhut, this little cult joint is known to most locals by its nickname, *Schmalznudel*, an oily type of doughnut that is the only thing served here. Best enjoyed with a pot of steaming coffee.

Wirtshaus in der Au Bavarian **€€**
(☎089-448 1400; Lilienstrasse 51; mains €9-20; ⏲5pm-midnight Mon-Fri, from 10am Sat & Sun; 🚊 Deutsches Museum) This traditional Bavarian restaurant has a solid 21st-century vibe but its the time-honoured dumpling that's the top speciality here, although carnvores might prefer the roast duck or another hearty menu item. Once a brewery, the space-rich dining room has chunky tiled floors, a lofty ceiling and a crackling fireplace in winter. When spring springs, the beer garden fills.

Wirtshaus Fraunhofer Bavarian **€€**
(☎089-266 460; www.fraunhofertheater.de; Fraunhoferstrasse 9; mains €7.50-19; ⏲4pm-1am; 🌶; 🚊 Müllerstrasse) With its screechy parquet floors, stuccoed ceilings, wood panelling and virtually no trace that the last century even happened, this wonderfully characterful inn is perfect for exploring the region with a fork. The menu is a seasonally adapted checklist of southern German favourites, but also features at least a dozen vegetarian dishes.

Vegelangelo Vegetarian **€€**
(☎089-2880 6836; www.vegelangelo.de; Thomas-Wimmer-Ring 16; mains €10-19; ⏲noon-2pm Tue-Thu, 6pm-late Mon-Sat; 🌶; 🚊 Isartor, 🚆 Isartor) Reservations are recommended at this petite vegie spot where Indian odds and ends, a piano and a small Victorian fireplace distract little from the superb meat-free cooking, all of which can be adapted to suit vegans. There's a menu-only policy Fridays and Saturdays (3/4 courses €24/30). Cash only.

Café Cord International **€€**
(☎089-5454 0780; www.cafe-cord.tv; Sonnenstrasse 19; mains €10-20; ⏲11am-1am Mon-Sat; **S** Karlsplatz, 🚊 Karlsplatz, 🚆 Karlsplatz) Clean-cut Cord is a good stop for a light lunch or coffee, or an ideal first stop on the club circuit. In summer the super-delicious global fare (mains €10 to €20) tastes best in the romantic, twinkle-lit courtyard.

Kochspielhaus International **€€**
(☎089-5480 2738; www.kochspielhaus.de; Rumfordstrasse 5; breakfast €10-16, mains €13-26; ⏲7am-8pm Sun & Mon, 6.30am-midnight Tue-Sat; **S** Fraunhoferstrasse) Attached to a gourmet bakery called Backspielhaus, this modern-country-style lair accented with massive candles packages only superfresh, top-quality ingredients into clever pasta, meat and fish dishes. Also a great spot for breakfast, especially in

Beer Halls & Beer Gardens

Beer drinking is not just an integral part of Munich's entertainment scene, it's a reason to visit. Here are some of our favourite places to knock back a couple or three:

Augustiner Bräustuben (089-507 047; www.braeustuben.de; Landsberger Strasse 19; 10am-midnight; Holzapfelstrasse) At this authentic beer hall inside the actual Augustiner brewery, the Bavarian grub is superb, especially the *Schweinshaxe* (pork knuckles). It's about 700m west of the Hauptbahnhof.

Hofbräuhaus (089-290 136 100; www.hofbraeuhaus.de; Am Platzl 9; 9am-11.30pm; S Marienplatz, Kammerspiele, Marienplatz) The ultimate cliché of Munich beer halls where tourists arrive by the busload but no one seems to mind.

Chinesischer Turm (089-383 8730; www.chinaturm.de; Englischer Garten 3; 10am-11pm; Chinesischer Turm, Tivolistrasse) This one's hard to ignore because of its English Garden location and pedigree as Munich's oldest beer garden (open since 1791).

summer when the white outdoor tables and benches beckon.

Drinking & Nightlife

Apart from the beer halls and gardens, Munich has no shortage of lively pubs. The Glockenbachviertel, the Gärtnerplatzviertel, Maxvorstadt and Schwabing are good places to nose around for fun.

Zephyr Bar Cocktail Bar

(www.zephyr-bar.de; Baaderstrasse 68; 8pm-1am Mon-Thu, to 3am Fri & Sat; S Fraunhoferstrasse) At one of Munich's best bars, Alex Schmaltz whips up courageous potions with unusual ingredients such as homemade cucumber-dill juice, sesame oil or banana-parsley purée. Cocktail alchemy at its finest, and a top gin selection to boot. No reservations.

Niederlassung Bar

(089-3260 0307; www.niederlassung.org; Buttermelcherstrasse 6; 7pm-1am Tue-Thu, to 3am Fri & Sat, to midnight Sun; S Fraunhoferstrasse, Isartor) From Adler Dry to Zephyr, this gin joint stocks an impressive 80 varieties of juniper juice in an unpretentious setting filled with books and sofas and humming with indie sounds. There's even a selection of different tonic waters to choose from. Happy hour from 7pm to 9pm and after midnight.

Atomic Café Club

(www.atomic.de; Neuturmstrasse 5; from 10pm Wed-Sat; Kammerspiele) This bastion of indie sounds with funky '60s decor is known for bookers with a knack for catching upwardly hopeful bands before their big break. Otherwise it's party time; long-running Britwoch is the hottest Wednesday club night in town.

Rote Sonne Club

(089-5526 3330; www.rote-sonne.com; Maximiliansplatz 5; from 11pm Thu-Sun; Lenbachplatz) Named for a 1969 Munich cult movie starring It-Girl Uschi Obermaier, the Red Sun is a fiery nirvana for fans of electronic sounds. A global roster of DJs keeps the wooden dance floor packed and sweaty until the sun rises.

Information

Tourist office Hauptbahnhof (089-2339 6500; www.muenchen.de; Bahnhofplatz 2; 9am-8pm Mon-Sat, 10am-6pm Sun)

Tourist office Marienplatz (089-2339 6500; www.muenchen.de; Marienplatz 2; 10am-7pm Mon-Fri, to 5pm Sat, to 2pm Sun)

Detour: Dachau Concentration Camp

About 16km northwest of central Munich, **Dachau (Dachau Concentration Camp Memorial Site; ☎08131-669 970; www.kz-gedenkstaette-dachau.de; Peter-Roth-Strasse 2a, Dachau; museum admission free; ⏰9am-5pm Tue-Sun)** opened in 1933 as the first Nazi concentration camp. All in all, it 'processed' more than 200,000 inmates, killing between 30,000 and 40,000. It is now a haunting memorial that will stay long in your memory. Expect to spend two to three hours exploring the grounds and exhibits. For deeper understanding, pick up an audioguide (€3.50), join a 2½-hour tour and watch the 22-minute English-language documentary at the main museum.

From the Hauptbahnhof (central train station) take the S2 to Dachau station (two-zone ticket, €5.20, 25 minutes), then catch bus 726 (direction: Saubachsiedlung) to the KZ-Gedenkstätte stop.

Getting There & Away

Air

Munich Airport **(MUC; www.munich-airport.de)** is about 30km northeast of town and linked to the Hauptbahnhof every 10 minutes by S-Bahn (S1 and S8, €10.40, 40 minutes) and every 20 minutes by the Lufthansa Airport Bus (€10.50, 45 minutes, between 5am and 8pm).

Note that Ryanair flies into Memmingen's Allgäu Airport **(FMM; www.allgaeu-airport.de)**, 125km to the west.

Bus

Buses, including the Romantic Road Coach, depart from Zentraler Omnibusbahnhof **(Central Bus Station, ZOB; Arnulfstrasse 21)** at S-Bahn station Hackerbrücke near the main train station.

Train

All services leave from the Hauptbahnhof, where Euraide **(www.euraide.de; Desk 1, Reisezentrum, Hauptbahnhof; ⏰10am-7pm Mon-Fri Aug-Apr)** is a friendly English-speaking travel agency.

Frequent fast and direct service includes trains to Nuremberg (€55, 1¼ hours), Frankfurt (€101, 3¼ hours), Berlin (€130, six hours) and Vienna (€91.20, four hours) as well as twice-daily trains to Prague (€69.10, six hours).

Getting Around

For information and trip planning, consult www.mvv.de.

BERCHTESGADEN

☎08652 / POP 7600

Steeped in myth and legend, the Berchtesgadener Land is almost preternaturally beautiful. Framed by six formidable mountain ranges and home to Germany's second-highest mountain, the Watzmann (2713m), its dreamy, fir-lined valleys are filled with gurgling streams and peaceful Alpine villages.

Much of the terrain is protected as the Nationalpark Berchtesgaden, which embraces the pristine Königssee, one of Germany's most photogenic lakes. Yet, Berchtesgaden's history is also indelibly entwined with the Nazi period, as chronicled at the disturbing Dokumentation Obersalzberg. The Eagle's Nest, a mountain-top lodge built for Hitler, is now a major tourist attraction.

Sights

Eagle's Nest Historic Site

(Kehlsteinhaus; ☎08652-2969; www.kehlsteinhaus.de; Obersalzberg; adult/child €16.10/9.30; ⏰buses 7.40am-4pm mid-May–Oct) The Eagle's Nest is a mountain-top retreat built as a 50th-birthday gift for Hitler. It took some 3000 workers only two years to carve the precipitous 6km-long mountain road, cut a 124m-long tunnel and a brass-panelled lift through the rock, and build the lodge itself (now a restaurant). It can only be reached by special shuttle bus from the Kehlsteinhaus bus station. Avoid peak hours (10am to 1pm).

On clear days, views from the top are breathtaking. If you're not driving, bus 838 makes the trip to the shuttle-bus stop from the Berchtesgaden Hauptbahnhof every half-hour.

At the mountain station, you'll be asked to book a spot on a return bus. Allow at least two hours to get through lines, explore the lodge and the mountain-top, and perhaps have a bite to eat. Don't panic if you miss your bus – just go back to the mountain-station kiosk and rebook.

Dokumentation Obersalzberg Museum

(☎08652-947 960; www.obersalzberg.de; Salzbergstrasse 41, Obersalzberg; adult/concession €3/free, audioguide €2; ⏲9am-5pm daily Apr-Oct, 10am-3pm Tue-Sun Nov-Mar, last entry 1hr before closing) In 1933 the quiet mountain village of Obersalzberg (3km from Berchtesgaden) became the second seat of Nazi power after Berlin, a dark period that's given the full historical treatment at this excellent exhibit. It documents the forced takeover of the area, the construction of the compound and the daily life of the Nazi elite. All facets of Nazi terror are dealt with, including Hitler's near-mythical appeal, his racial politics, the Resistance movement, foreign policy and the death camps.

Königssee Lake

(☎08652-963 696; www.seenschifffahrt.de; Schönau; return boat adult/child €13.90/7; ⏲boats 8am-5.15pm May–mid-Oct) Crossing the serenely picturesque, emerald-green Königssee makes for some unforgettable memories and once-in-a-lifetime photo opportunities. Cradled by steep mountain walls some 5km south of Berchtesgaden, the Königssee is Germany's highest lake (603m), with drinkably pure waters shimmering into fjordlike depths. Bus 841 makes the trip out here from the Berchtesgaden train station roughly every hour.

Escape the hubbub of the bustling lakeside tourist village of Schönau by taking an electric boat tour to **St Bartholomä**, a quaint onion-domed chapel on the western shore. At some point, the boat will stop while the captain plays a horn towards the Echo Wall – the sound will bounce seven times. From St Bartholomä, an easy trail leads to the wondrous **Eiskapelle** (Ice Chapel) in about one hour.

You can also skip the crowds by meandering along the lake shore. It's a nice and easy 3.5km return walk to the secluded **Malerwinkel** (Painter's Corner), a lookout famed for its picturesque vantage point.

Nationalpark Berchtesgaden

DANITA DELIMONT/GETTY IMAGES ©

Sleeping & Eating

Hotel Edelweiss Hotel **€€€**

(☎08652-979 90; www.edelweiss-berchtesgaden.com; Maximilianstrasse 2; d incl breakfast €200-236) Smack-dab in the town centre, the Edelweiss is Berchtesgaden's sleek new contender. The style is modern Bavarian, meaning a combination of traditional woodsy flair and such hip factors as a luxe spa, a rooftop terrace restaurant-bar with wonderful mountain views and an outdoor infinity pool. Rooms are XL-sized and most have a balcony.

Bräustübl Bavarian **€€**

(☎08652-976 724; www.braeustueberl-berchtesgaden.de; Bräuhausstrasse 13; mains €6.80-16; ⌚10am-1am) Past the vaulted entrance painted in Bavaria's white and blue diamonds, this cosy beer hall–beer garden is run by the local brewery. Expect a carnivorous feast with such favourite rib-stickers as pork roast and the house speciality: baked veal head (better than it sounds). On Friday and Saturday, a folkloric band kicks into knee-slapping action.

Tours

Eagle's Nest Tours Tour

(☎08652-649 71; www.eagles-nest-tours.com; Königsseer Strasse 2; adult/child €53/35; ⌚1.15pm mid-May–Oct) This highly reputable outfit offers a fascinating overview of Berchtesgaden's Nazi legacy.

Information

Tourist office (☎08652-896 70; www.berchtesgaden.com; Königsseer Strasse 2; ⌚8.30am-6pm Mon-Fri, 9am-5pm Sat, 9am-3pm Sun Apr–mid-Oct, reduced hours mid-Oct–Mar) Near the train station, this office has information about the entire Berchtegaden region.

Getting There & Away

Bus 840 connects the train stations in Berchtesgaden and Salzburg twice hourly (50 minutes).

Travelling from Munich by train involves a change to a bus at Freilassing (€32.80, 2½ hours).

ROMANTIC ROAD

From the vineyards of Würzburg to the foot of the Alps, the almost-400km-long Romantic Road (Romantische Strasse) is by far the most popular of Germany's themed holiday routes. It passes through more than two dozen villages and towns, the most famous being Rothenburg ob der Tauber and Füssen, home to Neuschwanstein, Germany's most famous castle.

Getting There & Around

Frankfurt and Munich are the most popular gateways for exploring the Romantic Road, especially if you decide to take the Romantic Road Coach (www.romanticroadcoach.de). From April to October this special service runs one coach daily in each direction between Frankfurt and Füssen (for Neuschwanstein) via Munich; the entire trip takes around 12 hours. There's no charge for breaking the journey and continuing the next day. Note that buses get incredibly crowded in summer.

Tickets are available for the entire route or for short segments. Buy them online or from travel agents, EurAide in Munich or Reisezentrum offices in larger train stations.

Rothenburg ob der Tauber

☎09861 / POP 11,000

In the Middle Ages, Rothenburg's town fathers built strong walls to protect the town from siege; today they are the reason the town is under siege from tourists. The most stereotypical of all German walled towns, Rothenburg can't help being so cute. Granted 'free imperial city' status in 1274, it's a confection of twisting cobbled lanes and pretty architecture enclosed by towered stone walls. Swarmed during the day, the underlying charm oozes out after the last bus leaves.

Sights

Jakobskirche Church

(Church of St Jacob; Klingengasse 1; adult/concession €2.50/1.50; ⌚9am-5.15pm Mon-Sat, 10.45am-5.15pm Sun) Rothenburg's majestic 500-year-old Lutheran parish church shelters the **Heilig Blut Altar** (Sacred

BRIAN LAWRENCE/GETTY IMAGES ©

Don't Miss
Neuschwanstein & Hohenschwangau Castles

Commissioned by Bavaria's most celebrated (and loopiest) 19th-century monarch, Ludwig II, Schloss Neuschwanstein rises from Alpine forests like a storybook illustration, dwarfing the king's teenage home of Hohenschwangau. Both castles must be seen on guided 35-minute tours (in German or English). Timed tickets are only available from the Ticket-Center at the foot of the castles and may be reserved online until two days prior to your visit (recommended). If visiting both castles on the same day, Hohenschwangau is scheduled first.

Schloss Neuschwanstein was reportedly the model for Disney's *Sleeping Beauty* castle. Ludwig II planned this sugary fairy-tale pile himself, with the help of a stage designer rather than an architect. He envisioned it as a giant set on which to re-create the world of Germanic mythology, inspired by the operatic works of his friend Richard Wagner. The most impressive room is the **Sängersaal** (Minstrels' Hall) the wall frescoes of which depict scenes from the opera *Tannhäuser*.

Other completed sections include Ludwig's Tristan and Isolde–themed bedroom, dominated by a huge Gothic-style bed crowned with intricately carved cathedral-like spires; a gaudy **artificial grotto** (another allusion to *Tannhäuser*); and the Byzantine-style **Thronsaal** (Throne Room) with an incredible mosaic floor containing over two million stones. The tour ends with a 20-minute film on the castle and its creator.

For the postcard view of Neuschwanstein, walk 10 minutes up to **Marienbrücke** (Mary's Bridge).

The castles are 4km outside the town of Füssen, which is served by regional train from Munich. From Füssen train station, bus 78 or 73 go the castles. It's possible to do this as a day trip if leaving Munich around 8am.

NEED TO KNOW

tickets 08362-930 830; www.neuschwanstein.de; Neuschwansteinstrasse 20, Hohenschwangau; each castle adult/concession/under 18yr €12/11/free, combination ticket €23/21/free; 9am-6pm Apr–mid-Oct, 10am-4pm mid-Oct–Mar

Blood Altar), a supremely intricate altarpiece by medieval master carver Tilman Riemenschneider (it's up the stairs behind the organ).

Rathausturm Historic Building

(Town Hall Tower; Marktplatz; adult/concession €2/0.50; ⌚9.30am-12.30pm & 1-5pm daily Apr-Oct, noon-3pm Sat & Sun Jan-Mar & Nov, 10.30-2pm & 2.30-6pm daily Dec) Climb the 220 steps of the medieval town hall to the viewing platform of the Rathausturm to be rewarded with widescreen views of the Tauber.

Stadtmauer Historic Site

(Town Wall) Follow in the footsteps of sentries on a walk along Rothenburg's original 15th-century town fortifications. A 2.5km stretch of it is accessible, but even a short walk 5m to 7m above the ground delivers tremendous views over the town's red roofs.

Mittelalterliches Kriminalmuseum Museum

(Medieval Crime & Punishment Museum; www.kriminalmuseum.eu; Burggasse 3; adult/concession €5/3.50; ⌚10am-6pm May-Oct, shorter hours Nov-Apr) Medieval implements of torture and punishment are on show at this gruesomely fascinating museum. Exhibits include chastity belts, masks of disgrace for gossips, a cage for cheating bakers, a neck brace for quarrelsome women and a beer-barrel pen for drunks. You can even snap a selfie of yourself in the stocks!

Sleeping & Eating

Altfränkische Weinstube Hotel **€€**

(☎09861-6404; www.altfraenkische.de; Klosterhof 7; d €75-118; 📶) This characterful inn has six romantic country-style rooms with exposed half-timber, bath-tubs and most with four-poster or canopied beds. From 6pm onwards, the tavern serves up sound regional fare (mains €7 to €16) with a dollop of medieval cheer.

Mittermeier Bavarian **€€**

(☎09861-945 430; www.villamittermeier.de; Vorm Würzburger Tor 7; mains €12-19; ⌚6-10.30pm Tue-Sat; P 📶) You'll sleep well in this smartly designed hotel just outside the town wall. The kitchen ninjas in the vaulted cellar restaurant pair punctilious craftsmanship with top-notch ingredients, sourced regionally whenever possi-

Würzburg Residenz

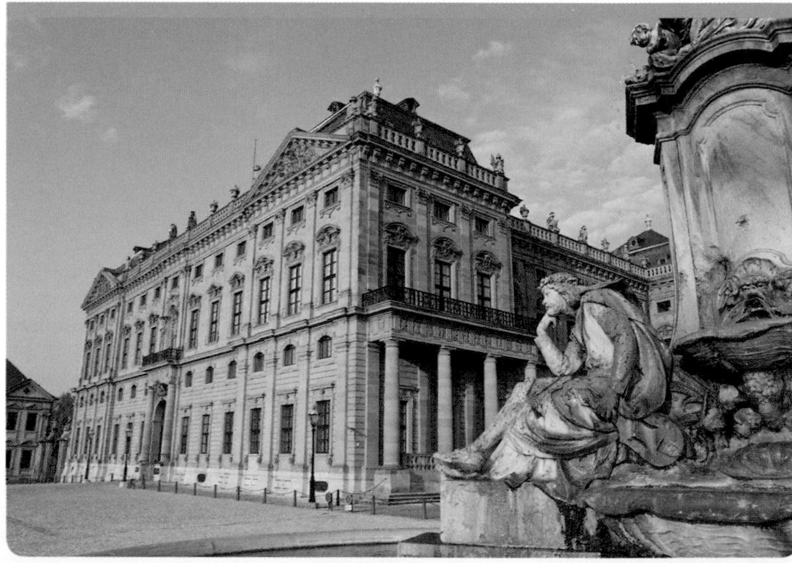

REINHARD DIRSCHERL/GETTY IMAGES ©

ble (dinner mains €22 to €38). The focus is on grills paired with creative sides and superb wines from Franconia and beyond. Breakfast costs €10.

Gasthof Butz German **€**
(☎09861-2201; Kapellenplatz 4; mains €7-15; ⏰11.30am-2pm & 6-9pm; 📶) For a quick, no-nonsense goulash, schnitzel or roast pork, lug your weary legs to this locally adored, family-run inn in a former brewery. In summer two flowery beer gardens beckon. It also rents a dozen simply furnished rooms (double €36 to €75).

Information

Tourist office (☎09861-404 800; www.tourismus.rothenburg.de; Marktplatz 2; ⏰9am-6pm Mon-Fri, 10am-5pm Sat & Sun May-Oct, 9am-5pm Mon-Fri, 10am-1pm Sat Nov-Mar) Offers free internet access.

Getting There & Away

Bus The Romantic Road Coach pauses in town for 45 minutes.

Train There are hourly trains to/from Steinach, a transfer point for service to Würzburg (€12.90, 1¼ hours).

Würzburg

☎0931 / POP 133,500

Tucked in among river valleys lined with vineyards, Würzburg beguiles even before you reach the city centre and is renowned for its art, architecture and delicate wines. For centuries the resident prince-bishops wielded enormous power and wealth, and the city grew in opulence under their rule. Its crowning glory is the Residenz, one of the finest baroque structures in Germany and a Unesco World Heritage Site.

Sights

Würzburg Residenz Palace
(www.residenz-wuerzburg.de; Balthasar-Neumann-Promenade; adult/concession/under 18yr €7.50/6.50/free; ⏰9am-6pm Apr-Oct, 10am-4.30pm Nov-Mar, 45-minute English tours 11am & 3pm, also 4.30pm Apr-Oct) The vast Unesco-listed Residenz, built by 18th-century starchitect Balthasar Neumann as the home of the local prince-bishops, is one of Germany's most important and beautiful baroque palaces. Top billing goes to the brilliant zigzagging **Treppenhaus** (Staircase), lidded by what still is the world's largest fresco, a masterpiece by Giovanni Battista Tiepolo depicting allegories of the four then-known continents (Europe, Africa, America and Asia). Most of the palace can be explored on your own.

The structure was commissioned in 1720 by Johann Philipp Franz von Schönborn, the prince-bishop unhappy with his old-fashioned digs up in Marienberg Fortress, and took almost 60 years to complete. Today the 360 rooms are home to government institutions, university faculties and a museum, but the grandest 40 have been restored for visitors to admire.

Besides the Grand Staircase, feast your eyes on the ice-white stucco-adorned **Weisser Saal** (White Hall) before entering the **Kaisersaal** (Imperial Hall), canopied by yet another impressive Tiepolo fresco. Other stunners include the gilded stucco **Spiegelkabinett** (Mirror Hall), covered with a unique mirrorlike glass painted with figural, floral and animal motifs (accessible by tour only).

In the residence's south wing, the **Hofkirche** (Court Church) is another Neumann and Tiepolo coproduction. Its marble columns, gold leaf and profusion of angels match the Residenz in splendour and proportions.

Entered via frilly wrought-iron gates, the **Hofgarten** (Court Garden; admission free; ⏰to dusk) is a smooth blend of French- and English-style landscaping teeming with whimsical sculptures of children, mostly by court sculptor Peter Wagner. Concerts, festivals and special events take place here during the warmer months.

The complex also houses collections of antiques, paintings and drawings in the Martin-von-Wagner Museum (no relation to Peter) and, handily, a winery in the atmospheric cellar, the **Staatlicher Hofkeller Würzburg**, that is open for tours with tasting.

Festung Marienberg Fortress
(tour adult/concession €3.50/2.50; tours 11am, 2pm, 3pm & 4pm Tue-Sun, also 10am & 1pm Sat & Sun mid-Mar–Oct, 11am, 2pm & 3pm Sat & Sun Nov–mid-Mar) Enjoy panoramic city and vineyard views from this hulking fortress, the construction of which was initiated around 1200 by the local prince-bishops who governed here until 1719. Dramatically illuminated at night, the structure was only penetrated once, by Swedish troops during the Thirty Years' War, in 1631. Inside, the **Fürstenbaumuseum** (closed November to mid-March) sheds light on its former residents' pompous lifestyle, while the **Mainfränkisches Museum** presents city history and works by local late-Gothic master carver Tilmann Riemenschneider and other famous artists.

The fortress is a 30-minute walk up the hill through the vineyards from the Alte Mainbrücke via the Tellsteige trail.

Sleeping & Eating

Hotel Zum Winzermännle Hotel €€
(0931-541 56; www.winzermaennle.de; Domstrasse 32; s €60-79, d €90-110; P) This family-run converted winery is a feel-good retreat in the city's pedestrianised heart. Rooms are well furnished if a little on the old-fashioned side; some among those facing the quiet courtyard have balconies. Communal areas are bright and often seasonally decorated. Breakfast costs €5.

Alte Mainmühle Franconian €€
(0931-167 77; www.alte-mainmuehle.de; Mainkai 1; mains €8-23; 9.30am-midnight) Tourists and locals alike cram into this old mill, accessed straight from the old bridge, to savour modern twists on Franconian classics (including popular river fish). In summer the double terrace beckons – the upper one delivers pretty views of the bridge and Marienberg Fortress; in winter retreat to the snug timber dining room. Year-round, guests spill out onto the bridge itself, wine glass in hand.

Backöfele Franconian €€
(0931-590 59; www.backoefele.de; Ursulinergasse 2; mains €7-19.50; noon-midnight Mon-Thu, to 1am Fri & Sat, to 11pm Sun) This old-timey warren has been spreading hearty Franconian food love for nearly 50 years. Find a table in the cobbled courtyard or one of four historic rooms, each candlelit and uniquely furnished with local flair. Featuring schnitzel, snails, bratwurst in wine, wine soup with cinnamon croutons, grilled meat and other local faves, the menu makes for mouth-watering reading. Bookings are recommended.

Christmas market (p568), Nuremberg

Getting There & Away

Bus The Romantic Road Coach stops next to the Hauptbahnhof.

Train Frequent trains run to Frankfurt (€35, 1¼ hours), Nuremberg (from €20.30, one hour) and Rothenburg ob der Tauber (via Steinach, €12.90, 1¼ hours).

NUREMBERG

☎0911 / POP 510,000

Nuremberg (Nürnberg) woos visitors with its wonderfully restored medieval Altstadt, its grand castle and, in December, its magical *Christkindlmarkt* (Christmas market).

The city played a major role during the Nazi years. It was here that the fanatical party rallies were held, the boycott of Jewish businesses began and the infamous Nuremberg Laws outlawing Jewish citizenship were enacted. After WWII the city was chosen as the site of the Nuremberg Trials of Nazi war criminals.

Sights

The city centre is best explored on foot, but the Nazi-related sights are a tram ride away.

Hauptmarkt — Square

This bustling square in the heart of the Altstadt is the site of daily markets as well as the famous *Christkindlsmarkt*. At the eastern end is the ornate Gothic **Frauenkirche** (church). Daily at noon crowds crane their necks to witness the clock's figures enact a spectacle called the *Männleinlaufen*. Rising from the square like a Gothic spire is the sculpture-festooned **Schöner Brunnen** (Beautiful Fountain). Touch the golden ring in the ornate wrought-iron gate if you want good luck.

Kaiserburg — Castle

(Imperial Castle; ☎0911-244 6590; www.kaiserburg-nuernberg.de; Auf der Burg; adult/concession incl Sinwell Tower €7/6, Palas & Museum €5.50/4.50; ⏰9am-6pm Apr-Sep, 10am-4pm Oct-Mar) This enormous castle complex above the Altstadt poignantly reflects Nuremberg's medieval might. Don't miss a tour of the residential wing (**Palas**) to see the lavish Knights' and Imperial Hall, a Romanesque double chapel and an exhibit on the inner workings of the

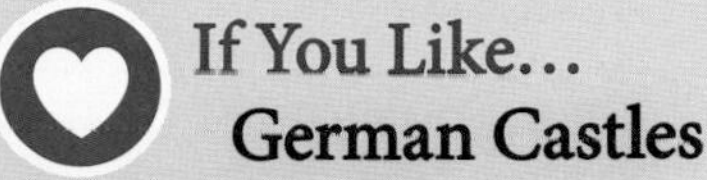

If You Like... German Castles

The twin castles of Neuschwanstein and Hohenschwangau are undoubtedly the most famous castles in Germany, but they're certainly not the only ones to explore.

1 WARTBURG

(☎03691-2500; www.wartburg-eisenach.de; Auf der Wartburg 1; tour adult/concession €9/5, museum & Luther study only €5/3; ⏰tours 8.30am-5pm Apr-Oct, 9am-3.30pm Nov-Mar, English tour 1.30pm) When it comes to medieval castles and their importance in German history, Eisenach's Wartburg is the mother lode. This huge medieval castle is where Martin Luther went into hiding in 1521 after being excommunicated and placed under papal ban. During his 10-month stay, he translated the New Testament from Greek into German, contributing enormously to the development of the written German language. Budget at least two hours: one for the guided tour, the rest for the museum and the grounds (views!).

2 SCHLOSS HEIDELBERG

(☎06221-658 880; www.schloss-heidelberg.de; adult/child incl Bergbahn €6/4, tours €4/2, audioguide €4; ⏰grounds 24hr, castle 8am-6pm, English tours hourly 11.15am-4.15pm Mon-Fri, 10.15-4.15pm Sat & Sun Apr-Oct, reduced tours Nov-Mar) Towering over the Altstadt (old town), Heidelberg's ruined Renaissance castle cuts a romantic figure, especially when illuminated at night and seen across the Neckar River. Attractions include the world's largest wine cask and fabulous views. Get there either via a steep, cobbled trail in about 10 minutes or by taking the cogwheel train from Kornmarkt station (tickets include Schloss entry). After 6pm you can stroll the grounds for free.

Right: Schloss Neuschwanstein (p561); Below: Cows grazing in the Black Forest region (p568)

Holy Roman Empire. This segues to the **Kaiserburg Museum**, which focuses on the castle's military and building history. Elsewhere, enjoy panoramic views from the **Sinwell Tower** or peer 48m down into the **Deep Well**.

Memorium Nuremberg Trials — Memorial

(☎0911-3217 9372; www.memorium-nuremberg.de; Bärenschanzstrasse 72; adult/concession incl audioguide €5/3; ⏰10am-6pm Wed-Mon) Göring, Hess, Speer and 21 other Nazi leaders were tried for crimes against peace and humanity by the Allies in Schwurgerichtssaal 600 (Court Room 600) of this still-working courthouse. Today the room forms part of an engaging exhibit detailing the background, progression and impact of the trials using film, photographs, audiotape and even the original defendants' dock. To get here, take the U1 towards Bärenschanze and get off at Sielstrasse.

Reichsparteitagsgelände — Historic Site

(Luitpoldhain; ☎0911-231 5666; www.museen-nuernberg.de; Bayernstrasse 110; grounds free, documentation centre adult/concession incl audioguide €5/3; ⏰grounds 24hr, documentation centre 9am-6pm Mon-Fri, 10am-6pm Sat & Sun) If you've ever wondered where the infamous black-and-white images of ecstatic Nazi supporters hailing their Führer were taken, it was here in Nuremberg. Much of the grounds were destroyed during Allied bombing raids, but enough remain to get a sense of the megalomania behind it, especially after visiting the excellent **Dokumentationszentrum** (Documentation Centre) served by tram 9 from the Hauptbahnhof.

Germanisches Nationalmuseum — Museum

(German National Museum; ☎0911-133 10; www.gnm.de; Kartäusergasse 1; adult/concession €8/5; ⏰10am-6pm Tue & Thu-Sun, to 9pm Wed) Spanning prehistory to the early 20th century, the Germanisches Nationalmuseum is the country's most important museum of German culture. It features works by German painters and sculptors, an archaeological collection, arms and armour, musical and scientific instruments, and toys.

 Sleeping

Hotel Drei Raben Boutique Hotel **€€€**

(**☎0911-274 380; www.hoteldreiraben.de; Königstrasse 63; d incl breakfast from €150;**) The design of this classy charmer builds upon the legend of the three ravens perched on the building's chimney stack, who tell stories from Nuremberg lore. Art and decor in the 'mythical theme' rooms reflect a particular tale, from the life of Albrecht Dürer to the first railway.

Hotel Elch Hotel **€€**

(**☎0911-249 2980; www.hotel-elch.com; Irrerstrasse 9; s/d from €57/70;**) This snug, romantic 12-room gem of a hotel occupies a 14th-century, half-timbered house near the Kaiserburg. The antique flair is offset by contemporary art, glazed terracotta bathrooms and multihued chandeliers. The downstairs restaurant specialises in schnitzel.

 Eating

Don't leave Nuremberg without trying its famous *Nürnberger Bratwürste* (finger-sized sausages). Order 'em by the half-dozen with *Meerrettich* (horseradish) on the side.

Goldenes Posthorn Franconian **€€**

(**☎0911-225 153; Glöckleinsgasse 2, cnr Sebalder Platz; mains €9-19; 11am-11pm;**) Push open the heavy copper door to find a real culinary treat that has hosted royals, artists and professors (including Albrecht Dürer) since 1498. You can't go wrong sticking with the miniature local sausages, but the pork shoulder and also the house speciality – vinegar-marinated ox cheeks – are highly recommended as well.

Christmas Markets

Beginning in late November every year, central squares across Germany are transformed into Christmas markets (*Christkindlmärkte,* also known as *Weihnachtsmärkte*). Folks stamp about between the wooden stalls, perusing seasonal trinkets (from hand-carved ornaments to plastic angels) while warming themselves with *Glühwein* (mulled, spiced red wine) and grilled sausages. Locals love 'em and, not surprisingly, the markets are popular with tourists, so bundle up and carouse for hours. Markets in Nuremberg, Dresden, Cologne and Munich are especially famous.

Hexenhäusle German €€
(☎0911-4902 9095; www.hexenhaeusle-nuernberg.com; Vestnertorgraben 4; mains €7-11; 🕐11am-11pm) The half-timbered 'Witches Hut' ranks among Nuremberg's most enchanting inns and beer gardens. Tucked next to a sturdy town gate at the foot of the castle, it serves the gamut of grilled fare and other Franconian rib-stickers with big mugs of local Zirndorfer and Tucher beer.

Information

Tourist office Hauptmarkt (☎0911-233 60; www.tourismus.nuernberg.de; Hauptmarkt 18; 🕐9am-6pm Mon-Sat year-round, 10am-4pm Sun Apr-Oct, closed Sun rest of the year) Sells the Nuremberg Card (€23) with two days of free museum entry and public transport.

Tourist office Künstlerhaus (☎0911-233 60; www.tourismus.nuernberg.de; Königstrasse 93; 🕐9am-7pm Mon-Sat, 10am-4pm Sun) Maps, info and advice.

Getting There & Around

Air Nuremberg airport (NUE; www.airport-nuernberg.de), 5km north of the centre, is served by the U-Bahn line U2 from the Hauptbahnhof (€2.50, 12 minutes).

Train Rail connections include Frankfurt (€55, two hours) and Munich (€55, 1½ hours).

BLACK FOREST

The Black Forest (Schwarzwald) gets its name from its dark evergreen canopy. Let winding backroads take you through misty vales, fairy-tale woodlands and villages that radiate earthy authenticity. It's not nature wild and remote, but bucolic and picturesque. And, yes, there are many, many places to buy cuckoo clocks..

Getting Around

Car One of Germany's most scenic roads is the Schwarzwald-Hochstrasse (B500), which meanders for 60km between Baden-Baden and Freudenstadt.

Train Regional trains link Alpirsbach, Schiltach, Hausach and other Black Forest villages. In Hausach, it connects with the Schwarzwaldbahn line, the route of which takes in Baden-Baden and Triberg.

Triberg

☎07722 / POP 4800

Sights

Triberger Wasserfälle Waterfall
(adult/concession/family €4/3/9.50; 🕐Mar-early Nov, 25-30 Dec) Niagara they ain't but Germany's highest waterfalls do exude their own wild romanticism. The Gutach River feeds the seven-tiered falls, which drop a total of 163m and are illuminated until 10pm.

Sleeping & Eating

Parkhotel Wehrle Historic Hotel €€€
(☎07722-860 20; www.parkhotel-wehrle.de; Gartenstrasse 24; d €155-179; P 📶 🏊) Hemingway once waxed lyrical about the trout he ordered at this venerable

restaurant (mains €13 to €32, open 6pm to 9pm daily, noon to 2pm Sunday) that's attached to a 400-year-old hotel with integrated spa. Often with a baroque or Biedermeier touch, quarters are roomy and beautifully furnished with antiques; the best have Duravit whirlpool tubs.

Café Schäfer Cafe **€**

(☎07722-4465; www.cafe-schaefer-triberg.de; Hauptstrasse 33; cakes €3-4; ⏰9am-6pm Mon, Tue, Thu & Fri, 8am-6pm Sat, 11am-6pm Sun) Confectioner Claus Schäfer uses the original 1915 recipe for black forest gateau to prepare this sinful treat that layers chocolate cake perfumed with cherry brandy, whipped cream and sour cherries and wraps it all in more cream and shaved chocolate. Trust us, it's worth the calories.

Information

Tourist office (☎07722-866 490; www.triberg.de; Wallfahrtstrasse 4; ⏰9am-5pm Mon-Fri) Inside the Schwarzwald-Museum.

RHINE VALLEY

Between Koblenz and Bingen, the Rhine cuts deeply through the Rhenish slate mountains. Nicknamed the 'Romantic Rhine', the stretch is justifiably a highlight for many Germany explorers. This is where forested hillsides cradle craggy cliffs and nearly vertical terraced vineyards. Idyllic villages appear around each bend, their neat half-timbered houses and church steeples seemingly plucked from the world of fairy-tales. High above the river, busy with barge traffic, are the famous medieval castles, some ruined, some restored, all vestiges from a mysterious past.

Although Koblenz and Mainz are logical starting points, the area can also be explored on a long day trip from Frankfurt.

Getting There & Around

Each mode of transport on the Rhine has its own advantages and all are equally enjoyable. Try combining several.

Boat From about Easter to October (winter services are very limited), passenger ships run by **Köln-Düsseldorfer** (KD; ☎0221-208 8318; www.k-d.com) link villages on a set timetable. You're free to get on and off as you like.

Car There are no bridges between Koblenz and Bingen but you can easily change banks by using a car ferry. There are five routes: Bingen–Rüdesheim, Niederheimbach–Lorch, Boppard–Filsen, Oberwese–Kaub and St Goar–Goarshausen.

Vineyards along the Moselle River (p571)

Detour: Baden-Baden

'So nice that you have to name it twice', enthused Bill Clinton about Baden-Baden, whose air of old-world luxury and curative waters have attracted royals, the rich and celebrities over the years – Bismarck, Queen Victoria and Victoria Beckham included.

This grand dame of German spa towns is as timeless as it is enduring. Baden-Baden's thermal baths – which put the 'Baden' (bathe) in Baden-Baden – are the main reason for a visit. The sumptuous 19th-century **Friedrichsbad** (07221-275 920; www.carasana.de; Römerplatz 1; 3hr ticket €25, incl soap-&-brush massage €37; 9am-10pm, last admission 7pm) is the most historic spa, but you'll have to abandon your modesty (and your clothes) to indulge. Alternatively, you can keep your bathing suit on at the glass-fronted **Caracalla Therme** (07221-275 940; www.carasana.de; Römerplatz 11; 2/3/4hr ticket €15/18/21; 8am-10pm, last admission 8pm) as you dip into the indoor and outdoor pools, grottoes and surge channels.

Postpamper, you can also head to the grand Kurhaus and its gilded **casino** (07221-30240; www.kurhaus-baden-baden.de; Kaiserallee 1; tour €5; tours 9.30am-noon Apr-Oct, 10am-noon Nov-Mar). Gents must wear a jacket and tie (available for rent), but there's no need to dress up for the 25-minute guided tour.

Baden-Baden is the northern starting point of the Schwarzwald-Hochstrasse (B500).

Bacharach

One of the prettiest of the Rhine villages, Bacharach conceals its considerable charms behind a 14th-century town wall. Beyond the thick arched gateways awaits a beautiful medieval old town graced with half-timbered town houses lining Oberstrasse, the main thoroughfare. There's no shortage of atmospheric places to eat and sample the local vintages.

For gorgeous views of village, vineyards and river, take a stroll atop the **medieval ramparts**, which are punctuated by guard towers. An especially scenic panorama unfolds from the **Postenturm** at the north end of town, from where you can also espy the filigreed ruins of the **Wernerkapelle**, a medieval chapel, and the turrets of the 12th-century hilltop **Burg Stahleck**, a castle turned youth hostel.

Another good place to stay is the **Rhein Hotel** (06743-1243; www.rhein-hotel-bacharach.de; Langstrasse 50; d incl breakfast €78-136; P ❄ 📶), which has 14 well-lit, soundproofed rooms with original artwork and a respected restaurant.

St Goar & St Goarshausen

These twin towns face each other across the Rhine. On the left bank, St Goar is lorded over by **Burg Rheinfels** (www.st-goar.de; adult/child €4/2; 9am-6pm mid-Mar–late Oct, to 5pm until 9 Nov), one of the largest and most impressive river castles. Its labyrinthine ruins reflect the greed and ambition of the local count who built the behemoth in 1245 to levy tolls on passing ships. Today an inexpensive ferry links St Goar with St Goarshausen and the most fabled spot along the Romantic Rhine, the **Loreley Rock**. This vertical slab of slate owes its fame to a mythical maiden whose siren songs are said to have lured sailors to their death in the river's treacherous currents.

A classy spot to spend the night is **Romantik Hotel Schloss Rheinfels** (06741-8020; www.schloss-rheinfels.de; d incl breakfast €130-245; P @ 📶 ≋), right by the castle. Its three restaurants enjoy a fine reputation but there are plenty more down in the village.

Braubach

Framed by forested hillsides, vineyards and Rhine-side rose gardens, the 1300-year-old town of Braubach, on the right bank, is centred on the small, half-timbered market square. High above are the dramatic towers, turrets and crenellations of the 700-year-old **Marksburg** (**☎02627; www.marksburg.de; adult/student/6-18yr €6/5/4; 10am-5pm late Mar-Oct, 11am-4pm Nov-late Mar**) which – unique among the Rhine fortresses – was never destroyed. Tours (in English at 1pm and 4pm from late March through early November) take in the citadel, the Gothic hall and the large kitchen, plus a grisly torture chamber.

Koblenz

Founded by the Romans, Koblenz sits at the confluence of the Rhine and Moselle Rivers, a point known as **Deutsches Eck** (German Corner) and dominated by a bombastic 19th-century statue of Kaiser Wilhelm I on horseback. On the right Rhine bank high above the Deutsches Eck – and reached by an 850m-long **Seilbahn** (**cable car; www.seilbahn-koblenz.de; return adult/child €9/4, incl fortress €11.80/5.60; 10am-6pm or 7pm Apr-Oct, to 5pm Nov-Mar**) – is the mighty fortress of **Festung Ehrenbreitstein** (**www.diefestungehrenbreitstein.de; adult/child €6/3, incl cable car €11.80/5.60, audioguide €2; 10am-6pm Apr-Oct, to 5pm Nov-Mar**). Views are great and there's a restaurant and a regional museum inside.

MOSELLE VALLEY

Like a vine right before harvest, the Moselle hangs heavy with visitor fruit. Castles and half-timbered towns are built along the sinuous river below steep, rocky cliffs planted with vineyards. It's one of Germany's most evocative regions, with stunning views revealed at every river bend. Unlike the Rhine Valley, it's spanned by plenty of bridges. The most scenic section unravels between Bernkastel-Kues and Cochem, 50km apart and linked by the B421.

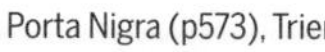

Porta Nigra (p573), Trier

HANS GEORG EIBEN/GETTY IMAGES ©

If You Like... Handsome & Historic Towns

If you've been smitten by the old towns of Rothenburg ob der Tauber and Nuremberg, you definitely won't want to miss these historic treasures.

1 **HEIDELBERG**
A mere hour's train ride from Frankfurt, Germany's oldest and most famous university town is renowned for its evocative half-ruined castle on a hill overlooking the Neckar River. Millions of visitors are drawn each year to this photogenic assemblage, thereby following in the footsteps of Mark Twain, who recounted his bemused observations in *A Tramp Abroad*.

2 **LÜBECK**
Compact and charming Lübeck makes for a great day trip from Hamburg. Looking like a pair of witches' hats, the pointed towers of its landmark Holstentor (Holsten Gate) form the gateway to its historic centre that sits on an island embraced by the arms of the Trave River. The town enjoys fame as Germany's marzipan capital.

3 **ERFURT**
A little river courses through this Instagram-pretty medieval pastiche of sweeping squares, time-worn alleyways, a house-lined bridge and lofty church spires. Martin Luther studied philosophy at its university before becoming a monk at the local monastery. It's a refreshingly untouristed spot and a quick 15-minute train ride from Weimar.

4 **BAMBERG**
Off the major tourist routes, Bamberg is one of Germany's most delightful and authentic towns. It has a bevy of beautifully preserved historic buildings, palaces and churches in its Unesco-recognised Altstadt (old town), a lively student population and its own style of beer. It's easily accessed from Würzburg.

Cochem

Easily reached by train or boat from Koblenz, Cochem is one of the most popular destinations on the Moselle thanks to its fairy-tale-like **Reichsburg** (**02671-255; www.burg-cochem.de; Schlossstrasse 36; tours adult/concession/child €5/4.50/3; 9am-5pm mid-Mar–Oct, 10am-3pm Nov & Dec, 11am, noon & 1pm Wed, Sat & Sun Jan–mid-Mar**). Like many others, the 11th-century original fell victim to frenzied Frenchmen in 1689, then stood ruined for centuries until a wealthy Berliner snapped it up for a pittance in 1868 and had it restored to its current – if not always architecturally faithful – glory. The 40-minute tours (in German but English leaflet available) take in decorative rooms reflecting 1000 years' worth of tastes and styles.

The **tourist office** (**02671-600 40; www.ferienland-cochem.de; Endertplatz 1; 9am-5pm Mon-Fri Apr-Oct, 9am-1pm & 2-5pm Mon-Fri Nov-Mar, 9am-3pm Sat May–mid-Jul, 9am-5pm Sat mid-Jul–Oct, 10am-3pm Sun Jul-Oct**) has information about the entire region.

Cochem is 55km from Koblenz via the scenic B327 and B49. Regional trains shuttling between Trier (€12.90, 45 minutes) and Koblenz (€11.30, 50 minutes) stop here as well.

Beilstein

Picture-perfect Beilstein is little more than a cluster of higgledy-piggledy houses surrounded by steep vineyards. Its historic highlights include the **Marktplatz** and the ruined hilltop castle **Burg Metternich** (views!). The **Zehnthauskeller** (**02673-900 907; www.zehnthauskeller.de; Marktplatz; 11am-evening Tue-Sun**) FREE houses a romantically dark, vaulted wine tavern owned by the same family that also runs two local hotels. There is no tourist office.

Bus 716 goes from Cochem to Beilstein (€3.65, 20 minutes) almost hourly in season, although the approach by boat is more scenic (€12, one hour).

Bernkastel-Kues

This charming twin town straddles the Moselle about 50km downriver from Trier and is close to some of the river's most famous vineyards. Bernkastel, on the right bank, is a symphony in half-timber, stone and slate, and teems with wine taverns. Get your heart pumping by hoofing it up to **Burg Landshut**, a ruined 13th-century castle on a bluff above town. Allow 30 minutes to be rewarded with glorious valley views and a cold drink at the beer garden.

The **tourist office** (☎06531-500 190; www.bernkastel.de; Gestade 6, Bernkastel; ⏰9am-5pm Mon-Fri, 10am-5pm Sat, 10am-1pm Sun May-Oct, 9.30am-4pm Mon-Fri Nov-Apr) is in Bernkastel.

Coming from Trier, drivers should follow the B53. Using public transport involves catching the regional train to Wittlich and switching to bus 300.

Trier

☎0651 / POP 106,700

Founded by the Romans around 16 BC as Augusta Treverorum, Trier became the capital of Roman Gaul in the 3rd century and the residence of Constantine the Great in the 4th century. To this day, you'll find more – and better preserved – Roman ruins here than anywhere else north of the Alps.

Sights

Porta Nigra Gate

(adult/student/child €3/2.10/1.50; ⏰9am-6pm Apr-Sep, to 5pm Mar & Oct, to 4pm Nov-Feb) This brooding 2nd-century city gate – blackened by time (hence the name, Latin for 'black gate') – is a marvel of engineering since it's held together by nothing but gravity and iron clamps.

Amphitheater Historic Site

(Olewiger Strasse; adult/concession/child €3/2.10/1.50; ⏰9am-6pm Apr-Sep, to 5pm Mar & Oct, to 4pm Nov-Feb) Trier's Roman

Trier

BRIGITTE MERZ/LOOK-FOTO/GETTY IMAGES ©

amphitheatre could accommodate 20,000 spectators for gladiator tournaments and animal fights. Beneath the arena are dungeons where prisoners sentenced to death waited next to starving beasts for the final showdown.

Kaiserthermen Historic Site

(Imperial Baths; Weberbachstrasse 41; adult/student/child €3/2.10/1.50; 9am-6pm Apr-Sep, to 5pm Mar & Oct, to 4pm Nov-Feb) Get a sense of the layout of this vast Roman thermal bathing complex with its striped brick-and-stone arches from the corner lookout tower, then descend into an underground labyrinth consisting of hot- and cold-water baths, boiler rooms and heating channels.

Trierer Dom Cathedral

(0651-979 0790; www.dominformation.de; Liebfrauenstrasse 12, cnr of Domfreihof; 6.30am-6pm Apr-Oct, to 5.30pm Nov-Mar) Trier's cathedral is considered the oldest bishop's church in Germany and looms above a palace built during Roman times. Today's edifice is a study in nearly 1700 years of church architecture, with Romanesque, Gothic and baroque elements. Intriguingly, its floor plan is that of a 12-petalled flower, a symbol of the Virgin Mary.

Sleeping

Hotel Deutscher Hof Hotel **€€**

(0651-977 80; www.hotel-deutscher-hof.de; Südallee 25; s/d from €60/75; P @) This comfortable value-priced pad a short walk south of the city centre oozes warmth and comfort in its softly lit and warmly decorated rooms. In summer there's a nice terrace for enjoying breakfast, while on colder days the sauna and steam baths beckon. Breakfast costs €8.

Hotel Villa Hügel Boutique Hotel **€€€**

(0651-937 100; www.hotel-villa-huegel.de; Bernhardstrasse 14; d incl breakfast €146-194; P @) A stylish, 33-room hillside villa where you can begin the day with sparkling wine at a lavish breakfast buffet and end it luxuriating in the 12m indoor pool and Finnish sauna. Rooms, decorated with honey-toned woods, are calming and create a sense of wellbeing. Served by buses 2 and 82.

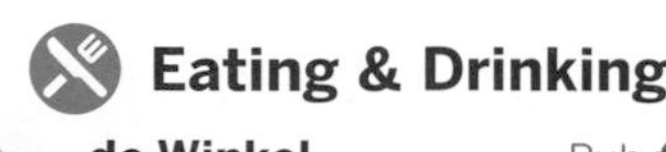

Eating & Drinking

de Winkel Pub **€**

(0651-436 1878; www.de-winkel.de; Johannisstrasse 25; mains €6-9.50; 6pm-1am Tue-Thu, to 2am Fri & Sat) Winny and Morris have presided over this locally adored watering hole for over 15 years. Join the locals for Pils and a bite, for instance the crispy chicken wings called 'Flieten' in Trier dialect.

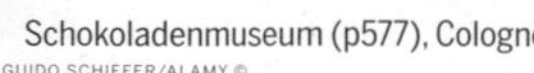

Schokoladenmuseum (p577), Cologne

GUIDO SCHIEFER/ALAMY ©

Weinstube Kesselstadt German €€

(☎0651-411 78; www.weinstube-kesselstatt.de; Liebfrauenstrasse 10; dishes €4.50-12; ⏰10am-midnight) Sampling the local wines is a great pleasure in this charming setting, in summer on the cathedral-facing terrace. The standard menu showcases quality products from the region and is augmented by specials starring seasonal bounty like mushrooms, game or asparagus. Order at the bar.

Zum Domstein Roman €€

(☎0651-744 90; www.domstein.de; Hauptmarkt 5; mains €9-19, Roman dinner €17-36; ⏰8.30am-midnight) At this old-timey restaurant you can either dine like an ancient Roman or feast on more conventional German and international fare. Roman dishes are based on the recipes of a 1st-century local chef named Marcus Gavius Apicius.

Information

Tourist office (☎0651-978 080; www.trier-info.de; ⏰9am-6pm Mon-Sat Mar-Dec, 10am-5pm Sun May-Oct, to 3pm Sun Mar, Apr, Nov & Dec, shorter hours Jan & Feb) Next to the Porta Nigra. Has excellent brochures in English and sells Moselle-area walking and cycling maps, concert tickets and boat excursions.

Getting There & Away

Frequent direct train connections include Koblenz (€22.10, 1½ to two hours), Cologne (€33, three hours) and Luxembourg (€17.30, 50 minutes).

Detour: Burg Eltz

At the head of the beautiful Eltz Valley, **Burg Eltz** (☎02672-950 500; www.burg-eltz.de; Wierschem; tour adult/student/family €9/6.50/26; ⏰9.30am-5.30pm Apr-Oct) is one of Germany's most romantic medieval castles. Never destroyed, this vision of turrets, towers, oriels, gables and half-timber has squatted atop a rock framed by thick forest for nearly 900 years and is still owned by the original family. The decorations, furnishings, tapestries, fireplaces, paintings and armour you see during the 45-minute tour are also many hundreds of years old.

By car, you can reach Burg Eltz via Munstermaifeld. Alternatively, take a boat or train to Moselkern village and approach the castle via a lovely 5km walk (or €24 taxi ride).

COLOGNE

☎0221 / POP 1 MILLION

Cologne (Köln) offers lots of attractions, led by its famous cathedral with filigree twin spires that dominate that the skyline. The city's museum landscape is especially strong when it comes to art but also has something in store for fans of chocolate, sports and Roman history.

Its people are well known for their joie de vivre and it's easy to have a good time right along with them year-round in the beer halls of the Altstadt.

Sights

Römisch-Germanisches Museum Museum

(Roman Germanic Museum; ☎0221-2212 4438; www.museenkoeln.de; Roncalliplatz 4; adult/concession €9/5; ⏰10am-5pm Tue-Sun) Sculptures and ruins displayed outside the entrance are merely the overture to a full symphony of Roman artefacts found along the Rhine. Highlights include the giant **Poblicius tomb** (AD 30–40), the magnificent 3rd-century **Dionysus mosaic**, and astonishingly well-preserved glass items. Insight into daily Roman life is gained from toys, tweezers, lamps and jewellery, the designs of which have changed surprisingly little since Roman times.

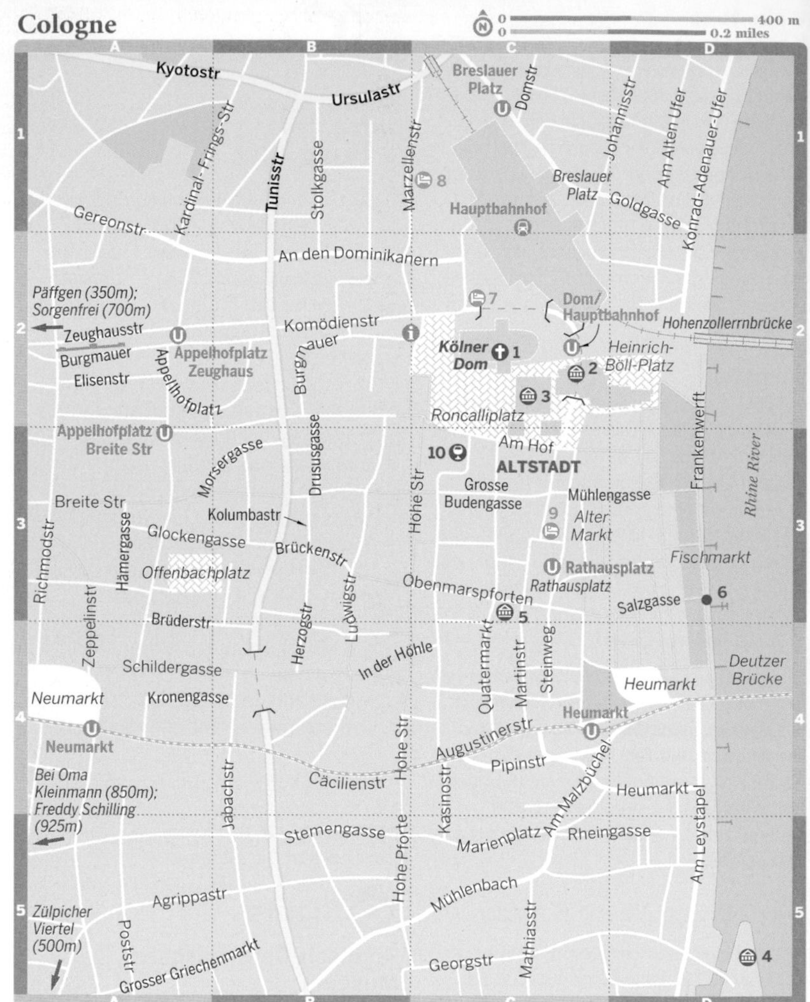

Museum Ludwig Museum

(☎0221-2212 6165; www.museum-ludwig.de; Heinrich-Böll-Platz; adult/child €11/7.50, special exhibits extra; ⏲10am-6pm Tue-Sun) A mecca of 20th-century art, Museum Ludwig presents a tantalising mix of works from all major phases. Fans of German expressionism (Beckmann, Dix, Kirchner) will get their fill here as much as those with a penchant for Picasso, American pop art (Warhol, Lichtenstein) and Russian avant-garde painter Alexander Rodchenko. Rothko and Pollock are highlights of the abstract collection, while Gursky and Tillmanns are among the reasons the photography section is a must-stop.

Wallraf-Richartz-Museum & Fondation Corboud Museum

(☎0221-2212 1119; www.wallraf.museum; Obenmarspforten; adult/concession €13/8; ⏲10am-6pm Tue-Sun, to 9pm Thu) A famous collection of European paintings from the 13th to the 19th centuries, the Wallraf-Richartz-Museum occupies a postmodern cube designed by the late OM Ungers.

Cologne

Don't Miss Sights
1 Kölner Dom C2

Sights
2 Museum Ludwig C2
3 Römisch-Germanisches Museum C2
4 Schokoladenmuseum D5
5 Wallraf-Richartz-Museum & Fondation Corboud C3

Activities, Courses & Tours
6 KD River Cruises D3

Sleeping
7 Excelsior Hotel Ernst C2
8 Station Hostel for Backpackers C1
9 Stern am Rathaus C3

Drinking & Nightlife
10 Früh am Dom C3

Works are presented chronologically, with the oldest on the 1st floor where standouts include brilliant examples from the Cologne School, known for its distinctive use of colour. The most famous painting is Stefan Lochner's *Madonna of the Rose Bower*.

Schokoladenmuseum Museum
(Chocolate Museum; 0221-931 8880; www.schokoladenmuseum.de; Am Schokoladenmuseum 1a; adult/concession/family €9/6.50/25; 10am-6pm Tue-Fri, 11am-7pm Sat & Sun, last entry 1hr before closing) At this high-tech temple to the art of chocolate-making, exhibits on the origin of the 'elixir of the gods', as the Aztecs called it, and the cocoa-growing process are followed by a live-production factory tour and a stop at a chocolate fountain for a sample.

Upstairs are departments on the cultural history of chocolate, advertising, and porcelain and other accessories. Stock up on your favourite flavours at the downstairs shop.

Tours

KD River Cruises Boat Tour
(0221-258 3011; www.k-d.com; Frankenwerft 35; adult/child €9.50/6; 10.30am-5pm Apr-Oct) One of several companies offering one-hour spins taking in the splendid Altstadt panorama; other options include brunch and sunset cruises.

Sleeping

Station Hostel for Backpackers Hostel €
(0221-912 5301; www.hostel-cologne.de; Marzellenstrasse 44-56; dm €17-20, s/d from €39/55;) Near the Hauptbahnhof, this is a hostel as hostels should be: central, convivial and economical. A lounge gives way to clean, colourful rooms sleeping one to six people. There's lots of free stuff, including linen, internet access, lockers, city maps and guest kitchen.

Stern am Rathaus Hotel €€
(0221-2225 1750; www.stern-am-rathaus.de; Bürgerstrasse 6; d incl breakfast €105-135;) This small, contemporary hotel has eight nicely spruced-up, luxuriously panelled rooms spread over three floors. It's in a quiet side street smack-dab in the Altstadt yet close to sights and plenty of restaurants. Kudos for the extra comfortable beds, the personalised service and the high-quality breakfast buffet.

Excelsior Hotel Ernst Hotel €€€
(0221-2701; www.excelsiorhotelernst.com; Trankgasse 1-5; d from €230;) Luxury is taken very seriously at this traditional hotel with a pedigree going back to 1863. Some of the plushly furnished rooms overlook the majestic Cologne cathedral. If that doesn't wow enough, perhaps a meal at the Michelin-starred restaurant will. Breakfast costs €32.

Eating & Drinking

There are plenty of beer halls and restaurants in the tourist-adored Altstadt, but for a more local vibe head to student-flavoured Zülpicher Viertel or the Belgisches Viertel, both in the city centre. Local breweries turn out a variety called Kölsch, which is relatively light and served in skinny 200mL glasses.

Freddy Schilling Burgers €
(0221-1695 5515; www.freddyschilling.de; Kyffhäuserstrasse 34; burgers €5.50-10; noon-

DAN HERRICK/GETTY IMAGES ©

Don't Miss
Kölner Dom

Cologne's geographical and spiritual heart – and its single-biggest tourist draw – is the magnificent Kölner Dom. With its soaring twin spires, this is the Mt Everest of cathedrals, jam-packed with art and treasures.

For an exercise fix, climb the 509 steps up the Dom's south tower to the base of the steeple that dwarfed all buildings in Europe until Gustave Eiffel built a certain tower in Paris. A good excuse to take a breather on your way up is the 24-tonne **Peter Bell** (1923), the largest free-swinging working bell in the world.

The Dom is Germany's largest cathedral and must be circled to truly appreciate its dimensions. Note how its lacy spires and flying buttresses create a sensation of lightness and fragility despite its mass and height. Soft light filters through the medieval stained-glass windows as well a much-lauded new one by contemporary artist Gerhard Richter in the transept.The pièce de résistance among the cathedral's bevy of treasures is the **Shrine of the Three Kings** behind the main altar, a richly bejewelled and gilded sarcophagus said to hold the remains of the kings who followed the star to the stable in Bethlehem where Jesus was born. The bones were spirited out of Milan in 1164 as spoils of war by Emperor Barbarossa's chancellor and instantly turned Cologne into a major pilgrimage site.

Other highlights include the **Gero Crucifix** (970), notable for its monumental size and an emotional intensity rarely achieved in those early medieval days; the **choir stalls** from 1310, richly carved from oak; and the **altar painting** (c 1450) by Cologne artist Stephan Lochner.

NEED TO KNOW

Cologne Cathedral; ☎0211-1794 0200; www.koelner-dom.de; tower adult/concession/family €3/1.50/6; ⏰6am-9pm Mon-Sat May-Oct, to 7.30pm Nov-Apr, 1-3.30pm Sun year-round, tower 9am-6pm May-Sep, to 5pm Mar-Apr & Oct, to 4pm Nov-Feb

10pm Sun-Tue, to 11pm Fri & Sat) A wholewheat bun provides a solid framework for the moist patties made with beef from happy cows and drizzled with Freddy's home-made 'special' sauce. Pair it with a side of Rosi's: small butter-and-rosemary-tossed potatoes.

Bei Oma Kleinmann German **€€**
(**☎0221-232 346; www.beiomakleinmann.de; Zülpicher Strasse 9; mains €13-21; ⏰5pm-1am Tue-Thu & Fri & Sat, to midnight Sun)** Named for its long-time owner, who was still cooking almost to her last day at age 95 in 2009, this perennially booked restaurant serves a mind-boggling variety of schnitzel, made either with pork or veal and paired with homemade sauces and sides. Pull up a seat at the small wooden tables for a classic Cologne night out.

Sorgenfrei Modern European **€€€**
(**☎0221-355 7327; www.sorgenfrei-koeln.com; Antwerpener Strasse 15; mains €17-35, 2-course lunch €17, 3-/4-course dinner €35/43; ⏰noon-3pm Mon-Fri, 6pm-midnight Mon-Sat)** A huge wine-by-the-glass menu is but one draw of this Belgische Viertel fine-dining treasure. Dishes are prepared with the same attention to detail yet lack of pretension found throughout this small restaurant. Hardwood floors encourage a casual vibe that goes well with salads and simple mains at lunch and more complex creations for dinner.

Päffgen Beer Hall
(**☎0221-135 461; www.paeffgen-koelsch.de; Friesenstrasse 64-66; ⏰10am-midnight Sun-Thu, to 12.30am Fri & Sat)** Busy, loud and boisterous, Päffgen has been pouring Kölsch since 1883 and hasn't lost a step since. In summer you can enjoy the refreshing brew and local specialities (€1.10 to €10.70) beneath starry skies in the beer garden.

Früh am Dom Beer Hall
(**☎0221-261 3215; www.frueh-am-dom.de; Am Hof 12-14; ⏰8am-midnight)** This warren of a beer hall near the Dom epitomises Cologne earthiness. Tuck into hearty meals (€2.50 to €20) sitting inside amid loads of knick-knacks or on the flower-filled terrace next to a fountain. It's also known for gut-filling breakfasts (€4.30 to €9.50).

ℹ Information

Tourist office (☎0221-346 430; www.cologne-tourism.com; Kardinal-Höffner-Platz 1; ⏰9am-8pm Mon-Sat, 10am-5pm Sun) Near the cathedral.

ℹ Getting There & Away

Air

About 18km southeast of the city centre, **Köln Bonn Airport (Cologne-Bonn Airport, CGN; ☎02203-404 001; www.koeln-bonn-airport.de; Kennedystrasse)** is connected to the Hauptbahnhof by the S-Bahn line S13 every 20 minutes (€2.80, 15 minutes).

Train

Services to and from Cologne are fast and frequent in all directions. A sampling: Berlin (€117, 4¼ hours), Frankfurt (€71, 1¼ hours), Düsseldorf (€11.30, 30 minutes), Bonn (€7.70, 30 minutes) and Aachen (€16.80, one hour). ICE trains leave for Brussels to connect with the Eurostar for London or Paris.

ℹ Getting Around

For public transport information and trip planning, consult www.vrs.de.

HAMBURG

☎040 / POP 1.8 MILLION

'The gateway to the world' might be a bold claim, but Germany's second-largest city and biggest port has never been shy. Hamburg has engaged in business with the world ever since it joined the Hanseatic League trading bloc back in the Middle Ages, and this 'harbourpolis' is now the nation's premier media hub and among its wealthiest cities.

Hamburg's maritime spirit infuses the entire city: from architecture to menus to the cry of gulls, you always know you're near the water. The city has given rise to vibrant neighbourhoods awash with multicultural eateries, as well as the gloriously seedy Reeperbahnparty and red-light district.

Sights

Rathaus — Historic Building

(040-428 312 064; Rathausmarkt 1; tours adult/under 14yr €4/free; tours half-hourly 10am-3pm Mon-Fri, to 5pm Sat, to 4pm Sun, English tours depend on demand; S Rathausmarkt, Jungfernstieg) Hamburg's baroque Rathaus (town hall) is one of Europe's most opulent, renowned for the Emperor's Hall and the Great Hall, with its spectacular coffered ceiling. The 40-minute tours take in only a fraction of this beehive of 647 rooms.

Speicherstadt — Neighbourhood

(Am Sandtorkai; 24hr; S Rödingsmarkt, Messberg) The seven-storey red-brick warehouses lining the Speicherstadt archipelago are a famous Hamburg symbol and the largest continuous warehouse complex in the world, recognised by Unesco as a World Heritage Site. Its distinctive architecture is best appreciated on a leisurely wander or a ride on a flat tour boat (called *Barkasse*). Many buildings contain shops, cafes and small museums.

Fischmarkt — Market

(Grosse Elbstrasse 9; 5-9.30am Sun Apr-Oct, 7-9.30am Sun Nov-Mar; 112 to Fischmarkt, Reeperbahn) Here's the perfect excuse to stay up all Saturday night. Every Sunday in the wee hours, some 70,000 locals and visitors descend upon the famous Fischmarkt in St Pauli. The market has been running since 1703, and its undisputed stars are the boisterous *Marktschreier* (market criers) who hawk their wares at full volume. Live bands also entertainingly crank out cover versions of ancient German pop songs in the adjoining *Fischauktionshalle* (Fish Auction Hall).

HafenCity — Neighbourhood

(040-3690 1799; www.hafencity.com; InfoCenter, Am Sandtorkai 30; InfoCenter 10am-6pm Tue-Sun; S Baumwall, Überseequartier) HafenCity is a vast new city quarter taking shape east of the harbour. When fully completed, it's expected to be home to 12,000 people and offer work space for 40,000. It's a showcase of modern architecture with the biggest eye-catcher being the Elbphilharmonie, a vast concert hall jutting into the harbour atop a protected tea-and-cocoa warehouse. After many delays, it's expected to open in 2017. For the low-down, visit the HafenCity InfoCenter, which also runs free guided tours.

Hamburger Kunsthalle — Museum

(040-428 131 200; www.hamburger-kunsthalle.de; Glockengiesserwall; adult/concession €12/6; 10am-6pm Tue, Wed & Fri-Sun, to 9pm Thu; S Hauptbahnhof) One of Germany's most prestigious art collections, the Kunsthalle displays works from the Middle Ages to today in two buildings. In the original brick one from 1869 you can admire old masters

Warehouses in the Speicherstadt district, Hamburg

(Rembrandt, Ruisdael), 19th-century Romantics (Friedrich, Runge) and classical modernist works (Beckmann, Munch). A stark white concrete cube – the Galerie der Gegenwart – showcases mostly German artists working since the 1960s, including Neo Rauch, Jenny Holzer, Candida Höfer and Reinhard Mucha.

Sleeping

Superbude St Pauli Hotel, Hostel €
(040-807 915 820; www.superbude.de; Juliusstrasse 1-7; dm/d from €16/60; @; S Sternschanze, Sternschanze, Holstenstrasse) The young and forever young mix and mingle without a shred of prejudice at this rocking design hotel-hostel combo that's all about living, laughing, partying and, yes, even sleeping well. All rooms have comfy beds and sleek private baths, breakfast is served until noon and there's even a 'rock star suite' with an Astra beer as a pillow treat.

Henri Hotel Hotel €€
(040-554 357 557; www.henri-hotel.com; Bugenhagenstrasse 21; r €98-138; ; S Mönckebergstrasse) Kidney-shaped tables, plush armchairs, vintage typewriters – the Henri channels the 1950s so successfully that you half expect to run into Don Draper. Its 65 rooms and studios are a good fit for urban lifestyle junkies who like the alchemy of modern comforts and retro design. For more elbow room get an L-sized room with a king-size bed.

25hours Hotel HafenCity Hotel €€
(040-855 870; www.25hours-hotel.de; Überseeallee 5; r €97-245; P; S Überseequartier) Funky decor, an infectious irreverence and postmodern vintage flair make this pad a top choice among global nomads. Sporting maritime flourishes, the decor channels an old-timey seaman's club in the lobby, the excellent restaurant and the 170 cabin-style rooms. Enjoy views of the emerging HafenCity neighbourhood from the rooftop sauna. Breakfast costs €14.

Cruising on the Cheap

Tthere's no need to fork over €18 for a cruise to see the port. Instead, hop on one of the public ferries for the price of a standard public-transport ticket (€3). The handiest line is ferry 62, which leaves from Landungsbrücken (pier 3) and travels west to Finkenwerder. Get off at the Dockland station to climb to the roof of this stunning office building shaped like a parallelogram for views of the container terminal, then continue to Neumühlen/Oevelgönne to look at old ships in the museum harbour and relax on the sandy Elbe beach with a beer from Strandperle (p583).

Hotel Wedina Hotel €€
(040-280 8900; www.hotelwedina.de; Gurlittstrasse 23; d incl breakfast €125-245; P@; S Hauptbahnhof) Margaret Atwood, Jonathan Franzen and Martin Walser are among the literary greats who've stayed at this lovable lair and left behind signed books. Rooms are spread over five brightly pigmented buildings that in different ways express the owners' love for literature, architecture and art. It's just a hop, skip and jump from the train station and the Alster lakes.

Eating

Fischbrötchenbude Brücke 10 Seafood €
(040-6504 6899; www.bruecke-10.de; Landungsbrücken, Pier 10; sandwiches €2.50-7.50; 10am-10pm Mon-Sat, 9am-10pm Sat; S Landungsbrücken, Landungsbrücken) There are a gazillion fish-sandwich vendors in Hamburg, but we're going to stick our neck out and say that this vibrant, clean and contemporary outpost makes the best. Try a classic *Bismarck* (pickled herring) or *Matjes* (brined) or treat yourself to a bulging shrimp sandwich.

Right: Alster River and the Rathaus (p580), Hamburg;
Below: Modern architecture in the HafenCity area (p580), Hamburg
(RIGHT) BEATE ZOELLNER/GETTY IMAGES ©; (BELOW) ARNE THAYSEN/GETTY IMAGES ©

Café Mimosa Cafe €

(☎040-3202 7989; www.cafemimosa.de; Clemens-Schultz-Strasse 87; mains €3.50-12; ⌚10am-7pm Tue-Sun; **S** St Pauli) This gem of a neighbourhood cafe is the go-to place for warm brioches, some of the yummiest cakes in town, plus daily changing lunch specials. Camp out inside among theatrical flourishes or grab a pavement table.

Café Koppel Vegetarian €

(www.cafe-koppel.de; Lange Reihe 66; mains €5-10; 🌶; **S** Hauptbahnhof) Set back from busy Lange Reihe, with a garden in summer, this vegie cafe is a refined oasis where you can hear the tinkling of spoons in coffee cups midmorning on the mezzanine floor. The menu could be an ad for the fertile fields of northern Germany as there are baked goods, salads, soups and much more made with fresh seasonal ingredients.

Altes Mädchen German €€

(☎040-800 077 750; http://altes-maedchen.com; Lagerstrasse 28b; mains €9-22; ⌚from noon Mon-Sat, from 10am Sun; **S** Sternschanze) The lofty red-brick halls of a 19th-century animal market have been upcycled into a hip culinary destination that includes a coffee roastery, a celebrity-chef restaurant, and this tarted-up brewpub with a central bar, in-house bakery and beer garden.

Erikas Eck German €€

(☎040-433 545; www.erikas-eck.de; Sternstrasse 98; mains €6-18; ⌚5pm-2pm; 🚇Sternschanze) This pit-stop institution originally fed hungry workers from the nearby abattoir (today the central meat market) and now serves wallet-friendly but waist-expanding portions of schnitzel and other trad German fare to a motley crowd of clubbers, cabbies and cops 21 hours a day.

Drinking & Entertainment

Partying in Hamburg concentrates on the Schanzenviertel and St Pauli south of here. Most people start the night in the former, then move on to the clubs and bars of the latter around midnight. Online sources: www.szene-hamburg.de and www.neu.clubkombinat.de.

Katze — Bar

(☎040-5577 5910; Schulterblatt 88; ⏰3pm-midnight Mon-Thu, 6pm-3am Fri, 1pm-3am Sat, 3pm-midnight Sun; S Sternschanze) Small and sleek, this 'kitty' (Katze means 'cat') gets the crowd purring for well-priced cocktails (best caipirinhas in town) and great music (there's dancing on weekends). It's one of the most popular among the watering holes on this main Schanzenviertel booze strip.

Strandperle — Bar

(☎040-880 1112; www.strandperle-hamburg.de; Oevelgönne 60; ⏰10am-11pm Mon-Fri, 9am-11pm Sat & Sun May-Sep, weather permitting, shorter hours otherwise; 🚌112) The mother of Hamburg's beach bars is a must for primo beer, burgers and people-watching. All ages and classes gather and mingle, especially at sunset, right on the Elbe as huge freighters glide past and you wiggle your toes in the sand. Get there by taking ferry 62 from Landungsbrücken or bus 112 from Altona station to Neumühlen/Oevelgönne.

Prinzenbar — Bar, Club

(Kastanienallee 20; S St Pauli, U Reeperbahn) With its cheeky cherubs, stucco flourishes and wrought-iron galleries, this intimate club has chapel looks but is in fact a former cinema that now hosts stylish electro parties, concerts, queer parties and indie nights in the heart of St Pauli.

St Pauli & the Reeperbahn

No discussion of Hamburg is complete without mentioning St Pauli, home to one of Europe's most (in)famous red-light districts. Sex shops, table-dance bars and strip clubs still line its main drag, the Reeperbahn, and side streets, but the popularity of prostitution has declined dramatically in the internet age. These days, St Pauli is Hamburg's main nightlife district, drawing people of all ages and walks of life to live music and dance clubs, chic bars and theatres.

In fact, street walkers are not even allowed to hit the pavement before 8pm and then are confined to certain areas, the most notorious being the gated Herbertstrasse (no women and men under 18 allowed). Nearby, the cops of the Davidwache police station keep an eye on the lurid surrounds. A short walk west is the side street called Grosse Freiheit, where the Beatles cut their teeth at the Indra Club (No 64) and the Kaiserkeller (No 36). Both are vastly different venues today, but there's a small monument to the Fab Four in a courtyard behind No 35.

Golden Pudel Club Live Music
(**040-3197 9930; www.pudel.com; St-Pauli-Fischmarkt 27; nightly; Reeperbahn**) In a 19th-century bootleggers' jail, this tiny bar-club is run by members of the legendary ex-punk band Die Goldenen Zitronen and is an essential stop on the St Pauli party circuit. Night after night it gets packed to the rafters for its countercultural vibe, quality bands and DJs, and relaxed crowd.

Molotow Live Music
(**040-430 1110; www.molotowclub.com; Holstenstrasse 5; Reeperbahn**) The legendary indie club still rocks on as hot and heavy as ever after moving to new digs after its Reeperbahn location was torn down in 2013.

Information

Tourist office Hauptbahnhof (**www.hamburg-tourism.de; Kirchenallee exit; 9am-7pm Mon-Sat, 10am-6pm Sun; S Hauptbahnhof, Hauptbahnhof**)

Tourist office St Pauli Landungsbrücken (**btwn piers 4 & 5; 9am-6pm Sun-Wed, to 7pm Thu-Sat ; S Landungsbrücken**) No hotel bookings.

Getting There & Away

Air

Hamburg's **airport** (**HAM; www.airport.de**) is linked to the city centre every 10 minutes by the S-Bahn line S1 (€3, 25 minutes). A taxi is €25.

Bus

The **Zentraler Omnibus Busbahnhof** (**ZOB, Central Bus Station; 040-247 576; www.zob-hamburg.de; Adenauerallee 78**), southeast of the Hauptbahnhof, has many domestic and international departures by Eurolines, Flixbus and other operators.

Train

Hamburg is a major train hub with four mainline train stations: the Hauptbahnhof, Dammtor, Altona and Harburg. Frequent trains serve Lübeck (€13.70, 45 minutes), Bremen (from €28, 55 minutes), Berlin-Hauptbahnhof (€78, 1¾ hours), Copenhagen (€85.40, 4¾ hours) and many other cities.

Getting Around

For information and trip planning, go to www.hvv.de. The city is divided into zones. Fare zone A covers the city centre, inner suburbs and airport.

SURVIVAL GUIDE

Directory A–Z

Accommodation

Reservations are a good idea, especially between June and September, around major holidays, festivals, cultural events and trade shows. Local tourist offices will often go out of their way to find something in your price range.

Unless noted, the following price ranges refer to a double room with private bathroom and breakfast in high season.

€ less than €80

€€ €80 to €170

€€€ more than €170

Discount Cards

Tourist offices in many cities sell 'Welcome Cards' entitling visitors to free or reduced admission on museums, sights and tours, plus unlimited local public transportation for the period of their validity (usually 24 or 48 hours).

Food

The following price categories are for the cost of a main course.

€ less than €8

€€ €8 to €17

€€€ more than €17

Gay & Lesbian Travellers

- Germany is a magnet for *schwule* (gay) and *lesbische* (lesbian) travellers, with the rainbow flag flying especially proudly in Berlin and Cologne, and with sizeable communities in Hamburg, Frankfurt and Munich.
- Generally speaking, attitudes towards homosexuality tend to be more conservative in the countryside, among older people and in the eastern states.

Legal Matters

- Drivers need to carry their driving licence at all times. The permissible blood-alcohol limit is 0.05%; stiff fines or a confiscated licence and even jail time are possible if caught driving over the limit.
- Drinking in public is not illegal, but please be discreet about it.
- Cannabis possession is a criminal offence and punishment may range from a warning to a court appearance.

Hamburger Kunsthalle (p580)

Money

- Cash is king in Germany, so it's best to always carry some with you and expect to pay in cash almost everywhere.
- ATMs (*Geldautomat*) linked to international networks such as Cirrus, Plus, Star and Maestro are widely available.
- Credit cards are becoming more widely accepted, but it's best not to assume that you'll be able to use one – enquire first.

TIPPING

Bar	5-10%
Hotel porter	€1 to €1.50 per bag
Room cleaners	€1-2 per night per person
Restaurant	5-10%
Toilet attendants	€0.50

Opening Hours

Banks 9am to 4pm Monday to Friday, extended hours usually on Tueday or Thursday

Bars 6pm to 1am

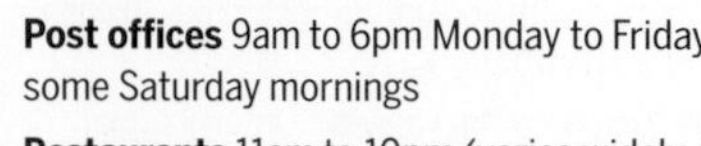

Cafes 8am to 8pm

Clubs 10pm to 4am

Post offices 9am to 6pm Monday to Friday, some Saturday mornings

Restaurants 11am to 10pm (varies widely, food service often stops at 9pm in rural areas)

Major stores and supermarkets 9.30am to 8pm Monday to Saturday (shorter hours in suburbs and rural areas, possible lunchtime break)

Public Holidays

In addition to the following nationwide holidays, individual German states observe additional (usually religious) holidays.

Neujahrstag (New Year's Day) 1 January

Ostern (Easter) Good Friday, Easter Sunday and Easter Monday

Christi Himmelfahrt (Ascension Day) Forty days after Easter

Maifeiertag/Tag der Arbeit (Labour Day) 1 May

Pfingsten (Whit/Pentecost Sunday & Monday) Fifty days after Easter

Tag der Deutschen Einheit (Day of German Unity) 3 October

Weihnachtstag (Christmas Day) 25 December

Zweiter Weihnachtstag (Boxing Day) 26 December

Telephone

German phone numbers consist of an area code (three to six digits) followed by the local number (three to nine digits).

Country code ☎49

International access code ☎00

Directory inquiries ☎11837 for an English-speaking operator (€1.99 per minute)

Visas

- EU nationals only need their passport or national identity card to enter, stay and work in Germany, even for stays over six months.
- Citizens of Australia, Canada, Israel, Japan, New Zealand, Poland, Switzerland and the US need only a valid passport but no visa if entering Germany as tourists for up to three months within a six-month period. Passports must be valid for another three months beyond the intended departure date.
- Nationals from other countries need a Schengen Visa.

Websites

German National Tourist Office (www.germany.travel)

Facts About Germany (www.tatsachenueber-deutschland.de) Reference tool on all aspects of German society.

Deutschland Online (www.magazinedeutschland.de) Insightful features on culture, business and politics.

Getting There & Away

Air

- Budget carriers, **Lufthansa** (www.lufthansa.com) and international airlines serve numerous German airports from across Europe and the rest of the world. Frankfurt and Munich are the hubs, but there are also sizeable airports in Berlin, Hamburg, Cologne/Bonn and Stuttgart, and smaller ones in Bremen, Dresden, Hanover, and Nuremberg.
- For details about individual airports, including information about getting to and from them, see the listings within the chapter.

Land

Bus

- Bus travel is becoming increasingly popular in Germany thanks to a new crop of companies offering good-value connections within Germany and beyond aboard comfortable buses with snack bars and free wi-fi. For routes, times and prices, check www.busliniensuche.de (also in English).
- The largest Europe-wide bus network is maintained by **Eurolines** (www.eurolines.com), a consortium of national bus companies.

Car & Motorcycle

- When bringing your own vehicle to Germany, you need a valid driving licence, car registration and proof of third-party insurance. All cars must display a nationality sticker unless they have official European plates. You also need to carry a warning (hazard) triangle and a first-aid kit.
- Most German cities now have environmental zones that may only be entered by vehicles (including foreign ones) displaying an *Umweltplakette* (emissions sticker). Check with your motoring assocaiton or buy one at www.umwelt-plakette.de.

Train

In Germany ticketing is handled by **Deutsche Bahn** (www.bahn.com). Seat reservations are essential during the peak summer season and around major holidays and recommended for Friday and Sunday travel. Eurail and Interrail passes are valid on all German national trains.

Sea

Germany's main ferry ports are Kiel, Lübeck and Travemünde in Schleswig-Holstein, and Rostock and Sassnitz (on Rügen Island). All have services to Scandinavia and the Baltic states. There are no direct ferries between Germany and the UK.

 Getting Around

Air

Unless you're flying from one end of the country to the other, say Berlin to Munich or Hamburg to Munich, planes are only marginally quicker than trains once you factor in the check-in and transit times.

Bus

- In some rural areas buses may be your only option for getting around without your own vehicle.
- In cities, buses generally converge at the *Busbahnhof* or *Zentraler Omnibus Bahnhof* (ZOB; central bus station), which is often near the Hauptbahnhof (central train station).
- Also see 'Bus' in the Getting There & Away sections of this chapter.

Car & Motorcycle

- Driving is on the right side of the road.
- No tolls are charged on public roads.
- Unless posted otherwise, speeds limits are 50km/h in cities, 100km/h on countryroads and no limit on the autobahn.
- To hire a car, you'll need to be at least 25 years old and possess a valid driving licence and a major credit card. Some companies lease to drivers between the ages of 21 and 24 for an additional charge. Automatic transmissions are rare and must be booked well in advance.

Local Transport

- Public transport is excellent within big cities and small towns and may include buses, trams (Strassenbahn), S-Bahn (light rail) and U-Bahn (underground/subway trains).
- Tickets cover all forms of transit, and fares are determined by zones or time travelled, sometimes both. Multiticket strips and day passes generally offer better value than single-ride tickets.
- Note that many tickets must be stamped before or upon boarding in order to be valid.

Train

- Germany's railway network is operated almost entirely by Deutsche Bahn, although there's a growing number of routes run by private companies.
- Of the several train types, ICE trains are the fastest and most comfortable. IC trains (EC if they cross borders) are almost as fast but older and less snazzy. RE and RB trains are regional. S-Bahn are suburban trains operating in large cities and conurbations.
- At most stations, you can store your luggage in a locker (*Schliessfach*). Larger ones may have a staffed left-luggage office (*Gepäckaufbewahrung*).
- Seat reservations for long-distance travel are highly recommended, especially if you're travelling on a Friday or Sunday afternoon, during holiday periods or in summer. Reservations can be made online and at ticket counters as late as 10 minutes before departure.
- ¨Buy tickets online (www.bahn.de, print-out required) or at stations from vending machines or ticket offices (Reisezentrum). Only conductors on ICE and IC/EC trains sell tickets on board at a surcharge.

Austria, Switzerland & the Czech Republic

If it's mountain scenery that inspires you, then Austria and Switzerland will seem like seventh heaven. This is a corner of Europe where Mother Nature has done her work on a grand scale: icy peaks, sheer cliffs and silver glaciers stand out against the open sky, providing the perfect mountain playground for skiers and snowboarders. While winter sports are the main attraction, there are plenty more reasons to visit: from the grand cities of Vienna and Salzburg to the sparkling waters of Lake Geneva.

Out to the east, the Czech Republic has emerged from behind the Iron Curtain to become one of Europe's most captivating places to travel. The charming city of Prague is packed with incredible architecture and historic sights, and further afield you could spend your time exploring the splendid castles of Konopiště and Karlštejn, hiking through the rolling Moravian countryside or sampling the world-class beer for which the Czech Republic is rightly renowned.

North face of the Eiger mountain, Switzerland
GRANT DIXON/GETTY IMAGES ©

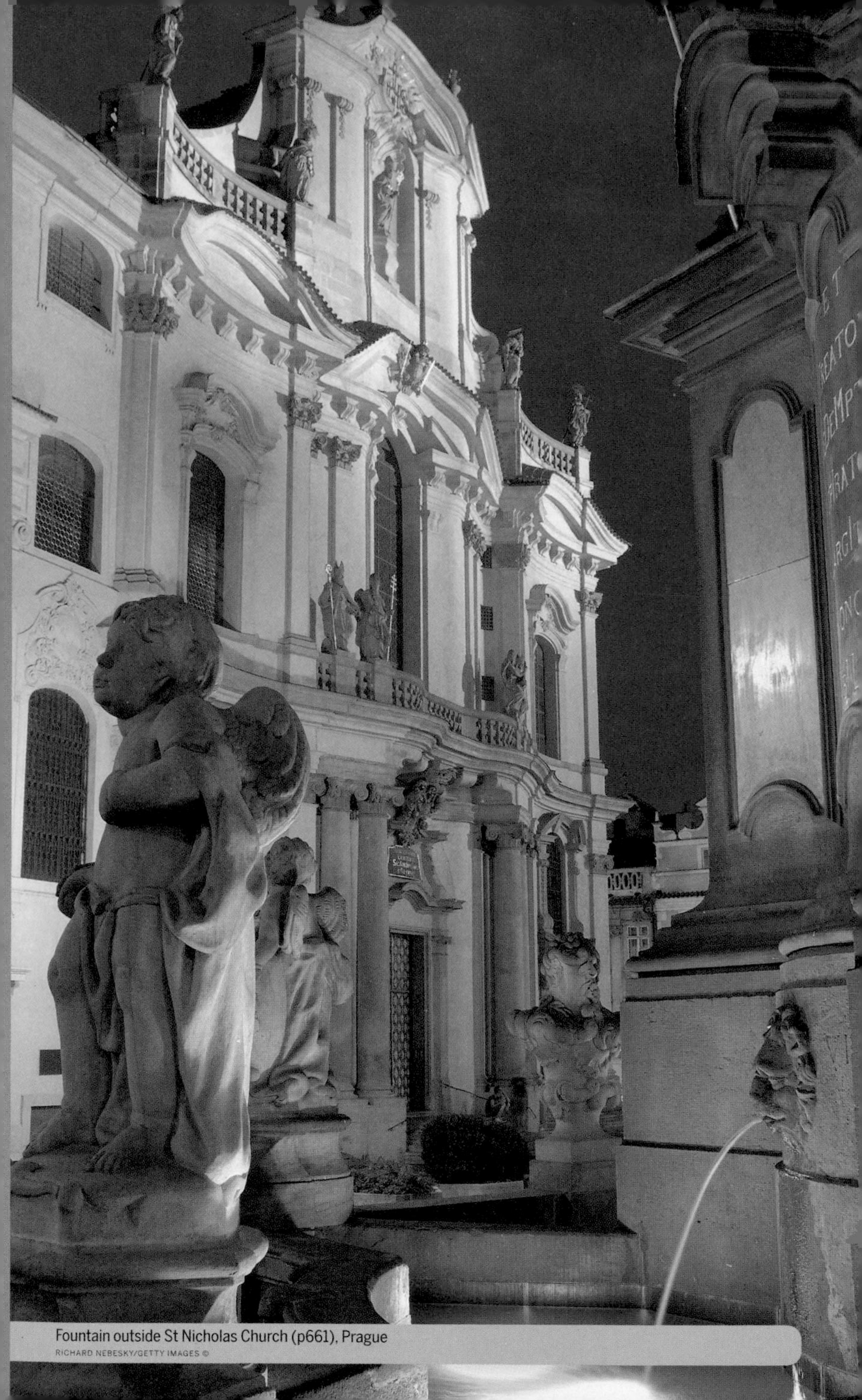

Fountain outside St Nicholas Church (p661), Prague

Austria, Switzerland & the Czech Republic

Austria, Switzerland & the Czech Republic Highlights

Salzburg

Salzburg (p616) has a lot more to offer than just Mozart and *The Sound of Music*. There's one of Austria's most atmospheric Altstadts to explore, for a start. Then there are boat trips down the Salzach, a wealth of baroque architecture to admire and a fantastic funicular ride up to the clifftop fortress of Festung Hohensalzburg, offering unforgettable views across Salzburg's higgledy-piggledy rooftops.

1

2 The Matterhorn, Zermatt

No mountain packs the same wow factor as the Matterhorn (p639). This sheer fang of ice, snow and rock stands in dramatic isolation above the town of Zermatt, and has been an irresistible draw for aspiring mountaineers since the sport began in the 19th century. You could just admire the view from the bottom, but those with a head for heights should catch Europe's highest cable car up to the cloud-top viewing platform at 3883m.

GREG ELMS/GETTY IMAGES ©

Vienna's Coffee Houses

3

There's one pastime the Viennese know how to do better than almost anyone else, and that's drink coffee (preferably accompanied by a thick slice of cake). The city's coffee houses (p610) have been the favourite haunts of intellectuals, impoverished artists and cultural types for centuries, and they're still by far the best places to take the city's pulse. Right: Interior of Café Sperl (p610)

D J BALL/GETTY IMAGES ©

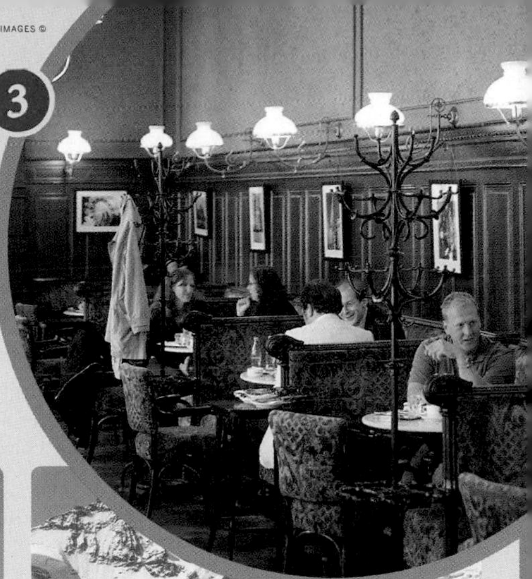

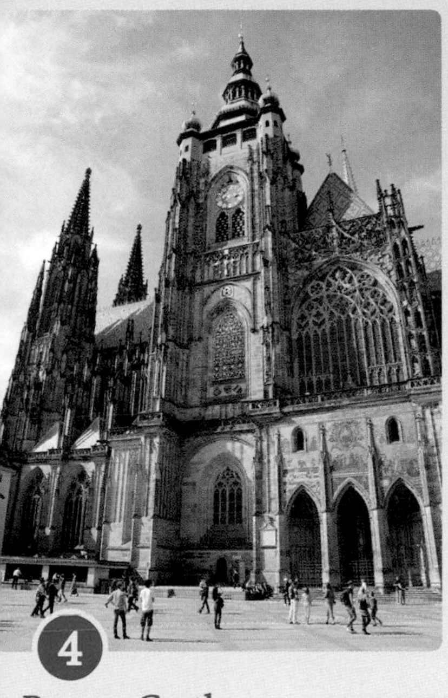

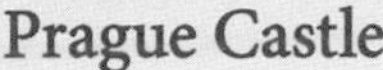

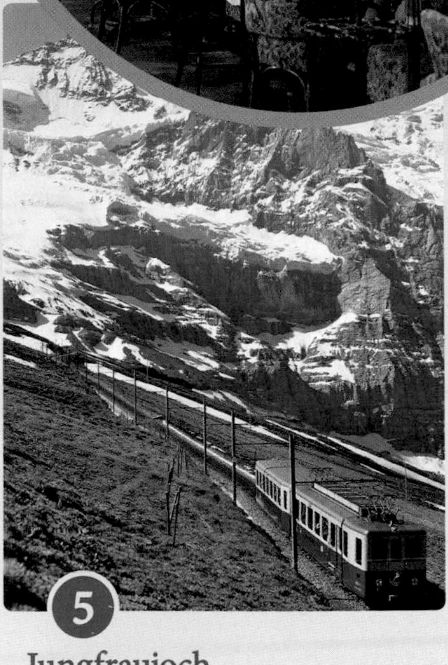

4

Prague Castle

Prague is littered with historical monuments, but in terms of sheer scale and ambition, Prague Castle (p659) definitely takes top prize. Overlooking the Vltava River, this mighty fortress covers a vast area of Prague's historic centre, and contains the city's largest house of worship, St Vitus Cathedral, within its crenellated walls. You'll need a whole day to do it justice, and don't miss a guided tour.

Above: St Vitus Cathedral (p654)

5

Jungfraujoch

You'll be king of the mountain at Europe's highest train station, Jungfraujoch (p647). At 3454m, this icy wonderland of glaciers inspires scores of people to make the journey, so it's a good idea to start early. Whatever you do, save the trip for a clear day – the ride's not worth the price of the ticket if all you see up there are clouds, so check the weather forecast before you set out.

Austria, Switzerland & the Czech Republic's Best...

Palaces & Chateaux

- **Hofburg** (p603) The might of the Austrian monarchy is summed up by this monumental Viennese palace.
- **Český Krumlov** (p674) The second-most famous Czech castle outside Prague.
- **Schloss Schönbrunn** (p599) The Habsburg dynasty's summer palace is a Unesco-listed treasure.
- **Schloss Hellbrunn** (p626) A palace renowned for its watery wonders.

Old Towns

- **Malá Strana** (p661) This rabbit warren of medieval streets is the place to lose yourself in Prague.
- **Salzburg** (p616) Winding alleyways, cobbled streets and photo ops aplenty.
- **Vienna** (p598) Re-enact some of those famous scenes from *The Third Man*.
- **Bern** (p641) Switzerland's dynamic capital conceals a much older heart.
- **Olomouc** (p671) This ancient Czech town is well off the tourist radar.

Epicurean Experiences

- **Swiss chocolate** Shop for something sweet and sinful in Geneva.
- **Coffee and cake** (p610) Practically an art form in the cafes of Vienna and Salzburg.
- **Beisln** (p607) These cosy Austrian beer dens are full of atmosphere: Vienna has some of the best.
- **Fondue** This cheesy indulgence is a Swiss speciality, especially in mountain towns like Zermatt.
- **Pilsner Urquell Brewery** (p670) Take a tipple at the Czech Republic's best-known beer factory.

Lofty Views

- **Gornergrat** (p639) Catch the cable car in Zermatt and behold the mighty Matterhorn.

- **Jungfraujoch** (p647) Gaze at the Eiger, Mönch and Jungfrau from Europe's highest train station.

- **Bergisel** (p627) Hold your nerve at the top of this gravity-defying ski jump in Innsbruck.

- **Matterhorn Glacier Paradise** (p639) Take Europe's highest-altitude cable car to gawp at 14 glaciers.

Left: Schloss Schönbrunn (p599), Vienna, Austria; **Above:** Schilthorn, Swiss Alps

Need to Know

ADVANCE PLANNING

- **Two months before** Reserve as early as possible in the Alps during the ski season.

- **One month before** Book hotels for summer travel in Prague, Vienna, Salzburg, Geneva and other big-ticket cities.

- **Two weeks before** Reserve tickets for the Staatsoper and the Spanish Riding School in Vienna.

RESOURCES

- **Österreich Werbung** (www.austria.info) Austria's national tourism authority.

- **Prague Information Service** (www.praguewelcome.cz) Official Prague info.

- **Czech Tourism** (www.czechtourism.com) Czech-wide travel planning from the state tourism body.

- **Switzerland Tourism** (www.myswitzerland.com) The full Swiss lowdown: accommodation, activities and more.

GETTING AROUND

- **Boat** Ferry services and cruise boats ply many Austrian and Swiss lakes.

- **Bus** Postbuses supplement regional train lines in Austria and Switzerland, and serve many smaller Czech towns and villages.

- **Car** Driving is best for rural areas, and pricey parking and incomprehensible one-way systems make Prague, Vienna, Salzburg and Zürich a no-no. *Vignettes* (motorway taxes) are charged on Austrian autobahns, and many tunnels incur a toll.

- **Train** Train services in all three countries are fast, frequent and efficient, although Switzerland really shines.

BE FOREWARNED

- **Czech manners** It's customary to say *dobrý den* (good day) when entering a shop, cafe or quiet bar, and *na shledanou* (goodbye) when leaving.

- **Mountain passes** Many road passes in Austria and Switzerland are closed in winter due to snowfall.

- **Scams** Prague pickpockets work the crowds at the Astronomical Clock, Prague Castle and Charles Bridge. Book a reputable taxi firm to avoid unscrupulous drivers.

Austria, Switzerland & the Czech Republic Itineraries

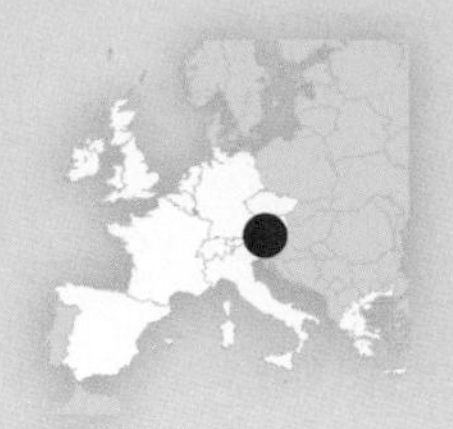

Take in the baroque beauty of Austria's top cities, then head for the stirring scenery of the Alps.

3 DAYS

BAROQUE BEAUTY

Prague to Vienna

Three days will give you just enough time to dip into two of Europe's must-see capitals. explore Austria's two must-see cities. Start with a day in ❶**Prague** (p654), a city that enthralls with its magnificent Renaissance squares, opulent palaces and happening nightlife fuelled by local brews. Tap into the cultural scene with a spin of Prague Castle, Charles Bridge, the Jewish Museum and Staré Město - the jewel among Europe's medieval Old Towns.

On day two catch the train to ❷**Vienna** (p598) a city that's been synonymous with culture and refinement since the days of the Habsburg empire. You'll need a full day to explore the incredible Hofburg and Schloss Schönbrunn palaces, which illustrate the immense wealth and political power this ancient dynasty wielded before being deposed in 1918 following the end of WWI.

INTO THE ALPS
Salzburg to Jungfrau

Revel in baroque architecture and the musical legacy of Mozart and The Sound of Music in ❶ **Salzburg** (p616), within reach of breathtaking mountain scenery. Spend at least a day exploring the attractions of ❷ **Salzkammergut** (p624), including the old salt mines and the ice caves. On day two, catch a train west to ❸ **Innsbruck** (p627), the capital of the Tyrol region and a thriving centre for outdoor sports. The Nordkettenbahnen whisks you via a funicular and two cable cars from the town centre to the tip of Hafelekar peak (2334m) in just 25 minutes. From here, the mighty Alps unfold all the way into Switzerland and France.

Fast and frequent trains run west from Innsbruck to ❹ **Zürich** (p648), a squeaky-clean city with a surprisingly lively heart, but the real scenery starts further south at ❺ **Interlaken** (p646), where you can paraglide, ice-climb, hike, ski or mountain bike the days away beneath the shadow of the Eiger, Mönch and Jungfrau peaks. Further south lies the ❻ **Jungfrau** (p647) region, where some of Europe's largest glaciers snake their way among the snow-dusted peaks.

Jungfrau peak (p647), Bernese Oberland
GLENN VAN DER KNIJFF/GETTY IMAGES ©

Discover Austria, Switzerland & the Czech Republic

At a Glance

- **Austria** (p598) Awash with imperial grandeur and sparkling lakes, not to mention numerous Mozart connections.
- **Switzerland** (p631) Famously efficient, this squeaky-clean nation is dominated by Europe's highest peaks.
- **Czech Republic** (p652) Baroque architecture, dramatic castles, world-class beer, and a fascinating post-Communist past.

Stephansdom, Vienna, Austria

AUSTRIA

For such a small country, Austria has made it big. This is, after all, the land where Mozart was born, Strauss taught the world to waltz and Julie Andrews grabbed the spotlight with her twirling entrance in *The Sound of Music*. This is where the Habsburgs built their 600-year empire, and where past glories still shine in the resplendent baroque palaces and chandelier-lit coffee houses of Vienna, Innsbruck and Salzburg. This is a perfectionist of a country and whatever it does – mountains, classical music, new media, castles, cake, you name it – it does exceedingly well.

Vienna

☎01 / POP 1.79 MILLION

Few cities in the world waltz so effortlessly between the present and the past like Vienna. Its splendid historical face is easily recognised: grand imperial palaces and bombastic baroque interiors, revered opera houses and magnificent squares.

But Vienna is also one of Europe's most dynamic urban spaces. A stone's throw from Hofburg (the Imperial Palace), the MuseumsQuartier houses some of the world's most provocative contemporary art behind a striking basalt facade. In the Innere Stadt, up-to-the-minute design stores sidle up to old-world confectioners, and Austro-Asian fusion restaurants stand alongside traditional *Beisln* (small taverns). Throw in the mass of green space within the confines of the city limits and the 'blue' Danube cutting a path east of the historical centre, and this is a capital that is distinctly Austrian.

Sights

If you're planning on doing a lot of sightseeing, consider purchasing the **Vienna Card** (48-/72-hour card €18.90/21.90) for unlimited travel plus discounts at selected museums, attractions, cafes and shops. It's available from hotels and ticket offices.

The City of Vienna runs some 20 **municipal museums** (www.wienmuseum.at), which are included in a free booklet available at the Rathaus (City Hall). Permanent exhibitions in all are free on the first Sunday of the month.

Many sights and attractions open slightly later in July and August, and close earlier from November to March.

Stephansdom — Church

(St Stephan's Cathedral; www.stephanskirche.at; 01, Stephansplatz; ⌚6am-10pm Mon-Sat, from 7am Sun, main nave & Domschatz audio tours 9-11.30am & 1-5.30pm Mon-Sat, 1-5.30pm Sun; M Stephansplatz) Vienna's Gothic masterpiece Stephansdom, or Steffl (Little Stephan) as it's nicknamed, is Vienna's pride and joy. A church has stood here since the 12th century, and reminders of this are the Romanesque **Riesentor** (Giant Gate) and **Heidentürme**. From the exterior, the first thing that will strike you is the glorious tiled **roof**, with its dazzling row of chevrons and Austrian eagle. Inside, the magnificent Gothic stone **pulpit** presides over the main nave, fashioned in 1515 by an unknown artisan.

Albertina — Gallery

(www.albertina.at; 01, Albertinaplatz 3; adult/child €11.90/free; ⌚10am-6pm Thu-Tue, to 9pm Wed; 👪; M Karlsplatz, Stephansplatz, 🚊D, 1, 2, 71 Kärntner Ring/Oper) Once used as the Habsburg's imperial apartments for guests, the Albertina is now a repository for the greatest collection of graphic art in the world. The permanent Batliner Collection – with paintings covering the period from Monet to Picasso – and the high quality of changing exhibitions are what really make the Albertina so worthwhile visiting.

Schloss Schönbrunn — Palace

(www.schoenbrunn.at; 13, Schönbrunner Schlossstrasse 47; Imperial Tour with audio guide adult/child €11.50/8.50, Grand Tour €14.50/9.50; ⌚8.30am-5.30pm; M Hietzing) The Habsburgs' overwhelmingly opulent summer palace is now a Unesco World Heritage Site. Of the palace's 1441 rooms, 40 are open to the public; the Imperial Tour takes you into 26 of these.

Kaisergruft — Church

(Imperial Burial Vault; www.kaisergruft.at; 01, Neuer Markt; adult/child €5/2.50; ⌚10am-6pm; M Stephansplatz, Karlsplatz, 🚊D, 1, 2, 71 Kärntner Ring/Oper) The Kaisergruft beneath the **Kapuzinerkirche** (Church of the Capuchin Friars) is the final resting place of most of the Habsburg royal family, including Empress Elisabeth.

Kunsthistorisches Museum — Museum

(Museum of Art History, KHM; www.khm.at; 01, Maria-Theresien-Platz; adult/under 19yr incl Neue Burg museums €14/free; ⌚10am-6pm Tue-Sun, to 9pm Thu; 👪; M Museumsquartier, Volkstheater) One of the unforgettable experiences of Vienna will be a visit to the Kunsthistorisches Museum, brimming with works by Europe's finest painters, sculptors and artisans. Occupying a neoclassical building as sumptuous as the art it contains, the museum takes you on a time-travel treasure hunt from classical Rome to Egypt and the Renaissance. If time is an issue, skip straight to the **Picture Gallery**, where you'll want to dedicate at least an hour or two to Old Masters.

MuseumsQuartier — Museum

(Museum Quarter; www.mqw.at; 07, Museumsplatz; ⌚information & ticket centre 10am-7pm; M Museumsquartier, Volkstheater) The MuseumsQuartier is a remarkable ensemble of museums, cafes, restaurants and bars inside former imperial stables designed by Fischer von Erlach. This breeding ground of Viennese cultural life is the perfect place to hang out and watch or meet people on warm evenings. With over 60,000 sq metres of exhibition space, the complex is one of the world's most ambitious cultural spaces.

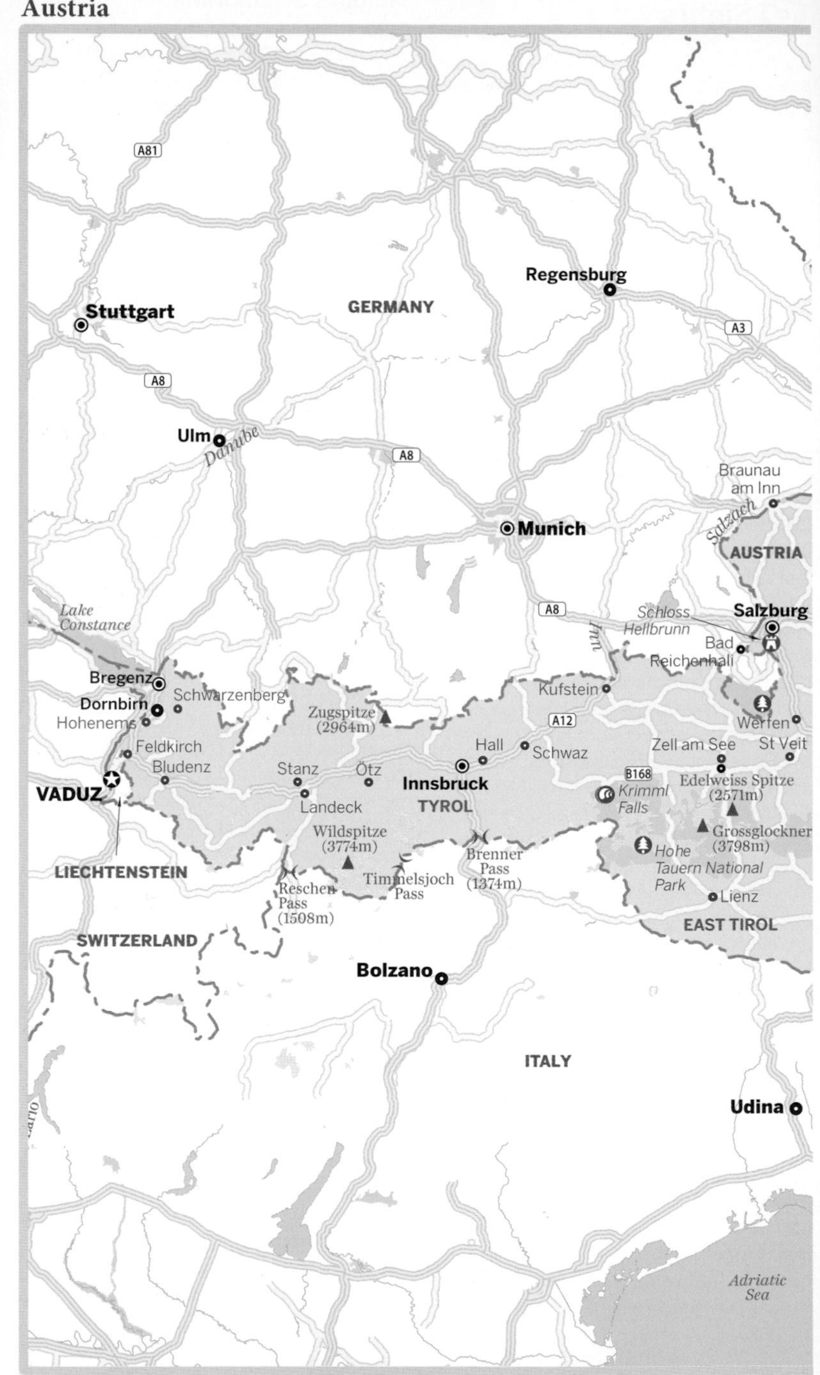
A81
GERMANY
Regensburg
Stuttgart
A3
A8
Ulm
Danube
A8
Braunau am Inn
Salzach
Munich
AUSTRIA
Lake Constance
A8
Inn
Schloss Hellbrunn
Salzburg
Bad Reichenhall
Bregenz
Dornbirn
Schwarzenberg
Kufstein
Zugspitze (2964m)
Hohenems
A12
Werfen
Feldkirch
Hall
Schwaz
Zell am See
St Veit
Bludenz
Stanz
Ötz
B168
Edelweiss Spitze (2571m)
VADUZ
Innsbruck
Krimml Falls
Landeck
TYROL
Wildspitze (3774m)
Grossglockner (3798m)
Brenner Pass (1374m)
Hohe Tauern National Park
LIECHTENSTEIN
Reschen Pass (1508m)
Timmelsjoch Pass
Lienz
EAST TIROL
SWITZERLAND
Bolzano
ITALY
Udina
Adriatic Sea

0 100 km
0 50 miles
CZECH REPUBLIC
20
R43
Brno
Drosendorf
Retz
Horn
Passau
Hollabrunn
Freistadt
Krems an der Donau
SLOVAKIA
Danube
UPPER AUSTRIA
Dürnstein
Stockerau
D2
Linz
Tulln
Traun
Melk
St Pölten
VIENNA
BRATISLAVA
A8
Ansfelden
A1
Schwechat
Wels
Perchtoldsdorf
Amstetten
Mödling
Neusiedl am See
THE SALZKAMMERGUT
Steyr
Baden bei Wien
Bad Vöslau
Gmunden
A1
A3
M1
Attersee
Nationalpark Kalkalpen
Wiener Neustadt
Eisenstadt
St Gilgen
Ebensee
Schneeberg (2076m)
Mariazell
Hoher Nock (1963m)
Neunkirchen
Bad Ischl
AUSTRIA
Gloggnitz
Neusiedler See
Bad Aussee
Eisenerz
Mürzzuschlag
Admont
S6
Oberpullendorf
B320
Stainach
Kapfenberg
BURGENLAND
A9
Haus
Radstadt
Leoben
Bruck an der Mur
Unzmarkt-Frauenburg
STYRIA
Oberwart
Judenburg
HUNGARY
Tamsweg
Bad Blumau
Köflach
Graz
Murau
Güssing
Rennweg
Voitsberg
CARINTHIA
Feldbach
Spittal an der Drau
St Veit an der Glan
Wolfsberg
A9
Bad Radkersberg
Feldkirchen
St Andrä
Ehrenhausen
Wörthersee
Völkermarkt
Villach
Klagenfurt
Drava
E57
A2
E59
Sava
Dráva
LJUBLJANA
SLOVENIA
ZAGREB
CROATIA
Kupa
Sava

Leopold Museum Museum

(www.leopoldmuseum.org; 07, Museumsplatz 1; adult/child €12/7, audio guide €3.50; 10am-6pm Wed-Mon, to 9pm Thu; M Museumsquartier, Volkstheater) The undoubted highlight of a visit to the MuseumsQuartier is the Leopold Museum, a striking gallery that showcases the world's largest collection of Egon Schiele paintings, alongside some fine Klimts and Kokoschkas.

MUMOK Gallery

(Museum Moderner Kunst, Museum of Modern Art; www.mumok.at; 07, Museumsplatz 1; adult/child €10/free; 2-7pm Mon, 10am-7pm Tue-Sun, to 9pm Thu; M Museumsquartier, Volkstheater, 49 Volkstheater) The dark basalt edifice and sharp corners of the Museum Moderner Kunst are a complete contrast to the MuseumsQuartier's historical setting. Inside, MUMOK is crawling with Vienna's finest collection of 20th-century art, centred on fluxus, nouveau realism, pop art and photo-realism.

Schloss Belvedere Palace, Gallery

(www.belvedere.at; adult/child Oberes Belvedere €12.50/free, Unteres Belvedere €11/free, combined ticket €19/free; 10am-6pm; M Taubstummengasse, Südtiroler Platz, D, 71 Schwarzenbergplatz) Belvedere is one of the world's finest baroque palaces, designed by Johann Lukas von Hildebrandt (1668–1745) for Prince Eugene of Savoy. The first of the palace's two buildings is the **Oberes Belvedere** (Upper Belvedere), showcasing Gustav Klimt's *The Kiss* (1908), the perfect embodiment of Viennese art nouveau, alongside other late-19th- to early-20th-century Austrian works. The lavish **Unteres Belvedere** (Lower Belvedere), with its richly frescoed **Marmorsaal** (Marble Hall), sits at the end of sculpture-dotted gardens.

Prater Park

(www.wiener-prater.at; M Praterstern) This large park encompasses meadows, woodlands, an amusement park (the Würstelprater) and one of the city's most visible icons, the **Riesenrad**. Built in 1897, this 65m-high Ferris wheel of *The Third Man* film fame affords far-reaching views of Vienna.

Secession Landmark, Gallery

(www.secession.at; 01, Friedrichstrasse 12; adult/child €9/5.50, audio guide €3; 10am-6pm Tue-Sun; M Karlsplatz) In 1897, 19 progressive artists swam away from the mainstream Künstlerhaus artistic establishment to form the Vienna Secession *(Sezession)*. Among their number were Klimt, Josef Hoffman, Kolo Moser and Joseph M Olbrich. Olbrich designed the new exhibition centre of the Secessionists, which combined sparse functionality with stylistic motifs. Its biggest draw is Klimt's exquisitely gilded *Beethoven Frieze*.

Haus der Musik Museum

(www.hdm.at; 01, Seilerstätte 30; adult/child €12/5.50, with Mozarthaus Vienna €17/7; 10am-10pm; ; M Karlsplatz, D, 1, 2 Kärntner Ring/Oper) The Haus der Musik is an interesting and unusual museum that manages to explain the world of sound in an amusing and highly interactive way (in English and German) for both children and adults. Exhibits are spread over four floors and cover everything from how sound is created through to Vienna's Philharmonic Orchestra and street noises.

Pestsäule Memorial

(Plague Column; 01, Graben; M Stephansplatz) Graben is dominated by the knobbly outline of this memorial, designed by Fischer von Erlach in 1693 to commemorate the 75,000 victims of the Black Death.

Sigmund Freud Museum House Museum

(www.freud-museum.at; 09, Berggasse 19; adult/child €9/4; 10am-6pm; M Schottentor, Schottenring, D Schlickgasse) Sigmund Freud is a bit like the telephone – once he happened, there was no going back. This is where Freud spent his most prolific years and developed his ground-breaking theories; he moved here with his family in 1891 and stayed until he was forced into exile by the Nazis in 1938.

Wien Museum Museum

(www.wienmuseum.at; 04, Karlsplatz 8; adult/under 19yr €8/free, 1st Sun of month free; 10am-6pm Tue-Sun; M Karlsplatz) The

BARRY WINIKER/GETTY IMAGES ©

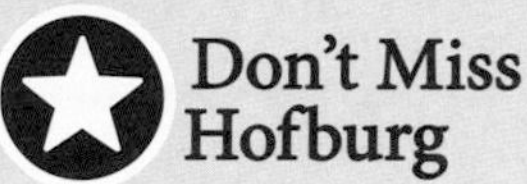

Don't Miss Hofburg

Nothing symbolises the culture and heritage of Austria more than its Hofburg, home base of the Habsburgs from 1273 to 1918. The oldest section is the 13th-century **Schweizerhof** (Swiss Courtyard), named after the Swiss guards who used to protect its precincts. The Renaissance **Swiss gate** dates from 1553. The courtyard adjoins a larger courtyard, **In der Burg**, with a monument to Emperor Franz II adorning its centre. The palace now houses the Austrian president's offices and a raft of museums.

The Hofburg owes its size and architectural diversity to plain old one-upmanship; new sections were added by the new rulers, including the early baroque **Leopold Wing**, the 18th-century **Imperial Chancery Wing**, the 16th-century **Amalia Wing** and the Gothic **Burgkapelle** (Royal Chapel).

NEED TO KNOW

Imperial Palace; www.hofburg-wien.at; 01, Michaelerkuppel; 1A, 2A Michaelerplatz, M Herrengasse, D, 1, 2, 71, 46, 49 Burgring

Wien Museum presents a fascinating romp through Vienna's history, from Neolithic times to the mid-20th century, putting the city and its personalities in a meaningful context. Exhibits are spread over three floors, including spaces for two temporary exhibitions.

Activities

The **Donauinsel** (Danube Island) features swimming areas and paths for walking and cycling. The **Alte Donau** is a landlocked arm of the Danube, a favourite of sailing and boating enthusiasts, swimmers, walkers, anglers and, in winter (when it's cold enough), ice skaters.

Central Vienna

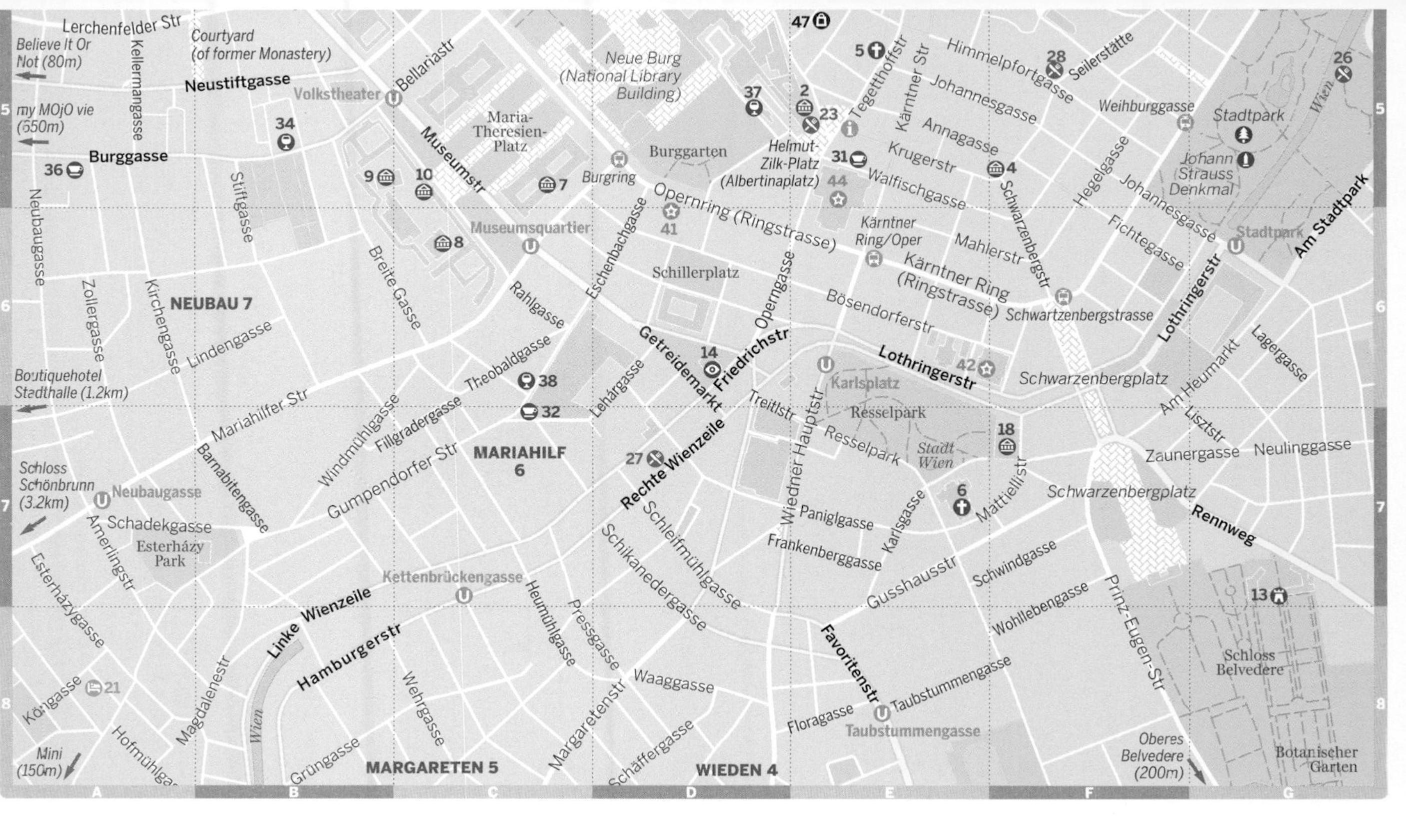
Lerchenfelder Str
Believe It Or Not (80m)
Courtyard (of former Monastery)
Kellermangasse
Neustiftgasse
Volkstheater
Bellariastr
my MOjO vie (650m)
Burggasse
34
36
Neue Burg (National Library Building)
Maria-Theresien-Platz
Museumstr
9
10
7
Burggarten
Burgring
37
2
23
Helmut-Zilk-Platz (Albertinaplatz)
31
44
Tegetthoffstr
Kärntner Str
47
5
Himmelpfortgasse
28
Seilerstätte
Johannesgasse
Annagasse
Krugerstr
4
Walfischgasse
Weihburggasse
Stadtpark
26
Wien
Johann Strauss Denkmal
Hegelgasse
Am Stadtpark
Neubaugasse
Stiftgasse
Museumsquartier
8
Breite Gasse
Eschenbachgasse
Opernring (Ringstrasse)
41
Kärntner Ring/Oper
Mahlerstr
Schwarzenbergstr
Fichtegasse
Stadtpark
Zollergasse
Kirchengasse
NEUBAU 7
Lindengasse
Rahlgasse
Schillerplatz
Operngasse
Kärntner Ring (Ringstrasse)
Bösendorferstr
Schwartzenbergstrasse
Lothringerstr
Boutiquehotel Stadthalle (1.2km)
Theobaldgasse
38
Getreidemarkt
14
Friedrichstr
Karlsplatz
42
Schwarzenbergplatz
Am Heumarkt
Lagergasse
Mariahilfer Str
Windmühlgasse
Fillgradergasse
32
Lehárgasse
Treitlstr
Resselpark
18
Lisztstr
Zaunergasse
Neulinggasse
Schloss Schönbrunn (3.2km)
Neubaugasse
Barnabitengasse
Gumpendorfer Str
MARIAHILF 6
27
Rechte Wienzeile
Wiedner Hauptstr
Resselpark
Stadt Wien
6
Mattiellistr
Rennweg
Schadekgasse
Amerlingstr
Esterházy Park
Schleifmühlgasse
Paniglgasse
Karlsgasse
Frankenberggasse
Schwindgasse
Esterházygasse
Kettenbrückengasse
Linke Wienzeile
Heumühlgasse
Schikanedergasse
Gusshausstr
Wohllebengasse
Prinz-Eugen-Str
13
Hamburgerstr
Pressgasse
Favoritenstr
Schloss Belvedere
Köngasse
21
Magdalenestr
Wehrgasse
Waaggasse
Margaretenstr
Taubstummengasse
Floragasse
Mini (150m)
Hofmühlgasse
Grüngasse
MARGARETEN 5
Schäffergasse
WIEDEN 4
Oberes Belvedere (200m)
Botanischer Garten
A
B
C
D
E
F
G
5
6
7
8

Central Vienna

Don't Miss Sights
- 1 Hofburg D4

Sights
- 2 Albertina E5
- 3 Burgtheater C3
- 4 Haus der Musik F5
- Kaisergruft .... (see 5)
- 5 Kapuzinerkirche E5
- 6 Karlskirche E7
- 7 Kunsthistorisches Museum C5
- 8 Leopold Museum C6
- 9 MUMOK B5
- 10 MuseumsQuartier C5
- 11 Pestsäule E4
- 12 Rathaus B3
- 13 Schloss Belvedere G7
- 14 Secession D6
- 15 Sigmund Freud Museum C1
- 16 Spanish Riding School D4
- 17 Stephansdom E4
- 18 Wien Museum F7

Sleeping
- 19 Hollmann Beletage F3
- 20 Hotel Rathaus Wein & Design A4
- 21 Pension Kraml A8
- 22 Pension Sacher E4

Eating
- 23 Bitzinger Würstelstand am Albertinaplatz E5
- 24 Figlmüller F4
- 25 Gasthaus Pöschl F4
- 26 Meierei im Stadtpark G5
- 27 Naschmarkt D7
- 28 Tian F5
- 29 Trzesniewski E4

Drinking & Nightlife
- 30 Café Leopold Hawelka E4
- 31 Café Sacher E5
- 32 Café Sperl C7
- 33 Dachboden B4
- 34 Das Möbel B5
- 35 Demel D4
- 36 Espresso A5
- 37 Palmenhaus D5
- 38 Phil C6
- Volksgarten ClubDiskothek .... (see 39)
- 39 Volksgarten Pavillon C4
- 40 Weinfach Vinothek & Bar G2

Entertainment
- 41 Burg Kino D6
- 42 Musikverein E6
- 43 Porgy & Bess F4
- 44 Staatsoper E5
- 45 Vienna Boys' Choir Tickets D4

Shopping
- 46 Bio-Markt Freyung D3
- 47 Dorotheum E5
- 48 Karmelitermarkt F1

Festivals & Events

Opernball — Ball

(www.wiener-staatsoper.at; Jan/Feb) Of the 300 or so balls held in January and February, the Opernball (Opera Ball) is number one. Held in the Staatsoper, it's a supremely lavish affair, with the men in tails and women in shining white gowns.

Wiener Festwochen — Arts

(www.festwochen.at; mid-May–late June) Wide-ranging program of arts from around the world.

Donauinselfest — Music

(https://donauinselfest.at; late Jun) Held over three days on a weekend in late June, the Donauinselfest features a feast of rock, pop, folk and country performers, and attracts almost three million onlookers. Best of all, it's free!

Viennale Film Festival — Film

(526 59 47; www.viennale.at; late Oct-early Nov) The country's best film festival features fringe and independent films from around the world. It is held every year, with screenings at numerous locations around the city.

Christkindlmärkte — Market

(www.christkindlmarkt.at; mid-Nov–25 Dec) Vienna's much-loved Christmas market.

Sleeping

my MOjO vie — Hostel €

(0676-551 11 55; http://mymojovie.at; 07, Kaiserstrasse 77; dm/d/tr/q €26/56/81/104; @; M Burggasse Stadthalle) An old-fashioned cage lift rattles up to these incredible backpacker digs. Everything you could wish for is here; design-focused dorms, a kitchen with free supplies, netbooks for surfing, guidebooks for browsing and even musical instruments for your own jam session.

Believe It Or Not Hostel €
(☎0676-550 00 55; www.believe-it-or-not-vienna.at; 07, Myrthengasse 10; dm €26-30; @ ; M Volkstheater) It may seem nondescript on the face of things, but you really won't believe what a cosy, homely hostel this is. We love the dorms with mezzanine-style beds, the laid-back lounge, kitchen with free basics and laptops for guest use.

Pension Kraml Pension €
(☎587 85 88; www.pensionkraml.at; 06, Brauergasse 5; s €35, d €48-78, tr €69-87, q €110-120; @ ; M Zieglergasse) Tucked peacefully down a backstreet five minutes' walk south of Mariahilfer Strasse, this family-run *pension* (guesthouse) looks back on 150 years of history and prides itself on old-school hospitality and comfort.

Rooms are surprisingly large, accommodating twin beds, bedside tables and a solid wardrobe, while leaving plenty of room for a close waltz.

Pension Sacher Pension €€
(☎533 32 38; www.pension-sacher.at; 01, Rothenturmstrasse 1; apt €100-152; ; M Stephansplatz) Filled with chintzy knick-knacks, florals and solid wood furnishings, these super-central, spacious apartments are lovingly kept by the Sacher family of chocolate-cake fame. There's everything you need to feel right at home and the views of Stephansdom are phenomenal.

Hotel Rathaus Wein & Design Boutique Hotel €€
(☎400 11 22; www.hotel-rathaus-wien.at; 08, Lange Gasse 13; s/d/tr €150/210/240; @ ; M Rathaus, Volkstheater) Each of the open-plan, minimalist-chic rooms at this boutique hotel is dedicated to an Austrian winemaker and the minibar is stocked with wines from the growers themselves.

Boutiquehotel Stadthalle Hotel €€
(☎982 42 72; www.hotelstadthalle.at; 15, Hackengasse 20; s €80-120, d €118-188; ;

Food Market Finds

The sprawling **Naschmarkt** (06, Linke & Rechte Wienzeile; 6am-7.30pm Mon-Fri, to 6pm Sat; M Karlsplatz, Kettenbrückengasse) is the place to *nasch* (snack) in Vienna. Stalls are piled high with meats, fruits, vegetables, cheeses, olives, spices and wine. There are also plenty of cafes dishing up good-value lunches, along with delis and takeaway stands.

Freyung Market (01, Freyungasse; 9am-6pm Fri & Sat; M Herrengasse, Schottentor) sells farm-fresh produce, as does the bustling **Karmelitermarkt** (02, Karmelitermarkt; 6am-7.30pm Mon-Fri, to 5pm Sat; M Taborstrasse, 2 Karmeliterplatz). Head to the Saturday farmers market at the latter for brunch at one of the excellent deli-cafes.

M Schweglerstrasse) Welcome to Vienna's most eco-aware hotel, which has a roof fragrantly planted with lavender. Bursts of purple, pink and peach enliven rooms that blend modern with polished antiques. An organic breakfast is served in the ivy-draped courtyard garden.

Hollmann Beletage Pension €€
(☎961 19 60; www.hollmann-beletage.at; 01, Köllnerhofgasse 6; d €159-229, tr €179-259, q €199-300, ste from €390; @ ; M Schwedenplatz, 1, 2 Schwedenplatz) This minimalist establishment offers style and clean lines throughout. A terrace and lounge where you can enjoy free snacks at 2pm are bonuses, as is the small hotel cinema and the free use of an iPad.

Eating

Vienna has thousands of restaurants covering all budgets and styles of cuisine, but dining doesn't stop there. *Kaffeehäuser* (coffee houses), *Beisln* (small taverns) and *Heurigen* (wine

CAROLIN VOELKER/GETTY IMAGES ©

Don't Miss Ringstrasse

One of the best deals in Vienna is a self-guided tour on tram 1 or 2 of the monumental Ringstrasse boulevard encircling much of the Innere Stadt, which turned 150 in 2015. For the price of a single ticket you'll take in the neo-Gothic **Rathaus** (City Hall; www.wien.gv.at; 01, Rathausplatz 1; guided tours 1pm Mon, Wed & Fri; M Rathaus, D, 1, 2 Rathaus) FREE, the Greek Revival–style parliament, the 19th-century **Burgtheater** (514 44 4140; www.burgtheater.at; 01, Dr-Karl-Lueger-Ring; tours adult/child €5.50/2; tours 3pm Sep-Jun; M Rathaus, D, 1, 2 Rathaus; pictured above) and the baroque **Karlskirche** (St Charles Church; www.karlskirche.at; Karlsplatz; adult/child €8/4; 9am-5.30pm Mon-Sat, 11.30am-5.30pm Sun; M Karlsplatz), among other sights.

taverns) are just as fine for a good meal. *Würstelstände* (sausage stands) are conveniently located on street corners and squares.

Trzesniewski Sandwiches €

(www.trzesniewski.at; 01, Dorotheergasse 1; bread & spread €1.20; 8am-7pm Mon-Fri, 9am-5pm Sat; M Stephansplatz) Possibly the finest sandwich shop in Austria, Trzesniewski has been serving spreads and breads to the entire spectrum of munchers for over 100 years.

Bitzinger Würstelstand am Albertinaplatz Fast Food€

(01, Albertinaplatz; sausages €1.70-4.30; 8am-4am; M Karlsplatz, Stephansplatz, Kärntner Ring/Oper) Vienna has many sausage stands but this one located behind the Staatsoper is hands down one of the best.

Mini Fusion €€

(159 54 483; www.minirestaurant.at; 06, Marchettigasse 11; mains €16-24; 11.30am-midnight; M Pilgramgasse) A slick, vaulted interior provides the backdrop for Hungarian cuisine with a pinch of global personality

at Mini. Starters like wild-boar soup warm you up nicely for bright, flavour-packed mains like swordfish in white-wine mushroom sauce. The two-course lunch is a snip at €7.90.

Meierei im Stadtpark Austrian **€€**
(☎713 31 68; http://steirereck.at; 03, Am Heumarkt 2a; set breakfasts €20-24, mains €11-20, 6-cheese selection €11; ⏰8am-11pm Mon-Fri, 9am-7pm Sat & Sun; 🌶; **M** Stadtpark) Embedded in the greenery of the Stadtpark, the Meierei serves a bountiful breakfast until noon. It's most famous, though, for its goulash served with leek roulade (€18), and its selection of 120 types of cheese.

Gasthaus Pöschl Austrian **€€**
(☎513 52 88; 01, Weihburggasse 17; mains €9-18; ⏰noon-midnight; **M** Stubentor) Close to pretty Franziskanerplatz, this small, wood-panelled *Beisl* brims with Viennese warmth and bonhomie. Austrian classics like *Tafelspitz* (boiled beef) and schnitzel are cooked to a T.

Figlmüller Bistro, Pub **€€**
(☎512 61 77; www.figlmueller.at; 01, Woll zeile 5; mains €13-23; ⏰11am-10.30pm; 📶; **M** Stephansplatz) The Viennese would simply be at a loss without Figlmüller. This famous *Beisl* has some of the biggest and best schnitzels in the business.

Tian Vegetarian **€€€**
(☎890 46 65; www.tian-vienna.com; 01, Himmelpfortgasse 23; 2-/3-course lunch €26/32, 4-/8-course evening menu €81-120; ⏰noon-midnight Mon-Sat; 🌶; **M** Stephansplatz, 🚋2 Weihburggasse) Stealthy charm meets urban attitude at this lounge-style, Michelin-starred restaurant which takes vegetarian cuisine to delicious heights. Lunch menus offer the best value; you can also enjoy a drink in the delightful wine bar.

Drinking & Nightlife

Weinfach Vinothek & Bar Wine Bar
(www.weinfach.at; 02, Taborstrasse 11a; ⏰5-10pm Tue-Sat ; 🚋2 Gredlerstrasse) This bright, modern wine store and bar extends the warmest of welcomes. The well-edited, 90-variety wine list traverses the entire Austrian spectrum and the sharing plates of local cheese and Carinthian salami are perfect for grazing. The clued-up staff arrange regular tastings and events.

Palmenhaus Bar
(www.palmenhaus.at; 01, Burggarten; ⏰11.30am-midnight Mon-Thu, 10am-1am Fri & Sat, 10am-11pm Sun; **M** Karlsplatz, Museums quartier, 🚋D, 1, 2, 71 Burgring) Housed in a beautifully restored Jungendstil palm house, the Palmenhouse opens onto a terrific garden terrace in summer.

Phil Bar
(www.phil.info; 06, Gumpendorfer Strasse 10-12; ⏰5pm-1am Mon, 9am-1am Tue-Sun; **M** Museumsquartier, Kettenbrückengasse) A retro bar, book and record store, Phil attracts a bohemian crowd happy to squat on kitsch furniture your grandma used to own. The vibe is as relaxed as can be.

Volksgarten Pavillon Bar
(www.volksgarten-pavillon.at; 01, Burgring 1; ⏰11am-2am Apr–mid-Sep; 📶; **M** Volkstheater, 🚋D, 1, 2, 71 Dr-Karl-Renner-Ring) Volksgarten Pavillon is a lovely 1950s-style pavilion with views of Heldenplatz.

Das Möbel Bar
(http://dasmoebel.at; 07, Burggasse 10; ⏰2pm-midnight Mon-Fri, from 10am Sat & Sun; 📶; **M** Volkstheater) Das Möbel wins points for its furniture, consisting entirely of one-off pieces produced by local designers – and everything is for sale.

Dachboden Bar
(http://25hours-hotels.com; 07, Lerchenfelder Strasse 1-3; ⏰2pm-1am Tue-Fri, noon-1am Sat, noon-10pm Sun; 📶; **M** Volkstheater) Housed in the circus-themed 25hours Hotel, Dachboden has big-top views of Vienna's skyline from its decked terrace. DJs spins jazz, soul and funk on Wednesday and Friday nights.

Pratersauna Club
(www.pratersauna.tv; 02, Waldsteingartenstrasse 135; ⏰club 9pm-6am Wed-Sun, pool 1-9pm Fri & Sat Jun-Sep; **M** Messe-Prater) Pool, cafe, bistro and club converge in a former sauna –

Coffee-House Culture

Vienna's legendary *Kaffeehäuser* (coffee houses) are wonderful places for people-watching, daydreaming and catching up on gossip or world news. Most serve light meals alongside mouth-watering cakes and tortes. Expect to pay around €8 for a coffee with a slice of cake. These are just five of our favourites.

Café Sperl (www.cafesperl.at; 06, Gumpendorfer Strasse 11; 7am-11pm Mon-Sat, 11am-8pm Sun; ; M Museumsquartier, Kettenbrückengasse) Gorgeous Jugendstil fittings, grand dimensions, cosy booths and an unhurried air. The must-try is *Sperl Torte,* an almond and chocolate cream dream.

Café Leopold Hawelka (www.hawelka.at; 01, Dorotheergasse 6; 8am-1am Mon-Sat, 10am-1am Sun; M Stephansplatz) Dark, moody and picture-plastered, this late 1930s coffee house was once the hang-out of artists and writers including Friedensreich Hundertwasser, Elias Canetti, Arthur Miller and Andy Warhol.

Demel (www.demel.at; 01, Kohlmarkt 14; 9am-7pm; 1A, 2A Michaelerplatz, M Herrengasse, Stephansplatz) An elegant, regal cafe near the Hofburg. Demel's speciality is the *Anna Torte,* a chocolate and nougat calorie-bomb.

Café Sacher (www.sacher.com; 01, Philharmonikerstrasse 4; 8am-midnight; M Karlsplatz, D, 1, 2, 71 Kärntner Ring/Oper) Fancy, chandelier-lit Sacher is celebrated for its *Sacher Torte,* a rich chocolate cake with apricot jam once favoured by Emperor Franz Josef.

Espresso (http://espresso-wien.at; 07, Burggasse 57; 7.30am-1am Mon-Fri, 10am-1am Sat & Sun; M Volkstheater, 49 Siebensterngasse/Kirchengasse) For a fresh take on the coffee-house scene, stop by this retro-cool blast from the 1950s, where hipsters linger over espressos with a kick and brunch.

these days, you'll sweat it up on the dance floor any given night.

Volksgarten ClubDiskothek Club
(www.volksgarten.at; 01, Burgring 1; cover from €6; 10pm-4am or later Tue & Thu-Sat; M Museumsquartier, Volkstheater, D, 1, 2, 71 Dr-Karl-Renner-Ring) A hugely popular club, superbly located near the Hofburg, Volksgarten serves a clientele eager to see and be seen.

Entertainment

Vienna is, and probably will be till the end of time, the European capital of opera and classical music.

Box offices generally open from Monday to Saturday and sell cheap (€3 to €6) standing-room tickets around an hour before performances.

Staatsoper Opera
(514 44 7880; www.wiener-staatsoper.at; 01, Opernring 2; M Karlsplatz, D 1, 2 Kärntner Ring/Oper) The Staatsoper is *the* premiere opera and classical-music venue in Vienna. Productions are lavish, formal affairs, where people dress up accordingly.

Musikverein Concert Venue
(505 81 90; www.musikverein.at; 01, Bösendorferstrasse 12; standing room €4-6, seats €25-89; box office 9am-8pm Mon-Fri, to 1pm Sat; M Karlsplatz) The opulent Musikverein holds the proud title of the best acoustics of any concert hall in Austria, of which the Vienna Philharmonic Orchestra makes excellent use.

Porgy & Bess Jazz
(512 88 11; www.porgy.at; 01, Riemergasse 11; around €18; concerts 7pm or 8.30pm; M Stubentor, 2 Stubentor) Quality is the

cornerstone of Porgy & Bess' continuing popularity. Its program is loaded with modern jazz acts from around the globe.

Burg Kino Cinema
(587 84 06; www.burgkino.at; 01, Opernring 19; M Museumsquartier, D, 1, 2 Burgring) The Burg Kino shows only English-language films. It has regular screenings of the *The Third Man*, Orson Welles' timeless classic set in post-WWII Vienna.

Shopping

In the alley-woven Innere Stadt, go to Kohlmarkt for designer chic, Herrengasse for antiques and Kärntnerstrasse for high-street brands. Tune into Vienna's creative pulse in the idiosyncratic boutiques and concept stores in Neubau, especially along Kirchengasse and Lindengasse.

Dorotheum Auction
(www.dorotheum.com; 01, Dorotheergasse 17; h10am-6pm Mon-Fri, 9am-5pm Sat; mStephansplatz) One of Europe's largest auction houses, it's as entertaining as visiting many of Vienna's museums.

Information

Tourist Info Wien (245 55; www.wien.info; 01, Albertinaplatz; 9am-7pm; ; M Stephansplatz, D, 1, 2, 71 Kärntner Ring/Oper) Vienna's main tourist office, with a ticket agency, hotel booking service, free maps and every brochure under the sun.

Getting There & Away

Boat

Fast hydrofoils travel eastwards to Bratislava (one way €20 to €35, 1¼ hours) daily from April to October. From May to September, they also travel twice weekly to Budapest (one way/return €109/125, 5½ hours). Bookings can be made through DDSG Blue Danube (www.ddsg-blue-danube.at).

Bus

Vienna currently has no central bus station. National Bundesbuses arrive and depart from several different locations, depending on the destination. Bus lines serving Vienna include Eurolines (0900 128 712; www.eurolines.com; Erdbergstrasse 200; 6.30am-9pm Mon-Fri; M Erdberg).

Car & Motorcycle

The Gürtel is an outer ring road that joins up with the A22 on the north bank of the Danube and the A23 southeast of town. All the main road routes intersect with this system, including the A1 from Linz and Salzburg, and the A2 from Graz.

Train

Vienna is one of central Europe's main rail hubs. Österreichische Bundesbahn (ÖBB, Austrian Federal Railway; www.oebb.at;) is the main operator. Sample destinations include Budapest (€29 to €37, 2½ to 3¼ hours), Munich (€93, 4½ to five hours), Paris (€51 to €142, 11½ to 13 hours), Prague (€49, 4¼ hours) and Venice (€49 to €108, seven to 11 hours). Vienna's main station is the Hauptbahnhof, formerly the Südbahnhof. Following a massive construction project, it became partially operational in December 2012 and is set for completion in 2015. In the meantime, some long-distance trains are being rerouted among the rest of Vienna's train stations, including the Westbahnhof and Wien Meidling. Further train stations include Franz-Josefs-Bahnhof (which handles trains to/from the Danube Valley), Wien Mitte and Wien Nord.

Getting Around

To/From the Airport

It is 19km from the city centre to Vienna International Airport (VIE; www.viennaairport.com) in Schwechat. The City Airport Train (CAT; www.cityairporttrain.com; return adult/child €19/free; departs airport 6.06am-11.36pm, departs city 5.36am-11.06pm) runs every 30 minutes and takes 16 minutes between the airport and Wien Mitte; book online for a €2 discount. The S-Bahn (S7) does the same journey (single €4.40), but in 25 minutes.

Taxis cost about €35.

Bicycle

Cycling is an excellent way to get around and explore the city – some 1200km of cycle tracks criss-cross the capital.

Vienna's city bike scheme is called Vienna City Bike (Vienna City Bike; www.citybikewien.at; 1st hour free, 2nd/3rd hours €1/2, per hour thereafter €4), with more than 120 bicycle stands across the city. A credit card is required to rent bikes – just swipe your card in the machine and follow the instructions (in a number of languages).

Imperial Entertainment

Founded over five centuries ago by Maximilian I as the imperial choir, the world-famous **Vienna Boys' Choir** (Wiener Sängerknaben; www.wienersaengerknaben.at) is the original boy band. These cherubic angels in sailor suits still hold a fond place in Austrian hearts. **Tickets** (533 99 27; www.hofburgkapelle.at; 01, Schweizerhof; Sun Burgkapelle performance €9-35; M Herrengasse) for their Sunday performances at 9.15am (late September to June) in the Burgkapelle (Royal Chapel) in the Hofburg should be booked around six weeks in advance. The group also performs regularly in the Musikverein.

Another throwback to the Habsburg glory days is the **Spanische Hofreitschule** (Spanische Hofreitschule; 533 90 31; www.srs.at; 01, Michaelerplatz 1; performances €31-190; 1A, 2A Michaelerplatz, M Herrengasse). White Lipizzaner stallions gracefully perform equine ballet to classical music. For **Morning Training** (adult/child/family €14/7/28; 10am-noon Tue-Fri Feb-Jun & mid-Aug–Dec) sessions, same-day tickets are available at the **visitor centre** (Michaelerplatz 1; 9am-4pm ; M Herrengasse) on Michaelerplatz.

Car & Motorcycle

Due to a system of one-way streets and expensive parking, you're better off using the excellent public-transport system.

Public Transport

Vienna's unified public-transport network encompasses trains, trams, buses, and underground (U-Bahn) and suburban (S-Bahn) trains. Free maps and information pamphlets are available from Wiener Linien (790 9100; www.wienerlinien.at).

All tickets must be validated at the entrance to U-Bahn stations and on buses and trams (except for weekly and monthly tickets). Singles cost €2.20. A 24-hour ticket costs €7.60, a 48-hour ticket €13.30 and a 72-hour ticket €16.50. Weekly tickets (valid Monday to Sunday) cost €16.20.

The Danube Valley

The stretch of Danube between Krems and Melk, known locally as the Wachau, is arguably the loveliest along the entire length of the mighty river. Both banks are dotted with ruined castles and medieval towns, and lined with terraced vineyards. Further upstream is the industrial city of Linz, Austria's avant-garde art and new-technology trailblazer.

KREMS AN DER DONAU

02732 / POP 24,085

Sitting on the northern bank of the Danube against a backdrop of terraced vineyards, Krems marks the beginning of the Wachau. It has an attractive cobbled centre, a small university, some good restaurants and the gallery-dotted Kunstmeile (Art Mile).

Sights

Kunsthalle Gallery

(www.kunsthalle.at; Franz-Zeller-Platz 3; admission €10; 10am-5pm Tue-Sun) The flagship of Krems' Kunstmeile, an eclectic collection of galleries and museums, the Kunsthalle has a program of small but excellent changing exhibitions.

Sleeping & Eating

Arte Hotel Krems Hotel **€€**

(71 123; www.arte-hotel.at; Dr-Karl-Dorrek-Strasse 23; s/d €109/159; P) This cutting-edge art hotel has 91 large, well-designed rooms scattered with big retro prints and patterns complementing the funky '60s-style furniture.

Hotel Unter den Linden Hotel €€
(☎82 115; www.udl.at; Schillerstrasse 5; s €67-87, d €90-118; 📶) This big, family-run hotel has knowledgeable and helpful owners, 39 bright, welcoming rooms and a convenient location in Krems itself.

Information

Krems Tourismus (☎82 676; www.krems.info; Utzstrasse 1; 🕘9am-6pm Mon-Fri, 11am-6pm Sat, 11am-4pm Sun, shorter hours in winter) Helpful office well stocked with info and maps.

Getting There & Away

Frequent daily trains connect Krems with Vienna's Franz-Josefs-Bahnhof (€15.90, one hour) and Melk (€12.70, 1½ hours).

The South

Austria's two main southern states, Styria (Steiermark) and Carinthia (Kärnten), often feel worlds apart from the rest of the country, both in climate and attitude. Styria is a blissful amalgamation of genteel architecture, rolling green hills, vine-covered slopes and soaring mountains. Its capital, Graz, is one of Austria's most attractive cities.

GRAZ

☎0316 / POP 269,997

Austria's second-largest city is probably its most relaxed and, after Vienna, its liveliest for after-hours pursuits. It's an attractive place with bristling green parkland, red rooftops and a small, fast-flowing river gushing through its centre. Architecturally, it has Renaissance courtyards and provincial baroque palaces complemented by innovative modern designs. The surrounding countryside, a mixture of vineyards, mountains, forested hills and thermal springs, is within easy striking distance.

Sights

Admission to all of the major museums with a 24-hour ticket costs €11/4 for adults/children.

Neue Galerie Graz Gallery
(www.museum-joanneum.at; Joanneumsviertel; adult/child €8/3; 🕘10am-5pm Tue-Sun; 🚊1, 3, 4, 5, 6, 7 Hauptplatz) The Neue Galerie is

Murinsel (p614), Graz, Austria

FRANZ MARC FREI/LOOK-FOTO/GETTY IMAGES ©

the crowning glory of the three museums inside the Joanneumsviertel museum complex. The stunning collection on level 0 is the highlight. Though not enormous, it showcases richly textured and colourful works by painters such as Ernst Christian Moser, Ferdinand Georg Waldmüller and Johann Nepomuk Passini. Egon Schiele is also represented here.

Kunsthaus Graz Gallery

(www.kunsthausgraz.at; Lendkai 1; adult/child €8/3; 10am-5pm Tue-Sun; 1, 3, 6, 7 Südtiroler Platz) Designed by British architects Peter Cook and Colin Fournier, this world-class contemporary-art space is a bold creation that looks something like a space-age sea slug. Exhibitions change every three to four months.

Schloss Eggenberg Palace

(Eggenberger Allee 90; adult/child €11.50/5.50; tours 10am-4pm Tue-Sun Palm Sun-Oct; 1 Schloss Eggenberg) Graz' elegant palace was created for the Eggenberg dynasty in 1625 by Giovanni Pietro de Pomis (1565–1633) at the request of Johann Ulrich (1568–1634). Admission is on a highly worthwhile guided **tour** during which you learn about the idiosyncrasies of each room, the stories told by the frescoes and about the Eggenberg family itself.

Murinsel Bridge

(4, 5 Schlossplatz/Murinsel, 1, 3, 6, 7 Südtiroler Platz) Murinsel is a constructed island-cum-bridge of metal and plastic in the middle of the Mur. This modern floating landmark contains a cafe, a kids' playground and a small stage.

Schlossberg Viewpoint

(1hr ticket for lift or funicular €2.10; 4, 5 Schlossbergplatz) FREE Rising to 473m, Schlossberg is the site of the original fortress where Graz was founded and is topped by the city's most visible icon – the Uhrenturn. Its wooded slopes can be reached by a number of bucolic and strenuous paths, but also by lift or Schlossbergbahn funicular. Take tram 4 or 5 to Schlossplatz/Murinsel for the lift.

Landeszeughaus Museum

(Styrian Armoury; www.museum-joanneum.at; Herrengasse 16; adult/child €8/3; 10am-5pm Mon & Wed-Sun; 1, 3, 4, 5, 6, 7 Hauptplatz) You won't need to have a passion for armour and weapons to enjoy what's on show at the Landeszeughaus. More than 30,000 pieces of glistening weaponry are housed here.

Burg Castle, Park

(Hofgasse; 30 Schauspielhaus, 1, 3, 4, 5, 6, 7 Hauptplatz) FREE Graz's 15th-century Burg today houses government offices. At the far end of the courtyard, on the left under the arch, is an ingenious **double staircase** (1499) – the steps diverge and converge as they spiral. Adjoining it is the **Stadtpark**, the city's largest green space.

Stift Melk, Austria

Detour: Melk

Stift Melk (Benedictine Abbey of Melk; www.stiftmelk.at; Abt Berthold Dietmayr Strasse 1; adult/child €10/5.50, with guided tour €12/7.50; 9am-5.30pm May-Sep, tours 11am & 2pm Oct-Apr) Of the many abbeys in Austria, Stift Melk is the most famous. Possibly Lower Austria's finest, the monastery church dominates the complex with its twin spires and high octagonal dome. The interior is baroque gone barmy, with regiments of smirking cherubs, gilt twirls and polished faux marble. The theatrical high-altar scene, depicting St Peter and St Paul (the church's two patron saints), is by Peter Widerin. Johann Michael Rottmayr created most of the ceiling paintings, including those in the dome.

In 1089 the Babenberg margrave Leopold II donated the castle to Benedictine monks, who converted it into a fortified abbey. Fire destroyed the original edifice, which was completely baroque-ified between 1702 and 1738 according to plans by Jakob Prandtauer and his disciple, Josef Munggenast.

Besides the monastery church, highlights include the Bibliothek (library) and the Marmorsaal (Marble Hall); both have amazing trompe l'œil-painted tiers on the ceiling (by Paul Troger) to give the illusion of greater height, and ceilings are slightly curved to aid the effect. Eleven of the imperial rooms, where dignitaries (including Napoleon) stayed, are now used as a somewhat overcooked concept museum.

A combined ticket with Schloss Schallaburg is €18. From around November to March, the monastery can only be visited by guided **tour** (11am and 2pm daily). Always phone or email ahead, even in summer, to ensure you get an English-language tour.

Sleeping

Hotel Daniel Hotel €

(711 080; www.hoteldaniel.com; Europaplatz 1; r €64-81; P ❄ @ ; 1, 3, 6, 7 Hauptbahnhof) The Daniel is a design hotel with slick, minimalist-style rooms and offers breakfast for €11. You can rent a Vespa or e-bike for €15 per day, or a Piaggio APE for €9 per hour.

Schlossberg Hotel Hotel €€

(80 70-0; www.schlossberg-hotel.at; Kaiser-Franz-Josef-Kai 30; s €115-135, d €150-185, ste €210-250; P @ ; 4, 5 Schlossbergbahn) Central but secluded, four-star Schlossberg is blessed with a prime location at the foot of its namesake. Rooms are well sized and decorated in the style of a country inn. The rooftop terrace with views is perfect for an evening glass of wine.

Hotel zum Dom Hotel €€

(82 48 00; www.domhotel.co.at; Bürgergasse 14; s €74, d €89-169, ste €189-294; P ❄ ; 30 Palais Trauttmansdorff/Urania, 1, 3, 4, 5, 6, 7 Hauptplatz) Ceramic art crafted by a local artist lends character to graceful Hotel zum Dom. The individually furnished rooms come either with steam/power showers or whirlpools, and one suite even has a terrace whirlpool.

Eating

With leafy salads dressed in delicious pumpkin-seed oil, fish specialities and *Pfand'l* (pan-grilled) dishes, Styrian cuisine is Austrian cooking at its light and healthy best. Stock up for a picnic at the **farmers markets** (6am-1pm Mon-Sat) on Kaiser-Josef-Platz and Lendplatz. For fast-food stands, head for Hauptplatz and Jakominiplatz.

Der Steirer Austrian, Tapas **€€**
(**☎703 654; www.dersteirer.at; Belgiergasse 1; tapas €2, lunch menu €7.90, mains €10-22.50; ⏲11am-midnight; ; 1, 3, 6, 7 Südtiroler Platz)** This Styrian neo-*Beisl* (bistro pub) and wine bar has a small but fantastic selection of local dishes, including a great goulash, and Austrotapas if you just feel like nibbling.

Landhauskeller Austrian **€€**
(**☎83 02 76; Schmiedgasse 9; mains €11.50-28.50; ⏲11.30am-midnight Mon-Sat; 1, 3 ,4, 5, 6, 7 Hauptplatz)** What started as a spit-and-sawdust pub in the 16th century has evolved into an atmospheric, medieval-style restaurant serving specialities such as its four different sorts of *Tafelspitz* (prime broiled beef).

Drinking

The bar scene in Graz is split between three main areas: around the university; adjacent to the Kunsthaus; and on Mehlplatz and Prokopigasse (dubbed the 'Bermuda Triangle').

La Enoteca Wine Bar
(**www.laenoteca.at; Sackstrasse 14; ⏲5-11pm Mon, 11.30am-11pm Tue-Fri, 10am-11pm Sat; 1, 3, 4, 5, 6, 7 Hauptplatz)** This small wine bar has an informal, relaxed atmosphere and courtyard seating, making it an ideal place to enjoy a Schilcher Sekt (sparkling rosé) with mixed antipasti.

Kulturhauskeller Bar, Club
(**Elisabethstrasse 30; ⏲9pm-5am Tue-Sat; 7 Lichtenfelsgasse)** The raunchy Kulturhauskeller is a popular student hang-out with a great cellar-pub feel and a Wednesday karaoke night.

Information

Graz Tourismus (**☎80 75; www.graztourismus.at; Herrengasse 16; ⏲10am-6pm; ; 1, 3, 4, 5, 6, 7 Hauptplatz)** Graz' main tourist office, with loads of free information on the city, and helpful and knowledgeable staff.

Getting There & Away

Air

Graz airport (**GRZ; ☎0316-29 020; www.flughafen-graz.at)** is located 10km south of the centre and is served by carriers including Air Berlin (**www.airberlin.com)**, which connects the city with Berlin.

Bicycle

Bicycle rental is available from Bicycle (**☎82 13 57; www.bicycle.at; Körösistrasse 5; per 24hr €10, Fri-Mon €16; ⏲7am-1pm & 2-6pm Mon-Fri)**.

Public Transport

Single tickets (€2.10) for buses, trams and the Schlossbergbahn are valid for one hour, but you're usually better off buying a 24-hour pass (€4.80).

Train

Trains to Vienna depart hourly (€37, 2½ hours), and six daily go to Salzburg (€48.20, four hours). International train connections from Graz include Ljubljana (€30 to €40, 3½ hours) and Budapest (€51 to €73, 5½ hours).

Salzburg

☎0662 / POP 147,825

The joke 'If it's baroque, don't fix it' is a perfect maxim for Salzburg; the tranquil Old Town burrowed below steep hills looks much as it did when Mozart lived here 250 years ago.

A Unesco World Heritage Site, Salzburg's overwhelmingly baroque old town is entrancing both at ground level and from Hohensalzburg fortress high above. Across the fast-flowing Salzach River rests Schloss Mirabell, surrounded by gorgeous manicured gardens.

If this doesn't whet your appetite, then bypass the grandeur and head straight for kitsch-country by joining a tour of *The Sound of Music* film locations.

Sights

The money-saving **Salzburg Card** (1-/2-/3-day card €27/36/42) gets you entry to all of the major sights and attractions, a free river cruise, unlimited use of public transport (including cable cars) plus numerous discounts on tours and events.

Don't Miss DomQuartier

Salzburg's historic centre shines more brightly than ever since the opening of the DomQuartier in May 2014. A single ticket (adult/child €12/4) gives you access to all five sights in the complex, including the Residenz (pictured above), Dommuseum and Erzabtei St Peter.

For more details, visit www.domquartier.at.

The card is half-price for children and €3 cheaper in the low season.

Festung Hohensalzburg Fort

(www.salzburg-burgen.at; Mönchsberg 34; adult/child/family €8/4.50/18.20, incl Festungsbahn funicular €11.30/6.50/26.20; 9am-7pm) Salzburg's most visible icon is this mighty 900-year-old cliff-top fortress, one of the biggest and best preserved in Europe. It's easy to spend half a day up here, roaming the ramparts for far-reaching views over the city's spires, the Salzach River and the mountains. The fortress is a steep 15-minute jaunt from the centre or a speedy ride in the glass **Festungsbahn funicular** (Festungsgasse 4).

Dom Cathedral

(Cathedral; Domplatz; donations accepted; 8am-7pm Mon-Sat, 1-7pm Sun) Gracefully crowned by a bulbous copper dome and twin spires, the Dom stands out as a masterpiece of baroque art. Bronze portals symbolising faith, hope and charity lead into the cathedral. In the nave, intricate stucco and Arsenio Mascagni's ceiling frescoes recounting the Passion of Christ guide the eye to the polychrome dome.

Residenz Palace

(www.domquartier.at; Residenzplatz 1; DomQuartier ticket adult/child €12/4; 10am-5pm Wed-Mon) The crowning glory of Salzburg's new DomQuartier, the Residenz is where the prince-archbishops held court in the 19th century. An audioguide tour takes

Salzburg

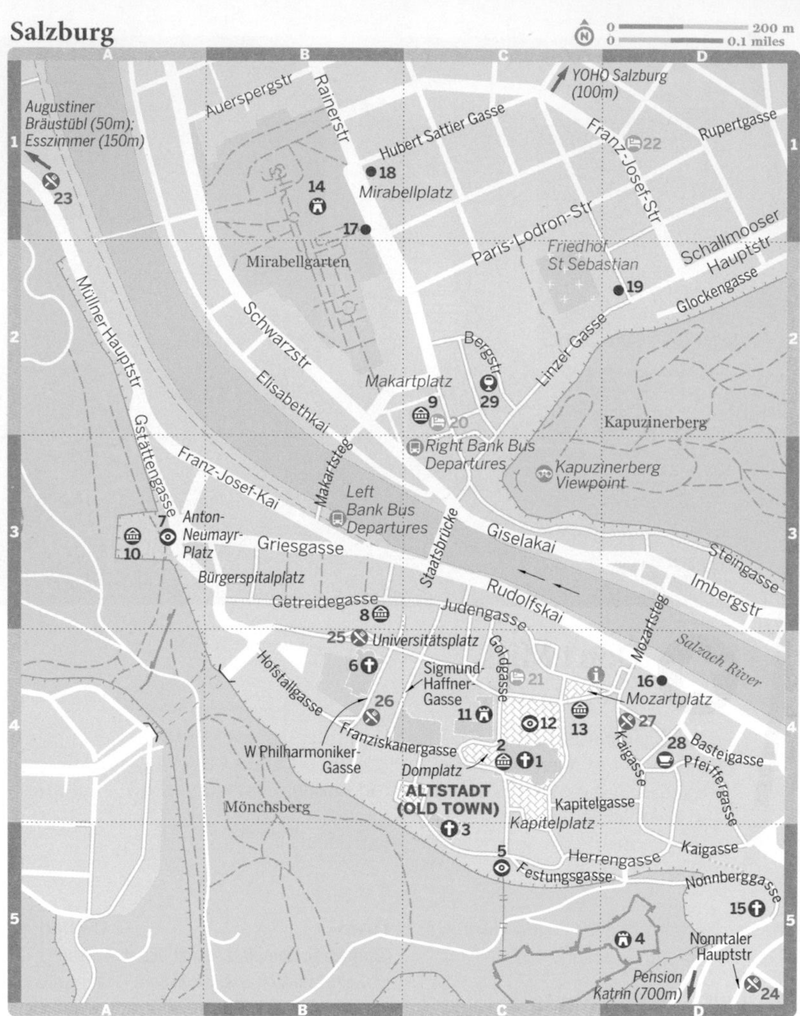

in the exuberant state rooms, lavishly adorned with tapestries, stucco and frescoes by Johann Michael Rottmayr. The 3rd floor is given over to the Residenz galerie, where the focus is on Flemish and Dutch masters. Must-sees include Rubens' *Allegory on Emperor Charles V* and Rembrandt's chiaroscuro *Old Woman Praying*.

Dommuseum Museum

(www.domquartier.at; Kapitelplatz 6; DomQuartier ticket adult/child €12/4; ⌚10am-5pm Wed-Mon) The Dommuseum is a treasure trove of sacred art. A visit whisks you past a cabinet of Renaissance curiosities crammed with crystals, coral and oddities such as armadillos and pufferfish, through rooms showcasing gem-encrusted monstrances, stained glass and altarpieces, and into the **Long Gallery**, which is graced with 17th- and 18th-century paintings, including Paul Troger's chiaroscuro *Christ and Nicodemus* (1739).

Salzburg

Sights

1 Dom ... C4
2 Dommuseum ... C4
3 Erzabtei St Peter ... C5
4 Festung Hohensalzburg ... D5
5 Festungsbahn Funicular ... C5
6 Kollegienkirche ... B4
7 Mönchsberg Lift ... A3
8 Mozarts Geburtshaus ... B3
9 Mozart-Wohnhaus ... C2
10 Museum der Moderne ... A3
11 Residenz ... C4
12 Residenzplatz ... C4
13 Salzburg Museum ... C4
14 Schloss Mirabell ... B1
15 Stift Nonnberg ... D5

Activities, Courses & Tours

16 Bob's Special Tours ... D4
17 Fräulein Maria's Bicycle Tours ... B1
18 Salzburg Panorama Tours ... B1
19 Segway Tours ... D2

Sleeping

20 Arte Vida ... C2
21 Hotel Am Dom ... C4
22 Hotel Mozart ... D1

Eating

23 Bärenwirt ... A1
24 Green Garden ... D5
25 Grünmarkt ... B4
26 Triangel ... B4
27 Zwettler's ... D4

Drinking & Nightlife

28 220 Grad ... D4
29 Enoteca Settemila ... C2

Erzabtei St Peter Church

(St Peter's Abbey; St Peter Bezirk 1-2; catacombs adult/child €2/1.50; church 8am-noon & 2.30-6.30pm, cemetery 6.30am-7pm, catacombs 10am-6pm) A Frankish missionary named Rupert founded this abbey church and monastery in around 700, making it the oldest in the German-speaking world. The cemetery is home to the **catacombs**, cave-like chapels and crypts hewn out of the Mönchsberg cliff face.

Residenzplatz Square

With its horse-drawn carriages, palace and street entertainers, this stately baroque square is the Salzburg of a thousand postcards. Its centrepiece is the **Residenzbrunnen**, an enormous marble fountain ringed by four water-spouting horses and topped by a conch-shell-bearing Triton.

Salzburg Museum Museum

(www.salzburgmuseum.at; Mozartplatz 1; adult/child €7/3; 9am-5pm Tue-Sun, to 8pm Thu) Housed in the baroque Neue Residenz palace, this flagship museum takes you on a fascinating romp through Salzburg past and present. Ornate rooms showcase everything from Roman excavations to prince-archbishop portraits. There are free guided tours at 6pm every Thursday.

Schloss Mirabell Palace

(Mirabellplatz 4; Marble Hall 8am-4pm Mon, Wed & Thu, 1-4pm Tue & Fri, gardens dawn-dusk) FREE Prince-Archbishop Wolf Dietrich had this splendid palace built for his mistress Salome Alt in 1606. Johann Lukas von Hildebrandt, of Schloss Belvedere fame, gave it a baroque makeover in 1721. The lavish **Marmorsaal** (Marble Hall), replete with stucco, marble and frescoes, is free to visit and provides a sublime backdrop for evening chamber concerts. For stellar fortress views, stroll the fountain-dotted gardens. *The Sound of Music* fans will naturally recognise the Pegasus statue and the steps where the von Trapps practised 'Do-Re-Mi'.

Mozarts Geburtshaus Museum

(Mozart's Birthplace; www.mozarteum.at; Getreidegasse 9; adult/child €10/3.50, incl Mozart-Wohnhaus €17/5; 9am-5.30pm) Wolfgang Amadeus Mozart, Salzburg's most famous son, was born in this bright-yellow townhouse in 1756 and spent the first 17 years of his life here.

Mozart-Wohnhaus Museum

(Mozart's Residence; www.mozarteum.at; Makartplatz 8; adult/child €10/3.50, incl Mozarts Geburtshaus €17/5; 9am-5.30pm) Mozart's one-time residence showcases family portraits, documents and instruments. An audio guide accompanies your visit, serenading you with opera excerpts. Alongside family portraits and documents, you'll find Mozart's original fortepiano.

Museum der Moderne Gallery
(www.museumdermoderne.at; Mönchsberg 32; adult/child €8/6; 10am-6pm Tue-Sun, to 8pm Wed) Straddling Mönchsberg's cliffs, this contemporary glass-and-marble oblong of a gallery stands in stark contrast to the fortress. The gallery shows first-rate temporary exhibitions of 20th- and 21st-century art. There's a free guided tour of the gallery at 6.30pm every Wednesday. The **Mönchsberg Lift (Gstättengasse 13; one-way/return €2.10/3.40, incl gallery €9.70/6.80; 8am-7pm Thu-Tue, to 9pm Wed)** whizzes up to the gallery year-round.

Stift Nonnberg Church
(Nonnberg Convent; Nonnberggasse 2; 7am-dusk) A short climb up the Nonnbergstiege staircase from Kaigasse or along Festungsgasse brings you to this Benedictine convent, founded 1300 years ago and made famous as *the* nunnery in *The Sound of Music*. You can visit the beautiful rib-vaulted church, but the rest of the convent is off limits.

Kollegienkirche Church
(Universitätsplatz; 8am-6pm) Johann Bernhard Fischer von Erlach's grandest baroque design is this late-17th-century university church, with a striking bowed facade. The high altar's columns symbolise the Seven Pillars of Wisdom.

Tours

If you would rather go it alone, the tourist office has four-hour iTour audio guides (€9), which take in big-hitters like the Residenz, Mirabellgarten and Mozartplatz.

Fräulein Maria's Bicycle Tours Bike Tour
(www.mariasbicycletours.com; Mirabellplatz 4; adult/child €30/18; 9.30am May-Sep, plus 4.30pm Jun-Aug) Belt out *The Sound of Music* faves as you pedal on one of these jolly 3½-hour bike tours, taking in film locations including the Mirabellgarten, Stift Nonnberg, Schloss Leopoldskron and Hellbrunn. No advance booking is necessary; just turn up at the meeting point on Mirabellplatz.

Salzburg Panorama Tours Bus Tours
(87 40 29; www.panoramatours.com; Mirabellplatz; office 8am-6pm) Boasts the 'original *Sound of Music* Tour' (€40) as well as a huge range of others, including Altstadt (Old Town)walking tours (€15), Mozart tours (€25) and Bavarian Alps and Salzkammergut excursions (€40).

BUCHBINDERE

Horse-drawn carriage, Salzburg, Austria

Segway Tours Tour

(www.segway-salzburg.at; Wolf-Dietrich-Strasse 3; City/Sound of Music tour €33/60; ⌚tours 10.30am, 1pm & 3pm Apr-Oct) These guided Segway tours take in the big sights by zippy battery-powered scooter. Trundle through the city on a one-hour ride or tick off *The Sound of Music* locations on a two-hour tour.

Bob's Special Tours Bus Tours

(☎84 95 11; www.bobstours.com; Rudolfskai 38; ⌚office 8.30am-5pm Mon-Fri, 1-2pm Sat & Sun) Minibus tours to *The Sound of Music* locations (€45), the Bavarian Alps (€45) and Grossglockner (€90). Prices include a free hotel pick-up for morning tours starting at 9am. Reservations essential.

Festivals & Events

Mozartwoche Music

(Mozart Week; www.mozarteum.at; ⌚late Jan) World-renowned orchestras, conductors and soloists celebrate Mozart's birthday with a feast of his music.

Salzburg Festival Arts

(Salzburger Festspiele; www.salzburgerfestspiele.at; ⌚late Jul-Aug) You'll need to book tickets months ahead for this venerable summer festival, running since 1920.

Sleeping

Haus Ballwein Guesthouse €

(☎82 40 29; www.haus-ballwein.at; Moosstrasse 69a; s €42-49, d €63-69, apt €98-120; P 📶) With its bright, pine-filled rooms, mountain views, free bike hire and garden, this place is big on charm. The largest, quietest rooms face the back and have balconies and kitchenettes. It's a 10-minute trundle from the Altstadt; take bus 21 to Gsengerweg.

YOHO Salzburg Hostel €

(☎87 96 49; www.yoho.at; Paracelsusstrasse 9; dm €20-24, s €41, d €67-77; @ 📶) Free wi-fi, secure lockers, comfy bunks, plenty of cheap beer and good-value schnitzels – what more could a backpacker ask for? Except, perhaps, a merry singalong with *The Sound of Music* screened daily

Local Knowledge

Salzburg

RECOMMENDATIONS FROM DANA HAMMETT, PROFESSIONAL OPERA SINGER AND TOUR GUIDE FOR FRAÜLEIN MARIA'S BICYCLE TOURS

1 SCHLOSS MIRABELL

Fans of *The Sound of Music* absolutely mustn't miss the gardens of Schloss Mirabell. Several key scenes were filmed here, most famously the sequences on the steps and around the fountain during 'Do-Re-Mi'. The rest of the park is gorgeous to explore, too – look out for the little gnome garden!

2 SCHLOSS HELLBRUNN

Another must-see for musical aficionados, where you can see the gazebo under which Liesl and Rolf sang 'I Am Sixteen, Going On Seventeen'. The grounds are also home to the famous Wasserspiele fountains and the oldest-known outdoor theatre in Austria, which is still sometimes used for performances in summer.

3 MUNCHSBERG

This rocky hill high above the city has one of the best views over Salzburg, which you can see in the film when Julie Andrews emerges from the monastery. At the top is the Museum der Moderne, which has a great restaurant, the M32, with a panoramic window over the city.

4 HOHENSALZBURG

Salzburg's castle is touristy, but catching the funicular to the top is just one of those experiences everyone should have! Nearby there's a trail to Nunnberg Abbey, which features in the film during scenes between Maria and the Reverend Mother.

5 KAPUZINERBERG

It's a bit off the beaten track, about 30 minutes walk from the centre, but the Kapuzinerberg is a lovely and little-known area of Salzburg. There's an old monastery there, the Franziskischloessl, with a sweet cloister.

If You Like... Austria's Natural Wonders

From glittering lakes to snowy mountains, Austria is blessed with glorious scenery.

1 EISRIESENWELT
(www.eisriesenwelt.at; adult/child €11/6, incl cable car €22/12; 9am-3.45pm May-Oct, to 4.45pm Jul & Aug) Billed as the world's largest accessible ice caves, Eisriesenwelt is a glittering ice empire spanning 30,000 sq metres and 42km of narrow passages burrowing deep into the heart of the mountains. Even if it's hot outside, entering the caves is like stepping into a deep freeze – bring warm clothing and sturdy footwear year-round. Photography is not permitted inside the caves.

2 KRIMMLER WASSERFÄLLE
(Krimml Falls; www.wasserfaelle-krimml.at; adult/child €3/1; ticket office 8am-6pm mid-Apr–Oct) Enshrouded in mist, arched by a rainbow, frozen solid – this waterfall always looks extraordinary, no matter the time of year. The **Wasserfallweg** (Waterfall Trail), which starts at the ticket office and weaves gently uphill through mixed forest, has numerous viewpoints with photogenic close-ups of the falls.

3 DACHSTEIN EISHÖHLE
(www.dachstein-salzkammergut.com; tour adult/child €14.30/8.30; core tour 9.20am-4pm May-late Oct) Near Hallstatt, Obertraun has the intriguing Dachstein Eishöhle. The caves are millions of years old and extend into the mountain for almost 80km in places.

(yes, *every* day). The friendly crew can arrange tours, adventure sports such as rafting and canyoning, and bike hire.

Pension Katrin Pension **€€**
(83 08 60; www.pensionkatrin.at; Nonntaler Hauptstrasse 49b; s €64-70, d €112-122, tr €153-168, q €172-188; P) With its flowery garden, bright and cheerful rooms and homemade goodies at breakfast, this *Pension* is one of the homiest in Salzburg. The affable Terler family keeps everything spick and span. Take bus 5 from the Hauptbahnhof to Wäschergasse.

Hotel Am Dom Boutique Hotel **€€**
(84 27 65; www.hotelamdom.at; Goldgasse 17; s €90-160, d €130-280;) Antique meets boutique at this Altstadt hotel, where the original vaults and beams of the 800-year-old building contrast with razor-sharp design features.

Arte Vida Guesthouse **€€**
(87 31 85; www.artevida.at; Dreifaltigkeitsgasse 9; s €59-129, d €86-140, apt €150-214;) Arte Vida has the boho-chic feel of a Marrakech riad, with its lantern-lit salon, communal kitchen and serene garden. Asia and Africa have provided the inspiration for the rich colours and fabrics that dress the individually designed rooms, all with DVD players and iPod docks.

Hotel Mozart Historic Hotel **€€**
(87 22 74; www.hotel-mozart.at; Franz-Josef-Strasse 27; s €95-105, d €140-155, tr €160-175; P) An antique-filled lobby gives way to spotless rooms with comfy beds and sizeable bathrooms at the Mozart.

Eating

Self-caterers can find picnic fixings at the **Grünmarkt (Green Market; Universitätsplatz; 7am-7pm Mon-Fri, 6am-3pm Sat)**.

Bärenwirt Austrian **€€**
(42 24 04; www.baerenwirt-salzburg.at; Müllner Hauptstrasse 8; mains €9.50-20; 11am-11pm) Sizzling and stirring since 1663, Bärenwirt combines a woody, hunting-lodge-style interior with a river-facing terrace. Go for hearty *Bierbraten* (beer roast) with dumplings, locally caught trout or organic wild-boar bratwurst. The restaurant is 500m north of Museumplatz.

Triangel Austrian **€€**
(84 22 29; Wiener-Philharmoniker-Gasse 7; mains €10-19; noon-midnight Tue-Sat) The menu is market fresh at this arty bistro, where the picture-clad walls pay

tribute to Salzburg Festival luminaries. It does gourmet salads, a mean Hungarian goulash with organic beef, and delicious homemade ice cream.

Green Garden Vegetarian **€€**

(☎84 12 01; Nonntaler Hauptstrasse 16; mains €9.50-14.50; ⌚noon-3pm & 5.30-10pm Tue-Sat;) The Green Garden is a breath of fresh air for vegetarians and vegans. Locavore is the word at this bright, modern cottage-style restaurant, pairing dishes like wild herb salad, saffron risotto with braised fennel and vegan fondue with organic wines in a totally relaxed setting.

Zwettler's Austrian **€€**

(☎84 41 99; www.zwettlers.com; Kaigasse 3; mains €9-18; ⌚4pm-2am Mon, 11.30am-2am Tue-Sat, 11.30am-midnight Sun) This gastropub has a lively buzz on its pavement terrace. Local grub such as schnitzel with parsley potatoes and goulash goes well with a cold, foamy Kaiser Karl wheat beer.

Esszimmer French **€€€**

(☎87 08 99; www.esszimmer.com; Müllner Hauptstrasse 33; 3-course lunch €38, tasting menus €75-118; ⌚noon-2pm & 6.30-9.30pm Tue-Sat) Andreas Kaiblinger puts an innovative spin on market-driven French cuisine at Michelin-starred Esszimmer. Eye-catching art, playful backlighting and a glass floor revealing the Almkanal stream keep diners captivated, as do gastro showstoppers inspired by the seasons. Buses 7, 21 and 28 to Landeskrankenhaus stop close by.

Drinking & Nightlife

Augustiner Bräustübl Brewery

(www.augustinerbier.at; Augustinergasse 4-6; ⌚3-11pm Mon-Fri, from 2.30pm Sat & Sun) Who says monks can't enjoy themselves? Since 1621, this cheery monastery-run brewery has been serving potent home-brews in stein tankards in the vaulted hall and beneath the chestnut trees in the 1000-seat beer garden.

Enoteca Settemila Wine Bar

(Bergstrasse 9; ⌚5-11pm Tue-Thu, from 3pm Fri & Sat) This bijou wine shop and bar brims with the enthusiasm and passion of Rafael Peil and Nina Corti. Go to sample their well-edited selection of wines, including Austrian, organic and bio dynamic ones, with *taglieri* (sharing

Schloss Mirabell (p619), Salzburg, Austria

No Tourist Trapp

Did you know that there were 10 (not seven) von Trapp children? Or that Rupert was the eldest (so long Liesl) and the captain a gentle-natured man? For the truth behind the Hollywood legend, stay at **Villa Trapp** (**☎63 08 60; www.villa-trapp.com; Traunstrasse 34; d €109-500**) in Aigen district, 3km southeast of the Altstadt. Marianne and Christopher have transformed the von Trapp's elegant 19th-century villa into a beautiful guesthouse, brimming with family heirlooms and snapshots. The villa sits in Salzburg's biggest private park.

plates of cheese and salumi from small producers).

220 Grad Cafe
(Chiemseegasse 5; ⌚9am-7pm Tue-Fri, to 6pm Sat) Famous for freshly roasted coffee, this retro-chic cafe serves probably the best espresso in town and whips up superb breakfasts.

Information

Many hotels and bars offer free wi-fi, and there are several cheap internet cafes near the train station. *Bankomaten* (ATMs) are all over the place.

Tourist Office (**☎889 87 330; www.salzburg.info; Mozartplatz 5; ⌚9am-7pm**) Helpful tourist office with a ticket-booking service.

Getting There & Away

Air

Low-cost airlines including Ryanair and easyJet serve Salzburg airport, 5.5km west of the city centre.

Buses

Buses depart from just outside the Hauptbahnhof on Südtiroler Platz. For bus timetables and fares, see www.svv-info.at and www.postbus.at.

Train

Fast trains leave frequently for Vienna (€51, 2½ hours) via Linz (€25, 1¼ hours). There is a two-hourly express service to Klagenfurt (€39, three hours). There are hourly trains to Innsbruck (€45, two hours).

Getting Around

To/From the Airport

Bus 2 runs from the Hauptbahnhof (€2.50, 19 minutes) to the airport. A taxi costs about €20.

Bicycle

Top Bike (**www.topbike.at; Staatsbrücke; per day €15; ⌚10am-5pm**) rents out bikes with half-price for kids. The Salzburg Card yields a 20% discount.

Car & Motorcycle

Parking places are limited and much of the Altstadt is pedestrian-only, so it's easier to leave your car at one of three park-and-ride points to the west, north and south of the city. The largest car park in the centre is the Altstadt Garage under Mönchsberg (€18 per day).

Bus

Bus drivers sell single (€2.50) and 24-hour (€5.50) tickets; these are cheaper when purchased in advance from machines (€1.70 and €3.40 respectively).

Salzkammergut

A wonderland of glassy blue lakes and tall craggy peaks, Austria's Lake District is a long-time favourite holiday destination. The peaceful lakes attract visitors in droves, who come to boat, fish, swim or just laze on the shore.

Bad Ischl is the region's transport hub, but Hallstatt is its true jewel. For info visit **Salzkammergut Touristik** (**☎0613-224 000; www.salzkammergut.co.at; Götzstrasse 12; ⌚9am-7pm**). The **Salzkammergut Card** (€4.90, available May to October) provides up to 30% discounts on sights, ferries, cable cars and some buses.

HALLSTATT

With pastel-hued homes, swans and towering mountains on either side of a glassy green lake, Hallstatt looks like some kind of greeting card for tranquillity. Boats chug lazily across the water from the train station to the village itself, which clings precariously to a tiny bit of land between mountain and shore.

Sights

Salzwelten Mine

(www.salzwelten.at; funicular return plus tour adult/child/family €26/13/54, tour only €19/9.50/40; 9.30am-4.30pm late Apr-late Oct) The fascinating Salzbergwerk is situated high above Hallstatt on Salzberg (Salt Mountain) and is the lake's major cultural attraction. The tour details how salt is formed and the history of mining, and takes visitors down into the depths on miners' slides – the largest is 60m, during which you have your photo taken.

Beinhaus Church

(Bone House; Kirchenweg 40; admission €1.50; 10am-6pm May-Oct) This small charnel house contains rows of neatly stacked skulls, painted with decorative designs and the names of their former owners. Bones have been exhumed from the overcrowded graveyard since 1600, and the last skull in the collection was added in 1995.

Hallstätter See Lake

(boat hire per hour from €11) You can hire boats and kayaks to get out on the lake, or scuba dive with the **Tauchclub Dachstein** (0664-88 600 481; www.dive-adventures.at; intro course from €35).

Sleeping & Eating

Pension Sarsteln Guesthouse €

(82 17; Gosaumühlstrasse 83; d €64-80, apt €70-120;) The affable Fischer family take pride in their little guesthouse, a few minutes' walk along the lakefront from central Hallstatt. The old-fashioned rooms are nothing flash, but they are neat, cosy and have balconies with dreamy lake and mountain views. Family-sized apartments come with kitchenettes.

Restaurant zum Salzbaron European €€

(82 63; Marktplatz 104; mains €16-23; 11.30am-10pm;) One of the best gourmet acts in town, the Salzbaron is perched alongside the lake inside the Seehotel Grüner Baum and serves a seasonal pan-European menu; local trout features strongly in summer.

Innsbruck (p627), Austria
JEREMY VOISEY/GETTY IMAGES ©

KEN GILLHAM/GETTY IMAGES ©

Don't Miss Schloss Hellbrunn

Built in the 17th century by bishop Markus Sittikus, this castle is mainly known for its ingenious trick fountains and water-powered figures. When the tour guides set them off, expect to get wet! Admission includes a tour of the baroque palace. Other parts of the garden (without fountains) are open year-round and are free to visit.

NEED TO KNOW

www.hellbrunn.at; Fürstenweg 37; adult/child/family €10.50/5/25; 9am-5.30pm, to 9pm Jul & Aug;

Information

Tourist Office (**82 08; www.dachstein-salzkammergut.at; Seestrasse 99; 9am-5pm Mon-Fri, to 1pm Sat**) Turn left from the ferry to reach this office. It stocks a free leisure map of lakeside towns, and hiking and cycling trails.

Getting There & Away

Hallstatt train station is across the lake. The boat service from there to the village coincides with train arrivals. About a dozen trains daily connect Hallstatt and Bad Ischl (€4.30, 27 minutes).

Tyrol

With converging mountain ranges behind lofty pastures and tranquil meadows, Tyrol (also Tirol) captures a quintessential Alpine panoramic view. Occupying a central position is Innsbruck, the region's jewel, while in the northeast and southwest are superb ski resorts. In the southeast, separated somewhat from the main state since part of South Tirol was ceded to Italy at the end of WWI, lies the protected natural landscape of the Hohe Tauern National Park, an Alpine wonderland of 3000m peaks, including the country's highest, the Grossglockner (3798m).

INNSBRUCK

0512 / POP 124,579

Tyrol's capital is a sight to behold. The mountains are so close that within 25 minutes it's possible to travel from the heart of the city to over 2000m above sea level. Summer and winter outdoor activities abound, and it's understandable why some visitors only take a peek at Innsbruck proper before heading for the hills. But to do so is a shame, for Innsbruck has its own share of gems, including an authentic medieval Altstadt, inventive architecture and vibrant student-driven nightlife.

Sights

The **Innsbruck Card** (€33/41/47 for 24/48/72 hours; half-price for children) gives one visit to Innsbruck's main sights and attractions, a return journey on lifts and cable cars, unlimited use of public transport including the Sightseer bus, and three-hour bike rental. It's available at the tourist office.

Hofkirche Church

(www.tiroler-landesmuseum.at; Universitätstrasse 2; adult/child €5/free; 9am-5pm Mon-Sat, 12.30-5pm Sun) Innsbruck's pride and joy is the Gothic Hofkirche, one of Europe's finest royal court churches. It was commissioned in 1553 by Ferdinand I, who enlisted top artists of the age such as Albrecht Dürer, Alexander Colin and Peter Vischer the Elder. Top billing goes to the empty **sarcophagus of Emperor Maximilian I** (1459–1519), a masterpiece of German Renaissance sculpture, elaborately carved from black marble.

Goldenes Dachl & Museum Museum

(Golden Roof; Herzog-Friedrich-Strasse 15; adult/child €4/2; 10am-5pm, closed Mon Oct-Apr) Innsbruck's golden wonder is this Gothic oriel, built for Emperor Maximilian I and glittering with 2657 fire-gilt copper tiles. An audio guide whizzes you through the history in the museum; look for the grotesque tournament helmets designed to resemble the Turks of the rival Ottoman Empire.

Hofburg Palace

(Imperial Palace; www.hofburg-innsbruck.at; Rennweg 1; adult/child €8/free; 9am-5pm) Demanding attention with its imposing facade and cupolas, the Hofburg was built as a castle for Archduke Sigmund the Rich in the 15th century, expanded by Emperor Maximilian I in the 16th century and given a baroque makeover by Empress Maria Theresia in the 18th century. The centrepiece of the lavish rococo state apartments is the 31m-long **Riesensaal** (Giant's Hall).

Bergisel Ski Jump

(www.bergisel.info; adult/child €9.50/4.50; 9am-6pm) Rising above Innsbruck like a celestial staircase, this glass-and-steel ski jump was designed by much-lauded Iraqi architect Zaha Hadid. It's 455 steps or a two-minute funicular ride to the 50m-high **viewing platform**, with a breathtaking panorama of the Nordkette range, Inntal and Innsbruck. Tram 1 trundles here from central Innsbruck.

Schloss Ambras Castle

(www.schlossambras-innsbruck.at; Schlosstrasse 20; adult/child/family €10/free/18; 10am-5pm;) Picturesquely perched on a hill and set among beautiful gardens, this Renaissance pile was acquired in 1564 by Archduke Ferdinand II, then ruler of Tyrol, who transformed it from a fortress into a palace. Don't miss the centrepiece **Spanische Saal** (Spanish Hall), the dazzling **armour collection** and the gallery's Velázquez and van Dyck originals.

Stadtturm Tower

(Herzog-Friedrich-Strasse 21; adult/child €3/1.50; 10am-8pm) Climb this tower's 148 steps for 360-degree views of the city's rooftops, spires and surrounding mountains.

DALE REUBIN/GETTY IMAGES ©

Don't Miss Free Guided Hikes

From late May to October, Innsbruck Information arranges daily guided hikes, from sunrise walks to half-day mountain jaunts. The hikes are free with a **Club Innsbruck Card**, which you receive automatically when you stay overnight in Innsbruck. Pop into the tourist office to register and browse the program.

Activities

Nordkettenbahnen Funicular

(www.nordkette.com; one way/return to Hungerburg €4.60/7.60, Seegrube €16.50/27.50, Hafelekar €18.30/30.50; ⏲Hungerburg 7am-7.15pm Mon-Fri, 8am-7.15pm Sat & Sun, Seegrube 8.30am-5.30pm daily, Hafelekar 9am-5pm daily) Zaha Hadid's space-age funicular runs every 15 minutes, whizzing you from the Congress Centre to the slopes in no time. Walking trails head off in all directions from **Hungerburg** and **Seegrube**. For more of a challenge, there is a downhill track for mountain bikers and two fixed-rope routes (*Klettersteige*) for climbers.

Inntour Adventure Sports

(www.inntour.com; Leopoldstrasse 4; ⏲9am-6.30pm Mon-Fri, to 5pm Sat & Sun) Based at Die Börse, Inntour arranges all manner of thrill-seeking pursuits, including canyoning (€80), tandem paragliding (€105), white-water rafting (€45) and bungee jumping from the 192m Europabrücke (€140).

Sleeping

The tourist office has lists of private rooms costing between €20 and €40 per person.

Nepomuk's Hostel **€**

(☎584 118; www.nepomuks.at; Kiebachgasse 16; dm/d €24 /58; 📶) Could this be backpacker heaven? Nepomuk's sure comes close, with its Altstadt location, well-stocked kitchen and high-ceilinged dorms with homely touches like CD players. The delicious breakfast in attached Cafe Munding, with homemade pastries, jam and fresh-roasted coffee, gets your day off to a grand start.

Pension Paula Guesthouse **€**
(292 262; www.pensionpaula.at; Weiherburggasse 15; s €35-46, d €60-70, tr/q €92/104; P) This *Pension* occupies an alpine chalet and has super-clean, homely rooms (most with balcony). It's up the hill towards the zoo and has great vistas across the city.

Hotel Weisses Kreuz Historic Hotel **€€**
(594 79; www.weisseskreuz.at; Herzog-Friedrich-Strasse 31; s €39-80, d €73-149; P @) Beneath the arcades, this atmospheric Altstadt hotel has played host to guests for 500 years, including a 13-year-old Mozart. With its wood-panelled parlours, antiques and twisting staircase, the hotel oozes history with every creaking beam. Rooms are supremely comfortable, staff charming and breakfast is a lavish spread.

Weisses Rössl Guesthouse **€€**
(583 057; www.roessl.at; Kiebachgasse 8; s €70-110, d €100-160; @) An antique rocking horse greets you at this 16th-century guesthouse. The vaulted entrance leads up to spacious rooms recently revamped with blonde wood, fresh hues and crisp white linen. The owner is a keen hunter and the restaurant (mains €10 to €18) has a meaty menu.

Eating

Markthalle Market **€**
(www.markthalle-innsbruck.at; Innrain; 7am-6.30pm Mon-Fri, to 1pm Sat) Fresh-baked bread, Tyrolean cheese, organic fruit, smoked ham and salami – it's all under one roof at this riverside covered market.

Cafe Munding Cafe **€**
(www.munding.at; Kiebachgasse 16; cakes €2-4; 8am-8pm) Stop by this 200-year-old cafe for delicious cakes – try the moist chocolate raspberry *Haustorte* or the chocolate-marzipan *Mozarttorte* – and freshly roasted coffee.

Typical South Tyrolean fare

Die Wilderin Austrian **€€**
(☎562 728; www.diewilderin.at; Seilergasse 5; mains €11-18; ⏰5pm-2am Tue-Sat, 4pm-midnight Sun) Take a gastronomic walk on the wild side at this modern-day hunter-gatherer of a restaurant, where chefs take pride in local sourcing and using top-notch farm-fresh and foraged ingredients. The menu sings of the seasons, be it asparagus, game, strawberries or winter veg. The vibe is urbane and relaxed.

Chez Nico Vegetarian **€€**
(☎0650-451 06 24; www.chez-nico.at; Maria-Theresien-Strasse 49; 2-course lunch €14.50, 7-course menu €60; ⏰6.30-10pm Mon & Sat, noon-2pm & 6.30-10pm Tue-Fri;) Take a petit bistro and a Parisian chef with a passion for herbs, *et voilà*, you get Chez Nico. Nicolas Curtil (Nico) cooks seasonal, all-vegetarian delights along the lines of smoked aubergine wonton and chanterelle-apricot goulash. You won't miss the meat, we swear.

Himal Asian **€€**
(☎588 588; Universitätsstrasse 13; mains €9.50-14.50; ⏰11.30am-2.30pm & 6-10.30pm Mon-Sat, 6-10pm Sun;) Friendly and intimate, Himal delivers vibrant, robust Nepalese flavours. Spot-on curries (some vegetarian) are mopped up with naan and washed down with mango lassis. The two-course €8.10 lunch is cracking value.

Drinking & Nightlife

Moustache Bar
(www.cafe-moustache.at; Herzog-Otto-Strasse 8; ⏰11am-2am Tue-Sun;) Playing Spot-the-Moustache (Einstein, Charlie Chaplin and co) is the preferred pastime at this retro bolthole, with a terrace overlooking pretty Domplatz and Club Aftershave in the basement.

Hofgarten Café Bar
(www.tagnacht.at; Rennweg 6a; ⏰7pm-4am Tue, Fri & Sat) DJ sessions and a tree-shaded beer garden are crowd-pullers at this trendy cafe-cum-bar set in the greenery of Hofgarten.

360° Bar
(Rathaus Galerien; ⏰10am-1am Mon-Sat) Grab a cushion and drink in 360-degree views of the city and Alps from the balcony that skirts this spherical, glass-walled bar. It's a nicely chilled spot for a coffee or sundowner.

Information

Innsbruck Information
(☎598 50; www.innsbruck.info; Burggraben 3; ⏰9am-6pm) Main tourist office with truckloads of info on the city and surrounds, including skiing and walking.

Jet d'Eau (p634), Geneva, Switzerland

Detour: Hohe Tauern National Park

If you thought Mother Nature pulled out all the stops in the Austrian Alps, Hohe Tauern National Park was her magnum opus. Straddling Tyrol, Salzburg and Carinthia, this national park is the largest in the Alps; a 1786-sq-km wilderness of 3000m peaks, Alpine meadows and waterfalls. At its heart lies **Grossglockner** (3798m), Austria's highest mountain, which towers over the 8km-long **Pasterze Glacier**, best seen from the outlook at **Kaiser-Franz-Josefs-Höhe** (2369m).

The 48km **Grossglockner Road** (www.grossglockner.at; Hwy 107; car/motorcycle €34.50/24.50; May-early Nov) from Bruck in Salzburgerland to Heiligenblut in Carinthia is one of Europe's greatest Alpine drives. A feat of 1930s engineering, the road swings giddily around 36 switchbacks, passing jewel-coloured lakes, forested slopes and wondrous glaciers.

If you have wheels, you'll have more flexibility, although the road is open only between May and early November, and you must pay tolls.

The major village on the Grossglockner Road is **Heiligenblut**, dominated by mountain peaks and the needle-thin spire of its 15th-century pilgrimage church. Here you'll find a **tourist office** (27 00; www.heiligenblut.at; Hof 4; 9am-noon & 2-6pm Mon-Fri, 3-6pm Sat & Sun), which can advise on guided ranger hikes, mountain hiking and skiing. The village also has a campsite, a few restaurants and a spick-and-span **Jugendherberge** (22 59; www.oejhv.or.at; Hof 36; dm/s/d €22/30/52; P @).

Bus 5002 runs frequently between Lienz and Heiligenblut on weekdays (€16.40, one hour), less frequently at weekends.

Getting There & Away

Air

EasyJet flies to Innsbruck Airport, 4km west of the city centre.

Car & Motorcycle

Heading south by car through the Brenner Pass to Italy, you'll hit the A13 toll road (€8). Toll-free Hwy 182 follows the same route, although it is less scenic.

Train

Fast trains depart at least every two hours for Bregenz (€37, 2½ hours), Salzburg (€45, two hours), Kitzbühel (€20.40, 1½ hours) and Munich (€41, 1¾ hours). There are several daily services to Lienz (€15.40, 3¾ hours).

Getting Around

Single tickets on buses and trams cost €1.80 from machines or €2 from the driver. A 24-hour ticket is €4.50. Bus F runs between the airport and Maria-Theresien-Strasse.

SWITZERLAND

Geneva

POP 189,000

The whole world seems to be in Geneva, Switzerland's second city. The UN, International Red Cross, World Health Organization – 200-odd governmental and non-governmental international organisations fill the city's plush hotels with big-name guests, feast on an incredible choice of cuisine and help prop up the overload of banks, jewellers and chocolate shops for which Geneva is known.

Switzerland

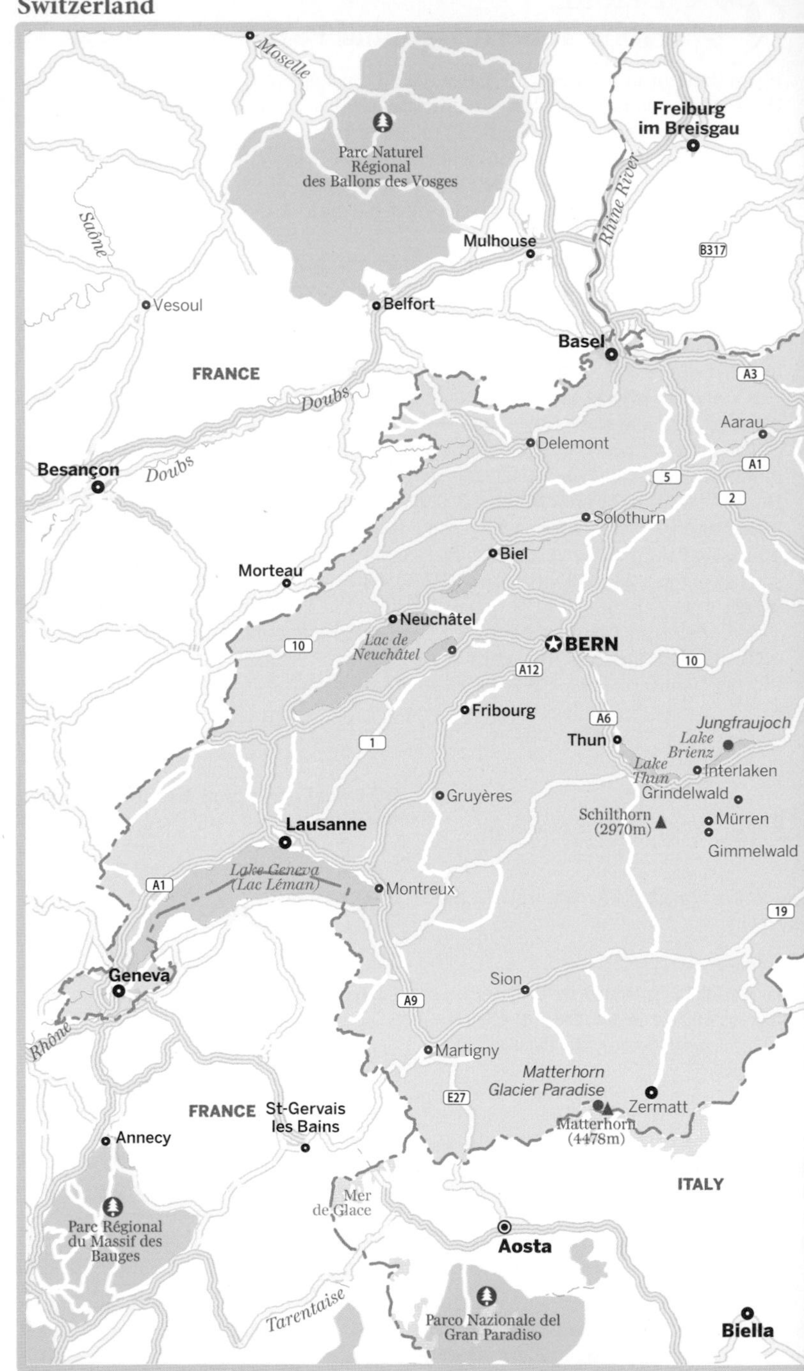

Moselle
Parc Naturel Régional des Ballons des Vosges
Freiburg im Breisgau
Rhine River
Saône
Mulhouse
B317
Vesoul
Belfort
Basel
FRANCE
A3
Doubs
Aarau
Delemont
A1
Besançon
Doubs
5
2
Solothurn
Biel
Morteau
Neuchâtel
10
Lac de Neuchâtel
BERN
10
A12
Fribourg
A6
Jungfraujoch
Thun
Lake Brienz
1
Lake Thun
Interlaken
Grindelwald
Gruyères
Schilthorn (2970m)
Mürren
Lausanne
Gimmelwald
Lake Geneva (Lac Léman)
A1
Montreux
19
Geneva
Sion
A9
Rhône
Martigny
Matterhorn Glacier Paradise
E27
Zermatt
FRANCE
St-Gervais les Bains
Matterhorn (4478m)
Annecy
ITALY
Mer de Glace
Parc Régional du Massif des Bauges
Aosta
Tarentaise
Parco Nazionale del Gran Paradiso
Biella

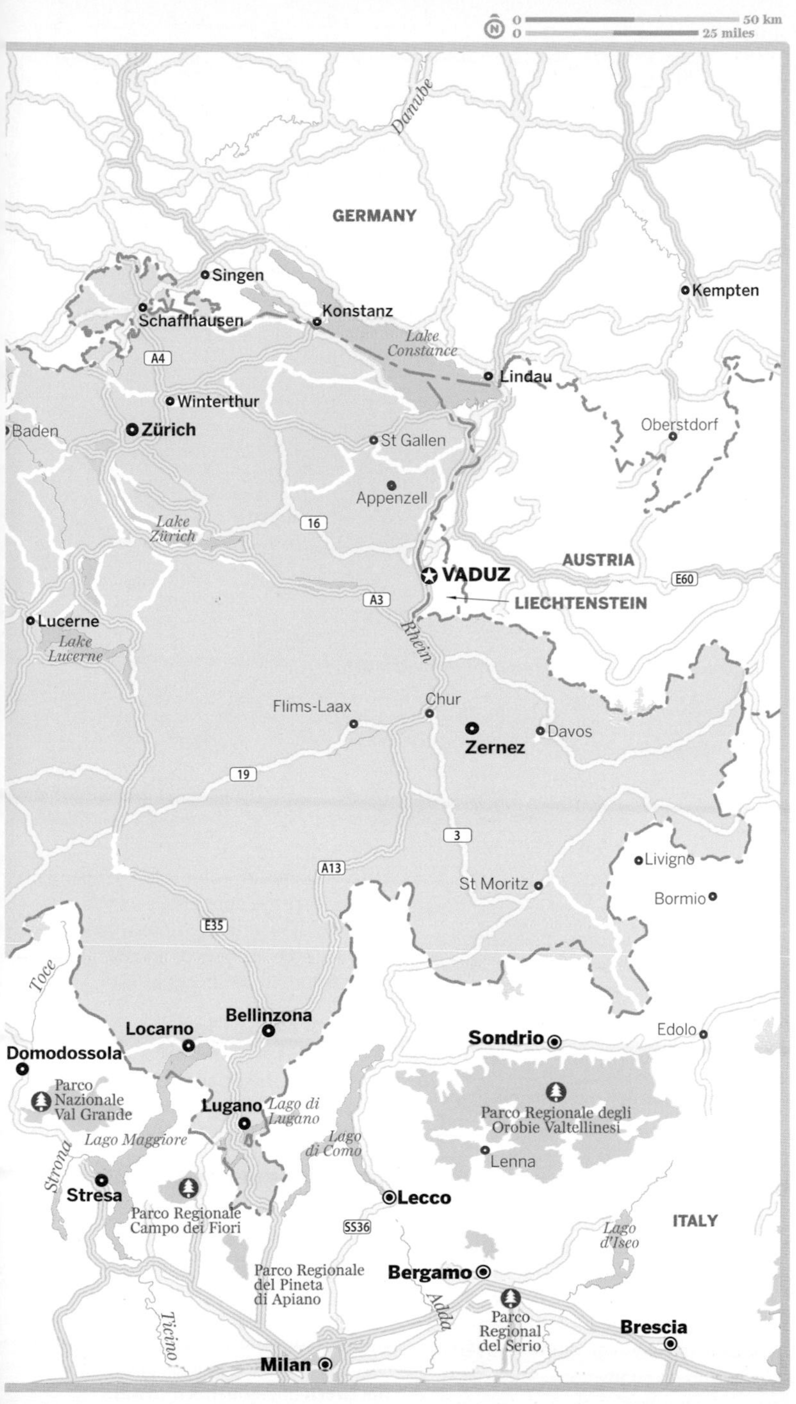
0 50 km
0 25 miles
GERMANY
Danube
Singen
Kempten
Schaffhausen
Konstanz
Lake Constance
A4
Lindau
Winterthur
Baden
Zürich
St Gallen
Oberstdorf
Appenzell
Lake Zürich
16
AUSTRIA
VADUZ
E60
A3
LIECHTENSTEIN
Lucerne
Lake Lucerne
Rhein
Flims-Laax
Chur
Zernez
Davos
19
3
Livigno
A13
St Moritz
Bormio
E35
Toce
Bellinzona
Locarno
Sondrio
Edolo
Domodossola
Parco Nazionale Val Grande
Lugano
Lago di Lugano
Parco Regionale degli Orobie Valtellinesi
Lago Maggiore
Lago di Como
Lenna
Strona
Stresa
Lecco
Parco Regionale Campo dei Fiori
ITALY
SS36
Lago d'Iseo
Parco Regionale del Pineta di Apiano
Bergamo
Adda
Parco Regional del Serio
Ticino
Brescia
Milan

Geneva

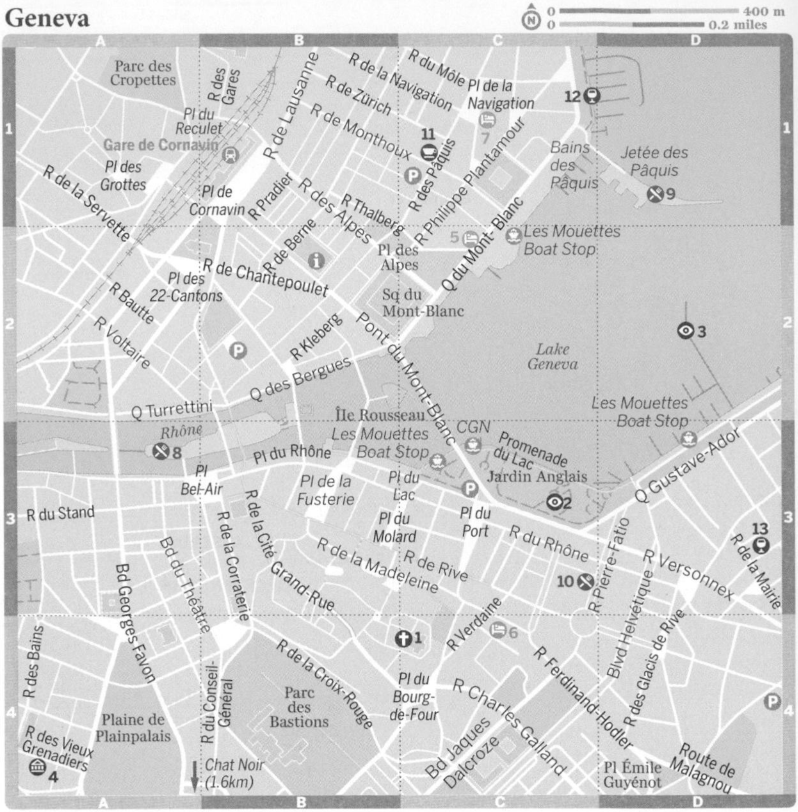

Sights

The city centre is so compact it's easy to see many of the main sights on foot. Begin your explorations on the southern side of Lake Geneva and visit the **Jardin Anglais** (Quai du Général-Guisan) to see the Horloge Fleurie. Crafted from 6500 flowers, the clock has ticked since 1955 and sports the world's longest second hand (2.5m).

Jet d'Eau — Fountain

(Quai Gustave-Ador) When landing by plane, this lakeside fountain is the first dramatic glimpse you get of Geneva. The 140m-tall structure shoots up water with incredible force – 200km/h, 1360 horsepower – to create the sky-high plume, kissed by a rainbow on sunny days. At any one time, 7 tonnes of water is in the air, much of which sprays spectators on the pier beneath. Two or three times a year it is illuminated pink, blue or another colour to mark a humanitarian occasion.

Cathédrale St-Pierre — Cathedral

(www.espace-saint-pierre.ch; Cour St-Pierre; admission free, towers adult/child Sfr5/2; 9.30am-6.30pm Mon-Sat, noon-6.30pm Sun Jun-Sep, 10am-5.30pm Oct-May) Begun in the 11th century, Geneva's cathedral is predominantly Gothic with an 18th-century neoclassical facade. Between 1536 and 1564 Protestant John Calvin preached here; see his seat in the north aisle. Inside the cathedral 77 steps spiral up to the attic – a fascinating glimpse at its architectural construction – from where another 40 lead to the top of the panoramic **northern** and **southern towers**.

Geneva

Sights

1 Cathédrale St-Pierre C4
2 Jardin Anglais C3
3 Jet d'Eau D2
4 Patek Phillipe Museum A4

Sleeping

5 Hôtel Beau-Rivage C2
6 Hôtel Bel'Esperance C4
7 Hotel Edelweiss C1

Eating

8 Brasserie des Halles de l'Île A3
9 Buvette des Bains D1
10 Le Relais d'Entrecôte C3

Drinking & Nightlife

11 Café des Arts C1
12 La Terrasse C1
13 Yvette de Marseille D3

In summer free carillon (5pm) and organ (6pm) concerts fill the cathedral and its surrounding square with soul.

Musée International de la Croix-Rouge et du Croissant-Rouge Museum

(www.redcrossmuseum.ch; Av de la Paix 17; adult/child Sfr15/7; 10am-6pm Tue-Sun Apr-Oct, 10am-5pm Tue-Sun Nov-Mar) Compelling multi media exhibits at Geneva's fascinating International Red Cross and Red Crescent Museum trawl through atrocities perpetuated by humanity. The litany of war and nastiness, documented in films, photos, sculptures and soundtracks, is set against the noble aims of the organisation created by Geneva businessmen and philanthropists Henri Dunant and Henri Dufour in 1864. Excellent temporary exhibitions command an additional entrance fee. Take bus 8 from Gare de Cornavin to the Appia stop.

Patek Phillipe Museum Museum

(022 807 09 10; www.patekmuseum.com; Rue des Vieux-Grenadiers 7; adult/child Sfr10/free; 2-6pm Tue-Fri, 10am-6pm Sat) This elegant museum by one of Switzerland's leading luxury watchmakers displays exquisite timepieces and enamels from the 16th century to the present.

Sleeping

When checking in, ask for your free public- transport ticket covering unlimited bus travel for the duration of your hotel stay.

Hôtel Bel'Esperance Hotel €

(022 818 37 37; www.hotel-bel-esperance.ch; Rue de la Vallée 1; s/d/tr/q from Sfr110/170/210/250; reception 7am-10pm; @) This two-star hotel is extraordinary value. Rooms are quiet and cared for, those on the 1st floor share a kitchen, and there are fridges for guests to store picnic supplies – or sausages – in! Ride the lift to the 5th floor to flop on its wonderful flower-filled rooftop terrace, complete with barbecue that can be rented (Sfr8).

Hotel Edelweiss Hotel €€

(022 544 51 51; www.hoteledelweissgeneva.com; Place de la Navigation 2; d Sfr160-400; @) Plunge yourself into the heart of the Swiss Alps with this Heidi-style hideout, very much the Swiss Alps *en ville* with its fireplace, wildflower-painted pine bedheads and big, cuddly St Bernard lolling over the banister. Its chalet-styled restaurant is a key address among Genevans for traditional cheese fondue.

Hôtel Beau-Rivage Historic Hotel €€€

(022 716 66 66; www.beau-rivage.ch; Quai du Mont-Blanc 13; d from Sfr515; P @) Run by the Mayer family for five generations, the Beau-Rivage is a 19th-century jewel dripping in opulence.

Eating

Eateries crowd Place du Bourg-de-Four, Geneva's oldest square, in the lovely Old Town. Otherwise, head down the hill towards the river and Place du Molard, packed with tables and chairs for much of the year. In Pâquis, there's a tasty line-up of more affordable restaurants on Place de la Navigation.

Buvette des Bains Cafeteria **€**
(**☎022 738 16 16; www.bains-des-paquis.ch; Quai du Mont-Blanc 30, Bains des Pâquis; mains Sfr14-16; ⏰7am-10.30pm)** Meet Genevans at this earthy beach bar – rough and hip around the edges – at lakeside pool, Bains des Pâquis. Grab breakfast, a salad or the *plat du jour* (dish of the day), or dip into a *fondue au crémant* (Champagne fondue). Dining is self-service on trays and alfresco in summer. In summer pay Sfr2/1 per adult/child to access the canteen, inside the pub.

Le Relais d'Entrecôte Steakhouse **€€**
(**☎022 310 60 04; www.relaisentrecote.fr; Rue Pierre Fatio 6; steak & chips Sfr42; ⏰noon-2.30pm & 7-11pm)** Key vocabulary at this timeless classic where everyone eats the same dish is *à point* (medium), *bien cuit* (well done) and *saignant* (rare). It doesn't even bother with menus, you just sit down, say how you like your steak cooked and wait for it to arrive – two handsome servings (!) pre-empted by a green salad and accompanied by perfectly crisp, skinny fries.

Brasserie des Halles de l'Île European **€€**
(**☎022 311 08 88; www.brasseriedeshallesdelile.ch; Place de l'Île 1; mains Sfr20-50; ⏰10.30am-midnight Sun & Mon, to 1am Tue-Thu, to 2am Fri & Sat)** At home in Geneva's old market hall on an island, this industrial-style venue cooks up a buzzing cocktail of after-work aperitifs with music, after-dark DJs and seasonal fare of fresh veggies and regional products (look for the Appellation d'Origine Contrôllée products flagged on the menu). Arrive early to snag the best seat in the house – a superb terrace hanging over the water.

Drinking & Nightlife

Pâquis, the district in between the train station and lake, is particularly well endowed with bars. In summer **La Terrasse (www.laterrasse.ch; Quai du Mont-Blanc 31; ⏰8am-midnight Apr-Sep)**, with wooden tables inches from the water, gets crammed.

Cathédrale St-Pierre (p634), Geneva, Switzerland

DBLIGHT/GETTY IMAGES ©

Three Languages

Located in the corner of Europe where Germany, France and Italy meet, Switzerland is a linguistic melting pot with three official federal languages: German (spoken by 64% of the population), French (19%) and Italian (8%). Swiss 'German' speakers write standard or 'high' German, but speak their own language: Schwyzertütsch has no official written form and is mostly unintelligible to outsiders.

A fourth language, Romansch, is spoken by less than 1% of the population, mainly in the canton of Graubünden. Derived from Latin, it's a linguistic relic that has survived in the isolation of mountain valleys. Romansch was recognised as a national language by referendum in 1938 and given federal protection in 1996.

English-speakers will have few problems being understood in the German-speaking parts. However, it is simple courtesy to greet people with the Swiss-German *grüezi* and to enquire *Sprechen Sie Englisch?* (Do you speak English?) before launching into English. In French Switzerland you shouldn't have too many problems either; in Italian-speaking Switzerland, people are more monolingual but you'll still encounter plenty of English-speakers.

For a dose of Bohemia, head to Carouge on tram 12. This shady quarter of 17th-century houses and narrow streets has galleries, hip bars and funky shops.

Café des Arts Cafe, Bar
(Rue des Pâquis 15; ⏲11am-2am Mon-Fri, 8am-2am Sat & Sun) As much a place to drink as a daytime cafe, this Pâquis hang-out lures a local crowd with its Parisian-style terrace and artsy interior. Food-wise, think meal-size salads, designer sandwiches and a great-value lunchtime *plat du jour*.

Yvette de Marseille Bar
(Rue Henri Blanvalet 13; ⏲5.30pm-midnight Mon & Tue, 5.30pm-1am Wed & Thu, 5.30pm-2am Fri, 6.30pm-2am Sat) No bar begs the question 'what's in the name?' more than this buzzy drinking hole. Urban and edgy, it occupies a mechanic's workshop once owned by Yvette. Note the garage door, the trap door in the floor where cars were repaired and the street number 13 (aka the departmental number of the Bouches-du-Rhône département, home to Marseille).

Chat Noir Club, Bar
(☎022 307 10 40; www.chatnoir.ch; Rue Vauthier 13; ⏲6pm-4am Tue-Thu, to 5am Fri & Sat) One of the busiest night spots in Carouge, the Black Cat is packed most nights thanks to its all-rounder vibe: arrive after work for an aperitif with selection of tapas to nibble on, and stay until dawn for dancing, live music and DJ sets.

Shopping

Designer shopping is wedged between Rue du Rhône and Rue de Rive; the latter has lots of chain stores. Grand-Rue in the Old Town and Carouge boast artsy boutiques.

Information

Tourist Office (☎022 909 70 00; www.geneve-tourisme.ch; Rue du Mont-Blanc 18; ⏲9am-6pm Mon-Sat, 10am-4pm Sun)

Getting There & Away

Air

Aéroport International de Genève (p681), 4km from town, has connections to major European cities and many others worldwide.

Boat

CGN (Compagnie Générale de Navigation; ☎0848 811 848; www.cgn.ch) operates a web of scenic steamer services from its Jardin Anglais jetty to other villages on Lake Geneva. Many only sail May to September, including those to/from Lausanne (Sfr64, 3½ hours). Eurail and Swiss Passes are valid on CGN boats or there is a one-day CGN boat pass (Sfr60).

Train

Trains run to major Swiss towns including at least every 30 minutes to/from Lausanne (Sfr21.80, 33 to 48 minutes), Bern (Sfr49, 1¾ hours) and Zürich (Sfr84, 2¾ hours).

International daily rail connections from Geneva include Paris by TGV (3¼ hours) and Milan (four hours).

Getting Around

To/From the Airport

Getting from the airport is easy with regular trains into Gare de Cornavin (Sfr2.50, eight minutes). Slower bus 10 (Sfr3.50) does the same 4km trip. A metered taxi costs Sfr35 to Sfr50.

Bicycle

Pick up a bike at **Genèveroule (www.geneveroule.ch)** on Place du Rhône: the first four hours are free, then it'sSfr2 per hour. Bring ID and a Sfr20 cash deposit. Find other Genèveroule stands at Bains des Pâquis, Place de l'Octroi in Carouge, and Place de Montbrillant.

Public Transport

Buses, trams, trains and boats service the city, and ticket dispensers are found at all stops. Most services are operated by **TPG (www.tpg.ch; Rue de Montbrillant; 7am-7pm Mon-Fri, 9am-6pm Sat)**. Typical tickets cost Sfr3.50 (one hour); a day pass is Sfr8 when purchased after 9am.

Valais

This is Matterhorn country, an intoxicating land that seduces the toughest of critics with its endless panoramic vistas and breathtaking views. Switzerland's 10 highest mountains – all over 4000m – rise to the sky here, while snow fiends ski and board in one of Europe's top resorts, Zermatt.

ZERMATT

POP 6000

Since the mid-19th century, Zermatt has starred among Switzerland's glitziest resorts. Today it attracts intrepid mountaineers and hikers; skiers who cruise at a snail's pace, spellbound by the scenery; and style-conscious darlings flashing designer togs in the lounge bars. But all are smitten with the **Matterhorn** (4478m),

Skier, Zermatt, Switzerland

Don't Miss Matterhorn Glacier Paradise

Views from Zermatt's cable cars are all remarkable, but the Matterhorn Glacier Paradise is the icing on the cake. Ride Europe's highest-altitude cable car to 3883m and gawp at 14 glaciers and 38 mountain peaks over 4000m from the **Panoramic Platform** (only open in good weather). Don't miss the **Glacier Palace**, an ice palace complete with glittering ice sculptures and an ice slide to swoosh down bum first. End with some exhilarating snow tubing outside in the snowy surrounds.

NEED TO KNOW

www.matterhornparadise.ch; adult/child Sfr99/49.50; ⌚8.30am-4.20pm

the Alps' most famous peak and an unfathomable monolith synonymous with Switzerland that you simply can't quite stop looking at.

Sights

Gornergratbahn Railway

(www.gornergrat.ch; Bahnhofplatz 7; one-way adult/child Sfr42/21; ⌚7am-9.50pm) Europe's highest cogwheel railway has climbed through picture-postcard scenery to **Gornergrat** (3089m) – a 30-minute journey – since 1898. Sit on the right-hand side of the little red train to gawp at the Matterhorn. Tickets allow you to get on and off en route; there are restaurants at Riffelalp (2211m) and Riffelberg (2582m). In summer an extra train runs once a week at sunrise and sunset – the most spectacular trips of all.

Activities

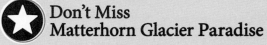

Zermatt is skiing heaven, with mostly long, scenic red runs, plus a smattering of blues for ski virgins and knuckle-whitening blacks for experts. The main skiing areas in winter are **Rothorn**,

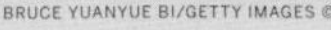
BRUCE YUANYUE BI/GETTY IMAGES ©

Don't Miss Glacier Express

You'll have a hard time avoiding the hype for the **Glacier Express** (www.glacierexpress.ch; one-way adult/child Sfr145/73), the train that links Zermatt with the eastern towns and resorts of Graubünden, including St Moritz (1st/2nd class Sfr262/149, eight hours). Although there is some stunning scenery of glacier-cleaved valleys and soaring peaks along the route, much of the run is down in valleys so don't expect non-stop scenic thrills. You can shorten the duration by starting at the rail hub of Brig instead of Zermatt or just doing the leg between St Moritz and Chur (another rail hub).

Swiss Cards cover the entire route, while Eurail and InterRail are good for about 50% of the fare.

Stockhorn and **Klein Matterhorn,** 350km of ski runs in all with a link from Klein Matterhorn to the Italian resort of Cervinia and a freestyle park with half-pipe for snowboarders. Summer skiing (20km of runs) and boarding (gravity park at Plateau Rosa on the Theodul glacier) is Europe's most extensive. It's Sfr82/122 for a one-/two-day summer ski pass.

Zermatt is also excellent for hiking, with 400km of summer trails through some of the most incredible scenery in the Alps; the tourist office has trail maps. For Matterhorn close-ups, nothing beats the highly dramatic **Matterhorn Glacier Trail** (two hours, 6.49km) from Trockener Steg to Schwarzsee; 23 information panels en route tell you everything you could possibly need to know about glaciers and glacial life.

Sleeping & Eating

Hotel Bahnhof Hotel €

(027 967 24 06; www.hotelbahnhof.com; Bahnhofstrasse; dm Sfr40-45, s/d/q from Sfr80/110/235; reception 8-11.30am & 4-7pm, closed May & Oct;) Opposite the train station, these five-star budget digs have comfy beds, spotless bathrooms and family-perfect rooms for four. Dorms (Sfr5 liner obligatory) are cosy and there's a stylish lounge with armchairs to flop in and books to read. No breakfast, but feel free to prepare your own in the snazzy, open-plan kitchen.

Snowboat International €

(027 967 43 33; www.snowboat.ch; Vispastrasse 20; mains Sfr19-26; noon-midnight) This hybrid eating-drinking, riverside address, with marigold yellow deckchairs sprawled across its rooftop sun terrace, is a blessing. When you tire of fondue, head here for barbecue-sizzled burgers (forget beef, try a lamb and goat's cheese or Indonesian chicken satay burger), superpower creative salads (the Omega 3 buster is a favourite) and great cocktails. The vibe? 100% fun and funky.

Chez Vrony Swiss €€

(027 967 25 52; www.chezvrony.ch; Findeln; breakfast Sfr28, mains Sfr23-45; 9.15am-5pm Dec-Apr & mid-Jun–mid-Oct) Ride the Sunnegga Express to 2288m then ski down blue piste 6 or summer-hike 15 minutes to Zermatt's tastiest slope-side address in the hamlet of Findeln. Keep snug in a cream blanket or lounge on a sheepskin-cushioned chaise longue and revel in the effortless romance of this century-old farmhouse with potted edelweiss on the tables, first-class Matterhorn views and exceptional organic cuisine.

Getting There & Around

Car

Zermatt is car free. Motorists have to park in Täsch (www.matterhornterminal.ch; 1st/subsequent day Sfr14.40/13.50) and ride the Zermatt Shuttle train (adult/child Sfr8/4, 12 minutes, every 20 minutes from 6am to 9.40pm) the last 5km to Zermatt.

Train

Trains run regularly between Zermatt and Brig – a major rail hub (Sfr32, 1½ hours), stopping at Visp en route. Zermatt is also the starting point of the popular Glacier Express to Graubünden.

Bern

POP 127,515

One of the planet's most underrated capitals, Bern is a fabulous find. With the genteel old soul of a Renaissance man and the heart of a high-flying 21st-century gal, the riverside city is both medieval and modern. The 15th-century Old Town is gorgeous enough to sweep you off your feet and make you forget the century (it's definitely worthy of its 1983 Unesco World Heritage Site status).

Sights

Bern's flag-bedecked **medieval centre** is an attraction in its own right, with 6km of covered arcades and cellar shops/bars descending from the streets. After a devastating fire in 1405, the wooden city was rebuilt in today's sandstone. The city has 11 **decorative fountains** (1545) depicting historical and folkloric characters. Most are along Marktgasse as it becomes Kramgasse and Gerechtigkeitsgasse, but the most famous lies in Kornhausplatz: the **Kindlifresserbrunnen** (Ogre Fountain) of a giant snacking...on children.

Zytglogge Clock Tower

(Marktgasse) Bern's most famous Old Town sight, this ornate clock tower once formed part of the city's western gate (1191–1256). Crowds congregate to watch its revolving figures twirl at four minutes before the hour, after which the chimes begin. Tours enter the tower to see the clock mechanism from May to October; contact the tourist office for details. The clock tower supposedly helped Albert Einstein hone his special theory of relativity, developed while working as a patent clerk in Bern.

Münster Cathedral

(www.bernermuenster.ch; Münsterplatz 1; tower adult/child Sfr5/2; 10am-5pm Mon-Sat, 11.30am-5pm Sun May–mid-Oct, noon-4pm Mon-Fri, 10am-5pm Sat, 11.30am-4pm Sun rest of year) Bern's 15th-century Gothic cathedral boasts Switzerland's loftiest spire (100m); climb the dizzying 344-step spiral staircase for vertiginous views. Coming down, stop by the **Upper Bells** (1356), rung at 11am, noon and 3pm daily, and the three 10-tonne **Lower Bells** (Switzerland's largest). Don't miss the main portal 's **Last Judgement**, which portrays Bern's mayor going to heaven, while his Zürich counterpart is shown into hell. Afterwards, wander through the adjacent **Münsterplattform**, a bijou cliff-top park with a sunny pavilion cafe.

Zentrum Paul Klee Museum

(031 359 01 01; www.zpk.org; Monument im Fruchtland 3; adult/child Sfr20/7, audio guide Sfr6; 10am-5pm Tue-Sun) Bern's answer to the Guggenheim, Renzo Piano's architecturally bold 150m-long wave-like edifice houses an exhibition space that showcases rotating works from Paul Klee's prodigious and often-playful career. Interactive computer displays and audio guides help interpret the Swiss-born artist's work. Next door, the fun-packed **Kindermuseum Creaviva** **(031 359 01 61; www.creaviva-zpk.org; Monument im Fruchtland 3; 10am-5pm Tue-Sun)** FREE lets kids experiment with hands-on art exhibits or create original artwork with the atelier's materials during the weekend **Five Franc Studio (www.creaviva-zpk.org/en/art-education/5-franc-studio; admission Sfr5; 10am-4.30pm Sat & Sun)**. Bus 12 runs from Bubenbergplatz direct to the museum.

Sleeping

Hotel Landhaus Hotel €

(031 348 03 05; www.landhausbern.ch; Altenbergstrasse 4; dm Sfr38, s Sfr80-130, d Sfr120-180, q Sfr200-220; P @) Fronted by the river and Old Town spires, this well-run boho hotel offers a mix of stylish six-bed dorms, family rooms and doubles. Its buzzing ground-floor cafe and terrace attracts a cheery crowd. Breakfast (included with private rooms) costs Sfr8 extra for dorm-dwellers.

Hotel Schweizerhof Luxury Hotel €€€

(031 326 80 80; www.schweizerhof-bern.ch; Bahnhofplatz 11; s Sfr284-640, d Sfr364-790; P @) This classy five-star hotel offers lavish accommodation with excellent amenities and service. A hop, skip and a jump from the train station, it's geared for both business and pleasure.

Eating & Drinking

Altes Tramdepot Swiss €€

(031 368 14 15; www.altestramdepot.ch; Am Bärengraben; mains Sfr18-37; 11am-12.30am) At this cavernous microbrewery, Swiss specialities compete against wok-cooked stir-fries for your affection, and the micro brews go down a treat: sample three different varieties for Sfr10.80, or four for Sfr14.50.

Café des Pyrénées Bar

(031 311 30 63; www.pyri.ch; Kornhausplatz 17; 9am-11.30pm Mon-Wed, to 12.30am Thu & Fri, 8am-5pm Sat) This Bohemian corner joint feels like a Parisian cafe-bar. Its central location near the tram tracks makes for good people-watching.

Information

Tourist Office (031 328 12 12; www.bern.com; Bahnhoftplatz 10a; 9am-7pm Mon-Sat, to 6pm Sun) On the street-level floor of the train station. City tours, free hotel bookings, internet access. There's also a branch near the bear park (031 328 12 12; www.bern.com; Bärengraben; 9am-6pm Jun-Sep, 10am-4pm Mar-May & Oct, 11am-4pm Nov-Feb).

Getting There & Around

Frequent trains connect to most Swiss towns, including Geneva (Sfr49, 1¾ hours), Basel (Sfr39, one hour) and Zürich (Sfr49, one hour).

Buses and trams are operated by **BernMobil** (www.bernmobil.ch); many depart from the western side of Bahnhoftplatz.

Central Switzerland & Bernese Oberland

These two regions should come with a health warning – caution: may cause breathlessness as the sun rises and sets over Lake Lucerne, trembling in the north face of Eiger and uncontrollable bouts of euphoria at the foot of Jungfrau.

LUCERNE

POP 79,500

Recipe for a gorgeous Swiss city: take a cobalt lake ringed by mountains of myth, add a medieval Old Town and sprinkle with covered bridges, sunny plazas, candy-coloured houses and waterfront promenades. Lucerne is bright, beautiful and has been Little Miss Popular since the likes of Goethe, Queen Victoria and Wagner savoured her views in the 19th century.

Sights

Lake Lucerne Region Visitors Card (**Vierwaldstättersee Gästekarte; www.luzern.com/visitors-card**) entitles visitors to discounts on various museums, sporting facilities, cable cars and lake cruises in Lucerne and the surrounding area. It's free: remember to have it stamped by your hotel.

Your first port of call should be the medieval **Old Town**, with its ancient rampart walls and towers. Wander the cobblestoned lanes and squares, pondering 15th-century buildings with painted facades and the two much-photographed covered bridges over the Reuss.

Kapellbrücke Bridge

(**Chapel Bridge**) You haven't really been to Lucerne until you have strolled the creaky 14th-century Kapellbrücke, spanning the Reuss River in the Old Town. The octagonal water tower is original, but its gabled roof is a modern reconstruction, rebuilt after a disastrous fire in 1993. As you cross the bridge, note Heinrich Wägmann's 17th-century triangular roof panels, showing important events from Swiss history and mythology. The icon is at its most photogenic when bathed in soft golden light at dusk.

Spreuerbrücke Bridge

(**Spreuer Bridge; btwn Kasernenplatz & Mühlenplatz**) Downriver from Kapellbrücke, this 1408 structure is darker and smaller but entirely original. Lore has it that this was the only bridge where Lucerne's medieval villagers were allowed to throw *Spreu* (chaff) into the river. Here, the roof panels consist of artist Caspar Meglinger's movie-storyboard-style sequence of paintings, *The Dance of Death*, showing how the plague affected all levels of society.

Kapellbrücke, Lucerne, Switzerland

Right: Zürich (p649), Switzerland;
Below: Kunsthaus (p649), Zürich, Switzerland

Lion Monument — Monument

(Löwendenkmal; Denkmalstrasse) By far the most touching of the 19th-century sights that lured so many British to Lucerne is the Lion Monument. Lukas Ahorn carved this 10m-long sculpture of a dying lion into the rock face in 1820 to commemorate Swiss soldiers who died defending King Louis XVI during the French Revolution. Mark Twain once called it the 'saddest and most moving piece of rock in the world'. For Narnia fans, it often evokes Aslan at the stone table.

Museum Sammlung Rosengart — Museum

(☎041 220 16 60; www.rosengart.ch; Pilatusstrasse 10; adult/student Sfr18/16; ⏰10am-6pm Apr-Oct, 11am-5pm Nov-Mar) Lucerne's blockbuster cultural attraction is the Sammlung Rosengart, occupying a graceful neoclassical pile. It showcases the outstanding stash of Angela Rosengart, a Swiss art dealer and close friend of Picasso. Alongside works by the great Spanish master are paintings and sketches by Cézanne, Klee, Kandinsky, Miró, Matisse and Monet. Standouts include Joan Miró's electric blue *Dancer II* (1925) and Paul Klee's child-like *X-chen* (1938).

Verkehrshaus — Museum

(Swiss Museum of Transport; ☎041 370 44 44; www.verkehrshaus.ch; Lidostrasse 5; adult/child Sfr30/15; ⏰10am-6pm Apr-Oct, to 5pm Nov-Mar; 👪) A great kid-pleaser, the fascinating interactive Verkehrshaus is deservedly Switzerland's most popular museum. Alongside space rockets, steam locomotives, bicycles and dugout canoes are hands-on activities such as flight simulators and broadcasting studios.

The museum also shelters a **planetarium (adult/child Sfr15/9)**; Switzerland's largest **3D cinema (www.filmtheater.ch; adult/child daytime Sfr18/14, evening Sfr22/19)**; and its newest attraction, the **Swiss Chocolate Experience (adult/child Sfr15/9)**, a 20-minute ride that whirls visitors through multimedia exhibits on the origins, history, production and distribution of chocolate, from Ghana to Switzerland and beyond.

 Sleeping

Backpackers Lucerne Hostel €
(041 360 04 20; www.backpackerslucerne.ch; Alpenquai 42; dm/d from Sfr33/78; reception 7-10am & 4-11pm;) Could this be backpacker heaven? Just opposite the lake, this is a soulful place to crash with art-slung walls, bubbly staff, a well-equipped kitchen and immaculate dorms with balconies. It's a 15-minute walk southeast of the station. There's no breakfast, but guests have kitchen access.

Hotel Waldstätterhof Hotel €€
(041 227 12 71; www.hotel-waldstaetterhof.ch; Zentralstrasse 4; s Sfr190, d Sfr290-315;) Opposite the train station, this hotel with faux-Gothic exterior offers smart, modern rooms with hardwood-style floors and high ceilings, plus excellent service.

The Hotel Hotel €€€
(041 226 86 86; www.the-hotel.ch; Sempacherstrasse 14; s/d ste from Sfr425/455;) This shamelessly hip hotel, bearing the imprint of architect Jean Nouvel, is all streamlined chic, with refined suites featuring stills from movie classics on the ceilings. Downstairs, Bam Bou is one of Lucerne's hippest restaurants, and the gorgeous green park across the street is a cool place to idle.

 Eating & Drinking

Grottino 1313 Italian €€
(041 610 13 13; www.grottino1313.ch; Industrie strasse 7; 2-course lunch menu Sfr20, 4-course dinner menu Sfr64; 11am-2pm & 6-11.30pm Mon-Fri, 6-11.30pm Sat, 9am-2pm Sun) Offering a welcome escape from Lucerne's tourist throngs, this relaxed yet stylish eatery serves ever-changing 'surprise' menus featuring starters like chestnut soup with figs, creative pasta dishes, meats cooked over an open fire and scrumptious desserts. The gravel-strewn, herb-fringed front patio is lovely on a summer afternoon, while the

Detour: Mountain Scenery

Among the several (heavily marketed) day trips from Lucerne, consider the one to 2132m-high **Mt Pilatus** (www.pilatus.com). From May to October, you can reach the peak on a classic 'golden round-trip'. Board the lake steamer from Lucerne to Alpnachstad, then rise with the world's steepest cog railway to Mt Pilatus. From the summit, cable cars bring you down to Kriens via Fräkmüntegg and Krienseregg, where bus 1 takes you back to Lucerne. The return trip costs Sfr97 (less with valid Swiss, Eurail or InterRail passes).

candlelit interior exudes sheer cosiness on a winter's evening.

Wirtshaus Galliker Swiss **€€**
(☎041 240 10 01; Schützenstrasse 1; mains Sfr21-51; ⏰11.30am-2pm & 5-10pm Tue-Sat, closed Jul–mid-Aug) Passionately run by the Galliker family for over four generations, this old-style, wood-panelled tavern attracts a lively bunch of regulars. Motherly waitresses dish up Lucerne soul food (rösti, *chögalipaschtetli* and the like) that is batten-the-hatches filling.

Rathaus Bräuerei Brewery
(☎041 410 52 57; www.braui-luzern.ch; Unter den Egg 2; ⏰11.30am-midnight Mon-Sat, to 11pm Sun) Sip home-brewed beer under the vaulted arches of this buzzy tavern near Kapellbrücke, or nab a pavement table and watch the river flow.

Information

Tourist Office (☎041 227 17 17; www.luzern.com; Zentralstrasse 5; ⏰9am-7pm Mon-Sat, 9am-5pm Sun May-Oct, 8.30am-5.30pm Mon-Fri, 9am-5pm Sat, 9am-1pm Sun Nov-Apr) Reached from Zentralstrasse or platform 3 of the Hauptbahnhof. Offers city walking tours. Call for hotel reservations.

Getting There & Around

Frequent trains serve Interlaken Ost (Sfr31, 1¾ hours), Bern (Sfr37, one hour), Lugano (Sfr58, 2½ hours) and Zürich (Sfr24, 50 minutes).

Trains also connect Lucerne and Interlaken East on the stunning GoldenPass Line via Meiringen (Sfr31, two hours).

SGV (www.lakelucerne.ch) operates boats (sometimes paddle steamers) on Lake Lucerne daily. Services are extensive. Rail passes are good for free or discounted travel.

INTERLAKEN

POP 5660

Once Interlaken made the Victorians swoon with its dreamy mountain vistas, viewed from the chandelier-lit confines of its grand hotels. Today it makes daredevils scream with its adrenalin-loaded adventures. Straddling the glittering Lakes Thun and Brienz (thus the name), and dazzled by the pearly whites of Eiger, Mönch and Jungfrau, the scenery here is exceptional.

Sights & Activities

Switzerland is the world's second-biggest adventure-sports centre and Interlaken is its busiest hub. Sample prices are around Sfr120 for rafting or canyoning, Sfr140 for hydrospeeding, Sfr130 to Sfr180 for bungee or canyon jumping, Sfr170 for tandem paragliding, Sfr180 for ice climbing, Sfr220 for hang-gliding, and Sfr430 for sky-diving. A half-day mountain-bike tour will set you back around Sfr25.

Harder Kulm Mountain
(www.harderkulm.ch) For far-reaching views to the 4000m giants, ride the **funicular** (adult/child return Sfr28/14; ⏰every 30 min 8.10am-6.25pm late Apr-Oct, plus 7-8.30pm Jul & Aug) to 1322m Harder Kulm. Many hiking paths begin here, and the vertigo-free can enjoy the panorama from the **Zweiseensteg** (Two Lake Bridge) jutting out above the valley. The wildlife park near the valley

BUENA VISTA IMAGE/GETTY IMAGES ©

Don't Miss Jungfraujoch

If the Bernese Oberland is Switzerland's Alpine heart, the Jungfrau region is where yours will skip a beat. Presided over by glacier-encrusted monoliths Eiger, Mönch and Jungfrau (Ogre, Monk and Virgin), the scenery stirs the soul and strains the neck muscles. Come summer, hundreds of kilometres of walking trails allow you to capture the landscape from many angles, but it never looks less than astonishing.

Jungfraujoch (3471m) is a once-in-a-lifetime trip and there's good reason why two million people a year visit Europe's highest train station. Clear good weather is essential for the trip; check www.jungfrau.ch or call ☎033 828 79 31 and don't forget warm clothing, sunglasses and sunscreen.

From Interlaken Ost, the journey time is 2½ hours each way (Sfr197.60 return, discounts with rail passes). The last train back sets off at 5.45pm in summer and 4.45pm in winter. However, from May through to October there's a cheaper Good Morning Ticket costing Sfr145 if you take the first train (which departs at 6.35am from Interlaken Ost) and leave the summit by 1pm.

station is home to Alpine critters, including marmots and ibex.

Sleeping

Backpackers Villa Sonnenhof Hostel €
(☎033 826 71 71; www.villa.ch; Alpenstrasse 16; dm Sfr39.50-47, s Sfr69-79, d Sfr110-148; P @) Sonnenhof is a slick combination of ultramodern chalet and elegant art nouveau villa. Dorms are immaculate, and some have balconies with Jungfrau views. There's also a relaxed lounge, a well-equipped kitchen, a kids' playroom and a leafy garden for mountain gazing. Special family rates are available.

Victoria-Jungfrau Grand Hotel & Spa Luxury Hotel **€€€**
(☎033 828 26 10; www.victoria-jungfrau.ch; Höheweg 41; d Sfr400-800, ste Sfr600-1000; P @ 📶 🏊) The reverent hush and impeccable service here (as well as the prices) evoke an era when only royalty and the seriously wealthy travelled. A perfect melding of well-preserved art nouveau features and modern luxury make this Interlaken's answer to Raffles – with plum views of Jungfrau, three first-class restaurants and a gorgeous spa to boot.

Eating

Sandwich Bar Sandwiches **€**
(Rosenstrasse 5; snacks Sfr4-9; 🕗7.30am-7pm Mon-Fri, 8am-5pm Sat) Choose your bread and get creative with fillings like air-dried ham with sun-dried tomatoes and brie with walnuts. Or try the soups, salads, toasties and locally made ice cream.

WineArt Mediterranean **€€**
(☎033 823 73 74; www.wineart.ch; Jungfraustrasse 46; mains Sfr24-59, 5-course menu Sfr59; 🕗4pm-12.30am Mon-Sat) This is a delightful wine bar, lounge, restaurant and deli rolled into one. High ceilings, chandeliers and wood floors create a slick, elegant backdrop for season-driven Mediterranean food. Pair one of 600 wines with dishes as simple as buffalo mozzarella and rocket salad and corn-fed chicken with honey-glazed vegetables – quality and flavour is second to none.

Information

Tourist Office (☎033 826 53 00; www.interlakentourism.ch; Höheweg 37; 🕗8am-7pm Mon-Fri, to 5pm Sat, 10am-4pm Sun Jul & Aug, 8am-noon & 1.30-6pm Mon-Fri, 9am-noon Sat rest of year) Halfway between the stations. There's a hotel booking board outside.

Getting There & Away

There are two train stations. Interlaken West is slightly closer to the centre and is a stop for trains to Bern (Sfr27, one hour). Interlaken Ost (East) is the rail hub for all lines, including the scenic ones up into the Jungfrau region and the lovely GoldenPass Line to Lucerne (Sfr31, two hours).

Zürich

POP 380,780

Zürich, Switzerland's largest city, is an enigma. A savvy financial centre with the densest public-transport system in the world, it also has a gritty, post-industrial edge that always surprises and an evocative Old Town, not to mention a lovely lakeside location.

Bahnhofstrasse, Zürich, Switzerland
TRAVELSTOCK4400/LOOK-FOTO/GETTY IMAGES ©

Sights

The cobbled streets of the pedestrian Old Town line both sides of the river, while the bank vaults beneath Bahnhofstrasse, the city's most elegant shopping street, are said to be crammed with gold. On Sundays all of Zürich strolls around the lake – on a clear day you'll glimpse the Alps in the distance.

Fraumünster Church
(www.fraumuenster.ch; Münsterhof; ⏲9am-6pm Apr-Oct, 10am-4pm Nov-Mar) The 13th-century cathedral is renowned for its stunning, distinctive stained-glass windows, designed by the Russian-Jewish master Marc Chagall (1887–1985). He did a series of five windows in the choir stalls in 1971 and the rose window in the southern transept in 1978. The rose window in the northern transept was created by Augusto Giacometti in 1945.

Kunsthaus Museum
(☎044 253 84 84; www.kunsthaus.ch; Heimplatz 1; adult/child Sfr15/free, Wed free; ⏲10am-8pm Wed-Fri, 10am-6pm Tue, Sat & Sun) Zürich's impressive fine-arts gallery boasts a rich collection of largely European art that stretches from the Middle Ages through a mix of old masters to Alberto Giacometti stick figures, Monet and Van Gogh masterpieces, Rodin sculptures and other 19th- and 20th-century art. Swiss Rail and Museum Passes don't provide free admission but the ZürichCard does.

Schweizerisches Landesmuseum Museum
(Swiss National Museum; www.musee-suisse.ch; Museumstrasse 2; adult/child Sfr10/free; ⏲10am-5pm Tue, Wed & Fri-Sun, 10am-7pm Thu) Inside a purpose-built cross between a mansion and a castle sprawls this eclectic and imaginatively presented museum. The permanent collection offers an extensive tour through Swiss history, with exhibits ranging from elaborately carved and painted sleds to household and religious artefacts to a series of reconstructed historical rooms spanning six centuries. The museum remains open while undergoing a major expansion; the new archaeology section and brand-new wing are slated to open in 2016.

Sleeping

SYHA Hostel Hostel €
(☎043 399 78 00; www.youthhostel.ch/zuerich; Mutschellenstrasse 114, Wollishofen; dm Sfr43-46, s/d Sfr119/140, all inc breakfast; @ 📶) A bulbous, Band-Aid pink 1960s landmark houses this busy hostel with 24-hour reception, dining hall, sparkling modern bathrooms and dependable wi-fi in the downstairs lounge. Breakfast features miso soup and rice alongside all the Swiss standards. It's about 20 minutes south of the Hauptbahnhof. Take tram 7 to Morgental, or the S-Bahn to Wollishofen, then walk five minutes.

Townhouse Boutique Hotel €€
(☎044 200 95 95; www.townhouse.ch; Schützengasse 7; s Sfr195-395, d Sfr225-425; 📶) With luxurious wallpapers, wallhangings, parquet floors and retro furniture, the 21 rooms in these stylish digs come in an assortment of sizes from 15 sq metres to 35 sq metres. Located close to the main train station, the hotel offers friendly service and welcoming touches including a DVD selection and iPod docking stations.

B2 Boutique Hotel & Spa Boutique Hotel €€€
(☎044 567 67 67; www.b2boutiquehotels.com; Brandschenkestrasse 152; s/d from Sfr330/380; @ 📶) A stone's throw from Google's European headquarters, this quirky newcomer in a renovated brewery is filled with seductive features. Topping the list are the stupendous rooftop jacuzzi pool, the spa and the fanciful library-lounge, filled floor to ceiling with an astounding 30,000 books (bought from a local antiquarian) on 13m-high shelves. Spacious rooms sport modern decor (including the odd bean-bag chair).

From the Hauptbahnhof, take tram 13 to Enge and walk five minutes west.

Zürich

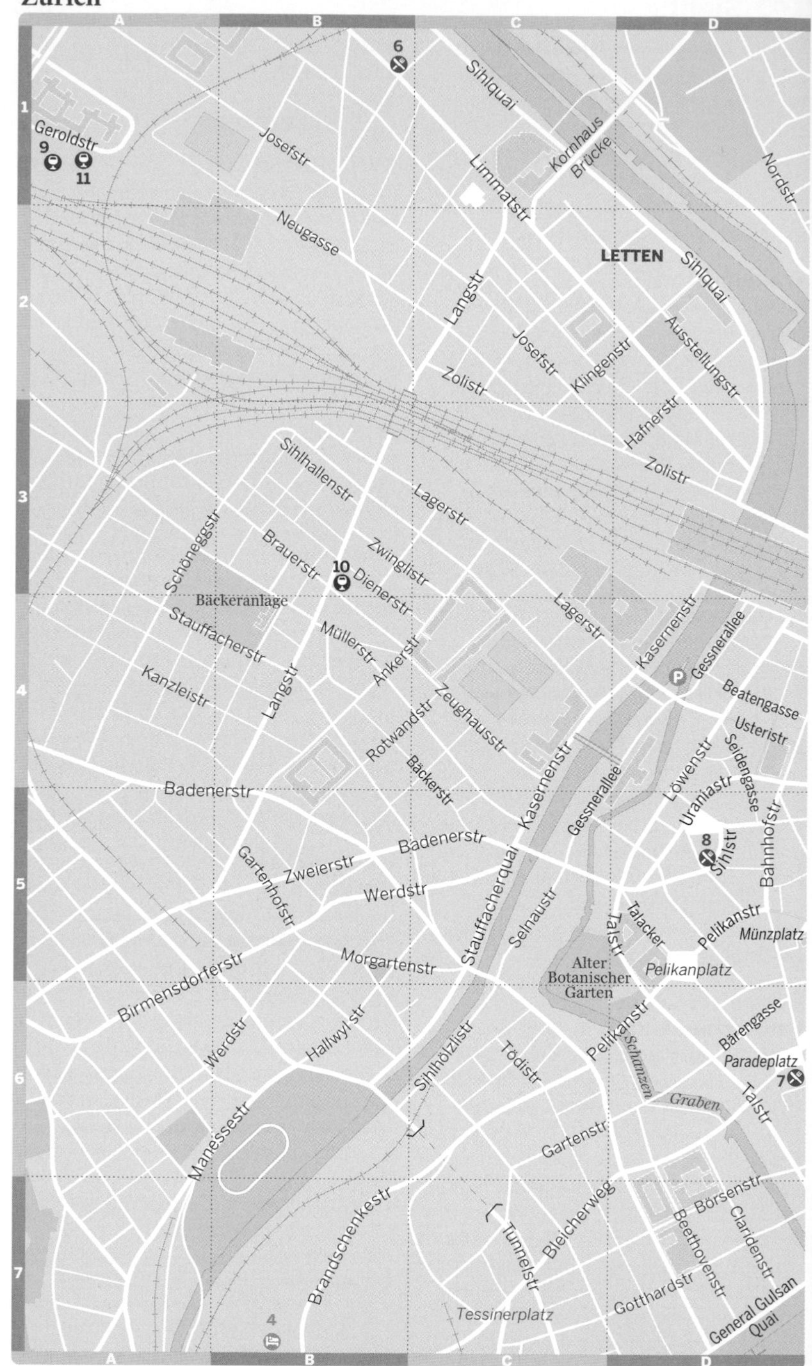
A
B
C
D
1
2
3
4
5
6
7
Geroldstr
Josefstr
Neugasse
Sihlquai
Limmatstr
Kornhaus Brücke
Nordstr
LETTEN
Langstr
Josefstr
Klingenstr
Ausstellungstr
Zolistr
Hafnerstr
Sihlhallenstr
Lagerstr
Schöneggstr
Brauerstr
Zwinglistr
Dienerstr
Bäckeranlage
Stauffacherstr
Müllerstr
Ankerstr
Kasernenstr
Gessnerallee
Beatengasse
Usteristr
Kanzleistr
Zeughausstr
Rotwandstr
Bäckerstr
Löwenstr
Seidengasse
Uraniastr
Badenerstr
Bahnhofstr
Sihlstr
Gartenhofstr
Zweierstr
Werdstr
Stauffacherquai
Selnaustr
Talacker
Talstr
Pelikanstr
Münzplatz
Morgartenstr
Alter Botanischer Garten
Pelikanplatz
Birmensdorferstr
Werdstr
Hallwylstr
Sihlhölzlistr
Tödistr
Schanzen
Graben
Bärengasse
Paradeplatz
Manessestr
Gartenstr
Brandschenkestr
Tunnelstr
Bleicherweg
Beethovenstr
Börsenstr
Claridenstr
Gotthardstr
General Gulsan Quai
Tessinerplatz

Zürich

Sights
1 Fraumünster E6
2 Kunsthaus F6
3 Schweizerisches Landesmuseum E3

Sleeping
4 B2 Boutique Hotel & Spa B7
5 Townhouse E4

Eating
6 Alpenrose B1
7 Café Sprüngli D6
8 Haus Hiltl D5

Drinking & Nightlife
9 Frau Gerolds Garten A1
10 Longstreet Bar B3
11 Supermarket A1

Eating

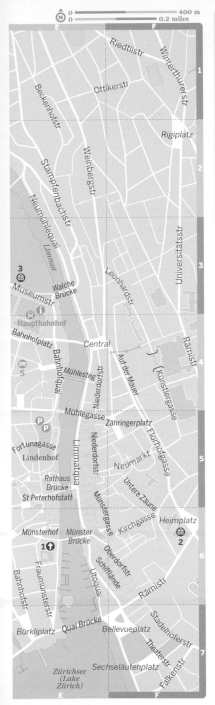

Haus Hiltl Vegetarian €

(**☎044 227 70 00; hiltl.ch; Sihlstrasse 28; per 100g takeaway/cafe/restaurant Sfr3.50/4.50/5.50; ⏰6am-midnight Mon-Sat, 8am-midnight Sun;**) Guinness-certified as the world's oldest vegetarian restaurant (established 1898), Hiltl proffers an astounding smorgasbord of meatless delights, from Indian and Thai curries to Mediterranean grilled veggies to salads and desserts. Browse to your heart's content, fill your plate and weigh it, then choose a seat in the informal cafe or the spiffier adjoining restaurant (economical take-away service is also available).

Café Sprüngli Sweets €

(**☎044 224 46 46; www.spruengli.ch; Bahnhofstrasse 21; sweets Sfr7.50-16; ⏰7am-6.30pm Mon-Fri, 8am-6pm Sat, 9.30am-5.30pm Sun**) Sit down for cakes, chocolate, coffee or ice cream at this epicentre of sweet Switzerland, in business since 1836. You can have a light lunch too, but whatever you do, don't fail to check out the heavenly chocolate shop around the corner on Paradeplatz.

Alpenrose Swiss €€

(**☎044 271 39 19; alpenrose.me; Fabrikstrasse 12; mains Sfr26-42; ⏰11am-midnight Wed-Fri, 6.15-11pm Sat & Sun**) With its timber-clad walls, 'No Polka Dancing' warning and multi-regional Swiss cuisine, the Alpenrose exudes cosy charm. Specialities include Ticinese risotto and *Pizokel*, a savoury kind of *Spätzli* from Graubünden – as proudly noted on the menu, they've served over 20,000kg of it over the past 20 years! Save room for creamy cognac parfait and other scrumptious desserts.

Drinking & Entertainment

Frau Gerolds Garten Bar

(www.fraugerold.ch; Geroldstrasse 23/23a; 11am-midnight Mon-Sat, noon-10pm Sun Apr-Oct, closed in bad weather;) Hmm, where to start? The wine bar? The margarita bar? The gin bar? Whichever poison you choose, this wildly popular recent addition to Zürich's summertime drinking scene is pure unadulterated fun. Overhung with multicoloured streamers and sandwiched between cheery flower beds and a screeching railyard, its outdoor seating options range from picnic tables to pillow-strewn terraces to a second-floor sundeck.

Longstreet Bar Bar

(044 241 21 72; www.longstreetbar.ch; Langstrasse 92; 6pm-late Wed-Fri, 8pm-4am Sat) In the heart of the Langstrasse action, the Longstreet is a music bar with a varied roll call of DJs. Try to count the thousands of light bulbs in this purple-felt-lined one-time cabaret.

Supermarket Club

(044 440 20 05; www.supermarket.li; Geroldstrasse 17; 11pm-late Thu-Sat) Looking like an innocent little house, Supermarket boasts three cosy lounge bars around the dance floor, a covered back courtyard and an interesting roster of DJs playing house and techno. Take a train from Hauptbahnhof to Hardbrücke.

Information

Zürich Tourism (044 215 40 00, hotel reservations 044 215 40 40; www.zuerich.com; train station; 8am-8.30pm Mon-Sat, 8.30am-6.30pm Sun)

Getting There & Away

Air

Zürich airport (p681), 10km north of the centre, is Switzerland's main airport.

Train

Direct trains run to Stuttgart (Sfr64, three hours), Munich (Sfr97, 4¼ hours), Innsbruck (Sfr77, 3½ hours) and other international destinations.

There are regular direct departures to most major Swiss towns, such as Lucerne (Sfr24, 45 to 50 minutes), Bern (Sfr49, one to 1¼ hours) and Basel (Sfr32, 55 minutes to 1¼ hours).

Getting Around

To/From the Airport

Up to nine trains an hour run in each direction between the airport and the main train station (Sfr6.60, nine to 14 minutes).

Bicycle

Züri Rollt (www.schweizrollt.ch) allows visitors to borrow or rent bikes from a handful of locations, including Velostation Nord across the road from the north side of the Hauptbahnhof. Bring ID and leave Sfr20 as a deposit. Rental is free if you bring the bike back on the same day and Sfr10 a day if you keep it overnight.

Public Transport

The comprehensive, unified bus, tram and SBahn public transit system **ZVV** (www.zvv.ch) includes boats plying the Limmat River. Short trips under five stops are Sfr2.60, typical trips are Sfr4.20. A 24-hour pass for the city centre is Sfr8.40.

CZECH REPUBLIC

Since the fall of communism in 1989 and the opening up of central and Eastern Europe, Prague has evolved into one of Europe's most popular travel destinations. The city offers an intact medieval core that transports you back 500 years. The 14th-century Charles Bridge, traversing two historic neighbourhoods, is one of the continent's most beautiful sights.

Outside the capital, castles and palaces abound – including the audacious hilltop chateau at Český Krumlov – which illuminate the stories of powerful

Czech Republic

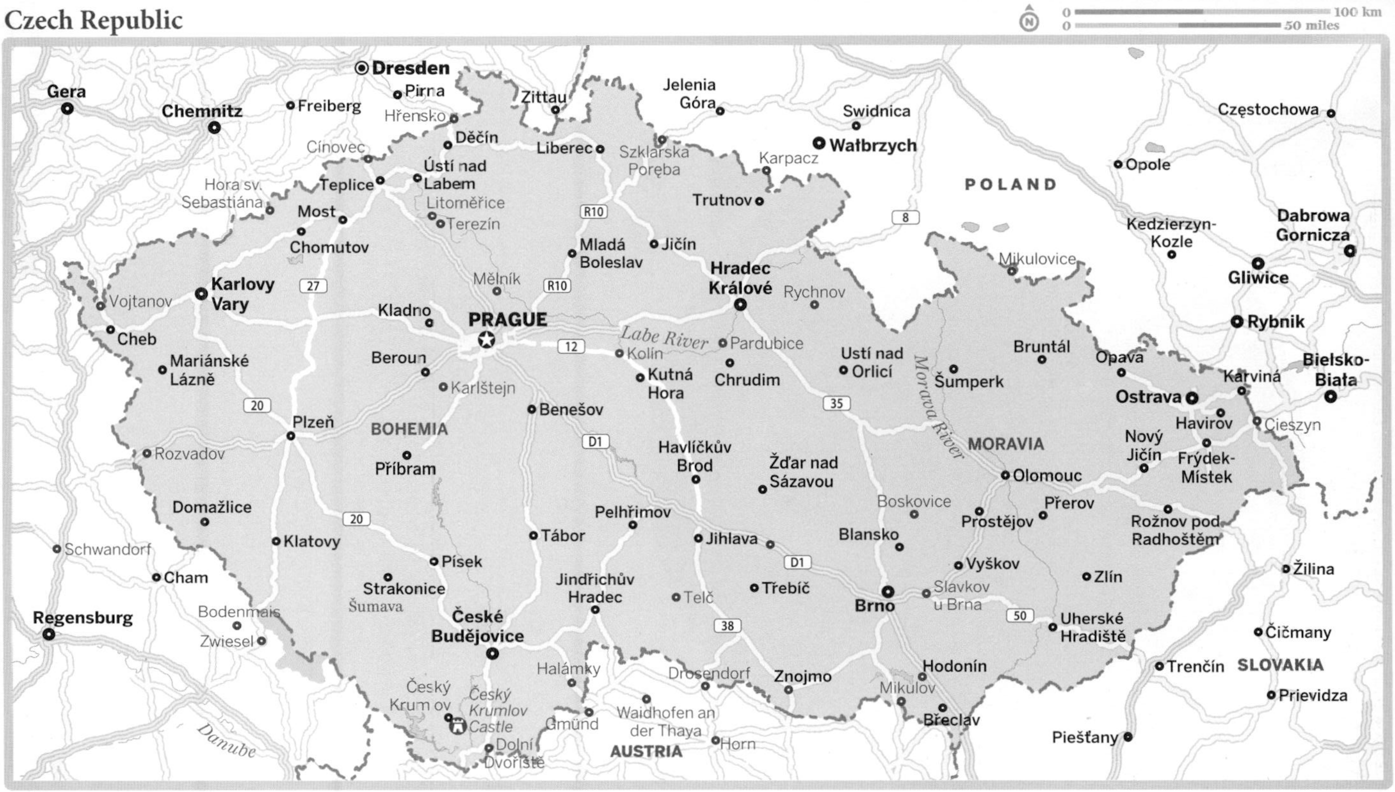

Right: Charles Bridge (p661) Prague, Czech Republic; **Below:** Astronomical Clock (p658), Prague, Czech Republic

(RIGHT) TANIALERRO/GETTY IMAGES ©; (BELOW) JONATHAN SMITH/GETTY IMAGES ©

dynasties whose influence was felt throughout Europe.

Prague

POP 1.24 MILLION

It's the perfect irony of Prague: you are lured here by the past, but compelled to linger by the present and the future. Fill your days with its illustrious artistic and architectural heritage, from Gothic and Renaissance to art nouveau and cubist. If Prague's seasonal legions of tourists wear you down, that's OK. Just drink a glass of the country's legendary lager, relax and rest reassured that quiet moments still exist: a private dawn on Charles Bridge, the glorious cityscape of Staré Město or getting lost in the intimate lanes of Malá Strana.

Sights

Prague nestles on the Vltava River, separating Hradčany (the Castle district) and Malá Strana (Lesser Quarter) on the west bank from Staré Město (Old Town) and Nové Město (New Town) on the east.

HRADČANY

Old Royal Palace Palace

(Starý královský palác; Map p660; admission with Prague Castle tour ticket; 9am-5pm Apr-Oct, to 4pm Nov-Mar; 22) The Old Royal Palace is one of the oldest parts of Prague Castle, dating from 1135. It was originally used only by Czech princesses, but from the 13th to the 16th centuries it was the king's own palace. At its heart is the grand Vladislav Hall and the Bohemian Chancellery, scene of the famous Defenestration of Prague in 1618.

St Vitus Cathedral Church

(Katedrála Sv Víta; Map p660; 257 531 622; www.katedralasvatehovita.cz; Third Courtyard, Prague Castle; admission with Prague Castle tour

ticket; 9am-5pm Mon-Sat, noon-5pm Sun Apr-Oct, to 4pm Nov-Mar; 22) It might appear ancient, but much of Prague's principal cathedral was completed just in time for its belated consecration in 1929. Its many treasures include the 14th-century mosaic of the Last Judgement above the Golden Gate, the baroque silver tomb of St John of Nepomuck, the ornate Chapel of St Wenceslas, and art nouveau stained glass by Alfons Mucha.

Lobkowicz Palace Museum
(Lobkovický palác; Map p660; 233 312 925; http://lobkowicz-palace.com; Jiřská 3; adult/concession/family 275/200/690Kč; 10am-6pm; 22) This 16th-century palace houses a private museum which includes priceless paintings, furniture and musical memorabilia. You tour with an audio guide dictated by owner William Lobkowicz and his family – this personal connection really brings the displays to life, and makes the palace one of the castle's most interesting attractions.

STARÉ MĚSTO

Staré Město is the city's oldest quarter and home to its main market, **Old Town Square (Staroměstské náměstí; Map p656; M Staroměstská)**, often simply called Staromák. The square has functioned as the centre of Staré Město since the 10th century.

Old Town Hall Historic Building
(Staroměstská radnice; Map p656; 236 002 629; www.staromestskaradnicepraha.cz; Staroměstské náměstí 1; guided tour adult/child 100/50Kč, incl tower 160Kč; 11am-6pm Mon, 9am-6pm Tue-Sun; M Staroměstská) Prague's Old Town Hall, founded in 1338, is a hotchpotch of medieval buildings acquired piecemeal over the centuries, presided over by a tall Gothic tower with a splendid Astronomical Clock. As well as housing Staré Město's main tourist information office, the town hall has several historic attractions, and hosts art exhibitions on the ground floor and the 2nd floor.

Central Prague

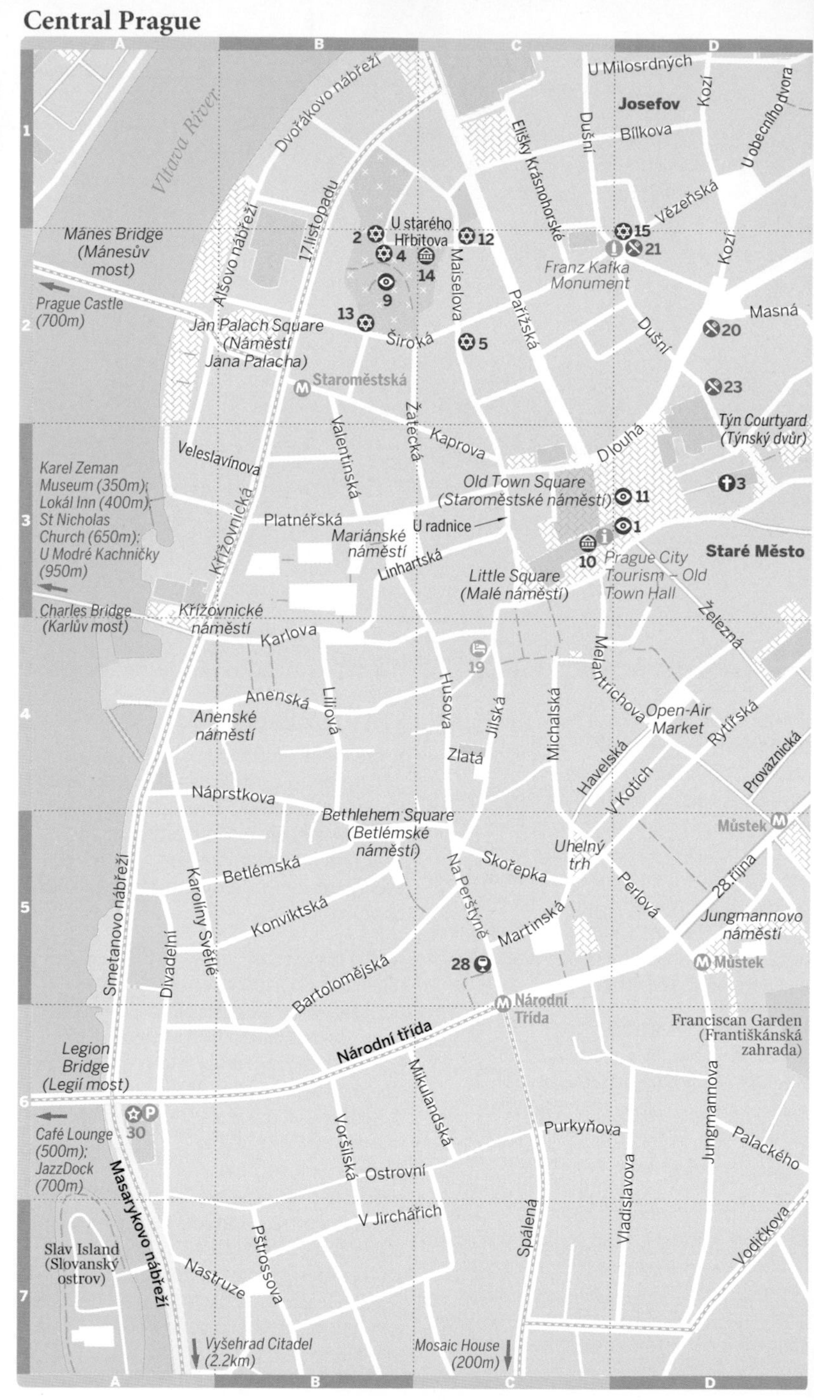

Josefov
Vltava River
Mánes Bridge (Mánesův most)
Prague Castle (700m)
Jan Palach Square (Náměstí Jana Palacha)
Staroměstská
Karel Zeman Museum (350m); Lokál Inn (400m); St Nicholas Church (650m); U Modré Kachničky (950m)
Charles Bridge (Karlův most)
Křížovnické náměstí
Old Town Square (Staroměstské náměstí)
Mariánské náměstí
U radnice
Little Square (Malé náměstí)
Prague City Tourism – Old Town Hall
Staré Město
Franz Kafka Monument
Týn Courtyard (Týnský dvůr)
Anenské náměstí
Bethlehem Square (Betlémské náměstí)
Open-Air Market
Uhelný trh
Můstek
Jungmannovo náměstí
Národní Třída
Franciscan Garden (Františkánská zahrada)
Legion Bridge (Legií most)
Café Lounge (500m); JazzDock (700m)
Slav Island (Slovanský ostrov)
Vyšehrad Citadel (2.2km)
Mosaic House (200m)
U starého Hřbitova
Národní třída
Masarykovo nábřeží

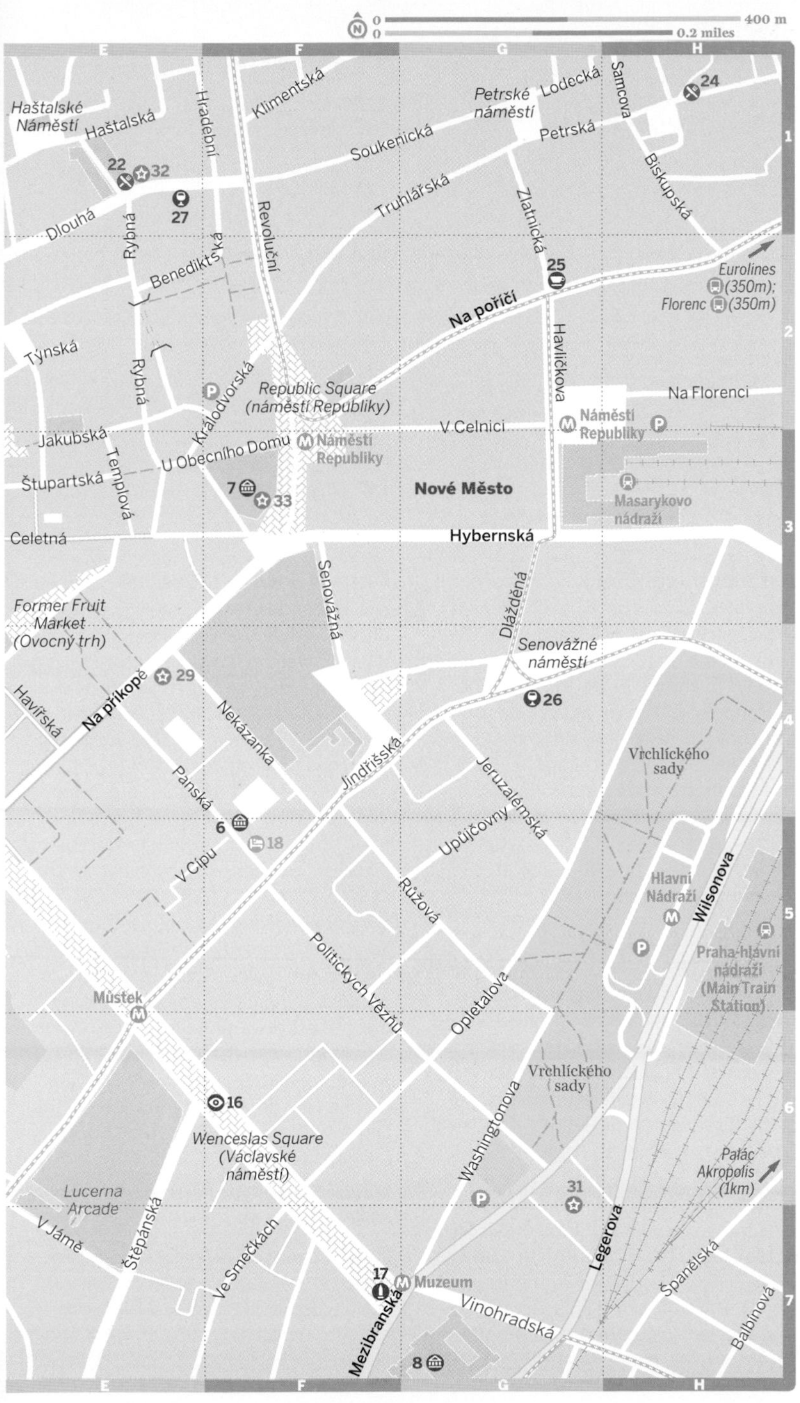
0
400 m
0
0.2 miles
E
F
G
H
Haštalské Náměstí
Haštalská
Hradební
Klimentská
Petrské náměstí
Lodecká
Samcova
24
Petrská
Soukenická
Biskupská
22
32
27
Dlouhá
Rybná
Revoluční
Truhlářská
Zlatnická
Benediktská
25
Eurolines (350m);
Florenc (350m)
Na poříčí
Týnská
Havlíčkova
Rybná
Kralodvorská
Republic Square (náměstí Republiky)
Na Florenci
Jakubská
V Celnici
Náměstí Republiky
Náměstí Republiky
Templová
U Obecního Domu
Štupartská
7
33
Nové Město
Masarykovo nádraží
Celetná
Hybernská
Senovážná
Dlážděná
Former Fruit Market (Ovocný trh)
Senovážné náměstí
29
Na příkopě
26
Havířská
Nekázanka
Jindřišská
Vrchlického sady
Panská
Jeruzalémská
6
18
Upůjčovny
V Cípu
Hlavní Nádraží
Wilsonova
Růžová
Politických Vězňů
Praha-hlavní nádraží (Main Train Station)
Můstek
Opletalova
Vrchlického sady
16
Washingtonova
Wenceslas Square (Václavské náměstí)
Palác Akropolis (1km)
31
Lucerna Arcade
V Jámě
Štěpánská
Ve Smečkách
Legerova
17
Muzeum
Španělská
Mezibranská
Vinohradská
Balbínova
8
1
2
3
4
5
6
7

Central Prague

Astronomical Clock — Historic Site

(Map p656; Staroměstské náměstí; chimes on the hour 9am-9pm; M Staroměstská) Every hour, on the hour, crowds gather beneath the Old Town Hall Tower to watch the Astronomical Clock in action. Despite a slightly underwhelming performance that takes only 45 seconds, the clock is one of Europe's best-known tourist attractions, and a 'must-see' for visitors to Prague. After all, it's historic, photogenic and – if you take time to study it – rich in intriguing symbolism.

Church of Our Lady Before Týn — Church

(Kostel Panny Marie před Týnem; Map p656; 222 318 186; www.tyn.cz; Staroměstské náměstí; suggested donation 25Kč; 10am-1pm & 3-5pm Tue-Sat, 10.30am-noon Sun Mar-Oct, shorter hours Nov-Feb; M Staroměstská) Its distinctive twin Gothic spires make the Týn Church an unmistakable Staré Město landmark. Like something out of a 15th-century – and probably slightly cruel – fairy tale, they loom over the Old Town Square, decorated with a golden image of the Virigin Mary made in the 1620s from the melted down Hussite chalice that previously adorned the church.

Prague Jewish Museum — Museum

(Židovské muzeum Praha; Map p656; 222 317 191; www.jewishmuseum.cz; Reservation Centre, U starého hřbitova 3a; ordinary ticket adult/child 300/200Kč, combined ticket incl entry to Old-New Synagogue 480/320Kč; 9am-6pm Sun-Fri Apr-Oct, to 4.30pm Nov-Mar; M Staroměstská) This museum consists of six Jewish monuments clustered together in Josefov.

An ordinary ticket gives admission to all six main monuments; a combined ticket includes the Old-New Synagogue as well. Admission to the Old-New Synagogue alone costs 200/140Kč. You can buy tickets at the Reservation Centre, the Pinkas Synagogue, the Spanish Synagogue and the shop opposite the entrance to the Old-New Synagogue. Queues tend to be shortest at the Spanish Synagogue. If you are pressed for time, the highlights are the Old-New Synagogue and the Old Jewish Cemetery.

Maisel Synagogue (Maiselova synagóga; Map p656; Maiselova 10)

Pinkas Synagogue (Pinkasova synagóga; Map p656; www.jewishmuseum.cz; Široká 3; incl in admission to Prague Jewish Museum)

CHRISTIAN KOBER/GETTY IMAGES ©

Don't Miss Prague Castle

Prague Castle – Pražský hrad, or just *hrad* to Czechs – is Prague's most popular attraction. Looming above the Vltava's left bank, its serried ranks of spires, towers and palaces dominate the city centre like a fairy-tale fortress. Within its walls lies a varied and fascinating collection of historic buildings, museums and galleries that are home to some of the Czech Republic's greatest artistic and cultural treasures.

NEED TO KNOW

Pražský hrad; Map p660; ☎224 372 423; www.hrad.cz; Hradčanské náměstí; grounds free, sights adult/concession short tour 250/125Kc, long tour 350/175Kc; ⏰grounds 5am-midnight Apr-Oct, 6am-11pm Nov-Mar, gardens 10am-6pm Apr & Oct, to 7pm May & Sep, to 9pm Jun-Aug, closed Nov-Mar, historic buildings 9am-5pm Apr-Oct, to 4pm Nov-Mar; Ⓜ Malostranská, 🚋22

Spanish Synagogue (Španělská synagóga; Map p656; www.jewishmuseum.cz; Vězeňská 1; incl in admission to Prague Jewish Museum)

Klaus Synagogue (Klauzová synagóga; Map p656; www.jewishmuseum.cz; U starého hřbitova 1)

Ceremonial Hall (Obřadní síň; Map p656)

Old Jewish Cemetery (Starý židovský hřbitov; Map p656; www.jewishmuseum.cz; Pinkas Synagogue, Široká 3; included in admission to Prague Jewish Museum).

There is also the **Old-New Synagogue** (Staronová synagóga; Map p656; www.jewishmuseum.cz; Červená 2; adult/child 200/140Kč), which is still used for religious services, and requires a separate ticket or additional fee.

In one of the most grotesquely ironic acts of WWII, the Nazis took over the management of the Prague Jewish

Prague Castle

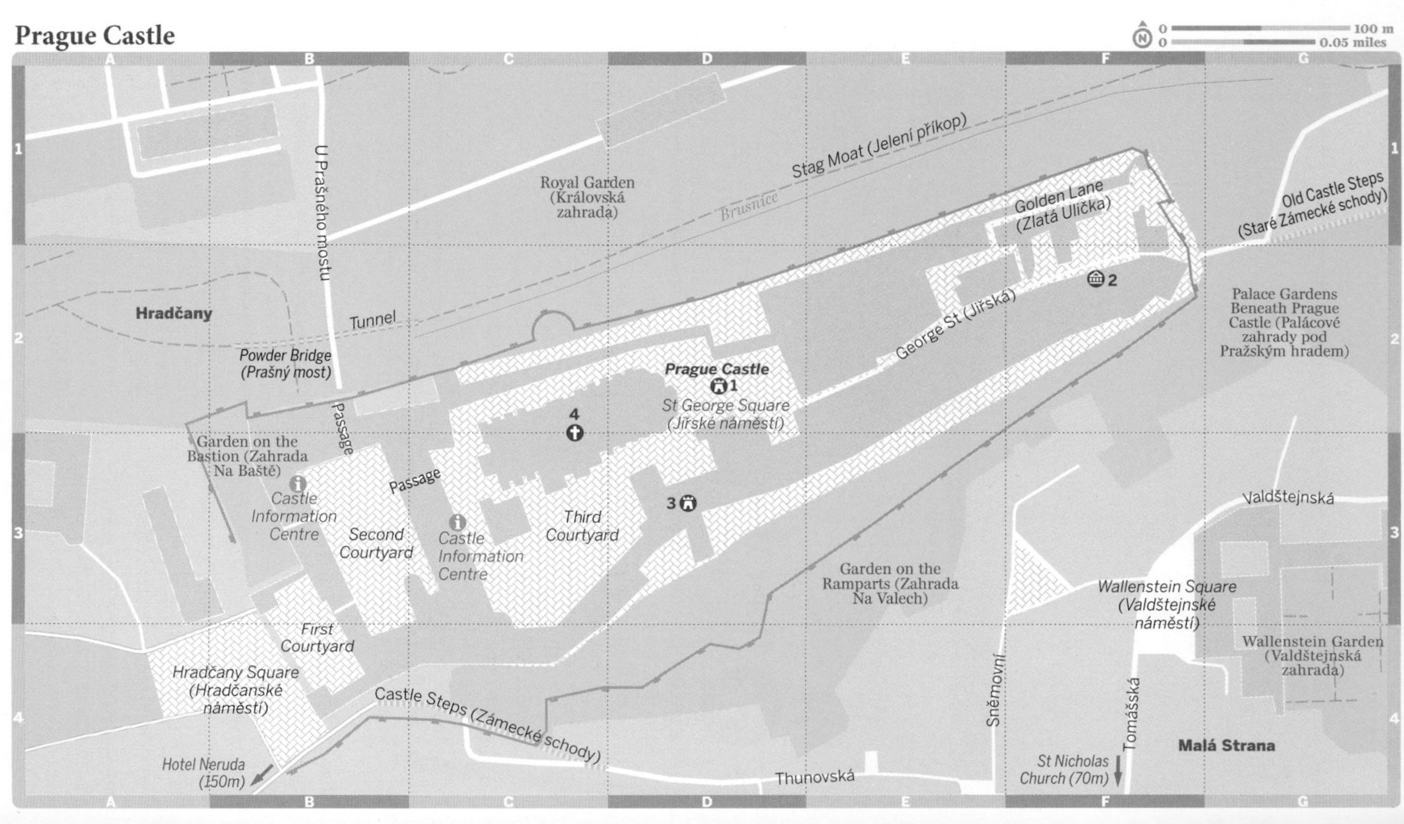

Prague Castle

Don't Miss Sights

1 Prague Castle D2

Sights

2 Lobkowicz Palace F2
3 Old Royal Palace D3
4 St Vitus Cathedral C2

Museum – first established in 1906 to preserve artefacts from synagogues that were demolished during the slum clearances in Josefov around the turn of the 20th century – with the intention of creating a 'museum of an extinct race'. They shipped in materials and objects from destroyed Jewish communities throughout Bohemia and Moravia, helping to amass what is probably the world's biggest collection of sacred Jewish artefacts and a moving memorial to seven centuries of oppression.

Municipal House Historic Building
(Obecní dům; Map p656; ☎222 002 101; www.obecnidum.cz; náměstí Republiky 5; guided tour adult/concession/child under 10yr 290/240Kč/free; ⏰public areas 7.30am-11pm, information centre 10am-8pm; M Náměstí Republiky) Restored in the 1990s after decades of neglect, Prague's most exuberant and sensual building is a labour of love, every detail of its design and decoration carefully considered, every painting and sculpture loaded with symbolism. The restaurant and cafe flanking the entrance are like walk-in museums of art nouveau design; upstairs are half a dozen sumptuously decorated halls that you can visit by guided tour.

MALÁ STRANA

Across the river from Staré Město are the baroque backstreets of Malá Strana, built in the 17th and 18th centuries by victorious Catholic clerics and nobles on the foundations of their Protestant predecessors' Renaissance palaces.

Charles Bridge Bridge
(Karlův most; ⏰24hr; 🚋17, 18 to Karlovy lázně, 12, 20, 22 to Malostranské náměstí) FREE Strolling across Charles Bridge is everybody's favourite Prague activity. However, by 9am it's a 500m-long fairground, with an army of tourists squeezing through a gauntlet of hawkers and buskers beneath the impassive gaze of the baroque statues that line the parapets. If you want to experience the bridge at its most atmospheric, try to visit it at dawn.

St Nicholas Church Church
(Kostel sv Mikuláše; ☎257 534 215; www.stnicholas.cz; Malostranské náměstí 38; adult/child 70/50Kč; ⏰9am-5pm Mar-Oct, to 4pm Nov-Feb; 🚋12, 20, 22) Malá Strana is dominated by the huge green cupola of St Nicholas Church, one of central Europe's finest baroque buildings. (Don't confuse it with the other Church of St Nicholas on Old Town Square.) On the ceiling, Johann Kracker's 1770 *Apotheosis of St Nicholas* is Europe's largest fresco (clever trompe l'œil technique has made the painting merge almost seamlessly with the architecture).

Karel Zeman Museum Museum
(Museum of Film Special Effects; ☎724 341 091; www.muzeumkarlazemana.cz; Saský dvůr, Saská 3; adult/child 200/140Kč; ⏰10am-7pm, last admission 6pm; 🚋12, 20, 22) Bohemia-born director Karel Zeman (1910–89) was a pioneer of movie special effects whose work is little known outside the Czech Republic. This fascinating museum, established by his daughter, reveals the many tricks and techniques he perfected, and even allows visitors a bit of hands-on interaction – you can film yourself on your smartphone against painted backgrounds and 3D models.

NOVÉ MĚSTO & VYŠEHRAD

Nové Město surrounds Staré Město on all sides and was originally laid out in the 14th century. Its main public area is **Wenceslas Square (Václavské náměstí; Map p656; M Můstek, Muzeum)**, lined with shops, banks and restaurants, and dotted by a statue of **St Wenceslas (sv Václav; Map p656; Václavské náměstí; M Muzeum)** on horseback. The **National Museum (Národní muzeum; Map p656; ☎224 497 111; www.nm.cz; Václavské náměstí 68; M Muzeum)**, which dominates the top of the square, is closed for long-term renovation.

Mucha Museum Gallery
(Muchovo muzuem; Map p656; ☎221 451 333; www.mucha.cz; Panská 7; adult/child 240/140Kč; ⏰10am-6pm; Ⓜ Můstek) This fascinating (and busy) museum features the sensuous art nouveau posters, paintings and decorative panels of Alfons Mucha (1860–1939), as well as many sketches, photographs and other memorabilia. The exhibits include countless artworks showing Mucha's trademark Slavic maidens with flowing hair and piercing blue eyes, bearing symbolic garlands and linden boughs.

Vyšehrad Citadel Fortress
(☎261 225 304; www.praha-vysehrad.cz; information centre at V pevnosti 159/5b; admission to grounds free; ⏰grounds 24hr; Ⓜ Vyšehrad) The Vyšehrad Citadel refers to the complex of buildings and structures atop Vyšehrad Hill that have played a role in Czech history for over 1000 years. While most structures date from the 18th century, the citadel is still viewed as the city's spiritual home. The sights are spread out over a wide area, with commanding views.

Festivals & Events

Prague Spring Classical Music
(www.festival.cz) The Czech Republic's biggest annual cultural event, and one of Europe's most important festivals of classical music.

Prague Fringe Festival Arts
(www.praguefringe.com) Eclectic action in late May and early June.

Christmas Market Market
1 to 24 December in the Old Town Square.

Sleeping

For better value stay outside of Staré Město and take advantage of Prague's excellent public-transport network.

Fusion Hotel Hostel, Boutique Hotel €
(Map p656; ☎226 222 800; www.fusionhotels.com; Panská 9; dm/d/tr from 400/2100/2700Kč; @📶; 🚋3, 9, 14, 24) Billing itself as an 'affordable design hotel', Fusion certainly

Czech beer

RICHARD NEBESKY/GETTY IMAGES ©

has style in abundance. From the revolving bar and spaceship-like UV corridor lighting, to the individually decorated bedrooms that resemble miniature modern-art galleries, the place exudes 'cool'. You can choose from the world's most stylish backpacker dorm, private doubles, triples and family rooms, and there's a Skype booth in the lobby.

Czech Inn Hostel, Hotel **€**
(**☎267 267 600; www.czech-inn.com; Francouzská 76, Vršovice; dm 260-450Kč, s/d 1320/1540Kč, apt from 3100Kč; P 🚭 @ 📶; 🚊4, 22)** The Czech Inn calls itself a hostel, but the 'boutique' label wouldn't be out of place. Everything seems sculpted by an industrial designer, from the iron beds to the brushed-steel flooring and minimalist square sinks. It offers a variety of accommodation, from standard hostel dorm rooms to good-value private doubles (with or without private bathroom) and apartments.

Mosaic House Hotel, Hostel **€€**
(**☎221 595 350; www.mosaichouse.com; Odborů 4; dm/tw from 370/2400Kč; 🚭 ❄ @ 📶; M Karlovo Náměstí)** A blend of four-star hotel and boutique hostel, Mosaic House is a cornucopia of designer detail, from the original 1930s mosaic in the entrance hall to the silver spray-painted tree branches used as clothes racks. The backpackers dorms are kept separate from the private rooms, but have the same high-quality decor and design, as does the in-house music bar and lounge.

Lokál Inn Inn **€€**
(**☎257 014 800; www.lokalinn.cz; Míšeňská 12; d/ste 3800/4900Kč; 🚭 📶; 🚊12, 20, 22)** Polished parquet floors and painted wooden ceilings abound in this 18th-century house designed by Prague's premier baroque architect, Kilian Dientzenhofer. The eight rooms and four suites are elegant and uncluttered, and the rustic, stone-vaulted cellars house a deservedly popular pub and restaurant run by the same folk as Lokál (p664), a popular Czech beer hall in Staré Město.

Local Knowledge

Prague's Architecture

RECOMMENDATIONS FROM MARTINA ŠVAJCROVÁ, PRAGUE INFORMATION SERVICE

1 PRAGUE CASTLE

For a millennium, Prague Castle has been a symbol of the Czech state. It was built in the 9th century for the princes and kings of Bohemia, but since 1918 it has served as the official seat of the Czech president. It's a mix of architectural styles – ecclesiastical, residential, military, regal – and it's one of the largest ancient castles in the world.

2 CHARLES BRIDGE & BRIDGE TOWERS

Prague's oldest and most iconic structure is Charles Bridge, begun by King Charles IV in 1357 and completed in 1402. The bridge's ends are fortified by towers – the smallest one is a relic of the 12th-century Judita's Bridge, the first stone bridge ever built in Prague. The bridge is also decorated by 30 saints, added between 1683 and 1928.

3 OLD TOWN HALL & THE ASTRONOMICAL CLOCK

Prague's town hall was established in 1338 to house the Staré Město (Old Town) authorities. The oldest part of the complex includes a beautiful tower, an oriel chapel and a fabulous astronomical clock, where the 12 apostles appear every hour between 9am and 9pm. The eastern wing was destroyed during the Prague uprising on 8 May 1945, and has never been rebuilt.

4 VYŠEHRAD

For astonishing views, this clifftop castle is one of the best-kept secrets in Prague. It began as a fort built around the 10th century, and briefly served as a residence for Czech royalty. Its notable buildings include the precious Romanesque rotunda of St Martin and the Gothic church of St Peter and Paul, but don't miss a walk around Vyšehrad cemetery, where many significant Czech personalities have been buried since 1869.

Savic Hotel Hotel **€€€**

(Map p656; 224 248 555; www.savic.eu; Jilská 7; r from 5200Kč; ; M Můstek) From the complimentary glass of wine when you arrive to the comfy king-size beds, the Savic certainly knows how to make you feel pampered. Housed in the former monastery of St Giles, the hotel is bursting with character and full of delightful period details including old stone fireplaces, beautiful painted timber ceilings and fragments of frescoes.

Eating

Eating in Prague's tourist areas is pricey, but cheaper eats are available just a block or two away.

Maitrea Vegetarian **€**

(Map p656; 221 711 631; www.restaurace-maitrea.cz; Týnská ulička 6; weekday lunch 115Kč, mains 145-165Kč; 11.30am-11.30pm Mon-Fri, noon-11.30pm Sat & Sun; ; M Staroměstská) Maitrea (a Buddhist term meaning 'the future Buddha') is a beautifully designed space full of flowing curves and organic shapes, from the sensuous polished-oak furniture and fittings to the blossom-like lampshades. The menu is inventive and wholly vegetarian, with dishes such as Tex-Mex quesadillas, spicy goulash with wholemeal dumplings, and pasta with smoked tofu, spinach and parmesan.

Lokál Czech **€**

(Map p656; 222 316 265; lokal-dlouha.ambi.cz; Dlouhá 33; mains 110-270Kč; 11am-1am Mon-Fri, noon-1am Sat, noon-10pm Sun; 5, 8, 24) Who'd have thought it possible? A classic Czech beer hall (albeit with slick modern styling); excellent *tankové pivo* (tanked Pilsner Urquell); a daily-changing menu of traditional Bohemian dishes; smiling, efficient, friendly service; and a nonsmoking area! Top restaurant chain Ambiente has turned its hand to Czech cuisine, and the result has been so successful that the place is always busy, mostly with locals.

Left: Old Town Square (p655) and Church of Our Lady Before Týn (p658), Prague, Czech Republic;
Below: Charles Bridge (p661), Prague, Czech Republic
(LEFT) JOHN FREEMAN/GETTY IMAGES ©; (BELOW) FRANK CHMURA/GETTY IMAGES ©

Café Lounge Czech **€**
(257 404 020; www.cafe-lounge.cz; Plaská 8; mains 120-390Kč; 7.30am-10pm Mon-Fri, 9am-10pm Sat, 9am-5pm Sun; ; 6, 9, 12, 20, 22) Cosy and welcoming, Café Lounge sports an art deco atmosphere, superb coffee, exquisite pastries and an extensive wine list. The all-day cafe menu offers freshly made salads and cornbread sandwiches, while lunch and dinner extends to dishes such as beef cheeks braised in red wine, or roast pike-perch with caraway seeds. Great breakfasts too (served until 11am weekdays, noon on weekends).

Kolkovna Czech **€€**
(Map p656; 224 819 701; www.kolkovna-restaurant.cz; V Kolkovně 8; mains 110-360Kč; 11am-midnight; ; M Staroměstská) Owned and operated by the Pilsner Urquell Brewery, Kolkovna is a stylish, modern take on the traditional Prague pub, with decor by top Czech designers, and posh (but hearty) versions of classic Czech dishes such as goulash, roast duck and Moravian sparrow, as well as the Czech favourite, roast pork knuckle. All washed down with exquisite Urquell beer, of course.

Sansho Asian, Fusion **€€**
(Map p656; 222 317 425; www.sansho.cz; Petrská 25; lunch mains 110-225Kč, 6-course dinner 850-950Kč; 11.30am-3pm & 6-11pm Tue-Thu, to 11.30pm Fri, 6-11.30pm Sat, last orders 10pm; ; 3, 8, 24) Friendly and informal best describes the atmosphere at this ground-breaking restaurant where British chef Paul Day champions Czech farmers by sourcing all his meat and vegetables locally. There's no menu: the waiter will explain what dishes are available, depending on market produce; typical dishes include curried rabbit, pork belly with watermelon salad, and 12-hour beef rendang.

Kalina French €€€

(Map p656; ☎222 317 715; www.kalinarestaurant.cz; Dlouhá 12; mains 330-720Kč; ⏰noon-3pm & 6-11.30pm Mon-Sat; 📶; 🚋5, 8, 24) Setting a trend for taking the best of fresh Czech produce and giving it the French gourmet treatment, this smart but unfailingly friendly little restaurant offers dishes such as duck pâté with rowan berries, smoked eel with beetroot and hazelnut, and roast wild boar with red wine and juniper. The set two-course lunch menu costs 330Kč.

U Modré Kachničky Czech €€€

(☎257 320 308; www.umodrekachnicky.cz; Nebovidská 6; mains 450-600Kč; ⏰noon-4pm & 6.30pm-midnight; 📶; 🚋12, 20, 22) A plush and chintzy 1930s-style hunting lodge hidden away on a quiet side street, 'At the Blue Duckling' is a pleasantly old-fashioned place with quiet, candlelit nooks perfect for a romantic dinner. The menu is heavy on traditional Bohemian duck and game dishes, such as roast duck with *slivovice* (plum brandy), plum sauce and potato pancakes.

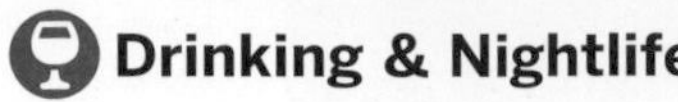

Drinking & Nightlife

Czech beers are among the world's best. The most famous brands are Plzeňský Prazdroj (Pilsner Urquell), Budvar and Prague's own Staropramen. Independent microbreweries and regional Czech beers are also becoming more popular in Prague.

U Medvídků Beer Hall

(At the Little Bear; Map p656; ☎224 211 916; www.umedvidku.cz; Na Perštýně 7; ⏰beer hall 11.30am-11pm, museum noon-10pm; 📶; Ⓜ Můstek, 🚋6, 9, 18, 22) The most micro of Prague's microbreweries, with a capacity of only 250L, U Medvídků started producing its own beer in 2005, though its trad-style beer hall has been around for many years. What it lacks in size, it makes up for in strength – the dark lager, marketed as X-Beer, is the strongest in the country, with an alcohol content of 11.8%.

Prague Beer Museum Pub

(Map p656; ☎732 330 912; www.praguebeermuseum.com; Dlouhá 46; ⏰noon-3am; 📶; 🚋5, 8, 14) Although the name seems aimed at the tourist market, this lively

Christmas market, Old Town Square (p655), Prague, Czech Republic

and always-heaving pub is very popular with Praguers. There are no fewer than 30 Czech-produced beers on tap (plus a beer menu with tasting notes to guide you). Try a sample board, a wooden platter with five 0.15L glasses containing five beers of your choice.

Café Imperial Cafe

(Map p656; ☎246 011 440; www.cafeimperial.cz; Na poříčí 15; ⏰7am-11pm; 📶; M Náměstí Republiky) First opened in 1914, and given a complete facelift in 2007, the Imperial is a tour de force of art nouveau tiling: the walls and ceiling are covered in original ceramic tiles, mosaics, sculptured panels and bas-reliefs, with period light fittings and bronzes scattered about. The coffee is good and there are cocktails in the evening.

Hoffa Cocktail Bar

(Map p656; ☎601 359 659; www.hoffa.cz; Senovážné náměstí 22; ⏰11am-2am Mon-Fri, 6pm-2am Sat & Sun; 📶; 🚋5, 9, 26) One of Prague's first entirely smoke-free bars, Hoffa matches clean air with clean design: a long (12m long!) bar fronts a room with sleek, functional decor and a wall of windows looking out onto Senovážné náměstí's fountain of dancing sprites. Friendly staff, accomplished cocktails and good snacks – there's even homemade lemonade and iced tea at lunchtime.

Cross Club Club

(☎736 535 010; www.crossclub.cz; Plynární 23; admission free-150Kč; ⏰cafe noon-2am, club 6pm-4am; 📶; M Nádraží Holešovice) An industrial club in every sense of the word: the setting in an industrial zone; the thumping music (both DJs and live acts); and the interior, an absolute must-see jumble of gadgets, shafts, cranks and pipes, many of which move and pulsate with light to the music. The program includes occasional live music, theatre performances and art happenings.

Entertainment

From dance to classical music to jazz, Prague offers plenty of entertainment options. Try the following ticket agencies to see what might be on during your visit and to snag tickets online: **Bohemia Ticket** **(Map p656; ☎224 215 031; www.bohemiaticket.cz/; Na příkopě 16, Nové Město; ⏰10am-7pm Mon-Fri, to 5pm Sat, to 3pm Sun)** and **Ticketstream** **(www.ticketstream.cz)**.

PERFORMING ARTS

National Theatre Opera, Ballet

(Národní divadlo; Map p656; ☎224 901 448; www.narodni-divadlo.cz; Národní třída 2; tickets 50-1100Kč; ⏰box offices 10am-6pm; 🚋6, 9, 18, 22) The much-loved National Theatre provides a stage for traditional opera, drama and ballet by the likes of Smetana, Shakespeare and Tchaikovsky, sharing the program alongside more modern works by composers and playwrights such as Philip Glass and John Osborne. The box offices are in the Nový síň building next door, in the Kolowrat Palace (opposite the Estates Theatre) and at the State Opera.

Prague State Opera Opera, Ballet

(Státní opera Praha; Map p656; ☎224 901 448; www.narodni-divadlo.cz; Wilsonova 4; tickets 180-1190Kč; ⏰box office 10am-6pm; M Muzeum) The impressive neo-rococo home of the Prague State Opera provides a glorious setting for performances of opera and ballet. An annual Verdi festival takes place here in August and September, and less conventional shows, such as Leoncavallo's rarely staged version of *La Bohème*, are also performed here.

Smetana Hall Classical Music

(Smetanova síň; Map p656; ☎222 002 101; www.obecnidum.cz; náměstí Republiky 5; tickets 300-600Kč; ⏰box office 10am-6pm; M Náměstí Republiky) The Smetana Hall, centrepiece of the stunning Municipal House (p661), is the city's largest concert hall, with seating for 1200. This is the home venue of the Prague Symphony Orchestra (Symfonický orchestr hlavního města Prahy), and also stages performances of folk dance and music.

LIVE MUSIC

Palác Akropolis Live Music

(☎296 330 911; www.palacakropolis.cz; Kubelíkova 27, Žižkov; admission free-200Kč; ⏰club

7pm-5am; ; 5, 9, 26 to Lipanska) The Akropolis is a Prague institution, a smoky, labyrinthine, sticky-floored shrine to alternative music and drama. Its various performance spaces host a smorgasbord of musical and cultural events, from DJs to string quartets to Macedonian Roma bands to local rock gods to visiting talent – Marianne Faithfull, the Flaming Lips and the Strokes have all played here.

Roxy Live Music
(Map p656; 224 826 296; www.roxy.cz; Dlouhá 33; admission Fri & Sat free-300Kč; 7pm-5am; 5, 8, 14) Set in the ramshackle shell of an art deco cinema, the legendary Roxy has nurtured the more independent and innovative end of Prague's club spectrum since 1987 – this is the place to see the Czech Republic's top DJs. On the 1st floor is NoD, an 'experimental space' that stages drama, dance, performance art, cinema and live music. Best nightspot in Staré Město.

Jazz Dock Jazz
(774 058 838; www.jazzdock.cz; Janáčkovo nábřeží 2, Smíchov; admission 150Kč; 4pm-3am; M Anděl, 7, 9, 12, 14) Most of Prague's jazz clubs are smoky cellar affairs – this riverside club is a definite step up, with clean, modern decor and a decidedly romantic view out over the Vltava. It draws some of the best local talent and occasional international acts. Go early or book to get a good table. Shows normally begin at 7pm and 10pm.

Information

The major banks are best for changing cash, but using a debit card in an ATM gives a better rate of exchange. Avoid *směnárna* (private exchange booths), which advertise misleading rates and have exorbitant charges.

Na Homolce Hospital **(257 271 111; www.homolka.cz; 5th fl, Foreign Pavilion, Roentgenova 2, Motol; 167, 168 to Nemocnice Na Homolce)** The best hospital in Prague, equipped and staffed to Western standards, with staff who speak English, French, German and Spanish.

Prague City Tourism – Old Town Hall **(Prague Welcome; Map p656; 221 714 444; www.prague.eu; Old Town Hall, Staroměstské náměstí 5; 9am-7pm; M Staroměstská)** The busiest of the Prague City Tourism branches occupies the ground floor of the Old Town Hall (enter to the left of the Astronomical Clock).

National Theatre (p667), Prague, Czech Republic

Relax Café-Bar (☎224 211 521; www.relaxcafebar.cz; Dlážděná 4; per 10min 10Kč; ⏰8am-10pm Mon-Fri, 2-10pm Sat; 📶; Ⓜ Náměstí Republiky) A conveniently located internet cafe. Wi-fi is free.

Getting There & Away

Train

Prague is well integrated into European rail networks and if you're arriving from somewhere in Europe, chances are you're coming by train. **Czech Railways** provides efficient train services to almost every part of the country. For an online timetable, go to http://jizdnirady.idnes.cz or www.cd.cz.

Most trains arrive at **Praha hlavní nádraží**. The station is accessible by public transport on metro line C.

There is regular rail service from Prague to and from Germany, Poland, Slovakia and Austria. Trains to/from the south and east, including from Bratislava, Vienna and Budapest, also stop at Brno's main train station.

Getting Around

To/From the Airport

To get into town from the airport, buy a full-price public-transport ticket (32Kč) from the **Prague Public Transport Authority** (DPP; ☎296 191 817; www.dpp.cz; ⏰7am-9pm) desk in the arrivals hall and take bus 119 (20 minutes; every 10 minutes, 4am to midnight) to the end of metro line A (Dejvická), then continue by metro into the city centre (another 10 to 15 minutes; no new ticket needed).

If you're heading to the southwestern part of the city, take bus 100, which goes to the Zličín metro station (line B).

There's also an **Airport Express** bus (50Kč; ⏰5am-10pm) that runs to Praha hlavní nádraží (main train station), where you can connect to metro line C (buy ticket from driver, luggage goes free).

AAA Radio Taxi (p670) operates a 24-hour taxi service, charging from 500Kč to 650Kč depending on the destination, to get to the centre of Prague. You'll find taxi stands outside both arrivals terminals. Drivers usually speak some English and accept credit cards.

Public Transport

Prague's excellent public-transport system combines tram, metro and bus services. It's operated by the **Prague Public Transport Authority** (DPP), which has information desks at Prague airport (7am to 10pm) and in several metro stations, including Muzeum, Můstek, Anděl and Nádraží Holešovice. The metro operates daily from 5am to midnight.

Tickets valid on all metros, trams and buses are sold from machines at metro stations (coins only), as well as at DPP information offices and many news-stands and kiosks. Tickets can be

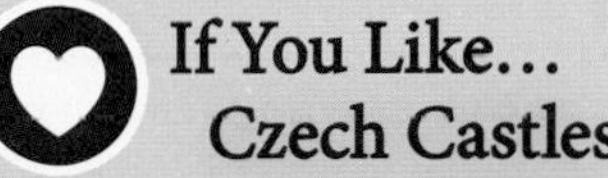

If You Like... Czech Castles

The magnificent castles in Prague and Český Krumlov draw the most visitors, but there are many more fortresses sprinkled across the Czech countryside.

1 KARLŠTEJN CASTLE
(Hrad Karlštejn; ☎tour booking 311 681 617; www.hradkarlstejn.cz; adult/child Tour 1 270/180Kč, Tour 2 300/200Kč, Tour 3 150/100Kč; ⏰9am-6.30pm Jul & Aug, 9.30am-5.30pm Tue-Sun May, Jun & Sep, to 5pm Apr, to 4.30pm Oct, to 4pm Mar, reduced hours Sat & Sun only Dec-Feb) Prague's most popular day trip is this medieval castle, 30km southwest of the capital and reachable by train. Karlštejn started life in 1348 as a hideaway for the crown jewels and treasury of the Holy Roman Emperor, Charles IV. After falling into disrepair over the centuries it was restored in the late 19th century. Visits are by guided tour only. Some tours must be reserved in advance by phone or via the castle website.

2 ŠPILBERK CASTLE
(Hrad Špilberk; ☎542 123 611; www.spilberk.cz; Špilberk 210/1; combined entry adult/concession 400/240Kč, casements only 90/50Kč, tower only 50/30Kč; ⏰9am-5pm Tue-Sun Oct-Apr, 9am-5pm daily May & Jun, 10am-6pm daily Jul-Sep; 🐾) Brno's spooky hilltop castle is considered the city's most important landmark. Its history stretches back to the 13th century, when it was home to Moravian margraves and later a fortress. Under the Habsburgs in the 18th and 19th centuries, it served as a prison. Today it's home to the **Brno City Museum**, with several temporary and permanent exhibitions.

purchased individually or as discounted day passes valid for one or three days.

A full-price individual ticket costs 32/16Kč per adult/senior aged 65 to 70 and is valid for 90 minutes of unlimited travel. For shorter journeys, buy short-term tickets that are valid for 30 minutes of unlimited travel. These cost 24/12Kč per adult/senior. One-day passes cost 110/55Kč per adult/senior; three-day passes cost 310Kč (no discount for seniors).

Taxi

Taxis are frequent and relatively inexpensive. The official rate for licensed cabs is 40Kč flagfall plus 28Kč per kilometre and 6Kč per minute while waiting. On this basis, any trip within the city centre – say, from Wenceslas Sq to Malá Strana – should cost around 170Kč. A trip to the suburbs, depending on the distance, should run from around 200Kč to 400Kč, and to the airport between 500Kč and 650Kč.

The following companies offer 24-hour service and English-speaking operators:

AAA Radio Taxi (☎14014, 222 333 222; www.aaataxi.cz)

City Taxi (☎257 257 257; www.citytaxi.cz)

Bohemia

The Czech Republic's western province boasts surprising variety. Český Krumlov, with its riverside setting and dramatic Renaissance castle, is in a class by itself. Big cities like Plzeň offer urban attractions like great museums and restaurants. The spa towns of western Bohemia, such as Karlovy Vary, were world famous in the 19th century and retain old-world lustre.

PLZEŇ

POP 173,000

Plzeň, the regional capital of western Bohemia and the second-biggest city in Bohemia after Prague, is best known as the home of the Pilsner Urquell brewery, but it has a handful of other interesting sights and enough good restaurants and night-time pursuits to justify an overnight stay. Most of the sights are located near the central square, but the brewery itself is about a 15-minute walk outside the centre.

Sights

Pilsner Urquell Brewery Brewery

(Prazdroj; ☎377 062 888; www.prazdrojvisit.cz; U Prazdroje 7; guided tour adult/child 190/100Kč; ⏰8.30am-6pm Apr-Sep, to 5pm Oct-Mar, English tours 12.45pm, 2.15pm & 4.15pm) Plzeň's most popular attraction is the tour of the Pilsner Urquell Brewery, in operation since 1842 and arguably home to the world's best beer. Entry is by guided tour only, with three tours in English available daily. Tour highlights include a trip to the old cellars (dress warmly) and a glass of unpasteurised nectar at the end.

Pilsner Urquell Brewery, Plzen, Czech Republic

Reservations are possible only for groups of 10 or more. Email the brewery to arrange.

Brewery Museum Museum

(☎377 224 955; www.prazdrojvisit.cz; Veleslavínova 6; guided tour adult/child 120/90Kč, English text 90/60Kč; ⌚10am-6pm Apr-Dec, to 5pm Jan-Mar) The Brewery Museum offers an insight into how beer was made (and drunk) in the days before Prazdroj was founded. Highlights include a mock-up of a 19th-century pub, a huge wooden beer tankard from Siberia and a collection of beer mats. All have English captions and there's a good English written guide available.

Underground Plzeň Tunnel

(Plzeňské historické podzemí; ☎377 235 574; www.plzenskepodzemi.cz; Veleslavínova 6; adult/child 100/70Kč; ⌚10am-6pm Apr-Dec, to 5pm Feb-Mar, closed Jan, English tour 1pm daily Apr-Oct) This extraordinary tour explores the passageways below the old city. The earliest were probably dug in the 14th century, perhaps for beer production or defence; the latest date from the 19th century. Of an estimated 11km that have been excavated, some 500m of tunnels are open to the public. Bring extra clothing (it's a chilly 10°C underground).

Techmania Science Centre Museum

(☎737 247 585; www.techmania.cz; cnr Borská & Břeňkova, Areál Škoda; adult/concession incl 3D planetarium 180/110Kč; ⌚8.30am-5pm Mon-Fri, 10am-6pm Sat & Sun; P 👪; 🚎15, 17) Kids will have a ball at this high-tech, interactive science centre, where they can play with infrared cameras, magnets and many other instructive and fun exhibitions. There's a 3D planetarium (included in the full-price admission) and a few full-sized historic trams and trains manufactured at the Škoda engineering works. Take the trolleybus; it's a hike from the city centre.

If You Like... Czech Architecture

Prague is justly famous for its architecture, but the crowds can take the shine off things. These little-visited towns are off the tourist radar, and make great places to experience the real Czech Republic.

1 OLOMOUC

Olomouc is a surprisingly majestic city, perhaps the most beautiful and authentic outside Prague. Around its stately streets you'll find an impressive castle, a Unesco-protected trinity column and one of the country's finest public squares. It's also famous for its cheese, *Olomoucký sýr,* reputedly the smelliest in the country. There are frequent trains from Prague and Brno.

2 TELČ

There are two reasons to visit Telč: its massive main square, lined by Renaissance and baroque burgers' houses, and its beautifully preserved Renaissance chateau, which can be visited on a guided tour. There's no train line, but around half-a-dozen buses run daily from Prague's Florenc bus station.

3 MIKULOV

In the heart of Moravian wine country, Mikulov is a wonderfully atmospheric town, surrounded by hills, adorned with an amazing hilltop Renaissance chateau and featuring a carefully restored Jewish Quarter. Little wonder that Czech poet Jan Skácel described it as a 'piece of Italy moved to Moravia by God's hand'. It's also an ideal base for sampling the local wines. Trains run to Brno and Bratislava.

Sleeping

Hotel Roudna Hotel €

(☎377 259 926; www.hotelroudna.cz; Na Roudné 13; s/d 1150/1400Kč; P @ 📶) Might very well be the city's best-value lodging. The exterior is not much to look at; but inside, rooms are well-proportioned, with high-end amenities such as flat screen TV,

Right: St Vitus Cathedral (p654), Prague, Czech Republic;
Below: Astronomical Clock (p658), Prague, Czech Republic

(RIGHT) NEIL FARRIN/GETTY IMAGES ©; (BELOW) JENIFOTO/GETTY IMAGES ©

minibar and desk. Breakfasts are fresh and ample. The reception is friendly. Note there's no lift. The hotel has an excellent steakhouse two doors down on the same street.

U Salzmannů Pension **€**

(377 235 476; www.usalzmannu.com; Pražská 8; s/d/ ste 1050/1450/2100Kč;) This pleasant pension, right in the heart of town, sits above a very good historic pub. The standard rooms are comfortable but basic; the more luxurious double 'suites' have antique beds and small sitting rooms, as well as kitchenettes. The pub location is convenient if you overdo it; to reach your bed, just climb the stairs.

Eating

Na Parkánu Czech **€**

(377 324 485; www.naparkanu.com; Veleslavínova 4; mains 100-200Kč; 11am-11pm Mon-Thu, to 1am Fri & Sat, to 10pm Sun;) Don't overlook this pleasant pub-restaurant, attached to the Brewery Museum. It may look a bit touristy, but the traditional Czech food is top rate, and the beer, naturally, could hardly be better. Try to snag a spot in the summer garden. Don't leave without trying the *nefiltrované pivo* (unfiltered beer). Reservations are an absolute must.

Aberdeen Angus Steakhouse Steak **€€**

(725 555 631; www.angussteakhouse.cz; Pražská 23; mains 180-400Kč; 11am-11pm;) For our money, this may be the best steakhouse in all of the Czech Republic. The meats hail from a nearby farm, where the livestock is raised organically. There are several cuts and sizes on offer; lunch options include a tantalising cheeseburger. The downstairs dining room is cosy; there's also a creekside terrace. Book in advance.

Information

City Information Centre (**Informační centrum města Plzně; ☎378 035 330; www.icpilsen.cz; náměstí Republiky 41; ⏰9am-7pm Apr-Sep, to 6pm Oct-Mar**) Plzeň's well-stocked and -staffed tourist information office is a first port of call for visitors. Can advise on sleeping and eating options, hands out free city maps, and has a wealth of brochures on what to see and do.

Getting There & Away

From Prague, eight trains (150Kč, 1½ hours) leave daily from the main station, *hlavní nádraží*. The train station is on the eastern side of town, 10 minutes' walk from nám Republiky, the Old Town Sq. From Prague, the bus service to Plzeň (100Kč, one hour) is frequent (hourly), relatively fast and inexpensive.

ČESKÝ KRUMLOV

POP 14,050

Outside of Prague, Český Krumlov is arguably the Czech Republic's only other world-class sight and must-see. From a distance, the town looks like any other in the Czech countryside, but once you get closer and see the Renaissance castle towering over the 17th-century townscape, you'll feel the appeal; this really is that fairy-tale town the tourist brochures promised. Český Krumlov is best as an overnight destination; it's too far for a comfortable day trip from Prague.

Sights

Castle Museum & Tower Museum, Tower

(**☎380 704 711; www.zamek-ceskykrumlov.eu; Zámek 59; combined entry adult/concession 130/60Kč, museum only 100/50Kč, tower only 50/30Kč; ⏰9am-6pm Jun-Aug, to 5pm Apr & May, to 5pm Tue-Sun Sep & Oct, to 4pm Tue-Sun Jan-Mar**) Located within the castle complex, this small museum and adjoining tower is an ideal option if you don't have the time or energy for a full castle tour. Through a series of rooms, the museum traces the castle's history from its origins through to the present day. Climb the tower for the perfect photo-op shots of the town below.

Don't Miss Český Krumlov State Castle

Český Krumlov's striking Renaissance castle, occupying a promontory high above the town, began life in the 13th century. It acquired its present appearance in the 16th to 18th centuries under the stewardship of the noble Rožmberk and Schwarzenberg families. The interiors are accessible by guided tour only, though you can stroll the grounds on your own.

Three main **tours** are offered: Tour 1 (one hour) takes in the opulent Renaissance rooms; Tour 2 (one hour) visits the Schwarzenberg portrait galleries and their 19th-century apartments. The Theatre Tour (40 minutes, 10am to 4pm Tuesday to Sunday May to October) explores the chateau's remarkable rococo theatre.

NEED TO KNOW

380 704 711; www.zamek-ceskykrumlov.eu; Zámek 59; adult/concession Tour 1 250/160Kč, Tour 2 240/140Kč, Theatre Tour 300/200Kč; 9am-6pm Tue-Sun Jun-Aug, to 5pm Apr, May, Sep & Oct

Egon Schiele Art Centrum — Museum

(380 704 011; www.schieleartcentrum.cz; Široká 71; adult/concession 120/70Kč; 10am-6pm Tue-Sun) This excellent private gallery houses a small retrospective of the controversial Viennese painter Egon Schiele (1890–1918), who lived in Krumlov in 1911, and raised the ire of townsfolk by hiring young girls as nude models. For this and other sins he was eventually driven out. The centre also houses interesting temporary exhibitions.

Museum Fotoateliér Seidel — Museum

(380 712 354; www.seidel.cz; Linecká 272; adult/concession 100/70Kč; 9am-noon & 1-5pm daily Apr & Oct-Dec, Tue-Sun Jan-Mar, 9am-noon & 1-6pm daily May-Sep) This photography museum presents a mov-

ing retrospective of the work of local photographers Josef Seidel and his son František. Especially poignant are the images recording early-20th-century life in nearby villages. In the high season you should be able to join an English-language tour; if not, let the pictures tell the story.

 Sleeping

Krumlov House Hostel €

(☎380 711 935; www.krumlovhostel.com; Rooseveltova 68; dm/d/tr 300/1000/1350Kč;) Perched above the river, Krumlov House is friendly and comfortable, and has plenty of books, DVDs and local information to feed your inner wanderer. Accommodation is in six-bed en suite dorms as well as private double and triple rooms or private, self-catered apartments. The owners are English-speaking and traveller friendly.

U Malého Vítka Hotel €€

(☎380 711 925; www.vitekhotel.cz; Radničnì 27; s/d 1200/1500Kč;) We like this small hotel in the heart of the Old Town. The simple room furnishings are of high-quality, hand-crafted wood, and each room is named after a traditional Czech fairy-tale character. The downstairs restaurant and cafe are very good too.

Hotel Konvice Hotel €€

(☎380 711 611; www.boehmer-waldhotels.de; Horní 144; s/d 1300/2000Kč;) Attractive old-fashioned hotel with romantic rooms and period furnishings. Many rooms, such as No 12, have impressive wood-beamed ceilings, and all have homey architectural quirks that lend atmosphere.

The service is reserved but friendly. The cook at breakfast is more than happy to whip up an egg on request (to go with the usual cold cuts and cheeses).

 Eating

Nonna Gina Italian €

(☎380 717 187; Klášteriní 52; pizzas 100-170Kč; 11am-10pm) Authentic Italian flavours from the Italian Massaro family feature in this pizzeria down a quiet lane. Grab an outdoor table and pretend you're in Naples. In winter the upstairs dining room is snug and intimate.

Hospoda Na Louži Czech €

(☎380 711 280; www.nalouzi.cz; Kájovská 66; mains 90-170Kč) Nothing's changed in this wood-panelled *pivo* (beer) parlour for almost a century. Locals and tourists pack Na Louži for huge plates of Czech staples such as chicken schnitzels or roast pork and dumplings, as well as dark (and light) beer from the Eggenberg brewery. Get the fruit dumplings for dessert if you see them on the menu.

Old Town Square (p655), Prague, Czech Republic

Krčma v Šatlavské Czech **€€**
(☎380 713 344; www.satlava.cz; Horní 157; mains 180-280Kč; ⌚11am-midnight) This medieval barbecue cellar is hugely popular with visitors, and your tablemates are much more likely to be from Austria or Asia than from the town itself, but the grilled meats served up with gusto in a funky labyrinth illuminated by candles are excellent and perfectly in character with Český Krumlov. Advance booking is essential.

Information

Infocentrum (☎380 704 622; www.ckrumlov.info; náměstí Svornosti 2; ⌚9am-7pm Jun-Aug, to 6pm Apr, May, Sep & Oct, to 5pm Nov-Mar) One of the country's best tourist offices. Good source for transport and accommodation info, maps, internet access (per five minutes 5Kč) and audio guides (per hour 100Kč). A guide for disabled visitors is available.

Getting There & Away

Buses are quicker and cheaper than trains. From Prague, **Student Agency** (☎841 101 101; www.studentagency.cz) coaches (195Kč, three hours) leave regularly from the Na Knížecí bus station at Anděl metro station (Line B).

From Prague (260Kč, 3½ hours), the train journey requires a change in České Budějovice.

SURVIVAL GUIDE

Directory A–Z

Accommodation

Austria

From simple mountain huts to five-star hotels fit for kings – you'll find the lot in Austria. Tourist offices invariably keep lists and details, and some arrange bookings for free or for a nominal fee. Some useful points:

- Book ahead for the high seasons: July and August and December to April (in ski resorts).

Left: Tyrol (p626), Austria;
Below: Cable car, Mt Pilatus (p646), Switzerland

- Some hostels and some rock-bottom digs have an *Etagendusche* (communal shower).
- *Privatzimmer* (private rooms) are cheap (often about €50 per double).
- In mountain resorts, high-season prices can be up to double the prices charged in the low season (May to June and October to November).
- Some resorts issue a *Gästekarte* (guest card) when you stay overnight, offering discounts on things such as cable cars and admission.

Some useful websites include the following:

Austrian Hotelreservation (www.austrian-hotelreservation.at)

Austrian National Tourist Office (www.austria.info)

Austrian Youth Hostel Association (www.oejhv.or.at)

Bergfex (www.bergfex.com)

Camping in Österreich (www.campsite.at)

Österreichischer Alpenverein (ÖAV, Austrian Alpine Club; www.alpenverein.at).

The following price indicators are for a standard double with bathroom in the high season. Prices include breakfast unless otherwise stated.

€ less than €80

€€ €80 to €200

€€€ more than €200

Switzerland

From palatial palaces and castles to mountain refuges, nuclear bunkers, icy igloos or simple hay lofts, Switzerland sports traditional and creative accommodation in every price range.

- The prices may seem steep – even the most inexpensive places are pricey compared with other parts of Europe. The upside is that standards are usually quite high.
- In Switzerland, many budget hotels have cheaper rooms with shared toilet and shower facilities. From there the sky is truly the limit. Breakfast buffets can be extensive and tasty but are not always included in room rates.

Rates in cities and towns stay constant most of the year. In mountain resorts prices are seasonal (and can fall by 50% or more outside high season):

Low season Mid-September to mid-December, mid-April to mid-June.

Mid-season January to mid-February, mid-June to early July, September.

High season July to August, Christmas, mid-February to Easter.

The following price ranges refer to a double room with a private bathroom, except in hostels or where otherwise specified. Quoted rates are for the high season and don't include breakfast unless otherwise noted.

$ less than Sfr170

$$ Sfr170 to Sfr350

$$$ more than Sfr350

Czech Republic

- The Czech Republic has a wide variety of accommodation options, ranging from luxurious hotels to simple pensions and camping grounds. Prague, Brno and Český Krumlov all have decent backpacker-oriented hostels.
- In Prague, hotel rates peak in spring and autumn, as well as around the Christmas and Easter holidays. Midsummer is considered 'shoulder season' and rates are about 20% cheaper.
- The capital is a popular destination, so be sure to book well in advance.

In this chapter we've used the following general price indicators (double room in high season):

€ less than 1600Kč

€€ 1600Kč to 3700Kč

€€€ more than 3700Kč

Business Hours

Hours are given for the high season and tend to decrease in the low season.

Austria

Banks 8am to 3pm Monday to Friday, to 5.30pm Thursday

Clubs 10pm to late

Post offices 8am to noon & 2pm to 6pm Monday to Friday, 8am to noon Saturday

Pubs 6pm to 1am

Cafes 7.30am to 8pm; hours vary widely

Restaurants Noon to 3pm, 7 to 11pm

Shops 9am to 6.30pm Monday to Friday, 9am to 5pm Saturday

Supermarkets 9am to 8pm Monday to Saturday

Switzerland

Banks 8.30am to 4.30pm Monday to Friday

Offices 8am to noon and 2pm to 5pm Monday to Friday

Restaurants Noon to 2pm and 6pm to 10pm

Shops 9am to 7pm Monday to Friday (sometimes with a one- to two-hour break for lunch at noon in small towns), 9am to 6pm Saturday. In cities, there's often shopping until 9pm on Thursday or Friday. Sunday sees some souvenir shops and supermarkets at some train stations open.

Czech Republic

Banks 8.30am to 4.30pm Monday to Friday

Bars 11am to midnight or later

Museums & castles Usually closed Monday year-round

Restaurants 11am to 10pm

Shops 8.30am to 6pm Monday to Friday, 8.30am to noon Saturday

Food

Austria

The following price ranges refer to a two-course meal excluding drinks.

€ less than €15

€€ €15 to €30

€€€ more than €30

Switzerland

The following price ranges refer to the average cost of a main meal.

$ less than Sfr25

$$ Sfr25 to Sfr50

$$$ more than Sfr50

Czech Republic

The following price indicators apply for a main meal.

€ less than 200Kč

€€ 200Kč to 500Kč

€€€ more than 500Kč

Discount Cards

Austria

International Student Identity Cards (ISIC) and European Youth Card (Euro<26; check www.euro26.org for discounts) will get you discounts at most museums, galleries and theatres. Admission is generally a little higher than the price for children.

Czech Republic

Swiss Museum Pass (www.museumspass.ch; adult/family Sfr155/277) Regular or long-term visitors to Switzerland may want to buy this pass, which covers entry to 480 museums countrywide.

Visitors' Cards Many resorts and cities have a visitors' card (*Gästekarte*), which provides benefits such as reduced prices for museums, pools, public transit or cable cars, plus free local public transport. Cards are issued by your accommodation.

Money

Austria

- Austria's currency is the euro.
- Some *Bankomaten* (ATMs) are 24 hours. Most accept at the very least Maestro debit cards and Visa and MasterCard credit cards.
- An approximate 10% tip is expected in restaurants. Pay it directly to the server; don't leave it on the table.

Switzerland

- Swiss francs are divided into 100 centimes (rappen in German-speaking Switzerland). There are notes for 10, 20, 50, 100, 200 and 1000 francs, and coins for 5, 10, 20 and 50 centimes, as well as for one, two and five francs. Euros are accepted by many tourism businesses.
- Exchange money at large train stations.
- Tipping is not necessary, given that hotels, restaurants, bars and even some taxis are legally required to include a 15% service charge in bills. You can round up the bill after a meal for good service, as locals do.

Czech Republic

- The best places to exchange money are banks, or use your credit or debit card to withdraw money as needed from ATMs.
- Never exchange money on the street and avoid private exchange offices, especially in Prague, as they charge exorbitant commissions.
- Keep small change handy for use in public toilets and metro-ticket machines.

Charles Bridge (p661), Prague, Czech Republic

Public Holidays

Austria

New Year's Day (Neujahr) 1 January

Epiphany (Heilige Drei Könige) 6 January

Easter Monday (Ostermontag) March/April

Labour Day (Tag der Arbeit) 1 May

Whit Monday (Pfingstmontag) Sixth Monday after Easter

Ascension Day (Christi Himmelfahrt) Sixth Thursday after Easter

Corpus Christi (Fronleichnam) Second Thursday after Whitsunday

Assumption (Maria Himmelfahrt) 15 August

National Day (Nationalfeiertag) 26 October

All Saints' Day (Allerheiligen) 1 November

Immaculate Conception (Mariä Empfängnis) 8 December

Christmas Day (Christfest) 25 December

St Stephen's Day (Stephanitag) 26 December

Switzerland

New Year's Day 1 January

Easter March/April (Good Friday, Easter Sunday and Monday)

Ascension Day 40th day after Easter

Whit Sunday & Monday Seventh week after Easter

National Day 1 August

Christmas Day 25 December

St Stephen's Day 26 December

Czech Republic

New Year's Day 1 January

Easter Monday March/April

Labour Day 1 May

Liberation Day 8 May

SS Cyril and Methodius Day 5 July

Jan Hus Day 6 July

Czech Statehood Day 28 September

Republic Day 28 October

Freedom and Democracy Day 17 November

Christmas 24 to 26 December

Telephone

Austria

Austrian telephone numbers consist of an area code followed by the local number.

Country code ☎41

International access code ☎00

Mobiles The network works on GSM 1800 and is compatible with GSM 900 phones. Phone shops sell prepaid SIM cards for about €10.

Public telephones Phonecards in different denominations are sold at post offices and *Tabak* (tobacconist) shops. Call centres are widespread in cities, and many internet cafes are geared for Skype calls.

Czech Philharmonic Orchestra

Switzerland

Country code ☎41

International access code ☎00

Telephone numbers Numbers with the code ☎0800 are toll-free; those with ☎0848 are charged at the local rate. Numbers beginning with ☎156 or ☎157 are charged at the premium rate.

Mobiles Mobile-phone numbers start with the code ☎076, ☎078 or ☎079. SIM cards are widely available from train-station ticket counters, exchange bureaux and mobile telephone shops. Several providers offer the same good deal: €20 for a SIM card that comes with €20 credit.

Czech Republic

Country code ☎420

Telephone numbers All Czech phone numbers have nine digits; dial all nine for any call, local or long distance.

Mobiles Mobile-phone coverage (GSM 900/1800) is excellent. If you're from Europe, Australia or New Zealand, your own mobile phone should be compatible. Purchase a Czech SIM card from any mobile-phone shop for around 500Kč (including 300Kč of calling credit). Local mobile-phone numbers start with the following; ☎601–608 and ☎720–779.

Public telephones Buy phonecards for public telephones from post offices and news-stands from 100Kč.

Visas

Austria, Switzerland and the Czech Republic are all part of the EU's Schengen area, and citizens of most countries can spend up to 90 days in those countries in a six-month period without a visa. See p772 for more details.

Getting There & Away

Air

Austria

Among the low-cost airlines, Air Berlin flies to Graz, Innsbruck, Linz, Salzburg and Vienna, easyJet to Innsbruck, Salzburg and Vienna, and Ryanair to Linz, Salzburg and Bratislava (for Vienna).

Following are the key international airports in Austria:

Blue Danube Airport Linz (☎7221-6000; www.linz-airport.at; Flughafenstrasse 1, Hörsching) Austrian Airlines, Lufthansa, Ryanair and Air Berlin are the main airlines servicing the Blue Danube Airport, 13km southwest of the centre.

Innsbruck Airport (INN; ☎0512-22 525; www.innsbruck-airport.com; Fürstenweg 180) EasyJet flies to Innsbruck Airport, 4km west of the city centre.

Salzburg Airport (☎858 00; www.salzburg-airport.com; Innsbrucker Bundesstrasse 95) Salzburg airport, a 20-minute bus ride from the city centre, has regular scheduled flights to destinations all over Austria and Europe.

Vienna International Airport (VIE; ☎01-7007 22 233; www.viennaairport.com) Vienna International Airport has good connections worldwide. The airport is in Schwechat, 18km southeast of Vienna.

Switzerland

The main international airports:

Aéroport International de Genève (GVA; www.gva.ch) Geneva airport is 4km from the town centre.

Zürich Airport (ZRH; ☎043 816 22 11; www.zurich-airport.com) The airport is 9km north of the centre, with flights to most European capitals as well as some in Africa, Asia and North America.

Czech Republic

Nearly all international flights arrive at **Václav Havel Airport Prague** (Prague Ruzyně International Airport; ☎220 111 888; www.prg.aero; K Letišti 6, Ruzyně; 🛜; 🚌100, 119). Flights to and from destinations outside the EU's Schengen zone use the airport's Terminal 1, which has standard passport and customs checks. Flights within the Schengen zone use Terminal 2 and are treated as domestic flights.

The national carrier **Czech Airlines** (www.czechairlines.com) has a good safety record and is a member of the Skyteam airline alliance.

Land

Austria

Bus

Buses depart from Austria for as far afield as England, the Baltic countries, the Netherlands,

Right: Swiss chocolates;
Below: Mountain railway, near Interlaken (p646), Switzerland
(RIGHT) / BRUCE YUANYUE BI/GETTY IMAGES ©; (BELOW) GLENN VAN DER KNIJFF/GETTY IMAGES ©

Germany and Switzerland. But most significantly, they provide access to Eastern European cities small and large – from the likes of Sofia and Warsaw, to Banja Luka, Mostar and Sarajevo.

Services operated by **Eurolines (www.eurolines.at)** leave from Vienna and from several regional cities.

Car & Motorcycle

There are numerous entry points into Austria by road from Germany, the Czech Republic, Slovakia, Hungary, Slovenia, Italy and Switzerland. All border-crossing points are open 24 hours.

Standard European insurance and paperwork rules apply.

Train

Austria has excellent rail connections. The main services in and out of the country from the west normally pass through Bregenz, Innsbruck or Salzburg en route to Vienna. Trains to Eastern Europe leave from Vienna. Express services to Italy go via Innsbruck or Villach; trains to Slovenia are routed through Graz.

For online timetables and tickets, visit the website of Austrian National Railways, **ÖBB (Österreichische Bundesbahnen; Austrian National Railways; ☎24hr hotline 05 1717; www.oebb.at)**. SparSchiene (discounted tickets) are often available when you book online in advance and can cost as little as a third of the standard train fare.

Switzerland

Bus

Eurolines (www.eurolines.com) has buses with connections across Western Europe.

Train

Switzerland is a hub of train connections to the rest of the Continent. Zürich is the busiest international terminus, with service to all neighbouring countries. Destinations include Münich (four hours), and Vienna (eight hours), from where there are extensive onward connections to cities in Eastern Europe.

- Numerous TGV trains daily connect Paris to

Geneva (three hours), Lausanne (3¾ hours), Basel (three hours) and Zürich (four hours).

- Nearly all connections from Italy pass through Milan before branching off to Zürich, Lucerne, Bern or Lausanne.
- Most connections from Germany pass through Zürich or Basel.
- Swiss Federal Railways accepts internet bookings, but does not post tickets outside of Switzerland.

Czech Republic

The Czech Republic has border crossings with Germany, Poland, Slovakia and Austria. These are all EU member states within the Schengen zone, meaning there are no longer any passport or customs checks.

Bus

The main international terminal is **Florenc Bus Station** (**ÚAN Praha Florenc; ☎900 144 444; www.florenc.cz; Křižíkova 2110/2b, Karlín; ⏲4am-midnight, information counter 6am-10pm; 📶; Ⓜ Florenc**) in Prague.

Leading international bus carriers include **Student Agency** (**☎bus information 841 101 101, nonstop info line 800 100 300; www.studentagency.cz; ÚAN Praha Florenc, Křižíkova 2110/2b**), operating comfortable, full-service coaches to major Czech cities as well as 60 destinations around Europe, and **Eurolines** (**☎245 005 245; www.elines.cz; ÚAN Praha Florenc, Křižíkova 2110/2b; ⏲6.30am-10.30pm Mon-Fri, 6.30am-9pm Sat; 📶; Ⓜ Florenc**), linking Prague to cities around Europe. Buy tickets online or at Florenc bus station.

Train

The country's main international rail gateway is **Praha hlavní nádraží** (**Prague main train station; ☎840 112 113; www.cd.cz; Wilsonova 8, Nové Město; Ⓜ Hlavní nádraží**). The station is accessible by public transport on metro line C.

There is regular rail service from Prague to and from Germany, Poland, Slovakia and Austria. Trains to/from the south and east, including from Bratislava, Vienna and Budapest, also stop at Brno's main train station.

In Prague, buy train tickets at **ČD Centrum** (**☎840 112 113; www.cd.cz; Praha hlavní nádraží, Wilsonova 8; ⏲3am-midnight; Ⓜ Hlavní nádraží**), located on the lower (street) level of the station. You can purchase train tickets for both domestic (*vnitrostátní jízdenky*) and international (*mezínárodní jizdenky*) destinations, as well as books couchettes and sleeping cars. Credit cards are accepted.

An adjoining travel agency, **ČD Travel** (**972 241 861; www.cdtravel.cz; Praha hlavní nádraží, Wilsonova 8; 9am-6pm Mon-Fri, 9am-2pm Sat Apr-Sep, 9am-5pm Mon-Fri Oct-Mar; M Hlavní nádraží**), can help work out complicated international connections.

Both InterRail and Eurail passes are valid on the Czech rail network.

River

Hydrofoils run to Bratislava and Budapest from Vienna; slower boats cruise the Danube between the capital and Passau. One of the major operators is **DDSG Blue Danube** (**www.ddsg-blue-danube.at**).

Getting Around

Air

Austria

The national carrier **Austrian Airlines** (**www.austrian.com**) offers several flights daily between Vienna and Graz, Innsbruck, Klagenfurt, Linz and Salzburg.

Bicycle

Austria

- All cities have at least one bike shop that doubles as a rental centre; expect to pay around €10 to €15 per day.
- Most tourist boards have brochures on cycling facilities and plenty of designated cycling routes within their region.
- You can take bicycles on any train with a bicycle symbol at the top of its timetable. For regional and long-distance trains, you'll pay an extra 10% on your ticket price. It costs €12 to take your bike on international trains.

Switzerland

Rent-a-Bike (**www.rentabike.ch**) allows you to rent bikes at 80 train stations in Switzerland. For an Sfr8 surcharge you can collect from one station and return to another.

Suisseroule (**Schweizrollt; www.schweizrollt.ch**) lets you borrow a bike for free or cheaply in places like Geneva, Bern and Zürich. Bike stations are usually next to the train station or central square.

Local tourist offices often have good cycling information.

Mozarts Geburtshaus (p619), Salzburg, Austria

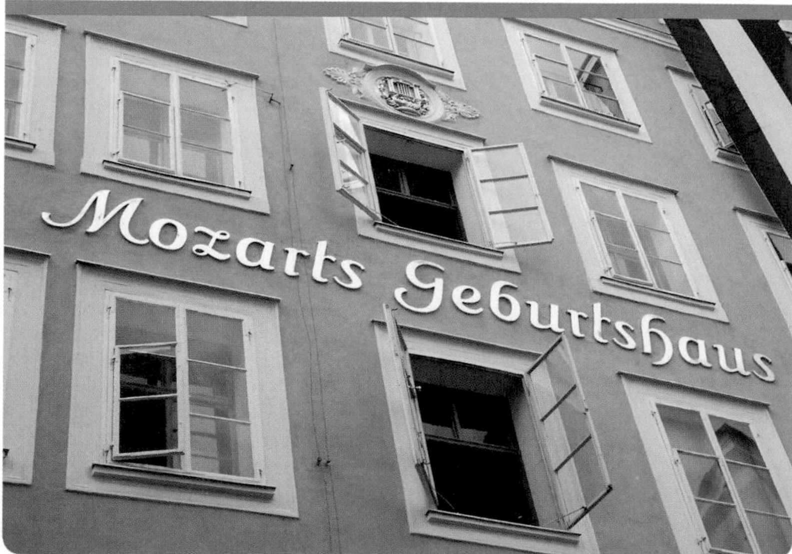

Boat

Austria

The Danube serves as a thoroughfare between Vienna and Lower and Upper Austria. Services are generally slow, scenic excursions rather than functional means of transport.

Switzerland

Ferries and steamers link towns and cities on many lakes, including Geneva, Lucerne, Lugano and Zürich.

Bus

Austria

Postbus (☎24hr 05 17 17; www.postbus.at) services usually depart from outside train stations. In remote regions, there are fewer services on Saturday and often none on Sunday. Generally, you can only buy tickets from the drivers.

Switzerland

- Yellow **post buses** (www.postbus.ch) supplement the rail network, linking towns to difficult-to-access mountain regions.
- Services are regular, and departures (usually next to train stations) linked to train schedules.
- Swiss national travel passes are valid.
- Purchase tickets on-board; some scenic routes over the Alps (eg the Lugano–St Moritz run) require advance reservations.

Czech Republic

- Buses are often faster, cheaper and more convenient than trains.
- Many bus routes have reduced frequency (or none) at weekends.
- Check bus timetables and prices at http://jizdnirady.idnes.cz.
- In Prague, many (though not all) buses arrive at and depart from the Florenc bus station. Be sure to double-check the correct station.
- Try to arrive at the station well ahead of departure to secure a seat. Buy tickets from the driver.

Car & Motorcycle

Austria

- A *Vignette* (toll sticker) is imposed on all motorways; charges for cars/motorbikes are €8.70/5 for 10 days and €25.30/12.70 for two months. *Vignettes* can be purchased at border crossings, petrol stations and Tabak shops. There are additional tolls (usually €2.50 to €10) for some mountain tunnels.
- Speed limits are 50km/h in built-up areas, 130km/h on motorways and 100km/h on other roads.
- Multinational car-hire firms Avis, Budget, Europcar and Hertz all have offices in majorcities. The minimum age for hiring small cars is 19 years, or 25 years for larger, 'prestige' cars. Customers must have held a driving licence for at least a year. Many contracts forbid customers to take cars outside Austria, particularly into Eastern Europe.
- Crash helmets are compulsory for motorcyclists.

Switzerland

- Headlights must be on at all times, and dipped in tunnels.
- The speed limit is 50km/h in towns, 80km/h on main roads outside towns, 100km/h on single-lane freeways and 120km/h on dual-lane freeways.
- Some minor Alpine passes are closed from November to May; check with the local tourist offices before setting off.

Czech Republic

- For breakdown assistance anywhere in the country, dial ☎1230.
- The minimum driving age is 18 and traffic moves on the right. Children under 12 are prohibited from sitting in the front seat.
- Drivers are required to keep their headlights on at all times. The legal blood-alcohol limit is zero.

Train

Austria

Austria has a clean, efficient rail system, and if you use a discount card it's very inexpensive.

Fares Fares quoted here are for 2nd-class tickets.

Information ÖBB (p682) is the main operator, supplemented with a handful of private lines. Tickets and timetables are available online.

RailJet It's worth seeking out RailJet train services connecting Vienna, Graz, Villach, Salzburg, Innsbruck, Linz and Klagenfurt, as they travel up to 200km/h.

Reservations In 2nd class within Austria this costs €3.50 for most express services; recommended for travel on weekends.

Travellers with disabilities Use the 24-hour ☎05-17 17 customer number for special travel assistance; do this at least 24 hours ahead of travel (48 hours ahead for international services). Staff at stations will help with boarding and alighting.

Depending on the amount of travelling you intend to do in Austria, rail passes can be a good deal. The following rail passes are available:

Eurail Austria Pass This handy pass is available to non-EU residents; prices start at €129 for three days' unlimited 2nd-class travel within one month. See the website at www.eurail.com for all options.

Interrail Passes are for European residents and include One Country Pass Austria (three/four/six/eight days €131/154/187/219). Youths under 26 receive substantial discounts. See www.interrail.eu for all options.

Vorteilscard Reduces fares by at least 45% and is valid for a year, but not on buses (adult/under 26 years/senior €99/19/2). Bring a photo and your passport or ID.

Switzerland

The Swiss rail network combines state-run and private operations. The **Swiss Federal Railway** (www.sbb.ch) is abbreviated to SBB in German, CFF in French and FFS in Italian.

- All major train stations are connected to each other by hourly departures, at least between 6am and midnight.
- Second-class seats are perfectly acceptable, but cars are often close to full. First-class carriages are more comfortable, spacious and have fewer passengers.
- Ticket vending machines accept most major credit cards from around the world.
- The SBB smartphone app is an excellent resource and can be used to store your tickets electronically.
- Check the SBB website for cheap Supersaver tickets on major routes.
- Most stations have 24-hour lockers (small/large locker Sfr6/9), usually accessible from 6am to midnight.
- Seat reservations (Sfr5) are advisable for

Left: Hallstatt (p624), Austria;
Below: Cable car near Solden, Tyrol (p626), Austria

longer journeys, particularly in the high season.

Convenient discount passes make the Swiss transport system even more appealing. On extensive travel within Switzerland the following national travel passes generally offer better savings than Eurail or InterRail passes:

Swiss Pass This entitles the holder to unlimited travel on almost every train, boat and bus service in the country, and on trams and buses in 41 towns, plus free entry to 400-odd museums. Reductions of 50% apply on funiculars, cable cars and private railways. Different passes are available, valid between four days (Sfr272) and one month (Sfr607).

Swiss Flexi Pass This pass allows you to nominate a certain number of days – from three (Sfr260) to six (Sfr414) days – during one month when you can enjoy unlimited travel.

Half-Fare Card As the name suggests, you pay only half the fare on trains with this card (Sfr120 for one month), plus you get some discounts on local-network buses, trams and cable cars.

Czech Republic

- Czech Railways provides efficient train services to almost every part of the country.
- For an online timetable, go to http://jizdnirady.idnes.cz or www.cd.cz.

Greece

Greece is an absolutely essential stop on any European trip, despite its well-publicised money troubles. The economy may be in a mess, but the elements that have always drawn people here are still very much in evidence: gorgeous beaches, paradisaical islands, great food and, of course, several thousand years' worth of ancient history.

Athens is the inevitable starting point, home to the nation's greatest Grecian monuments including the Acropolis and its landmark new museum. You'll find plenty of ancient history to explore further afield, from oracle's caves to abandoned amphitheatres. But the past is far from Greece's only selling point. Wanderers can island-hop to their hearts content, from Santorini to the faraway Aegean Islands, while gastronomes feast on ouzo and octopus, and beach addicts dive into the sapphire blue waters of the Mediterranean. There are many different sides to Greece – the hard part is deciding which one to experience first.

Ancient Delphi (p711)

Greece
MACEDONIA
Kavadarci
Prilep
Ohrid
Lake Ohrid
Ljubojno
Prespa Lakes
Florina
Edessa
Gianitsa
Kilkis
Sidirokastro
Drama
Seres
Strymnas (Truma)
E75
E79
E90
Thessaloniki
Naoussa
Kristalopigi
ALBANIA
Sazan Island
Kastoria
Ptolemaida
Veria
Alexandria
Kozani
Katerini
E90
Meteora
Mt Olympus (2917m)
E65
Ionian Sea
Corfu
Corfu Town (Kerkyra)
Paxies
Ioannina
E92
Meteora
Kalambaka
Tirnavos-x
Larisa
Igoumenitsa
Arahthos
Trikala
Volos
Alonnisos
E951
Karditsa
Arta
E75
Skiathos
Skopelos
Loutra Edipsou
Preveza
Lamia
E952
Strofylia
Lefkada
Lefkada
Agios Kostantinos
Kymi
Mytikas
Lefkada
Evia
Astakos
Ithaki
Agrinio
Aheloös
Mt Parnassos
E75
Halkida
Messolongi
Delphi
Kefallonia
Patra
Argostoli
ATHENS
E55
Kyllini
Corinth
Piraeus
Zakynthos
Amaliada
Lavrio
Zakynthos
Mycenae
Aegina
Pyrgos
Olympia
Epidaurus
Methana
Nafplio
Galatas
Ionian Sea
E65
Hydra
Spetses
Sparta
Kalamata
Geraki
Mystras
Pylos
Gythio
Monemvasia
Areopoli
Gefyra
Neapoli
Kythira
Antikythira
MEDITERRANEAN SEA
Kastelli
Hania
Paleohora
1 Acropolis
2 Acropolis Museum
3 Meteora
4 Knossos
5 Santorini

BULGARIA
Zlatograd
0
200 km
0
100 miles
N
İstanbul
Kavala
E90
Alexandroupolis
Keşan
Sea of Marmara
Kocaeli (İzmit)
Limenas
Thasos
The Dardanelles
Samothraki
Gallipoli Peninsula
Bursa
Gökçeada
Çanakkale
Myrina
Limnos
Bozcaada
Balıkesir
Edremit
TURKEY
Lesvos
Mytilini
Skyros
Manisa
Psara
Chios
İzmir
Chios
Çeşme
Aegean Sea
Karystos
Aydin
Büyük Menderes River
Denizli
Gavrio
Andros
Samos
Kea
Tinos
Ikaria
Kythnos
Renia
Mykonos
Syros
Mt Kythnos (113m)
Patmos
Bodrum Peninsula
Gökova (Akyaka)
Leros
Naxos
Paros
Kalymnos
Kos
Datça Peninsula
Bozburun Peninsula
Amorgos
Kos
Milos
Ios
Symi
Santorini (Thira)
Astypalea
Rhodes Town
Tilos
Anafi
Rhodes
5
Aegean Sea (Egë Denızı)
Lindos
Kattavia
Olymbos
Karpathos
Pigadia
Kassos
Rethymno
Iraklio
MEDITERRANEAN SEA
Crete
4
Sitia
Agios Nikolaos
Hora Sfakion

Greece Highlights

Acropolis

The Acropolis (p700) is a masterpiece of classical architecture and an absolutely essential item on any Athens itinerary. The complex was largely developed during the rule of Pericles, and even experiencing its part-ruined state will transport you back into the glory of Greece from long ago. Below: Parthenon

1

2 Acropolis Museum

It may have taken over three decades to bring to fruition, but Athens has finally got the archaeological museum (p698) it's always deserved. Prominently positioned in the shadow of the Acropolis, the museum has been specially designed to house the nation's greatest ancient treasures and provide fascinating historical context to the real-life ruins themselves.

Meteora

3

The dramatic rock pinnacles at Meteora (p713) grace many a Grecian postcard, but nothing compares to seeing them for yourself. Inhabited by monks since the 11th century, these rocky spires are still home to a string of peaceful monasteries, best seen in the light of the setting sun. You can travel between them by road, but hiking the ancient paths provides a much more authentic pilgrimage. Right: Agias Triados monastery

4

Knossos

The capital of Minoan Crete, Knossos (p725) is another essential attraction for aficionados of ancient history. According to legend, the city was once the site of the infamous Labyrinth inhabited by the beastly half-man, half-bull known as the Minotaur. Whatever the truth of the story, it's still a stunning sight – but you'll need to get there early to avoid the crowds. Above: Palace of Knossos

5

Santorini

With its ancient ruins, seaside ports and rugged hillsides, Greece is irresistibly photogenic – but nowhere quite compares to Santorini (p719) in the scenery stakes. This idyllic island overlooks a glittering caldera formed by a prehistoric volcanic explosion, and its clifftop churches, stark white buildings and azure waters are a photographer's dream come true. Above: Oia (p720), Santorini

Greece's Best...

Ancient Sites

- **Parthenon, Athens** (p701) The mother of all Doric structures, completed in 438 BC.
- **Temple of Olympian Zeus, Ancient Olympia** (p699). The spiritual home of the Olympic Games.
- **Temple of Athena, Delphi** (p711) Where ancient Greeks once consulted the Oracle.
- **Knossos, Crete** (p725) The legendary lair of the Minotaur was rediscovered in 1900.
- **Mycenae** (p709) This ancient cityscape is a must for archaeology buffs.

Old-World Towns

- **Athens Old Town** (p698) Plaka and Monastiraki are brimming with antiquated atmosphere.
- **Nafplio, Peloponnese** (p714) Elegant houses and seaside mansions; Nafplio is made for wandering.
- **Rhodes Town** (p729) Protected by massive 12m-thick walls, this is a medieval gem.
- **Corfu Town** (p732) A tangle of winding alleyways and hidden plazas, overlooked by fortresses.
- **Hania** (p724) Crete's most picturesque town is a photographer's dream.

Island Getaways

- **Naxos** (p717) Sparkling beaches and marbled hills make for one of the loveliest islands of the Cyclades.
- **Rhodes** (p729) Stroll the fantastic old-town then go beach-hopping.
- **Santorini** (p719) Fall for the cliffside houses and azure waters of this vivid, volcanic island.
- **Mykonos** (p715) Bronze with the fabulous people and then party the night away.
- **Corfu** (p732) Dine on Venetian-inspired cuisine and explore cypress-lined coves.

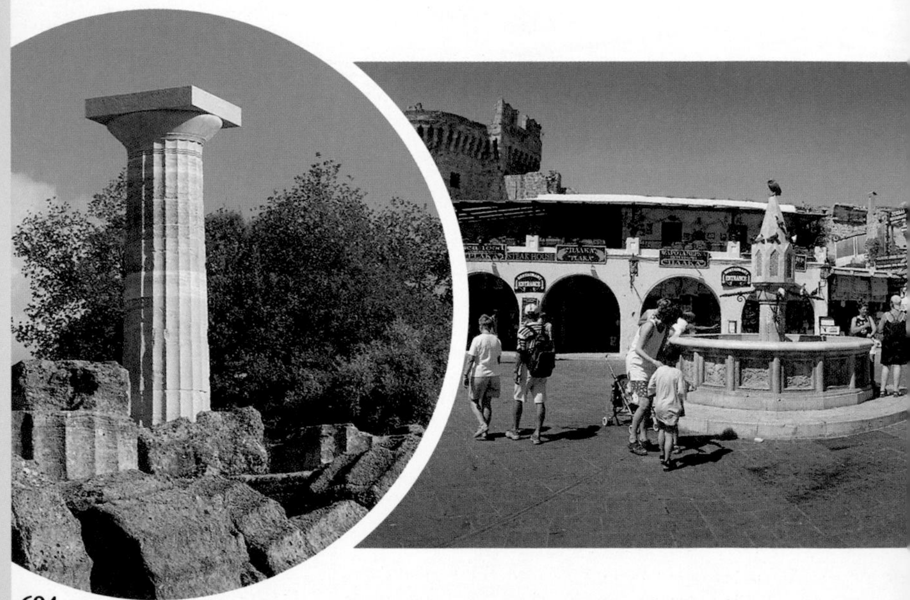

Geological Sights

- **Santorini's black beaches** (p719) Santorini's ink-black sand is a reminder of the island's volcanic origins.
- **Samaria Gorge** (p728) Hike through this spectacular canyon on the island of Crete.
- **Mt Olympus** (p709) The home of the gods, and now a hikers' paradise.
- **Meteora's pinnacles** (p713) A strange formation of rock spires, now topped by medieval monasteries.

Left: Temple of Olympian Zeus (p699), Ancient Olympia; **Above:** Old Town, Rhodes, (p729)

Need to Know

ADVANCE PLANNING

- **As far as possible ahead** Book popular ferry routes, especially in high summer.
- **At least a month ahead** Top hotels are generally booked out in the high season, so reserve as early as you can.
- **When you arrive** The €12 Acropolis ticket covers entry to several other Athens ancient sites.

RESOURCES

- **Greek National Tourist Organisation** (www.visitgreece.gr, www.discovergreece.com) Known as EOT within Greece.
- **Ministry of Culture** (www.culture.gr) Crammed with cultural information.
- **Ancient Greece** (www.ancientgreece.com) Handy online guide to the ancient world.
- **Greek Ferries** (www.openseas.gr) Essential resource for island-hoppers.

GETTING AROUND

- **Boat** Nearly every island has a boat service, but timetables are notoriously erratic – sailings can be cancelled at short notice due to bad weather.
- **Bus** Often the only option for reaching smaller towns and villages.
- **Car** Allows for maximum freedom, but Greece's roads require nerves of steel. Scooters are a good option on many islands.
- **Train** Greece's train network is limited to two main lines (connecting Athens with the Peloponnese and northern Greece), plus a few small branch lines.

BE FOREWARNED

- **Theft** Watch out for pickpockets in crowded spots, especially in big cities such as Athens, at markets and in popular tourist areas. Never leave your belongings unattended on the beach.
- **Toilets** Public toilets in Greece are rare, and many can't handle toilet paper!
- **Driving** Take extra care – Greece has the highest road-fatality rate in Europe.
- **Ferries** Sailings are extremely weather dependent, so it pays to be flexible with your travel plans.

Greece Itineraries

With its mystic temples and magnificent ruins, travelling through Greece often feels like a journey through time. This wonderful country allows your imagination to truly wander.

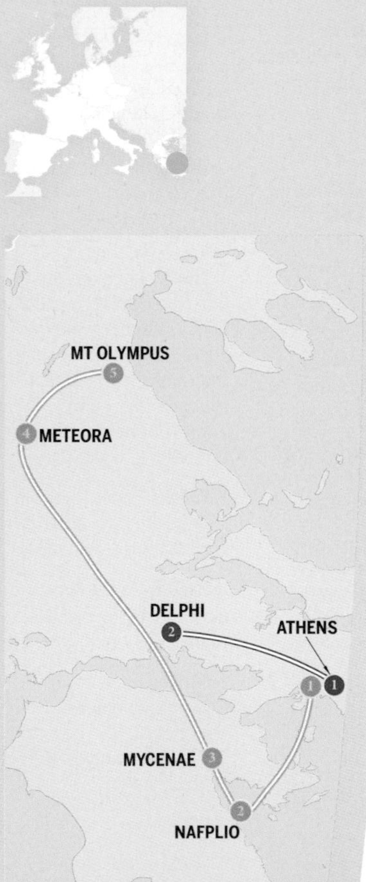

ANCIENT WONDERS

Athens to Delphi

For an introduction to the world of ancient Greece, nowhere compares with ❶**Athens** (p698). Magnificent monuments are scattered across the city, but for the historical background it's sensible to start at the Acropolis Museum, which brings together the surviving art treasures unearthed at the nearby Acropolis. In the afternoon, hike up to the Parthenon and Ancient Agora, and spend the evening exploring some of Athens' atmospheric tavernas. Spend the following day seeing the rest of Athens, including the National Archaeological and Benaki Museums, and finish with a visit to the Temple of Olympian Zeus and the Panathenaic Stadium.

On day three, take a trip north to ❷**Delphi** (p711) and feel the potent spirit on the slopes of Mt Parnassos. The ancient Greeks considered this the centre of the world. You can follow in the pilgrims' footsteps along the Sacred Way, which leads uphill to the Temple of Apollo. Nearby is another impressive ruin, the 20-column Sanctuary of Athena.

Top Left: Statues at Ancient Agora (p699), Athens; **Top Right:** Climbing stairs to a monastery at Meteora (p713)

MANSIONS & MONASTERIES

Athens to Thessaloniki

With five days at your disposal, you can venture out from ❶ **Athens** (p698) on some fantastic day trips. A couple of hours west is ❷ **Nafplio** (p714) and its smart hillside mansions tumbling down towards the sparkling Mediterranean. The best views are from the Venetian Palamidi Fortress, which dates back to the early 18th century.

An hour from Nafplio is another unmissable relic of the ancient world, the ruined city of ❸ **Mycenae** (p709), once one of the most powerful in ancient Greece. Try to imagine the sights and sounds that would have greeted you as you walk through the monumental Lion's Gate, the city's main entrance, and one of the largest surviving ancient sculptures in Greece.

On day three make a pilgrimage to the bewitchingly beautiful rock-top monasteries of ❹ **Meteora** (p713). Take a bus up to the summit and work your way back down or walk the ancient paths; you can usually visit at least four of the religious communities in a day.

Spend the last couple of days exploring the sacred home of the gods, ❺ **Mt Olympus** (p709), which is criss-crossed by stunning hiking trails, or head back to Athens and make a quick jaunt out to one of Greece's marvelous islands.

Discover Greece

At a Glance

Museum of the Ancient Agora, Athens

DENNIS K. JOHNSON/GETTY IMAGES ©

ATHENS ΑΘΗΝΑ

POP 3.8 MILLION

Ancient and modern, with equal measures of grunge and grace, bustling Athens is a heady mix of history and edginess. Iconic monuments mingle with first-rate museums, lively cafes and alfresco dining, and it's downright fun. With Greece's financial difficulties Athens has revealed its more restive aspect, but take the time to look beneath the surface and you'll discover a complex metropolis full of vibrant subcultures.

History

Athens' golden age, the pinnacle of the classical era under Pericles (r 461–429 BC), came after the Persian Empire was repulsed at the battles of Salamis and Plataea (480–479 BC). The city has passed through many hands and cast off myriad invaders, from Sparta to Philip II of Macedon, the Roman and Byzantine Empires, and, most recently, the Ottoman Empire. In 1834 Athens superseded Nafplio as the capital of independent Greece.

Sights

Due to the financial difficulties in Greece, which became acute starting in 2010, opening hours, prices and even the existence of some establishments have fluctuated much more than usual.

Acropolis Museum Museum

(☎210 900 0901; www.theacropolismuseum.gr; Dionysiou Areopagitou 15, Makrygianni; adult/child €5/free; ⏰8am-4pm Mon, to 8pm Tue-Sun, to

10pm Fri Apr-Oct, 9am-5pm Mon-Thu, to 10pm Fri, 9am-8pm Sat & Sun Nov-Mar; M Akropoli) The long-awaited Acropolis Museum opened with much fanfare in 2009 in the southern foothills of the Acropolis. Ten times larger than the former on-site museum, the imposing modernist building brings together the surviving treasures of the Acropolis, including items formerly held in other museums or storage, as well as pieces returned from foreign museums. The restaurant has superb views (and is surprisingly good value) and there's a fine museum shop.

Ancient Agora — Historic Site

(☎210 321 0185; http://odysseus.culture.gr; Adrianou; adult/child €4/free, free with Acropolis pass; ⏰11am-3pm Mon, from 8am Tue-Sun; M Monastiraki) The heart of ancient Athens was the Agora, the lively, crowded focal point of administrative, commercial, political and social activity. Socrates expounded his philosophy here, and in AD 49 St Paul came here to win converts to Christianity. The site today is a lush, refreshing respite with beautiful monuments and temples, and a fascinating museum.

Roman Agora & Tower of the Winds — Ruin

(☎210 324 5220; cnr Pelopida & Eolou, Monastiraki; adult/child €2/1, free with Acropolis pass; ⏰8am-3pm; M Monastiraki) The entrance to the Roman Agora is through the well-preserved **Gate of Athena Archegetis**, which is flanked by four Doric columns. It was erected sometime during the 1st century AD and financed by Julius Caesar. The well-preserved, extraordinary **Tower of the Winds** was built in the 1st century BC by a Syrian astronomer named Andronicus.

National Archaeological Museum — Museum

(☎210 821 7717; www.namuseum.gr; 28 Oktovriou-Patision 44, Exarhia; adult/concession €7/3; ⏰1-8pm Mon, 8am-8pm Tue-Sat, 8am-3pm Sun Apr-Oct, 1-8pm Mon, 9am-4pm Tue-Sun Nov-Mar; M Viktoria, 🚎2, 4, 5, 9 or 11 Polytechnio stop) One of the world's most important museums, the National Archaeological Museum houses the world's finest collection of Greek antiquities. Treasures offering a view of Greek art and history, dating from the Neolithic era to classical periods, include exquisite sculptures, pottery, jewellery, frescoes and artefacts found throughout Greece. The exhibits are displayed largely thematically and are beautifully presented.

Athens Discounts

The €12 ticket at the Acropolis (valid for four days) includes entry to the other significant ancient sites: Ancient Agora, Roman Agora, Keramikos, Temple of Olympian Zeus and the Theatre of Dionysos.

Enter the sites free on the first Sunday of the month from November to March, and on certain holidays. Anyone aged under 18 years or with an EU student card gets in free.

Temple of Olympian Zeus — Ruin

(☎210 922 6330; adult/child €2/free, free with Acropolis pass; ⏰8am-8pm Apr-Oct, 8.30am-3pm Nov-Mar; M Syntagma, Akropoli) You can't miss this striking marvel, smack in the centre of Athens. It is the largest temple in Greece and was begun in the 6th century BC by Peisistratos, but was abandoned for lack of funds. Various other leaders had stabs at completing it, but it was left to Hadrian to complete the work in AD 131. In total, it took more than 700 years to build.

Benaki Museum — Museum

(☎210 367 1000; www.benaki.gr; Koumbari 1, cnr Leoforos Vasilissis Sofias, Kolonaki; adult/child €7/free, free Thu; ⏰9am-5pm Wed & Fri, to midnight Thu & Sat, to 3pm Sun; M Syntagma, Evangelismos) Greece's finest private museum contains the vast collection of Antonis Benakis, accumulated during 35 years of avid collecting in Europe and Asia. The collection includes Bronze Age finds from Mycenae and Thessaly;

(Continued on page 706)

Don't Miss
Acropolis

No monument encapsulates the glory and mystery of the ancient world better than the Acropolis, which stands on the top of a hill high above Athens and is visible right across the city. For many scholars, it's the most important ancient monument in the Western world.

210 321 0219

http://odysseus.culture.gr

adult/concession/child €12/6/free

8am-8pm Apr-Oct, to 5pm Nov-Mar

M Akropoli

History

People lived on the Acropolis until the late 6th century BC, but in 510 BC the Delphic oracle declared that the Acropolis should be the province of the gods. When all the buildings were reduced to ashes by the Persians on the eve of the Battle of Salamis (480 BC), Pericles set about rebuilding a city purely of temples. The present-day Acropolis is what remains of this great project; although much has been lost, it still offers a wonderfully atmospheric glimpse into the world of the ancient Greeks.

Parthenon

The Parthenon epitomises the glory of ancient Greece. Completed in 438 BC, it's unsurpassed in grace and harmony. To achieve the appearance of perfect form, columns become narrower towards the top and the bases curve upward slightly towards the ends – effects that make them look straight when viewed from below. It's a demonstration of the truly remarkable understanding the ancient Greeks had of the fundamental rules of geometry, and how they could be applied in the real world.

Theatre of Dionysos

On the southern slope of the Acropolis, the importance of theatre in the everyday lives of ancient Athenians is made manifest in the enormous Theatre of Dionysos. Built between 340 and 330 BC on the site of an earlier theatre dating to the 6th century BC, it held 17,000 people.

Local Knowledge

Acropolis

RECOMMENDATIONS FROM CATHERINE TRIANTIS, PROFESSIONAL TOURIST GUIDE

1 PARTHENON

This is the crowning achievement of Greek architecture. Walk around the temple to get a feel for its geometry. Stop at the northeastern corner to see the curves of the building. By looking at the eastern steps, you can see them gradually ascend and then descend, forming a curve.

2 THE ERECHTHEION

Have a look at each side of this ornate and architecturally unique temple, characterised by elegance, grace and elaborate decoration. The most interesting side is the porch of the caryatids with six female Korae statues. Although the statues are copies, the artists' craftsmanship is evident in the transparency of the clothing and unique hairstyles.

3 VIEWS OF ATHENS

The Acropolis offers an aerial view of the city. To the north you'll see Plaka and the Ancient Agora; to the east, the Temple of Olympian Zeus, Hadrian's Arch and the National Gardens; to the south, the new Acropolis Museum and Filopappou Hill; and to the west, the Athenian Observatory.

4 THE MONUMENT'S PAST

Built to protect the Acropolis after the Persian Wars in 479 BC, the massive northern fortification walls were made from columns taken from the sites of earlier temples. Look closely to spot hints of colour on these columns – almost everything was rendered with colour in the past.

5 TEMPLE OF ATHENA NIKE

An absolute jewel, this temple was dedicated to the victory goddess, Athena Nike, and contained a wingless statue of her to keep her from flying away from Athens and therefore keeping the city victorious.

The Acropolis

Cast your imagination back in time, two and a half millennia ago, and envision the majesty of the Acropolis. Its famed and hallowed monument, the Parthenon, dedicated to the goddess Athena, stood proudly over a small city, dwarfing the population with its graceful grandeur. In the Acropolis' heyday in the 5th century BC, pilgrims and priests worshipped at the temples illustrated here (most of which still stand in varying states of restoration). Many were painted brilliant colours and were abundantly adorned with sculptural masterpieces crafted from ivory, gold and semiprecious stones.

As you enter the site today, elevated on the right, perches one of the Acropolis' best-restored buildings: the diminutive **Temple of Athena Nike** ❶. Follow the Panathenaic Way through the Propylaia and up the slope toward the Parthenon – icon of the Western world. Its **majestic columns** ❷ sweep up to some of what were the finest carvings of their time: wraparound **pediments, metopes and a frieze** ❸. Stroll around the temple's exterior and take in the spectacular views over Athens and Piraeus below.

As you circle back to the centre of the site, you will encounter those renowned lovely ladies, the **Caryatids** ❹ of the Erechtheion. On the Erechtheion's northern face, the oft-forgotten **Temple of Poseidon** ❺ sits alongside ingenious **Themistocles' Wall** ❻. Wander to the Erechtheion's western side to find Athena's gift to the city: **the olive tree** ❼.

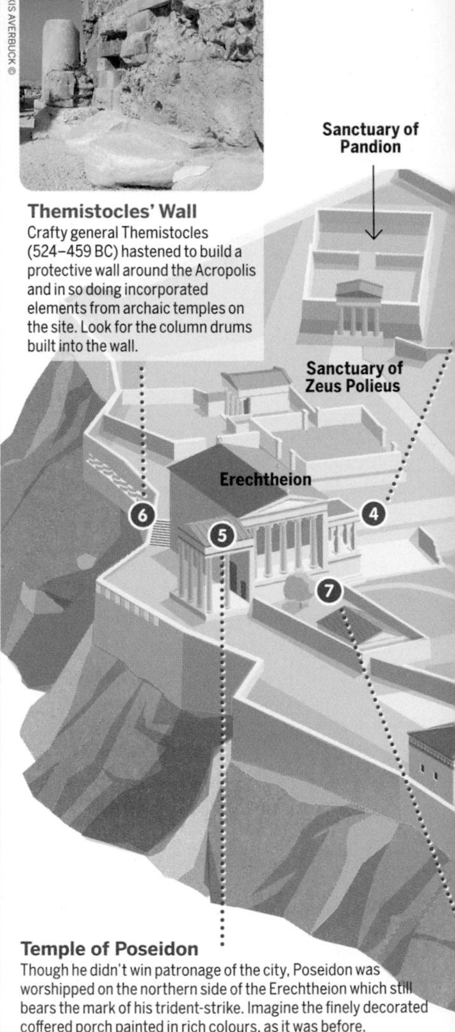

Themistocles' Wall
Crafty general Themistocles (524–459 BC) hastened to build a protective wall around the Acropolis and in so doing incorporated elements from archaic temples on the site. Look for the column drums built into the wall.

Temple of Poseidon
Though he didn't win patronage of the city, Poseidon was worshipped on the northern side of the Erechtheion which still bears the mark of his trident-strike. Imagine the finely decorated coffered porch painted in rich colours, as it was before.

TOP TIP

» **The Acropolis** is a must-see for every visitor to Athens. Avoid the crowds by arriving first thing in the morning or late in the day.

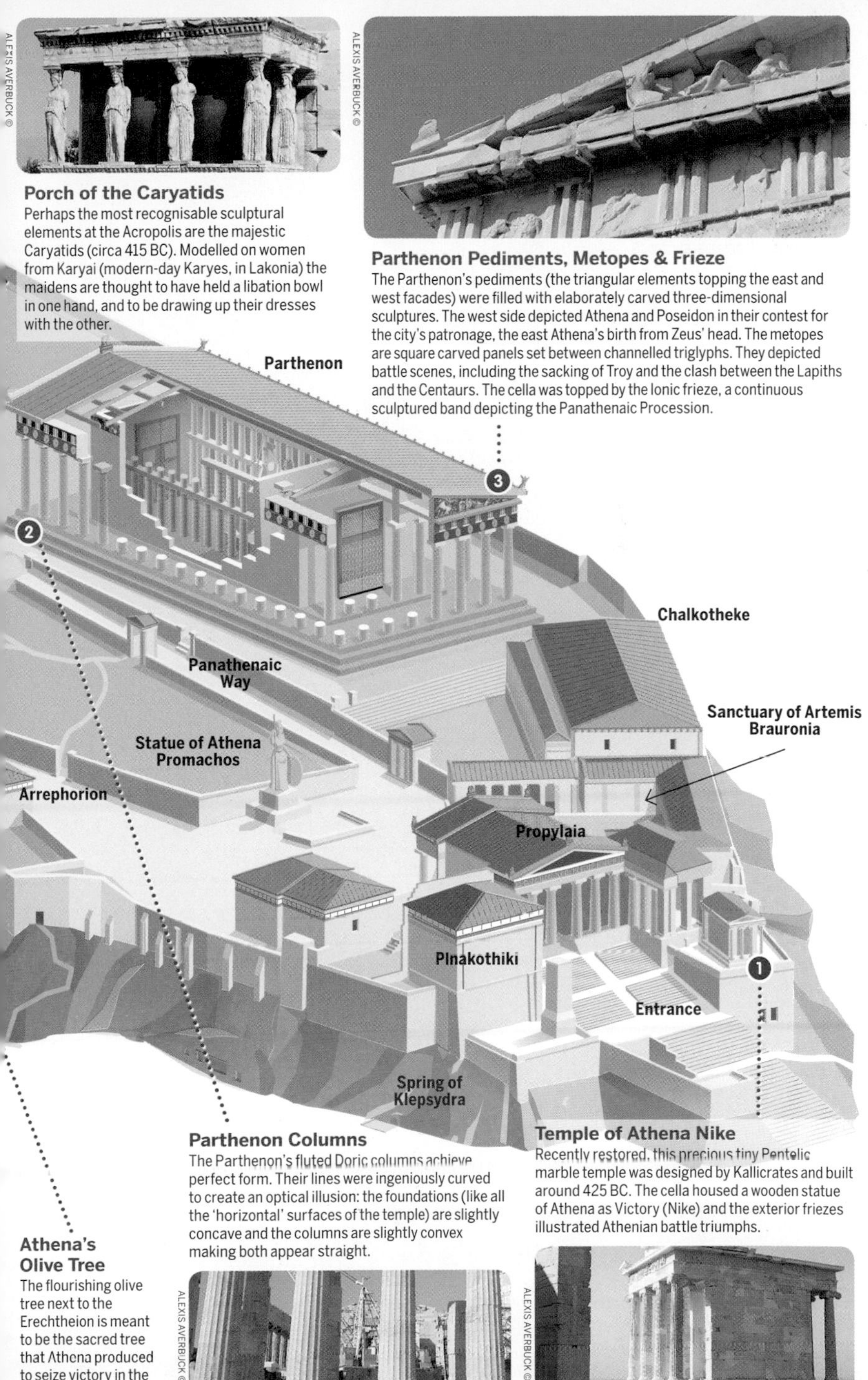

Porch of the Caryatids
Perhaps the most recognisable sculptural elements at the Acropolis are the majestic Caryatids (circa 415 BC). Modelled on women from Karyai (modern-day Karyes, in Lakonia) the maidens are thought to have held a libation bowl in one hand, and to be drawing up their dresses with the other.

Parthenon Pediments, Metopes & Frieze
The Parthenon's pediments (the triangular elements topping the east and west facades) were filled with elaborately carved three-dimensional sculptures. The west side depicted Athena and Poseidon in their contest for the city's patronage, the east Athena's birth from Zeus' head. The metopes are square carved panels set between channelled triglyphs. They depicted battle scenes, including the sacking of Troy and the clash between the Lapiths and the Centaurs. The cella was topped by the Ionic frieze, a continuous sculptured band depicting the Panathenaic Procession.

Parthenon Columns
The Parthenon's fluted Doric columns achieve perfect form. Their lines were ingeniously curved to create an optical illusion: the foundations (like all the 'horizontal' surfaces of the temple) are slightly concave and the columns are slightly convex making both appear straight.

Temple of Athena Nike
Recently restored, this precious tiny Pentelic marble temple was designed by Kallicrates and built around 425 BC. The cella housed a wooden statue of Athena as Victory (Nike) and the exterior friezes illustrated Athenian battle triumphs.

Athena's Olive Tree
The flourishing olive tree next to the Erechtheion is meant to be the sacred tree that Athena produced to seize victory in the contest for Athens.

Central Athens

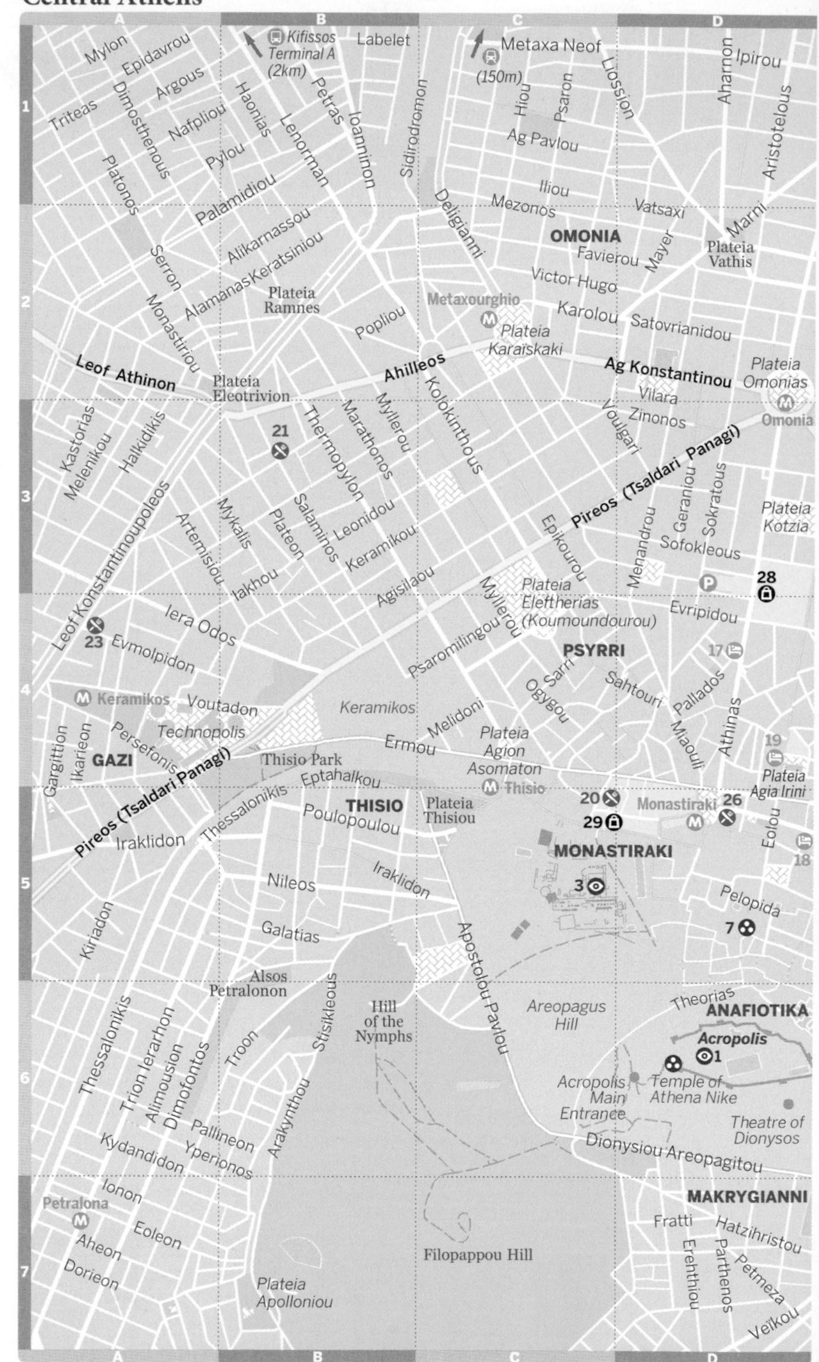

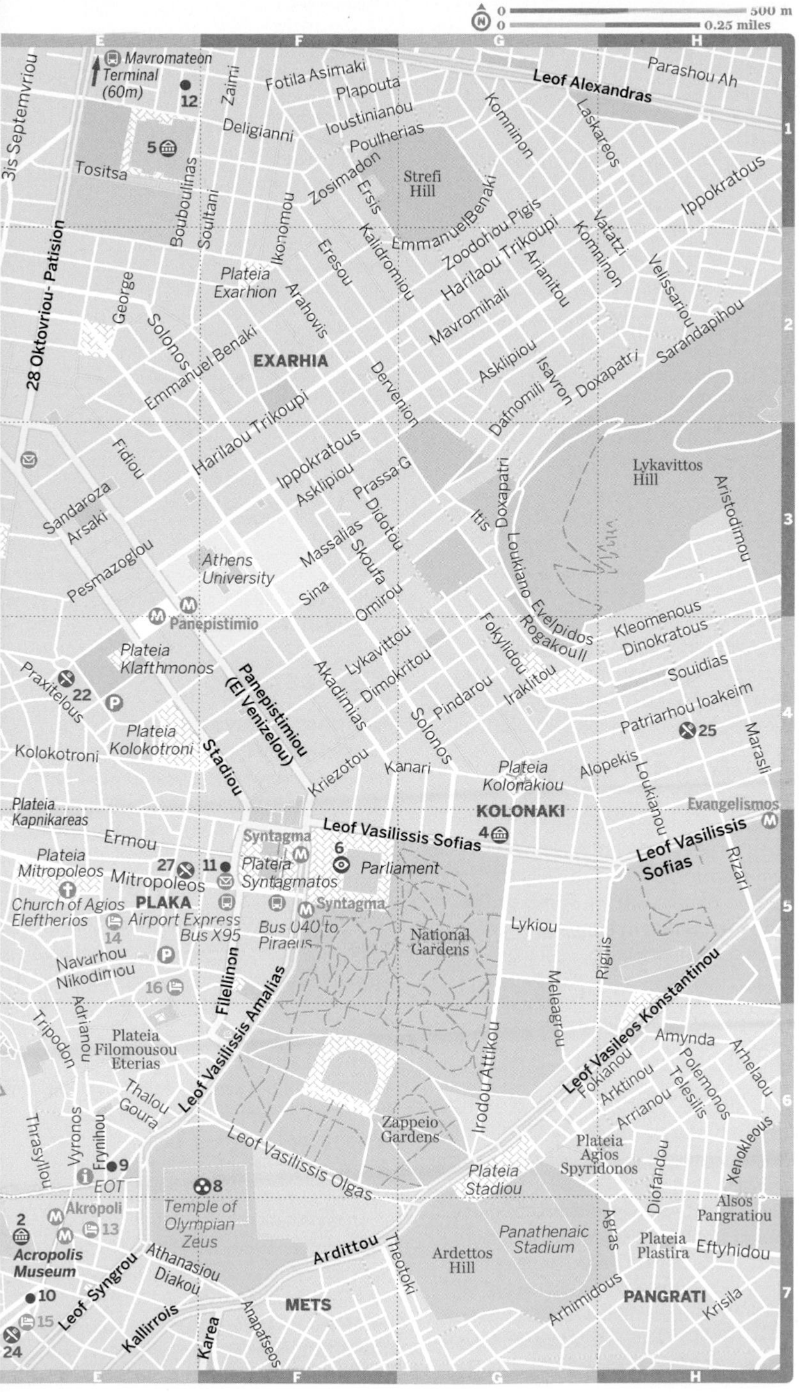
0
500 m
0
0.25 miles
EXARHIA
KOLONAKI
PLAKA
METS
PANGRATI
Mavromateon Terminal (60m)
Strefi Hill
Lykavittos Hill
Athens University
Panepistimio
Plateia Klafthmonos
Plateia Kolokotroni
Plateia Exarhion
Plateia Kapnikareas
Plateia Mitropoleos
Church of Agios Eleftherios
Syntagma
Plateia Syntagmatos
Parliament
Airport Express Bus X95
Bus 040 to Piraeus
National Gardens
Plateia Kolonakiou
Evangelismos
Plateia Filomousou Eterias
Zappeio Gardens
EOT
Akropoli
Acropolis Museum
Temple of Olympian Zeus
Plateia Stadiou
Panathenaic Stadium
Ardettos Hill
Plateia Agios Spyridonos
Alsos Pangratiou
Plateia Plastira
28 Oktovriou- Patision
3is Septemvriou
Leof Alexandras
Panepistimiou (El Venizelou)
Stadiou
Leof Vasilissis Sofias
Leof Vasilissis Amalias
Leof Vasileos Konstantinou
Leof Vasilissis Olgas
Leof Syngrou
Ermou
Mitropoleos
Filellinon
Irodou Attikou
Arditou
Kallirrois
GREECE ATHENS

Central Athens

Don't Miss Sights
1 Acropolis ... D6
2 Acropolis Museum ... E7

Sights
3 Ancient Agora ... C5
4 Benaki Museum ... G5
5 National Archaeological Museum ... E1
6 Parliament & Changing of the Guard ... F5
7 Roman Agora & Tower of the Winds ... D5
8 Temple of Olympian Zeus ... F6

Activities, Courses & Tours
9 Athens Segway Tours ... E6
10 Athens: Adventures ... E7
11 CitySightseeing Athens ... F5
12 Trekking Hellas ... E1

Sleeping
13 Athens Backpackers ... E7
14 Central Hotel ... E5
15 Hera Hotel ... E7
16 Hotel Adonis ... E5
17 Hotel Cecil ... D4
18 Plaka Hotel ... D5
19 Tempi Hotel ... D4

Eating
20 Café Avyssinia ... C5
21 Funky Gourmet ... B3
22 Kalnterimi ... E4
23 Kanella ... A4
24 Mani Mani ... E7
25 Oikeio ... H4
26 Thanasis ... D5
27 Tzitzikas & Mermingas ... E5

Shopping
28 Athens Central Market ... D3
29 Monastiraki Flea Market ... C5

(Continued from page 699)

works by El Greco; ecclesiastical furniture brought from Asia Minor; pottery, copper, silver and woodwork from Egypt, Asia Minor and Mesopotamia; and a stunning collection of Greek regional costumes.

Parliament & Changing of the Guard Building
(Plateia Syntagmatos; M Syntagma) FREE In front of the parliament building on Plateia Syntagmatos, the traditionally costumed *evzones* (guards) of the **Tomb of the Unknown Soldier** change every hour on the hour. On Sunday at 11am, a whole platoon marches down Vasilissis Sofias to the tomb, accompanied by a band.

Tours

The usual city tours exist like open-bus **CitySightseeing Athens** (210 922 0604; www.city-sightseeing.com; Plateia Syntagmatos, Syntagma; adult/child €15/6.50; every 30min 9am-8pm; M Syntagma), **Athens Segway Tours** (210 322 2500; www.athenssegway-tours.com; Eschinou 9, Plaka; 2hr tour €59; M Akropoli) or the volunteer **This is My Athens** (www.thisisathens.org). Get out of town on the cheap with **Athens: Adventures** (210 922 4044; www.athensadventures.gr). Hike or kayak with **Trekking Hellas** (210 331 0323; www.trekking.gr; Saripolou 10, Exarhia; M Viktoria).

Festivals

Hellenic Festival Performing Arts
(www.greekfestival.gr; Jun-Sep) The ancient theatre at Epidavros and Athens' Theatre of Herodes Atticus are the headline venues of Greece's annual cultural festival featuring a top line-up of local and international music, dance and theatre.

Sleeping

Book well ahead for July and August.

PLAKA

Central Hotel Business Hotel €€
(210 323 4357; www.centralhotel.gr; Apollonos 21, Plaka; d/tr incl breakfast from €105/150; ; M Syntagma) This stylish hotel has been tastefully decorated in light, contemporary tones. It has comfortable rooms with all the mod cons and good bathrooms. There is a lovely roof terrace with Acropolis views, a small spa and sun lounges. As its name suggests, Central Hotel is in a great location between Syntagma and Plaka.

Hotel Adonis Hotel €€

(☎210 324 9737; www.hotel-adonis.gr; 3 Kodrou St, Plaka; s/d/tr incl breakfast €70/88/105; ❄@📶; Ⓜ Syntagma) This comfortable pension on a quiet pedestrian street in Plaka has basic, clean rooms with TVs. Bathrooms are small but have been excellently renovated. Take in great Acropolis views from 4th-floor rooms and the rooftop terrace where breakfast is served. No credit cards.

MONASTIRAKI

Tempi Hotel Hotel €

(☎210 321 3175; www.tempihotel.gr; Eolou 29, Monastiraki; d/tr €55/65, s/d without bathroom €37/47; ❄📶; Ⓜ Monastiraki) Location and affordability are the strengths of this older, family-run place on pedestrian Eolou. Front balconies overlook Plateia Agia Irini, the scene of some of Athens' best nightlife, and side views get the Acropolis. Basic rooms have satellite TV, but bathrooms are primitive. Top-floor rooms are small and quite a hike. There is a communal kitchen.

Plaka Hotel Hotel €€

(☎210 322 2096; www.plakahotel.gr; Kapnikareas 7, cnr Mitropoleos, Monastiraki; d incl breakfast €125-200; ❄📶; Ⓜ Monastiraki) It's hard to beat the Acropolis views from the rooftop garden, as well as those from top-floor rooms. Tidy rooms have light timber floors and furniture, and satellite TV, though bathrooms are on the small side. Though called the Plaka Hotel, it's actually closer to Monastiraki.

Hotel Cecil Hotel €€

(☎210 321 7079; www.cecilhotel.gr; Athinas 39, Monastiraki; s/d/tr/q incl breakfast from €60/65/95/120; ❄@📶; Ⓜ Monastiraki) This charming old hotel on busy Athinas has beautiful high moulded ceilings, polished timber floors and an original cage-style lift. The simple rooms are tastefully furnished, but don't have fridges. Two connecting rooms with a shared bathroom are ideal for families.

MAKRYGIANNI

Athens Backpackers Hostel €

(☎210 922 4044; www.backpackers.gr; Makri 12, Makrygianni; dm incl breakfast €24-29, 2-/4-/6-person apt €95/125/155; ❄@📶; Ⓜ Akropoli) The popular rooftop bar with cheap drinks and Acropolis views is a major drawcard of this modern and friendly Australian-run backpacker favourite, right near the Acropolis metro. There's a barbecue in the courtyard, a well-stocked kitchen and a busy social scene. Spotless dorms with private bathrooms and lockers have bedding, but use of towels cost €2. The same management runs well-priced modern apartments nearby.

Hera Hotel Boutique Hotel €€

(☎210 923 6682; www.herahotel.gr; Falirou 9, Makrygianni; d incl breakfast €120-165, ste €225;

View of the Acropolis (p700), Athens
THOMAS STANKIEWICZ/GETTY IMAGES ©

; (M Akropoli) This elegant boutique hotel, a short walk from the Acropolis and Plaka, was totally rebuilt, but the formal interior design is in keeping with the lovely neoclassical facade. There's lots of brass and timber, and stylish classic furnishings. The rooftop garden, restaurant and bar have spectacular views.

Eating

In addition to mainstay tavernas, Athens has upscale eateries (wear your most stylish togs at night). Eat streets include Mitropoleos, Adrianou and Navarchou Apostoli in Monastiraki, the area around Plateia Psyrri, and Gazi, near Keramikos metro.

The fruit and vegetable market, **Athens Central Market** (Varvakios Agora; Athinas, btwn Sofokleous & Evripidou; 7am-3pm Mon-Sat; M Monastiraki, Panepistimio, Omonia), on Athinas is opposite the meat market.

SYNTAGMA & MONASTIRAKI

Kalnterimi Taverna €

(210 331 0049; www.kalnterimi.gr; Plateia Agion Theodoron, cnr Skouleniou, Monastiraki; mains €6-9; noon-midnight; M Panepistimio) Find your way behind the Church of Agii Theodori to this hidden open-air taverna offering Greek food at its most authentic. Everything is fresh cooked and delicious: you can't go wrong. Hand-painted tables spill onto the footpath along a pedestrian street and give a feeling of peace in one of the busiest parts of the city.

Tzitzikas & Mermingas Mezedhes €

(210 324 7607; Mitropoleos 12-14, Syntagma; mezedhes €6-11; noon-11pm; M Syntagma) Greek merchandise lines the walls of this cheery, modern *mezedhopoleio* that sits smack in the middle of central Athens. It serves a tasty range of delicious and creative *mezedhes* (like the honey-drizzled, bacon-wrapped cheese one) to a bustling crowd of locals.

Thanasis Souvlaki €

(210 324 4705; Mitropoleos 69, Monastiraki; gyros €2.50; 8.30am-2.30am; M Monastiraki) In the heart of Athens' souvlaki hub, at the end of Mitropoleos, Thanasis is known for its kebabs on pitta with grilled tomato and onions.

Café Avyssinia Mezedhes €€

(210 321 7047; www.avissinia.gr; Kynetou 7, Monastiraki; mains €10-16; 11am-1am Tue-Sat, to 7pm Sun; M Monastiraki) Hidden away on colourful Plateia Avyssinias, in the middle of the flea market, this bohemian *mezedhopoleio* gets top marks for atmosphere, food and friendly service. It specialises in regional Greek cuisine, from warm fava to eggplants baked with tomato and cheese, and has a great selection of ouzo, *raki* (Cretan firewater) and *tsipouro* (a distilled spirit similar to ouzo but usually stronger).

MAKRYGIANNI

Mani Mani Greek €

(210 921 8180; www.manimani.com.gr; Falirou 10, Makrygianni; mains €9-15; 2.30-11.30pm Mon-Fri, from 1pm Sat, 1-5.30pm Sun, closed Jul & Aug; M Akropoli) Head upstairs to the relaxing, cheerful dining rooms of this delightful modern restaurant, which specialises in regional cuisine from Mani in the Peloponnese. The ravioli with Swiss chard, chervil and cheese, and the tangy Mani sausage with orange are standouts. Almost all dishes can be ordered as half portions (at half-price), allowing you to sample widely.

KERAMIKOS & GAZI

Kanella Taverna €

(210 347 6320; Leoforos Konstantinoupoleos 70, Gazi; dishes €7-10; 1.30pm-late; M Keramikos) Homemade village-style bread, mismatched retro crockery and brown-paper tablecloths set the tone for this trendy, modern taverna serving regional Greek cuisine. Friendly staff serve daily specials such as lemon lamb with potatoes, and an excellent zucchini and avocado salad.

Funky Gourmet Mediterranean €€€

(210 524 2727; www.funkygourmet.com; Paramithias 3, cnr Salaminas, Keramikos; set menu from €70; 7.30-11.30pm Tue-Sat;

Ⓜ Metaxourgio) Noveau gastronomy meets fresh Mediterranean ingredients at this Michelin-starred restaurant. Elegant lighting, refinement and sheer joy in food make this a worthwhile stop for any foodie. The degustation menus can be paired with wines. Book ahead.

KOLONAKI

Oikeio Mediterranean **€**
(☎ 210 725 9216; Ploutarhou 15, Kolonaki; mains €7-13; ⏲ 1pm-2.30am Mon-Sat; Ⓜ Evangelismos) With excellent home-style cooking, this modern taverna lives up to its name (meaning 'homey'). It's decorated like a cosy bistro on the inside, and tables on the footpath allow people-watching without the normal Kolonaki bill. Pastas, salads and international fare are tasty, but try the *mayirefta* (ready-cooked meals) specials such as the excellent stuffed zucchini. Book ahead.

Drinking & Entertainment

Kolonaki has a mind-boggling array of cafes off Plateia Kolonakiou on Skoufa and Tsakalof. Another cafe-thick area is Adrianou, along the Ancient Agora.

Athenians know how to party. Expect people to show up after midnight. Head to Monastiraki (around Plateia Agia Irini, Plateia Karytsi or Kolokotroni), Gazi (around Voutadon and the Keramikos metro station) or Kolonaki (around Ploutarhou and Haritos or Skoufa and Omirou) and explore!

Gay bars cluster in Gazi near the railway line on Leoforos Konstantinoupoleos and Megalou Alexandrou, as well as Makrygianni, Psyrri, Metaxourghio and Exarhia. Check out www.athensinfoguide.com or www.gayguide.gr.

For events listings try: www.breathtakingathens.gr, www.elculture.gr, www.tickethour.com, www.tickethouse.gr, www.ticketservices.gr. The Kathimerini supplement inside the *International Herald Tribune* contains event listings and

If You Like... Ancient Greece

The Acropolis might be Greece's most famous ancient ruin, but there are hundreds more sites to uncover.

1 **EPIDAVROS**
(☎ 27530 22009; adult/concession €6/3; ⏲ 8am-7pm) In its day Epidavros, 30km east of Nafplio, was famed as a place of healing. Visitors came great distances to this gorgeous sanctuary of Asclepius (god of medicine) to seek a cure for their ailments. Today visitors flock here for its amazingly well-preserved theatre, a venue for Classical Greek theatre during the Hellenic Festival.

2 **ANCIENT MYCENAE**
(☎ 27510 76585; adult/concession €8/4; ⏲ 8am-8pm Apr-Oct, to 3pm Nov-Mar) In the foothills of Mt Agios Ilias and Mt Zara 25km north of Nafplio stand the mighty ruins of Ancient Mycenae. Highlights include the magnificent Lion Gate, Grave Circle A where priceless golden treasures were excavated from the royal tombs, and Agamemnon's and Clytemnestra's tombs.

3 **MYSTRAS**
(☎ 23315 25363; adult/concession €5/3; ⏲ 8am-8pm Apr-Sep, to 5.30pm Aug, to 3pm Nov-Mar) This former capital of the Byzantine Empire is the single most compelling set of medieval ruins in Greece. Duck into the ruins of palaces, monasteries and churches, most of them dating from between 1271 and 1460, and surrounded by verdant olive and orange groves.

4 **ANCIENT OLYMPIA**
(☎ 26240 22517; adult/concession €6/3, site & museum €9/5; ⏲ 8am-8pm Apr-Oct, to 3pm Nov-Mar) The Olympic Games took place here for at least 1000 years, up until in AD 393. Picture the sweaty, oiled-up athletes waiting inside the original stadium, the jostling crowds and the women and slaves watching from nearby Hill of Kronos.

5 **MT OLYMPUS**
The cloud-covered lair of the Ancient Greek pantheon, awe-inspiring Mt Olympus, fires the visitor's imagination today, just as it did for the ancients who venerated it.

a cinema guide. In summer, dance clubs move to the beachfront near Glyfada.

Shopping

Shop for cool jewellery, clothes, shoes, and souvenirs such as backgammon sets, hand-woven textiles, olive-oil beauty products, worry beads and ceramics. Find boutiques around Syntagma, from the Attica department store past Voukourestiou and on Ermou; designer brands and cool shops in Kolonaki; and souvenirs, folk art and leather in Plaka and Monastiraki.

Monastiraki Flea Market Market

(Adrianou, Monastiraki; daily; M Monastiraki) This traditional market has a festive atmosphere. Permanent antique and collectables shops are open all week, while the streets around the station and Adrianou fill with vendors selling jewellery, handicrafts and bric-a-brac.

Information

Dangers & Annoyances

- Though violent street crime remains relatively rare, travellers should be alert on the streets, especially at night, and beware the following:
- Streets surrounding Omonia have become markedly seedier, with an increase in prostitutes and junkies; avoid the area, especially at night.
- Watch for pickpockets on the metro and at the markets.
- When taking taxis, ask the driver to use the meter or negotiate a price in advance. Ignore stories that the hotel you've chosen is closed or full: they're angling for a commission from another hotel.
- Bar scams are commonplace, particularly in Plaka and Syntagma. Beware the over-friendly!
- With the recent financial reforms in Greece have come strikes in Athens (check http://livingingreece.gr/strikes). Picketers tend to march in Plateia Syntagmatos.

Emergency

Visitor Emergency Assistance (112) Toll-free 24-hour service in English.

SOS Doctors (1016, 210 821 1888; 24hr) Pay service with English-speaking doctors.

Internet Resources

Official visitor site (www.breathtakingathens.gr)

Evzones (guards) at the Tomb of the Unknown Soldier (p706), Athens

Detour: Delphi ΔΕΛΦΟΙ

Modern Delphi and its adjoining ruins hang stunningly on the slopes of Mt Parnassos overlooking the shimmering Gulf of Corinth.

According to mythology, Zeus released two eagles at opposite ends of the world and they met here, thus making Delphi the centre of the world. By the 6th century BC, **Ancient Delphi** (22650 82312; www.culture.gr; site or museum adult/child €6/free, combined €9; 8am-3pm, longer hr summer) had become the Sanctuary of Apollo. Thousands of pilgrims flocked here to consult the middle-aged female oracle who sat at the mouth of a fume-emitting chasm. Wars, voyages and business transactions were undertaken on the strength of these prophecies. From the entrance, take the **Sacred Way** up to the **Temple of Apollo**, where the oracle sat. From here the path continues to the well-preserved **theatre** and **stadium**.

Opposite the main site and down the hill some 100m, don't miss the **Sanctuary of Athena** and the much-photographed **Tholos**, a 4th-century-BC columned rotunda of Pentelic marble.

Six buses a day go to Athens Liossion Terminal B (€15.50, three hours).

Money

Banks surround Plateia Syntagmatos.

Tourist Information

EOT (Greek National Tourist Organisation; 210 331 0347, 210 331 0716; www.visitgreece.gr; Dionysiou Areopagitou 18-20, Makrygianni; 8am-8pm Mon-Fri, 10am-4pm Sat & Sun May-Sep, 9am-7pm Mon-Fri Oct-Apr; M Akropoli) Free Athens map, transport information and *Athens & Attica* booklet.

Athens City Information Kiosk (Airport) (210 353 0390; 8am-8pm; M Airport) Maps, transport information and all Athens info.

Getting There & Away

Air

Modern Eleftherios Venizelos International Airport (ATH; 210 353 0000; www.aia.gr), 27km east of Athens.

Boat

Most ferries, hydrofoils and high-speed catamarans leave from the massive port at Piraeus. Some depart from smaller ports at Rafina and Lavrio.

Bus

Athens has two main intercity KTEL (14505; www.ktel.org) bus stations: Liossion Terminal B (210 831 7153; Liossion 260, Thymarakia; M Agios Nikolaos), 5km north of Omonia with buses to central and northern Greece (Delphi, Meteora), and Kifissos Terminal A (210 512 4910; Kifisou 100, Peristeri; M Agios Antonios), 7km north of Omonia, with buses to Thessaloniki, the Peloponnese, Ionian Islands and western Greece. KTEL website and tourist office have timetables.

Buses for destinations in southern Attica leave from the Mavromateon Terminal (210 880 8000, 210 822 5148; cnr Leoforos Alexandras & 28 Oktovriou-Patision, Pedion Areos; M Viktoria), about 250m north of the National Archaeological Museum.

Car & Motorcycle

The airport has car rental, and Syngrou, just south of the Temple of Olympian Zeus, is dotted with car-hire firms, though driving in Athens is treacherous.

Train

Intercity trains to central and northern Greece depart from the central **Larisis train station**, about 1km northwest of Plateia Omonias. For the

Island in a Day

For islands within easy reach of Athens, head to the Saronic Gulf. **Aegina** (*eh*-yee-nah; www.aeginagreece.com), just a half hour from Piraeus is home to the impressive **Temple of Aphaia** (☎22970 32398; adult/child €4/free; ⏰8am-3pm), said to have served as a model for the construction of the Parthenon. The catwalk queen of the Saronics, **Hydra** (*ee*-drah; www.hydra.gr, www.hydraislandgreece.com) is a delight, an hour and a half from Piraeus. Its picturesque horseshoe-shaped harbour town with gracious stone mansions stacked up the rocky hillsides is known as a retreat for artists, writers and celebrities. There are no motorised vehicles – apart from sanitation trucks – leading to unspoilt trails along the coast and into the mountains.

From Hydra, you can return to Piraeus, or carry on to Spetses and the Peloponnese (Metohi, Ermione and Porto Heli). Check Hellenic Seaways (www.hsw.gr) and Aegina Flying Dolphins (www.aegeanflyingdolphins.gr).

Peloponnese, take the suburban rail to Kiato and change for other OSE services, or check for available lines at the Larisis station.

Getting Around

To/From the Airport

Bus

Tickets cost €5. Twenty-four-hour services:

Plateia Syntagmatos Bus X95, 60 to 90 minutes, every 15 minutes (the Syntagma stop is on Othonos)

Piraeus Port Bus X96, 1½ hrs, every 20 minutes

Terminal A (Kifissos) Bus Station Bus X93, 35 minutes, every 30 minutes

Metro

Blue line 3 links the airport to the city centre in around 40 minutes; it operates from Monastiraki from 5.50am to midnight, and from the airport from 5.30am to 11.30pm. Tickets (€8) are valid for all public transport for 70 minutes. Fare for two or more passengers is €14 total.

Taxi

Fixed fares are posted. Expect day/night €35/50 to the city centre, and €47/65 to Piraeus. Both trips often take at least an hour, longer with heavy traffic. Check www.athensairporttaxi.com for more info.

Public Transport

The metro, tram and bus system makes getting around central Athens and to Piraeus easy. Athens' road traffic can be horrendous. Get maps and timetables at the tourist offices or **Athens Urban Transport Organisation** (OASA; ☎185; www.oasa.gr).

Tickets & Passes

Tickets good for 70 minutes (€1.20), a 24-hour/5-day travel pass (€4/10) are valid for all forms of public transport except for airport services, the 3-day tourist ticket (€20) includes airport transport. Bus/trolleybus-only tickets cannot be used on the metro. Children under six travel free; people under 18 and over 65 pay half-fare. Buy tickets in metro stations, transport kiosks, or most *periptera* (street corner kiosks). Validate the ticket in the machine as you board.

Bus & Trolleybus

Buses and electric trolleybuses operate every 15 minutes from 5am to midnight.

Piraeus From Syntagma and Filellinon to Akti Xaveriou catch Bus 040; from Omonia end of Athinas to Plateia Themistokleous, catch Bus 049.

Metro

Trains operate from 5am to midnight (Friday and Saturday to around 2am), every three to 10 minutes. Get timetables at www.stasy.gr.

PAOLO CORDELLI/GETTY IMAGES ©

Don't Miss

Meteora ΜΕΤΕΩΡΑ

Meteora (meh-*teh*-o-rah) should be a certified Wonder of the World with its magnificent late-14th-century monasteries perched dramatically atop enormous rocky pinnacles. Try not to miss it. The tranquil village of **Kastraki**, 2km from Kalambaka, is the best base for visiting.

While there were once monasteries on all 24 pinnacles, only six are still occupied: **Megalou Meteorou** (Grand Meteoron; ☎24320 22278; ⏰9am-5pm Wed-Mon Apr-Oct, to 4pm Thu-Mon Nov-Mar), **Varlaam** (☎24320 22277; ⏰9am-4pm Sat-Thu Apr-Oct, closed Thu Nov-Mar), **Agiou Stefanou** (☎24320 22279; ⏰9am-1.30pm & 3.30-5.30pm Tue-Sun Apr-Oct, 9.30am-1pm & 3-5pm Nov-Mar), **Agias Triados** (Holy Trinity; ☎24320 22220; ⏰9am-5pm Fri-Wed Apr-Oct, 10am-3pm Fri-Tue Nov-Mar), **Agiou Nikolaou Anapafsa** (Monastery of St Nikolaou Anapafsa; ☎24320 22375; ⏰9am-3.30pm Sat-Thu Nov-Mar, to 2pm Apr-Oct) and **Agias Varvaras Rousanou** (⏰9am-6pm Thu-Tue Apr-Oct, to 2pm Nov-Mar). Admission is €3 for each monastery and strict dress codes apply (no bare shoulders or knees and women must wear skirts; borrow a long skirt at the door if you don't have one). Walk the footpaths between monasteries, drive the back asphalt road, or take the bus (€1.20, 20 minutes) that departs from Kalambaka and Kastraki at 9am, and returns at 1pm (12.40pm on weekends).

From Kalambaka **train station** (☎24320 22451; www.trainose.gr), trains run to Athens (regular/IC €18-29, 5½/4½ hours, both twice daily) and Thessaloniki (€15.20, four hours, one daily). You may need to change in Paleofarsalos.

Taxi

Taxis are generally reasonable, with small surcharges for port, train and bus station pick-ups, baggage over 10kg or radio taxi. Insist on a metered rate (except for posted flat rates at the airport).

Athina 1 (☎210 921 2800)

Train

Fast suburban rail (☎1110; www.trainose.gr) links Athens with the airport, Piraeus, the outer regions and the northern Peloponnese. It connects to the metro at Larisis, Doukissis Plakentias and Nerantziotissa stations, and goes from the airport to Kiato.

PELOPONNESE

Nafplio ΝΑΥΠΛΙΟ

POP 14,200

Elegant Venetian houses and neoclassical mansions dripping with crimson bougainvillea cascade down Nafplio's hillside to the azure sea. Vibrant cafes, shops and restaurants fill winding pedestrian streets. Crenulated Palamidi Fortress perches above it all. What's not to love?

Sights

Palamidi Fortress Fort

(☎27520 28036; adult/concession €4/free; ⏲8am-6.45pm May–mid-Oct, to 3pm mid-Oct–Apr) This vast and spectacular citadel, reachable either by punishingly steep ascent on foot or a short drive, stands on a 216m-high outcrop of rock with all-encompassing views of Nafplio and the Argolic Gulf. It was built by the Venetians between 1711 and 1714, and is regarded as a masterpiece of military architecture in spite of being successfully stormed in one night by Greek troups in 1822, causing the Turkish garrison within to surrender without a fight.

Peloponnese Folklore Foundation Museum Museum

(☎27520 28947; www.pli.gr; Vasileos Alexandrou 1; admission €2; ⏲9am-2pm Wed-Mon) Established by the philanthropic owner, Nafplio's award-winning museum is a beautifully arranged collection of folk costumes and household items from Nafplio's 19th and early 20th century history. Be wowed by the intricate embroidery of traditional costume and the heavy silver adornments, admire the turn-of-the-century couture and see if you can spot a horse-tricycle. The gift shop sells high-quality local crafts.

Sleeping

The Old Town is *the* place to stay, but it has few budget options. Friday to Sunday the town fills and prices rise; book ahead.

Sanctuary of Athena (p711), Delphi

Amfitriti Pension Pension **€€**
(☎27520 96250; www.amfitriti-pension.gr; Kapodistriou 24; d incl breakfast from €60; ❄📶) Quaint antiques fill these intimate rooms in a house in the Old Town. You can also enjoy stellar views at its nearby sister hotel, **Amfitriti Belvedere**, which is chock full of brightly coloured tapestries and emits a feeling of cheery serenity.

Eating

Antica Gelateria di Roma Gelateria **€**
(☎27520 23520; www.anticagelateria.gr; cnr Farmakopoulou & Komninou; ice cream from €2.50; ⏰10am-11pm) The only 'true' gelato shop in Nafplio is still holding back the competition. Italian gelati maestros Marcello, Claudia or Monica Raffo greet you with: '*Bongiorno* – this is an *Italian* gelati shop!' Only natural and local ingredients are used and it's all made on the premises.

Getting There & Away

KTEL Argolis Bus Station (☎27520 27423; www.ktel-argolidas.gr; Syngrou) has the following services:

Athens €13.10, 2½ hours, hourly (via Corinth)

Epidavros €2.90, 45 minutes, two Mon-Sat

Mycenae €2.90, one hour, three daily

CYCLADES ΚΥΚΛΑΔΕΣ

The Cyclades (kih-*klah*-dez) are Greek islands to dream about. Named after the rough *kyklos* (circle) they form around the island of Delos, they are rugged outcrops of rock in the azure Aegean, speckled with white cubist buildings and blue-domed Byzantine churches.

Some of the islands, such as Mykonos and Santorini, have seized tourism with great enthusiasm. Prepare to battle the crowds if you turn up at the height of summer.

Mykonos ΜΥΚΟΝΟΣ

POP 10,190

Sophisticated Mykonos glitters happily under the Aegean sun, shamelessly surviving on tourism. The island has something for everyone, with marvellous beaches, romantic sunsets, chic boutiques, excellent restaurants and bars, and its long-held reputation as a mecca for gay travellers.

Sights & Activities

The island's most popular beaches are on the southern coast. **Platys Gialos** has wall-to-wall sun lounges, while nudity is not uncommon at **Paradise Beach**, **Super Paradise**, **Agrari** and gay-friendly **Elia**.

Hora Town
(Mykonos Town) Mykonos Town is a captivating labyrinth that's home to chic boutiques and whiter-than-white houses decked with bougainvillea and geraniums, plus a handful of small museums and photogenic churches. **Little Venice**, where the sea laps up to the edge of the restaurants and bars, and Mykonos' famous hilltop **windmills** should be high on the must-see list.

Sleeping

Carbonaki Hotel Boutique Hotel **€€**
(☎22890 24124; www.carbonaki.gr; 23 Panahrantou, Hora; s/d/tr/q from €120/142/180/206; ❄📶) This family-run boutique hotel in central Mykonos is a delightful oasis with bright, comfortable rooms, relaxing public balconies and sunny central courtyards. Chill out in the jacuzzi and small sauna. Some wheelchair access and great low-season discounts.

Manto Hotel Hotel **€€**
(☎22890 22330; www.manto-mykonos.gr; Evagelistrias 1, Hora; s/d incl breakfast from €60/85; ⏰year-round; ❄📶) Buried in the heart of Hora, cheerful Manto is an excellent affordable option (for Mykonos), with well-kept colourful rooms, some with

Mykonos

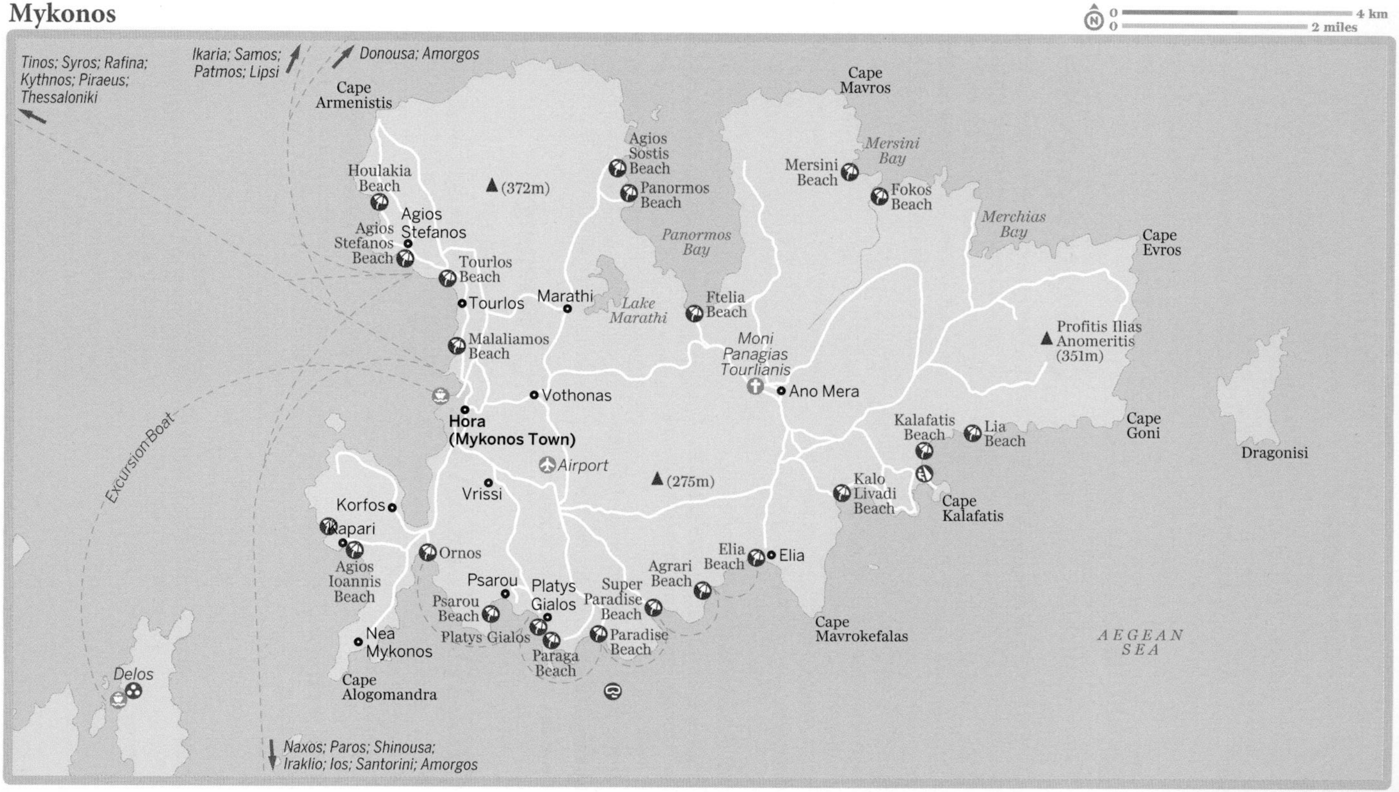

0 — 4 km
0 — 2 miles

Tinos; Syros; Rafina; Kythnos; Piraeus; Thessaloniki
Ikaria; Samos; Patmos; Lipsi
Donousa; Amorgos
Cape Armenistis
Houlakia Beach
(372m)
Agios Sostis Beach
Panormos Beach
Cape Mavros
Mersini Bay
Mersini Beach
Fokos Beach
Merchias Bay
Cape Evros
Agios Stefanos
Agios Stefanos Beach
Tourlos Beach
Tourlos
Marathi
Lake Marathi
Panormos Bay
Ftelia Beach
Profitis Ilias Anomeritis (351m)
Malaliamos Beach
Moni Panagias Tourlianis
Ano Mera
Vothonas
Hora (Mykonos Town)
Excursion Boat
Airport
Kalafatis Beach
Lia Beach
Cape Goni
Dragonisi
(275m)
Vrissi
Kalo Livadi Beach
Cape Kalafatis
Korfos
Kapari
Agios Ioannis Beach
Ornos
Elia Beach
Elia
Agrari Beach
Psarou
Platys Gialos
Super Paradise Beach
Psarou Beach
Platys Gialos
Paradise Beach
Paraga Beach
Nea Mykonos
Cape Mavrokefalas
AEGEAN SEA
Delos
Cape Alogomandra
Naxos; Paros; Shinousa; Iraklio; Ios; Santorini; Amorgos

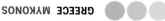

Detour: Delos ΔΗΛΟΣ

Southwest of Mykonos, the island of **Delos** (**22890 22259; museum & sites adult/child €5/free; 8am-8pm Apr-Oct, to 3pm Nov-Mar**) is the Cyclades' archaeological jewel.

According to mythology, Delos was the birthplace of Apollo – the god of light, poetry, music, healing and prophecy. The island flourished as an important religious and commercial centre from the 3rd millennium BC, reaching its apex of power in the 5th century BC.

Ruins include the **Sanctuary of Apollo**, containing temples dedicated to him, and the **Terrace of the Lions**. These proud beasts were carved in the early 6th century BC using marble from Naxos to guard the sacred area. The original lions are in the island's **museum**, with replicas on the original site. The **Sacred Lake** (dry since 1926) is where Leto supposedly gave birth to Apollo and his twin sister Artemis, while the **Theatre Quarter** is where private houses were built around the **Theatre of Delos**.

Boats from Mykonos to Delos (€18 return, 30 minutes) go between 9am and 5pm in summer, and return between noon and 8pm. In Mykonos Town (Hora) buy tickets at the old wharf kiosk or at travel agents. Sometimes in summer boats go from Tinos and Naxos.

balconies, an inviting breakfast room and friendly owners.

Eating

Nautilus Greek **€€**
(**22890 27100; www.nautilus-mykonos.gr; Kalogera 6, Hora; mains €11-16; 7pm-1am Mar-Nov**) The whitewashed terrace spills out onto the street and Greek fusion dishes incorporate top ingredients.

M-Eating Mediterranean **€€€**
(**22890 78550; www.m-eating.gr; Kalogera 10, Hora; mains €15-26; 7pm-midnight**) Attentive service and relaxed luxury are the hallmarks of this creative restaurant specialising in fresh Greek products prepared with flair. Sample anything from tenderloin stuffed with Metsovo cheese to shrimp ravioli with crayfish sauce. Don't miss the Mykonian honey pie, or for beer lovers the Volcano microbrew from Santorini.

Getting There & Around

Air

There are daily flights connecting Mykonos airport (JMK) to Athens, plus a growing number of international flights winging in directly from May to September. The airport is 3km southeast of the town centre; €1.60 by bus from the southern bus station, €9 by taxi.

Boat

Year-round ferries serve mainland ports Piraeus (€35, 4¾hr, 1-2 daily) and Rafina (sometimes quicker if you are coming directly from Athens airport), and nearby islands, Tinos and Andros. In the high season, Mykonos is well connected with all neighbouring islands, including Paros and Santorini.

Naxos ΝΑΞΟΣ

POP 12,089

The largest of the Cyclades islands, Naxos could probably survive without tourism – unlike many of its neighbouring islands. Green and fertile, Naxos produces olives, grapes, figs, citrus, corn and potatoes.

Naxos Town (Hora), on the west coast, is the island's capital and port.

Sights

Kastro
Neighbourhood

(Naxos Town) Behind the waterfront, get lost in the narrow alleyways scrambling up to the spectacular hilltop 13th-century *kastro*, where the Venetian Catholics lived. You'll get super views, and there's a well-stocked **archaeological museum** (☎22850 22725; adult/child €3/free; ⏰8am-3pm Tue-Sun).

Temple of Apollo
Archaeological Site

(The Potara) FREE From Naxos Town harbour, a causeway leads to Palatia Islet and the striking, unfinished Temple of Apollo, Naxos' most famous landmark. Simply two marble columns with a crowning lintel, it makes an arresting sight, and people gather at sunset for views back to Naxos' whitewashed houses and 13th-century *kastro* on the hilltop.

Temple of Demeter
Temple

(Dimitra's Temple; ☎22850 22725; ⏰8.30am-3pm Tue-Sun) FREE Surrounded by mountains, and gleaming in a gorgeous verdant valley sweeping to the sea, the impressive Temple of Demeter remains remarkably powerful. The ruins and reconstructions are not large, but they are historically fascinating, and the location is unparalleled – it's clear that this is a place for the worship of the goddess of the harvest. The site museum holds additional reconstructions of temple features. Signs point the way from the village of **Sangri** about 1.5km south to the site.

BEACHES

The popular beach of **Agios Georgios** is just a 10-minute walk south from the main waterfront. **Agia Anna Beach**, 6km from town, and **Plaka Beach** are lined with accommodation and packed in summer. Beyond, wonderful sandy beaches.

VILLAGES

A hire car or scooter will help reveal Naxos' dramatic and rugged landscape. The **Tragaea region** has tranquil villages, churches atop rocky crags and huge olive groves. Between Melanes and Kinidaros are the island's famous **marble quarries**. You'll find two ancient abandoned **kouros** (youth) statues, signposted a short walk

Paradise Beach (p715), Mykonos

from the road. Little **Apiranthos**, perches on the slopes of **Mt Zeus** (1004m), the highest peak in the Cyclades, and has a few intermittently-open museums. The historic village of **Halki**, one-time centre of Naxian commerce, is well worth a visit.

 Sleeping

Nikos Verikokos Studios Hotel €

(☎22850 22025; www.nikos-verikokos.com; Naxos Town; s/d/tr €40/50/60; ⏲year-round; ❄📶) Friendly Nikos maintains immaculate rooms in the heart of the old town. Some have balconies and sea views, most have little kitchenettes. They offer port pickup with pre-arrangement.

Hotel Glaros Boutique Hotel €€

(☎22850 23101; www.hotelglaros.com; Agios Georgios Beach; d €115-125, ste from €150; ⏲Apr-Oct; ❄@📶) Edgy yet homey, simple yet plush, this well-run and immaculate hotel has a seaside feel with light blues and whites and handpainted wooden furnishings. Service is efficient and thoughtful and the beach is only a few steps away. Breakfast is €7.

 Eating

Meze 2 Seafood €

(☎22850 26401; Harbour, Naxos Town; mains €6-13; ⏲noon-midnight Apr-Oct) It would be easy to dismiss this waterfront restaurant as a tourist trap, but don't. Its Cretan and Naxian menu and fantastic service make it stand out from the bunch. The seafood is superb; try stuffed squid, grilled sardines, fisherman's *saganaki* (seafood baked with tomato sauce and feta) or mussels in ouzo and garlic. The salads are creative and filling, particularly the Naxian potato salad. Yum!

L'Osteria Italian €€

(☎22850 24080; Naxos Town; mains €10-15; ⏲7pm-midnight) This authentic Italian eatery is tucked in a small alley uphill from the harbour and beneath the *kastro* walls. Plunk yourself down in the relaxed courtyard and prepare to be gastronomically wowed. The menu changes daily with dishes like salmon lasagne and homemade ravioli. Need we say more?

 Getting There & Around

Air

Naxos airport (JNX) has daily flight connections with Athens. The airport is 3km south of town; no buses – a taxi costs €15, or arrange hotel pickup.

Boat

Myriad high season daily ferry and hydrofoil connections to most Cycladic islands and Crete, plus Piraeus ferries (€31, five hours) and catamarans (€48, 3¾ hours). Reduced in winter.

Car & Motorcycle

Having your own wheels is a good option on Naxos. Car (€45-65) and motorcycle (€25-30) rentals are readily available in Naxos Town.

Santorini (Thira) ΣΑΝΤΟΡΙΝΗ (ΘΗΡΑ)

POP 13,500

Stunning Santorini is unique and should not be missed. The startling sight of the submerged caldera almost encircled by sheer lava-layered cliffs – topped off by clifftop towns that look like a dusting of icing sugar – will grab your attention and not let it go. If you turn up in high season, though, be prepared for relentless crowds and commercialism – Santorini survives on tourism.

Sights & Activities

FIRA

Santorini's vibrant main town with its snaking narrow streets full of shops and restaurants perches on top of the caldera; the stunning caldera views from Fira are unparalleled.

The exceptional **Museum of Prehistoric Thira** (☎22860 23217; Mitropoleos, Fira; admission €3; ⏲8.30am-3pm Tue-Sun), which has wonderful displays of artefacts predominantly from ancient Akrotiri, is two blocks south of the main square.

Santorini (Thira)

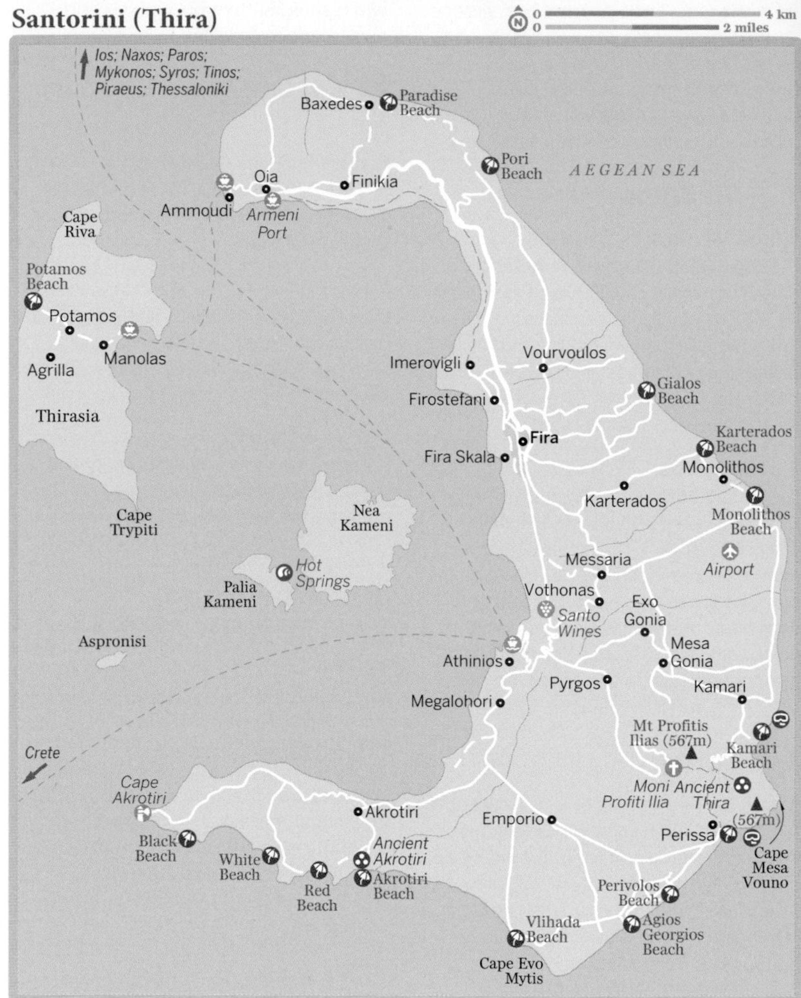

AROUND THE ISLAND

At the north of the island, the intriguing village of **Oia** (ee-ah), famed for its postcard sunsets, is less hectic than Fira and a must-visit. Its caldera-facing tavernas are superb spots for brunch. There's a path from Fira to Oia along the top of the caldera that takes three to four hours to walk; otherwise take a taxi or bus.

Excavations in 1967 uncovered the remarkably well-preserved Minoan settlement of **Akrotiri** (☎22860 81366; adult/child €5/free; ⏰8am-3pm Tue-Sun) at the south of the island, with its remains of two- and three-storey buildings. Akrotiri has recently reopened to the public after a seven-year hiatus.

Santorini's black-sand **beaches** of **Perissa**, **Perivolos**, **Agios Georgios** and **Kamari** sizzle – beach mats are essential. **Red Beach**, near Ancient Akrotiri, has impressive red cliffs and smooth, hand-sized pebbles submerged under clear water.

On a mountain between Perissa and Kamari are the atmospheric ruins of **Ancient Thira** (admission €4; 8am-2.30pm Tue-Sun), first settled in the 9th century BC.

Of the surrounding islets, only **Thirasia** is inhabited. Visitors can clamber around on volcanic lava on **Nea Kameni** then swim into warm springs in the sea at **Palia Kameni**. Many excursions get you there; small boats are at Fira Skala port.

Sleeping

Hotel Keti Hotel **€€**
(22860 22324; www.hotelketi.gr; Agiou Mina, Fira; d/tr from €115/140;) Hotel Keti is one of the smaller 'sunset view' hotels in a peaceful caldera niche. Its attractive traditional rooms are carved into the cliffs. Half of the rooms have jacuzzis. Two-night minimum in high season.

Aroma Suites Boutique Hotel **€€€**
(22860 24112, 6945026038; www.aromasuites.com; Agiou Mina, Fira; d €175-220;) Overlooking the caldera at the quieter southern end of Fira, and more accessible than similar places, this boutique hotel has charming service and plush, beautiful rooms. Built into the side of the caldera, the traditional interiors are made all the more lovely with strong colour touches, canopied beds, local art, books and stereos. Balconies offer a feeling of complete seclusion.

Eating

Krinaki Taverna **€€**
(22860 71993; www.krinaki-santorini.gr; Finikia; mains €10-20; noon-late) All-fresh, all-local ingredients go into top-notch dishes at this homey taverna in tiny Finikia, just east of Oia. Local beer and wine, plus a sea (but not caldera) view.

Ta Dichtia Seafood **€€**
(22860 82818; www.tadichtia.com; Agios Georgios-Perivolos Beach; mains €9-20; noon-11pm) The quintessential seaside taverna with fresh fish daily and soft sand at your feet.

Selene Modern European **€€€**
(22860 22249; www.selene.gr; Pyrgos; mains €20-35; restaurant 7-11pm, bistro noon-11pm Apr-Oct) Meals here aren't just meals – they're a culinary experience. When a menu contains phrases like 'scented Jerusalem artichoke velouté', you know it's

Church at Fira (p719), Santorini

DAVID C TOMLINSON/GETTY IMAGES ©

Crete

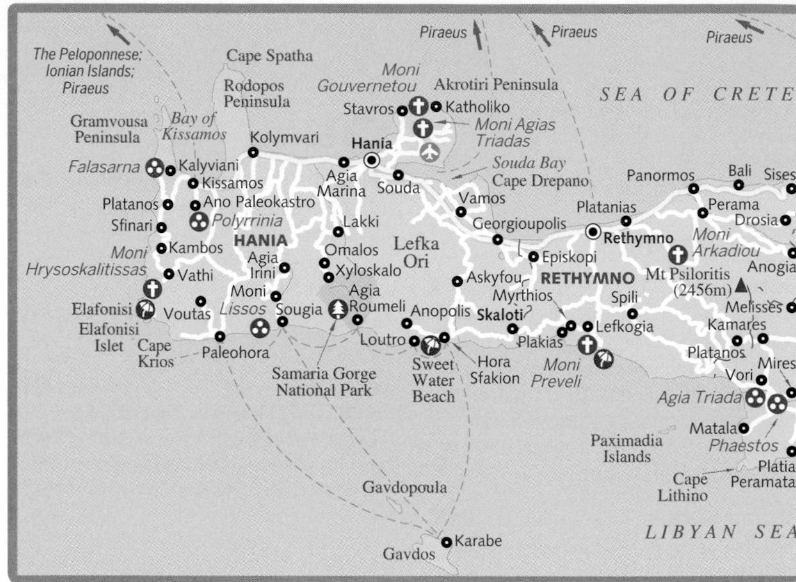

not going to be run-of-the-mill. The chef uses local products wherever possible and is continually introducing new dishes. You'll now find a museum here along with a more moderately priced wine and meze **bistro**, and full-day **cooking classes**.

Information

There is no tourist office. Try the website www.santorini.net for more information.

Getting There & Around

Air

Santorini airport (JTR) has daily flight connections with Athens, plus a growing number of domestic destinations and direct international flights from all over Europe. The airport is 5km southeast of Fira; frequent buses (€1.50) and taxis (€15).

Boat

There are daily ferries (€33.50, nine hours) and fast boats (€60, 5¼ hours) to Piraeus; daily connections in summer to Mykonos, Ios, Naxos, Paros and Iraklio; and ferries to the smaller islands in the Cyclades. Large ferries use Athinios port, where they are met by buses and taxis.

Car & Motorcycle

A car or scooter is a great option on Santorini. There are plenty of places to rent them (from €30 per day).

CRETE ΚΡΗΤΗ

POP 550,000

Crete is Greece's largest and most southerly island and its size and distance from the rest of Greece give it the feel of a different country. The rugged mountainous interior, dotted with caves and sliced by dramatic gorges, offers rigorous hiking and climbing.

While Crete's proud, friendly and hospitable people have enthusiastically embraced tourism, they continue to fiercely protect their traditions and culture – and it is the people that remain a major part of the island's appeal.

Crete was the birthplace of Minoan culture, Europe's first advanced civilisation, which flourished between 2800 and 1450 BC.

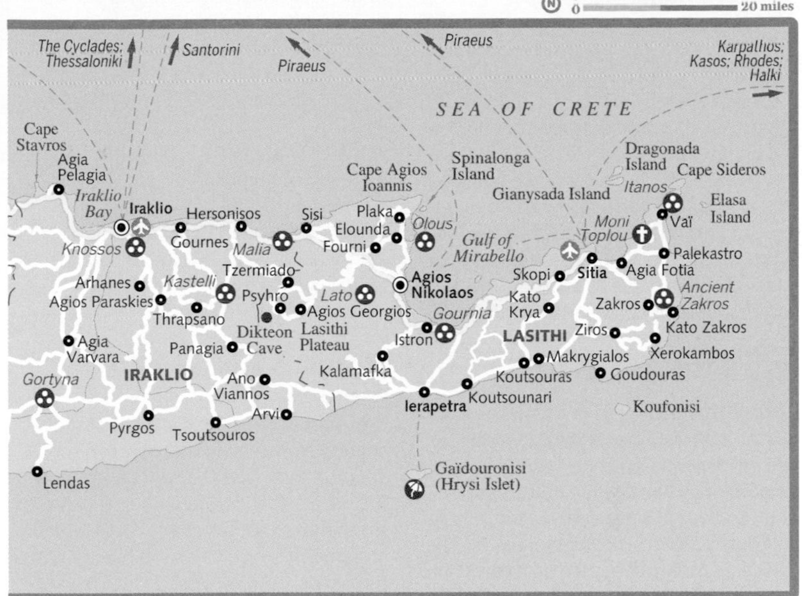

Iraklio ΗΡΑΚΛΕΙΟ

POP 174,000

Iraklio (ee-*rah*-klee-oh; often spelt Heraklion), Crete's capital and economic hub, is a bustling modern city and the fifth-largest in Greece.

Iraklio's harbours face north with the landmark **Koules Venetian Fortress**. Plateia Venizelou, known for its **Lion (Morosini) Fountain**, is the heart of the city, 400m south of the old harbour up 25 Avgoustou.

Sights & Activities

Heraklion Archaeological Museum Museum

(http://odysseus.culture.gr; Xanthoudidou 2; adult/non-EU students/child €6/3/free, incl Knossos €10; 8am-8pm Apr-Oct, 11am-5pm Mon, 8am-3pm Tue-Sun Nov-Mar) This outstanding museum is one of the largest and most important in Greece. There are artefacts spanning 5500 years from neolithic to Roman times, but it's rightly most famous for its extensive Minoan collection. The beautifully restored museum makes a gleaming showcase for the artefacts, and greatly enhances any understanding of Crete's rich history. Don't skip it.

The treasure trove includes pottery, jewellery, sarcophagi, plus several famous frescoes from the sites of Knossos, Phaestos, Zakros, Malia and Agia Triada.

Cretan Adventures Outdoors

(28103 32772; www.cretanadventures.gr; Evans 10, 3rd fl) This well-regarded local company organises hiking tours, mountain biking and extreme outdoor excursions.

Sleeping

Kronos Hotel Hotel €

(2810 282240; www.kronoshotel.gr; Sofokli Venizelou 2; s/d €49/60;) After a thorough makeover this waterfront hotel pole-vaulted to the top of the budget hotel category. Rooms have double-glazed windows to block out noise, as well as balconies, phone, a tiny TV and a fridge. Some doubles have sea views (€66).

Lato Boutique Hotel Boutique Hotel **€€**
(**☎28102 28103; www.lato.gr; Epimenidou 15; d incl breakfast €84-117;** ❄@📶) Iraklio goes Hollywood – with all the sass but sans attitude – at this mod boutique hotel overlooking the old harbour, easily recognised by its jazzy facade. Rooms here sport rich woods, warm reds and vinyl floors, plus custom furniture, pillow-top mattresses, a playful lighting scheme and a kettle for making coffee or tea. Back rooms overlook a modernist metal sculpture.

Eating

Ippokambos Seafood **€€**
(**Sofokli Venizelou 3; mains €6-13; ⏰noon-midnight Mon-Sat;** 📶) Locals give this unpretentious *ouzerie* an enthusiastic thumbs up and we are only too happy to follow suit. Fish is the thing here, freshly caught, simply but expertly prepared and sold at fair prices. In summer, park yourself on the covered waterfront terrace.

Getting There & Around

Air

Flights from Iraklio's **Nikos Kazantzakis International Airport** (**HER; ☎general 28103 97800, info 28103 97136; www.heraklion-airport.info**) serve Athens, Thessaloniki and Rhodes plus destinations all over Europe. The airport is 5km east of town. Bus 1 travels between the airport and city centre (€1.20) every 15 minutes from 6.15am to 10.45pm.

Boat

Daily ferries service Piraeus (€39, eight hours), and catamarans head daily to Santorini and continue on to other Cycladic islands. Ferries sail east to Rhodes (€28, 14 hours) via Agios Nikolaos, Sitia, Kasos, Karpathos and Halki.

Phaestos & Other Minoan Sites ΦΑΙΣΤΟΣ

Phaestos (**☎28920 42315; adult/child €4/free, incl Agia Triada €6/free; ⏰8am-8pm May-Oct, 8am-3pm Nov-Mar**), 63km southwest of Iraklio, is Crete's second-most important Minoan site. While not as impressive as Knossos, Phaestos (fes-*tos*) is still worth a visit for its stunning views of the surrounding Mesara plain and Mt Psiloritis (2456m; also known as Mt Ida). Eight buses a day head to Phaestos from Iraklio's Bus Station B (€7, 1½ hours).

Other important Minoan sites can be found at **Malia**, 34km east of Iraklio, where there's a palace complex and adjoining town, and **Zakros**, 40km southeast of Sitia, the last Minoan palace to have been discovered, in 1962.

Hania XANIA

POP 54,000

Crete's most romantic, evocative and alluring town, Hania (hahn-*yah*; often spelt Chania) is the former capital and the island's second-largest city. There is a rich mosaic of Venetian and Ottoman architecture, particularly in the area of the old harbour, which lures tourists in droves.

Sights

Venetian Harbour Historic Quarter
FREE A stroll around the old harbour is a must for any visitor to Hania. Pastel-coloured historic homes and businesses line the harbour, zig-zagging back into narrow lanes lined with shops. The entire area is ensconced in impressive **Venetian fortifications**, and it is worth the 1.5km walk around the sea wall to the **Venetian lighthouse**. On the eastern side of the inner harbour the prominent **Mosque of Kioutsouk Hasan** (also known as the Mosque of Janissaries) houses regular exhibitions.

Archaeological Museum Museum
(**☎28210 90334; Halidon 30; adult/child €3/free; ⏰8am-8pm Mon-Fri, to 3pm Sat & Sun**) Hania's Archaeological Museum is housed in the superb 16th-century Venetian Church of San Francisco that became a mosque under the Turks, a movie theatre in 1913 and a munitions depot for the Germans during WWII. The museum houses a well-displayed collection of finds from western Crete dating from the neolithic to the

MARCO SIMONI/GETTY IMAGES ©

Don't Miss Knossos

Crete's most famous historical attraction is the Palace of Knossos (k-nos-*os*), 5km south of Iraklio, and the grand capital of Minoan Crete. Excavation started in 1878 with Cretan archaeologist Minos Kalokerinos, and continued from 1900 to 1930 with British archaeologist Sir Arthur Evans. The setting is evocative and the ruins and re-creations impressive, incorporating an immense palace, courtyards, private apartments, baths, lively frescoes and more.

NEED TO KNOW

28102 31940; adult/child €6/free, incl Heraklion Archaeological Museum €10; 8am-8pm May-Oct, to 5pm Nov-April

Roman eras. Artefacts from 3400 to 1200 BC include tablets with Linear A script. There is also exquisite pottery from the Geometric Age (1200–800 BC) and a case of bull figurines.

Agora Market

(www.chaniamarket.com; Municipal Market; 8am-3pm or 4pm Mon-Sat) Hania's famous covered market is a good-value place for self-caterers to stock up on supplies, as well as stop for lunch. It's also good for take-home purchases such as spices, honey, olive oils and wines.

Sleeping

Ionas Hotel Hotel **€€**

(28210 55090; www.ionashotel.com; cnr Sarpaki & Sorvolou; s/d/ste incl breakfast from €95/100/120;) One of the new breed of boutique hotels in the quieter Splantzia quarter, Ionas is housed in an historic building with contemporary interior design and friendly owners. The nine rooms are kitted out with all mod cons and share a terrace. Original touches include a Venetian archway in the entrance, and walls from the mid-16th century.

Palace of Knossos

THE HIGHLIGHTS IN TWO HOURS

The Palace of Knossos is Crete's busiest tourist attraction, and for good reason. A spin around the partially and imaginatively reconstructed complex (shown here as it was thought to be at its peak) delivers an eye-opening peek into the remarkably sophisticated society of the Minoans, who dominated southern Europe some 4000 years ago.

From the ticket booth, follow the marked trail to the **North Entrance** 1 where the Charging Bull fresco gives you a first taste of Minoan artistry. Continue to the Central Court and join the queue waiting to glimpse the mystical **Throne Room** 2, which probably hosted religious rituals. Turn right as you exit and follow the stairs up to the so-called Piano Nobile, where replicas of the palace's most famous artworks conveniently cluster in the **Fresco Room** 3. Walk the length of the Piano Nobile, pausing to look at the clay storage vessels in the West Magazine. Circle back and descend to the **South Portico** 4, beautifully decorated with the Cup Bearer fresco. Make your way back to the Central Court and head to the palace's eastern wing to admire the architecture of the **Grand Staircase** 5 that led to what Evans imagined to be the royal family's private quarters. For a closer look at some rooms, walk to the south end of the courtyard, stopping for a peek at the **Prince of the Lilies fresco** 6, and head down to the lower floor. A highlight here is the **Queen's Megaron** 7 (Evans imagined this was the Queen's chambers), playfully adorned with a fresco of frolicking dolphins. Stay on the lower level and make your way to the **Giant Pithoi** 8, huge clay jars used for storage.

South Portico
Fine frescoes, most famously the Cup Bearer, embellish this palace entrance anchored by a massive open staircase leading to the Piano Nobile. The Horns of Consecration recreated nearby once topped the entire south facade.

Fresco Room
Take in sweeping views of the palace grounds from the west wing's upper floor, the Piano Nobile, before studying copies of the palace's most famous artworks in its Fresco Room.

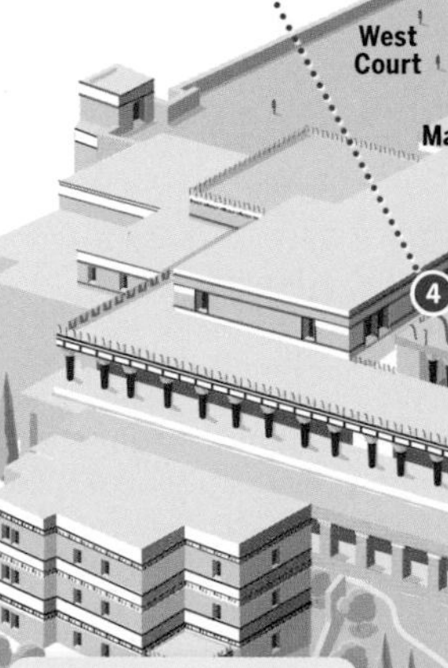

FOOD TIP

Save your appetite for a meal in the nearby Iraklio Wine Country, amid sunbaked slopes and lush valleys. It's just south of Knossos.

Prince of the Lilies Fresco
One of Knossos' most beloved frescoes was controversially cobbled together from various fragments and shows a young man adorned in lilies and peacock feathers.

PLANNING

To beat the crowds and avoid the heat, arrive before 10am. Budget one or two hours to explore the site thoroughly.

ANDREA SCHULTE-PEEVERS ©

Throne Room

Sir Arthur Evans who began excavating the Palace of Knossos in 1900, imagined the mythical King Minos himself holding court seated on the alabaster throne of this beautifully proportioned room. However, the lustral basin and griffin frescoes suggest a religious purpose, possibly under a priestess.

ANDREA SCHULTE-PEEVERS ©

North Entrance

Bulls held a special status in Minoan society as evidenced by the famous relief fresco of a charging beast gracing the columned west bastion of the north palace, which harboured workshops and storage rooms.

Grand Staircase

The royal apartments in the eastern wing were accessed via this monumental staircase sporting four flights of gypsum steps supported by columns. The lower two flights are original. It's closed to the public.

Giant Pithoi

These massive clay jars are rare remnants from the Old Palace period and were used to store wine, oil and grain. The jars were transported by slinging ropes through a series of handles.

ANDREA SCHULTE-PEEVERS ©

Queen's Megaron

The queen's room is among the prettiest in the residential eastern wing thanks to the playful Dolphin Fresco. The adjacent bathroom (with clay tub) and toilet are evidence of a sophisticated drainage system.

ANDREA SCHULTE-PEEVERS ©

Samaria Gorge ΦΑΡΑΓΓΙ ΤΗΣ ΣΑΜΑΡΙΑΣ

The **Samaria Gorge** (☎28210 67179, 28210 45570; adult/child €5/free; ⏲7am-sunset May–late-Oct) is one of Europe's most spectacular gorges and a superb hike. Walkers should take rugged footwear, food, drinks and sun protection for this strenuous five- to six-hour trek.

You can do the walk as part of an excursion tour, or independently by taking the Omalos bus from the main bus station in Hania (€6.90, one hour) to the head of the gorge at Xyloskalo (1230m). It's a 16.7km walk (all downhill) to Agia Roumeli on the coast, from where you take a boat to Hora Sfakion (€10, 1¼ hours) and then a bus back to Hania (€7.60, 1½ hours). You are not allowed to spend the night in the gorge, so you need to complete the walk in a day.

Casa Leone Boutique Hotel **€€**
(☎28210 76762; www.casa-leone.com; Parodos Theotokopoulou 18; d/ste incl breakfast from €135/160; ❄ wifi) This Venetian residence has been converted into a classy and romantic family-run boutique hotel. The rooms are spacious and well appointed, with balconies overlooking the harbour. There are honeymoon suites, with classic drape-canopy beds and sumptuous curtains.

Eating & Drinking

Look beyond the waterfront tourist-traps for some of the best eats on the island. The Splantzia neighbourhood is popular with discerning locals. Nightclubs dot the port and atmpospheric **Fagotto Jazz Bar** (☎28210 71877; Angelou 16; ⏲7pm-2am) has occasional live music.

Taverna Tamam Mediterranean **€€**
(☎28210 96080; Zambeliou 49; mains €7-12; ⏲noon-midnight or 1am; wifi ✎) This excellent, convivial taverna in a converted Turkish bathhouse fills with chatting locals at tables spilling out onto the street. Meals incorporate mid-Eastern spices, and include tasty soups and a superb selection of vegetarian specialities.

To Maridaki Cretan **€€**
(☎28210 08880; Daskalogianni 33; dishes €7-12; ⏲noon-midnight Mon-Sat) This modern seafood *mezedhopoleio* (mezedhes restaurant) is not to be missed. In a cheerful, bright dining room, happy visitors and locals alike tuck into impeccable, local seafood and Cretan specialties. Ingredients are fresh, the fried calamari is to die for, the house white wine is crisp and delicious, and the complimentary panacotta to finish the meal is transcendent. What's not to love?

Information

For more information visit the Hania website (www.chania.gr).

Getting There & Away

Air

There are several flights a day between Hania airport (CHQ) and Athens, plus a number of flights to Thessaloniki each week. The airport is 14km east of town on the Akrotiri Peninsula. Taxis to town cost €20; buses cost €2.30.

Boat

Nightly ferries sail between Piraeus (€35, nine hours) and the port of Souda, 9km southeast of Hania. Frequent buses (€1.65) and taxis (€10) connect town and Souda.

DODECANESE ΔΩΔΕΚΑΝΗΣΑ

Strung out along the coast of western Turkey, the 12 main islands of the Dodecanese (*dodeca* means 12) have suffered a turbulent past of invasions and occupations that have endowed them with a fascinating diversity.

The islands themselves range from the verdant and mountainous to the rocky and dry. While Rhodes and Kos host highly developed tourism, the more remote islands await those in search of traditional island life.

Rhodes ΡΟΔΟΣ

POP 98,000

Rhodes (Rodos in Greek) is the largest island in the Dodecanese. According to mythology, the sun god Helios chose Rhodes as his bride and bestowed light, warmth and vegetation upon her. The blessing seems to have paid off, for Rhodes produces more flowers and sunny days than most Greek islands.

Getting There & Away

Air

There are plenty of flights daily between Rhodes' **Diagoras airport** (RHO) and Athens, plus less-regular flights to Karpathos, Kastellorizo, Thessaloniki, Iraklio and Samos. The airport is on the west coast, 16km southwest of Rhodes Town; 25 minutes and €2.20 by bus, €22 by taxi.

Boat

There are daily ferries from Rhodes to Piraeus (€59, 13 hours). Most sail via the Dodecanese north of Rhodes, but at least twice a week there is a service via Karpathos, Crete and the Cyclades.

In summer, catamaran services run up and down the Dodecanese daily from Rhodes to Symi, Kos, Kalymnos, Nisyros, Tilos, Patmos and Leros.

RHODES TOWN

POP 56,000

Rhodes' capital is Rhodes Town, on the northern tip of the island. Its **Old Town**, the largest inhabited medieval town in Europe, is enclosed within massive walls and is a joy to explore. To the north is **New Town**, the commercial centre.

Sights

A wander around Rhodes' World Heritage–listed Old Town is a must. It is reputedly the world's finest surviving example of medieval fortification, with 12m-thick walls.

Palace of the Grand Masters (p730), Rhodes Town

IAN CUMMING/GETTY IMAGES ©

The Knights of St John lived in the **Knights' Quarter** in the northern end of the Old Town.

The cobbled **Odos Ippoton** (Ave of the Knights) is lined with magnificent medieval buildings, the most imposing of which is the **Palace of the Grand Masters** (22410 23359; admission €6; 8.30am-3pm Tue-Sun), which was restored, but never used, as a holiday home for Mussolini.

The 15th-century Knight's Hospital now houses the **Archaeological Museum** (22410 65256; Plateia Mousiou; admission €6; 8am-3pm Tue-Sun).

The pink-domed **Mosque of Süleyman** at the top of Sokratous, was built in 1522 to commemorate the Ottoman victory against the knights, then rebuilt in 1808.

Sleeping

Mango Rooms Pension €
(22410 24877; www.mango.gr; Plateia Dorieos 3, Old Town; d/tr €60/72;) Set in a square in Old Town, these are spotless, simple rooms with safety deposit box, fridge and bathroom. Downstairs is a restaurant and internet cafe.

Marco Polo Mansion Boutique Hotel €€
(22410 25562; www.marcopolomansion.gr; Agiou Fanouriou 40, Old Town; d incl breakfast €80-180; Apr-Oct;) We love the vivid style in this 15th-century former Ottoman official's house; with its heavy antique furniture and Eastern rugs, and stained-glass windows washing the oxblood walls in blue light. The rooms are spectacularly romantic with huge beds, and tasteful furnishings. Try the split-level ex-harem bedroom. There's a top **restaurant**, too!

Eating

Inside the walls, Old Town has it all in terms of touts and over-priced tavernas trying to separate less-savvy tourists from their euro. The back alleys tend to throw up better-quality eateries and prices.

To Meltemi Taverna €€
(Kountourioti 8; mains €10-15; noon-6pm;) With wide sea views and just yards from the beach, this breezy taverna has a cosy, nautically themed interior, or you can dine on the semi-alfresco terrace. Staff are charming and the menu swimming in feisty salads, salted mackerel, calamari and octopus.

Pizanias Taverna €€
(22410 22117; Sofokleous 24; mains €8-18; noon-midnight Feb-Oct) This atmospheric little taverna tucked back into the heart of Old Town is known for its fresh seafood and delicious fava. Dine under the trees and the night sky.

Information

For more information, see **Rodos** (www.rodos.gr).

Tourist Information Office (EOT; 22410 44335; www.ando.gr/eot; cnr Makariou & Papagou; 8am-2.45pm Mon-Fri) Brochures, maps, transport information and *Rodos News*, a free English-language newspaper.

Kos ΚΩΣ

POP 19,872

Captivating Kos, only 5km from the Turkish peninsula of Bodrum, is popular with history buffs as the birthplace of Hippocrates (460–377 BC), the father of medicine. The island also attracts an entirely different crowd – sun-worshipping beach lovers from northern Europe who flock here during summer.

Sights

Asklepeion Archaeological Site
(22420 28763; adult/child €4/free; 8am-7.30pm Tue-Sun) On a pretty pine- and olive-grove-clad hill 4km southwest of Kos Town stand the extensive ruins of the renowned healing centre which taught the principles of Hippocrates' way. Doctors and healers come from all over the world to visit.

Castle of the Knights Fortress
(22420 27927; Kos Town; admission €4; 8am-2.30pm Tue-Sun) Reach the once

impregnable Castle of the Knights by crossing a bridge over Finikon from **Plateia Platanou**. The castle, which had massive outer walls and an inner keep, was built in the 14th century and separated from the town by a moat (now Finikon). Damaged by an earthquake in 1495 and restored in the 16th century, it was the knights' most stalwart defence against the encroaching Ottomans.

Ancient Agora Ruin

(Kos Town) FREE The ancient agora, with the ruins of the **Shrine of Aphrodite** and **Temple of Hercules**, is an open site south of the Castle of the Knights. A massive 3rd-century-BC stoa, with some reconstructed columns, stands on its western side.

Sleeping

Hotel Afendoulis Hotel **€**

(22420 25321; www.afendoulishotel.com; Evripilou 1, Kos Town; s/d €30/50; Mar-Nov;) Peaceful Afendoulis has unfailingly friendly staff and sparkling rooms with white walls, small balconies, flat-screen TVs, hairdryers, and spotless bathrooms. Downstairs there's an open breakfast room and flowery terrace with wrought-iron tables and chairs for enjoying the feast of homemade jams and marmalades.

Hotel Sonia Hotel **€€**

(22420 28798; www.hotelsonia.gr; Irodotou 9, Kos Town; s/d/tr €45/60/75; year-round;) On a peaceful street, this pension has sparkling rooms with parquet floors, flat-screen TVs, fridges, chic bathrooms and an extra bed if you need it. There's a relaxing communal verandah with wrought-iron chairs, spacious private balconies, and a decent library. Room 4 has the best sea view.

Eating

H2O International **€€**

(22420 47200; www.kosaktis.gr; Vasileos Georgiou 7, Kos Town; mains €10-20; 11am-midnight;) The city's glitziest waterfront eatery at Kos Aktis Art Hotel is patronised by fashionistas and makes for a great stop for a healthy lunch or dinner, out on the decked terrace facing Bodrum. Choose from bruschetta, grilled

Plateia Platanou, Kos

veg, battered shrimp, chicken risotto, or simply plump for a sundowner mojito.

Getting There & Around

Air

There are daily flights to Athens from Kos' Ippokratis airport (KGS), which is 28km southwest of Kos Town. Get to/from the airport by bus (€4) or taxi (€30).

Boat

Kos has services to Piraeus and all islands in the Dodecanese, the Cyclades, Samos and Thessaloniki. Local passenger and car ferries run to Pothia on Kalymnos from Mastihari. In summer excursion boats depart daily for Bodrum in Turkey (€20 return, one hour).

IONIAN ISLANDS ΤΑ ΕΠΤΑΝΗΣΑ

The idyllic cypress- and fir-covered Ionian Islands stretch down the western coast of Greece from Corfu in the north to Kythira, off the southern tip of the Peloponnese. Mountainous, with dramatic cliff-backed beaches, soft light and turquoise water, they're more Italian in feel, offering a contrasting experience to other Greek islands. Invest in a hire car to get to small villages tucked along quiet back roads.

Corfu ΚΕΡΚΥΡΑ

POP 122,700

Many consider Corfu, or Kerkyra (*ker*-kih-rah) in Greek, to be Greece's most beautiful island – the unfortunate consequence of which is that it's overbuilt and often overrun with crowds.

Getting There & Away

Air

Ioannis Kapodistrias Airport (CFU; ☎26610 89600; www.corfu-airport.com) is 2km southwest of Corfu Town. Olympic Air, Aegean Airlines and Astra Airlines fly daily to Athens and a few times weekly to Thessaloniki. Sky Express operates seasonal routes to other Ionian Islands and Crete (but beware the strict baggage policy). Charter planes and budget airlines fly internationally in summer. Bus 19 serves the airport (€1.50), taxis cost €7-10.

Boat

Ferries go to Igoumenitsa (€10, 1½ hours, hourly). In summer daily ferries and hydrofoils go to Paxi, and ferries to Italy (Bari, Brindisi and Venice) also stop in Patra (€35, six hours), some stop in Kefallonia and Zakynthos. Petrakis Lines goes to Saranda, Albania.

CORFU TOWN

POP 31,360

Built on a promontory and wedged between two fortresses, Corfu's Old Town is a tangle of narrow walking streets through gorgeous Venetian buildings.

Beach at Paleokastritsa, Corfu

Sights

Palaio Frourio Fortress
(Old Fortress; ☎26610 48310; adult/concession €4/2; ⏱8am-8pm Apr-Oct, 8.30am-3pm Nov-Mar) Constructed by the Venetians in the 15th century on the remains of a Byzantine castle and further altered by the British, this spectacular landmark offers respite from the crowds and superb views of the region. Climb to the summit of the inner outcrop which is crowned by a lighthouse for a 360-degree panorama. The gatehouse contains a Byzantine museum.

Palace of St Michael & St George Palace
Originally the residence of a succession of British high commissioners, this palace now houses the world-class **Museum of Asian Art** (☎26610 30443; www.matk.gr; adult/child incl audioguide €3/free, with Antivouniotissa Museum & Old Fortress €8; ⏱8.30am-3.30pm Tue-Sun), founded in 1929. Expertly curated with extensive, informative English-language placards, the collection's approximately 10,000 artefacts collected from all over Asia include priceless prehistoric bronzes, ceramics, jade figurines, coins and works of art in onyx, ivory and enamel. Additionally, the palace's throne room and rotunda are impressively adorned in period furnishings and art.

Church of Agios Spyridon Church
(Agios Spyridonos; ⏱7am-8pm) FREE The sacred relic of Corfu's beloved patron saint, St Spyridon, lies in an elaborate silver casket in the 16th-century basilica.

Sleeping

Bella Venezia Boutique Hotel €€
(☎26610 46500; www.bellaveneziahotel.com; N Zambeli 4; s/d incl breakfast from €120/125;) In a neoclassical former girls' school, the Venezia has comfy rooms and an elegant ambience. Conscientious staff welcome you, and the gazebo breakfast room in the garden is delightful.

Hermes Hotel Hotel €€
(☎26610 39268; www.hermes-hotel.gr; Markora 12; s/d/tr from €55/65/75;) In a busy part of the new town, overlooking the market, Hermes offers simple, tidy rooms with double glazing, which are especially atmospheric in the old wing.

Eating

To Tavernaki tis Marinas Taverna €
(☎69816 56001; 4th Parados, Agias Sofias 1; mains €6-16; ⏱noon-midnight) Restored stone walls, smooth hardwood floors and cheerful staff lift the ambience of this taverna a cut above the rest. Check daily specials or choose anything from *mousakas* (baked layers of eggplant or zucchini, minced meat and potatoes topped with cheese sauce) or grilled sardines to steak. Accompany it all with a dram of ouzo or *tsipouro* (a spirit similar to ouzo).

La Cucina Italian €€
(☎26610 45799; cnr Guilford & Moustoxidou; ⏱7-11pm) Every detail is cared for at this intimate bistro, from the hand-rolled *tortellonis* to the inventive pizzas and murals on the walls.

AROUND THE ISLAND

To fully explore all regions of the island your own transport is best. Much of the coast just north of Corfu Town is overwhelmed with beach resorts, the south is quieter, and the west has beautiful, if popular, coastline. The **Corfu Trail** traverses the island north to south.

In **Kassiopi**, **Manessis Apartments** (☎26610 34990; http://manessiskassiopi.com; Kassiopi; 4-person apt €70-100;) offers water-view apartments. Don't miss a dinner at one of the island's best tavernas, **Klimataria** (Dellos; ☎26610 71201; mains €8-14; ⏱7pm-midnight) in Benitses.

To gain an aerial view of the gorgeous cypress-backed bays around **Paleokastritsa**, the west coast's main resort, go to the quiet village of **Lakones**. Further south, good beaches surround tiny **Agios Gordios**.

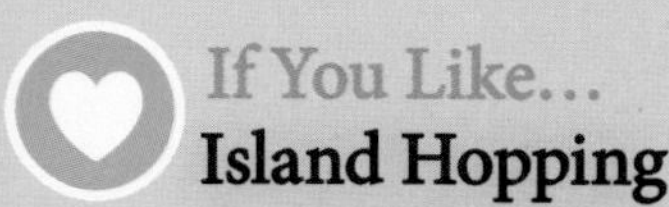

If You Like... Island Hopping

If you've fallen for the laid-back pace of life on the Ionian Islands, then you're in luck – Greece has plenty more island archipelagos to explore.

1 **AEGEAN ISLANDS**
These far-flung islands are strewn across the northeastern Aegean. **Samos** was an important centre of Hellenic culture. **Lesvos**, or Mytilini as it is often called, is the third-largest of the Greek Islands, and produces half the world's ouzo, while little **Chios** is ideal if you want to escape the crowds. There are regular flights from Athens, plus seasonal boats from the Cyclades and Dodecanese.

2 **CYCLADES**
Most people never make it beyond Mykonos and Santorini, but the Cyclades have lots of other fascinating islands. **Naxos** is the largest and lushest; **Paros** is known for its beaches and terraced hills; **Ios** is the island for party animals. All can be reached by ferry from Piraeus on the mainland and Iraklio on Crete.

3 **DODECANESE**
Beyond the main islands, traditional Greek culture still holds sway. To the north of Rhodes, **Symi** is home to the ancient Monastery of Panormitis, while the mountainous island of **Karpathos**, midway between Crete and Rhodes, is a scenic island with a cosy port and more than 40 unspoilt villages. Tourism remains low-key except in July and August, when the island goes mad. Both can be easily reached from Rhodes.

SURVIVAL GUIDE

Directory A–Z

Accommodation

Hotels Range from basic business lodgings to high-end boutique extravaganzas.

Pensions & Guesthouses Often include breakfast and are usually owner-operated.

Domatia Rooms for rent; owners greet ferries and buses shouting 'room!'

Youth hostels In most major towns and on some islands.

Campgrounds Generally open April to October; standard facilities include hot showers, kitchens, restaurants and minimarkets, often a swimming pool; see **Panhellenic Camping Association** (☎21036 21560; www.greececamping.gr). Wild camping forbidden.

Mountain refuges Listed in *Greece Mountain Refuges & Ski Centres*, available free from EOT and EOS (Ellinikos Orivatikos Syndesmos, Greek Alpine Club) offices.

Price Ranges

'High season' is usually in July and August. If you turn up in the 'middle' or 'shoulder seasons' (May and June; September and October) expect to pay significantly less. During 'low season' (late October to late April) prices can be up to 50% cheaper, but a lot of places, especially on the islands, virtually close their shutters for winter.

Prices quoted in listings are for high season (usually July and August) and include a private bathroom.

€ less than €60

€€ €60 to €150

€€€ more than €150

Business Hours

Banks 8am-2.30pm Mon-Thu, 8am-2pm Fri

Cafes 10am-midnight

Post offices 7.30am-2pm Mon-Fri (in cities 7.30am-8pm Mon-Fri, 7.30am-2pm Sat)

Restaurants 11am-3pm & 7pm-1am (varies greatly)

Supermarkets 8am-8pm Mon-Fri, 8am-3pm Sat

Food

Price ranges in our reviews are based on the average cost of a main dish:

€ under €10

€€ €10-20

€€€ over €20

Gay & Lesbian Travellers

The church plays a significant role in shaping society's views on issues such as sexuality, and homosexuality is generally frowned-upon.

It is wise to be discreet and to avoid open displays of togetherness. That said, Greece is a popular destination for gay travellers.

Athens has a busy gay scene that packs up and heads to the islands for summer, with Mykonos famous for its bars, beaches and hedonism, and Skala Eresou on Lesvos something of a pilgrimage for lesbians.

Money

ATMs Everywhere except the smallest villages.

Bargaining While souvenir shops will generally bargain, prices in other shops are normally clearly marked and non-negotiable; accommodation is nearly always negotiable outside peak season, especially for longer stays.

Cash Currency is king at street kiosks and small shops, and especially in the countryside.

Changing currency Banks, post offices and currency exchange offices are all over the places; exchange all major currencies.

Credit cards Generally accepted, but may not be on smaller islands or in small villages.

Tipping The service charge is included on the bill in restaurants, but it is the custom to 'round up the bill'; same for taxis.

Public Holidays

New Year's Day 1 January

Epiphany 6 January

First Sunday in Lent February

Greek Independence Day 25 March

Good Friday/Easter Sunday March/April

May Day (Protomagia) 1 May

Feast of the Assumption 15 August

Ohi Day 28 October

Christmas Day 25 December

St Stephen's Day 26 December

Telephone

Maintained by Organismos Tilepikoinonion Ellados, known as OTE (o-*teh*). Public phones are everywhere, take all phonecards and are easy to use; pressing the 'i' button brings up the operating instructions in English.

For directory inquiries within Greece, call ☎131 or 132; for international directory inquiries, it's ☎161 or ☎162.

Chios village, Chios, Aegean Islands

Mobile Phones

Mobile phones are a must-have in Greece. If you have a compatible GSM phone from a country with a global roaming agreement with Greece, you'll be able to use your phone there.

There are several mobile service providers in Greece; **CosmOTE** (www.cosmote.gr) has the best coverage. You can purchase a Greek SIM card for around €20.

Phone Codes

Telephone codes are part of the 10-digit number within Greece. The landline prefix is ☎2 and for mobiles it's ☎6.

Phonecards

All public phones use OTE phonecards; sold at OTE offices and street kiosks. Phonecards come in €3, €5 and €10 versions; local calls cost €0.30 for three minutes. Discount-card schemes are available, offering much better value for money.

Time

Greece is in the Eastern European time zone: two hours ahead of GMT/UTC and three hours ahead on daylight-saving time (last Sunday in March through last Sunday in October).

Toilets

Greek plumbing can't handle toilet paper: anything larger than a postage stamp will cause a blockage. Put your used toilet paper, sanitary napkins and tampons in the small bin provided next to every toilet.

Tourist Information

Greek National Tourist Organisation (www.gnto.gr, www.visitgreece.gr, www.discovergreece.com)

Travellers with Disabilities

Most hotels, museums and ancient sites are not wheelchair accessible; the uneven terrain is an issue even for able-bodied people. Few facilities exist for the visually or hearing impaired. Check out www.greecetravel.com/handicapped.

Visas

Generally not required for stays up to 90 days. Member of the Schengen Convention.

ℹ Getting There & Away

Air

Most visitors arrive by air, mostly into Athens. There are 17 international airports in Greece; most handle only summer charter flights to the islands.

Sea

Check ferry routes and schedules online at www.greekferries.gr and www.openseas.gr.

Fishing boats, Ithaki, Ionian Islands

If you are travelling on a rail pass, check to see if ferry travel between Italy and Greece is included. Some ferries are free, others give a discount.

 Getting Around

Boat

Ferries come in all shapes and sizes, from state-of-the-art 'superferries' that run on the major routes, to ageing open ferries that operate local services to outlying islands.

Newer high-speed ferries, catamarans and hydrofoils are slashing travel times, but cost much more.

Tickets can be bought at the last minute at the dock, but in high season, some boats may be full – plan ahead.

The Greek Ships app for smartphones can be used for real-time tracking to see if your ferry is going to turn up on time – search for 'Greek Ships' in your app store.

Bus

Long-distance buses are operated by KTEL (www.ktel.org).

Car & Motorcycle

A great way to explore areas in Greece that are off the beaten track, but be careful – Greece has the highest road-fatality rate in Europe.

The Greek automobile club, **ELPA** (www.elpa.gr), generally offers reciprocal services to members of other national motoring associations. If your vehicle breaks down, dial ☎104.

EU-registered vehicles are allowed free entry into Greece for six months without road taxes being due; a green card (international third party insurance) is all that's required.

Rental cars

Available just about anywhere in Greece, you'll get better rates with local rental-car companies than with the big multinational outfits. Check the insurance waivers closely; check how they can assist in case of a breakdown.

High-season weekly rates start at about €280 for the smallest models, dropping to €175 in winter – add tax and extras. Major companies will request a credit-card deposit.

Minimum driving age in Greece is 18, but most car-hire firms require a driver of 21 or over.

Mopeds & Motorcycles

These are available for hire everywhere. Regulations stipulate that you need a valid motorcycle licence stating proficiency for the size of motorcycle you wish to rent – from 50cc upwards.

Mopeds and 50cc motorcycles range from €10 to €25 per day or from €25 per day for a 250cc motorcycle. Outside high season, rates drop considerably.

Road Rules

- Drive on the right.
- Overtake on the left (not all Greeks do this!).
- Compulsory to wear seatbelts in the front seats, and in the back if they are fitted.
- Drink-driving laws are strict; a blood alcohol content of 0.05% incurs a fine of around €150 and over 0.08% is a criminal offence.

Public Transport

Taxi

Taxis are widely available and reasonably priced. Yellow city cabs are metered; rates double between midnight and 5am. Grey rural taxis do not have meters; settle on a price before you get in.

Train

Check the Greek Railways Organisation website (www.trainose.gr) for current schedules. Greece has only two main lines: Athens north to Thessaloniki and Alexandroupolis, and Athens to the Peloponnese.

Europe In Focus

View of San Giorgio Maggiore, Venice (p401), Italy

Europe Today

European Parliament, Brussels

> *Eurovision...this one-of-a-kind musical marathon is allegedly Europe's most-watched non-sporting event*

belief systems
(% of population)

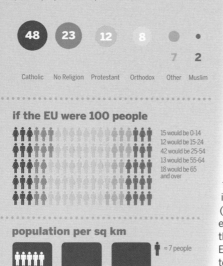

7 2

Catholic No Religion Protestant Orthodox Other Muslim

if the EU were 100 people

15 would be 0-14
12 would be 15-24
42 would be 25-54
13 would be 55-64
18 would be 65 and over

population per sq km

≈ 7 people

EUROPE AFRICA NORTH AMERICA

Economic Challenges

The effects of the 2008 financial crash, which led to the 2009 European debt crisis, continue to echo to this day. Growth throughout the EU has been sluggish, with many countries dipping in and out of recession. Unemployment figures across many European nations remain high, especially in Spain and Greece, where about one in four people are currently without work, rising to around one in two people aged under 25.

Although the euro stabilised after a series of multi-billion-euro rescue packages for Greece, Ireland, Portugal and Spain, the currency is still subject to uncertainty. In 2015, the Swiss franc 'unpegged' from the euro, resulting in an immediate 30% increase in its relative value (with some later correction). Also in 2015, an extension of Greece's bailout was granted in the hope of keeping the country within the Eurozone, to avoid a Greek exit (aka 'Grexit'), and to avoid other debt-saddled countries following suit. And the European Central Bank launched massive quantitative easing (QE) measures

ZIUTOGRAF/GETTY IMAGES ©

involving money printing and bond buying, pumping over €1 trillion into the economy in an effort to resuscitate it.

Reconciling countries' divergent needs, however, remains a tough problem to solve.

State of the Union

Where Europe should be headed as a political entity remains a burning question for EU nations. Deeper integration is necessary to address current issues but means individual nations have to relinquish further powers to the EU parliament. It's a controversial proposition, especially in countries with significant numbers of eurosceptic voters, such as the UK. Its conservative Tory party has promised to hold an 'in/out' referendum on UK membership of the EU by the end of 2017 if it holds power.

EU membership also raises questions about democratic representation: in exchange for their financial bailouts, financially strapped countries have been forced to follow the political will of Brussels, often in direct contradiction to the wishes of their own constituents and, in some cases, the platforms on which their governments were elected.

Greener Europe

On a brighter note, many European countries are making significant efforts to combat climate change. Increasingly, high-speed rail services provide an eco-friendly alternative to short-haul flights, green spaces flourish in urban areas, share-bicycle schemes are becoming prevalent in cities and towns, and vehicle emissions are being reduced with more electric and hybrid engines and biofuels. Two of Europe's most congested cities, London and Paris, both plan to ban pollution-prone diesel vehicles from 2020.

The Eurovision Issue

And on a lighter note, every May, Europe's international song contest sparks the same debates. Is the voting system rigged? Should acts sing in English or in their own language? Above all, why are the songs invariably so awful?

Each country is allowed to enter one song, and is then allowed to pick their favourites of their competitors'. Inevitably this leads to accusations of 'block voting' (neighbouring countries tending to vote for each other, for example). Confusingly, too, several non-European countries are allowed to enter. The host city, with a few exceptions, is in the winner country of the previous year, with cities competing domestically for the honour and associated tourism boost.

This one-of-a-kind musical marathon has been screened every year since 1956, making it the longest-running television show of its kind, and allegedly Europe's most-watched non-sporting event.

History

Caryatids of the Erechtheion (p701), the Acropolis, Greece

JEAN-PIERRE LESCOURRET/GETTY IMA

Europe is a place where history seems to seep into every corner. It's literally everywhere you look: in the tumbledown remains of Greek temples and Roman bathhouses, in the fabulously ostentatious architecture of French chateaux and Austrian castles, and in the winding streets and broad boulevards of its many stately cities. Understanding Europe's long and often troubled history is a crucial part of figuring out what makes this continent tick.

Prehistory

The first settlers arrived in Europe around two million years ago, but it wasn't until the end of the last major ice age between 12,000 BC and 8000 BC that humans really took hold. As the glaciers and ice sheets retreated, hunter-gatherer tribes extended their reach northwards in search of new land. Some of Europe's earliest human settlements were left behind by Neolithic tribes.

4500–2500 BC

Neolithic tribes build burial tombs, barrows, stone circles and alignments across Europe, including Stonehenge and Carnac.

Greeks & Romans

Europe's first great civilisations developed in Mycenae (about 90km southwest of Athens) and ancient Crete, but it was the Greeks and the Romans who left the most enduring mark. The civilisation of ancient Greece emerged around 2000 BC and made huge leaps forward in science, technology, architecture, philosophy and democratic principles. Many of the writers, thinkers and mathematicians of ancient Greece, from Pythagoras to Plato, still exert a profound influence to this day.

Then came the Romans, who set about conquering most of Europe and devised the world's first republic. At its height, Roman power extended all the way from Celtic Britain to ancient Persia (Iran). The Romans' myriad achievements are almost too numerous to mention: they founded cities, raised aqueducts, constructed roads, laid sewers and built baths all over the continent, and produced a string of brilliant writers, orators, politicians, philosophers and military leaders.

Dark Ages to Middle Ages

By the 4th century AD, the Greek and Roman Empires had seen their golden ages come and go. Greece had been swallowed by Macedonia, led by Alexander the Great, then by Rome itself in AD 146. Meanwhile, Rome's empire-building ambitions eventually proved too much, and a series of political troubles and military disasters resulted in the sacking of Rome (in 410) by the Goths. Although Roman emperors clung onto their eastern Byzantine empire for another thousand years, founding a new capital at Constantinople, Rome's dominance over Western Europe was over. A new era, the Dark Ages, had begun.

The next few centuries were marked by a series of conflicts in which the various kingdoms of the European mainland sought to gain political and strategic control. In 711AD, the Moors – Arabs and Berbers who had converted to the Islamic religion prevailing throughout northern Africa – crossed the Straits of Gibraltar, defeating the Visigothic army. They went on to rule the Iberian Peninsula for almost 800 years, until the fall of Granada in 1492, leaving behind a flourishing architectural, scientific and academic legacy. Meanwhile, in 768, Charlemagne, King of the Franks, brought together much of Western Europe under what would become known as the Holy Roman Empire, and an alliance of Christian nations sent troops to reclaim the Holy Land from Islamic control in a series of campaigns known as the Crusades.

Renaissance & Reformation

Europe's troubles rumbled on into the 14th and 15th centuries. In the wake of further conflicts and political upheavals, as well as the devastating outbreak of the Black Death (estimated to have wiped out somewhere between one-third and two-thirds

2500–500 BC
Ancient Greeks break new ground in technology, science, art and architecture.

1st century BC–4 AD
The Romans conquer much of Europe. The Roman Empire flourishes under Augustus and his successors.

410
The sacking of Rome by the Goths brings an end to Roman dominance.

The Best... Ancient Ruins

1 Acropolis (p702), Greece

2 Colosseum (p375), Italy

3 Stonehenge (p98), England

4 Pompeii (p441), Italy

5 Alignements de Carnac (p216), France

of Europe's population), control over the Holy Roman Empire passed into the hands of the Austrian Habsburgs, a political dynasty that was to become one of the continent's dominant powers. Meanwhile, the Italian city-states of Genoa, Venice, Pisa and Amalfi consolidated their control over the Mediterranean, establishing trading links with much of the rest of Europe and the Far East, and embarking on some of the first journeys in search of the New World.

In the mid-15th century, a new age of artistic and philosophical development broke out across the continent. The Renaissance encouraged writers, artists and thinkers to challenge the accepted doctrines of theology, philosophy, architecture and art. The centre of this artistic tsunami was Florence, Italy, where such inspirational figures as Michelangelo and Leonardo da Vinci made great strides in art and architecture. Another epoch-changing development was under way in Germany, thanks to the invention of the printing press by Johannes Gutenburg in around 1440. The advent of 'movable type' made printed books available to the masses for the first time.

While the Renaissance challenged artistic ideas, the Reformation dealt with questions of religion. Challenging Catholic 'corruption' and the divine authority of the Pope, the German theologian Martin Luther established his own breakaway branch of the Church, to which he gave the name 'Protestantism', in 1517. Luther's stance was soon echoed by the English monarch Henry VIII, who cut ties with Rome in 1534 and went on to found his own (Protestant) Church of England, sowing the seeds for centuries of conflict between Catholics and Protestants.

The New World

The schisms of the Church weren't the only source of tension. The discovery of the 'New World' in the mid-16th century led to a colonial arms race between the major European nations, in which each country battled to lay claim to the newly discovered lands – often enslaving or killing the local populace in the process.

More trouble followed during the Thirty Years' War (1618–48), which began as a conflict between Catholics and Protestants and eventually sucked in most of Europe's principal powers. The war was ended by the Peace of Westphalia in 1648, and Europe entered a period of comparative stability.

1066
William the Conqueror defeats the English King Harold at the Battle of Hastings.

1340s-1350s
The Black Death reaches its peak in Europe, killing between 30% and 60% of Europe's population.

15th century
The Italian Renaissance brings about a revolution in art, architecture and science.

The Enlightenment

The Enlightenment (sometimes known as 'The Age of Reason') is the name given to a philosophical movement that spread throughout European society during the mid- to late-17th century. It emphasised the importance of logic, reason and science over the doctrines of religion. Key figures included the philosophers Baruch Spinoza, John Locke, Immanuel Kant and Voltaire, as well as scientists such as Isaac Newton.

The Enlightenment also questioned the political status quo. Since the Middle Ages, the majority of Europe's wealth and power had been concentrated in the hands of an all-powerful elite, largely made up of monarchs and aristocrats. This stood in direct contradiction to one of the core values of the Enlightenment – equality. Many thinkers believed it was an impasse that could only be solved by revolution.

Things came to a head in 1789 when armed mobs stormed the Bastille prison in Paris, thus kick-starting the French Revolution. The Revolution began with high ideals, inspired by its iconic slogan of *liberté, egalité, fraternité* (liberty, equality, brotherhood; a phrase that still graces French €1 and €2 coins). Before long things turned sour and heads began to roll. Hardline republicans seized control and demanded retribution for centuries of oppression. Scores of aristocrats met their end under the guillotine's

Fontana dei Quattro Fiumi (p379), Piazza Navona, Rome

1517
Martin Luther nails his demands to the church door in Wittenburg, sparking the Reformation.

1789
France becomes a republic following the French Revolution. Numerous aristocrats are executed by guillotine.

18th & 19th centuries
The Industrial Revolution transforms European society.

The Best... Royal Palaces

1 Windsor Castle (p108), England

2 Château de Versailles (p202), France

3 Hofburg (p603), Austria

4 Palacio Real (p287), Madrid

5 Prague Castle (p659), Czech Republic

blade, including the French monarch Louis XVI, who was publicly executed in January 1793 in Paris' Place de la Concorde, and his queen, Marie-Antoinette, killed in October that year.

The Reign of Terror between September 1793 and July 1794 saw religious freedoms revoked, churches closed, cathedrals turned into 'Temples of Reason' and thousands beheaded. In the chaos, a dashing young Corsican general named Napoleon Bonaparte (1769–1821) seized his chance.

Napoleon assumed power in 1799 and in 1804 was crowned Emperor. He fought a series of campaigns across Europe and conquered vast swathes of territory for the French empire but, following a disastrous campaign to conquer Russia in 1812, his grip on power faltered and he was defeated by a coalition of British and Prussian forces at the Battle of Waterloo in 1815.

Industry, Empire & WWI

Having vanquished Napoleon, Britain emerged as Europe's predominant power. With such innovations as the steam engine, the railway and the factory, Britain unleashed the Industrial Revolution and, like many of Europe's major powers (including France, Spain, Belgium and the Austro-Hungarian empire), set about developing its colonies across much of Africa, Australasia and the Middle and Far East.

Before long these competing empires clashed again, with predictably catastrophic consequences. The assassination of the heir to the Austro-Hungarian Empire Franz Ferdinand in 1914 led to the outbreak of the Great War, or WWI, as it came to be known. By the end of hostilities in 1918, huge tracts of northern France and Belgium had been razed and over 16 million people across Europe had been killed.

In the Treaty of Versailles, the defeated powers of Austro-Hungary and Germany lost large areas of territory and found themselves crippled with a massive bill for reparations, sowing seeds of discontent that would be exploited a decade later by a young Austrian painter by the name of Adolf Hitler.

WWII

Hitler's rise to power was astonishingly swift. By 1933 he had become Chancellor and, as the head of the Nazi Party, assumed total control of Germany. Having spent much of the 1930s building up a formidable war machine, assisting General Franco's nationalist

1914
The assassination of Archduke Franz Ferdinand leads to the outbreak of WWI (1914–18).

1939–45
WWII rages across Europe, devastating many cities. After peace is declared, much of Eastern Europe falls under communist rule.

1957
The European Economic Community (EEC) is formed by a collection of Western European countries.

forces during the Spanish Civil War, Hitler annexed former German territories in Austria and parts of Czechoslovakia, before extending his reach onwards into Poland in 1939.

The occupation of Poland proved the final straw. Britain, France and its Commonwealth allies declared war on Germany, which had formed its own alliance of convenience with the Axis powers of Italy and Japan. Hitler unleashed his blitzkrieg on an unsuspecting Europe, and within a few short months had conquered huge areas of territory across Eastern and central Europe, forcing the French into submission and driving the British forces to a humiliating retreat at Dunkirk. Europe was to remain under Nazi occupation for the next six years.

The Axis retained the upper hand until the Japanese attack on Pearl Harbor forced a reluctant USA into the war in 1941. Hitler's subsequent decision to invade Russia in 1941 proved to be a catastrophic error, resulting in devastating German losses that opened the door for the Allied invasion of Normandy in June 1944.

After several months of bitter fighting, Hitler's remaining forces were pushed back towards Berlin. Hitler committed suicide on 30 April 1945 and the Russians took the city, crushing the last pockets of German resistance. By 8 May Germany and Italy had unconditionally surrendered to the Allied powers, bringing the war in Europe to an end.

Hall of Mirrors, Versailles (p202), France
DENNIS JOHNSON/GETTY IMAGES ©

1989
The fall of the Berlin Wall heralds the downfall of oppressive regimes across much of Eastern Europe.

1993
The Maastricht Treaty leads to the formation of the EU.

2002
Twelve member states of the EU ditch their national currencies in favour of the euro.

The Best... Historic Landmarks

1 Nelson's Column (p61), London

2 Place de la Bastille (p187), Paris

3 Berlin Wall (p532)

4 Alhambra (p346), Granada

5 D-Day Beaches (p210), France

The Iron Curtain

Differences of opinion between the Western powers and the communist Soviet Union soon led to a stand-off. The USSR closed off its assigned sectors, including East Berlin, East Germany and much of Eastern Europe, which heralded the descent of the Iron Curtain and the beginning of the Cold War. This period of political tension and social division in Europe lasted for 40 years.

The Cold War era came to an end in 1989, when popular unrest in Germany resulted in the fall of the Berlin Wall. Germany was reunified in 1990; a year later the USSR was dissolved. Shortly afterwards Romania, Bulgaria, Poland, Hungary and Albania had implemented multiparty democracy. In Czechoslovakia (now the Czech Republic and Slovakia), the so-called Velvet Revolution brought about the downfall of the communist government through mass demonstrations and other nonviolent means.

Europe United

Elsewhere in Europe, the process of political and economic integration has continued apace since the end of WWII. The formation of the European Economic Community (EEC) in 1957 began as a loose trade alliance between six nations, but since its evolution into the European Union (EU) when the 1992-signed Treaty of Maastricht came into effect in 1993 its core membership has expanded to 28 countries. Six other countries – Albania, Iceland, Macedonia, Montenegro, Serbia and Turkey – are slated for admission over the next few years ; Bosnia & Herzegovina and Kosovo are potential candidates. Another key development was the implementation of the Schengen Agreement in 1995, which abolished border checks and allowed EU citizens to travel freely throughout member states (with the notable exceptions of the UK and Ireland).

Even more momentous was the adoption of the single currency of the euro on 1 January 1999 as a cashless accounting currency; euro banknotes and coins have been used since 1 January 2002. To date, 19 countries have joined the Eurozone, while the UK, Denmark and Sweden have chosen to retain their national currencies. In future any new states joining the EU will be required to adopt the euro as a condition of entry. It's a hot topic, especially since the financial crash in countries including Greece and Spain, which has required richer nations (principally France and Germany) being called on to bail out several of their more indebted European neighbours.

2009–
Europe is rocked by a series of financial crises, leading to costly bailouts for Ireland, Greece, Portugal and Spain.

2014
Scotland votes on and rejects becoming a fully independent nation and so remains part of the United Kingdom

2015
Greece defaults on loan payments. Bailout proposals with tough conditions trigger riots and Greek banks close..

Family Travel

Family outside the Museo Guggenheim (p304), Spain

DOMINIC BONUCCELLI/GETTY IMAGES ©

Travelling with kids can be one long adventure or a nonstop nightmare. The key to fun and rewarding family travel is planning – organising your European trip together is not just an excellent way to avoid any unwelcome surprises on the road, it will also get everyone excited about the adventure ahead.

Travel

In general, Europe is an incredibly family-friendly place to travel, but distances can be long, so it's a good idea to break up the trip with things to see and do en route. Traffic is at its worst during holiday seasons, especially between June and August, and journey times are likely to be much longer during this period. Trains can be a great option for family travel – kids will have more space to move around, and you can pack books, puzzles and computer games to keep them entertained.

Children and young people qualify for cheap travel on most public transport in Europe (usually around 50% of the adult fare). Look out for railcards and passes that open up extra discounts – many cities offer passes that combine entry to sights and attractions with travel on public transport.

The Best... Kids' Experiences

1 Disneyland Paris (p208)

2 The Making of Harry Potter (p94), near London

3 Park Güell (p323), Barcelona

4 Jungfraujoch (p647), Switzerland

5 Haus der Musik (p602), Vienna

Sights & Attractions

Most attractions offer discounted entry for children (generally for 12 years and under, although this varies). If you can, try to mix up educational activities with fun excursions they're guaranteed to enjoy – balance that visit to the Tate Modern or the Louvre with a trip to the London Aquarium or a day at Disneyland Paris, for example. The number one rule is to avoid packing too much in – you'll get tired, the kids will get irritable and tantrums are sure to follow. Plan carefully and you'll enjoy your time much more.

Hotels & Restaurants

It's always worth asking in advance whether hotels are happy to accept kids. Many are fully geared for family travel, with children's activities, child-minding services and the like, but others may impose a minimum age limit to deter guests with kids. Family-friendly hotels will usually be able to offer a large room with two or three beds to accommodate families, or at least neighbouring rooms with an adjoining door.

Dining out *en famille* is generally great fun, but again, it's always worth checking to see whether kids are welcome – generally the posher or more prestigious the establishment, the less kid-friendly they're likely to be. Many restaurants offer cheaper children's menus, usually based around simple staples such as steak, pasta, burgers and chicken. Most will also offer smaller portions of adult meals.

If your kids are fussy, buying your own ingredients at a local market can encourage them to experiment – they can choose their own food while simultaneously practising the local lingo.

Need to Know

- **Changing facilities** Found at most supermarkets and major attractions.
- **Cots and highchairs** Available in many restaurants and hotels, but ask ahead.
- **Health** Generally good, but pack your own first-aid kit to avoid language difficulties.
- **Kids' menus** Widely available.
- **Nappies (diapers)** Sold everywhere, including pharmacies and supermarkets.
- **Strollers** It's easiest to bring your own.
- **Transport** Children usually qualify for discounts; young kids often travel free.

Visual Arts

Galleria degli Uffizi (p419), Florence, Italy

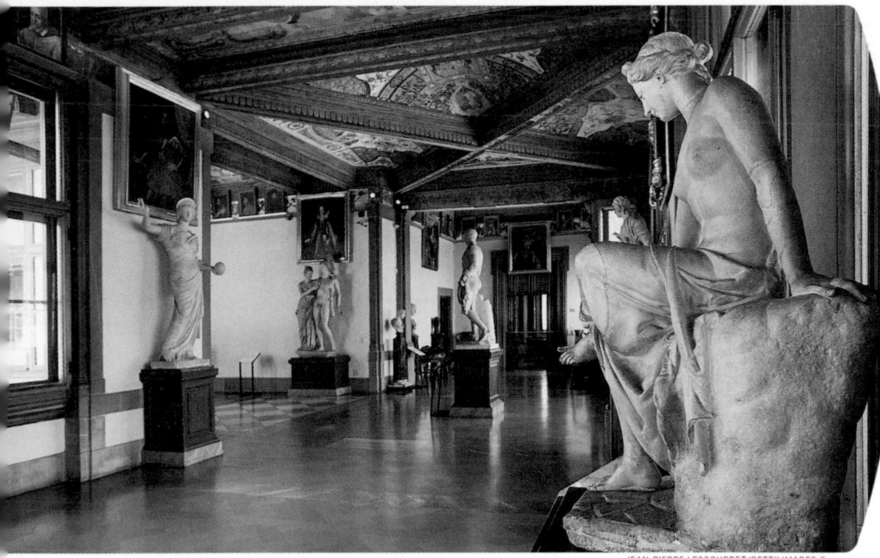

Europe's artistic legacy is exceptional. Many of the major art movements of the last millennium began in Europe, and you'll find some of the world's top artistic institutions, containing priceless masterworks, dotted across the continent.

Ancient Art

Art was a crucial part of everyday life for ancient civilisations: decorative objects were a sign of status and prestige, while statues were used to venerate and honour the dead, and monuments and temples lavishly decorated in an attempt to appease the gods.

You'll find sculptures and artefacts from early civilisations in all Europe's top art museums, including the British Museum, the Louvre in Paris and the Acropolis Museum in Athens. Perhaps the most famous ancient artwork is the *Venus de Milo* at the Louvre, thought to have been created between 130 BC and 100 BC by the master sculptor Alexandros of Antioch.

Medieval Art

During the Middle Ages, the power of the Church and its importance as an artistic patron meant that the majority of medieval

The Best... Modern Art Galleries

1 Tate Modern (p65), London

2 Museu Picasso (p317), Barcelona

3 MUMOK (p602), Vienna

4 Centre Pompidou (p182), Paris

5 SMAK (p503), Ghent

art dealt with religious subjects. The Old Testament, the crucifixion, the apostles and the Last Judgment were common topics. Some of the finest medieval artworks are actually woven into the fabric of Europe's churches in the form of frescoes painted onto panels or walls.

Flemish and German painting produced several important figures during the period, including Jan van Eyck (c1390–1441) and Hans Memling (c1430–94), known for their lifelike oils, and Hieronymus Bosch (1450–1516), known for his use of fantastic imagery and allegorical concepts.

The Renaissance

The Renaissance marked Europe's golden age of art. Artists such as Leonardo da Vinci (1452–1519), Michelangelo (1475–1564), Raphael (1483–1520), Titian (c1488/90–1576) and Botticelli (1445–1510) introduced new techniques, colours and forms into the artistic lexicon, drawing inspiration from the sculptors and artists of the classical world.

Landscape and the human form gained increasing importance during the Renaissance. Michelangelo's masterpiece, *David,* is often cited as the perfect representation of the human figure (despite the fact that the artist deliberately distorted its proportions to make it more pleasing to the eye). The sculpture is now displayed at the Galleria dell'Accademia in Florence. Florence's Galleria degli Uffizi contains the greatest collection of Italian Renaissance art.

In the wake of the Renaissance came the great names of the baroque period, epitomised by the Italian artist Caravaggio (1571–1610) and the Dutch artists Rembrandt (1606–69), Rubens (1577–1640) and Johannes Vermeer (1632–75). The baroque artists employed light and shadow *(chiaroscuro)* to heighten the drama of a scene and give their work a photographic intensity.

Romanticism & Impressionism

During the 18th century, Romantic artists such as Caspar David Friedrich (1774–1840) and JMW Turner (1775–1851) explored the drama of the natural landscape – cloud-capped mountains, lonely hilltops, peaceful meadows and moody sunsets. Other artists, such as Théodore Géricault (1791–1824) and Eugène Délacroix (1798–1863), drew inspiration from French history and prominent people of the day. One of Spain's most important artists, Francisco Goya (1746–1828), covered everything from royal portraits to war scenes, bullfight etchings and tapestry designs.

During the late 19th century, artists such as Claude Monet (1840–1926), Edgar Degas (1834–1917), Camille Pissarro (1830–1903), Edouard Manet (1832–83) and Pierre-Auguste Renoir (1841–1919) aimed to capture the general 'impression' of a scene rather than its naturalistic representation (hence the name of their movement, 'Impressionism').

Their bold experiments with light, colour and form segued into that of their successors, the post-Impressionists such as Paul Cézanne (1839–1906), Vincent van Gogh (1853–90) and Paul Gauguin (1848–1903).

From Fauvism to Conceptual Art

The upheavals of the 20th century inspired many new artistic movements. The fauvists were fascinated by colour, typified by Henri Matisse (1869–1954), while the cubists, such as Georges Braque (1882–1963) and Pablo Picasso (1881–1973), broke their work down into abstract forms, taking inspiration from everything from primitive art to psychoanalysis.

The dadaists and surrealists took these ideas to their illogical extreme, exploring dreams and the subconscious: key figures include Réné Magritte (1898–1967) from Belgium, Max Ernst (1891–1976) from Germany, and Joan Miró (1893–1983) and Salvador Dalí (1904–89) from Spain.

After 1945 abstract art became a mainstay of the West German scene, with key figures such as Joseph Beuys (1921–86) and Anselm Kiefer (1945–) garnering worldwide reputations. After reunification, the New Leipzig School achieved success at home and abroad with figurative painters such as Neo Rauch generating much acclaim.

The late 20th century and 21st century to date have introduced many more artistic movements: abstract expressionism, neoplasticism, minimalism, formalism and pop art, to name a few. One of the most controversial movements has been conceptual art, which stresses the importance of the idea behind a work rather than its aesthetic value. Britain has a particularly vibrant conceptual art scene: key names such as Tracy Emin (1963–) the Chapman Brothers (Dinos, 1962– and Jake, 1966–), Rachel Whiteread (1963–), Mark Wallinger (1959–) and Damien Hirst (1965– ; famous for his pickled shark and diamond-encrusted skull) continue to provoke controversy.

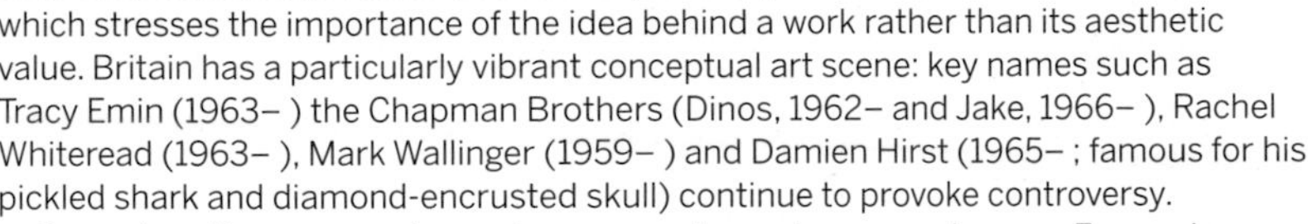

Several exciting new modern art museums have also opened across Europe in recent decades. Particularly noteworthy are the Tate Modern in London, installed in a former power station beside the Thames, and the Centre Pompidou-Metz in France, an offshoot of the landmark Parisian museum.

The Best... National Art Museums

1 National Gallery (p61), London

2 Musée du Louvre (p184), Paris

3 Galleria degli Uffizi (p419), Florence

4 Rijksmuseum (p468), Amsterdam

5 Museo del Prado (p286), Madrid

Architecture

Erechtheion (p701), the Acropolis, Athens, Greece

DENNIS K. JOHNSON/GETTY IMAGES

With an architectural heritage stretching back seven millennia, Europe is one long textbook for building buffs. From Greek temples to venerable mosques and modern skyscrapers, this fascinating and complex architectural environment is bound to be one of the main highlights of your visit.

The Ancient World

Europe's oldest examples of architecture are the many hundreds of stone circles, henges, barrows, burial chambers and alignments built by Neolithic people between 4500 BC and 1500 BC. The most impressive examples of these ancient structures are at Carnac in Brittany and, of course, Stonehenge in the southwest of England.

No one is quite sure what the purpose of these structures was, although theories abound. Some say they could be celestial calendars, burial monuments or tribal meeting places, although it's generally agreed these days that they served some sort of religious function.

Greek & Roman Architecture

Several ancient cultures have left their mark around the shores of the Mediterranean, including the Minoans (in Crete), the Etruscans (in present-day Tuscany), the Mycenaeans (in the northeast Peloponnese) and, of course, the ancient Greeks and Romans. Athens is the best place to appreciate Greece's golden age: the dramatic monuments of the Acropolis illustrate the ancient Greeks' sophisticated understanding of geometry, shape and form, and set the blueprint for many of the architectural principles that have endured to the present day.

The Romans were even more ambitious, and built a host of monumental structures designed to project the might and majesty of the Roman Empire. Roman architecture was driven by a combination of form and function – structures such as the Pont du Gard in southern France show how the Romans valued architecture that looked beautiful but also served a practical purpose. Rome has the greatest concentration of architectural treasures, including the famous Colosseum, but remains of Roman buildings are scattered all over the continent.

The Best... Gothic Landmarks

1 Cathédrale de Notre Dame (p179), Paris

2 Reims Cathedral (p218), France

3 Kölner Dom (p578), Germany

4 Canterbury Cathedral (p94), Britain

5 St Vitus Cathedral (p654), Prague

Romanesque & Gothic Architecture

The solidity and elegance of ancient Roman architecture echoed through the 10th and 11th centuries in buildings constructed during the Romanesque period. Many of Europe's earliest churches are classic examples of Romanesque construction, using rounded arches, vaulted roofs, and massive columns and walls.

Even more influential was the development of Gothic architecture, which gave rise to many of Europe's most spectacular cathedrals. Tell-tale characteristics include the use of pointed arches, ribbed vaulting, great showpiece windows and flying buttresses. The famous cathedrals situated in Cologne, Reims and Notre-Dame in Paris are ideal places to see Gothic architecture in action.

Renaissance & Baroque Architecture

The Renaissance led to a huge range of architectural experiments. Pioneering Italian architects such as Brunelleschi, Michelangelo and Palladio shifted the emphasis away from Gothic austerity towards a more human approach. They combined elements of classical architecture with new building materials, and specially commissioned sculptures and decorative artworks. Florence and Venice are particularly rich in Renaissance buildings, but the movement's influence can be felt right across Europe – the showy chateaux in France's Loire Valley, for example, bear many hallmarks of the Renaissance movement.

Architectural showiness reached its zenith during the baroque period, when architects pulled out all the stops to show off the wealth and prestige of their clients. Baroque buildings are all about creating drama, and architects often employed swathes of craftsmen and used the most expensive materials available to create the desired effect. The lavish country estate of Castle Howard in northern England, Paris' Hôtel des Invalides

The Best... Modern Buildings

1 Museo Guggenheim (p304), Bilbao

2 The Shard (p72), London

3 Musée des Civilisations de l'Europe et de la Méditerranée (p252), Marseille

4 Reichstag Dome (p529), Berlin

5 Markthal Rotterdam (p487), Rotterdam

and practically all of Salzburg's buildings showcase the ostentation and expense that underpinned baroque architecture.

The Industrial Age

The 19th century was the great age of urban planning, when the chaotic streets and squalid slums of many of Europe's cities were swept away in favour of grand squares and ruler-straight boulevards. This was partly driven by an attempt to clean up the urban environment, but it also allowed architects to redesign the urban landscape to suit the industrial age, merging factories, public buildings, museums and residential suburbs into a seamless whole. One of the most obvious examples of urban remodelling was Baron Haussmann's reinvention of Paris during the late 19th century, which resulted in the construction of the city's great boulevards and many of its landmark buildings.

Nineteenth-century architects began to move away from the showiness of the baroque and rococo periods in favour of new materials such as brick, iron and glass. Neo-Gothic architecture was designed to emphasise permanence, solidity and power, reflecting the confidence of the industrial age. It was an era that gave rise to many of Europe's great public buildings, including many landmark museums, libraries, city halls and train stations.

The 20th Century

By the turn of the 20th century, the worlds of art and architecture had both begun to experiment with new approaches to shape and form. The flowing shapes and natural forms of art nouveau had a profound influence on the work of Charles Rennie Mackintosh in Glasgow, the Belgian architect Victor Horta and the Modernista buildings of Spanish visionary Antonio Gaudí. Meanwhile, other architects stripped their buildings back to the bare essentials, emphasising strict function over form: Le Corbusier, Ludwig Mies van der Rohe and Walter Gropius are among the most influential figures of the period.

Functional architecture continued to dominate much of mid-20th-century architecture, especially in the rush to reconstruct Europe's shattered cities in the wake of two world wars, although the 'concrete box' style of architecture has largely fallen out of fashion over recent decades. Europeans may have something of a love-hate relationship with modern architecture, but the best buildings eventually find their place – a good example is the inside-out Centre Pompidou in Paris, which initially drew howls of protest but is now considered one of the icons of 20th-century architecture.

More recently, the fashion for sky-high skyscrapers seems to have caught on in several European cities, especially London, where a rash of multistorey buildings have recently been completed, all with their own nickname (the Walkie Talkie, the Cheesegrater and so on). Topping them all is the Shard, which became the EU's highest building at 309.6m when it was completed in 2013.

Regardless of whether you approve of the more recent additions to Europe's architectural landscape, one thing's for sure – you won't find them boring.

Food & Drink

Spaghetti alle Vongole, Italy

LONELY PLANET/GETTY IMAGES ©

Europe is united by its passion for eating and drinking with gusto. Every country has its own flavours, incorporating olive oils and sun-ripened vegetables in the hot south, rich cream and butter in cooler areas, fresh-off-the-boat seafood along the coast, delicate river and lake fish, and meat from fertile mountains and pastures. Each country has its own tipples, too, spanning renowned wines, beers, stouts and ciders, and feistier firewater.

Britain & Ireland

Britain might not have a distinctive cuisine, but it does have a thriving food culture, with a host of celebrity chefs and big-name restaurants. Britain's colonial legacy has also left it with a taste for curry – a recent poll suggested the nation's favourite food was chicken tikka masala.

Traditional Dishes

The Brits love a good roast, traditionally eaten on a Sunday and accompanied by roast potatoes, vegetables and gravy. The classic is roast beef with Yorkshire pudding (a crisp batter puff), but lamb, pork and chicken are equally popular. 'Bangers and mash' (sausages and mashed potato) and fish and chips (battered cod or haddock served with thick-cut fried potatoes) are also old favourites.

Specialities in Scotland include haggis served with 'tatties and neeps' (potato and

A European Breakfast

Frühstuck, desayuno, petit déjeuner – every country has its own take on breakfast.

In Britain and Ireland, the classic cooked breakfast ('fry-up') consists of eggs, bacon, sausages, mushroom, black pudding (blood sausage), fried bread, beans and tomatoes.

The Mediterranean approach is lighter. Spaniards usually start the day with coffee and a *tostada* (piece of toast) or *pastel/bollo* (pastry), while the French opt for coffee and a baguette with jam, a croissant or a *pain au chocolat*. Italians prefer a cappuccino and *cornetto* (Italian croissant) at a cafe.

The biggest breakfasts are served in Germany, Austria and Switzerland, where you could survive for the entire day purely on what's served up on the breakfast table – breads, cakes, pastries, cold meats, cheeses, cereals and fruit. *Gut essen* indeed!

turnip). Traditional Welsh dishes include *cawl* (broth, usually with lamb and leeks) and *bara lafwr* (savoury scones made with oatmeal and seaweed).

Ireland's traditional dishes reflect the country's rustic past: look out for colcannon (mashed potato with cabbage), coddle (sliced sausages with bacon, potato and onion) and boxty (potato pancake), plus classic Irish stew (usually made with lamb or mutton).

Cheese

Britain's favourite cheese is cheddar – a matured hard cheese with a pungent flavour – but there are many others, including Wensleydale, Red Leicester and Stilton.

Drinks

The traditional British brew is ale, served warm and flat in order to bring out the hoppy flavours. It's an acquired taste, especially if you're used to cold, fizzy lagers.

Ireland's trademark ale is stout – usually Guinness, although in Cork stout can mean a Murphy's or a Beamish, too.

Scotland and Ireland are both known for whisky-making, with many distilleries open for tours and tasting sessions. Note that in Scotland it's always spelled whisky; it's only in Ireland that you add the 'e'.

France

Each French region has its distinctive dishes. Broadly, the hot south favours dishes based around olive oil, garlic and tomatoes, while the cooler north tends towards root vegetables, earthy flavours and creamy or buttery sauces. The French are famously unfussy about which bits of the animal they eat – kidney, liver, cheek and tongue are as much of a delicacy as a fillet steak or a prime rib.

Traditional Dishes

Bouillabaisse is the signature southern dish; it's a saffron-scented fish stew that's best eaten in Marseille. It is served with spicy rouille sauce, gruyère cheese and croutons.

The Alps are the place to try fondue, hunks of toasted bread dipped into cheese sauces. Brittany and Normandy are big on seafood, especially mussels and oysters. Lyon's small local restaurants *(bouchons)* are renowned for their piggy dishes, particularly *andouillette,* a sausage made from pig intestines.

Central France prides itself on its hearty cuisine, including *foie gras* (goose liver), *boeuf bourgignon* (beef cooked in red wine), *confit de canard* (duck cooked in preserved fat) and *truffes* (black truffles).

Cheese

Charles de Gaulle's famous quip that it was impossible to 'govern a country which has two hundred and forty-six varieties of cheese' speaks volumes about how much the French love their *fromages*. The big names are camembert, brie, Livarot, Pont l'Évêque and Époisses (all soft cheeses); Roquefort and Bleu d'Auvergne (blue cheeses); and Comté, cantal and gruyère (hard cheeses).

Drinks

France is Europe's biggest wine producer. The principal regions are Alsace, Bordeaux, Burgundy, Languedoc, the Loire and the Rhône, all of which produce reds, whites and rosés. Then, of course, there's Champagne – home to the world's favourite bubbly, aged in centuries-old cellars beneath Reims and Épernay.

The Best... Foodie Experiences

1 Tucking into a Sunday roast in a British pub

2 Nibbling on a light-as-air *macaron* in Paris (p193)

3 Choosing tapas in Madrid (p296)

4 Eating crispy pizza in a real Roman pizzeria (p386)

5 Indulging in coffee and cake in a Vienna cafe (p610)

Italy

Italian cuisine is dominated by the twin staples of pizza and pasta, which have been eaten in Italy since Roman times. A full meal comprises an *antipasto* (starter), *primo* (pasta or rice dish), *secondo* (usually meat or fish), *contorno* (vegetable side dish or salad), *dolce* (dessert) and coffee. When eating out it's OK to mix and match any combination.

Traditional Dishes

Italian pasta comes in numerous shapes, from bow-shaped *farfalle* to twisty *fusilli,* ribbed *rigatoni* and long *pappardelle*. Italian pasta is made with durum flour, which gives it a distinctive *al dente* bite; the type of pasta used is usually dictated by the type of dish being served (ribbed or shaped pastas hold sauce better, for example).

Italian pizza comes in two varieties: the Roman pizza with a thin crispy base, and the Neapolitan pizza, which has a higher, doughier base. The best are always prepared in a *forno a legna* (wood-fired oven). Flavours are generally kept simple – the best pizza restaurants often serve only a couple of toppings, such as *margherita* (tomato and mozzarella) and *marinara* (tomato, garlic and oregano).

Cheese

Like the French, the Italians pride themselves on their cheeses, especially prestigious varieties such as Parmesan, ricotta and mozzarella.

Drinks

Italy's wines run the gamut from big-bodied reds such as Piedmont's Barolo, to light white wines from Sardinia and sparkling *prosecco* from the Veneto.

The Netherlands & Belgium

Traditional Dishes

The Netherlands' colonial legacy has given the Dutch a taste for Indonesian and Surinamese-inspired meals like *rijsttafel* (rice table): an array of spicy dishes such as braised beef, pork satay and ribs, all served with white rice.

Other Dutch dishes to look out for are *erwertensoep* (pea soup with onions, carrots, sausage and bacon), *krokotten* (filled dough balls that are crumbed and deep-fried) and, of course, *friet* (fries). Here they're thin, crispy and eaten with mayonnaise rather than ketchup (tomato sauce).

The iconic Belgian dish is *mosselen moules* – a steaming cauldron of shell-on mussels, typically accompanied by *frites* (fries) and cold beer. Other dishes include *balekkes/bouletten* (meatballs), *vlaamse stoverij/carbonade flamande* (beer-based beef casserole) and *waterzooi* (creamy chicken or fish stew), often accompanied by *stoemp* (veg-and-potato mash).

Cheese

The Dutch are keen on cheese: the best known varieties are edam and gouda, sometimes served as bar snacks with mustard.

Drinks

Beer is the tipple of choice. Small Dutch brewers like Gulpen, Haarlem's Jopen, Bavaria, Drie Ringen and Leeuw are all excellent. You'll find an even bigger choice in Belgium:

Sweet Treats

From pralines to puddings, Europe specialises in foods that are sweet, sticky and sinful. Germans and Austrians have a particularly sweet tooth – treats include *Salzburger nockerl* (a fluffy soufflé) and *Schwarzwälder kirschtorte* (Black Forest cherry cake), plus many types of *apfeltasche* (apple pastry) and *strudel* (filled filo pastry). The Brits are another big cake-eating nation – a slice of cake or a dunked biscuit is an essential teatime ritual.

The Italians are famous for their *gelaterie* (ice-cream stalls; the best will be labelled *produzione propria,* indicating that it's handmade on the premises). Most Greek desserts are variations on pastry soaked in honey, such as *baklava* (thin layers of pastry filled with honey and nuts).

But it's the French who have really turned dessert into a fine art. Stroll past the window of any *boulangerie* (bakery) or patisserie and you'll be assaulted by temptations, from creamy *éclairs* (filled choux buns) and crunchy *macarons* (macaroons) to fluffy *madeleines* (shell-shaped sponge cakes) and wicked *gâteaux* (cakes).

Go on – you know you want to.

look out for dark Trappist beers, golden beers such as Duuvel and the champagne-style lambic beers brewed around Brussels.

Jenever (gin) is a favourite in the Netherlands.

Spain

Spain's cuisine is typical of the flavours of Mediterranean cooking, making extensive use of herbs, tomatoes, onions, garlic and lashings of olive oil.

Traditional Dishes

The nation's signature dish is paella, consisting of rice and chicken, meat or seafood, simmered with saffron in a large pan. Valencia is considered the spiritual home of *paella*.

Spain also prides itself on its ham and spicy sausages (including *chorizo, lomo* and *salchichón*). These are often used in making the bite-size Spanish dishes known as tapas (or *pintxos* in the Basque region). Tapas is usually a snack, but it can also be a main meal – three or four dishes is generally enough for one person.

Cheese

Spain has fewer world-famous cheeses than its neighbours in France and Italy, but there are still plenty worth trying. *Manchego* is perhaps the best known, a semi-hard sheep's cheese with a buttery flavour, often used in tapas.

Drinks

Spain boasts the largest area (1.2 million hectares) of wine cultivation in the world. La Rioja and Ribera del Duero are the principal wine-growing regions.

Cakes in a patisserie, Paris, France
JODIE WALLIS/GETTY IMAGES ©

Greece

Greece is known for its seafood. As with its Mediterranean neighbours, garlic, tomatoes and olives (either whole or as olive oil) feature heavily.

Traditional Dishes

The Greek form of tapas is *mezedhes* (shortened to *meze*): common dishes include grilled octopus, kalamata olives, meatballs, fried sausages and fava beans, served with dips such as hummus (chickpeas), taramasalata (cod roe) and tzatziki (yoghurt, garlic and cucumber).

In Greece, large kebabs are known as *gyros,* while *souvlaki* is made from small cubes of meat cooked on a skewer; both are served in pitta bread with salad and sauces.

Cheese

Greece's main cheese is feta. Its strong, salty flavour is a key ingredient in many dishes and salads. *Halloumi* is a chewy cheese that is often pan-fried or grilled.

Drinks

The potent aniseed-flavoured spirit of ouzo is traditionally mixed with water and ice (turning it a cloudy white). Similar traditions exist in the south of France (where *pastis* is the tipple) and Italy *(grappa)*.

TIJEN EROL/GETTY IMAGES

Grilled *halloumi* cheese

Vegetarians & Vegans

Vegetarians will have a tough time in many areas of Europe – meat eating is still the norm, and fish is often seen as a vegetarian option. However, you'll usually find something meat-free on most menus, though don't expect much choice. Vegans will have an even tougher time – cheese, cream and milk are integral ingredients in most European cuisines.

Vegetable-based *antipasti* (starters), tapas, meze, pastas, side dishes and salads are good ways of providing a meat-free meal. Shopping for yourself in markets is a good way of trying local flavours without having to compromise your principles.

Germany, Austria and Switzerland

The Germanic nations are all about big flavours and big portions. *Wurst* (sausage) comes in hundreds of forms, and is often served with *sauerkraut* (fermented cabbage).

Traditional Dishes

The most common types of Wurst include *Bratwurst* (roast sausage), *Weisswurst* (veal sausage) and *Currywurst* (sliced sausage topped with ketchup and curry powder). Austria's signature dish is *Wiener Schnitzel* (breaded veal cutlet) but schnitzel in general (usually featuring pork) are also popular in Germany.

Other popular mains include *Rippenspeer* (spare ribs), *Rotwurst* (black pudding), *Rostbrätl* (grilled meat) and *Putenbrust* (turkey breast). Potatoes are served as *Bratkartoffeln* (fried), *Kartoffelpüree* (mashed), Swiss-style *rösti* (grated then fried) or *Pommes Frites* (French fries).

The Swiss are known for their love of fondue and the similar dish of *raclette* (melted cheese with potatoes).

Cheese

Emmental and gruyère are the best-known Swiss cheeses, while the Germans are known for their hard cheeses – especially *Allgäu Emmentaler* and *Bergkäse* (mountain cheese).

Drinks

Beer is the national beverage. *Pils* is the crisp pilsner Germany is famous for, often slightly bitter. *Weizenbier* is made with wheat instead of barley malt and served in a tall, 500mL glass. *Helles bier* is light beer, while *Dunkles bier* is dark.

Germany is principally known for white wines – inexpensive, light and intensely fruity. The Rhine and Moselle Valleys are the largest wine-growing regions.

The Art of the Sandwich

There's no such thing as a simple sandwich in Europe. In the UK, a sandwich is usually made with two square slices of bread; across the Channel in France and Belgium, they make their sandwiches using a long baton-shaped baguette.

The Italians favour *panini,* pocket-shaped bread served piping hot. The pitta, a flat bread served widely in Greece, is a close relation.

Czech Republic

Traditional Dishes

Like many nations in Eastern Europe, Czech cuisine revolves around meat, potatoes and root vegetables, dished up in stews, goulashes and casseroles. *Pečená kachna* (roast duck) is the quintessential Czech restaurant dish, while *klobása* (sausage) is a common beer snack. A common side dish is *knedliky,* boiled dumplings made from wheat or potato flour.

Cheese

The Czechs are not renowned for their cheese, though you'll probably try *nakládaný hermelín,* a marinated soft cheese covered in a white rind, at least once.

Drinks

The Czechs have a big beer culture, with some of Europe's best *pivo* (beer), usually lager style. The Moravian region is the up-and-coming area for Czech wines.

Survival Guide

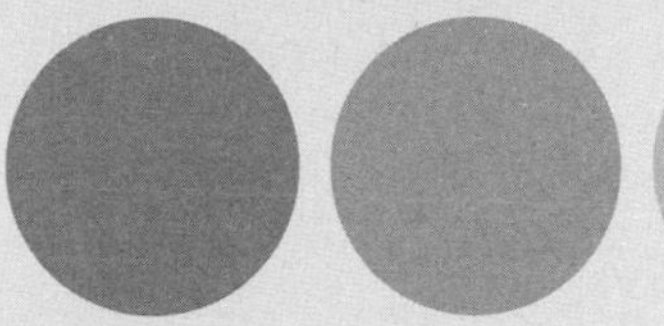

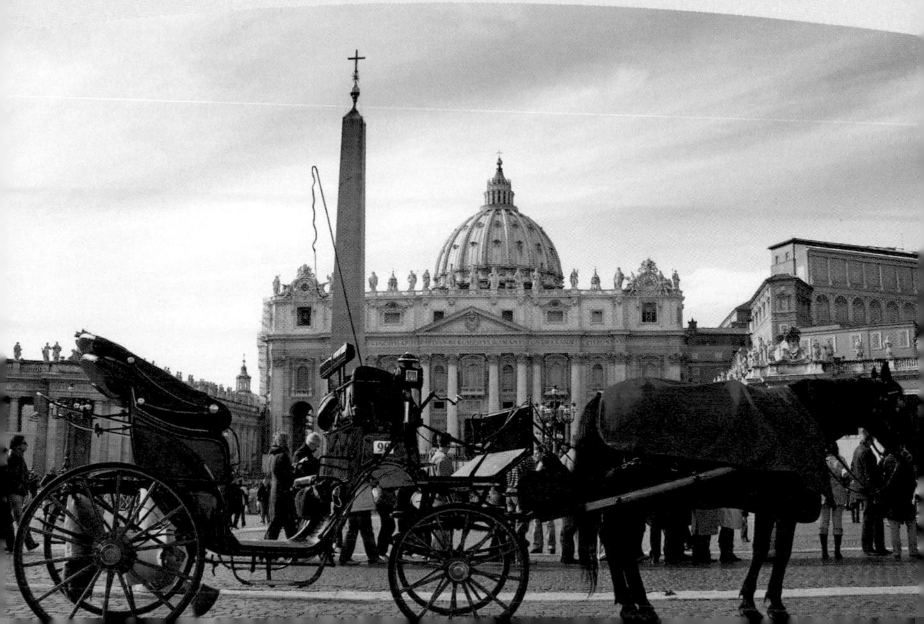

St Peter's Square (p374), Rome, Italy

Directory

Climate

London

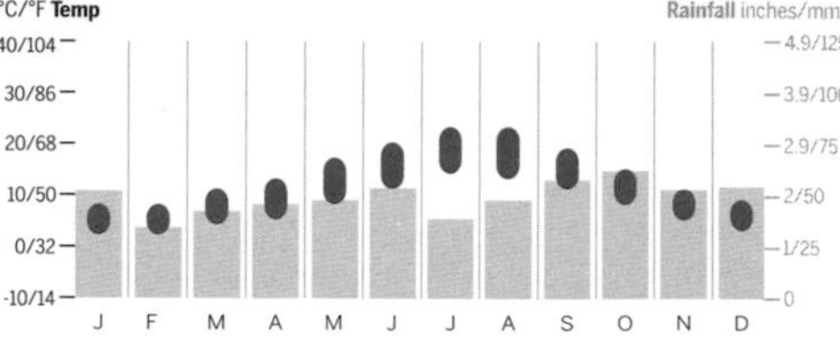

Madrid

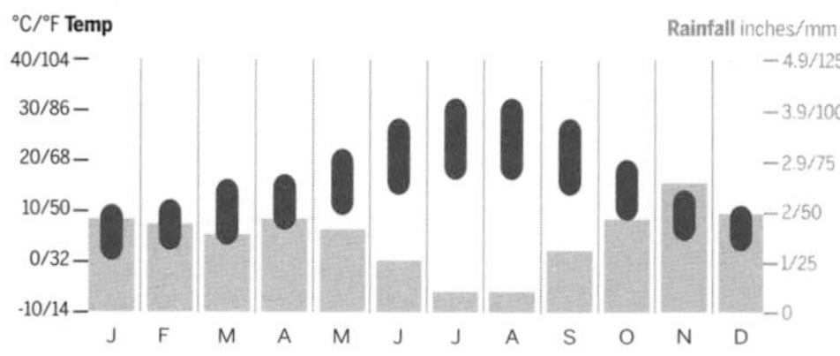

Prague

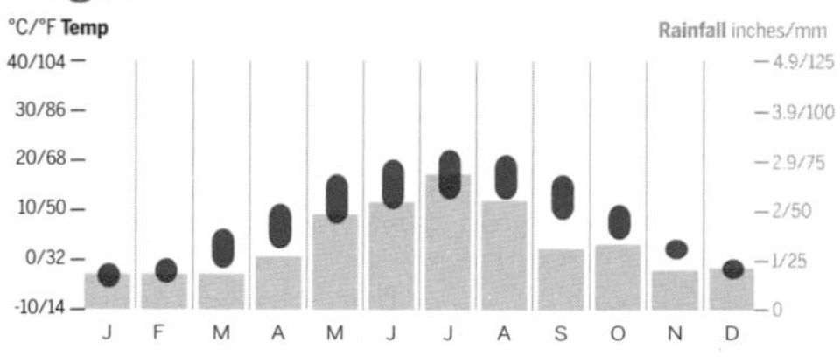

Accommodation

Price Ranges

Rates are for high season and often drop outside high season by as much as 50%. High season in ski resorts is usually between Christmas and New Year and around the February to March winter holidays.

Reservations

During peak holiday periods, particularly Easter, summer and Christmas – and any time of year in popular destinations such as London, Paris and Rome – it's wise to book ahead. Most places can be reserved online.

B&Bs & Guesthouses

Guesthouses (pension, *gasthaus, chambre d'hôte* etc) and B&Bs (bed and breakfasts) offer comfort at a reasonable price.

B&Bs in the UK and Ireland often aren't really budget accommodation – even the lowliest tend to have midrange prices and there is a new generation of 'designer' B&Bs which are positively top end.

Book Your Stay Online

For more accommodation reviews by Lonely Planet authors, check out lonelyplanet.com/hotels. You'll find independent reviews, as well as recommendations on the best places to stay. Best of all, you can book online.

Hotels

Hotels are usually the most expensive accommodation option, though at their lower end there is little to differentiate them from guesthouses or even hostels.

Cheap hotels around bus and train stations can be convenient for late-night or early-morning arrivals and departures, but can be sleazy. Check the room beforehand and make sure you're clear on price and what it covers.

Discounts for longer stays are usually possible and hotel owners in southern Europe *might* be open to a little bargaining if times are slack. In many countries it's common for business hotels (usually more than two stars) to slash their rates by up to 40% on Friday and Saturday nights.

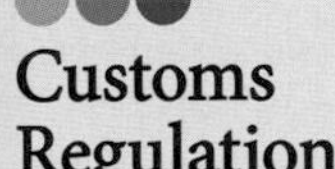

Customs Regulations

The European Union (EU) has a two-tier customs system: one for goods bought duty-free to import to or export from the EU, and one for goods bought in another EU country where taxes and duties have already been paid.

- Entering or leaving the EU, you are allowed to carry duty-free: 200 cigarettes, 50 cigars or 250g of tobacco; 2L of still wine plus 1L of spirits over 22% alcohol or another 2L of wine (sparkling or otherwise); 50g of perfume, 250cc of eau de toilette.

- Travelling from one EU country to another, the duty-paid limits are: 800 cigarettes, 200 cigars, 1kg of tobacco, 10L of spirits, 20L of fortified wine, 90L of wine (of which not more than 60L is sparkling) and 110L of beer.

Discount Cards

Rail Passes

If you plan to visit more than a few countries, or one or two countries in-depth, you might save money with a rail pass.

Student Cards

The International Student Identity Card (www.isic.org), available for students, teachers and under-26s, offers thousands of worldwide discounts on transport, museum entry, youth hostels and even some restaurants. Apply for the cards online or via issuing offices, which include **STA Travel** (www.statravel.com).

For under-26s, there's also the **Euro<26** (www.euro26.org). Many countries have raised the age limit for this card to under 30.

Electricity

Europe generally runs on 220V, 50Hz AC, but there are exceptions. The UK runs on 230/240V AC, and some old buildings in Italy and Spain have 125V (or even 110V in Spain). If your home country has a vastly different voltage you will need a transformer for delicate and important appliances.

The UK and Ireland use three-pin square plugs. Most of Europe uses the 'europlug' with two round pins. Greece, Italy and Switzerland use a third round pin in a way that the two-pin plug usually – but not always in Italy and Switzerland – fits. Buy an adapter before leaving home.

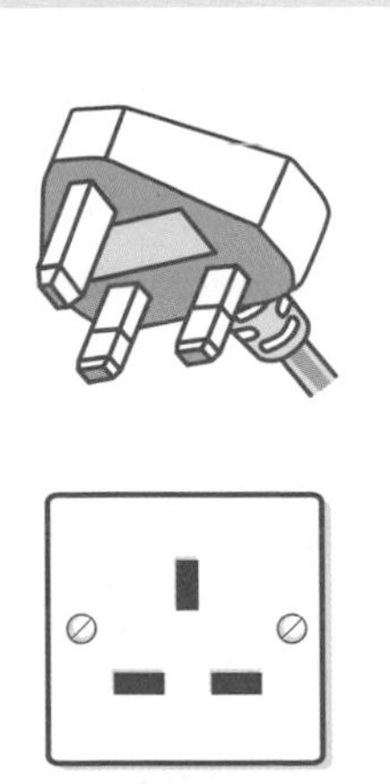

230V/50Hz

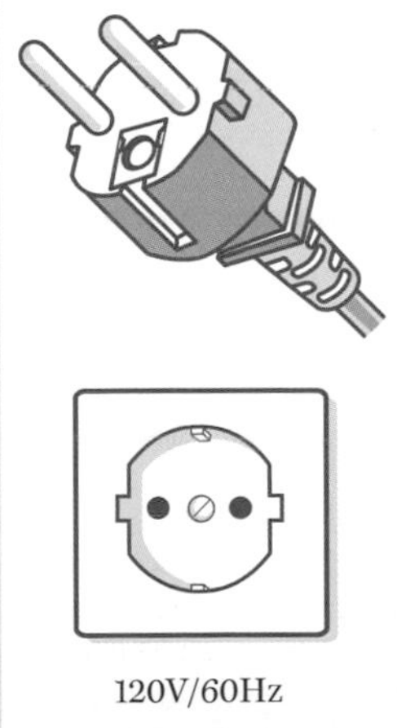

120V/60Hz

230V/50Hz

Gay & Lesbian Travellers

Across Western Europe you'll find very liberal attitudes towards homosexuality. London, Paris, Berlin, Munich, Amsterdam, Madrid and Lisbon have thriving gay communities and pride events. The Greek islands of Mykonos and Lesvos are popular gay beach destinations. Gran Canaria and Ibiza in Spain are big centres for both gay clubbing and beach holidays.

Health

Good health care is readily available in Western Europe and, for minor illnesses, pharmacists can give valuable advice and sell over-the-counter medication. They can also advise if you need specialised help and point you in the right direction. The standard of dental care is usually good.

No jabs are necessary for Europe. However, the World Health Organization (WHO) recommends that all travellers be covered for diphtheria, tetanus, measles, mumps, rubella and polio, regardless of their destination. Since most vaccines don't produce immunity until at least two weeks after they're given, visit a physician at least six weeks before departure.

Tap water is generally safe to drink in Western Europe. Do not drink water from rivers or lakes as it may contain bacteria or viruses.

Condoms are widely available in Europe, however emergency contraception may not be, so take the necessary precautions.

Insurance

It's foolhardy to travel without insurance to cover theft, loss and medical problems. There are a wide variety of policies, so check the small print.

Some policies specifically exclude 'dangerous activities', which can include scuba diving, motorcycling, winter sports, adventure sports or even hiking.

Check that the policy covers ambulances or an emergency flight home.

Worldwide travel insurance is available online at www.lonelyplanet.com/travel-insurance. You can buy, extend and claim online anytime – even if you're already on the road.

Internet Access

Internet access varies enormously across Europe. In most places, you'll be able to find wireless (wi-fi, also called WLAN in some countries), although whether it's free varies greatly.

Where the wi-fi icon appears, it means that the establishment offers free wi-fi that you can access immediately, or by asking for the access code from staff.

Access is generally straightforward, although a few tips are in order. If you can't find the @ symbol on a keyboard, try Alt Gr + 2, or Alt Gr + Q. Watch out for German keyboards, which reverse the Z and the Y positions. Using a French keyboard is an art unto itself.

Where necessary in relevant countries, click on the language prompt in the bottom right-hand corner of the screen or hit Ctrl + Shift to switch between the Cyrillic and Latin alphabets.

Legal Matters

You can generally purchase alcohol (beer and wine) from between 16 and 18 (usually 18 for spirits), but if in doubt, ask. Although you can drive at 17 or 18, you might not be able to hire a car until you're 25.

Cigarette-smoking bans in bars and r-estaurants and other public places are increasingly common across Europe so ask before lighting up.

Drugs are often quite openly available in Europe, but that doesn't mean they're legal. The Netherlands is most famed for its liberal attitudes, with *coffeeshops* openly selling cannabis even though the drug is *not* technically legal. However, a blind eye is generally turned to the trade as the possession and purchase of small amounts (5g) of 'soft drugs' (ie marijuana and hashish) is allowed and users won't be prosecuted for smoking or carrying this amount. Don't take this relaxed attitude as an invitation to buy harder drugs; if you get caught, you'll be punished. Since 2008 magic mushrooms have been banned in the Netherlands.

In Belgium, the possession of up to 5g of cannabis is legal, but selling the drug isn't, so if you get caught at the point of sale, you could be in trouble. Switzerland has also decriminalised possession of up to 10g of marijuana.

Getting caught with drugs in other parts of Europe can lead to imprisonment.

If in any doubt, err on the side of caution, and don't even think about taking drugs across international borders.

Useful Web Resources

Currency Conversions (www.xe.com) Up-to-the-second exchange rates for hundreds of currencies.

Lonely Planet (www.lonelyplanet.com/thorntree) On Lonely Planet's message board you can usually get your travel questions answered by fellow travellers in a matter of hours.

Money Saving Expert (www.moneysavingexpert.com) Excellent tips on the best UK travel insurance, mobile phones and bank cards to use abroad. The flight-checker facility shows the latest cheap flights available.

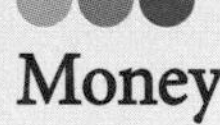

Money

ATMs

Across major European towns and cities international ATMs are common, but you should always have a back-up option, as there can be glitches. In some remote areas, ATMs might be scarce, too.

Much of Western Europe now uses a chip-and-pin system for added security. You will have problems if you don't have a four-digit PIN number and might have difficulties if your card doesn't have a chip. Check with your bank.

If your card disappears and the screen goes blank before you've even entered your PIN, don't enter it – especially if a 'helpful' bystander tells you to do so. If you can't retrieve your card, call your bank's emergency number, before leaving the ATM, if you can.

Credit Cards

Visa and MasterCard/Eurocard are more widely accepted in Europe than Amex and Diners Club; Visa (sometimes called Carte Bleue) is particularly strong in France and Spain.

There are, however, regional differences in the general acceptability of credit cards; in Germany for example, it's rare for restaurants to take credit cards. Cards are not widely accepted off the beaten track.

To reduce the risk of fraud, always keep your card in view when making transactions; for example, in restaurants that do accept cards, pay as you leave, following your card to the till. Keep transaction records and either check your statements when you return home, or check your account online while still on the road.

Letting your credit-card company know roughly where you're going lessens the chance of fraud – or of your bank cutting off the card when it sees (your) unusual spending.

Debit Cards

It's always worthwhile having a Maestro-compatible debit card, which differs from a credit card in deducting money straight from your bank account. Check with your bank or MasterCard (Maestro's parent) for compatibility.

Exchanging Money

Euros, US dollars and UK pounds are the easiest currencies to exchange. You may have trouble exchanging some lesser-known ones at small banks.

Importing or exporting some currencies is restricted or banned, so try to get rid of any local currency before you leave. Get rid of Scottish pounds before leaving the UK; nobody outside Britain will touch them.

Most airports, central train stations, big hotels and many border posts have banking facilities outside regular business hours, at times on a 24-hour basis. Post offices in Europe often perform banking tasks, tend to open longer hours and outnumber banks in remote places.

Taxes & Refunds

When non-EU residents spend more than a certain amount (around €75) they can usually reclaim any sales tax when leaving the country.

Making a tax-back claim

is straightforward. First, make sure the shop offers duty-free sales (often a sign will be displayed reading 'Tax-Free Shopping'). When making your purchase, ask the shop attendant for a tax-refund voucher, filled in with the correct amount and the date. This can be used to claim a refund directly at international airports, or stamped at ferry ports or border crossings and mailed back for a refund.

Tipping & Bargaining

Tipping has become more complicated, with 'service charges' increasingly added to bills. In theory this means you're not obliged to tip. In practice that money often doesn't go to the server and they might make it clear they still expect a gratuity. Don't pay twice. If the service charge is optional, remove it from the bill and pay a tip. If the service charge is not optional, don't tip.

Travellers Cheques

It's become more difficult to find places that cash travellers cheques. That said, having a few cheques is a good back-up.

Safe Travel

Travelling in Europe is usually very safe. The following outlines a range of general guidelines.

Discrimination

In some parts of Europe travellers of African, Arab or Asian descent might encounter unpleasant attitudes that are unrelated to them personally. In rural areas travellers whose skin colour marks them out as foreigners might experience unwanted attention.

Attitudes vary from country to country. People tend to be more accepting in cities than in the country.

Druggings

Although rare, some drugging of travellers does occur in Europe. Travellers are especially vulnerable on trains and buses where a new 'friend' may offer you food or a drink that will knock you out, giving them time to steal your belongings.

Gassings have also been reported on a handful of overnight international trains. The best protection is to lock the door of your compartment (use your own lock if there isn't one) and to lock your bags to luggage racks, preferably with a sturdy combination cable.

If you can help it, never sleep alone in a train compartment.

Pickpockets & Thieves

Theft is definitely a problem in parts of Europe and you have to be aware of unscrupulous fellow travellers. The key is to be sensible with your possessions.

- Don't store valuables in train-station lockers or luggage-storage counters and be careful about people who offer to help you operate a locker. Also be vigilant if someone offers to carry your luggage.
- Don't leave valuables in your car, on train seats or in your room. When going out, don't flaunt cameras, laptops and other expensive electronic goods.
- Carry a small day pack, as shoulder bags are an open invitation for snatch-thieves. Consider using small zipper locks on your packs.
- Pickpockets are most active in dense crowds, especially in busy train stations and on public transport during peak hours. Be careful in these situations.
- Spread valuables, cash and cards around your body or in different bags.
- A money belt with your essentials (passport, cash, credit cards, airline tickets) is usually a good idea. However, so you needn't delve into it in public, carry a wallet with a day's worth of cash.
- Having your passport stolen is less of a disaster if you've recorded the number and issue date or, even better, photocopied the relevant data pages. You can also scan them and email them to yourself. If you lose your passport, notify the police immediately to get a statement and contact your nearest consulate.
- Record the serial numbers of travellers cheques and carry photocopies of your credit cards, airline tickets and other travel documents.

Scams

Most scams involve distracting you – either by kids running up to you, someone asking for directions or spilling something on you – while another person steals your wallet.

In some countries you may encounter people claiming to be from the tourist police, the special police, the super-secret police, whatever. Unless they're wearing a uniform and have good reason for accosting you, treat their claims with suspicion.

Needless to say, never show your passport or cash to anyone on the street. Simply walk away. If someone flashes a badge, offer to accompany them to the nearest police station.

Unrest & Terrorism

Civil unrest and terrorist bombings are rare in Europe, but they do occur. Attacks by ETA (the Basque separatist group in Spain and France) and attacks by Muslim extremists in the UK, France and Spain have all occurred in recent years. Keep an eye on the news and avoid areas where any flare-up seems likely.

Telephone

If your mobile phone is European, it's often perfectly feasible to use it on roaming throughout the Continent.

If you're coming from outside Europe, it's usually worth buying a prepaid local SIM in one European country. Even if you're not staying there long, calls across Europe will still be cheaper if they're not routed via your home country and the prepaid card will enable you to keep a limit on your spending. In several countries you need your passport to buy a SIM card.

In order to use other SIM cards in your phone, you'll need to have your handset unlocked by your home provider. Even if your phone is locked, you can use apps such as 'whatsapp' to send free text messages internationally wherever you have wi-fi access, or Skype to make free international calls whenever you're online.

Europe uses the GSM 900 network, which also covers Australia and New Zealand, but is not compatible with the North American GSM 1900 or the totally different system in Japan and South Korea. If you have a GSM phone, check with your service provider about using it in Europe. You'll need international roaming, but this is usually free to enable.

You can call abroad from almost any phone box in Europe. Public telephones accepting phonecards (available from post offices, telephone centres, news stands or retail outlets) are virtually the norm now; coin-operated phones are rare if not impossible to find.

Without a phonecard, you can ring from a telephone booth inside a post office or telephone centre and settle your bill at the counter. Reverse-charge (collect) calls are often possible. From many countries the Country Direct system lets you phone home by billing the long-distance carrier you use at home. These numbers can often be dialled from public phones without even a phonecard.

Emergency Numbers

The phone number ☎112 can be dialled free for emergencies in all EU states. See individual countries for country-specific emergency numbers.

Time

Europe is divided into four time zones. From west to east these are:

UTC (Britain, Ireland, Portugal) GMT (GMT+1 in summer)

CET (the majority of European countries) GMT+1 (GMT+2 in summer)

EET (Greece, Turkey, Bulgaria, Romania, Moldova, Ukraine, Belarus, Lithuania, Latvia, Estonia, Kaliningrad, Finland) GMT+2 (GMT+3 in summer)

MSK (Russia) GMT+3 (GMT+4 in summer)

At 9am in Britain it's 1am (GMT/UTC minus eight hours) on the US west coast, 4am (GMT/UTC minus five hours) on the US east coast, 10am in Paris and Prague, 11am in Athens, midday in Moscow and 7pm (GMT/UTC plus 10 hours) in Sydney.

In most European countries, clocks are put forward one hour for daylight-saving time on the last Sunday in March, and turned back again on the last Sunday in October.

The Schengen Area

Twenty-six European countries are signatories to the Schengen Agreement, which has effectively dismantled internal border controls between them. They are Austria, Belgium, Czech Republic, Denmark, Estonia, Finland, France, Germany, Greece, Iceland, Italy, Hungary, Latvia, Liechtenstein, Lithuania, Luxembourg, Malta, the Netherlands, Norway, Poland, Portugal, Slovenia, Slovakia, Spain, Sweden and Switzerland.

Citizens of the US, Australia, New Zealand, Canada and the UK only need a valid passport to enter these countries. However, other nationals, including South Africans, can apply for a single visa – a Schengen visa – when travelling throughout this region.

Non-EU visitors (with or without a Schengen visa) should expect to be questioned, however perfunctorily, when first entering the region. However, later travel within the zone is much like a domestic trip, with no border controls.

If you need a Schengen visa, you must apply at the consulate or embassy of the country that's your main destination, or your point of entry. You may then stay up to a maximum of 90 days in the entire Schengen area within a six-month period. Once your visa has expired, you must leave the zone and may only re-enter after three months abroad. Shop around when choosing your point of entry, as visa prices may differ from country to country.

If you're a citizen of the US, Australia, New Zealand or Canada, you may stay visa-free a total of 90 days, during six months, within the entire Schengen region.

If you're planning a longer trip, you need to inquire personally as to whether you need a visa or visas. Your country might have bilateral agreements with individual Schengen countries allowing you to stay there longer than 90 days without a visa. However, you will need to talk directly to the relevant embassies or consulates.

While the UK and Ireland are not part of the Schengen area, their citizens can stay indefinitely in other EU countries, only needing paperwork if they want to work long term or take up residency.

Travellers with Disabilities

Cobbled medieval streets, 'classic' hotels, congested inner cities and underground subway systems make Europe a tricky destination for people with mobility impairments. However, the train facilities are good and some destinations boast new tram services or lifts to platforms.

Accessible Europe (www.accessibleurope.com) Specialist European tours with van transport.

Lonely Planet (www.lonelyplanet.com/thorntree) Share experiences on the Travellers With Disabilities branch of the Thorn Tree message board.

Mobility International Schweiz (www.mis-ch.ch) Good site (only partly in English) listing 'barrier-free' destinations in Switzerland and abroad, plus wheelchair-accessible hotels in Switzerland.

Mobility International USA (www.miusa.org) Publishes guides and advises travellers with disabilities on mobility issues.

DisabledGo.com (www.disabledgo.com) Detailed access information to thousands of venues across the UK and Ireland.

Society for Accessible Travel & Hospitality (SATH; www.sath.org) Reams of information for travellers with disabilities.

Visas

- Citizens of the USA, Canada, Australia, New Zealand and the UK need only a valid passport to enter nearly all countries in Europe, including the entire EU.
- Transit visas are usually cheaper than tourist or business visas but they allow only a very short stay (one to five days) and can be difficult to extend.
- All visas have a 'use-by' date and you'll be refused entry afterwards. In some cases it's easier to get visas as you go along, rather than arranging them all beforehand. Carry spare passport photos (you may need from one to four for each visa).
- Consulates are generally open weekday mornings (if there's both an embassy and a consulate, you want the consulate).
- Because regulations can change, double-check with the relevant embassy or consulate before travelling.

Women Travellers

- Women might attract unwanted attention in rural Spain and southern Italy, especially Sicily, where many men view whistling and catcalling as flattery. Conservative dress can help to deter lascivious gazes and wolf whistles; dark sunglasses help avoid unwanted eye contact.
- Marriage is highly respected in southern Europe, and a wedding ring can help, along with talk about 'my husband'. Hitchhiking alone is not recommended anywhere.
- **Journeywoman** (www.journeywoman.com) maintains an online newsletter about solo female travels all over the world.

Transport

Getting There & Away

Flights, tours and rail tickets can be booked online at lonelyplanet.com/bookings

Entering Europe

All countries require travellers to have a valid passport, preferably with at least six months between the time of departure and the passport's expiry date.

EU travellers from countries that issue national identity cards are increasingly using these to travel within the EU, although it's impossible to use these as the sole travel documents outside the EU.

Some countries require certain nationalities to buy a visa allowing entry between certain dates.

Air

Airports & Airlines

To save money, it's best to travel off-season. This means, if possible, avoid mid-June to early September, Easter, Christmas and school holidays.

Regardless of your ultimate destination, it's sometimes better to pick a recognised transport 'hub' as your initial port of entry, where high traffic volumes help keep prices down. The busiest, and therefore most obvious, airports are London, Frankfurt, Paris and Rome. Sometimes tickets to Amsterdam, Athens, Barcelona, Berlin, İstanbul, Madrid and Vienna are worth checking out.

Most of the aforementioned gateway cities are also well serviced by low-cost carriers that fly to other parts of Europe.

Getting Around

In most European countries, the train is the best option for internal transport. Check the websites of national rail systems as they often offer fare specials and national passes that are significantly cheaper than point-to-point tickets.

Air

Airlines

In recent years low-cost carriers have revolutionised European transport. Most budget airlines have a similar pricing

Climate Change & Travel

Every form of transport that relies on carbon-based fuel generates CO_2, the main cause of human-induced climate change. Modern travel is dependent on planes which might use less fuel per kilometre per person than most cars but travel much greater distances. The altitude at which aircraft emit gases (including CO_2) and particles also contributes to their climate change impact. Many websites offer 'carbon calculators' that allow people to estimate the carbon emissions generated by their journey and, for those who wish to do so, to offset the impact of the greenhouse gases emitted with contributions to portfolios of climate-friendly initiatives throughout the world. Lonely Planet offsets the carbon footprint of all staff and author travel.

system – namely that ticket prices rise with the number of seats sold on each flight, so book as early as possible to get a decent fare.

Some low-cost carriers – Ryanair being the prime example – have made a habit of flying to smaller, less convenient airports on the outskirts of their destination city, or even to the airports of nearby cities, so check the exact location of the departure and arrival airports before you book.

Departure and other taxes (including booking fees, checked-baggage fees and other surcharges) soon add up and are included in the final price by the end of the online booking process – usually a lot more than you were hoping to pay – but with careful choosing and advance booking you can get excellent deals.

In the face of competition from low-cost airlines, many national carriers have decided to drop their prices and/or offer special deals. Some, such as British Airways, have even adopted the low-cost model of online booking, where the customer can opt to buy just a one-way flight, or can piece together their own return journey from two one-way legs.

For a comprehensive overview of which low-cost carriers fly to or from which European cities, check out the excellent www.flycheapo.com.

Air Passes

Various travel agencies and airlines offer air passes, such as SAS's Visit Scandinavia/Nordic Air Pass (www.flysas.com). Check with your travel agent for current promotions.

Bicycle

Much of Europe is ideally suited to cycling. Popular cycling areas include the whole of the Netherlands, the Belgian Ardennes, the west of Ireland, the upper reaches of the Danube in southern Germany and anywhere in northern Switzerland or the south of France.

Wearing a helmet is not compulsory in most countries, but is certainly sensible.

Rental & Purchase

It is easy to hire bikes throughout most of Europe. Many Western European train stations have bike-rental counters. It is sometimes possible to return the bike at a different outlet so you don't have to retrace your route. Hostels are another good place to find cheap bike hire.

Boat

Several different ferry companies compete on the main ferry routes, resulting in a comprehensive but complicated service. The same ferry company can have a host of different prices for the same route, depending on the time of day or year, validity of the ticket and length of your vehicle. Vehicle tickets usually include the driver and often up to five passengers free of charge.

It's worth booking ahead where possible as there may be special reductions on off-peak crossings and advance-purchase tickets. On English Channel routes, apart from one-day or short-term excursion returns, there is little price advantage in buying a return ticket versus two singles.

Rail-pass holders are entitled to discounts or free travel on some lines. Food on ferries is often expensive (and lousy), so it is worth bringing your own. Also be aware that if you take your vehicle on board, you are usually denied access to it during the voyage.

Lake and river ferry services operate in many countries, Austria and Switzerland being just two. Some of these are very scenic.

Bus

International Buses

Often cheaper than trains, sometimes substantially so, long-distance buses also tend to be slower and less comfortable. However in Portugal, Greece and Turkey, buses are often a better option than trains.

Europe's biggest organisation of international buses operates under the name Eurolines (www.eurolines.com), comprised of various national companies. A Eurolines Pass (www.eurolines.com/en/eurolines-pass) is offered for extensive travel, allowing passengers to visit a choice of 53 cities across Europe over 15 or 30 days. In the high season (mid-June to mid-September) the pass costs €315/405 for those aged under 26, or €375/490 for those 26 and over. It's cheaper in other periods.

Busabout (www.busabout.com) offers a hop-on hop-off service around Europe, stopping at major cities. Buses are often oversubscribed, so book each sector to avoid being stranded. It departs every two days from May to the end of October.

National Buses

Domestic buses provide a viable alternative to trains in most countries. Again, they are usually slightly cheaper and somewhat slower. Buses are generally best for short hops, such as getting around cities and reaching remote villages, and they are often the only option in mountainous regions.

Reservations are rarely necessary. On many city buses you usually buy your ticket in advance from a kiosk or machine and validate it on entering the bus.

Europe's Border Crossings

Border formalities have been relaxed in most of the EU.

In line with the Schengen Agreement, there are officially no passport controls at the borders between Austria, Belgium, Czech Republic, Denmark, Estonia, Finland, France, Germany, Greece, Iceland, Italy, Hungary, Latvia, Liechtenstein, Lithuania, Luxembourg, Malta, the Netherlands, Norway, Poland, Portugal, Slovakia, Slovenia, Spain, Sweden and Switzerland. Sometimes, however, there are spot checks on trains crossing borders, so always have your passport. The UK, which is an EU country but a nonsignatory to Schengen, maintains border controls over traffic from other EU countries (except Ireland, with which it shares an open border), although there is no customs control.

Car & Motorcycle

Travelling with your own vehicle gives flexibility and is the best way to reach remote places. However, the independence does sometimes isolate you from local life. Also, cars can be a target for theft and are often impractical in city centres, where traffic jams, parking problems and getting thoroughly lost can make it well worth ditching your vehicle and using public transport. Various car-carrying trains can help you avoid long, tiring drives.

Fuel

- Fuel prices can vary enormously (though fuel is always more expensive than in North America or Australia).
- Unleaded petrol is available throughout all of Europe. Diesel is usually cheaper, though the difference is marginal in Britain, Ireland and Switzerland.
- Ireland's Automobile Association maintains a webpage of European fuel prices at www.theaa.ie/AA/Motoring-Advice/Petrol-Prices.aspx.

Motorcycle Touring

Europe is made for motorcycle touring, with quality winding roads, stunning scenery and an active motorcycling scene. Just make sure your wet-weather motorcycling gear is up to scratch.

- Rider and passenger crash helmets are compulsory everywhere in Europe.
- Austria, Belgium, France, Germany and Spain require that motorcyclists use headlights during the day;

in other countries it is recommended.

- On ferries, motorcyclists rarely have to book ahead as they can generally be squeezed on board.
- Take note of the local custom about parking motorcycles on pavements (sidewalks). Though this is illegal in some countries, the police often turn a blind eye provided the vehicle doesn't obstruct pedestrians.

Rental

- Renting a car is ideal for people who will need cars for 16 days or less. Anything longer, it's better to lease.
- Big international rental firms will give you reliable service and good vehicles. National or local firms can often undercut the big companies by up to 40%.
- Usually you will have the option of returning the car to a different outlet at the end of the rental period, but there's normally a charge for this and it can be very steep if it's a long way from your point of origin.
- Book early for the lowest rates and make sure you compare rates in different cities. Taxes range from 15% to 20% and surcharges apply if rented from an airport.
- If you rent a car in the EU you might not be able to take it outside the EU, and if you rent the car outside the EU you will only be able to drive within the EU for eight days. Ask at the rental agencies for other such regulations.
- Make sure you understand what is included in the price (unlimited or paid kilometres, tax, injury insurance, collision damage waiver etc) and what your liabilities are. We recommend taking the collision damage waiver, though you can probably skip the injury insurance if you and your passengers have decent travel insurance.
- The minimum rental age is usually 21 years and sometimes 25. You'll need a credit card and to have held your licence for at least a year.
- Motorcycle and moped rental is common in some countries, such as Italy, Spain, Greece and southern France.

Road Conditions & Road Rules

- Conditions and types of roads vary across Europe. The fastest routes are generally four- or six-lane highways known locally as motorways, autoroutes, autostrade, autobahnen etc. These tend to skirt cities and plough through the countryside in straight lines, often avoiding the most scenic bits.
- Some highways incur tolls, which are often quite hefty (especially in Italy, France and Spain), but there will always be an alternative route. Motorways and other primary routes are generally in good condition.
- Road surfaces on minor routes are unreliable in some countries (eg Greece or Ireland), although normally they will be more than adequate.
- Except in Britain and Ireland, you should drive on the right. Vehicles brought to the Continent from any of these locales should have their headlights adjusted to avoid blinding oncoming traffic (a simple solution on older headlight lenses is to cover up a triangular section of the lens with tape). Priority is often given to traffic approaching from the right in countries that drive on the right-hand side.
- Speed limits vary from country to country. You may be surprised at the apparent disregard for traffic regulations in some places (particularly in Italy and Greece), but as a visitor it is always best to be cautious. Many driving infringements are subject to an on-the-spot fine. Always ask for a receipt.
- European drink-driving laws are particularly strict. The blood-alcohol concentration (BAC) limit when driving is usually between 0.05% and 0.08%.

Local Transport

European towns and cities have excellent local-transport systems, often encompassing trams as well as buses and metro/subway/underground-rail networks.

Most travellers will find areas of interest in European cities can be easily traversed by foot or bicycle. In Greece and Italy, travellers sometimes rent mopeds and motorcycles for scooting around a city or island.

Taxi

Taxis in Europe are metered and rates are usually high. There might also be supplements for things such as luggage, time of day, location of pick-up and extra passengers.

Good bus, rail and

underground-railway networks often render taxis unnecessary, but if you need one in a hurry, they can be found idling near train stations or outside big hotels. Lower fares make taxis more viable in some countries such as Spain, Greece, Portugal and Turkey.

Train

Comfortable, frequent and reliable, trains are *the* way to get around Europe.

- Many state railways have interactive websites publishing their timetables and fares, including www.bahn.de (Germany) and www.sbb.ch (Switzerland), which both have pages in English. Eurail (www.eurail.com) links to 28 European train companies.
- The very comprehensive, The Man in Seat 61 (www.seat61.com) is a gem, while the US-based Budget Europe Travel Service (www.budgeteuropetravel.com) can also help with tips.
- European trains sometimes split en route to service two destinations, so even if you're on the right train, make sure you're also in the correct carriage.
- A train journey to almost every station in Europe can be booked via Voyages-sncf.com (http://uk.voyages-sncf.com/en), which also sells InterRail and other passes.

Express Trains

Eurostar (www.eurostar.com) links London's St Pancras International station, via the Channel Tunnel, with Paris' Gare du Nord (2¼ hours, up to 25 a day) and Brussels' international terminal (one hour 50 minutes, up to 12 a day). Some trains also stop at Lille and Calais in France. From December 2016, Eurostar trains will also link Amsterdam Centraal Station with London St Pancras, with stops at Schiphol airport and Rotterdam Centraal Station (and Antwerp and Brussels in Belgium), with an Amsterdam–London journey time of around four hours.

The train stations at St Pancras International, Paris, Brussels and Amsterdam are much more central than the cities' airports. So, overall, the journey takes as little time as the equivalent flight, with less hassle.

Eurostar in London also sells tickets onwards to some Continental destinations. Holders of Eurail and InterRail passes are offered discounts on some Eurostar services; check when booking.

Within Europe, express trains are identified by the symbols 'EC' (EuroCity) or 'IC' (InterCity). The French TGV, Spanish AVE and German ICE trains are even faster, reaching up to 300km/h. Supplementary fares can apply on fast trains (which you often have to pay when travelling on a rail pass), and it is a good idea (sometimes obligatory) to reserve seats at peak times and on certain lines. The same applies for branded express trains, such as the Thalys (between Paris and Brussels, Bruges, Amsterdam and Cologne), and the Eurostar Italia (between Rome and Naples, Florence, Milan and Venice).

If you don't have a seat reservation, you can still obtain a seat that doesn't have a reservation ticket attached to it. Check which destination a seat is reserved for – you might be able to sit in it until the person boards the train.

International Rail Passes

If you're covering lots of ground, you should get a rail pass. But do some price comparisons of point-to-point ticket charges and rail passes beforehand to make absolutely sure you'll break even. Also shop around for rail-pass prices as they do vary between outlets. When weighing up options, look into cheap deals that include advance-purchase reductions, one-off promotions or special circular-route tickets, particularly over the internet.

Normal point-to-point tickets are valid for two months, and you can make as many stops as you like en route; make your intentions known when purchasing and inform train conductors how far you're going before they punch your ticket.

Supplementary charges (eg for some express and overnight trains) and seat reservation fees (mandatory on some trains, a good idea on others) are not covered by rail passes. Always ask. Note that European rail passes also give reductions on Eurostar, the Channel Tunnel and on certain ferries.

Pass-holders must always carry their passport with them for identification purposes. The railways' policy is that passes cannot be replaced or refunded if lost or stolen.

Non-European Residents

Eurail (www.eurail.com) passes can be bought only by residents of non-European countries and should be purchased before arriving in Europe.

The most comprehensive of the various Eurail passes is the 'Global Pass' covering 28 countries. While the pass is valid on some private train lines in the region, if you plan to travel extensively in Switzerland, be warned that the many private rail networks and cable cars, especially in the Jungfrau region around Interlaken, don't give Eurail discounts. A Swiss Pass or Half-Fare Card might be an alternative or necessary addition.

The pass is valid for a set number of consecutive days or a set number of days within a period of time. Those under 26 years of age can buy a Eurail Youth pass, which only covers travel in 2nd-class compartments. Those aged 26 and over must buy the full-fare Eurail pass, which entitles you to travel 1st class.

Alternatively, there is the Select pass, which allows you to nominate four bordering countries in which you wish to travel, and then buy a pass allowing five, six, eight or 10 travel days in a two-month period. The five- and six-day passes offer an attractive price break, but for more expensive options, the continuous pass becomes better value.

Regional Passes cover two bordering countries, but you might want to ensure that they are good value given your travel plans. There are also Eurail National Passes for just one country.

Two to five people travelling together can get a Saver version of all Eurail passes for a 15% discount.

European Residents

InterRail (www.interrail.eu) offers passes to European residents for unlimited rail travel through 30 European and North African countries (excluding the pass-holder's country of residence). To qualify as a resident, you must have lived in a European country for six months.

While an InterRail pass will get you further than a Eurail pass along the private rail networks of Switzerland's Jungfrau region (near Interlaken), its benefits are limited. A Swiss Pass or Half-Fare Card might be a necessary addition if you plan to travel extensively in that region.

For a small fee, European residents can buy a Railplus Card, entitling the holder to a 25% discount on many (but not all) international train journeys. It is available from counters in main train stations.

National Rail Passes

National rail operators might also offer their own passes, or at least a discount card, offering substantial reductions on tickets purchased (eg the Bahn Card in Germany or the Half-Fare Card in Switzerland).

Look at individual train operator sites via http://uk.voyages-sncf.com/en/ to check. Such discount cards are usually only worth it if you're staying in the country a while and doing a lot of travelling.

Overnight Trains

There are usually two types of sleeping accommodation: dozing off upright in your seat or stretching out in a sleeper. Again, reservations are advisable, as sleeping options are allocated on a first-come, first-served basis. Couchette bunks are comfortable enough, if lacking in privacy. There are four per compartment in 1st class, six in 2nd class.

Sleepers are the most comfortable option, offering beds for one or two passengers in 1st class, or two or three passengers in 2nd class. Charges vary depending upon the journey, but they are significantly more costly than couchettes.

Security

Sensible security measures include always keeping your bags in sight (especially at stations), chaining them to the luggage rack, locking compartment doors overnight and sleeping in compartments with other people. However, horror stories are very rare.

Language

Don't let the language barrier get in the way of your travel experience. This section offers basic phrases and pronunciation guides to help you negotiate your way around Europe. Note that in our pronunciation guides, the stressed syllables in words are indicated with italics.

To enhance your trip with a phrasebook (covering all of these languages in much greater detail), visit **lonelyplanet.com**. Lonely Planet iPhone phrasebooks are available through the Apple App store.

CZECH

Hello.	*Ahoj.*	*uh*·hoy
Goodbye.	*Na shledanou.*	*nuh*·skhle·duh·noh
Yes./No.	*Ano./Ne.*	*uh*·no/ne
Please.	*Prosím.*	*pro*·seem
Thank you.	*Děkuji.*	*dye*·ku·yi
Excuse me.	*Promiňte.*	*pro*·min'·te
Help!	*Pomoc!*	*po*·mots

Do you speak English?
Mluvíte anglicky? — *mlu*·vee·te *uhn*·glits·ki
I don't understand.
Nerozumím. — *ne*·ro·zu·meem
How much is this?
Kolik to stojí? — *ko*·lik to *sto*·yee
I'd like ..., please.
Chtěl/Chtěla bych . . ., prosím. (m/f) — khtyel/*khtye*·luh bikh . . . *pro*·seem
Where's (the toilet)?
Kde je (záchod)? — gde ye (*za*·khod)
I'm lost.
Zabloudil/ Zabloudila jsem. (m/f) — *zuh*·bloh·dyil/ *zuh*·bloh·dyi·luh ysem

DUTCH

Hello.	*Dag.*	dakh
Goodbye.	*Dag.*	dakh
Yes.	*Ja.*	yaa
No.	*Nee.*	ney
Please.	*Alstublieft.*	al·stew·*bleeft*
Thank you.	*Dank u.*	dangk ew
Excuse me.	*Excuseer mij.*	eks·kew·*zeyr* mey
Help!	*Help!*	help

Do you speak English?
Spreekt u Engels? — spreykt ew *eng*·uhls
I don't understand.
Ik begrijp het niet. — ik buh·*khreyp* huht neet
How much is this?
Hoeveel kost het? — hoo·*veyl* kost huht
I'd like ..., please.
Ik wil graag . . . — ik wil khraakh . . .
Where's (the toilet)?
Waar zijn (de toiletten)? — waar zeyn (duh twa·*le*·tuhn)
I'm lost.
Ik ben verdwaald. — ik ben vuhr·*dwaalt*

FRENCH

Hello.	*Bonjour.*	bon·zhoor
Goodbye.	*Au revoir.*	o·rer·vwa
Yes.	*Oui.*	wee
No.	*Non.*	non
Please.	*S'il vous plaît.*	seel voo play
Thank you.	*Merci.*	mair·see
Excuse me.	*Excusez-moi.*	ek·skew·zay·mwa
Help!	*Au secours!*	o skoor

Do you speak English?
Parlez-vous anglais? — par·lay·voo ong·glay
I don't understand.
Je ne comprends pas. — zher ner kom·pron pa
How much is this?
C'est combien? — say kom·byun
I'd like ..., please.
Je voudrais . . ., s'il vous plaît. — zher voo·dray . . . seel voo play
Where's (the toilet)?
Où sont (les toilettes)? — oo son (lay twa·let)
I'm lost.
Je suis perdu(e). (m/f) — zhe swee·pair·dew

GERMAN

Hello.	*Guten Tag.*	*goo*·ten taak
Goodbye.	*Auf Wiedersehen.*	owf *vee*·der·zey·en
Yes.	*Ja.*	yaa
No.	*Nein.*	nain
Please.	*Bitte.*	*bi*·te
Thank you.	*Danke.*	*dang*·ke
Excuse me.	*Entschuldigung.*	ent·*shul*·di·gung
Help!	*Hilfe!*	*hil*·fe

Do you speak English?
Sprechen Sie Englisch? shpre·khen zee *eng*·lish
I don't understand.
Ich verstehe nicht. ikh fer·*shtey*·e nikht
How much is this?
Was kostet das? vas *kos*·tet das
I'd like ..., please.
Ich hätte gern . . ., bitte. ikh *he*·te gern . . . *bi*·te
Where's (the toilet)?
Wo ist (die Toilette)? vaw ist (dee to·a·*le*·te)
I'm lost.
Ich habe mich verirrt. ikh *haa*·be mikh fer·*irt*

ITALIAN

Hello.	*Buongiorno.*	bwon·*jor*·no
Goodbye.	*Arrivederci.*	a·ree·ve·*der*·chee
Yes.	*Sì.*	see
No.	*No.*	no
Please.	*Per favore.*	per fa·*vo*·re
Thank you.	*Grazie.*	*gra*·tsye
Excuse me.	*Mi scusi.*	mee *skoo*·zee
Help!	*Aiuto!*	a·*yoo*·to

Do you speak English?
Parla inglese? *par*·la een·*gle*·ze
I don't understand.
Non capisco. non ka·*pee*·sko
How much is this?
Quanto costa? *kwan*·to *ko*·sta
I'd like ..., please.
Vorrei . . ., per favore. vo·*ray* . . . per fa·*vo*·re
Where's (the toilet)?
Dove sono (i gabinetti)? *do*·ve *so*·no (ee ga·bee·*ne*·ti)
I'm lost.
Mi sono perso/a. (m/f) mee *so*·no *per*·so/a

GREEK

Hello.	Γεια σου.	yia su
Goodbye.	Αντίο.	a·*di*·o
Yes.	Ναι.	ne
No.	Οχι.	*o*·hi
Please.	Παρακαλώ.	pa·ra·ka·*lo*
Thank you.	Ευχαριστώ.	ef·kha·ri·*sto*
Excuse me.	Με συγχωρείτε.	me sing·kho·*ri*·te
Help!	Βοήθεια!	vo·*i*·thia

Do you speak English?
Μιλάς Αγγλικά; mi·*las* ang·gli·*ka*
I don't understand.
Δεν καταλαβαίνω. dhen ka·ta·la·*ve*·no
How much is this?
Πόσο κάνει; *po*·so *ka*·ni
I'd like ..., please.
Θα ήθελα . . ., παρακαλώ. tha *i*·the·la . . . pa·ra·ka·*lo*
Where's (the toilet)?
Που είναι (η τουαλέτα); pu *i*·ne (i tu·a·*le*·ta)
I'm lost.
Έχω χαθεί. *e*·kho kha·*thi*

SPANISH

Hello.	*Hola.*	*o*·la
Goodbye.	*Adiós.*	a·*dyos*
Yes.	*Sí.*	see
No.	*No.*	no
Please.	*Por favor.*	por fa·*vor*
Thank you.	*Gracias.*	*gra*·thyas
Excuse me.	*Disculpe.*	dees·*kool*·pe
Help!	*¡Socorro!*	so·*ko*·ro

Do you speak English?
¿Habla inglés? *a*·bla een·*gles*
I don't understand.
No entiendo. no en·*tyen*·do
How much is this?
¿Cuánto cuesta? *kwan*·to *kwes*·ta
I'd like ..., please.
Quisiera . . ., por favor. kee·*sye*·ra . . . por fa·*vor*
Where's (the toilet)?
¿Dónde están (los servicios)? *don*·de es·*tan* (los ser·*vee*·thyos)
I'm lost.
Estoy perdido/a. (m/f) es·*toy* per·*dee*·do/a

Behind the Scenes

Author Thanks

CATHERINE LE NEVEZ

Thanks first and foremost to Julian, and to all who provided insights, information and good times during this gig. Huge thanks too to Destination Editor Kate Morgan and everyone at LP. As ever, *merci encore* to my parents, brother, belle-sœur and neveu.

Acknowledgments

Climate map data adapted from Peel MC, Finlayson BL & McMahon TA (2007) 'Updated World Map of the Köppen-Geiger Climate Classification', *Hydrology and Earth System Sciences*, 11, 163344.

Illustrations pp68-9, pp76-7, pp114-5, pp122-123, pp128-129, pp138-9, pp180-1, pp184-5, pp204-5, pp212-13, pp250-1, pp268-9, pp288-9, pp314-15, pp324-5, pp338-9, pp344-5, pp348-9, pp370-1, pp406-7, pp420-1, pp442-3, pp702-3, pp726-7 by Javier Zarracina.

p139 Sphere Within a Sphere, Sfera con sfera, 1982-83, bronze, ø 200 cm, Berkeley Library, Trinity College, University of Dublin.

Cover Photographs: Front: Bavaria, Germany, HP Huber/4Corners; Back: Provence, France, Cornelia Dorr/4Corners.

This Book

This 4th edition of Lonely Planet's *Discover Europe* guidebook was coordinated by Catherine Le Nevez, and was written and researched by Alexis Averbuck, Mark Baker, Kerry Christiani, Emilie Filou, Duncan Garwood, Anthony Ham, Catherine Le Nevez, Sally O'Brien, Andrea Schulte-Peevers, Helena Smith and Neil Wilson. This guidebook was produced by the following:

Destination Editor Kate Morgan
Product Editors Elin Berglund, Tracy Whitmey
Senior Cartographer Valentina Kremenchutskaya
Book Designer Wendy Wright
Assisting Editors Charlotte Orr, Ross Taylor
Cover Researcher Campbell McKenzie
Thanks to Imogen Bannister, Sasha Baskett, Jorjit S Bhullar, Sarah Billington, Gladys Chua, Elizabeth Jones, Kate Mathews, Catherine Naghten, Luna Soo, Lyahna Spencer, Tony Wheeler

SEND US YOUR FEEDBACK

We love to hear from travellers – your comments keep us on our toes and help make our books better. Our well-travelled team reads every word on what you loved or loathed about this book. Although we cannot reply individually to postal submissions, we always guarantee that your feedback goes straight to the appropriate authors, in time for the next edition. Each person who sends us information is thanked in the next edition, the most useful submissions are rewarded with a selection of digital PDF chapters.

Visit **lonelyplanet.com/contact** to submit your updates and suggestions or to ask for help. Our award-winning website also features inspirational travel stories, news and discussions.

Note: We may edit, reproduce and incorporate your comments in Lonely Planet products such as guidebooks, websites and digital products, so let us know if you don't want your comments reproduced or your name acknowledged. For a copy of our privacy policy visit lonelyplanet.com/privacy.

Index

A

B

000 Map pages

C

000 Map pages

D

E

F

G

000 Map pages

H

I

J

K

L

M

000 Map pages

000 Map pages

Q

R

S

T

000 Map pages

U

V

W

Y

Z

How to Use This Book

These symbols give you the vital information for each listing:

- Telephone Numbers
- Opening Hours
- Parking
- Nonsmoking
- Air-Conditioning
- Internet Access
- Wi-Fi Access
- Swimming Pool
- Vegetarian Selection
- English-Language Menu
- Family-Friendly
- Pet-Friendly
- Bus
- Ferry
- Metro
- Subway
- London Tube
- Tram

All reviews are ordered in our authors' preference, starting with their most preferred option. Additionally:

Sights are arranged in the geographic order that we suggest you visit them, and within this order, by author preference.

Eating and Sleeping reviews are ordered by price range (budget, mid-range, top end) and within these ranges, by author preference.

Look out for these icons:

FREE No payment required

A green or sustainable option

Our authors have nominated these places as demonstrating a strong commitment to sustainability – for example by supporting local communities and producers, operating in an environmentally friendly way, or supporting conservation projects.

Map Legend

Sights
- Beach
- Buddhist
- Castle
- Christian
- Hindu
- Islamic
- Jewish
- Monument
- Museum/Gallery
- Ruin
- Winery/Vineyard
- Zoo
- Other Sight

Activities, Courses & Tours
- Diving/Snorkelling
- Canoeing/Kayaking
- Skiing
- Surfing
- Swimming/Pool
- Walking
- Windsurfing
- Other Activity/Course/Tour

Sleeping
- Sleeping
- Camping

Eating
- Eating

Drinking
- Drinking
- Cafe

Entertainment
- Entertainment

Shopping
- Shopping

Information
- Post Office
- Tourist Information

Transport
- Airport
- Border Crossing
- Bus
- Cable Car/Funicular
- Cycling
- Ferry
- Monorail
- Parking
- S-Bahn
- Taxi
- Train/Railway
- Tram
- Tube Station
- U-Bahn
- Underground Train Station
- Other Transport

Routes
- Tollway
- Freeway
- Primary
- Secondary
- Tertiary
- Lane
- Unsealed Road
- Plaza/Mall
- Steps
- Tunnel
- Pedestrian Overpass
- Walking Tour
- Walking Tour Detour
- Path

Boundaries
- International
- State/Province
- Disputed
- Regional/Suburb
- Marine Park
- Cliff
- Wall

Population
- Capital (National)
- Capital (State/Province)
- City/Large Town
- Town/Village

Geographic
- Hut/Shelter
- Lighthouse
- Lookout
- Mountain/Volcano
- Oasis
- Park
- Pass
- Picnic Area
- Waterfall

Hydrography
- River/Creek
- Intermittent River
- Swamp/Mangrove
- Reef
- Canal
- Water
- Dry/Salt/Intermittent Lake
- Glacier

Areas
- Beach/Desert
- Cemetery (Christian)
- Cemetery (Other)
- Park/Forest
- Sportsground
- Sight (Building)
- Top Sight (Building)

EMILIE FILOU

France Emilie was born in Paris and spent most of her childhood holidays roaming the south of France. She now lives in London, where she works as a freelance journalist specialising in development issues in Africa. She still goes to France every year for holidays and loves feasting on local market products, especially cheese and wine. See more of Emilie's work on www.emiliefilou.com; she tweets at @emiliefilou.

Read more about Emilie at:
auth.lonelyplanet.com/profiles/emiliefilou

DUNCAN GARWOOD

Italy Duncan is a British travel writer based near Rome. Since he moved to Italy in 1997, he has travelled extensively in his adopted homeland and worked on about 30 Lonely Planet guides including *Rome, Sardinia, Sicily,* and *Italy's Best Trips.*

Read more about Duncan at:
auth.lonelyplanet.com/profiles/duncangarwood

ANTHONY HAM

Spain In 2001 Anthony fell in love with Madrid on his first visit to the city. Less than a year later, he arrived on a one-way ticket, with not a word of Spanish and not knowing a single person. Having recently passed the 10-year mark in Madrid, he still adores his adopted city. Anthony also writes about and photographs Spain, Scandinavia, Africa and the Middle East for newspapers and magazines around the world.

Read more about Anthony at:
auth.lonelyplanet.com/profiles/anthony_ham

SALLY O'BRIEN

Switzerland Since moving to Switzerland in 2007, Sally has revelled in swimming the country's lakes and rivers, snowboarding down its astounding mountains, scoffing its cheese and chocolate, and quaffing local-secret wines. Writing about this dreamy country for Lonely Planet and heading out on the road with her family to explore every last corner of her adopted home only adds to the fun.

Read more about Sally at:
auth.lonelyplanet.com/profiles/swissingaround

ANDREA SCHULTE-PEEVERS

Germany Born and raised in Germany and educated in London and at UCLA, Andrea has travelled the distance to the moon and back in her visits to some 75 countries and now makes her home in Berlin. She's written about her native country for two decades and authored or contributed to some 80 Lonely Planet titles, including *Germany* and *Berlin*.

Read more about Andrea at:
auth.lonelyplanet.com/profiles/andreaschultepeevers

HELENA SMITH

Belgium Helena Smith is a travel writer and photographer, who also blogs about food and community at eathackney.com.

NEIL WILSON

Britain & Ireland Neil's first experiences of Ireland were a sailing trip to Kinsale in 1990 and a tour of Northern Ireland's Antrim coast in 1994. Since then he has returned regularly for holidays, hiking trips and guidebook research – this time around he climbed Mt Brandon and six of Connemara's Twelve Bens. Neil is a full-time travel writer based in Edinburgh, Scotland, and has written around 50 guidebooks, including working on the last five editions of Lonely Planet's *Ireland* guide.

Read more about Neil at:
auth.lonelyplanet.com/profiles/neilwilson

Our Story

A beat-up old car, a few dollars in the pocket and a sense of adventure. In 1972 that's all Tony and Maureen Wheeler needed for the trip of a lifetime – across Europe and Asia overland to Australia. It took several months, and at the end – broke but inspired – they sat at their kitchen table writing and stapling together their first travel guide, *Across Asia on the Cheap*. Within a week they'd sold 1500 copies. Lonely Planet was born.

Today, Lonely Planet has offices in Melbourne, London and Oakland, with more than 600 staff and writers. We share Tony's belief that 'a great guidebook should do three things: inform, educate and amuse'.

Our Writers

CATHERINE LE NEVEZ

Coordinating Author, the Netherlands Catherine's wanderlust kicked in when she first roadtripped across Europe, including the Netherlands, aged four, and she's been returning to this spirited, *gezellig* country ever since, completing her Doctorate of Creative Arts in Writing, Masters in Professional Writing, and post-grad qualifications in Editing and Publishing along the way. Catherine has worked as a freelance writer for many years and during the past decade or so she's written scores of Lonely Planet guidebooks and articles covering destinations all over Europe and beyond.

Read more about Catherine at:
auth.lonelyplanet.com/profiles/catherine_le_nevez

ALEXIS AVERBUCK

Greece Alexis lives in Hydra, Greece, takes regular reverse R&R in Athens, and makes any excuse she can to travel the isolated back roads of her adopted land. A travel writer for two decades, Alexis has lived in Antarctica for a year, crossed the Pacific by sailboat and written books on her journeys through Asia and the Americas. She's also a painter - visit www.alexisaverbuck.com.

Read more about Alexis at:
auth.lonelyplanet.com/profiles/alexisaverbuck

MARK BAKER

Czech Republic Based permanently in Prague, Mark has lived and worked in eastern Europe for more than 20 years, first as a journalist for The Economist Group and then for Bloomberg News and Radio Free Europe/Radio Liberty. He travels frequently throughout the region. In addition to this book, Mark is co-author of the Lonely Planet guides *Prague*, *Slovenia*, and *Romania & Bulgaria*.

Read more about Mark at:
auth.lonelyplanet.com/profiles/markbaker

KERRY CHRISTIANI

Austria Ever since her first post-grad trip to Austria, Kerry has seized every available chance to travel to the country of Mozart, Maria and co. Picking the cream of Vienna's coffee houses, glimpsing September snow in the Alps above Innsbruck and finding out the truth about the von Trapps in Salzburg kept her busy for this edition. Kerry has authored/co-authored some 20 guidebooks, including Lonely Planet's *Austria*, *Germany* and *Switzerland*. She tweets at @kerrychristiani and lists her latest work at www.kerrychristiani.com.

Read more about Kerry at:
auth.lonelyplanet.com/profiles/kerrychristiani

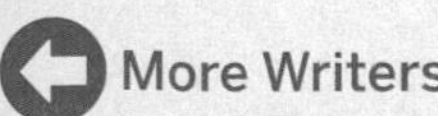

More Writers

Published by Lonely Planet Publications Pty Ltd
ABN 36 005 607 983
4th edition – Dec 2015
ISBN 978 1 74321 400 8

10 9 8 7 6 5 4 3 2 1
Printed in China